Offset Lithographic Technology

Fourth Edition

Kenneth F. Hird

Charles E. Finley

Publisher

The Goodheart-Willcox Company, Inc.

Tinley Park, Illinois

www.g-w.com

Cover image: Getty Images RF/ James Lauritz

The Goodheart-Willcox Company, Inc. Brand Disclaimer: Brand names, company names, and illustrations for products
and services included in this text are provided for educational purposes only and do not represent or imply endorsement or
recommendation by the author or the publisher.

The Goodheart-Willcox Company, Inc. Safety Notice: The reader is expressly advised to carefully read, understand, and apply
all safety precautions and warnings described in this book or that might also be indicated in undertaking the activities and
exercises described herein to minimize risk of personal injury or injury to others. Common sense and good judgment should also be
exercised and applied to help avoid all potential hazards. The reader should always refer to the appropriate manufacturer's technical
information, directions, and recommendations; then proceed with care to follow specific equipment operating instructions. The
reader should understand these notices and cautions are not exhaustive.

The publisher makes no warranty or representation whatsoever, either expressed or implied, including but not limited to equipment,
procedures, and applications described or referred to herein, their quality, performance, merchantability, or fitness for a particular
purpose. The publisher assumes no responsibility for any changes, errors, or omissions in this book. The publisher specifically
disclaims any liability whatsoever, including any direct, indirect, incidental, consequential, special, or exemplary damages resulting,
in whole or in part, from the reader's use or reliance upon the information, instructions, procedures, warnings, cautions, applications,
or other matter contained in this book. The publisher assumes no responsibility for the activities of the reader.

Colophon

Offset Lithographic Technology was composed and paginated in InDesign® software, using Palatino for
body text and Broadway and Helvetica as display faces. The book was run through the Prinergy Prepress
Workflow System. The book body was printed on 45# New Page Publisher's Matte using 4/C process on a 4/C
MAN Roland web press in 48-page signatures. Cover printing was done on Type II film-laminated material
using 4/C process on a 4/C Heidelberg Speedmaster sheetfed press. Binding is adhesive case bind hardcover.

Library of Congress Cataloging-in-Publication Data

Hird, Kenneth F.
     Offset lithographic technology / Kenneth F. Hird, Charles E. Finley. -- 4th ed.
          p. cm.
     Includes index.
     ISBN 978-1-60525-068-7
     1. Offset printing. I. Finley, Charles. II. Title.
     Z252.5.O5H57   2010
     686.2'315--dc22

                                        2008041011

Introduction

The printing industry has seen immense technological growth and changes in the past 20 years. Electronics and computer technologies have completely changed the complexion of the industry. Most manual processes have been eliminated from the preprinting, printing, and finishing stages of production. Original manuscript and art can be created on personal computers and sent over the Internet to the publisher or production house. Once the layout and design are completed, the files can be downloaded to the printer, who in turn, can send them to remote plants for distributed printing.

Many time-consuming, waste-producing processes have also been eliminated from the work flow. Scanners and digital cameras are used to produce electronic images. These images can be modified, color corrected, screened, and printed with or without film or plate production. Dry-film processors and laser-based platesetters produce film and plates without the chemistry required in conventional processing.

The smallest offset duplicators and the largest web offset presses use computer technology to run, monitor, and adjust everything from ink densities to web tension. These computer systems are programmed to alert the operator to potential problems and even shut down the press if necessary. These advances and improvements, along with the conventional methods, have made offset lithography a mature combination of processes and techniques. There are many career opportunities for those who have the necessary skills and educational background. *Offset Lithographic Technology* has been designed and organized to teach you about offset lithography methods and processes as they are used by professionals in the industry.

The printing industry is not limited to the pressroom. Printed products usually begin with an idea from an author or artist before entering numerous production phases. Many professional and technical people are required to produce the printed materials we often take for granted.

Student Workbook

The fast pace of technological change in the printing industry presents a special challenge to you, as well as to your instructor. Tomorrow's jobs will be different from today's, requiring new applications and skills. As a consequence, today's professional must have a thorough knowledge of the principles and practices related to offset lithography. The *Offset Lithographic Technology Workbook* offers a variety of questions and activities to enhance your understanding and technical skills. The workbook supplements the textbook by integrating academic concepts with technical applications using a practical, workplace approach.

About the Authors

Kenneth Hird learned the printing trade as an apprentice for Campbell Publishing Company in San Jose, California. During the Korean War, he served aboard the aircraft carriers USS *Gilbert Islands* and USS *Lake Champlain*. His career spans 15 years in the printing industry and 34 years in graphic arts and printing education.

Hird has a bachelor's degree from San Jose State University, a master's degree from the University of Northern Iowa, and a doctorate from Utah State University. He began a teaching career at William Howard Taft High School in Woodland Hills, California. After nine years at the high school, Hird moved on to Kirkwood Community College in Cedar Rapids, Iowa, where he established a vocational printing-trades program. Five years later, he accepted a professorship at California State University, in Los Angeles, where he was involved in industrial technology, printing management, and graphic communications technology programs.

He also had some involvement in his wife Nancy's quick-printing business in San Dimas, California.

Hird has had three other textbooks published in the graphic arts and printing-technology field. He and his wife now live in Arizona, where they enjoy hiking, desert exploration, and flying light planes.

Charles E. Finley is retired from having taught for 36 years. After teaching at two high schools, he was a professor of graphic communications at Columbus State Community College from 1976 to 2004. He completed his bachelor's and doctorate degrees at Ohio University, his master's degree at Union College, and additional coursework at Rochester Institute of Technology, Michigan State University, Ball State University, and the Ohio State University. Finley is the author of two other books and several articles in *American Printer* and has taught several seminars at Rochester Institute of Technology. He received the Teaching Excellence Award at Columbus State; has been listed four times in *Who's Who Among America's Teachers*; and is a member of the International Graphic Arts Education Association (IGAEA), Phi Kappa Phi, and the National Association of Scholars. Finley is a consultant to the printing industry.

Acknowledgments

The authors and publisher wish to express their appreciation to the following individuals, companies, and organizations for their cooperation in furnishing photographs, line art, and technical information used in this book:

A.B.Dick Co.
ACCEL Graphic Systems
Agfa-Gevaert Inc.
American ColorScans
American Roller Company
ANSCO Graphic Arts Products
Atco Printing
ATF Davidson Co.
Baker Perkins Limited
Baldwin Technology
Baum USA
Boise Cascade Paper Group
Bowling Green State University, Visual
    Communication Technology Program
Brandtjen & Kluge, Inc.
Buckeye Printing and Mailing Solutions
ByChrome Co.
Caprock Developments, Inc.
Center for Metric Education, Western
    Michigan University
Champion Manufacturing Company, Inc.
Chapman Corp.
Chemco, Inc.
Color Graphics, Los Angeles
Columbus Bride Magazine
Corel, Inc.
Crane Lake Visitor and Tourism Bureau
Daytona Beach Convention and Visitors Bureau
Decco, Inc.
Diagraph®
Didde Graphic Systems Corp.
Dover Flexo Electronics, Inc.
Duplo USA
Dynagram
DynaStrip
E.I. DuPont de Nemours and Co.
Eastman Kodak Co.
EMA
Enco Products
EPG, Inc.
Ferris State University, Printing and Imaging
    Technology Management
Fireworks
Flint Ink Corp.
Flying Color
Franklin Estimator
Fuji Photo Film USA, Inc.
General Binding Corp.
Gentner Electronics Corp.
Gerber Systems Corp.
Goerz Optical Co.
Goss International Corporation
Graphic Arts Technical Foundation (GATF)
Graphpros
Gretag Macbeth, New Windsor, NY
Gutenberg Museum, Mainz
Hagen Systems, Inc.
Hamada

Hammer Packaging
Hammermill Paper Co.
Harris Corp.
Heidelberg, Inc.
Hilton Head Convention and Visitors Bureau
Hi-Temp Products Co.
Hopkins Printing
HP/Indigo
IDESCO Corp.
Industrial Chemical Measurement Co.
International Paper Co.
I-Trap
Jack Klasey
Jalema Inc., Filing Systems Division
JetPlate Systems
John F. Cuneo Co.
John N. Schaedler, Inc.
Jomac, Inc.
Justrite Manufacturing Co.
J. Walker
Kimberly-Clark Corp.
Kissimmee–St. Cloud Convention and Visitors
    Bureau
Kodak NexPress
Koenig & Bauer
Koh-I-Noor Rapidograph, Inc.
Lab Safety Supply
Leslie Paper Co.
Letraset, Inc.
Linotype-Hell
Lithographics, Inc.
Logic Associates, Inc.
Lucid Dream Software, Inc.
Man Roland, Inc.
Matt Cook
Matthias Bauerle GrmbH
McCain Manufacturing Corp.
MeadWestvaco
Michael Orr and Associates for Corning
    Museum of Glass
Micro Essential Laboratory, Inc.
Microtek Lab, Inc.
Miehle Products, Graphic Systems Division
Millcreek Mall
Minolta Corporation
MixMasters, Inc.
Monaco Systems, Incorporated
Monotype Systems
Multigraphics
National Association for Printing Leadership
National Association of Printers and
    Lithographers (NAPL)
National Association of Printing Ink
    Manufacturers (NAPIM), Inc.
National Soy Ink Information Center
nuArc Company, Inc.
Ohaus Corp.
Ohio Blow Pipe

Omnitrade Industrial/Omni Adast
Orobotech, Inc.
Pantone, Inc.
Pederson Group
Polychrome Corp.
Presstek, Inc.
Prime Systems, Inc.
Printer's Software, Inc.
Printing Consulting, Inc.
PXP Ohio
Raden® C Inc.
Robertson Photo-Mechanix, Inc.
Rockwell International
Rust-Oleum Corporation
Ryobi Xpedx Impact Group
S.D. Warren Co.
Safety-Kleen
Sakurai USA, Inc.
Screen USA
Sierra Pacific Power Co.
SIG Packaging Technology
SIMCO
SkillsUSA
Smithsonian Institute
Smurfit-Stone
Southwestern Publishing Co.
Special Products Engineering Co.
Standard Finishing Systems
Step-by-Step Graphics Magazine
Stouffer Graphic Arts Equipment Co.
Strachan Henshaw Machinery, Inc.
SWOP
TEC Systems
Tensor Group, Inc.
The Ink Well
The Think Tank Group Inc. for the Pittsburgh
    Chamber Music Society
3M Company
T. Lewis
Tobias Associates, Inc.
Torit® Products
U.S. Copyright Office
U.S. Government Printing Office
Ultimate Technographics, Inc.
Van Son Holland Ink Corp.
Varn Products Company, Inc.
Vaughan & Bushnell Manufacturing
Vijuk Equipment, Inc.
Virkotype Corp.
Walden-Mott Corp.
Walden's Paper Catalog
Wolverine Corporation
Xante
Xeikon
Xerox Corp.
X-Rite, Incorporated
Zipf Lock Co.

Brief Contents

Contents

Section II
Content Creation

Section V
The Printing Business and Career Opportunities

Offset Lithographic Technology is an easy-to-understand, up-to-date book summarizing the operations involved in the production of printed materials using offset lithography. Various fonts and typefaces are used throughout this textbook to identify important terms and highlight figure references. A variety of special notices are used throughout this textbook. These notices contain cautions, technical information, and references to pertinent information in other parts of the text. The notices are identified by color. The textbook uses design features that facilitate learning, including large type and short line widths. Over 1000 images (photographs, drawings, and line illustrations) are used throughout the textbook to assist you in understanding the material that has been presented.

Features of the Textbook

Cautions identify situations that can cause physical injury or damage to equipment and tools, if proper procedures are not followed or if safety measures are not observed.

Figure References within the body of the text and in the captions are printed in bold red type. This makes them easy to locate and identify.

Notes might contain references to another section of the text or supplemental information relating to the procedure or system being explained.

Key Terms appear in bold-italic type where they are defined. These terms are identified when they are introduced and are included in the glossary.

Learning Objectives appear at the beginning of each chapter. These objectives identify the topics covered and goals to be achieved in the chapter. By reading the learning objectives before and after completing the chapter, you will know what to expect to learn and then make sure you have met each objective.

Chapter Introductions provide an interesting transition into each chapter and often point out the practical value of learning the material.

Sample page excerpts

.92   Section II   Content Creation

Caution

Some ink-jet and laser printers use agents that can be irritating or toxic. Laser toner can be an irritant to the respiratory tract and eyes. MSDSs are available from the toner vendor or manufacturer.

Digital Proofers

A proof is a preliminary copy of a job still in production, serving as a sample for the customer and a visual specification for the press operator. A *hard proof* is a tangible sheet made directly from digital files, generated directly from film, or from digital proof press. A *soft proof* is the image appearing on the computer monitor. Cost and the exact elements in question (such as color, text flow, or positional errors) determine the types of proofs requested at various stages of prepress production.

Digital proofs are generated by outputting files on a high-resolution, high-quality printer. See **Figure 13-18.** Depending on the system's capabilities, digital proofs can simulate results from any type of printing press. For digital proofs to replace film-generated proofs, however, they must accurately represent all the features of the traditional proof, including color fidelity, traps and overprints, representative screening, and quality in fine line details. Customers often require proofs that accurately represent color and halftone reproduction. Comparatively inexpensive digital proofs can be produced and used to indicate the location of page

Figure 13-18. High-resolution proofers can closely simulate the colors that will appear on the press sheet. (HP/Indigo)

elements a... approximate color and service bureaus, however, use closely predict the colors to produce dig proofing systems sheets. These proofs can be used as ce proofs used to define what the clie from the finished job. Used in conju color-management system, digital-pro can simulate the *dot gain* expected on digital-output device is connected to the *image processor (RIP)* that runs the ima will output halftone patterns identical to will appear on the final sheet.

It is important for many customers to halftone dots that will be printed on the Customers once previewed the halftone-dot because traditional analog proofs were made the same films that made the printing plate. digital proofs do not, however, contain halfto The viewer might not be able to determine if t will be a problem with the screening of an image, the text embedded in the image. A digital halfto proofer, such as the Kodak Approval or Polaro PolaProof® system, is able to simulate the halfton dots, resolution, screen angles, and dot gain, as w as the traditional analog proofs.

Through the use of modems and the Internet, *remote proofing* allows a printer to send digital files to an out-of-town client. Files can be viewed on a monitor (soft proofing) or output to a high-quality proofing device, similar to the one the printer or service bureau uses. The printer and the customer can efficiently transmit and receive electronic files that permits both soft proofing and hard proofing at the client's location. This proofing is software provider, printing company, and client to simultaneously view, mark up, and make notes displayed on their respective monitors. See **Figure 13-19.**

Note

Soft proofing should not be used for proofing color reproduction. Hard copies should be generated on a digital proofing device to provide a better color match. All devices (from the service bureau, publisher, and printer) should be calibrated for accurate and consistent results.

Forest, Fibers, Formation, and Finish

The paper in the photograph is nearing the end of its production. Its journey began, however, in a distant forest. Selected trees were harvested and sent to pulp mills, where the wood was reduced to individual fibers. After the fibers were refined, they were formed into a sheet. This formation was critical to the sheet's quality. Next, the sheet received a finish—perhaps textured or glossy. The photograph was taken at this point. This chapter takes the student on a more detailed study of paper—its manufacture, physical properties, classifications, and uses. The graphic designer who selects the paper, the planner who orders it, and the press operator who prints on it need a solid understanding of paper.

(Smurfit-Stone)

Chapter 18
Paper

Key Terms

absorbency
alkaline paper
antique finish
baronial envelope
blank
bleaching
bond paper
book paper
bristol
business paper
cancellation method
carbonless bond paper
category
chemical-mechanical pulp
chemical pulp
chipping
classification
coated back (CB)
coated front (CF)
coated front-and-back (CFB)
coated groundwood paper
coated offset paper
combination cut
cover paper
cut size
deckle edge
digester
dimensional stability
dull finish
eggshell

label paper
linting
long-grain paper
machine finish
machine finished
matte finish
mechanical pulp
mineral paper
news
offs
opac
opaq
oxyge
paper
paper c
Picking
pick resi
piling
postconsu
powdering
Preconsum
pulping
recycled pap
recycled pulp
refiner groun
refining stage
scumming
sheets per carton
ain paper
tree

owance
eight
ight
ering

fold strength
forming wire
fourdrinier machine
gloss finish
grain
groundwood pulping
hardwood tree
hickey
index bristol
internal sizing

...rmal-mechanical
pulp (TMP)
totally chlorine-free
(TCF) bleaching
twin-wire paper machine
uncoated offset paper
universal basic size
utility paper
vellum finish
washer
watermark
wet

Learning Objectives

When you have completed the reading and assigned activities related to this chapter, you will be able to do the following:

- Summarize the papermaking process and list the various stages involved.
- Identify paper requirements for sheetfed and webfed presses.
- Give examples of various paper properties and explain how they affect a paper's printability.
- List the paper classifications and indicate their print quality, and runnability.
- Explain basic size, substance weight, ream weight, and M weight (Mwt).
- Describe the various sizes and envelopes.
- Determine the

Summaries highlighting the material covered in each chapter are included. This feature serves as a learning aid.

Review Questions are included at the end of each chapter. These questions can be used to evaluate your comprehension of the chapter material.

Skill-Building Activities are included at the end of each chapter. These activities relate to the material covered in the chapter. They can be used to expand your knowledge, as well as to increase your math, communication, and leadership skills.

The **Appendices** include resources (names, addresses, and Web sites, if available), examples of typefaces, tables of metric and customary units of measurement, and examples of electronic Photoshop applications.

The **Index** is very detailed and serves as a valuable reference tool.

The **Glossary** summarizes the terminology presented in the textbook and contains over 1000 entries.

---

58   Section I   Introduction to Offset Lithographic Technology

Summary

Safety and health issues are the responsibility of every student or employee working in a printing facility. All printing firms must follow the safety guidelines OSHA has established. Knowledge of safety colors, machine lockout devices, and tagout devices is essential to making your work area a safe and enjoyable place to be. Following recommended procedures for storing and using chemicals, solvents, and flammable liquids helps prevent physical injury and fire.

Noise abatement is a factor in all printing facilities. All workers and students should wear the proper ear protection to prevent hearing damage or loss. Good housekeeping, preventive maintenance, and education are the key elements to a good fire protection plan. This includes the proper disposal of hazardous materials and the recycling of appropriate materials whenever possible.

Review Questions

Please do not write in this book. Write your answers on a separate sheet of paper.

1. What are the five OSHA-specified hazard areas?
2. Of what use are safety color codes?
3. What purpose does OSHA serve?
4. How can on-the-job physical injuries resulting from mechanical hazards be controlled?
5. What should an operator do before working on any electrical equipment?
6. What is the purpose of a lockout device?
7. How are lockout and tagout procedures applied?
8. Name the personal protection devices that could be used in three different situations.
9. List five guidelines for handling tools and materials properly.
10. Define the term *flash point.*
11. What information can be found on an MSDS?
12. What are the recommended procedures for storing and using toxic and flammable liquids?
13. How can noise be properly controlled in a printing facility?
14. What is the maximum allowable dBA exposure limit for an eight-hour day?
15. List five ways fires can be prevented and controlled in the printing industry.

16. List the four color, letter, and shape designations used to identify the types of material on which fire extinguishers can be used.
17. Why is it dangerous to use water on an electrical fire?
18. List three guidelines for safely operating computer equipment.
19. What is meant by the statement "Safety is your responsibility"?

Skill-Building Activities

1. Design a safety inspection form suitable for the lab in which you are working. Conduct a safety inspection using the form. Prepare a written or oral report.
2. Invite a local fire department official to discuss fire drill procedures and fire prevention. Ask the official to demonstrate the proper use of fire extinguishers in the graphic arts lab.
3. Invite the school nurse or another health official to demonstrate first aid procedures for each kind of accident that might occur in a printing facility (electrical shock, cuts, poisoning, burns, and chemical spills).
4. As a class activity, design a bulletin board or other type of display with a "Safety in the Printing Industry" theme. Sources for visual aid materials include OSHA, the local labor department, the school health office, and local printing plant safety representatives.
5. Ask the school nurse or another health official to assist the class in assembling a first aid kit for the lab. Be sure all required items are obtained and in good condition. Place the first aid kit in a prominent location in the graphic arts lab.

Appendix B
Typefaces

There are five classifications of typefaces, and within each classification, there are both obvious and subtle differences that make each style unique. Several typefaces are presented here, grouped by classification. First, look for the one or more characteristics that make each typeface distinct. Why is Bauer Bodoni a modern serif typeface, but Caslon 540 and Cheltenham are old-style serif typefaces? What differences distinguish Helvetica from Swiss 721? As you study these type designs, refer to the components identified below for features to compare.

Ascender line
Uppercase, or capital, character
Lowercase characters
Waistline
Baseline
Descender

Closed counter

...ng typefaces, using the correct terminology ensures effective communication.

Glossary

material by ...
...stic of being ...
...n in which the ...the paper were a ...
...folds in which ...
...arity in which ...white, gray, an...
...82
...76

adjacent: bordering. (16)
alcohol dampening system: a dampening system that uses alcohol in the fountain solution. (20)
alkaline paper: paper that has a pH above 7. (18)
American-British system: a system of print measurement used throughout North America and Great Britain. (3)
American Standard Code for Information Interchange (ASCII): an ind... representing text (let... and sets of ...

...d code
...tion,
...attributes
...tone

...nting press and ...g from the side or ...
antifoaming agent: a silicone-based fluid or emulsion added to a fountain solution to reduce the tendency of the solution to foam or bubble. (19)

...g the ...ening lacquer to ...bility). (17)

...at a 45 ...the former folder. (23)

Index

accordion fold, 648–649
achromatic vision, 364–365
acid, 476–477
    conductivity, 477
actinic light, 252–253
adaptation, 363–364
additive color system, 352–353
additive plates, 392–393
    processing, 405–406
additives, 462–463
adhering page elements, 186–187
adjacent, 364–365
adjusting image, 588
administrative positions, 686–687
air and vacuum control, 571
airborne hazards, 48
alcohol dampening, 526–527
    Dahlgren units, 526
    Varn Kompac units, 526–527
    alcohol solutions, 531–533
    alcohol-free operations, 532
alkaline paper, 444–445
    alternatives, 532
American-British system, 63
American Standard Code for Information Interchange (ASCII), 171
AM screening, 238–239

...s stacker, 573–575

A Part of the Digital World

Anyone can spend money on a magazine, but it is even better to be among those people who earn money from the magazine—people who contributed to its production. Young people who belong to the Digital Generation are well suited to the printing and publishing industries. Computers are used to input both words and photographic images and integrate them into beautiful documents, such as magazines, posters, brochures, and books.

Computer networks allow a printing company to receive digital files from clients across the nation. Once received, these images can be digitally manipulated, and a digital proof can be sent to the client for approval. Plates for the press shown here can be digitally imaged.

Even the press itself can be operated from a computer console. The electronic device in the upper right of the photograph supplies data to the computer to maintain production quality.

Management uses computers to schedule the various departments and track production. A walk through a modern printing facility will reveal computer monitors in every department, but computers are nothing more than tools. Computers need people to tell them what to do, and that is how this book enters the picture. As part of a graphic communications curriculum, this book can help prepare students for a rewarding career in the digital world of printing and publishing.

(Koenig & Bauer)

Chapter 1
The Printing Industry

Key Terms

commercial printing
direct lithography
electronic prepress
flatbed press
flexography
gravure
in-plant printing
letterpress
nonimpact printing
offset lithography

packaging
platen press
prepress service bureau
printing
production house
publishing industry
quick printing
rotary press
screen printing
substrate

Learning Objectives

When you have completed the reading and assigned activities related to this chapter, you will be able to do the following:

◆ Describe why the printing industry is considered to be a strong industry.

◆ Identify several types of business enterprises that make up the printing industry.

◆ Define the six basic printing processes.

◆ Explain the principle of offset lithography.

◆ List the basic steps in the offset lithography printing process.

◆ Discuss the primary difference between direct and indirect lithography.

◆ Summarize how photography influenced the development of offset lithography.

◆ Name typical products manufactured with the offset lithography process.

The technical definition of *printing* is the production of multiple copies of images and words to transfer an impression onto paper, plastic, metal, glass, or cloth. A more complete view of printing lies with an awareness of the marvelous ways that the marriage of information and images enhances our everyday lives. Magazines, books, CD covers, food packaging, maps, posters, and electronic circuit boards are a small sampling of the diverse products on which many people have come to rely.

We live in a world defined by high technology. Scientists explore space and announce breakthroughs in medicine, engineers devise methods of creating structures undreamed of just one generation earlier, and the Internet allows people to access information instantly from around the world. None of these achievements could have come about, however, without printing—the world's first means of mass communication.

How important is printing? At the end of the second millennium, panels of experts from many fields were charged with ranking the most influential people of the last one thousand years. Included in the top ten were famous greats such as Galileo, Sir Isaac Newton, William Shakespeare, Charles Darwin, Karl Marx, Copernicus, and Sigmund Freud, but the number one spot consistently went to Johannes Gutenberg, who made all other modern-day fields of endeavor possible through the invention of movable type and, therefore, printing.

Since Gutenberg's first press was invented around 1450, the printing industry has evolved technologically to keep pace with society's demands to know more and know it sooner, to the point that the printing and publishing industries' functions are nearly all digital. Images can be scanned in Georgia, digitally transmitted to be enhanced and merged with text in Quebec, and digitally transmitted to Arizona for platemaking and printing for a client in New York. Students who are very comfortable with a computer mouse in their hand will be right at home in today's printing industry.

Many people's image of the printing industry is limited to what goes on in the pressroom—putting ink on paper. Actually, printed products begin with an idea from an author, designer, or anyone with a need to communicate visually, before entering numerous production phases. See **Figure 1-1.** Once the idea has emerged, it will move through production stages in which a wide range of both professional and technical people are required to bring about the near-magic process of modern-day printing. Several of these production stages are introduced in this chapter

Figure 1-1. Printed products often begin with the customer's explanation to the graphic designer of what the design is intended to communicate. Copy is written, images are created, and the design takes form. After the customer approves the design, production begins.

and will be covered in more detail later in the textbook. In addition, all the dominant methods of printing in use today are described briefly in this chapter.

The Purpose of the Printing Industry

The primary purpose of the printing industry is to create and manufacture products that communicate visually. See **Figure 1-2.** Most businesses would be unable to function without some form of graphic communications because everyone is a consumer of printed products. We are consumers of printed products when we purchase magazines, buy food wrapped in printed containers, glance at billboards, read the instruments on our automobiles' dashboards, spot decorative T-shirts, or even read this textbook.

The printing industry is constantly developing higher-quality and more efficient ways to meet the demands of our growing population. This industry is one of the largest manufacturing organizations in the world. The printing industry's sales income and number of employees rank it as one of the largest industries in the United States.

There are more than 38,000 printing establishments in the United States. This figure represents the largest number of American firms engaged in any one type of manufacturing process. These establishments range in size from fewer than 20 employees to well over 500, and they collectively employ more than 1 million people.

Figure 1-2. The printing industry creates and manufactures a huge range of products that communicate visually. Examples include hang tags, books, CD covers, candy wrappers, ink pens, table tents, labels, promotional folders, magazines, plastic sample containers, postage stamps, coffee cups, and plastic name tags.

Printing is a strong industry. Nearly every year, more products are manufactured than in the previous year. As a result, present and future employment opportunities are excellent. In fact, the most often cited challenge facing printing companies is finding qualified employees. Chapter 27 discusses career opportunities in the printing industry.

Divisions of the Printing Industry

The product diversity of the printing industry is so enormous that the industry is often referred to as the *printing, publishing, and packaging industry.* Also, the industry encompasses a wide range of businesses, including everything from the actual printers to equipment manufacturers, sales and service groups, suppliers of materials, and specialized production facilities. See **Figure 1-3.** Careers exist in these areas as well, so each of these segments of the industry will be described briefly.

Commercial printing involves printing a large variety of products. General commercial printing companies do not specialize in a single product. These

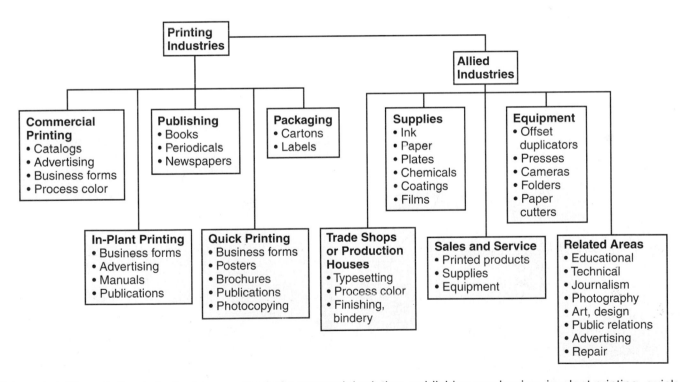

Figure 1-3. The printing industry is composed of commercial printing, publishing, packaging, in-plant printing, quick printing, and allied industries. Good careers can be found in all these sectors.

printing: the production of multiple copies of images and words with the use of another surface to transfer an impression to a substrate.

commercial printing: an important segment of the graphic communications industry, encompassing all sizes and types of printing operations, ranging from small local shops with one or two employees to large companies with several plant locations and hundreds or thousands of employees. This industry segment is dominated by one printing process, offset lithography.

companies serve their customers by manufacturing many different products, such as catalogs, advertisements, business forms, and posters. Other commercial printing companies might limit their range of products; for example, they might not print business cards or forms.

The *publishing industry* is composed of thousands of companies that produce textbooks, newspapers, magazines, and many other printed products. Many companies specialize in the production and marketing of books. Most publishers do not own their own printing facility, so they usually contract with printing companies that specialize in books or magazines.

Packaging refers to labels, boxes, tags, juice cartons, wrappers, plastic bags, and other containers. See **Figure 1-4.** Companies that specialize in packaging printing produce the hundreds of different containers we use every day. The package items are used to contain, preserve, protect, identify, and decorate the products or give instructions for use.

One of the seldom-seen areas of printing is in-plant printing. This area saw tremendous growth in the 1970s and 1980s. *In-plant printing* is defined as any printing operation that is owned by and serves the needs of a single company or corporation. For example, an insurance company, a large hospital, a governmental agency, or a university might have its own printing facility. These operations typically produce in-house business forms, time cards, booklets, instruction manuals for products they manufacture, and other business-related materials. Printed materials that cannot be produced internally are printed at commercial facilities.

One of the fastest-growing areas in the printing industry is *quick printing*. See **Figure 1-5.** Quick printing shops are usually located in high-traffic areas; often depend on walk-in business; and are limited to small offset presses (called *offset duplicators*), photocopiers (also called *xerography*), and digital imaging systems. Quick printers generally specialize in comparatively simple, short-run jobs; however, rapid advancements in computer technology and imaging systems have expanded their capabilities. Pressruns can be as small as one hundred or as large as several thousand.

Every type of printing facility requires supplies, such as paper, ink, printing plates, chemicals, and film, on a daily basis. Printers generally order supplies from firms specializing in these products. Supplies account for over one-half of the production cost for most printed products. Printers are especially careful when selecting and using printing supplies because the supplies are not only expensive, but also are critical to the quality of the printed product. Therefore, suppliers need knowledgeable and articulate people to represent them and service the printing companies that are their customers.

Equipment makes up a large and important investment for every type of printing facility. Presses, computers (hardware and software), scanners, imaging devices, folders, and paper cutters are necessary and expensive pieces of equipment. Because printers must

Figure 1-4. Examples of printed packaging products include box wraps; juice containers; cardboard; metal soda pop cans; paper, plastic, and foil candy wrappers; batteries; metal containers; labels for plastic and glass bottles; seed packets; and corrugated cardboard.

Figure 1-5. Quick printing, one of the most visible sectors of the printing industry, relies heavily on walk-in business. (Atco Printing)

consider the purchase of new or used equipment carefully, equipment manufacturers and dealers must have technically savvy and personable representatives.

A printing firm that is not equipped to do a particular phase of the printing process relies on an outside source called a ***production house*** or ***prepress service bureau***. Once referred to as *trade shops*, these firms specialize in work such as graphic design, process color separations, platemaking, specialized presswork (for example, printing on balloons), and finishing operations (embossing or hot-foil stamping, for instance). The printing firm subcontracts services from a production house and adds a percentage of markup to the job when billing the customer.

Several related areas of the printing industry contribute services that are essential to the printing process. Artists, graphic designers, and photographers provide creative services in the form of visual ideas and images. See **Figure 1-6.** Authors, editors, and journalists prepare copy. Educators prepare people for careers in the industry. Engineers, technicians, and scientists plan and produce new processes, equipment, and materials.

Major Printing Processes

The six major printing processes commonly used today are letterpress, gravure, screen printing, flexography, nonimpact printing, and offset lithography. You might wonder why there are so many methods of printing, and the answer lies with the wide range of situations printers face. Each of these printing processes is well designed for a certain type of *substrate* (the surface receiving the ink), the size or shape of the object to be printed, the length of the run, or the client's budget. Although this book is concerned primarily with ***offset lithography***, the other major printing processes are explained to provide an understanding of the industry at large and the major role of offset lithography.

The printing processes are grouped according to the nature of the plates they use. All plates are comprised of image and nonimage areas. Image areas carry ink, and nonimage areas do not carry ink. Physical printing processes use plates in which the image and nonimage areas are physically different. For this reason, the image and nonimage areas must be different from one another in some crucial way. For example, the image areas might be chemically different from or physically higher or lower than the nonimage areas.

Physical Printing Processes

Two physical printing processes use plates with image areas that are physically higher than the nonimage areas. The plates are called *relief plates*. These relief processes are letterpress and flexography.

Letterpress is the oldest of the printing processes. The ancient Chinese printed with letterpress by carving away the nonimage areas from a wooden block to create plates that were used like rubber stamps. Nearly 2000 years later, around 1455, letterpress printing made a huge leap forward when the German goldsmith Johannes Gutenberg invented movable metal type and made printing a much faster

Figure 1-6. Product photography is one of many professional areas related to the printing industry. (American ColorScans)

publishing industry: the sector of the printing industry specializing in producing books, booklets, catalogs, journals, and magazines.

packaging: the sector of the printing industry specializing in producing items that contain objects.

in-plant printing: a printing operation that is part of a company, a corporation, or an association.

quick printing: a printing establishment specializing in producing short-run jobs quickly on offset duplicators or digital presses.

production house: a business specializing in one area of printing production, such as prepress or finishing.

prepress service bureau: a business specializing in prepress operations such as page composition and image manipulation.

substrate: any surface to be printed to which ink will adhere. This surface is the material being printed on.

offset lithography: a printing method in which inked images are offset, or transferred, from one surface to another.

letterpress: the process of printing from a raised surface.

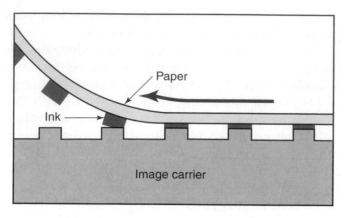

Figure 1-7. In letterpress printing, ink is applied to a raised, or relief, printing surface and then transferred to paper or a different substrate.

and, therefore, less expensive alternative to the handwritten books and documents Europe had depended on up to that point. See **Figure 1-7.** For the next 350 years, nearly all printing was done by letterpress, and until the 1960s, letterpress was used extensively.

In letterpress printing, pastelike ink is applied to the raised image areas of the plate. Paper is then pressed against the plate, transferring the ink to the paper. This pressure must be carefully regulated to avoid embossing the paper or other substrate or creating a slight amount of ink squeeze around the edges of type elements.

Several types of letterpress machines have evolved over the past 500 years. These machines include the platen press, flatbed press, and rotary press. See **Figure 1-8.**

- On a *platen press*, a flat plate is mounted on the flatbed of the press, and a platen (a flat metal surface that holds the sheet of paper) closes over the inked typeform. Pressure is then exerted to transfer the ink from the type to the paper.

- On a *flatbed press*, the typeform is placed on the flatbed of the press, which slides under the rotating impression cylinder carrying the paper.

- A *rotary press* uses a rotating plate cylinder, a rotating impression cylinder, and a web (continuous ribbon) of paper. The web receives the image as it passes between the two cylinders.

The use of letterpress printing began a sharp decline in use around 1960, primarily because it requires a great deal of makeready time that can be very costly. Letterpress printing is now mostly limited to specialty work, such as fine art prints and posters. In fact, letterpress machines seldom carry ink at all and are used mainly in finishing operations, such as embossing, scoring, and hot-foil stamping.

Flexography is another printing process that uses relief plates. The major difference between flexography and letterpress is that, in flexography, the plates are flexible and made of a rubber or photopolymer material. Flexography became popular in the 1950s because the flexible plate material can print on a variety of both absorbent and nonabsorbent substrates used in packaging, including metal foil and the clear polyethylene film used to make bread and paper towel wrappers, without snagging or tearing the material. Corrugated boxes are another large market for flexography because the raised image areas are flexible enough to avoid crushing the corrugated material. Flexography is also used to print candy wrappers, shopping bags, milk cartons, cereal boxes, gift wrap, wallpaper, and many other goods.

In the flexographic process, the plates are affixed to cylinders of various circumferences and use very fast-drying, liquid ink delivered by only two rollers. See **Figure 1-9.** Flexographic printing can usually be identified under a magnifying glass by a thin halo appearing around type and other images.

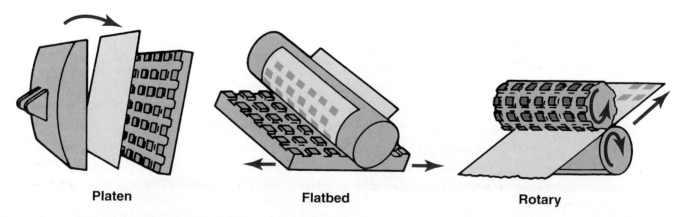

Platen   **Flatbed**   **Rotary**

Figure 1-8. Letterpress printing presses are made in a variety of designs, including platen, flatbed, and rotary. (Eastman Kodak Co.)

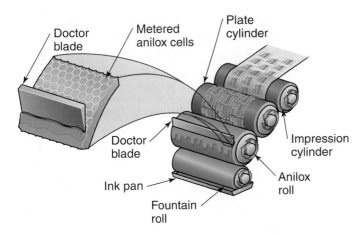

Figure 1-9. The inking system on a flexographic press uses an anilox roll engraved with tiny cells. (Agfa-Gevaert Inc.)

Gravure is an intaglio (in-TAL-yo) method of printing, which means the image areas are physically below the plate surface. Gravure plates are computer-engraved cylinders with tiny cells, or minute depressions, that accept and hold the liquid ink and deposit it onto the substrate. The plate cylinder is immersed in a fountain of liquid ink, and as the cylinder rotates, a doctor blade scrapes off the excess ink. See

Figure 1-10. The ink remaining in the cells is then transferred when it contacts the substrate.

Gravure printing is recognizable under a magnifying glass because all the type consists of dots, resulting in images that have a ragged or rough-textured outline. These dots result from the fact that ink is carried in individual cells. Gravure printing produces the richest four-color tonal range of all the printing processes, yet the high cost of preparing the plate cylinder usually requires the very long runs typical of publications, postage stamps, wallpaper, and packaging printing.

Screen printing is a process in which the image area is physically open, thereby allowing ink to flow through the image areas of a stencil and onto the substrate. This type of printing uses a stencil attached to a porous mesh to form the image carrier. The liquid ink is forced through this mesh and the stencil openings onto the substrate surface below with a squeegee. See **Figure 1-11.** Screen printing is characterized by a thicker film transfer than other processes and is used to print on a wide range of substrates, such as paper, metal, plastic, glass, wood, cork, and laminates.

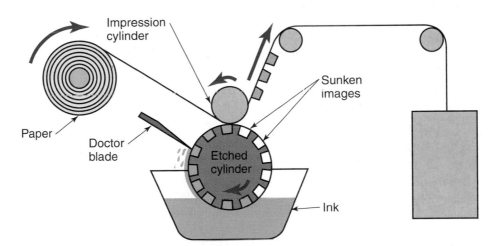

Figure 1-10. Gravure prints from sunken images on the printing surface of a copper cylinder. (National Association of Printing Ink Manufacturers, Inc.)

platen press: a type of letterpress in which both the form and the substrate remain flat during printing.

flatbed press: a lithographic press on which lithographic stone rests on a flat bed.

rotary press: a printing press that uses two cylinders rotating in the same direction.

flexography: a direct rotary printing method that uses flexible relief image plates of rubber or photopolymer material and relatively thin-bodied, resin-solvent or water-based inks.

gravure: a printing process that uses engraved cylinders or cylinder-mounted plates to carry the image.

screen printing: a printing process that uses a squeegee to force ink through a porous fabric covered by a stencil that blocks the nonimage areas.

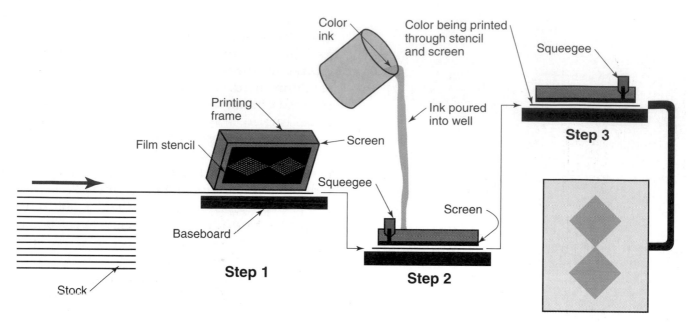

Figure 1-11. Screen printing uses a stencil attached to a porous mesh screen to form the image carrier. Ink is forced through the stencil image area and mesh screen, onto the substrate surface. (National Association of Printing Ink Manufacturers, Inc.)

Although screen printing makes up a small percentage of the printing processes in use today, it is very important to the industry because of its diverse applications. Almost any substrate, in almost any shape or size, can be printed on with the screen method. Screen printing is commonly used today in billboard and poster printing, as well as with substrates that are not flat, such as automobile dashboards, three-ring binder covers, T-shirts, and cylindrical objects (for example, mascara tubes).

Nonimpact Printing

The digital world has introduced methods of printing directly from electronic files without the need to create a physical plate. Examples of *nonimpact printing* are toner-based photocopiers and thermal, inkjet, and laser printers. These technologies bring two major advantages: production time is greatly reduced, and the image can be changed while the job is being printed. At this point, nonimpact-printing methods are most appropriate for short-run jobs, but evolving technology continues to expand their capabilities.

Chemical Printing Processes

Although the printing processes discussed to this point are very different from one another, they share the characteristic that the image and nonimage areas of their plates are physically different from one another. Offset lithography, in contrast, is a chemical printing process because the image and nonimage areas of a lithographic plate are different in their chemical composition. The result is that these areas react very differently from one another when they are placed in contact with water and then ink.

There are many types of printing processes, but offset lithography is the most widely used in the printing industry. U.S. government statistics indicate that offset lithography is used to produce over 70% of commercial and publication printing in the United States (excluding packaging, textiles, and specialty products such as wallpaper). Unlike physical processes, offset lithography uses a printing plate with a flat surface. Because of chemical differences, ink adheres only to the image areas of the plate. Offset lithography is recognizable under a magnifying glass by sharp, clean type images and exceptional color and black-and-white halftone reproduction capabilities. The offset lithography printing process is also known as *photo-offset lithography, offset, photo-offset,* and *lithography.* For consistency, the term *offset lithography* is used throughout this book.

Lithographic principles

Offset lithography is also called *planography* because the printing areas are on the same plane as the surface of the printing plate. See **Figure 1-12.** Offset lithography is based on the principle that water and grease do not readily mix. During printing, the image areas accept only the lithographic ink, and the nonimage areas accept only water.

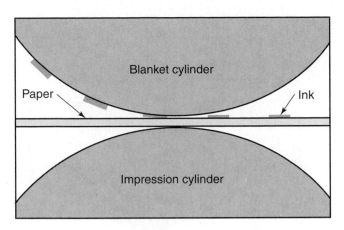

Figure 1-12. As the paper passes through the cylinders on an offset press or duplicator, the image is offset to the paper's surface. (A.B.Dick Co.)

Offset printing plates are imaged through various photographic, electronic, and chemical processes. These imaging processes make the image area of the plate receptive to the lithographic ink and the nonimage area receptive only to water. As the printing plate rotates on the press, the nonimage area receives water (fountain solution) from the press dampening system. The plate also receives ink from the ink fountain. Under proper conditions, the ink coats only the image areas of the plate.

Offset lithography is also unique among the printing processes because the image on the plate is not printed directly onto the substrate. Instead, the image is transferred from the plate on the plate cylinder to a rubber blanket on another cylinder,

called the *blanket cylinder*. The rubber blanket then transfers, or offsets, the image to the paper by gentle pressure from another cylinder, called the *impression cylinder*. This process is shown in **Figure 1-13**.

Lithography is well suited to print on the comparatively rough surface of newsprint and other uncoated paper because this process uses a rubber blanket, instead of a rigid metal plate, to transfer ink to the substrate. The blanket is able to compress and make a more uniform contact with the tiny valleys of the paper's surface. Lithographic printing is also compatible with printing on metal, as well as all types of paper and the cardboard used for cereal boxes. Most magazines, newspapers, books, calendars, postcards, maps, and catalogs and a large percentage of packaging are printed with offset lithography.

Waterless lithography

Traditionally, offset lithography uses a dampening system to wet the printing plate. There is a comparatively new method of offset lithography, however, that does not use dampening solution. This method is called *waterless offset printing*, and it will be described in detail later in the book.

The History of Offset Lithography

The printing process known as *offset lithography* dates back over 200 years. Alois Senefelder of Munich, Germany invented lithography in 1796. Senefelder's invention was based on the principle that oil or grease and water do not readily mix.

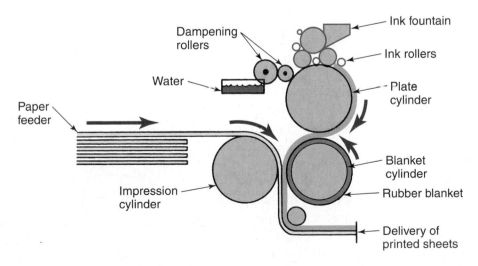

Figure 1-13. In offset printing, the image on the plate is transferred to the rubber blanket on the blanket cylinder. The rubber blanket then transfers, or offsets, the image to the paper.

nonimpact printing: a method of printing in which the substrate is never in contact with the plate.

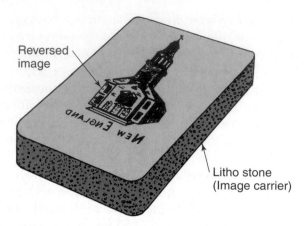

Figure 1-14. Alois Senefelder drew type and other designs with a greasy, crayonlike liquid on Bavarian limestone. This process became known as *lithography*.

Figure 1-15. Words lettered in reverse on lithographic stones are readable on the printed sheets.

Using a slab of porous limestone as a plate, Senefelder sketched a design with a greasy, crayonlike material, which adhered to the stone. See **Figure 1-14.** The entire surface of the stone was then wet with a rag containing a mixture of water and gum arabic. Only the blank (nonimage) areas accepted this solution, while the greasy image areas repelled it. A grease-based ink was then applied to the entire plate surface with a roller. Because grease and water do not mix, the ink did not transfer to the moist blank areas. When a sheet of paper was pressed against the surface of the stone, a print of the design was made.

The lithographic stone Senefelder used was a slab of Bavarian limestone. He used this stone because it had qualities that were especially good for lithographic printing. The stone absorbed grease readily, was porous enough to hold moisture, and provided a smooth printing surface. Even today, artists make lithographic prints by painting Bavarian limestone with a liquid similar to what Senefelder used and then wetting and inking the stone before pressing a sheet of paper against the stone's surface.

Senefelder had to draw his letters on the stone backward. The letters were then readable on the printed sheets. See **Figure 1-15.** Later, a new method was tried. The artist first drew the image onto a thin sheet of paper, and the image was pressed against and transferred to the stone. The image could then be printed from the stone. This transfer method, however, did not always impart a clear image to the stone. Thus, the most popular method was drawing the image directly onto the stone.

As might be expected, lithographic stone is heavy and bulky. Before being used, the stones have to be carefully cut and processed. The top of the stone has to be very smooth and level. The bottom of the stone also has to be smooth and parallel to the top. The stone surface has to be prepared by being grained with sand and then with pumice and an emery stone.

The First Lithographic Presses

The first lithographic press was known as a *flatbed press* because the lithographic stone rested on a flat bed in the press. See **Figure 1-16.** The press could produce about one thousand impressions a day. Later, automatic dampening and inking rollers were made for the presses. A cylinder for carrying the paper also was added. The lithographic stone was placed on the flatbed of the press. This bed moved back and forth under the dampening and inking rollers and then

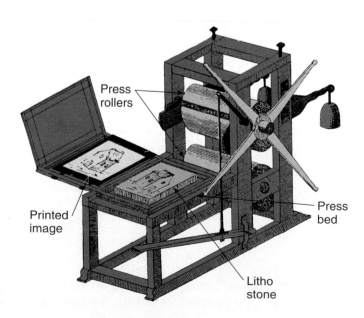

Figure 1-16. The first lithographic press was known as a flatbed press because the lithographic stone rested on a flat bed in the press.

under the cylinder carrying the paper. The cylinder turned at the same speed as the bed moved and pressed the paper firmly against the stone to make the impression. These presses were the forerunners of the high-speed offset presses used today. Black-and-white lithographic printing processes were too slow and expensive to compete with the well-established letter-press printing process. Lithography became more popular, however, with the invention of aluminum and zinc printing plates, which could absorb grease and water just like the lithographic stone and, because they were light and flexible, could also easily be wrapped around a printing press cylinder.

The rotary press resulted from experiments with lightweight metal plates and consists of two cylinders rotating in the same direction. See **Figure 1-17.** One cylinder holds the plate, and the other holds the paper. On a rotary press, a printer can produce about one thousand impressions per hour, instead of the one thousand impressions per day that can be produced on the flatbed press.

Once the rotary press became more common, lithography was well on its way to becoming a significant method of printing, but the word *offset* had not yet been introduced. It is important to remember that nearly all the lithographic printing up to this time had been done by ***direct lithography***, which is to say that the image was transferred directly from the stone or metal plate to the paper. The lone exception was an indirect, or offset, lithographic printing process that had been used to print on tin.

In 1903, over 100 years after Senefelder's invention of lithography, a New Jersey lithographer named Ira Rubel developed an offset press designed for indirect lithography. See **Figure 1-18.** On Rubel's new press design, the inked plate transferred the image to a rubber-covered cylinder, called the *blanket cylinder,* which then transferred the image to the paper. Oddly enough, the image quality actually improved when the plate did not print to the paper directly. Also, adding an intermediate blanket cylinder meant images could be right reading on the plate, eliminating the nuisance of having to create them backward on the plate in order for them to appear right reading on the paper. The creation of the blanket cylinder added the word *offset* to lithography because the image was offset to another cylinder, rather than printed directly to the paper.

The Invention of Photography

In 1839, the French painter Louis Jacques Mandé Daguerre developed a process for producing permanent photographic images. George Eastman (the founder of Eastman Kodak Company), however, first made photography practical. In the late 1800s, he standardized camera sizes and produced roll film to fit the cameras. See **Figure 1-19.**

Printing type in black ink on white paper is a simple proposition because letters consist entirely of black. On the plate, these letters are simply made image areas, so they pick up black ink and transfer the ink to the paper. Printing photographs, however, is quite different because they consist of not only black and white, but also the several dozen tones of gray in between. The question then becomes how to print tones of gray using only black ink. To appreciate the early printers' dilemma, try to create gray with only a black marker.

The ability to print photographs was made possible in 1886 with the invention of the halftone screen, which converts photographs into a format that allows them to be printed. The first halftone screen was made from two sheets of glass containing numerous equally spaced, parallel, scribed (scratched) lines. The negatives were cemented together with their lines at right angles.

When the original photograph is rephotographed through the glass screen, the image is broken into hundreds of tiny dots in different sizes, called *halftone dots.* On the printing press, each halftone dot prints in black, but the combinations of tiny black dots and tiny white areas between them merge to create the illusion of gray to the naked eye. An area dominated by large black

Figure 1-17. A rotary lithographic press passes the sheet between two revolving cylinders—a plate cylinder and an impression cylinder. (Gutenberg Museum, Mainz)

direct lithography: a lithographic printing process in which the printed impressions are made on the paper directly from the stone, metal stone, or plate.

Figure 1-18. Ira Rubel is shown standing beside the offset press he designed for indirect lithography. (Smithsonian Institute)

Figure 1-19. In the late 1800s, George Eastman standardized camera sizes and produced roll film for home cameras. (Eastman Kodak Co.)

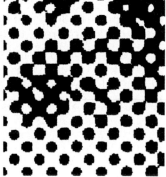

Figure 1-20. A halftone is made up of many small dots of varying sizes, which print in a solid color, giving the illusion of light, medium, and dark areas in the picture. (T. Lewis)

Note

Chapter 11 contains detailed information on halftone photography.

dots appears as dark gray, and an area dominated by small black dots appears as light gray. See **Figure 1-20.** Today, both black-and-white and color photographs are converted into halftone dots for reproduction in books, magazines, and other printed materials. The halftone screen added to the versatility of offset lithography (and the other printing processes), making it possible to reproduce both type and photographs.

Offset Duplicators

During World War II, rapid movements of troops required the distribution of maps showing the current placement of troops. The result of this need for fast reproduction of simple images brought about the technology of offset duplicators, which made the quick printing segment of the industry, mentioned earlier in the chapter, possible. See **Figure 1-21.** These small offset presses have been greatly improved over the years to keep pace with increasing customer demands for more sophisticated design and better quality in quick printing.

With improvements in photographic processes and offset printing plate materials, more sophisticated offset press designs followed. Multicolor sheetfed offset presses (for individual pieces of paper) and web offset presses (for a large roll of paper) were designed. See **Figure 1-22** and **Figure 1-23.** Most printers, both small and large, print with offset lithography.

Figure 1-22. Commercial offset printers commonly use modern, high-speed sheetfed offset presses. (Heidelberg, Inc.)

Figure 1-21. Duplicators, such as the one illustrated here, are small offset presses used by many quick printers and in-plant operations. (Buckeye Printing and Mailing Solutions)

Figure 1-23. Magazines and catalogs are usually printed on presses large enough to fill a room. (Heidelberg, Inc.)

Electronic Systems

Up to this point, discussion has revolved around the many methods of putting ink on paper or some other substrate. The preparation of the images to be printed, however, must precede the presswork. In all the printing processes today, these preliminary stages, which are collectively called *prepress*, depend on computer technology.

Offset lithography technology continues to expand rapidly, due largely to advances in computer technology and automated production systems. Digital systems have penetrated every stage of the printing process—from the author's manuscript preparation to platemaking and the actual running of the press. Digital technology has become so dominant in prepress operations that the steps prior to presswork are referred to as ***electronic prepress***. Electronic design and imaging systems increase output and decrease the time and expense of designing.

Electronic prepress includes several steps, or stages: typesetting, digital imaging, image assembly, platemaking, and proofing. All can be performed digitally. Typesetting can be performed with word processing software to input and format copy (also known as *text*). In addition to the ability to use the computer's keyboard to input text, you can also use scanners and optical character recognition (OCR) software to input text from existing hard copy.

After the text has been generated, the next stage—known as *digital imaging*—creates, manipulates, and arranges the photographs and other graphic elements to create the final product. Computer graphic software allows artwork to be created digitally and photographs to be altered. Desktop publishing software is used to integrate text, art, and photographs. The digital work flow in prepress allows great flexibility for making changes—even minutes before a pressrun.

Although digital prepress has greatly reduced the use of film to capture and transfer images, some production houses and printers still use computer-equipped process camera systems. Though film is still used, it is increasingly imaged electronically, instead of with cameras. Therefore, most of the work associated with image assembly is now done electronically, using imposition software. For example, the pages of a 16-page booklet can be generated, imaged, arranged in proper position, and output as a single piece of film from which the plate can be exposed—all electronically.

Sending digital data from the computer directly to a plate-imaging device is called *computer-to-plate (CTP) technology*, or *direct-to-plate (DTP) technology*.

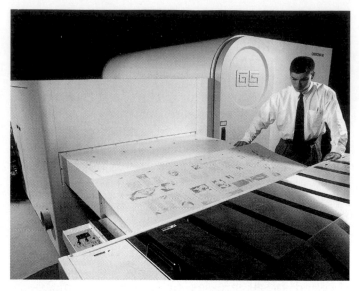

Figure 1-24. CTP systems bypass film entirely by imaging the plate directly. (Gerber Systems Corp.)

See **Figure 1-24.** By imaging directly to the plate, these computer systems eliminate the need for film. The greatest advantages of CTP technology include the reduction of makeready time; the elimination of most, if not all, chemical processing; and the ability to easily make last-minute changes.

Proofs can be generated directly from film (conventionally), run off on a proof press, or made directly from digital files. The customer's needs determine what type of proof will be acceptable. There are several methods for making proofs from both film and digital data. Some proofs are capable of highly accurate predictions of how the job will look when it comes off the press.

Many digital proofing systems can compensate for such factors as ink hues, color contamination, color changes during platemaking and the pressrun, and the paper's color and ink absorption. Some systems can also simulate dot patterns and the dot gain expected on final output. See **Figure 1-25.**

Computerized Production Control

Nearly every aspect of a modern printing facility is computer controlled or assisted. Computerized systems used to monitor ink and paper consumption and waste during the pressrun improve efficiency. Electronic scanners are installed on offset presses to evaluate and adjust ink coverage and color reproduction. These systems are fully computerized and are especially useful in monitoring complex functions on high-speed offset presses.

Electronic job tickets can be used to follow the work from inception to delivery. The data compiled

Figure 1-25. Digital proofs can closely match the colors of the press sheet because the proofs are imaged from the same digital data that will later image the plates.

from the prepress production phases, the pressrun, and the finishing end can be used to evaluate the productivity level of the facility. This data can also be used to predict a customer's needs in the future.

Quality control software packages are used to monitor and control the color and appearance of printed sheets. These systems use optical sensors, computer hardware and software, and various types of electronic equipment and controls. Computerized systems provide fast, accurate color measurement data for purposes of quality control.

Computer software allows the operator of postpress (or finishing) equipment to input data and program the machines to cost-effectively cut and fold each particular job. Robotic technology can also be used in conjunction with computerized cutters and folders to load and unload paper. Young people who have an interest in an ultrahigh-tech area are well suited for the printing industry.

To Learn More about the Industry

Magazines, catalogs, and Web sites are more than just good sources of information about the printing industry. These sources provide an excellent method of becoming acquainted with the whole enterprise. You can find many industry-related magazines and catalogs at your school or community library. If you want to contact a particular magazine, look for the address in the masthead or check to see if there is a Web site on the Internet. A list of useful resources is given in Appendix A. Skilled personnel are needed at every stage of the printing process to perform high-quality color printing on fast precision presses.

Summary

Printing is the production of multiple copies of images and words with the use of another surface to transfer an impression to a substrate. This production can be used to place inked images, such as the words on this page, onto a substrate, such as paper, plastic, metal, glass, or cloth. Initially, Gutenberg's invention of the printing press allowed the reproduction and circulation of written material on a level that far exceeded what the hands of the medieval scribes could achieve. Today, technological advances and the development of various printing processes allow production of everything from textbooks to greeting cards on an extremely large scale. The printing industry encompasses a wide range of operations, including everything from printing to equipment manufacturers, suppliers of materials, and specialized production houses.

Digital technology has greatly enhanced the capabilities and efficiency of the three stages of printing production: prepress (imaging), press, and postpress (finishing). To survive in this highly competitive environment, printing companies need workers with a broad range of skills and knowledge. Specifically, companies need workers who can use computer software and other equipment, analyze problems, make decisions, and have a solid understanding of the entire production process.

A well-rounded education is essential for a career in the printing industry. The digital age requires workers to enter the printing industry with higher skill and knowledge levels than their predecessors had. Current workers must continually upgrade their skills to remain competitive in the job market.

electronic prepress: the steps prior to printing that use computers and digital technology.

Review Questions

Please do not write in this book. Write your answers on a separate sheet of paper.

1. Why is the printing industry considered to be a strong industry?

2. A printing operation that is owned by and serves the needs of a single company or corporation is referred to as a(n) _____ printing facility.

3. List at least ten segments making up the printing, publishing, and packaging industry.

4. There are five major printing processes (other than nonimpact) in the printing industry. List and briefly describe each.

5. In relief and intaglio methods of printing, the image and nonimage areas of the plate are _____ different from one another.

6. Offset lithography is based on the principle that _____ and _____ do not readily mix.

7. Most books and magazines are printed by the _____ printing process.
   A. gravure
   B. lithographic
   C. screen
   D. nonimpact

8. Identify three types of cylinders used on an offset press.

9. The process of stone lithography was invented by _____.

10. The original lithographic stones were made of _____.

11. Limestone accepts _____ easily.

12. The first lithographic presses were known as _____ presses.

13. A(n) _____ is made of two cylinders rotating in the same direction.

14. Ira Rubel developed a press designed for _____ printing.

15. What is the difference between direct lithography and indirect lithography?

16. Photography, used together with the _____ screen, added to the versatility of offset lithography.

17. The steps prior to printing (presswork) are now often referred to as _____.

Skill-Building Activities

1. Using your local or school library, write a one-page report describing the contributions Senefelder and Rubel made to offset lithography.

2. Visit a local offset lithography firm and observe the several kinds and sizes of offset presses. Ask printing technicians about the functions of the presses, the kind of work done, and sheet sizes. Prepare a short report on your findings.

3. In your school, home, or community, find samples of offset printing. Prepare a bulletin board display with the samples.

4. George Eastman (the founder of Eastman Kodak Company) first made photography practical. Prepare an outline of his experiences and adventures in the field of photography.

5. Research and prepare a visual example of the halftone screen process.

The operation of a Heidelberg digital offset press is explained to a printing student. (Ferris State University)

Safety Benefits Everyone

American business and industry once contained hazards that no longer even exist. Advances in technology and the 1971 establishment of the Occupational Safety and Health Administration (OSHA) eliminated these hazards. During the last 30 years, workplace-related injuries and illnesses have been reduced by 40%. For example, the clear guard shown in this photograph of a booklet stitcher helps to prevent operator injury. The guard is in place while the machine is running, and lifting the guard stops the machine.

Preventing workplace injuries benefits everyone. Employees enjoy a safe working environment. Management enjoys several advantages—increased production that is not interrupted by injury, reduced insurance costs, and the many benefits of having happy employees.

Just as everyone benefits from workplace safety, everyone must contribute to the effort. Management and employees must be aware of their roles in promoting safety. This chapter acquaints the student with many issues and practices involved in advancing safety and health in the workplace.

(Heidelberg, Inc.)

Chapter 2
Safety and Health

Key Terms

barrier guard
decibel (dBA)
dust collector
ergonomics
flash point
infrared (IR) light
ink mist
laser beam
lockout device
main disconnect (master)
   switch
material safety data sheet
   (MSDS)
mercury vapor lamp
nip point
Occupational Safety and
   Health Administration
   (OSHA)

personal protective
   equipment
pulsed xenon lamp
   (PXA)
respiratory protection
   device
safety color code
skin protection device
static eliminator
tagout device
ultraviolet (UV)
   radiation
volatile organic
   compound (VOC)

Learning Objectives

When you have completed the reading and
assigned activities related to this chapter, you will
be able to do the following:

- List and explain factors that make a safety and
  health program successful.

- Demonstrate safe work habits that help prevent
  on-the-job physical injuries.

- Identify and explain the application of lockout
  and tagout devices.

- Select the proper personal protection devices
  for specific situations.

- Practice proper material and tool handling, as
  well as proper techniques for lifting.

- State the recommended procedures for storing
  and using toxic and flammable liquids.

- Describe proper noise control and means of
  preventing ear damage.

- Give examples of means for fire prevention
  and control.

- Discuss safe practices to be used when
  operating computer equipment.

- Explain ways in which printing facilities can
  minimize damage to the environment.

Safety and health are important considerations in the printing industry. This fact holds true for school graphic arts programs, training laboratories, small printing operations, and large printing firms. Many accidents are caused by carelessness and ignorance and can be prevented if all employees are well informed in preventive and predictive safety measures.

The wide variety of processes performed in a printing facility creates great potential for injury, illness, or death. It is vital for workers to know basic safety procedures. Most printing operations provide safety and health programs based on the five safety hazard areas specified by the *Occupational Safety and Health Administration (OSHA)*. The five OSHA-specified hazard areas are mechanical, chemical, noise, fire, and light. Each area is not exclusive, and there is often a great deal of overlap.

Planning a Safe Working Environment

Planning for safety starts with an organized safety and health program dedicated to accident prevention. This type of program can be used to recognize, evaluate, and control potential hazards in the workplace. An effective safety program begins with informed students and employees. Safety and health programs are often tailored to suit individual operations. The most effective programs include all five OSHA-specified areas and topics such as personal protection and first aid.

To ensure the success of the safety and health program, management leadership is essential. The person assigned responsibility for the safety and health of the facility must have the authority to enforce the program, and everyone in the establishment must be aware of the plan. A safe operation depends on all personnel being properly informed of potential hazards, accident prevention measures, and the proper first aid response.

Safety Tours

Students entering a graphic arts program and employees new to a printing facility should be given the opportunity to review all relevant safety documents and be given a safety tour of the facilities in which they are working. See **Figure 2-1**. The safety tour should include information indicating inherent dangers, such as presses, paper cutters, folders, stitchers, and chemical hazards. The locations and use of master switches, emergency stop buttons, fire extinguishers, fire alarms, and first aid kits should be stressed. In addition, items such as *safety color codes* should be emphasized and explained in detail.

Safety Color Codes

In an effort to make educational, training, and working facilities safer, safety color codes have been developed. See **Figure 2-2**. Safety color codes have been established to alert and inform students and workers to take precautionary action around potential hazards. With proper implementation, color codes help improve personal safety and minimize the possibility of injury during the operation and use of tools, equipment, and machinery.

Varying standards designate the safety colors and how they should be used for specific purposes. See **Figure 2-3**. There are many potential safety hazards in a printing facility or graphic arts lab. If you have any questions regarding the safety colors used in your facility, you should discuss their application with your supervisor or instructor.

Personal Conduct

Safety is the responsibility of every person. Students and employees should be properly trained in all safety procedures and regulations before beginning work. It is not uncommon for instructors or supervisors to administer written safety tests before allowing students or employees to begin working.

Unsafe conduct and work habits by workers or students should be reported and corrected immediately. The offender should be informed that this type of behavior could result in removal from the lab or dismissal from the job. Horseplay of any kind should never be allowed.

Safety Regulations

OSHA governs the safety and health of workers in the United States. Besides developing and enforcing job safety and health regulations, the agency also works to educate employers and employees. All types of businesses and industrial firms are required to comply with OSHA regulations or face severe penalties.

Although OSHA regulations apply to all types of businesses, many industry-specific regulations have been developed. The following guidelines apply to offset lithography operations, but they are just a brief summary of safety precautions that should be followed. These regulations, in their entirety, can be found at any OSHA office. Careful adherence to regulations, good housekeeping, and a healthy attitude toward safety can make the facility a safe and pleasant place to work.

Figure 2-1. Most safety guards and danger zones in the pressroom are painted with safety colors. These colors serve to warn workers of potential hazards.

Mechanical Hazards

Oftentimes, on–the–job physical injuries are the result of mechanical hazards. These hazards can be controlled. The following regulations should be followed:

- Machines must be properly guarded.
- Lockout and tagout devices must be used during maintenance.
- Workers must use *personal protective equipment*.
- Materials, tools, and equipment must be handled safely.

Machine guards

Safety in a printing facility requires awareness of the many types of potential hazards. The reciprocating, rotating, shearing, and pinch–pointing actions of the types of machinery used in the printing industry present many mechanical hazards. See **Figure 2-4.** Consequently, proper placement of machine guards is important for the operator's protection.

Occupational Safety and Health Administration (OSHA): the agency of the U.S. Department of Labor that promotes and enforces safe and healthful working conditions. This administration also educates employers and employees about industrial hazards.

safety color code: a color code established to alert and inform students and workers to take precautionary action around potential hazards.

personal protective equipment: various types of eye, ear, respiratory, and skin protection devices used to prevent physical injury.

Color	Indication	Applications
Safety Red	Danger or Stop	Identify hazards that can cause death or serious injury. Identify safety cans or containers of combustible or flammable materials (the name of contents should also be on the can or container). Mark stop buttons, stop bars, or electrical switches for the emergency stopping of machinery. Identify fire equipment or the area where fire equipment is located.
Safety Orange	Warning	Identify hazardous parts of machines/equipment. Mark hazardous machine parts that may cut, crush, or electrically shock and may cause serious injury or even death. Emphasize hazards such as open or removed guards and shields, exposed gears or belts, or any other unguarded moving parts. Identify exposed parts of pulleys, gear rollers, cutting devices, etc. Identify levers of machine tools which must not be moved while the machine is operating.
Safety Yellow	Warning	Mark physical hazards that can cause a person to stumble, trip, fall, or become caught in or under, or strike-against. Identify storage cabinets for flammable materials (cabinets should be clearly labeled "Flammable, Keep fire away"). Identify containers for explosives, corrosives, or unstable materials by painting them yellow or have a yellow band at least one-quarter the height of the container around the middle (contents should be painted on the container). Identify adjustable levers, knobs, or control wheels which may be adjusted while the machine is operating. Yellow lines should be painted on the floor to designate Equipment Operator Zones for operators of fixed-power equipment and Keep Clear Zones in front of fire and first-aid equipment and electrical panels, etc.
Safety Green	Safety	Show the location of first-aid kits and equipment, safety showers, and emergency exits.
Safety Blue	Safety information	Warn people not to start, use, or move equipment that is being serviced. Provide mandatory information for the wearing of protective clothing and/or equipment such as hard hats, goggles, gloves, etc.
Safety Purple	Radiation hazards	Used in areas where radioactive materials are stored, handled, or where an area has been contaminated with radioactive material.
Safety Gray	Work areas	May be used on floors or work areas around machines and for metal bench tops.
Safety Black or Safety White		Safety Black or Safety White or combination of the two indicates traffic and housekeeping areas. Safety White lines on the floor indicate aisles and stairways.
Fluorescent Colors and Other Reflective Materials	Danger spots in dark areas	Used for stripes on stair railings and risers to make them visible in the dark. Arrows that indicate the direction of exits and fire escapes. Marking electrical switch plates so they may be seen in the dark.
Piping Systems	Marked at point of use to indicate the materials carried by the pipe.*	Safety Red w/Safety White lettering on fire extinguisher materials. Safety Yellow w/Safety White lettering for flammables, explosives, chemically active substances, extreme temperatures, and pressure fluids (steam and hot water). Safety Green w/Safety White lettering on cold water pipes. Safety Blue w/Safety White lettering for compressed air or other inert gases at low pressure.

*All pipes should be identified by the appropriate colors. Rubber and flexible synthetic hoses and pipes should not be painted.

Figure 2-2. Many manufacturers and users of equipment follow the same color-coding standards. Many color-coding recommendations have also been incorporated into the OSHA standards.

Figure 2-3. Fluorescent paint can be used to help workers identify exits during power outages. (IDESCO Corp.)

Caution

Never use any piece of equipment unless you have demonstrated your ability to operate the machine safely to the instructor's or supervisor's satisfaction.

Machine guards protect the operator, as well as other workers in the facility. The guards serve to prevent flying fragments from cutting, smashing, or hitting parts of the human body. Guards also protect equipment from damage from foreign objects.

Machine guarding is necessary wherever hazardous machine parts are within reach of the operator. Guards should be in place over all points of operation. These points of operation include cylinders, shears, rollers, gears, clamps, drills, punches, fasteners, shafting, pulleys, cutters, flywheels, chains, and belts.

Most machines used in the printing industry are equipped with some type of guarding. See **Figure 2-5.** Equipment should not be used if guards are missing, broken, or out of adjustment. Likewise, guards should not be removed to perform an operation or running adjustments.

Reciprocating and rotating motions create hazards at the point of operation and the points where power or motion is being transmitted from one part to another. Bodily contact with any rotating part is dangerous and can lead to serious injury or even death. Loose clothing or hair can be drawn into the equipment and cause severe injury. Therefore, long hair should be tied back or worn under a cap, and no jewelry should be worn when operating equipment.

Specialized types of guarding are used on some machines. For instance, a common control device used on paper cutters requires both hands of the operator to be on the operating controls. See **Figure 2-6.** A paper cutter blade is very sharp, and all precautions should be taken to avoid injury when cutting stock or changing the blade. Movable or hinged **barrier guards** are often used to keep a person out of the operating area. If the guard is not in its proper position, power is cut off to the machine.

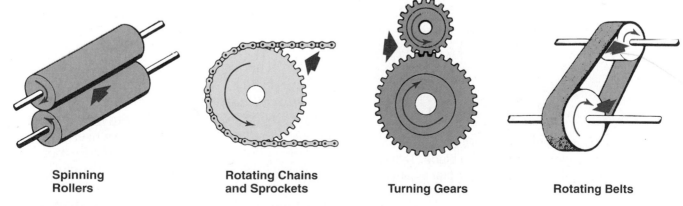

Spinning Rollers

Rotating Chains and Sprockets

Turning Gears

Rotating Belts

Figure 2-4. Mechanisms found in a printing facility can cause serious physical injury.

barrier guard: a plastic or metal safety barrier covering a point of operation on machinery.

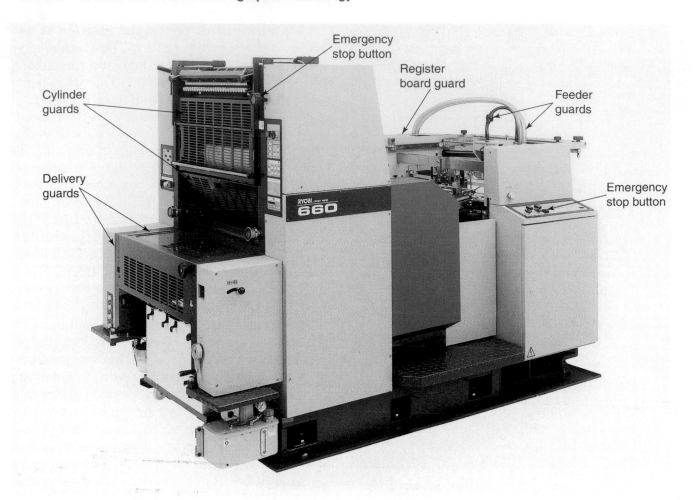

Figure 2-5. Safety guards should always be kept in place while the machine is operating.

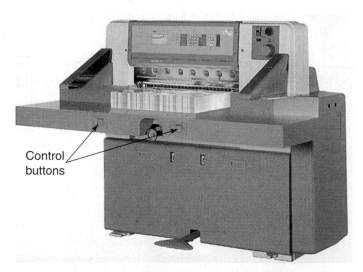

Figure 2-6. Both control buttons on this cutter must be pressed at the same time to operate the blade. This type of dual mechanism ensures that the operator's hands cannot be near the blade when cutting. (Heidelberg, Inc.)

Caution

When operating a power paper cutter, never bypass the safety device requiring both hands to be used to operate the blade. Turn the machine off. Use the proper safety procedures to correct any problems or malfunctions.

Electrical considerations

The school graphic arts lab or commercial printing facility should have an accessible *main disconnect (master) switch* that allows all power to machinery and small appliances to be turned off when the lab or facility is not in use. Emergency disconnect buttons or switches should be installed at every machine location. These allow anyone to turn off the power in case of emergency or malfunction. In the industry, these buttons are sometimes referred to as *panic buttons*.

Frayed and damaged electrical cords, plugs, and switches should be replaced. A local inspection agency should periodically inspect all cords, plugs, and switches. All electrical components must comply with existing electrical codes. Grounded (three–prong) plugs and outlets should be used throughout the facility.

Avoid locating electrical equipment near sinks or water pipes. Even a minor mishap in such an area could cause a severe shock or electrocution. Additional safety measures, such as the installation of ground-fault circuit interrupter (GFCI) outlets, should be taken.

Lockout and tagout devices should be used whenever a piece of equipment is being serviced. *Lockout devices* use a key or combination lock to hold an energy–isolating device (such as a manually operated circuit breaker) in the off position to prevent the machine from energizing. A *tagout device* is a prominent warning attached to an energy-isolating device. No attempt to restore power at a tagged power box should be made until repairs are completed and the person who placed the tag has removed it. See **Figure 2-7.**

Personal protective equipment

The use of personal protective equipment should not be taken lightly. Personal comfort or vanity should not take precedence over safety concerns. Operators should never wear watches, rings, ties, medallions, bracelets, scarves, or loose clothing while working with machinery. Long hair should be tied up, and cleaning cloths should not be left dangling out of your pocket. Personal protective equipment includes various types of eye, ear, respiratory, and skin protection devices. Certain operations, such as press, bindery, and storage, typically require foot protection.

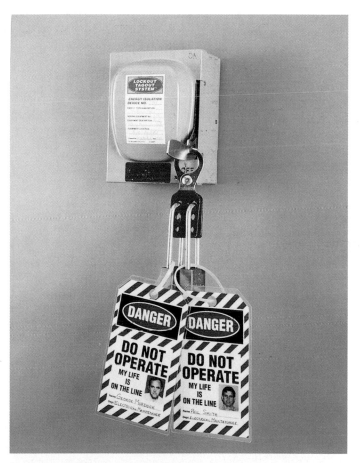

Figure 2-7. Lockout devices and tags are used to prevent the operation of machinery that is damaged or being serviced. The tags often provide a space for the authorized person's name and sometimes a photograph. (IDESCO Corp.)

main disconnect (master) switch: a switch that allows all power to machinery and small appliances to be turned off when a facility is not in use.

lockout device: a key or combination-type lock to hold an energy-isolating device in the off position to prevent the machine from energizing.

tagout device: a prominent warning attached to an energy-isolating device to prevent power from being restored to a particular circuit.

- **Eye protection devices.** Includes safety goggles, glasses, and face shields. Eye protection should be worn when operating any type of machine that can cause material to fly and strike workers. This protection should also be worn when preparing or working with any type of chemicals.

- **Ear protection devices.** Includes earplugs, earmuffs, moldable inserts, and noise-reducing headsets. Ear protection should be worn when sound levels exceed permissible levels.

- *Respiratory protection devices.* Includes respirators and dust masks. Respiratory protection devices should be worn when airborne particles create respiratory hazards, such as *ink mists* and chemical vapors.

- *Skin protection devices.* Includes rubber, leather, or plastic gloves, aprons, and boots and full safety suits. Skin protection devices should be worn when working with or cleaning up chemicals and solvents that can cause minor irritation or severe bodily damage. See **Figure 2-8.** At the very least, aprons and gloves should be worn to keep your hands and clothes clean.

First aid kits and equipment

Even if the proper personal protective devices are worn, accidents do happen. It is important that everyone working in a printing facility be trained in basic first aid. First aid kits should be visible and easily accessible, and they should be checked and stocked on a regular basis.

In addition to first aid kits, equipment such as eye and face wash units should be installed in work areas where hazardous chemicals are used. See **Figure 2-9.** Emergency telephone numbers should be posted in a prominent location near the lab or office telephone.

Proper material and tool handling

You can avoid physical injury by correctly handling materials and tools, practicing good housekeeping, and following basic safety rules. When lifting materials, you should keep your knees bent and your back straight. Leaning over while lifting is poor practice and causes you to use your back rather than your legs to lift. Follow the tips for safe lifting in **Figure 2-10.** If materials are too heavy or bulky to lift, use a dolly or request assistance. See **Figure 2-11.**

Whether you are using hand tools or power equipment, you should use the tool only for the job it was intended to do. Tools should be kept clean and in good working condition and stored in the appropriate storage cabinet. Following these simple rules helps prevent physical injury and damage to equipment.

Good housekeeping habits also help maintain a safe working environment. Floors should be kept clean, dry, and clear of obstacles. Spills should be cleaned up immediately, and cleaning materials

Figure 2-8. The proper type of personal protection equipment provides the worker with effective resistance to chemicals. (Kimberly-Clark Corp.)

Figure 2-9. The eye and face water wash unit is designed to furnish first aid to chemical splash victims. (Lab Safety Supply)

Tips for Safe Lifting	
Clear a pathway	Before you move things from one place to another, be sure you have a clear pathway.
Check weight	Check the object's weight to see if you will need help lifting it.
Request help	Ask for help from another person if you need it, or use mechanical lifting equipment.
Keep your back straight	Your back should be straight and vertical to the ground.
Lift with your knees	If you can, bend your knees when lifting; don't stoop over the object.
Keep objects close to your body	Always bring the object as close to your body as possible.
Tighten your stomach	Tighten your stomach muscles. This helps your back stay in balance.
Deliver carefully	Use care when you put the object down. Follow the same guidelines as you would for lifting.

Figure 2-10. Prevent painful back injuries by following these tips for safe lifting.

should be disposed of properly. Nonskid mats, adhesive strips, or coating materials can be applied to the floor around work areas. See **Figure 2-12.**

Safety rules have been designed to protect personnel and prevent damage to equipment. You should never use or adjust any equipment unless you have been properly trained to do so. If you are unsure of the proper use of any piece of equipment, do not be afraid to ask your instructor or supervisor for instruction.

Equipment such as forklifts and air compressors can cause serious harm if not handled properly. Only certified drivers should operate forklifts, and riders should never be permitted. Many forklifts use an audible backup warning signal to alert other workers of their presence.

Compressed air should never be used to clean off clothes or do general cleanup work. An air nozzle can force air through the skin and into the bloodstream, creating a condition that can cause death. The careless release of compressed air can also stir up paper dust, making breathing difficult and causing eye irritation.

Figure 2-11. Using the proper equipment to lift and move materials prevents physical injury and spills. The skid turner illustrated on the bottom is used to lift and turn over a pallet of paper. (Kimberly-Clark Corp.; Vijuk Equipment, Inc.)

respiratory protection device: a mask that prevents harmful matter from entering the respiratory system.

ink mist: tiny droplets making up a spray, fog, or mist of ink, created as rotating press rollers throw tiny droplets of ink into the air.

skin protection device: gloves or other clothing that protects the skin from contact with harmful materials.

Figure 2-12. Nonskid mats, adhesive strips, or coating materials are used to prevent workers from slipping or falling. (Rust-Oleum Corporation)

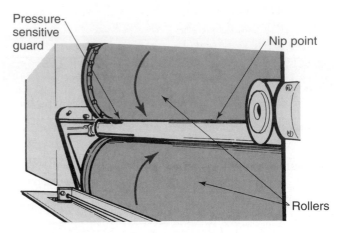

Figure 2-13. Nip points occur where two rollers come together. The rollers illustrated use a pressure-sensitive guard that shuts off the press if anything is pulled into the nip point.

Caution

When operating a compressed air nozzle, do not exceed 30 psi (200 kPa). Also, always wear eye protection. Insertion of an air nozzle into body cavities with subsequent activation of air pressure can cause serious injury or even death.

Printing facilities require workers to follow basic safety rules. These facilities also require workers to take added safety precautions. When operating a printing press or bindery or finishing equipment, people should keep the following factors in mind:

- Check to make sure all guards are in place.
- Never turn on a machine unless all tools have been removed from it and all mechanisms have been set correctly.
- Make sure no one is near the machine before starting it.
- Hands should be kept clear of any point of operation while the machine is running.
- Do not try to grab paper, perform adjustments, lubricate parts, or do anything that places your hands near rollers, *nip points*, drills, punches, or cutting blades while the machine is running. See **Figure 2-13.**
- Always work with an assistant when cleaning or operating machinery.
- While working around operating machinery, people should not wear long sleeves (except if they are snug fitting), bulky sweaters, pants with cuffs, jewelry, medallions, necklaces, ties, watches, rings, bracelets, scarves, or other loose items.
- Keep long hair tied back or tucked under a hair net to prevent it from being caught in machinery.
- The floor of the facility should always be kept clean of liquids and debris.
- Hands should be washed before eating or drinking to remove any toxic products.

Chemical Hazards

As production processes in the printing industry have progressed from manual to electronic methods, chemical use has been greatly reduced. Toxic materials are, however, still being used and produced as by-products. The first defense against toxic materials is to know the types of chemicals being used and the hazards involved. Certain substances are more harmful than others. The amount of exposure to a toxic substance and the duration of exposure affect the degree of harm the substance can cause.

Hazard communication programs

OSHA requires employers to keep a list of all hazardous chemicals used on their premises, maintain files of *material safety data sheets (MSDSs)* on the chemicals, and train their employees to use the chemicals and respond properly should an accident occur. Printers must also have a thorough labeling program so chemicals can be readily identified. An MSDS gives the chemical name; common name; hazardous components; and name, address, and telephone number of the manufacturer. See **Figure 2-14.** Employees must have access to MSDS files, and the sheets must be complete. The label on the product itself should indicate the potential hazards (such as flammability, medical, health, and exposure limits) and give detailed handling instructions. Product labels also include information that might be useful to firefighters.

Note

MSDSs must be readily available. An MSDS includes very specific information. This sheet is extremely useful if a medical emergency occurs.

MSDSs are part of OSHA's Hazard Communication program (HCP), which in turn, is part of the Hazard Communication Standard (HCS). The program is directed at the "right to know" of all employees. The responsibility of both the HCP and the HCS is to inform employees as to the various chemicals in the plant, the dangers inherent in using each of them, and the proper response if there is an accident. The idea behind the right-to-know regulation is to develop a universal warning system.

The MSDSs are of no value unless they get into the hands of the right people. It is a supplier's responsibility to provide data sheets to product dealers, who in turn, make sure the printers receive copies. Printers should, therefore, be aware that complete data sheets must be provided with chemicals and kept on file in the printing facility.

OSHA requires employers who use chemicals in their facilities to educate their employees. Employers must have a written educational program, and training must be done at regular intervals. Educational programs must include information on the potential hazards of the chemicals, how to use the chemicals, how to dispose of the chemicals, what personal protective equipment should be worn when handling the chemicals, and how to administer proper first aid in case of spills. See **Figure 2-15.** Employers must clearly label any hazardous material

MATERIAL SAFETY DATA SHEET | DATE PREPARED 3/07

HI-TEMP PRODUCTS CO. 14936 GROVER ST. OMAHA, NEBRASKA 68144	EMERGENCY PHONE NUMBER 1-402-333-8323 1-402-359-5796	TELEPHONE NUMBER FOR INFORMATION 1-402-330-3344

1 PRODUCT NAME: HT 0801 AKRYA Cut

+ HEALTH	1
^ FIRE	0
* REACTIVE	0

HAZARD RATING
0 – LEAST
1 – SLIGHT
2 – MODERATE
3 – SERIOUS
4 – SEVERE

2 PRECAUTIONARY STATEMENT FROM PRODUCT LABEL

WARNING

WEAR SAFETY GLASSES. MAY CAUSE EYE IRRITATION. IF EYE IRRITATION OCCURS, FLUSH EYES FOR 15 MINUTES WITH WATER. IF SWALLOWED, DO NOT INDUCE VOMITING. DRINK WATER OR MILK. IN EITHER CASE, CALL A PHYSICIAN IMMEDIATELY. REFER TO MSDS FOR CHEMICAL HAZARDOUS INFORMATION.

KEEP OUT OF THE REACH OF CHILDREN.

3 HAZARDOUS COMPONENTS OSHA – >

INGREDIENTS	%	CAS NO.	PEL/TLV ppm[a]	PEL/TLV mg/m^3	TWA ppm[a]	TWA mg/m^3	STEL[c] ppm[a]	STEL[c] mg/m^3	CEILING ppm[a]	CEILING mg/m^3
ISOPROPYL ALCOHOL	<3	67-63-0			400	983	500	1230		

4 PHYSICAL/CHEMICAL CHARACTERISTICS

Boiling Point	212° F	Specific Gravity (H20=1)	N/A
Vapor Pressure (mm Hg.)	N/A	Melting Point	N/A
Vapor Density (Air = 1)	N/A	Evaporation Rate (Butyl Acetate = 1)	N/A
Solubility in water	MISCIBLE		

Appearance and Odor PURPLE THICK EMULSION, BANANA ODOR

5 Fire and Explosion Hazard Data

Flash Point N/A | Flammable Limits N/A | LEL N/A | UEL N/A

Extinguishing Media WATER TO COOL DOWN CONTAINERS

Special Fire Fighting Procedures N/A DIRECT FLAME FROM BUTANE TORCH

WILL NOT IGNITE MATERIAL.

Unusual Fire and Explosion Hazards N/A

6 HEALTH HAZARD INFORMATION – SIGNS AND SYMPTOMS OF EXPOSURE

SKIN: MAY IRRITATE SKIN, CAUSE LIGHT REDDENING IN PATIENTS WITH PREEXISTING SKIN DISORDERS.
EYES: MAY CAUSE EYE IRRITATION, BURNING, AND REDNESS.

SWALLOWING: MAY CAUSE MOUTH AND THROAT IRRITATION, BURNING, AND POSSIBLE ABDOMINAL DISCOMFORT OR NAUSEA.
BREATHING: PROLONGED BREATHING OF MIST MAY IRRITATE NASAL PASSAGES.

7 EMERGENCY AND FIRST AID PROCEDURES

ON SKIN: WASH WITH SOAP AND WATER. IF IRRITATION PERSISTS, SEEK MEDICAL ATTENTION.

IN EYES: FLUSH EYES WITH PLENTY OF RUNNING WATER FOR 15 MINUTES, LIFTING EYELIDS OCCASIONALLY. GET IMMEDIATE MEDICAL ATTENTION.

SWALLOWED: CALL A PHYSICIAN IMMEDIATELY. DO NOT INDUCE VOMITING. IF CONSCIOUS, DRINK PLENTY OF WATER OR MILK.

BREATHED: REMOVE TO FRESH AIR. GIVE ARTIFICIAL RESPIRATION IF NOT BREATHING. SEEK IMMEDIATE MEDICAL ATTENTION.

8 TOXICITY DATA

ORAL: N/A | DERMAL: N/A

INHALATION: N/A

CARCINOGENICITY: NOT CONSIDERED TO BE A CARCINOGEN BY IARC.

NTP? N/A IARC MONOGRAPHS? N/A OSHA REGULATED? N/A

9 PERSONAL PROTECTION

VENTILATION: LOCAL OR MECHANICAL EXHAUST.
RESPIRATORY PROTECTION: IF NECESSARY, WEAR A PARTICLE MASK OR AN OSHA APPROVED MASK FOR MIST CONCENTRATIONS.
EYE PROTECTION: WEAR GOGGLES OR SAFETY GLASSES.
SKIN AND PROTECTIVE CLOTHING: WEAR RUBBER GLOVES.

10 HAZARDOUS REACTIVITY

STABILITY:	UNSTABLE?		CONDITIONS TO AVOID: N/A
	STABLE?	X	

INCOMPATIBILITY: N/A

HAZARDOUS BYPRODUCTS: N/A

HAZARDOUS POLYMERIZATION:	MAY OCCUR		CONDITIONS TO AVOID: N/A
	WILL NOT OCCUR	X	

Figure 2-14. MSDSs vary in design but usually include the same types of information. (Hi-Temp Products Co.)

nip point: the point where two rollers come together.

material safety data sheet (MSDS): a sheet that gives the chemical name and the name, address, and telephone number of the manufacturer.

used in the printing facility. The labels must include the following:

- The name of the chemical.
- The word *caution*, *warning*, or *danger*.

Safety Can

Waste Container

Figure 2-15. Safety cans with flame arrestors should be used when transferring flammable liquids. Flammable debris should be placed in approved waste containers. Oily or ink-soaked rags should never be stored in a container that does not meet fire safety requirements. (Justrite Manufacturing Co.)

- A brief description of the major hazards, such as "extremely flammable."
- Measures for avoiding possible hazards, such as "wash hands thoroughly after handling."
- First aid instruction, in the event of exposure to the chemical.
- How to extinguish a fire caused by the chemical.
- Information for treatment by medical personnel.
- Directions for handling and storage.

Offset lithographic chemicals and agents

The types of chemicals and chemical agents posing hazards to workers in the printing industry are commonly classified as solvents, platemaking chemicals, ink mists, gases, fumes, and dust. Although this list might sound intimidating, some of these hazards do not exist in most printing plants. None are a threat if they are handled properly.

Chemical handling and disposal

Historically, the printing industry has had to dispose of waste chemicals that were used to develop plates, clean ink from the press during washup, and clean machine parts. In addition, used dampening solution and waste ink needed to be disposed of properly. In the last 10 years, however, there has been a great reduction in the volume of waste chemistry.

Several years ago, dampening solutions commonly contained isopropyl alcohol (IPA), some of which evaporated and contaminated the air in the pressroom. Today, propylene glycol and other alcohol substitutes are more environmentally friendly than IPA, but they still contain chemicals that must be disposed of at some point. In addition, dampening solutions become contaminated with ink residue, paper particles, and other impurities. One method of reducing the volume of waste dampening solution is to filter out these impurities, instead of replacing the solution.

The platemaking process is a potential source of hazardous waste. Although some systems use no harmful chemistry, some direct imaging processes place silver or a strong alkaline exceeding the limits of the local sewer system into the wastewater. In this situation, the chemistry must be collected and stored as a hazardous material.

The most common source of hazardous waste in a lithographic printing facility is the solvent used to wash ink from the press. These solvents are usually used with rags to clean the press, and the contaminated rags must then be stored as hazardous material. The rags need to be placed into covered containers so fumes from the solvent do not escape.

After most of the solvent has been removed, the rags are stored in Department of Transportation (DOT)–approved drums and eventually removed from the printing facility by an industrial laundry service. Recovered solvent can then be distilled to produce clean solvent that can be reused. Solvent recycling can be performed within the printing facility or off-site.

Although there are nontoxic cleaning solvents available, many blanket and roller washes contain *volatile organic compounds (VOCs)*. VOCs are compounds emitted from organic chemicals contained in certain liquids or solids. The term *volatile* refers to the ease of evaporation. Examples of materials that emit VOCs are paints, cleaning supplies, permanent markers, adhesives, correction fluids, carbonless paper, and alcohol. Workers can protect themselves when cleaning a press by wearing personal protective equipment and properly handling washes. As the solvents evaporate, however, VOCs can pass into the air, and breathing these solvent vapors can be very harmful. Many vapors do not give off a strong odor, and students and workers should not rely on their sense of smell to warn them.

Some solvents are more harmful than others. Solvents that should not be used include benzene, carbon tetrachloride, gasoline, chloroform, and carbon disulfide. When possible, solvents that are less irritating to the skin, are noninjurious to offset rollers and blankets, are nonflammable, or have a high flash point should be used.

A solvent's *flash point* is the lowest temperature at which the solvent emits vapors that will ignite if exposed to an open flame or spark. For example, kerosene is relatively safe, with a flash point as low as 100°F (38°C), while gasoline has a low flash point of only –40°F (–40°C). This means that gasoline ignites or supports combustion as low as –40°F (–40°C). For this reason, gasoline should never be used as a solvent for washing ink from a press. Instead, a blanket wash with a flash point over 150°F is the safer choice.

Harmful vapors are not limited to the use of cleaning solvents. Some types of shrink-wrap film used in the bindery can cause employees to suffer from a condition known as *meatpacker's asthma*. This condition results from inhaling hydrogen chloride gas emitted during the heat-shrinking process. To diminish the possibility of inhaling harmful vapors, working areas should be well ventilated, and employees who work near concentrations of hazardous fumes should wear approved respiratory equipment. See **Figure 2-16.**

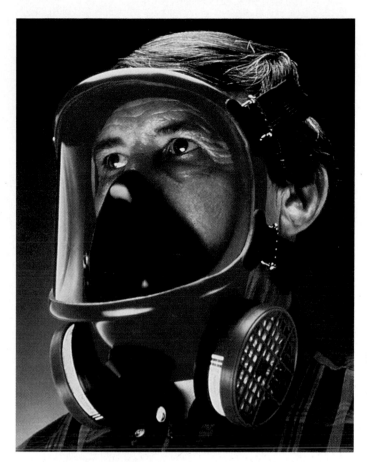

Figure 2-16. An expert must select the proper respirator for each situation.

Caution

You should never attempt to identify a solvent by sniffing it. Inhaling harmful vapors can cause serious physical injury or even death.

Platemaking chemicals

Platemaking chemicals can irritate the skin and cause burns. To prevent physical harm when processing lithographic plates, a platemaker should always wear the proper personal protective equipment and keep the following factors in mind when working with potentially hazardous platemaking chemicals:

volatile organic compound (VOC): an organic compound that significantly participates in photochemical reactions and is released as hazardous emissions. A VOC eventually vaporizes and reacts with the atmosphere and sunlight to create smog and other pollutants.

flash point: the lowest temperature at which a solvent emits vapors supporting combustion if exposed to an open flame.

- Wearing an apron prevents chemicals from staining clothing and seeping through to the skin.
- Rubber or plastic gloves protect the hands from chemical burns. Gloves should be inspected for tears and holes before beginning work.
- Face shields and splash goggles are the best form of eye and face protection.
- Never wear contact lenses when working with chemicals. If splashed in the eyes, chemicals can seep under the lenses and cause severe burning.
- Do not store food or beverages in the same area as platemaking chemicals.
- Properly labeled and stored platemaking chemicals pose less risk.
- When processing offset plates by hand, follow the manufacturer's recommended procedure.
- Be sure bottle caps are tight before shaking containers.
- Clean up spilled chemicals or oil immediately. Using an oil-absorbent cleanup product keeps the work area dry and slip free without press contamination. See **Figure 2-17.**
- Make sure there are adequate mechanical exhaust ventilation and a supply of clean air available where chemicals are used or stored.

Caution

When diluting platemaking chemicals, always pour the acid into the water. Never add water to a concentrated acid. Doing so can produce a dangerous splattering of the acid.

Airborne hazards

Besides the solvent vapors roller and blanket washes emit, pressroom personnel should be aware of hazards from ink mists, gases, fumes, and dust. Ink mists are created as rotating press rollers throw tiny droplets of ink into the air. These droplets are small enough for unprotected press operators to inhale. Ink mists often contain harmful pigments, polymers, plasticizers, resins, and solvents. On some types of presses, face shields and respirators should be worn for protection. Harmful gases such as ozone (O_3) are emitted from the breakdown of VOCs found in solvents, carbon arcs, some antistatic devices, and ultraviolet (UV) ink-curing units. Acids and molten materials can emit harmful fumes.

A large amount of dust can accumulate in a printing facility. Printing press antisetoff powders

Figure 2-17. Chemical-sorbent materials often come in portable dispensers. Most sorbent materials are designed to fit under equipment, around corners, and into tight areas. These materials are also designed not to leave granules or dust residue, reducing cleanup time and preventing contamination. (3M Company)

and the vast amount of paper used for printing can create dust. When inhaled, microscopic dust particles can lodge in the lung tissue, causing respiratory disease and lung damage. Systems for controlling dust, providing adequate ventilation, and scrubbing the air should be installed in all printing facilities. See **Figure 2-18.**

Figure 2-18. Filtration systems vary in size and design. This mist collector can achieve filtration efficiencies of up to 99%. The collector also features a pressure-differential gauge that indicates when maintenance is required. (Torit® Products)

Noise Hazards

Printing, binding, and finishing equipment creates loud noise. Excessive noise in a printing facility can reduce the efficiency of the facility's workforce, interfere with clear communications, and cause permanent hearing damage. The first step in protecting students and employees from hearing loss is to control the sound level of noise created in the plant. This is often done by modifying machines and installing sound barriers or sound-absorbing materials to the facility. When it is not possible to reduce the noise to an acceptable level, all employees must wear the proper ear protection. See **Figure 2-19.**

Sound levels are expressed in units called *decibels (dBA)*. OSHA has established permissible noise levels and time periods industry personnel can be exposed to the noise. The chart in **Figure 2-20** compares typical sound intensities to those found in a printing facility, as well as the maximum exposure limits. The maximum allowable exposure for an employee is 90 dBA of continuous noise for eight hours. If noise levels are higher than 90 dBA, employee exposure must be shortened, per OSHA regulations.

Figure 2-19. Ear protection is often needed in the pressroom and bindery area of an offset lithography plant. Protective devices for ears include headsets, earmuffs, moldable inserts, and earplugs.

Fire Hazards

Printing industry employees must be alert to situations that can cause fire. Good housekeeping, preventive measures, and education are the key elements to a sound fire protection plan. The National Fire Protection Association lists the following as major problem areas in the printing industry:

- Flammable debris left on floors and around equipment-operating areas—safety trash containers should be used for this purpose.
- Low flash point cleaning solvents for presses— solvents with a flash point of over 100°F (38°C) should be used.
- Static electricity accumulation on presses—*static eliminators* should be installed on all presses.
- Oily cloths left outside cans with self-closing lids–cans with self-closing lids should be used for disposal of solvent-soaked and oily cloths.
- Flammable ink and solvent storage—ink and solvent cans should be stored in a safety cabinet when not in use.
- Greasy metal parts and tools should be cleaned in a special parts–cleaner machine.
- Paper dust from bindery and press areas—*dust collectors* should be installed in these areas.
- Scrap paper accumulation—all scrap paper should be placed in bins.
- Setoff spray powder accumulation, with possibility of dust cloud formation and ignition— avoid this condition.

Sprinkler systems and hoses

The invention and installation of sprinkler systems have greatly reduced the chance of tragic industrial fires. Sprinkler systems also reduce the amount of potential water and fire damage by isolating the fire to a specific area. If the sprinkler system is not properly maintained, however, its presence is of no use. Along with regular inspection by local fire departments, all sprinkler system components should be regularly serviced by a

decibel (dBA): a unit of measure for stating sound levels.

static eliminator: a press attachment used to reduce the amount of static developing on a press because of low relative humidity and the movement of paper over metal surfaces. This attachment is also used to eliminate ink setoff or paper-feeding problems.

dust collector: a vacuum system that captures airborne dust and removes it to a storage compartment.

Permissible Noise Exposure

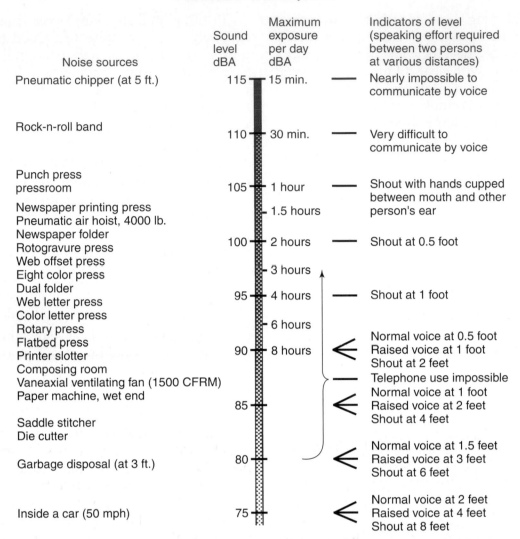

Figure 2-20. OSHA determines permissible noise exposures. When employees are subjected to sound exceeding the levels prescribed, employees must wear the proper ear protection.

facility's maintenance department. Although sprinkler systems vary, most operate under the same principles and use the same basic components.

Exterior fire department connections and hose systems should also be examined regularly. See **Figure 2-21.** The connections should be properly marked and easily accessible. Hose lines and valves should never be obstructed or blocked. Hoses should be checked regularly for rot, mildew, and other damage. The hoses should never be used for anything but periodic testing and fire fighting. Hydrants should also be flushed and tested to make sure they operate.

Fire extinguishers

All printing facilities use flammable and combustible materials. Therefore, fire prevention is a crucial part of plant safety programs. Students and employees should be aware of fire extinguisher locations, evacuation routes, and the proper response in case of a fire.

The proper fire extinguishers should be located near potential hazard areas. See **Figure 2-22.** Extinguishers should be easily accessible and properly charged.

Types of fires

As indicated in **Figure 2-22,** there are four general types of fires—Class A, Class B, Class C, and Class D. It is important to know the different classes of fires because, depending on the material burning, different means of controlling and extinguishing the fire must be used. For example, water is ideal for putting out a paper fire. When used on an electrical fire, however, water can cause additional damage to electrical equipment or electrocution because the water conducts electricity.

Figure 2-21. Fire department connections should be properly marked and easily accessible.

Caution

In order to extinguish an electrical fire, the power source must be turned off!

Water cannot be used on flammable liquids, such as gasoline, because it might disperse the liquid, causing the fire to spread. Such liquids burn at the surface, where the vapors are given off. Therefore, smothering or blanketing the burning liquid is the best technique for extinguishing the fire.

Light Hazards

Light hazards include light sources that can cause damage to a person's skin or eyes. These hazards also include insufficiently lit work and storage areas. Light sources commonly used in the printing industry include UV radiation, infrared (IR) light, laser beams, pulsed xenon lamps (PXAs), mercury vapor lamps, and ozone lights.

Ultraviolet (UV) radiation is used for curing ink and exposing plates. Although UV light rays are not visible to the human eye, they can be harmful to the eyes and skin. Damage from UV rays can be prevented by wearing the proper eye protection and clothing and avoiding exposure.

Caution

Most platemakers operate at extremely high voltage. The platemaker should always be unplugged when the bulbs or lamps are replaced or repairs are made.

Infrared (IR) light is often used in ink-drying and ink-curing devices. Similar to UV light, IR light can cause eye and skin burns with extensive exposure. *Laser beams* are commonly used for plate exposure and are potentially harmful. Although the rays used in the printing industry might not be able to cut through metal, they can cause a great deal of damage to unprotected skin and eyes.

Potentially harmful sources of light also include *pulsed xenon lamps (PXAs)* and *mercury vapor lamps* used on antisetoff devices. The proper eye protection devices must be worn. See **Figure 2-23.**

Exposure lamps used in cameras and platemakers can reach extremely high temperatures. Care should be taken when working around them or changing the bulbs. The bulbs should be allowed to cool down completely before being changed.

To avoid tripping or falling, lights should be turned on when working with machines, at workstations, and when entering stockrooms. This, of course, is not true when the process prohibits illumination, such as in darkrooms. Insufficient lighting can also cause undue strain on your eyes.

Ergonomic Hazards

The awareness of *ergonomics* has increased greatly. Manufacturers, employers, and consumers have dedicated a great deal of time and money to the science of fitting the job to the worker. Although OSHA does not yet regulate ergonomic issues, many types of workstations have been redesigned to meet the physical needs of the worker. See **Figure 2-24.** Properly designed workstations help workers remain healthy, increase productivity, and prevent accidents.

ultraviolet (UV) radiation: a range of electromagnetic radiation lying outside the visible spectrum. In the printing industry, UV rays are used for producing various types of proofs, curing ink, or exposing plates.

infrared (IR) light: a range of the electromagnetic spectrum that serves as a source of heat.

laser beam: a beam of nearly parallel and monochromatic light moving in phase.

pulsed xenon lamp (PXA): a primary light source in graphic arts photography. This source provides a constant output with a spectral composition resembling sunlight.

mercury vapor lamp: an enclosed light source that produces radiation by passing an electrical current through gaseous mercury.

ergonomics: the study of equipment design that improves convenience, ease of use, and operator comfort.

Fire Extinguishers and Fire Classifications

Fires	Type	Use	Operation
Class A Fires Ordinary Combustibles (Materials such as wood, paper, textiles.) *Requires... cooling-quenching* A (triangle)	**Soda-acid** Bicarbonate of soda solution and sulfuric acid	Okay for use on A Not for use on B C D	Direct stream at base of flame.
Class B Fires Flammable Liquids (Liquids such as grease, gasoline, oils, and paints.) *Requires...blanketing or smothering* B (square)	**Pressurized Water** Water under pressure	Okay for use on A Not for use on B C D	Direct stream at base of flame.
Class C Fires Electrical Equipment (Motors, switches, and so forth.) *Requires... a nonconducting agent* C (circle)	**Carbon Dioxide (CO$_2$)** Carbon dioxide (CO$_2$) gas under pressure	Okay for use on B C Not for use on A D	Direct discharge as close to fire as possible, first at edge of flames and gradually forward and upward.
	Foam Solution of aluminum sulfate and bicarbonate of soda	Okay for use on A B Not for use on C D	Direct stream into the burning material or liquid. Allow foam to fall lightly on fire.
Class D Fires Combustible Metals (Flammable metals such as magnesium and lithium.) *Requires...blanketing or smothering* D (star)	**Dry Chemical**	Multi-purpose type / Ordinary BC type Okay for: A B C / B C Not okay for: D / A D	Direct stream at base of flames. Use rapid left-to-right motion toward flames.
	Dry Chemical Granular type material	Okay for use on D Not for use on A B C	Smother flames by scooping granular material from bucket onto burning metal.

Figure 2-22. The classification system for fire extinguishers uses letter, color, and shape designations to denote the type of material on which the extinguisher can be used.

Figure 2-23. Wearing the proper protection device prevents damage to your eyes from chemical splashes, airborne particulates, and potentially harmful light sources.

Environmental Considerations

The Chemical Manufacturers Association (CMA) established environmental protection principles. Many printing industry vendors (companies that sell supplies and equipment to printers) incorporate these principles into daily business operations. Called *Responsible Care (RC)*, the initiative includes the following codes of practice:

- Establish community awareness and emergency response programs at every facility.
- Ensure that research and development operations protect the environment at all stages of chemical development and use.
- Protect workers and the environment during manufacturing operations.
- Ensure the transport of chemical products in a manner minimizing environmental risks.
- Track the distribution of chemical products.
- Address all options related to hazardous waste management.

Federal Regulations

Along with the safety and health guidelines OSHA established, the federal government has established many environmental protective regulations. The Environmental Protection Agency (EPA) enforces most of these regulations. The Clean Air Act Amendments (CAAA) and Clean Water Act (CWA) significantly affect printing establishments.

The CAAA regulates toxic emissions and air pollution controls. The CWA regulates the discharge of pollutants into U.S. waters, regulates water pollution control, and enforces industrial laundry guidelines. See **Figure 2-25.** In addition, local communities place restrictions on the volume of certain chemicals

---

Computer Sense

- Use a chair with adjustable back support. Your feet should touch the floor, and your thighs should be parallel with the floor.

- Place light sources perpendicular to your computer, so they will not shine in your eyes or reflect on the monitor. If there is a glare problem, install a glare screen or three-sided hood.

- Use an antistatic cloth to keep dust and fingerprints off the monitor's glass.

- Inspect and clean the computer's exhaust fan slot periodically.

- Position the monitor 16″ to 30″ away from your eyes, depending on what is comfortable. The angle between your eyes and the monitor should be 0 to 45. It should be 4″ to 8″ lower than eye level, so you are looking slightly down toward it. It should be tilted slightly up as if it were a book or magazine.

- When typing from copy, keep it as close to the monitor as possible to prevent swiveling your gaze back and forth.

- Take periodic breaks, at least 15 minutes every two hours.

- Make an effort to blink frequently. If necessary, use artificial tears to keep your eyes moist.

Figure 2-24. To promote safety and reduce health hazards relating to computer workstations, keep this information in mind.

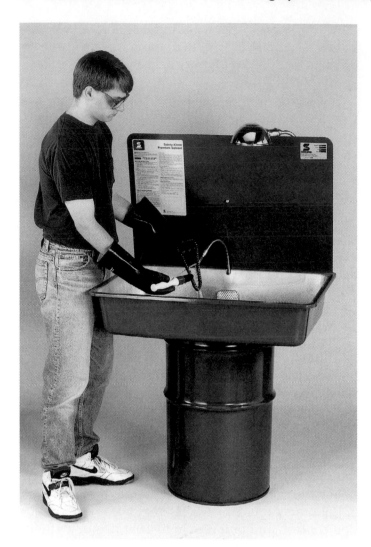

Figure 2-25. A parts cleaner combines state-of-the-art separation technology with improved solvents to help minimize waste and reduce disposal costs. (Safety-Kleen)

Shop Towels, Rags, and Gloves

Before the enactment and enforcement of federal and state laws on clean air, clean water, and other environmental factors, cloth shop towels, rags, and gloves were placed in the trash and hauled away to landfills. Now, that practice is against the law, and offenders are subject to fines and criminal prosecution. As a result of the new environmental laws, "industrial dry cleaning laundries" now clean and recycle shop towels, rags, and gloves, using solvents instead of water for cleaning. The laundries meet all the requirements for environmental compliance.

Contaminated shop towels, rags, and gloves are picked up from the printing facility in drums the DOT has approved and are taken to the laundry. After a thorough cleaning, the waste residue from the laundry operation is removed by DOT-licensed haulers and incinerated at facilities the EPA has licensed. By using the cleaning services, printers save from 30% to 50% of the money spent annually for new towels, rags, and gloves. Industrial laundries also dispose of worn-out towels, rags, and gloves.

Helping the Environment

Manufacturers of printing supplies and equipment have taken the responsibility of developing new environmentally friendly technologies and materials. The printing industry is meeting these challenges by taking action on the following issues:

- Negotiating long-term contracts for the purchase of recycled paper, thereby allowing suppliers to speed up research, development, and production of recycled paper.

- Establishing cooperative research and development relationships with paper and ink suppliers to ensure new and more environmentally friendly products.

- Investing in air and water quality control equipment that meets and exceeds current and future standards.

- Recycling preconsumer waste paper, inks, solvents, and other materials and supporting paper-recycling programs at the plant and community level.

that can enter their wastewater treatment facilities. Printing companies must become acquainted with these limits.

For detailed information on the CAAA and CWA, as well as other environmental regulations, contact your local, state, or federal EPA office. The phone number and address of your local EPA office can be found in the telephone directory. The Internet is also a good source for reviewing the most current regulations.

- Training employees to consider the environmental implications of all manufacturing processes and material purchases.
- Establishing sound environmental company policies.

Everyone talks about being committed to preserving our environment. In order for our good intentions to have any effect, however, we must take action. Here are some simple tips to reduce waste, increase efficiency, and positively affect the environment:

- **Use recycled paper.** A lot has been done to improve the quality of recycled papers. Today's recycled papers have stronger fiber characteristics and fewer problems on press than their predecessors did. The costs have come down to be competitive with nonrecycled papers.

- **Know what is environmentally smart and what is not.** By establishing a close relationship with your suppliers, you can keep abreast of the developments in environmentally friendly printing materials. There is a variety of recycled papers, vegetable-based inks, and water-based glues already available, with new products coming on the market all the time.

- **Recycle at school, work, and home.** With so many recyclable products, there is no reason not to recycle. Set up a recycling center at the school or office for paper, aluminum and other cans, and corrugated boxes. Check with your local trash collection company about picking up recyclable materials.

- **Perform environmental audits.** Regularly assessing a facility's compliance with environmental regulations helps keep the facility in compliance and protect the environment.

Safety Is Your Responsibility

Unsafe machines, work areas, and procedures are the cause of many accidents. Take time to inspect all equipment and work areas. Never assume an area is safe because there are no large machines or toxic chemicals.

Periodic inspections are one of the most important aspects of a successful safety and health program. When unsafe conditions exist, take immediate action to correct and eliminate them. A sample safety inspection checklist is shown in **Figure 2-26.**

Safety Inspection List					
Date: _____		Area: _____			
Inspectors: _____					
	Satisfactory	Unsatisfactory	Not Applicable	Dangerous	Remarks
Housekeeping					
General impression					
Clean and orderly work areas					
Desks and tables—orderly					
Waste containers—adequate/orderly					
Proper materials available for housekeeping					
Maintenance schedules used					
Properly marked aisles					
Warnings and cautions posted					
Containers labeled					
Storage space—adequate/orderly					
Chairs—in good condition					
—properly used					
Ladders—inspection current					
—in good condition					
Personal Protection Equipment					
Eye protection					
Ear protection					
Foot protection					
Head protection					
Protective clothing					
Respiratory equipment					
Security					
Personal valuables—lockers provided					
Locks—adequate					
Electrical Equipment					
Inspection current					
Cords—in good condition					
—away from aisles					
Tampering—no evidence of					
Panel boxes—properly enclosed/locked					
Lighting—adequate					
Lighting—emergency adequate					
Machines and Equipment					
Operators trained					

Figure 2-26. A safety inspection checklist should be used when performing periodic inspections.

Guards—adequate				
Attire—appropriate for job				
Jewelry—appropriate for job				
Computers/keyboards—properly placed				
Work space—adequate				
Storage				
Ladders and stools—adequate				
Heavy objects—near floor level				
File cabinets—secured or weighted				
—open drawers do not block				
Aisles—not blocked or cluttered				
Waste containers—adequate/orderly				
Tripping and/or Slipping Hazards				
Carpets and mats—in good condition				
Floors—clean and in good condition				
Fire Safety				
Waste paper disposal				
Other trash disposal				
Flammable liquid storage				
Exits—not blocked, properly marked				
Fire extinguishers—inspection current				
Other fire hazards (specify)				
Administration				
Safety program				
Education				
Incentives				
Procedures				
Record keeping				
Accident and injury				
Emergency evacuation plan				
Job hazard analysis				

Other observations and explanantion of items needing attention

_____

_____

_____

_____

_____

_____

_____

Figure 2-26. *(Continued)*

Summary

Safety and health issues are the responsibility of every student or employee working in a printing facility. All printing firms must follow the safety guidelines OSHA has established. Knowledge of safety colors, machine lockout devices, and tagout devices is essential to making your work area a safe and enjoyable place to be. Following recommended procedures for storing and using chemicals, solvents, and flammable liquids helps prevent physical injury and fire.

Noise abatement is a factor in all printing facilities. All workers and students should wear the proper ear protection to prevent hearing damage or loss. Good housekeeping, preventive maintenance, and education are the key elements to a good fire protection plan. This includes the proper disposal of hazardous materials and the recycling of appropriate materials whenever possible.

Review Questions

Please do not write in this book. Write your answers on a separate sheet of paper.

1. What are the five OSHA–specified hazard areas?
2. Of what use are safety color codes?
3. What purpose does OSHA serve?
4. How can on–the–job physical injuries resulting from mechanical hazards be controlled?
5. What should an operator do before working on any electrical equipment?
6. What is the purpose of a lockout device?
7. How are lockout and tagout devices applied?
8. Name the personal protection devices that could be used in three different situations.
9. List five guidelines for handling tools and materials properly.
10. What information can be found on an MSDS?
11. Define the term *flash point*.
12. What are the recommended procedures for storing and using toxic and flammable liquids?
13. How can noise be properly controlled in a printing facility?
14. What is the maximum allowable dBA exposure limit for an eight–hour day?
15. List five ways fires can be prevented and controlled in the printing industry.
16. List the four color, letter, and shape designations used to identify the types of material on which fire extinguishers can be used.
17. Why is it dangerous to use water on an electrical fire?
18. List three guidelines for safely operating computer equipment.
19. What is meant by the statement "Safety is your responsibility"?

Skill-Building Activities

1. Design a safety inspection form suitable for the lab in which you are working. Conduct a safety inspection using the form. Prepare a written or oral report.
2. Invite a local fire department official to discuss fire drill procedures and fire prevention. Ask the official to demonstrate the proper use of fire extinguishers in the graphic arts lab.
3. Invite the school nurse or another health official to demonstrate first aid procedures for each kind of accident that might occur in a printing facility (electrical shock, cuts, poisoning, burns, and chemical spills).
4. As a class activity, design a bulletin board or other type of display with a "Safety in the Printing Industry" theme. Sources for visual aid materials include OSHA, the local labor department, the school health office, and local printing plant safety representatives.
5. Ask the school nurse or another health official to assist the class in assembling a first aid kit for the lab. Be sure all required items are obtained and in good condition. Place the first aid kit in a prominent location in the graphic arts lab.

Press rooms are extremely noisy during a pressrun. It is important to wear hearing protection whenever you are in the press area. (3M Company)

Keeping It Real

Words can go only so far in communicating events, ideas, and desires. In sports, it is not enough to say that a team won easily or by a close margin. People want to know the score. Individual players' performances are quantified—measured with numbers, not words. Words such as *tall, old, huge, good,* and *awesome* can vary in meaning when different people use them. Descriptions are less vague when they are accurately quantified. The ancient Greeks tried to quantify facial beauty by determining the ideal mathematical ratios of certain features, such as the eyes to the face.

In both graphic design and printing, communication is improved with numbers. Instead of asking for type that is "sort of big but not too crowded," you can specify "48 point with 8-point leading." Paper is not just "lightweight" or "thick"; it is described as "Sub. 16 or 12 point," respectively. A printed photograph's image quality could be described as "not bad," but a more useful description is the number of dots in a linear inch. A computer's speed and storage space are expressed numerically in gigahertz and gigabytes.

In fact, digital technology has increased the need for math and measurements. As an example, color has traditionally been described with words such as *blue, warm, bright, pastel,* or even *nice*. The densitometer shown here is analyzing the color accuracy of a press sheet by numerically measuring the density of the inks used to print it. Colorimeters go a step further by quantifying any color by measuring its value in three dimensions. Of the thousands of colors out there, no two colors have the same three values.

Chapter 3
Math and Measurement

Key Terms

American-British system
ascender
basic size
basis weight
binary digit (bit)
caliper
color depth
colorimeter
copyfitting
densitometer
descender
Didot system
dot pitch
dots per inch (dpi)
E gauge
grade
holding dimension
International Organization
  for Standardization
  (ISO)
International System of
  Units (SI) metric system
ISO series
leading
line gauge
lines per inch (lpi)
Mediaan system
micrometer

M weight
nominal weight
nonpareil
paper caliper
paper size
photometer
pica
picture element (pixel)
pixels per inch (ppi)
point
point size
point system
proportion scale
ream
reflection densitometer
reproduction size
resolution
sampling rate
scaling
scanning densitometer
screen
screen angle
sizing
spectrodensitometer
spectrophotometer
standard size
transmission densitometer
U.S. Customary system

Learning Objectives

When you have completed the reading and assigned activities related to this chapter, you will be able to do the following:

◆ Differentiate between the U.S. Customary system and the International System of Units (SI) metric system.

◆ Use the point system of type measurement.

◆ Explain how paper varies in size, weight, and thickness.

◆ Define *image resolution*, based on the device being used to display or output the image.

◆ Summarize the use of proportional scales, screens, and color measurements in the reproduction of images.

Precise measurement standards and good math skills are extremely important in the printing industry. Quality printed products cannot be produced with inaccurate measurements, and profits cannot be realized with inaccurate calculations. Everyone involved in the production process must have good math skills and a basic understanding of the most commonly used systems of measurement:

- Graphic designers must determine space limitations, accurate margins, type sizes, and proper image *resolution*.
- Camera and scanner operators must be able to calculate resolution values, measure chemicals, and size images.
- Press operators must be able to measure ink, determine how much paper will be needed, and determine the proper press speed.
- The production manager must schedule press time, purchase paper, and evaluate which printing facility would be the most practical.
- The estimator must use accurate cost analysis and proven methods of pricing printed products.

Digits, Hands, Feet, and Inches

Systems of measurement developed out of the necessity to describe quantities and values. Items for sale had to be quantified in a common form to buy or trade material goods, land, and animals. Terms for quantifying materials had to be something everyone could understand. For this reason, many of the first measuring terms referred to parts of the human body. For instance, the distance spanned by four fingers was known as *four digits*. The hand was also a common measuring unit, representing about 4″. The length of a forearm was once called a *cubit*, or six palms, and the length of a person's foot represented a distance of about 12″.

Of course, most people do not have the same size feet or hands. Measurements one person made would not always equal those another made. These differences made it difficult to trade items on a fair scale—hence, the need for standardized systems of measurement.

Standardized Systems of Measurement

The measurement units used most often in the United States belong to the *U.S. Customary system*. This system originated in the 1200s and is also referred to as the *U.S. Conventional system* or *English*

system. The U.S. Customary system was derived from the English system of weights and measures and includes units such as inches, feet, gallons, and pounds.

Although the U.S. Customary system is still widely used in the United States, most nations use the *International System of Units (SI) metric system* (the *Système International d'Unités*, or simply, the metric system). The metric system was first created in the 1790s and is, by far, the simplest system of measurement. This system was originally developed with the meter as the standard unit of length, the gram as the standard unit of mass, and the liter as the standard unit of capacity.

The metric system is a decimal number system in which all units increase or decrease in size by tens. See **Figure 3-1.** This type of number system makes calculations easier. Also, the metric system uses only seven base units to make all types of measurement, whereas the U.S. Customary system has more than twenty.

The United States legalized the metric system in 1866 as a standard for weights and measures. The system has remained largely unused in U.S. industry, however, despite the Metric Conversion Act signed in 1975. This Act established a national policy to coordinate conversion to metric standards. Most products manufactured or used in the United States list both conventional and metric measurements.

Measurement Conversions

It is sometimes necessary to convert to or from metric values because there is still widespread use of U.S. Customary measures in the printing industry. For instance, if a chemical quantity is given in liters and the equipment uses mixture ratios in quarts, one of the values has to be converted to the other system. A conversion chart can be used to change a metric value to a conventional value or a conventional value to a metric value. See **Figure 3-2.** Values are converted from one system to another by multiplying known quantities by a given number. Along with understanding the U.S. Customary system and the SI metric system, people working in the graphic communication and printing industries must understand the *point system*.

The Point System

The point system is a system of measurement common only to the graphic communication and printing industries. This system developed from the need of typographers to standardize type

Base Units of the SI Metric System
Length = meter (m)
Mass = kilogram (kg)
Time = second (s)
Electric current = ampere (A)
Temperature = Kelvin (K) or degree Celsius (°C)
Amount of substance = mole (mol)
Luminous intensity = candela (cd)

Common Prefixes	Increase or Decrease in Metric Unit
giga (G)	1,000,000,000 (one billion)
mega (M)	1,000,000 (one million)
kilo (k)	1,000 (one thousand)
hecto (h)	100 (one hundred)
deka (da)	10 (ten)
deci (d)	0.1 (one-tenth)
centi (c)	0.01 (one-hundreth)
milli (m)	0.001 (one-thousandth)
micro (μ)	0.000001 (one-millionth)

Figure 3-1. The prefixes listed in the bottom table are added to most of the seven base units to increase or decrease metric units. The most commonly used prefixes are *centi-*, *kilo-*, and *milli-*.

measurement. The point system dates from early handset metal type, where the sizes of type cast by type founders were graduated on a uniform *point* scale. Each size is described by its number of points, or *point size*. Originally, the point size referred to the height of the body on which the type was cast. See **Figure 3-3.** A point measures approximately 1/72 of an inch, or 0.0138".

At one time, there were three point systems in use worldwide—the Didot system, the Mediaan system, and the American-British system. The *Didot system* is still used in Europe and has largely replaced the *Mediaan system*. Most European countries, however, are moving to purely metric measurements. The *American-British system* is used throughout North America and Great Britain. This system is more commonly referred to as the *point system*.

Determining point size

Point size does not solely refer to the size of the letter or character. Originally, point size described the length of the piece of metal on which a letter was cast. The actual size of the character printed was slightly smaller than the metal block. Consequently, the point size includes white space above and below the characters. This space allows room for line spacing, ascenders, and descenders. *Ascenders* are portions of certain letters that extend above a lowercase *x*. For example, *d*, *b*, *f*, *k*, *h*, *l*, and *t* have ascenders. *Descenders* are portions of certain letters that extend below a lowercase *x*. Examples of letters with descenders are *g*, *j*, *p*, *q*, and *y*.

Due to variances of white space above and below the characters of different designs of type, it is often necessary to use an *E gauge* or similar measuring device to determine point size. See **Figure 3-4.** The E gauge has a series of capital *E* characters, with point sizes indicated for each character. The correct point size can be determined by placing the gauge flat over a line of type and matching the character *E* closest in size to the characters in the line. Type size can

resolution: a means of quantifying an image's sharpness of clarity.

U.S. Customary system: the system of weights and measures used in the United States. This system establishes the values of units such as inches, feet, ounces, pounds, and gallons.

International System of Units (SI) metric system: the modern version of the metric system, based on seven internationally recognized units of measure.

point system: a system of print measurement used throughout the printing industry in the United States.

point: a principal unit of measure for type and line spacing equal to approximately 1/72 of an inch, or 0.0138".

point size: the vertical measurement used to identify or specify the size of a typeface. This measurement is roughly from the top of the ascender to the bottom of the descender.

Didot system: a system of print measurement used primarily in the European printing industry.

Mediaan system: a system of print measurement used primarily in Belgium.

American-British system: a system of print measurement used throughout North America and Great Britain.

ascender: the part of a type character extending above the body height.

descender: the part of a type character extending below the body height.

E gauge: a device used to measure point sizes and leading of printed type.

When You Know	Multiply by	To Find
Torque		
pound-inch	0.11298	newton-meters (N•m)
pound-foot	1.3558	newton-meters (N•m)
Light		
foot-candles	1.0764	lumens/meters^2 (m/m^2)
Speed		
miles per hour (mph)	1.6093	kilometers per hour (kph)
Force		
kilograms (k)	9.807	newtons (N)
ounces (oz)	0.278	newtons (N)
pounds (lb)	4.448	newtons (N)
Power		
horsepower (hp)	0.746	kilowatts (kW)
Pressure or Stress		
inches of water	0.2491	kilopascals (kPa)
pounds per square inch (psi)	6.895	kilopascals (kPa)
Energy or Work		
British thermal units (Btu)	1.55.0	joules (J)
foot-pounds	1.3558	joules (J)
kilowatt-hours	3600000.0	joules (J)
Length		
inches	25.4	millimeters
inches	2.54	centimeters
feet	0.3048	meters
feet	30.48	centimeters
yards	0.9*	meters
miles	1.6*	kilometers
Weight		
grains	15.4*	grams
ounces	28.0*	grams
ounces	.028*	kilograms
pounds	0.45*	kilograms
tons	.9*	tonnes
Volume		
fluid ounces	30.0*	milliliters
cups	0.24*	liters
pints	0.47*	liters
quarts	0.95*	liters
gallons	3.8*	liters
cubic inches	0.02*	
cubic feet	0.03*	cubic meters
cubic yards	0.76*	cubic meters
Area		
square inches	6.5*	square centimeters
square feet	0.09*	square meters
square yards	0.8*	square meters
square miles	2.6*	square kilometers
acres	0.4*	hectares
Temperature		
Fahrenheit (F)	5/9 (after subtracting 32)	Celsius

*approximate

Figure 3-2. Conversion charts can be used to change values from one measuring system to another.

Figure 3-3. The pieces of metal type illustrated here vary in size.

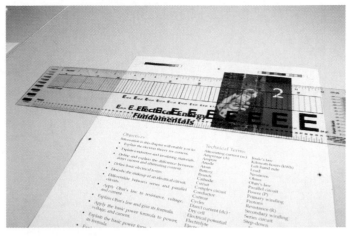

Figure 3-4. An E gauge is a measuring device for different point sizes of type and leading.

also be determined by taking two lowercase letters, one with an ascender and one with a descender, and aligning them side by side. The distance from the top of the highest ascender to the bottom of the lowest descender will be the approximate point size of the type body.

Comparing two typefaces having the same point size, but different body heights, makes it easier to see how letter height can differ. The copy in **Figure 3-5** is printed in two different typefaces. Both typefaces are 24-point type, but the actual size of the letters is different.

The amount of vertical space between lines of type is also measured in points and is called *leading*. An E gauge has a series of line-spacing grids marked with point sizes that can be used to approximate leading. See **Figure 3-6.** When the gauge is placed over several lines of type, the grid that most closely matches the spacing between the lines indicates the leading point size.

Determining line lengths

Line lengths or widths are given in picas and points. A *pica* measures approximately 1/6", or 0.166 mm. Twelve points equal a pica, and six picas equal approximately one inch (0.996"). See **Figure 3-7.** A *line gauge* is an instrument used to measure type sizes and line lengths in picas or inches. Line gauges typically measure up to 72 picas (approximately 12"). One side of the gauge is marked in inches, and the other side is marked in picas and *nonpareils* (units equal to one-half of a pica).

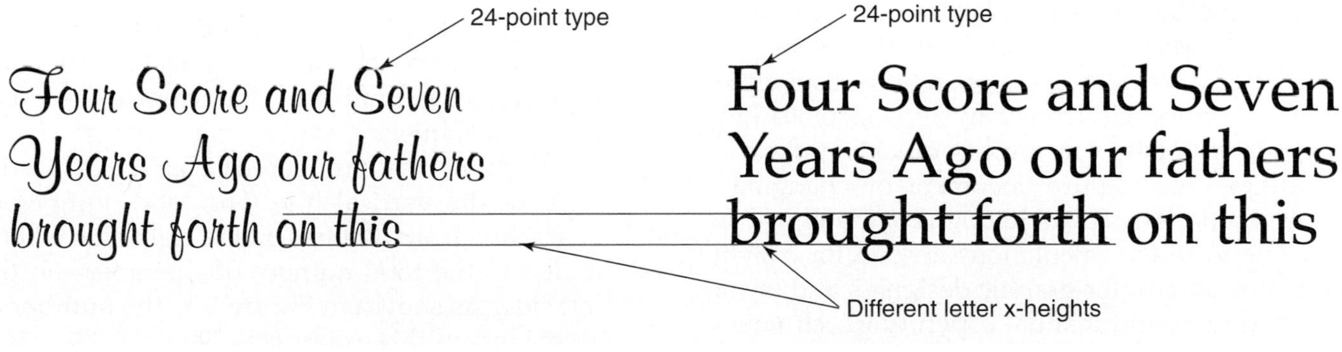

24-point type

Four Score and Seven Years Ago our fathers brought forth on this

24-point type

Four Score and Seven Years Ago our fathers brought forth on this

Different letter x-heights

Figure 3-5. Letter height of different typefaces printed at the same point size can vary greatly.

leading: the vertical distance separating each line of typeset copy, measured in points from one line to the next.

pica: a principal unit of measurement of the point system equal to 0.166˝.

line gauge: a device used to measure type sizes and line widths in picas or inches.

nonpareil: a unit of measure of the point system equal to one-half pica.

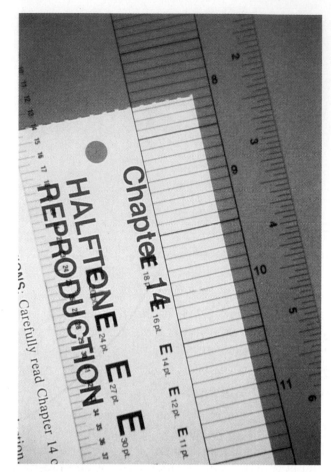

Figure 3-6. These lines represent the amount of vertical space that lines of text type require when they are set in the labeled point sizes.

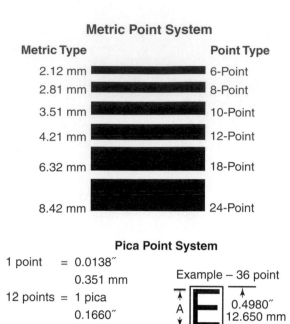

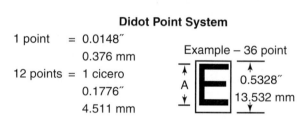

Figure 3-7. Equivalent measures for the metric, pica, and Didot point systems.

Copyfitting

Copyfitting is the process of fitting copy, or text, into a specific amount of space. This process can be done by altering type size, leading, line length, or character spacing. Typically, the person laying out the product determines how, or if, copy will fit into the layout.

Like many other prepress operations, copyfitting is now performed electronically. Type size, leading, line length, and letterspacing can quickly and easily be modified on an entire document by changing a few specifications (specs). Although computers can be used to perform the calculations needed for copyfitting, it is important for graphic designers and layout artists to understand manual copyfitting techniques. The most common method involves counting the number of characters in a given body of text. Follow the procedure outlined here when manually copyfitting typewritten manuscript, using the Courier typestyle:

1. To determine the number of characters in the text, begin by drawing a vertical line through the printed copy at the end of the shortest full line. See **Figure 3-8.**

2. Count the number of characters in a single line to the left of the vertical line. Include all characters, spaces, and punctuation.

3. Multiply the number of characters in one line by the number of full lines.

4. If there is a partial line, count the number of characters it contains and add this number to the total from the preceding step. This total represents the number of characters to the left of the vertical line.

5. Next, count the number of characters to the right of the vertical line. The total number of characters from all lines on the right side is then added to the total number of characters on the left side. As shown in **Figure 3-8,** the number of characters in this example is 290.

Once the number of characters in the text is determined, a type style and size are selected for the text. The line length and character size for the text, in picas, must then be determined. Typeface tables or catalogs showing different sizes of type and the number of characters per pica are commonly used. See **Figure 3-9.** Suppose you wish to set type in a 10-point sans serif typeface with a line length of 18

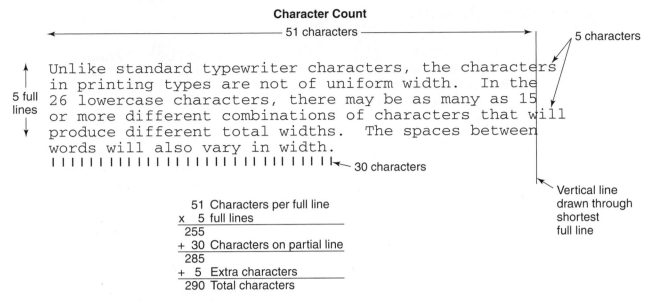

Figure 3-8. The number of characters in a block of text can be determined by drawing a vertical line though the shortest full line of copy and counting characters on both sides of the line.

Lower case alphabet 157 pts.
Characters per pica 2.2

14 pt.

THE EARLY PRINTERS CAST THE
They instructed some local black

Lower case alphabet 136 pts.
Characters per pica 2.5

12 pt.

THE EARLY PRINTERS CAST THEIR OWN
They instructed some local blacksmith

Lower case alphabet 117 pts.
Characters per pica 2.9

10 pt.

THE EARLY PRINTERS CAST THEIR OWN TYPES
They instructed some local blacksmith to make
the iron frames or chases in which the types

Lower case alphabet 93 pts.
Characters per pica 3.7

8 pt.

THE EARLY PRINTERS CAST THEIR OWN TYPES, MADE INK
They instructed some local blacksmith to make the iron
frames or chases in which the types are confined for

Lower case alphabet 88 pts.
Characters per pica 3.8

6 pt.

THE EARLY PRINTERS CAST THEIR OWN TYPES, MADE INK
They instructed some local blacksmith to make the iron frames
or chases in which the types are confined for printing, and
either made or designed the wooden cases and stands that

Figure 3-9. Typeface tables or catalogs list the number of characters per pica for different typestyles.

picas and there are 310 total characters in the text. The following steps are used to determine the space required for the text:

1. Referring to **Figure 3-9,** find the number of characters in 10-point type that will fill one pica of space. Multiply that figure (2.9) by the line length to find the number of characters in an 18-pica line:

   $2.9 \times 18 = 52.2$ characters per line

2. Find the number of typeset lines by dividing the total number of characters in the text by the number of characters per line:

   $310 \div 52 = 5.96$, or 6 lines (always round up here)

3. To find the total depth of the text, multiply the point size (type plus leading) by the number of typeset lines:

   $10 \times 6 = 60$ points

4. Convert the measure from points to picas. One pica is equal to 12 points.

   $60 \div 12 = 5$ picas

The text will measure 5 picas deep and 18 picas wide. This example is for type that is set solid. If leading is added, the amount of leading space in points must be added to the type size. If the type is set as 10 points with 2 points of leading (10/12), the calculation is as follows:

10-point type + 2-point leading = 12 points
12 points × 6 lines = 72 points
$72 \div 12 = 6$ picas

The depth of the text, with leading added, would be 6 picas. The text would measure 6 picas deep and 18 picas wide.

copyfitting: the process of fitting copy or text into a specific amount of space.

Paper—Size, Weight, and Thickness

Paper is manufactured for many purposes and in many sizes. Along with knowing which type of paper will best suit a particular job, printers must understand variances in size, thickness, and weight. Paper is very costly, and there should be as little waste as possible. The printer must be able to determine how much paper is needed and how to cut and size the paper. The following is a brief description of the information and steps needed to determine these factors. For more detailed information on paper production, qualities, and calculations, refer to Chapter 18.

Paper Sizes

Paper mills have agreed on **standard sizes** to which paper is cut and sold to printing companies. This variety allows printers to order paper (called *stock*) to match the requirements of their presses and their customers' needs. **Paper sizes** are designated in length and width dimensions. Each classification of paper (such as business, cover, and book) is assigned a **basic size**, which usually determines the available sizes. For example, the basic size of business paper is 17″ × 22″. Commonly found sizes for business papers are 17″ × 22″ (the basic size), 22″ × 34″ (twice the basic size), 11″ × 17″ (half the basic size), and 8 1/2″ × 11″ (one-quarter of the basic size). See **Figure 3-10.** Standard sizes often satisfy a particular end-use requirement. For example, bond paper is often purchased at 17″ × 22″ because, when this size is cut into quarters, it produces four sheets that are 8 1/2″ × 11″, which is the normal size for letterheads.

Grade	Basic Size
Bond	17″ × 22″ (432 mm × 559 mm)
Book	25″ × 38″ (635 mm × 965 mm)
Offset	25″ × 38″ (635 mm × 965 mm)
Cover	20″ × 26″ (508 mm × 660 mm)
Text	25″ × 38″ (635 mm × 965 mm)

Figure 3-10. Some commonly used grades of paper and their basic sizes. Conventional dimensions (inches) can be converted to metric dimensions (mm) by multiplying the inches by 25.4 and rounding off to the nearest whole millimeter.

Standard envelope sizes

Envelopes are classified by size and distinguished by styles serving a special use. See **Figure 3-11.** Business envelope sizes are usually designated by number. The most commonly used size is a Number 10, which measures 4 1/8″×9 1/2″. Window envelopes are available in the same size and are generally used for invoices or statements.

Envelopes used for wedding announcements and invitations or other formal occasions commonly measure 5″ × 6″. Open-end envelopes are larger types used for mailing reports, pamphlets, magazines, and other materials. Common sizes are 9″ × 12″ and 8 3/4″ × 11 1/4″.

International Organization for Standardization (ISO) paper sizes

The **International Organization for Standardization (ISO)** has developed standard metric sizes for paper. The sizes, known as the **ISO series**, are given in both SI metric units (mm) and U.S. Customary units (inches). ISO sizes are commonly grouped into the following three series:

- **A series.** Used for general printing requirements.
- **B series.** Used for posters.
- **C series.** Used for postcards, folders, and envelopes.

Envelope Style

Commercial	Window
Text	Booklet, open-side
Baronial	Banker's flat and wallet flap
	Banker's flat and wallet flap
Clasp	Open end

Figure 3-11. Each style and size of envelope fits a specific purpose. (Leslie Paper Co.)

The A-series and B-series paper sizes are rectangular. Their sizes are based on the ratio of the two sides having the proportion of one to the square root of two (1:1.416). In the A series, for example, A3 is half the area of A2 and double the area of A4. The A series has the unique advantage that the proportion of height to width remains the same, regardless of size. See **Figure 3-12.**

The ISO A- and B-series paper sizes are considered to be trimmed sizes. There are other series, however, used to classify sizes for normal trims, bleed work, and extra trims. See **Figure 3-13** and **Figure 3-14.** Although 8 1/2″ × 11″ is still thought of as a standard letterhead and brochure size in the United States, ISO promoters have adopted the A4 size, which is 8 1/4″ × 11 1/2″.

Note

To convert conventional paper sizes to metric, multiply the number of inches by 25.4 and round off to the nearest whole millimeter. The following is an example:

8 1/2″ × 25.4 = 215.9 mm = 216 mm
11″ × 25.4 = 279.4 mm = 279 mm

The familiar 8 1/2″ × 11″ size is equal to approximately 216 mm × 279 mm.

ISO Sizes	Metric (mm)	Conventional (″)
A0	841 × 1189	33.11 × 46.81
A1	594 × 841	23.39 × 33.11
A2	420 × 594	16.54 × 23.39
A3	297 × 420	11.69 × 16.54
A4	210 × 297	8.27 × 11.69
A5	148 × 210	5.83 × 8.27
A6	105 × 148	4.13 × 5.83
A7	74 × 105	2.91 × 4.13
A8	52 × 74	2.05 × 2.91
A9	37 × 52	1.46 × 2.05
A10	26 × 37	1.02 × 1.46

ISO Sizes	Metric (mm)	Conventional (″)
B0	1000 × 1414	39.37 × 55.67
B1	707 × 1000	27.83 × 39.37
B2	500 × 707	19.68 × 27.83
B3	353 × 500	13.90 × 19.68
B4	250 × 353	9.84 × 13.90
B5	176 × 250	6.93 × 9.84
B6	125 × 176	4.92 × 6.93
B7	88 × 125	3.46 × 4.92
B8	62 × 88	2.44 × 3.46
B9	44 × 62	1.73 × 2.44
B10	31 × 44	1.22 × 1.73

Figure 3-13. ISO A- and B-series metric and conventional paper sizes. Both the ISO A- and B-series paper sizes are based on the same ratio (1:1.416). (Center for Metric Education, Western Michigan University)

standard size: a commonly available sheet dimension.

paper size: a metric or conventional measurement that describes the length and width dimensions of paper.

basic size: the size of a sheet of a particular grade of paper at which its basis weight is determined.

International Organization for Standardization (ISO): the organization that sets international standards on products, services, and testing in nearly all industries.

ISO series: the standard sizes of paper set by the ISO.

ISO-A Size Paper

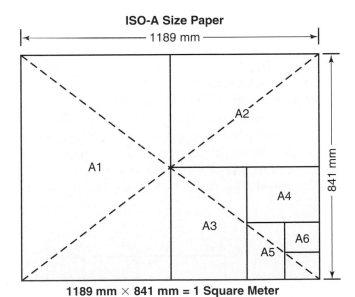

1189 mm × 841 mm = 1 Square Meter

Figure 3-12. The ISO A-series size of paper is based on the area of one square meter. Each cut reduces the size of the sheet to 50% of the previous size; for example, the size of A2 is double that of A3. (Center for Metric Education, Western Michigan University)

ISO Sizes for Normal Trims		
ISO Size	**Metric (mm)**	**Conventional (″)**
RA0	860 × 1220	33.66 × 48.03
RA1	610 × 860	24.02 × 33.86
RA2	430 × 610	16.93 × 24.02
ISO Sizes for Bleed Work or Extra Trims		
ISO Size	**Metric (mm)**	**Conventional (″)**
SRA0	900 × 1280	35.43 × 50.39
SRA1	640 × 900	25.20 × 35.43
SRA2	450 × 640	17.72 × 25.20

Figure 3-14. Trimmed ISO paper sizes for normal trims, bleed work, and extra trims. (Center for Metric Education, Western Michigan University)

Press dimensions also influence paper sizes. Nearly all printing presses are manufactured outside of the United States, and their sizes are expressed in metric terms. For instance, printers will commonly call a multicolor Heidelberg offset press a *40-inch press*, but it is actually 102 cm, or about 40 1/4″, wide. A press of this size prints 25″ × 38″ paper with no difficulty, but it is capable of printing a sheet as large as 70 cm × 100 cm (approximately 27 1/2″ × 39 3/8″). This is the preferred sheet size in Europe and other parts of the world.

ISO envelope sizes

The ISO has also established standard sizes for envelopes. The sizes for ISO A-series paper are compatible with the sizes for ISO-C envelopes. See **Figure 3-15.** These sizes are designed to hold the A-series sheets unfolded or folded. For example, an A1 sheet will fit unfolded into a C1 envelope. If it is folded in half, the sheet will fit in a C2 envelope.

Paper Weight

Most *grades* of paper are known by their basis weight. The ***basis weight*** is a measure of the number of pounds in a ream of paper cut to its basic size. For example, when identifying paper by its basis weight and grade, you would refer to it as *20-pound bond* or *70-pound book*. A ***ream*** of 20-pound bond consists of 500 sheets of 17″ × 22″ writing paper and weighs 20 pounds. A ream of 70-pound book paper, containing 500 sheets measuring 25″ × 38″ in size, weighs 70 pounds.

The basis weight is indicated after the dimensions:

$$17″ × \underline{22″}—20$$
$$25″ × \mathbf{38″}—70$$

The paper grain direction is often indicated by an underlined dimension (22″) or a bold-type dimension (**38″**). If an *M* appears after the weight, it means the weight refers to a quantity of 1000 sheets, rather than 500. For example, 25″ × 38″—140M describes a quantity of 1000 sheets of 25″ × 38″ book paper, weighing 140 pounds.

Paper dealers often provide paper manufactured in other than common sizes. These are listed in tables from the manufacturer. The tables usually list prices per thousand sheets. For example, a 20-pound bond paper could be listed as 17″ × 22″—40M. The *M* represents a quantity of 1000.

The approximate ream weight of an irregular-size paper can be determined by multiplying the sheet length by the width. This will determine the square inch area of the irregular-size sheet. Multiply this figure by the weight factor the manufacturer provides to determine the ream weight. To find the ***M weight*** (weight of 1000 sheets), multiply by two.

When using the U.S. Customary system of measurement, paper weight is expressed by pound-weight per ream or caliper. When using a metric weight system, paper weight is expressed in grams per square meter (g/m²). Factors for converting

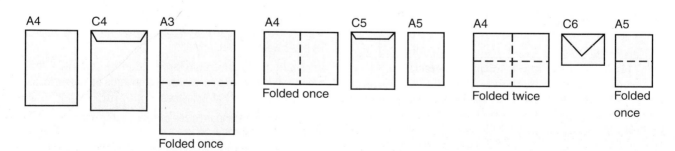

A4   C4   A3   A4   C5   A5   A4   C6   A5

Folded once

Folded once   Folded twice   Folded once

Figure 3-15. ISO A-series paper and ISO C-series envelopes have compatible sizes. The envelopes are designed so A-series paper will fit into different envelopes, folded or unfolded.

Grade of Paper	Conventional Size (″)	Conventional to Metric	Metric to Conventional
Book	25 × 38	1.480	0.675
News	24 × 36	1.627	0.614
Writing	12 × 22	3.760	0.266
Cover	20 × 26	2.704	0.370
Cardboard	22 × 28	2.282	0.438

Figure 3-16. Use these factors for converting paper weights from conventional or metric units.

conventional weights of paper to metric units are listed in **Figure 3-16.** The conversion factors for changing from conventional weights of 500 sheets to g/m^2 are listed in the third column. The conversion factors for changing weights from g/m^2 to conventional weights are listed in the fourth column.

Using the conversion factors shown, a ream of coated book paper would be expressed as 100 g/m^2, or 67.5 lbs. (100 × 0.675). A ream of good writing paper would be listed as 85 g/m^2, or 22.61 lbs. (85 × 0.266). A rough conversion of U.S. Customary to ISO metric for basic weight can be made by multiplying the weight in pounds by 1.5. For example, a 50-pound book paper is about the same as 75 g/m^2.

Nominal weight is the basis weight actually specified when ordering paper. This weight is the target weight in manufacturing. The actual basis weight varies somewhat from the nominal weight, due to variations in moisture content and other variables in the papermaking process.

Paper Thickness

Papers are also available in various thicknesses, according to their classification and weight. A paper's thickness is its *caliper.* Several types of devices are available for measuring caliper. A caliper gauge, a device that works similarly to a *micrometer* with broader feet, measures a paper's thickness. See **Figure 3-17.** In America, *paper caliper* is expressed in thousandths of an inch, also referred to as *points.* This book was printed on paper that is approximately 3/1000″ (or three points thick).

Image Measurement

The advancement of computer technology in the printing industry has revolutionized the approach to the production and manipulation of visual images. Traditional methods used in operations such as film processing and color separation have been replaced with electronic methods. Highly advanced software programs allow the quick and easy enlargement, reduction, modification, and reproduction of images. Although many of the measurements once taken

Figure 3-17. A paper caliper reveals this hockey card to be 14 points thick.

by hand are now computed electronically, people employed in the industry must understand how and why various calculations are made.

grade: a means used to identify and categorize the hundreds of different types of paper.

basis weight: the weight, in pounds, of a ream of paper cut to the basic size for a particular grade of paper.

ream: for most types of paper, 500 sheets of paper of a single size.

M weight: the figure representing the weight of 1000 sheets of a paper in the size listed.

nominal weight: the basis weight specified when ordering paper.

caliper: the thickness of a sheet of paper, measured in thousandths of an inch or in points.

micrometer: a device that measures the thickness of thin objects, such as paper.

paper caliper: a device used to measure paper thickness.

Resolution

One of the most important measurements of an image is its resolution. Resolution describes the visual quality of an image and is a measure of elements defining the image. An image will have a resolution measurement whether it is in electronic or printed format. In computer imaging, the term *resolution* can mean a variety of different things. The term's meaning depends on the image and the particular aspect of a graphics system you are discussing. It is important to be able to discern what type of resolution is being discussed and whether or not the resolution is adequate. If the proper resolution is not used, the result will not be what the customer expects.

Computer screens

When discussing computer screens, resolution can refer to both the color depth and intensity of the displayed image or to the number of *picture elements (pixels)* displayed per unit of length. Bit depth (or *color depth*) refers to the number of colors that can be displayed on a monitor. The number of bits used to describe each screen pixel determines the number of colors that can be displayed. A *binary digit (bit)* is the smallest piece of information a computer uses. The pixel is the smallest indivisible point of display on a computer monitor. Therefore, the unit for color-depth measurement is bits per pixel.

If a monitor has a color depth of one bit per pixel, it can describe only two colors (black and white). A monitor with a color depth of 24 bits per pixel, however, can describe over 16 million colors. Color depth is an important consideration when buying monitors. Someone working in the editorial or finance department would not require a color depth of 24 bits per pixel, whereas a graphic artist or the image-setter operator would benefit greatly from the higher-resolution monitor. See **Figure 3-18.**

A computer screen's resolution is also measured by the number of *pixels per inch (ppi)* or *lines per inch (lpi)*. Monitor resolution is commonly expressed as the number of rows and columns of the monitor's pixel array. For example, a 640 × 480 monitor has 640 pixels across and 480 pixels down. By comparison, a high-resolution monitor rated at 1600 × 1200 pixels is able to display a resolution of 1600 pixels

1 Bit   8 Bits   24 Bits

Figure 3-18. A monitor with a color depth of 1 bit is limited to displaying only type and other line art, while a monitor with an 8-bit color depth can display a gray scale image. A color image requires a color depth of 24 bits or more.

horizontally and 1200 pixels vertically. The greater the ppi is, the better the resolution will be.

The term *lpi* also indicates the number of dots in an image. The lpi of an image is similar to the ppi or *dots per inch (dpi)* of the image. The number of lines in an inch will equal the number of dpi because lines are also composed of pixels and dots. The greater the lpi or dpi is, the greater the resolution and the sharper the image will be.

The type of image being described can also determine the meaning of screen resolution. When describing vector displays, screen resolution refers to the number of horizontal lpi. When describing raster displays, screen resolution refers to the number of horizontal and vertical pixels that can be displayed. *Dot pitch* is the measure of the diameter of an individual pixel. A monitor with a dot pitch of 0.32, for example, is composed of pixels 0.32 mm in diameter.

Scanners

Electronic scanners are identified by a measure of dpi for image resolution. A laser printer rated at 600 dpi can produce a resolution of 600 dots for each horizontal or vertical inch. A scanner that scans images at 1200 dpi can produce a file with an image resolution of 1200 dpi.

The term *pixel* is also used to refer to the smallest point a scanner can detect. This is the same as the *sampling rate* of the scanner. See **Figure 3-19.** A scanner that takes 600 samples per inch (or 600 distinct points of imaging each inch) can be said to have a resolution of 600 ppi or dpi.

Almost all the images used in printed publications are manipulated electronically. Negatives, slides, transparencies, photos, paintings, line drawings, type, and even printed images are scanned electronically for

Figure 3-19. Compare the difference in the image when the image is scanned at one resolution and at twice that resolution. Observe that the higher scan resolution provides greater detail.

picture element (pixel): the smallest indivisible point of display on a computer monitor.

color depth: the number of distinct colors that can be represented by a piece of hardware or software.

binary digit (bit): the smallest piece of information used by a computer, consisting of either the number *1* or the number *0*.

pixels per inch (ppi): the number of pixels making up a digital image. Also referred to as dots per inch (dpi).

lines per inch (lpi): a term used to describe screen ruling, computer screen resolution, and image resolution.

dots per inch (dpi): a measure of the resolution of a computer monitor, a scanner, or an output device.

dot pitch: the measure of the diameter of an individual pixel.

sampling rate: in digitizing of images, the frequency with which points are recorded. In scanning, the sampling rate is measured as the number of samples taken per inch (or per mm), both horizontally and vertically.

use in printed materials. The quality of the scanned image depends on the type of scanner and its sampling rate.

The Warren Standard indicates that there is a simple way to govern how images should be scanned. Doubling the line screen at which the image will be printed provides the number of dpi at which the image should be scanned. Scanning at different resolutions and saving as different formats will change the file size and the amount of storage space needed. See **Figure 3-20**.

Output devices

Resolution is also used to describe output devices. Output devices such as laser printers and imagesetters generate images composed of many tiny dots. Resolution is determined by measuring how many of these dots can fit in a unit of linear distance. Commonly, dpi is used as a measure of output resolution, but a preferable measure is the number of detectable line pairs per inch or lpi. This is because the dots are often deliberately made to overlap to produce a better image.

The resolution (in dpi) required of a scanned image depends on the halftone screen value in lpi at which it will be printed and the scaling percentage. In short, fine screenings and significant enlargements require higher resolution. The following is a useful formula for calculating the optimum dpi:

$$\text{dpi resolution} = (\text{lpi} \times 1.5) \times \frac{\text{reproduction width}}{\text{original width}}$$

For example, if a 4" × 6" color print is to be enlarged to 8" wide and printed with a 150-line *screen*, its minimum scanning resolution should be the following:

$$\text{dpi resolution} = (\text{lpi} \times 1.5) \times \frac{\text{reproduction width}}{\text{original width}}$$

$$\text{dpi resolution} = (150 \times 1.5) \times \frac{8}{4}$$

File Sizes at Various Resolutions								
		Bitmap		**Grayscale**		**RGB**		**CMYK**	
35mm:	120 dpi	3	kb	19	kb	57	kb	76	kb
	170 dpi	6	kb	38	kb	114	kb	152	kb
	220 dpi	9	kb	64	kb	191	kb	254	kb
	300 dpi	15	kb	118	kb	353	kb	470	kb
	400 dpi	27	kb	210	kb	628	kb	838	kb
	600 dpi	60	kb	471	kb	1.38	Mb	1.84	Mb
4" × 5":	120 dpi	36	kb	282	kb	844	kb	1.10	Mb
	170 dpi	72	kb	565	kb	1.65	Mb	2.21	Mb
	220 dpi	119	kb	946	kb	2.77	Mb	3.69	Mb
	300 dpi	220	kb	1.72	Mb	5.15	Mb	6.87	Mb
	400 dpi	391	kb	3.05	Mb	9.16	Mb	12.2	Mb
	600 dpi	879	kb	6.87	Mb	20.6	Mb	27.5	Mb
8" × 10":	120 dpi	141	kb	1.10	Mb	3.30	Mb	4.39	Mb
	170 dpi	283	kb	2.21	Mb	6.62	Mb	8.82	Mb
	220 dpi	473	kb	3.69	Mb	11.1	Mb	14.8	Mb
	300 dpi	879	kb	6.87	Mb	20.6	Mb	27.5	Mb
	400 dpi	1.53	Mb	12.2	Mb	36.6	Mb	48.8	Mb
	600 dpi	3.43	Mb	27.5	Mb	82.4	Mb	109.9	Mb

Figure 3-20. Scanning an image at different dpi and in different formats will result in a wide range of file sizes. (S.D. Warren Co.)

dpi resolution = (225) × 2
dpi resolution = 450 dpi

Although the term *pixel* is often used to refer to the individual dots making up an image output from a digital device, these pixels, or dots, are more correctly known as *spots*.

Photography-Related Measurement

Images are usually enlarged or reduced by certain percentages for use in on-screen or printed reproduction. Traditionally, image size was manipulated photographically. Traditional methods used in halftone photography rely on measuring scales, halftone screens, and process cameras. The layout person and camera operator have to understand the fundamentals of proportion in order to correctly reproduce images. Although computer imaging has eliminated the need for traditional processes, it is important to understand the fundamentals of proportion.

Sizing

The operation of preparing illustrations for enlargement or reduction is known as *sizing*, or *scaling*. When preparing images, it is important to remember that enlargements tend to magnify defects in the original, and reductions usually reduce defects and sharpen the detail. For most purposes, artwork and photographs are reduced to retain detail.

Enlargements and reductions are proportional. This means a photograph or drawing will have its same proportions when reduced or enlarged. For example, a 3″ × 5″ photograph reduced 50% will then measure 1 1/2″ × 2 1/2″. A reduction will reduce the width, as well as the height. An enlargement will increase both the width and the depth. It is important to remember that the image will also retain its shape. A rectangle will reproduce as a smaller or larger rectangle, and a square will reproduce as a smaller or larger square.

When sizing a photograph or drawing, one of its two dimensions is called the *holding dimension*. The holding dimension is extremely important to the layout. If a photograph is being reduced to fit a column that is 15 picas wide, the holding dimension is the width of the photograph. See **Figure 3-21**. If the height of the column is the critical factor, it becomes the holding dimension.

To illustrate the concept, imagine reducing a 4″ × 6″ photograph to a width of 3″. The width becomes the holding dimension because both the original (old)

Figure 3-21. If this cropped photograph is sized so the reproduction width becomes 15 picas, the width becomes the holding dimension, and the reproduction height is determined by calculation. If the reproduction height is known, however, the height is the holding dimension, and the reproduction width is calculated. (Diagraph®)

and reproduction (new) widths are known. When the three known values are placed into the formula, the reproduction height becomes the unknown:

$$\frac{4″}{6″} = \frac{3″}{x}$$

4x = 18
x = 4.5″

The proportion scale

One way of calculating enlargements and reductions is the proportion-scale method. A *proportion scale* is a simple calculator made up of a wheel that revolves on a circle. See **Figure 3-22**. The measurements on the smaller, inside wheel represent the dimensions of the original art. The measurements

screen: a ruled screen used to change continuous tone photographs into dotted halftones for printing.

sizing (scaling): the process of reducing or enlarging an image.

holding dimension: as part of the sizing process, the new dimension that is known.

proportion scale: a device used to determine the percentage of reduction or enlargement an image requires, based on a ratio of the size of the original to the size it needs to fit.

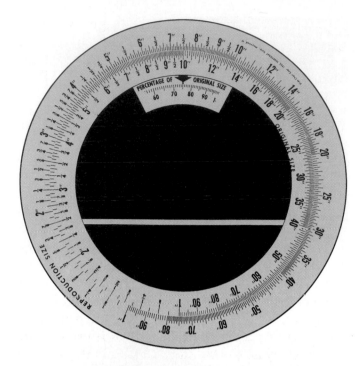

Figure 3-22. A proportional scale is used to determine the limit of image enlargement or reduction. (ANSCO Graphic Arts Products)

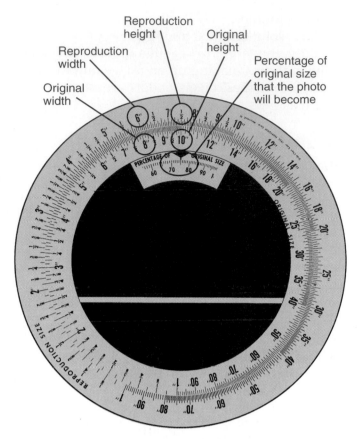

Figure 3-23. In this example, the holding dimension's original width is 8″. This dimension will be reduced to 6″. The 75% reproduction size will reduce the remaining dimension from 10″ to 7 1/2″. (ANSCO Graphic Arts Products)

on the outside wheel refer to the dimensions of the art after scaling. This outside scale is known as the *reproduction size*.

To size the art, line up the holding dimension on the inside scale with the desired size on the reproduction scale. The percentage of original size appears in the window opening. Assume a photo is 8″ wide and 10″ deep. The photo must be scaled to fit a space 6″ wide. The holding dimension is, then, the width of the photo, or 8″. The proportion scale is used in the following manner:

1. Locate the original width of the artwork on the inner wheel scale, as shown in **Figure 3-23.** This would be 8″ in our example.
2. Turn the wheel and match the original width with the desired new width, 6″. The new width is found on the outer scale. See **Figure 3-23.**
3. Read the percentage figure under the arrow in the window opening of the scale. Refer to **Figure 3-23.**
4. To find the new depth of this artwork, locate 10″ (the original depth) on the original-size scale. Read the new depth, which lines up opposite on the reproduction-size scale. The depth is 7 1/2″.

A proportion scale can be used to determine percentages for both the length and width of an image in either conventional or metric units. A reproduction size of 100% indicates the image will be reproduced at the same size, while a reproduction size of 50% indicates the image will be reduced by half its original size. See **Figure 3-24.**

The diagonal-line method

The diagonal-line method can also be used for projecting image enlargement or reduction. With this method, the diagonal of a rectangle or square is used to see the final results of making an enlargement or reduction. See **Figure 3-25.** Enlargements and reductions are proportional, which means, if a photograph or drawing is narrow in width and long in depth, it will have these same proportions when it is reduced. Follow the steps below when using the diagonal-line method:

1. Determine the space allowed for the photograph or artwork on the comprehensive or rough layout.
2. Place a sheet of vellum paper over the photograph and hinge it to the back with tape.
3. Place a piece of transparent-acetate film between the photo and overlay sheet. This will protect the photo from damage.

Original size

Reduced size

50%

50%

A 50% reduction

Figure 3-24. A reduction in size will reduce width and depth proportionately.

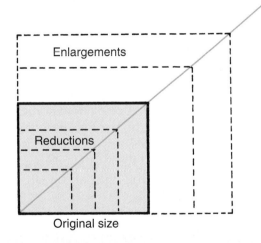

Enlargements

Reductions

Original size

Figure 3-25. The diagonal line is used to see the results of an enlargement or reduction.

4. Draw lines on the vellum sheet to show the image area of the photo to be reduced. This might be the entire photo or a cropped section. Use a T square and triangle. The corners must be square.

5. Draw a diagonal line from the lower-left corner to the top-right corner. Use a straightedge.

6. On the baseline, measure and mark the desired new width on the photo.

7. Draw a vertical line from the baseline to the diagonal line. This shows the reduced photo width. This line must be exactly 90° to the baseline.

8. Draw a horizontal line at the point where the new-width vertical line crosses the diagonal line. This line will then show the new height. Use a T square to make the line parallel with the baseline.

The same method can be used to enlarge a photo or artwork. Just extend the baseline to the right beyond the first photo width. Do the same to the diagonal line. Determine the new width or height. Draw the correct vertical and horizontal lines. The lines must intersect with the extended diagonal line.

The percentage of enlargement or reduction can also be found by mathematical calculations. To calculate the percentage, divide the desired reproduction size by the size of the original copy. The length of the sides can be stated in inches, millimeters, or picas. These calculations are shown in **Figure 3-26.**

The width and depth of rectangular areas enlarge or reduce in direct proportion to each other. If the original copy is 3″ wide and 6″ deep and the 3″ width has to be reduced to 2″, how deep is the reduced copy? The following statement of proportion is used:

original width/desired width = original depth/ desired depth

3″/2″ = 6″/desired depth

3″ × desired depth = 12″

desired depth = 4″

Screens

Halftone photography screens are used to change continuous tone photographs into dotted halftones for printing. Screens are measured in lpi in conventional units and lines per centimeter in metric units. The lpi of a halftone screen is equal to the number of halftone dots per linear inch. Thus, a screen described as 175-line would contain 175 rows and 175 columns of dots, or 30,625 dpi.

Screen sizes below 75 lpi are considered to be coarse, while sizes above 133 lpi are considered fine. The greater the number of lines is, the finer the screen will be. Conventional screen sizes can be converted to metric units by dividing the lpi by 2.54. To convert metric screen sizes to lpi, multiply the number of lines per centimeter by 2.54.

Different *screen angles* are used when making color separations for each of the four subtractive

reproduction size: the size of an image after the sizing process, not to be confused with the original size.

screen angle: the angular relationship of halftone screens used in making black-and-white halftones and color separations for four-color printing.

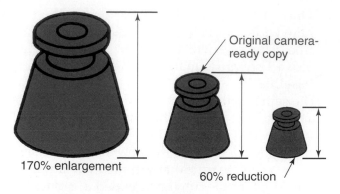

170% enlargement

60% reduction

Original camera-ready copy

Enlargement Calculations

$$\frac{\text{Length of enlarged side}}{\text{Length of same side on original}} = \frac{17}{10} = \begin{array}{l}170\% \text{ of}\\ \text{original size}\end{array}$$

Reduction Calculations

$$\frac{\text{Length of reduced side}}{\text{Length of same side on original}} = \frac{6}{10} = \begin{array}{l}60\% \text{ of}\\ \text{original size}\end{array}$$

Figure 3-26. Mathematical calculations can be used to determine a reduction or enlargement. To find percentage, divide the desired reproduction size by the size of the original.

primaries. Screen angles are measured in degrees. A scale giving the screen angles for each color is shown in **Figure 3-27.** The line patterns on each screen have a specific angular relationship to prevent a moiré pattern (an unwanted dot pattern). To print properly, each separation must have the correct screen angle:

- 105° for cyan.
- 75° for magenta.
- 90° for yellow.
- 45° is normally used for black.

Color Measurement

Precise standardized measurement is needed to maintain consistency in color reproduction. Various measuring instruments have been designed for use in the printing industry. Some measure density, some measure color values, and others measure light waves. The most common color-measuring instruments are spectrophotometers, densitometers, colorimeters, and spectrodensitometers.

Spectrophotometers

The *spectrophotometer* is the most accurate type of color-measurement device. A *photometer* is used to measure light intensity. The prefix *spectro-* indicates that the instrument is capable of measuring light of different colors or wavelengths. Most of the

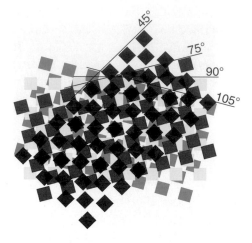

Figure 3-27. Each of the four primary printing colors requires a specific screen angle. This enlargement shows the superimposed cyan, magenta, yellow, and black halftone screens.

spectrophotometers used in the printing industry are limited to reading light waves in the visible spectrum.

Densitometers

Densitometers compute the light-stopping or light-absorption ability of an image or surface material. See **Figure 3-28.** Simply stated, densitometers compute the density, or darkness, of an image. The basic difference between a color densitometer and a spectrophotometer is in the bandwidth of light being used. A densitometer uses red, green, and blue filters to isolate broad bands of light. A spectrophotometer uses a prism to spread the light and a slit to isolate narrow bands of light.

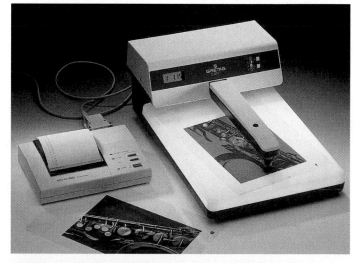

Figure 3-28. Depending on the type being used, densitometers can be used on negative or positive transparencies, photographs, or printed images. (Gretag Macbeth, New Windsor, NY)

Depending on the type being used, densitometers can be used on negative or positive transparencies, photographs, or printed images. *Reflection densitometers* measure the amount of light bouncing off a photographic print or printed sheet at a 90° angle. See **Figure 3-29**. *Transmission densitometers* measure the fraction of light conveyed through a negative or positive transparency without being absorbed or scattered. Combination densitometers measure both reflection and transmission densities.

A *scanning densitometer* is used to scan print-control strips located in the margin of printed sheets as they enter the delivery pile of the press. See **Figure 3-30**. Any color problems that might be occurring on the sheets are instantly indicated on the scanning device.

Colorimeters

Colorimeters measure and compute color values in a way that models vision. These instruments measure colors quantitatively; that is, they measure them numerically. A colorimeter identifies a color by indicating how much red, green, and blue are present. The colorimeter allows the user to match colors more precisely than to judge them visually.

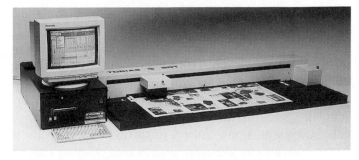

Figure 3-30. Scanning densitometers are used to measure the color bars on printed sheets and bring problems to the immediate attention of the press operator. (Tobias Associates, Inc.)

Spectrodensitometers

Spectrodensitometers serve all the functions of a spectrophotometer, densitometer, and colorimeter. This single instrument measures color value and optical density. Many of these instruments can also be used to measure paper attributes and special colors.

spectrophotometer: the most accurate type of color-measurement device. A spectrophotometer measures light intensity and different colors or wavelengths of light.

photometer: a device used to measure light intensity.

densitometer: a color-measurement device that computes the light-stopping or light-absorption ability of an image or a surface material.

reflection densitometer: an electronic device used to measure the amount of light that bounces, or reflects, off a photographic print or printed sheet at a 90° angle.

transmission densitometer: an electronic instrument that measures the fraction of incident light conveyed through negative or positive transparency without being absorbed or scattered.

scanning densitometer: an electronic instrument installed on press that uses a photocell to accurately measure the amount of light reflected from or through different tone values.

colorimeter: a color-measurement device that measures and compares the hue, purity, and brightness of colors in a manner modeling vision.

spectrodensitometer: a color-measurement device that serves all the functions of a spectrophotometer, densitometer, and colorimeter in a single instrument.

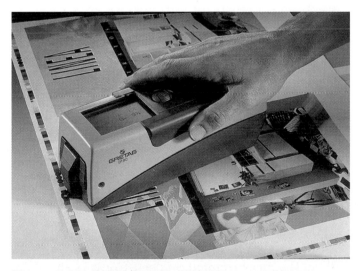

Figure 3-29. Reflection densitometers vary by manufacturer, but most offer all the functions needed for prepress and print production in a single unit. (Gretag Macbeth, New Windsor, NY)

Summary

Precise measurement standards and good math skills are extremely important in the printing industry. Everyone involved in the production process must have good math skills and a basic understanding of the most commonly used systems of measurement. The creation of standardized systems of measurement allowed goods and services to be traded and sold on an equal basis. In the printing industry, standardized systems of measurement allow materials such as paper and envelopes to be used and produced in similar sizes on an international basis. This allows printers to order stock to match the requirements of their presses and customers to buy paper and paper products according to their needs.

The advancement of computer technology in the printing industry has revolutionized the approach to the production and manipulation of visual images. People involved in the industry should have some knowledge of resolution requirements for images, scanners, and output devices. These people should also understand photoconversion measurement, including the use of proportion scales, halftone screens, and color-measurement devices.

Review Questions

Please do not write in this book. Write your answers on a separate sheet of paper.

1. What are the two most commonly used systems of measurement?
2. Using the conversion chart in **Figure 3-3**, convert the values listed below.
   A. 2″ = _____ mm
   B. 4 meters = _____ yards
   C. 12 quarts = _____ liters
   D. 24 milliliters = _____ fluid oz.
   E. 550 lbs. = _____ kilograms
   F. 79°F = _____ °C
3. A point measures approximately _____ of an inch.
4. Originally, to what did the point size of a piece of type refer?
5. The point size of a character includes _____ above and below the character.
6. _____ is the vertical space between lines of type.
7. The pica is approximately _____ of an inch.
8. Different types of paper are known as _____ and are classified with a basic size.
9. What is the basis weight of paper?
10. How many sheets of paper are in a ream?
11. List the three ISO series and the uses for each.
12. The various thicknesses of paper are called _____.
13. What is nominal weight?
14. The unit for color-depth measurement is _____.
15. What does it mean if a monitor has a screen-resolution rating of 640 × 480?
16. What is dot pitch?
17. What are the screen angles used when making color separations for the four subtractive primaries?
18. Identify the four most common color-measuring instruments.
19. What does the prefix *spectro-* indicate?
20. _____ densitometers measure the amount of light bouncing off a photographic print or printed sheet at a 90° angle.

Skill-Building Activities

1. Using a line gauge and an E gauge, measure the elements on page 74 of this text and answer the following questions. Give your answers in both metric- and point-system units.
   A. What is the inside margin?
   B. What is the outside margin?
   C. How much space is there between columns?
   D. What are the measurements of **Figure 3-20**?
   E. How much space is there between the heading and the body text?
2. Gather a variety of materials, including solids and liquids. Using various tools, measure the materials and compare the accuracy of the measurement devices. Convert all measurements to metric units and compile a brief report of your findings. Use charts and graphs where applicable.

3. Choose one of the following topics to research and create an illustrated report. If possible, use a computer for layout and design.
    - The origin of measurement systems.
    - The history of the SI metric system.
    - The history of the ISO.
    - The evolution of the process color-separation methods.

4. In a group of two or three students, gather a variety of printed material. Determine the number of typefaces used on each piece of material. Measure type sizes and compare typefaces having the same point size but different character heights.

5. A 30-page manuscript typed on an elite typewriter contains 22 lines per page. An elite typewriter produces 12 characters per inch. Each line of the manuscript contains about 83 characters. The manuscript will be composed in 9-point Times Roman type. This type contains 3.0 characters per pica. Each line of type will be 20 picas wide. Between lines, 1-point leading will be used. How many typeset lines will there be altogether? What will their total depth be in picas? Show your calculations.

6. Convert inches to metric units:
    A. Convert 2″ to millimeters.
    B. Convert 4 1/2″ to millimeters.
    C. Convert 5 3/4″ to centimeters.
    D. Convert 7 1/4″ to centimeters.

7. Calculate the weight of the following orders of paper:
    A. The weight of 500 sheets of 17″ × 22″ Substance 20 bond paper is _____ pounds.
    B. The weight of 500 sheets of 17″ × 22″ Substance 24 bond paper is _____ pounds.
    C. The weight of 500 sheets of 11″ × 17″ Substance 20 bond paper is _____ pounds.
    D. The weight of 1M sheets of 17″ × 22″ Substance 20 bond paper is _____ pounds.
    E. The weight of 3000 sheets of 8 1/2″ × 11″ Substance 24 bond paper is _____ pounds.
    F. The weight of 4500 sheets of 11″ × 17″ Substance 20 bond paper is _____ pounds.

Getting Down to Business

When many people think about the printing industry, images might come to mind of people operating presses and other equipment. Less visible are the thousands of people who plan and manage production, predict the cost of the job, schedule the work flow, acquire materials, and work with clients to ensure that each job conforms to expectations. These front office jobs add to the wide range of types of employment available in the printing industry.

Whether a printing facility has 15 or 150 employees, all the business functions must be performed. In small companies, one person might handle more than one function. In larger companies, employees tend to specialize.

As is the case in nearly all jobs in a modern printing facility, order entry, estimating, planning, customer service, purchasing, inventory control, and accounting are computerized. In fact, special software allows people throughout the company to share data and communicate with a common network. Even customers and suppliers can be given access to this network. Therefore, the person in this photograph could be performing any of these functions. This chapter will acquaint you with some of these jobs and explain the benefits of software that allows instant communication within organizations.

(Heidelberg, Inc.)

Chapter 4
Cost Estimating and Production Planning

Key Terms

budgeted hourly rate
  (BHR)
buyout
cost center
estimating
fixed cost
job costing
job ticket
management information
  system (MIS)
outside purchase
production standard
variable cost

Learning Objectives

When you have completed the reading and
assigned activities related to this chapter, you will
be able to do the following:

- Outline the steps an estimator takes to price a
  printing job.
- Explain the budgeted hourly cost-rate method
  of estimating offset printing.
- Summarize the function of production
  standards in an offset-printing firm.
- Identify typical cost centers and rates in an
  offset-printing plant.
- Describe the importance of job costing.
- Discuss the role of management information
  systems (MISs) in production planning.

Customers typically request an estimate before they award a job to a particular printing company because price is often a consideration when selecting a printer. The estimator prepares an estimate—a prediction of the cost of producing the job, plus a profit—based on job specs the customer supplies. If the customer accepts the estimate, the production-planning function must begin. Production planning involves devising the route the job will take as it moves through the plant, as well as making arrangements for acquiring the necessary materials. Developing and executing the plan is made easier with management information software. The value of management information software is that it allows many different functions within the company to communicate and access the same database. The estimating and planning functions are at the heart of a printing company's success.

The Estimating Procedure

When customers are in the process of choosing a printing company to produce an upcoming job, the price is nearly always a significant factor in the decision, and often, it is the primary factor. Therefore, customers typically submit a set of job specs to a few printing companies and request the price for each company to print the job. At this point, the estimating process begins.

Estimating is a complex process of predicting the costs of producing a job based on client-submitted specs, including the desired quantity, dimensions, type of paper, and number of ink colors, along with many other factors pertaining to the job. In printing, as well as in other manufacturing operations, the cost estimate plus the profit margin equals the selling price. For this reason, the cost estimate is the basis for the price, and an accurate prediction of costs is critical. Accurate, reality-based estimates must be made because an estimate that is too high is likely to result in the job going to a competitor, while an estimate that is too low will probably cause the company to take a loss on the job. Clearly, the cost estimate is crucial to the success of the printing company. The only jobs not requiring an estimate are the rare instances in which the customer agrees in writing to pay whatever the job costs turn out to be.

Estimators are people who prepare the estimate by studying the client-supplied specs for a proposed job, devising a plan for producing the job, and calculating the costs for producing the job according to that plan. Accurate estimates are based on data gathered from all aspects of the operation. Estimators

work with prepress, press, bindery, and shipping personnel. Therefore, the estimators must understand the capabilities of the equipment and services in the plant. Estimators are also liaisons between sales and production, helping the sales representatives bid competitively. The estimator might even produce a variety of estimates to help a client determine the most economical way to produce the best product. See **Figure 4-1.**

The most accurate method of predicting costs for a proposed job is to identify the operations involved in its production. For example, a simple job, such as 500 business cards, might require time spent in prepress preparing the digital file and plate, time spent on the press, time spent cutting the individual cards from a larger press sheet, and time spent boxing the finished cards. Each of these stages in the job's production is a *cost center*. The total of each cost center's requirements plus the cost of materials will yield the total cost.

The estimator must use a systematic approach to arrive at the most likely cost for producing each proposed job. The following steps generally are used to price a printing job:

1. Secure accurate specs for the proposed job. Prepare a layout or dummy.
2. Plan the sequence of operations involved in the job.
3. Determine the time required to complete each cost center.
4. Determine the production cost for each cost center and total them.
5. Determine the amount of each required material and its cost.

Figure 4-1. An estimator calculates the costs involved in production, often with several variations so the customer can make an informed decision.

6. Add the markup of material cost.
7. Total the costs and add a profit.
8. Prepare a quotation for the customer.

Specifications (Specs)

The estimating procedure begins with the estimator's careful review of the specs for the potential job. The specs are supplied by the customer and listed on a form often called a *Request for Quote (RFQ)*. Typical specs included on an RFQ are the quantity to be printed, the dimensions of the job, the type of paper or other substrate to be printed on, the number of inks and their colors, the number of folds, the method of binding (if appropriate), the method of packaging, and any other factors influencing the cost. For example, an RFQ for booklets might look similar to this:

> 25,000 6″ × 9″ 16-page booklets with separate cover. Text on Sub. 50 Sabre uncoated offset stock; covers printed on Sub. 100 Skylark gloss coated cover stock. Two inks (reflex blue and black) printed on text pages; process inks (CMYK) on both sides of the cover. Saddle stitch, shrink-wrap in bundles of 100. Pages to be supplied on CD.

Sequence of Operations

The estimator's job is to analyze these customer-supplied specs for indications of which cost centers will be involved in producing the job, how much time the job will be at each cost center, and how much material will be required. The next step is to plan a sequence of operations for the job as the job moves through production. In the sample job specs for the booklet, the text pages and cover appear to have been built by the customer. If they were prepared properly, the job can go directly to image assembly and then to platemaking. After the plates are made, the job will be run on one or more presses. In postpress, the press sheets will be trimmed on a cutter, folded on a folder, bound by a gatherer-stitcher-trimmer (GST), and then bundled and shrink-wrapped. It is obviously important for the estimator's sequence of operations to include all necessary cost centers, or the estimate will be inaccurate.

Some estimators use a worksheet to write all costs during the estimating process. See **Figure 4-2.** Such a worksheet outlines the requirements of a job and indicates the sequence of operations. Computer-assisted estimating software programs have worksheets resembling these forms.

Several estimators organize the worksheet around production departments, such as scanning, image assembly, and presswork. A layout or dummy is sometimes prepared to help the estimator visualize the job. Regardless of how the worksheet is set up, it should include all major production operations.

Cost Centers

A cost center is a production workstation that costs money to maintain. The *budgeted hourly rate (BHR)*, or hourly charge, will include both fixed and variable costs associated with each cost center. *Fixed costs* are those expenses incurred even when the cost center is not in operation. Examples of fixed costs include rent, heating and cooling, lighting, equipment depreciation, insurance, and taxes. In contrast, *variable costs* vary in proportion to the volume of production. Examples include labor and electrical power. A companion to the BHR is a cost center's production standard. A *production standard* is a measurement of the cost center's productivity and can be expressed as the amount of time required to perform a particular operation or the amount of output that can be expected. **Figure 4-3** reveals that, for a job of average difficulty, a Hamada 665CD requires .25 hours to prepare the press, .14 hours of running time per 1000 press sheets, and .20 hours to wash up the ink and gum the plate. These production standards can be used to predict the total amount of time a given job will spend on this press. This time requirement can then be multiplied by the BHR to reveal the press cost for the job.

estimating: the process of determining the approximate costs of a printed job, based on quality and quantity specs.

cost center: a production operation that costs money to maintain.

budgeted hourly rate (BHR): the cost determined from all fixed and variable costs, based on the hourly operation of a particular cost or production center.

fixed cost: a cost rate that remains constant, regardless of production output in the cost center.

variable cost: a cost rate generated by items such as labor and utilities, when production occurs in a cost center.

production standard: an hourly value representing the average output of a particular operating area under specified conditions.

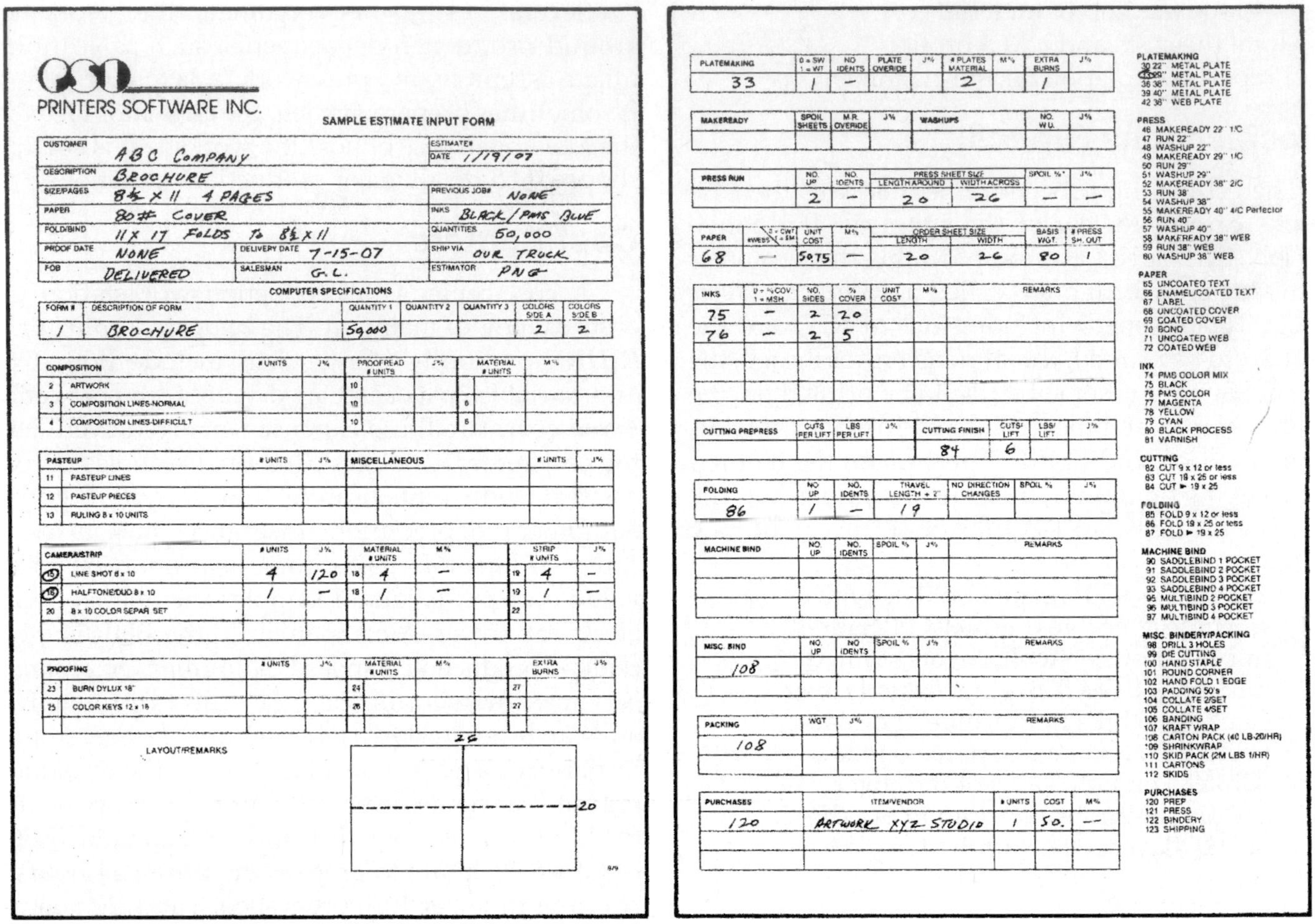

PRINTERS SOFTWARE INC.

SAMPLE ESTIMATE INPUT FORM

CUSTOMER: ABC COMPANY		ESTIMATE#:	DATE: 1/19/07
DESCRIPTION: BROCHURE			
SIZE/PAGES: 8½ × 11 4 PAGES		PREVIOUS JOB#: NONE	
PAPER: 80# COVER		INKS: BLACK/PMS BLUE	
FOLD/BIND: 11 × 17 FOLDS TO 8½ × 11		QUANTITIES: 50,000	
PROOF DATE: NONE	DELIVERY DATE: 7-15-07	SHIP VIA: OUR TRUCK	
FOB: DELIVERED	SALESMAN: G.L.	ESTIMATOR: PNG	

COMPUTER SPECIFICATIONS

FORM #	DESCRIPTION OF FORM	QUANTITY 1	QUANTITY 2	QUANTITY 3	COLORS SIDE A	COLORS SIDE B
1	BROCHURE	50,000			2	2

COMPOSITION	# UNITS	J%	PROOFREAD # UNITS	J%	MATERIAL # UNITS	M%
2 ARTWORK			10			
3 COMPOSITION LINES-NORMAL			10		6	
4 COMPOSITION LINES-DIFFICULT			10		6	

PASTEUP	# UNITS	J%	MISCELLANEOUS	# UNITS	J%
11 PASTEUP LINES					
12 PASTEUP PIECES					
13 RULING 8 × 10 UNITS					

CAMERA/STRIP	# UNITS	J%	MATERIAL # UNITS	M%		STRIP # UNITS	J%
15 LINE SHOT 8 × 10	4	120	18 4	—		19 4	—
16 HALFTONE/DUO 8 × 10	1	—	18 1	—		19 1	—
20 8 × 10 COLOR SEPAR. SET						22	

PROOFING	# UNITS	J%	MATERIAL # UNITS	M%		EXTRA BURNS	J%
23 BURN DYLUX 18"			24			27	
25 COLOR KEYS 12 × 18			26			27	

LAYOUT/REMARKS

26

20

PLATEMAKING	0 = SW 1 = WT	NO IDENTS	PLATE OVERIDE	J%	# PLATES MATERIAL	M%	EXTRA BURNS	J%
33	1	—			2		1	

MAKEREADY	SPOIL SHEETS	M.R. OVERIDE	J%	WASHUPS	NO. W.U.	J%

PRESS RUN	NO. UP	NO. IDENTS	PRESS SHEET SIZE LENGTH AROUND	PRESS SHEET SIZE WIDTH ACROSS	SPOIL %*	J%
	2	—	20	26	—	—

PAPER	# WEBS / 3 = CWT 1 = SM	UNIT COST	M%	ORDER SHEET SIZE LENGTH	ORDER SHEET SIZE WIDTH	BASIS WGT.	# PRESS SH. OUT
68	—	50.75	—	20	26	80	1

INKS	0 = %COV. 1 = MSH	NO. SIDES	% COVER	UNIT COST	M%	REMARKS
75	—	2	20			
76	—	2	5			

CUTTING PREPRESS	CUTS PER LIFT	LBS PER LIFT	J%	CUTTING FINISH	CUTS/ LIFT	LBS/ LIFT	J%
				84	6		

FOLDING	NO UP	NO. IDENTS	TRAVEL LENGTH + 2"	NO DIRECTION CHANGES	SPOIL %	J%
86	1	—	19			

MACHINE BIND	NO. UP	NO. IDENTS	SPOIL %	J%	REMARKS

MISC. BIND	NO. UP	NO. IDENTS	SPOIL %	J%	REMARKS
108					

PACKING	WGT	J%	REMARKS
108			

PURCHASES	ITEM/VENDOR	# UNITS	COST	M%
120	ARTWORK XYZ STUDIO	1	50.	—

PLATEMAKING
30 22" METAL PLATE
33 29" METAL PLATE
36 38" METAL PLATE
39 40" METAL PLATE
42 38" WEB PLATE

PRESS
46 MAKEREADY 22" 1/C
47 RUN 22"
48 WASHUP 22"
49 MAKEREADY 29" 1/C
50 RUN 29"
51 WASHUP 29"
52 MAKEREADY 38" 2/C
53 RUN 38"
54 WASHUP 38"
55 MAKEREADY 40" 4/C Perfector
56 RUN 40"
57 WASHUP 40"
58 MAKEREADY 38" WEB
59 RUN 38" WEB
60 WASHUP 38" WEB

PAPER
65 UNCOATED TEXT
66 ENAMEL/COATED TEXT
67 LABEL
68 UNCOATED COVER
69 COATED COVER
70 BOND
71 UNCOATED WEB
72 COATED WEB

INK
74 PMS COLOR MIX
75 BLACK
76 PMS COLOR
77 MAGENTA
78 YELLOW
79 CYAN
80 BLACK PROCESS
81 VARNISH

CUTTING
82 CUT 9 × 12 or less
83 CUT 19 × 25 or less
84 CUT ► 19 × 25

FOLDING
85 FOLD 9 × 12 or less
86 FOLD 19 × 25 or less
87 FOLD ► 19 × 25

MACHINE BIND
90 SADDLEBIND 1 POCKET
91 SADDLEBIND 2 POCKET
92 SADDLEBIND 3 POCKET
93 SADDLEBIND 4 POCKET
95 MULTIBIND 2 POCKET
96 MULTIBIND 3 POCKET
97 MULTIBIND 4 POCKET

MISC. BINDERY/PACKING
98 DRILL 3 HOLES
99 DIE CUTTING
100 HAND STAPLE
101 ROUND CORNER
102 HAND FOLD 1 EDGE
103 PADDING 50's
104 COLLATE 2/SET
105 COLLATE 4/SET
106 BANDING
107 KRAFT WRAP
108 CARTON PACK (40 LB-20/HR)
109 SHRINKWRAP
110 SKID PACK (2M LBS 1/HR)
111 CARTONS
112 SKIDS

PURCHASES
120 PREP
121 PRESS
122 BINDERY
123 SHIPPING

Figure 4-2. Example of an estimator's worksheet. Worksheets come in many formats, and individual printing firms generally prepare the worksheets to meet their particular needs. (Printer's Software, Inc.)

Calculating Production Costs

To understand how the BHRs and production standards are used to calculate production costs, consider calculating the press cost for the following job specs: 10,000 8 1/2″ × 11″ letterheads printed on one side and in one ink color. The job will be estimated for the Ryobi 2800CD, which can print on a sheet as large as 12″ × 17″, as **Figure 4-4** shows. The job can be assumed to be average in its difficulty, and the printing company in this scenario has a 75% productivity rate. Therefore, the appropriate BHR for the Ryobi 2800CD is $85.23. The 10,000 letterheads will require only 5000 press sheets because a 12″ × 17″ sheet can contain two 8 1/2″ × 11″ pages. According to **Figure 4-3,** the Ryobi 2800CD requires .15 hours to print 1000 press sheets, so the press will need .75 hours to print the 5000 press sheets (.15 × 5 = .75 hrs.). These .75 hours of running time added to the .30 hours of makeready time and .33 hours of washup time equal 1.38 hours of total press time. At $85.23 an hour, the presswork cost is expected to be $117.62 (1.38 hrs. × $85.23 = $117.62).

Material Markup

Printing companies incur several costs associated with acquiring, storing, and moving the paper, ink, plates, and other materials needed to produce a job. These costs include the personnel time involved in ordering, receiving, and assigning the materials; warehousing costs; and the expense of replacing damaged materials. To recover these costs, printing companies apply a markup percentage to these materials, which becomes part of the estimate. For example, a company that applies a 12% markup to materials would add $84.00 to a $700.00 delivery of paper (.12 × $700 = $84). Therefore, the client would be charged $784.00. It should be understood that this $84 is not profit. The $84 merely reflect the actual costs of procuring and warehousing the material.

	Makeready Time (in Hours)			Running Time per 1000 Press Sheets			Washup Time
	Simple	Average	Difficult	Simple	Average	Difficult	(in Hours)
One-Color Offset Presses							
A.B. Dick 360	.20	.25	.40	.15	.19	.22	.35
A.B. Dick 8920	.20	.25	.40	.14	.20	.25	.34
Ryobi 2800CD	.25	.30	.45	.14	.15	.18	.33
A.B. Dick 9910	.20	.25	.40	.14	.20	.25	.34
Heidelberg Quickmaster QM46-1	.15	.20	.25	.15	.20	.25	.15
Two-Color Offset Presses							
Hamada 665CD	.20	.25	.30	.13	.14	.15	.20
Hamada H234CX	.15	.20	.25	.12	.13	.14	.20
Ryobi 3302H	.33	.50	.75	.14	.15	.18	.50
Sakurai Oliver 258	.20	.25	.30	.10	.11	.12	.15
Four-Color Offset Presses							
Ryobi 3304	.50	.75	1.00	.14	.15	.18	.75
Heidelberg Speedmaster SM52-4	.33	.50	.80	.07	.09	.13	1.0
Digital Imaging Presses							
A.B. Dick Colour (Basic)	.10	.10	.10	.14	.14	.14	2.0
Heidelberg Quickmaster 46-4 DI	.06	.06	.06	.13	.17	.25	.50
Presstek/Ryobi 3404 DI	.33	.40	.50	.17	.17	.17	1.00

Figure 4-3. Production standards reveal the average amount of time required to perform press functions.

Outside Purchases

The cost of subcontracting outside materials, supplies, and services—called *outside purchases*, or *buyouts*—is also part of the overall cost. Examples of outside services include graphic design, photography, color separations, and specialty bindery work, such as embossing and hot-foil stamping. When preparing the estimate, outside purchase costs are usually marked up similarly to material costs.

outside purchase: a service or material contracted to be performed or supplied by another company.

buyout: the cost of subcontracting outside materials, supplies, and services.

Name of Cost Center	Maximum Sheet Size	Investment in Equipment	Cost per Hour at Varying Productivity Levels		
			60%	75%	85%
One-Color Offset Presses					
A.B. Dick 360	11" × 17"	$15,800	$82.52	$70.58	$62.15
A.B. Dick 8920	11.7" × 17"	$18,500	$108.21	$86.85	$76.25
Ryobi 2800CD	12" × 17"	$22,500	$106.47	$85.23	$75.33
Ryobi 3200CD	13.39" × 17.72"	$28,000	$107.17	$86.67	$75.74
A.B. Dick 9910	13.5" × 17.75"	$25,295	$111.73	$89.46	$78.51
Heidelberg Quickmaster QM46-1	18.13" × 13.5"	$49,500	$112.43	$89.55	$79.56
Two-Color Offset Presses					
Hamada 665CD	11.75" × 17"	$26,000	$115.52	$92.31	$81.94
Hamada H234CX	13.36" × 17.75"	$80,000	$127.33	$102.43	$90.78
Ryobi 3302H	13.39" × 17.72"	$88,000	$128.44	$103.32	$90.16
Sakurai Oliver	17.75" × 22.75"	$240,000	$163.83	$131.48	$115.21
Four-Color Offset Presses					
Ryobi 3304	13.39" × 17.72"	$250,000	$180.36	$144.66	$127.51
Heidelberg Speedmaster SM52-4	14.5" × 20.5"	$615,000	$259.52	$207.26	$183.45
Digital Imaging Presses					
A.B. Dick Colour (Basic)	12" × 18"	$149,000	$142.64	$114.42	$100.73
Heidelberg Quickmaster 46-4 DI	18.13" × 13.38"	$465,000	$224.37	$179.41	$158.58
Presstek PAX DI	15" × 20.5"	$650,000	$278.32	$221.78	$195.84

Figure 4-4. BHRs for each cost center are based on each machine's share of insurance, heating, lighting, maintenance, depreciation, and labor costs. Shown are BHRs for several small presses.

Calculating Profit

The word *profit* is short for *profit on sales*. Therefore, profit is a percentage of the selling price, not the cost. The following is the formula for calculating the selling price that will result in a profit of a certain percentage of the selling price:

$$\frac{\text{total cost}}{1.0 - \text{profit percentage (expressed as a decimal)}} = \text{selling price}$$

For example, to calculate the selling price for a job with a total cost of $3600 and a desired profit percentage of 14%, use the following equation:

$$\frac{\$3600}{1.0 - .14} = \text{selling price}$$

$$\frac{\$3600}{.86} = \text{selling price}$$

$$\$4186.05 = \text{selling price}$$

The selling price of $4186.05 reflects a 14% profit margin.

Quotations

All job specs and special requirements must be noted for inclusion in the final price quotation. See **Figure 4-5.** The quotation describes the terms of the job and serves as a contract between the printing firm and client. Once the client submits to and accepts the terms and cost of the job, the price is considered firm, and the client does not pay more than the quoted price unless the specs are changed during production. The customer is given a stated number of days to accept the quotation before it becomes void.

Job Costing and Analysis

Printing companies should record the actual cost to produce each job, a procedure called *job costing*. Once the job cost is known, the cost can be compared to the estimate. This postproduction analysis will reveal the actual amount of profit. In addition, the analysis can identify trouble spots in production or errors in the estimating procedure. The expense of comparing the estimate to the job cost can more than pay for itself by improving production and preventing the estimator from repeating mistakes.

Printing companies that do not feel compelled to follow up every job should evaluate any jobs requiring special handling, material, labor, or other elements. Four steps are involved in the follow-up procedure:

1. **Prepare the initial estimate.** The follow-up system begins with a carefully prepared estimate. All figures, data, and calculations are recorded in readable form. Notes and cross-referencing of work for later checking are important. Some estimators find that following up is simplified if they add an extra column to their worksheet for entry of follow-up data.

2. **Produce the job and collect data.** In this phase, the estimator keeps careful records of production time and costs. Copies of invoices are made and posted to particular jobs. All shop personnel must understand the importance of keeping careful records of the actual time spent on each job. The personnel should record all labor time, material, downtime, waste, buyouts, and supplies. One convenient way to do this is to assign a charge number to each job in the shop and charge all materials, labor, and supplies to this number.

3. **Review estimates and compare actual costs.** Estimates of production times in each cost center, as well as materials and outside purchases, are compared with invoices, bills, and payroll. This accounting can be done a day or two after the job has been finished or weeks later, but the sooner the follow-up is performed, the better the accounting will be, because important details are still close at hand. A comparison will reveal the amount of profit that the company made on that job. It can also indicate procedures to be improved.

4. **Make changes and adjustments in practices.** It is not enough to discover errors in the estimate's calculations or problems in production. Both the estimator and the production system must make corrections to prevent similar occurrences in the future. If the problem is out-of-date production standards, production personnel must update this data.

Computer software can be a valuable tool for performing postproduction analysis. Spreadsheet software is ideal for this function. If the estimator prepares the cost estimate using a spreadsheet, an additional column can be provided for entering actual costs later. A third column should be added to record any deviation. The estimator then enters a simple formula that provides the percentage of deviation between actual and estimated costs. The analysis is closed out by having the spreadsheet software calculate the average deviation of each element on the estimate.

Even estimates that do not result in the printing company being awarded the job can be useful to management. An assessment of estimates that did not turn into jobs can reveal that the company is not competitive for jobs with certain specs. Often, this situation is due to owning equipment that is better suited to either long-run or short-run jobs, or the situation could be due to inexperience in working with certain design requirements. In either case, management can then consider changing production capabilities or directing the sales staff to seek out jobs for which the company is better suited.

job costing: the process of comparing the estimated production times and costs to the actual production times and costs.

BENZONIA LITHO

1669 White Birch Lane / Lakewood, NH 48689

Date _____

QUOTATION FOR:

We are pleased to submit this quote for the following:

Description: _____

_____

Quantity: _____   Size: _____

Paper Stock: _____

_____

Colors of Ink: _____

_____

Binding: _____

_____

Delivery: _____

Price: _____

Benzonia Litho

By _____

(See Printing Trade Customs on back)

Figure 4-5. A printing company's quotation form contains not only the price, but also the job specs.

Production Planning

Once the estimate is calculated and the client accepts the quotation, production can begin. A work order, or *job ticket*, is drawn up from the estimate. See **Figure 4-6.** The job ticket lists the cost centers involved in producing the job and charts the job's progress through the production stages. This ticket moves with the job through production and communicates the client's specs to production personnel. The job ticket can be a sheet of paper or an envelope, or it can be part of an electronic file that can be accessed by computer throughout the plant.

Job No. | **Job Ticket** | **Delivery Date:**

Invoice to:

Customer _____
Address _____
City _____ State ____ Zip _____
Contact _____ Phone _____

Date billed _____
Customer no. _____
P.O. no. _____
Ordered by _____
Sales rep. _____ No. _____

□ Quoted $ _____
□ Price open
□ Est. sell price $
Can sell ____%overs/
_____%unders
□ Prod. coord. _____

Date written _____ by _____
Date checked _____ by _____
Date planned _____ by _____
Date scheduled _____ by _____
Credit approved _____ by _____
Mat's. purchased _____ by _____

Job specs.

Item	Quantity	Description	Flat size	Finish size	Invoice amount

Type/art

□ Set changes only   □ Set entire job
□ Paste-up   □ Create mechanicals
_____
_____
_____

Prep

□ Exact repeat   □ Change repeat   Previous job no. _____ Drawer no. _____
□ Camera ready   □ Composite film furnished   □ Loose film furnished
□ Seps furnished
_____
_____
_____

Proofs: □ None ___ Blueline(s) □ ___ Colorkeys □ Chromalin/proof to: _____ □ Press check: ____ □ Sales rep. □ Customer □ Prod. coord. Notify ___ Phone ___

Paper

Item	Form(s)	Basis wt.	Description	Suplr.	Order date	Due in	Lot no.	No. sheets	Size/grain	Cut to	Pieces out	Final pieces
									×	×		
									×	×		
									×	×		
									×	×		
									×	×		
									×	×		
									×	×		
									×	×		

Sheet-fed press

Item	Form(s)	No. up	Layout	Press	Front inks(s) No.	Front inks(s) Colors	Back inks(s) No.	Back inks(s) Colors	Gross sheets	Makeready allowance	Run-waste allowance	Net count required	Net yield

Bindery

Folding instructions

Item	Form(s)	Fold type	Net yield

□ Saddlestitch ___ Wires on ___ Side: Net yield _____
□ Perfect bind on _____ side: Net yield _____
□ Drill ____ Holes ____″ Diam. _____″ Ctr to ctr ___ side
□ Trim to size
□ Other _____

□ Pad ___ side, per ___
□ Round corner
□ Eyelet
□ Side switch ___ wires

Vendors

□ Film/seps _____
□ Dies _____
□ Die cut/emboss _____
□ Type _____
□ Bindery _____
□ Other _____

Mailing

Class: _____
Permit no. _____
□ PS labels ___ Up: qty ___
□ Cheshire ___ Up: qty ___
□ UPS: shippers no. ___
□ Fed Ex: shippers no. ___

Packaging

□ Band _____
□ Wrap _____
□ Shrink _____
□ Box _____
□ Labels furnished ___
□ Labeling instr. ___
_____
□ Special skids ___

Ship to

Note: All jobs ship freight collect unless pre-approved:
(prepaid approval by _____)

Ship via: _____

Art & Samples

□ Do not return art
□ Art and _____ samples
To: _____
_____
_____ Samples to:
_____
_____ Samples to:
_____

Figure 4-6. A job ticket includes the specs, details of the production plan, needed materials, notes to production employees, and a section where production times are recorded.

job ticket: an electronic form or a paper form used to track costs for labor, materials, and press time of a given printing job.

A scheduler matches the requirements of a job to the available equipment, materials, labor, and time and prepares a detailed job schedule. Job scheduling is an important production control task. Each printing job must be integrated into the overall shop schedule. The flow of jobs is continually adjusted to react to such delays as paper jams, equipment breakdowns, lack of materials, and clients not returning proofs. After the job has been completed, the business office generates a bill for the client. The job is then removed from the production schedule.

Each printing job that comes into a printing company creates its own paper trail. The trail begins with a sales representative bringing in a Request for Estimate (RFE) describing the potential job. See **Figure 4-7.** Using information on the RFE, the

REQUEST FOR ESTIMATE

Date: _____ Sales rep: _____ Estimate due by: _____

Client:_____ Contact: _____

Address:_____ City, State, Zip: _____

Phone: _____Budget or formal estimate? _____

Job title: _____

Quantities: _____

Number of pages or sheets: _____ Self cover or separate cover: _____

Finish size:_____ Size with bleeds: _____

Paper stock: cover _____ text _____

Prepress requirements:

    Will customer supply complete digital file?_____

    Page layout software used: _____

    Number of images to be scanned: _____

    Imaging to be performed by printer:_____

    _____

    Proofs required:_____

Press requirements:

    Number of sides to be printed:_____

    Number of colors on front: _____ Number of colors on back: _____

Postpress requirements:

    Folding: _____

    Numbering:_____ Die cutting: _____

    Embossing: _____ Scoring: _____

    Perforating: _____ Laminating: _____

    Binding method:_____

Packing and delivery: _____

Other instructions: _____

_____

_____

_____

Figure 4-7. An RFE is submitted by the client and lists the job specs.

estimator generates an estimate. If the client accepts the estimate, the planner, who creates a production plan, reviews the estimate. The scheduler uses copies of the production plan for each job to create and post a grid showing the location of each job and where it will be next. See **Figure 4-8.** During the day, various people go to the schedule board to check on the progress of one or more jobs. Meanwhile, inventory control and purchasing use information on the production plan to determine which needed materials are already on hand and which and how much of the materials will need to be ordered.

On the shop floor, production workers, from prepress through press and postpress, record on each job ticket their starting and ending times for working on the job. These entries will serve as a basis for determining the job's actual cost. If a client calls to check on a job's progress, the customer service representative (CSR) will likely need to confer with the scheduler to get the needed update. Also, if a client calls to make a change in the job, the CSR will probably complete a change order, which is created to communicate the change to the appropriate personnel. See **Figure 4-9.** For example, a request for another 5000 copies will not only change the schedule, but this request will likely require more paper to be ordered.

After production has been completed, someone in management can compile information from several job tickets that will go into reports on productivity

Figure 4-8. A schedule board displays the status of each job in production for several days.

or profitability, to help guide top management's long-term decision making. The weaknesses in this system are the redundancy and wasted time in transferring information from one form to another and the likelihood of crucial information—such as a change order—not reaching all concerned personnel. Typically, this kind of miscommunication results in having to rework some or all of the job.

The application of computers in printing operations has expanded from design to management.

Job Number: _3149_   Date _Oct. 24_

Customer: _Betsie Industries_

Job description: _32-page catalog_

Proof: _____

Quantity: _Increase from 25,000 to 35,000_

Size: _____

Stock: _Extra stock ordered 10-24_

Binding: _____

Ink color: _Pantone 180 to Pantone 215 - ordered 10-24_

Delivery date: _____

Deliver to: _____

Figure 4-9. A change-order form is needed when the client makes a change in the job after production has begun.

Today, computer-based *management information systems (MISs)* are used to link all aspects of production to a single database and nearly eliminate the paper trail described earlier. A printing company with MIS software facilitates the access to and sharing of information, including estimating, order entry, production planning, inventory control, change orders, shop floor data, financial transactions, and sales records.

Although the paper trail just described is still very common within the printing industry, companies with an MIS link employees through an electronic network that allows people to communicate through a common database. An estimator can copy information from the digital RFE into the estimating module without retyping it. The planner can access the estimate, either copy or modify it to reflect current conditions, and send a message to inventory control to check on the availability of the needed materials. Purchasing can be advised of what needs to be ordered. The scheduler enters the job onto the plant's electronic schedule, which people throughout the plant can access and view. Production workers record their beginning and ending times for each job electronically—perhaps by scanning the individual bar code on each job ticket with a wand. See **Figure 4-10.** Sensors on press and bindery equipment report production status, waste, materials, unscheduled stops, current production speed, and progress toward job completion. By collecting data as soon as it is known, the status of the operation can be quickly assessed, and any problems can be immediately corrected.

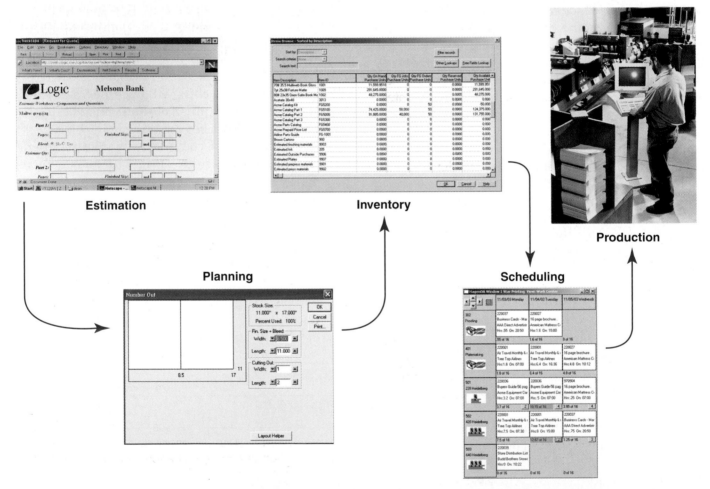

Estimation

Inventory

Production

Planning

Scheduling

Figure 4-10. Many printing companies' MIS software allows customers to submit an RFE over the Internet. The planning module of an MIS allows employees to access job information from any computer workstation. The inventory control module indicates the amounts of materials, such as paper, ink, and plates, as well as printed materials to be shipped to clients over a period of time. The scheduling module replaces the schedule board and allows employees to access the schedule at any designated computer workstation. The colors indicate the number of hours scheduled. At each stage of production, workers can both enter and access data, contributing to the MIS. (Logic Associates, Inc.; Franklin Estimator; Hagen Systems, Inc.)

A CSR can send change orders directly to the appropriate people and later check to see that the change was made. Also, CSRs can check on the progress of a given job without having to leave their desks. Management can use MIS software to create reports by sifting through the accumulated data from hundreds of jobs. Clearly, many printing companies have used MIS software to make information more accessible and streamline communication throughout the plant. Whether information is carried and shared on paper or electronically, the smoothness of its movement represents a major factor in efficiency, productivity, and profitability.

Automatic data collection is the key to an MIS. Several benefits to the company quickly become obvious. Worker productivity increases when operators at each workstation enter and access data from a computer screen, rather than writing the data out longhand. Job tracking is more efficient and accurate. Actual job data can be compared to the original estimate for a careful postproduction analysis of costs. Future estimates can be adjusted based on the information. Clients benefit as well. A CSR can instantly access a job on a computer screen and immediately advise a customer of progress, delays, or delivery dates.

Summary

Estimating is a complex process of determining approximate costs based on quality and quantity specs. A cost center is a production operation that costs money to maintain. Cost rate is the expense of operating a specific cost center per hour. Budgeted hourly cost rate is a popular method of estimating, determined from fixed and variable costs and buyouts, based on the hourly operation of a particular cost or production center.

A quotation describes the terms of the job. Once the terms and cost of the job have been submitted to the customer, the price is considered firm. Any jobs requiring special handling, material, labor, or other elements should be evaluated in the postproduction phase.

Follow-up estimates should be performed a few days after a job is completed. The goal is to determine the percentage of deviation between estimated and actual costs of a job. Future adjustments in pricing can then be made. MISs are used in production planning, inventory control, financial transactions, and sales records. Automatic data collection is the key to an MIS.

Review Questions

Please do not write in this book. Write your answers on a separate sheet of paper.

1. Briefly discuss the various steps an estimator takes to price a printing job.
2. Estimators use a(n) _____ to write all costs when estimating a job.
3. The _____ is the expense of operating a specific cost center per hour.
4. _____ costs remain, independent of whether or not work is being produced.
5. _____ costs are generated only when production occurs in the cost center.
6. What is the purpose of production standards?
7. Give two examples of cost centers.
8. What do you call costs for outside materials, supplies, and services, such as layout and design, artwork, color separations, or bindery?
9. Calculate the 15% markup on an order of paper costing $760.
10. Calculate the selling price that would generate a 14% profit on a job costing $3000 to produce.
11. A(n) _____ describes the terms of a printing job and serves as a contract between the printing firm and customer.
12. The _____ examines the deviation between estimated and actual costs.
13. Why are follow-up estimates important?
14. _____ are used to link several functions, such as production planning, inventory control, financial transactions, and sales records.
15. Why is it important for managers to receive data from the shop floor, such as machine counts, unscheduled stops, and the time a job spends in each cost center?

---

management information system (MIS): a computer-based management tool used to assess data in production planning, inventory control, financial transactions, and sales records.

Skill-Building Activities

1. Calculate the press cost to print 18,000 11″ × 17″ posters printed in two colors on one side. Use the A.B. Dick 360 and assume 60% productivity. The nature of the job will require two difficult passes through the press, two difficult makereadies, and two washups. Also, note that this press can accommodate only one poster.

2. Calculate the cost for the same job described in Activity #1 if it were run on the Ryobi 3302 two-color press, which will be able to print both colors in one pass, with one washup and one makeready.

3. Prepare a worksheet and quotation sheet for a substantial printing job in your facility. Have your instructor check the calculations and quoted price.

4. Make a list of the cost centers in your graphic arts facility. Describe the cost centers in a short written report.

5. In groups of two or three students, prepare a worksheet and quotation for a substantial printing job in your graphic arts facility. Use the data to prepare an oral report on estimating for the class.

Printing presses are one of the largest investments of a printing company. (Heidelberg, Inc.)

Staying Legal

Have you ever heard the old joke, "My uncle always dreamed of making big money. The only trouble is that he made it about a quarter of an inch too big"? Although everyone knows counterfeiting money is illegal, there are other aspects of the law that printers and their clients must be aware of.

The printing industry has created a set of policies that protect printing companies and make clear the roles the companies and their clients play. Referred to as the *Printing Trade Customs*, these provisions cover a wide range of topics and are typically printed on the back of job estimates and contracts. When these policies are presented to customers before jobs go into production, many misunderstandings are prevented.

(The Ink Well)

Chapter 5
Trade Customs, Organizations, and Laws

Key Terms

closed shop
copyright
copyright infringement
counterfeit
fair use
Graphic Communications
   Trade Customs
Graphic Design Trade
   Customs
labor union
made for hire
obscene literature
open shop
Printing Trade Customs
software piracy

Learning Objectives

When you have completed the reading and assigned activities related to this chapter, you will be able to do the following:

- ◆ Describe the purpose of trade customs in the printing and graphic communications industries.
- ◆ Explain the purpose of printing industry labor unions.
- ◆ Discuss printing industry trade associations.
- ◆ Give examples of items that can be copyrighted.
- ◆ Identify the three elements in a copyright notice.
- ◆ Name items that cannot be legally reproduced.

The printing industry is governed by accepted standards and organizations. Most authors, graphic designers, printers, and publishers are diligent in terms of their responsibility and ethical considerations with regard to the manufacture of printed materials. Members of the printing and graphic communications industries have formed trade organizations, associations, and standards to establish outlines allowing the following:

- Standard business practices.
- Materials to be bought and sold in common dimensions.
- Data transfer in compatible formats.
- Better regulation compliance and fair industry representation.
- Maintenance of fair wages and labor practices.
- Sharing of technical expertise, new processes, and methods of operation.

Anyone involved in the production process of printed materials should have a working knowledge of industry-accepted standards. This chapter summarizes some of the most important aspects of trade customs, labor unions, trade associations, and copyright laws.

Trade Customs

The business practices most commonly used in the printing industry are called *Printing Trade Customs*, or *Graphic Communications Trade Customs*. These trade customs were originally established at the annual convention of the United Typothetae of America in 1922. The United Typothetae of America was a group of printers formed in 1887 for mutual support within the industry.

The Printing Trade Customs cover such matters as proofs, alterations, press overruns, delivery, and terms of payment. The trade customs are revised periodically to accommodate technological advances and shifts in practices between printers and print buyers. A thorough understanding of the trade customs under which work is being contracted protects both the printer and the customer. See **Figure 5-1.**

The customs are useful for protecting the printer's rights and ideas. For example, if a customer includes material copyrighted by a third party, the printer cannot be held responsible. If a customer takes one printer's creative ideas and has another printer print the job, the original printer would have a right to compensation.

Customers are also protected from problems that can arise during the production process. For example,

Figure 5-1. All parties involved should have a clear understanding of the contract before any work is begun.

if the printer fails to provide proofs as agreed upon and runs the job without final customer approval, it is unlikely the customer would be responsible for payment. This protection would be extremely important if the job is inadequate or greatly flawed.

Many printers reproduce the Printing Trade Customs and submit them to a customer. This is especially important when a bid or quotation is given in written form. Printers often print the Printing Trade Customs on the back of contracts, quotation forms, invoices, or letterheads. The Printing Trade Customs in general use in the industry are shown in **Figure 5-2.**

The general terms and conditions for sales within the graphic design sector of the graphic communications industry are called **Graphic Design Trade Customs.** See **Figure 5-3.** These terms and conditions define specific areas of responsibility between the graphic designer and the customer. The Graphic Design Trade Customs were initially developed in 1983 for the International Design by Electronics Association. These trade customs are usually printed on the back of estimates and quotes for design projects. Graphic designers also make use of commercial contracts to define the scope of work, schedule, costs, and terms of payment. When a contract is silent with respect to one or more practices, the trade customs are used to interpret the understanding of the parties.

Although the terms *business practices* and *trade customs*, as presented here, reflect the common practices of the printing industry, they are not mandatory practices. Many printers and graphic designers operate their businesses under these general guidelines with provisions for customers' wishes, relationships with potential customers, and other competitive issues. Some firms modify the trade customs by adding a rider or additional stipulations. **Figure 5-4**

Printing Trade Customs	
Quotation	A quotation not accepted within 30 days may be changed.
Orders	Acceptance of orders is subject to credit approval and contingencies such as fire, water, strikes, theft, vandalism, and other causes beyond the provider's control. Canceled orders require compensation for incurred costs and related obligations.
Experimental Work	Experimental or preliminary work performed at customer's request will be charged to the customer at the provider's current rates. This work cannot be used without the provider's written consent.
Creative Work	Sketches, copy, dummies, and all other creative work developed or furnished by the provider are the provider's exclusive property. The provider must give written approval for all use of this work and for any derivation of ideas from it.
Accuracy of Specifications	Quotations are based on the accuracy of the specifications provided. The provider can requote a job at time of submission if copy, film, tapes, disks, or other input materials do not conform to the information on which the original quotation was based.
Preparatory Materials	Artwork, type, plates, negatives, positives, tapes, disks, and all other items supplied by the provider remain the provider's exclusive property.
Electronic Manuscript or Image	It is the customer's responsibility to maintain a copy of the original file. The provider is not responsible for accidental damage to media supplied by the customer or for the accuracy of furnished input or final output. Until digital input can be evaluated by the provider, no claims or promises are made about the provider's ability to work with jobs submitted in digital format, and no liability is assumed for problems that may arise. Any additional translating, editing, or programming needed to use customer-supplied files will be charged at prevailing rates.
Alterations/Corrections	Customer alterations include all work performed in addition to the original specifications. All such work will be charged at the provider's current rates.
Prepress Proofs	The provider will submit prepress proofs along with original copy for the customer's review and approval. Corrections will be returned to the provider on a "master set" marked "OK," "OK with corrections," or "Revised proof required" and signed by the customer. Until the master set is received, no additional work will be performed. The provider will not be responsible for undetected production errors if (a) proofs are not required by the customer; (b) the work is printed per the customer's OK; (c) requests for changes are communicated orally.
Press Proofs	Press proofs will not be furnished unless they have been required in writing in the provider's quotation. A press sheet can be submitted for the customer's approval as long as the customer is present at the press during makeready. Any press time lost or alterations/corrections made because of the customer's delay or change of mind will be charged at the provider's current rates.
Color Proofing	Because of differences in equipment, paper, inks, and other conditions between color proofing and production pressroom operations, a reasonable variation in color between color proofs and the completed job is to be expected. When variation of this kind occurs, it will be considered acceptable performance.
Overruns or Underruns	Overruns or underruns will not exceed 10% of the quantity ordered. The provider will bill for actual quantity delivered within this tolerance. If the customer requires a guaranteed quantity, the percentage of tolerance must be stated at the time of quotation.

Figure 5-2. The printer and the customer must be fully aware of the graphic communications and printing business practices and trade customs. For a more detailed explanation of these customs, contact the NAPL or the Printing Industries of America (PIA).

Printing Trade Customs (Graphic Communications Trade Customs): the trade customs originally established in 1922 covering such matters as proofs, alterations, press overruns, delivery, and terms of payment.

Graphic Design Trade Customs: the general terms and conditions for sales within the graphic-design sector of the graphic-communications industry.

Printing Trade Customs	
Customer's Property	The provider will only maintain fire and extended coverage on property belonging to the customer while the property is in the provider's possession. The provider's liability for this property will not exceed the amount recoverable from the insurance. Additional insurance coverage may be obtained if it is requested in writing and if the premium is paid to the provider.
Delivery	Unless otherwise specified, the price quoted is for a single shipment, without storage, FOB provider's platform. Proposals are based on continuous and uninterrupted delivery of the complete order. If the specifications state otherwise, the provider will charge accordingly at current rates. Charges for delivery of materials and supplies from the customer to the provider or from the customer's supplier to the provider are not included in quotations unless specified. Title for finished work passes to the customer upon delivery to the carrier at shipping point or upon mailing of invoices for the finished work or its segments, whichever occurs first.
Production Schedules	Production schedules will be established and followed by both the customer and the provider. In the event that production schedules are not adhered to by the customer, delivery dates will be subject to renegotiation. There will be no liability or penalty for delays due to state of war, riot, civil disorder, fire, strike, accidents, action of government or civil authority, or other causes beyond the control of the provider. In such cases, schedules will be extended by an amount of time equal to delay incurred.
Customer-Furnished Materials	Materials furnished by customers or their suppliers are verified by delivery tickets. The provider bears no responsibility for discrepancies between delivery tickets and actual counts. Customer-supplied paper must be delivered according to specifications furnished by the provider. These specifications will include correct weight, thickness, pick resistance, and other technical requirements, Artwork, film, color separations, special dies, tapes, disks, or other materials furnished by the customer must be usable by the provider without alteration or repair. Items not meeting this requirement will be repaired by the customer or by the provider at the provider's current rates.
Outside Purchases	Unless otherwise agreed in writing, all outside purchases as requested or authorized by the customer are chargeable.
Terms/Claims/Liens	Payment is net cash 30 calendar days from date of invoice. Claims for defects, damages, or shortages must be made by the customer in writing no later than 10 calendar days after delivery. If no such claim is made, the provider and the customer will understand that the job has been accepted. By accepting the job, the customer acknowledges that the provider's performance has fully satisfied all terms, conditions, and specifications. The provider's liability will be limited to the quoted selling price of defective goods, without additional liability for special or consequential damages. As security for payment of any sum due under the terms of an agreement, the provider has the right to hold and place a lien on all customer property in the provider's possession. This right applies even if credit has been extended, notes have been accepted, trade acceptances have been made, or payment has been guaranteed. If payment is not made, the customer is liable for all collection costs incurred.
Liability	Disclaimer of Express Warranties: Provider warrants that the work is as described in the purchase order. The customer understands that all sketches, copy, dummies, and preparatory work shown to the customer are intended only to illustrate the general type and quality of the work. They are not intended to represent the actual work performed. Disclaimer of Implied Warranties: The provider warrants only that the work will conform to the description contained in the purchase order. The provider's maximum liability, whether by negligence, contract, or otherwise, will not exceed the return of the amount invoiced for the work in dispute. Under no circumstances will the provider be liable for specific, individual, or consequential damages.

Figure 5-2. *(Continued)*

Printing Trade Customs	
Indemnification	The customer agrees to protect the provider from economic loss and any other harmful consequences that could arise in connection with the work. This means that the customer will hold the provider harmless and save, indemnify, and otherwise defend him/her against claims, demands, actions, and proceedings on any and all grounds. This will apply regardless of responsibility for negligence.
	Copyrights. The customer also warrants that the subject matter to be printed is not copyrighted by a third party. The customer also recognizes that because subject matter does not have to bear a copyright notice in order to be protected by copyright law, absence of such notice does not necessarily assure a right to reproduce. The customer further warrants that no copyright notice has been removed from any material used in preparing the subject matter for reproduction.
	To support these warranties, the customer agrees to indemnify and hold the provider harmless for all liability, damages, and attorney fees that may be incurred in any legal action connected with copyright infringement involving the work produced or provided.
	Personal or Economic Rights. The customer also warrants that the work does not contain anything that is libelous or scandalous or anything that threatens anyone's right to privacy or other personal or economic rights. The customer will, at the customer's sole expense, promptly and thoroughly defend the provider in all legal actions on these grounds as long as the provider (a) promptly notifies the customer of the legal action; and (b) gives the customer reasonable time to undertake and conduct a defense.
	The provider reserves the right to use his or her sole discretion in refusing to print anything he or she deems illegal, libelous, scandalous, improper, or infringing upon copyright law.
Storage	The provider will retain intermediate materials until the related end product has been accepted by the customer. If requested by the customer, intermediate materials will be stored for an additional period at additional charge. The provider is not liable for any loss or damage to stored material beyond what is recoverable by the provider's fire and extended insurance coverage.
Taxes	All amounts due for taxes and assessments will be added to the customer's invoice and are the responsibility of the customer. No tax exemption will be granted unless the customer's "Exemption Certificate" (or other official proof of exemption) accompanies the purchase order. If, after the customer has paid the invoice, it is determined that more tax is due, then the customer must promptly remit the required taxes to the taxing authority or immediately reimburse the provider for any additional taxes paid.
Telecommunications	Unless otherwise agreed, the customer will pay for all transmission charges. The provider is not responsible for any errors, omissions, or extra costs resulting from faults in the transmission.

Figure 5-2. *(Continued)*

shows an example of a rider used with the basic trade customs. The National Association of Printers and Lithographers (NAPL) developed this rider. Riders are important because they can determine responsibilities and greatly affect the outcome of a job.

Organizations

Several organizations are affiliated with the printing industry. Some organizations are labor unions that represent employees. Other organizations are trade associations that enhance education and training. A trade association's membership can be made up largely of employees or companies.

Labor Unions

A *labor union* is an organization of workers formed to advance its members' interests concerning wages, benefits, and working conditions. Labor unions were first formed in the United States around 1800. The first printing-related union was the International Typographical Union (founded in 1852).

labor union: an organization of workers formed to advance its members' interests concerning wages, benefits, and working conditions.

Graphic Design Trade Customs	
Estimate	An estimate is a preliminary projection of cost, which is not intended to be binding. Estimates are based upon prevailing wages and the anticipated hours of work and cost of materials and supplies necessary to produce work in accordance with preliminary copy, style, and specifications and are not binding upon the graphic designer unless a firm quotation has been issued.
Quotation	A quotation is a fixed price for producing a given project. A quotation is firm unless otherwise specified. Quotations are subject to acceptance within thirty (30) days and are based on the cost of labor and materials on the date of the quote. If changes occur in the cost of materials, labor, or other costs prior to acceptance, the right is reserved to change the price quotes. Subsequent projects will be subject to price revision if required. Quotations do not include alterations or applicable sales tax unless otherwise specified.
Alterations	Alteration charges are incurred by a client when a change is made to approved layout, approved manuscript, mechanicals or disk produced correctly, or any new work not within the original specifications.
Overtime	Overtime is work performed by the graphic designer in excess of the work schedule of the project. Overtime may be charged at the graphic designer's prevailing rates for this service.
Copyright/ Ownership	Creative work, such as sketches, illustrations, layouts, designs, icons, logos, etc., produced on paper, computer disks, or any other medium are protected from the moment they are created under the 1976 Copyright Act. Until the graphic designer transfers ownership rights in writing, all creative work remains the property of the graphic designer. There can be no unauthorized use of the graphic designer's work. Purchase orders issued after the completion of creative work claiming the client's ownership of creative work are not valid unless agreed upon by both parties.
Experimental Work	Experimental or preliminary work performed at the client's request will be charged at current rates and may not be used by the client until the graphic designer has been reimbursed in full for the work performed. All experimental work performed by a graphic designer without authorization of the client is not billable.
Condition of Copy	If original copy, disk or manuscript, furnished by the client to the graphic designer differs from that which has been originally described and consequently quoted, the original quotation shall be amended, or a new quotation will be issued.
Production Schedules	Production schedules will be established and adhered to by client and graphic designer, providing that neither shall incur any liability or penalty for delays due to state of war, riot, civil disorder, fire, labor trouble, strikes, accidents, energy failure, equipment breakdown, delays of supplies or corners, action of government or civil authority, and acts of God or other causes beyond the control of client or graphic designer. When production schedules are not adhered to by the client, final delivery date(s) will be subject to renegotiation.
Client's Property	The graphic designer will maintain fire, extended coverage, vandalism, malicious mischief, and sprinkler leakage insurance covering all property belonging to the client while such property is in the graphic designer's possession. The graphic designer's liability for such property shall not exceed the amount recoverable from such insurance. Client's property of extraordinary value shall not be specially protected, unless the client identifies the property as requiring extraordinary coverage.
Outright Purchase vs. Reproduction Rights	These terms should be established at the time of purchase. Outright purchase gives the buyer physical possession of the artwork, disk, or negatives, while reproduction rights and related copyright interests require the return of the original to the graphic designer. Outright purchase does not give to the buyer commercial or private reproduction rights or any other copyright interests unless so stipulated in the purchase agreement. The matter of first reproduction rights with subsequent reproduction rights subject to additional compensation should be clearly understood at the time of purchase.
Reuse and Extended Use of Artwork, Disks, or Negatives	Artwork, disks, or negatives purchased for a specific use cannot be reused or adapted for other purposes than originally planned without additional compensation to the graphic designer. If this possibility exists at the time of purchase, it should be so stated and the price adjusted accordingly. If reuse or adaptation occurs after purchase, and the client has not acquired the copyright, the client should negotiate reasonable additional compensation with the graphic designer. Whenever adaptation requires the services of a graphic designer, and the graphic designer has performed to the client's satisfaction, the graphic designer should be given the opportunity to revise the graphic designer's own work.

Figure 5-3. The Graphic Design Trade Customs.

Graphic Design Trade Customs	
Markups	Any services or goods such as typography, printing, photography, etc., or materials used specifically for the completion of a given project will be billed to the client with an appropriate markup. This markup is a handling fee only, and unless otherwise agreed, does not include any professional or management fees.
Speculation	Graphic designs or layouts should not be asked for on speculation by a client. Design contents are considered speculation, except for educational or philanthropic purposes.
Terms	By requesting work either verbally, in writing, or by purchase order, the client agrees to the graphic designer's terms of payment and applicable late charges on unpaid balances. Payment shall be in conformance with the quotation or invoice unless otherwise specified in writing. Disputes over invoices must be made by the client in writing within a period of fifteen (15) days after the client's receipt of the invoice. Failure to make a claim within the stated period shall constitute acceptance and an admission that the client agrees with the invoice submitted. If only a portion of the invoice is in dispute, it is the client's responsibility to pay that portion within the terms of the invoice.
Liability	The graphic designer is only liable for the correction of the graphic designer's errors made during the production process. The ultimate proofing prior to printing is always the client's responsibility unless the graphic designer accepts this responsibility in written agreement. In any instance, the graphic designer will not be liable for more than the design and mechanical costs of a job in dispute.
Indemnification	The client shall indemnify and hold harmless the graphic designer from any and all losses, costs, expenses, and damages (including court costs and reasonable attorney fees) on account of any and all manner of claims, demands, actions, and proceedings that may be instituted against the graphic designer on grounds alleging that the graphic designer unknowingly violated any copyright or any proprietary right of another. Any materials such as photographs, photostats, transparencies, drawings, paintings, maps, diagrams, etc., furnished by the client to the graphic designer should not infringe on the copyright or proprietary right of any third party. The graphic designer is indemnified against any liability due to the client's failure to obtain correct usage rights on those materials. Any false statements knowingly or unknowingly given to the graphic designer by the client to be used as factual information to promote a product or service shall remain the client's sole responsibility for substantiation and all other purposes.
Print Management/ Press Inspections	If a graphic designer performs a press inspection for a client, the client's responsibility for proofing remains in effect. If the client has signed a printer's blueline proof, the graphic designer is not responsible for any errors reflected in the approved blueline. If the graphic designer approves color on a press proof or any other color proof, the graphic designer is only responsible for approving color acceptable by industry standards. The printer is responsible for ensuring that the subsequent press run matches the color within acceptable standards of the proof approved by the graphic designer.

Figure 5-3. *(Continued)*

Labor union members are required to pay dues. These dues usually fund life and medical insurance, retirement and death benefits, and minimal wages when a union goes on strike. Members are expected to walk on the picket line when contract disputes are unsettled and the union calls a strike.

A company that hires only union members is called a *closed shop*. A nonunion company is called an *open shop*. In some cases, the workers in an open shop can be members of a labor union.

Many people will argue that unions are necessary and extremely useful, while others might argue that unions are detrimental to industry. As with most things, labor unions have good and bad points. Whether you decide to work in a union or nonunion shop is a personal matter requiring careful consideration.

Trade Associations

Trade associations are made up of individual employees or organizations within the printing industry, and they exist to serve their memberships. An example of an organization made up mostly of employees is the International Association of Printing House Craftsmen (IAPHC), which is dedicated to the development of individuals and the enhancement of the printing industry. The IAPHC has chapters throughout the United States and the world. Examples of associations made up mostly of

■■■■■■□□□□

closed shop: a company that hires only union members.

open shop: a nonunion company.

Rider

Falcone Publishing will accept orders for printing, binding and other book manufacturing services upon the following understandings and agreements of Customer:

Risk of loss and insurance coverage on material supplied by Customer and on work produced and billed by Falcone Publishing or delivered, including film and unfinished as well as finished books, are Customer's responsibilities. Customer releases and forever discharges Falcone Publishing and its employees from any and all claims or causes of action whatsoever founded upon loss of or damage to such material or work, if such loss or damage is caused by fire or other insurable peril, whether or not attributable to the fault or negligence of Falcone Publishing, its employees, or agents, and whether or not Customer has obtained insurance coverage therefore. Insurable perils are those perils such as sprinkler leakage, explosion, riot/civil commotion and building collapse, in addition to fire and such other risks that are insurable under the standard form of ALL RISKS insurance currently in use.

Falcone Publishing prices are based on the present cost of materials involved and Falcone Publishing current labor rates. If there are any changes in the cost of materials, or in Falcone Publishing scale of wages prior to the completion of any portion of this work, said increases or decreases will be reflected in Falcone Publishing charges for that portion of the work.

All applicable personal property, sales, use of other taxes now in effect or hereafter imposed on this sale and on the use or ownership of the finished goods covered by this proposal, shall be filled as an extra and will be borne by the Customer.

It is understood that five percent (5%) overrun or underrun of a single binding shall constitute complete delivery and that Falcone Publishing charges are based upon quantities delivered.

No agreements or instructions shall be binding upon Falcone Publishing unless accepted in writing by Falcone Publishing. Printing orders shall specify the quantity of each title to be printed at one run; binding orders, the quantity of each title to be bound at one time. Falcone Publishing retains the right to reject Customer's order based on any proposal, without liability, upon mailing Purchaser written notice of such rejection within thirty (30) days after Falcone Publishing receives it. Once accepted, orders cannot be cancelled by Customer except on terms that will compensate Falcone Publishing for all expenses incurred for materials purchased, services performed and unrecovered production time attributable thereto.

Falcone Publishing warrants articles manufactured by it will conform to specifications and be free from defects in workmanship and materials attributable to the labor performed and materials furnished by Falcone Publishing which render the articles unmerchantable. THERE ARE NO WARRANTIES THAT EXTEND BEYOND THOSE STATED. In the event of breach of warranty, Customer's exclusive remedy and Falcone Publishing liability and responsibility will be limited, at Falcone Publishing option, (a) to repairing or replacing such defective articles at no cost to the Customer, or (b) if such repairing or replacing is not practicable, then to reimbursing Customer for the cost of any paper or other materials furnished for such articles by Customer and for the cost of labor and materials furnished by Falcone Publishing and paid for by Customer, including shipping, upon receiving actual notice of the nature of the defect and the quantity involved. In no event shall Falcone Publishing be liable for consequential damages resulting from breach of warranty or any other default.

It is understood that all Customer-owned material, paper, sheets or books remaining in Falcone Publishing custody, will be subject to a five percent (5%) inventory shrinkage allowance for each year said material is in Falcone Publishing possession.

Customer agrees to indemnify and hold Falcone Publishing harmless from all loss, damage and expense (including attorney's fees) incurred by Falcone in defending against any claim alleging that Falcone Publishing has libeled or violated the privacy of any individual or has infringed any copyright or contributed to such wrongs, by reason of Falcone Publishing performance in accordance with Customer's order or instructions.

Falcone Publishing shall not be liable for any default or delay which is due to any act or neglect of Customer or Customer's agents or employees, or which is due to a shortage of materials or energy, labor difficulties, flood, fire, governmental action or control, a delay of common carriers, act of God or any cause beyond Falcone's control. Should Falcone Publishing performance be delayed by any one or more of such occurrences it may be completed as soon as practicable after such disabilities have ceased, but Falcone Publishing shall give reasonable notice to Customer of the delay.

Falcone Publishing acceptance of Customer's order shall result in a contract made in Illinois and shall be construed according to Illinois Law.

Customer hereby agrees that this Rider is incorporated as part of Customer's Purchase Order # _____ dated _____ and any other order that may be placed with respect to the subject matter thereof, and supercedes any terms and conditions in conflict herewith.

_____　Dated: _____
Customer
By: _____　　　Title: _____

Figure 5-4. An example of a rider designed to be used with the basic trade customs. (National Association of Printers and Lithographers)

companies are the Printing Industry of America/ Graphic Arts Technical Foundation (PIA/GATF) and the National Association of Printing Leadership. The main purpose of trade associations is to assist members and contribute to their welfare. Some of the services include training programs; scholarship funds; the sharing of technical expertise, new processes, and methods of operation; and fair representation to the government on industry-related issues.

Printing-industry associations can work together to establish guidelines, such as the Printing Trade Customs, or standards for production practices. Most of these standards are not mandatory. By following them, however, production tends to flow much better—especially if several facilities or companies are involved in a job.

A listing of industry-related associations is provided in Appendix A. Most of the associations listed provide publications that will help you learn more about the association itself and the printing industry. Use the Internet to search for company Web sites or write to the addresses provided.

Laws and Legal Restrictions

There are legal restrictions in the United States regulating what can be printed. Printers must be alert to possible violations of the law. Those printers who are in doubt about a printing job generally consult a lawyer. The most common legal problems relate to copyrights, photocopying, software piracy, counterfeiting, and the publication of obscene literature.

Copyrights

According to Title 17 of the U.S. Code, a *copyright* establishes the exclusive legal right to reproduce, publish, and sell "original works of authorship [that] are fixed in any tangible medium of expression." Copyrightable works include pieces that fall into the following categories:

- Literary works.
- Musical works, including any accompanying words.
- Dramatic works, including any accompanying music.
- Pantomimes and choreographic works.
- Pictorial, graphic, and sculptural works.
- Motion pictures and other audiovisual works.
- Sound recordings.
- Architectural works.

Printers and copy-service shops should have a form for customers to sign, releasing the printer from liability of copyright infringement. *Copyright infringement* is the unauthorized use of copyrighted work. This type of release form can be extremely valuable, since conviction on a charge of copyright infringement can be quite costly.

Just as copyrights can protect a wide range of works, trademarks can be protected when they become registered. A trademark is any name, figure, word, letter, or symbol that a manufacturer, service provider, or merchant has adopted to identify its product or service. A trademark used to identify a service, rather than a product, can also be referred to as a *service mark*.

A registered trademark is protected from unauthorized use, known as *trademark infringement*. The ® symbol indicates that a trademark is registered. The ™ symbol indicates that trademark rights are claimed, although the trademark has yet to be registered. Unregistered trademarks have some protection, but only in limited geographical areas.

Copyright notices

A copyright notice can take a number of forms. See **Figure 5-5**. This notice should contain the word *copyright*, abbreviation *Copr.*, or symbol ©. The name of the copyright owner and year of publication should follow the word or symbol.

© Falcone Publishing 2007

Copyright Falcone Publishing 2007

`Copr. Falcone Publishing`

© FP

Copr. FP 2007

Figure 5-5. Copyright notices can take on a number of forms.

copyright: the exclusive legal right to reproduce, publish, and sell original works of authorship existing in print or another tangible form of expression.

copyright infringement: the unauthorized use of copyrighted work.

Copyright coverage

Copyright law influences everyone involved in the production and distribution of information. Permission should be obtained, or credit should be given, whenever there is a question of ownership. Providing a simple credit line can often prevent many legal problems among the printer, customer, and copyright holder.

Copyrightable works

The U.S. Copyright Office defines *copyrightable works* as "original works of authorship fixed in any tangible medium of expression." These works include literary works, dramatic works, pantomimes, choreographic works, pictorial works, graphic works, sculptural works, motion pictures, other audiovisual works, and sound recordings. The U.S. Copyright Office has a variety of forms that can be ordered through the mail or downloaded from the Internet. See **Figure 5-6.**

Duration of copyright

Before 1978, copyright in the United States was limited to 28 years, plus an additional 28 years upon renewal. The current copyright law extends the renewal term from 28 to 47 years for copyrights that were subsisting on January 1, 1978, making these works eligible for a total term of protection of 75 years. For works created after January 1, 1978, copyright in the United States lasts for the lifetime of the designer, creator, or author and extends for 50 years after the person dies. In the case of anonymous works, pseudonymous works, and works *made for hire*, the copyright lasts 75 years from the date of publication or 100 years from the time of completion of the work, whichever is sooner.

International protection

There is no such thing as an international copyright that will automatically protect an author's writings throughout the world. Protection against unauthorized use in a particular country depends on the national laws of that country. Most countries do offer protection to foreign works under certain conditions, however, and international copyright treaties and conventions have greatly simplified these conditions. For a list of countries that maintain copyright relations with the United States, contact the U.S. Copyright Office.

Photocopying

There are exceptions to the law that allow duplication of copyrighted materials without written permission or copyright infringement. These exceptions are known as the *fair use* provisions of the law. The most common example of fair use is in education. According to copyright law, educators can do the following:

- Produce single copies of a chapter of a book, an article from a periodical, a short story, an essay, a poem, a chart, a graph, or a diagram for research or class preparation.
- Produce multiple copies (one per student) if copying "meets the tests of brevity and spontaneity" and carries a notice of copyright.

Copyright law also states that educators cannot do the following:

- Photocopy consumable works, such as workbooks or worksheets.
- Copy publications as a substitute for buying books.
- Copy to replace or create selected literary pieces or passages.
- Charge students more than the actual cost of copying.

Software Piracy

Software piracy, or the use of unlicensed computer software programs, is a serious matter that can lead to large fines and lawsuits for copyright infringement. An End-User License Agreement (EULA) protects software manufacturers. A EULA covers the legal conditions under which software products can be installed and used. The Business Software Alliance (BSA) enforces the proper licensing of computer software within businesses, government agencies, schools, and nonprofit groups. The association oversees piracy through enforcement programs in countries throughout North America, Europe, Asia, and Latin America.

There are a number of ways software piracy occurs. A company might distribute a single copy to a number of employees instead of obtaining a site license or multiple copies. This type of violation is similar to purchasing a book and making multiple copies for distribution. Employees can commit software piracy by copying software for use at home.

It is important for companies to establish good software management. Copies of software should be kept by a responsible party and distributed in the proper manner. Site licenses and multiple copies should be purchased and used in accordance with purchasing agreements the manufacturer provides. See **Figure 5-7.**

Copyright Office fees are subject to change. For current fees, check the Copyright Office website at www.copyright.gov, write the Copyright Office, or call (202) 707-3000.

Form TX
For a Nondramatic Literary Work
UNITED STATES COPYRIGHT OFFICE

REGISTRATION NUMBER

_____

TX   TXU
EFFECTIVE DATE OF REGISTRATION

_____
Month   Day   Year

DO NOT WRITE ABOVE THIS LINE. IF YOU NEED MORE SPACE, USE A SEPARATE CONTINUATION SHEET.

1 TITLE OF THIS WORK ▼

PREVIOUS OR ALTERNATIVE TITLES ▼

PUBLICATION AS A CONTRIBUTION If this work was published as a contribution to a periodical, serial, or collection, give information about the collective work in which the contribution appeared.   **Title of Collective Work ▼**

If published in a periodical or serial give: Volume ▼   Number ▼   Issue Date ▼   On Pages ▼

2 a NAME OF AUTHOR ▼

DATES OF BIRTH AND DEATH
Year Born ▼   Year Died ▼

Was this contribution to the work a "work made for hire"?
☐ Yes
☐ No

AUTHOR'S NATIONALITY OR DOMICILE
Name of Country
OR { Citizen of ▶_____
Domiciled in▶_____

WAS THIS AUTHOR'S CONTRIBUTION TO THE WORK
Anonymous?   ☐ Yes ☐ No
Pseudonymous?   ☐ Yes ☐ No
If the answer to either of these questions is "Yes," see detailed instructions.

NATURE OF AUTHORSHIP Briefly describe nature of material created by this author in which copyright is claimed. ▼

NOTE

Under the law, the "author" of a "work made for hire" is generally the employer, not the employee (see instructions). For any part of this work that was "made for hire" check "Yes" in the space provided, give the employer (or other person for whom the work was prepared) as "Author" of that part, and leave the space for dates of birth and death blank.

b NAME OF AUTHOR ▼

DATES OF BIRTH AND DEATH
Year Born ▼   Year Died ▼

Was this contribution to the work a "work made for hire"?
☐ Yes
☐ No

AUTHOR'S NATIONALITY OR DOMICILE
Name of Country
OR { Citizen of ▶_____
Domiciled in▶_____

WAS THIS AUTHOR'S CONTRIBUTION TO THE WORK
Anonymous?   ☐ Yes ☐ No
Pseudonymous?   ☐ Yes ☐ No
If the answer to either of these questions is "Yes," see detailed instructions.

NATURE OF AUTHORSHIP Briefly describe nature of material created by this author in which copyright is claimed. ▼

c NAME OF AUTHOR ▼

DATES OF BIRTH AND DEATH
Year Born ▼   Year Died ▼

Was this contribution to the work a "work made for hire"?
☐ Yes
☐ No

AUTHOR'S NATIONALITY OR DOMICILE
Name of Country
OR { Citizen of ▶_____
Domiciled in▶_____

WAS THIS AUTHOR'S CONTRIBUTION TO THE WORK
Anonymous?   ☐ Yes ☐ No
Pseudonymous?   ☐ Yes ☐ No
If the answer to either of these questions is "Yes," see detailed instructions.

NATURE OF AUTHORSHIP Briefly describe nature of material created by this author in which copyright is claimed. ▼

3 a YEAR IN WHICH CREATION OF THIS WORK WAS COMPLETED   This information must be given ◀ Year in all cases.

b DATE AND NATION OF FIRST PUBLICATION OF THIS PARTICULAR WORK   Complete this information ONLY if this work has been published.   Month ▶_____ Day▶_____ Year▶_____   ◀ Nation

4 COPYRIGHT CLAIMANT(S) Name and address must be given even if the claimant is the same as the author given in space 2. ▼

APPLICATION RECEIVED

ONE DEPOSIT RECEIVED

TWO DEPOSITS RECEIVED

See instructions before completing this space.

TRANSFER If the claimant(s) named here in space 4 is (are) different from the author(s) named in space 2, give a brief statement of how the claimant(s) obtained ownership of the copyright. ▼

FUNDS RECEIVED

DO NOT WRITE HERE
OFFICE USE ONLY

MORE ON BACK ▶ · Complete all applicable spaces (numbers 5-9) on the reverse side of this page.
· See detailed instructions.   · Sign the form at line 8.

DO NOT WRITE HERE
Page 1 of _____ pages

Figure 5-6. Applications are available for every type of copyrightable work. (U.S. Copyright Office)

made for hire: a work an employee created or a work that has been specially ordered or commissioned, in writing, as a contribution to a collective work.

fair use: exceptions to the law that allow duplication of copyrighted materials without written permission or copyright infringement.

software piracy: the use of unlicensed computer software programs.

EXAMINED BY	FORM TX
CHECKED BY	
☐ CORRESPONDENCE Yes	FOR COPYRIGHT OFFICE USE ONLY

DO NOT WRITE ABOVE THIS LINE. IF YOU NEED MORE SPACE, USE A SEPARATE CONTINUATION SHEET.

PREVIOUS REGISTRATION Has registration for this work, or for an earlier version of this work, already been made in the Copyright Office?

☐ Yes ☐ No If your answer is "Yes," why is another registration being sought? (Check appropriate box.) ▼

a. ☐ This is the first published edition of a work previously registered in unpublished form.

b. ☐ This is the first application submitted by this author as copyright claimant.

c. ☐ This is a changed version of the work, as shown by space 6 on this application.

If your answer is "Yes," give: **Previous Registration Number** ▶   **Year of Registration** ▶

5

DERIVATIVE WORK OR COMPILATION

Preexisting Material Identify any preexisting work or works that this work is based on or incorporates. ▼

Material Added to This Work Give a brief, general statement of the material that has been added to this work and in which copyright is claimed. ▼

a   **6**

See instructions before completing this space.

b

DEPOSIT ACCOUNT If the registration fee is to be charged to a Deposit Account established in the Copyright Office, give name and number of Account.

Name ▼   **Account Number** ▼

a   **7**

CORRESPONDENCE Give name and address to which correspondence about this application should be sent.   Name/Address/Apt/City/State/Zip ▼

b

Area code and daytime telephone number ▶   Fax number ▶

Email ▶

CERTIFICATION* I, the undersigned, hereby certify that I am the

Check only one ▶

☐ author

☐ other copyright claimant

☐ owner of exclusive right(s)

☐ authorized agent of _____

of the work identified in this application and that the statements made by me in this application are correct to the best of my knowledge.

Name of author or other copyright claimant, or owner of exclusive right(s) ▲

8

Typed or printed name and date ▼ If this application gives a date of publication in space 3, do not sign and submit it before that date.

_____ Date ▶ _____

Handwritten signature ▼

_____

Certificate will be mailed in window envelope to this address:	Name ▼	**YOU MUST:** · Complete all necessary spaces · Sign your application in space 8
	Number/Street/Apt ▼	**SEND ALL 3 ELEMENTS IN THE SAME PACKAGE:** 1. Application form 2. Nonrefundable filing fee in check or money order payable to *Register of Copyrights* 3. Deposit material
	City/State/Zip ▼	**MAIL TO:** Library of Congress Copyright Office 101 Independence Avenue SE Washington, DC 20559-6222

9

*17 *USC* §506(e): Any person who knowingly makes a false representation of a material fact in the application for copyright registration provided for by section 409, or in any written statement filed in connection with the application, shall be fined not more than $2,500.

Form TX – Full   Rev: 11/2006   Print: 11/2006 – 30,000   Printed on recycled paper   U.S. Government Printing Office: 2006-xx-xxx/60,xxx

Figure 5-6. *(Continued)*

Figure 5-7. A purchasing agreement governs the use of software.

Counterfeiting

To *counterfeit* means to imitate or copy closely with the intent to deceive. Most people associate counterfeiting with the illegal reproduction of money and works of art. See **Figure 5-8.** Keep in mind that any request for printing or photographing, in part or whole, or the supplying of materials for any work that might seem to violate any part of federal regulations should be reported at once.

If the proposed work is legally permissible, you will be so informed. If the work is illegal, you will be far better off having had no part in it. Never proceed on the assumption that something similar to what is requested has been publicly distributed with permission. Prior violations might have gone unnoticed or be under investigation at the time.

Obscene Literature

Obscene literature is material considered offensive to morality or virtue. The printing of articles,

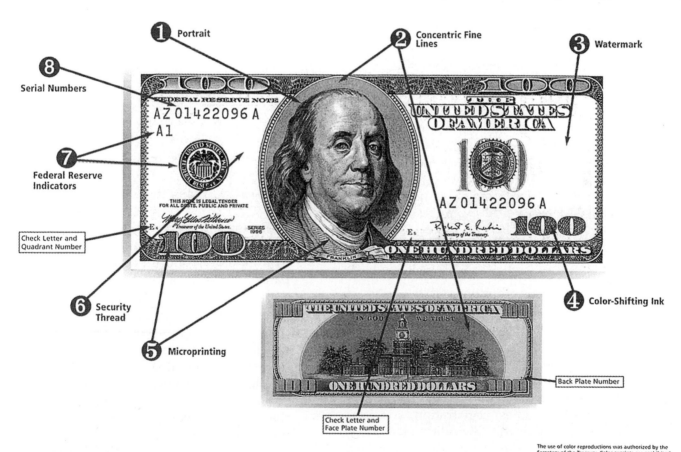

Figure 5-8. Special features have been added to U.S. currency to deter counterfeiting. Photographic reproductions are permissible, provided the items are reproduced in black and white and are less than 3/4 or greater than 1 1/2 times the size.

counterfeit: to imitate or copy closely with the intent to deceive.

obscene literature: material considered offensive to morality or virtue.

drawings, or photographs that might be classified as obscene requires careful legal review. The printer's attorney should review the material in question and possibly contact the proper governmental agency before any potentially obscene printing is undertaken.

To define what is obscene is sometimes difficult. In the 1960s, the U.S. Supreme Court declared that "to be obscene any printed matter must be utterly without redeeming social value." This ruling resulted in an increase in pornographic publications because nearly any work can be construed to have at least a trace of redeeming social value.

In 1973, the U.S. Supreme Court declared that individual communities could establish their own standards for obscenity. The Supreme Court also ruled that a work in question could be judged obscene if, taken as a whole, it lacks serious literary, artistic, political, or scientific value. By looking at each work as a whole, instead of searching for a trace of value, the Supreme Court made it easier for a work to be judged obscene. Allowing communities to set their own standards, however, created the potential for material judged to not be obscene in one region to be judged obscene in another region. Therefore, printers were faced with an increased likelihood of printing something that could be declared obscene somewhere. This risk became one reason for most printers to refuse to print certain materials. Other reasons include the objection of some employees to work on jobs they consider obscene and the risk to the printing company's reputation within its own community.

Rights of the Printer

Printers should also understand the importance of protecting their own works by copyright. Works created by artists, designers, and writers for the printer for personal distribution and sale should bear copyright notice. Examples include artwork on calendars and greeting cards.

Literature is available from the U.S. Copyright Office clearly explaining the copyright procedure. This literature can be useful in helping a printer answer basic customer questions on application for copyright, deposit of copies, registration, and fees. When discussing copyright law with customers, there is a point at which the printer should advise a customer to consult with an attorney regarding legal restrictions and obligations.

Business Trade Secrets

Information technology secrets, referred to as *business trade secrets*, are less safe today than at any other time in the history of business and industry. The commercial value of business secrets has been brought to light in a number of lawsuits large corporations have filed. Each of these cases demonstrates the extraordinary lengths to which owners and managers of companies will go to protect these secrets.

The victims of these corporate thefts told Congress they needed additional protection for trade secrets. They noted that the U.S. economy is becoming more dependent on intellectual property for competitive advantage, and this property is getting easier to steal. With the computer's power to copy and transmit information, intangible assets can be expropriated more easily than ever—often without arousing immediate attention. The victim is not immediately aware of the theft because the original is still in place.

Urged by business and industry, the U.S. Congress enacted the Economic Espionage Act (EEA) of 1996, which makes the theft of business secrets a federal offense. When espionage can be established, the EEA prescribes prison sentences of up to 15 years and fines of up to $500,000. Prosecutors can also seize property used in commission of the crime.

Before the enactment of the EEA, the legal definition of a business secret was ambiguous. To help determine what is covered under the law, the definition has been refined in the EEA:

All forms and types of financial, business, scientific, technical, economic, or engineering information, including patterns, plans, compilations, program devices, formulas, designs, prototypes, methods, techniques, processes, procedures, programs or codes, whether tangible or intangible, and whether or how stored, compiled, or memorialized physically, electronically, graphically, photographically, or in writing if: (A) the owner thereof has taken reasonable measures to keep such information secret; and (B) the information derives independent economic value, actual or potential, from not being generally known to, and not being readily ascertainable through proper means by, the public. (Unified Trade Secrets Act, Sec. 18 U.S.C. [section] 1839 [3])

For example, a printing company theoretically can get in trouble with the law simply by hiring a salesperson who brings a Rolodex® file from a past employer. The contents on that Rolodex file might be deemed business secrets. If they are, and if the new hire uses them to the detriment of his former employer, it could amount to a federal offense.

Patents apply only to inventions (and only to novel, useful, and nonobvious ones). Business secrets, by contrast, can apply to mere ideas and information. Their all-inclusive nature can mislead companies into believing everything they have is secret. This is not true. Making sure valuable information will have business secret status is not difficult. For example, in the case of the printing salesperson, the Rolodex file list could be made more clearly a business secret if it included details learned during the salesperson's employment. These details could include such things as a client's taste in clothing, reading matter, or food.

Summary

Organized members of the printing and graphic communications industries established the Printing Trade Customs to help companies establish similar business practices. The Printing Trade Customs protect the customer and printer from unfair business practices. These customs cover such matters as proofs, alterations, press overruns, delivery, and terms of payment.

Labor unions are also a part of the printing industry. These unions serve their members to help establish and maintain fair wages, benefits, and good working conditions. In addition to unions, there are a number of trade associations also serving the people who work in the printing industry. These associations provide members with a variety of services, including training programs; scholarship funds; the sharing of technical expertise, new processes, and methods of operation; and fair representation to the government on industry-related issues.

There are legal restrictions in the United States regulating what can be printed. The most common legal problems printers encounter relate to copyrights, photocopying, software piracy, counterfeiting, and the publication of obscene literature. To avoid problems, printers should remain current on these types of legal issues and be alert to possible violations of the law.

Review Questions

Please do not write in this book. Write your answers on a separate sheet of paper.

1. List at least four reasons members of the printing and graphic communications industries have formed trade organizations, associations, and standards.
2. Business practices in the printing industry are called _____.
3. What are some of the benefits of membership in a labor union?
4. A company that hires only union members is called a(n) _____.
5. A nonunion company is called a(n) _____.
6. Briefly explain the main purpose of printing industry trade associations.
7. Into what eight categories do copyrightable works fall?
8. What is copyright infringement?
9. Which one of the following is *not* an acceptable copyright notice format?
   A. © Falcone Publishing 2001
   B. Copr. Falcone Publishing 2001
   C. Copyright Falcone Publishing 2001
   D. 2001 Falcone Publishing
10. How long is a copyright in effect on a work created on or after January 1, 2001?
11. Exceptions to copyright law that allow duplication of copyrighted materials without written permission or copyright infringement are known as _____ provisions of the law.
12. Identify three items that cannot be legally reproduced.
13. What is software piracy?
14. In 1973, the U.S. Supreme Court ruled that the standards for judging obscenity could be drawn up by the _____.
15. The _____ of 1996 makes theft of business secrets a federal offense.

Skill-Building Activities

1. In a group of two to four students, prepare a display showing different copyrighted material and material that is not copyrightable. Label the samples for the benefit of those who will see the display. After getting permission, place the display in the library or a busy part of the school.
2. Write a research paper on counterfeiting. Include historical information and obtain or create illustrations if possible.

The Evolution of Our Alphabet

The earliest examples of graphic communication are paintings on the walls of caves. The oldest were made over 37,000 years ago. These crude drawings represented people, animals, and objects that were part of those civilizations. Called *pictographs*, these drawings were limited to images of physical objects. Pictographs were limited to a one-to-one ratio with reality. For example, to communicate that a herd contained 120 deer, one would have to draw 120 deer. The need to communicate more abstract concepts, such as father, happiness, pride, and hunger, brought about drawings called *ideographs*, symbols representing more than their actual images. Modern-day ideographs include the shape of the heart to communicate love and the skull and crossbones on a label to represent poison.

Many ideographs gave new meanings to old pictographic symbols. For example, the pictographic symbols for an ox and a house evolved into the ideographic symbols representing food and shelter, respectively. Although this ability to convey abstract ideas visually was a major enhancement of written communication, ideographic languages such as the Egyptians' hieroglyphics soon became cumbersome because a new symbol had to be created every time a new thing or idea came along. In time, written languages consisted of several hundred characters and were still growing.

This problem was solved around 900 BC, when the Phoenician civilization devised a written language based on sounds. The Phoenicians took some of their ideographic symbols and reassigned them to represent sounds. The symbol for food, called *aleph*, took on the *A* sound, and the symbol for shelter, called *beth*, became the symbol for the *B* sound. With this amazing breakthrough, the Phoenicians were able to write about any subject with fewer than 40 symbols.

The ancient Greeks adopted the Phoenician system 600 years later, but they altered the letterforms to improve their aesthetics. The Phoenician letters *aleph* and *beth* were rotated to make them symmetrical, and they became *alpha* and *beta*, the first two letters of the Greek alphabet and the basis for the word *alphabet*. Centuries later, the ancient Romans also adopted the sound-based system for written communication, but not without giving most of the characters another makeover. The resulting Roman alphabet has better visual unity because the characters are different enough to avoid confusion, but not so different as to seem foreign to one another. In addition, the Romans gave their letters both thick and thin strokes and flared extensions at the end of strokes, called *serifs*. Amazingly, Roman letter design has remained intact for over 2000 years. Later developments included the addition of three new letters and the development of small (lowercase) letters, italics, and punctuation.

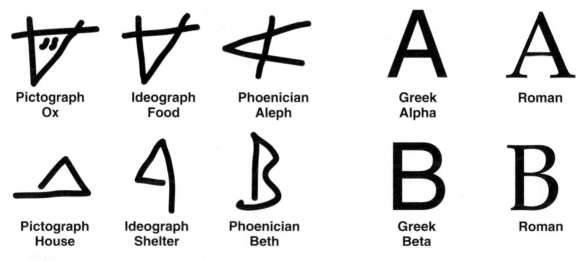

Pictograph Ox   **Ideograph Food**   **Phoenician Aleph**   **Greek Alpha**   **Roman**

Pictograph House   **Ideograph Shelter**   **Phoenician Beth**   **Greek Beta**   **Roman**

Phoenician 900 BC

Greek 300 BC

A B C D E F G H I K L M N O P Q R S T U V W X Y Z

Roman 400 BC

Chapter 6
Principles of Typography

Key Terms

bitmap font
body type
centered format
closed counter
cursive typeface
decorative typeface
digital font
dingbat
diphthong
display type
em
em quad
em space
en
en quad
flush left/ragged right
    format
flush right/ragged left
    format
font
font library
gothic
initial character
justified format
kerning
legibility
letterspacing
ligature
line spacing
lowercase letter
modern serif typeface
old-style serif typeface
one-person proofing
open counter
page description language
    (PDL)

Postscript® font
    technology
proofreader's mark
proofreading
ragged
readability
reverse type
Roman
runaround format
sans serif
script typeface
serif typeface
skew
small cap
square-serif typeface
text type
tracking
transitional serif
    typeface
TrueType® font
    technology
two-person proofing
type
typeface
typeface classification
type family
type series
typesetting format
typography
unit system
uppercase letter
vector font
word spacing

Learning Objectives

When you have completed the reading and assigned activities related to this chapter, you will be able to do the following:

◆ Summarize the basic functions and goals of typography.

◆ Distinguish the differences among typefaces, fonts, families, and series.

◆ Identify and explain basic letter and typeface elements.

◆ List and identify the basic typeface classifications.

◆ Use the point system to measure point size and determine the actual height of typeset characters.

◆ Distinguish between text type and display type.

◆ Define *leading* and indicate its purpose.

◆ Explain the differences and applications of various digital fonts.

◆ Differentiate among the various typesetting formats.

◆ Select and use typefaces with the most effective physical characteristics for a specific printed piece.

Graphic designers are in the business of making decisions—decisions regarding the size and shape of the printed piece; the ink colors and paper finish; the selection, cropping, and placement of photographs; and more. The most critical design decisions, however, usually revolve around the selection and use of type. The reason for this is that the client's budget often cannot afford the expense of hiring artists and photographers. Often, the designer's image options are limited to what can be done with type. The mishandling of type can ruin a design. In contrast, the proper handling of type can create striking images that communicate both words and an appropriate mood. See **Figure 6-1.**

Thousands of typefaces are available to graphic designers and printers. In fact, there are more typefaces than can be counted because new ones are continually created. See **Figure 6-2.** This astonishing variety of typefaces can be a boundless resource to the perceptive and informed designer or a sea of confusion to the novice. The more that beginning

designers understand about type and typography, the more effectively they will be able to use these powerful graphic elements. The key to success is to become familiar with the typeface classifications, visual effects, and nomenclature so intelligent decisions can be made as to which type treatment best communicates the verbal and visual messages of the printed piece.

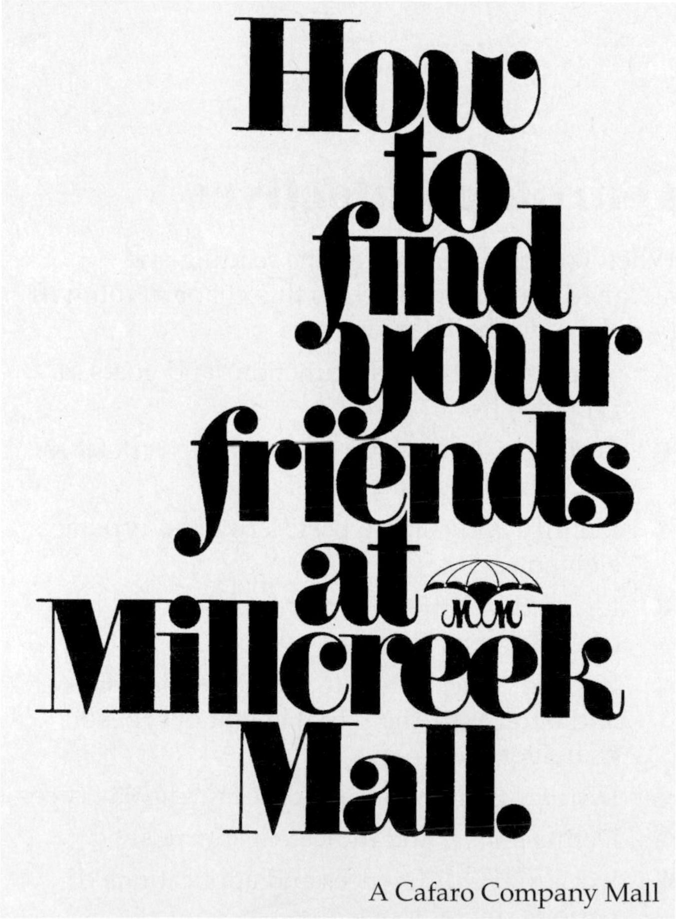

Type and Typography

The characters, figures, and punctuation marks used in printed messages are called *type*. The selection and arrangement of type in the design is *typography*. Typography has two basic functions. The first is to convey a message concisely, quickly, and with little effort from the reader, and the second is to enhance the mood or feel of the design.

From the outset, the terms *legibility* and *readability* must be understood. *Legibility* measures the ease and speed with which short phrases can be read accurately. For the large type in advertisements, posters, book titles, and signage, legibility is critical. Too often, though, amateur designers choose *typefaces* that are striking but lack legibility, and type that is not read easily fails to communicate well.

Type set in a large volume, such as the body copy of books, magazines, and newspapers, must not only be legible but also highly readable. *Readability* measures the ability of a large body of type to be read without tiring the reader's eyes. Type that is very legible in small amounts might not be very readable when set in long lengths. These distinctions will be examined later in the chapter.

Figure 6-1. The typographic treatments of the front panel of this folder do much more than merely communicate verbal meaning. The nesting of the words and the careful vertical alignment of certain letters impart unity and a cozy, informal style to the design. (Millcreek Mall)

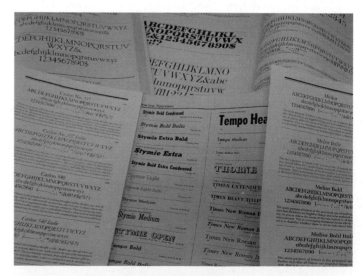

Figure 6-2. The graphic designer can choose from thousands of typefaces when creating a printed piece.

Effective typography begins with the selection of the appropriate typefaces for communicating the message to the reader. This process includes considerations of the nature of the message, type of reader, printing process, and kind of paper or other substrate to be used. Typographic success requires an understanding of typeface characteristics, type measurement, and the various typographic formats available. When a graphic designer uses type well, it can be the only element of a design—functioning without the need for photographs or other art. In fact, the ability to allow type alone to carry a design is a sign of an excellent graphic designer.

In this chapter, we will explore the primary typeface classifications, as well as what distinguishes typefaces from one another. You will become familiar with typographic terminology. By the end of this chapter, you will understand the rules for using type effectively and the reasons behind those rules.

Typefaces, Fonts, Families, and Series

The terms *typeface, type font, type family,* and *type series* are often used interchangeably. These terms do, however, have distinct meanings that cannot be switched without inviting confusion and production errors. It is especially important for graphic designers to use these terms properly when communicating with people who work in prepress, as well as clients and other designers.

Typefaces

A typeface is a specific style with its own combination of design features such as shape, stroke, and weight, which distinguish one typeface from another. These distinctions can be obvious or subtle, as shown in **Figure 6-3.** A typeface interprets the characters of the alphabet with a particular style and an individual set of design rules. The term *typeface* originally referred to the face (or printing surface) of three-dimensional metal type. See **Figure 6-4.** Today, hundreds of electronic versions of traditional and newly developed typefaces are available.

Note

Although originally having different meanings, the terms *typeface* and *font* have become blurred because word processing and desktop-publishing software screen menus erroneously use the word font in place of *typeface* or *typestyle*. In truth, a *font* is a *typeface* in a particular size, weight, and structure.

Wagtf

Wagtf

Wagtf

Wagtf

Figure 6-3. Although this grouping of typefaces might appear at first to contain the same style, closer inspection will reveal many subtle differences in stroke thickness, design features, and proportion. When type is set in large volumes, these small distinctions become collectively significant and affect the overall impression of the printed piece.

Figure 6-4. Most typographic terminology originated when type was carried on raised areas of metal. Note that the size of the actual letter is only a portion of the size of the type.

type: the letters and other characters (numerals and punctuation) used in printed messages.

typography: the selection and arrangement of type to be used in the design of a printed piece.

legibility: the ease with which a typeface can be read immediately.

typeface: a type family narrowed down to a specific weight and width.

readability: a measure of how difficult or easy it is to read several pages of printed matter before eye fatigue begins.

Typefaces differ radically in detail, and each has design strengths and weaknesses. Some are made narrow for space requirements, others are designed for high readability, and some are intended to grab attention or create a mood. It is nearly impossible, however, for a typeface to have all these strengths. For example, narrow or ornamental typefaces usually lose readability. Nonetheless, if a typeface design is well chosen, the type will impart a mood in harmony with the message, while the reader is still able to recognize each character quickly. See **Figure 6-5.**

Typefaces are visually as full of accent, impact, and tonalities as human voices. Details such as the relative sizes of the characters, how tightly the lines of type are packed together, what weight and force the characters carry, and whether the strokes get thinner in the curves of the characters influence a reader's reactions to a printed piece. These features contribute to how easily the typeface can be read. See **Figure 6-6.** Research has found that a typestyle's influence on the reader is often subconscious, but this influence has very real results, as measured by whether paragraphs continue to be read or are skipped over, the amount of reading time required, and the readers' retention of the content. The key to making good typographic decisions and effectively specifying those decisions is to become knowledge-able about the design, function, classification, and terminology of type.

Type Fonts

A *font* is the complete alphabet in a particular typeface and point size. It includes all characters available, such as uppercase and lowercase letters, numerals, punctuation marks, ligatures, diphthongs, dingbats, and other symbols. See **Figure 6-7.** A useful image for understanding a font is the single typeface and size available on a typewriter.

In the early days of hand-set type, a font's characters were carried in two large wooden drawers or cases. The capital letters were in the case that, when in use, was placed above the case carrying the small letters. From this use, we got the terms *uppercase letters* (such as A, B, and C) and *lowercase letters* (such as a, b, and c). *Ligatures* are combinations of characters into one unit, such as fi or fl, and they also date back to the days of metal type. *Diphthongs* are combinations of vowels, such as æ and œ. *Dingbats* (or wingdings) are ornamental designs (such as ✇, ⇨, and ✄) used to illustrate and attract attention to specific text matter. Some fonts might include *small caps*, which are uppercase letters slightly smaller than the normal capitals of the font.

New and improved!

New England Historical

FRONTIER RANCH

Renaissance Festival

Soft and Silky

Deb's Daycare

Broadway Classics

Uptown Boutique

Cartoon Classics

You are cordially invited

Road-tested tough

Figure 6-5. To realize the importance of choosing the right typeface for a given message, imagine switching the typefaces with the words shown in these examples.

UNUSUAL STYLES CAN BE ILLEGIBLE.

UNUSUAL STYLES CAN BE ILLEGIBLE.

UNUSUAL STYLES CAN BE ILLEGIBLE.

Figure 6-6. Legibility is highest with traditional typefaces, such as the first two shown. Variations such as a thicker stroke, italics, or a condensed style often reduce legibility.

ABCDEFGHIJKLMNOPQRSTUV
WXYZabcdefghijklmnopqrstuvwxyz.,
;:"'?/—-_1234567890

Figure 6-7. A font is a collection of the entire alphabet and punctuation marks in a certain typeface and size. This font is 16-point Garamond. Garamond in another size is a different font.

Type Families

A *type family* is a collection of a typeface and its variations, based on weight (light or bold), structure (condensed or expanded), and stress (italic or Roman). See **Figure 6-8.** A type family typically consists of the original font, as well as light, bold, extra bold, italic, condensed, and expanded faces. Very popular typefaces often have a large type family and can include additional variations, such as bold italic, condensed italic, bold condensed italic, bold expanded, outline, and reverse.

Size	
6	ABCDEFGHIJKLMNOPQRSTUVWXYZ
8	ABCDEFGHIJKLMNOPQRSTUVWXYZ
10	ABCDEFGHIJKLMNOPQRSTUV
12	ABCDEFGHIJKLMNOPQR
14	ABCDEFGHIJKLMNOP
18	ABCDEFGHIJKLM
24	ABCDEFGHIJ
30	ABCDEFG
42	ABCDE
48	ABCD
60	ABC

Figure 6-9. A type series consists of all sizes available in one typeface.

Type Series

A *type series* is the range of sizes available for a specific typeface in a specific type family. For example, one series might include all the sizes available in Times Roman medium, while another series might include all the sizes available in Helvetica. See **Figure 6-9.**

Garamond Light
Garamond Book
Garamond Bold
Garamond Ultra
Garamond Light Italic
Garamond Book Italic
Garamond Bold Italic
Garamond Ultra Italic
Garamond Light Condensed
Garamond Book Condensed
Garamond Bold Condensed
Garamond Ultra Condensed
Garamond Light Condensed Italic
Garamond Book Condensed Italic
Garamond Bold Condensed Italic
Garamond Ultra Condensed Italic

Figure 6-8. A type family consists of variations on a type design. Popular type designs such as Garamond have large families.

font: a type family narrowed down to a specific weight, width, and point size.

uppercase letter: a capital letter.

lowercase letter: a "small" letter of the alphabet.

ligature: a combination of characters in one unit.

diphthong: the combination of two letters in a single graphic and single sound.

dingbat: an ornamental design used to illustrate and attract attention to specific text matter.

small cap: an uppercase letter slightly smaller than the normal capitals of the font.

type family: a collection that includes a typeface and its variations.

type series: the range of point sizes available for a specific font of a specific typeface in a specific type family.

Type Design Options

Typefaces vary in several ways. See **Figure 6-10.** An important consideration in type selection is a typeface's use of proportion, the design element revolving around size relationships. There are many proportion applications in typography: the height and width of the characters; the thickness of the strokes; and the ascender, descender, and x-height spaces. See **Figure 6-11** and **Figure 6-12** for a listing and illustration of several character elements. The use of these design elements distinguishes one typeface from the thousands of others. These distinctions might be glaringly obvious or very subtle, but their combined effect determines the typography's effectiveness in a particular situation. Two of these elements are the closed counter and the open counter. A *closed counter* is an entirely closed area within a character.

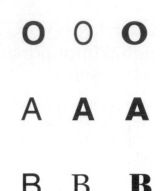

Figure 6-10. Several variations in typeface design are structure, stroke or weight, and stroke variation. The three uppercase Os are shown in different structures, the proportion of width-to-height. The three As vary in stroke thickness. The three Bs reflect three degrees of stroke contrast—none, modest, and great.

Ascender	In lowercase characters, the upper stroke, as in *b*, *d*, *h*, and *k*.
Baseline	The imaginary line along the bottom of the body height of characters, sometimes referred to as the x-height line.
Boldface	Type characterized by heavier weight than the "plain" versions of the characters. Commonly referred to as *bold*. (bold vs. not bold, or plain)
Counter	Refers to areas inside the loops of type characters, as in *D*, *O*, and *Q*.
Descender	In lowercase characters, the downstroke, as in *y*, *p*, and *g*.
Hairline stroke	The thin lines forming the elements of a character.
Heavy stroke	The heavy lines forming the elements of a character.
Italic	Type that slants to the right. Sometimes italic is referred to as *oblique*.
Character height	The distance from top to bottom of the lowercase letters, not including the ascenders and descenders. Also referred to as *body height* or *x-height*.
Lowercase	The small characters in type, as distinguished from uppercase or capitals, sometimes referred to as *lc*.
Serifs	Thin strokes at the ends of the main character strokes.
Set width	The distance from the left to right sides of an individual type character.
Stem	The vertical stroke of a character, such as in lowercase *d*, *h*, *k*, *l*, and *t*.
Stress	The slant or posture of a character, such as italic typefaces.
Uppercase	These are capital, or cap, characters.
Waist line	An imaginary line drawn along the top of body height letters.

Figure 6-11. An understanding of these typographic terms is fundamental to effectively communicating typographic specs.

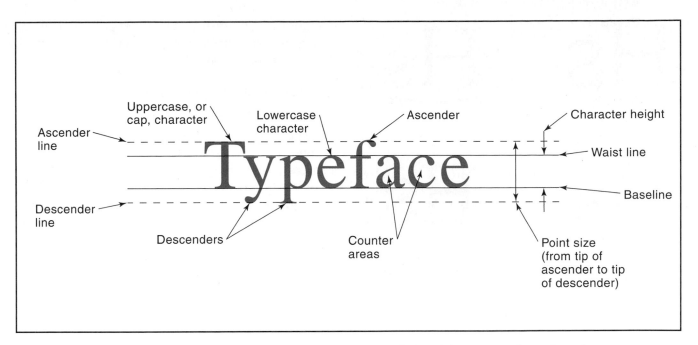

Figure 6-12. The anatomy of type includes many components that distinguish one type from the others.

An *open counter* is a partially enclosed area within a character. For example, the letters *a* and *e* contain both an open counter and a closed counter.

Typeface Classifications

Even though there are thousands of typeface designs in the Western world, all are grouped into five *typeface classifications* (or races): serif, square serif, sans serif, script and cursive, and decorative. Understanding the characteristics of these classifications is essential for selecting, describing, and locating type for a printed piece. Type catalogs usually group typestyles by these classifications. The numerous typefaces in Appendix B are representative of these classifications.

Serif, or Roman, Typefaces

Serif typefaces are named for the flared extensions at the end of their strokes, called *serifs*. See **Figure 6-13.** Another name for this classification is *Roman*, the ancient civilization that created the serif. Besides the serifs, another important feature of serif typefaces is the stroke variation, the combination of thin and thick strokes in every character. Serifs can be straight or bracketed.

Serifs significantly improve readability in two ways. First, their extending outward creates a subtle linkage between the characters of a word and helps the horizontal path of the eye. Second, serifs help to distinguish characters that otherwise share similar design elements. See **Figure 6-14.**

The look of most serif typefaces has stood the test of time because these typefaces are patterned after the classic Roman designs. These typefaces are easily read because of their serifs and stroke variation, as well as their open, round, and wide design. A serif typeface is usually selected for large bodies of type, such as books and magazine articles, because the serifs and stroke variation improve readability, or the ease of reading long passages.

Serif typefaces are further categorized as old style, transitional, or modern. See **Figure 6-15.** *Old-style serif typefaces* most closely resemble the original Roman letters. They feature little contrast between the thick and thin strokes within each letter, and the serifs are somewhat pointed and heavily bracketed. The *transitional serif typefaces* were patterned

closed counter: a portion of a letter consisting of a closed loop.

open counter: a portion of a letter consisting of a loop that is incomplete (not closed).

typeface classification: a basic category into which typefaces are grouped.

serif typeface: any typeface containing traditional (not square) serifs.

Roman: a typestyle based on the capital letters the ancient Romans cut into stone monuments.

old-style serif typeface: a typeface with little contrast between thick and thin lines and pointed serifs that generally slant or curve and extend outward at the top of the capital *T* and the bottom of the capital *E*.

transitional serif typeface: a Roman typeface with characteristics of both old-style and modern typefaces.

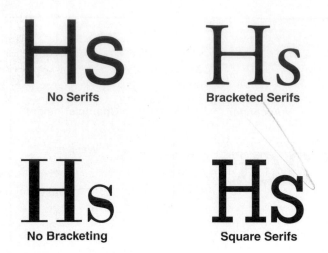

Figure 6-13. Serifs greatly influence letters. Clockwise from the top left, the type is set with no serifs, serifs with bracketing, square serifs, and serifs with no bracketing. The bracketing is most obvious at the top of the *H*.

d b d b

Figure 6-14. Note that a lowercase *d* and *b* are mirror images in the typeface without serifs. In the Roman typeface, however, the serif at the top of the stem points away from the closed counter in the *b*, but it is over the closed counter in the *d*. At the bottom of the stem, the *b* has no serif, but the *d* does. The serifs help prevent tired eyes from confusing the two letters.

after the old-style designs, but with refinements that were possible due to improvements in paper, ink, and plate material that allowed finer thin strokes and sharper serif points. Continued advances in printing technology and the arrival of even smoother paper brought about *modern serif typefaces*. The serifs are typically very thin, straight, unbracketed, and rectangular at the ends. The strong stroke contrast is due to the thin strokes being finer than was technologically possible earlier.

Square-Serif Typefaces

Square-serif typefaces (also known as *slab-serif typefaces*, *block typefaces*, or *Egyptian typefaces*) are geometric in design, and their appearance in 1825 represented a sharp rejection of the classic Roman letters. Square-serif characters have square, or blocked, serifs and comparatively uniform strokes. See **Figure 6-16.** Square-serif typefaces reflect more boldness than elegance. Therefore, they are used in display lines to impart a sense of rugged strength or the Old West. These typefaces are also commonly used with college athletic team logos.

Sans Serif Typefaces

Type design made another radical shift in the late 1800s and early 1900s with the widespread adoption of typestyles with no serifs at all. Named *sans serif* (*sans* is French for *without*), these designs embraced the twentieth century's taste for clean, simple lines and no decoration. See **Figure 6-17.** Sans serif typefaces are also known as *gothics*, due to their early popularity in northern Europe. These typefaces have little or no stroke contrast.

Script and Cursive Typefaces

Script and cursive typefaces are intended to represent handwriting. *Script typefaces* are designed so adjoining characters will actually touch. The characters of *cursive typefaces* do not join. See **Figure 6-18.**

Both scripts and cursives contain thin and thick strokes. These variations result from pen designs and the natural pressure variations exerted in penmanship.

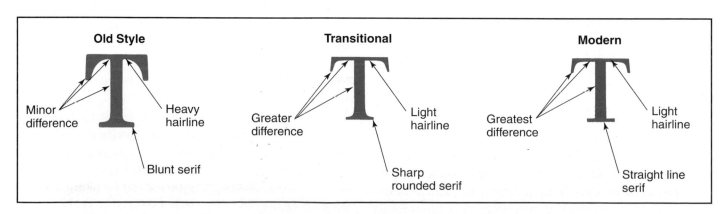

Figure 6-15. The three subclassifications of Roman typefaces are old style, transitional, and modern. The most distinguishing characteristics are the stroke variations and serifs.

Bernard Bold Condensed

Playbill

Boton

Figure 6-16. Square-serif typefaces can evoke a contemporary or historical mood.

Myriad

Avalon

Lucinda Sans

News Gothic MT

Figure 6-17. Sans serif typefaces lack serifs and feature minimal or no stroke variation. Their simplicity of form gives them a modern look.

Ex Ponto Regular

Paradise Plain

Kastler Italic

Brush Script

Figure 6-18. Script typefaces are designed to resemble handwriting with joining characters. Cursive typefaces also resemble handwriting, but they have noticeable gaps between characters.

Script and cursive typefaces should never be set in all uppercase letters or letterspaced because the awkward character combinations are difficult to read.

Decorative Typefaces

The *decorative typeface* classification consists of those typefaces that do not fit any other classification. *Novelty typeface, occasional typeface,* and *miscellaneous typeface* are other terms used to describe this highly diverse classification that includes ornamental and greatly exaggerated designs, along with typefaces appropriate only to convey a very specialized mood. Decorative typefaces are not intended to be used as text matter. These typefaces are commonly used in logos and other advertising applications. **Figure 6-19** shows some examples of decorative typefaces.

PORTAGO ITC TT

DESDEMONA

CHI TOWN

BUDMO JIGGLER

Old English Text

Figure 6-19. Typefaces classified as decorative do not qualify for any of the other classifications and seldom share common features. Notice that they can range from the unique to the ridiculous and often are used as logos. Due to their unorthodox look, however, they can lack legibility and should be used sparingly.

modern serif typeface: a Roman typeface showing great variation in stroke thickness; thin, straight, and somewhat rectangular serifs; and a very strong contrast between the thin and thick lines of the characters.

square-serif typeface: any typeface containing serifs that do not come to a sharp or rounded point.

sans serif: a typeface with no serifs and little or no contrast in the thickness of character strokes.

gothic: a sans serif typeface.

script typeface: a typeface designed to imitate handwriting with characters that touch.

cursive typeface: a typeface imitating handwriting with characters that do not touch.

decorative typeface: a typeface classification consisting of typefaces that do not fit any other classification.

Type Size and Measurement

In the world of metal type, the type size is the height of the piece of metal holding the letter. The letter itself occupies only a portion of this piece of metal. Therefore, an uppercase *R* set in 24 points will not actually be 24 points. Refer back to **Figure 6-4.** Instead, the height of an uppercase character will be roughly 2/3 of its specified point size. For example, uppercase characters set in 48-point type will actually appear approximately 32 points high ($48 \times 2/3 = 32$). Accordingly, an uppercase headline measuring 32 points high was probably set in 48-point type. A point is 1/72 of an inch because there are 72 points in an inch. Also, a pica contains 12 points, and an inch contains six picas.

Type sizes that are 12 points and smaller are referred to as **text type**, **body type**, or *body text*. Type sizes from 9 to 12 points are usually used for newspapers and books. Typefaces that are 14 points and larger are referred to as **display type**. These sizes of type are usually used as headlines and subheadings.

Leading

Inserting additional space between lines of type is called *leading*, or **line spacing**. The purpose of leading is to make type matter easier to read by separating the lines. The optimum amount of leading depends on the type's column width, point size, and x-height. Type set in wide columns or large sizes generally requires more leading than narrow lines and small typefaces do. Also, typefaces with large x-heights require more leading. Examples of type set solid and with various points of leading added are shown in **Figure 6-20.**

When you are specifying leading for typesetting, two numbers are written—the type size and line size (type plus leading). For example, if 9-point type is to be set with 1-point leading, it is set 9 on 10, which is specified as 9/10 on the manuscript copy. Type to be set with no leading would be marked 9/9. Today's typesetting systems have the capability of reducing spacing so characters can actually overlap, a treatment called *negative leading*, or *minus leading*. Refer back to **Figure 6-1.** The specs might be written as 36/30 (36 on 30). This notation means the space between lines is to be reduced by 6 points.

X-Height Proportions

One way typefaces vary in their design is the proportion of the x-height to the type size. Some type designers allocate a comparatively large amount of space to the x-height, while others are more conservative. Because x-heights can vary greatly, two typefaces can be set in the same size but appear very different in size. See **Figure 6-21.** Therefore, typefaces with large x-heights, such as Helvetica, are

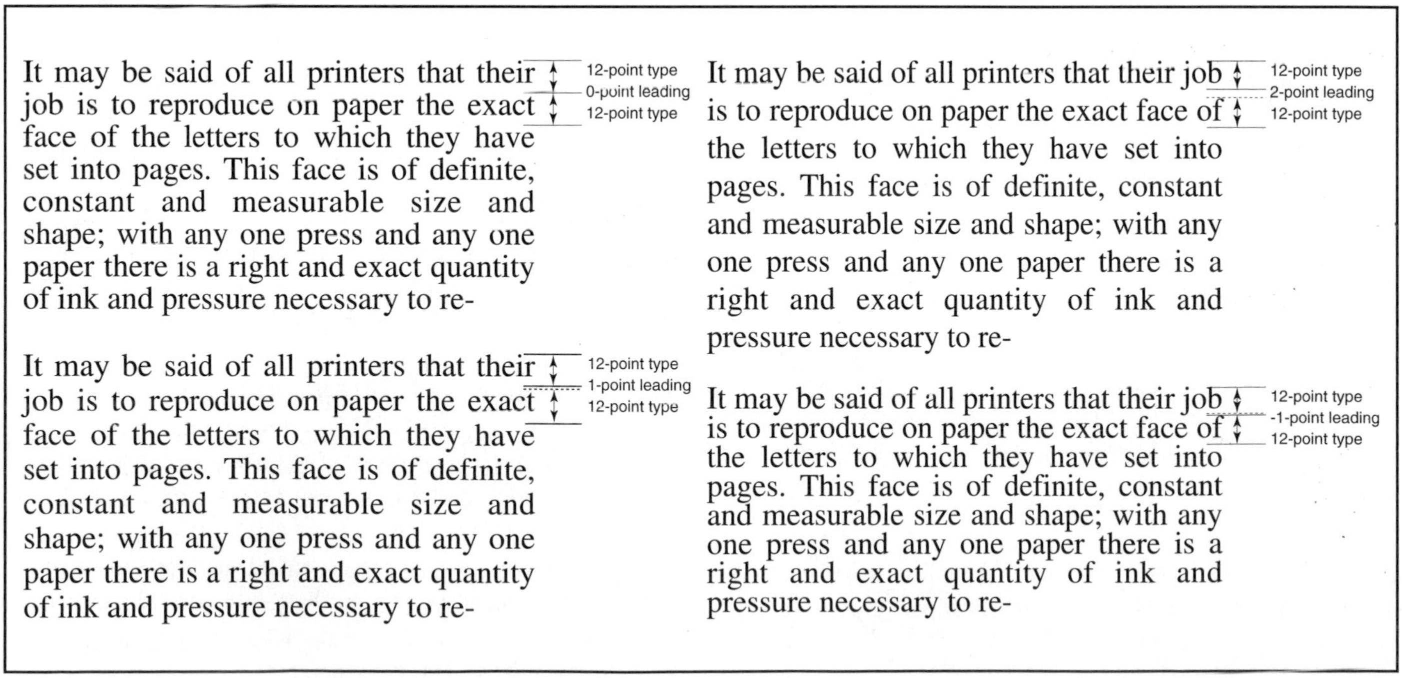

It may be said of all printers that their job is to reproduce on paper the exact face of the letters to which they have set into pages. This face is of definite, constant and measurable size and shape; with any one press and any one paper there is a right and exact quantity of ink and pressure necessary to re-

12-point type
0-point leading
12-point type

It may be said of all printers that their job is to reproduce on paper the exact face of the letters to which they have set into pages. This face is of definite, constant and measurable size and shape; with any one press and any one paper there is a right and exact quantity of ink and pressure necessary to re-

12-point type
1-point leading
12-point type

It may be said of all printers that their job is to reproduce on paper the exact face of the letters to which they have set into pages. This face is of definite, constant and measurable size and shape; with any one press and any one paper there is a right and exact quantity of ink and pressure necessary to re-

12-point type
2-point leading
12-point type

It may be said of all printers that their job is to reproduce on paper the exact face of the letters to which they have set into pages. This face is of definite, constant and measurable size and shape; with any one press and any one paper there is a right and exact quantity of ink and pressure necessary to re-

12-point type
-1-point leading
12-point type

Figure 6-20. Leading controls how much space separates one line of type from another. In these examples, type has been set solid and with 1-point, 2-point, and negative leading.

dxp dxp **dxp**

Figure 6-21. A major difference among these three typefaces set in the same size is the proportionality among the ascender, descender, and x-height spaces. Typefaces with large x-heights have less white space between the baseline and the x-height of the next line of type, so the lines of type appear to be closer together. More leading is needed to compensate for this effect.

especially well suited for highway signs and other applications requiring that they are legible from significant distances. At the same time, typefaces with small x-heights can work well in long bodies of copy because the extra white space above and below the letters with neither ascenders nor descenders will cause the lines to appear farther apart. In this sense, typefaces with small x-heights seem to come with their own leading built in and do not require as much leading as those with larger x-heights.

Ems and Ens

In the days of metal type, pieces of metal that carried no images occupied the spaces between words. The basic spacer occupied a square and was called an *em quad*. Em quads were as high as the type size being used and, being a square, were the same width. See **Figure 6-22**. The em quad got its name by being equal to the width of the capital *M*

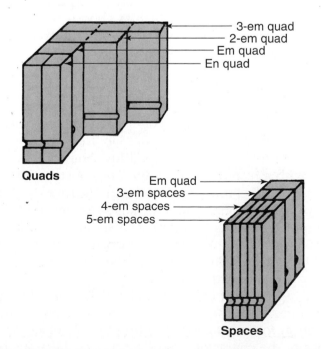

Figure 6-22. Quads and spaces were used with metal type for indenting paragraphs and spacing between words.

in an early typeface, and it was the standard indention of a paragraph. Today, paragraph indentation in desktop-publishing software is usually specified in *ems*. With the em as the basis, wider and narrower pieces of metal were also made. An *en quad* (or *en*) is half the width of an em quad. *Em spaces* are even narrower. The 3-em space (1/3 em), 4-em space (1/4 em), and 5-em space (1/5 em) are typically used as *word spacing*.

The Unit System

All typesetting methods are based on a counting system specifying type sizes and spacing. From the time of the ancient Romans, some type characters have been wider than others. In other words, type has proportional spacing. Type designers use a universal **unit system** to determine character width and spacing. In the unit system, the em is broken into 54 units, and each character's width is measured in units, with wide letters such as *M* and *W* consisting of more units than more narrow letters such as *R* and *I*. See **Figure 6-23**.

text type: a typeface that is 13 points or smaller and usually used for newspapers and books.

body type: type sizes ranging from 4-point through 12-point used for setting straight matter.

display type: a typeface that is 14 points or larger and usually used for headlines, subheadings, and decks added below main headlines in newspapers and magazines.

line spacing: additional space inserted between lines of type to make the type matter easier to read. Also referred to as *leading*.

em quad: a nonprinting body in the shape of a square of the type size being used.

em: a printer's unit of area measurement equal in width and height to the letter *M* in any selected type body size. This unit is commonly used as an abbreviation of the pica em, in which the em is equivalent to 12 points.

en quad: an increment equal to half the width of an em quad, used for space between words.

en: a printer's unit of measurement equal to the same height, but half the width, of the em. This unit is sometimes used to specify the area of composition, as its value closely approximates the number of characters in the text.

em space: a nonprinting fixed space equal in width to the point size of a font. This space is used for indenting paragraphs and aligning type columns.

word spacing: the spacing between words.

unit system: a counting system used with typesetting methods that specifies type sizes and spacing.

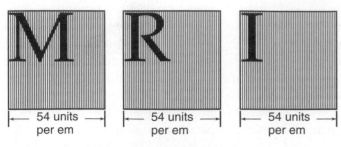

Figure 6-23. In computer typesetting, the em is usually divided into 54 units. Wide letters consist of more units than do more narrow letters.

In most desktop-publishing programs, *letterspacing* (the space between characters) can be modified. Type can be set with regular, loose, or tight letterspacing to achieve more consistent spacing than results automatically. *Kerning* is the term for the process of manually adjusting the space between certain character pairs. See **Figure 6-24.** Spacing between words in typeset lines is referred to as *word spacing.* Depending on the program being used, many different variations in word spacing can be achieved either manually or automatically.

Patents and Licenses

Patents and licenses protect a number of typefaces. Companies such as Linotype and Monotype secured original patents on many of the typefaces they had cast in hot metal. These patents exist today, even though many of the original typefaces are used in digital-fonts libraries. Some of the most popular protected typefaces have been nearly replicated as look-alikes. See **Figure 6-25.** Often, the name of the near replica is similar to that of the original design.

You should be aware that *digital fonts* are software and are subject to strict licensing agreements. Professional practice honors font license agreements. It is the responsibility of users to maintain licensed versions of the fonts used at their location.

VAIL
VAIL

Figure 6-24. Kerning allows spacing to be reduced between selected characters, while maintaining normal spacing between others. Here, the *V* and *A* are too far apart before kerning.

Typography
Typography

Figure 6-25. Many popular typefaces have been closely replicated. To distinguish between Helvetica (top) and Arial, study the end stroke of the *a*, the angle of the bottom of the *y*, and the angle of the top of the *r*.

Copyrights

Traditionally, copyright law did not protect typefaces. Typefaces were viewed as merely functional representations of letters or characters, lacking the creative qualities needed for copyright protection. Similarly, digitized typefaces were lacking in original authorship. In 1992, however, the U.S. Copyright Office suggested that computer programs generating typefaces can obtain copyright protection. The 1992 regulation states, "computer programs designed for generating typeface in conjunction with low resolution and other printing devices may involve original computer instructions entitled to protection."

Digital Fonts

Technological advancements in digital typesetting have given the graphic designer a vast array of typefaces from which to choose. Typefaces represented and stored as digitized electronic data are referred to as *digital fonts.* Digital fonts exist as bitmaps or outlines.

A *bitmap font* is a set of typographic characters existing as a collection of pixels (rectangular dots) rather than as outline fonts, or mathematical descriptions of lines and curves. Bitmap fonts were the original type format developed for computer monitors with a resolution of 72 dpi. The construction of a bitmapped character is shown in **Figure 6-26.** For proper display on the monitor, it is necessary that the computer contains a bitmap of each point size of the typeface. If the computer does not contain the proper bitmaps, it will simply enlarge the pixels, resulting in a jagged on-screen image.

A *vector font* (also outline, scalable, or fill font) generates type characters and symbols from mathematical formulas corresponding to the curves and lines of the characters, as opposed to collections of dots. See **Figure 6-27.** Vector fonts simulate the paths

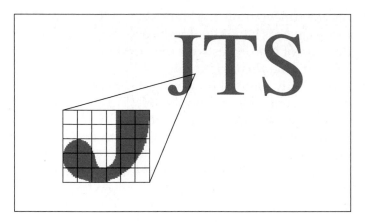

Figure 6-26. Characters in a bitmap font are formed as a collection of dots called *pixels*.

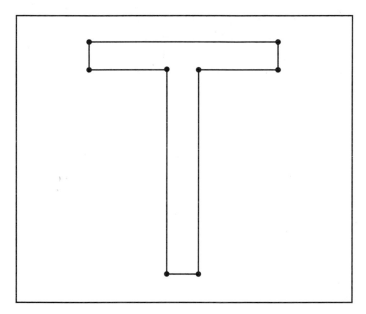

Figure 6-27. Outline fonts generate type characters and symbols from mathematical formulas corresponding to the curves and lines of the characters.

a pen would follow along the outside edge of a type character to produce a particular character or symbol. Outline fonts can be scaled easily and can output at whatever resolution the output device is capable of printing. Scaling is a computer function that allows altering the size of an image or a font proportionately. PostScript® and TrueType® font technologies are examples of vector-font libraries.

Unlike a bitmap, outlines can be scaled up or down or rotated in almost any direction without creating distortion or jagged edges. Only one outline is required to represent a specific character in any size or design of type. Outline fonts offer the artist increased flexibility for more typefaces, point sizes, and rotational possibilities. In addition, vector fonts

require less memory than bitmap fonts do, because vector fonts do not require storage of each image in a range of sizes.

One early breakthrough in computerized-typeface technology was Apple's **TrueType® font technology**, fully scalable fonts operating from a single file format, as opposed to the older format, where both printer and screen font files were needed. Although TrueType fonts were originally developed for use with Macintosh® computers, Microsoft has worked jointly with Apple to develop the most recent versions. Hence, TrueType support is built into both operating systems. TrueType fonts can be used for both bitmapped screen display and vector-based output. These fonts are now used primarily with word processing programs, however, and are usually replaced with **PostScript® font technology** for high-quality output.

PostScript technology is a page description language (PDL) that Adobe Systems, Inc. invented. A **page description language (PDL)** consists of software commands that, when translated through a special device, form the desired image on an output device. PostScript fonts use both a bitmap font and a special PostScript file describing the outlines and fills of the typeface. The PostScript and bitmap files are both necessary for correct display and printing.

letterspacing: the spacing placed between individual characters.

kerning: the process of adjusting the space between certain character pairs to minimize gaps for the best appearance and readability.

digital font: a typeface represented and stored as digitized electronic data.

bitmap font: a set of typographic characters existing as a collection of dots, rather than as outline fonts.

vector font: type characters and symbols generated from mathematical formulas corresponding to the curves and lines of the characters, as opposed to collections of dots. This font is similar to an outline font, in that it can be proportionally sized and rotated.

TrueType® font technology: a fully scalable font operating from a single file format, as opposed to the older format in which both printer and screen font files were needed. This technology was originally developed by Apple.

PostScript® font technology: a PDL Adobe Systems, Inc. developed that enables imagesetters different companies have developed to interpret electronic files from any number of personal computers and off-the-shelf programs.

page description language (PDL): a software program consisting of commands that, when translated through a special device, form the desired image on an output device.

PostScript commands are used with type and other images and enable the user to integrate text matter with graphics. The main advantage of PostScript technology is that the code becomes a raster or bitmap in an interpreter in the output device, not the computer, allowing for device independence. Device independence is the ability to generate virtually identical output on devices made by different manufacturers that can interpret PostScript commands.

Many companies offer CD-ROMs with huge *font libraries*. Agfa offers a CD-ROM for Macintosh-computer and Windows®–operating system users called the *Creative Alliance Library*, which offers over 1000 of the most contemporary typefaces available. Type designers and foundries from around the world produced many of the typefaces included.

Typesetting Formats

A *typesetting format* refers to any one of several ways in which type can be displayed on the printed page. The formats are flush left/ragged right, flush right/ragged left, centered, justified, and runaround. See **Figure 6-28.**

The *flush left/ragged right format* has the type aligned evenly on the left side of the column and *ragged* (uneven) on the right side. When using this format, words should not be hyphenated because the division of words destroys the effect of the irregular contour. The *flush right/ragged left format* has the copy evenly aligned on the right side of the column and unevenly aligned on the left. This format is not as commonly used as flush left because it is difficult for the reader to follow and return to uneven lines on the left.

The *centered format* has the type centered on the page or column, resulting in uneven line lengths. This format has the same disadvantage as flush right/ragged left type. Centered type has no uniform left edge to which the reader's eye can return.

In the *justified format*, lines are aligned on both the left and right edges of the column or page. This textbook is set with a justified column format. To achieve uniform line lengths, the extra space that ordinarily would appear at the end of shorter lines is distributed between the words in the line. Therefore, word spacing varies from line to line, sometimes creating distracting open areas. Maintaining a minimum column width of 39 characters can avoid excessive open areas.

The *runaround format* (also called *wraparound format*) flows around the contour of illustrations and

Since the printed word is intended primarily to be read, it is essential that the type should be of a size to produce maximum legibility. If type is too small, it very quickly creates eye strain and fatigue. If it is too large, it spreads out upon too great an area on the retina of the eye to be perceived quickly.

Flush Left/Ragged Right

Since the printed word is intended primarily to be read, it is essential that the type should be of a size to produce maximum legibility. If type is too small, it very quickly creates eye strain and fatigue. If it is too large, it spreads out upon too great an area on the retina of the eye to be perceived quickly.

Flush Right/Ragged Left

Since the printed word is intended primarily to be read, it is essential that the type should be of a size to produce maximum legibility. If type is too small, it very quickly creates eye strain and fatigue. If it is too large, it spreads out upon too great an area on the retina of the eye to be perceived quickly.

Centered

Since the printed word is intended primarily to be read, it is essential that the type should be of a size to produce maximum legibility. If type is too small, it very quickly creates eye strain and fatigue. If it is too large, it spreads out upon too great an area on the retina of the eye to be perceived quickly.

Justified

Figure 6-28. Type can be set in various formats. Keep in mind that some formats negatively affect the legibility of the text matter.

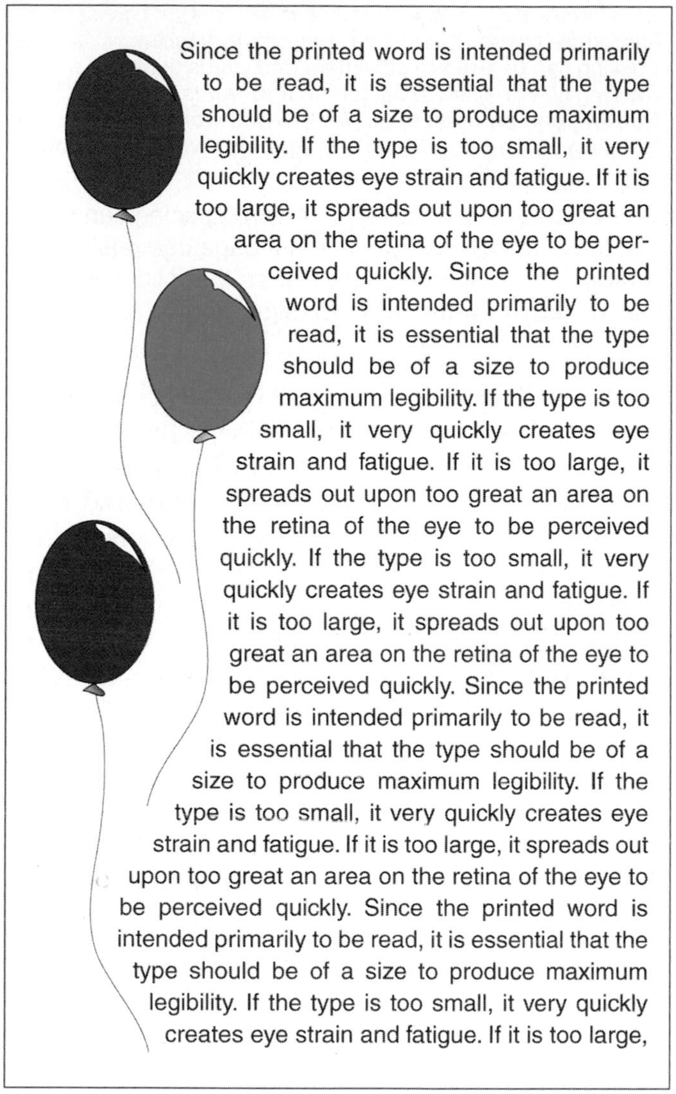

Since the printed word is intended primarily to be read, it is essential that the type should be of a size to produce maximum legibility. If the type is too small, it very quickly creates eye strain and fatigue. If it is too large, it spreads out upon too great an area on the retina of the eye to be perceived quickly. Since the printed word is intended primarily to be read, it is essential that the type should be of a size to produce maximum legibility. If the type is too small, it very quickly creates eye strain and fatigue. If it is too large, it spreads out upon too great an area on the retina of the eye to be perceived quickly. If the type is too small, it very quickly creates eye strain and fatigue. If it is too large, it spreads out upon too great an area on the retina of the eye to be perceived quickly. Since the printed word is intended primarily to be read, it is essential that the type should be of a size to produce maximum legibility. If the type is too small, it very quickly creates eye strain and fatigue. If it is too large, it spreads out upon too great an area on the retina of the eye to be perceived quickly. Since the printed word is intended primarily to be read, it is essential that the type should be of a size to produce maximum legibility. If the type is too small, it very quickly creates eye strain and fatigue. If it is too large,

Figure 6-29. Runarounds require a great deal of planning and execution to avoid bad breaks with the text, as well as awkward word spacing.

logos. When it runs around a jagged illustration, the runaround is often called a *skew*. Runarounds should be used sparingly to avoid annoying the reader. See **Figure 6-29.**

Typeface Selection Considerations

Design novices typically select too many features for effective communication because desktop-publishing programs are loaded with several fonts and design capabilities. The vast array of typefaces, sizes, shadows, patterns, and decorations can overwhelm both the beginner and the design itself. It is tempting to go overboard and use so many typographic gimmicks that a hodgepodge results, instead of an effective design. See **Figure 6-30.** To avoid

Beulah Lake
Canoe Livery &
Fᴜn **Center**

Beulah Lake
Canoe Livery &
Fun Center

Figure 6-30. Beginning graphic designers often use too many typefaces, with the result that the type body lacks unity. Applying proper restraint will create a design that has adequate contrast and maintains unity.

excessive typographic gimmicks, several factors that must be carefully considered when selecting and using typefaces for a printed piece include legibility, readability, appropriateness, leading, word spacing, letterspacing, tracking, reverse type, and the use of initial characters.

Generally, highly readable typefaces were designed to be used as text matter, and others were intended as display type, such as headlines. In the case of decorative typefaces, the type designers might or might not have had legibility in mind when they created the characters, so judgment is necessary to ensure a design does not fail because of inappropriate

font library: a collection of fonts, either on a computer's hard drive or available for purchase on a CD or another storage device.

typesetting format: a way in which type can be displayed or set on the printed page.

flush left/ragged right format: a typesetting format with the type aligned evenly on the left side of the page and ragged on the right side.

ragged: type aligned unevenly on the right or left side.

flush right/ragged left format: a typesetting format with the copy evenly aligned on the right side of the column and uneven on the left.

centered format: a typesetting format centered on the page or column, resulting in uneven line widths.

justified format: a typesetting format in which the lines are aligned on both the left and right edges of the column or page.

runaround format: a typesetting format in which text flows or contours around illustrations and logos.

skew: text that contours around a jagged illustration.

MUSEUM

LITTLE

GIMMICKS

Figure 6-31. Examples of typographic pitfalls include using an inappropriate typeface for a word, setting a script typeface in all caps, and using a typeface that is difficult to read.

type. Legibility refers to the speed at which the reader can identify type characters and the ease with which the display type can be read. **Figure 6-31** gives some examples of typographic pitfalls.

The intended message and audience determine the appropriateness of a typeface for a particular printed piece. Some typefaces are said to "speak" in a normal tone. Others "shout" their message. Some typefaces remind the reader of a historical era, while others convey the impression of newness. In addition, a particular typeface can suggest characteristics such as ruggedness, femininity, masculinity, formality, or pure fun. For example, banks and insurance companies often use a classic serif typeface in their logos to suggest permanence and dependability, and computer companies commonly use a sans serif logo to convey state-of-the-art expertise.

Poor word spacing can reduce readability. Typefaces with high levels of readability can be read in long bodies of text type without tiring the reader. Lines with narrow word spacing appear to run together and are difficult to read, whereas excessive word spacing makes the lines appear choppy. If the spacing between words is noticeably uneven, a displeasing effect and lack of unity reduce the readability. See **Figure 6-32.**

Desktop-publishing programs often have a feature called *tracking*, which allows the user to control the letterspacing and word spacing together. The user can choose from very tight, tight, normal, loose, and very loose tracking. See **Figure 6-33.**

Too much word spacing

Better word spacing

Figure 6-32. Excessive word spacing impairs readability.

Tracking can be used to set letters and words very tight.
Tracking can be used to set letters and words tight.
Tracking can be used to set letters and words normal.
Tracking can be used to set letters and words loose.
Tracking can be used to set letters and words very loose.

Figure 6-33. Letterspacing and word spacing can be adjusted simultaneously with most page composition programs, such as the QuarkXPress™ application, PageMaker© software, and InDesign© software.

Reverse type refers to type that drops out of the background and assumes the color of the paper. See **Figure 6-34.** This technique commonly is used to add contrast, gain the reader's attention, and stress the importance of the message. Reverse type is difficult to read and should be used sparingly. Excessive use of reverse type reduces readability, especially if the type is extremely small or printed on a glossy paper. Also, the thin strokes of serif typefaces can be overwhelmed by the surrounding darkness and seem to disappear. For this reason, boldface type and sans serif typefaces work best for reversing.

An *initial character* is a larger first letter in a body of copy. See **Figure 6-35.** This character is set in display type for emphasis or to serve a decorative function. Initial characters are often used to begin chapters of a novel and feature articles in magazines or other periodicals. These characters are often used to break up the monotony of long, narrow columns of text.

When initial characters are used, alignment must be carefully considered. For example, a wide gap between the initial character and the remainder of the word is often ungainly. In addition, the space around the initial should be in balance with the initial character. Initial-character alignment and spacing formats are shown in **Figure 6-36.**

Typographic Guidelines

With the thousands of typefaces from which to choose, designers have the potential to make the right combinations of style, weight, and stress to add interest to a promotional piece, impart unity and structure to complicated pieces, and aid reader comprehension. Too many typefaces or typefaces that do not combine well can hinder communication. Keep the following points in mind when selecting typefaces:

- Maintain design harmony by using just enough typographic change.

The typeface and color used for reverse type greatly affect its readability. This is even more apparent when a small type size is used.

The typeface and color used for reverse type greatly affect its readability. This is even more apparent when a small type size is used.

The typeface and color used for reverse type greatly affect its readability. This is even more apparent when a small type size is used.

The typeface and color use for reverse type greatly affect its readability. This is even more apparent when a small type size is used.

Figure 6-34. The readability of reverse type can suffer if this type is used excessively, the type is too small, or a bold color that does function well in the background is used. Because the thin strokes of many serif typefaces tend to disappear when reversed, sans serif typefaces usually reverse better.

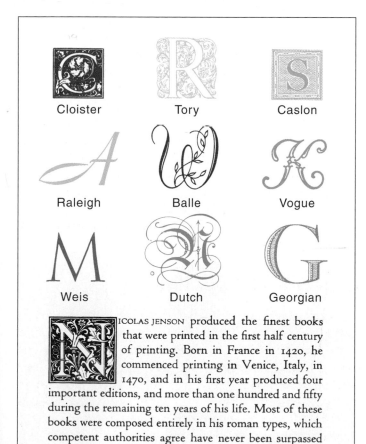

Cloister   Tory   Caslon

Raleigh   Balle   Vogue

Weis   Dutch   Georgian

NICOLAS JENSON produced the finest books that were printed in the first half century of printing. Born in France in 1420, he commenced printing in Venice, Italy, in 1470, and in his first year produced four important editions, and more than one hundred and fifty during the remaining ten years of his life. Most of these books were composed entirely in his roman types, which competent authorities agree have never been surpassed

Figure 6-35. Initial characters are used for decorative emphasis. The sample paragraph shows the effective application of an initial character in conjunction with text matter.

- Most documents need from two to three typefaces to guide the reader and aid comprehension. Different style headlines and subheads can be used to create the necessary hierarchy. Rarely is there a need for more than four typefaces in a single piece.
- Combining two sans serif or two serif typefaces is confusing to the reader because they appear similar, but not identical. Only very different designs should be combined on a page. Typefaces similar in design hardly ever work well together.
- Strong contrasts are usually not a problem.
- Making information clearer, improving visual relationships, and creating contrast are valid reasons for combining typefaces.

tracking: a feature of computer-typesetting programs that allows the user to control the character and word spacing together.

reverse type: type that drops out of the background and assumes the color of the paper.

initial character: a larger first character in a body of copy set in display type for emphasis or to serve a decorative function.

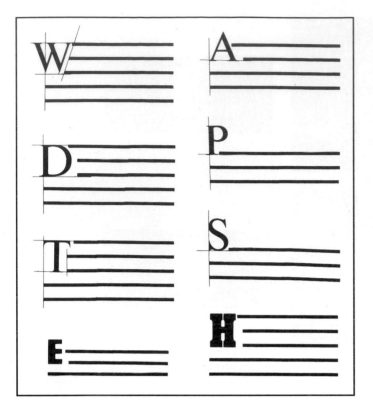

Figure 6-36. The space around the initial should always be in balance with the initial character.

- Staying within a typeface family can ensure acceptable levels of contrast, make complicated graphics simpler, and make an otherwise bland page more appealing. In addition, consistent use of the same family will impart unity to the design.

- The bigger the design contrast is, the better the mix will be. The safest out-of-family contrast is a serif typeface with a sans serif typeface. Typically, the display type is sans serif, and the text is serif.

- Mixing two very different designs from the serif type category can create a pleasing effect. Examples are mixing an old-style serif and a square serif and mixing a transitional serif typeface with a script.

- Electronically distorting or modifying a typeface is seldom a good idea. Electronic distortions are generally not as effective as the original design and tend to look amateurish. The result is usually out of harmony with the original design because it is not an integrated design variation.

Note

Some samples of popular typefaces are included in Appendix B. The typefaces show the date of origin and the company or person responsible for their designs.

Proofreading

Regardless of how attractive or "correct" a layout is, typographical errors (typos) will distract the reader from the message and hurt the piece's credibility, as the reader might question the accuracy of the information and the author's knowledge of the subject. The printed material should be proofread carefully before going to press to minimize, if not eliminate, typos. *Proofreading* is the process of checking for typesetting errors and marking them for correction.

In traditional typesetting situations, a manuscript was edited and marked for type size and design before being sent to the typesetter. Today, copy is often proofread after the layout has been completed and before the customer signs off on the proofs. When proofreading material, the proofreader checks for such things as correct word hyphenations, spelling, style consistency, and copy omissions or repetitions. It should be noted that the proofing aids available with word processing and desktop-publishing software will point out many typing errors, but they will miss many others. If the typo creates another word (for example, *ton* for *town*), the mistake will go uncaught. In addition, the suggested alternative spellings can be for another word altogether. For these reasons, reliance on computer proofing is a mistake.

Proofreading can be performed by one person or two people. *One-person proofing* (or comparison proofing) is used primarily to find major problems such as copy omission, incorrect sequence, or copy duplication. This proofing is most suitable for small jobs with little copy, because switching back and forth from proof to copy can be troublesome. *Two-person proofing* uses a reader and a marker and is the best proofreading method when accuracy and speed are important. This method is frequently used with larger jobs, such as a textbook. See **Figure 6-37.**

Figure 6-37. The two-person proofing system requires the reader to work with an assistant.

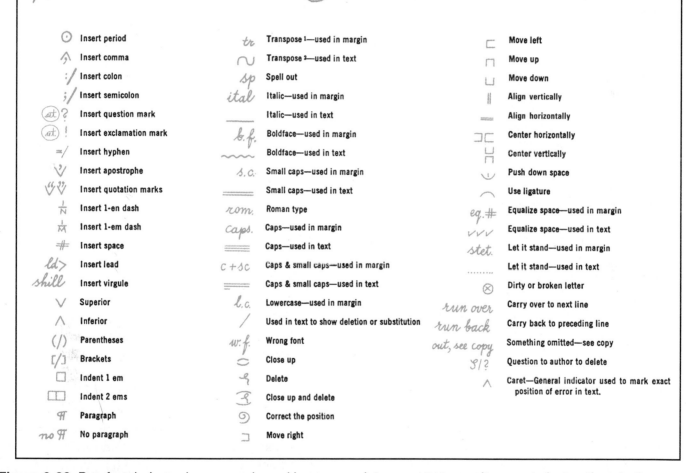

PROOF SYMBOLS USED TO CORRECT ERRORS IN LINES OF TYPE

⊙ Change this to a period, It marks the

A comma, inserted here will make more

Machinecast is a compound word when

The printers work is most interesting

Place a colon here, this is a place to

Semi-colon, one should be inserted here

Quotation marks are called "quotes by

Delete, or take out, a characters marked

The meeting was held in Columbus, O.

THE LINES AFTER CORRECTIONS HAVE BEEN MADE

Change this to a period. It marks the

A comma, inserted here, will make more

Machine-cast is a compound word when

The printer's work is most interesting

Place a colon here: this is a place to

Semi-colon; one should be inserted here

Quotation marks are called "quotes" by

Delete, or take out, a character marked

The meeting was held in Columbus, Ohio

Symbol	Meaning	Symbol	Meaning	Symbol	Meaning
⊙	Insert period	tr	Transpose 1—used in margin	⊏	Move left
⋀	Insert comma	∾	Transpose 2—used in text	⊓	Move up
:/	Insert colon	sp	Spell out	⊔	Move down
;/	Insert semicolon	ital	Italic—used in margin	‖	Align vertically
?	Insert question mark	—	Italic—used in text	=	Align horizontally
!	Insert exclamation mark	b.f.	Boldface—used in margin	⊐⊏	Center horizontally
=/	Insert hyphen	∼	Boldface—used in text		Center vertically
⋁	Insert apostrophe	s.c.	Small caps—used in margin	⌣	Push down space
""	Insert quotation marks		Small caps—used in text	⌢	Use ligature
⊥/N	Insert 1-en dash	rom.	Roman type	eq.#	Equalize space—used in margin
⊥/M	Insert 1-em dash	caps	Caps—used in margin	∨∨∨	Equalize space—used in text
#	Insert space		Caps—used in text	stet.	Let it stand—used in margin
ld>	Insert lead	c+sc	Caps & small caps—used in margin		Let it stand—used in text
shill	Insert virgule		Caps & small caps—used in text	⊗	Dirty or broken letter
⋁	Superior	l.c.	Lowercase—used in margin	run over	Carry over to next line
⋀	Inferior	/	Used in text to show deletion or substitution	run back	Carry back to preceding line
(/)	Parentheses	w.f.	Wrong font	out, see copy	Something omitted—see copy
[/]	Brackets	⌒	Close up	?/?	Question to author to delete
□	Indent 1 em	⌿	Delete	⋀	Caret—General indicator used to mark exact position of error in text.
□□	Indent 2 ems	⌿	Close up and delete		
¶	Paragraph	⟲	Correct the position		
no ¶	No paragraph	⊐	Move right		

Figure 6-38. Proofreader's marks are a universal language printers use to transmit accurate instructions to the person doing the typesetting or layout.

The symbols used to show when something is to be deleted, added, or changed are called *proofreader's marks.* Proofreader's marks are universally used symbols that identify and explain copy errors and changes. **Figure 6-38** shows common proofreader's marks.

proofreading: the process of checking for typesetting errors and marking them for correction.

one-person proofing: proofreading during which one person is responsible for reading both the galley and the manuscript.

two-person proofing: proofreading during which one person reads the manuscript aloud, while another person compares what is heard to what is being read on the galley.

proofreader's mark: a symbol used on manuscript or proof to show when something is to be deleted, added, or changed.

Summary

A thorough understanding of the basic functions and goals of typography will help you produce effective printed pieces. To properly select and arrange type on a printed piece, you must be able to distinguish the differences among typefaces, type series, fonts, and families; identify the basic typeface classifications; and explain basic character and typeface elements. You should also be able to apply sound design considerations when specifying text and display type and use the most effective text format.

To be able to estimate space requirements and limitations, graphic designers and printers must understand the point system. Being able to properly measure point sizes and determine the actual height of typeset characters contributes to accurate typesetting. You must also be able to apply the proper leading, letterspacing, word spacing, and tracking methods when laying out text matter.

All material should be proofread and corrected before going to print. Numerous typos will distract the reader, regardless of how attractive or "correct" a layout is. Typos might cause the reader to question the accuracy of the information and the author's knowledge of the subject at hand.

Review Questions

Please do not write in this book. Write your answers on a separate sheet of paper.

1. _____ involves the selection and arrangement of type for a proposed printed piece.
2. What are the two main functions of typography?

Matching questions: For Questions 3 through 9, match each description on the left with the correct term on the right.

3. A specific style with its own combination of design features, such as shape, stroke, and weight.
4. The complete assortment of characters available in a certain typeface and size.
5. A combination of characters into one unit, such as *fi* and *fl*.
6. A combination such as æ or œ.
7. An ornamental design used to illustrate and attract attention to specific text matter.

A. Diphthong.
B. Type family.
C. Typeface.
D. Type series.
E. Ligature.
F. Font.
G. Wingding.

8. A collection of a typeface and its variations, relative to weight, stress, and structure.
9. The range of point sizes available for a specific typeface.
10. Distinguish between a closed counter and an open counter.
11. List the five basic typeface classifications.
12. _____ are the fine end strokes of Roman typefaces.
    A. Serifs
    B. Points
    C. Descenders
    D. Stems
13. _____ typefaces are geometric in design, have blocked serifs, and have reasonably uniform strokes.
14. Designed to imitate handwriting, _____ typefaces actually join.
15. Typefaces that do not fit any other classification are referred to as _____.
16. What units are used to measure the size of type?
17. Typefaces 12 points and smaller are referred to as _____.
18. What is the purpose of leading?
19. The unit system divides the em quad into _____ equal increments.
20. _____ is the process of adjusting the space between certain character pairs to minimize gaps for the best appearance.
21. A(n) _____ font is a set of typographic characters existing as a collection of dots.
22. A(n) _____ font generates type characters and symbols from mathematical formulas corresponding to the curves and lines of the characters.
23. What is type scaling?
24. Why was the introduction of TrueType fonts a breakthrough in computer-typeface technology?
25. What is the main advantage of PostScript technology?
26. What is the type format that generates lines of equal length?

27. The display type for an ad promoting a rodeo or frontier-town recreation would likely come from which type classification? Explain your thinking.

28. Why is it essential for copy to be proofread before going to print?

Skill-Building Activities

1. Gather samples of serif, sans serif, square-serif, script, and decorative typefaces from printed publications. Paste your samples on 8 1/2" × 11" paper. Create a chart including the following categories: typeface classification, point size, leading, and format. Include columns for legibility and appropriateness and rate these two items on a scale of 1–10 (1 being the highest). Have your instructor review your work.

2. Form groups of three or four students. Using a variety of printed publications, find 10 samples of initial letters. Paste your samples to a sheet of 8 1/2" × 11" paper. Have each member of the group evaluate the samples on the basis of readability and alignment. Write the evaluations in report form. Have your instructor review your work.

3. Using a word processing or page composition program, write and design a one-page public relations article extolling the benefits of your school's printing or graphic communications program. Create your layout using the following restrictions:
   • Two-column, justified format.
   • One serif and one sans serif typeface.
   • Two levels of headings.
   • One initial letter at the beginning of the copy (can be a different typeface).
   • Insert dingbats (wingdings) for a bulleted list.
   • One image (line art or continuous tone).
   When you have completed, have your instructor check your work.

It's Not about the Designer

The graphic designer shown here is working with a brightly colored illustration for a design. This designer might not like the illustration. Even if he created it himself, he might not like it at all. The reason graphic designers routinely use illustrations, typestyles, colors, and photographs they do not personally like underscores a fundamental design principle: it's not about the designer. It is about the intended audience.

The designer might be 35 years old and prefer detailed art and deep, rich colors. If he is designing materials for second-grade children who usually like very simple art and bright, saturated colors, however, he must put aside his personal preferences and design for the children. This approach is part of the discipline of design.

Many young people confuse being creative with being free to do whatever comes to mind. In truth, successful graphic designers are not free spirits because they realize they have been hired to help a client communicate the client's message to the client's audience. They understand that it's not about the designer.

Chapter 7
Graphic Design

Key Terms

artwork
balance
booklet
broadside
brochure
chroma
color
color harmony
color wheel
communication model
comprehensive layout
　(comp)
continuous tone art
contrast
cropping
design
folder
graphic design
halftone copy
harmony
hue
intermediate color
layout
leaflet
line

line art
line copy
primary color
production stage
proportion
psychology of color
requisite of design
rhythm
rough layout
rule
secondary color
shade
shape
signature
signature imposition
size
specifications (specs)
texture
thumbnail sketch
tint
tone
unity
value
white space

Learning Objectives

When you have completed the reading and assigned activities related to this chapter, you will be able to do the following:

- Illustrate the communication model.
- Explain the role of the graphic designer.
- Summarize the stages of design.
- List and explain the elements and requisites of graphic design.
- Discuss the dimensions of color.
- Name and describe the types of color harmony.
- Identify the different types of artwork.
- Describe how to prepare illustrations for printing.

Graphic design is a process involving the arrangement and organization of graphic elements in a manner pleasing to the eye and conducive to clear communication. The primary goal of graphic design is to communicate the intended message to the intended audience. The term *graphic design* is used almost exclusively to mean the activity of designing materials to be printed. As more material is created for more than one medium, however, this term is also applied to materials designed for electronic reproduction, such as the Internet and interactive CDs.

In graphic design, the primary goal is effective communication with the audience. The importance of this concept cannot be overstated because beginning designers have a strong tendency to design for themselves—using typefaces, art, and colors they like. The intended audience, however, might be in a different age, gender, or geographic group than that of the designer and respond very differently to the design. Many people are drawn to graphic design because of what they perceive to be the freedom to create, only to quickly learn about the discipline necessary to ignore their personal instincts and design for the intended audience.

A second lesson that beginning designers usually must learn is that the design carries the message, but the design is not the message itself. For this reason, the design should be unobtrusive and not overpower the message. Graphic designers look to the basic communication model to guide their efforts in distinguishing among the various elements of the communication process because they are communicators.

Effective graphic design—like all forms of communication—results from applying the concepts of the **communication model**. As shown in **Figure 7-1**, the communication model consists of a sender and a receiver. For the graphic designer, the sender is likely to be the client, and the receiver is the recipient of the brochure, poster, book, or other printed piece being designed. The sender usually determines the message, and the medium is the printed piece carrying the message. The final component of the communication model is the feedback loop, which gives the sender some insight into how well the message was received. Often, feedback will reveal noise, which is anything that interferes with receiving the message. Noise can be small type, inappropriate art, offensive colors, typographic errors, or anything else that distracts readers from the message.

For example, an entertainment company might wish to promote an upcoming concert by printing some posters. In this scenario, the company is the sender, the posters are the medium, and people who see the posters (the medium) are the receivers. The message is not only the "who, what, where, and when" information about the concert, but also the motivation to attend the concert. This motivation can be achieved through the choice of type, art, and colors, and the receiver drives these design choices. That is, the poster's type, art, and colors likely would be appropriate to the type of music at the concert—gospel, rock, jazz, Dixieland, hip-hop, or classical—and the intended audience. The feedback loop might result from asking ticket buyers, "How did you hear about the concert?"

The graphic designer is not part of the communication model. Successful designers do not use their personal favorite typefaces and colors. Instead, they show the discipline to focus on what would likely work well with the intended audience. To accomplish this goal, designers also consider the purpose of the piece, the printing process involved, and the client's budget.

This chapter covers the primary elements and basic requisites of design. The elements of design represent what is in the designer's toolbox. As the name implies, the requisites of design are qualities required of a design. Without one or more of the requisites, one might have a layout (an arrangement of art and type), but still not a design. These concepts will be explored in this chapter.

The Design Process

For many people, the terms *design* and *layout* are synonymous, but these terms represent different stages in the process. The term **design** refers to the manner in which the design elements are selected and arranged to produce a certain result or effect. The

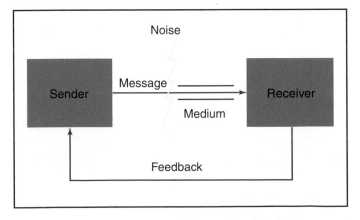

Figure 7-1. An understanding and application of the communication model is the basis of all effective communication—including graphic communication.

term *layout* refers to the actual combining of these elements onto paper or a digital file. Traditionally, different people performed these tasks. The designer would sketch out a rough dummy, which would act as a guide for a graphic artist, who would produce the pasteup containing the actual type and art. Today, these role distinctions have blurred, as designers can use desktop-publishing software to work through the design visually and build the electronic file in an integrated process. See **Figure 7-2.**

The purpose of the printed piece helps determine its design. For example, a company's business card can make the first printed impression on a potential client. See **Figure 7-3.** The card's design should reflect two considerations. First, it should be in harmony with the company's letterhead and envelopes. Second, it should create a positive image of the organization.

As in any creative process, graphic designers have found that following a sequence of stages produces the best results, with a minimum of confusion and wasted effort. Designers generally prepare layouts in three stages: thumbnail sketches, rough layout, and comprehensive layout (comp). The first step in designing a printed piece is to prepare *thumbnail*

Figure 7-2. The distinctions between the design and prepress production functions can become blurred in the digital world. (HP/Indigo)

sketches, miniature pencil sketches in the same shape and proportion as the piece being planned. Even designers who prepare the files for their designs electronically have learned that sketching thumbnails on paper is the most efficient way of exploring a wide range of potential design solutions.

Figure 7-3. Even a design project as basic as a business card contains a wealth of possibilities. These four designs convey different moods, despite containing the same basic elements.

graphic design: a process that involves the arrangement and organization of graphic elements in a manner pleasing to the eye and conducive to clear communication.

communication model: a diagram identifying the components of communication and the sequence it follows.

design: the manner in which materials are selected and arranged on a printed page to produce a certain result or effect.

layout: a drawing, a sketch, or another plan indicating how a printed piece will look, including the placement of text, illustrations, and other page elements.

thumbnail sketch: a small rendering in the same shape and proportion as the printed piece being planned.

Thumbnail sketches contain very little detail. Boxes or irregular shapes represent art, wavy lines represent display type, and horizontal lines represent body copy. See **Figure 7-4.** The key to optimizing the potential of the thumbnail stage is to make the first thumbnail and then change a single component of it when making the second thumbnail. Continue with this process by changing one element of the second thumbnail to make the third one. Using a modification of the last thumbnail to make the next one prevents time lost coming up with a new idea, keeps the creative momentum going, and ensures a systematic approach toward the best design.

By representing elements instead of rendering them, the designer can easily create six thumbnail sketches in a minute. This speed is important because the goals of the thumbnail stage are to amass several options and enable the designer to explore a broad spectrum of possibilities. The lack of detail is acceptable because no one sees the thumbnails except the designer. Typically, fifty thumbnail sketches are made in pencil, and the one with the most potential is then used to prepare a *rough layout*.

The chosen thumbnail sketch is prepared as a rough layout, either in pencil or electronically. See **Figure 7-5.** The rough layout is the same size as the proposed printed piece. Display type appears as it will in the finished piece. Body type is represented by neatly drawn horizontal *lines* of the correct line length or electronically represented by random characters in the correct typestyle and size. The size and position of art are accurate. The art's content is represented as accurately as possible. Designs that look fine as thumbnail sketches often require modification during the rough layout stage, as details are added.

The completed rough layout is then shown to the client for a reaction. Typically, changes will be requested. Allowance for this reality is the reason for a modest investment of time during this stage.

Usually, client approval of the rough layout is followed by putting the job into production. Some clients require a more detailed representation of the intended piece, however—the comp. The *comprehensive layout (comp)* is an actual replica of how the final printed piece will appear. See **Figure 7-5.**

Figure 7-4. In order for thumbnails to serve as the launching point of an effective design, they must flow quickly. The thumbnails shown result from minimal alteration of the previous thumbnail and lack detail.

Rough Layout

Comp

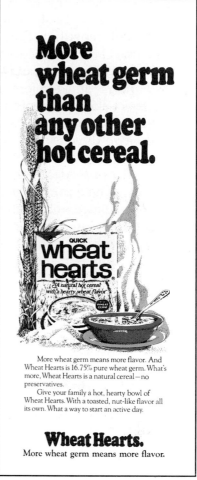

Finished Product

Figure 7-5. After the thumbnail that is judged to have the most potential is chosen, it is the basis for the rough layout. At this stage, detail is added to the art and display type, but body type is represented by straight lines. A comp is a highly detailed—and therefore, expensive—rendering closely resembling how the printed product will look. Colors are included using colored pencils, felt pens, or tempera paints. Note how closely the comprehensive resembles the finished product.

The layout shows the actual typestyles, type sizes, illustrations, logos, colors, and border elements. These layouts, if rendered by hand, usually are drawn using colored felt pens or pencils on the same paper stock intended for the job. Computer-generated comps have greater potential to replicate the final job and greatly reduce the cost.

The Elements of Design

A graphic artist deals with a variety of visual elements, such as copy, illustrations, and border elements, within a given amount of space. Good design serves both purposeful and aesthetic functions and usually employs a variety of design elements, as well as many principles of design. Basic elements of design include lines, shapes, tone, texture, size, white space, and color.

Lines, or **rules**, are one of the most basic design elements and serve several design functions. The style or personality of a printed piece can be changed through variations in line width, form, and length. The basic types of lines—straight and curved—can be used to generate several subtypes, such as spiral, zigzag, and meandering. Therefore, lines can suggest

rough layout: a sketch or an enhanced thumbnail of a page design or layout depicting a somewhat accurate representation of the final size and position of all page elements.

line: a long narrow mark that can be straight or curved.

comprehensive layout (comp): a detailed drawing of how the final printed piece will appear.

rule: an object formed by directly connecting two points. This object is one of the most basic design elements.

moods, such as loose and free, sharp and severe, fancy, or delicate. Lines can be static or indicate motion and energy through repetition. See **Figure 7-6.**

When lines are combined, they can form *shapes*, such as the rectangle, circle, and triangle, which can be combined and modified to form more intricate shapes that can attract attention, represent objects, and otherwise communicate in a nonverbal fashion. Although shapes are two-dimensional images in the printed piece, they can be made to appear three-dimensional by adding sides or shades of gray. See **Figure 7-7.**

When creating a printed piece, the psychological meanings associated with each shape can be used as a basis for the design. Circles can be used to convey a feeling of closeness or protection or to imply a sense of infinity. Triangles are commonly used as pointing devices to direct the eye flow across the design and also can be arranged haphazardly to portray a sense of conflict or action. Square objects or shapes tend to be associated with a feeling of honesty or equality.

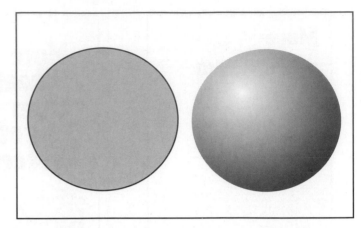

Figure 7-7. Two-dimensional shapes can be made to appear three-dimensional by skillfully changing the color values or shades of gray.

Figure 7-6. Lines are powerful tools for a graphic designer. Their strokes, thickness, shapes, and arrangement can impart many moods. Examples of lines include bold, geometric, precise, curved, delicate, action, whimsical, and shaded.

Figure 7-8. Shapes can be used as components of the layout or as the overall design of the printed piece. The first newspaper advertisement design merely lets the elements conform to the shape of the format. Two different treatments utilize many shapes to add interest, and the irregular shapes of the overall designs help to distinguish them from adjacent ads. Which one do you prefer?

Shapes can be used either as components of the layout or as the overall design of the printed piece. See **Figure 7-8.**

Tone is the degree of darkness of an image. Tone variation can add emphasis to a shape and prevent monotony across the design. In single-color printing, middle tones (grays) can be achieved by combining black and white strokes or tiny black and white dots. See **Figure 7-9.**

In graphic design, *texture* concerns the surface characteristics of the printed piece or an element in the design. Physical texture (or tactile texture) can result from the substrate's actual surface (smooth or rough) or from the raised images achieved through embossing, hot-foil stamping, or thermographic printing. Optical texture can be achieved by printing a pattern of tones suggesting texture. See **Figure 7-10.**

Size is a measure of the area an image occupies in the design. Designers use size to establish priority. Large images often attract attention. Designers also use size to prevent redundancy and monotony across the design by varying the relative sizes of elements.

White space is the total amount of nonimage area on a page and includes the gutters, margins, and space on either side of typographic characters. This space (also called *negative space*) is a necessary, useful, and highly effective design element. See **Figure 7-11.** White space not only helps distinguish the design's elements from one another, but it is crucial to imparting an overall shape to the design.

Color is of great importance when planning and designing a printed product, and color decisions involve both the ink and the substrate. Used appropriately, color contributes visual impact and enhances communication. See **Figure 7-12.** Used poorly, color is a waste of the client's money and can actually reduce the design's effectiveness.

The Requisites of Design

Many people consider themselves to be designers merely because they think they know what looks good. In truth, graphic design—like architecture—is a discipline that is both technical and aesthetic. Just as not any person who lays out a poster qualifies as a designer, neither does the poster itself necessarily qualify as a design. The *requisites of design* are

shape: an elementary form, such as the square, circle, and triangle.

tone: lightness or general quality of a color. To tone is to alter a color by adding some of its complement.

texture: the visual surface characteristics and appearance of an element in a layout.

size: in graphic design, the dimensions of an element within a design.

white space: the total amount of nonimage area on a page.

color: a visual sensation produced in the brain when the eye views various wavelengths of light.

requisite of design: a characteristic that is a necessary component of a design.

Figure 7-9. Middle tones—whether created with black and white lines or dots—add depth to line art. This design uses lines to achieve a rich range of tones.

Figure 7-10. Texture can create a mood by softening or intensifying a design's background, or it can emphasize a design element. (Hilton Head Convention and Visitors Bureau)

Figure 7-11. In addition to type and art, white space can also be used as a design element.

requirements of designs. If one or more is missing, the poster is a layout, but not a design.

If a person sits in front of a computer keyboard and randomly strikes a number of keys, the result might or might not produce actual words. Similarly, if the same person is given several pieces of wood in various shapes and sizes to randomly place onto a tabletop, the resulting arrangement might or might not qualify as a design. In other words, just as not any combination of letters qualifies as a word, not any combination of lines, shapes, tones, textures, and colors qualifies as a design. The requisites of design are those qualities required of a true design, and they are proportion, balance, unity, contrast, rhythm, and harmony.

Proportion

In design, *proportion* is about the comparative size of the design's elements and dimensions. Good proportion results in pleasing size relationships among the display type, text-type blocks, photographs, other art, and dimensions of the piece itself.

Outside Panel   **Inside Panels**

Figure 7-12. The front and back of a two-sided job should match in their use of color and overall look. Both the outside panel and opened-up inside panels of this folder use contrasting warm and cool colors to stimulate interest.

Even in a very simple design, there are several design decisions involving proportion. To demonstrate this point, imagine designing a menu cover containing a single word. See **Figure 7-13.** As shown, a square format provides no relief from the monotony of four equal sides. Yet, in the slender format, the height overpowers the width. The third format achieves good proportion by using a 3:2 ratio between the height and width. This classic 3:2 ratio, known as the *Regular Oblong*, and the 5:3 ratio, known as the *Golden Oblong*, were devised by the ancient Greeks and have been used ever since to avoid poor proportion.

Placement of the word *MENU* brings a second proportion issue. If the word is centered vertically, the menu cover will be visually broken into two equal parts, which will create monotony. See **Figure 7-14.** At the same time, if the word is placed near the top, the area beneath the word will dwarf the area above it. If the word is placed 5/8 of the distance from the bottom, however, the areas above and below will be different, but still proportional. This point, known as the *Line of Golden Proportion*, has 5 units below it and 3 units above. Hence, this point benefits from the classic 5:3 ratio.

The size of the word *MENU* presents a third proportion decision. If the word is set very large, the left and right margins will be too small to be in proportion with the top and bottom margins. See **Figure 7-15.** A better solution is to create a copy block that creates three distinct, but still proportional, margins. Designers avoid proportion problems when they ensure that size ratios stay in the 3:2 and 5:3 ranges. For example, nearly all photographs, books, magazines, letterhead stationery, posters, postcards, and direct-mail pieces stay near these ratios.

Balance

Balance describes the even distribution of visual weight to create a pleasing visual effect. In formal balance, the elements on the page are horizontally symmetrical. Centering elements—repeating

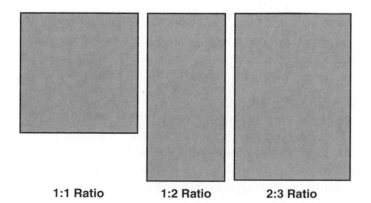

1:1 Ratio   **1:2 Ratio**   **2:3 Ratio**

Figure 7-13. The width-to-height ratio of a menu, poster, or magazine can be monotonous, overwhelming, or in good proportion.

proportion: the pleasing relationship between the elements on the printed page and the general dimensions of the page itself.

balance: the even distribution of images to create a pleasing visual effect.

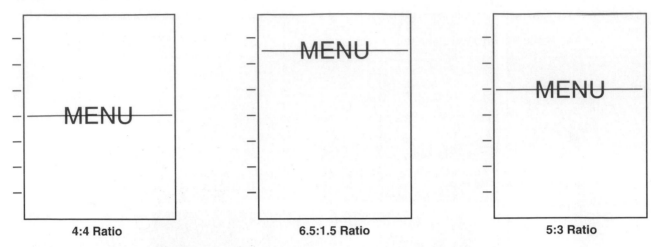

4:4 Ratio   6.5:1.5 Ratio   5:3 Ratio

Figure 7-14. The placement of a single line of type within a format is an opportunity to effectively handle proportion. In this application, proportion is the ratio of the space above and below the center of the type.

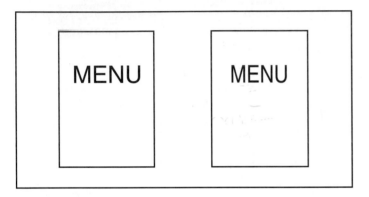

Figure 7-15. The size ratio of the block of type to the format and the resultant margins around the type are examples of design decisions involving proportion. In the menu on the left, the side margins are too small to be in proportion with the top and bottom margins. The margins around the word in the second menu are in better mathematical proportion to one another.

elements in size, tone, and shape on both sides—is an easy way to achieve formal balance. Informal balance allows elements to be placed asymmetrically, as long as the visual weight of the two sides is nearly equal. This style is less traditional than formal balance. Informal balance allows more variety in the placement of the elements on the page because it is less rigid. See **Figure 7-16.**

Achieving vertical balance involves an awareness of the following optical illusion: when a single line of type or art is placed on the actual center of a page, it will appear to be slightly below the center. See **Figure 7-17.** Items balanced against the optical center, which is approximately 10% above the actual center, will make the design appear balanced.

Unity

Unity is what holds the design together visually by creating continuity and controlling contrast. One of the most obvious traits of amateur graphic design is a lack of unity. Without unity, the elements lack the visual connection to hold the design together. Beginning designers often lay out the elements as if they were placing furniture in a room—starting in the corners. This approach usually results in trapped white space near the center, where it divides the layout into two or more groupings, and unity is lost. A better approach is to begin near the optical center and work outward so extra white space is on the outside, where it serves the useful purpose of helping to define the shape of the design. A long-standing guideline is white space should surround, not separate. Another means of achieving unity is to frame the design with a border or connecting element. See **Figure 7-18.**

A design's typography can greatly enhance its unity. When a design's type includes members of the same family, a common look moves through the design and links its elements. Emphasis is achieved by varying the size, weight, color, and orientation. See **Figure 7-19.**

Contrast

Contrast is required if the design is to avoid excessive repetition and monotony. Just as it is boring to listen to someone who speaks in a monotone, materials that lack visual variety are equally boring. If no element immediately stands out to arrest the reader's attention, the entire design might be skipped over. Contrast is achieved by using different sizes, weights, or colors of type and art to emphasize one or more elements and add interest to the printed page. See **Figure 7-20.** An element can also be contrasted by being placed away from the others.

Worth the investment

Asg gjosl a pshjod a iuosda hapz iosa a plxcops iens oucnnsso a fos goos josl a pshjod a iuosda hapz iosa a plxcops iens oucnnsso a fos goosjosl a pshjod a iuosda hapz iosa a plxcops iens oucnnsso a fos goosjosl a pshjod a iuosda hapz iosa a plxcops iens oucnnsso a fos goosjosl a pshjod a iuosda hapz iosa a plxcops iens oucnnsso a fos goos.

Formal Balance

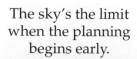

The sky's the limit when the planning begins early.

Ask about establishing a trust fund.

GRISWOLD
— National Bank —

**Formal Balance with a Photo
That Is Assymetrical in Content**

Worth the investment

Asg gjosl a pshjod a iuosda hapz iosa a plxcops iens oucnnsso a fos goos josl a pshjod a iuosda hapz iosa a plxcops iens oucnnsso a fos goosjosl a pshjod a iuosda hapz iosa a plxcops iens oucnnsso a fos goosjosl a pshjod a iuosda hapz iosa a plxcops iens oucnnsso a fos goosjosl a pshjod a iuosda hapz iosa a plxcops iens oucnnsso a fos goos.

Informal Balance

Informal Balance

Figure 7-16. Both formal and informal balance can produce highly effective designs. Although the top two designs consist of the same elements, they carry different moods. The design in the lower-left corner shows how informal balance is appropriate for the motion of athletics. Although the design in the lower-right corner is formally balanced, the informal balance of the photograph's content infuses the ad with energy.

unity: the proper balance of all elements in an image so a pleasing whole results and the image is viewed as one piece.

contrast: the principle of design that adds interest and emphasis to the printed page by using different sizes and weights of type and art, using a second ink color, underlining type, or shading backgrounds.

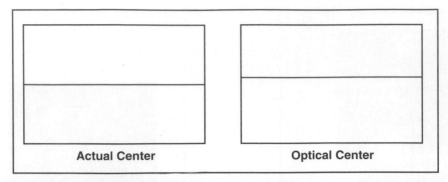

Figure 7-17. A line of type or other element placed on the actual center of a layout will appear to be too low. The optical center is slightly higher than the actual center and is a better point of reference for establishing vertical balance.

Haphazard Placement

Unifying Placement

Unifying Border

Unifying Typeface

Figure 7-18. Unity can be achieved by three different means—element placement, typography, and framing. The haphazard placement of the ad's elements creates a scattered look. Unifying the elements by their placement creates more interest through the outline of their collective pattern and makes it easier for the reader's eye to take in all of the design. Using a frame and variations of a single typeface—boldface, capitals, and boldface capitals—holds this single-color design together. The white space on the outside, the uniform typeface, and the color red unify this fashion ad. (Kissimmee-St. Cloud Convention and Visitors Bureau)

Figure 7-19. Although the display type elements vary in size, weight, color, and even orientation, using a single typeface (Avenir) unifies the design. (Michael Orr and Associates for Corning Museum of Glass)

Figure 7-20. Contrast is achieved when a norm is established, which a single element stands out against. Options include size, shape, color, and placement. Although the six photographs have the same shape, the large one is dominant. The square pizza stands out from the round ones. Both size and color emphasize one word. In this magazine article about a nonconformist, the page design reinforces the story's content.

The first step in achieving contrast is to decide which element will receive top priority. Once priorities have been established, the next question is the degree of contrast to use. Although inadequate contrast is visually boring, excessive contrast results in the elements appearing so unrelated that the design loses unity. Therefore, the designer must take a middle path, blending contrast and unity. See **Figure 7-21.**

Rhythm

In music, rhythm measures the movement of sound. In graphic design, *rhythm* measures the movement of the eye across the page. This movement includes the path the reader's eye takes across the page (sequence), as well as the rate of flow across the individual elements. The size, shape, placement, and content of an element influence eye flow. See **Figure 7-22.** The eye tends to move quickly across or down a long photograph, but it moves more slowly across or down the same area if the area consists of separate photographs. Triangles tend to serve as pointing devices, and circles slow the eye more than any other shape.

Although the path the eye takes across the page cannot be controlled, it certainly can be influenced. For this reason, effective designers create a natural path that will increase readers' time spent with the design and awareness of the design's main points. The starting point of this path is the focal point, typically located in the upper-left quadrant of the page. From the focal point, the path should follow the shortest and most direct path possible to touch the most important elements—perhaps the headline, photos, and logo. See **Figure 7-23.**

Harmony

The choice and placement of elements appropriate to the message, one another, or the theme of the message is called *harmony*. Referring to the

Figure 7-21. This design strikes an effective blend of contrasting colors, tones, lines, typestyles, and textures. Despite their contrast, the curved and straight lines carry the eye along, serve as axes for the type, and hold the design together. (Crane Lake Visitor and Tourism Bureau)

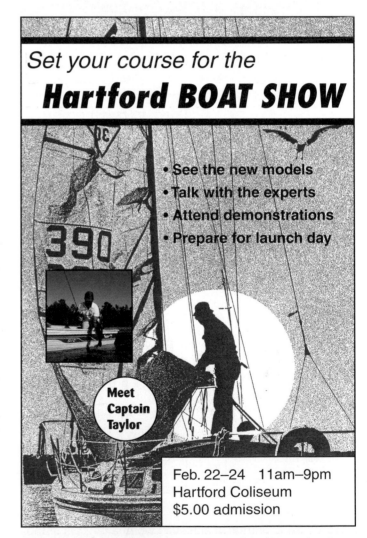

Figure 7-22. The lines of the sailboat's mast and sail create a path the other design elements straddle. The result is a logical sequence for the reader's eye.

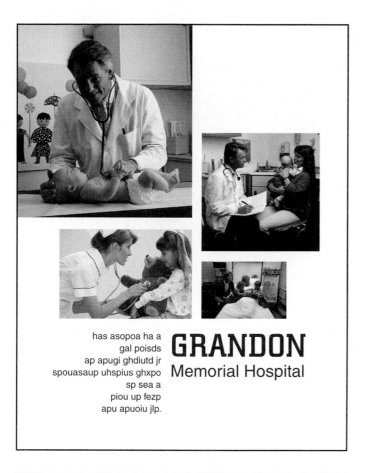

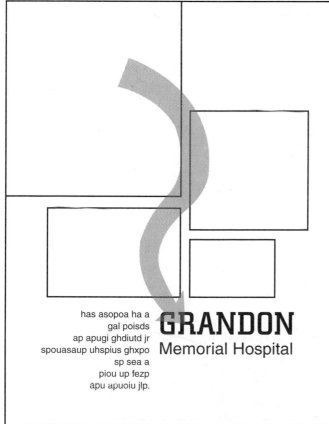

Figure 7-23. Observe the natural and compact path the reader's eye can follow when rhythm is part of the design.

communication model, layouts lacking harmony include elements that do not work well together, with the result that more than one message is sent, which produces noise. See **Figure 7-24.** Each of the elements should support the others, and none of the elements should appear inappropriate or unnecessary. Harmony problems arise when elements are not appropriate to the message. Informal typefaces or art used to convey a formal message or a delicate typestyle carrying a message about strength and durability are examples of harmony problems.

Using Color

The application of color can greatly impact a design's effectiveness—for better or worse. Used wisely, color can add interest, create a mood, and enhance communication. See **Figure 7-25.** Used poorly, color can confuse, contradict, and detract from the message. Decisions regarding the use of color should be approached similarly to decisions regarding the use of any other design element: How will it advance the message? Graphic designers must resist the urge to use a favorite color and, instead, exercise the discipline to consider the effect on the intended receiver.

The Psychology of Color

Making the right color decisions often involves an awareness of the *psychology of color*, which deals with the effect colors and their combinations have on people. A combination of factors, including physiological, psychological, and cultural, influence people's reactions to color. Color can be used to create an overall mood. Red, orange, and yellow are referred to as *warm colors* because they resemble fire. See **Figure 7-26.** Warm colors can reinforce a message dealing with physical or emotional warmth. These colors tend to advance toward the reader and, therefore, seldom make good background colors when used in their pure form. Because bright reds often have a stimulating effect on people, they are usually

rhythm: the state of design created with the repetition of similar elements in a design. Rhythm is the flow or movement of the individual elements in a design.

harmony: the state of design achieved when the placement of elements do not clash with one another or with the theme of the message.

psychology of color: the knowledge of proper color combinations and applications.

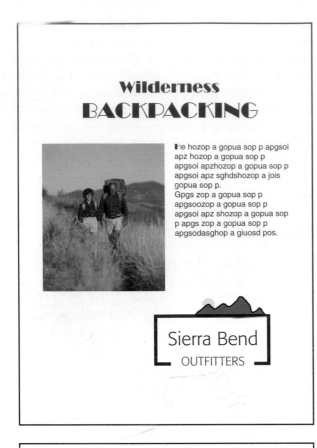

Figure 7-24. Harmony is missing when art or typography that is inappropriate to other elements or the message is used. A formal, elegant typestyle is wrong for an ad on backpacking. An ornate border or a delicate border is inappropriate for camping equipment. The light type is a good match for light lines of the art. The bold type of the design about energy is in harmony with the strong lines of the windmill art.

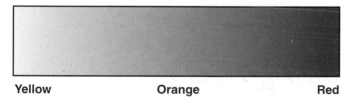

Figure 7-25. The blue sky, golden sand, and green of the model's dress and logo brighten this design. Similar colors are used on the cover of the promotional piece. (Daytona Beach Convention and Visitors Bureau)

Yellow	Orange	Red

Figure 7-26. Used in their pure forms, warm colors resemble fire, are bold, and tend to advance.

not the best choice when a calming mood is desired. Red is, however, a highly effective accent color that works very well with black. See **Figure 7-27.**

Blues and greens are referred to as *cool colors* because of their association with clear skies, clean water, and vegetation. Cool colors function well as background colors and enhance photographs of metal and snow scenes. See **Figure 7-28.** Blues and greens should not be used with photographs of inappropriate subjects, however, such as people's faces or most foods. These colors are inappropriate for people's faces because flesh tones are not green or blue—except in the case of sickness or death. Blue and green are also inappropriate for most foods. Blueberries are one of the only blue foods, and green is usually indicative of moldy food, except for foods such as green beans and peas.

Figure 7-27. The front panel of this promotional piece demonstrates the vibrancy and power of warm colors against a black background. (The Think Tank Group Inc. for the Pittsburgh Chamber Music Society)

Figure 7-28. A blue duotone can make a black-and-white photograph appear cold.

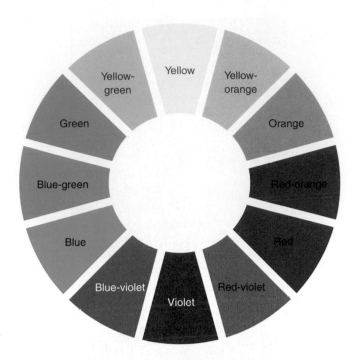

Figure 7-29. The color wheel includes primary, secondary, and intermediate colors.

The Dimensions of Color

Although it is impossible to precisely describe the appearance of a color verbally, it is useful to arrange adjacent colors in what is known as the *color wheel*. See **Figure 7-29.** The relationships among the basic colors are readily apparent when viewing the color wheel. Red, blue, and yellow are termed *primary colors* because the other colors can be formed by mixing two of them. Orange, green, and violet are referred to as *secondary colors* because they are formed from mixing equal amounts of two primary colors. For example, orange is located midway between yellow and red because it results from mixing equal amounts of those two colors. The remaining colors are *intermediate colors* because they result from mixing equal amounts of a primary color and its neighboring secondary color. For example, equal amounts of yellow and green produce yellow-green. The color wheel is the foundation of a systematic approach to describing and using color.

Albert Munsell devised a system in the early 1900s to reduce confusion because color can be difficult to describe verbally. The Munsell system describes color in three dimensions, or attributes—hue, value, and chroma (HVC). *Hue* describes a color's placement on the color wheel. *Value* is the lightness or darkness of a color. *Chroma* indicates the saturation, or purity, of a color. See **Figure 7-30.** The Munsell system augments the basic color wheel by revealing how changes in value create new colors. See **Figure 7-31.** The center ring contains the hues of the original color wheel. The colors of the inner ring result from the addition of white to each hue and are called *tints*. The outer ring consists of darker values, called *shades*, which are created by adding black to the original hues.

The use of tints and shades greatly expands the color choices for the graphic designer. When black is added to green in varying percentages, a range of dark green colors is created. When white is added to green in varying percentages, a range of light green colors is created. See **Figure 7-32.** By using a single ink color in various combinations with black to create shades, a design can appear to have more colors than the two actually being used. Similarly, using a single color in various screen tints creates the appearance of multiple inks by using the white paper as the tinting medium. Because printing extra ink colors requires additional plates and added press cost, designers can use tints and shades to maximize the effect of one or two inks when the client's budget is limited.

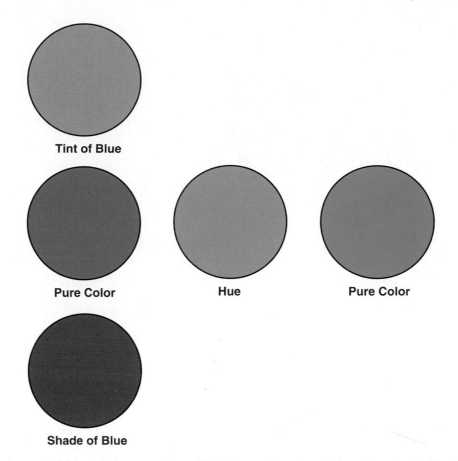

Tint of Blue

Pure Color   **Hue**   **Pure Color**

Shade of Blue

Figure 7-30. A color's chroma is highest in its purest form. High chroma is reduced when it is mixed with white to produce a tint, black to produce a shade, or another color to produce a hue. Therefore, a color's chroma is reduced through contamination.

Color Harmonies

Color harmony is the combining of two or more colors in a design to achieve a pleasing effect on the viewer. The key to color harmony is choosing the proper hues, tones, placement, and proportion. A good choice of colors can be ruined if the colors are not used well in the design.

Decades of research have established that people like the combination of colors that are either similar or very different in hue. The color wheel serves as the framework for designating color harmonies. See **Figure 7-33.** *Analogous* color harmony consists of using colors on the same part of the color wheel. For example, using red with either red-orange or red-violet is analogous harmony. *Complementary* color harmony combines colors that are opposite one another, such as red and green or yellow and violet. *Split-complementary* color harmony matches a color with one adjacent to the complement. Examples include yellow with blue-violet or red-violet. *Triad* harmony results from using three colors connected by an equilateral triangle. *Monochromatic* color harmony uses a color with shades and tints made from that color. An example of monochromatic color

color wheel: a circle containing colors in positions reflective of the colors' relationships to one another.

primary color: in additive color formation, a main color on the color wheel (red, yellow, or blue).

secondary color: in additive color formation, a color (orange, green, or violet) created by the combination of two primary colors.

intermediate color: in additive color formation, colors (yellow-green, blue-green, blue-violet, red-violet, red-orange, and yellow-orange) created by combining primary colors and secondary colors.

hue: the color perceived by the eye and determined by the dominant wavelengths reflected or transmitted.

value: the lightness or darkness of a color as measured against a scale running from white to black.

chroma: the intensity or strength of a color and its saturation.

tint: the alteration of a color created by adding white to the color.

shade: the alteration of a color created by adding black to the color.

color harmony: the selection of two or more colors that produce a visually pleasing sensation.

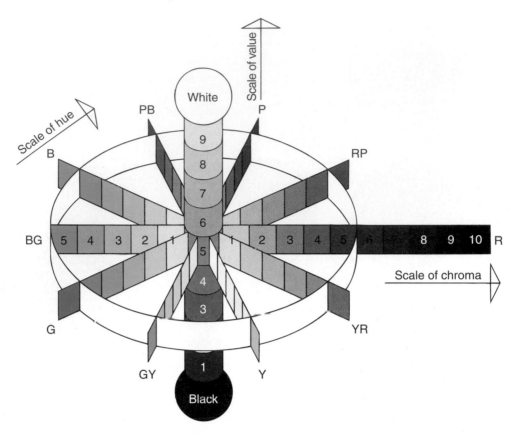

Figure 7-31. The Munsell system of color classification describes a color in terms of its HVC.

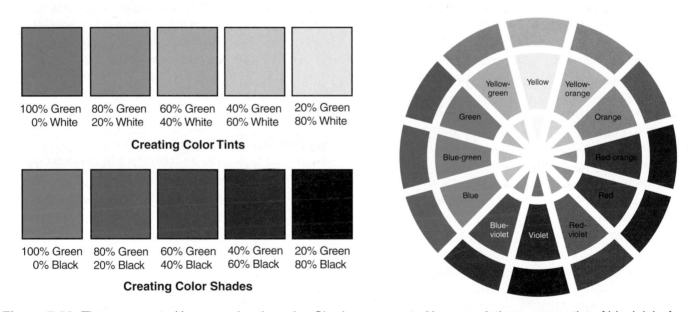

Creating Color Tints

| 100% Green 0% White | 80% Green 20% White | 60% Green 40% White | 40% Green 60% White | 20% Green 80% White |

Creating Color Shades

| 100% Green 0% Black | 80% Green 20% Black | 60% Green 40% Black | 40% Green 60% Black | 20% Green 80% Black |

Figure 7-32. Tints are created by screening the color. Shades are created by overprinting a screen tint of black ink. An augmented color wheel includes screens and tints.

harmony is the use of bright red with two tints—one that creates mauve and one that creates pink. See **Figure 7-34.** Monochromatic color harmony allows the budget-conscious graphic designer to judiciously use one ink color to create the appearance of several ink colors.

Types of Artwork

The two main types of *artwork* are line art and continuous tone art. *Line art* consists of solid lines on a white or contrasting background. For this reason, it consists entirely of lines and includes pen-and-ink

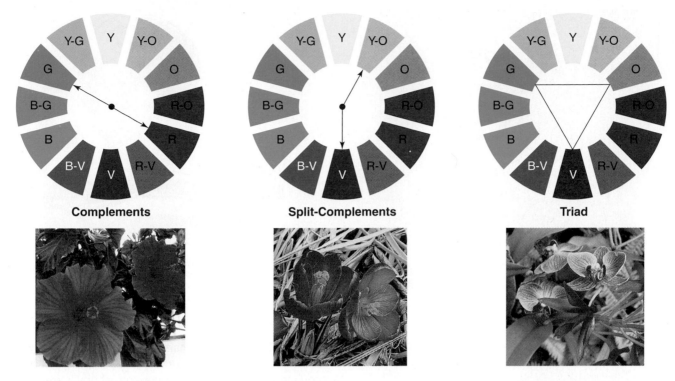

Figure 7-33. Color harmonies achieve pleasing color combinations by working with similarities (analogous and monochromatic) and opposites (complements, split-complements, and triad). Shown here are examples of complementary, split-complementary, and triad harmony.

drawings, diagrams, clip art, and type composition. Line art consists of only two tones—black and white. This art has no tone variations, except those the artist's pen makes. See **Figure 7-35.** Notice how the varying line densities and use of solid black provide tonal variations.

Continuous tone art contains gradations of tone varying from light to dark. These gradations are created by changing the amount of density. Black-and-white photographs, along with single-color watercolor, charcoal, and airbrush art, are good examples of continuous tone because they have middle tones (grays), as well as black and white. The existence of middle tones greatly complicates the printing of continuous tone art. In fact, only line art was reproduced during the first 400 years of printing.

The challenge in printing continuous tone art lies in the fact that printing plates are comprised of only two areas—image areas that carry ink and nonimage areas that do not carry ink. Middle tones do not fit into either category. Therefore, continuous tone art must be converted to tiny image and nonimage areas so small they appear gray to the casual observer. See **Figure 7-36.** Using a magnifying glass or a loupe will reveal this optical illusion. The areas appearing to be gray actually consist of halftone dots that are either solid black or white.

Line art and continuous tone art require very different preparations for printing. Usually, the graphic designer desires a faithful reproduction of the original art, which means the art is intended to appear in print just as it appears in its original form. A faithful reproduction of line art requires no conversion to image and nonimage areas because it already is in that form. A faithful reproduction of continuous tone art, however, does require the conversion to halftone dots in order to create the appearance of middle tones. Therefore, line art is considered *line copy*. Continuous tone art is considered *halftone copy*. Line copy is not to be converted to halftone dots. Halftone copy must be converted to halftone dots. See **Figure 7-37.**

artwork: any illustration matter, including hand lettering, that is not text.

line art: type or a drawing with no grays or middle tones.

continuous tone art: an image containing one or more gray tones.

line copy: artwork with no tone variations consisting of solid lines on a white or contrasting background, including pen-and-ink drawings, diagrams, and type composition.

halftone copy: a photograph or another image that must be broken into halftone dots in order to reproduce it in the printing process.

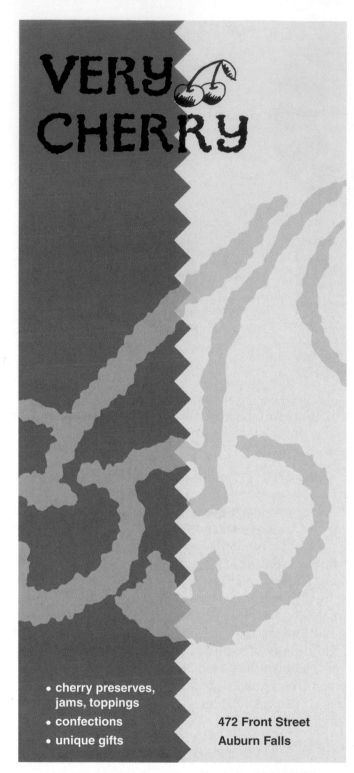

Figure 7-35. Line art consists strictly of black and white. Although they contain no grays, middle tones can be simulated by varying the relationship of black areas to white areas. Techniques an artist can use to accomplish tonal variations include varying line densities, using cross-hatching, and using tiny dots that create a screen tint.

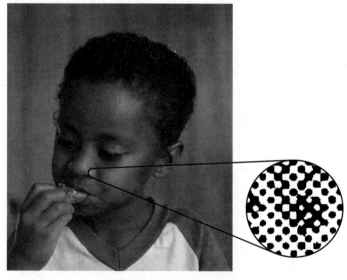

Figure 7-36. Examples of halftone copy include photographs, charcoal art, watercolors, and airbrush art. To be reproduced by printing, this copy must be screened into halftone dots.

Figure 7-34. The use of red and two screen tints of red gives this design a depth and richness beyond the capability of black and red alone.

On occasion, a graphic designer will not desire a faithful reproduction of a photograph. For example, if the desired effect is ultrahigh contrast, the middle tones of a photograph can be eliminated if the photograph is not converted to halftone dots. In this instance, continuous tone art becomes line copy. See **Figure 7-38.**

The grays of halftone copy were first converted to halftone dots through the use of halftone screens. Photographs can now be scanned or downloaded directly to the computer from digital cameras and then converted to halftone dots digitally. Chapter 11 discusses halftone reproduction in detail.

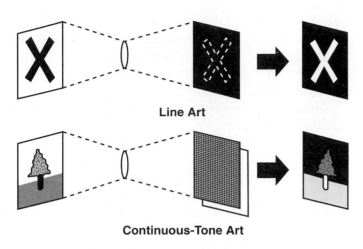

Line Art

Continuous-Tone Art

Figure 7-37. Line art is viewed as line copy. That is, line art is copied to film without being screened into dots. Continuous tone art is normally viewed as halftone copy. That is, a halftone screen placed over the film breaks continuous tone art into halftone dots. The assumption in both instances is that the client wants a faithful reproduction of the original.

The Production Process

After client approval, the design is ready to enter the *production stage*. At this point, designers need to either perform much of the prepress themselves or generate *specifications (specs)* directing the people who will produce the job. To perform either function, designers must understand the basics of printing production. These topics include typographic specs, the cropping and scaling of art, the handling of line and halftone copy, and signature imposition.

Type Specifications (Specs)

As has been stated, one of the most important elements of a design is the type. The primary objective of typography is to transform the original manuscript into a legible, visually interesting, functional, pleasing, and inviting medium. Body type that is too small, line lengths that are too long or too short, or typefaces that lack readability can cause eye fatigue and cause the reader to turn the page or put down the brochure. Display type needs to arrest the reader's attention and invite interest in the body type, which in turn must permit a smooth flow of the reader's eye from line to line.

Figure 7-38. If the designer desires a photograph to lose its middle tones, the photograph is not broken into halftone dots, and all tones go to either black or white.

production stage: a collection of functions that occur to a design as part of getting the design printed.

specifications (specs): written information relating to typestyle, type sizes, and line or column width for a project.

The written information relating to type design, type sizes, and line or column width is referred to as the *specs* for a project. A spec sheet, or style sheet, lists the specs to be used in a job. The spec sheet serves as the bridge between the graphic designer and the people who will produce the job because it communicates how the type is to look. See **Figure 7-39.** For this reason, spec sheets must answer every typographic question that could come up during production—including the amount of indentation for paragraphs, any words to be set in bold or italics, the amount of leading, and the type of bullets that should be used.

Cropping Artwork

It is very common to select only a portion of a photograph or an illustration for use in a publication, and the selection and identification of the part of the illustration to be used is *cropping.* Cropping is an important design tool. This selection can direct the reader to the portion of the art that best communicates the message, and it eliminates the distraction (noise) of other images. Cropping also alters the proportion of the art to fit the available layout space. See **Figure 7-40.**

Images being prepared for reproduction with a process camera should be mounted on white illustration board with rubber cement to keep the artwork rigid and smooth. Images being sent out of house to be scanned can be mounted on white paper with drafting tape. In either case, crop marks are placed in the margins, not in the image area. These marks should be made with a grease pencil or similar marker that will not damage the art. If the margins cannot be marked, a sheet of vellum paper should be fastened to the back of the artwork and then folded over the front. Marks on the vellum paper can then be drawn to outline the part of the art to be reproduced.

The use of scanners and software that allows image manipulation has greatly simplified the ability to crop images. Once the image is in digital format, the prepress operators can crop, enlarge, or reduce the image. Software also allows the "repair" of creases or other flaws in the original artwork. For more information on electronic imaging, refer to Chapter 14.

Scaling Artwork

In addition to cropping, it is often necessary to alter the size of the original art. Drawings and photos can be enlarged or reduced to fit the space available in a layout. The operation of preparing illustrations for enlargement or reduction is known as *scaling* (or sizing). For example, if a drawing measures 4" × 6" and the design space is only 2" × 3", the photo would

---

Specifications for *Offset Lithographic Technology*   October 30, 2008

Trim: 8-1/2″ × 11″
Gutter: 4p3
Bottom Margin: 3p6
Thumb Margin: 3p
Top Margin: 2p6 to the base of the running head, 4p to the top of the first line of text
2 column format: 21 × 1p6 × 21
Length of text column: 43p9

4 color process

Colors used in text:

OLT blue	90C	OLT red	100M	OLT yellow	0C
	40M		100Y		100Y
					0K

All text copy prints in black unless otherwise stated in the style specifications.

Chapters are always to start a new left.

Typefaces used: Palatino, Helvetica (all in roman, bold, italic and/or bold italic), Broadway BT, Symbol, Zapf Dingbats SWA.

Front Matter: To come

Running Heads:
Left hand page:
344   Section I   Introduction to Offset Lithographic Technology
(page number flush left in 9pt. Helvetica Bold)   (Section # and Title flush left in 9pt. Helvetica Bold)

Right hand page:
Chapter 3   Measurement   345
(Chapter number and title flush left 9pt. Helvetica Bold)   (page number flush right in
                                                          9pt. Helvetica Bold)

Chapter opener takes a drop folio, 9pt. Helvetica Bold, prints black, flush right on the outside margin, the baseline of the number is 2p below the normal text bed.

Chapter Opening Graphic/number/title: See layout example
Case Studies:

Figure 7-39. The spec sheet for a promotional piece can consist of the manuscript marked up by the designer. A sheet for an entire book lists the typographic conventions to be followed. Here is the spec sheet for this book.

Figure 7-40. Cropping is an important part of the communication process because it helps to define the message and eliminate distractions.

Figure 7-41. Scaling alters the size of a photograph or other art, while maintaining the proportions of width and height.

have to be reduced to half its original size, or by 50%. In **Figure 7-41,** a photograph needs be enlarged to 250% of its original size to fill one column of this book.

The key to specifying art for scaling is to mark the percentage that will produce the correct dimensions. Dividing the reproduction (desired) dimension by the original dimension provides the appropriate percentage. Therefore, a 5″-high photograph that needs to become 7 1/2″ to fit a space would be marked 150%.

Enlargements can magnify defects in the original, whereas reductions tend to minimize defects and sharpen detail. For most purposes, artwork and photographs are reduced to retain detail. Refer to Chapter 3 to review methods and steps used for scaling images.

Note

When you are supplying the dimensions of a photograph, piece of art, or finished job, the width is expressed first. Therefore, 5″ x 7″ should be read as 5″ wide and 7″ high.

Handling Artwork

Original artwork should be protected against dirt and fingerprints. The art can be mounted on a sheet of paper with drafting tape or rubber cement. Paper clips should never be used to attach notations to artwork. Drafting tape, Post-it® notes, or rubber cement should be used instead. The face of the illustration can be covered with a vellum paper overlay. The reproduction size, crop marks, or other notations can be written on the paper background or on the

vellum before it is attached to the artwork. Writing on paper placed on top of art might leave an impression of the writing on the photo or drawing. These types of marks or indentations might be picked up by the camera or scanner and be reproduced along with the image.

Signature Imposition

Designing magazines, booklets, or books requires an awareness of signatures. A *signature* is a single sheet carrying several of the publication's pages. When folded, the signature becomes a portion of the publication. A publication can consist of a single signature or dozens of signatures, depending on the number of pages on a signature and the number of pages in the publication itself. See **Figure 7-42.** Each side of a signature is called a *flat,* and the flat with the signature's lowest page number is the front flat. The proper placing of pages onto signatures is known as *signature imposition.*

Signatures are of interest to graphic designers who wish to maximize the publication's budget by placing pages requiring extra expense (such as a different color of ink) onto the same signature or even on the same flat. By planning to group pages with the same production requirements, the designer limits the number of signatures requiring the extra

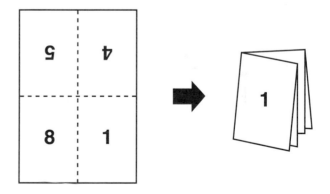

Figure 7-42. Books and booklets consist of signatures that begin as flat sheets printed with pages. After being folded, the pages appear in order. A signature can contain 4, 8, or 16 pages.

cropping: a method used to identify the part of an illustration to be used.

signature: a folded printed sheet in a sequence of 4, 8, 16, 32, or 64 pages.

signature imposition: arranging pages so they will appear on a press sheet in the proper position and so, when the sheet is folded, the pages will be in the proper sequence.

expense. The challenge in publication planning is to distinguish between the reader's spread and the printer's spread. A reader's spread is the pair of pages the reader sees when opening the finished publication. A printer's spread is the pair of adjacent pages as they appear on the signature before it is folded. See **Figure 7-43.** By making what is referred to as a *folding dummy*, the designer can see which pages will be on the same signature and flat. For example, if a second color is required on one page of a flat, that color can be used on the other pages of that flat without additional cost.

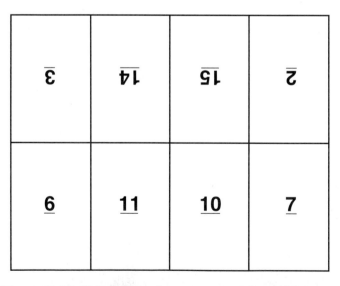

Figure 7-43. This folding dummy was made to show the placement of pages onto a 16-page signature. The numbers are underlined to reveal the top of the pages after the dummy is unfolded. Books with as many pages as *Offset Lithographic Technology* consist of dozens of signatures. A printer's spread consists of the two adjacent pages on the flat. In this example, pages 2 and 15 make up a printer's spread.

Categories of Printed Advertising Materials

Too many people—especially graphic designers and other people who should know better—use terms such as *brochure, card, folder, leaflet,* and *booklet* as if these terms were synonymous. In fact, each term applies to a specific type of printed piece. It is important that people in the field become familiar with the meanings of these terms.

Unfolded Single Sheets

Cards are small flat pieces printed on cover-weight paper. Business cards are usually 3 1/2"×2" so they can fit into traditional-sized holders. Variations on business-card design include a vertical format and oversize cards that fold once to the 3 1/2" × 2" size. Counter cards are usually larger than business cards and, as the name implies, are typically placed in a short pile on a retail counter, but they can also be placed on bulletin boards or mailed in envelopes. These cards are usually printed on both sides.

Leaflets, or fliers, are also single sheets that can be printed on one or both sides but not folded. These sheets are printed on lighter-weight paper—usually 40- or 50-pound offset or 20-pound bond. Leaflets are commonly handed out at intersections, placed on windshields, or stapled to telephone poles.

Folded Single Sheets

Folders are the sheets folded into two or more panels. These sheets usually contain two or more folds and, therefore, three or more panels on each side of the piece. A folder with three parallel folds consists of eight panels—four on each side. Folders might also consist of a combination of parallel and right-angle folds, and the way they unfold plays an important role in how the message is presented to the receiver.

The number of folds appearing in the finished piece might not be the number of folds the piece received during production. For example, if you produce an eight-panel folder by folding an 11" × 8 1/2" sheet of paper in half and then folding it in half a second time with a parallel fold, when it is opened up, it will have three folds. The paper received, however, only two folds.

Broadsides are sheets of paper typically 17" × 22" or larger that have been folded down to fit into an envelope. Therefore, broadsides are usually part of an elaborate mailing—such as a magazine subscription direct mail campaign. As with folders, the method in which the broadside opens determines the sequence in which the message is received.

Bound Pieces

Booklets (also known as *pamphlets*) consist of two or more sheets bound together—probably saddle stitched. Pamphlets are printed as signatures. A single sheet folded once produces a 4-page signature. A second fold at a right angle to the first will produce an 8-page signature. The body of a 32-page booklet could consist of two 16-page signatures or four 8-page signatures. The separate cover would be a 4-page signature, and all the signatures would be inserted, stitched, and trimmed.

None of these terms is misused as often as *brochure*. When asked, "Would you like one of our brochures?" you are likely to receive a folder, a booklet, or even a leaflet. Just as very few cars are limousines and very few boats are yachts, very few printed pieces are brochures. In truth, a brochure is a large, elaborate, and very expensive oversized booklet. The unit cost of an actual brochure is at least a dollar. Features that add to the cost are large dimensions; heavyweight text pages; heavily embossed cover stock; the use of translucent or deckle-edged paper; and elaborate design features, such as hot-foil stamping, embossing, lamination, and die cutting. Actual brochures are very rare and certainly not placed out for passersby to take. Brochures are commonly part of a sophisticated marketing campaign for expensive real estate or another high-ticket purchase.

Summary

The primary concern with printed pieces is the communication of ideas. An ongoing awareness of the communication model is useful when beginning the design process. The requisites of design guide the use of elements, such as lines, shapes, texture, and color, to blend the verbal and the visual into a coherent statement. A layout that lacks one or more of the design requisites, however, will likely detract from the message and impair communication.

Color can have a positive or negative effect on a design. Matters of color preference require that the intended audience be considered when selecting color. Color selection and specification revolve around the dimensions of color—HVC. Combining colors to achieve color harmony imparts a pleasing effect to the design.

After having moved through the design stages and gaining client approval, the design is ready to be prepared for production—a process that involves supplying type specs and marking art for cropping and scaling. Designers are also aware of the stages involved in production. They know the difference between line and halftone copy, and they understand signature imposition.

Review Questions

Please do not write in this book. Write your answers on a separate sheet of paper.

1. Sketch the communication model and label the components.
2. What is the role of a graphic designer?
3. What are the three stages of graphic design?
4. Name the basic elements of design.
5. How can texture or the appearance of texture be created in a printed piece?
6. In graphic design, _____ refers to the pleasing relationship between the size of the elements on the printed page and the general dimensions of the page itself.
7. In _____ balance, an equal amount of each major element is positioned on either side of an imaginary centerline.
8. _____ balance allows much variety in the placement of elements on the page.
9. How can contrast be achieved in a design?
10. Identify and define the requisites of design.
11. The selection and placement of elements so they do not clash with one another or the theme of the message is called _____.
12. Relative to the dimensions of color, explain HVC.
13. What type of color harmony uses two colors directly across from one another on the color wheel?

leaflet: a folded flier intended for free distribution.

folder: a folded, single sheet of paper, printed on two sides.

broadside: a large, single sheet of paper, printed on two sides and folded down.

booklet: a small book, particularly a brochure.

brochure: a large elaborate booklet with features such as string binding, embossing, translucent paper, hot-foil stamping, or heavy paper and costing over a dollar per copy to produce.

14   What are two factors that might influence a person's color preferences?

15.   _____ art consists of solid lines on a white or contrasting background.

16.   _____ art contains gradations of tone varying from light to dark.

17.   How are illustrations prepared for printing?

18.   What type of information does a spec sheet provide?

19.   The method used to identify the portion of an illustration to appear in print is called _____.

20.   The arrangement of a magazine's pages so they will be in the proper sequence after the sheet is printed and folded is known as _____.

21.   Distinguish between a reader's spread and a printer's spread.

22.   Compare the following categories of advertising pieces: folder, brochure, leaflet, and booklet.

Skill-Building Activities

1.   From good-quality magazines, obtain one printed advertising example for each of the design requisites: proportion, balance, unity, harmony, contrast, and rhythm. Share your examples with class members. Which of the design requisites was most difficult to identify? Why?

2.   Prepare thumbnail sketches, rough layouts, and comps for a poster advertising the offset lithography program in your school. Prepare a final layout using a page composition program. Ask your instructor to comment on the design selected.

3.   In groups of two to four students, conduct a visual color experiment among the graphic arts class members. Obtain several different magazine advertisements or other printed products containing substantial amounts of color. Ask members of the class to view the printed products and give their responses as to how the colors influence their feelings about each piece. Compare responses of all the class members. What interesting results were revealed?

4.   Find a printed sample of a poster or flier used in the school library or counseling office. Prepare thumbnail sketches and a rough layout for what you think would be a more effective design. Consult with other class members and see if your design has greater appeal than the original printed piece. If not, try to determine where your design might be improved.

5.   Prepare a display including a card, leaflet, folder, brochure, and booklet. Warning: a true brochure will be the most difficult to find.

Advanced scale systems are used to count the number of sheets in the paper lift right at the jogging table. This eliminates the need for estimating the number of sheets by height and prevents miscalculations and waste. (Heidelberg, Inc.)

It's Always Been about Communicating

The very first graphic communicators applied images of animals on cave walls around 37,000 years ago. Graphic design began, however, when people began to make decisions about how the elements of a design would be coordinated to enhance the message. Gutenberg invented movable type, but he did not invent graphic design. Before 1440, all books and other documents were created by hand, but decisions were already being made regarding matters of proportion, balance, contrast, unity, and harmony.

The first page shown is a page from a medieval prayer book penned in Latin on animal skin by a Flemish scribe in the fifteenth century. Notice the pencil guidelines drawn to define the margins. Similar to today's books, the greatest margin is at the bottom, followed by the outside, inside, and top margins. Baseline guides were drawn for each of the 16 lines of type. The decision was made to add contrast by highlighting certain capital letters with blue and red ink, as well as burnished gold.

The second page is from a book on astronomy. Although it resembles the first page, this page was printed on a press in 1482. Many elements of book design that medieval scribes created remain, such as proportional margins and initial letters. The new technology of printing has, however, eliminated pencil guidelines, allowed smaller type, and produced uniform line lengths. Today's digital software and sophisticated presses permit much more elaborate design elements, but the designer's basic goal remains the same—to enhance communication.

Chapter 8
Text Composition

Key Terms

American Standard
  Code for Information
  Interchange (ASCII)
binary system
byte
codex
cold-type composition
compact disc–recordable
  (CD-R)
composition
conventional prepress
digital camera
digital videodisc (DVD)
disk
gigabyte (GB)
graphics tablet
hand composition
hard disk drive (hard
  drive)
hot-type composition

jukebox
keyboard
kilobyte (KB)
megabyte (MB)
memory
modem
phototypesetting
pocket CD
random-access memory
  (RAM)
repurposing
scanner
touch pad
trackball
type specifications
  (specs)
video digitizer
word processing
  software

Learning Objectives

When you have completed the reading and
assigned activities related to this chapter, you will
be able to do the following:

- Describe the impact of movable type on mass
  communication.

- Trace the historical development of typographic
  image–generation technology.

- Explain the difference between hot-type
  composition and cold-type composition.

- Define *photocomposition* and explain the concept
  on which it is based.

- Discuss the binary system as it relates to
  processing and storage of information by
  computers.

- Give examples of various input devices used in
  electronic composition.

- Summarize the capabilities of the numerous
  digital storage devices.

- Produce a text document with word processing
  software.

The term *composition* refers to the production and organization of all images and type to be placed in a layout. Although electronic desktop publishing has essentially replaced manual composition methods, you should still be familiar with these processes. These methods are still used for small quantities of display composition or for making changes for reprinting material mounted on layout boards. This chapter briefly reviews the history of text composition and explains several types of manual and electronic type- and page composition methods.

Composition is the first of several stages included in *conventional prepress*—the nondigital means of preparing copy for printing. Very briefly, these four stages are as follows:

1. **Composition.** Images are generated as galleys and arranged onto mechanicals.
2. **Camera.** Mechanicals are photographed to generate films.
3. **Image assembly.** Films are positioned onto flats.
4. **Platemaking.** Flats are used to expose images onto plates.

The creation of the plates to be used for printing is the final stage of prepress.

Clay Tablets to Movable Type

The history of the written word can be traced to about 3000 BC. The Sumerians used a triangle stylus to press characters from the cuneiform alphabet into clay tablets. The clay tablets were dried and fired for longevity, and some even had clay envelopes. As you might imagine, the transportation and distribution of these tablets was extremely limited.

As new civilizations and languages developed, people created other types of substrates and means of writing. Scrolls were made from animal skins, papyrus, and parchment. Tablets were made from stone, wax, and wood. Before the first century BC, the Greeks and Romans used wax tablets framed and backed with wood. These tablets were joined with cords, similar to a three-ringed binder, and called a *codex*. Although codices were a great improvement to clay tablets, the discovery of papermaking in China during the first century made the writing and dissemination of ideas on a larger scale more feasible.

Though paper was being made throughout Europe by the thirteenth century, all manuscripts were still being handwritten. This was a time-consuming process, and the availability of books was limited to the monasteries where the books were written. Around 1450, however, Johannes Gutenberg's invention of movable type changed the production of books forever. The Chinese and Koreans had used wood-block type as early as 1041 AD, but Gutenberg invented a type mold that made

printing from individual pieces of metal type practical for the first time. See **Figure 8-1.** Gutenberg's invention ensured an adequate supply of uniformly cast characters that would last through numerous printings. His typeface was designed to imitate the handwritten characters people of the time expected to see. See **Figure 8-2.** For the next 400 years,

Figure 8-1. Gutenberg's fifteenth-century invention of carrying raised letters on individual blocks of metal made the first information technology possible. This technology was dominant for over 300 years.

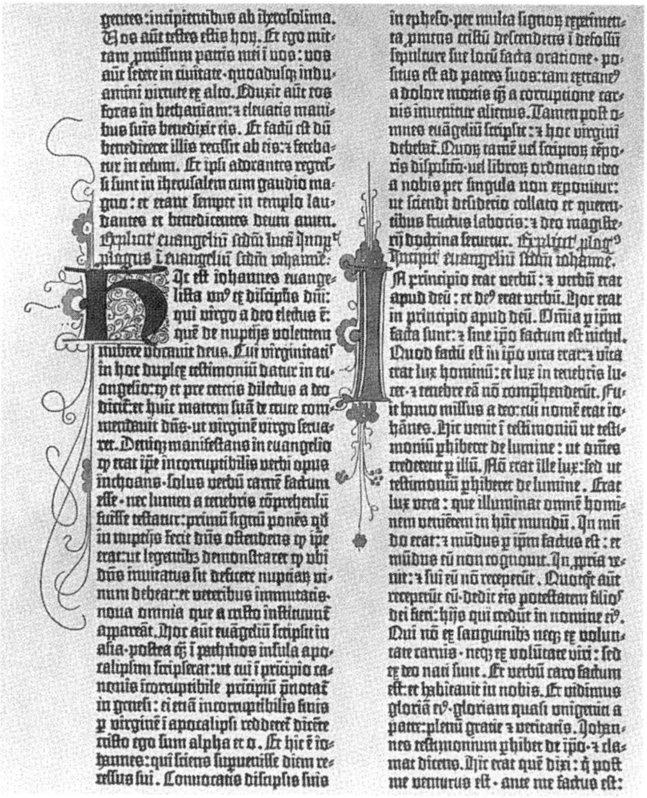

Figure 8-2. Gutenberg's invention of movable type made the printing of a great quantity of books possible. This page is from Gutenberg's 42-line Bible and demonstrates that the first books were designed to look similar to the handwritten manuscripts people were accustomed to.

hand-set metal type was the only method for publishing. His invention created the original medium of mass communication.

Type Composition

Gutenberg used molten metal to form the pieces of type, hence the term *hot-type composition*. Hot type was composed first by hand and then by machines, such as Ottmar Mergenthaler's automated Linotype™ machine. See **Figure 8-3**. The Linotype machine was lightning fast in comparison with hand-set type because it is operated with a *keyboard*, and it is still considered one of the world's 10 greatest inventions. Linotype machines dominated until the 1960s. Today, the various methods of type composition are referred to as *cold-type composition*. **Cold-type composition**, or two-dimensional type, refers to all typesetting that does not use molten metal to cast

images. This composition involves the production of images on paper or film and uses such methods as hand composition, photocomposition, and electronic composition.

Hand Composition

Before desktop publishing, **hand composition** of display type involved techniques such as pressure-sensitive type, which consists of wrong-reading characters printed on the back of translucent plastic sheets. Individual letters are transferred to a surface by aligning them and pressing against the top of the plastic sheet. See **Figure 8-4**.

Photocomposition

In text composition, photocomposition, or **phototypesetting**, is the setting of type by exposing letters onto photographic paper or film and then

Figure 8-3. Beginning in 1886, Linotype machines automated the process by casting lines of raised type called *slugs*. Linotype machines were much faster than hand-set type and allowed larger amounts of type to be set inexpensively.

composition: the production and organization of all images and type to be placed in a layout.

conventional prepress: preparing images for platemaking without using electronic software.

codex: a wax tablet framed and backed with wood and joined with cords on which the Greeks and Romans wrote.

hot-type composition: a typesetting method in which molten metal is used to form pieces of type.

keyboard: a computer input device based on the original typewriter keyboard arrangement.

cold-type composition: all typesetting that does not use molten metal to cast images.

hand composition: a typesetting method that creates images by using preprinted type and lettering machines.

phototypesetting: the setting of type or the preparation of copy for printing using photographic paper or film.

1—Remove protective blue backing sheet and place lettering sheet over a predrawn guideline. Letters transfer most easily when a burnisher is used. Position lines under letters on your predrawn guideline. This ensures both vertical and horizontal alignment.

2—Transfer letter by rubbing lightly with burnisher. Work diagonally from the top left of the letter to the bottom right. The letter will appear to turn gray as it transfers.

Figure 8-4. The sheet of pressure-sensitive type is positioned over the receiving surface, and the letter is rubbed. Burnishing makes the transferred image adhere properly to the base. (Letraset, Inc.)

developing the material. Photochemical methods were first used in the 1960s and were a great improvement over the hot-type machines such as the Linotype. Photocomposition methods were widely used for over 30 years, but they saw rapid displacement by digital imaging in the early 1990s.

By carrying the letters on a strip of film and projecting them onto paper, the operator can enlarge or reduce the typeface without changing the filmstrip. See **Figure 8-5.** A change in typestyle, however, probably requires a different filmstrip. In a later development, laser light formed individual characters that were projected onto the photographic paper or film. See **Figure 8-6.** This technology is not to be confused with laser printers used today.

Each advancement in cold-type composition allowed type to be set at faster speeds. The commonality among these advancements was that their output was images exposed to photosensitive paper that needed to be chemically processed. Afterward, these strips of paper, called *galleys*, needed to be pasted up to form the mechanical.

Electronic Composition

Electronic composition uses computer software to generate and compose text and graphic images. This type of composition has practically eliminated the need for hand composition methods. Most manuscripts are typed in word processing or desktop-publishing software. Continuous tone and line

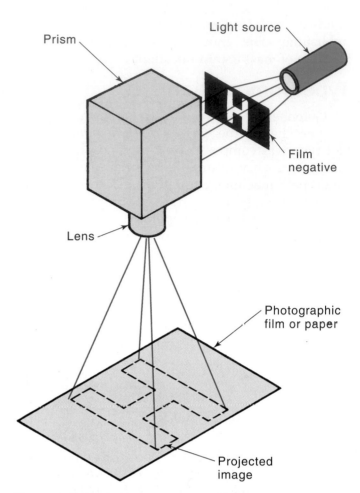

Figure 8-5. In projection phototypesetting, light is projected through a filmstrip or disk and onto light-sensitive paper, which is then developed similarly to any other photopaper.

art can be created on-screen, photographed with a digital camera, or captured with a scanner. Software also allows the user to easily correct and manipulate text and images. After a file is built, it can be sent to the printer on diskettes or CDs or transmitted digitally. The following sections explain computer basics, components, and programs used in electronic composition. A more detailed explanation of the electronic prepress processes is given in Chapter 13.

Computer basics

A computer is an electronic device that, by means of stored instructions and information, performs complex computing tasks. The information and instructions are stored in digital form using a **binary system** in which all data consists of only two numbers, or digits: *1*s and *0*s. The computer actually recognizes two states, rather than numbers: on and off (the presence or absence of an electrical charge). The number *1* is used to represent an on state, and *0* represents off.

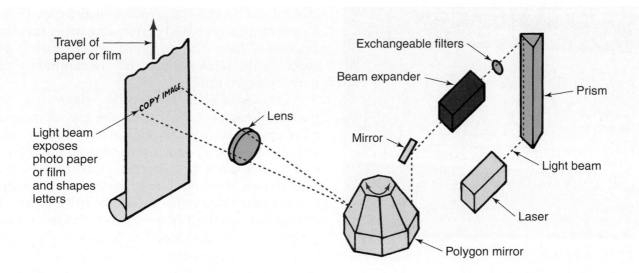

Figure 8-6. One type of phototypesetting system uses a laser beam to directly "write" an image onto the photographic paper or film.

The individual *1*s and *0*s are called *bits*, which is an abbreviation for *binary digits*. Bits are combined into groups of eight digits, or *bytes*. There are 256 possible combinations of *1* and *0* in an eight-digit byte (such as *11111111* or *00000000*). A *kilobyte (KB)* equals about a thousand (1024) bytes. A *megabyte (MB)* equals about a million (1,048,576) bytes. A *gigabyte (GB)* equals 1024 MB, or about a billion bytes.

A special code called the *American Standard Code for Information Interchange (ASCII)* was devised to assign a specific meaning to each combination of *1*s and *0*s in an eight-digit byte. ASCII provides a way to digitally store and process letters, numbers, punctuation marks, and symbols. When the letter *J* is pressed on a keyboard, for example, it is converted to a specific combination of *1*s and *0*s. Different combinations are assigned for the capital and lowercase forms of each letter. Once it is in digital form, the information can be processed in the computer's circuits and stored as electrical or magnetic charges.

Computer components

All computers, from the smallest laptop to the largest mainframe, require a means of inputting, processing, storing, and outputting information. The devices used to perform these functions might vary from system to system. The different methods and devices used for input, processing, storage, and output are described in the following sections.

Input devices

Text and graphics information can be acquired in a number of ways. Input devices can use manual or electronic methods to acquire data. Some of the most common input devices include the keyboard, mouse, digitizing tablet, touch pad, trackball, video digitizer, modem, scanner, and digital camera.

A keyboard is the most common device used to input data into the computer. Most computer keyboards are based on the standard-typewriter, QWERTY-keyboard layout. See **Figure 8-7**. The characters *Q, W, E, R, T,* and *Y* are in a row near the top-left corner. Most computer keyboards have a separate numeric keypad resembling the keypad of a simple calculator. The keypad's clustering of keys allows faster input than the number keys on the top row of the keyboard do.

There are a number of keys on a computer that are not found on typewriters. For example, there is usually a delete key to remove characters or graphic images. The cursor keys on the keyboard allow you to move the cursor on the monitor. A cursor is used to indicate on the screen where information is being

binary system: a mathematical system based on two numbers (*1*s and *0*s) and used by computers.

byte: a group of eight digits, or bits.

kilobyte (KB): about one thousand (1024) bytes.

megabyte (MB): about one million (1,048,576) bytes.

gigabyte (GB): one billion bytes.

American Standard Code for Information Interchange (ASCII): an industry-standard code representing text (letters, numbers, punctuation, and sets of basic commands) but not style attributes (bold, italic, and underlined).

Figure 8-7. A computer keyboard closely resembles the keyboard on a standard typewriter.

placed. The cursor can be moved up, down, left, or right using the cursor keys.

A mouse is a small, rolling input device used in conjunction with the keyboard. When a mouse is moved on the work surface, the movement sensors output electrical signals to the computer that move the cursor on the monitor. The buttons on the top of the mouse allow data manipulation. Computer mice are available in a variety of designs, including those ergonomically designed to fit left-handed people. These mice are sloped at an angle so it feels more natural clicking with the index finger of the left hand.

A *graphics tablet*, or digitizing tablet, is an electronic pen and "paper." The tablet is an electronic drawing board on which a stylus can be moved. The stylus is usually a mouselike pointing device or a pen-type device. The movements of the stylus on the pad are recorded and stored electronically. Graphic tablets vary in their pressure sensitivity and their susceptibility to interference by metal desks or nearby metal objects.

Similar to a digitizing tablet, a *touch pad* controls the position of the cursor when a fingertip is moved over a pressure-sensitive pad. The pad registers the direction of the movement and transmits this information as electrical signals to the computer, which converts the information to digital information that moves the cursor correspondingly. An accompanying button usually allows the touch pad to function identically to a mouse. Touch pads are often found on laptop computers.

A *trackball* is a mounted, movable ball that can be rotated to move and position the cursor. This ball is likened to an upside-down mouse—because the mouse also uses a rotatable ball—except the trackball rotates in a stationary base and does not move

around a surface. A trackball might also have buttons for selecting objects and performing other functions. Trackballs have the advantage of requiring little space on the work surface and are commonly used with laptop computers.

A *video digitizer* works in conjunction with the small cameras that sit on the top of computer monitors by converting analog (continuous) video signals into digital data. Conventional video frames can be converted to computer graphics, which are then shown at a high rate of speed on the computer's monitor to give the illusion of full motion. The QuickTime® application program is a video software program Apple developed to be used to play back compressed video images on a standard Macintosh computer. Video for Windows is the Microsoft version of the QuickTime program that allows compressed video images to be played on desktop computers running the Microsoft Windows operating system.

The term *modem*, an abbreviation for *modulator/demodulator*, refers to an electronic device that converts (modulates) digital computer data into a form that can be transmitted along telephone lines. A modem receives these transmitted signals from over the phone line and converts (demodulates) them back to digital data. This device also controls the speed at which data is transmitted.

Scanners are electronic devices that measure color densities of an original image, store those measurements as digital information, manipulate or alter the data, and use the manipulated data to create four-color separations. See **Figure 8-8.** A scanner's imaging quality depends on many variables, including the dynamic range, resolution, quality of optics, light source used, number of bits per color, and aperture. Differences in these variables explain why the sharpness of any given resolution varies from one scanner to another.

Depending on the type of scanner, almost any type or size of original can be scanned, including film negatives or transparencies, photographic prints, printed media, drawings, graphs, and text. Scanners do not distinguish text from illustrations. They represent all images as bitmaps. Therefore, scanned text cannot be edited without OCR software to translate the image into ASCII characters. Scanners are discussed in Chapter 13.

Digital cameras function in much the same way as conventional cameras, except digital cameras capture and store the visual images as digital data. These cameras are available in a variety of styles and sizes. Many are similar in appearance to the familiar 35 mm camera or the conventional studio

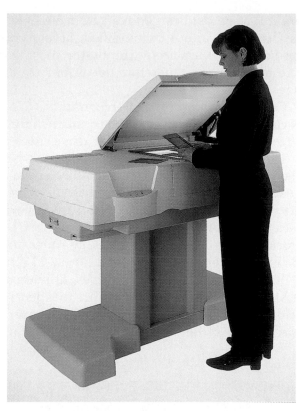

Figure 8-8. Scanners have been designed to capture all types of media, including film negatives and positives, photographic prints, printed media, drawings, graphs, and text. (Fuji Photo Film USA, Inc.)

Figure 8-9. Digital cameras can be very small or larger with more resolution, increased optical zoom, or greater storage capability. When they are hardwired to the computer, or when their removable storage disk is plugged into the computer, digital cameras become input devices.

camera. See **Figure 8-9.** The photographer can choose a digital camera or camera back (for attachment to a conventional camera) from an ever-increasing number of designs. Once the pictures have been taken, the images are stored within the camera, stored on an external disk, or directly downloaded from the camera to a computer. From the computer, the images can be analyzed, manipulated, imported into a layout, or output to a printer.

Storage devices

Computer systems come with a certain amount of physical memory, usually referred to as *main memory*, or *random-access memory (RAM)*. RAM is the short-term memory the computer uses to store information in process. Systems can be updated, and memory capabilities can be increased, to support additional programs. Besides being capable of running programs, a computer must have some means for storing and transmitting data.

The term *memory* identifies data storage that comes in the form of chips, while the word *storage* is used for memory that exists on tapes or disks. Although compression methods can be used to reduce file size, most page composition files remain very large. Fortunately, there are many types of storage devices available that accommodate large files. Storage devices vary in size (physical and memory), access capabilities, speed, reusability, and integrity. Storage capacity is measured in KB, MB, and GB. The computer system and type of files being used determine the necessary capacity and means of storage.

graphics tablet: an input device by which pictographic data can be manually entered into a computer in a way comparable to drawing.

touch pad: an input device typically found on laptop computers to move the cursor by sliding a fingertip across the surface of the pad.

trackball: a mounted, movable ball that can be rotated to move and position the cursor on a computer screen.

video digitizer: a component that converts analog video signals into digital data.

modem: an electronic device that converts digital computer data into a form that can be transmitted along telephone lines. A modem also receives transmitted signals from over the phone line and converts them back to digital data.

scanner: an electronic imaging device that measures color densities of an original, stores those measurements as digital information, manipulates or alters the data, and uses the manipulated data to create color separations.

digital camera: a camera that uses arrays of photosites to convert light into electrical signals and then into digital data.

random-access memory (RAM): the short-term memory a computer uses to store information in process.

memory: computer data storage that comes in the form of chips.

A *disk* is a round plate on which data can be encoded, and there are two basic types: magnetic and optical. Magnetic disks store data as videotape does. Data are encoded as microscopic magnetized needles on the disk's surface. These data can be recorded and erased on a magnetic disk any number of times. Magnetic disks come in a number of different forms, including hard and floppy.

The *hard disk drive (hard drive)* is a machine that reads data from and writes data to a hard disk. Hard drives are usually built into the computer system. See **Figure 8-10.** The hard drive contains one or more permanent aluminum hard disks coated with a magnetic material. The aluminum disks are rotated very quickly, and a read-and-write head moves over the disk surface, which contains densely packed magnetic tracks. The read-and-write head is used to read (retrieve) or write (record) information as the magnetic tracks spin past the head.

Caution

Hard disks store data as magnetic pulses, and stray magnetic fields from heavy motors or other equipment can erase data, as can static electricity. Vibrations or particles of smoke or dust can also cause the heads to bounce or crash into the media and scramble the data. Use proper storage habits to maintain data integrity.

Unlike hard disks, which use electromagnetism to encode data, optical disk drives use a laser to read and write data. These disks come in three forms: CD-ROM; write once, read many (WORM); and erasable optical (EO). CD-ROMs are read-only disks. See

Figure 8-11. The data can be read from a CD-ROM, but a CD-ROM cannot be modified, be erased, or accept new data. CDs are currently the most stable storage medium and, therefore, ideal for long-term storage.

WORM, or *compact disc–recordable (CD-R)*, disks can be written once and then read any number of times. You need a special disk drive, however, to write data onto a WORM disk. This type of media storage is inexpensive and reliable. Due to the inability of these disks to be edited, however, a number of disks will need to be disposed of when they are used for backup of works in progress.

Pocket CDs are miniature CDs, measuring 3 1/8" in diameter. See **Figure 8-12.** These CDs hold 210 MB of data, sit in most CD drives, fit into some Sony Mavica® digital cameras, and are inexpensive.

Although *digital videodiscs (DVDs)* are the same size as CDs, they can hold up to 4.7 GB of data.

Figure 8-11. CDs are ideal for long-term storage because they are a very stable storage medium.

Figure 8-10. The hard drive contains one or more permanent aluminum hard disks coated with a magnetic material. This system includes a Redundant Array of Independent Disks (RAID) configuration and a CD drive.

Figure 8-12. A pocket CD is a smaller version of the standard CD.

These disks are most useful in storing huge files, such as a motion picture. DVDs require a DVD driver, but a DVD driver can also read CDs.

Photographers using digital cameras use a removable storage device known as a *Personal Computer Memory Card International Association (PCMCIA) card*. PCMCIA cards, or PC cards, were originally designed for adding memory to portable computers. The PCMCIA standard has been expanded several times, and the cards are now suitable for use with many types of devices, including digital cameras and scanners.

Removable Universal Serial Bus (USB) storage devices include the flash drive, ThumbDrive™ device, jump drive, and USB drive. These solid-state storage devices are very small and plug into a computer's USB port. The flash drive and ThumbDrive device are available in a wide range of data capacities. The jump drive serves as a reader for Memory Stick® media, multimedia, or other memory cards commonly used with digital cameras. All three of these removable hard drives have exceptional capacities for their tiny size, which can be compared with a car key or one-third of a carpenter's pencil. In addition, these drives work with both PC and Macintosh operating systems.

Many printers and service bureaus use a *jukebox* to store and access the information they keep on hundreds of CDs and magneto-optical (MO) media. CD and MO jukeboxes function in much the same way as music jukeboxes. These jukeboxes can be used to organize image files, text files, or files of textbook and magazine pages.

Caution

Whether sending files to the service bureau on disk or through a modem, backup copies should always be made as a precaution. Files should be backed up on a regular basis.

Power supply

Once a system is installed and running, the power supply is often forgotten. When the electrical power supply is disrupted, however, the digital work flow grinds to a halt. When computers lose power without warning, hours of work can be lost. In addition, no work can be done until power is restored. An uninterruptible power supply (UPS) will save time and prevent work-flow interruptions during power drops and blackouts.

Desktop computers can use a small battery supply that keeps the system running for at least five minutes in the event of a power loss. The battery supply gives users enough time to save their work and shut their

computers down properly. Some UPS systems also protect the computer from power surges more effectively than power strips. Larger systems using a server should have both a battery backup and a generator. The battery should supply enough power to keep the system running until the generator starts.

Word processing software

Word processing software is used for electronic typesetting. The text of a document is input and formatted through the use of a computer keyboard. After text files are created in a word processing program, they can be imported into a page composition program, where the type can be integrated with photographs and other art.

Text can also be input by scanning lines of type with OCR software, which will convert each letter to ASCII code. Although this conversion will cause the format codes, such as boldface and italics, to be lost, the sequence of letters and punctuation will be saved just as if they had been keyboarded. Type scanned with OCR software can be edited and formatted with word processing software. Type scanned without OCR software, however, is merely captured as line images and cannot be altered later.

Control methodologies

Setting type with a word processing program is similar to using a typewriter's keyboard. The ability to change the type's face, style, weight, and stress; edit type; and save the type as a text file, however, greatly enhances the capability of the typist. Understandably, the freedom to control these typographic features requires a more sophisticated range of options and terminology for the typesetter to understand than is required to use a typewriter.

disk: a round flat plate on which information for a computer is stored.

hard disk drive (hard drive): a device that reads data from and writes data to a hard disk. These drives are usually built into the computer system. A hard drive contains one or more permanent aluminum, hard disks coated with a magnetic material.

compact disc–recordable (CD-R): a computer storage disk that can be written to once and then read any number of times.

pocket CD: a compact disc that is 3 1/8″ in diameter, in contrast to a larger CD, which is 4 5/8″ in diameter.

digital videodisc (DVD): a very high-capacity optical storage disk that is the same size as a CD but can hold six times as much data.

jukebox: a device used to store and access information from a collection of electronic storage devices, such as CDs, MOs, and DVDs.

word processing software: a computer application for creating and editing text in various typestyles, sizes, and formats.

Control over the appearance of the type is achieved through selecting from several options displayed in various locations, including the menu bar, the tool bar, scroll bars, and menus. See **Figure 8-13.** The typesetter accesses these options by navigating through these locations with the mouse and clicking on the appropriate icon (symbol). In addition to navigating through these locations with the mouse, the typesetter can make selections from the keyboard with keyboard commands by holding down both the control key and another key. See **Figure 8-14.** The ruler appearing beneath the tool bars can be used to establish the column width for the text block and also set the tab stops, which will control how far the first line of paragraphs will be indented and set the tabs for tables or other text matter requiring tabbing. See **Figure 8-15.** Indentation and other paragraph specs can also be made by clicking on the appropriate menu bar item and then selecting the appropriate dialog box, which is a window displayed to solicit a response from the typesetter. See **Figure 8-16.**

Figure 8-13. The menu bar, tool bar, and scroll bars are features of all word processing software screens.

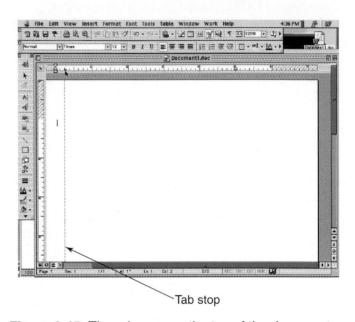

Figure 8-15. The ruler across the top of the document window can be used for setting tabs and paragraph indentation.

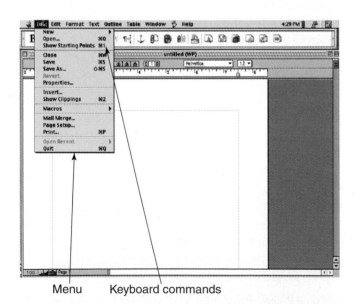

Figure 8-14. Commands can be executed by using the mouse to open a menu and highlighting the command or by using the keyboard commands shown on the right side of the menu.

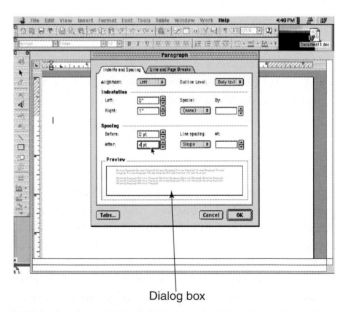

Figure 8-16. A dialog box provides the means to input specs or other commands with the keyboard. In this example, four points of spacing are being placed after each paragraph.

Creating text files

To demonstrate some of the basic functions of word processing software, the text type for a promotional folder will be set. These text blocks and other art will then be assembled to create a mechanical in Chapter 9. As is the custom in typesetting, the typesetter will follow the graphic designer's *type specifications (specs)*, the markings on the manuscript communicating how the type is to appear (such as size, style, and format). See **Figure 8-17**. Unfortunately, the term *font* is used in word processing software to denote the typeface. As was explained in Chapter 6, the term *font* refers to a typeface in a particular size. In word processing software, the typeface and size are selected separately, so the term *font* is used in error. See **Figure 8-18**. Page margins will already be set to a default value, but the size of page margins can be changed by accessing the proper dialog box for the software being used.

A necessary step in typesetting is text formatting—the assigning of the typeface, weight (regular or bold), stress (Roman or italic), and other options, such as underlining. The type format (flush left, flush right, justified, or centered) also can be selected from a dialog box or the tool bar. Following the manuscript's type specs, the correct typeface (under the font heading) and size are assigned—in this example, 12-point Helvetica, set flush left. See **Figure 8-19**. After these lines have been set, the headings are highlighted individually and set in boldface. Changes in type size can also be made. Other text blocks within the manuscript are typeset as specified. Other typefaces and sizes are used. Some lines are centered, and others are set flush right. See **Figure 8-20**.

Some word processing programs include a spelling and grammar checker that identifies words that seem to be misspelled and phrases that seem to be in error. See **Figure 8-21**. Not all perceived grammatical and spelling errors are actually wrong, and many typing errors are not caught. In short, the spelling and grammar checker feature is no substitute for proofreading.

A mistaken editing command or other error can be remedied if the undo icon is selected immediately after the error is made. Many changes can be made to the galley by using the edit feature on the menu bar. The edit feature allows a highlighted letter, word, phrase, sentence, or paragraph to be cut and pasted or copied and pasted elsewhere. The paste command can be used repeatedly to generate several copies of the same text matter.

The find-and-replace feature allows a reoccurring change to be made quickly to a lengthy body of type. For example, if a client decided to substitute *road* with *highway* in a magazine article, the changes could be time-consuming if *road* appears 27 times. With the find-and-replace feature, the word *road* is entered into the find what field, and the word *highway* is entered into the replace with field. The software can then make the replacement throughout the article or highlight each use of the word *road* and give the typesetter the opportunity to make the replacement or move on to the next *road*.

During the typesetting function, type matter should be saved periodically to prevent the loss of material if the computer crashes or loses power. After the galley has been completed, it should be saved as a document. The document should be saved onto the computer's hard drive, a storage disk, or both.

Books, journal articles, reports, and other formal documents often require a rather elaborate hierarchy of headings. When preparing such a document, each text element on the page should be identified by a specific name. For example, this paragraph was formatted, or tagged, as body text in a word processing program. See **Figure 8-22**. Other styles, or tags, used in this textbook are Head 1, Head 2, and Head 3. The text files retain the style names when they are imported into a page composition program. This allows the designer to maintain the hierarchy of heads, text, and captions the author has created.

Text files that have been formatted with a word processing program must be stored and transmitted as binary files to preserve the formatting. If the text file is saved as an ASCII file, all formatting will be lost. The text can, however, still be repurposed. *Repurposing* is reusing content intended for one medium by reformatting it for another. When a word processing program does not recognize a text file, the program might offer the user the option of converting the file to its ASCII format. The formatting will be lost, but the copy will remain usable.

Page Composition

After the type files for a document have been created with a word processing program, the next step is to either output the type to a sheet of paper

type specifications (specs): directions written on rough layout or on a manuscript informing the compositor about alphabet style, series, size, and amount of leading, or space between lines.

repurposing: reusing content intended for one medium by reformatting it for another.

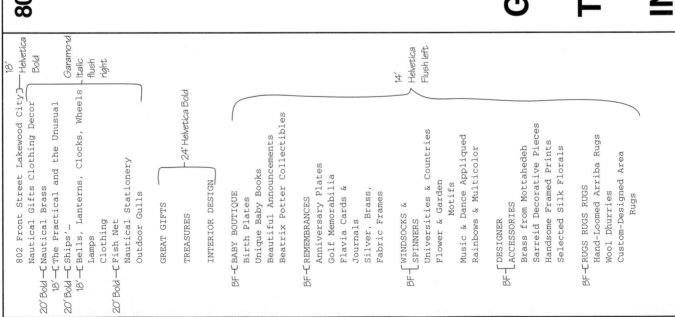

Figure 8-17. The specs on a manuscript reflect the graphic designer's vision for the type and communicate the proper requirements to the typesetter.

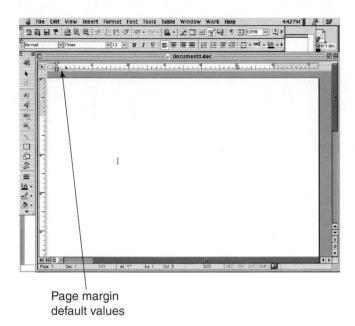

Page margin
default values

Figure 8-18. Setting type usually begins by opening a new document with default settings.

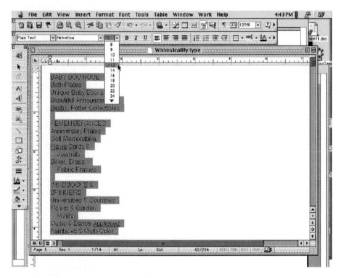

Figure 8-19. Type can be assigned a typestyle, size, and format by being highlighted before a menu selection is made. This type is being set in 12-point Helvetica.

that can be trimmed and pasted up to create camera-ready art or bring this type into a page composition program, such as PageMaker software, the QuarkXPress application, or InDesign software. With both conventional and electronic prepress, the type will be integrated with other page elements,

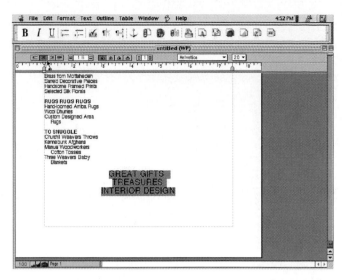

Figure 8-20. Letters and words can be highlighted and then assigned a format. These three lines are being centered.

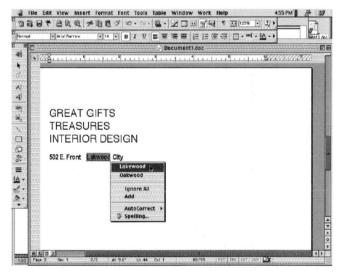

Figure 8-21. Many word processing programs underline misspelled words and can then suggest alternative spellings. Proper nouns and other correctly spelled words not programmed into the software will also be underlined.

such as photographs and illustrations. In subsequent chapters, the text blocks created in this chapter will become part of a two-panel folder. Conventional composition will be demonstrated in Chapter 9, and electronic page composition will be examined in Chapter 15.

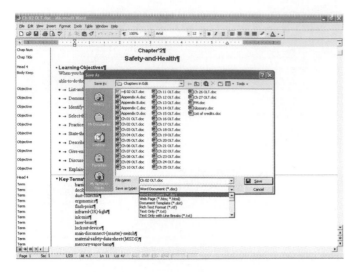

Figure 8-22. When preparing documents with multiple levels of headings, it is possible to establish specs for each heading level and then select the desired level for each heading used.

Summary

Composition is the production and organization of all images and type to be placed in a layout. Although electronic desktop publishing has essentially replaced manual composition methods, these processes are still used for small quantities of display composition or for making changes to manually prepared jobs that need to be reprinted. Electronic computer-imaging processes have become indispensable tools for graphic arts designers and technicians within the prepress area of the printing industry. The use of computers has eliminated production stages and dramatically sped up prepress production by giving workers the freedom to manipulate text matter and all types of graphics with ease and overall control.

Review Questions

Please do not write in this book. Write your answers on a separate sheet of paper.

1. What are the four stages of conventional prepress?

2. What were the main advantages of Gutenberg's invention of movable type?

3. Outline the chronological progress of typographic image–generation technology.

4. _____ composition is any form of typesetting that does not use molten metal to cast images.

5. What method of typesetting creates type images by exposing light-sensitive paper to light?

6. Explain the meaning of the term *binary system*.

7. Define the terms *bit, byte, kilobyte, megabyte,* and *gigabyte.*

8. Identify and describe four types of input devices.

9. What is the complete term for a computer's short-term memory?

10. Summarize the differences between a CD and a CD-R.

11. What is the benefit of converting scanned type to ASCII code?

12. List four input devices used in electronic composition.

13. Describe two methods of setting paragraph indentations with word processing software.

14. Explain the find-and-replace function within word processing software.

15. Summarize the processes of saving a text file to a storage disk in the PC and Macintosh platforms.

16. Distinguish between the capabilities of word processing software and page composition software.

Skill-Building Activities

1. Using the materials available to you, compose a single- or double-page spread with copy and display type, as well as a piece of line copy. Use one of the various hand composition methods first, and then use electronic composition. Compare the time involved, as well as the quality of the finished pieces.

2. With a partner, collect print samples from at least four different types of computer printers. Compare the features, quality of output, and prices of these printers. Prepare a summary report of your findings for the class.

3. In groups of two or three students, determine what types of graphic arts software packages are being used in three or four printing firms in your community. Prepare a summary report of your findings for the class.

4. Select one of the events listed below and
    prepare a 300-word report summarizing its
    effect on graphic communication technologies:
    - Ancient scrolls.
    - Woodblocks.
    - Movable metal type.
    - Linotype machines.
    - Phototypesetters.
    - Word processing software.

Why It's Called
Conventional

Gutenberg's movable type was the basis of printing for over 500 years. By 1970, the practice of assembling lines of metal type had largely given way to computer typesetting and assembling strips of paper carrying the text. Although assembling metal strips is very different from assembling paper strips, both methods require people who are skilled with their hands. This is called *conventional prepress* because, although type is set digitally, the page is assembled manually.

As shown in this photograph, the key to conventional page composition is the proper use of tools, such as the T square and triangle, in placing and aligning type and other images. This chapter will acquaint you with not only the tools and procedures of page composition, but also the principles of good page makeup. People who have learned conventional page composition have an advantage when they later learn digital page composition.

Chapter 9
Conventional Page Composition

Key Terms

bleed
camera-ready art
commercial register
copy preparation
cover flap
dimension line
dummy
hairline register
halftone-block method
halftone-outline method
halftone-positive method
masking film
mechanical
nonregister
one-piece copy
overlay
page composition
screen tint
spot color
template

Learning Objectives

When you have completed the reading and assigned activities related to this chapter, you will be able to do the following:

◆ Position register marks.
◆ Prepare a mechanical using traditional composition methods.
◆ Distinguish among the classes of registration.
◆ Explain the circumstances when each of the methods of handling halftones is appropriate.
◆ Compare spot color and process color.

Text files are first generated with word processing software. Afterward, the type might need to be integrated with photographic or other art before the document is complete. Assembling all these elements, or components, is referred to as *page composition*, or *page layout*.

Historically, there have been three eras of page composition. From the invention of movable type around 1450 through the first half of the twentieth century, the hot-type method of page composition prevailed. Hot-type composition consists of positioning raised metal type with wood blocks or metal plates that carry the raised images of line art or photographs.

By 1970, hot type largely had given way to cold type, in which type, line, and photographs are generated onto sheets of paper that can be trimmed, carefully positioned, and adhered to a large piece of paper to produce a mechanical, or pasteup. The completed mechanical is then photographed to produce a photographic negative, which is stripped into position and used to expose a plate. This system of photographing a mechanical is referred to today as *conventional prepress*.

By 1995, the cold-type era generally had been replaced with the digital (or electronic) era. Digital page composition creates or combines type, line art, and photographic images consisting of binary code. After all elements have been generated and assembled, this binary code can be sent to one of several output devices that can generate a proof, a sheet of film that can expose a plate, or the actual plate itself.

Although most prepress work is performed digitally today, conventional prepress still exists. Some printing companies are equipped with both conventional and digital prepress systems because their customers bring in both types of images. See **Figure 9-1.** In many instances, conventional page assembly actually can be faster than preparing the same document with page composition software, and conventional prepress can serve as a backup system when the digital network becomes dysfunctional. Page composition systems were created to parallel many of the steps in conventional prepress. Therefore, an awareness of conventional prepress is a useful preparation for learning digital prepress.

Once the manuscript and images have been created, they must be assembled in accordance with the designer's dummy. **Copy preparation** is the procedure of placing and adhering images onto a heavy sheet of paper to form **camera-ready art**, which later is photographed to produce films used to create the plate. The copy-preparation function is commonly known as *pasteup*.

Most type and related visual elements are now assembled electronically. Some situations, however, require hand assembly of type, borders, and artwork. The page elements are assembled on an art board to

Figure 9-1. Customers can bring in the job as either conventional mechanical art or a digital file.

produce a **mechanical**. See **Figure 9-2.** When manually preparing copy, remember that the final printed product will be only as good as the accuracy and quality of the mechanical. Cleanliness and sharp mechanical image elements are essential for high-quality printing. For preparing a mechanical, a good work surface and several tools and accessories are required. The most common pasteup tools are triangles, scissors, art knives, rulers, tweezers, burnishers, nonreproducing blue-ink pens, black-ink pens, T squares, erasers, tape, compasses, and dividers.

Figure 9-2. A completed mechanical contains all line copy, provisions for halftone copy, register marks, fold marks, trim marks, and instructions.

The Basics of Copy Preparation

A light table or drawing board is used as a work surface. The working edge of the table or drawing board must be straight. The *base sheet* on which the page elements will be placed should be a heavy sheet of coated paper, cut approximately 2–3" (50–75 mm) larger on all four sides than the finished size of the printed piece being pasted up, thereby providing enough space for marginal information, corner marks, center marks, and register marks.

Aligning and Squaring the Base Sheet and Dummy

The copy-preparation artist works from a dummy, which the customer or graphic designer supplies. The *dummy* is a piece of paper indicating the placement of each page element and also carrying instructions regarding ink colors, reverses, overprints, and screen tints. See **Figure 9-3**. Although a dummy might be very informal in its appearance, it should

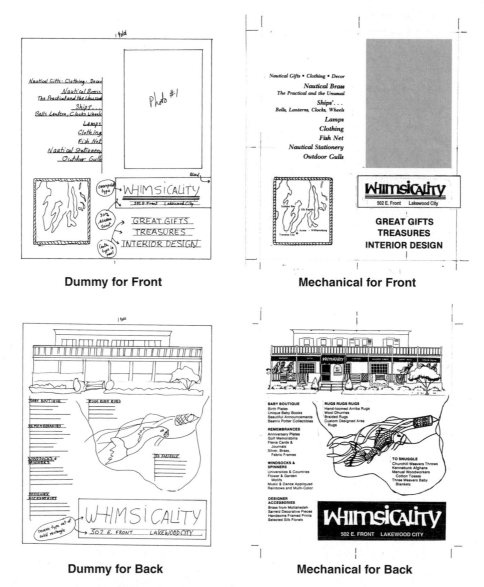

Dummy for Front

Mechanical for Front

Dummy for Back

Mechanical for Back

Figure 9-3. The dummy is prepared by the graphic designer and serves as the blueprint for preparing the mechanical. These mechanicals are for the two sides of a folder.

page composition (copy preparation): the process of properly arranging the various elements, or components of a page, (such as type and illustrations) that make up a printed page.

camera-ready art: copy that has been prepared for exposure in the camera, in preparation for platemaking.

mechanical: the camera-ready page elements assembled on an art board. A mechanical is the paperboard on which camera-ready page elements are mounted.

dummy: a folded sheet of paper representing the finished job.

be exact and thorough concerning the job's specs. The first steps in beginning a mechanical are to find and mark the center of both the dummy and the base sheet with nonphoto blue ink and place the two sheets next to one another because the dummy holds the key to what the customer wants. The centers are then aligned, and a horizontal border of the dummy and the top or bottom edge of the base sheet are squared with a T square before the sheets are taped at the top and bottom. See **Figure 9-4.** This pattern of taping allows type galleys to be slipped under either sheet to preview how well the set type fits the area allocated for it.

Laying in Guidelines

Guidelines on the base sheet indicate the job's dimensions, columns, and margins and where page elements are to be placed. These lines are drawn in nonreproducing blue so they will not show up on the negative or printing plate. The film used to photograph the mechanical is not sensitive to cyan light. See **Figure 9-5.** Horizontal guidelines are made with a T square, and vertical guidelines are made with a T square and triangle combination.

These guidelines should include vertical and horizontal centerlines, as well as fold marks, dimension lines, or borders to be created. **Dimension lines** define the finished size of the job. Guidelines also can indicate where to place elements needing to be aligned. Images extending beyond the edge of the final printed page are called **bleeds**, and bleed lines are drawn in nonreproducing blue, 1/8″ outside the dimension lines, to provide a target for any elements that must bleed.

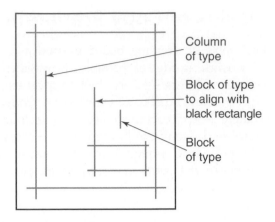

Figure 9-5. Examination of the dummy reveals where guidelines should be drawn to help place page elements needing to be aligned with one or more other elements. The nonreproducing blue guidelines on this base sheet derive from the dummy in Figure 9-4.

Inking Black Lines and Borders

After guidelines are in place, they are used to indicate the placement of trim marks, fold marks, rules, or any borders to be inked with a black-ink pen. See **Figure 9-6.** All inking should be made before any type galleys are placed onto the base sheet because the wax or other adhesive can cause the ink to skip.

Positioning and Adhering Page Elements

In most instances, body and display copy comes on sheets of paper called *galleys*. Line illustrations are provided as inked drawings. A uniform layer of

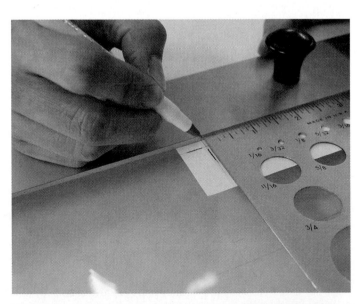

Figure 9-6. Corner marks, borders, and all other inked images are placed onto the base sheet before any waxed elements are. In this photograph, the corner marks are inked over the light-blue dimension lines.

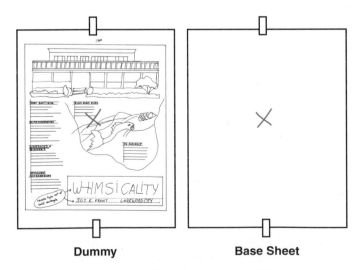

Dummy   **Base Sheet**

Figure 9-4. The center of the design and the center of the base sheet are marked, and the two sheets are positioned alongside one another with the centers aligned.

wax is applied to the back of these sheets, and they are placed onto a sheet of paperboard called a *cutting board*. See **Figure 9-7.** Starting with the images on the top of the design, each page element is individually trimmed out of its galley and positioned onto the base sheet. The T square is placed on the appropriate image of the dummy so it indicates the placement of that page element on the base sheet. See **Figure 9-8.** After the page element has been positioned and squared, it is burnished—that is, pressure is applied to greatly increase adhesion to the base sheet.

Handling Halftones

In order for the middle tones of halftone copy to be reproduced in print, they must be broken into a pattern of fine dots of various sizes, called *halftones*. To ensure this separate treatment, original photographs are not placed on the mechanical. Instead, one of three methods is commonly used to handle halftone copy—the halftone-block, halftone-outline, or halftone-positive method.

In the ***halftone-block method***, black or red masking material made of paper or plastic is placed onto the mechanical where halftone copy is to be printed. See **Figure 9-9.** The material is cut to the size of the halftone art and adhered with wax or rubber

Figure 9-8. The T square is used to ensure that each element is placed onto the base sheet in line with the art on the dummy.

cement to the base sheet. Separate negatives are made of the mechanical (which is line copy) and halftone copy. The masking material on the base sheet becomes a transparent window in the line negative when it is photographed and processed. The halftone negative of the continuous-tone copy is then taped behind the clear window of the line negative. This method also requires line and halftone images to be converted to films and assembled, before a proof showing both can be made for the client.

In the ***halftone-outline method***, the copy-prep artist inks a border on the base sheet to define the size and placement of a photograph or other halftone art. The mechanical is then photographed to produce a line negative. Using the border as a guide, the stripper then cuts out an area of the film to produce a window for the halftone negative.

The ***halftone-positive method*** (or screened print) begins with the preparation of a halftone-positive print from the original continuous tone copy. The halftone-positive print looks similar to the

Figure 9-7. Wax is applied to the back of each galley. In the lower right of this photograph, an already-waxed galley sits on its cutting board.

dimension line: a line drawn in nonphoto blue indicating where type, art, or any other page element is to be placed on a mechanical.

bleed: a printed image extending to the trim edge of a sheet or page.

halftone-block method: the method that uses masking film or black construction paper to indicate the position of photographs on the pasteup base material.

halftone-outline method: a method used to locate the position of photographs on the pasteup base material.

halftone-positive method: a technique for integrating line and halftone copy onto a mechanical during page composition.

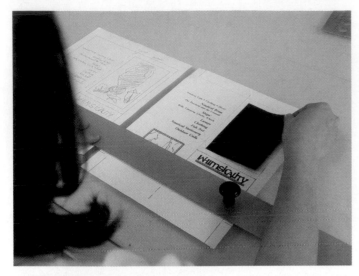

Figure 9-9. A black area cut to the reproduction size of the halftone will create a clear area on the line negative that will hold the halftone negative.

original continuous-tone art, but it has been converted into thousands of halftone dots simulating the grays of the original. See **Figure 9-10.** Any halftone positives are positioned and adhered to the base sheet, and the entire mechanical is photographed as line copy because halftone positives—similar to type—are composed entirely of black and white. Using halftone positives allows the client to see both type and photographs in place on the mechanical, instead of having to wait until a proof is made from films that were made from photographing the mechanical. Halftone positives must be made with comparatively coarse screens, however, which means the halftone dots might be visible to the reader. When finer

screening is required, one of the other two methods is used. The process of converting continuous-tone art to halftone dots is covered in detail in Chapter 11.

Creating Overlays

The simplest kind of mechanical prepared for multicolor printing involves a design in which images in different colors do not overlay or otherwise touch—for example, a design in which the body-type print is to be printed in blue ink and the display type is to be printed in red ink. All the type and other line art can be placed onto the base sheet because the red and blue images do not touch. The film negative resulting from photographing the mechanical can still generate two separate plates by a masking procedure described in Chapter 12.

When the design calls for images in the two colors to touch, however, either the red or blue images need to be placed in register on an overlay. The *overlay* is a transparent sheet attached at the top of the base sheet that carries elements requiring separate treatment from other elements on the mechanical. See **Figure 9-11.** Overlays are required when elements requiring separate treatment are in contact with other elements. Examples include elements in different colors touching one another, type overprinted on a screen tint, or type reversed out of a dark background. *Masking film,* a material with a clear plastic base and a thinner red or amber-colored emulsion layer, is usually used to make overlays. Areas intended to print are created where the emulsion layer is left intact on the clear base. Type

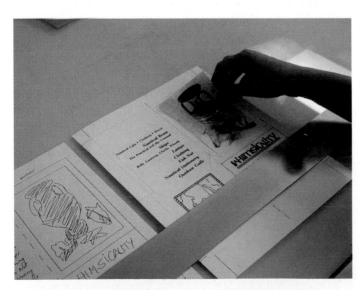

Figure 9-10. A halftone positive can be prepared and positioned onto the base sheet if a fine screen value is not needed.

Figure 9-11. Images that require separate treatment and touch other images must be carried on an overlay. In this photograph, the three red vertical stripes on the transparent overlay will be printed in a second color, and the logo will be reversed from the dark background.

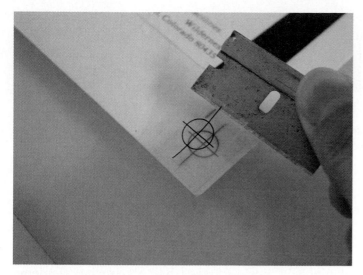

Figure 9-12. An overlay requires register marks to be placed on diagonal corners of the base sheet and overlay. When positioned properly, it will appear as if there is only one register mark.

and other art can be adhered to the clear base after the emulsion layer has been removed.

Placing Register Marks

When using masking film, a piece the same size as the base sheet should be cut. The film is attached to the base sheet at the top with a single piece of masking tape, with the emulsion (dull side) facing upward. The design area is then outlined with an art knife, and the unwanted or nonimage areas of film are removed. *Register marks* are placed in two diagonal corners of the base sheet. The overlay is lowered over the base sheet, and the register marks are then positioned precisely over the register marks on the base sheet. See **Figure 9-12.**

After both the base sheet and overlay have been completed, they are photographed separately. The two pieces of resulting film are then used to expose different plates. For example, a two-color job requiring an overlay generates two negatives—one of the base sheet's images and one of the overlay's images. Each piece of film will be prepared and used to expose a separate plate. The register marks will help the press operator know when images from both plates are precisely in place.

The three categories of register in common use are commercial register, hairline register, and nonregister. The use of *commercial register* allows for variations in overlapping or adjacent colors of 1/100″ or one row of dots. *Hairline register* requires that no overlap or white space be allowed between the edges of touching elements. The least exacting category is

nonregister, which applies to jobs in which no colors overlap or touch, so no register marks are needed.

One-Piece Copy

As was explained, overlays are not necessary in the preparation of a two-color job if the different colors do not touch. In these instances, the color breaks (separations) can be indicated on a single tissue overlay, a process called *one-piece copy*. In the case of a two-color job, for example, two identical film negatives are made from the mechanical. On the first negative, clear images that are not to print in the first color are masked so they do not transfer to the plate. On the second negative, images on the mechanical that were not masked on the first negative are masked. The result is that each plate carries only images appropriate to it.

Screen Tints

A common design technique is to use screen tints to expand the range of colors from a single ink color. A *screen tint* is a fine screen that creates a pattern of uniform dots simulating a middle tone. See **Figure 9-13.** Screen tints differ from halftone screens because screen tints generate dots of a consistent size. The resulting tone pattern of dots on the finished product is usually also referred to as a *screen tint*.

When a design calls for a screen tint, the mechanical must include a black or red area defining the size and shape of the area to be made up of dots. The dark area on the mechanical will become a clear

overlay: a transparent sheet (similar to acetate) to which second-color image elements are attached. The overlay is attached at the top of the pasteup base.

masking film: a material with a thin ruby- or amber-colored emulsion on a thicker sheet of clear plastic, creating a clear area when a film negative is exposed.

commercial register: an industry standard that does not allow more than 1/100″ of variation between adjacent colors.

hairline register: the register setup in which no overlap or white space is allowed to show where elements touch.

nonregister: the least exacting color registration in which allowance is made for several different colors to be completely independent of each other.

one-piece copy: a mechanical with no overlay.

screen tint: the mechanical or electronic special effect added to certain areas of a layout to add contrast, emphasis, or color or to subdue a background image.

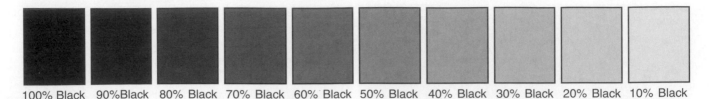

| 100% Black | 90%Black | 80% Black | 70% Black | 60% Black | 50% Black | 40% Black | 30% Black | 20% Black | 10% Black |

Figure 9-13. Screen tints use tiny black and white areas to create the illusion of gray. Examine each value shown above with a magnifying glass to see how increases in the percentage of black produce darker grays. The value is a measurement of the percentage of black.

area on the resulting film negative. When the plate is exposed, light will pass through the clear area of the film and be broken into dots by the screen tint that has been placed between the film and the plate. If the screen tint carries either overprinted or reversed type or art, an overlay will carry either the screen tint area or the other image. See **Figure 9-14.**

Mechanical Cleanliness

All excess wax, rubber cement, eraser residue, and dirt must be removed from the surface of the

Figure 9-14. The screen tint called for in the design goes onto an overlay because type on the base sheet will be overprinted.

mechanical. Unremoved rubber cement is easy to see if the mechanical is held at an angle to the light. This part of cleanup is important because unwanted elements will be photographed along with the image elements. Check to see that all image elements are secure and have not moved. An item-by-item comparison with the dummy will reveal any missing elements.

Keying Illustrations

Before the mechanical is sent to the camera department, it must be prepared for conversion to negative form. Continuous tone photographs provided with the mechanical are marked to designate their locations on the page. For example, the page number and letter might be marked as "1-A," "1-B," and "1-C," for identification. This process is known as *keying*. The halftones are keyed to the mechanical in the exact spaces they will occupy.

Spot Colors

Spot color is an ink color other than black or a color resulting from overprinting the process colors (cyan, magenta, and yellow). A spot color is achieved by mixing inks off press to achieve the desired hue and value, instead of achieving the same hue and value by overlaying the process colors onto the sheet on press. Spot colors are commonly used with black ink to add contrast, create initial interest, highlight important information, and accent line art. If the spot color is being used as a second color (in addition to black), two plates are needed—one for the black and one for the spot color. See **Figure 9-15.** The use of spot color to supplement black ink without the expense of four-color printing was more common prior to the 1990s. In the 1990s, increased reader expectations and the reduced cost of printing full-color publications caused a decrease in the use of two-color printing. Spot colors are increasingly used today to augment the process colors, however, requiring presses that can print five or more colors with a single pass.

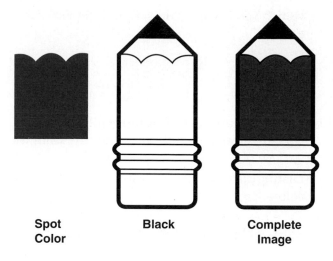

Spot Color **Black** **Complete Image**

Figure 9-15. Images to be printed in a second color that touch images to be printed in the first color must be placed on an overlay. Each image will be carried on a separate plate, and the two images will be printed in register on the press.

Cover Flaps

Mechanicals with complex design features might require a translucent *cover flap* to identify how certain elements are to be handled and carry other instructions. See **Figure 9-16.** Examples of typical cover-flap communications include screen-tint values, elements to be reversed or overprinted, elements to be printed in a second color, and areas to receive embossing or die cutting. The cover sheet is taped to the back of the mechanical. If the mechanical contains an overlay, the cover sheet is taped below the point where the overlay is taped.

Templates

A *template* is a framework on which multi-page documents are created. For example, a 48-page booklet will likely have consistent exterior margins, gutters, and placement of headers and page numbers. To achieve consistency without having to draw the same guidelines on every base sheet, the copy-preparation artist will likely create a template of a 2-page spread that will sit under the base sheet. The illumination of the light table allows the guidelines of the template to show through the base sheet and serve as guides for placement of the page elements. To enhance contrast, templates are often drawn in red, green, or another bright color. After a 2-page spread is completed, the base sheet is removed and replaced with a new base sheet for the next 2-page spread.

Figure 9-16. A cover flap carries instructions on how complex jobs will be printed. Screen-tint values, reverses, overprints, and desired colors are typically explained on cover flaps.

Summary

Conventional page composition is the manual preparation of camera-ready art by assembling type, art, and other images onto a sheet of heavy paper. This process, usually known as *copy preparation*, involves the use of tools including a light table, a T square, a triangle, art knives, scissors, ink pens, and burnishers. The copy-preparation artist works from a customer-supplied dummy indicating where each element is to be placed. Guidelines are drawn in nonphoto blue to assist in placing page elements. Borders and other lines that must be drawn in ink are placed on the mechanical before pieces of paper with text and art elements are positioned and adhered to the mechanical.

spot color: a color added to a layout to add interest, highlight important information, accent line art, and create duotones.

cover flap: a thin sheet of paper taped to the top of a mechanical to protect the mechanical or carry instructions.

template: a reusable form incorporating all the master pages and other formatting for a document.

Halftones and screen tints can be handled in different ways, depending on the screen expectations of the customer. Mechanicals requiring page elements that touch one another to be printed in different colors or receive any other separate treatment must have an overlay carrying one of the elements. Register marks are placed on both the base sheet and overlay to assist bringing the two images into registration later in production. A completed mechanical must carry all the images to be printed on that page, as well as instructions regarding the ink colors to be used to print them and any special instructions (such as reverses). Mechanicals must be clean and made with a concern for detail because they are photographed.

Review Questions

Please do not write in this book. Write your answers on a separate sheet of paper.

1. Assembling type and art elements to build a document is known as _____ .

2. Assembling type and art elements manually by placing and adhering these images onto a sheet of paper is known as _____.

3. What is camera-ready art?

4. The sheet of paper or board carrying the assembled images is known as a _____.

5. The copy-prep artist works from a customer-supplied _____, a drawing of the job as it should appear when completed.

6. Why is nonreproducing blue used to print or draw guidelines on the layout sheet or board?

7. Why must halftone copy be photographed separately from line copy?

8. A(n) _____ is a transparent sheet to which second-color image elements are attached.

9. Where should register marks be placed on a mechanical?

10. _____ register allows for 1/100" variations in the overlapping of color images.

11. _____ register is used when image elements must touch but not overlap where colors meet.

12. _____ describes a job in which no images in different colors overlap.

13. A screen tint is used to simulate a(n) _____ tone.

14. Which screen tint value creates the darkest area?
    A. 20%.
    B. 80%.
    C. 40%.
    D. 35%.

15. Why is it important to remove all excess wax, rubber cement, pencil lines, and dirt from the surface of the mechanical?

16. Distinguish between process colors and spot colors.

Skill-Building Activities

1. Design a small advertisement and write display and text type for it. Include at least one border in the design, as well as a piece of line art you can generate or acquire as clip art. Output the galley of type, and then wax it, as well as the line art. Following your dummy, prepare a mechanical for the advertisement.

2. Examine the examples of screen tints shown in **Figure 9-13.** Use a magnifying glass (loupe) to examine printed jobs containing screen tints and try to identify their percentage values by comparing them. Compare your answers with the labeled screen tints to check on your accuracy, or show your answers to your instructor.

The IAPHC's Web site (http://www.iaphc.org) is a useful resource for people involved with the printing industry.

The Original Image Capture

In conventional prepress, assembled pages are called *camera-ready copy* because the next step in production is to record those images on film. In this photograph, type and similar copy are being positioned for photographing. These test target images are being used to determine the ideal exposure for line copy.

After exposure, the film will be processed, and the images will be assessed for quality. Well-exposed images will not deviate from the original images.

Type will not become thicker or thinner. Serifs and other tiny details will be preserved. Any loss of detail will result in poor printing because these films will be used to expose the printing plates.

This chapter will describe the process camera and explain how to use test images to determine proper exposure. Process cameras are seldom used in today's digital world. Many printing companies still use them, however, when clients bring in camera-ready art.

(3M Company)

Chapter 10
Process Cameras and Line Photography

Key Terms

antihalation coating
base
bellows extension
blue-sensitive material
choke
color sensitivity
contacting film
contact printing
contact vacuum frame
control strip
copyboard
copyboard light
darkroom
daylight film
developing
dry film
duplicating film
emulsion
exposure index
fixing
focal length (FL)
focusing controls
fog
f-stop
graphic arts film
gray scale
gray scale method
ground glass
horizontal camera
inspection method

iris diaphragm
lens
lensboard
light integrator
line negative
line photography
log E curve
mask
orthochromatic material
panchromatic (pan) film
process camera
pulsed xenon
quartz-iodine lamp
rapid access film
safelight
sensitivity guide
silverless film
spherical aberration
spread
stop bath
stopping
time-and-temperature
   method
trap
tungsten filament
vacuum back
vertical camera
washing
wedge spectrograph

Learning Objectives

When you have completed the reading and assigned activities related to this chapter, you will be able to do the following:

- Describe the purpose of a process camera and distinguish between design types.
- List and describe common darkroom equipment and related accessories.
- Practice safe procedures while working in the darkroom.
- Discuss the differences among orthochromatic, panchromatic (pan), and silverless films.
- Name the various graphic arts films and photographic papers and describe their uses.
- List and describe the various classifications of line copy.
- Establish proper camera settings for making line negatives through a series of tests.
- Expose and develop line negatives to acceptable standards.
- Summarize the purpose and use of the camera gray scale, as it relates to line photography.
- Prepare the camera for a same-size reproduction, an enlargement, and a reduction.
- Establish exposure calibrations for contact printing.
- Give examples of typical kinds of equipment and materials used in contact printing.
- Identify common methods of contact printing and methods of application.

The era of digital prepress has greatly reduced the use of the process camera to capture images. The traditional role of the process camera is to record the images of camera-ready art onto photographic, high-contrast film, which will be used to expose plates. Increasingly, printing companies are receiving digital files, instead of mechanicals, from their customers. In these cases, there are no images to photograph. Although digital prepress does not involve process cameras, some companies still use their cameras. Also, a familiarity with the use of these cameras provides an excellent base of knowledge for learning the software that digitally performs the same functions of the process camera.

Process Cameras

Graphic arts photography is a photomechanical process used to produce film negatives or positives for offset lithography. The negatives can be line, halftone, right reading, or reverse reading, depending on the process and final output. The special graphic arts *process camera* converts camera-ready copy into sharp, high-contrast films, which are then used to prepare printing plates for the press. See **Figure 10-1**. The process *lens* on the camera is constructed to give optimum resolution with flat, or two-dimensional, copy. In contrast, the lens on a regular camera is made to photograph three-dimensional subject matter.

Types of Process Cameras

Process cameras are either horizontal or vertical cameras. A *horizontal camera* requires two rooms to accommodate it. The image to be captured is placed on the part of the camera on one side of a wall, and the film receiving the image is in a light-tight room on the other side of the wall. The wall allows the operator to position and process the film under controlled lighting and illuminate the image with bright lighting. A horizontal process camera is constructed in a horizontal line, or with a camera track parallel with the floor. The parts of a horizontal process camera are illustrated in **Figure 10-2**.

A *vertical camera* is smaller and can be contained in a single room. Typically, the room contains *safelights* so the film can be loaded into the camera without the film being exposed. A vertical process camera is constructed in a vertical line, with the lens facing the floor. The parts of a vertical process camera are illustrated in **Figure 10-3**. Vertical cameras are useful in areas where space is restricted.

Light Sources

Process cameras require special lighting arrangements to expose film. The spectral distribution of light for the various common graphic arts process-camera light sources varies widely. Light sources used with process cameras include pulsed xenon, tungsten filament, and quartz-iodine. The illumination from each of these light sources varies in intensity (the amount of light) and kind of light (the degree of the visible spectrum).

Pulsed xenon (ZEE-non) is similar to the electronic flashtube used in photography. The PXA is designed to light, or pulse, with each half cycle of alternating current applied. The quality of light pulsed xenon produces closely resembles natural light. PXAs are clean and not affected by voltage fluctuations. The level of light is constant. No warm-up time is required. The main disadvantage of pulsed-xenon lighting is the high initial cost of installation.

A *tungsten filament* is used in regular lightbulbs. The same metal is used in some lamps for the process camera. The *quartz-iodine lamp* uses a tungsten filament inside a quartz-glass envelope. The envelope is the glass shell over the filament. Tungsten, which makes an incandescent source of light, is generally inexpensive, clean, and easy to operate.

Quartz-iodine lamps provide even illumination of the image and do not grow dimmer with age. These lamps are used primarily for black-and-white photography and as a source of illumination for platemaking equipment. Quartz-iodine lamps have greater light intensity than tungsten-filament lamps. When a quartz-iodine lamp burns out, all the lamps on the camera should be replaced to ensure even illumination.

Figure 10-1. A mechanical is being loaded onto the copyboard of a vertical process camera, which is used to capture two-dimensional images onto film.

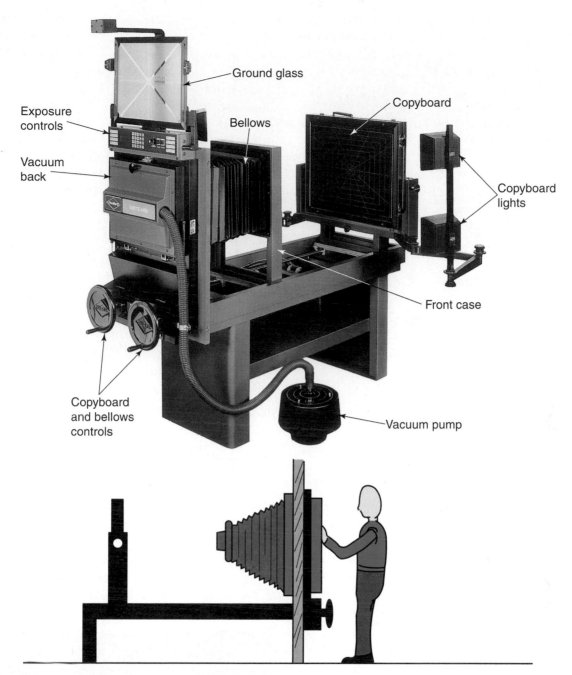

Figure 10-2. The components of a horizontal process camera are labeled. The ground glass, exposure controls, vacuum back, vacuum pump, and controls are on one side of a wall, and the rest of the camera is on the other side.

process camera: a special graphic arts camera designed to photograph two-dimensional copy and produce high-contrast films used to prepare printing plates.

lens: the part of a camera through which light passes and is focused on the film.

horizontal camera: a process camera that has a side-to-side optical axis.

vertical camera: a process camera that has an up-and-down optical axis.

safelight: a special darkroom lamp emitting illumination under which light-sensitive materials can be handled without danger of fogging through exposure to light.

pulsed xenon: a light source designed to light, or pulse, with each half cycle of alternating current applied.

tungsten filament: a photographic light source that uses the same metal found in regular lightbulbs.

quartz-iodine lamp: a photographic light source that provides even illumination at the film plane and does not grow dimmer with age. This lamp is used primarily for black-and-white photography and as a source of illumination for platemaking equipment.

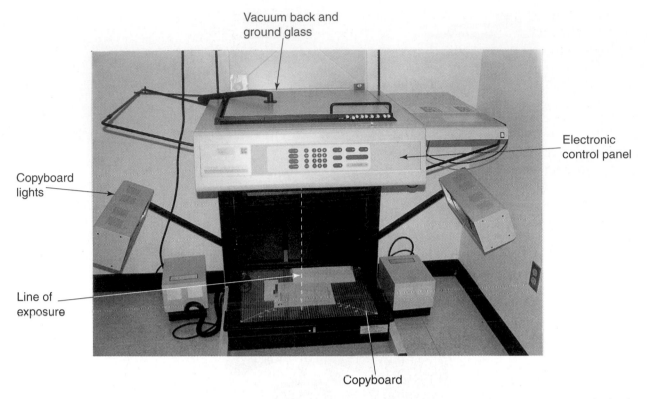

Vacuum back and
ground glass

Electronic
control panel

Copyboard
lights

Line of
exposure

Copyboard

Figure 10-3. A vertical camera projects light down to the copyboard, and the light reflects upward through the lens.

Caution

Do not touch the process-camera lamps. The bulbs might be extremely hot and can cause severe burns. The trace amount of acid in your fingers can also damage the surface of the lamp and cause it to refract light away from the copyboard.

Process-Camera Components

Regardless of camera size or design, the method and function of the controls are basically the same. There are approximately seven components common to all process cameras. These include the copyboard, copyboard lights, lensboard, bellows extension, ground glass, vacuum back, and focusing controls.

The *copyboard* is the part of the process camera on which the copy to be photographed is positioned. See **Figure 10-4.** This board has a large flat surface with a hinged glass cover to hold the copy during exposure. The copyboard is mounted on a track so it can be moved forward and backward for reductions and enlargements.

The *copyboard lights* are the source of illumination of the copy. On most process cameras, the lights are attached so they stay with the copyboard when it is moved forward or backward on the track

for reduction or enlargement settings. By moving with the copyboard, the amount of illumination of the image remains constant. Copyboard lights are generally positioned at a 45° angle to the copyboard.

The *lensboard* contains the lens and is also mounted on a track so it can be moved forward and backward during reductions and enlargements. The most critical part of the camera is the lens. This part is composed of several curved and polished glass

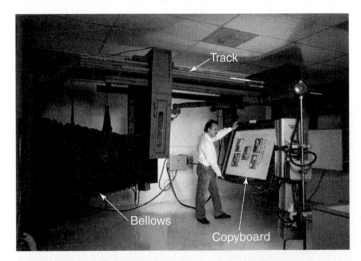

Track

Bellows

Copyboard

Figure 10-4. A large overhead horizontal process camera is used for exceptionally large pieces of camera copy. The operator has loaded the copyboard and is rotating it into position for exposure.

circles mounted in a cylinder called a *lens barrel*. The lens gathers reflected or transmitted light from the copy. The light is then projected onto the camera back, where the film is positioned. The curved surface of the lens causes light to converge (focus) on the film. See **Figure 10-5.**

The loss of focus at the outer edges of the lens is referred to as **spherical aberration**. High-quality lenses are precisely ground to avoid these image distortions. Process-camera lenses are also coated to reduce what is known as *flare*—any stray light that reaches the photographic *emulsion* during exposure. Stray light will reduce the contrast of the negative.

The lens barrel also contains the **iris diaphragm**. This diaphragm is a device that restricts light passage by reducing the size of the opening. The diameter of the iris is measured in **f-stops**, which will be explained later.

The **bellows extension** is an accordion-shaped component that forms a light tunnel from the lens to the film plane (surface). This extension is attached to the lensboard. The accordion arrangement of the bellows is designed to allow the lensboard to be moved for reductions and enlargements. The bellows should be checked periodically for cracks and breaks, which can cause light leaks. Periodically, the bellows extension should be cleaned internally with a hand-held vacuum cleaner to remove dust and dirt.

Most process cameras are equipped with a **ground glass** to assist the camera operator in positioning and focusing the image. See **Figure 10-6.** The ground glass is attached to the rear camera case and is usually mounted in a hinged frame so it can be swung out of the way when not in use.

When in the viewing position, the ground-glass surface is on the same plane as the film during

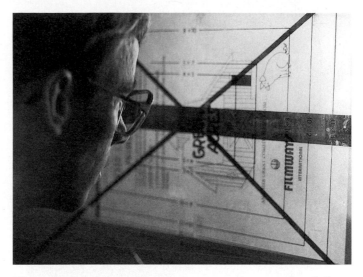

Figure 10-6. A process-camera operator can check the position and focus of an image on the ground glass.

exposure. Some cameras have a separate ground-glass attachment stored in a compartment below the camera back. To use this type of glass, the camera operator removes the glass from the compartment and places it in position on the camera back for viewing purposes.

The **vacuum back**, similar to the ground glass, is hinged to the rear case of the camera. See **Figure 10-7.** The dull, black-colored vacuum back has markings on it to show the proper position for standard film sizes.

copyboard: the part of the process camera on which the copy to be photographed is positioned.

copyboard light: the source of illumination for copy being photographed with a process camera.

lensboard: the part of a process camera that acts as the carrier of the lens.

spherical aberration: the loss of focus when the outer edges of the process lens transmit light.

emulsion: a gelatin or collodion solution holding light-sensitive salts of silver in suspension.

iris diaphragm: the device on a process camera for restricting light gradually from the outer edges of the ends toward the center.

f-stop: a fixed size at which the aperture of a lens can be set, the value of which is determined by the ratio of the aperture to the focal length (FL) of the lens.

bellows extension: an accordion-shaped component on a process camera that forms a light tunnel from the lens to the film plane.

ground glass: a process-camera component used to assist the camera operator in positioning and focusing the image.

vacuum back: a process-camera component at the rear of the camera that uses a vacuum device to hold the photographic film in position during the exposure.

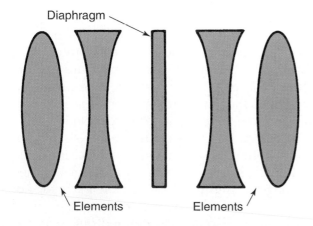

Figure 10-5. The precisely ground curves of these four individual lenses work together to focus the image onto the film. (Goerz Optical Co.)

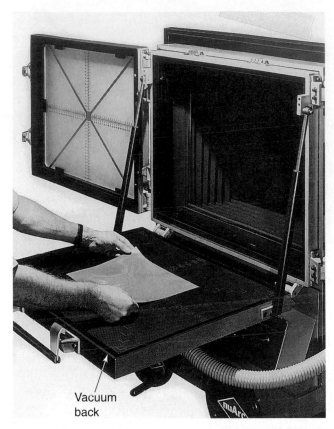

Figure 10-7. The vacuum back is used to hold film in position during exposure. (nuArc Company, Inc.)

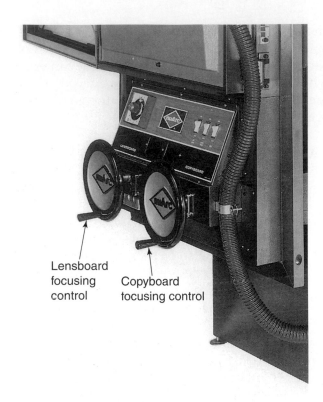

Figure 10-8. The copyboard and lensboard focusing controls are located at the rear camera case. (nuArc Company, Inc.)

A series of holes or narrow channels in the vacuum back are connected to a vacuum chamber. With the vacuum pump turned on, the photographic film is held in position during the exposure. The vacuum back can also be fitted with register pins that accommodate prepunched film register systems.

The lensboard and copyboard *focusing controls* are located at the rear camera case. See **Figure 10-8.** Each control consists of a dial that runs a sliding tape with percentages printed on it. When reducing or enlarging copy size on a process camera, the copyboard and lensboard tapes must be set at the same percentage size. For a reduction, the lensboard moves closer to the vacuum back to reduce the image size. For an enlargement, the lensboard moves away from the vacuum back to enlarge the image size.

Controlling the Image Quality

These seven primary components of the process camera function to direct and focus the correct amount of light reflected from the image being photographed onto a sheet of film. When they are used properly, the film receives the image without distortion. Controlling the quantity and quality of the light striking the film involves several considerations, and most involve the size of the aperture, which the f-stop setting determines. The camera operator controls the aperture size by selecting the *f-stop* setting. See **Figure 10-9.**

The larger the f-stop number is, the smaller the opening of the iris will be. Each larger f-stop number allows one-half of the previous amount of light to go through the lens and, therefore, doubles the exposure time. For example, an 8-second exposure at f/11 would require a 16-second exposure at f/16 or a 32-second exposure at f/22.

The lens speed is the minimum amount of exposure time required at the lens's largest aperture, which admits the maximum amount of light. Most graphic arts process cameras have f-stops of f/8, f/11, f/16, f/22, f/32, and f/45. The lenses are ground so the sharpest focus and most effective f-stop is two f-stops from the lens's largest aperture.

Light from the copyboard is collected by the lens and restricted by the aperture of the iris. When the opening of the iris is small, such as f/32, it causes the light to bend or diffract around the edges of the iris. The image is slightly distorted on its outer edges. As a result, this fuzziness might be transferred to the film in the camera. As pointed out earlier, each higher f-stop number (smaller aperture) doubles the exposure time and increases the diffraction of light.

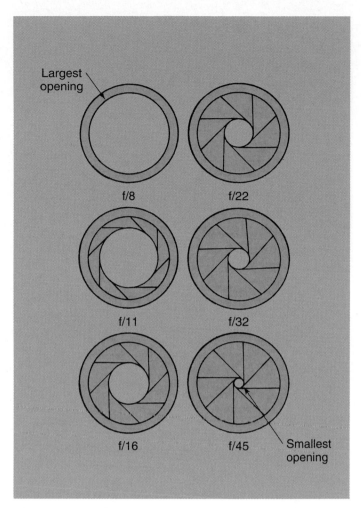

Figure 10-9. The lens speed is determined by the largest opening of the iris, which admits the maximum amount of light. (A.B.Dick Co.)

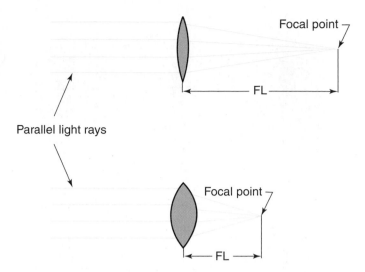

Figure 10-10. The lens manufacturer determines FL by aiming parallel rays of light at a lens and then measuring the distance from the center of the lens to a spot where the light rays converge at infinity. (Robertson Photo-Mechanix, Inc.)

Therefore, long exposure times at small apertures should be avoided.

The *focal length (FL)* of a lens is the distance from the lens's center to the film, when the camera is focused for the maximum image reduction (infinity). See **Figure 10-10.** Process-camera lenses have relatively long FLs and, therefore, are slow, compared to short-FL, high-speed lenses.

Enlargements and reductions of the focused image are determined by moving the lensboard and copyboard. These movements should be made in FL ratios to each other, if the image is to remain in focus. When the lens is moved closer to the film, the image size is reduced. When the lens is moved farther from the film, the image size is enlarged. See **Figure 10-11.**

When the size of the original image is either reduced or enlarged, the distance from the film plane of both the copyboard and the lensboard must be altered in order for the image on the film to be the desired size and in focus. Fortunately, the focusing controls simplify this process. One control moves the lensboard, and the other moves the copyboard. The key factor is the desired percentage of the original copy. For example, if an 8″-wide piece of line art needs to be enlarged to 12″ wide, both controls are set to 150%.

Light integrators

A *light integrator* is similar to a light meter because it is capable of making certain that the exposure is correct for originals of any given density. Achieving correct exposure is necessary because of the large number of variables involved, such as the film, type of illumination, distance from the copy to the lens, ambient light, and voltage fluctuations. In addition, a light integrator ensures that if a halftone negative must be reshot, consistent results can be obtained because these variables can be quantified. Light integrators are either built into the camera or stand-alone units. Most light integrators have a programmable memory that allows certain

focusing controls: the wheels on the process camera controlling the distance of the lens and the copyboard from the film plane.

focal length (FL): the distance from the lens's optical center to the film, when the image is in focus.

light integrator: a device, similar to a light meter, that is capable of making certain that the exposure is correct for originals of any given density.

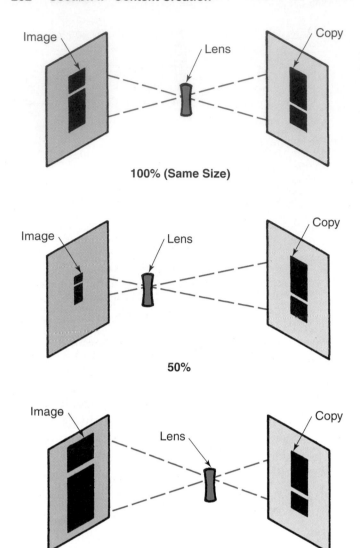

100% (Same Size)

50%

150%

Figure 10-11. When the lens is moved closer to the film, the image size is reduced. When the lens is moved farther from the film, the image size is enlarged.

combinations of exposures to be stored if they are used frequently. This memory also allows for color balance and precise exposure times and light amplitude.

Densitometers

A *densitometer* is an electronic device that allows for the tonal evaluation of copy of all kinds. This device is not truly a part of the process camera. See **Figure 10-12.** The densitometer permits the operator to achieve more even illumination, however, across the film plane. Although light might appear at the copyboard to provide even illumination, the light on the film plane does not. In most cases, the edges are denser than the center.

Using the densitometer with white paper in the copyboard and clear glass in place of the ground glass, density readings can be taken of the image.

Figure 10-12. A transmission densitometer measures the density (darkness) of film by measuring the amount of light passing through the film. (Hopkins Printing)

The results are recorded for various lens settings. Illumination can then be adjusted accordingly to achieve zero tonal variation.

Darkroom Layout and Equipment

A *darkroom* consists of a specially lighted room for processing light-sensitive photographic materials. Most darkrooms have basically the same types of layout, equipment, and accessories. The processing of photographic materials requires development, stopping, fixing, and washing. The darkroom must be lighttight because all the operations in a darkroom involve the use of light-sensitive materials.

The essential element of a good darkroom layout is utility. A typical darkroom layout is shown in **Figure 10-13.** In most cases, an automatic film processor replaces a processing sink and trays. Most darkrooms are planned for movement of work from left to right. The major components of a darkroom generally include a lighttight entrance, a film processor (or a processing sink and trays), safelights, a contact vacuum frame, a film dryer, and ventilation equipment.

Darkroom entrances

To protect light-sensitive paper and film, it is essential to be able to enter and leave a darkroom

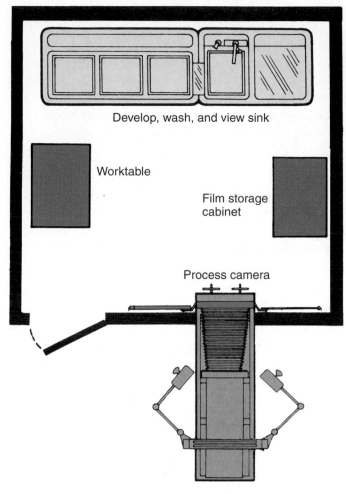

Figure 10-13. This darkroom layout shows a horizontal camera through the wall, as well as a sink for tray developing. An automatic film processor eliminates the need for a sink. (nuArc Company, Inc.)

without admitting light. The construction of double doors or light locks makes this possible. In addition, the walls of entrances and passageways to the darkroom are painted with a special paint color to prevent reflection of light around the entrance. There are three basic types of darkroom entrances. These include open-passage, double-door, and revolving-door entrances:

- The open-passage entrance provides both easy access and good ventilation. Easy access is important when people are carrying packages of film and plates. The size of the entrance depends on the size of the photographic materials used and space allocations.

- A double-door entrance can be used when floor space is at a premium. With this opening, heavy single or double curtains can replace one or both of the doors. If two solid doors are used, it is necessary to place a light-trapped vent in the wall of the passageway. This relieves the changes in air pressure that opening and closing the doors causes.

- A revolving-door entrance consists of two cylinders, the one with the smaller diameter fitting into the larger one. Revolving doors are used where space is limited. These doors can also be used to connect other darkrooms and contacting rooms to form a central facility.

Caution

Use extreme caution when entering and exiting the darkroom.

Processing sinks

The processing sink provides a place to hold the processing trays. See **Figure 10-14.** This sink is generally fitted with a source of fresh running water and a means to dispose of used chemicals. Processing sinks are made primarily of fiberglass or stainless steel. Automatic, thermostatically controlled mixing valves provide for the control of water. These valves operate by mixing warm and cold water to obtain the desired temperature. The mixing valves are capable of mixing water to temperatures accurate to within ± 0.5°F. Plastic, fiberglass, stainless-steel, or hard-rubber trays hold the chemicals during the development cycle. At least three trays are required—one each for the developer, stop bath, and fixer.

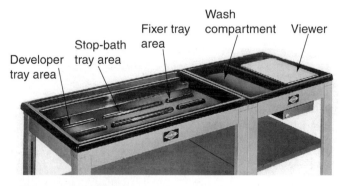

Figure 10-14. This processing sink accommodates developing, stop bath, and fixing trays. A built-in wash compartment and lighted viewing area are included. (nuArc Company, Inc.)

darkroom: a specially lighted room for processing light-sensitive photographic materials.

developing: a film-processing step that basically dissolves the light-exposed area of the film.

Safelights

The handling of photosensitive materials must be done under safelight conditions or, in some cases, in total darkness. Safelights should be located where most of the *developing* activity occurs. This is generally over the sink and near the film storage area. Safelights can be plugged directly into a wall, attached to a wall, or hung from the ceiling. The correct filters and correct-wattage bulbs for the safelights should be used in the darkroom.

Caution

> Ruby-red bulbs should never be used because, even though they look red, they often transmit light to which orthochromatic films are sensitive.

Any photographic material will *fog* (expose) if left too long under safelight illumination. This is because non-color-sensitive materials have some sensitivity to green, yellow, and red light. For example, all Kodak safelight filters, when used with the recommended bulb and at the recommended distance, are safe for at least 30 seconds. This assumes dry photographic materials are being used. The safe time is longer for materials in the developing tray.

Figure 10-15. A photographic film processor is used for automatic processing of film materials. This processor eliminates the need for a processing sink, trays, and related utensils.

Automatic film processors

An *automatic film processor* is used for fast, consistent processing of film materials. See **Figure 10-15.** This processor eliminates the need for a processing sink, trays, and related utensils. These machines allow for the control of all variables and reduce the chance of human error. Film processors accept the film after it has been exposed.

Film dryers

For tray processing, a film dryer is useful. See **Figure 10-16.** The majority of film dryers are of the forced-air type. This means they operate very similarly to a hair dryer in blowing hot air over the film surface. Film drying time is reduced to a matter of seconds.

Ventilation

The proper control of darkroom ventilation is important for several reasons. The health, safety, and efficiency of the camera department personnel must be considered. Temperature and humidity must be controlled to avoid adverse effects on film materials. If the air is too dry, film has a tendency to attract static accumulations.

Incoming air should pass through filters to remove dust particles. The airflow should be in sufficient volume to change the air in the darkroom 6–10 times an hour. Air should be pumped in, rather than out. This will prevent dust from entering through the windows and doors.

Graphic Arts Film

Graphic arts film is a transparent or translucent acetate or plastic base with a light-sensitive coating. The light-sensitive coating is a photographic emulsion containing gelatin and silver salts. The sensitivity of the silver salts to light is the basis of the photographic process. Photographic paper is similar to film, but it is opaque. This paper is normally used for producing high-resolution text matter and line art. Graphic arts film can be classified by its color sensitivity, contrast, and film speed.

Figure 10-16. A film dryer can be useful when tray-processing photographic film materials. This compact unit operates very similar to a hair dryer in blowing hot air over the film surface. (Decco, Inc.)

Film structure

Whatever their chemical differences, all films are constructed to include the same general components—the base, emulsion, and antihalation layer. These basic components are shown in **Figure 10-17.** The film's *base* is generally made from cellulose-, ester-, or polystyrene-based material. The emulsion is bonded to the base and contains the light-sensitive silver halide (silver salts) that forms the image after development. The other side of the base is covered with an *antihalation coating*, which prevents light from reflecting back to the emulsion side of the film during exposure.

Color sensitivity

The *color sensitivity* of a light-sensitive material describes the type of light that will expose the emulsion. This sensitivity refers to the visible area of the electromagnetic spectrum that will cause a chemical change in a particular silver-halide emulsion. A wedge

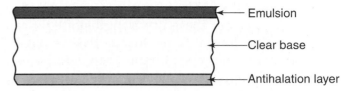

Figure 10-17. Graphic arts film contains a thick, clear base with a light-sensitive emulsion on one side and an antihalation layer on the other side.

spectrogram is used to illustrate a film's reaction to light across the visible spectrum. A spectrogram is similar to a diagram used to describe a light-source output. **Figure 10-18** shows a wedge spectrogram used to describe the relative sensitivity of the human eye to the visible spectrum.

The idea of color sensitivity is better explained by example. The human eye cannot see X rays, which are usually considered a form of light, but are technically a form of energy. X rays can, however, be recorded on

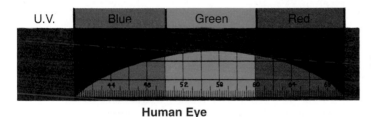

Human Eye

This wedge spectrogram illustrates the sensitivity of the human eye in relationship to the visible spectrum of blue, green, and red.

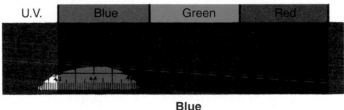

Blue

Blue-sensitive photographic-film materials record high-densities from blue materials, but very little from the green or red end.

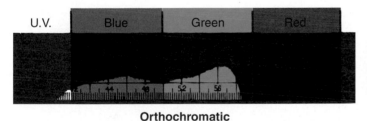

Orthochromatic

Orthochromatic photographic-film materials are sensitive to all colors, except red.

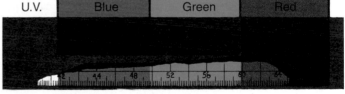

Panchromatic

Panchromatic photographic-film materials come closest to the sensitivity of the human eye since they are sensitive to all visible colors.

Figure 10-18. The human eye and three different types of film have different sensitivities to wavelengths of light.

fog: a photographic defect in which a deposit of silver either locally or entirely veils the image. This defect is due either to the action of stray light or to improperly compounded chemical solutions.

graphic arts film: any type of film used to capture an image in conventional prepress.

base: an alkaline fountain solution.

antihalation coating: an application to the back of film that prevents light from reflecting back to the emulsion during exposure.

color sensitivity: a measure of how receptive a material is to the colors of light.

certain types of films. The human eye is also blind to IR and UV rays, but these wavelengths of light can be recorded on special films. Just as the eye has its limitations as to the type of light it can perceive, the same is true of light-sensitive materials.

Film emulsions

The three basic types of light-sensitive emulsions are blue sensitive, orthochromatic, and panchromatic (pan). **Blue-sensitive materials** are known as *color-blind* or *monochromatic*. On a negative, these materials record high densities from blue materials, but they record very little from the green or red ends. **Orthochromatic materials** are sensitive to all areas of the visible spectrum, except red. The **panchromatic (pan) films** come closest to the sensitivity of the human eye. See **Figure 10-18.** These films are sensitive to all visible colors.

Types of film

There are several different types of film available for graphic arts photography. Each of these films has specific characteristics and uses:

- **Silverless film** uses a diazo compound in its light-sensitive emulsion. This film can be used in subdued light, but it requires bright light to make effective exposures. The development process can be either dry (gas) or wet (liquid).

- **Contacting film** is used to produce contact reproductions of negatives or positives. This means the film can be used to make negatives from positives or positives from negatives.

- **Duplicating film** is used to produce copies of negatives or positives (negative from negative and positive from positive).

- **Rapid access film** is used to produce negatives with a process camera and contact negatives and film positives using a contact vacuum frame.

- **Daylight film** is used with very high-intensity light sources. The emulsion is not very sensitive to light. Most of these films are intended for use in emulsion-to-emulsion contacting. A base-to-emulsion contact will create a poor-quality reproduction.

- **Dry film** (or recoding film) requires no chemical processing. This film is imaged with data from electronic files and then used to make printing plates. Although its composition varies by manufacturer, dry film uses a layer of carbon particles between a polyester base on an adhesive topcoat. When the laser strikes the film, it changes the carbon's adherence. The top layer can then be pulled off, leaving imaged pixels behind.

Film manufacturers provide a *wedge spectrograph* for evaluating each of their films. See **Figure 10-19.** The most accurate negatives are obtained when the peak sensitivity of a film's spectrograph corresponds with the peak output of a light source. For example, **Figure 10-20** illustrates how tungsten light has its lowest output in the range that orthochromatic film has its peak sensitivity. A pulsed-xenon light source would produce better results.

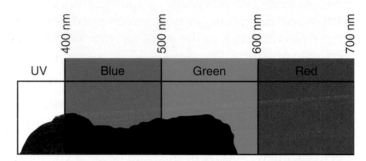

Figure 10-19. Film manufacturers provide a wedge spectrograph for evaluating each of their films. This wedge shows that the light sensitivity of orthochromatic film is highest in the green and blue portions of the visible spectrum. (Eastman Kodak Co.)

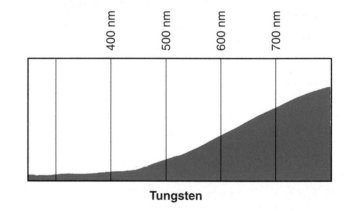

Tungsten

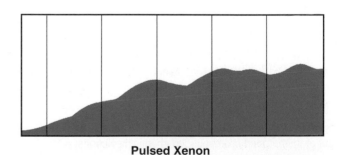

Pulsed Xenon

Figure 10-20. Notice that tungsten light emits large amounts of red light (between 600 and 700 nm). Orthochromatic film is not sensitive to red light, however, as seen in **Figure 10-19.** For this reason, process cameras do not use tungsten lights.

Film contrast

The difference between the lightest and darkest portions of an original photographic image creates contrast on the film. If this difference is great, the contrast is considered high. For example, snow compared to coal is high in contrast, just as black type on white paper is high in contrast. To reproduce the original, the proper-contrast film must be used. Line copy, which is high in contrast, requires a high-contrast film. Halftones are reproduced by photographing the continuous tone original through a halftone contact screen onto a high-contrast film.

Contrast is described by a film's characteristic curve, also called a *log E curve*. A simple characteristic curve can be drawn for any film by photographing a step scale. The density of each step of the original and film negative is measured. The results are plotted on a graph similar to the one in **Figure 10-21.**

Film speed

All film materials require a different amount of light to cause a chemical change in the emulsion. This measured amount of light is referred to as the film's *speed*. Emulsions requiring little light are called *fast*, and emulsions requiring comparatively strong light are called *slow*. These terms become almost meaningless because there are so many different materials, each requiring a different amount of light.

An ***exposure index*** is used to classify the speed for each film manufactured because there are so many types of light-sensitive materials. A film-speed number, called *ISO*, is assigned to each film—the higher the number, the faster the film. For example, a film with an ISO rating of 25 will require twice as much light to create an image as does a film with an ISO of 50. The exposure index of a particular film is assigned as a function of the kind of light source used to expose it.

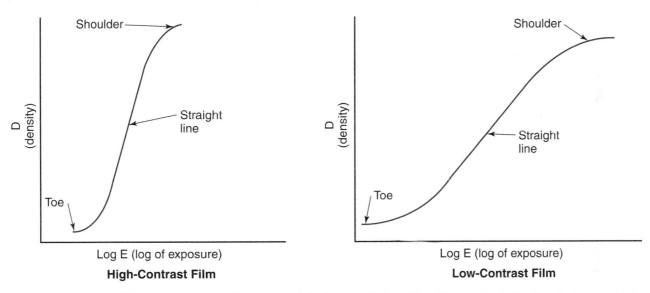

Figure 10-21. The log E curve consists of a toe, straight line, and shoulder. The main distinction between high-contrast and low-contrast film is the steepness of the curve.

blue-sensitive material: a light-sensitive material that records high densities from blue materials, but very little from green or red light.

orthochromatic material: a light-sensitive material sensitive to all areas of the visible spectrum, except red.

panchromatic (pan) film: film that is sensitive to the colors visible to the human eye.

silverless film: graphic arts film that uses a diazo compound in its light-sensitive emulsion.

contacting film: graphic arts film used to produce contact reproductions of negatives or positives.

duplicating film: graphic arts film used to produce exact copies of negatives or positives.

rapid access film: graphic arts film used to produce negatives with a process camera and contact negatives and film positives with a contact vacuum frame.

daylight film: graphic arts film used with very high-intensity light sources.

dry film: graphic arts film that requires no chemical processing. This film is imaged with data from electronic files and a laser.

wedge spectrograph: a device that splits a beam of light into the beam's spectrum. The spectrograph varies the intensity of the light passing through the entrance slit by moving an optical wedge.

log E curve: a graphical representation of the contrast capabilities of graphic arts film.

exposure index: a means of classifying the speed of film.

Film processing

Developing is a process that dissolves the light-exposed area of the film's emulsion by reducing the silver salts in the emulsion. *Stopping* is used to halt the developing action. With development completed, the film is placed in a *stop bath* solution for about 10 seconds. *Fixing* is used to make the developed image stable and permanent. *Washing* is used to remove any remaining processing chemicals.

Caution

Proper eye protection (safety glasses or goggles) should be worn when mixing chemicals.

The chemistry used in processing should be compatible with the type of film. Developer is generally purchased in concentrated liquid or powder form. The stop bath is prepared by mixing 1 oz (29.5 ml) of 28% glacial acetic acid with each 32 oz (944 ml) of water. Fixer is generally purchased in concentrated liquid or powder form.

Caution

Darkroom chemicals should be stored in plastic or stainless-steel containers on low shelves, where they can be reached easily.

Caution

Do not use concentrated, glacial acetic acid. This acid can cause serious burns, irritation, and even blindness if allowed to come in contact with skin, eyes, or clothes.

Manual processing

There are three generally accepted methods of controlling the film during the developing step. In the *inspection method*, the operator waits until development is nearly complete. The negative is then lifted briefly from the developer and viewed in front of an inspection safelight. By observing the density of the black background, a judgment is made when development should be stopped. In the *time-and-temperature method*, the film is developed for the exact length of time and at the solution temperature the film manufacturer recommends. In the *gray scale method*, control of development can easily be

monitored. A *gray scale* is a series of continuous tone rectangles of increasing darkness placed on the periphery of the copy as it is placed onto the copyboard. See **Figure 10-22**. The image of the gray scale develops with the film because the scale is photographed with the copy, and the operator can monitor the development of the film by observing the progressive darkening of the steps on the gray scale as the film develops in the tray. When the desired step turns black (usually solid step four), development is stopped by placing the film in the stop bath.

Caution

Always clean up water and chemicals from the floors and working surfaces in and around the darkroom.

Automatic processing

When a large amount of film negatives has to be processed, an automatic film processor is used to develop, fix, wash, and dry the film by carrying it through the stages at a constant speed. See **Figure 10-23**. Developer concentration and temperature combine with transport speed to control developer activity.

Control of the processor is achieved with the use of a process *control strip*—a sheet of film about 4″ × 10″ with a preexposed gray scale image on it. Control strips are used to give the operator an accurate indication of the condition of the chemistry in the processor. Processor calibration is usually performed the first thing in the morning and every two hours thereafter.

Line copy image

When processed, the negative is opaque (dark) in the areas that were white on the original copy. The negative is transparent (light) in the areas that were black on the original copy. The areas of the film that were struck by reflected light rays were intensified in the developing process. These are the areas that show as dense, black areas on the negative. The areas of the film that received NO reflected light are washed away as a result of the processing. They become the transparent (image) areas of the negative.

Figure 10-22. A sensitivity guide is placed alongside line-copy originals on the copyboard of the process camera.

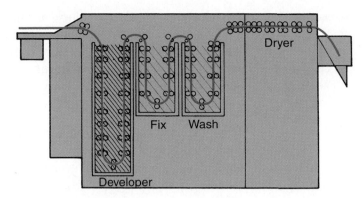

Figure 10-23. Automatic film processors are used when large quantities of film are handled. (Agfa-Gevaert Inc.)

Line Photography

In *line photography*, original single-color or single-tone camera copy is reproduced on film. In other words, line photography is limited to capturing line art—images consisting entirely of black and white. These images do not contain shades of gray, as in continuous tone photography. Examples of line art include type, inked drawings, reversals, screen tints, and screened prints. The film negatives line photography produces are called *line negatives*.

Line Copy

As was explained in Chapter 7, there are two classifications of art. Line art consists entirely of black and white tones, and continuous tone art contains middle tones (grays) as well. There are two classifications of copy. Line copy is an image that will be captured without a halftone screen, and halftone copy is an image for which a halftone screen will be used. The distinction is that art describes the nature of the image, while copy describes how the image will be handled.

Nearly all the time, line copy is limited to line art. Graphic designers sometimes, however, want the middle tones removed from a black-and-white photograph to impart an ultrahigh contrast. To achieve this effect, the photographic image is captured without a halftone screen, and the high-contrast film converts all middle tones to either black or white. In this situation, continuous tone art becomes line copy.

Types of line copy

All typeset composition is classified as line copy. The words you are reading and the inked drawing shown in **Figure 10-24** are examples of line copy. Inked drawings are traditionally prepared by drawing on white paper or illustration board with black ink. This type of image can, however, also be drawn on a computer.

Figure 10-24. An artist uses a pen and ink to render a line drawing. Exceptional detail can be achieved in such drawings. The appearance of grays is achieved with a combination of closely placed black and white lines. (Koh-I-Noor Rapidograph, Inc.)

Both reversed line images and screen tints qualify as line copy. See **Figure 10-25**. Although screen tints create the appearance of gray, they actually consist of no more than black and white. Similarly, a halftone

stopping: a film-processing step used to halt the developing action.

stop bath: a film-processing solution consisting of a mild solution of acetic acid and water used to immediately stop the action of the developer.

fixing: a step of film development used to make the developed image stable and permanent.

washing: a step in the film-development process used to remove any remaining processing chemicals.

inspection method: a method for determining the proper amount of development for exposed film by observing detail during development.

time-and-temperature method: a method for determining the proper amount of development for exposed film by relying on the film manufacturer's recommendations.

gray scale method: a method for determining the proper amount of time of development for exposed film by using a gray scale and monitoring when the desired step becomes totally black.

gray scale: a measuring device, supplied on film as continuous tones, used to obtain consistent exposure and development of graphic arts film and offset plates.

control strip: a sheet of film (about 4″ × 10″) with a preexposed gray scale image used to determine the condition of the chemicals in an automatic film processor.

line photography: original single-color or single-tone camera copy reproduced on film without continuous tones.

line negative: a film negative produced by line photography.

Figure 10-25. Examples of typical line art include all type—in positive and reversed forms—and art consisting of dots and lines—screen tints and halftone positives.

positive (or screened print) made from an original continuous tone photograph is line copy because it consists of only black and white dots.

The processing procedure

Line copy is generally positioned so the image is upside-down on the camera copyboard. This procedure allows the operator to check the copy on the ground glass, where it will be right side up and right reading, because the lens inverts the image. The film is placed in the camera back, with the emulsion side facing the camera lens.

When the camera lights are turned on, light is reflected from the white areas of the copy, through the camera lens, and projected onto the film. The black image areas do not reflect significant amounts of light. The contrast between the white base and black images of the copy forms the image on the film.

When processed, the negative is opaque in the areas that were white on the original copy. The negative is transparent in the areas that were black on the original copy. The areas of the film struck by reflected light rays were intensified in the developing process.

These are the areas showing as dense, black areas on the negative. The areas of the film that received no reflected light are washed away as a result of the processing and become the transparent (image) areas of the negative.

The basic exposure procedure

Good line photography results from accurate camera focus, exposure time, and care in film processing. The following test-exposure procedure is recommended to achieve the highest-quality line negatives:

1. Select a piece of line copy containing various line images, such as in **Figure 10-26.** This is referred to as a *line-copy target*.
2. Clean both sides of the copyboard glass. Use a graphic arts glass cleaner.
3. Place the line-copy target upside-down on the camera copyboard. A **sensitivity guide** (gray scale) should be placed next to the copy. See **Figure 10-27.**
4. Set the camera for same-size (100%) reproduction.
5. Set the lens for the best f-stop. Each film manufacturer recommends a setting for optimum results. An aperture of f/16 or f/22 is common. For the purposes of this test, set the lens at f/16.

Note

The process of determining the best f-stop is described at the end of this test-shot sequence.

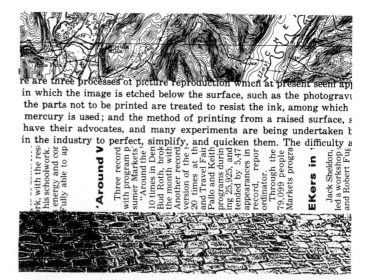

Figure 10-26. A line test negative should reveal a line width and the shape of small image areas as sharp as in the original copy. (Eastman Kodak Co.)

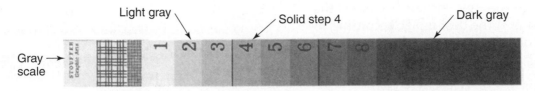

Figure 10-27. In the gray scale method, the operator observes the number sections get darker as the black moves from high-numbered patches toward step number one. When the desired step (usually number four) becomes a solid black, development is halted by placing the film into the stop bath.

6. The control-arm setting on the aperture scale should match the percentage of enlargement or reduction of the copy. In this test, the size is 100%.
7. Position the camera lights. The proper angle of the lights is very important. Make sure the camera lights are pointing toward the center of the copyboard.
8. Focus the copy on the ground glass.
9. Place a sheet of orthochromatic film on the camera back. Turn on the vacuum and make sure the film is smooth, flat, and dust free. The dull side of the film is the emulsion side and should face the lens when the camera back is closed. Handle the film by the edges to avoid fingerprints in the image area.
10. Cut a piece of black construction paper measuring a little wider than, and at least as long as, the sheet of film. This is called a *mask*.
11. Place the mask over the film so there is an uncovered 1″ strip across the top of the film. Close the camera back and make the exposure. All exposures in the test series should be made at the same f-stop setting, at the same size.
12. Open the camera back, leaving the vacuum pump on, and move the mask down about 1″. Close the camera back and make the next test exposure in the series.
13. Repeat this procedure until about six exposures have been made. **Figure 10-28** illustrates the mask-exposure procedure.

Note

Select a series of exposure times in which each successive exposure represents a uniform increase over the last exposure—for example, 3, 6, 9, 12, and 15 seconds. This is easier to time than a more complicated logarithmic series, such as 5, 8, 12, and 18.

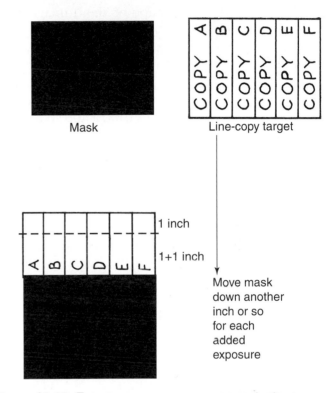

Figure 10-28. For process-camera exposure tests, a mask procedure is recommended for best results and accurate line-copy exposure times. (Eastman Kodak Co.)

14. Turn off the vacuum pump and remove the film from the camera back.
15. Develop and fix the test film. Develop to a solid step four. After a short wash, squeegee the film on a piece of glass in the darkroom. Examine the film over a light table using a magnifier of about 10-power magnification.

sensitivity guide: a narrow, calibrated, continuous tone gray scale with each tone scale numbered. In a platemaking operation, the sensitivity guide is exposed on a sensitized press plate with the rest of the work. The device measures the tone values represented on the plate.

mask: in line photography, a piece of black construction paper (or similar light-blocking material) placed over the film when making test strips.

After producing a line test negative, select the exposure that produced the best image according to the following criteria:

- The black areas should be dense enough so light can barely be seen through the film.
- There should be no pinholes in the solid black areas.
- The transparent areas should be clean and clear.
- The edges of the image should be as sharp as in the original copy.
- The line width and shape of small image areas should be as sharp as in the original copy, especially in the serif areas of Roman type.

The appearance of an undcrexposed segment can result even after correct exposure, if the developer is too cold or improperly mixed. This appearance can also result if the development time is too short.

Pinholes and Fogging

If the camera room or darkroom is dusty, and if the relative humidity is too low (air is too dry), the film will attract dust particles. These dust particles cast tiny shadows during exposure, which leave unexposed pinholes in the negative. Pinholes are unwanted tiny clear areas in the negative. Dirt on the copyboard glass and specks in the copy can also cause pinholes. Such unwanted spots (holes) can be eliminated from the negative by painting with film opaque. Fog is a condition resembling overexposed film, but it is caused by stray light or flare from a dirty lens.

The Final Negative

By selecting the best-resolution strip in the test negative, the correct exposure time has been determined. A full piece of film can be exposed. If the same conditions are duplicated, good line negatives should result each time because all the variables have been eliminated.

After getting a good negative, the details of how it was made should be recorded. These details include the type of film, exposure time, developer, and development time. By duplicating the conditions and procedures of the test, good negatives of any line copy can be made without additional testing. The gray scale will show the correct development with the same camera, lens aperture, film, and conditions.

Occasionally, a large piece of line copy might require a different light position for even illumination. If the lights are moved farther away, the exposure time must be increased. Similarly, the exposure must be adjusted for enlargements and reductions, as shown in **Figure 10-29**.

Reproduction Size	Suggested Exposure-Time Factor	
	Lights Attached to Copyboard	Copyboard Moves, Lights Do Not
200%	2.40	2.00
175%	2.00	1.70
150%	1.60	1.40
125%	1.30	1.20
100%	1.00	1.00
90%	.92	.92
80%	.85	.84
70%	.75	.75
60%	.68	.67
50%	.60	.60
40%	.52	.55
30%	.44	.50
20%	.38	.50

Figure 10-29. Camera reductions and enlargements require adjusted exposure times for best results. This information should be placed near the process camera. (Stouffer Graphic Arts Equipment Co.)

Determining the Best Aperture

The previous test determined the correct exposure time for a line shot. You must also determine the best aperture for the camera. Lenses are manufactured to be sharpest at one f-stop. This f-stop should always be used for line shots. To determine the best f-stop, use the following procedurc to make a series of test exposures:

1. Set the camera for same-size reproduction.
2. Position the copy used in the previous test on the copyboard.
3. Place a large sheet of film in the camera back. Position the film for exposure in the upper-right corner. Mask the remainder of the film. Set the exposure time for 10 seconds.
4. Expose the film at the largest f-stop.
5. Reposition the film and make each additional exposure in a clockwise pattern.
6. Reduce the f-stop for each exposure. Do not change the exposure time.
7. Process the film by the tray method. Select the sharpest image by using the magnifier. Always use the f-stop that produced the sharpest image.

Sensitivity Guides

A sensitivity guide, or gray scale, should be included along with the copy for every line shot. Refer back to **Figure 10-27.** The gray scale is actually an aiming device used during the development stage. This scale represents a visual description of the logarithmic density scale. Each step on the scale equals a specific measurable density.

Gray scales are available in several forms. The number of steps is arbitrary. Most camera operators use the 12-step gray scale. The opposed gray scale can also be used. See **Figure 10-30.**

- The Stouffer 12-step gray scale contains 12 steps, in blocks ranging from a neutral white to a dense black. As the exposed negative begins to develop, step one fills in (blackens). Within seconds, step two fills in, and so forth. Generally, step four is used as an aim point for normal black-and-white line-copy development.

- The opposed gray scale is used for quick visual reference for checking exposure and development changes. The term *break* is used to describe the point at which a line negative appears to have lost most of the separation between the steps. The break shows a major shift in density. Therefore, the opposed gray scale will look different at the break, as exposure is adjusted to suit the kind of copy.

The test exposure that gives the best negative from good line copy will be the proper aim point for a fairly wide range of copy conditions. Due to differences in shop conditions and operations, experience in using the opposed gray scale will soon establish the most suitable visual reference. Once the best reference point on the guide has been established for different types of copy and conditions, results can be interpreted quickly, with repeatability and consistency.

The guide should be checked against moderately overexposed or underexposed films during development. This comparison will result in more reliable corrections in development time. When development progresses to the point where the guide shows the proper break, the film should have a good image. This is because you will have adjusted the development time to compensate for the exposure error. Extreme overexposure or underexposure of the film will not respond well to development compensation, and the exposure will need to be adjusted.

Reductions and Enlargements

It is often necessary to reduce or enlarge line copy to make it fit a given area. There are two basic methods for setting the camera to make reductions and enlargements. These are the constant-aperture exposure method and constant-time exposure method.

The constant-aperture exposure method

A high degree of control can be achieved by using the constant-aperture exposure method. The length of exposure time is varied to fit the desired reproduction size. The lens aperture, called the *f-stop*, is held constant for the desired reproduction size.

To use this method, determine the basic exposure time at 100% for the camera you are using. The procedure was described earlier in this chapter. For purposes of this explanation, assume the basic 100% exposure was made at f/16, with an exposure of 10 seconds.

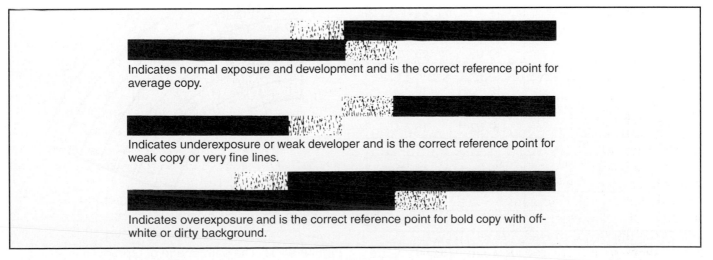

Indicates normal exposure and development and is the correct reference point for average copy.

Indicates underexposure or weak developer and is the correct reference point for weak copy or very fine lines.

Indicates overexposure and is the correct reference point for bold copy with off-white or dirty background.

Figure 10-30. The opposed gray scale gives an accurate indication as to normal, underexposed, or overexposed line negatives. (Eastman Kodak Co.)

Figure 10-31 shows the new exposure time for various reproduction sizes. It is assumed that the camera lights are attached to the copyboard and that they move with it. In this example, assume a 70% reduction is required. Read across the chart from the 70% reproduction size to the column for 10 seconds of basic exposure. The new exposure time is shown as 7 1/4 seconds.

The constant-time exposure method

The manual diaphragm control, with its percentage bands, is frequently used with the constant-time exposure method for making film negatives. Every exposure is made for the same

length of time. The lens aperture is changed to admit more light for an enlargement and less light for a reduction. To use the constant-time method, you must know the basic exposure time and best f-stop for 100% reproductions. The procedure for determining these figures was described earlier.

The following example is given to illustrate the constant-time exposure method. Assume the basic exposure time is 10 seconds at the f/16 diaphragm-control percentage band. We also assume the process camera has a manual diaphragm control and percentage-calibrated tapes. The copy is 4"×8". A reduction of 50% is required. The procedure is as follows:

1. Determine the percentage of reproduction. The percentage is generally indicated on the copy. You might be required to determine the percentage.
2. Make the correct camera settings for this exposure.
3. Set the timer for 10 seconds (basic length of exposure).
4. Set the camera tapes for lensboard and copyboard extensions at 50% reproduction size.
5. Set the diaphragm-control pointer at 50% on f/16.
6. The reproduction size of 50% at f/16 will automatically reduce the lens aperture from f/16 to f/22, as shown in **Figure 10-32.**

The 50% reproduction will actually be made at an aperture of f/22. The length of exposure will, however, remain constant at 10 seconds. An exposure of 10 seconds at f/22 admits less light through the lens than an exposure of 10 seconds at f/16. As you can see by this example, it takes less light for the 50% reproduction.

Reproduction Size Required	Same-Size Basic Exposure Time		
	10 Seconds	**20 Seconds**	**30 Seconds**
300%	40	80	120
275%	35	70	105 1/2
250%	30 1/2	61 1/4	92
225%	26 1/2	53	79
200%	22 1/2	45	67 1/2
175%	19	38	57
150%	15 1/2	31	47
125%	12 1/2	25	38
100%	10	20	30
95%	9 1/2	19	28 1/2
90%	9	18	27
85%	8 1/2	17	25 1/2
80%	8	16 1/4	24 1/4
75%	7 1/2	15	23
70%	7 1/4	14 1/2	21 1/2
65%	6 3/4	13 1/2	20 1/2
60%	6 1/2	12 3/4	19 1/4
55%	6	12	18
50%	5 3/4	11 1/4	17
45%	5 1/4	10 1/2	15 3/4
40%	5	10	15
35%	4 1/2	9	13 1/2
30%	4 1/4	8 1/2	12 3/4
25%	4	8	12
20%	3 1/2	7 1/4	10 3/4

Figure 10-31. Exposure times for reductions and enlargements using the constant-aperture exposure method. (Eastman Kodak Co.)

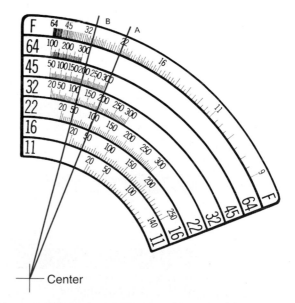

Figure 10-32. The percentage of reproduction size is determined by setting the diaphragm-control pointer, timer, and lensboard and copyboard extensions.

Contact Printing

Images on film can be transferred to either another piece of film or a different light-sensitive material through *contact printing*—a process involving placing the piece of film carrying the image over and in direct contact with the receiving material. A *contact vacuum frame* is used to make same-size reproductions on film or photographic paper. See **Figure 10-33**. A sheet of glass is lowered to hold the two sheets together, a vacuum is created to enhance the contact, and an exposure is made using a point-source light. If the original piece of film is a negative, either a positive or a second negative can be created, depending on the receiving material. The film or photo-print paper can be processed manually in trays or with an automatic processor. Contact printing is a photomechanical process with many applications:

- Making film positives from film negatives. (A film positive is the reverse of a negative. The image is black, and the nonimage area is transparent.)
- Making film negatives from film positives.
- Changing the image orientation from right reading to wrong reading and vice versa.
- Making photo-print proofs of negatives and positives.
- Making screened-halftone photo prints for use in pasteup.

- Using tint screens to make tint blocks of various percentages.
- Making spreads and chokes.
- Making duplicate negatives or positives for multiple printing on one printing plate.
- Making negatives and positives for color-separation printing.

Contact-printing equipment

Contact printing involves the use of three pieces of equipment. These are the vacuum frame, point-source light, and transformer. The transformer includes a light-intensity control, a timer, and an on-and-off switch. The contact-printing equipment is generally set up in a separate darkroom adjacent to the camera darkroom. This arrangement makes it possible for personnel in both darkroom areas to work independently, thereby avoiding accidental exposure of light-sensitive materials.

The vacuum frame is set up so the lamp will illuminate the entire glass of the frame. The lamp is hung directly overhead at a distance of 4′–5′ from the frame. The amount (intensity) of light at the frame and the time it is on determine exposure. A transformer is used to adjust the intensity of the light.

The Inverse Square Law of Light shows that the distance between the light and the film affects the intensity of the light striking the film. See **Figure 10-34**. To achieve proper exposure, the light source should be the prescribed distance from the frame and regulated by a variable voltage transformer, creating longer, more accurate, and easier-to-control exposures.

Contact-printing films

Two general types of reproducing materials are used for contacting. Contact film is made especially for contact printing and will produce positives from negatives or negatives from positives. This film is blue sensitive, and because the film emulsion is photographically slow, it can withstand a large amount of safelight illumination. Duplicating film is used to make negatives from negatives and positives from positives. Duplicate negatives or positives are required when assembling film for multiple images on one printing plate.

Figure 10-33. A vacuum contact frame is used to make same-size contact prints on film or paper. (nuArc Company, Inc.)

contact printing: a photographic process in which a film negative or positive is placed in direct vacuum contact over a sheet of film or photo-print paper.

contact vacuum frame: a frame used to make prints, negatives, positives, spreads, and chokes by holding the negative or positive in vacuum contact with the photographic material being made.

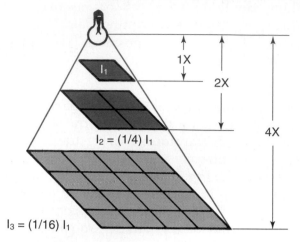

The Inverse Square Law of Light
Intensity (I) of light on a plane is inversely proportional to square of distance (X) of that plane from light source. (I = k/X²)

I_1

1X

2X

$I_2 = (1/4) I_1$

4X

$I_3 = (1/16) I_1$

Figure 10-34. This example of the Inverse Square Law of Light demonstrates that the distance between the light and the film affects intensity. Here is an example of a film manufacturer's characteristic-curve data sheet for use with an orthochromatic film. (E.I. DuPont de Nemours and Co., Eastman Kodak Co.)

The film emulsions used for most contact printing are slower than those used in process photography. This means more light is needed to expose the film. Contact-printing films have good emulsion density and are available in several thicknesses. Photo-print papers are available in a variety of finishes and contrasts for various purposes, including contact printing.

Good contact printing results from using accurate time, light intensity, and processing techniques. The step off procedure, similar to the one used in line photography, can be used to determine optimum exposure. This procedure must be performed for each type of film and photo-print paper being used.

The contact-printing procedure

Before contact-printing operations begin, the vacuum frame and point-source light should be checked, making certain that the glass on the vacuum frame is clean. The image to be transferred can be on either a film negative or a film positive. If a film negative is used, the resulting image will be positive. If a film positive is used, the resulting image will be negative. The receiving material can be a second piece of contact film or a sheet of photopaper.

An emulsion-to-emulsion contact

The most accurate image transfer is achieved when the original film (either a negative or positive) and the receiving film are oriented emulsion-to-emulsion. See **Figure 10-35.** An emulsion-to-emulsion contact is used between an original piece of film and a sheet of proof paper or a plate. When the emulsions are in contact with one another, the projected light cannot stray while moving through the clear base layer. An emulsion-to-emulsion contact will, however, alter the reading orientation of the receiving film. For example, if the original film's image is wrong reading on the emulsion side, the receiving film will be right reading on the emulsion side.

A base-to-emulsion contact

If the receiving film will be used later to expose a plate, its images cannot be right reading when looking at the emulsion, and an emulsion-to-emulsion contact cannot be made. In this situation, the original film (wrong reading on the emulsion side) is placed with the emulsion up, over the receiving film, with its emulsion up as well. See **Figure 10-36.** After development, the receiving film will be wrong reading on the emulsion side, similar to the original film. The film can then be used to make a right-reading plate.

Making duplicates

Up to this point, film negatives have been exposed to contact film to produce film positives, or film positives have been exposed to contact film to produce film negatives. There are instances, however, when it is necessary to duplicate (or dupe) film negatives or positives—that is, produce a negative from a negative or a positive from a positive. For example, four negatives of the same image might be needed to expose

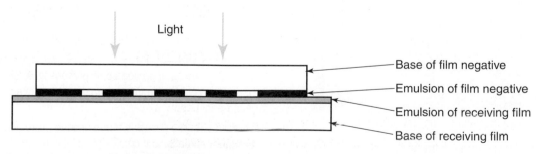

Light

Base of film negative

Emulsion of film negative

Emulsion of receiving film

Base of receiving film

Figure 10-35. An emulsion-to-emulsion contact exposure.

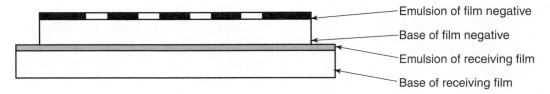

Figure 10-36. Contacting a film emulsion negative to the base.

the image onto a plate that will print four images at a time. See **Figure 10-37**. Film duplicates are made by exposing onto duplicating film, which loses density when light strikes.

Spreads and chokes

Contact printing can be used for the purpose of widening or thinning a particular image area on the copy. A *spread*, or fat, is the process of widening an image. A *choke*, or skinny, is the process of thinning

an image. Enlarging an image is necessary when adjoining images are printed in two different colors, to prevent a white gap from appearing due to the tiniest misregistration on the press. If the surrounded (foreground) image is enlarged to create the *trap* (overlap), the process is referred to as a *spread*. If the background image is enlarged to create the trap, the process is referred to as a *choke*. See **Figure 10-38**. The term *choke* is derived from the fact that the enlargement of the background image results from reducing

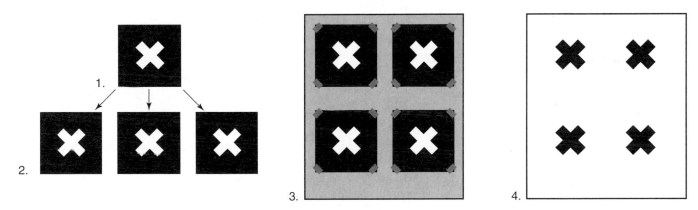

Figure 10-37. Duplicate negatives are often made for multiple-image plates. In this example, an original film negative is used to produce three duplicate negatives, which are arranged with the original onto a flat that will produce an offset plate, which will then be able to print four images onto each press sheet.

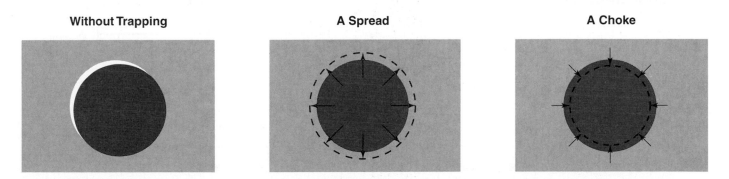

Figure 10-38. Without trapping, two adjoining colors will likely produce a white gap when printed. A spread will create a trap by expanding the foreground image into the background image. A choke will expand the background image into the foreground image.

spread: a print made in a contact-printing frame that makes the original image slightly larger.

choke: a print made in a contact-printing frame that makes the original image slightly smaller.

trap: an allowance of color overlap in multicolor printing. This allowance helps prevent gaps between colors.

Figure 10-39. In this example, the image of the type was spread on the yellow plate to overlap the blue background area.

(choking) the foreground image. The lighter of the two adjoining colors is usually chosen to be enlarged because the enlarging of an image produces soft edges. Spreads are always made from an original negative, while chokes are made from original positives.

One of the most common uses of a spread involves an image being reversed out of the background color and printed in a second color. See **Figure 10-39.** To ensure that all parts of the two images make contact when printed on the press, the yellow image shown in the example is made slightly larger than the reversed image it will fill. To accomplish this enlargement, the image is spread by placing a clear plastic spacer between the original negative and the receiving film. See **Figure 10-40.** A *diffuser sheet* often is used over the frame to help scatter the light and enhance the spreading of the image.

Figure 10-41 illustrates the use of an original negative to make a spread negative on duplicating film. This figure shows the use of an original positive to make a choked positive on duplicating film. If a reversed image is required for a spread or choke,

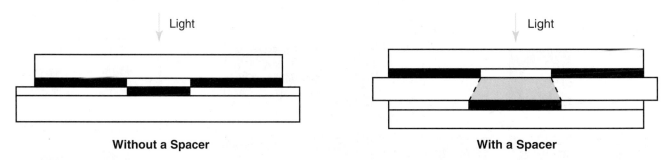

Figure 10-40. In an emulsion-to-emulsion orientation, the image is transferred with no change in size. With an acetate spacer in place, the light moving through the open image areas of the original negative spreads out to create a larger image.

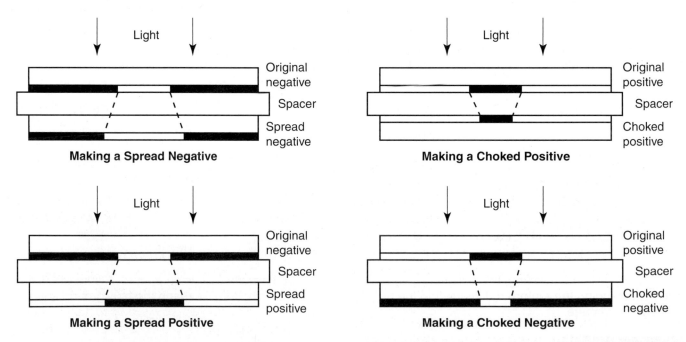

Figure 10-41. There is a method for spreading or choking to produce a negative or positive. Note the method of preparing a spread negative on duplicating film from an original negative. The original positive is used to prepare a choked positive on duplicating film. The original negative is used to prepare a spread positive. A choked negative on contact film is prepared from an original positive. (Eastman Kodak Co.)

contact film is used. **Figure 10-41** also demonstrates a spread positive made from an original negative using contact film. This figure shows a choked negative made from an original positive using contact film, as well.

Summary

Graphic arts photography is a photomechanical process used to produce film negatives or positives for offset lithography. Although the use of process cameras is diminishing as a result of electronic technology, conventional photography is still being used. Process cameras are designed for reproduction of two-dimensional copy and differ from conventional cameras primarily by the type of lens they use. These cameras are either vertical or horizontal in design. Process cameras require special lighting to expose film and might use light sources such as pulsed xenon, tungsten filament, and quartz-iodine.

Regardless of camera size or design, the method and function of the controls are similar. The seven basic components of a process camera are the copyboard, copyboard lights, lensboard, bellows extension, ground glass, vacuum back, and focusing controls. A darkroom is needed for processing light-sensitive photographic materials. Most darkrooms have the same basic types of layouts, equipment, and accessories. The processing of photographic materials requires development, stopping, fixing, and washing.

Graphic arts film is a transparent or translucent acetate or plastic base with a light-sensitive coating. This film is normally used for producing high-resolution text matter and line art. Whatever their chemical differences, all films are constructed to include the same general components. Films vary by the type of emulsion and the type of light to which they are sensitive.

Line photography involves the use of a graphic arts process camera to reproduce single-tone copy on film. There are no continuous tones in line photography. Examples of line copy include type matter, inked drawings, reversals, screen tints, and screened prints.

Good line photography results from accurate camera focus, exposure time, and care in film processing. This is usually accomplished by initially conducting a series of test exposures to determine the optimum type of film, exposure time, developer, and development time. These tests must be performed under controlled conditions in order to eliminate all variables. By subsequently duplicating the conditions and procedures of the test results, high-quality negatives can be achieved.

It is frequently necessary to make line-copy reductions and enlargements. There are two generally accepted methods used to set the process camera for this purpose. These include the constant-aperture and constant-time exposure methods. Of the two, the constant-aperture method provides the highest degree of control and accuracy.

Same-size contact printing is done by placing a film negative or positive in direct contact over a sheet of film or photo-print paper in a vacuum contact frame. Contact printing is typically used to produce items such as film duplicates, film and photo-print positives and reverses, screened-halftone photo prints, tint screens and blocks, spreads, and chokes. Special films are used for making contact prints. Good contact printing results from using accurate time, light intensity, and processing techniques.

Review Questions

Please do not write in this book. Write your answers on a separate sheet of paper.

1. A process-camera lens is made to give best results with flat, or _____, copy.

2. A process camera installed with the film-holder end on the other side of the wall from the bellows is referred to as a(n) _____ camera.

3. The large flat surface with a hinged glass cover holding the original copy during the exposure is called the _____.

4. The _____ lights act as the source of illumination of the copy on a process camera.

5. The process-camera lens is made of several optical glass elements assembled into a lens _____.

6. Unwanted light reflected from objects or bellows-light leaks is called _____.

7. The accordion-shaped tunnel channeling light from the lens to the film plane is called the _____.

8. Most process cameras are equipped with a(n) _____ to assist the camera operator in positioning and focusing the image.

9. The size of the opening the process-camera diaphragm produces is referred to as the _____ number.

10. Why is a light integrator often used on a process camera?

11. Density readings of original copy can be measured with a(n) _____.

12. Why is it necessary to handle photosensitive materials under a safelight or in complete darkness?

13. Name and describe three components of a darkroom.

14. What is one way to stay safe while working in the darkroom?

15. The ventilating system in a darkroom should be capable of changing the air _____ times an hour.

16. The _____ sensitivity of a light-sensitive material describes the type of light that will expose its particular emulsion.

17. _____ films are sensitive to the same range of visible light as the human eye.

18. Define four types of graphic arts film and explain their uses.

19. The characteristic curve of a particular film describes its _____.

20. Film _____ refers to the specific amount of light that will cause a chemical change in the emulsion of a particular film.

21. After development is completed, the film is placed in a(n) _____ for about 10 seconds.

22. There are no _____ tones in line photography.

23. Which of the following is *not* an example of line copy?
    A. Inked drawing.
    B. Screen tint.
    C. Photograph.
    D. Typeset composition.

24. Good line photography results from accurate camera focus, _____ time, and care in film processing.

25. To establish proper camera settings for making line negatives, after the correct exposure time is found, how is the best aperture determined?

26. What can cause pinholes on line negatives?

27. A camera _____ guide is an aiming device used during the developing of film.

28. When making enlargements or reductions, a high degree of control can be achieved by using the _____ aperture method.

29. Contact printing is used to make _____ reproductions on film or photographic paper.

30. How is same-size contact printing done?

31. Explain three typical kinds of equipment or materials used in contact printing.

32. In contact-printing operations with contact film, a film negative produces a(n) _____, and a film positive produces a(n) _____.

33. List two common methods of contact printing.

34. _____ and _____ are names given to the processes of widening and thinning particular images on the copy.

Skill-Building Activities

1. Describe the term *focal length (FL)* and illustrate the way in which the FL of a lens is determined.

2. Illustrate how enlargements and reductions are made by changing the bellows (lensboard) and copyboard extensions on the process camera.

3. Draw a cross-sectional view of a piece of ortho litho film and label the various parts.

4. Make a wall chart for the darkroom showing the content and order of trays for hand-processing film.

5. Make a chart illustrating the color sensitivity of orthochromatic and pan films.

6. If there is a film processor available in the lab, make the necessary preparations to operate the machine. These steps include the processing of control strips to check for proper chemical balance according to the manufacturer's specs.

7. Make a chart using examples of various kinds of line copy. Label each example and place the chart near the process-camera work area.

8. Make a chart listing common filter factors. Place the chart near the process-camera area.

9. Prepare the required developer, stop bath, fixer, and running-water wash for processing line negatives.

10. Expose and process a test negative to determine the correct exposure time on your process camera.

11. With a partner, expose and process a line negative using copy your instructor supplies.

12. Prepare a photographic-paper contact print from a halftone negative. Prepare a negative from a positive.

Designed for the high-quality commercial printing and packaging markets, this large-format press will handle sheets up to 56″ in width at printing speeds as high as 13,000 sheets per hour. It can be configured with up to eight printing units and can be networked via fiber optics with other pressroom units and operations. (Man Roland, Inc.)

Making the Conversion

Shown here are an original photograph and a striking variation that was made from it. This effect, a three-tone posterization, was created with a process camera by exposing the original image to different pieces of film and at different exposure times. In this example, the lightest portions of the original image remain white, slightly darker portions are printed in yellow ink, midtones are printed in red ink, and the shadow areas are printed in black ink.

Posterizations represent only one of many ways photographs can be dramatically manipulated with a process camera and special screens, filters, and multiple exposures. Process cameras are mostly used, however, to convert original photographs into the thousands of tiny halftone dots required for printing. This chapter will explain these various conversions.

Chapter 11
Halftone and Special-Effects Photography

Key Terms

AM screening
basic density range (BDR)
conventional screen
duotone
elliptical dot screen
fake duotone
flash exposure
FM screening
halftone
halftone screen
highlight area
line shot
midtone area
moiré pattern
photomechanical transfer
   (PMT) gray contact
   screen
posterization
screen ruling
shadow area
shadow exposure
square dot screen
stochastic screening
tonal range
tone break

Learning Objectives

When you have completed the reading and assigned activities related to this chapter, you will be able to do the following:

- Define *halftone*.
- Describe the different screen colors and dot shapes.
- Discuss the terms *highlight*, *midtone*, and *shadow*—both in negative and positive (print) form.
- Use a halftone-exposure calculator to determine exposure times for various types of original continuous tone copy.
- Explain several methods used to improve shadow details.
- Create graphic appeal by using special-effects screens.
- Summarize the process of producing different classifications of posterizations.
- Discuss duotones and explain the methods of producing them.

As mentioned in Chapter 10, nearly all image reproduction is now done electronically. For this reason, the capture of photographic and other continuous tone art is usually performed with a scanner. Some printing firms, however, still use the conventional halftone process. This chapter describes how continuous tone photographs are prepared photomechanically with the halftone process because many of the principles of halftone image capture are common to both methods. Special-effects photography is a form of image manipulation intended to enhance either line or halftone copy. Although these effects are usually performed electronically, the photographic methods are presented in this chapter.

The Halftone Process

The halftone process is a procedure in which a continuous tone original is converted to a pattern of dots in varying sizes, or more accurately, a *halftone*. As discussed in Chapter 7, continuous tone art contains gradations of tone (grays) varying from light to dark. These gradations are created by changing the amount of density (or darkness). After conversion to halftone dots, continuous tone art is no longer a continuous tone image. The result of the conversion can be seen by examining a photograph that has been printed in a book or magazine with a magnifying glass or loupe. The tiny halftone dots that vary in size and create the illusion of gray become apparent. See **Figure 11-1**. This conversion of actual

grays to tiny black and white areas that create the appearance of grays is necessary because a printing press can only print solid-ink image areas. Phrased differently, a press carrying black ink can either transfer that ink to a portion of the paper and create a black area or *not* transfer it, and that portion of the paper will remain white. Therefore, the press cannot create an actual gray. Instead, it prints tiny black dots that combine with the tiny unprinted areas to create the illusion of gray.

This amazing conversion of a continuous tone image to halftone dots is performed with a *halftone screen*. The halftone dots that make up an image vary in size according to the tonal (darkness) levels in the original art they represent. The dots in the dark areas of an image are large and cover more area than those in the light areas. The dots representing the light areas are small. **Figure 11-2** shows the halftone-dot areas of very different tones. The halftone dots vary in size, but the dpi is uniform across the photograph. In other words, the different tones result from the percentage of ink coverage, not from the number of black dots.

Halftone photography makes the printed reproduction of continuous tone photographs, paintings, and drawings possible. If the areas or dots are small enough, the eye will not perceive the dot pattern, but it will see the mixture of ink dots and unprinted specks of white paper as varying tones of color. If this conversion to halftone dots is performed skillfully, the printed photograph will appear to be identical to the original continuous tone image.

Figure 11-1. A magnifying glass reveals that photographs appearing in printed materials are composed of thousands of tiny black dots creating the illusion of gray. The dot size determines the tone.

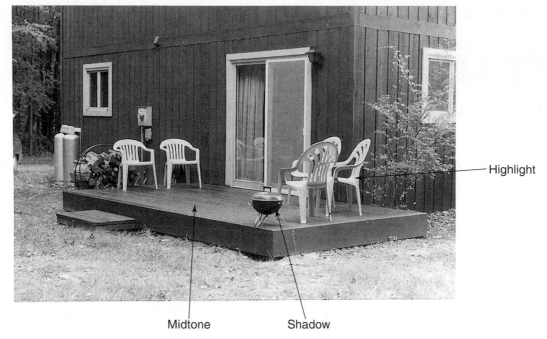

Highlight

Midtone

Shadow

Figure 11-2. Photographs consist of highlight, midtone, and shadow areas. Control of the dot size in each area is crucial to reproducing an original photograph's subtle tones.

Note

When printing in full color, it is necessary to make a halftone negative for each of the colors being printed. Therefore, a color photograph will be converted into four different halftone images: one each for the cyan, magenta, yellow, and black inks that will be used to print it.

Halftone Dots

The invention of the photograph in the 1800s presented a real problem for printers because photographs contain grays. Before photography, there was only line copy—black and white. Imagine printing a "For Sale" sign with black ink on white paper. If the sign carries no photograph, the black ink has to reproduce only the jet-black type. If the "For Sale" sign carries a black-and-white photograph, however, the same black ink must now reproduce all the grays in the picture.

In truth, the black ink only creates the illusion of those grays. The images in the photograph are broken into thousands of halftone dots of various sizes, but all these dots are too tiny to be seen as dots. Instead, they blend with the white areas between them to create the visual sensation of gray. The effect is the same as if black paint is added to white paint to produce gray paint. Dark grays are simulated by

printing black dots that occupy a high percentage of the area. For example, an 80% dot covers 80% of the paper, with only 20% remaining unprinted. A 40% dot covers only half as much as the 80% dot and appears half as dark. Halftone dots allow the wide range of grays in the photograph to be reproduced with only black ink.

Percent dot sizes

The dot sizes are specified as percentages of ink density on a printed sheet. Dots in the *shadow area* of a halftone image should be around 95%. The *midtone area* dots should be between 30% and 70%. The dots in the *highlight areas* should be around 5%.

When evaluating a halftone negative, the percentages are reversed. An area in the negative containing 90% dots (90% black area and 10% clear) produces a 10% black dot in the positive, or print. See **Figure 11-3.**

halftone: a continuous tone copy formed as a series of fine dots of various sizes and densities.

halftone screen: a sheet of film or clear, flexible plastic with a diffused pattern of dots on it.

shadow area: the area of least density in a halftone negative. This area is the darkest area on the positive, or printed image.

midtone area: the area of an image falling between the highlight and shadow areas.

highlight area: the darkest area of a negative consisting of small, clear openings in an otherwise solid area. This area is the lightest area on the positive, or printed image.

Halftone Scale Percent Dot Areas

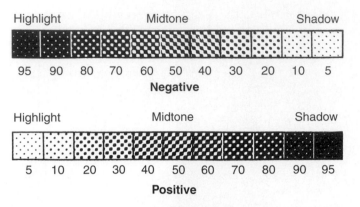

Highlight   Midtone   Shadow

95 90 80 70 60 50 40 30 20 10 5

Negative

Highlight   Midtone   Shadow

5 10 20 30 40 50 60 70 80 90 95

Positive

Figure 11-3. Dots of varying sizes represent the shadow and highlight areas of a negative or positive.

Resolution

Halftone screens are measured in lpi. The lpi of a halftone is equal to the number of halftone dots per linear inch. For example, a screen described as 166 lpi contains 166 rows and 166 columns of dots, which produces 27,556 dots per square inch. The lpi of a halftone is a measure of its resolution. The higher the lpi is, the greater the resolution and the sharper the image will be. See **Figure 11-4.** The lpi of a halftone is also referred to as its *screen ruling* (or *line screen*).

Halftone Screens

The major difference between line photography and halftone photography is the use of the halftone screen. A halftone screen is a sheet of film or clear, flexible plastic with a vignette (diffused) pattern of dots on it. Looking at the screen with a magnifier reveals a soft, out-of-focus pattern of diffused dots and corresponding spaces. See **Figure 11-5.** The halftone screen is always placed in contact with the film and is commonly referred to as a *halftone contact screen*, or simply, a *contact screen*.

Note

A special prescreened film can also be used to make halftones. The film is exposed to the contact-screen pattern during manufacture. The pattern remains a latent image on the film until the film is used to photograph continuous tone copy and developed. The developed negative is a halftone of the original copy.

Lowest lpi

Slightly Higher lpi

Higher lpi

Highest lpi

Figure 11-4. Compare the reproduction quality of this image at various screen rulings.

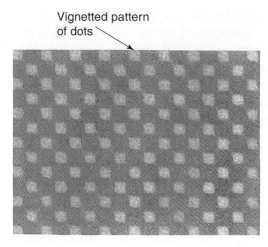

Figure 11-5. A contact screen is a precision pattern of vignetted or diffused dots on a flexible support, such as polyester. A vignetted area appears as a soft, out-of-focus pattern of diffused dots and corresponding spaces. (Eastman Kodak Co.)

A halftone screen is used in direct contact with the light-sensitive film. See **Figure 11-6.** A vacuum setup is used because it is essential that this be the closest possible contact. To provide a good vacuum seal, the screen must be at least 1″ (25.4 mm) larger on all four edges than the film being exposed.

To create a halftone negative, the reflected light from the original art passes through the halftone screen and exposes the film with the dot pattern from the screen. See **Figure 11-7.** The lightest areas of the continuous tone copy reflect the largest amounts of light to the halftone screen. A large amount of light is able to penetrate more of the screen's density than is a smaller amount of light, which would be reflected from a darker portion of the copy. In this manner, the light reflected from white areas of the original creates larger halftone dots on the film negative than the light reflected from darker portions does. See **Figure 11-8.** Contact screens are used for making halftone negatives on a process camera for black-and-white reproduction from reflective copy. These screens are also used in color-separation

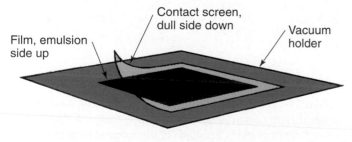

Figure 11-6. The halftone screen is placed over the light-sensitive film, emulsion to emulsion. (Eastman Kodak Co.)

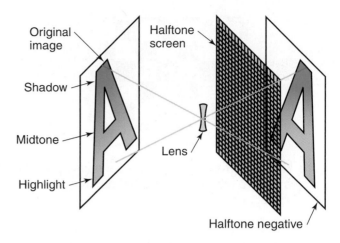

Figure 11-7. The light must pass through the screen to expose the film with its dot pattern.

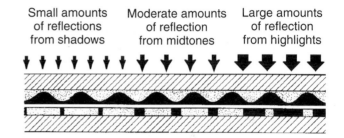

Figure 11-8. Halftone dots of different sizes are created because the density of a halftone screen varies with every dot. Large amounts of light reflected from light areas of the original photograph are able to penetrate moderate densities that smaller amounts of light from dark areas cannot penetrate. Large amounts of light create large dots, and small amounts of light create small dots on the negative.

photography—the process of creating halftone negatives for printing a full-color photograph.

Types of screens

A **square dot screen** produces square, midtone dots that join all four corners as the dots reach 50% size. See **Figure 11-9.** When the four corners of the square dot join, the density of that midtone area jumps slightly, resulting in a small tone break across the 50% dot. A **tone break** refers to an uneven blend

screen ruling: the number of ruled grid lpi on a halftone screen.

square dot screen: a halftone screen producing square dots that join in all four corners, as the dots reach 50% midtone size.

tone break: an uneven blend of the dots in the 50% region of a halftone.

Figure 11-9. A conventional square dot halftone screen produces square midtone dots. (Eastman Kodak Co.)

of the dots in the 50% region. The square dot screen is commonly referred to as a *conventional screen*.

The *elliptical dot screen* produces diamond or oval dots that join only two opposite corners as the dots reach 50% size. See **Figure 11-10.** The tone gradation across the 50% dots is smoother with elliptical dots than with square dots because only two corners join. The primary difference between a square dot screen and an elliptical dot screen is found in the midtones of a halftone reproduction.

The *magenta screen* is a purplish shade of red. The screen's coloring serves as a filter that usually limits its use to black-and-white original copy. Magenta contact screens can be used with magenta or yellow color-compensating filters to compress or extend the screen range and improve tone reproduction.

The *gray screen* is used in color separation, when a colored screen would affect the color. The silver or gray color is neutral and will not alter the effect of the color-separation filters. The *photomechanical transfer (PMT) gray contact screen* is used for making screened paper prints. This type of screen has an extralong screen range to maintain tonal separation and detail in the shadow areas of a screened print.

Screen angles

When printing a photograph in more than one ink color, the rows of halftone dots for each color must be

Figure 11-10. Elliptical dot screens produce diamond or oval midtone dots. (Eastman Kodak Co.)

placed at different angles to the horizontal. Printing the halftones at different screen angles eliminates moiré patterns, which occur when the dots of one color interfere with those of another color. A *moiré pattern* is an undesirable wavelike or checkerboard pattern visible across the halftone or screened image. See **Figure 11-11.** Moiré patterns are usually caused by overlapping one dot pattern over another. For example, screening a photograph that had already been screened will likely produce a moiré pattern.

Moiré patterns are kept minimal in full-color (process) printing when the magenta, cyan, yellow, and black screens are 30° from each other. It is not possible, however, to rotate all four screens 30° from each other because there is only a total of 90° in which to rotate them. For this reason, a standard set of screen angles has been devised. Printers typically use the screen angles specified in the Specifications for Web Offset Publications (SWOP) specs. See **Figure 11-12.** The usual screen angles consist of black at 45°, magenta at 75°, yellow at 90°, and cyan at 105°. Although they are not mandated as such, the SWOP specs are accepted as printing-industry standards.

The SWOP system places the three darkest inks 30° apart, with the yellow placed 15° away. For example, the black can be at 45°, the magenta at 75°, the cyan at 105°, and the yellow at 90°. The yellow can function on a different angle differential because it is the lightest color and is less likely to create a moiré. It is often acceptable to place the yellow on the

Figure 11-11. A moiré pattern is an undesirable wavelike or checkerboard pattern visible across the image. A directional misalignment of the dot pattern of the original halftone print and the dot pattern of the halftone screen used for rescreening usually causes it.

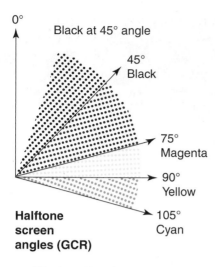

Black as Dominant Color

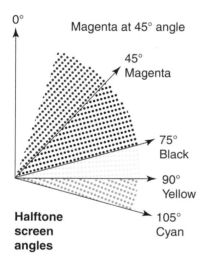

Magenta as Dominant Color

Figure 11-12. On the top, black is the dominant color because it is placed at the 45° angle. On the bottom, magenta replaces black as the dominant color at the 45° angle. (SWOP)

same angle as the cyan or, depending on the dominant colors in the reproduction, on the same angle as the magenta. This alignment has the advantage of spacing all the angles by 30° and eliminating the moiré that can occur between yellow and the other colors.

It is desirable to have the dominant color (magenta, in most cases) on the 45° angle. Screen angles for one- and two-color printing should follow the same guidelines, with the black at 45°. Depending on the application, the screen angles might vary from these specs. Only an experienced color separator, however, should do this.

Positive and negative screens

Either positive or negative contact screens can be used to make halftones. Positive screens are required to make halftone positives for indirect color separation. Negative screens (magenta or gray) are most often used to make halftone negatives. These screens are made with a built-in highlight exposure. This ensures good tonal separation with normal continuous tone copy. The three main characteristics that must be considered when evaluating a halftone negative are the highlight, midtone, and shadow areas.

Highlight areas

The highlight areas are the lightest parts of the original art and, therefore, the darkest parts of the negative. Highlight areas of the negative consist of small, clear openings in an otherwise solid dark area. See **Figure 11-13.**

Midtone areas

The halftone dots in the range of 30%–70% make up the midtones of the negative. See **Figure 11-14.** This is the area where the small black dots are increasing in size until they connect to form the 50% dots. At this point, the clear, open areas are equal in size to the black dots and form a checkerboard pattern. The 50% area is less obvious with an elliptical dot screen than with a conventional square dot screen. Between 50% and 70%, the open areas decrease in size, as the connected black dots increase in size.

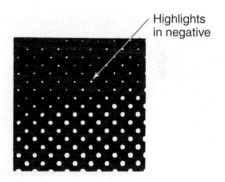

Figure 11-13. The highlights in a halftone negative consist of small, clear openings in an otherwise solid black area. (Eastman Kodak Co.)

conventional screen: a halftone screen that produces a square dot.

elliptical dot screen: a halftone screen with diamond or oval dots that join only two opposite corners, as the dots reach 50% size.

photomechanical transfer (PMT) gray contact screen: a halftone screen used for making screened paper prints.

moiré pattern: an undesirable wavelike or checkerboard pattern visible across a halftone or screened image. This pattern is usually caused by a misalignment of screens.

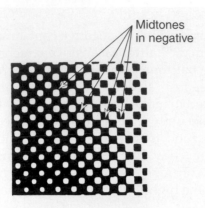

Figure 11-14. The midtones in a halftone negative consist of 30%–70% dots. (Eastman Kodak Co.)

Shadow areas

The areas of least density in the halftone negative are the shadow areas. Dots in the shadow areas range from tiny, pinpoint black dots to a dot value of about 30%. See **Figure 11-15.** Shadow dots print as 70% to 99% in the reproduction image. As in the case of the highlight dot, it is impossible to specify the exact size the shadow dot should attain. Dot size is dependent on the individual printing conditions and paper stock.

Identifying the 50% Dot

Identifying the 50% dot is a relatively simple matter with a screen that has a conventional square dot. See **Figure 11-16.** Identifying the 50% dot on an elliptical dot halftone is another matter. The dots join on two diagonally opposite corners at less than 50% and on the other two corners at more than 50%. See **Figure 11-17.** The 50% dot will have two corners well joined and two corners not quite joined. The width of the joined corners will be approximately equal to the

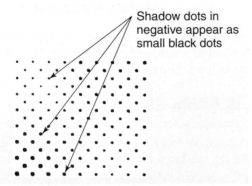

Figure 11-15. The shadow dots in a halftone negative range in size from tiny, pinpoint dots to a dot value of about 30%. Shadow dots print as 70% to 99% in the reproduction image. (Eastman Kodak Co.)

Figure 11-16. The 50% dot from a conventional square dot screen can be identified as a checkerboard pattern. (Eastman Kodak Co.)

Figure 11-17. The 50% dot from an elliptical dot screen is joined on two opposite corners. (Eastman Kodak Co.)

separation of the unjoined corners. Until a person becomes skilled in recognizing the patterns, the best method is to make a quick check with a densitometer. The table in **Figure 11-18** reveals that the 50% dot area should have a density reading of 0.30—with either an elliptical dot screen or a square dot screen.

Tonal Range

Original copy for halftone reproduction represents a *tonal range* from the whitest highlights, through varied grays, to the black of the shadows. A good black-and-white photograph has a range of densities from paper white to a 1.7-density black or slightly darker. The entire tonal range of the original can seldom be reproduced on the printed sheet. Solid, printing-press, black ink yields a density of about 1.40 to 1.60 (compared to a solid 2.0 black) on coated paper and usually less on uncoated papers. The loss of some of the tones of the original might occur in the highlights, in the shadows, or as a fairly uniform compression (reduction) of the tonal range.

The usual alternative is to reproduce the highlights through midtones as accurately as possible and accept the necessary loss of detail in the shadows. In the process, the highlight, midtone, and shadow areas are controlled with multiple exposures. A *main* (detail) exposure is always used. A second exposure,

Conversion from Density Readings to Percent Dot Area			
Integrated Halftone Density	Percent Dot Areas	Integrated Halftone Density	Percent Dot Areas
.004	1	.310	51
.009	2	.319	52
.013	3	.328	53
.018	4	.337	54
.022	5	.347	55
.027	6	.357	56
.032	7	.366	57
.036	8	.377	58
.041	9	.387	59
.046	10	.398	60
.051	11	.409	61
.056	12	.420	62
.061	13	.432	63
.066	14	.444	64
.071	15	.456	65
.076	16	.468	66
.081	17	.482	67
.086	18	.495	68
.092	19	.509	69
.097	20	.523	70
.102	21	.538	71
.108	22	.553	72
.114	23	.569	73
.119	24	.585	74
.125	25	.602	75
.131	26	.620	76
.137	27	.638	77
.143	28	.658	78
.149	29	.678	79
.155	30	.699	80
.161	31	.721	81
.168	32	.745	82
.174	33	.770	83
.181	34	.796	84
.187	35	.824	85
.194	36	.854	86
.201	37	.886	87
.208	38	.921	88
.215	39	.959	89
.222	40	1.000	90
.229	41	1.046	91
.237	42	1.097	92
.244	43	1.155	93
.252	44	1.222	94
.260	45	1.301	95
.268	46	1.398	96
.276	47	1.522	97
.284	48	1.699	98
.292	49	2.000	99
.301	50		

Figure 11-18. This chart shows the percentage of dot areas converted to density readings. For example, a 90% dot area should have a density reading of 1.000. (Eastman Kodak Co.)

the *flash exposure*, is usually required to enhance dots in the shadow area. A *no-screen exposure* is used where additional highlight contrast is desired. The flash and no-screen exposures are explained later.

Tone control

Different types of contact screens vary in the way they control the tonal range of the negative. Therefore, a more detailed discussion of screen characteristics should prove helpful. Highlight, midtone, and shadow areas of a halftone are interdependent. Each element cannot be manipulated without affecting the others.

The flash and no-screen exposures affect one part of a tone scale more than another part. The whole scale is affected, however, with the characteristics of the contact screen determining the relative amount of effect. A contact screen is limited as to the range or amount of the original continuous tone copy it can convert to tones.

Basic density range (BDR)

The ability of a contact screen to reproduce tones depends on many factors. These include such things as light source, exposure and development techniques, and other camera and darkroom variables. Given a fixed set of working conditions, however, a contact screen is capable of reproducing a specific range of tones.

Disregarding variables, a single camera exposure of a gray scale through the contact screen to a sheet of film will result in a measure of the screen's specific range of tones. The tonal-range capability of the contact screen is called the **basic density range (BDR)**, or screen range. The following procedure is recommended to determine the BDR of a contact screen:

1. Place a calibrated gray scale in the camera copyboard. See **Figure 11-19.** Set the controls for making a same-size (100%) reproduction.
2. Cover a sheet of orthochromatic film with a selected contact screen, emulsion to emulsion.

tonal range: the range of tones in an original continuous tone image or a halftone reproduction, expressed as the difference between the areas of maximum and minimum density.

flash exposure: a nonimaging, yellow light exposure made through a halftone screen. This exposure is used to enhance the dots in the shadow regions of the halftone negative.

basic density range (BDR): the tonal-range capability of a halftone screen.

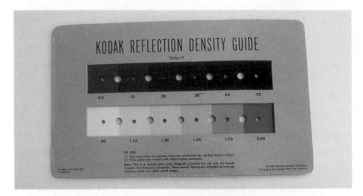

Figure 11-19. A reflection-density guide is a calibrated gray scale used for halftone photography.

3. Expose a halftone negative of the gray scale. Try an exposure of 30 seconds at f/16, if two 1500-watt PXAs are set 4' from the copy.
4. Process the film and evaluate the resulting test negative. Refer to Chapter 10 for the film-processing procedure.

On the test negative, locate the halftone dots representing typical highlight and shadow dots as you would want them in the highlights and shadows of your halftone negatives. **Figure 11-20** illustrates a test negative of a reflection-density guide. If this is similar to your negative, you might select the dots in the 0.20 step as typical highlight dots and the dots in the 1.30 step as typical shadow dots.

Halftone-exposure calculators

A halftone-exposure calculator is a device that simplifies finding the proper exposure. See **Figure 11-21.** The basic principle of this calculator applies only to reproducing copy "as is" or as you see it. It is extremely accurate if calibrations and procedures are done with control and if exposures and processing are handled carefully. The greater the control of the variables is, the greater the accuracy of the calculator will be.

Modifying the BDR

For the halftone negative to represent all tones in the copy, the BDR must be modified to equal the density range of the copy. To lengthen the BDR, use a flash exposure. To shorten the BDR, use a no-screen exposure. A flash exposure is a yellow-light exposure made through the halftone screen. This exposure is used to enhance the dots in the shadow regions of the halftone negative and affects the entire emulsion surface uniformly. The flash exposure can also be referred to as a *shadow exposure*.

A no-screen exposure is a very brief white-light exposure of the highlight areas of an image without the use of a halftone screen. This exposure is used to increase the highlight contrast and detail of the camera copy, while not affecting the dots in

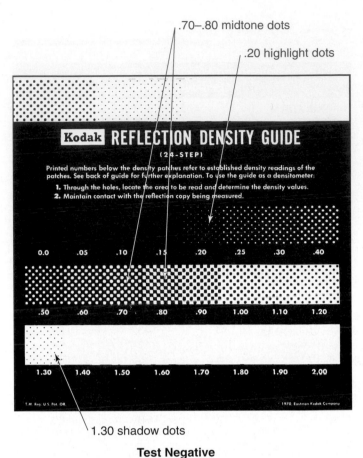

Test Negative

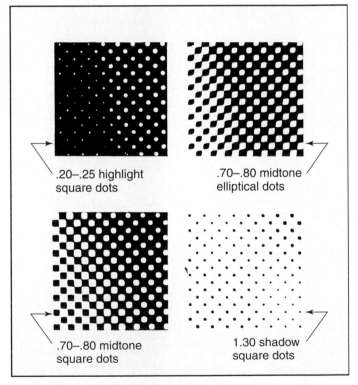

Test Negative Magnified

Figure 11-20. An example of a test negative of a reflection-density guide, indicating the desired dot sizes for highlight, midtone, and shadow dots. Magnified portions of the test negative can be used to compare the square dot and elliptical dot midtone structure. (Eastman Kodak Co.)

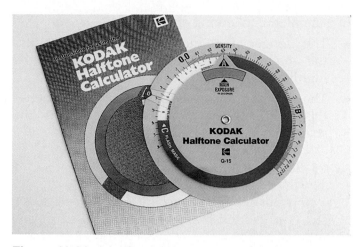

Figure 11-21. A halftone-exposure calculator provides an easy way to calculate halftone exposures.

the shadow areas. A no-screen exposure is usually slightly less than 10% of the main exposure time. This exposure is also called a *bump exposure*.

In most cases, the BDR falls short of the range of the original photograph, known as the *copy-density range (CDR)*, requiring a flash exposure. If the BDR is exactly equal to the CDR, the copy can be reproduced with a main exposure alone. The example below illustrates this rule:

$$
\begin{array}{r}
1.10 \text{ BDR} \\
- \underline{1.10 \text{ CDR}} \\
0.00
\end{array}
$$

It becomes essential for the camera operator to establish a basic flash exposure because each piece of copy requires a different flash exposure to match the range of tones on the original. The flash-exposure table in **Figure 11-22** shows the difference

Basic Flash	0.10	0.20	0.30	0.40	0.50
10	2.00	3.75	5.00	6.00	6.75
11	2.25	4.00	5.50	6.50	7.50
12	2.50	4.50	6.00	7.25	8.25
13	2.75	4.75	6.50	7.75	8.75
14	3.00	5.25	7.00	8.50	9.50
15	3.25	5.50	7.50	9.00	10.25
16	3.25	6.00	8.00	9.50	11.00
17	3.50	6.25	8.50	10.25	11.50
18	3.75	6.75	9.00	10.75	12.25
19	4.00	7.00	9.50	11.50	13.00
20	4.00	7.50	11.00	12.00	13.50

Figure 11-22. A flash-exposure table shows the difference in exposure times for various copy and screen ranges, once the basic time has been established. This table should be posted next to the process camera.

in exposure times once the basic time is established. As every piece of continuous tone copy varies, the difference between the copy and screen ranges will fluctuate, and so should the flash exposure. The camera operator should post a flash-exposure table next to the camera.

The darkroom flashing lamp should be equipped with a filter holder that will accept a neutral-density (ND) filter. See **Figure 11-23**. ND filters complement the flashing lamp's normal yellow filter. These filters can be used to shorten the flash-exposure time, allow better control of the exposure time, and make it easier to duplicate exposure times accurately.

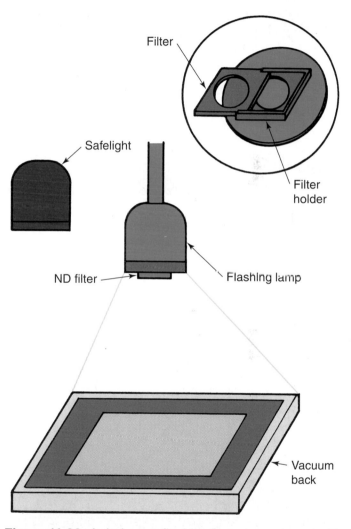

Figure 11-23. A darkroom flashing lamp is equipped with a filter holder that will hold ND filters. These filters can be used to shorten flash-exposure time.

shadow exposure: a yellow light exposure made through a halftone screen after the main exposure, in making a halftone. This exposure is used to enhance the dots in the shadow regions of the halftone negative and to improve detail.

Note

Newton's rings (concentric bands of light) might become a problem with the gray contact screen when using an ND filter. If Newton's rings become a problem, try flashing without the filter.

Local printing conditions will determine the most useful BDR values. The table in **Figure 11-24** will serve as a rough guide. The modified BDR is shown at the top of the table. Underneath each value is a rough guide to its effect on the tone scale when printed on various papers. The table includes high-reflectance (HR) papers, such as clay-coated papers; normal-reflectance (NR) papers, such as offset paper; and low-reflectance (LR) papers, such as newsprint.

In general, the following effects will be noted:

- The longer the modified BDR, the better the shadow detail and the more loss in the highlights.
- The shorter the modified BDR, the better the highlight detail and the more loss in the shadows.

Note

To find out how each modification affects the actual printability of the negatives, make plates for the offset press. Make press proofs of the test negatives on the paper normally used. Compare the press proofs, instead of the negatives.

Effect of Modified BDR on Tone Reproduction					
Modified BDR	.75 and below	.80–.90	.95–1.10	1.15–1.30	1.35 and higher
Effect on Tone Reproduction	Greatly accentuates the highlight detail on all stocks.	Tends to accentuate highlight detail on HR stock. Greatly accentuates highlight detail on NR and LR stocks.	Satisfactory highlight detail on HR and NR stocks. Accentuates highlight detail on LR stock.	Accentuates shadow detail on HR stock. Satisfactory highlight detail on NR and LR stocks.	Greatly accentuates shadow detail on all stocks.
Approximate Placement of 50% Dot on Gray Scale (When the Highlight Dot Is in the .00 Step)	.40 and below	.40–.50	.50–.60	.60–.70	.70 and higher

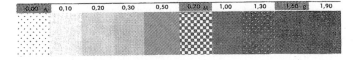

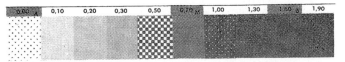

The 50% dot will appear at about the 0.70 step when the modified BDR is about 1.25 to 1.35.

The 50% dot will appear at about the 0.50 step when the modified BDR is about 0.90 to 1.00.

Figure 11-24. Modifying the BDR of various kinds of copy is sometimes necessary under certain conditions. The type of paper, ink, and press and the purpose of the printed piece are considerations when modifying the BDR of the copy. The 50% dot is used to illustrate a modified BDR effect. (Eastman Kodak Co.)

Applying the modified BDR

Assume you have worked out how to obtain the several modified BDRs under your conditions. You will have recorded the procedure for each BDR. Proceed as follows:

1. Determine the paper on which the printing is to be done: HR, NR, or LR.
2. Study the photograph being reproduced to determine if one portion of the tonal scale needs improvement. From the table in **Figure 11-24,** select the modified BDR indicating that particular improvement on your paper.
3. Expose the negative, using the contact screen and technique that gave you the indicated BDR. Add the flash required.

You will find that a large number of your negatives call for normal exposures. In relatively few cases, you will have to apply extreme measures. This is the result of the design of the negative magenta and gray contact screens.

Making Halftone Negatives

The steps in making a halftone negative are illustrated in **Figure 11-25.** This procedure assumes the original copy is normal or near average. Many photographs, however, are poorly made. The photograph might have no highlight detail or be dark and muddy. It might have a density range shorter than that of the contact screen.

Before making a halftone negative, let us review what you will need, in the way of equipment and supplies:

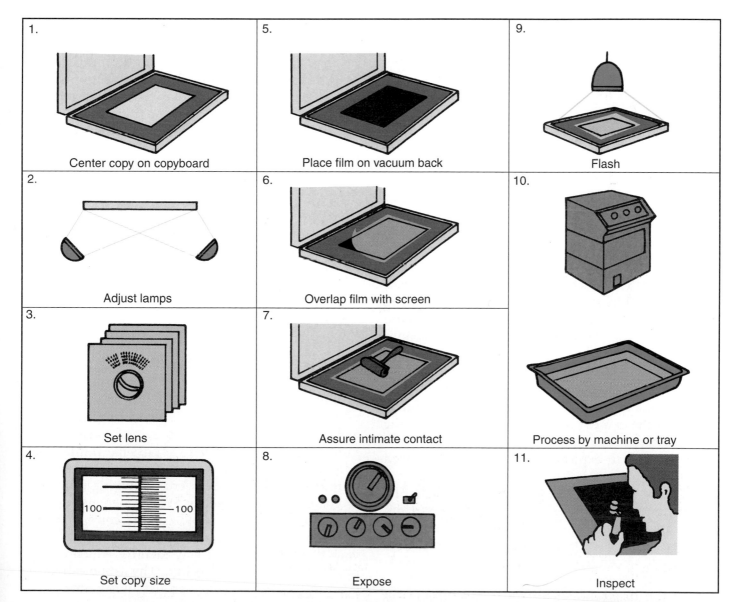

1. Center copy on copyboard	5. Place film on vacuum back	9. Flash
2. Adjust lamps	6. Overlap film with screen	10.
3. Set lens	7. Assure intimate contact	Process by machine or tray
4. Set copy size	8. Expose	11. Inspect

Figure 11-25. The major halftone reproduction steps are illustrated. The procedure shown assumes that the original continuous tone copy is normal, or average. (Chemco, Inc.)

- Darkroom.
- Process camera.
- Flash lamp (if not built into the camera).
- Contact screen (magenta or gray, 133 line).
- Litho-ortho film.
- Processing trays and sink or film processor and processing chemicals.
- Reflection-density guide, Kodak Q-16.
- Halftone calculator, Kodak Q-15.
- 10× or 12× magnifier.

To make a halftone negative, apply what you have just learned by following these steps. Before you begin, determine the correct main- and flash-exposure times.

1. Clean the copyboard glass on both sides.
2. Place a piece of black-and-white continuous tone copy upside down in the copyboard with a 12-step gray scale beside it.
3. Set the bellows and copyboard extensions for same-size reproduction.
4. Set the lens for the same f-stop as used in line work at 100%.
5. Adjust the lights for proper angles.
6. Set the main exposure time.
7. Turn off the overhead white lights and turn on the red safelights.
8. Select the correct litho-ortho film box and remove a sheet. Cut the sheet to the proper size, if required.
9. Open the camera back and position the piece of film.
10. Position the contact screen over the film, emulsion side to emulsion side. The contact screen must be at least 1″ larger on all four sides than the film. See **Figure 11-26**. This is to ensure good vacuum contact.
11. Turn on the vacuum pump.
12. Close the vacuum back.
13. Press the exposure button and expose the film.
14. Open the camera back, but do not turn off the vacuum or remove the contact screen.
15. Set the flash-exposure timer for the required time.
16. Make the flash exposure with yellow light. The halftone screen remains in position over the film during exposure.
17. Turn off the vacuum pump and remove the contact screen and film from the camera back. Replace the contact screen in its container.
18. Set the darkroom timer for 2 3/4 minutes in readiness for film development.

Figure 11-26. The halftone contact screen is positioned over the unexposed film, emulsion to emulsion. A contact screen must be at least 1″ larger on all four sides than the film. (nuArc Company, Inc.)

19. Process the exposed film in the same way as described for line-negative work. The developing solutions should be fresh and maintained at 68°F (20°C). Move the film back and forth during the developing cycle.
20. After the negative has been stopped, fixed, and washed, squeegee the acetate side. Hang the film to dry in a dust-free area of the darkroom or process it in a film dryer.
21. Examine the halftone negative on a light table. An acceptable negative should give a 90% dot in the highlights and a 10% dot in the shadows. It might be necessary to adjust exposure times slightly and try again.

Troubleshooting

By establishing a troubleshooting system, many common darkroom problems can be easily fixed or eliminated. The troubleshooting system should take exposure, temperature, processing, handling techniques, and product types into consideration. Eliminate as many variables as possible. If this rule is adhered to, problems that arise resulting from poor or unusual copy can be overcome with a minimum of changes in the system. When changes must be made to meet the demands of the copy, only one change should be put into practice at a time. In this way, the operator can easily identify which change produced the desired result. The troubleshooting chart in **Figure 11-27** can be a useful resource.

Problem	Cause	Remedy
Image develops slowly	A. Material underexposed	A. Check lens opening, lamp position, and exposure setting. When determining exposure, allow for halftone screen. If necessary, use gray rather than magenta screen to reduce length of exposure.
Highlight dots plugged up	A. Material overexposed B. Too much bump C. Developer too warm D. Too much agitation of developer	A. Reduce main exposure. B. Reduce or eliminate the no-screen exposure. C. Cool to 68°F. D. Agitate less vigorously.
Highlight dots too open	A. Underexposure B. Inactive chemistry C. Developer cold	A. Increase main exposure. B. Try a no-screen exposure for 5% of the main exposure to pinch up highlights. C. Increase agitation of chemistry. Warm to 68°F.
No shadow dot	A. Not enough flash B. Not enough main exposure C. Too much developer activity D. Exhausted developer E. Developer too cold	A. Increase flash exposure. B. Increase main exposure (this will also affect highlights). C. Slow down developer agitation to give shadow dots a chance to come up. If necessary, try to still develop for a third of the developing time. D. Dispose of properly and replace with fresh chemistry. E. Warm to 68°F.
Shadow dots weak in areas adjacent to highlights	A. Developer losing strength	A. Dispose of properly and replace with fresh developer.
Fingerprints	A. Chemistry impregnated in fingers of operator B. Fingerprints in original photo	A. Make sure hands are fully dry before handling new film. Use powder or rubber gloves. B. Try to clean the original with film cleaner. Change angle of copy in copyboard, where lights will strike from a different angle.

Figure 11-27. Troubleshooting charts for halftone work are useful when displayed near the camera and darkroom area.

Stochastic Screening

As has been explained, moiré patterns can be a problem when printing color photographs. A method of creating halftone negatives that avoids the threat of moiré patterns is randomly placed halftone dots. In conventional halftones, the halftone dots vary in size, or amplitude, but have the same density, or spacing between them. *Stochastic screening* is a type of electronic screening using dots that are all the same size but vary in frequency or pattern. Varying the distance between the dots creates the illusion of tone variances. See **Figure 11-28.** There are more dots in darker areas and fewer dots in lighter areas. Stochastic screening cannot be accomplished photographically. Although it is an electronic process,

stochastic screening is explained in this chapter because it is a method of creating halftones.

The term *stochastic* deals with probability, arising from the distribution of random variables. There are no screen angles with which to be concerned because the dots in a stochastic screen are randomly placed. The overall distribution is important, not the placement of the individual dots. For this reason, the term *line screen*, or *lpi*, which describes the uniform distance between the dots in a conventional halftone, has no application in stochastic screening.

stochastic screening: a type of electronic halftone screening using dots that are all the same size but varying in frequency or pattern.

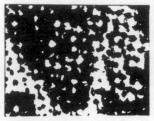

Conventional Halftone Screening	Stochastic Halftone Screening

Figure 11-28. Unlike conventional halftone screening, stochastic halftone screening has no visible dot pattern. Notice the difference in these two enlargements. (Linotype-Hell)

Conventional halftone dots are referred to as *AM screening* because they create tone values through AM. This means the size of the dot varies. Stochastic halftone dots are referred to as *FM screening* because they create tone values through FM. This means the number (or frequency of occurrence) of dots varies.

On the printing press, the stochastic screen tone will print consistently and render more detail. There is no interference or moiré, and the contrast is well defined. The press operator has less trouble achieving and maintaining this detail and reaching optimum ink density. This technology allows up to 15% more ink to be used, resulting in a more striking reproduction.

Another advantage to the random dot placement is smoother tone rendering over the complete tonal scale. With conventional halftone dots, eventually two dots will touch, blending into a larger mass, as the tonal value increases. This effect leads to tone jumps, causing ink buildup on the press and reduced quality. Stochastic screening exhibits no tone jumps at specific points, due to the very small size and careful distribution of the dots.

The largest application of stochastic screening is in the reproduction of high-quality images. Examples include fine-art reproductions, art subjects, fabrics, and objects with regularly repeating or geometric patterns susceptible to moiré. Another application is scientific and medical imaging, where fine detail can be reproduced at a lower resolution or on coarser paper.

Special-Effects Photography

As discussed in previous chapters, there are many ways to create and generate text and art. Just as most current image generation is electronic, most image manipulation is performed electronically. Special effects are used on type and images for emphasis, to add color, and to help convey a mood or message. Regardless of whether conventional or electronic methods are used to manipulate images, image alteration serves the same purpose.

Special-effects photography refers to the creative side of darkroom photography. There are a number of photomechanical methods available for producing special effects, including halftone screens, line shots, posterization, and duotones. The equipment found in most offset-lithography darkrooms can be used for special-effects photography. The most important pieces of equipment are the process camera and contact-printing frame with a point-source light.

Special-Effects Screens

As discussed earlier in this chapter, halftone (contact) screens are placed in direct contact with the film before exposure. Standard halftone screens create the dots needed to print images so they simulate the original continuous tone art. Special halftone screens can be used to apply unusual patterns to images and copy. These screens create a variety of effects, including mezzotint, circular, wavy line, and vertical straight line. See **Figure 11-29.**

When using special patterns on an image, remember that some artwork lends itself to a desired effect better than other artwork. Patterns such as the concentric circles in **Figure 11-30** can be used to draw the viewer's attention to one part of an image. Once applied, the special-effects contact screen essentially creates a line conversion, and the image can be easily manipulated without distorting tone gradations.

Special-effects screens are used when a full tonal range is important and a pattern or texture is desired. **Figure 11-31** shows how a contact screen can be used to impart a linen pattern. The effectiveness of special-effects screens depends on how well the design will enhance communication.

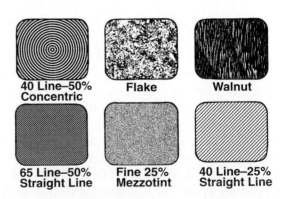

40 Line–50% Concentric	Flake	Walnut
65 Line–50% Straight Line	Fine 25% Mezzotint	40 Line–25% Straight Line

Figure 11-29. Halftone screens are available in a variety of patterns. (John N. Schaedler, Inc.)

Figure 11-30. A concentric-circle special-effects screen can be used to single out one item in a photograph. This example shows a person in a crowd being singled out. (Chemco, Inc.)

Figure 11-31. A linen pattern is one of many treatments that can be imparted to a photograph. (ByChrome Co.)

Line Shots

As was explained in Chapter 7, reproducing continuous tone art, such as a photograph, requires a screening to break the various tones of the original art into thousands of halftone dots that create the illusion of grays. Therefore, a faithful reproduction of continuous tone art requires the art to be treated as halftone copy. If no halftone screen is used, the photograph receives a *line shot*, and the high-contrast nature of lithographic film will eliminate the middle tones and convert the photograph to strictly black and white. See **Figure 11-32.** Although the loss

Faithful Reproduction

Line Shot

Figure 11-32. A faithful reproduction of a black-and-white photograph requires a screen. If the photograph is treated as line copy and a screen is not used, the high-contrast nature of orthochromatic film causes the middle tones to be recorded as either black or white. This effect is referred to as a *line shot*.

AM screening: producing a conventional halftone with equally spaced dots of various sizes.

FM screening: a type of electronic halftone screening using dots that are all the same size but varying in frequency or pattern.

line shot: an image captured with a process camera without the use of a halftone screen, usually used for line copy, such as text and line drawings, and occasionally used to reduce an original photograph to only black and white.

of middle tones would destroy the visual message of most photographs, other photographs can be visually strengthened when reduced to only two tones. In fact, a line shot can convert a photograph into an image resembling a pen-and-ink drawing. See **Figure 11-33.**

Posterization

Posterization is the conversion of a continuous tone image to a high-contrast image with one or more middle tones. See **Figure 11-34.** In other words, a line shot becomes a posterization when one or more middle tones are added. When posterized photomechanically, high-contrast film is used to produce a line negative. Posterizations are classified according to the number of colors (inks) and tones reproduced on the final press sheet.

A posterization is prepared photomechanically by increasing the exposure to approximately three times the normal line-copy exposure. A second tone can be added to the print by making a negative with the exposure reduced by approximately one-half. This records the midtones of the original copy and adds detail to the print. More colors can be added to record the highlight areas of the original. It is necessary to prepare a negative for each color. With conventional litho film, the negative can be stripped into position in the flat for exposure to the offset plate. Posterizations can also be performed digitally in an image manipulation program by specifying a set number of gradient steps.

Original Photograph

Line Shot

Figure 11-33. Used with an appropriate photograph, a line shot can resemble a pen-and-ink drawing.

Original Photograph

Posterization

Figure 11-34. A posterization adds one or more midtones to a line shot. The result can be increased detail.

Figure 11-35. A duotone combines the interest of color with the contrast of black ink on white paper. (Strachan Henshaw Machinery, Inc.)

Figure 11-36. A fake duotone lacks the contrast of a duotone because it is no more than a halftone image printed over a uniform block of a second color. (Strachan Henshaw Machinery, Inc.)

Duotones

A *duotone* is a two-color halftone produced by overprinting images made from two halftone negatives made from the same photograph. See **Figure 11-35.** The two negatives (screens) are made to different specs. One negative emphasizes highlights, and the other emphasizes shadows. Most duotones are produced by using black ink and another color of ink. Sometimes a dark color other than black is used with a light color, to be more spectacular than using black and another color.

In preparing a duotone, the primary negative (the darker color) is exposed and processed for nearly normal contrast. The negative should favor detail in the shadows and have only partial highlights. The second negative (the lighter color), must have a contact screen angled at 30° to the first, to prevent a moiré. A moiré will result from two negatives with tones printing directly over one another.

A *fake duotone* is produced from a single halftone and a uniform block of a color, instead of two halftone screens. See **Figure 11-36.** The fake duotone can be created to simulate a color-and-black duotone or a color-on-color duotone. This duotone is an inexpensive way to add the appearance of color to a printed piece. The fake duotone lacks contrast, however, because no portion of the photograph can be lighter than the screen tint.

posterization: the conversion of a continuous tone image to a high-contrast image with only a few distinct tones. This conversion can be performed photomechanically with high-contrast film or electronically in an illustration program, by specifying a set number of gradient steps.

duotone: a two-color halftone produced with two halftone negatives made from the same photograph.

fake duotone: a photograph printed in black ink over an area (usually a rectangle) printed in a color.

Summary

Halftone photography is a special photographic procedure used almost exclusively by the printing industry. This photography is used to convert continuous tone copy into a series of halftone dots. It is necessary to convert these images into dots in order to print them with an offset press. The dots and paper give the viewer the illusion of a continuous array of tones.

Traditionally, halftones are created photomechanically with the use of a process camera and halftone screens. It is often necessary to perform various tests to determine the best screen-and-exposure combination. Many variables, including the lpi the screen contains, determine the reproduction quality of a halftone image.

Stochastic screening is a method of producing halftone dots not aligned in rows, but instead placed randomly. With stochastic screening, tone darkness is not determined by the size of the halftone dots, but by the number of dots in an area of the photograph. Stochastic screening eliminates the problem of moiré patterns.

Photographic images can be manipulated to produce special effects. These effects include special halftone screens, line shots, posterizations, and duotones. Used appropriately, special effects can enhance a photograph and strengthen its visual impact.

Review Questions

Please do not write in this book. Write your answers on a separate sheet of paper.

1. What is a halftone?
2. _____ copy consists of a range of gray (gradations of tone).
3. Name two types of original copy that should be prepared as halftones.
4. Halftone dot sizes are specified as percentages of _____ on a printed sheet.
5. What does it mean when the printer says the work will be printed with a 155-line screen?
6. Which halftone dots on a printed reproduction are the largest?
   A. Highlight.
   B. Midtone.
   C. Shadow.
   D. Elliptical.
7. The _____ contact screen is a purplish red.
8. A gray screen is used in direct color separation because it is neutral in color and will not affect the _____ filters.
9. What is a moiré pattern? What causes a moiré pattern?
10. When preparing a halftone, why is it best to begin with an original continuous tone image and not a printed halftone?
11. The halftone dots in the range from 30%–70% comprise the _____ of the negative.
12. Why is it better to use an elliptical dot screen for copy with soft midtone vignetting?
13. The areas of least density in the halftone negative are the _____ areas. Dots in these areas range from tiny, pinpoint dots to a dot value of about 30%.
14. Explain the tonal-range capability of a halftone contact screen.
15. The tonal capability of the contact screen is called the _____.
16. If the BDR is 1.10 and the CDR is .95, _____ exposure should be used.
    A. a bump
    B. a flash
    C. both a bump and flash
    D. no
17. Describe the function of a flash exposure.
18. Explain the purpose of a no-screen exposure.
19. ND filters can be used to _____ (shorten/lengthen) flash-exposure time.
20. The _____ (shorter/longer) the modified BDR is, the better the shadow detail and the more loss in the highlights will be.
21. The _____ (shorter/longer) the modified BDR is, the better the highlight detail and the more loss in the shadows will be.
22. What is stochastic screening?
23. Special _____ can be used to photomechanically apply unusual patterns to images and copy.
24. Describe a photograph that could be visually enhanced if it was printed with a concentric-patterned screen, instead of with halftone dots.
25. A line shot of a black-and-white photograph produces an image with no _____.

26. _____ is an electronic or photomechanical special effect that converts a continuous tone image to a high-contrast image with one or more distinct tones.

27. A duotone is a two-color halftone produced with two halftone _____ made from the same black-and-white photograph, but at different _____.

28. Summarize the methods of producing duotones.

Skill-Building Activities

1. Prepare a display of printed halftone samples from magazines and newspapers. Label each sample with its correct screen ruling (such as 85, 100, 120, 133, or 150).

2. Prepare satisfactory halftone negatives, using main and flash exposures. Check each of the halftone negatives with a 10× or 12× magnifier over a light table.

3. Prepare a satisfactory halftone negative from an already-printed coarse-screened halftone print. You must avoid producing a moiré pattern when angling the contact screen.

4. After a demonstration by your instructor, determine the correct main- and flash-exposure times for a halftone.

5. Over a period of several days, look in magazines and other printed materials for examples of line shots, posterizations, and duotones.

6. Obtain a black-and-white photograph suitable for a three-tone posterization. Prepare the posterization with care and note whether the correct detail was obtained.

7. Obtain a black-and-white photograph. Use a suitable special-effects contact screen to prepare a negative. Prepare a paper contact proof of the special-effects halftone.

8. Obtain a black-and-white photograph suitable for a duotone. Use an appropriate contact screen to prepare both negatives. Make color proofs of the negatives and note whether the correct detail was attained.

Everything in Its Place

After camera-ready art has been captured onto film, the films must be arranged so they will appear where they should on the plate. Without this precise placement, pages in a book would appear crooked, out of order, or upside down. Photographs would be backward or in the wrong place. In this photograph, carefully measured lines are being drawn to act as guides for the placement of the film.

This highly skilled task of arranging films is known as *image assembly*, or merely *stripping*. Image assembly revolves around the use of tools, manual dexterity, and precision and is a part of conventional prepress. Although most image assembly is performed digitally, the principles of where images must be imposed on the plate have not changed. In fact, people who understand conventional image assembly usually make an easy transition into the digital world. For this reason, the principles of imposition are in this chapter.

(Color Graphics, Los Angeles)

Chapter 12
Conventional Image Assembly and Imposition

Key Terms

actinic light
axis
bleed image
blueline
butterfly
collimator
color bar
complementary flat
conventional image
   assembly
creep
diazo proofing material
Dylux® proofing material
flat
folding dummy
form
goldenrod paper
image assembly
imposition
layout line
layout table
lead edge
lip
main flat
masking flat
masking sheet
negative film assembly

nonactinic light
paper gripper margin
parallax error
pinhole
pin register system
plate bend
positive film assembly
press sheet
register mark
register pin
register punch
right-reading side
screen angle indicator
single-side imposition
star target
step-and-repeat film
   assembly
stripper
trim edge
work-and-back
   imposition
work-and-flop
   imposition
work-and-tumble
   imposition
work-and-turn
   imposition

Learning Objectives

When you have completed the reading and assigned activities related to this chapter, you will be able to do the following:

◆ Define *imposition* and *image assembly*.

◆ Describe the four primary imposition layouts used in offset lithography.

◆ Give examples of the equipment, tools, and materials the stripper commonly uses.

◆ Explain the importance of a reliable registration system for film assembly.

◆ Use a pin register system to prepare a work-and-tumble job.

◆ Discuss the steps required to manually prepare a single-color flat.

◆ Identify the additional steps required to prepare a complementary flat.

◆ Create a folding dummy and use it to impose an eight-page signature.

Image assembly is the process of positioning images so they appear where they need to be on the printing plate and, by extension, on the press sheet. This positioning is at the heart of optimizing the capabilities of the press and postpress functions. Poor image assembly wastes paper, machine time, and money. In contrast, well thought-out image assembly reduces both production time and material costs.

This assembly can be performed conventionally with film images on light tables, or it can be performed electronically at a computer with special imposition software. Increasingly, image assembly is being performed electronically. Many offset-printing companies, however, continue to use manual methods of imposition and film assembly. Also, it is widely believed that the best way to learn the principles is to perform image assembly conventionally. This chapter will explain conventional image assembly. The use of electronic imposition is presented in Chapter 15.

The act of *conventional image assembly*, commonly referred to as *stripping*, is the process of positioning images by accurately positioning and fastening film negatives or positives to a masking sheet. The procedure is also known as *film assembly* because the images are on pieces of film, and the person who performs this function is called a *stripper*. See **Figure 12-1.**

The *masking sheet* is a thick sheet of paper or plastic holding the films in place. This sheet is the same size as the offset plate used for the job and does not transmit blue light. The completed masking sheet with its taped-on films is called a *flat*. After completion, the flat is placed over a plate, and light passes through the clear areas of the film images to expose the plate.

Imposition Principles

Imposition is the pattern of images arranged so they will be in proper position on the press sheet. Estimators, job planners, and image assemblers must be very familiar with the basic types of imposition so the best type is selected. The type of imposition used depends on the size of the *press sheet* and the size and design of the finished piece. The four basic types of imposition (or press layouts) used in printing are single-side, work-and-back (or sheetwise), work-and-turn, and work-and-tumble imposition. The following explanation is limited to flat-sheet imposition. Signature imposition, used when printing books and magazines, is presented later in the chapter because it is more complex.

Single-Side Imposition

Single-side imposition is used when printing one-sided pieces, such as labels, posters, forms, letterhead stationery, and business cards. This imposition is a good place to begin when learning imposition principles because it is the least complex. The images are arranged to print as many as practical on each press sheet, with considerations for paper-grain direction, paper grippers, and bleed images. Paper-grain direction influences imposition if the client has specified the grain direction of the final piece. For example, business cards should always be imposed so the paper grain runs in the long dimension, or the cards will lack stiffness. As shown in **Figure 12-2,** 12 business cards measuring 3 1/2″ × 2″ can be printed on an 8 1/2″ × 11″ press sheet, but if the press sheet

Figure 12-1. *Stripping, image assembly,* and *film assembly* are terms for the manual positioning of film negatives or positives onto a masking sheet.

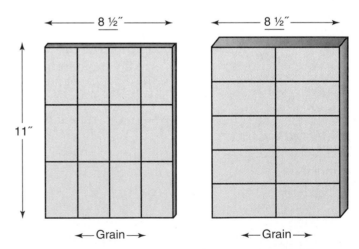

Figure 12-2. An 8 1/2″ × 11″ press sheet can yield 10 or 12 business cards, depending on the imposition. In this situation, the grain direction of the press sheet dictates the 10-up imposition to produce grain-long cards. Reminder: the underlined dimension is the grain direction.

is grain short, the finished cards will be grain short and lack stiffness. A better imposition for this job is to print 10 cards on each press sheet to ensure that the finished cards are grain long and have the expected stiffness. The first imposition is referred to as a *12-up imposition*, and the second is called a *10-up imposition*.

Paper grippers influence imposition if the graphic designer has placed images so close to the edge that the metal, fingerlike grippers holding the **lead edge** of the press sheet during printing interfere with the images being printed. As shown in **Figure 12-3,** two 5 1/2″ × 8 1/2″ fliers can be printed on an 8 1/2″ × 11″ press sheet (a two-up imposition). The design allows an adequate amount of unprinted margin on the lead edge for the 3/16″ paper grippers. If the graphic designer had placed a border within 1/8″ of the flier's edges, however, the paper grippers would cover an image area of the press sheet and prevent printing. The fliers would have to be run with a one-up imposition, if printing on a larger press sheet is not an option, and after printing, the extra paper would be trimmed away. **Bleed images** also influence imposition by requiring extra space on the press sheet. If the graphic designer of the 5 1/2″ × 8 1/2″ flier described above had chosen to bleed images, a two-up imposition would require bleed margins on the outside of the press sheet and gutters between the images, as well as extra paper grippers. See **Figure 12-4.**

Work-and-Back Imposition

Imagine that the same 5 1/2″ × 8 1/2″ flier is two sided—blue ink on the front and red ink on the back. This design change obviously requires the card to

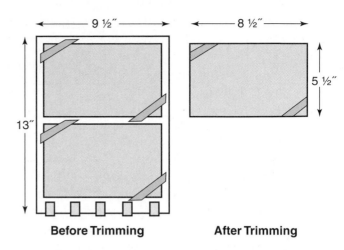

Before Trimming   **After Trimming**

Figure 12-4. Bleed images require extra paper for not only the grippers, but for the bleeds as well.

be printed on both sides, and one method of doing this is **work-and-back imposition** (or sheetwise). On work-and-back layouts, the first side of the press sheet is printed. The sheet is then turned over, left to right, and sent back through the press to be printed with a different plate. See **Figure 12-5.** Phrased differently, the press sheets are worked through the press and then flipped to be printed on the back with a new plate—hence, the term *work-and-back imposition*. The press's paper gripper uses the same leading edge during both passes because the press sheets are turned left to right. After the two passes through the press, the press sheets are cut in half.

image assembly: the process of manually or electronically positioning and assembling line and halftone films into their proper places for exposure during platemaking.

conventional image assembly: the manual positioning and attaching of films to a flat, with the purpose of exposing the films' images to a plate.

stripper: the person who handles the task of film assembly.

masking sheet: the thick sheet of paper or plastic that holds the negatives or positives.

flat: a complete masking sheet, with its taped-on film negatives or positives.

imposition: the arrangement of pages so they will be in the proper sequence after the sheet is printed and folded.

press sheet: a large sheet of paper printed on the front and back.

single-side imposition: image assembly for a job to be printed on one side only.

lead edge: the part of a sheet entering the printing press first.

bleed image: a printed image extending to the trim edge of a sheet or page.

work-and-back imposition: positioning films for a two-sided job in which the fronts will be carried on one plate and the backs will be carried on a different plate.

Adequate Gripper Margin   **Inadequate Gripper Margin**

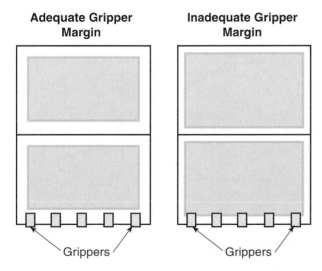

Grippers   Grippers

Figure 12-3. Two 5 1/2″ × 8 1/2″ fliers can be printed on an 8 1/2″ × 11″ press sheet if the margin can accommodate the paper grippers. If the margin on the lead edge is insufficient, only a one-up imposition is possible without a larger press sheet.

Plate #1

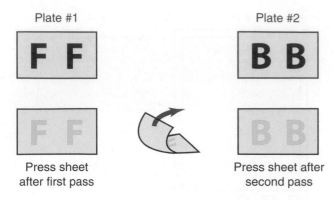

Plate #2

Press sheet
after first pass

Press sheet after
second pass

Figure 12-5. Work-and-back jobs are printed on both sides. The fronts are printed on the first pass, the press sheets are turned over, and the backs are printed with a new plate during the second pass.

Whereas a one-sided job might be described as a five-up imposition, if the job is two sided, its imposition is termed a *five-up, work-and-back imposition*. See **Figure 12-6.**

Work-and-Turn Imposition

To continue with the 5 1/2″ × 8 1/2″, two-sided flier, imagine the colors are the same—blue on both sides. If it is printed with a work-and-back imposition, two plates are needed—one for the front images and one for the back images. The entire job can be printed with only a single plate, however, if it is set up with a ***work-and-turn imposition***, because the design calls for the same color to be printed on both sides.

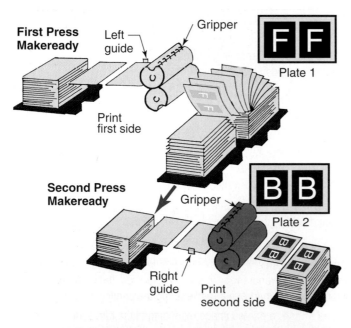

Figure 12-6. In this two-up, work-and-back imposition, one plate carries the fronts, and a second plate carries the backs. Work-and-back imposition is always used when the colors on the two sides are not the same.

In a work-and-turn layout, a single plate carries both the fronts and backs of the job. One half of the plate carries fronts, and the other half carries backs. See **Figure 12-7.** The fronts are on the left-hand side of the plate, and the backs are on the right. The line separating front and back (the *axis*) is parallel to the direction of travel into the press. This orientation is important because, after the front of the card is printed, the press sheets are turned left to right on this axis. The printed side of the press sheet is now facing down, and the front and back have changed positions. See **Figure 12-8.** The upside-down fronts are now on the right-hand side of the pile of paper, and the backs are now on the left. As the second pressrun is made, the front images on the same plate will be printed on the left side of the press sheet, and they will be behind the backs that were printed on the first pass. At the same time, the back images on the plate will be printed on the right side of the press sheet, and they will be behind the fronts that were printed on the first pass. The finished cards will look the same as if they had been printed in a work-and-back imposition, but the number of plates is cut in half, along with the plate costs. Therefore, work-and-turn imposition is the preferred imposition plan for two-sided jobs if the ink color or colors on the front and back of the job are the same, the paper's front and back surfaces are the same, and the number of images on the plate is even.

Work-and-Tumble Imposition

Work-and-tumble imposition is similar to work-and-turn imposition. One half of the plate carries fronts, and the other half of the plate carries

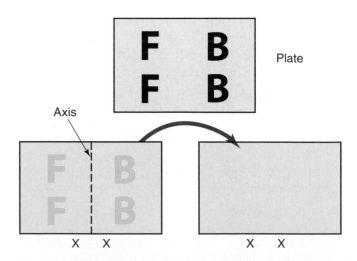

Figure 12-7. In a work-and-turn imposition, the same plate can print both sides of the press sheet because the plate carries both fronts and backs.

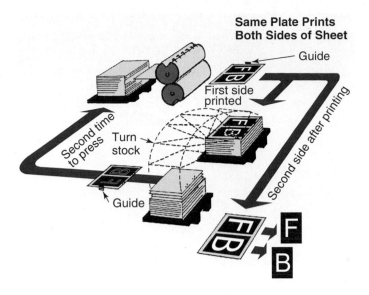

Same Plate Prints Both Sides of Sheet

Figure 12-8. A work-and-turn imposition requires the press sheet to be turned side-to-side after the first pass through the press. This motion is required because the axis is parallel to the direction of travel.

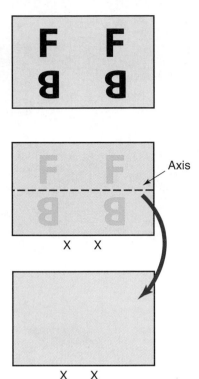

Figure 12-9. A work-and-tumble imposition is similar to a work-and-turn imposition because the plate carries both fronts and backs. The press sheet is tumbled head over heels, however, after the first pass through the press because the axis is perpendicular to the direction of travel.

backs. The key difference is the orientation of the axis relative to the direction of travel of the sheet to the press. With work-and-tumble impositions, the axis is perpendicular to the direction of travel to the press. See **Figure 12-9.** The sheets are printed on the first side and then tumbled (from top to bottom) before the second side of the sheet is printed. The reduced plate costs of work-and-turn imposition are also realized with work-and-tumble imposition. The lead edge during the first pass becomes the trailing edge during the second pass, because the sheets are tumbled instead of turned. Therefore, if a job's design necessitates adding extra gripper space to the lead edge, this addition must be added twice. See **Figure 12-10.**

The word *out* is used to describe both work-and-tumble and work-and-turn impositions—as in, a *six-out, work-and-tumble imposition*—because both plans use plates that carry both front and back images. Also, the job requirements for work-and-turn jobs apply to work and tumble: an even number of images on the plate, uniform colors on the front and back, and a uniform paper finish. The essential difference between work-and-turn and work-and-tumble impositions is the orientation of the axis—the centerline separating fronts from backs. Work-and-tumble imposition is also called ***work-and-flop imposition.*** Shown in **Figure 12-11** are several impositions with their labels, to assist you in becoming familiar with them. Xs are traditionally used to indicate the lead edge.

Equipment and Tools

Most of the work of the stripper is done at what is called a *light table.* See **Figure 12-12.** The working surface is translucent and lighted from below. The light shines through the film negatives so they can be positioned accurately on the flat. Light tables are equipped with working edges that allow for the precise drawing of lines with a T square and triangle.

Layout tables are used to accurately prepare layouts or check finished flats. See **Figure 12-13.** Most layout tables are equipped so the stripper can make

work-and-turn imposition: a layout producing two or more identical, perfected pieces using one printing plate in two impositions.

axis: in design, a line actually drawn and used as the origin of dimensions in an effective representation. In image assembly, the axis is the line separating the front images from the back images in a work-and-turn or work-and-tumble imposition.

work-and-tumble imposition (work-and-flop imposition): a layout similar to a work-and-turn imposition, in which the press-sheet size must be twice the size of the finished signature sheet, but in which the axis is perpendicular to the direction of travel.

layout table: a table used to prepare layouts or check finished flats.

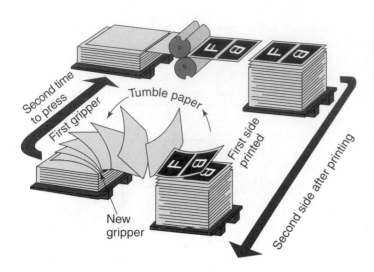

Fold

Figure 12-10. The tumbling of the press sheet between passes requires a different lead edge for each pass. If extra gripper space is needed, it will be needed on each lead edge.

micrometer adjustments when preparing layouts. The tables might have space to store ruling and film-scribing devices, tools, flats, films, and other necessary materials.

Register punches are devices used to make perfectly aligned holes on the masking sheet and printing plate. See **Figure 12-14.** *Registration* (alignment) is controlled by holding the flats in the same position during film assembly and platemaking. *Register pins* are used to hold the punched sheets

Figure 12-12. A light table's illumination helps strippers see the clear image areas. A T square and triangle ensure that images are properly aligned.

Figure 12-13. A lineup table guides the alignment of images during film assembly. This table is useful when working on several masking sheets with the same reference lines. (Flying Color)

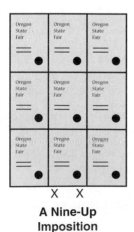
A Nine-Up Imposition

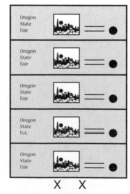
A Five-Up, Work-and-Back Imposition

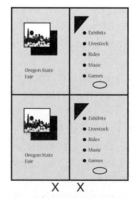
A Four-Out, Work-and-Turn Imposition

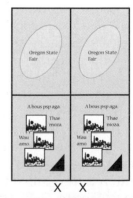
A Four-Out, Work-and-Tumble Imposition

Figure 12-11. Several impositions are shown here. The first imposition is for a one-sided job, and the others are for two-sided jobs.

Figure 12-14. A register punch creates holes on the masking sheets and printing plate that ensure precise positioning.

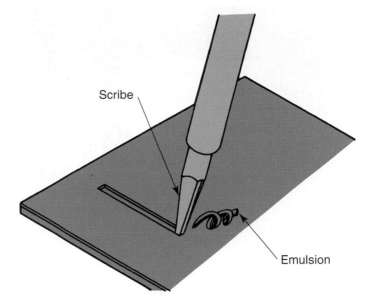

Scribe

Emulsion

Figure 12-16. Scribing is the physical removal of a portion of a film negative's emulsion.

in place for film assembly and platemaking. See **Figure 12-15.**

A *T square* and *triangle* are needed to make **layout lines** and to cut and position negatives and masking materials. Most of the T squares and triangles used for film assembly are made of stainless steel. Loupes (magnifying glasses) are used to examine film negatives and register marks. Damaged negatives or positives can be detected more easily, and register marks on color flats can be more accurately positioned, using a magnifier. The **collimator** is an optical instrument useful when the visible line of sight is straight. The stripper can use a collimator to make sure **register marks** are properly aligned when two or more overlays are used. The collimator eliminates **parallax error**, an illusion that can result from a change in the viewing angle.

Transparent areas on negatives transmit light to produce a printing image. Wherever the blackened emulsion is removed from film, light can pass through to expose the offset plate. To manually produce rules, grids, or borders on a negative, strips of emulsion can be shaved away with a *scribing tool* to form transparent lines. See **Figure 12-16.** *Opaquing solution* is applied to pinholes, scratches, or other unwanted clear areas.

Screen angle indicators are used to determine the screen angles of halftones and screen tints. See **Figure 12-17.** When a halftone or tint area overlaps, the screen angle indicator is useful for determining the correct angle to eliminate an objectionable moiré pattern. See **Figure 12-18.**

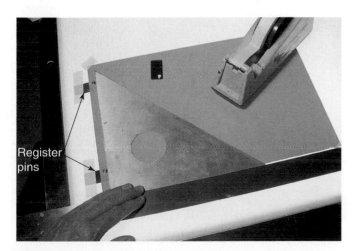

Register pins

Figure 12-15. Register pins inserted through the punched holes are taped to the light table to standardize the placement of different flats.

register punch: a device used to make perfectly aligned holes on the masking sheet and printing plate.

register pin: a holding device used to hold punched sheets in place for film assembly and platemaking.

layout line: a straight line drawn on a masking sheet to assist the stripper in placing images.

collimator: an optical instrument used to make sure register marks are properly aligned when two or more overlays are used.

register mark: a design or shape placed in the nonimage areas of negatives, positives, color separations, and plates to ensure correct register.

parallax error: an illusion that can result from a change in the viewing angle.

screen angle indicator: a device used to determine the screen angles of halftones and screen tints.

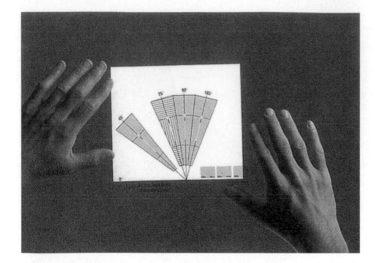

Figure 12-17. The stripper uses a screen angle indicator to improve the quality of the image. (Graphic Arts Technical Foundation)

Goldenrod paper is used as masking paper when preparing flats. This paper's name comes from its yellow-orange color. Goldenrod paper allows **nonactinic light** (rays from fluorescent and incandescent bulbs) to penetrate the paper so the images on the film can be seen during film assembly. The paper does not allow **actinic light**, which causes photochemical changes, to affect the plate when the exposure is made. Plastic masking-sheet material is used where extreme accuracy in black-and-white or color printing is required. Paper or plastic masking sheets are cut the same size as the offset-printing plate.

Masking paper is often purchased with preprinted guidelines (top, side, and bottom margins and a centerline) to meet the size requirements of a specific press. Goldenrod, unprinted paper and plastic masking material are available in various sizes and can be cut to meet plate specs. See **Figure 12-19.** Preprinted masking sheets are seldom used for larger offset-press sizes.

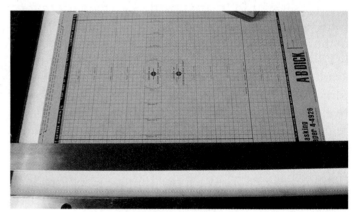

A Preprinted Sheet

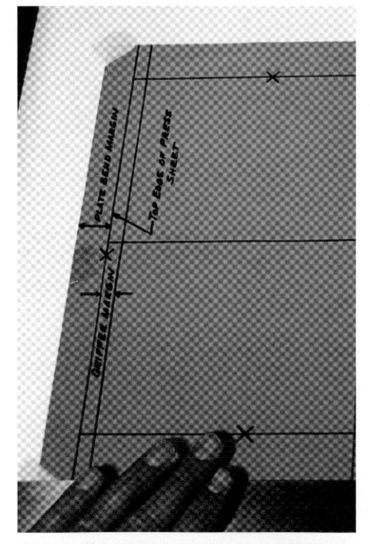

Figure 12-18. Incorrect screen angles in multicolor halftones can cause a moiré—an unwanted pattern across the image.

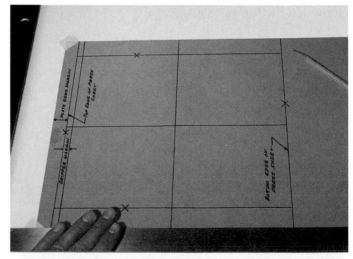

A Plain Sheet

Figure 12-19. Preprinted masking sheets are prepared for a particular model of press. Plain masking sheets are more versatile, but they require more preparation.

The Pin Register System

The term *register* describes the placement of one image in relation to another image. For example, a job printed with two colors requires the colors to be in proper alignment with one another. A *pin register system* uses punched holes and metal pins at various stages of production to ensure that the final printed piece is in accurate register. See **Figure 12-20.** This system works best if the flats and plates are punched identically and the offset press is fitted with a matching set of pins to receive the plate. In a pin register system, the acetate or plastic masking sheets are first punched on a two- or three-hole pin register punch. Some punches have self-centering devices that automatically ensure accurate alignment.

Register pins are available in many sizes and styles. See **Figure 12-21.** These pins are taped to the surface of the light table. The first masking sheet is placed in position and fitted over the register pins. After the first flat is stripped, the flats carrying images to be printed in an additional color are pinned over the first flat. See **Figure 12-22.** The light table's backlighting allows images on the second flat to be positioned, with images on the first flat being visible.

The pin register system is needed when a job's design requires more than one flat to hold all the images going onto a plate. If the design is simple, all images can be carried on a single flat. Screen

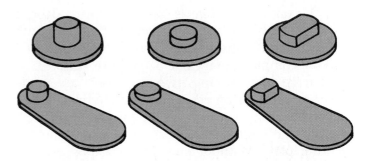

Figure 12-21. Several types of register pins.

Figure 12-22. Jobs requiring more than one masking flat for a single plate are punched together and placed over pins that allow the flats to be removed and repositioned in register with one another.

tints, reverses, overprints, and halftones, however, are common examples of design features requiring one or more additional flats. When more than one flat is needed for a plate, the first is known as the *main flat* (or *master flat*). Any additional flat is a *complementary flat*.

goldenrod paper: yellow-orange masking paper used for preparing flats.

nonactinic light: rays from fluorescent and incandescent bulbs.

actinic light: light rays that cause photochemical changes. This light is used to harden light-sensitive offset plate emulsions.

pin register system: a system that uses punched holes and mechanical devices to produce an accurate register. This register system allows multiple overlays to be created in precise register.

main flat: the flat carrying most of the images, when a complementary flat is needed.

complementary flat: a film-assembly method in which the line negatives and halftone negatives are stripped separately.

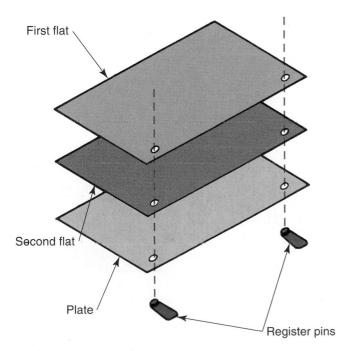

Figure 12-20. With a pin register system, the flats and plate are punched to keep them in alignment during exposure.

For example, if type is to be overprinted on a photograph, the halftone negative can be placed onto the main flat. The line negative with the type is placed onto the complementary flat. See **Figure 12-23.**

During platemaking, two exposures are made onto one plate using register pins. The platemaker makes the first exposure, using the main flat with the halftone negative to "burn" the image into the printing plate. Without moving the exposed plate, the main flat is removed, and the complementary flat containing the type is placed in register over the plate. A second exposure is made to expose the type onto the plate.

Manual Film Assembly

The basic steps in stripping a flat and making an offset plate are illustrated in **Figure 12-24.** The film-assembly process is generally handled in the following way. Film negatives and positives are prepared by the camera department or electronic

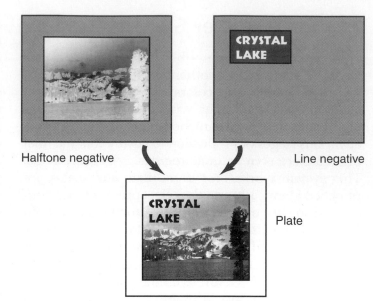

Figure 12-23. A halftone and overprint require two flats—one to carry the halftone negative and one to carry the type to be overprinted. The two images are exposed on the plate in separate operations.

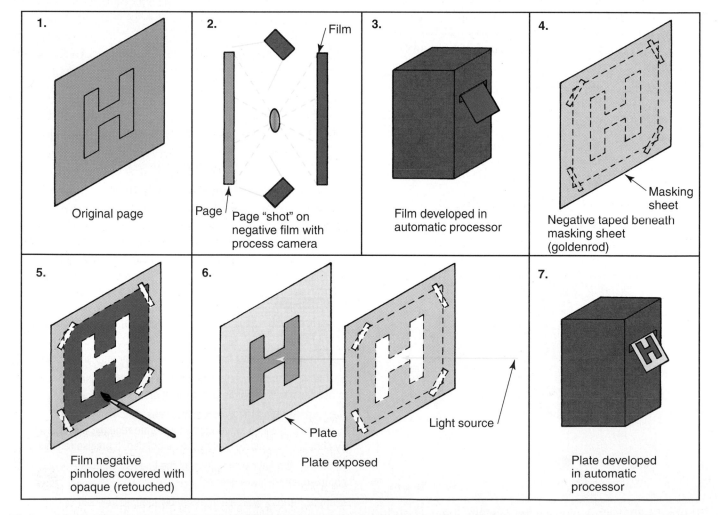

Figure 12-24. The mechanical is photographed to capture the image on film, which is developed to create a negative. The stripper positions and tapes the negative to a masking sheet and removes a portion of the masking sheet to open up the clear image. The completed flat is exposed to a plate, which is then developed.

means. The developed film is taped, emulsion side up, onto a ruled masking sheet in the positions indicated on the layout. Assembly takes place on a light table.

The stripped-up flat is turned over on the light table so it is right reading (the words and images can be read from left to right). This places the base side of the film up and the emulsion side of the film down. The stripper cuts out sections of the masking sheet, exposing the desired elements on the film below it. *Pinholes* in the negative are retouched with an opaque.

The assembled flat is placed over a sensitized offset plate in the platemaker, and a high-intensity light exposes the plate. The plate is developed with processing chemicals that bring out the image. This action causes the image to be ink receptive on the offset press. See **Figure 12-25.**

Negative Film Assembly

Negative film assembly refers to the preparation of a flat containing film negatives. The same two-sided folder for which mechanicals were prepared in Chapter 9 will be stripped up on the following pages. An examination of the negatives produced from those mechanicals reveals the corner marks defining the final size, the fold marks, the boundary of the screen tint that will bleed off one side, and the area for the halftone negative. See **Figure 12-26.** The job can be run two out, work and tumble on an 11″ × 17″ press sheet because the dimensions of the finished job are 7 1/2″ × 8 5/8″ before folding.

Inspecting and trimming films

The films to be stripped should be examined for size and quality using a magnifying glass. Inspection is very important with halftone negatives. Scissors

Figure 12-26. These film negatives make up the front and back images for a one-color folder. The ruled box below the window defines a screen tint.

are used to trim the films, leaving at least 1/2″ (12 mm) margin around the image or work area. Crop and trim marks should not be cut off, and if the negative image is to bleed (extend to the *trim edge* of the sheet), the negative should not be trimmed until it is taped in place on the masking sheet.

Positioning and ruling the masking sheet

The stripper's first task is to place on the light table a yellow or orange-colored masking sheet that is the same size as the plate. The masking sheet is placed so the lines of type are parallel to the T square, to simplify checking their alignment. The *lead edge* is usually nearest the stripper. For duplicator-size presses, the lead edge is the short dimension, and for larger presses, the lead edge is the long dimension. See **Figure 12-27.** After the first *masking flat* is in place on the glass, the stripper makes layout lines with a ballpoint pen on the masking sheet to indicate the lead edge, plate-bend margin, paper gripper margin, and other lines. See **Figure 12-28.** Images cannot sit too close to the lead edge of the masking sheet for two reasons. First, the plate will be bent at both the

Figure 12-25. A finished offset plate produced in an automatic plate processor.

pinhole: a small unwanted transparent opening on a film negative that forms a small dot-size image on the printing plate.

negative film assembly: the preparation of flats containing film negatives.

trim edge: the outside dimensions of the finished printed piece.

masking flat: a flat used to cover certain images and prevent their exposure during platemaking.

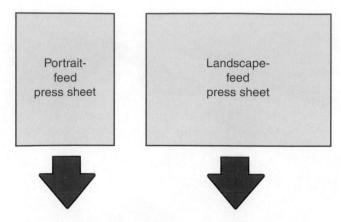

Figure 12-27. The short dimension is the lead edge on press sheets for duplicator and other portrait-feed presses. The long dimension is the lead edge for larger, landscape-feed presses.

Figure 12-28. After the masking flat is affixed to the light table, the stripper rules several lines that will guide the placement of the films.

lead and back edges in order to be clamped to the plate cylinder of the press. This portion of the plate's lead edge is called the *plate bend*. See **Figure 12-29.** Second, as the press sheet enters the press, a set of metal fingers in the impression cylinder, called *grippers*, holds the sheet's lead edge. For this reason, strippers draw a second line to define the *paper gripper margin* and ensure that no images are placed within this margin. See **Figure 12-30.** A centerline is drawn from the center of the lead edge, using the triangle in conjunction with the T square, after the plate-bend and paper gripper margins are drawn. See **Figure 12-31.** Lines are also drawn to define the press sheet and show where it will contact the blanket. See **Figure 12-32.** The axis of the press sheet

is drawn one-half the distance from the plate-bend line to the opposite edge of the press sheet, because the job will have a two-out, work-and-tumble imposition. See **Figure 12-33.** Next, the dimensions of the finished job are drawn. See **Figure 12-34.**

Stripping

Film assembly is done by working with the films either emulsion side up or emulsion side down. The emulsion-up film-assembly method is preferred when stripping more than one negative on a masking sheet, as is the case in our example. To find the emulsion side of film, remember that the

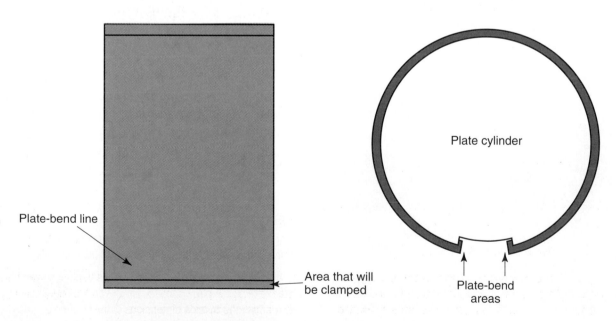

Figure 12-29. An offset plate is bent and clamped to the plate cylinder at both ends. The portion of the plate clamped at the lead edge—the plate bend—is marked on the masking sheet with a solid line.

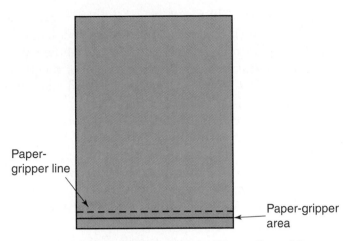

Figure 12-30. A broken line marks the portion of the press sheet the paper grippers will hold.

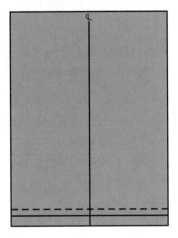

Figure 12-31. The centerline begins at the lead edge and defines the center of both the plate and the press sheet.

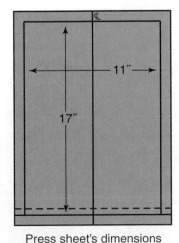

Press sheet's dimensions

Figure 12-32. The dimensions of the press sheet are drawn. The length begins at the plate-bend line, and the width is measured outward in both directions from the centerline.

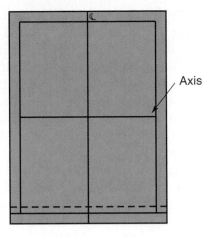

Figure 12-33. The axis for this work-and-tumble imposition is drawn halfway across the sheet's length.

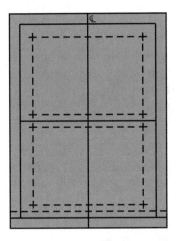

Figure 12-34. Working outward from the centerline and the axis, the dimensions of the two folders are ruled in place.

emulsion side is duller than the base side and the type is wrong reading when the emulsion side is up. The emulsion-up method of film assembly is outlined in the following steps:

1. Remove all tape and dirt from the glass surface of the light table. Clean the surface with a cloth and recommended glass cleaner. Avoid using any cleaner containing ammonia because ammonia tends to leave the glass surface too slippery for tape to adhere properly. Gather all necessary tools and supplies. Use soap and water to clean the T square, triangles, and other measuring tools.

plate bend: the portion of a plate that is bent to be clamped onto the plate cylinder. A plate bend is also the portion of a flat corresponding to the plate-bend area of the plate.

paper gripper margin: the area on the lead edge of a press sheet that grippers hold during printing.

2. Select two masking sheets (unruled) that are the same size as the plate to be used and punch them.

3. Line up the first masking sheet with the upper edge of the T square. The lead edge should be toward you, and the end with the punched holes should be away from you. For convenience in reaching the entire masking sheet, the lead edge of the masking sheet should be close to you. Fasten the masking sheet to the light table by placing register pins in the punched holes and taping the pins to the glass. See **Figure 12-35.** Work from diagonal corners when taping, smoothing the masking sheet before taping each corner.

4. Identify the lead edge of the masking sheet by drawing Xs along the lead edge (left side) of the masking sheet.

5. Draw a solid line 11/16″ (18 mm) from the lead edge of the masking sheet to define the plate bend.

6. Draw a broken line 5/16″ (8 mm) away from and parallel to the solid plate-bend line. The space between the lead-edge line and the second line represents the paper gripper margin. Remember that none of the image area of a negative can be positioned in the gripper margin.

7. Measure the width of the masking sheet and draw a centerline through the middle, perpendicular to the gripper-margin line. Label it "CL" at the top.

8. Draw a line representing the length of the press sheet (17″). Be sure to measure from the solid plate-bend line.

9. Draw the remaining edges of the press sheet, representing its width (11″). Half of the width (5 1/2″) will be on either side of the centerline.

10. Draw the axis of the press sheet halfway across the length of the press sheet.

11. Allowing a 1/2″ (12 mm) gutter at the axis, draw dimension lines showing the exact size and position of the finished pieces. Extend the lines approximately 1″ (25 mm) beyond the corners of the rectangle to assist in positioning the negatives.

12. When all the layout lines have been drawn, position the negatives with the emulsion side up. See **Figure 12-36.** Align the corner marks (or trim marks) at the four corners of each negative with the dimension lines drawn on the masking sheet.

13. Using a T square and triangle, carefully square the negatives. Hold the negative firmly in position with one hand, while using the other hand to reach for the red litho tape.

14. Place a 1″ (25 mm) piece of red litho tape at each corner of the film negatives and, depending on their length, one piece along the center of each side of the negatives. Use a minimal number of pieces of tape to hold the negative in place. Excessive tape prevents good contact between the film and offset plate during platemaking. The tape should be at least 1/8″ (3 mm) from any image.

15. Place the halftone negative (emulsion up) over the window. Align it so it is cropped properly and tape it to the line negative. See **Figure 12-37.**

Figure 12-35. While attached to the masking sheet, the register pins are aligned with the T square and taped to the light table.

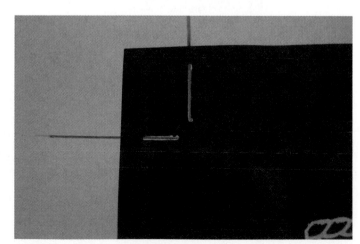

Figure 12-36. The corner marks on the negatives are lined up with the dimension lines on the masking flat, and the corners are taped.

Figure 12-37. The halftone negative is placed in the clear window.

16. After all films have been taped in position, make a triangular-shaped cut along the centerline at the gripper edge of the masking sheet to identify both the lead edge and the center of the plate. See **Figure 12-38.** This mark will help the press operator center the plate on the press.

17. Once all negatives have been taped in place, remove the masking sheet from the register pins and turn it over on the light table. At this point, the film's emulsion is against the glass. With a sharp knife, open up the image areas by cutting away the portions of the masking sheet covering them—without cutting through the clear base layer of the film negative. Be sure to open up the corner marks, as well as any other images that need to be printed. A small sheet of clear acetate inserted between the negative and goldenrod

Figure 12-38. A triangle is notched at the centerline to mark the center of the plate.

paper can be used to add greater protection to the negative during cutting. Open up the holes at least 1/8″ (3 mm) larger than the image areas. Allow the masking sheet to cover as much of the nonimage areas of the negative as possible to provide additional protection to the plate during exposure and reduce the time later spent covering unwanted openings and scratches with opaque.

Caution

Always use a sharp art-knife blade. Do not force the cut. Handle the knife carefully. The blade is extremely sharp and can cause serious injury.

18. Small unwanted transparent openings, called *pinholes*, and scratches are often found on film negatives. These must be covered, or they will show up on the offset plate as images. Also, some negatives might contain image areas you do not wish to print. These areas must be covered with opaque before the flat is sent to the platemaking department. Retouching with opaque is usually done after the windows have been cut.

    Cover all pinholes and scratches on the *right-reading side* (base side) of the film negative with opaque whenever possible. Examine the negative for pinholes and scratches on the light table with the emulsion side down. Use a fine art brush to apply the thinned opaque. See **Figure 12-39.** Care must be taken not to get opaque solution on the image areas of the negative. Label this main flat "1 of 2."

19. With the main flat complete, the next task is to prepare the complementary flat, which will carry the clear rectangle for the screen tint. Return the main flat (emulsion up) to the register pins.

20. Place the second masking flat over the main flat and the register pins. Recall that both masking sheets were punched together in step two.

21. With the light table on, look through the second masking sheet and locate the rectangular border below the halftone.

22. Place a 4 1/2″ × 1 1/2″ piece of red masking film (emulsion up) over the rectangle and tape it to the masking sheet. See **Figure 12-40.**

23. With the T square and triangle, use the rectangular border as a guide to cut through the thin red layer of the masking film. Cut down the middle of the lines forming the rectangle.

right-reading side: the side of a negative that allows type to be read easily.

Figure 12-39. A stripper covers any imperfections in the negatives with opaque to block unwanted light from reaching the plate or proofing material. (Bowling Green State University, Visual Communication Technology Program)

Figure 12-40. A piece of red masking film is taped to the complementary flat and over the ruled box defining the screen-tint area.

24. Carefully remove the red film from the inside of the rectangle.
25. Lift the complementary flat from the register pins, turn it over, and open up the rectangular window by cutting an opening in the masking sheet 1/8" larger than the window. See **Figure 12-41.** This window will define the size of the screen tint.
26. Label the completed complementary flat "2 of 2." Both flats will be exposed, one at a time, to the same plate. This complementary flat will be used with a screen to create the screen tint.

Some strippers who prepare single negative flats for duplicator-size presses use the emulsion-down, negative film-assembly method. During the film-assembly operation, the negative is kept right-reading side up on the light table. This method is not practical when stripping more than one negative on a single masking sheet, especially for large presses. Steps in the emulsion-down, negative film-assembly method are outlined as follows:

1. Place the film negative on the light-table surface with the emulsion side of the negative against the glass surface. See **Figure 12-42.** The negative will be right reading. The side of the negative near the lead edge of the masking sheet should be placed away from you.
2. Tape the negative to the light table with small pieces of masking tape.
3. Place a preruled masking sheet over the negative in the correct position. See **Figure 12-43.** The printed lines on the masking sheet should face up. Since the masking sheet is translucent, you can align it with the film images.
4. When the masking sheet is in position over the negative, hold it firmly with one hand. Cut two small oblong windows in the masking sheet at

Figure 12-41. The complementary flat is turned over, and a portion of it is removed to open up the window.

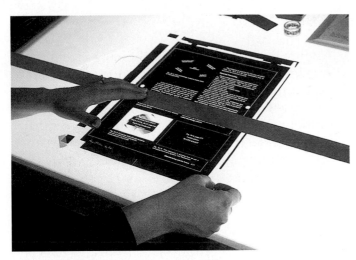

Figure 12-42. In emulsion-down film assembly, the film negative is placed on a light table with the emulsion side against the glass surface. The negative appears right reading.

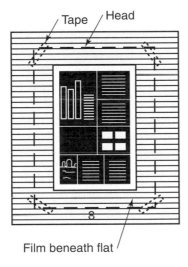

Figure 12-43. A flat for an emulsion-down form containing two pages of an eight-page signature.

opposite sides, top and bottom. Cut over the film negative, but outside the image area. Be careful not to cut through the negative.
5. While still holding the masking sheet down firmly against the negative, place a piece of red litho tape over each window and press firmly.
6. Cut two more windows at the other sides of the negative and place tape over them. Continue to hold the masking sheet down firmly against the negative.
7. Remove the masking tape used to hold the film negative to the light-table surface.
8. Turn the masking sheet over.
9. Place a 1″ (25 mm) piece of red litho tape at each corner of the film negative and one piece along the center of each side of the negative.

10. With the art knife, cut away the goldenrod paper covering the image areas of the negative. Cut the windows at least 1/8″ (3 mm) larger than the image areas.
11. Cover all pinholes and scratches on the right-reading side of the negative with opaque.
12. Make a wedge-shaped cut along the centerline at the gripper edge of the preruled masking sheet.

Positive Film Assembly

The procedure for **positive film assembly**, or stripping positive, varies slightly from negative film assembly. The positive flat might consist of one or more individual film positives. These are taped to a transparent (film) plastic base the size of the press plate. It is also common practice for the camera department to prepare a single film positive consisting of several different positive images. The composite film positive is the same size as the press plate. The basic steps for positive film assembly are as follows:
1. Tape a sheet of layout material larger than the press plate to the light table. The layout material usually consists of ink-receptive, matte acetate or white paper. This provides the base for a master layout. See **Figure 12-44.**

Note

Another method of preparing a master layout is to make a film positive of the layout. Make sure accuracy is maintained during film processing.

2. Draw all layout lines on the master-layout sheet. These include press-sheet and image limits and gripper, center, trim, fold, and cut marks. All the layout lines normally used in negative film assembly are included for positive film assembly. See **Figure 12-45.**
3. Tape a sheet of transparent plastic (film base) in register over the layout. The transparent plastic must be the same size as the press plate. This plastic replaces the masking sheet used in negative stripping.
4. Use cellulose tape to adhere the film positives, emulsion side up, to the transparent plastic. This is done by accurately aligning the positives with the layout underneath.

positive film assembly: the preparation of flats containing film positives.

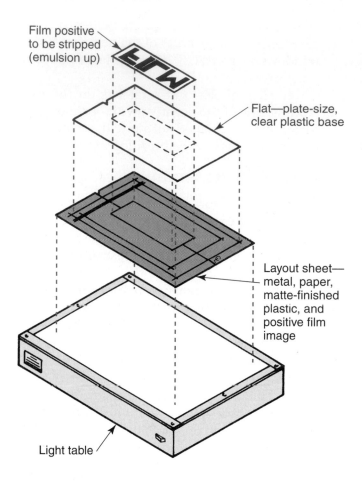

Film positive to be stripped (emulsion up)

Flat—plate-size, clear plastic base

Layout sheet—metal, paper, matte-finished plastic, and positive film image

Light table

Figure 12-44. This schematic illustrates the basic elements and steps in positive film assembly.

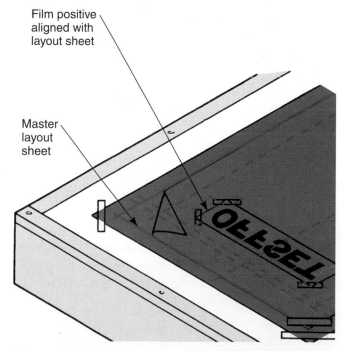

Film positive aligned with layout sheet

Master layout sheet

Figure 12-45. Layout lines used in negative film assembly are included in positive film assembly.

Note

All film positives must be of the same thickness so film-to-plate contact is uniform during exposure in the platemaker. All adjoining film positives should be butted, rather than overlapped, at the joints. A minimum of thin, transparent cellulose tape should be used to fasten the film positives to the plastic base.

5. Remove the complete flat from the layout sheet. Carefully inspect the flat over a lighted table, and cover image pinholes, defects, or scratches with opaque in the usual manner. Remove dust and dirt with film cleaner and a soft brush.

Signature Imposition

A signature is a folded piece of paper containing pages that will become part of a book or booklet. Signature imposition can appear more complex than the flat-sheet imposition already presented because a signature consists of at least 4 pages or as many as 32 pages, depending on the capacity of the press sheet. This textbook is a good example of how 16-page signatures can be bound together to form a complete volume.

Each signature starts out as a large sheet of paper, printed front and back, called a *press sheet*. The group of pages printed on each side of the press sheet is called a *form* (or *flat*). The front form contains the lowest page number within the signature, and the back form is the other side. The pages on each form are imposed so, when the signatures are folded, trimmed, and bound, they are in the correct sequence for reading. A 16-page signature, for example, has 8 pages printed on one side and 8 pages printed on the other side. See **Figure 12-46.**

There are two keys to understanding signature imposition. The first is to see each form as the unit counted. That is, count the number of forms on the signature, instead of the number of pages. See **Figure 12-47.** The second key is to make a *folding dummy*. When unfolded, the folding dummy displays the position of each page in the signature and also indicates each page's orientation to the other pages. See **Figure 12-48.**

To make a dummy, use a blank sheet of paper the same size as the press sheets to be used for the job. The sheet is then folded as many times as the actual press sheet will be folded during production. A single fold will create a four-page signature, and each subsequent fold will double the number of pages.

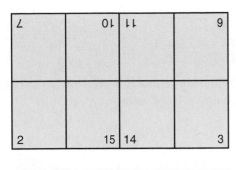

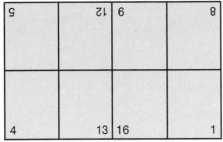

Figure 12-46. A 16-page signature consists of two 8-page flats. The front flat contains the lowest page number of the signature.

For example, to create an eight-page dummy, fold the sheet in half and then in half again. Number each page and cut a notch through the tops of the folds. See **Figure 12-49.** When the sheet is unfolded, the sequence of the pages is a guide for image assembly, and the notches will indicate the top edge (head) of each page.

Figure 12-48. A folding dummy is a representation of the signature. A sheet of paper is folded as the printed press sheet will be folded, a notch is cut, and the pages are numbered.

Multisignature Publications

Books, booklets, and magazines usually require more than one signature. For example, a 104-page magazine would likely consist of six 16-page signatures and an 8-page signature. These signatures must be bound together, and the binding method greatly influences the page sequence. As a result, the binding method is simulated when making the folding dummy for the entire publication.

Bound publications, such as books, booklets, catalogs, and magazines, can be bound using several

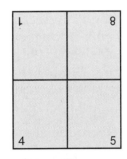

8-Page Signature
One-Up, Work-and-Back
Imposition

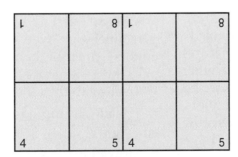

8-Page Signature
Two-Up, Work-and-Back
Imposition

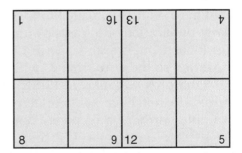

16-Page Signature
One-Up, Work-and-Back
Imposition

Figure 12-47. Shown here are an 8-page signature printed with a one-up, work-and-back imposition; an 8-page signature printed with a two-up, work-and-back imposition; and a 16-page signature printed with a one-up, work-and-back imposition.

form: a group of pages printed on each side of the press sheet.

folding dummy: a sheet of paper folded as the job will be folded in production. This sheet serves as a prototype.

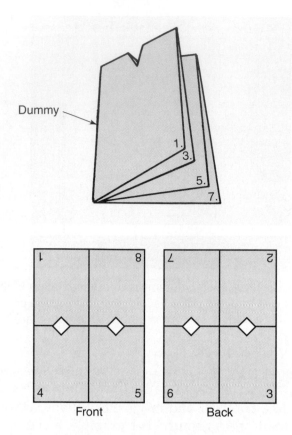

Dummy

Front   Back

Figure 12-49. When opened, the dummy shows both the placement and orientation of the pages. The notches represent the head of each page.

Figure 12-50. Signatures that will receive perfect binding or case binding are gathered.

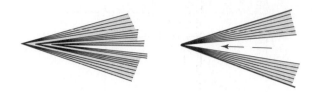

Figure 12-51. Signatures that will receive saddle stitching are inserted.

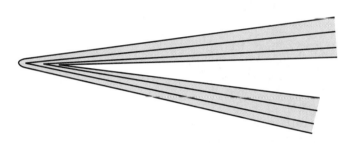

Figure 12-52. Signatures to be saddle stitched require a lip. Therefore, the final fold must be off center.

methods. Paperback books, large catalogs, and magazines receive perfect binding, while hardback books receive case binding. Signatures are gathered before binding. See **Figure 12-50.** Signatures that will be gathered have sequential page numbers.

Many publications are saddle stitched (stapled). Saddle-stitched publications require the signatures to be inserted so the wire stitches will hold together all the signatures. See **Figure 12-51.** Most inserted signatures do not have sequential page numbers. For example, consider a 64-page booklet consisting of four 16-page signatures. The first 16-page signature contains the first 8 pages and the last 8 pages of the booklet. In all saddle-stitched publications, only the inside signature has sequential pages. For this reason, a folding dummy for the entire publication must be made to learn the page sequence for each signature.

The signatures to be saddle stitched must be folded to create a *lip* (also lap, or pickup). A lip is an extension of either the first or last half of a signature that is needed for the assembling of the signatures. See **Figure 12-52.** To create a lip, the final fold of the

signature is off center, and imposition must provide for this feature. The placement on the signature for the lip allowance is dependent on how the signature is folded.

Anatomy of a Signature

Image assembly, binding, and finishing personnel—as well as graphic designers and editors—must be knowledgeable about the various parts of a signature. See **Figure 12-53.** Familiarize yourself with the following signature elements:

- **Head.** The top portion or edge of the signature.
- **Thumb edge.** The edge where the signature is spread to turn the pages.
- **Bind edge.** The outside edge opposite the thumb edge. This edge is the same as the saddle or spine edge, forming the backbone of the finished volume.
- **Gutter.** The inside of the bind or saddle edge.
- **Open edge.** A side that is not folded, so the pages can be opened without cutting or trimming.
- **Closed edge.** A side that is folded and must be cut or trimmed to open the pages.
- **Foot.** The bottom of the signature.

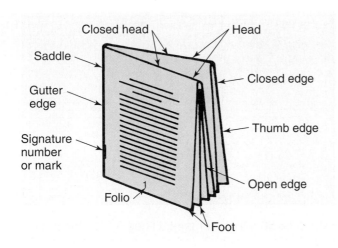

Figure 12-53. Elements of a folded signature.

- **Signature number or mark.** A mark printed on the spine or saddle edge to designate the sequence of the signatures. This number ensures the signatures are in the correct order for binding.
- **Folio.** Each page number in the volume.
- **Front folio.** The lowest page number in each signature. After the page size has been determined, 1/8″ to 1/4″ extra is added for trim on the top, side, and bottom of each page. Trim takes into consideration the amount of paper removed or cut from the three outside edges to make them even after the signature is folded.

In addition to trim allowance, provision must be made for creep. This allowance is made when planning a thick saddle-stitched magazine or book. *Creep* is the effect that occurs when a signature is folded and the inside pages extend past the outside pages. See **Figure 12-54.** Due to creep, the inside center pages will trim out smaller in size, because they extend farther out than the outside signature pages. The paper's caliper and the number of folds determine the degree of creep that will occur. Creep especially affects saddle-stitched books, because all the signatures are inserted.

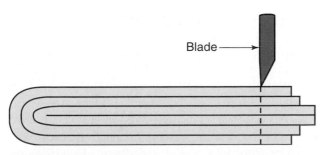

Figure 12-54. Creep occurs when the pages inside a signature extend farther than the outside pages do. The blade removes extra paper to give a book or magazine a finished appearance.

Signature Image Assembly

When stripping a job requiring two or more film negatives, the emulsion-up method is preferred. Only the major differences between signature image assembly and flat-sheet assembly are detailed here because the assemblies are similar. This sample job is the first 16-page signature of a 4″ × 5 1/4″ 240-page catalog that will be gathered. No lip is required because the catalog will be gathered.

1. Cut a masking sheet to press-plate size. Place its long edge parallel to the edge of the table nearest you. Align it with a T square. Label the bottom edge with Xs to indicate it as the lead edge.
2. Register pins are not needed because there will be no complementary flat, and tape can fasten the masking sheet to the glass surface.
3. Draw two Xs along the lead edge.
4. Draw the two lines identifying the plate-bend and paper gripper areas.
5. Measure the width of the masking sheet and draw a vertical centerline through the middle, perpendicular to the gripper margin. Label it "CL" at the top.
6. Draw the two layout lines representing side margins of the press sheet. Measure from the centerline out to both side margins.
7. Measure from the plate-bend line, and draw a line representing the press sheet's length.
8. Using the full-size folding dummy as a guide, draw lines where the sheet will be folded and label the fold lines at the bind edge with a *B*. See **Figure 12-55.** Inside each of these areas will be a page, as well as the extra paper that is removed when the bound signature is trimmed.
9. From the B lines, measure the 4″ page width in both directions and draw vertical lines representing the face trims. See **Figure 12-56.**
10. Note the horizontal-fold line containing the diamond-shaped notches on the folding dummy. Draw a horizontal line 1/4″ above it (H1) and a second horizontal line 1/4″ below it (H2). These lines indicate the pages' head trims. See **Figure 12-57.**

lip: an allowance made for the gripper to pick up and open signatures during saddle-stitching assembly. A lip is also the amount of overlap of one-half of a folded signature. This amount is needed for the feeding of signatures into a GST.

creep: a pushing out on the inside of a folded signature or group of signatures, caused by the thickness of the paper.

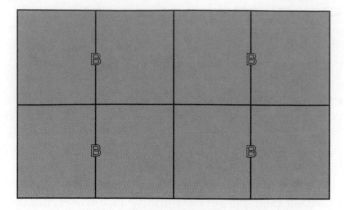

Figure 12-55. After drawing fold lines, label the bind-edge folds with a *B*.

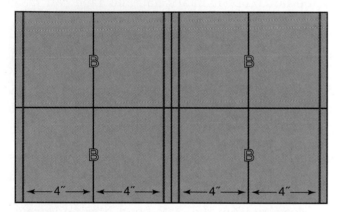

Figure 12-56. Working out from the B folds in both directions, draw vertical lines 4″ (the page width).

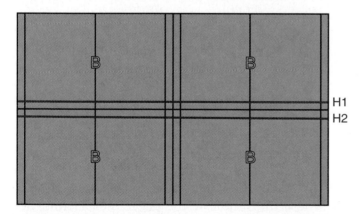

Figure 12-57. Draw horizontal lines 1/4″ above and below the centerline. These lines (H1 and H2) mark the heads of the eight pages.

11. Draw a horizontal line (F1) across the top of the flat 5 1/2″ from line H1. Perform the same function with line B, which will produce line F2. See **Figure 12-58.** These lines indicate the foot (bottom) of each page.

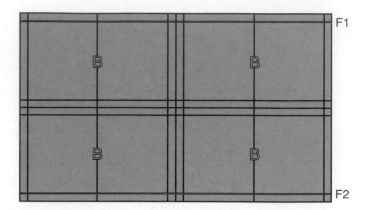

Figure 12-58. Draw horizontal lines 5 1/4″ (the page height) away from the head of each page. These lines (F1 and F2) mark the foot of each page.

12. Using the folding dummy as a guide, position the film negatives of each page, emulsion side up. If the negatives contain corner marks, align them with the guidelines defining the pages. See **Figure 12-59.**
13. Use the T square to position and align the negatives one at a time. Remember that half of the negatives will be upside down.
14. When several negatives are being stripped close together, the film edges should not overlap because overlapping usually creates contact problems during platemaking. The edges of the film should be butted together, rather than overlapped. See **Figure 12-60.**
15. After the negatives have been taped in place, make a wedge-shaped cut along the centerline on the lead edge of the masking sheet. This is a reference for the platemaking and press departments.
16. Turn the combined masking sheet and negatives over on the light table, and cut windows to expose the image areas.
17 Cover any pinholes and scratches on the right-reading side of the film negatives with opaque.
18. Perform the same function with a new masking sheet for the signature's other flat.

Quality-Control Devices

The use of quality-control devices addresses the quality of images and accuracy of registration. Available through the Graphic Arts Technical Foundation, these registration devices are usually stripped onto the trailing edge of flats. A common quality-control device is a *star target*. See **Figure 12-61.** The star target is a circular pattern of wedges used to detect slurring (smearing) of ink on the printed sheets. Other devices include the sensitivity guide, which is a gray scale used to gauge film and plate

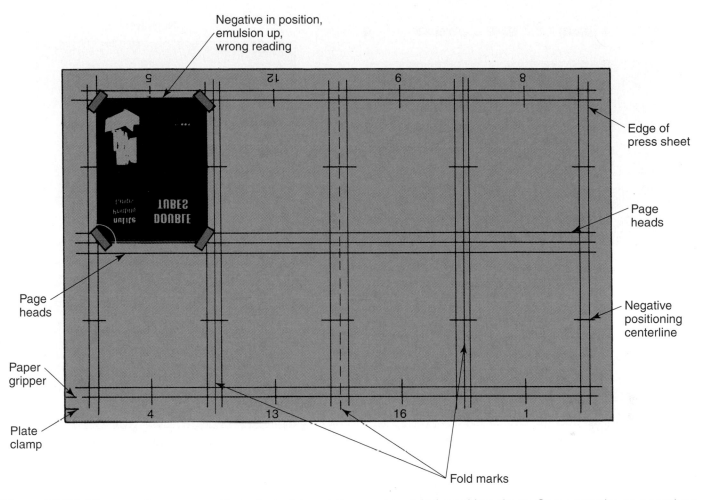

Figure 12-59. Film negatives are positioned emulsion side up over a ruled masking sheet. Corner marks on negatives are used for precise positioning within page areas. (nuArc Company, Inc.)

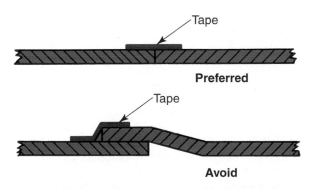

Figure 12-60. Film edges should not overlap when several negatives are stripped close together. The edges of film should be butted and taped together.

Figure 12-61. A star target reveals when slur, dot gain, or doubling occurs during printing. (Graphic Arts Technical Foundation)

exposure; the dot-gain scale, used to gauge the dot areas of halftones; the slur gauge; and the *color bars* (or color gauge), used to maintain accurate color on the press. See **Figure 12-62.**

Step-and-Repeat Film Assembly

Printing two or more copies of the same job on a single sheet is economical because press time is shortened. This can be accomplished with *step-and-repeat film assembly*, in which one negative is exposed to a plate in two or more positions. See **Figure 12-63.**

star target: a circular pattern of lines on a color bar, primarily used to detect ink slur.

color bar: a strip of colors printed in the trim area of a press sheet containing a variety of quality-control devices.

step-and-repeat film assembly: the means by which multiple images from a single image are exposed onto a printing plate in two or more positions.

Figure 12-62. A color gauge indicates color consistency across the press sheet.

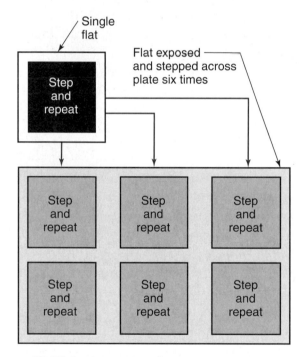

Figure 12-63. In the step-and-repeat process, one negative is used to expose a series of images on a single offset plate.

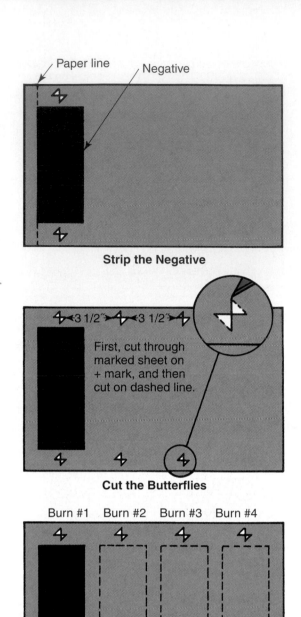

Figure 12-64. The butterfly step-and-repeat method. In this example, a single negative is stripped on the masking sheet in the usual manner, positioned for a four-up form. Butterflies are cut in the masking sheet on 3 1/2″ (8.9 cm) centers for precise registration. A second masking sheet (large enough to cover the entire plate) is laid out with windows cut where the negative will be exposed. Butterflies are cut to correspond with the first flat. During exposure, the masking sheet containing the negative is registered over one window at a time in a second masking sheet, while other windows are covered.

Step-and-repeat machines that automatically reposition the image are commonly used for this purpose. In this procedure, one negative is used to step and repeat a series of images on a single offset plate. Business cards are typically printed in this way.

When a machine is not available, the following procedure can be used to step and repeat a job for most purposes. Strip the negative on a masking sheet in the usual way. Cut register marks, called *butterflies*, in the masking sheet. See **Figure 12-64.**

Butterflies are used to position the flat for each exposure to the plate. Lay out another masking sheet, large enough to cover the entire plate, for as many exposures of the image as desired. Cut windows in the sheet wherever the negative is to be exposed, and cut corresponding register marks in both sheets so the negative will be positioned accurately.

During exposure, the masking sheet containing the negative is placed over one of the windows (in register) in the other masking sheet. The extra windows are covered. This process is repeated until the negative has been exposed over each of the windows. Two other variations for step-and-repeat layouts are illustrated in **Figure 12-65.**

Multiple-Color Film Assembly

If the printed piece is to include two or more colors that do not touch one another, all the negatives for the job can be stripped onto one main flat. The images will be selectively exposed to their respective plates with the use of masking flats. Masking flats

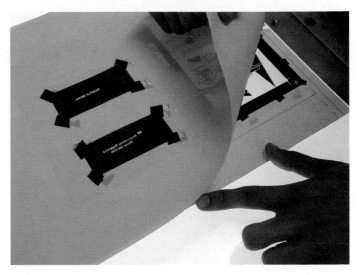

Figure 12-66. Masking flats are made to selectively mask images that do not belong on a given plate.

are masking sheets that do not carry films. Instead, they have openings that permit selected images on the main flat to be exposed to the appropriate plate. See **Figure 12-66.** All other images on the film are masked. A separate masking flat is needed for each ink color. The dummy should indicate the colors that illustrations and type are to be printed.

For example, consider a job to be printed in black and blue. Register crosses are marked in diagonal corners of this main flat. The main flat is then turned over on the light table.

The stripper traces register marks on this sheet and cuts out small register windows at the center of the register marks to expose the register cross. Each part of the flat that is to print in black is cut open to form window openings in the goldenrod. The stripper marks the flat "black flat."

Another sheet of goldenrod is placed over the main flat. Each part of the flat that is to print in blue is cut open to form window openings. Register marks are included, as they were for the preceding flat. The stripper marks this flat "blue flat."

During platemaking, the master flat is taped to the plate. The goldenrod sheet with the window openings for the black flat is registered over the master flat. The plate, when exposed and developed, will contain all the images to print in black ink.

A second unexposed plate is placed in the exposure unit. The operator tapes the master flat to this plate. The goldenrod sheet with the window openings for the blue flat is registered over the master flat.

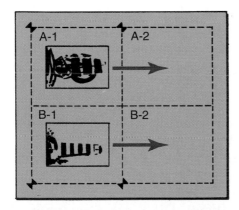

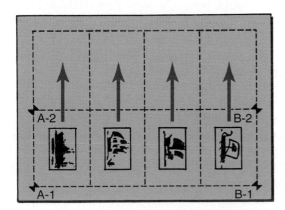

Figure 12-65. Two variations of the butterfly step-and-repeat method. The platemaker moves A-1 and B-1 to positions A-2 and B-2 for the second exposure. Uncovered portions of the plate are masked off as each exposure is made.

butterfly: a register mark cut in a masking sheet.

The plate, when exposed and developed, will contain all the images to print in blue ink.

If more than two colors are required, this method can be adapted to include separate flats for each color. This requires a precise system of registration. A pin register system is used for this purpose.

Sometimes the job calls for simple color work. If the colors do not overlap, a single flat containing hinged masks for each color can be used. While each color plate is being exposed, the other colors are masked out. See **Figure 12-67.**

Proofing Flats

When a job has been stripped and checked, it is ready for platemaking. Before the plates are prepared, proofs are made of each flat. The purpose of proofing is to check for imposition and register errors and obvious typos. The proof also gives the customer an opportunity to check and approve the job. The operations described here apply only to manual methods of single-color proofing. Three common types of proofs for single-color flats are blueline, diazo, and Dylux® media.

Blueline Proofs

As its name implies, *blueline* has a blue image, since blueprint paper is used for making the proof. The paper is coated with an organic iron compound that changes structure when light strikes it. Blueline

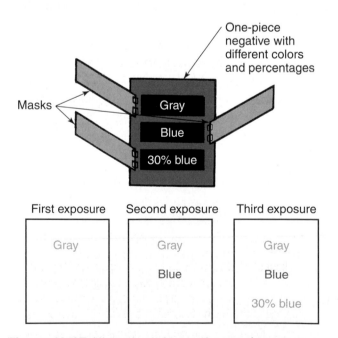

Figure 12-67. Hinged masks can be used to expose different color images or plates at different times. This method saves the stripper from preparing a separate flat for each color.

paper is exposed through the negative flat on a plate-maker. The emulsion is developed in water until cleared. This emulsion is then fixed with a diluted hydrogen-peroxide solution and dried. Blueprint paper is not dimensionally stable, and the image tends to lighten with age. To make a blueline proof, follow these steps, working under subdued- or yellow-light conditions:

1. Cut a piece of blueline paper a little larger than the negative image area to be proofed.
2. Lay the piece of blueline paper on the bed of the platemaker, emulsion side up.
3. Place the negative flat on top of the blueline paper, emulsion side down. Turn on the vacuum pump and expose the image for the recommended time. Test exposures must be made to determine the correct exposure time.
4. Remove the exposed blueline paper. Place it in a plate-processing sink.
5. Develop the blueline paper with water, allowing the image to become dark.
6. Rinse with water and squeegee.
7. Fix the blueline proof with a mild solution of hydrogen peroxide.
8. Rinse with plain water and squeegee.
9. Blot the blueline proof between sheets of newsprint paper and hang to dry.

Diazo Proofs

With *diazo proofing material,* a positive image is produced when the material is exposed to a flat composed of transparent film positives. Similarly, a negative image is produced from film negatives. The exposure is made on a platemaker, and the exposed emulsion is developed when placed in contact with ammonia fumes. Diazo paper is relatively dimensionally stable because it is not moistened during processing. Although it is economical, diazo paper is not made specifically for proofing flats.

Dylux Proofs

Single-color proofs can be prepared by using *Dylux® proofing material* and exposing the material through an overhead filter. The finished proof is cleared (made insensitive to light) with a second filter. See **Figure 12-68.** No wet processing is required to prepare these proofs.

Figure 12-68. A Dylux proof is a good indicator of how well the images were assembled because it is made from the same flats that will make the plates.

Summary

The film-assembly department is responsible for the imposition or layout of pages to form printed signatures. Several methods are used to print signature sheets on sheetfed or web presses. These include sheetwise, work-and-turn, and work-and-tumble imposition.

Conventional film assembly involves positioning film negatives and positives on a masking sheet. As the name implies, negative film assembly involves the preparation of flats containing film negatives. Similarly, positive film assembly involves the preparation of flats containing film positives. A stripper uses the imposition layout to position the film materials in the correct sequence on a masking sheet.

Single- and multiple-page film assembly involves different jobs that are grouped, or ganged, to fill a single press sheet. Complementary flats are used for exposing a single plate, while multicolor flats are used for exposing separate press plates. Register pins and tabs are used to ensure accurate registration of images on one or more flats. Flats are proofed before platemaking to check for imposition errors, register errors, obvious typos, and customer satisfaction. Three common types of proofs for single-color flats are blueline, diazo, and Dylux media.

Review Questions

Please do not write in this book. Write your answers on a separate sheet of paper.

1. The arrangement of pages so they will be in proper sequence after the sheet is printed and folded is _____.
2. Positioning and fastening film negatives or positives to a masking sheet is called _____.
3. The edge of the sheet entering the press first is the _____.
4. On _____ impositions, the first side of the press sheet is printed with one plate. The sheets are then turned over, left to right, and sent through again to be printed with a second plate.
5. A two-sided flier printed with four fronts on one plate and four backs on a second plate with the axis parallel to the direction of travel is a(n) _____ , work-and-_____ imposition.
6. A two-sided flier printed with two fronts on one plate and two backs on the same plate with the axis parallel to the direction of travel is a(n) _____, work-and-_____ imposition.
7. What is an advantage of a work-and-turn or work-and-tumble imposition over a work-and-back imposition?
8. Most of the stripper's work is done at a(n) _____ table.
9. Name and explain the function of a few of the tools a stripper uses.
10. The _____ is used to eliminate parallax error when checking the alignment of images.
11. What happens if the masking sheet does not prevent actinic rays from reaching the plate?
12. Why is a reliable registration system important for film assembly?
13. How do you use a pin register system to prepare a work-and-tumble job?

blueline: a light-sensitive proof with a blue image, used for proofing single-color flats. This proof is a single-color photographic proof exposed from film negatives prior to platemaking and used primarily to evaluate pagination and the location or omission of page elements.

diazo proofing material: a proofing material with a positive image produced from transparent film positives or negatives.

Dylux® proofing material: a dry-processed proof for single-color printing.

14. The stripper prepares _____ flats when reverses, overprints, or screen tints must appear together on a page.

15. The preparation of flats consisting of film negatives is _____ film assembly.

16. Lines the stripper draws to indicate the center of the sheet, the outline of the press sheet, and the trim size are _____.

17. The distance between the lead edge of the sheet of paper and where the printed image begins is called the _____.

18. The emulsion-_____ film-assembly method is preferred when stripping more than one negative on a masking sheet.

19. No part of the _____ area of a negative can be positioned in the gripper margin when stripping a flat.

20. Briefly discuss the additional steps required to prepare a complementary flat.

21. How is positive film assembly performed?

22. A group of pages printed on each side of a signature is called a(n) _____.

23. The top and bottom of a book's pages are called the _____ and _____, respectively.

24. Printing two or more copies of the same job on a single press sheet requires _____ film assembly.

25. Quality-control devices are located on the _____ edge of the press sheet.

Skill-Building Activities

1. Prepare a flat for the duplicator using the emulsion-down film-assembly method. Attach the negatives. Open the masking sheet around the image areas. Cover all pinholes with opaque. Check the flat for accuracy by making a blueline proof.

2. Prepare a flat for the duplicator using the emulsion-up film-assembly method. Attach the negatives. Open the masking sheet around the image areas. Cover all pinholes with opaque. Check the flat for accuracy by making a blueline proof.

3. Prepare a set of flats in which the main flat contains the line work and the complementary flat contains at least one halftone. Check the flats for register by making a proof.

4. With a partner, prepare flats for a two-sided print job that must be folded, inserted, stitched, and trimmed. Make a folding dummy for the job before starting the film-assembly operation.

5. Prepare a set of flats for a three- or four-color printing job. If possible, use a punch register system for this activity.

6. Acquire several copies of the same printed piece. Arrange them onto a press sheet to represent their imposition for printing, and then adhere them with rubber cement. Allow for any necessary bleeds and the gripper margin. Label the imposition. Perform this activity for other printed pieces with different finished sizes and designs with different bleed requirements.

7. Use the pin register system to prepare a job to be run work and tumble.

A web press can be constructed to feed from one or more rolls at the same time. Depending on the design, web presses can print on one or both sides of the web. (Heidelberg, Inc.)

1s and 0s

This chapter represents the shift the printing industry has made from a conventional work flow to an electronic work flow. Instead of images being made on paper pasted in place, photographically captured onto film, assembled onto flats, and transferred to plates, images and data are carried by the digits *1* and *0*. Binary code drives the digital world. *Binary* refers to these two values (*1* and *0*) indicating whether an electrical switch is open or closed. Each *1* or *0* is a *bit*, a term made from *binary* and *digit*.

Binary code is similar to Morse code, which alternates periods of sound and silence. In binary code, combinations of *1s* and *0s* represent numbers, letters, and symbols. For example, *893* is *1101111101* in binary code.

The graphic designer shown here is working with a photograph on her monitor. If the image was scanned, the scanner not only captured the image, but it also converted the image to binary code. As the designer manipulates the image, the software she is using is writing new code that will define the new pixels. Binary code will merge the photograph into a document and carry it across the Internet to the printing company that will prepare digital proofs and digitally expose the plates.

(Heidelberg, Inc.)

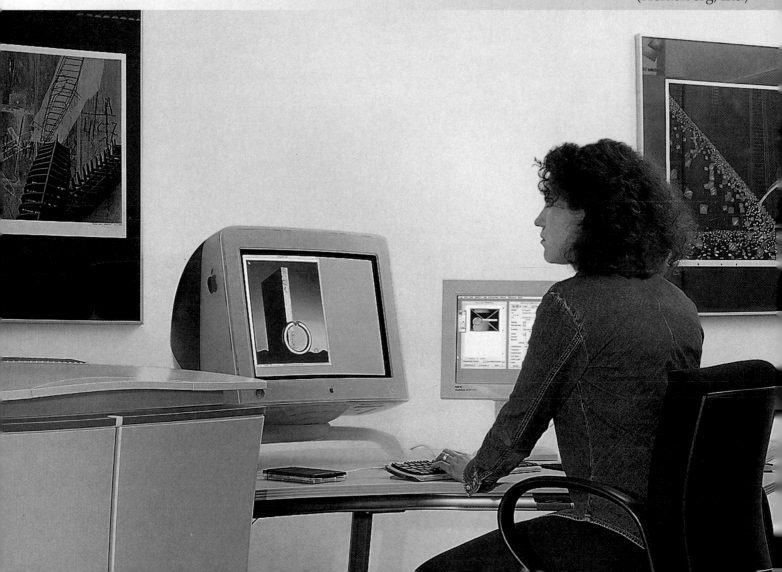

Chapter 13
Electronic Work Flow

Key Terms

analog image
automatic picture
  replacement (APR)
bit depth
bitmap graphic
cathode-ray tube (CRT)
  monitor
computer platform
Computer Ready Electronic
  File (CREF) II guidelines
computer-to-plate (CTP)
  technology
continuous ink-jet printer
contract proof
cross-platform
desktop publishing
digital image
digital imaging (DI)
  technology
digital printing
digital proof
digital toner-based press
  technology
dot gain
dot matrix printer
draw program
drop-on-demand ink-jet
  printer
dye sublimation printer
Encapsulated PostScript
  (EPS) file
engine speed
hard proof
hardware
image manipulation
  program
imagesetter
imagesetting system
ink-jet printer
International Cooperation
  for Integration of
  Prepress, Press, and
  Postpress (CIP3)
Internet
interpreter
Job Definition Format (JDF)

laser printer
laser proof
liquid crystal display
  (LCD) monitor
output device
output service bureau
page composition
  program
paint program
piezoelectric ink-jet
  printer
plasma display monitor
platesetter
portable document
  format (PDF)
preflighting
prepress service
printer
Print Production
  Format (PPF)
proof
raster image processor
  (RIP)
rasterization
remote proofing
repeatability
service bureau
soft proof
software
thermal ink-jet printer
thermal printer
uninterruptible power
  supply
variable data printing
  (VDP)
vector graphic
What You See Is What
  You Get (WYSIWYG)
What You See Is
  What You Print
  (WYSIWYP)
word processing
  program
World Wide Web
  (WWW)

Learning Objectives

When you have completed the reading and assigned activities related to this chapter, you will be able to do the following:

❧ Distinguish between analog form and digital form.

❧ State the functions of word processing, page composition, and illustration programs.

❧ Explain the functions of PDLs.

❧ Summarize the functions of Print Production Format (PPF) and Job Definition Format (JDF).

❧ Cite the definition of *preflighting* and explain its importance to prepress production.

❧ Describe the basic creation, transmission, and output of electronic media.

❧ List proofing methods used in the printing industry.

❧ Identify the basic functions of raster image processors (RIPs), imagesetters, and platesetters.

❧ Define *digital printing*.

Although type has been set electronically since the 1970s, all prepress functions could not be performed electronically (digitally) until the 1990s. Today, digital cameras and scanners are capturing images that can be manipulated and integrated with typographic data and other data to form entire documents. These documents then can be imposed and imaged to plates already mounted on the press. This range of very different functions requires several software packages, as well as a wealth of knowledge. It is now common, however, for a printing company's entire prepress work flow to be electronic. New technology is always accompanied by new demands for technological expertise and an awareness of how that expertise can be applied in everyday situations to enhance quality and improve productivity.

Distinguishing Analog from Digital

In the printing industry, most images enter the work flow in analog form and are converted into digital form somewhere along the line of production. The principle features of an *analog image* are that it is continuous (similar to a curved line) and that it can vary in density (similar to the tones of a watercolor painting or an original photograph). A *digital image*, however, consists of tiny cells on a very fine grid. See **Figure 13-1**. Binary code—a combination of *1*s and *0*s—determines whether a given cell is empty or filled, which indicates whether an electrical switch is open or closed. Each of these distinct cells, called *pixels*, represents a variance in tone or color of the original image. Pixels are arranged in rows and columns to form a grid. Each pixel is assigned a set of numbers to designate position, brightness, and

color. Whereas an analog image can contain one or more actual gray tones, a digital image must simulate grays by interspersing black pixels with empty areas within the grid.

Some of the most common types of analog images are continuous tone images, such as slides, paintings, and photographs. Before entering the digital work flow, continuous tone images must be converted to a digital form. This conversion process is accomplished primarily with the use of electronic scanners.

Making the Transition to Digital

Once the first printing press was invented around 1450, mass reproduction of printed materials became feasible. Image reproduction was limited, however, to type and black-and-white line drawings. Color could be added to illustrations only by hand. Although the invention of photography in the 1800s made it possible to capture photographic images, reproducing these images on a printing press was not possible until the invention of the halftone screen in 1886. By using a halftone screen to break a photograph's continuous tones into black and white dots of various sizes, the printer could print photographic images, as well as type.

For over 100 years, the conversion of photographs into halftone images was performed by a photographic process. The invention and development of photomechanical scanning, however, produced a new means of image reproduction—electronic scanners. See **Figure 13-2**. In the twenty-first century, scanners have largely replaced basic photographic reproduction methods. When computers and digital technology were introduced, the printing industry experienced some of its greatest changes since the introduction of movable type. Personal computers have replaced cumbersome typesetting machines. Scanners and digital cameras have replaced process cameras. Printing plates and film can be imaged and automatically processed with electronic devices. Materials that once moved through production as mechanicals and film now typically move from one process to another in electronic form. The work flow has become almost completely digital. To implement and maintain a digital work flow, all people involved in the production process must understand the creation, transmission, manipulation, and output of electronic media.

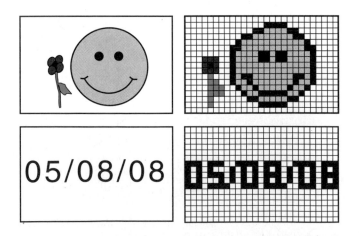

Figure 13-1. Both the smiley face and the numbers on the left are in analog form. The same images are on the right in digital form.

Figure 13-2. Electronic scanners are quickly replacing process cameras for image capture in the printing industry. (Fuji Photo Film USA, Inc.)

The Digital Work Flow

Manuscript and images might begin the work flow in one platform and type of software and enter the layout and output stages in another. Each time data is transferred or converted, its integrity might be compromised. New problems might be introduced. It is the responsibility of the publisher, prepress house, and printer to make sure the electronic data of a project maintains its integrity while moving through the work flow. File formats should be discussed and agreed on before the project begins, to prevent problems as the job moves through each step of production.

Computer Platforms

Ideally, every piece of electronic equipment and computer-software package would be compatible and allow data to move seamlessly through a production sequence including customers, advertising agencies, publishers, service bureaus, and printers. Unfortunately, this is not the current situation because jobs are created with a variety of software packages and on different platforms and then stored in a variety of physical and digital formats. Too often, the result of this mix is a series of problems, with files not being compatible with subsequent software or output devices. For this reason, it is necessary to be familiar with computer platforms and operating systems. A *computer platform* is the basic computer architecture, or hardware, a particular model uses. The major platforms in use today are the PC (a computer using the Microsoft® Windows operating system) and the Macintosh computer.

Computer platforms are defined by the specific operating system a particular computer or specialized system software uses. The operating system is used to install, manage, and access other software programs. The most common operating systems are the Windows operating system, Macintosh OS X™ operating system, and UNIX® system. Many *service bureaus* use a particular platform to process their work. Many others, however, maintain at least one computer station to access and translate files from their customers' operating systems.

The term *cross-platform* is used to describe programs, formats, or devices that work on different platforms. Power Mac® computers can read files written on PC platforms. Software is available that allows PC platforms to read Macintosh programs. It is also possible to connect peripheral devices designed for a certain platform to most other systems.

Software Programs

Software is the computer program, or instructions, used to direct the functions of a computer. This program is used for word processing, page composition, image creation and manipulation, imposition, and other applications in the printing and publishing industries. There are many types of software. Developers are constantly upgrading their products to improve capability, adaptability, and performance. With this range of software products, it is important that each product is used in programs for which it was intended. For example, text creation (writing) and editing should be done in a *word processing program*. The text can then be imported into a *page composition program*.

---

analog image: an image created by variations in voltage or density, instead of digitized numerical values.

digital image: an image created by a unique combination of numerical values known as *bits*.

computer platform: the basic computer architecture, or hardware, a particular model uses.

service bureau: a supplier providing services such as high-resolution scanning or film output.

cross-platform: the capacity to function with two or more computer platforms, such as the Microsoft Windows operating system, Linux® software, and Mac OS® operating system software.

software: a computer program that initiates the functions of a computer, such as word processing, page composition, and image creation and manipulation.

word processing program: computer software that allows the user to compose the text, or body matter, of a page.

page composition program: computer software that allows the user to determine the page size and format and to assemble the page elements.

Word processing programs

Word processing programs allow the user to compose the text (type) of a page. Examples include the Microsoft Word program, the AppleWorks® program, and the WordPerfect® program. Although many word processing programs include applications for both text and graphics formatting, it is better to use word processing programs strictly for text entry and editing. Completed text files later can be imported into a page composition program.

Paint programs

Paint programs create or transform images into bitmap graphics. A *bitmap graphic*, or raster graphic, is a pattern of dots or pixels arranged on a grid. The number of bits in a pixel is referred to as the *bit depth* and is greatly influenced by the demands of the art. Line-art images, such as a black-and-white line drawing, are represented by pixels (dots) consisting of only one bit. This bit is a single digit—either a *0* or a *1*—representing either black or white. The pixels shown on the left in **Figure 13-3** consist of only the black and white tones sufficient to create line art. In contrast, the image on the right contains pixels in black and white, as well as various shades of gray. These pixels consist of 8 bits (digits). For example, *00000000* represents pure white, *00000001* represents nearly white, *00000010* represents a slightly darker tone, and so on. The 256 possible combinations, therefore, permit 256 tones (black, white, and 254 grays) to represent a black-and-white photograph on a computer monitor. The pixels making up a color photograph need 24 bits—8 bits for each of the primary colors: red, green, and blue (RGB).

By zooming in on an area of a bitmap image, the rows and columns of dots are more visible. The size, shape, and color of a bitmap image are edited by filling in or emptying the squares on the grid. See **Figure 13-4.** Editing bitmaps is easy. Bitmaps cannot, however, be enlarged or reduced indefinitely. Their output resolution is limited by the size of the pixel matrix (grid). When bitmaps are enlarged excessively, aliasing occurs, in which the edges of curved lines become ragged because they are composed of step-like shapes called *jaggies* that do not create a smooth line. Antialias algorithms can produce smoother curved lines through a filtering technique.

Draw programs

Instead of seeing images as a series of individual dots, *draw programs* use straight and curved lines to produce shapes called *vector graphics*. **Vector graphics** (also known as *object-oriented graphics*) are represented as mathematical formulas (algorithms) defining all the shapes in the images, as well as their placements on a page. See **Figure 13-5.** Vector

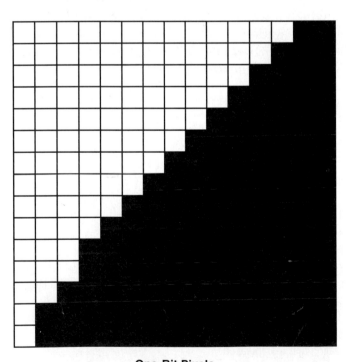

One-Bit Pixels

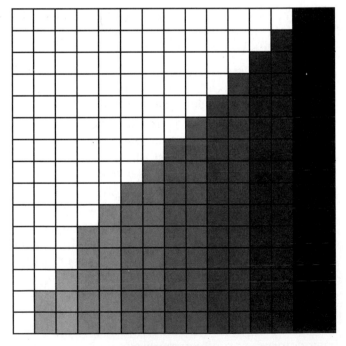

Eight-Bit Pixels

Figure 13-3. Pixels consisting of only one bit are sufficient for producing type or other black-and-white images. The gray scale demands of halftones require eight-bit pixels.

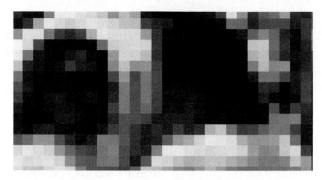

Figure 13-4. Bitmap images consist of pixels that fill a grid. Pixels can be black, white, gray, or a color.

Figure 13-5. Vector images are made from mathematical formulas.

graphics have two distinct advantages over bitmap graphics. These graphics are more flexible than raster graphics because they can be greatly enlarged and still remain sharp. Enlarging a bitmap image merely enlarges the pixels making up the image, with the result that the pixels can become visible and jagged. Enlarging a vector graphic creates a different formula that redraws the graphic in the new size, so curved lines remain curved. In addition, vector-graphic files require less computer memory than bitmap files, which must control the position of each dot, or pixel. As a result, vector graphics can print faster than bitmap graphics. Draw programs are also referred to as *drawing programs*, *illustration programs*, or *design programs*. The Adobe® Illustrator® program, CorelDRAW® suite, and Freehand® program are examples of software packages containing paint and draw capabilities.

Image manipulation programs

Image manipulation programs (also known as *image-editing programs* or *photo-editing programs*) are paint programs that generate bitmap, or raster,

graphics. The more advanced programs allow the manipulation of almost any aspect of an image. The designer can use tools in the program to crop, change color and contrast, and remove or replicate images. Some programs include a means of creating composites. The Adobe Photoshop® editor is an example of an image manipulation program.

Page composition programs

A page composition program, such as the QuarkXPress program, PageMaker software, or InDesign software, is used to electronically integrate the files that very different types of software produce. For example, a design might include text files created with a word processing program, vector graphics created with a drawing program, and bitmap graphics created with a paint or photo-editing program. See **Figure 13-6.** Page composition programs are capable of understanding the different languages that produced the various elements being integrated into the document and translating them into a common language defining the entire ad, poster, flier, or magazine. Page composition software allows the user to determine the page size and format and to assemble all the elements according to the design.

Translating Files

After the page composition software has generated a finished document, the file is translated into a PDL. A PDL describes the page as a series of verbal codes that various **output devices**, such as high-resolution color proofers, imagesetters, and platesetters, can interpret. In other words, a PDL directs the imaging the output device performs. A PDL allows a page composition program to print directly from

paint program: computer software that allows the user to create original bitmap graphics or manipulate existing ones.

bitmap graphic: a digital representation of an image created with pixels arranged in rows and columns.

bit depth: the number of bits used to represent each pixel of an image.

draw program: a software program used to produce and manipulate vector graphics.

vector graphic: an electronic image represented as mathematical formulas that define all the shapes in the image, as well as their placements on a page.

image manipulation program: a graphics program providing a variety of special features for altering bitmap images.

output device: a target for information held in the central computer unit.

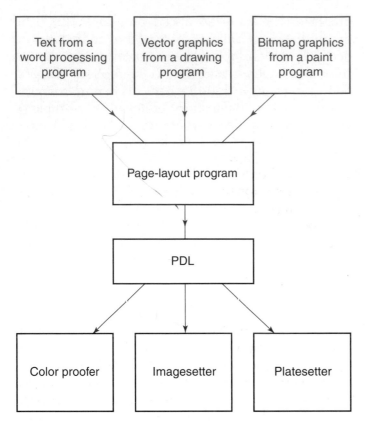

Figure 13-6. Page composition software can read the languages of word processing, vector-graphic, and bitmap-graphic software and integrate these images into a document. The next step is for the document to be converted into a PDL, which will use a series of commands to verbally describe the document to whatever output device is selected.

its files and be device independent—that is, capable of working with more than a device from a certain manufacturer. A commonly used PDL is PostScript technology.

PostScript technology was invented by Adobe Systems, Inc. and has evolved greatly over the years. This technology allows for device independence because manufacturers include a PostScript interpreter as part of their software programs and output devices. An *interpreter,* a computer program residing on a controller board in the printer, receives the PostScript page descriptions and translates them line by line into patterns of dots for printing or pixels for on-screen display. An *Encapsulated PostScript (EPS) file* is a PostScript file including (encapsulating) a low-resolution representation of the document that can appear on the monitor during various prepress stages, such as electronic imposition.

One of the most recent advances in PDLs is Adobe Systems, Inc.'s *portable document format (PDF)*. PDF evolved out of PostScript technology. A PDF file encapsulates all the information needed to output a job from a digital file—fonts, text, and images. In other words, PDF files allow the efficient delivery of digital documents from the content creator to the output provider by bridging the software languages used at each end of the process. In addition, because the file format is device independent, it facilitates the efficient sharing and viewing of documents, regardless of the platform on which the documents were created. Images can be viewed in a zoom mode and edited before output to a proofer, an imagesetter, or a platesetter.

PDF files are simple, are compact, and can move between platforms such as PCs, Macintosh computers, and UNIX systems. Individual pages within a PDF file can easily be replaced, altered, and printed without creating the need to reprocess connected pages. The PDF was designed to support CD-ROMs, Internet- and intranet-page production, digital-printing technologies, and the digital work flow of *computer-to-plate (CTP) technology*, or *direct-to-plate (DTP) technology*. This format was also created with repurposing in mind. Companies can use PDF files to easily recycle the content of their print media for use on their Web pages.

Job tickets can be incorporated into a project using PDF files. Everyone who has access to the file can easily view and modify the job-ticket specs. The PDF is also a good *preflighting* tool. The user is warned if not all elements are present when the file is created.

PDF files are quickly becoming the industry standard for delivering compressed digital files. These files preserve the document's original layout, fonts, and graphics so files can be transferred between media. PDF publishing also eliminates the film-proofing stage.

Integrating All of Production

Compatibility problems between hardware and software hampered the evolution of electronic work flow. Many printing facilities found that data had to be reentered when a job moved from one system to another. Although certain functions became electronic, other functions remained conventional. In addition, electronic functions were written in different languages, so they could not be connected. In response to this growing problem, several vendors formed the *International Cooperation for Integration of Prepress, Press, and Postpress (CIP3)*. Created in 1995 and based in Switzerland, CIP3 brought together many of the main vendors of hardware and software used around the world in the printing industry.

With its members working collaboratively, CIP3 produced *Print Production Format (PPF)*, a format allowing information input at the beginning of a job's production to flow seamlessly from one workstation to the next. With PPF, it became possible for data on a job to move from prepress to press and onto post-press operations. For example, imagine an 8 1/2″ × 11″ flier created in prepress with page composition software and electronically imposed so each press sheet will carry four fliers (four-up). After the plates are imaged and sent to the pressroom, the press operator no longer must determine which areas of the plate will need the most ink and accordingly set the ink keys on the press. Instead, the ink keys can be set automatically with data from the software that imaged the plate. Similarly, prepress data can communicate the location of the press sheets' trim marks to automatically program the guillotine cutter. In this scenario, digital data is created in one software package and passed on to other software packages equipped with the ability to read PPF.

In 2001, CIP3 evolved into the International Cooperation for Integration of Process, Prepress, Press, and Postpress (CIP4). PPF evolved into *Job Definition Format (JDF)*. Similar to PPF, JDF is a standard method of communication that eliminates the need for data to be reentered as a job moves from one system to another during production. JDF can create an even longer seamless electronic work flow, however, which can begin with the customer's specs submitted to the printer as the basis of getting a cost estimate.

The three main capabilities of JDF are the job ticket, work-flow organization, and device control and automation. The job-ticket component describes the job's design in exact detail. As the job-ticket component describes the product, the work-flow organization describes the process that will be necessary to create the product. The device control-and-automation component actually commands each software package and piece of hardware involved in producing the job. Several companies have created JDF work flows integrating software and hardware produced by manufacturers that are members of CIP4.

Desktop Publishing

Desktop publishing is a general term used to describe the process of creating and assembling pages on a computer. Initially, desktop publishing was used only for business correspondence and for creating brochures, fliers, and short-run newsletters. Today, however, desktop-publishing systems are the basis for all electronic prepress. See **Figure 13-7.** Stand-alone personal computers are used to produce art, copy, and page composition. When connected to powerful servers and various output devices, personal computers can be used to assemble pages (imposition), generate film, create printing plates, and control digital presses. In other words, all prepress functions can be performed digitally.

Most printed products follow a basic order of production from inception to publication. Personal computers equipped with appropriate software are used during every step of the process. For example, in the production of a book, the author writes the copy on a personal computer. After the edit is complete and the author has reviewed the manuscript, the publisher gives the author's copy in the form of a text file to its in-house production department or to a service bureau for page makeup. Art is prepared and integrated with the text, in accordance with the specs of the book designer.

Initially, the pages are output as inexpensive *laser proofs* and sent to the publisher and author for review of the art and layout and to make any

interpreter: a computer program residing on a controller board in the printer.

Encapsulated PostScript (EPS) file: a file format used to transfer PostScript-image information from one program to another and for outputting to an imagesetter.

portable document format (PDF): a file format Adobe Systems developed for representing documents in a manner that is independent of the original program software, hardware, and operating system used to create those documents.

computer-to-plate (CTP) technology: a combination platemaking and printing process that allows plates to be imaged directly from electronic data.

preflighting: an orderly review of files to identify things that might cause problems during prepress operations or at the output stage.

International Cooperation for Integration of Prepress, Press, and Postpress (CIP3): an association working to produce systems for digital documents that can be created in prepress and used to set up press and finishing devices.

Print Production Format (PPF): a format that allows data input at the beginning of a job's production to be read by several workstations throughout the job's production.

Job Definition Format (JDF): a format that allows data input by customers seeking an estimate to be used by workstations involved in the job's production.

desktop publishing: the process of creating and assembling pages on a desktop computer.

laser proof: a proof created on a laser printer.

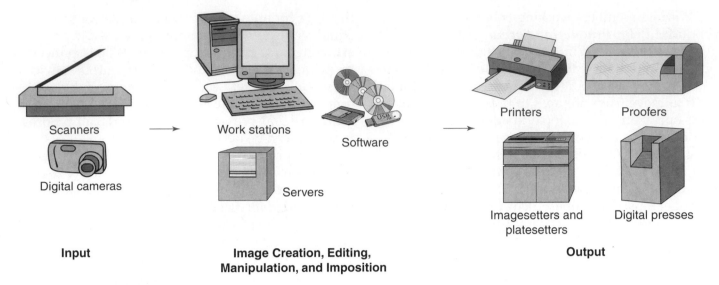

Input   Image Creation, Editing, Manipulation, and Imposition   Output

Figure 13-7. The basic stages of electronic prepress are input (image capture); image creation, editing, manipulation, and imposition; and output.

necessary changes. After the publisher reviews the corrections and approves the work, the files are translated into PostScript format and sent to the printer to generate film or plates. In the case of short runs, the files can go directly to a digital press. Long-run jobs require a nondigital press. This press is likely to be computer operated, however, as will the postpress finishing and binding operations.

Power Supply

Once a system is installed and running, the power supply is often forgotten. When the electrical power supply is disrupted, however, the digital work flow grinds to a halt. When computers lose power without warning, hours of work might be lost. In addition, no work can be done until power is restored. An *uninterruptible power supply* will save time and prevent work-flow interruptions during power drops and blackouts.

Desktop computers can use a small battery supply that keeps the system running for at least five minutes in the event of a power loss. The battery supply will give users enough time to save their work and shut the computers down properly. Some uninterruptible power-supply systems also protect the computer from power surges more effectively than power strips do. Larger systems that use a server should have both a battery backup and a generator. The battery should supply enough power to keep the system running until the generator starts.

Service Bureaus

Many publishers do not have an in-house production department that can scan high-resolution images or output film, so they must contract this type of work to a service bureau. A service bureau provides a link between publishers or advertising agencies and printers. See **Figure 13-8.** In the decades before digital prepress, trade shops served as this link and provided services such as manual page composition, line photography, halftone production, and film assembly. The digital revolution in the graphic communications industry, however, forced many trade shops to either go out of business or expand into electronic technology.

Some service bureaus offer a full range of *prepress services* and include everything from page composition to high-end scanning and raster-image processing. This type of service bureau is referred to as a *prepress service*. A prepress service provides specific services (such as scanning images) for customer use. This service can also produce a project from page layout and design to film production. Service bureaus that limit their services to high-resolution output from PostScript files are usually referred to as *output service bureaus*.

When contracting prepress work, it is important to identify who is responsible for each step of the project. Maintaining open communication among the client, service bureau, and printer enhances a smooth digital work flow. Also, it ensures faster problem solving.

Figure 13-8. Service bureaus provide a variety of services. Smaller shops might provide copying services and short-run printing. Regardless of whether the job is output to an imagesetter, platesetter, or digital press, desktop-publishing software is the basis for file preparation. (Buckeye Printing and Mailing Solutions)

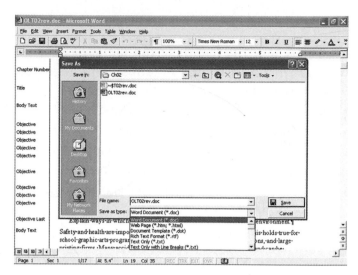

Figure 13-9. Most word processing programs allow the user to save a file in various formats. In this instance, the file is being saved as a Microsoft Word document.

File Formats

Digital files represent many hours of labor. For this reason, extreme care must be paid to the format in which the data will be stored. All prepress programs store jobs in their own proprietary formats. The job files are converted to PostScript technology for imaging or for input into another program. The capability to convert a system's data format to and from various standards is extremely important.

Caution

Digital data can become damaged or corrupted. Always back up your files on a regular basis. When you make backup copies, you are copying your files to a second medium as a precaution, in case the first medium, such as your computer's hard drive, fails or is destroyed.

Text files are fairly versatile. Many word processing programs allow the user to save a file in various formats. See **Figure 13-9.** The data from a text file can also be saved in its ASCII format and imported into any word processing program. The styles might be lost, but the text can be reformatted for use in an incompatible program. File formats for graphic images, however, are not as flexible.

The file format of a graphic image is important because it determines how much the image can be manipulated and how well it can be reproduced. Graphic images should be saved in a manner that makes them editable, so they can be reused, repurposed, and continuously adapted. If an image cannot be edited, it can be reused only as originally created. For example, if a company's catalog is properly designed and formatted, the company could merely edit the file to produce the next catalog, without having to begin a new job. In addition, files created for printed materials can be repurposed to be used on the company's Web site. Extensive knowledge of a program's capabilities and open communication among the client, service bureau, and printer will best determine the type of file formats that should be used for any given job.

File-Naming Conventions

Carefully naming files helps to keep work organized. A standard convention for naming might be created in-house or supplied by the service bureau or printer that will receive the job. Regardless of the method chosen, consistent application of the

uninterruptible power supply: a battery that supplies temporary power to a computer when there is a power loss.

prepress service: a service bureau offering a full range of prepress services, including everything from manual page composition to high-end scanning and RIPping.

output service bureau: a supplier generally specializing in PostScript output, rather than in a broader range of color separation and prepress service.

convention is required to ensure prompt access to files. The computer platform might limit the type of characters and the length of the file names. Along with the platform's built-in limitations, there are several general rules that should be followed:

- File names should not begin with a space.
- Each file name should be unique.
- Only alphanumeric characters should be used. The use of symbols should be avoided.
- The appropriate file extensions should be used to identify file type, such as .tif or .eps.

To avoid confusion, revised files should not be submitted with the same name as the original file. *Automatic picture replacement (APR)* or Open Prepress Interface (OPI) files, however, should not be renamed because the name of the file serves as the link to the high-resolution image. Changing the name will cause delays while the link is reestablished. Refer to Chapter 14 for additional information on file types and APR.

Preflighting

After an electronic file has been created, there are many items to be preflighted before it can continue through production and onto output. Preflighting is an orderly review of files to identify potential problems that could occur during production. A service bureau or printer will routinely preflight files received from clients to check for missing or incompatible file components. If problems are found, clients are usually contacted and offered the option of correcting the file themselves or incurring the time delays and added expense of having the service bureau or printer correct the file. In either event, correcting errors at this point is much less expensive than doing so well into production. Therefore, it is prudent for clients to preflight their files before submitting them for production. Developing a preflighting chart similar to the one in **Figure 13-10** will enhance a smooth digital work flow. Desktop-publishing programs might include preflighting tools that alert the user to potential problems. More robust preflight software, such as the FlightCheck® program, not only lists errors and omissions, but it can also indicate their locations and recommend solutions.

The client, service bureau, and printer should discuss file format and preparation to make the preflighting go smoothly. If the files are prepared properly, all parties involved will save time and money. Some of the most commonly recurring problems with customer-furnished files are the following:

- No laser proofs supplied.
- Incorrect page sizes.
- Inadequate image bleeds.
- Scans supplied in wrong file format or with resolution that is too high or too low.
- Files defined with incorrect color (red, green, and blue versus cyan, magenta, yellow, and black).
- Missing or corrupt fonts, images, trapping, or graphics.

Preflighting includes the printing of composite hard copies and color separations. The printer or service bureau can refer to the hard copies when they encounter problems.

Once the separations and composites are printed, all the graphics should be linked. Page composition programs allow the user to select link options as the art is imported. Linking art files makes it easier to handle the files. If a file becomes corrupted, only that piece of art will need to be replaced. If all the graphics are embedded in the document file and one piece of art is corrupted, the entire page or project will have to be recreated.

To prevent art from printing as low-resolution images or bitmap placeholders, check to make sure every graphic used in the file is in the proper folder. The original art files should be included in a separate directory if the linked graphics are in an uneditable format. Print the directories for each folder and indicate the total number of folders included for the project. Include a letter outlining specific aspects of the job. The letter should outline the software and fonts used, trapping requirements, print specs, and any other important information.

To avoid the omission of data, prepare a checklist to verify both mechanical and electronic materials. See **Figure 13-11**. The checklist should help verify that all graphic, font, and color components are present and correct. The Scitex Graphic Arts Users Association (SGAUA) publishes the *Computer Ready Electronic File (CREF) II guidelines* to improve prepress productivity. Professionals recommend consulting the CREF II guidelines before beginning any prepress work.

File Repair

Files that become damaged or corrupted usually cannot be opened, causing the data they contain to become unavailable. Virus attacks, broken downloads, improper system shutdown, bad sectors in

Before preparing the file…	Is your service provider's hardware and software (including versions) compatible?
	Do output capabilities meet your needs?
	What different types of media can be supported?
	What compression programs are supported?
	What fonts used in the file does the service provider support?
	Who will do trapping on files?
	Should the file be prepared as a printer or reader spread?
Acceptable graphic formats	Submit only tagged image file format (TIFF), PDF, and EPS file formats, regardless of platform.
	Convert color graphics from RGB to cyan, magenta, yellow, and black (CMYK), including nested or embedded elements.
	Duotones and files with embedded clipping paths must be supplied as EPS files.
Proofs	Supply a composite proof (either laser or color) of the final file provided for output.
	For color jobs, supply separated laser proofs of each color with identification on each sheet the application created.
Is the output file correct?	Have all application, source, and EPS files been included?
	Are all PostScript technology–type fonts used in the file included?
	Have you removed any extraneous versions or files from the medium that do not pertain to the job being output?
	Did you include complete fonts for modified typefaces and give them a name different from the library font?
	Were all the for position only (FPO) images for APR named with the same names as the scanned images?
Things that don't always appear as they seem	Laser proofs of the same file do not always output the same way on an imagesetter or a platesetter.
	Monitor images do not match hard-proof images.
	All digital-proofing devices do not output color hues and values the same way.
File preparation	In draw programs, have you limited anchor points to the smallest number possible to minimize RIPping problems?
	Have you correctly used the actual font in the Font menu, rather than incorrectly using the Style menu for typestyles (such as bold or italic)?
	Have you established crop marks correctly from the Page Setup or Preferences menu?
	Have you included overwork for bleeds outside the crop area?
Items to make sure are included	Include the job sheet with the submitted file showing the following:
	Applications used (including version number)
	File names
	Directories
	Folders
	Fonts
	Due dates
	List a contact name including both business and after-hours phone numbers.
	Make a backup copy of the file to retain for yourself.

Figure 13-10. There are many items to consider and check before beginning a job and sending it to a service provider or printer. Develop a preflighting chart to help your staff maintain a smooth digital work flow.

automatic picture replacement (APR): a process by which high-resolution image files are automatically substituted for low-resolution image files at output time.

Computer Ready Electronic File (CREF) II guidelines: the guidelines the SGAUA publishes to improve prepress productivity.

Usually included in the base cost	Installing fonts listed on the order form and included with the job.
	Setting up applications to run the customer file, based on client-supported information.
	Cursory file examination for obvious problems seen on the monitor.
	Quality control to meet specified printing requirements.
	Final image output.
	Redo, due to vendor error.
Not usually included in the base cost	Trapping.
	File editing, including conversion of RGB to CMYK.
	Creating laser proofs not supplied with the file.
	Additional time, due to incomplete files or missing elements.
	Color proofing of final film or output.

Figure 13-10. *(Continued)*

CDs or DVDs, media corruption, and malfunctioning software can cause damage. Damaged files can often be repaired either by digitally sending the file to a data-repair and -recovery service or by purchasing file-repair software. File-repair software often is created to repair a certain file format (such as .zip files), a certain medium (such as CDs and DVDs), or files of certain applications (such as Microsoft Office software or the AppleWorks application program). Software also can be purchased that recovers graphics files that were accidentally deleted from applications such as Adobe InDesign software and Photoshop editor, the QuarkXPress application, and Paint Shop Pro® software.

Output Devices

After the file has been properly prepared, it is sent to an output device, which is any device receiving and displaying output from a computer. There is a wide range of output devices to meet several applications. Examples of output devices include computer monitors; ink-jet, laser, and toner-based printers; proofers; imagesetters; and platesetters. Output devices can transfer data onto a substrate such as paper, photopaper, film, or a printing plate.

Monitors

The software used for word processing and page layout on computer systems provides a *What You See Is What You Get (WYSIWYG)* display on the monitor. Monitors used for page layout are large enough (17"–21" diagonal measure) to display an entire page or even two pages. Smaller monitors (14" and 15") used primarily for word processing and general computer use require scrolling across and up and down to see a full page displayed in actual size.

Resolution and dot pitch are also issues of major importance when choosing a monitor. Monitor resolution (the ability to show fine detail) is stated in the number of pixels lined up across and down the screen. A typical high-resolution monitor has 1280 pixels across the screen and 1024 pixels top-to-bottom, usually stated as 1280 × 1024. Monitors used in graphic design typically have resolutions ranging from 1024 × 768 to 2048 × 1536.

Dot pitch is a measurement of the vertical distance between rows of pixels on the monitor. The distance is stated in decimal fractions of a millimeter, with the image quality becoming crisper as the fraction becomes smaller. A common dot-pitch measurement on monitors for general computer use is 0.28, but 0.26 dot pitch is often preferred for graphics applications.

The color monitor uses the additive color system to form the images on the screen. This system is based on combinations of RGB light. The final output to the printing press, however, will be in the colors of the subtractive color system (cyan, magenta, yellow, and black). It is difficult to accurately represent the subtractive colors on-screen without color-management software because colors on a monitor are displayed in RGB. The monitor display created using this type of software is termed *What You See Is What You Print (WYSIWYP)*.

Checklist for the Designer		✔
1. Check pasteboard items	• Crops and trim size okay. • Bleeds okay. • Fold, die-cut, and perforation marks okay. • Registration mark offset okay.	
2. Check FPOs and keylines	• All FPOs labeled correctly. • All key lines okay.	
3. Check separations	• All plates check okay. • Plates to be printed: _____	
4. Check traps	• Type traps okay. • Page layout–graphics trap okay. • Imported-graphics trap okay. • Disregard, vendor will do trapping.	
5. Copy files to transfer disk	• Page-layout document(s) copied. • Imported graphics copied. • Editable graphics copied. • Nested graphics copied. • Imported scans copied. • Fonts specified by actual name in document. • Screen fonts copied. • Fonts copied per license agreement. • Transfer disk tracked to vendor.	
6. Test transfer-disk files (print proofs)	• Final composite proof with printer's marks. • Final separations with printer's marks.	
7. Collate and mark up final proofs	• Composite proof labeled, notated, stapled.	
8. Prepare traditional art	• Matching art for each FPO on hand. • Art labeled with correct identifier per FPO. • Scaling and cropping information for art noted. • All art collected in labeled envelope.	
9. Prepare instructions	• Read-me documents written and included. • Output/Checklist report included. • Vendor's work order completed. • Copies made for internal records.	
10. Final transmittal package complete	• Instructions, reports, work orders. • Transfer disk. • Composite and separation proofs. • Traditional-art envelope.	

Figure 13-11. Following checklists when verifying the completeness of prepress materials reduces the chances of an oversight.

What You See Is What You Get (WYSIWYG): the ability of computers to display text, graphics, color, and other page elements almost exactly the way they will print.

What You See Is What You Print (WYSIWYP): software that adjusts printers and other output devices to output the same colors seen on the monitor.

Cathode-ray tube (CRT) monitors

A stream of electrons (negatively charged particles) directed onto a phosphor coating on the inside surface of the screen generates images on the face of the *cathode-ray tube (CRT) monitor*. See **Figure 13-12.** Monochrome monitors use a single electron beam that fires a continuous stream of electrons at the back of the display screen. The arrival of electrons on one of the phosphor atoms causes that portion of the screen to light up. Focusing lenses and deflection plates constantly control the position of the electron beam, ensuring image quality. A color monitor uses three electron beams to produce tiny RGB lights (dots) that combine to form a full-color display. Wide-screen CRTs must grow in depth because CRT monitors depend on electrons being able to reach the entire screen, making CRT monitors box-shaped and bulky.

Liquid crystal display (LCD) monitors

In their natural state, liquid-crystal molecules transmit light through two sheets of polarized glass. When a liquid-crystal molecule is heated, it rotates and ceases to twist the light. Therefore, a black-and-white *liquid crystal display (LCD) monitor* consists of a coating of liquid crystals between two thin sheets of polarized glass. See **Figure 13-13.** Also included are vertical columns of tiny wires on one side of the liquid crystal and horizontal rows of tiny wires on the other side. To rotate a given liquid crystal, a small electric charge is sent down the column passing behind the liquid crystal. A ground is established on the row passing in front of the liquid crystal. When

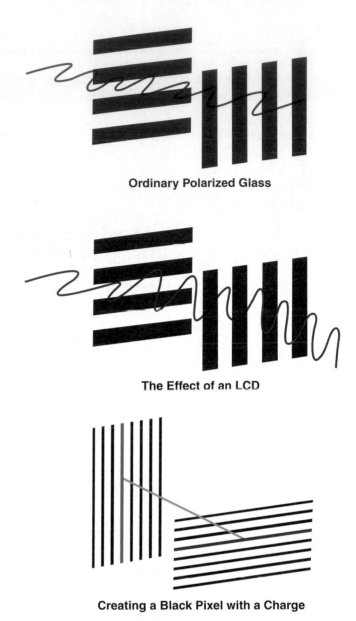

Ordinary Polarized Glass

The Effect of an LCD

Creating a Black Pixel with a Charge

Figure 13-13. LCD technology involves two sheets of polarized glass that prevent light from passing through. With ordinary polarized glass, light waves passing through the first polarized sheet of glass vibrate on a horizontal plane, but the vertical orientation of the second sheet of glass blocks them. An LCD places thousands of liquid crystals between the two sheets of glass. The crystals rotate the light waves so they vibrate vertically and pass through the second sheet of glass to light that portion of the screen. When an electrical charge moves through one of the tiny vertical wires against the back glass (blue wire) and one of the horizontal wires against the second glass (red wire), the current moves through the liquid crystal (green wire). The LCD no longer twists the light, which the second polarized sheet of glass then blocks. This pixel on the monitor now appears black.

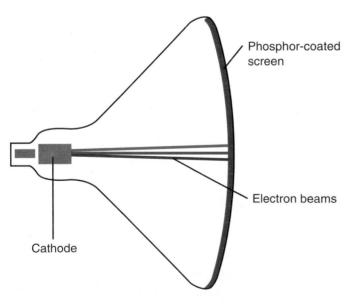

Phosphor-coated screen

Electron beams

Cathode

Figure 13-12. The images on the screen of a CRT monitor are generated from beams of electrons striking phosphors on the inside of the screen.

the charge arrives near the liquid crystal, it moves through the crystal to get to the ground wire. The voltage rotates the liquid crystal and causes the crystal not to twist the light. The result is a dark area on the screen. Grays are created by sending smaller charges that rotate the liquid crystal only slightly—thereby allowing some light to pass. In fact, LCD monitors can show 256 levels of light transmission and, therefore, 256 grays per pixel. Each pixel in a color LCD monitor is made up of three subpixels (RGB).

Plasma display monitors

The concept of subpixels being activated by a small electric current passing from one wire to another is also at the heart of *plasma display monitors*. Instead of each subpixel being a liquid crystal, however, it is a cell containing plasma, a gas consisting mostly of electrons and uncharged atoms. See **Figure 13-14.** When an electrical charge passes through the cell, the electrons collide with the atoms and cause them to emit UV light, which strikes a phosphor coating. The stimulated phosphors emit visible light. Similar to the LCD monitor, each pixel of a plasma display monitor consists of three subpixels. One contains blue phosphors, one contains green phosphors, and one contains red phosphors. Similar to the LCD, the voltage levels passing through each subpixel control the intensity of the RGB lights that determine the color of each pixel. At present, plasma display technology is mostly used to produce the large-screen television screens that hang on a wall. As the plasma display technology matures, however, plasma display monitors are expected to become more common.

Printers

Printers are electronic devices that output digital information onto a substrate such as paper. Printer resolution is measured in dpi. A *dot matrix printer* is a low-quality output device that prints dots to form an image. Images are formed by the ends of thin wires striking an inked ribbon and transferring a dot of ink to the paper. The images have rough edges because of the dot structure. Resolution is low (100 dpi or fewer). This type of printer can be used to print both text matter and art. Material printed

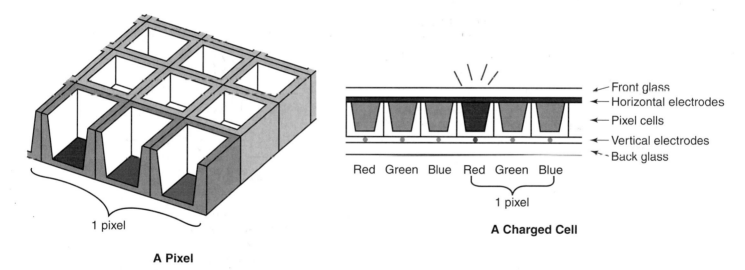

A Pixel

A Charged Cell

Figure 13-14. Each pixel in a plasma monitor consists of three tiny cells (RGB) containing a gas sensitive to electrical charges. The pattern of cells is sandwiched between two sheets of glass, one with vertical columns of electrodes (wires) and one with horizontal electrodes. When an electrical charge passes through one vertical wire and one horizontal wire, the cell at the wires' intersection is charged with an electrical current. The cell lights up. In this drawing, a cell with red phosphorous gas has been charged. The pixel will emit red light.

cathode-ray tube (CRT) monitor: a large vacuum tube with an inside surface that is a flat screen on which images appear when light is selectively allowed to strike it.

liquid crystal display (LCD) monitor: a flat screen on which images appear by the rotation of selected liquid crystals.

plasma display monitor: a flat screen on which images appear when electrons strike selected cells and cause the creation of UV light, which in turn, creates visible light.

printer: an electronic device that outputs digital information onto a substrate, such as paper.

dot matrix printer: a low-quality output device that prints dots to form an image.

on a dot matrix, however, is not of professional-level quality. Dot matrix printers are also comparatively slow, with a speed that ranges from approximately 50 to 200 characters per second.

The *ink-jet printer* forms images with a printhead containing nozzles that shoot tiny dots of ink onto the substrate. Most ink-jet printers are *drop-on-demand ink-jet printers* and use either heat (thermal ink-jets) or electricity (piezoelectric ink-jets) to squeeze ink out of the printhead nozzles at selected moments. *Thermal ink-jet printers* use an electric charge to generate heat, which creates an air bubble in the ink chamber that, in turn, forces the ink out of the nozzle. The bubble's rapid expansion can cause the ink to splatter when it reaches the page, however, and reduce image quality. See **Figure 13-15.** The *piezoelectric ink-jet printers* use an electrical pulse to bend a piezocrystal, which distorts and squeezes the ink reservoir. This type of method controls the ink more precisely and helps eliminate splatter. See **Figure 13-16.** *Continuous ink-jet printers* emit a steady stream of droplets that receive electrical charges. The charges direct the droplets to the appropriate spots on the substrate or to a recycling trough. Designed more for speed than image quality, continuous ink-jet printers are often used to print lot numbers, as well as date and time information, on packages at speeds of over 1000 per minute.

Laser printers operate very similarly to photocopying machines in that electrical charges are used to attract toner material to a drum. This type of printer has a built-in computer, called a *controller,* which translates vector data from the computer into thousands of tiny dots (bitmap images) for printing. A laser then uses this pattern of dots to project a pulse of light for each bitmap dot. See **Figure 13-17.** These pulses of light strike a mirror that pivots slowly to distribute the pulses across a drum, which either a corona wire or a charged roller positively charges. As the laser's pulses of light move across the rotating drum, they discharge the drum's image areas. After this treatment, the drum surface consists of negatively charged image areas and positively charged nonimage areas. Positively charged toner particles are then rolled against the entire drum. Only the negatively charged image areas, however, lift the particles onto the drum. The paper with its toner images next passes between Teflon® surface coating–coated, heated rollers that fuse (melt) the powder dots onto the paper to produce a permanent image. As the drum continues to rotate, a strong light discharges it completely, which prepares it to receive the next page of images. Full-color laser printers successively apply cyan, magenta, yellow, and black (CMYK) toners to a charged drum. A printer's *engine speed* refers to the maximum number of pages per minute the printer can output in full- or single-color mode.

Laser printers have three advantages over ink-jet printers. First, the laser is able to move across the page faster and, therefore, print faster. Second, although a laser printer costs more than an ink-jet printer to purchase, toner is much less expensive to replace than ink. Third, laser printers can generate images with greater detail.

Thermal printers use the thermal transfer process to output color images. The thermal transfer process creates printed images using colored wax

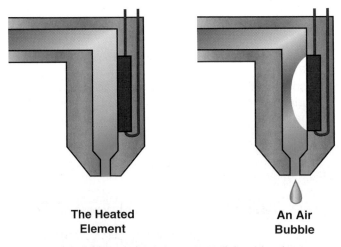

The Heated Element   **An Air Bubble**

Figure 13-15. Thermal ink-jet printers are also known as *bubble-jet printers* because the jet of ink is triggered when a brief electric current heats a small element, which immediately produces an air bubble in the ink reservoir, forcing out a tiny drop of ink.

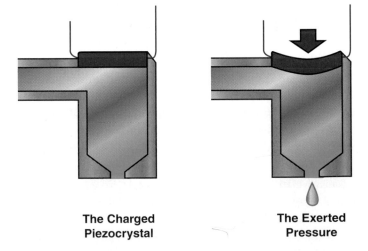

The Charged Piezocrystal   **The Exerted Pressure**

Figure 13-16. In a piezoelectric ink-jet printer, a brief electrical charge is sent through a piezocrystal, which is immediately bent. The pressure exerted into the ink reservoir forces out a tiny ink drop.

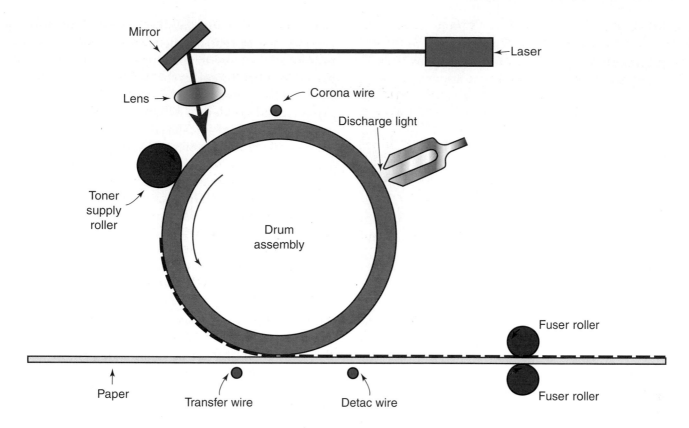

Figure 13-17. After a corona wire charges the surface of the drum assembly, a laser beam imparts a negative charge to the image areas so they will attract the positively charged toner particles. The transfer wire gives an even stronger negative charge to the paper so it will attract the toner from the drum. A detac wire discharges the paper before it moves between hot rollers that melt the toner.

melted and fused to special coated papers. The wax, or ink sheet, contains strips of cyan, magenta, and yellow, and sometimes black, colorants that the printhead vaporizes or melts onto the substrate. In most thermal applications, each color prints in a separate pass of the printing head. The thermal transfer process can be very expensive because the entire ink sheet is used, regardless of how much color is removed in the process. Thermal printers are generally used for prepress color proofing and other professional-presentation applications.

Dye sublimation printers use a form of heat-transfer printing to create high-quality continuous tone images. These printers produce photographic-quality, digital color *proofs* using a sublimable dye (one that moves directly from a solid state to a gaseous state, without moving through a liquid state). The image is first imprinted in reverse on a carrier sheet and then transferred to the receiving sheet by placing it in direct contact with the carrier and subjecting it to a high temperature for a short time. After the substrate has cooled, the release paper is peeled away. The image will have transferred to the substrate.

ink-jet printer: a computer output device that forms images with a printhead containing nozzles that shoot tiny dots of ink onto the substrate.

drop-on-demand ink-jet printer: a device that emits tiny drops of ink when commanded by digital data.

thermal ink-jet printer: a device that emits tiny drops of ink through the use of heat.

piezoelectric ink-jet printer: a device that emits tiny drops of ink when the ink chamber is squeezed.

continuous ink-jet printer: a device that emits a steady stream of tiny drops of ink.

laser printer: a medium- to high-quality computer output device that uses a laser beam to polarize images on the drum.

engine speed: the maximum number of pages per minute the printer can output in full- or single-color mode.

thermal printer: a computer output device that uses the thermal transfer process to output color images.

dye sublimation printer: an electronic output device that produces photographic-quality digital color proofs using a sublimable dye.

proof: a prototype of the printed job made digitally from electronic data, photochemically from film and dyes, or photomechanically from plates.

Caution

Some ink-jet and laser printers use agents that can be irritating or toxic. Laser toner can be an irritant to the respiratory tract and eyes. MSDSs are available from the toner vendor or manufacturer.

Digital Proofers

A proof is a preliminary copy of a job still in production, serving as a sample for the customer and a visual specification for the press operator. A *hard proof* is a tangible sheet made directly from digital files, generated directly from film, or run off on a proof press. A *soft proof* is the image appearing on the computer monitor. Cost and the exact elements in question (such as color, text flow, or positional errors) determine the types of proofs requested at various stages of prepress production.

Digital proofs are generated by outputting files on a high-resolution, high-quality printer. See **Figure 13-18.** Depending on the system's capabilities, digital proofs can simulate results from any type of printing press. For digital proofs to replace film-generated proofs, however, they must accurately represent all the features of the traditional proof, including color fidelity, traps and overprints, representative screening, and quality in fine line details.

Customers often require proofs that accurately represent color and halftone reproduction. Comparatively inexpensive digital proofs can be produced and used to indicate the location of page

elements and approximate color. Many printers and service bureaus, however, use high-resolution proofing systems to produce digital proofs that closely predict the colors that will appear on the press sheets. These proofs can be used as *contract proofs*, proofs used to define what the client can expect from the finished job. Used in conjunction with a color-management system, digital-proofing systems can simulate the *dot gain* expected on press. If the digital-output device is connected to the same *raster image processor (RIP)* that runs the imagesetter, it will output halftone patterns identical to those that will appear on the final sheet.

It is important for many customers to see the halftone dots that will be printed on the press. Customers once previewed the halftone-dot pattern because traditional analog proofs were made from the same films that made the printing plate. Many digital proofs do not, however, contain halftone dots. The viewer might not be able to determine if there will be a problem with the screening of an image and the text embedded in the image. A digital halftone proofer, such as the Kodak Approval or Polaroid PolaProof® system, is able to simulate the halftone dots, resolution, screen angles, and dot gain, as well as the traditional analog proofs.

Through the use of modems and the Internet, *remote proofing* allows a printer to send digital files to an out-of-town client. Files can be viewed on a monitor (soft proofing) or output to a high-quality proofing device, similar to the one the printer or service bureau uses. The printer and the customer can efficiently transmit and receive electronic files in a matter of minutes. On-line proofing is software that permits both soft proofing and hard proofing at the client's location. This proofing allows the service provider, printing company, and client to simultaneously view, mark up, and make notes displayed on their respective monitors. See **Figure 13-19.**

Note

Soft proofing should not be used for proofing color reproduction. Hard copies should be generated on a digital proofing device to provide a better color match. All devices (from the service bureau, publisher, and printer) should be calibrated for accurate and consistent results.

Figure 13-18. High-resolution proofers can closely simulate the colors that will appear on the press sheet. (HP/Indigo)

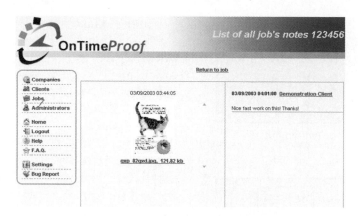

Figure 13-19. On-line proofing allows clients to view a proof and communicate with the provider immediately. Note the customer's comment on the right of the screen. (Lucid Dream Software, Inc.)

Imagesetters and Platesetters

After the proof has been approved, the job can continue onto the making of printing plates, which requires either an imagesetter or a platesetter. An *imagesetter* is a high-resolution output device that takes bitmap data and produces either film or polyester printing plates. See **Figure 13-20.** Imagesetters

Figure 13-20. Imagesetters use a laser to expose a bitmap image directly to either film or polyester plate material. (Monotype Systems)

use a laser to record the images line by line to a light-sensitive material (such as film or a plate), thereby eliminating the pasteup, camera, and image-assembly stages of prepress. See **Figure 13-21.** The intensity of the laser beam controls dot size. The size of the press and, therefore, the press's printing plates usually determine the size of the imagesetter. For example, a 25″ × 38″ press needs an imagesetter that can output a piece of film large enough to cover that area.

There are two basic types of imagesetters—capstan and drum. See **Figure 13-22.** Capstan imagesetters feed a roll of film or polyester plate material forward past a laser that moves laterally. This coordinated movement allows the laser to expose the entire page before the material is cut off and output to either a lighttight cassette or an in-line processor. In drum imagesetters, a cylindrical drum holds the receiving material. Internal-drum imagesetters hold the material stationary, while the laser spins in the center of the drum and directs its light outward to expose the page. The less common external-drum imagesetter holds the material on the outside of the drum. As the drum spins, the material is moved past a stationary laser.

To ensure high-quality output and repeatability, especially with color separations, special attention must be given to calibration and maintenance of the imagesetter. *Repeatability* is the ability of an imagesetter or other device to achieve exactly the same

hard proof: a proof printed onto a sheet of paper or other material.

soft proof: a proof displayed on a computer screen.

digital proof: a proof generated by outputting files on a high-resolution, high-quality printer, rather than from film separations.

contract proof: a color proof representing the appearance of the finished printed product that the printer and the client agreed on.

dot gain: the optical increase in the size of a halftone dot during prepress operations or the mechanical increase in halftone-dot size that occurs as the image is transferred from plate to blanket to paper.

raster image processor (RIP): a hardware-software combination that interprets digital data into an array of dots (a bitmap), which can be output through an imagesetter marking engine.

remote proofing: sending a digital image across the Internet to a proofer located in a different location.

imagesetter: a high-resolution output device that takes bitmap data generated by a RIP and writes it to film, paper, or printing plates, using a laser that writes the data line by line.

repeatability: the ability of an imagesetter or another device to achieve exactly the same results each time, given the same data. This ability is a critical specification for accurate color-film separations.

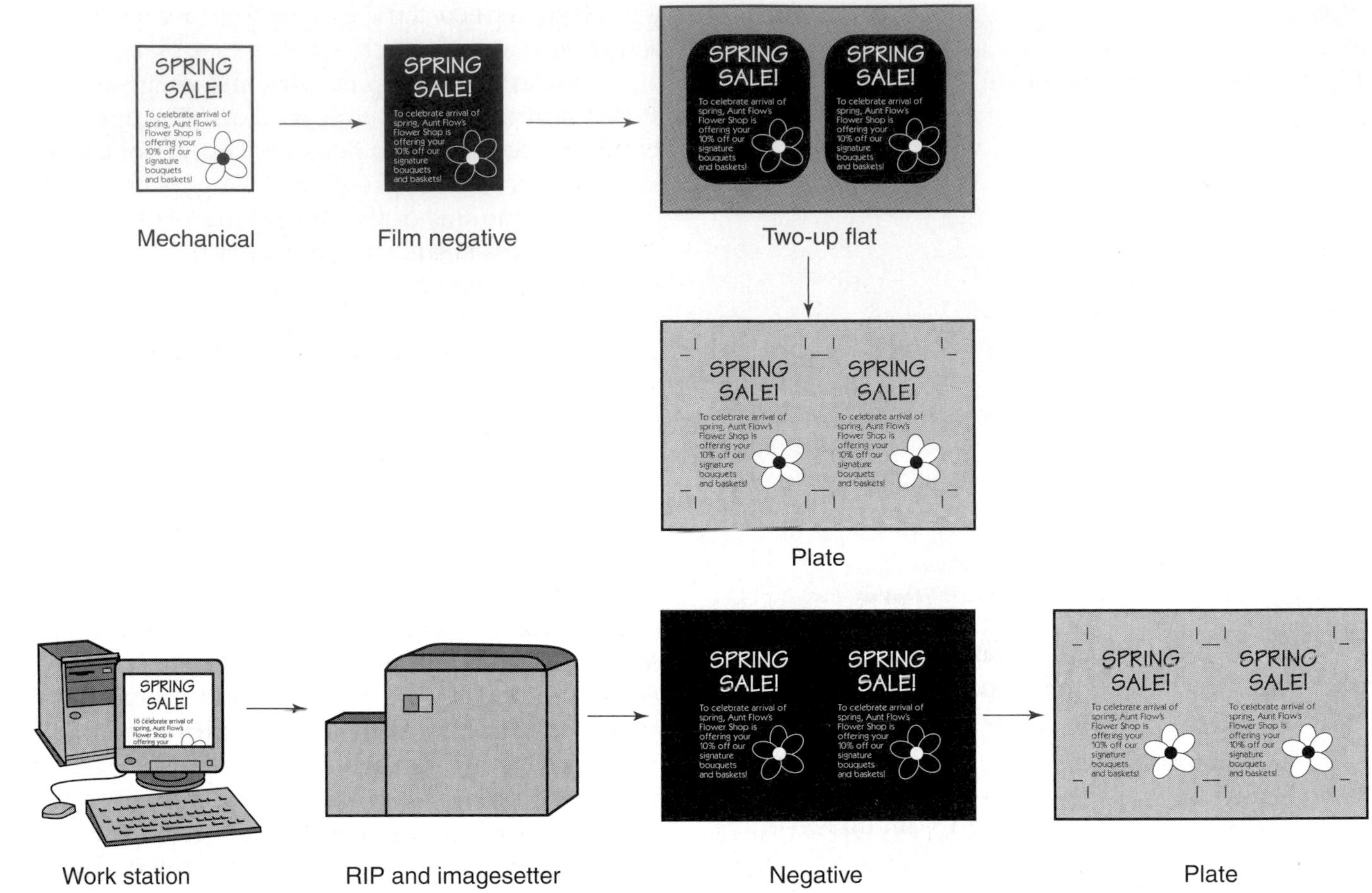

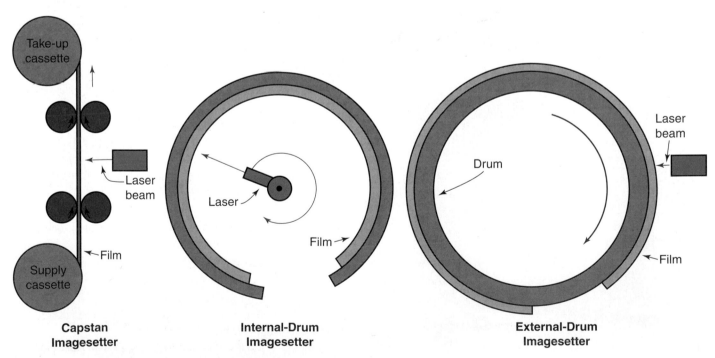

Figure 13-21. An imagesetter replaces the copy preparation, camera, and stripping functions and permits a digitally imposed file to be imaged directly to a single sheet of film that will expose the plate.

Figure 13-22. Capstan imagesetters advance film or polyester plate material vertically, while a laser moves horizontally to expose the material. Internal-drum imagesetters hold the receiving material stationary, while the laser spins inside. External-drum imagesetters hold the film against the outside of a drum that spins in front of the laser.

results each time, given the same data. Imagesetters are manufactured by a number of companies and differ in speed, precision, resolution, screening technology, and media capability.

Printers who want to produce durable metal plates without using film can use a technology in which the digital data is imaged directly to the plate. Known as *CTP systems* or *DTP systems*, this technology uses platesetters that work similarly to imagesetters, in that RIPs produce bitmap data, which directs the laser's beam onto a light-sensitive emulsion. The emulsion is on a sheet of metal, however, instead of a sheet of film. See **Figure 13-23**. *Platesetters* consist of a plate-material storage area, a transport system that positions a single plate for imaging, a laser, an in-line processor, and the ability to punch plates for mounting on a specific press.

There are three categories of platesetters. They greatly resemble the categories of imagesetters. Flatbed platesetters function similarly to capstan imagesetters. That is, the plate moves past a stationary visible-light laser. Internal-drum platesetters use a stationary laser of either visible or invisible light to expose a plate held inside a revolving drum. External-drum platesetters use several stationary laser beams to expose a plate held against the outside of a revolving drum. These platesetters are well suited to imaging plates 40″ and larger in the long dimension. Some systems subject imaged plates to high temperatures to increase image durability. CTP systems are capable of delivering high-resolution plates with excellent image registration because every plate is a master plate created from the same digital data.

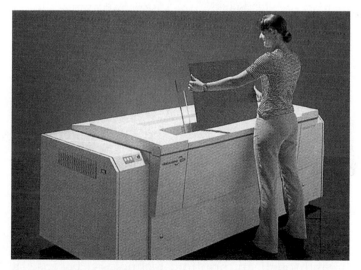

Figure 13-23. Platesetters function as imagesetters do, except they eliminate the need for film by exposing directly to plate material.

Raster Image Processors (RIPs)

An *imagesetting system* consists of an imagesetter and its RIP. A RIP is a hardware-software combination that translates PostScript technology's description of the page into the bitmap images that will make up the page on the printing plates. Phrased differently, the RIP translates the language of the page-layout software into the language driving imagesetters and platesetters. A hardware RIP is dedicated to working with a specific model of imagesetter. A software RIP can be adapted to a different model.

All computer-generated output is composed of small dots. The RIP converts a vector image, such as type or other line art, into the pattern of dots needed to generate the output. The processor also generates halftone dots by combining several smaller cells or grid units. See **Figure 13-24**. The RIP determines what value each pixel or spot of output should possess. The conversion of a vector image to a raster image is called *RIPping*, or *rasterization*. Essentially, an interpreter in the *hardware* converts a PostScript file into a display list, which is then converted into a bitmap describing the page. Most PostScript output devices have a RIP built into the hardware. RIPs are powerful devices that allow the viewing of screened images before they are output, are capable of driving more than one output device, and can screen halftones to minimize or eliminate moiré patterns.

Many RIPs can also perform dot-gain calibration. Dot gain is the optical increase in the size of a halftone dot during prepress operations or the mechanical increase in halftone-dot size that occurs as the image is transferred from plate to blanket to paper. This gain can cause shifts in color during four-color printing because increased dot size increases the amount of ink placed on the substrate. Although dot gain is inevitable in printing, it can be controlled by starting with a smaller dot on the plate. RIPs can be calibrated to allow for the anticipated dot gain for a particular job.

platesetter: the platemaking component of a CTP system, used to image plates containing paginated text and graphics.

imagesetting system: an imagesetter and its RIP.

rasterization: the process of converting mathematical and digital information into a series of dots by an imagesetter or a platesetter for the production of film or plates.

hardware: the basic computer architecture a particular model uses.

25-Cell Resolution Grid

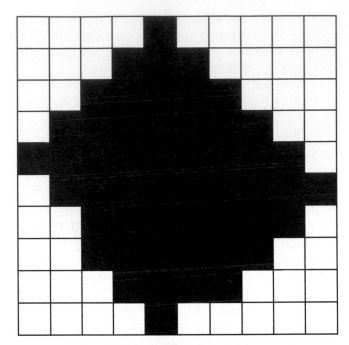

100-Cell Resolution Grid

Figure 13-24. A RIP converts continuous tone images into a pattern of tiny dots, forming halftone dots. A halftone dot made from a 25-cell resolution grid is coarser than a dot made with a 100-cell resolution grid.

As will be explained in more detail in Chapter 20, the digital files that drive imagesetters and platesetters can also reduce the time required to prepare the press for printing the job. By analyzing where the plate will be imaged and the ink coverage that different portions of the plate require, software applications can determine the fountain-key settings on the press and actually set them automatically. The fountain keys control the amount of ink going into each zone of the plate. Areas with greater concentrations of images receive more ink.

Automated Ink Control

The digital data that drives the imaging of the plate is now shared with the pressroom. Historically, the press operator would examine the plate and set controls (called *ink keys*) to ensure that areas of the plate received just the right amount of ink. Portions of the plate with twice as much image area would receive twice as much ink as portions of the plate with half the image area. In the 1990s, plate scanners were developed that could move across the plate, assess the demand for ink, and set the ink fountain controls automatically. Now, the digital data from the RIP that image the plate can also apply the same information about where the image areas appear to set the ink keys automatically. The result is less time spent making the press ready for the run.

Digital Printing

Digital printing is any method of printing in which the imaging of the plate occurs on the press. Digital-printing technology is a product of the 1990s and includes two processes—direct imaging presses and toner-based presses. *Digital imaging (DI) technology* images plates that already have been mounted on the press. Although DI is CTP technology built into the press, it is usually referred to as *direct-to-press (DTPr)* or *computer-to-press (CTPr)*, instead of CTP. See **Figure 13-25.** Advantages to DI presses are shorter production time, reduced labor costs, more cost-effective short runs, and greater registration control. A disadvantage is the limitation to the size of the press sheets. DI presses are discussed in Chapter 20.

Digital toner-based press technology uses lasers or light-emitting diodes (LEDs) to impart an electrical charge to image areas of a plate. The charged areas attract liquid or solid toner material, which is then transferred to the paper. See **Figure 13-26.** The main advantage of digital toner-based technology is *variable data printing (VDP)*, or variable information printing (VIP)—the ability to reimage the plate between impressions. This technology is a major breakthrough in printing technology because it allows each printed sheet to be unique. See **Figure 13-27.** Although VIP is currently limited to comparatively

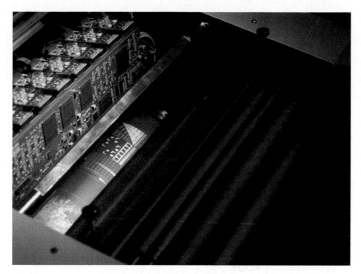

Figure 13-25. DI technology allows the imaging of plates after they are in place on the press. (Presstek, Inc)

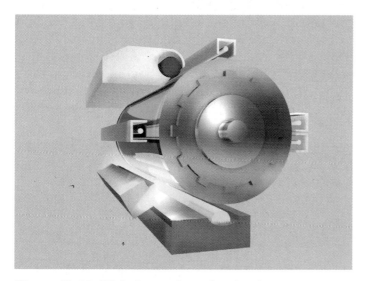

Figure 13-26. Digital toner-based technology uses electrostatic principles to charge the image areas of the plates. (Xeikon)

small press sheets, the potential impact of this technology is astonishing. For example, a national magazine could tailor the advertisements and articles in each individual copy to the interests of each individual subscriber.

Before digital printing, traditional offset printing and systems based on color laser printers or electrostatic copiers were the only methods of fulfilling short-run color-printing needs. Unfortunately, traditional offset printing was too expensive for short runs. The quality of laser printers and copiers was inadequate. Today, digital-printing technologies make the cost of single-color and four-color short runs more affordable. For example, Xerox, Toshiba, and Canon manufacture high-speed toner-based

Figure 13-27. Variable-image printing permits each sheet of a pressrun to be different. These consecutive press sheets were printed with different images because the plates were reimaged during each revolution.

electrostatic-copier systems that print from digital files. See **Figure 13-28.**

Digital printing offers quick turnaround times and a great flexibility because there is no need for producing film and plates, thus shortening makeready time and allowing inexpensive last-minute changes. Individual pages can be customized during print runs. Content such as names and addresses can be changed for split runs.

This printing also enables many more companies to use distributed printing on a local, national, or worldwide basis. Distributed digital printing allows the client to send electronic files to a printing operation near the point of distribution, thereby reducing time and shipping costs. For example, the file for a brochure can be sent electronically to a service bureau or printer near a trade-show location a few days before the event. The brochure can then be printed and delivered directly to the trade show. Digital files can also be sent to remote locations to make plates.

digital printing: any reproduction technology that receives electronic files and uses spots (or dots) for replication.

digital imaging (DI) technology: the hardware and software that images a plate on the press.

digital toner-based press technology: a type of DI in which the image is imparted to the plate by electrically charging image areas that attract toner material.

variable data printing (VDP): a type of digital printing that allows different type and images to be printed on consecutive press sheets because the plate is reimaged between impressions.

Figure 13-28. Some copy machines can be connected to a server or personal computer and used for small print runs. (Heidelberg, Inc.)

Publishers can use digital-printing technologies to extend the life of their products and build new sources of revenue. When unsure of a product, a publisher can use digital printing to produce one-color books in small runs ranging from 1 to 1000.

Digital printing can also be used to reprint books that would otherwise be out of print, without increasing the publisher's inventory.

Although digital printing eliminates many of the time-consuming and expensive steps involved in traditional printing, it has not fully achieved the quality traditional printing provides. Most digital presses do not yet produce the rich, deep look of material printed on a traditional offset press. Digital presses are not replacements for conventional presses. They are, however, designed for the types of jobs that are impractical or impossible to do on their traditional counterparts.

The Internet

One of the most significant advances in digital technology is the ability to transfer documents electronically. A graphic designer in one location can use a computer, telephone line, and modem to transfer camera-ready documents directly to a printer's computer across town, across the country, or anywhere in the world. Today, most companies use the *Internet* to communicate, transfer documents, and sell their products and services. See **Figure 13-29.**

Figure 13-29. Printing companies can use the Internet to advertise, accept orders, send out proofs, and communicate with clients during production. (Lithographics, Inc.)

The Internet is a worldwide computer network, in which numerous smaller networks and individual computers are connected to each other. Originally developed for the military, the Internet has become a tool for communication, business, and education that people all over the world use.

The *World Wide Web (WWW)*, or the Web, is the fastest growing part of the Internet. The Web is a highly interlinked collection of hypertext servers that facilitate the sharing and display of text, graphics, sound, animation, and video files among computers around the world. Search engines such as the Yahoo!® search engine and Google™ search engine make it easy to locate specific information on the Web. Web pages can be used to share information, as well as to sell products.

Printing companies are also using the Internet for business-to-business (B2B) file sharing. For example, a printing company or digital photographer can send a poor-quality photograph over the Internet to ColorCentric or a similar company, with specific instructions for color correction. Within 24 hours, the image will be returned with increased contrast, a removed color cast, or another requested adjustment.

Summary

The introduction of computers and digital technology generated some of the greatest changes in the printing industry since the introduction of movable type. Materials that once moved through production as pasteup copy and film now move through production as binary code. The work flow has become almost completely digital. All people involved in the production process must understand their roles and responsibilities in maintaining this work flow.

Problems often occur because of differences in computer platforms and software. By establishing standards to which all parties in a project must conform, many of these problems can be eliminated. The client should also use an established preflighting regimen to identify items that might cause problems during prepress operations or at the output stage. The digital work flow is made up of several electronic devices, including scanners, proofers, imagesetters, platesetters, and digital presses.

Digital printing and the Internet have had a great deal of influence on the printing industry. The quality of digital printing, however, has not surpassed the quality traditional printing provides. Electronic communication is not replacing printed materials. Clients, service bureaus, and printers can use these technologies to their advantage. Digital printing can be used to enter new printing markets, build new sources of revenue, and reprint small quantities of books that would otherwise be out of print. The Internet and WWW can be used to communicate, transfer documents, and sell products and services.

Review Questions

Please do not write in this book. Write your answers on a separate sheet of paper.

1. Compare analog form and digital form.
2. What is a computer platform? Give two examples.
3. _____ is the computer program, or instructions, that initiate the functions of a computer, such as word processing, page composition, and image creation and manipulation.
4. _____ programs allow the user to compose the text, or body matter, of a page.
5. Bitmap graphics can be created or manipulated using a(n) _____ program.
6. _____ programs are used to produce and manipulate vector graphics.
7. _____ graphics are represented by mathematical formulas.
8. A(n) _____ program allows the user to determine the page size and format and to assemble the page elements.
9. A(n) _____ describes the page as a series of codes that output devices, such as RIPs and imagesetters, can interpret.
10. What does *JDF* stand for, and what is its function?
11. _____ is an orderly review of files to identify things that might cause problems during prepress operations or at the output stage.
12. Printers, proofers, and monitors are examples of _____ devices.
13. Printer resolution is measured in _____.
14. The _____ printer forms images with a printhead containing nozzles that shoot tiny dots of ink onto the substrate.

Internet: a worldwide computer network in which smaller networks and individual computers are connected to each other by means of a complex system of routers and gateways.

World Wide Web (WWW): an interlinked collection of pages corresponding to files on widely separated computers.

15. A(n) _____ printer operates on the same basic principle as a photocopying machine.

16. The maximum number of pages per minute a printer can output in full- or single-color mode is its _____.

17. _____ printers create images by heating pigment materials that move directly from a solid state to a gaseous state.

18. Distinguish between a hard proof and a soft proof.

19. What purpose does a contract proof serve?

20. Why is it important for customers to see the halftone dots on a proof?

21. A(n) _____ generates the bitmap data that drives imagesetters and platesetters.

22. Compare and contrast imagesetters and platesetters. In what ways are they similar? How are they different?

23. What is digital proofing?

24. _____ technology allows the reimaging of the plate between impressions.

Skill-Building Activities

1. Obtain samples of material printed from various types of output devices (a laser printer, a bubble-jet printer, an ink-jet printer, and a dye sublimation printer). Perform a visual comparison. Examine the materials with a loupe.

2. Contact a local service bureau or printer. Arrange a visit to the production facility. Ask which parts of production are digital. Is PPF or JDF used? What technological plans exist?

3. Contact a local service bureau or printer and ask for copies of old proofs and, if possible, a copy of the finished product. Ask the person to identify the various types of proofs used. Compare the quality of each type of proof and its emulation of the final product.

4. Make arrangements to visit a local daily or weekly newspaper. During your visit, find out what types of software are used for text, graphics, and page composition. Prepare a brief report of your findings.

5. Contact a local quick or commercial printer who has a short-run, four-color printing facility. Prepare a list of questions covering the firm's entry into the short-run market and the types of clients serviced. Ask for several copies of typical short-run jobs. Prepare a brief report of your findings.

Newspapers that are ready for delivery stream off this two-story web-offset press. While two operators check for quality, two others monitor press operation. (Heidelberg)

Playing with Pixels

In an electronic work flow, image capture is performed with scanners and digital cameras. This chapter will explain how these devices work. Also, this chapter will examine concepts such as interpolation, resolution, dynamic range, and bit depth.

The large photograph below is an original image, which was first scanned and then digitally altered with image manipulation software. Shown below it are three examples of how this software can use filters to electronically enhance a photographic image. In addition to filters, this chapter will discuss other mechanisms for manipulating images.

(Omnitrade Industrial/Omni Adast)

Find Edges Filter   **Mezzotint Filter**   **Difference-Clouds Filter**

Chapter 14
Electronic Image Capture and Manipulation

Key Terms

artifact
automatic trap
Bayer filter pattern
cast removal
charge-coupled device (CCD)
choke trap
cloning stamp
color level
curve adjustment
descreening
drum scanner
dynamic range
filter
flatbed scanner
for position only (FPO) image
gray scaling
healing brush
intelligent character recognition (ICR)
interpolated resolution
interpolation
laser

Newton's rings
Open Prepress Interface (OPI)
optical character recognition (OCR)
optical resolution
patch tool
photomultiplier tube
photo retouching
resampling
rotary scanner
spread trap
tagged image file format (TIFF)
tagged image file format for image transfer (TIFF/IT-P1)
tone compression
trapping
tungsten-halogen lamp
unsharp masking (USM)
xenon lamp

Learning Objectives

When you have completed the reading and assigned activities related to this chapter, you will be able to do the following:

◆ Explain the advantages and limitations of different types of digital cameras.

◆ Summarize interpolation and its applications.

◆ Distinguish between optical zoom and digital zoom.

◆ Compare a scanner's bit depth and dynamic range.

◆ Contrast optical resolution and interpolated resolution.

◆ Identify the types of light-gathering sensors used in DI devices.

◆ Name the various types of scanners.

◆ Describe types of scanner software applications.

◆ State several software applications used for image manipulation.

◆ List and define several image manipulation functions available with bitmap photo-editing software.

◆ Describe several methods used to improve shadow details in color separations.

◆ Define and explain the different types of traps.

◆ Discuss Open Prepress Interface (OPI) and the use of for position only (FPO) images.

Within the digital work flow, the capture, creation, and manipulation of images usually precedes the integration of these images with page composition software. That is, images that digital cameras and scanners capture are manipulated with the Photoshop editor, CorelDRAW suite, Paint Shop Pro software, or similar software, before they are imported into programs such as PageMaker software, the QuarkXPress application, or InDesign software. Although page composition software can perform some image manipulation, these functions are usually best handled with programs made specifically for them. A few image manipulation functions can be performed either during scanning or later, with appropriate software. This chapter will examine many of the options available to prepress operators in capturing and manipulating images.

Digital Cameras

As digital cameras become less expensive and more popular, they are playing an increasing role in prepress production. The digital camera's RGB-to-CMYK conversion capabilities allow its image files to bypass scanning and color-separation procedures and move directly into the production flow. Digital cameras vary in size, design, quality, and performance. See **Figure 14-1.** Digital cameras capture light images and convert them into electrical charges and then into digital data. The wide range of digital cameras is extensive because they vary in sensor technology, color-capture mechanisms, image resolution, image storage, zoom capabilities, and cost.

Sensor Technology

Digital cameras use rows of light sensors called *photosites* to transform light energy (photons) into electrical energy (electrons). Increased light energy striking a photosite results in increased levels of electrons, which are then transformed into digital data. Most cameras use the same charge-coupled device (CCD) technology used in flatbed scanners for their photosites. A *charge-coupled device (CCD)* is a solid-state chip that converts light into electrical charges, which are, in turn, converted by an analog/digital (A/D) adapter into digital data in the form of pixels. Some digital cameras use the easily mass-produced *complementary metal oxide semiconductors (CMOSs)* as their photosites, however, to lower the cost. Although much less expensive than CCD sensors, CMOSs are less sensitive to light and produce poorer-quality pixels. It is expected, though, that CMOS technology will continue to improve and become more commonly used in digital cameras.

Color-Capture Mechanisms

No photosites are able to distinguish colors of light. Therefore, photosites must be used with filters to isolate the color being measured. Digital cameras used in studio photography typically use a trilinear CCD array. See **Figure 14-2.** Digital cameras can also use a spinning disk containing RGB filters to allow each photosite to capture the image with three

Figure 14-1. Digital cameras are available in a wide range of capabilities and prices. Shown here are, from left, a digital single-lens reflex camera, a camera that writes to mini CDs, and a camera that fits into a pocket. All three provide images with good resolution.

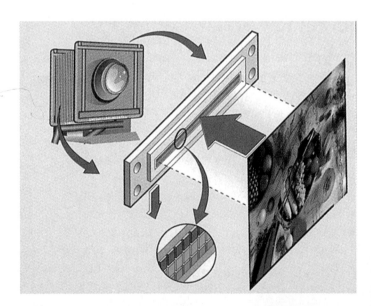

Figure 14-2. High-end cameras used in studio photography often use a trilinear CCD array, three rows of photosites (RGB) that move across the film plane to make the exposure. Product photography can capture an image with an exposure for each of the three primary colors because the subject is stationary.

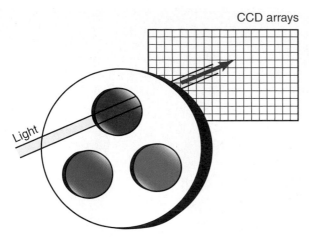

Figure 14-3. A spinning-disk camera requires three exposures. At this precise moment, the red light is being captured. The subject must be stationary for this type of camera.

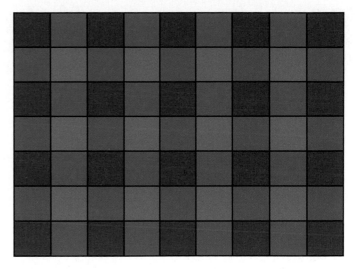

Figure 14-5. A Bayer filter consists of several arrays of photosites behind a fixed pattern of alternating RGB filters. Each photosite records only the color of its filter.

separate exposures—once through each filter. See **Figure 14-3.** With each method, each color is recorded, but not at the exact same moment. Therefore, neither the camera nor the image can move during the three exposures—making this design impractical outside of the photographic studio.

High-quality digital cameras that are appropriate for normal applications use a beam splitter to send the image to three sensors, each behind a different-colored filter, to measure the amount of red, green, or blue light passing through the filter. See **Figure 14-4.** Although the image quality is excellent, cameras with beam splitters are both expensive and cumbersome.

Bayer Filter Patterns

Less expensive and less bulky digital cameras use a system that permanently places a blue, green, or red filter over each photosite. A *Bayer filter pattern*

alternates horizontal rows of red and green filters with rows of blue and green filters. See **Figure 14-5.** Behind each filter is a photosite, which receives the amount of light passing through the filter. The number of green-receiving photosites is greatest to compensate for human vision's being less sensitive to green light than it is to red and blue light. Although each pixel reads only one of the three colors of light, special software averages the amount of light that falls adjacent to a particular photosite to calculate the likely amounts of all three light colors making up that tiny portion of the image.

For example, consider a tiny portion of the rows of photosites receiving the entire image. See **Figure 14-6.** Photosite C-3 receives only red light because it is covered with a red filter. Adjacent photosites C-2 and C-4 are receiving green light, however, while adjacent photosites D-2 and B-4 are receiving blue light. Through a process known as *interpolation*, the amount of light the neighboring green and blue photosites receive is used to calculate the amount of green and blue light the red filter removed over photosite C-3. By combining the measured value of red light and the interpolated values of green and blue light, the actual color of the tiny portion of the

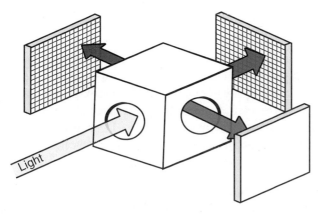

Figure 14-4. Beam-splitter digital cameras can record moving subjects, but they are both expensive and cumbersome.

charge-coupled device (CCD): an array of light-sensitive, solid-state receptors that react electronically when exposed to light.

Bayer filter pattern: a mosaic of tiny color filters arranged in two array patterns that alternate in rows.

interpolation: the increase of image resolution by the addition of new pixels throughout an image.

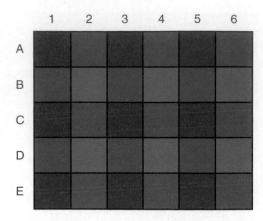

	1	2	3	4	5	6
A						
B						
C						
D						
E						

Figure 14-6. A small section of a Bayer filter.

photograph photosite C-3 represents can be established. Accurate color interpolation is possible because each photosite represents such a tiny portion of the photograph. There is a photosite for each pixel, and even a camera with a modest 640×480 resolution has over 300,000 pixels, each created by its own photosite.

Image Resolution

The image resolution of a digital camera is a measurement of the amount of detail that can be captured, and image resolution is determined by the number of pixels, which is determined by the number of photosites. Resolution is expressed by the number of pixels arranged horizontally, followed by the number of pixels arranged vertically. Very low–resolution cameras with 256 × 256–pixel resolution capture an image with roughly 65,000 photosites. Although 65,000 might seem like a lot of pixels, an enlargement of the image to 8″ × 10″ will make the pixels quite visible and the photographic quality unacceptable. See **Figure 14-7.** Higher-resolution cameras, such as 1600 × 1200, contain the nearly 2 million pixels (or 2 megapixels) required for maintaining image quality in enlargements of 8″ × 10″ and larger. The term *megapixel* refers to the number of millions of pixels constituting an image. For example, 7.7 megapixels is 7,700,000 pixels.

Increasingly, digital cameras contain software that enhances the image resolution attained by the number of photosites. Interpolation allows digital cameras to capture an image at one level of resolution and then divide the pixels into more pixels when the image is greatly enlarged. For example, a camera with 4.4 megapixels (million photosites) might be able to interpolate an image to 8.3 megapixels. There are different levels of sophistication among interpolation software, however, which produce different levels of image quality. The distinct edges between

Complete Image

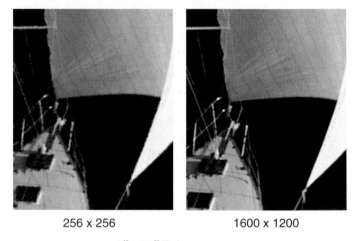

256 x 256   1600 x 1200

8″ x 10″ Enlargements

Figure 14-7. A portion of a 65,000-pixel image (left) and a nearly 2 million–pixel image (right) after being enlarged to 8″ × 10″.

contrasting images can be softened because interpolation increases the number of pixels by creating new pixels from the averages of adjacent pixels' colors. See **Figure 14-8.** Interpolation cannot generate detail that was not captured initially. Therefore, the most important factor in achieving high resolution is the camera's number of photosites.

Image Storage

After an image is captured, it can be stored within the camera's built-in memory and then transferred to a computer, or it can be stored on a

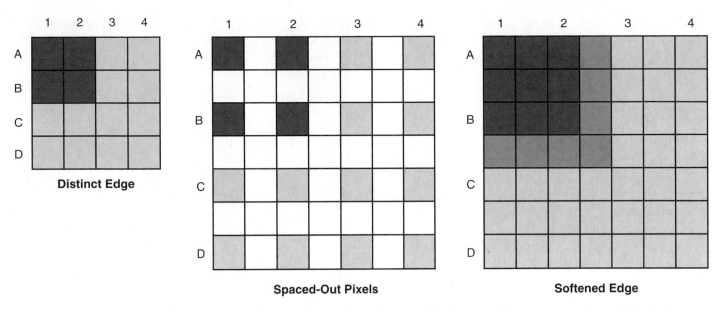

Figure 14-8. The edge between a dark object and its light background is sharp in this representation of 16 pixels. Digital zoom enlarges the image by spacing out the pixels. Interpolation creates new pixels, which are averages of their neighboring pixels, to fill in the gaps. Notice that the edge has become softened.

removable storage device. A camera's built-in memory can limit the number of photographs that can be taken to as few as six, depending on the images' resolution. Once filled, the memory's images must be downloaded to a computer or erased before more photographs can be taken.

Greater image capacity is available with a removable storage device. Although these devices come in many formats and capacities, they share the function of transferring digital images by being removed from the camera and plugged into the computer. Some of the most common formats are the CompactFlash® card, Microdrive® media, SmartMedia® card, Secure Digital® card, and Memory Stick® media. These small devices come with different capacities, with some holding as much as 4 GB. Some Sony Mavica cameras write to a 175-MB CD. Larger professional cameras can use PCMCIA PC cards, which have a capacity of several GBs.

Compression allows a digital image to be converted to data requiring considerably less memory, thereby permitting more images to be stored. Limited-capacity storage media are dependent on compression. Joint Photographic Experts Group (JPEG) is a file format that allows compression and, therefore, is the file format used in most digital cameras. *Tagged image file format (TIFF)*, the other file format used for photographic images, does not allow image compression.

Zoom Capabilities

Many conventional cameras can be fitted with a telephoto or zoom lens that enlarges the subject by extending the focal length (FL). Similarly, most digital cameras can extend the FL with a feature called *optical zoom*. The amount of optical zoom is indicated with a number revealing the maximum power of the optics. For example, 2× zoom will double the size of the image, and 3× zoom will triple it.

Cameras often have a feature called *digital zoom*, in which interpolation is used to create new pixels after the original pixels are moved apart to enlarge the photo. Refer back to **Figure 14-8**. The effect of digital zoom can also be achieved with image manipulation software, such as the Photoshop editor, by cropping a photograph and enlarging it. The results might be disappointing because interpolation can cause image edges to lose sharpness.

Cost

Digital cameras can cost less than $200 or more than $4000. The least expensive digital cameras are compact, have low resolution (640 × 480 or lower), and have no optical zoom. Inexpensive cameras are well suited for people who wish to e-mail their photographs or post them on the Internet because these applications seldom require high resolution.

tagged image file format (TIFF): a bitmap file used for exchanging raster images between applications.

Photographers who wish to print their images in sizes such as 5″ × 7″ or 8″ × 10″ will be better served by investing in cameras with optical zoom and a resolution of 5.0 megapixels or more.

Electronic Scanners

A scanner is an electronic device that can capture analog images, such as type or other line art, black-and-white photographs, color photographs and art, or black-and-white or color film, and convert them to digital data. This device can also create color separations by measuring the color densities of an original image, using special software to manipulate the data to create RGB or CMYK images. Scanners vary in size, design, quality, and performance. They all function, however, in approximately the same way. Scanners expose the analog art with light and measure the amounts of RGB light reflected off or transmitted through the object. These measurements are converted into the digital data representing the image.

Depending on the type of scanner, almost any type or size of original can be scanned. This includes film negatives, transparencies, photographic prints, printed media, drawings, graphs, and text copy. Many scanners allow the operator to specify the type of color separations—RGB or CMYK—to be made. Scanners come in several designs, including drum, flatbed, and film and slide scanners.

The main differences among scanners are the resolution capability and the quality of the light-gathering sensors. To understand how scanners function and to judge their capabilities require a grasp of some terms. These terms are *resolution, dpi, bit depth,* and *dynamic range.*

Resolution

Resolution determines the ability to show fine detail. The resolution quality of a scanned image is determined by the number of dpi and the bit depth. The dpi of an image represents the number of pixels making up the image. See **Figure 14-9.** The greater the dpi is at the time an image is scanned, the greater the amount of detail and the better the resolution will be. Dpi can also be referred to as *ppi.* Chapter 3 contains the formula for calculating the minimum scanning resolution for a given image, based on the scaling percentage and the halftone screen value (lpi) used.

Figure 14-9. The image on the top was reproduced with a dpi of 60. The improvement in quality is clearly visible when the image is reproduced with a much higher dpi of 216.

Bit depth

The bit depth of an image is defined by the number of bits used to make up each pixel. As was explained in Chapter 3, a pixel can be made up of one bit or several bits. A pixel consisting of only one bit can be either black or white, while a pixel consisting of more bits can combine various combinations of their being "on" or "off" to create exponentially more tones of gray or colors. Each additional bit multiplies the number of possible grays or colors by two. Therefore, a pixel with a bit depth of four can record 16 different tones, and one with a bit depth of eight can record up to 256 tones. An analogy can be made between bit depth and a wall, with the top of the wall representing black and its base representing white. With no steps, a person can either stand on the wall or at its base, with no points in between. Adding steps to the wall allows a person to stand at various points between the top and the bottom, and these intervals represent grays. See **Figure 14-10.** More steps (greater bit depth) permit the capture of more tones of gray.

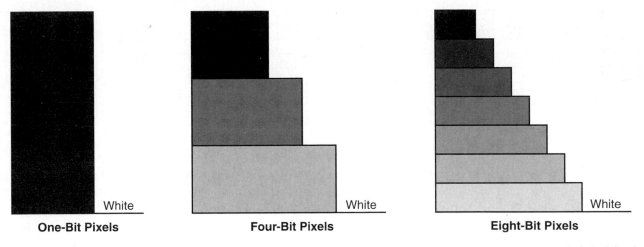

Figure 14-10. One-bit pixels can display only black or white. Four-bit pixels can display 16 tones, and eight-bit pixels can display 256 tones. Greater bit depth increases the range of tones exponentially.

Dynamic range

A scanner's bit depth defines its capability of recording tonal variations, but its pixels cannot record more than the scanner's dynamic range can see. *Dynamic range* is the difference between the *Dmin* and *Dmax* (whitest and blackest) tones a scanner can capture. A wide dynamic range gives a scanner the ability to capture details in the very light tones (highlights) and very dark tones (shadows) of the original image. It is critical that a scanner's dynamic range is greater than the dynamic range of the scanned image.

The dynamic range of both a scanner and copy is measured against a scale from 0.0 to 4.0, with 0.0 representing pure white (Dmin) and 4.0 representing the darkest black (Dmax). A scanner with a Dmax of 2.9 and a Dmin of 0.4 has a dynamic range of 2.5 (2.9 − 0.4 = 2.5). A dynamic range of 2.5 is capable of capturing the range of color photographic prints, which have a dynamic range of less than 2.0. This range is, however, unable to capture all the tones of a film negative (with a potential dynamic range of 2.7) or a color transparency (with a potential dynamic range of 3.1).

To summarize the relationship between bit depth and dynamic range, a scanner's bit depth is its ability to record the tones and colors the dynamic range can recognize. Dynamic range is largely determined by the quality of the scanner's light-gathering sensors and is a key factor in determining the scanner's cost. This range is also referred to as *density range*.

Optical and interpolated resolution

A scanner's **optical resolution** is a measure of the maximum resolution at which the scanner can capture an image using its optics alone. Optical resolution is properly specified in dpi in both horizontal and vertical directions (600 × 1200), but it is commonly given in the horizontal direction only. Very often, images are scanned at one size with the intent of being greatly enlarged before being printed. Unfortunately, the overall image is made larger by enlarging the individual pixels, with the result that they can become visible and greatly impair image quality. The problem is that the number of pixels in the original image is inadequate for displaying the image after considerable enlargement. One solution is to increase the number of pixels with interpolation software to maintain resolution. **Interpolated resolution** (also known as *digital resolution*) is a measure of the maximum resolution at which a scanner can capture an image, using its optics in combination with the software. Software is available in three basic levels of sophistication, delivering three different levels of quality. See **Figure 14-11.** Interpolation can, however, result in softer edges and fuzzier detail at the edge of very different values. The resultant softness in interpolated images can be reduced by applying unsharp masking (USM) software, which is explained later in this chapter.

dynamic range: the range of tones of an image or the difference between the minimum and maximum tones a scanner can capture, as measured on a scale of 0.0 to 4.0.

optical resolution: a measure of the maximum resolution at which a scanner can capture an image using its optics alone, exclusive of software interpolation.

interpolated resolution: a measure of the maximum resolution at which a scanner can capture an image using its optics in combination with interpolation software.

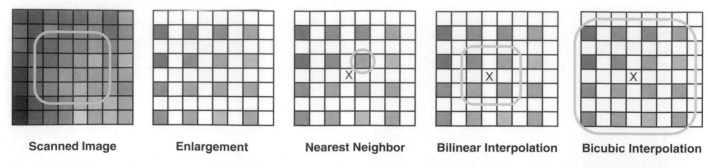

| Scanned Image | Enlargement | Nearest Neighbor | Bilinear Interpolation | Bicubic Interpolation |

Figure 14-11. Interpolation can be performed with different degrees of sophistication. To enlarge the picture, 16 pixels of a scanned image are spread out. Nearest neighbor merely duplicates a neighboring pixel. Bilinear interpolation averages the tonal value of the 4 surrounding pixels. Bicubic interpolation averages the surrounding 16 pixels to supply the best image.

Light-Gathering Sensors

Just as the lens quality and film used in a camera determine the quality of the negatives and photographs, the light-gathering sensor determines the bit depth and dpi a scanner can produce. The most common light-gathering sensors in use today are the photomultiplier tube and the CCD. A *photomultiplier tube* is composed of highly sensitive photocells. The photocells transform variations in light into electric currents, which are converted to digital form in a process called *sampling*. In electronic prepress production, *drum scanners* are the only DI devices that use photomultiplier tubes. Flatbed, handheld, and film or slide scanners—as well as digital cameras—use light-gathering sensors known as *CCDs*.

Note

Most analog electrical devices and light sources require at least a few minutes to reach a stable operating temperature. It is best to allow the scanner an adequate amount of time to warm up before performing any scans.

Light Sources

Common types of light sources used in scanners are xenon lamps, tungsten-halogen lamps, fluorescent lamps, and lasers. The light source is generally held in a sealed compartment to shield the other parts of the scanner from heat and to eliminate flare. See **Figure 14-12.**

- A *xenon lamp* is a high-pressure, gas-discharge lamp that emits a constant high-intensity light. This lamp provides a high concentration of light in a small area.

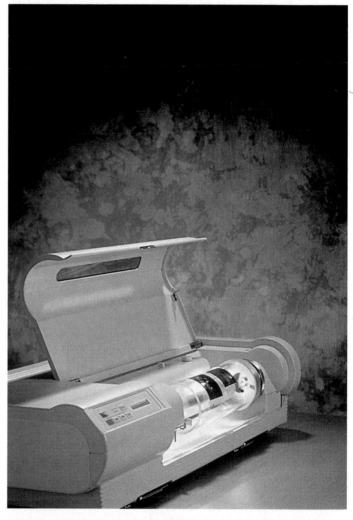

Figure 14-12. The light source is generally held in a sealed compartment to shield the other parts of the scanner from heat and to eliminate flare. (Screen USA)

- The *tungsten-halogen lamp* is a low-voltage, high-current tungsten light. The halogen gas prevents the vaporized filament materials from depositing on the walls of the lamp and dimming its output.

- A *laser* produces consistent, parallel rays of light that can be easily controlled. This light source offers a high concentration of light and is much cooler than other light sources.

Types of Scanners

A drum scanner, or rotary scanner, scans images mounted on a rotating drum. The drum spins quickly in front of a sensor unit or analyzing head. Depending on the scanner's design, the sensor unit might be stationary, or it might move alongside the spinning drum. See **Figure 14-13.**

Caution

Originals can be damaged when mounted on a drum. A duplicate should be made for drum scanning rare or precious originals, or a flatbed scanner should be used for imaging the materials.

A *flatbed scanner* uses a flat glass bed and a linear CCD array to digitize images. A linear CCD array allows the scanner to capture an image in a single pass. The media is placed on the glass bed, or scan area. Depending on the scanner design, either the bed or the CCD array moves. See **Figure 14-14.** A magnetic image holder can be used on some scanners to eliminate the glass between the image and the optics. This helps preserve sharpness and reduce distortion and *Newton's rings*.

Handheld scanners are small devices you move across the paper or image by hand. These scanners

Figure 14-14. Some flatbed scanners use a built-in drawer for scanning transparent materials. Reflective materials are placed facedown on the glass bed. (Microtek Lab, Inc.)

are typically used for scanning small amounts of text and *for position only (FPO) images*. They are impractical if you need to scan a large amount of text or graphics. Handheld scanners are usually limited to black-and-white reflective copy.

Film and slide scanners are designed specifically for digitizing images from various types of film. Film scanners use a CCD array to capture images. These scanners are usually small enough to fit on a desktop. See **Figure 14-15.** The imaging speed and resolution capabilities of handheld and film scanners depend on the quality of their light-gathering sensors.

photomultiplier tube: a light-gathering sensor composed of highly sensitive photocells that transform variations in light into electric currents.

drum scanner: an electronic imaging device that uses a rotating drum and photomultiplier tubes to digitize images.

xenon lamp: a high-pressure, gas-discharge lamp that emits a constant high-intensity light.

tungsten-halogen lamp: a low-voltage, high-current tungsten light.

laser: a device that produces intense, single-wavelength, unidirectional beams of light.

flatbed scanner: an electronic imaging device in which the original is placed on a flat glass bed and a CCD is used to digitize images.

Newton's rings: an undesirable color pattern resulting from interference between the exposure light and its reflected beam from the closely adjacent surface.

for position only (FPO) image: a copy of a graphic image placed on a mechanical or in an electronic layout to indicate placement, but not used for reproduction.

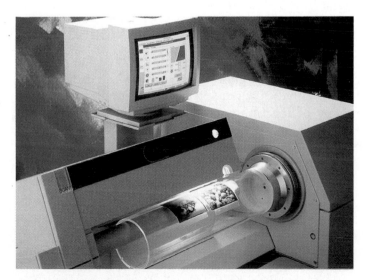

Figure 14-13. The copy is wrapped around the cylinder of a drum scanner.

Figure 14-15. Film scanners are usually small enough to sit on a desk. (Minolta Corporation)

Scanner Maintenance

The buildup of ink and other chemicals on the scanner components can cause permanent damage and poor image quality. The buildup of some chemicals can even permanently damage the rubber on rollers, belts, and pulleys. If many carbon copies or toner-printed documents are being scanned, the rollers and other contact surfaces can accumulate stray particles that will not easily come off with glass cleaner. Damaged components can lead to misfeeds, skews, and paper jams. Most scanner manufacturers offer cleaning kits, which include special cleaning fluids and lint-free cloths to remove buildup.

Isopropyl alcohol can be used to clean the roller surfaces of most scanners. This alcohol should be used only in emergencies or after testing its effect on the plastic or rubber rollers. Test its effect by placing a small drop on one roller. If the scanner uses replaceable rollers and you have an old set, test the alcohol on them. If the alcohol does not damage the roller, moisten a lint-free cloth with the alcohol and gently rub the rollers clean. The alcohol will dissolve the particles of toner and ink. Let the rollers dry completely before resuming scanning.

Feeding Documents into the Scanner

All paper clips and staples should be removed from documents before feeding them into the scanner. These sharp objects can scratch optics and tear rubber components along the paper path, causing streaks, noise, and skews. Many older flatbed scanners output paper originals at the bottom of the machine, whereas newer models output to the top. Outputting to the top eliminates the need for the operator to bend over and retrieve the media. If someone is operating the scanner all day long, the ease of loading, unloading, and retrieving jams should be considered.

Some scanners use a vacuum double-feed detector, similar to those used on high-speed check readers. Vacuum sensors located on either side of the paper path pull the paper toward them. If the paper covers one sensor and not the other, it is moved on. If both sensors are covered, the scanner stops and alerts the operator to the double feed.

Most double-feed detection methods use rollers and belts to move the paper and measure the length or thickness of the paper. The vacuum method allows the user to mix media of different sizes and thicknesses in the feeder tray. Even more advanced double-feed detection systems use an ultrasonic device, which listens for sound from one side of the document to the other.

A Scanner's Software Applications

The electronic scanner has become the primary means of image generation for use in a digital work flow. With the proper software, a scanner can perform many of the image-correction and image manipulation processes highly skilled technicians once performed. Most scanner software programs will prompt the operator for information to determine the correct settings for the image appearance, image condition, desired results, desired effects, printing process, paper stock, press gain, and screening. See **Figure 14-16.** The scanner's artificial intelligence uses these input characteristics to analyze the image and automatically adjust the raw scan. The software will also determine which tools to use in the appropriate order to give the requested output characteristics.

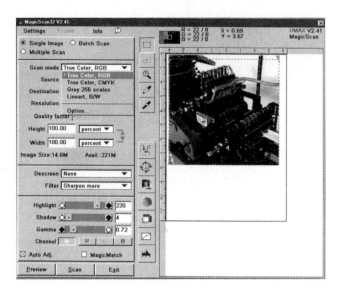

Figure 14-16. Most scanner software programs will prompt the operator for information to determine the appropriate settings.

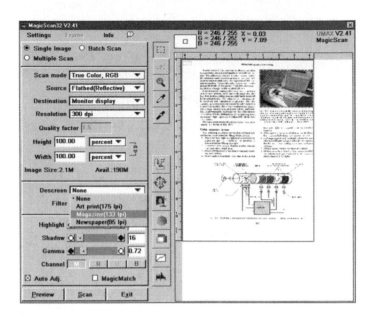

Figure 14-18. Using the descreening option will prevent moiré patterns.

When a scanner is used to scan copy or text, the type will be captured as bitmap images, unless the scanner can perform OCR. *Optical character recognition (OCR)* is an imaging process that electronically reads typewritten or printed pages and saves the copy in its ASCII format. The text can be imported into a word processing program and edited. See **Figure 14-17.** An imaging process known as *intelligent character recognition (ICR)* is used to recognize handwritten material.

Although it is best to perform scans with continuous tone originals, it might be necessary to scan a printed image. If you scan a printed halftone image, the final image might contain a moiré pattern. This can be avoided by increasing the resolution of the image and manipulating the line screen or by using the software's *descreening* application. In halftone photography, eliminating the printed dot pattern is called *rescreening.* See **Figure 14-18.**

Unsharp masking (USM) is the process of adjusting tonal contrast where light and dark tones come together at the edges of an image to create a sharper image. The scanner performs USM through special software, which analyzes the tonal values of pixels along the edges of the image. The software adjusts the tonal values on either side of the edge to exaggerate the contrast along the edge. See **Figure 14-19.** More advanced programs allow the user to adjust the degree of USM by specifying the number of pixels that should be modified.

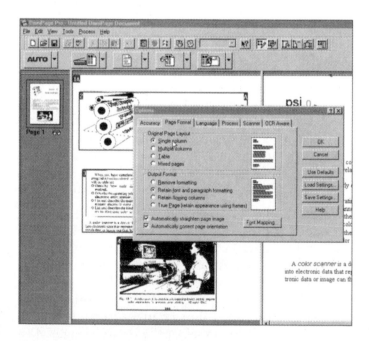

Figure 14-17. Most OCR software includes page segmentation, zone definition, image cleanup and enhancement, and format retention.

optical character recognition (OCR): an imaging process that electronically reads typewritten or printed pages and saves the copy in its ASCII format.

intelligent character recognition (ICR): an imaging process that electronically reads handwritten material.

descreening: an electronic means of eliminating or minimizing the halftone-dot pattern of a scanned printed image.

unsharp masking (USM): the increase of tonal contrast where light and dark tones come together at the edges of an image to create a sharper image.

Figure 14-19. Of the two reproductions shown here, USM was applied to the image on the left. The difference is most apparent on the labels on the hammer and the shirt's buttons. (Vaughan & Bushnell Manufacturing)

Image Manipulation

After an image has been captured with either a scanner or a digital camera, it can be manipulated electronically in several ways. Several programs can perform image manipulation, and the desired effect determines which software is appropriate. Basically, there are bitmap (or paint) programs and vector-graphic (or draw) programs. After the image is manipulated, it is usually imported into page composition software for integration with the other content of the document.

Image manipulation programs typically allow the user to crop, change color and contrast, combine images, and add or remove visual information. For example, the user can eliminate background clutter and erase images within a photograph. Although many drawing programs allow some graphics editing, image manipulation programs should be used to make extensive changes.

Many images are produced with a combination of vector and bitmap software programs. That is, vector art can be created and then imported into a bitmap program for added effects. After all graphics are completed, they and the text files that were generated with word processing software can be integrated into a page composition program.

Using Image Manipulation Programs

Some of the most commonly used programs are the Adobe Photoshop editor, Macromedia® Freehand application, CorelDRAW suite, Corel® Paint Shop Pro software, and Adobe Illustrator program. The programs used depend on the functions needed. Most image-editing programs offer similar tools and applications and allow changes to be made to a single area, multiple areas, or the entire image. Most programs will also allow you to work in layers, apply filters, paint and erase, and apply masks.

Working in layers

Layers in an illustration program can be thought of as a stack of clear acetate sheets. Each sheet contains one or more objects. The sheets are transparent wherever there is no object, and you can see through to the sheet below. See **Figure 14-20.**

It is easier to modify parts of an image without affecting all aspects of the art, by working in layers. Most programs allow the user to blend between layers, create and modify layer masks, link layers, and merge layers. Separate layers take up storage space, so they should be merged or flattened when the image is finished.

Applying filters

The same types of special effects created with special halftone screens and screen tints can be created electronically with a wide array of *filters.* Filters are used to apply textures and patterns to images. See **Figure 14-21.** Commonly used filters can blur, distort, or stylize a photograph. Artistic filters can convert a photograph to resemble a pencil, watercolor, solarized, or embossed image.

Most programs allow the user to preview the effect of a filter. A fade command can reduce the effect of a filter. Too often, beginning designers use filters excessively. As is the case with all

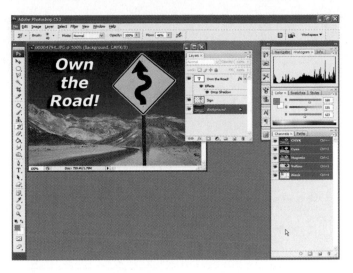

Figure 14-20. The background photograph is on one layer, and the type is on a second layer. By working in layers, it is easier to modify parts of an image without affecting other elements of the art.

graphic-design decisions, the message intended for the receiver should always guide the use of these filters.

Painting and erasing

Most image manipulation programs provide paint features similar to those provided in paint and draw programs. The user can create and add color to

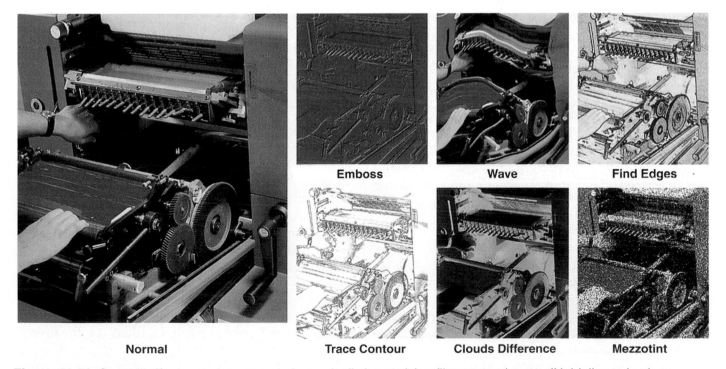

Normal   Emboss   Wave   Find Edges

Trace Contour   Clouds Difference   Mezzotint

Figure 14-21. Special effects can be created electronically by applying filters to an image. (Heidelberg, Inc.)

filter: colored material, usually glass or acetate, blocking some wavelengths of the light spectrum and letting others through.

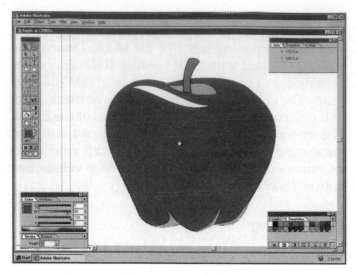

Figure 14-22. Most image manipulation programs provide paint features similar to those provided in paint and draw programs.

Figure 14-23. Electronic masks are used to isolate an area, to protect it from changes being made to the rest of the image.

images. See **Figure 14-22.** Other tools allow the user to erase portions of the image, adjust color values, and create gradations.

Applying masks

Just as photographic masks are used to block certain areas of a negative or photopaper, electronic masks are used to isolate an area, to protect it from changes being made to the rest of the image. Semitransparent masks enable the user to partially affect an area of an image. See **Figure 14-23.**

Image Manipulation with Bitmap Programs

After images are captured, they usually require some preparation before they are ready to be integrated into the publication. These modifications might be as modest as changing the size of the image to fit the layout or as complex as removing a portion of a photograph. In some instances, the image is worked with to prepare it for platemaking and presswork.

Cropping

Determining and indicating which portion of the photograph will be printed is cropping. It is wise to crop an image early in the production sequence to prevent useless data from taking up file space. Cropping can be performed with scanning or image-editing software. This modification is usually performed with a click-and-drag movement of the mouse. See **Figure 14-24.** In addition to removing unwanted images, cropping allows a photograph to be reshaped to conform to the space allocated in a layout.

Sizing

Enlarging or reducing a photograph is traditionally referred to as *scaling*, but *sizing* is the term used in the digital world. After an image has been cropped, it is usually sized by typing either the desired width or height in the appropriate field of a dialog box. The software can then calculate the other dimension that will maintain the proportions of the cropped image. See **Figure 14-25.** Scaling merely modifies the spacing of the image's pixels to fit the new dimensions. This modification changes neither the number of pixels in the image nor the file size.

Resampling

If an image is scanned at a resolution twice the number of lpi that will be used during platemaking, the file will contain excessive data and use unnecessary storage space. **Resampling** can save file space by reducing the image resolution to 1.5 times the lpi of the printing plate. For example, a photograph that will be printed with 150 lpi should have a document size of approximately 225. Resampling is usually performed by typing the desired resolution in the same dialog box as sizing.

Tone compression

As was explained in Chapter 11, the tonal range of an original photograph is likely to be greater than the tonal range that can be achieved on an offset press. The tonal range of a scanned color-transparency image can be as high as 3.0, which is significantly greater than the 1.8 tonal range that can be achieved on an offset press. For this reason, *tone compression* must be applied to the image to bring

Original Image   **Cropped Image**

Figure 14-24. Photo cropping is performed by clicking on the Crop tool and then performing a click-and-drag move with the marquee. (Corel, Inc.)

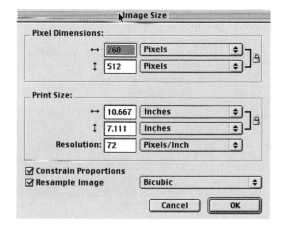

Figure 14-25. A dialog box is used to change the image's dimensions. Resizing is sometimes accompanied with a change in resolution, to maintain image quality. (Fireworks)

its tonal range closer to the press capability. Tone compression greatly reduces the lost detail in the highlight and shadow areas. This compression is a function of photo-editing software.

Cast removal

Color photographs taken under unbalanced light sources, such as incandescent and fluorescent lighting, often acquire an orange hue or a green hue. *Cast removal* can remedy the off-color nature of the photograph by creating better color balance. This removal can be performed with photo-editing software. See **Figure 14-26.**

Color-level adjustment

The process ink colors CMYK are referred to as *color channels* in most photo-editing software. *Color levels* allow color modification by either adjusting one channel at a time or adjusting all four collectively. Adjustments can be made to the highlights, midtones, and shadows by moving the input- or output-level sliders. See **Figure 14-27.** For example, dragging the shadow (black) input slider to the right darkens a photograph's shadows, and dragging the highlight (white) input slider to the left lightens highlights—thereby increasing contrast. The same adjustments to the highlight and shadow sliders of the output levels, however, have the opposite effects on lightness and contrast.

resampling: in image manipulation, reducing the file size of an image by lowering the resolution.

tone compression: a reduction of the tonal range of an original image to make the image compatible with the capabilities of a press or an output device.

cast removal: the removal of an excessive amount of a color from a photograph or another digital image.

color level: an image manipulation tool that allows adjustment of the tonal range and contrast of a bitmap image by using sliders to change the values of highlights, midtones, and shadows.

Before Cast Removal

After Cast Removal

Figure 14-26. The photograph on the left was taken with film or a digital camera setting inappropriate to the light source, giving it a bluish cast. On the right, the cast has been removed with a photo-editing application.

Original Image

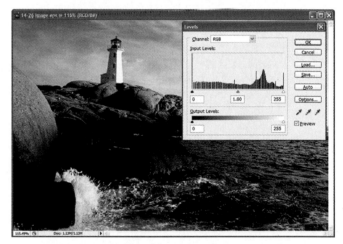

Increased Contrast

Figure 14-27. An original photograph and its histogram within the Levels dialog box. The image's darkness and lack of contrast are due to the histogram's ending well short of its potential. Also shown is the same photograph after moving the histogram to the right.

Curve adjustment

The diagonal line representing a photograph's density, from its darkest shadow through the midtones and highlights, can be altered with *curve adjustment*. Making adjustments to a photograph by modifying its lightness or darkness at the 1/4 tone, midtone, and 3/4 tone correspond to the 25%, 50%, and 75% dot values of a halftone photograph. Both color and black-and-white photographs can have their tones and contrast greatly enhanced. See **Figure 14-28.** In the example shown, a washed-out image, which could have resulted from a poor image capture with either the camera or scanner, is greatly improved by moving the entire curve upward and toward darkness. Adjusting the density of a specific color channel (red, green, or blue) of a color photograph can alter the overall color, as well as its density. For example, reducing the red channel can remove the sunburned look from a person's face.

Posterization

As was explained in Chapter 11, a posterization is the conversion of a continuous tone image to a high-contrast image with one or more middle tones. See **Figure 14-29.** In other words, a line shot becomes a posterization when one or more middle tones are added. Posterizations are classified according to the number of colors (inks) and the number of tones reproduced on the final press sheet.

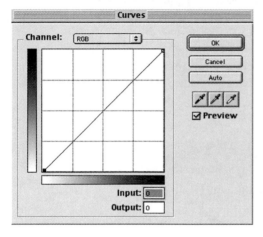

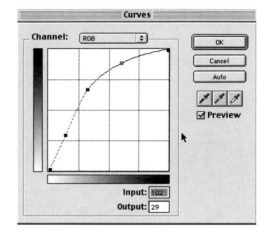

Original Image   Adjusted Curve

Figure 14-28. An original photograph with poor contrast and its straight tonal curve. The same photograph is shown after a shifting of the curve's 1/4, midtone, and 3/4 points.

Photo retouching

Artifacts are visible imperfections in a digital photograph or other image, usually resulting from file compression or an inadequate hardware and software combination. *Photo retouching* can be performed with various tools. The *cloning stamp* is used to cover a target (unwanted) area of a photograph with pixels from a source area. The covering pixels are placed on a second layer, but the appearance is that the unwanted image has been replaced. Repetitive cloning is commonly used to cover large portions of a photograph. See **Figure 14-30.** The healing brush and patch tool are advanced versions of the cloning stamp because they not only capture the color of the source area, but also match the new pixels to the color, texture, and lightness of the pixels surrounding the target area. The *patch tool* uses a lasso to identify the area to be covered and the area to cover it. This tool covers pixels with pixels from another area of the image. The *healing brush* uses a point source to identify the area to be carried to another part of the image. Also, the healing brush tool allows the pixels moved into a different part of the image to assume the contour and lighting of the area being covered. In this sense, the healing brush

curve adjustment: an image manipulation tool that allows the lightness and darkness of a digital photograph to be modified at the 1/4-tone, halftone, and 3/4-tone levels of the image by altering a diagonal line.

artifact: a visible defect within a digital photograph.

photo retouching: a photo-editing tool that alters all or part of a digital photograph.

cloning stamp: an image manipulation tool that covers selected pixels with selected pixels from another area of the photograph.

patch tool: an image manipulation tool that can be used to cover selected pixels with pixels from another area of the photograph. This tool can be used in conjunction with the healing brush.

healing brush: a photo-editing technique that improves the blending of pixels that have been placed over pixels with the patch tool.

Original Image

Tone Levels
Reduced

High-Contrast Image

Figure 14-29. A digital posterization is performed by experimenting with the number of value levels. An original black-and-white photograph is shown here. The wide range of tone levels is reduced to only four. The result is a more dramatic image with heightened contrast.

Original Image

Missing Boulder

Figure 14-30. The boulder in the original photograph can be covered with pixels copied from neighboring areas. The result is a missing boulder.

is more sophisticated and produces an alteration that looks less fake. See **Figure 14-31.**

Gray scaling

The process of converting a color photograph to a monochromatic image is *gray scaling.* Continuous tone photographs—both black-and-white and color—contain an almost unlimited number of tones. Computers, however, can represent only a limited number of shades of gray (typically 16–256). An image might be scanned as a gray scale image or converted with an image manipulation program. See **Figure 14-32.** Appendix D contains three images composed by combining and manipulating elements from two or

more photographs. These three composites demonstrate many capabilities of image manipulation software.

Image Manipulation with Vector-Graphic Programs

Drawing software programs, such as the Freehand application, the Adobe Illustrator program, and the CorelDRAW suite, generate vector, or object-oriented, graphics. Instead of the bitmap art of image-editing or paint programs, vector graphics are based on mathematical formulas. That is, a combination of menu choices and movements with the mouse create vector points, which define both straight and curved lines, as well as their positioning. Mathematically

Area to Be Covered **Area to Be Placed on Top** **Altered Image**

Figure 14-31. The Healing and Patch tools capture not only the color of the source pixels, but their texture as well. In this example, the area to be covered and the area to be placed over it are defined. The result is a seamlessly altered image.

Figure 14-32. Compare the four-color image on the left to the gray-scaled version on the right. (Omnitrade Industrial/ Omni Adast)

based curves, known as *Bezier curves*, are shaped by clicking onto a handle and moving the mouse. See **Figure 14-33.**

Unlike bitmap graphics, vector graphics are resolution independent. Whether reproduced at high or low resolution, a curved line within a vector graphic looks the same, with no jaggies. Also, vector graphics maintain their quality after being scaled, rotated, and reshaped.

The mathematical formulas work with the PostScript PDL to generate each stroke of a design,

as well as to craft every subtle curve of each letter of type. For this reason, vector graphics are well suited to charts, graphs, drawings, and type. See **Figure 14-34.** Drawing programs can convert vector art to bitmap art when bitmap art is required to achieve a certain effect.

The toolbox of a drawing program reveals many of its capabilities. See **Figure 14-35.** Selection tools define

gray scaling: the process of converting a continuous tone image to a monochromatic image with varying shades of gray.

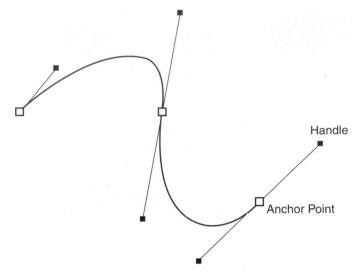

Figure 14-33. Vector-graphic (Bezier) curves are shaped by moving the handles with the mouse.

Soliday Enterprises				
Qnty	Model	Description		Price
Special Instructions				
Delivery				

Figure 14-34. A business form is an excellent example of the use of grids.

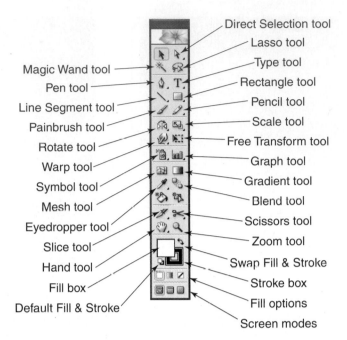

Figure 14-35. The range of capabilities of a drawing program can be seen in the toolbox.

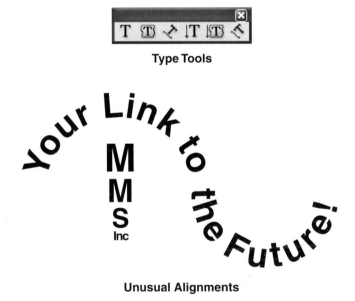

Figure 14-36. Type tools allow unorthodox treatments, such as curved and vertical alignment.

which images or parts of images will be manipulated. Type tools allow type to be aligned vertically or follow a curved line. See **Figure 14-36.** Pen tools draw lines and control the handles manipulating curved lines. Basic shape tools create the outlines of objects such as rectangles, circles, ovals, polygons, rectangular grids, spirals, and stars. These outlines can then be filled uniformly or with a gradient. See **Figure 14-37.**

Trapping

Although adjacent images in different colors look fine on a computer monitor, they are not yet ready for printing. A technique called *trapping* is used to create a small area of overlap, or trap, between these adjacent colors and prevent gaps of white between objects that need to be printed in tight register. See **Figure 14-38.** Trapping is necessary because slight misregistration will occur even under the best possible conditions during a pressrun. Properly

Figure 14-37. A basic shape can be created and filled with a gradient screen.

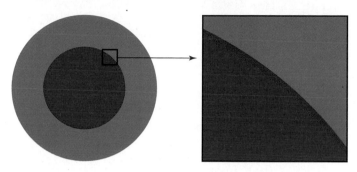

Figure 14-38. Trapping, the slight overlapping of different-colored images, is required to maintain registration on press.

performed trapping creates enough overlap to avoid a white gap without generating a third color. For example, an excessive trap of cyan over yellow would create a visible green line. See **Figure 14-39.**

Conventional trapping is performed by placing a clear spacer sheet between a film negative and the receiving film. The separation of the two films by the spacer allows the light to expand and produce an image slightly larger than the original. Although trapping is usually performed electronically today, the principles and the effect are the same.

Types of Traps

Traps can be spreads or chokes, depending on whether the foreground or background is the darker color. In most cases, the lighter of the two colors is spread into the darker color because the spread color acquires a soft edge. A *spread trap* is created by expanding the foreground into the darker background color. Vector (illustration) programs that are limited to one type of trapping usually use spread traps. *Choke traps* are performed by expanding the background under a darker foreground image. See **Figure 14-40.**

Automatic traps require one or more colors present in both the foreground and background. The shared color prevents any white line being created due to misregistration on press. In the example shown in **Figure 14-41,** three ink colors—yellow, magenta, and cyan—comprise the brown background, and the blue letter in the foreground uses only magenta and cyan. The magenta and cyan are common colors.

Trapping Procedures

Trapping can be performed automatically in some illustration programs by applying a trap filter. A trap filter should be used only for simple objects, where

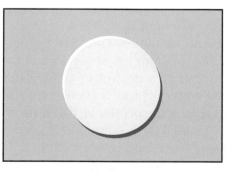
No Trap

Appropriate Trap

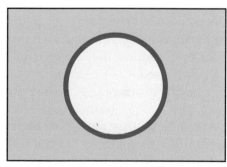
Excessive Trap

Figure 14-39. Two colors printed with no trap are likely to show a white gap. An appropriate trap allows subtle misregistration on press without a white gap. An excessive trap creates an obvious third color.

trapping: how well one color overlaps another without leaving a white space between the two or generating a third color.

spread trap: a trap created by spreading the foreground over the background color. This trap is used when a lighter object knocks out of a darker background.

choke trap: a trap performed by spreading the background under the foreground object.

automatic trap: a trap set by building art with common colors.

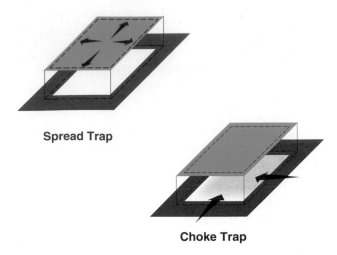

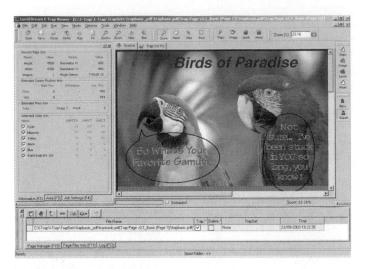

Figure 14-40. Spread traps result when the foreground (blue rectangle) expands into the background. Choke traps result when the background image (red frame) expands into the foreground.

Figure 14-42. Sophisticated software programs are able to generate a range of traps within highly complex images. (Lucid Dream Software, Inc.)

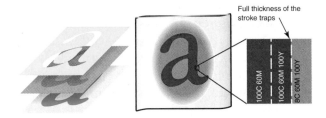

Figure 14-41. An automatic trap can be achieved when the foreground and background images share one or more colors. Even with subtle misregistration, there will be no white gap.

parts can be selected and trapped individually. Trap filters do not work with gradients or patterns. Most image manipulation programs provide an alternative trapping method that allows more complex work to be performed.

Electronic trapping can be performed with vector software, page composition software, or software dedicated to this task. See **Figure 14-42.** Graphics with EPS formatting (explained later) should be trapped before they are imported into a page composition program because this type of program is likely not capable of trapping EPS art. The most common method of trapping within an illustration program is to add a stroke on each element and set the stroke to overprint. The stroke should be twice the width of the desired trap. When a stroke is specified to overprint, the adjoining color will be trapped beneath the outside half. It is best to perform trapping after the images (graphics and type) are scaled to their final size. If the images must be enlarged or reduced, trapping will need to be recreated because the amount of trapping will increase or decrease when the object is scaled.

Factors that must be considered when applying traps to type include everything from the kind of paper to pressroom conditions. These variables are extremely important when applying traps to type because spreading or choking might cause character distortion. Applying process colors to type at small point sizes should be avoided because any amount of misregistration can make the text difficult to read. If it is necessary to trap type, always remember that smaller type requires a smaller trap to prevent distortion.

Text can also be trapped by first converting it to outlines and then placing a copy behind the original. A trap can then be created as with any other graphic object. Text can no longer be edited when converted to outlines because it is no longer type, but a graphic.

Trapping can be an extremely complex process. The party responsible for trapping should be determined at the beginning of a project to ensure that traps are performed correctly and prevent a myriad of problems. In most cases, the printer will determine if any trapping is needed and supply the correct parameters or values that should be applied.

Trapping Software

Many printing companies prefer their clients to defer the trapping function to their prepress departments, which can perform the function with specialized software. Trapping software includes many features that assist the procedure and enhance the printed images. A highlight tool can be used to assist the viewer in viewing and determining the traps within an image. See **Figure 14-43.**

In addition, the sophistication of trapping software permits choices in the trapping technique used.

Highlighting Activated

Highlighting Not Activated

Figure 14-43. In this detail from the image seen in **Figure 14-42,** highlighting enhances the prepress operator's view of the trapped areas. The same detail is shown without the highlighting tool activated. (Lucid Dream Software, Inc.)

For example, miter trapping produces better-defined images by altering the angle of the intersecting lines and the degree of overlapping. See **Figure 14-44.** Miter trapping is a feature that can be activated where appropriate.

File Formats

Graphics files are divided into two types—object oriented (vector) and bitmap (raster). There are, however, many file formats used to produce graphic images. The file format of a graphic image is important because it will determine how much manipulation can be done to the image and how well the image will be reproduced. Graphic images should be editable so they can be reused, repurposed, and continuously adapted. The two most widely used file formats are the TIFF and EPS technology.

Object-oriented graphics are often used for line drawings, logos, or any image requiring smooth, crisp edges. One of the benefits of object-oriented graphics is that these graphics can be enlarged, reduced, or distorted without loss of detail or sharpness. Object-oriented graphics are commonly referred to as *vector graphics.*

Bitmap graphics are usually pictures or photographic-type images, such as those captured with a scanner. As explained in Chapter 13, a bitmap

Miter Trapping Activated

Miter Trapping Not Activated

Figure 14-44. Miter trapping controls the angle of the ends of the intersecting lines. The same traps are shown without a miter trap. (Lucid Dream Software, Inc.)

graphic is made up of a collection of pixels arranged on a grid. The value of each pixel is stored in one or more bits of data, and each pixel is encoded as a single binary digit.

Unlike object-oriented graphics, bitmap graphics cannot be enlarged without affecting image quality. As the image increases in size, the squares of the grid increase in size, reducing clarity. It is important to plan for the final output size when scanning a bitmap image, to have enough information, or detail, to meet the output requirements. Bitmap graphics are usually larger files than object-oriented graphic files, since more information is required to reproduce the image.

Tagged Image File Format (TIFF)

Scanners and software commonly use the TIFF to save bitmap images and reproduce photographs and other continuous tone images. TIFF is also used for exchanging raster images between applications. TIFF files can be exchanged among several platforms, including Mac OS operating system software, DOS, PC, and the UNIX system.

The *tagged image file format for image transfer (TIFF/IT-P1)* is a device-dependent format that incorporates high-end capabilities for describing demanding four-color documents, including specs for printing presses. TIFF/IT-P1 was designed to improve the flow of data within high-end color electronic prepress systems (CEPSs). The profile one (P1) component was added when the ISO accepted the format for consideration as an international standard. TIFF/IT-P1 is the file format of choice for magazine publishers and their advertisers, for delivering the files of advertisements.

EPS Format

The EPS technology is used to transfer PostScript files between PostScript devices and is one of the most stable of the file formats used in outputting to an imagesetter or a platesetter. The EPS format is very reliable for graphic images because it handles both vector and bitmap images. This format allows inclusion of low-resolution previews for screen display and non-PostScript printing. It is possible to display just a box with the file name of an image, instead of the image itself. EPS files also allow the inclusion of *Open Prepress Interface (OPI)* comments (explained below). The OPI file format allows the replacement of low-resolution images in files from one system with high-resolution image files from another.

Other File Formats

Each type of file format varies in the way images are saved, how they can be modified, and how well they will reproduce. File formats determine aspects such as image placement, resolution, color, and background. Other common file formats include the Windows metafile (WMF), picture (PICT), Desktop Color Separation (DCS), and the Graphics Interchange Format (GIF)™ standard. Extensive knowledge of your 'programs' capabilities and open communication among the publisher, service bureau, and printer will best determine the type of file formats that should be used for any given job.

PICT is the standard data format on Macintosh platforms. PICT2 is an expanded file format that is more appropriate for use in multimedia presentations than printing. WMF is the Windows operating system version of PICT. Both PICT and WMF can store vector and bitmap graphics.

JPEG and GIF files are not usually used in the printing industry. Although the JPEG file format can compress a photograph to as little as 5% of its original size, the compression process eliminates some data and degrades the image quality. Both JPEG and GIF file formats are more appropriate to posting photographs on the Internet.

Open Prepress Interface (OPI)

OPI is a work-flow protocol in which high-resolution images are stored on a server and low-resolution files with corresponding names are placed in the layout. The low-resolution files are considered FPO images. Changes (such as cropping, scaling, positioning, or coloring) made to the FPO image are sent back to the server. When the page is output to an imagesetter, the high-resolution image replaces the low-resolution one. The changes made to the FPO image are also made to the high-resolution image before output.

Caution

The FPO images should never be opened with image-editing software and saved in a different format.

OPI files should not be renamed. The file name of the low-resolution and high-resolution images serves as a link between the two. Changing the name will cause delays while the link is reestablished.

To reduce the chance for error, all artwork should be properly sized and rotated before it is scanned. The low-resolution images should be placed in the layout at 100% size and 0° rotation. Although the FPO images can be cropped without creating problems, they should not be resized. Resizing can create problems when the images are swapped. After scanning, resizing should be kept to a maximum of ±20% to prevent loss in quality. If the image must be rotated or resized drastically, it should be rescanned.

OPI is useful for increasing processing speed while working on a project and for limiting high-resolution traffic on a network. This saves time and avoids storage problems, which are created when working with large files created by high-resolution images. OPI can also be called *APR*.

Repurposing

As digital communication continues to mature, images are increasingly repurposed. That is, images are modified to function in a new application or medium. With these versatile file formats and PDLs, companies can easily use materials created primarily for use in a catalog or brochure for publication on their Web sites.

Summary

Digital cameras can be used to digitize images. Although the nature of camera use (handheld and mobile) places several limitations on digital cameras, technological advances are closing the gap. The quality of digital cameras is determined by the technology involved in image sensing, color capture, resolution, and zooming.

Most art enters the production process in analog form and must be converted to digital form before it can be placed in a layout. Scanners are the predominant means of digitizing images. Digital cameras use the same type of imaging process as flatbed scanners do. Combined with personal computers and advanced software programs, scanners prepare images in a fraction of the time conventional photographic processes require.

Almost any type or size of original can be scanned. This includes film negatives, transparencies, photos, printed media, drawings, graphs, and text copy. Many scanners allow the operator to specify what type of color separation is to be made and make a variety of corrections before the scan has been completed. Scanners come in several designs, including drum, flatbed, handheld, and film or slide scanners. The main differences among scanners are the resolution capability, bit depth, and type of light-gathering sensors they use.

A wide array of special effects can be created with most vector or photo-editing programs. These effects include gradations, posterizations, image editing, and trapping. Object-oriented graphic art consists of lines defined by mathematical formulas found in drawing (illustration) programs. Bitmap art consists of dots and is generated by paint and photo-editing software.

Many file formats are used to produce graphic images. The file format of a graphic image is important because it will determine how much manipulation can be done to the image and how well the image will be reproduced. Graphic images should be editable so they can be reused, repurposed, and continuously adapted.

Review Questions

Please do not write in this book. Write your answers on a separate sheet of paper.

1. Identify advantages of certain types of digital cameras.
2. Explain the role interpolation plays in the function of a Bayer filter pattern of photocells.
3. _____ allows a digital image to be converted to data that requires less memory.
4. Distinguish between optical zoom and digital zoom.
5. Analog images, such as a photograph or document, can be captured as digital data by a(n) _____.
6. The greater the _____ is, the smoother the gradation and the more colors or gray scales a scanner can represent.
7. _____ refers to the difference between the minimum and maximum tones a scanner can capture.
8. Describe the roles a scanner's dynamic range and bit depth play.

tagged image file format for image transfer (TIFF/IT-P1): a device-dependent format used for describing four-color documents, including specs for printing presses.

Open Prepress Interface (OPI): a work-flow protocol in which high-resolution images are stored on a server and low-resolution files with corresponding names are placed in the layout.

9. The maximum resolution at which a scanner can capture an image without interpolation is the scanner's _____ resolution.

10. What is interpolation, as it applies to scanners?

11. The lack of sharpness resulting from interpolation can be improved by using the _____ feature of image manipulation software.

12. What types of scanners use photomultiplier tubes as photosites?

13. What type of photosite is used in flatbed scanners?

14. What are the two basic types of scanners?

15. When scanning text, _____ software translates the copy into ASCII characters.

16. List three software applications used for image manipulation.

17. Name several image manipulation functions available with bitmap photo-editing software.

18. What software feature can correct the poor color balance of a color photograph taken under the wrong light?

19. Discuss two methods used to improve shadow details in color separations.

20. State the different types of traps.

21. Summarize OPI and the use of FPO images.

Skill-Building Activities

1. Prepare a schematic showing the operational features of a flatbed or drum scanner.

2. Obtain a black-and-white photograph suitable for a three-tone posterization and a four-tone posterization. Prepare the posterizations with care and note whether the correct detail was obtained.

3. Obtain a black-and-white photograph. Use a suitable special-effects contact screen to prepare a negative. Prepare a paper contact proof of the special-effects halftone.

4. Using the same image from Activity 3, scan the photograph. Import the image into an illustration program and apply a filter similar to the special-effects screen used in Activity 3. Compare the final image (from film or printer output) to the contact proof from Activity 3.

5. Using a scanned image and an electronic page composition program, design a two-color radio-station bumper sticker. The copy should include the call letters of the station and a suitable slogan. The size of the sticker is 3 1/2″ × 10″.

6. Obtain a black-and-white photograph suitable for a duotone. Use an appropriate contact screen to prepare both negatives. Make color proofs of the negatives and note whether the correct detail was attained.

A pallet of printed and folded signatures sits in front of the GST that will bind them to the other signatures and cover and then trim them on three sides to complete a magazine. (Hopkins Printing)

Getting It All Together

After the text files, photographs, and other images have been prepared, they must be imported into and arranged within the document. This function is called *page composition*. Chapter 9 looked at how a promotional piece is composed conventionally, and this chapter shows how to prepare the same document on the computer.

After a document has been prepared, it must be imposed in the pattern it will occupy on the printing plates. In this photograph, the monitor displays four documents as they will appear on the plates. The top row of images will be printed behind the bottom row of images. In other words, the job has received a work-and-tumble imposition. This chapter discusses the imposition software that performs the image-assembly function.

(Heidelberg, Inc.)

Chapter 15
Electronic Page Composition and Image Assembly

Key Terms

font report
font set
format
journalistic convention
library
master page
orphan
page composition software
picture box
ruler
ruler guide
style sheet
text box
widow

Learning Objectives

When you have completed the reading and assigned activities related to this chapter, you will be able to do the following:

- State the function of page composition software.
- Identify the function of basic tools within a page composition program's toolbox.
- Summarize how to create guidelines, text boxes, and picture boxes.
- Describe the importation of text and graphic images into a document.
- Discuss the value of creating style sheets and master pages.
- Define the basic terms of newsletter layout.
- Explain the linking function.
- Give examples of the functions of font-utility software.
- Paraphrase the basic steps of electronic image assembly.

In an electronic work flow, the text and graphics that were created digitally are integrated to produce a complete document, such as a business card, folder, newspaper, or magazine, with page composition software. Image-assembly software is then used to digitally arrange the documents in the positions they will occupy on the printing plate. Both of these functions are part of the prepress department. In conventional prepress, these functions were performed manually, but they can be performed electronically in less time and with greater precision.

Electronic Page Composition

After text has been created in word processing software, photographic images have been prepared with photo-editing software, and illustrations have been prepared with vector (drawing) software, these elements can be integrated into a document with page composition (layout) software. *Page composition software* allows the importation and placement of various page elements within a document such as a newsletter, a magazine, or an advertisement. See **Figure 15-1.**

Page composition software gave birth to the concept of desktop publishing in 1985, with the introduction of Aldus® PageMaker software. Although the limited memory of 1985 computers greatly restricted the use of photographs and illustrations within a document, the immediate enthusiasm for the concept generated rapid development of both hardware and software. The Corel VENTURA® program, Adobe FrameMaker® software, QuarkXPress application, and Adobe InDesign software were introduced later, but they became popular because of their greatly expanded range of capabilities. Today, large documents with elaborate graphics are universally prepared electronically for printing.

Page Composition Functions

Although the primary function of page composition software is to assemble images that might have been created or manipulated with other software, most page-layout programs are also capable of generating text and basic graphic images. Drawing; typesetting; cropping and scaling photographs; and applying fills, gradients, and colors are examples of these capabilities. An examination of the InDesign toolbox reveals the many available functions. See **Figure 15-2.** The function of the Shear tool can be seen in **Figure 15-3. Figure 15-4** shows the capabilities of the Gradient tool.

Figure 15-1. Even a design as basic as this one employs several functions within page composition software. A horizontal text box was created and rotated 90° to create the rectangle holding the words *Cape Camden* and bleeding off three sides. The words were made yellow, and the background was made blue. A picture box was created, and the photograph was placed in it. A second text box was created for the text below the photograph.

Clearly, page composition software is highly capable of preparing a wide range of documents—including fliers, advertisements, promotional folders, posters, newsletters, magazines, and books. Not only can it import type files and vector graphics, but it can also generate these images. In this chapter, two very different documents will be created with page composition software to demonstrate some of the capabilities of this software.

Creating a Two-Panel Folder

The steps involved in producing a mechanical on a light table for a two-panel folder to promote a specialty store were presented in Chapter 9. See **Figure 15-5.** In this chapter, the same folder will be produced electronically with the QuarkXPress application to demonstrate some of the basic procedures and functions of page composition software.

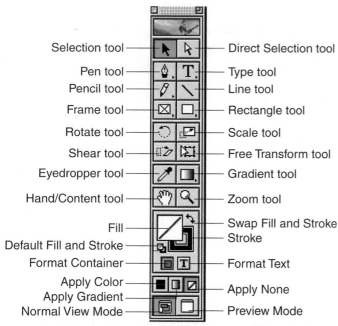

Tools	Functions
Selection	Selects one or more objects for moving or other work.
Direct Selection	Selects a portion of an object.
Pen	Draws straight or curved vector paths indicating boundaries.
Type	Creates text.
Pencil	Creates free-form paths that can be erased or smoothed later.
Line	Produces straight lines.
Frame	Creates frames to hold text or graphic images.
Rectangle	Creates rectangles or squares.
Rotate	Allows an object to be rotated by either typing in the desired angle or clicking and dragging.
Scale	Enlarges or reduces the size of an object.
Shear	Permits an object to be angled and distorted to create the appearance of being three-dimensional.
Free Transform	Allows several transformations—such as scaling, shearing, and rotating—on an object.
Eyedropper	Permits attributes such as color, stroke, and fill to be copied from one page element and applied to another.
Gradient	Alters the attributes of an object's gradient fill.
Scissors	Cuts vector lines.
Hand (or Content)	Moves a document within the document window (The action resembles scrolling).
Zoom	Enlarges or reduces the document.
Fill	Fills an object with a color, gradient, or pattern.
Swap Fill and Stroke	Transposes the color of an object's fill and stroke.
Default Fill and Stroke	Returns the Fill and Stroke tool to its default values—black stroke and no fill.
Stroke	Applies attributes, such as color, to a stroke.
Format Container and Format Text	Apply the fill and stroke functions to either an active frame or its text.
Apply Color	Applies a selected color to the stroke or fill of an object.
Apply Gradient	Applies a selected gradient to an object's fill or stroke.
Apply None	Places a transparent fill within an object.
View Mode	Switches between visible and invisible guides, grids, and margins.

Figure 15-2. Many of the capabilities of page composition software are shown in the toolbox.

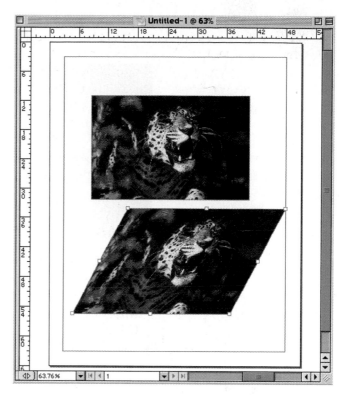

Figure 15-3. A photograph before and after shearing. Shearing can be used to form the sides of a box or other three-dimensional object being imaged.

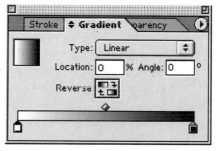

Linear Gradient

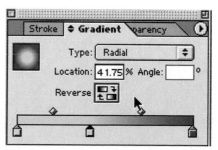

Radial Gradient

Figure 15-4. The gradient tool can create linear and radial gradients.

page composition software: an application that creates layouts for any type of document by positioning text and graphic elements.

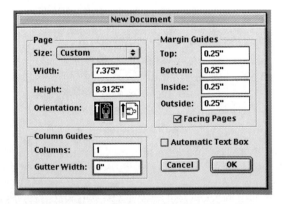

Figure 15-5. The digital equivalent of this conventional mechanical can be prepared with page composition software.

Whether you are preparing pages conventionally or electronically, the first step is to study the dummy and devise a plan. Preparing an electronic mechanical begins by establishing the document's parameters. In the New Document dialog box, several settings are entered, including the folder's width and height, the number of columns, and the outside margins. See **Figure 15-6.** The *rulers* across the top and left side of the Document window can display either picas or inches.

Figure 15-6. The dimensions, margins, and columns are established for a new job in the New Document dialog box. This job will be 7 3/8″ × 8 5/16″ with 1/4″ margins.

Clients can submit some materials measured in fractions of inches, and the decimal equivalent is what needs to be input to the software. In addition, clients might submit some materials measured in picas and other materials measured in inches. Both situations can be simplified with a conversion chart kept nearby when building documents. See **Figure 15-7.**

In traditional copy preparation, nonphoto-blue guidelines are placed on the base sheet to assist with the placement and alignment of elements. In electronic page composition, these blue lines, which will not print, are called *ruler guides*, or *guides*. Within the View menu, ruler guides can be shown or hidden. The placement of ruler guides for the two-panel folder begins with measuring the distances from the left side and top of the dummy to each type block, photograph, or piece of art. A vertical ruler guide is created by clicking on the vertical ruler, dragging the blue line the proper distance on the horizontal ruler, and then releasing the mouse button. Similarly, a horizontal ruler guide is made by clicking on the horizontal ruler and dragging to the desired point on the vertical ruler. For this job, six vertical and four horizontal ruler guides were made to assist in the placement of type and graphic elements. See **Figure 15-8.**

Page composition applications include dozens of keyboard shortcuts that allow tools to be selected and functions to be performed without using the mouse

Inches	Decimal	Picas	Points
1/16	0.0625	0p4.5	4.5
1/8	0.125	0p9	9
3/16	0.1875	1p1.5	13.5
1/4	0.25	1p6	18
5/16	0.3125	1p10.5	22.5
3/8	0.375	2p3	27
7/16	0.4375	2p7.5	31.5
1/2	0.5	3p	36
9/16	0.5625	3p4.5	40.5
5/8	0.625	3p9	45
11/16	0.6875	4p1.5	49.5
3/4	0.75	4p6	54
13/16	0.8125	4p10.5	58.5
7/8	0.875	5p3	63
15/16	0.9375	5p7.5	67.5
1	1.0	6p	72

Figure 15-7. A conversion chart provides instant decimal, pica, and point equivalents of inch fractions.

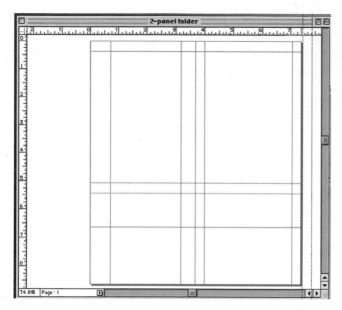

Figure 15-8. Nine ruler guides were electronically drawn to assist in the placement of text and graphic elements. Note that these lines are in the traditional nonphoto blue required in conventional mechanicals.

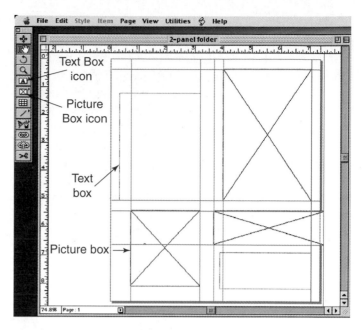

Figure 15-9. Picture boxes are placed onto the document to hold photographs and vector graphics. Text boxes hold blocks of type. The picture boxes are marked with large *X*s.

or touch pad. These keyboard commands are usually the same for both Windows operating systems and Macintosh computers. In some instances, however, they are different.

Referring to the dimensions on the dummy, text boxes and picture boxes are created. A ***text box*** defines the dimensions and placement of a block of type. Clicking on the Rectangle Text Box tool icon activates the tool. The cursor is then placed where the upper-left corner of the text box is to be, and the mouse is clicked and dragged until a rectangle that is the desired size is created. A ***picture box*** is created to hold photographs and imported graphic images, and it is made the same way, except the Rectangle Picture Box tool is clicked. InDesign software uses the same box for either text or a picture. Three picture boxes (indicated with crossing diagonal lines) and two text boxes were made for this document. See **Figure 15-9.**

Text and graphic images can then be imported into these boxes with the Get Text or Get Picture command. Text can be keyboarded directly, instead of imported, and also edited at this point in production. An examination of **Figure 15-10** reveals that three lines of type have been placed in a text box. The Measurements palette near the bottom of the screen displays the distance of the upper-left corner of the text box from the upper-left corner of the document because the box has been clicked on. This box is 4.014″ from the origin on the x-axis and 7.072″ from the origin on the y-axis. The W and H values display the width and height of the text box.

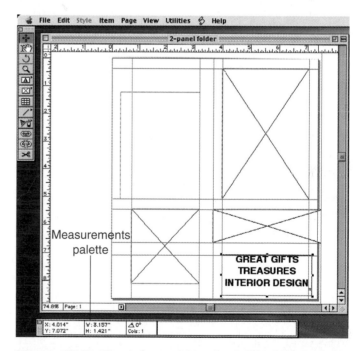

Figure 15-10. Three lines of type have been imported into a text box. Note that the x- and y-coordinates of the upper-left corner of the text box and the dimensions of the text box are shown in the Measurements palette.

ruler: a representation of a conventional ruler showing increments of linear measurement.

ruler guide: a light blue line that is not output to a printer, but assists in the placement of type or graphic elements during page composition.

text box: a closed figure of any shape used to position text.

picture box: a closed figure of any shape used to position a graphic element.

The scanned image of the black-and-white photograph is opened in a photo-editing program to verify that its resolution is adequate before importing it into the document. See **Figure 15-11.** The logo is brought into a paint program, and a customer-specified second color is applied to the background using the RGB sliders in the Color palette. See **Figure 15-12.** The logo can then be imported into the document. This form of color selection could have been performed in page composition software. If the customer specified the spot color with a Pantone number, the color selection can be performed within page composition software by entering that number into a dialog box. Selecting a color in any program is done only for proofing purposes. The ink color the press operator loads into the press determines the actual color appearing on the finished product.

A map that had been created in a drawing program is then imported and placed in a second picture box. See **Figure 15-13.** After the logo and the remaining text are placed in their respective boxes, the front of the folder is complete. See **Figure 15-14.** The preparation of the second side can begin.

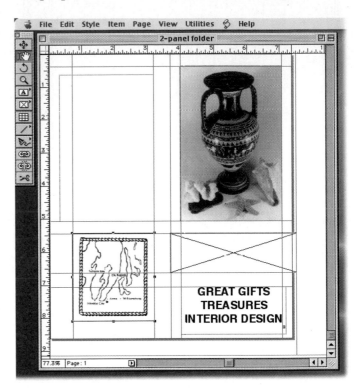

Figure 15-13. At this point, two picture boxes have been filled with a photograph and a map.

Figure 15-11. The scanned black-and-white photograph is opened up in a photo-editing program to verify that the resolution is adequate.

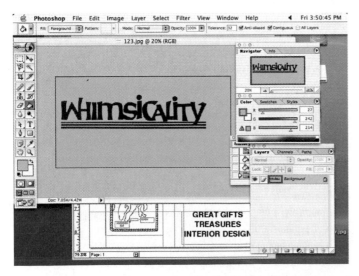

Figure 15-12. A spot color is applied to the logo's background in a paint program before the logo is imported into a picture box.

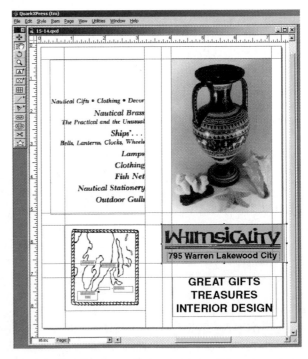

Figure 15-14. The front of the folder will be complete when the galley on the left is straightened.

Producing a Publication

Page composition software is also used to prepare newsletters, magazines, booklets, books, catalogs, and any other publication consisting of pages within signatures. When the job involves signatures, the pages should be built as reader's spreads—the pairs of pages the reader will see together. The software facilitates this procedure by arranging the pages in two-page spreads. See **Figure 15-15.** It is important to view the publication as a series of two-page spreads because that is how the reader will view it.

Establishing the publication's format

It is important that the appearance of all the pages be consistent in basic format and typography because they are part of a single publication. Two software features can be used to impart these commonalities to each page in an efficient manner. These features are master pages and the style sheet.

Page composition software usually allows the creation of *master pages*, which are the result of placing design features common to most pages on each page in advance of the actual building of those pages. For example, master pages usually indicate the placement, typestyle, and size of page numbers, as well as the name of the publication or chapter. See **Figure 15-16.** In the example shown, red rules are placed across the top and bottom of each page, and the issue date and page numbers are positioned at the bottom of each page of a newsletter. Notice that the page orientation of the title and page numbers varies between even-numbered pages (always the left-hand page of the reader's spread) and odd-numbered pages (always the right-hand page of the reader's spread). These page elements would probably be deleted from the first page of a newsletter or the first page of a book's chapters. Establishing master pages saves considerable production time because it saves the repetitive task of creating these page elements on each page.

An efficient tool for handling a publication's typography is the *style sheet,* a set of specs for the typographic elements of the publication. A style sheet allows the specs for different levels of headlines and

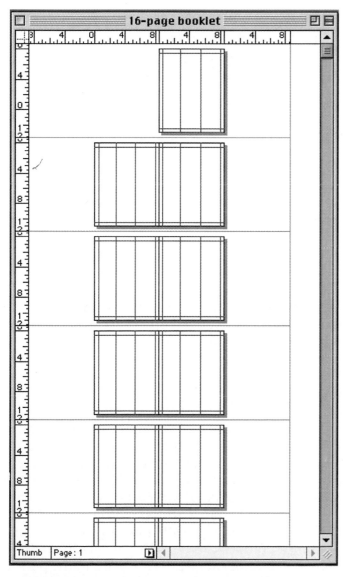

Figure 15-15. To assist the page composition of publications, pages can be displayed and built as reader's spreads.

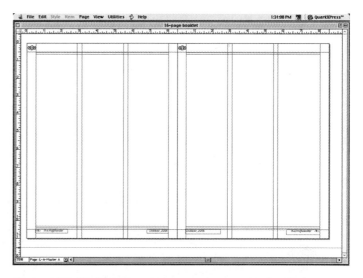

Figure 15-16. Master pages can be created with features common to most pages within a publication.

master page: a page composition–program feature that can be set up to include the page geometry, typography, and other elements of a page that will recur in a document.

style sheet: a formatting tool used in page-composition programs that combines a number of attributes, such as type size, alignment, and other factors.

subheads, as well as photographs' captions and other page elements, to be stored and applied instantly as the document is being built. For example, imagine a newsletter that uses headlines in three different levels—one, two, and three. The specs of a level-one headline are entered into the style sheet. See **Figure 15-17.** As shown in this example, every level-one headline will be 30-point Helvetica bold. When a level-one headline is specified, the text is highlighted, the style sheet menu is activated, and then the level-one headline is selected and automatically applied. By creating and using a style sheet for each publication, production time is significantly reduced. Both word processing and page composition software have style-sheet capabilities.

Preparing a newsletter

Page composition software usually includes templates. Templates are basic formats that can be selected to establish the basic design and serve as the foundation for the publication. See **Figure 15-18.**

Newsletter terminology

An aspect of producing newsletters is being able to communicate with clients who are likely to have a background in journalism, which has its own terminology. Knowing these terms will prevent confusion when working with a client-supplied dummy. A newsletter's *format* is its basic appearance—including the number of columns on a page, the typefaces used, the margin sizes, whether the text is set justified or flush left, and the headline styles. See **Figure 15-19.** Headlines (also known as *heads*) can be set up style or down style. With up-style heads, the first letter of most words is capitalized, while with down-style heads, only the first letter of the first word and proper nouns are capitalized.

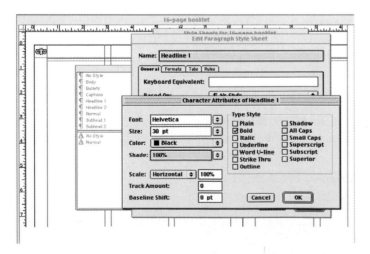

Figure 15-17. A style sheet can be prepared to speed the process of assigning specs to type elements.

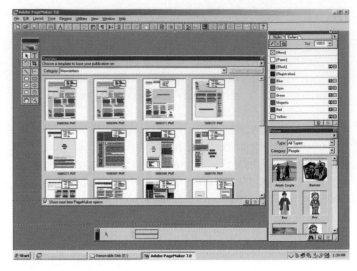

Figure 15-18. Page composition software usually offers a collection of templates that can serve as the basis of a newsletter.

There are several types of headlines. A banner head runs across the entire page. A smaller and shorter head called a *kicker* augments some heads. Kickers sit over the mainline, are approximately one-half the height of the mainline, and have the opposite structure of the mainline. If the mainline is italicized, the kicker is not. In addition, the mainline is indented. A reverse kicker is larger than the mainline, but the other rules still apply. If a head was written too short, it can be centered and placed within a 3/4 box. Headlines used in several issues are called *standing heads* and should be retrieved from the software's library, rather than created each time they are used. A headline's width is measured in columns. See **Figure 15-20.**

A photograph is usually referred to as a *cut*, a term born in a time when newspaper illustrations were woodcuts, and is represented on the dummy with a single diagonal line. Similar to headlines, a cut's width is usually measured in columns. The lines of type describing the pictures are cutlines, and they are normally a different typeface than the one used for the stories. See **Figure 15-21.** Typically, the body copy is a serif typeface, and the cutlines are sans serif. Large (display) type accompanying a cut and its cutline is an attention line, and it signals to the reader that the cut is not part of a story. In other words, an attention line is used with cuts that do not have their own headlines. Although they look like headlines, cutlines can be informal and do not have to contain a verb. An ident is the name of the person in the cut.

Informal Format

Formal Format

Figure 15-19. An informal format with down-style headlines and flush-left body type is on the left. A more formal format with up-style headlines and justified body type is on the right. Both newsletters are in three columns.

One-Column, Two-Line Head	Marketing announces fourth-quarter plans
Two-Column, One-Line Head	Marketing announces fourth-quarter plans
Kicker and Mainline	*Four-year appointment made* Bautista named to head commission
Reverse Kicker and Mainline	Just in time *Pediatric department takes delivery of new computers*
Head with ¾ Box	Highway funding plan studied
Standing Head	NCAA SCORES

Figure 15-20. Types of headlines include a one-column, two-line head; a two-column, one-line head; a kicker and its mainline; a reverse kicker and its mainline; a head with a 3/4 box; and a standing head.

format: the form, dimensions, and general structure of a publication.

A Cutline

As part of a last Saturday's spring-cleanup project, Lake Township residents fed brush into a chipper along White Birch Trail. The chips will be used on township playgrounds and hiking trails.

An Attention Line

Up, up, and away

Several colorful hot air balloons took to the sky at the start of the eighth annual Mesa Verde BalloonFest last Sunday. Seventeen contestants from five states traveled from east of Mesa Verde to Lanark. The winner was Kenny Tarmac.

An Ident

Arlen Wharsey

Figure 15-21. Cutlines describing the cuts accompany the cuts that are part of a story. Human interest and other cuts that are not part of a story also have an attention line. This attention line is centered. There are several formats for attention lines. An ident only identifies the photograph's subject.

The nameplate is the name of the newsletter in its official typeface, and it is part of the masthead, the collection of type and graphics traditionally found at the top of the first page. A masthead that is not always at the top of the page is a floating mast. The staff block is the listing of staff members and their titles, and it often contains a small version of the nameplate. The name of the person who wrote the story is the byline, and the jump line is used to tell the reader where to find the portion of a story that was jumped to another page.

Journalistic conventions

Journalistic conventions define what is considered traditional newspaper and newsletter design. These conventions hold that the columns of a rectangular story align across the top and bottom. If a story consisting of 30 lines of type is placed in three columns, the logical approach is to place 10 lines in each column. If the story has 28 lines, however, the columns will be uneven. Although newsletters with highly informal formats permit the last column to be short, more formal newsletters require the extra space to be distributed between the paragraphs of the story. The first lines of paragraphs in the short columns are highlighted, and the Space Before field is used to add points of space between paragraphs. This method of leading out the short columns until they align with the longest column should be subtle. That is, the extra space should be distributed throughout the column instead of placed in one spot. See **Figure 15-22.**

Even if a three-column story consists of 30 total lines, some extra spacing might be needed to avoid widows and orphans. A *widow* is the last line of a paragraph appearing at the top of a column. Many clients will want widows eliminated from the newsletter because very short widows give the appearance of uneven columns. See **Figure 15-23.** In the example shown, observe how one adjustment can eliminate a widow and correct a short column. Space is added before the paragraphs in the first column, with the result that the last line of the column moves over to the top of the second column. The widow is eliminated, and the last line of the second column is moved to the third column, which is no longer short. Similar to the word processing programs discussed in Chapter 6, page composition programs are capable of performing kerning. In some instances, widows can be corrected by reducing the space between letters of one or more lines so more words fit into the lines. An *orphan* is the first line of a paragraph, if it is at the bottom of a column. Although orphans are not considered as undesirable as widows, they are dealt with in a similar manner.

The October meeting was convened at 2:00 p.m. on Saturday. Members of the organization's finance committee voted 27-8 to increase funding for the proposed study.

The vote followed a second discussion that revolved around usage fees to be collected from boaters who launch at the Weldon facility.

Seventeen committee members voiced concerns regarding the likelihood of boaters choosing to launch at the Colfax facility

instead of paying the surcharge. They suggested that the usage fees be applied in July.

Still other members suggested that such a change in activity is unlikely because of the close proximity of the Weldon boat ramp to the marina. It was their concern that the increased user fees would not generate more income. Instead, they would merely inconvenience and annoy boaters.

Uneven Lines
(11 Lines in Left Column, 10 Lines in Right Column)

The October meeting was convened at 2:00 p.m. on Saturday. Members of the organization's finance committee voted 27-8 to increase funding for the proposed study.

The vote followed a second discussion that revolved around usage fees to be collected from boaters who launch at the Weldon facility.

Seventeen committee members voiced concerns regarding the likelihood of boaters

choosing to launch at the Colfax facility instead of paying the surcharge. They suggested that the usage fees be applied in July.

Still other members suggested that such a change in activity is unlikely because of the close proximity of the Weldon boat ramp to the marina. It was their concern that the increased user fees would not generate more income. Instead, they would merely inconvenience and annoy boaters.

Even Lines

Figure 15-22. If the number of lines in a multicolumn story is uneven, most newsletters require the extra space to be added between paragraphs.

The newsletter shown in **Figure 15-19** will be built with Adobe InDesign software. Guidelines are created to establish the columns and margins of the newsletter. See **Figure 15-24.** A frame is created for the masthead, which is imported from the *library*. InDesign software can hold type in either a frame or a text box. The spot color used to print the nameplate is chosen in the Swatch Options dialog box and established as a color for this document. See **Figure 15-25.** Text boxes are created for the headlines, stories, and cutline. A frame is created for the cut. The headlines are imported from the customer's word processing files, highlighted, and identified as first-level headlines in the style sheet. The one-column cut is placed into the third column. The text of the first story is imported into the first frame and then *threaded* to the second and third frames. See **Figure 15-26.** In the QuarkXPress application, this flowing of text is referred to as *linking*.

Font Management

Word processing, drawing, image manipulation, and page composition programs provide a selection of typefaces under the heading Fonts. All typefaces used in a document file sent to a commercial printer must be available to the printer so the imagesetter or platesetter can image them. Without the proper files, the printer is forced to substitute the missing typefaces with available typefaces. Typeface substitution can not only change the appearance of the document, but it can also cause the document to be reflowed, hyphenated words that had been at the end of lines

journalistic convention: an accepted practice newspapers and other publications use, regarding typography and page layout.

widow: the last line of a paragraph at the top of a column of type.

orphan: the first line of a paragraph at the bottom of a column of type.

library: a set of reference resources.

The October meeting was convened at 2:00 p.m. on Saturday. Members of the organization's finance committee voted 27-8 to increase funding for the proposed study.

The vote followed a second discussion that revolved around usage fees to be collected from boaters who launch at the Weldon facility.

Seventeen committee members voiced concerns regarding the likelihood of boaters choosing to launch at the Colfax facility instead of paying the surcharge. Local hardware merchant Ernie Fergler suggested that the usage fees be applied in July, after the Summer Festival and the June Extravaganza.

Still other members suggested that such a change in activity is unlikely because of the close proximity of the Weldon boat ramp to the marina. It was their concern that the increased user fees would not generate more income. Instead, they would merely inconvenience and annoy boaters.

Two Widows Before Correction

The October meeting was convened at 2:00 p.m. on Saturday. Members of the organization's finance committee voted 27-8 to increase funding for the proposed study.

The vote followed a second discussion that revolved around usage fees to be collected from boaters who launch at the Weldon facility.

Seventeen committee members voiced concerns regarding the likelihood of boaters choosing to launch at the Colfax facility instead of paying the surcharge. Local hardware merchant Ernie Fergler suggested that the usage fees be applied in July, after the Summer Festival and the June Extravaganza.

Still other members suggested that such a change in activity is unlikely because of the close proximity of the Weldon boat ramp to the marina. It was their concern that the increased user fees would not generate more income.

Instead, they would merely inconvenience and annoy boaters.

No Widows After Correction

Figure 15-23. Widows are corrected by moving lines from one column to another and then placing the extra space between paragraphs.

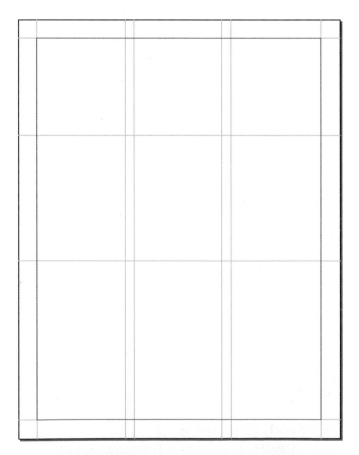

Figure 15-24. Columns and margins are established according to the format of each newsletter. The horizontal guidelines will help place headlines and ads.

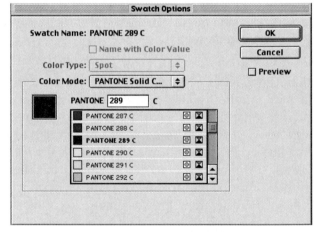

Swatch Options Dialog Box

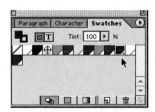

Color Swatch

Figure 15-25. The spot color that has been specified for the masthead is selected in the Swatch Options dialog box. The color is then placed into the color swatch for the publication.

The plus sign

The link icon

Figure 15-26. After the masthead, headlines, text boxes, and cut are in place, the first story is placed in the first text box and threaded to the second column. The red plus sign at the bottom of the second column indicates there is still more text. To continue the threading, the plus sign is clicked on. The link icon then appears and is dragged to the next column. When the mouse button is released, the remaining text appears.

to appear within the lines, and kerning and tracking to be lost. Font-utility software, such as Adobe Type Manager® software, Adobe Type Reunion® software, Symantec™ Suitcase, and FontMinder™ software, is useful for managing, collecting, and transferring fonts.

Adobe Type Manager software uses PostScript outline fonts to generate bitmap typefaces in any size. Adobe Type Reunion software collects variations of a given typeface into a single pop-up menu. For example, Palatino can be listed with other members of the Palatino family, such as Palatino bold, Palatino italic, and Palatino bold italic—thereby making typeface selection more efficient.

All font-utility programs allow the creation of a *font set*, a list of the typefaces used for a given document. With a font set, typefaces can be selected from a list of only those being used in the document. This saves the time needed to scroll repeatedly down the potentially long list of fonts loaded on the computer.

Printing companies and service bureaus that receive electronic files recommend that a font report accompanies the job. A *font report* is a list of typefaces used in the document, including any fonts within imported EPS graphics. Page composition programs, such as the QuarkXPress application, InDesign software, and PageMaker software, can generate font reports.

Electronic Image Assembly

Imposition software has become the preferred method of imposition and image assembly because of its speed, accuracy, and flexibility. Electronic image assembly of complex jobs can be performed in less than half the time conventional stripping requires. The latest electronic CTP process allows for automatic imposition and image assembly of pages. Intermediate film and masking sheets are eliminated.

As you learned, manual imposition is the process of positioning images on a printing plate. Imposition includes placing a business card's image on six locations of a plate, as well as positioning pages on a signature that will become part of a book. Digital imposition computerizes this process, eliminating the

font set: the font list for a document. These sets can be created for individual jobs, and only the set needed can be activated.

font report: a list of the typefaces used in a document.

film-assembly process. See **Figure 15-27.** Although some page composition software can perform very basic imposition functions, more demanding imposition requires sophisticated imposition software. The primary benefit of electronic imposition is it is much faster than manual imposition.

Dedicated imposition software has many useful features. Users might be able to fold a virtual dummy on screen. Page-number sequence, page orientation, and folding marks can be automatically applied. Options for controlling creep and bleeds can be determined quickly. See **Figure 15-28.**

Software programs enable users to impose, preview, edit, proof, color separate, and print in a single application. See **Figure 15-29.** The imposition

can be output directly as a multipage signature to an imagesetter, a platesetter, a proofer, or a digital printer with all marks in position.

Software performs the same functions the stripper performed in traditional image assembly—but in much less time. The dimensions of the finished job and the edges containing bleeds are entered into a dialog box. The number of images that will be placed on the press sheet, the imposition pattern, and the space allowance for gutters are also entered, and the configuration is displayed. See **Figure 15-30.** Trim and bleed marks, as well as their dimensions, can also be established. Allowances for plate bend and paper grippers must be made.

When a signature to be folded and become part of a publication is imposed, the placement of each page is displayed. See **Figure 15-31.** Next, the properly named and formatted documents are imposed onto the press sheet. The display shows the text and graphics in place, as well as the colors. Two-sided jobs are automatically displayed alongside one another.

Standard templates can be accessed quickly from an imposition library, or original templates can be created and added to the library. Some imposition software allows the creation of a digital folding dummy. See **Figure 15-32.**

After the job has been successfully imposed, it is ready to be sent to an output device for imaging. The output device might be a wide-format proofer, an imagesetter, or a platesetter. In any event, imposition is one of the final stages of prepress. If the imposed images are sent to an imagesetter, a single sheet of film with all the images in the correct position will be generated. See **Figure 15-33.** This film will be the

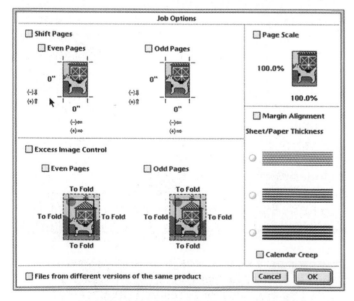

Figure 15-27. This software enables users to perform press and postpress settings in the imposition stage. (Heidelberg, Inc.)

Figure 15-28. Job options can be accessed from a single dialog box. (Ultimate Technographics, Inc.)

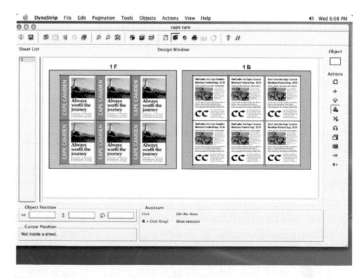

Figure 15-29. The QuarkXPress document seen at the beginning of this chapter is shown imposed in a six-up, work-and-back imposition. (DynaStrip)

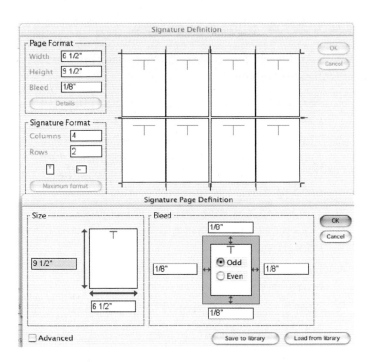

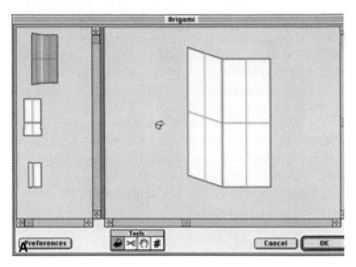

Figure 15-32. Software allows the user to create a folding dummy on screen. (Ultimate Technographics, Inc.)

Figure 15-30. Many specs of an imposed job are established in the Signature Definition dialog box. Included here are the page size, the 4 × 2 pattern, the placement and width of the bleed gutters, and the trim marks. Once created, this template can be saved for use with another job. (DynaStrip)

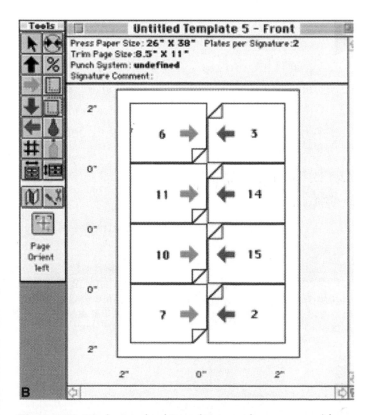

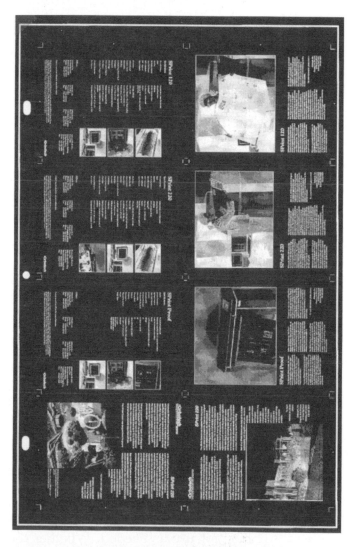

Figure 15-31. A standard template can be accessed from the imposition library. (Ultimate Technographics, Inc.)

Figure 15-33. Electronic image assembly allows an imagesetter to output film with correctly positioned images that are ready for exposure to an offset printing plate. The same digital file can also be output to a platesetter, thereby eliminating film. (Orobotech, Inc.)

same size as the plate and will be used to expose the plate. More advanced systems use a DTP system, in which the output device is a platesetter that generates the plate directly—eliminating the need for film. DTPr systems image plates after they have been loaded onto the plate cylinders of the press.

A completed document should be converted to a file format that is device independent and, for that reason, portable enough for any output device to read. Adobe InDesign software can export directly to a PDF. The QuarkXPress application can save a page as an EPS.

Summary

In an electronic work flow, page composition software, such as PageMaker software, the QuarkXPress application, and InDesign software, has replaced the light table and art knife of the copy-prep artist. This powerful tool is able to perform the dozens of functions required to produce the full range of materials printed today. Basically, page composition software imports both type and graphics and arranges them according to the dummy the customer supplies.

The software functions similarly to the conventional process it replaces. The dimensions of the document are established, and nonphoto-blue guidelines are created to help align the boxes that are made to hold the text, photographs, and art making up the document. Both spot and process colors can be specified through various methods. Images on the same page that touch, but require separate treatment, are placed on separate layers. It is important that the people who produce newsletters are aware of journalistic conventions so the documents conform to the customer's expectations, especially because so many organizations print their own newsletters.

After each page of a document is completed, image-assembly software electronically imposes the pages. To impose a job is to arrange pages in the best pattern to optimize the capacity of the printing plate. Imposition programs are able to perform the same functions strippers, who arranged films onto masking sheets, once handled, in less time and more accurately. Allowances have to be made for plate bend, paper grippers, and creep. Jobs commonly produced by a shop—such as business cards—can be imposed quickly if templates are created and stored in a library for use as needed. Whether the imposed file is to be sent to a proofer, an imagesetter, a platesetter, or a digital press, it should be converted to a PDF file format. Any output device that receives a PDF will accurately read it because a PDF is device independent.

Review Questions

Please do not write in this book. Write your answers on a separate sheet of paper.

1. Text and graphics can be imported and integrated into page _____ software.
2. The text box holding the yellow words *Cape Camden* in **Figure 15-1** was horizontal when the words were typed. What tool was then used to make the text box vertical?
3. The blue lines that assist in the correct placement of text and graphic images are known as _____.
4. How are guidelines, text boxes, and picture boxes created?
5. A(n) _____ box is created to hold photographs and vector graphics.
6. How is a picture box indicated?
7. Describe the procedure for importing a photograph into a document.
8. If a 2″-wide and 4 1/2″–high text box is placed 3 1/2″ to the right and 1 1/2″ below the upper-left corner of the document, what are the X, Y, W, and H values within the Measurements palette?
9. What is the benefit of creating and using master pages?
10. What is a template?
11. Define *cutline* and *attention line*.
12. Cite the definitions of *widow* and *orphan*.
13. What is one method for choosing a spot color for a digital document?
14. Explain the steps involved in getting the text type of a news story to flow into four text boxes.
15. What is the value of using font-utility software?
16. _____ image assembly computerizes the process of combining pages on a signature, eliminating manual film assembly.
17. What are the basic steps of electronic image assembly?
18. Distinguish between DTP and DTPr.

Skill-Building Activities

1. Create a chart displaying the icons in the toolbox of a page composition software package and explaining the function of each.

2. Design a small two-color poster including display type, text type, vector graphics, and a photograph. Generate each element in its appropriate software and import the elements into a page composition software package.

3. Create a style sheet for a newsletter.

4. Collect at least 12 newsletters from different organizations and assess their formats.

5. Collect at least five different daily newspapers and assess their typographic formats—headlines, cutlines, and attention lines. Look for examples of kickers, reverse kickers, and standing heads. Look for places in the papers where the nameplate appears.

6. With the same collection of daily newspapers, assess the ability of the newspapers to avoid widows.

7. Redesign the masthead for your school's newspaper.

8. Choose three templates from a page composition software package and fill them in with text and photographs.

9. Pick up several copies of a promotional piece and paste them on a press sheet to reflect an imposition plan. Be sure to allow for bleed images and the gripper area.

Avoiding Color Drift

Chapter 7 discusses choosing and matching colors. After the graphic designer has specified the colors to be used in a printed piece, however, the task of generating those exact colors and maintaining them throughout production falls to the production personnel. The challenge arises because colors typically become altered as the job moves through the electronic maze of scanners, page composition software, proofers, and platesetters, to the press itself.

Before people can faithfully reproduce color, they must understand its science, as well as how to measure and manage it.

In this photograph, a proof of a scarf's image is compared with the actual scarf. Fortunately, human color perception is not the only method of judging color. Production personnel have many sophisticated tools for maintaining precise color, and this chapter will explain them.

(Heidelberg, Inc.)

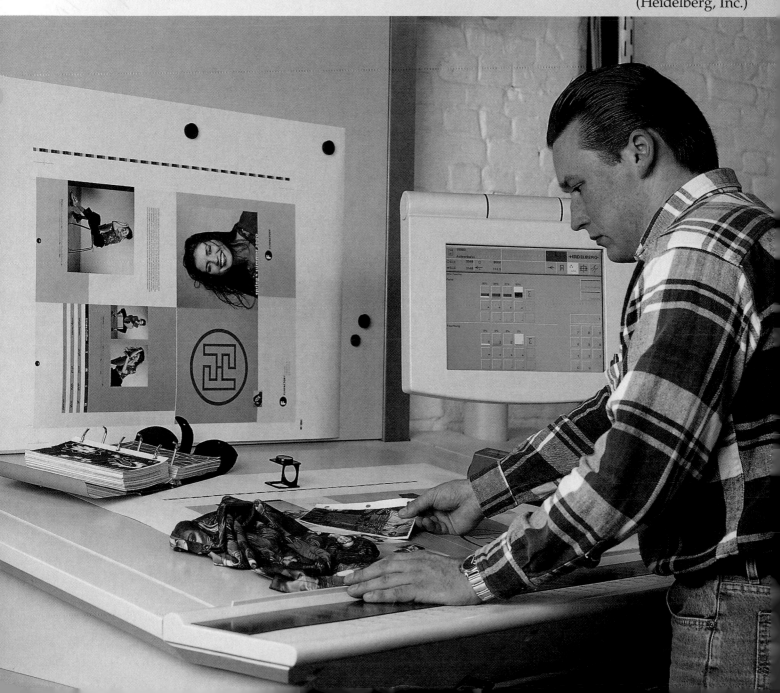

Chapter 16
Color Science, Reproduction, and Management

Key Terms

achromatic vision
additive color system
adjacent
black printer
brightness
calibrate
CIELAB system
colorant
color blindness
color drift
color gamut
Color-Key® proof
color management
   software (CMS)
color separation
color sequence
color space
color temperature
contract color proof
cyan
cyan, magenta, yellow, and
   black (CMYK)
dichromatic vision
dot gain compensation
electromagnetic spectrum
electronic color separation
General Requirements
   for Applications in
   Commercial Offset
   Lithography (GRACoL)
gray component
   replacement (GCR)
G7
hi-fi color
input resolution
International Color
   Consortium (ICC)
International Commission
   on Illumination (CIE)
International Commission
   on Illumination (CIE)
   chromaticity diagram

International
   Commission on
   Illumination (CIE)
   XYZ value
lightness
magenta
Matchprint® proof
metamerism
nanometer (nm)
output resolution
output size
Pantone Matching
   System® standard
photographic color
   separation
pigment
prepress proof
press proof
process color
process color printing
profile
proof press
registration
resizing
saturation
sharpening
Specifications
   for Newsprint
   Advertising
   Production (SNAP)
Specifications for Web
   Offset Publications
   (SWOP®) specs
subtractive color system
tristimulus
undercolor addition
   (UCA)
undercolor removal (UCR)
viewing booth
visible spectrum
vision fatigue
yellow

Learning Objectives

When you have completed the reading and assigned activities related to this chapter, you will be able to do the following:

❖ Explain the basic principles of color perception.

❖ Summarize additive and subtractive color formation.

❖ Describe the relationship between primary and secondary colors.

❖ Discuss the basic principles of color separation.

❖ Give examples of how variables such as vision deficiencies and external conditions affect color perception.

❖ Define *color space* and the dimensions of color.

❖ Distinguish among hue, saturation, and brightness (HSB); International Commission on Illumination (CIE) XYZ; CIE xyY; and CIELAB.

❖ Identify various color-measurement instruments.

❖ List the various types of proofs used in the printing industry.

❖ Explain the basic methods of color correction.

❖ Summarize color sequencing.

❖ Describe the color-management function.

Color plays many significant roles in our everyday lives. In addition to beautifying our environment, the use of color can greatly enhance communication. As an element of design, color can add contrast and visual impact, as well as lend realism and create a specific mood. See **Figure 16-1.**

Research indicates that well-applied color in print media is more effective than just black and white. Even printed pages with no illustrations can be more attractive if one or two colors are added to the layout. Fortunately, with advances in technology, press designs, and ink composition, the addition of color to many publications is now practical and economical.

Although color has the potential to enhance communication, it also has the potential to impair communication. Similar to typography, color can be mishandled. Color can be excessive, distracting, or inappropriate to the message or the reader. When used poorly, color becomes an expensive form of visual noise. Also similar to typography, an awareness of color's properties enhances the effective use of color. One of the challenges of color reproduction is maintaining color consistency throughout the production process. To accomplish this goal, everyone from the graphic designer to the press operator should have a basic understanding of color theory.

Understanding Color

Even a very basic understanding of color involves some physics, anatomy, and psychology. Color is not a thing as much as it is a phenomenon. This phenomenon is light energy generated at a source and traveling in waves, which ultimately stimulate receptors in the brain. Therefore, the type of light source, the behavior of the light during its travel, and the color sensitivity of the viewer collectively determine perception of color.

The Interaction of Light and Pigments

Light, radio waves, X rays, gamma rays, and microwaves are part of the *electromagnetic spectrum* because they all travel in waves. Their different wavelengths—the distances from peak to peak of their wave patterns—determine the differences in their properties. See **Figure 16-2.** Moving from left to right on the electromagnetic spectrum, the wavelengths become longer. Wavelengths are measured by the *nanometer (nm)*, which is one billionth of a meter, so even the longest wavelengths in the electromagnetic spectrum are very tiny distances. Near the middle of the electromagnetic spectrum are wavelengths producing light. Although most of this light is invisible, the human eye is sensitive to a narrow band known as the *visible spectrum*. Within this visible spectrum, differences in wavelength determine the light's color. Roughly speaking, wavelengths between 400 and 500 nm produce blue light, wavelengths between 500 and 600 nm produce green light, and wavelengths between 600 and 700 nm produce red light.

In the seventeenth century, Sir Isaac Newton discovered that a beam of sunlight passing through a prism is refracted, or bent, into separate bands of colors because the wavelength determines how much the light is bent. See **Figure 16-3.** This discovery revealed that the white (colorless) light emitted from the sun and other sources, such as fluorescent and incandescent lights, actually consists of several colors of light. Color does not exist, however, until the natural balance within the visible spectrum is broken. In other words, color results from some of

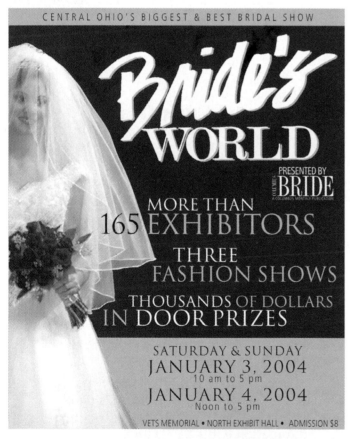

Figure 16-1. Well-chosen and well-placed color can greatly enhance a design's stopping power, appeal, and ability to communicate. The red background and bouquet infuse contrast to the neutral black, white, and gray tones of this ad. Red reinforces the mood of love and romance because of its traditional connection to Valentine's Day. (*Columbus Bride* Magazine)

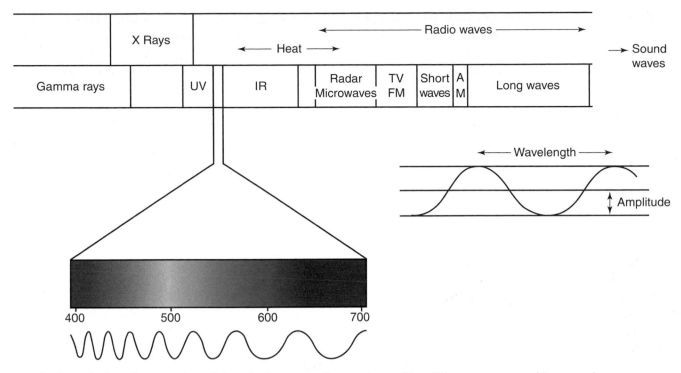

Figure 16-2. Light is only a portion of the electromagnetic spectrum. The difference among X rays, microwaves, broadcast waves, and light is their wavelengths, the distances from peak to peak. Within the visible spectrum, wavelength determines the color of light. Visible light includes wavelengths ranging from 400 nm to 770 nm.

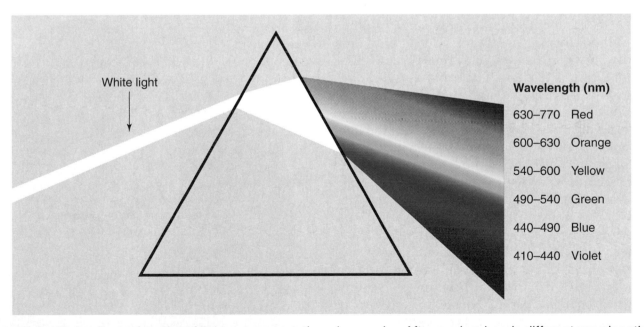

Figure 16-3. When all wavelengths of light are present, there is no color. After a prism bends different wavelengths of light by different degrees, the various colors making up white light can be seen.

electromagnetic spectrum: the entire range of wavelengths of electromagnetic radiation, extending from gamma rays to radio waves.

nanometer (nm): a unit of measurement equal to one-billionth of a meter.

visible spectrum: the portion of electromagnetic waves visible to humans.

wavelengths of light being removed. For example, if all wavelengths of light between 400 and 600 nm are removed, only the wavelengths between 600 and 700 nm (red) remain. A person looking at this light experiences the sensation of red.

As strange as it might seem at first, color is a phenomenon resulting from the interaction of light and pigments. A *pigment* is any material that absorbs light. When light falls on most objects, pigments within the object absorb certain wavelengths of light and reflect others. For example, when white light strikes a red apple, pigments within the apple's skin absorb the blue and green light (400–600 nm), and the light not absorbed is reflected. The apple appears red because the reflected light represents the red end of the spectrum. Similarly, when sunlight strikes green grass, pigments within the grass absorb the red and blue light and reflect only the green light. To continue, the pigments in the paint of a blue car absorb the red and green light and reflect only the blue. In short, we see only the reflected light.

How We See Color

The light-sensitive nerve cells of the retina known as *rods* and *cones* determine our sense of light and color. There are about 12 million rods and 7 million cones in the human eye. The rods detect only light intensity, but the cones detect intensity, as well as wavelength. The wavelength determines color.

The ability to be stimulated by various combinations of blue, green, and red light allows humans to perceive a multitude of colors derived from the light waves entering the eye. For example, despite *yellow*'s pure appearance, it is not a pure color. There is no retinal receptor sensitive to yellow light. The color yellow is perceived through the combined activity of the red-sensitive and green-sensitive cones. That is, equal amounts of red light and green light form yellow.

Just as the wavelengths of light entering the eye determine the color, the amount of light entering the eye determines **brightness**. Brightness is often referred to as **lightness** or *luminosity* and can be defined as a value indicating how light or dark a color is. Light of 550 nm appears green. Whether it is a dark green or a light green depends on the amount of 550 nm light. The perception of color depends on both the quantity (amount) and quality (wavelengths) of light striking the receptors in an observer's eyes.

The Additive Color System

People who work with light realize they can produce any desired color by combining only three

colors of light—RGB. To illustrate this point, imagine three spotlights of these three colors. If they are directed onto a white surface so they create the pattern shown in **Figure 16-4,** three new colors—cyan, magenta, and yellow (CMY)—result. Still other colors result from varying the intensity of one of the spotlights. For example, equal amounts of red and green light produce yellow. If the green light's brightness is reduced, however, the red dominates, and the yellow shifts toward orange. When equal amounts of RGB light are overlapped, the result is white because the original components of white light have been reunited. Varying the brightness of the three overlapping colors of light, however, creates hundreds of colors—such as purple, teal, tangerine, russet, salmon, pink, beige, and citrine.

Producing a range of colors by combining RGB light in various ratios is known as the **additive color system**. The lighting at concerts and theatrical productions uses the additive system, and this system is also used to produce the colors on a television screen and computer monitor. RGB are known as the *primary colors*—the colors from which all

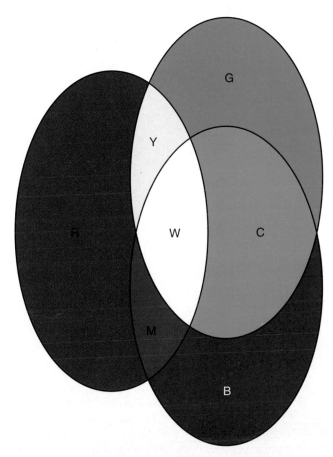

Figure 16-4. Combining equal amounts of RGB light produces white (no color). Combining light involves the additive system. (Southwestern Publishing Co.)

others can be made—because the additive system requires only these colors of light. Combining colors in the additive system always creates a lighter color because light is being added. For example, *magenta* is lighter than either red or blue.

Although the additive color system is at work generating a full range of colors on television screens and computer monitors by combining dots of RGB light, the additive system is restricted to applications combining light. Artists who work with paints and printers who work with ink mix pigments, not light. A different system of creating color is needed.

The Subtractive Color System

Most people who create color work with the *subtractive color system* because their colors are created by mixing pigments. Pigments produce color by absorbing (or subtracting) light. This subtractive system is the opposite of the additive system, in which new colors are created by adding light. Artists using watercolors, children using crayons, and printers using inks are all examples of pigments being used to create colors by selectively absorbing light. Light that has been absorbed is subtracted from the light reflected to the viewer. See **Figure 16-5**. As explained earlier, green grass gets its color because its pigments absorb the red and blue light and reflect only the green light. Similarly, a blue car contains pigments absorbing the red and green light and reflecting only the blue.

The primary colors are different because the subtractive color system works differently than the additive system. In the subtractive system, the primary colors are CMY. See **Figure 16-6**. These colors are all that are necessary to print the wide

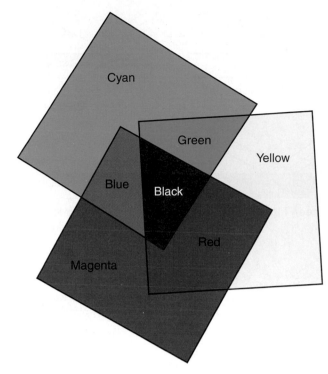

Figure 16-6. As part of the subtractive system, the pigments used in inks absorb light. Therefore, overlapping pigments produces darker colors. Mixing the magenta, yellow, and cyan subtractive primaries in pairs forms RGB. Mixing all three produces black.

range of colors on any magazine cover because they are primary colors.

The key to the subtractive system is that each of its primary colors—CMY—absorbs roughly one-third of the white light striking it. Overlapping any two of the process colors absorbs two-thirds of the white light and reflects only one-third to the viewer. Overlapping all three absorbs nearly all the light, producing nearly black. See **Figure 16-7**.

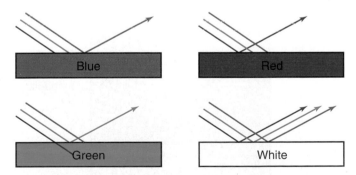

Figure 16-5. Color results from the interaction of light and pigments. Blue ink absorbs the red and green light and reflects the blue light. Green grass absorbs the red and blue light and reflects the green light. Red paint absorbs the green and blue light and reflects only the red light. White reflects nearly all the light and has no color because it contains no pigments. Black has no color because it reflects no light.

pigment: a colorant that does not dissolve, but spreads as tiny particles through liquids or other substances, such as ink.

yellow: a color whose hue bears a resemblance to that of ripe lemons or sunflowers or is that of the part of the spectrum lying between green and orange. This color is light with a wavelength of 570–580 nm.

brightness: a value indicating how light or dark a color is.

lightness: the degree to which colors reflect light.

additive color system: the forming of colors by combining RGB light in various proportions.

magenta: a purplish-red color made by combining equal amounts of red and blue light. This color is a primary color of the subtractive color system.

subtractive color system: the forming of colors by combining CMY pigments.

Yellow

Blue Light Absorbed

Green and Blue Light Absorbed

Magenta

Green Light Absorbed

Blue and Red Light Absorbed

Cyan

Red Light Absorbed

Green and Red Light Absorbed

Figure 16-7. When only the blue light is absorbed, green light and red light are reflected, and the observer perceives yellow. When only green light is absorbed, blue light and red light are reflected to produce magenta. When only red light is absorbed, green light and blue light are reflected. Overlapping magenta and yellow inks absorb both green and blue light and reflect red light. Overlapping cyan and yellow inks absorb both blue and red light and reflect green light. Overlapping magenta and cyan inks absorb both green and red light and reflect blue light.

- An area of *cyan* printed on a page absorbs the red wavelengths of light and reflects back only the blue and green wavelengths forming the color cyan.

- An area of magenta absorbs green and reflects back the blue-red combination (magenta).

- A yellow area absorbs blue light and reflects the red and green wavelengths forming yellow.

- An area printed with black ink (or a black made by combining equal parts of pure CMY) absorbs nearly all the wavelengths. In the same way, a white paper surface reflects all the wavelengths, producing white light.

- Any two of the three subtractive primaries (CMY) can be mixed together in equal proportions to form the additive primaries (RGB). When mixed, cyan and magenta inks absorb both red and green light and reflect only blue. Magenta and yellow combined absorb green and blue light and reflect only red. Yellow and cyan together absorb red and blue light and reflect only green.

As a result of this relationship between the additive and subtractive systems, the primary colors of the subtractive system are the secondary colors of the additive system, and the secondary colors of the subtractive system are the primary colors of the additive system.

Process Color Printing

In *process color printing*, only the three subtractive primary colors (plus black) produce hundreds of colors that are mixed visually, rather than physically. Tiny, closely spaced dots of CMY ink in varying sizes absorb and reflect the different wavelengths of light to produce different colors. The dot size of each ink color controls the amount of color used in a given area. These dots can be seen by looking at any color photograph in this book or a magazine through a magnifying glass. The size of the dots varies to achieve the desired color in each area of the image. See **Figure 16-8.**

As was explained, black can be formed by mixing equal quantities of the subtractive primaries, CMY. In actual practice, however, commercially economical inks are contaminated and do not absorb the full one-third of the light as intended. See **Figure 16-9.** As a result, all three primaries reflect some light. Instead of producing the black that would result with pure CMY inks, real-world inks produce a very dark brown. To achieve a true black, printers use black ink as a fourth ink color. An examination of **Figure 16-10** reveals the greater contrast and sharper detail achieved with the addition of black ink.

In descriptions of color systems, black is designated with the letter *K*. Thus, the four *process colors* are cyan, magenta, yellow, and black (CMYK). Using

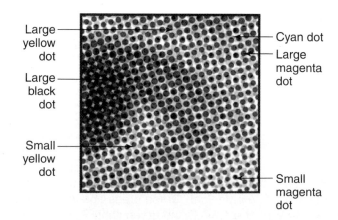

Large yellow dot

Cyan dot

Large magenta dot

Large black dot

Small yellow dot

Small magenta dot

Figure 16-8. This enlargement of a color photograph, which was printed in a book, reveals that the hundreds of colors in the photograph were reproduced with only four colors of ink. (X-Rite, Incorporated)

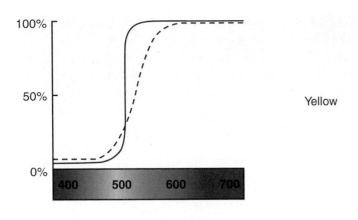

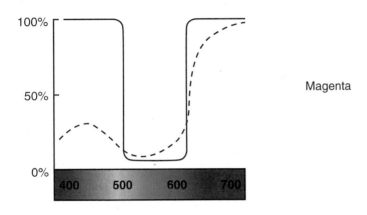

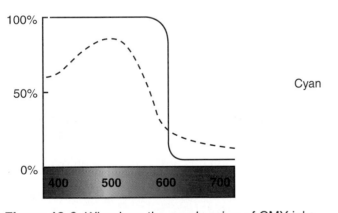

Figure 16-9. Why does the overlapping of CMY inks not produce a true black? Contamination of commercial process inks prevents each ink from absorbing all the light it should. The percentages of visible light reflection are shown as they should be (solid lines) and as they actually are (dotted lines).

black as the fourth color ensures a truer printed black and faster ink-drying time because the presence of black ink requires less of the other three inks. A near black created overlapping the other three colors requires a heavier (and thus slower drying) ink deposit on the paper. Using black ink is also more cost-effective because this ink is less expensive than the color inks.

Color Separation

Color separation is the process of dividing the colors of multicolored original art into the subtractive primary colors and black. See **Figure 16-11**. Traditionally, the *cyan, magenta, yellow, and black (CMYK)* color separations are output as films, which are used to prepare printing plates. Separations can also be made directly to plates electronically. The methods of separating a color photograph into CMYK images have changed greatly since the 1970s, when photographic techniques were dominant. During the late 1970s, photographic methods began to be replaced by large drum scanners, which then gave way in the 1990s to the much smaller flatbed scanners in use today. Although the photographic methods have been replaced in commercial operations, they remain useful in teaching the concepts of color separation because all methods rely on colored filters to distinguish colors in the original art.

Photographic Separation

Photographic color separation can be performed with originals that are either color prints or transparencies. The end product is a set of four halftone negatives, which are used to expose the four CMYK plates. The image is projected through a filter, which transmits the complementary color of the plate being made and absorbs the other colors. For example, to create the negative exposing the cyan plate, a red filter is placed between the original and the film.

It seems strange to students that a red filter is used to make a record of the cyan. The trick to

cyan: a greenish-blue color formed by combining green and blue light. This color is a primary color of the subtractive color system.

process color printing: the printed reproduction of full-color images using the transparent inks of CMYK. This color printing is printing from a series of two or more plates in halftone to produce other colors and shades.

process color: one of the three ink colors (CMY) used for printing full-color materials.

color separation: the process of dividing the colors of a multicolored original into the subtractive, or printing, primaries and black. The CMYK color separations are made into films and used to prepare printing plates.

cyan, magenta, yellow, and black (CMYK): the four process colors.

photographic color separation: separating a full-color photograph or piece of art into the process colors of CMY to film, with the use of color filters.

**The Three-Color Process-
Printing Method**

**The Four-Color Process-
Printing Method**

Figure 16-10. The three-color process-printing method uses yellow, magenta, and cyan process color inks. In this method, black is not used as a printing color. The four-color process-printing method uses yellow, magenta, cyan, and black color inks. The black ink increases density range and improves shadow detail in halftones.

Figure 16-11. These four process printers were created electronically. When the images are combined and printed, they create the four-color image on the right.

understanding the process is to realize that, if the output is film, the film is a negative. Similar to all negatives, it must be the tonal opposite of the plate. That is, it must be clear where the plate is dark. Therefore, in order for the cyan plate to be a record of where the cyan is, the negative must be a record of where the cyan is not. An examination of **Figure 16-4** reveals that cyan is the result of combining equal amounts of green and blue light—or everything but red light. A red filter transmits red light and holds back the green and blue light that make cyan. For this reason, the resulting negative is a record of where everything except cyan is, and the plate it exposes becomes a record of where the cyan is. See **Figure 16-12.**

Following the same principle, the blue filter is used to produce the yellow negative. If an exposure is made with a blue filter, only the blue elements of the copy pass through and expose the film. The black, or exposed, areas of the negative represent the blue areas of the original color copy. The unexposed, or clear, areas of the negative represent the yellow light the blue filter absorbed. When the negative's image transfers to the plate and becomes a positive image, the plate is dark where the original art contains yellow.

The green filter is used to produce the magenta printer. Only the green elements of the copy pass through the green filter and expose the film. The

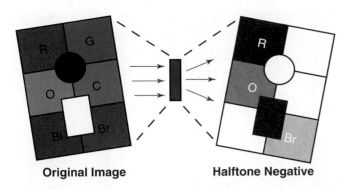

Original Image   **Halftone Negative**

Figure 16-12. When the cyan color-separation negative is made, a red filter absorbs the green and blue light reflected from the art and transmits only the red. The red and white areas cause those areas of the film to become black because they reflect large amounts of red light. The green, cyan, blue, and black areas do not expose the negative because they reflect no red light. For this reason, these areas remain clear. Both orange and brown create halftone dots because small amounts of red light are in these areas. The negative must be the tonal opposite of the plate it will produce later. Therefore, the negative must be a record of where the cyan light is not, so the plate will be a record of where the cyan is. In truth, the negative would be backward and upside-down, relative to the original, but this orientation was not used, to avoid confusing the reader.

exposed areas of the negative represent the green areas of the original. The unexposed areas represent the blue and red light waves the filter absorbed. When the image is printed in positive form with magenta ink (a green-light absorber), only the blue and red light waves reflect. The viewer sees the color magenta. The filter is the complementary (opposite) color of the ink color the plate carries.

The ***black printer***, often referred to as the *skeleton printer* or *detail printer*, can be created by using a neutral density filter, which absorbs small amounts of light across the visible spectrum. This printer is created with white light. Printing a black ink over the three primaries improves and enhances shadow details of the reproduction. The black printer also adds contrast and helps compensate for CMY misregister.

Electronic Separation

Electronic color separation can occur at a high-end drum or flatbed scanner if the output of the scanner is CMYK. A more likely procedure, however, is for the scanner to output an RGB file to a computer workstation for the actual conversion to CMYK with separation and image manipulation software, such as the Adobe Photoshop editor. After the separations are made, they are typically imported into

page-layout software and combined with type and any other images on the page. These files are then sent to a RIP, which translates the information into the raster language of dots (bitmaps) instructing the output device to produce either films or plates.

Using Color-Separation Software

There are several basic considerations in creating professional color separations. These separations should have the proper output resolution, sizing, dot-gain allowance, shadow details, color correction, sharpening, and output format. The *input resolution* describes the ppi of the image as it was created during the scanning operation. The *output resolution* describes the ppi of the image after the RGB-to-CMYK conversion, however, and is the resolution that moves on to the next prepress stage. The output resolution should be 150% of the line value because excessively high resolution merely adds unnecessary data that takes up storage space and reduces operating speed. **Figure 16-13** shows suggested output resolutions for eight screen values.

A photograph's *output size* should equal its size when printed. This *resizing* should occur before the actual separation is performed. For example, imagine that a 10 2/3″ × 7 1/9″ photograph is scanned at 72 ppi and needs to be printed at 7″ × 5″, at 133 lpi. In the Image Size dialog box of the Photoshop editor, the document size represents the input dimensions and resolution. See **Figure 16-14**. The file size is 1.13 MB. To perform the resizing, the smaller of the new dimensions (5″) and the new resolution (200 dpi) are entered, while the Constrain Proportions button is checked. After the changes, the file size is nearly four times as large because of the much-higher, new resolution. The photograph is then cropped so the width becomes 7″. The file size is slightly smaller because of the cropping. At this point, the image's size and resolution are consistent with how it will be printed on press.

black printer: the black component image of process color printing.

electronic color separation: the process of separating the process colors and black with an electronic imaging system.

input resolution: the amount of detail a digital image contains.

output resolution: the amount of detail in an image that a monitor, a printer, or another output device can produce.

output size: the dimensions a digital image becomes when output to a monitor or printer.

resizing: altering the height and width of a digital image, such as a photograph or another graphic.

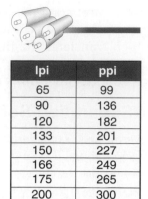

lpi	ppi
65	99
90	136
120	182
133	201
150	227
166	249
175	265
200	300

Figure 16-13. This chart shows the suggested output resolutions (ppi) for eight screen values. Each resolution is approximately 150% of the screen value (lpi).

One constant of the printing process is that halftone dots become larger in diameter during the printing process. The degree of this growth, referred to as *dot gain*, is measured by the difference in size. For example, a 40% dot that becomes a 60% dot experiences a dot gain of 20%. Total dot gain consists of mechanical dot gain—the actual growth of the dot— and optical dot gain—a shadow caused by reflected light. A densitometer measures total dot gain because it reads both mechanical and optical dot gain.

Dot gain creates three problems. Larger dots cause the image to appear darker than intended. Extra darkness causes a loss of detail in the midtones and shadows. When dot gain is inconsistent among the CMYK process colors, color shift occurs. As the name suggests, color shift is a deviation from the original and, therefore, intended color. For example, if the magenta dots grow more than the cyan and yellow dots, skin tones in a photograph move toward red and produce a sunburned look.

This gain occurs in both the prepress and press stages. In conventional platemaking, a 50% dot on the film might grow 5%, to become a 55% dot on the plate. As the dot is transferred from the plate to the blanket and from the blanket to the substrate, the pressure squeezes the dot and causes it to expand further. Depending on the absorbency of the substrate, the dot expands still more if the ink moves outward in the paper's fibers. Press factors that determine the amount of dot gain are ink tack, viscosity, and temperature; the ink-film thickness; and the blanket hardness.

Although dot gain occurs across an entire image, it is most severe in the midtones. See **Figure 16-15.** This pattern is because midtone dots have the greatest circumference and, therefore, the greatest potential for growth. *Dot gain compensation* (also known as

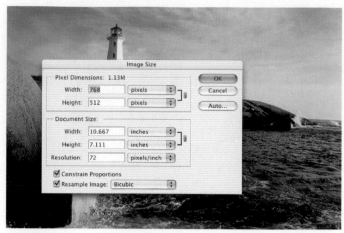

Image Scanned at 72 dpi

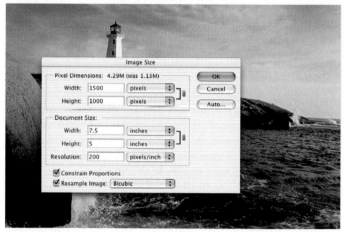

Height Reduced and Resolution Increased

Photograph Cropped

Figure 16-14. This 10.667″ × 7.111″ image was scanned at 72 dpi. After it was reduced to its desired height and its resolution was increased to 200 dpi, the file size grew by more than three times. The cropping tool eliminates unwanted portions of the photograph and brings the width to its proper size. The pixels eliminated by cropping reduce the file size somewhat.

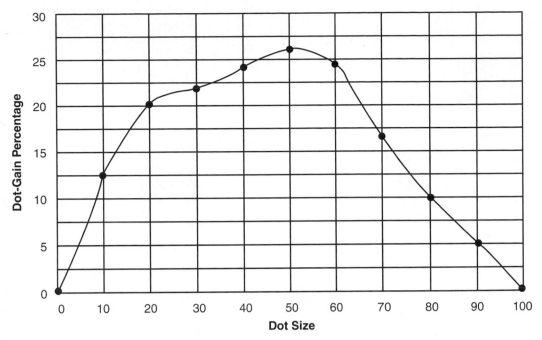

Figure 16-15. The curved line represents the growth of the dot size on the printed sheet. For example, a 10% dot on the plate will grow by 12½ percentage points to become a 22½% dot.

pinch back) occurs in prepress by creating a smaller dot on the film or plate than is needed on the paper.

As was explained earlier in the chapter, commercial CMY inks lack the purity to absorb all the light required for them to create a true black when the three colors are superimposed. Instead, they produce a dark brown. For this reason, black ink is used to create a true black where needed in a photograph.

A second benefit of printing with black ink is its ability to reduce the total amount of ink-film thickness on the paper. Even if process inks were pure enough to produce a true black, printing solid CMY on the same area to create black requires three times as much ink as black ink alone does. For example, if combining 100% cyan, 100% magenta, and 100% yellow produced a true black, the same tone could be produced with 100% black alone. In the same manner, 50% screens of CMY would produce a middle gray, but so does a 50% screen of black only. By using extra black ink in the printing of color photographs, less CMY ink is used, with a decrease in total ink used.

Excessive ink application increases ink costs, slows drying time, and creates problems with ink transfer and image quality. A solid application of all four process inks on the same area of the press sheet produces a 400% coverage. A total-ink percentage limit can be set and achieved by increasing the amount of black ink and reducing the amount of the other three inks for an overall reduction in ink coverage because this much ink can create many

problems. Not only is less ink used, but CMY inks are more expensive than black ink. The most common methods used to produce this effect are undercolor removal (UCR), gray component replacement (GCR), and undercolor addition (UCA).

Undercolor removal (UCR) reduces the amount of CMY applied to the shadow areas and replaces it with an appropriate amount of black. When black replaces equal amounts of CMY, the same effect is achieved with less ink. See **Figure 16-16**. All three inks overlap in the darkest shadows because 400% total ink coverage is being allowed. The power of UCR is demonstrated when the total-ink limit is lowered to 300%. See **Figure 16-17**. The increase in black ink in the shadows improves shadow densities without altering the colors in the image. See **Figure 16-18**. ***Gray component replacement (GCR)*** carries the concept of UCR to a higher level. Whereas UCR replaces CMY inks with black in only the shadow

dot gain compensation: a reduction of the size of dots on a printing plate in anticipation that the size of the dots will grow when they are transferred to the substrate.

undercolor removal (UCR): a technique used to reduce the amount of CMY in shadows and neutral areas of an image and replace it with an appropriate amount of black.

gray component replacement (GCR): an electronic technique used to substitute black ink for calculated amounts of CMY inks to produce a clearer, less muddy image.

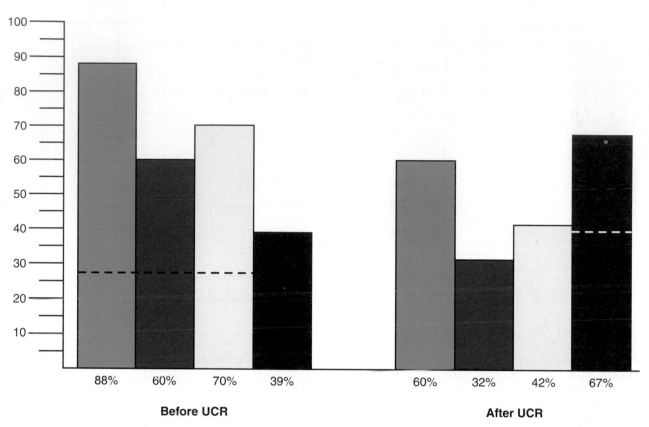

Before UCR **After UCR**

Figure 16-16. UCR replaces equal amounts of the CMY inks with black ink to reduce the total amount of ink used and reduce drying time. In this example, 28% of the CMY (broken line) was removed, and the black was increased by 28% for a net reduction in total ink.

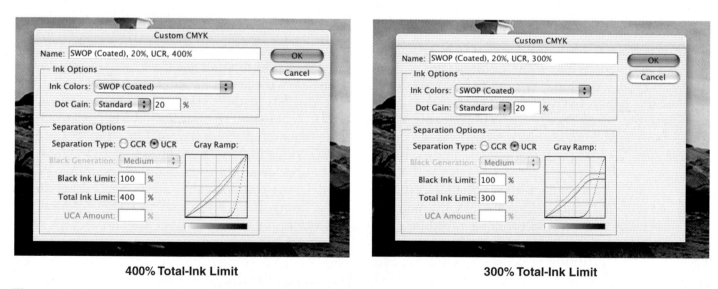

400% Total-Ink Limit **300% Total-Ink Limit**

Figure 16-17. When the total-ink limit is left at 400%, UCR does not significantly reduce ink usage. When the total-ink limit is reduced to 300%, the curve for black begins its rise earlier, and the CMY inks do not exceed 75% in even the darkest shadows.

Printed Photograph **CMY Only** **Black Only**

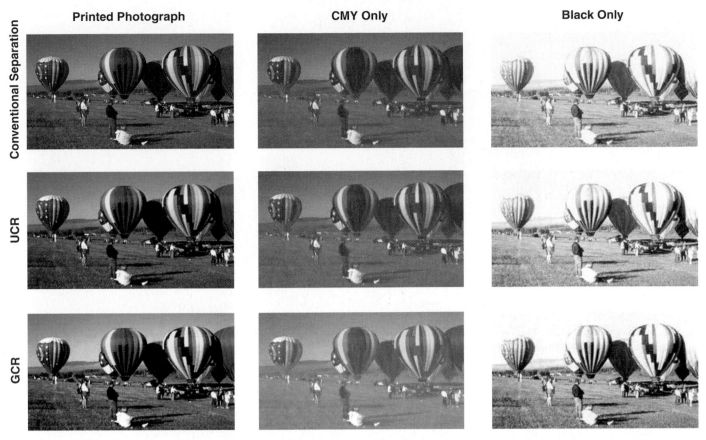

Figure 16-18. The top image received a conventional separation. The CMY inks make up nearly all the highlight and midtone areas, and black ink is used in only the dark shadows. In the second row, the same photograph relies less on the CMY inks and more on the black ink to form the shadows because it received UCR. When GCR is used instead of UCR, even less CMY inks are used in the midtones and shadows. A large amount of black replaces them.

areas, GCR uses black as a substitute for calculated amounts of CMY inks wherever they are used to create a neutral gray in shadows and midtones. See **Figure 16-19.** *Undercolor addition (UCA)* is a means of lightening dark areas of a reproduction and adding warmth or coolness to the dark areas. UCA is the opposite of UCR because it adds CMY back into the shadow area, after removing some of the black. The color added to the black and neutral areas adds warmth. See **Figure 16-20.** The amount of UCA is set in its own field at the bottom of the Custom CMYK dialog box. See **Figure 16-21.**

After specs have been made for the image's output resolution, size, dot gain, and shadow details, the conversion should be made from RGB to CMYK. Just as some image manipulations are best performed in RGB, sharpening is best handled in CMYK. Enhancing the perception of detail by increasing the contrast of an image is known as *sharpening*, and this enhancement should be applied to the image late in the sequence. Although USM is a feature of most scanners, it can also be performed in photo-editing software. See **Figure 16-22.**

Separating with a Spot Color

When CMYK separations are created, there are four separations—one for each color. When a spot color or specialty ink is going to be used in the printing, a fifth separation must be created. Most major page-layout and illustration programs have this capability. All the user needs to do is select one color from the available color-matching systems or create a new color and define it as spot rather than process. This additional color can then be applied to the layout or image. The procedure is the same for a one- or two-color job that does not use CMYK. The colors must always be defined as spot colors to come out on their own separations. The steps below describe one way to create a separation for a specialty

undercolor addition (UCA): a means of lightening dark areas of a reproduction and adding warmth or coldness to the dark areas by adding CMY to the shadow areas after removing some of the black.

sharpening: the software function of creating the illusion of greater sharpness by increasing the contrast at the edges within an image.

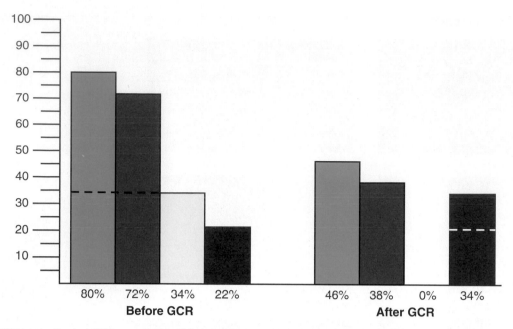

Figure 16-19. GCR is similar to UCR, except black ink replaces a greater amount of the three process inks. Black halftone dots become larger, and the halftone dots of the three process inks become smaller in the midtones, as well as in the shadows.

Before UCA

After UCA

Figure 16-20. UCA is used to increase the warmth in shadows or otherwise replace neutral tones with some color.

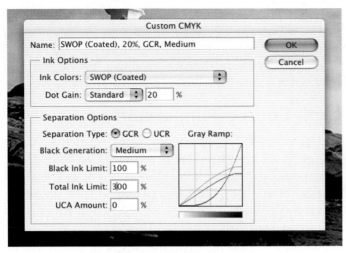
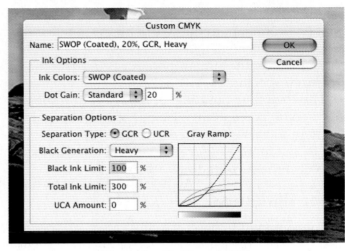

Medium Application of GCR

Heavy Application of GCR

Figure 16-21. GCR can be applied to different degrees. A medium application of GCR lowers the curve of the CMY inks. A heavy application of GCR lowers the CMY curves to an even greater degree because the black curve begins to replace the other three colors in much lighter tones.

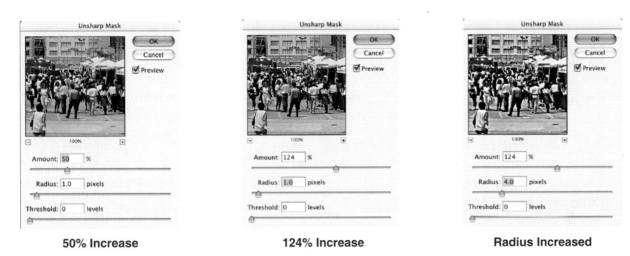

50% Increase   **124% Increase**   **Radius Increased**

Figure 16-22. Note the effect of USM values on this photograph. On the left, the amount of increase is 50%. In the center, the amount of increase is 124%, and the radius is 1.0 pixels. On the right, the radius is increased to 4.0 pixels.

ink or process color. The process varies according to the software and type of ink being used.

1. Convert the image to CMYK, if necessary.
2. Select the areas where the specialty ink will print.
3. Turn the special channel into a spot-color channel.
4. To avoid oversaturation, you might have to decrease the CMYK plates' coverage where the specialty ink will appear.
5. Save the file for output.

Viewing Color Variables

Although the viewing of color is taken for granted, human physiology actually makes the process both complex and inconsistent. The color a person experiences is dependent on many variables. These variables include the eye's tendency to adapt and be affected by adjacent colors, as well as the fact that color perception varies among people.

Adaptation

The adjustment the human eye makes to light conditions is called *adaptation*. When the eyes experience low light for some time, dark adaptation occurs, which means the cones and rods grow more sensitive and light appears brighter. In a similar manner, eyes adapt to the color of light in much the same way, a phenomenon called *chromatic adaptation*. In other words, the human eye adjusts to adapt to the surrounding light.

The colors surrounding, or **adjacent** to, a subject affect color perception. Placing one color against a different background color causes the color to look different. See **Figure 16-23.** A color also looks brighter if the surroundings are dark.

Color Blindness

To compound these variables, not all people view colors in the same way. If people do not have the necessary pigmentation in the cones of their retinas, some light entering the eye is not absorbed fully and not perceived. For example, if some blue-absorbing pigment is missing from a person's cones, that person does not see all wavelengths of blue light. This condition, known as **color blindness**, occurs in varying degrees in 1% of females and 8% of males and causes people to see colors differently.

Color blindness is the inability to distinguish among colors. A person with normal vision has cones that respond to all three of the additive primary colors. A color-blind person lacks one type of cone, two types of cones, or all three types of cones. Most color-blind people have **dichromatic vision** and can see only yellows and blues. They confuse reds with greens and some reds or greens with some yellows. The very few people who are completely color-blind have **achromatic vision** and see only in shades of white, gray, and black.

Vision fatigue is caused by overuse of the vision system and can impair color judgment. Random retinal impulses and involuntary rapid eye movements keep the vision system perpetually active and are essential to accurate vision. Visual acuity suffers when an image becomes optically fixed on the retina. Part of the function of eye movement is to sweep the

light pattern over the receptors to continually signal to the mind the presence of the image. Viewing a saturated color for an extended time causes a second color to appear different because vision fatigue subtracts some of the first color from the image.

Light-Source Temperature

As was explained earlier, light from the sun is made up of roughly equal amounts of RGB light. As a result of this balance, the sunlight is colorless. Sources of artificial light are not as balanced, however, and they produce light with colors, depending on the **color temperature** of the light source.

The concept of color temperature is based on the fact that all objects change color when heated sufficiently. For instance, when metal is heated to high levels, the light emitted changes from red to orange, yellow, and then white. Similarly, various light sources operate at different temperatures and emit light of various colors. **Figure 16-24** lists the approximate color temperatures of common light sources, including the sun, fluorescent lights, household incandescent lightbulbs (tungsten), and candles. The color of light is measured in degrees Kelvin (K).

Color temperature is important in color viewing because the same object viewed under light sources of different temperatures appears different. If you are reading this page under direct sunlight, you see the bright white of the paper. If you are reading this page by candlelight, you see it as a warm yellow. Similarly, because fluorescent lights emit high amounts of green light and incandescent bulbs emit high levels of red light, an object's color likely does not look the same when seen under these different sources.

This phenomenon of a color's shifting under different light sources is known as **metamerism**. Metamerism creates problems when a printer is trying to match a customer-supplied color swatch. The press sheet might match the swatch under the lights of the pressroom, but it might not match when the customer views the finished job in her office. See **Figure 16-25.** Metamerism can be avoided by viewing proofs and press sheets under light sources with consistent color temperature. A common technique is to use **viewing booths** to evaluate color. A viewing booth generating 5000-K light provides color-balanced lighting closely resembling natural light from the sun. See **Figure 16-26.** For this reason, the printing industry has established daylight 5000 K (D_{50}) light as the standard for viewing and assessing color. A second commonly used standard is daylight 6500 K (D_{65}).

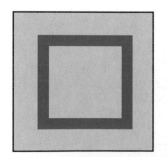

Figure 16-23. The adjacency effect makes a color viewed against a light background appear darker. When the same color is viewed against a dark background, it appears lighter.

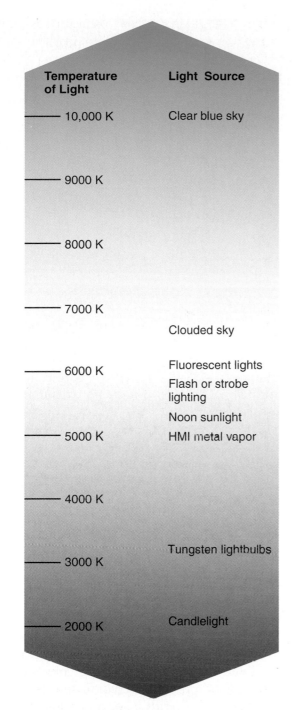

Figure 16-24. Approximate color temperatures of some common light sources.

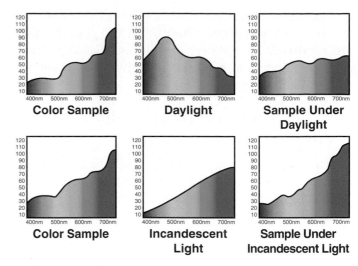

Figure 16-25. Metamerism causes a color to look different under different light sources. A color with a large amount of red reflects large amounts of red light under incandescent light because large amounts of red light are present to be reflected. The same color appears very different under daylight because there is much less red light to be reflected. (X-Rite, Incorporated)

Figure 16-26. Viewing booths with RGB-balanced light are located near the press for comparing original and printed copies. The customer should view proofs under the same type of lighting. (Heidelberg, Inc.)

adjacent: bordering.

color blindness: the inability to tell colors apart.

dichromatic vision: a vision irregularity in which a person can see only yellows and blues.

achromatic vision: a vision irregularity in which a person can see only in shades of white, gray, and black.

vision fatigue: the tiring of the eyes from excessive reading.

color temperature: a means of evaluating color using the temperature to which a black object would need to be heated to produce light of a certain wavelength (or color).

metamerism: the phenomenon of a color appearing differently under light sources with different color balances.

viewing booth: a viewing area with color-balanced lighting so anyone viewing the same printed materials is seeing them under the same lighting conditions.

Defining Color

In addition to the color-viewing variables just examined, there is also the problem of labeling colors. Although there are dozens of words identifying and describing color, words are not nearly precise enough to identify the thousands of available colors. A color one person describes as blue-green might be called *greenish-blue* or *aqua* by another. People have studied the science of color in an attempt to measure it objectively and describe it numerically because much more precise color definition and classification are required. For this reason, various systems have been developed to establish a universal system for color classification.

The Pantone Matching System® Standard

In 1963, Lawrence Herbert came up with the idea of creating a book of standardized colors and formulas for mixing inks to match a client's sample. Until this point, color matching was trial and error, and it was difficult to meet a client's needs. Herbert designed the *Pantone Matching System® standard*, based on the major group of pigment colors (such as reds, yellows, greens, and blues) common to the printing industry, and it became the first color standard accepted in the printing industry. With the Pantone® Formula Guide, a customer or graphic designer can select a color from over 1000 swatches and specify the color's number to the printer, who in turn, can mix inks according to the Pantone formula to achieve the desired color. See **Figure 16-27.**

Today, the Pantone Matching System standard is the most widely used system in the graphic-communications industry. Using a variety of manuals, books, and software products, designers, clients, and printers can effectively communicate color selections over long distances. The manuals and books provide color simulations, names, and mixing formulas. Software programs allow press operators to more accurately match colors a client created and approved on a computer monitor.

Dimensions of Color

It is impossible to verbally describe the appearance of a color in absolute terms. It is possible, however, to describe a color's appearance in terms of its three dimensions: *hue, saturation, and brightness (HSB)*. The HSB dimensions are simply different terms for the characteristics hue, chroma, and value—which were explained in Chapter 7.

According to the HSB color model, the hue is the color the eye perceives. In other words, it is what a person describes as red, green, yellow, or blue. Hues are represented as stations on the color wheel. The dominant wavelengths reflected or transmitted to the eye determine hue. If an ink's pigments absorb blue and green light and reflect red light, its hue is red. Brightness is often referred to as *lightness* or *luminosity* and is defined as a value indicating how light

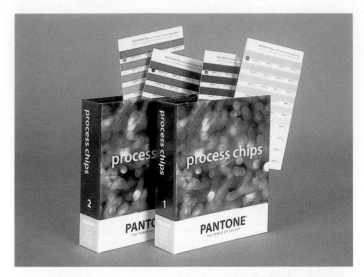

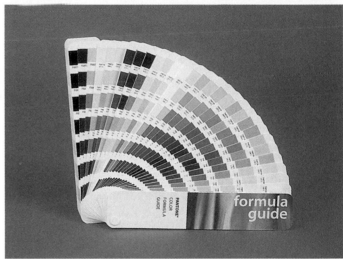

Figure 16-27. There is a variety of products to help avoid problems when reproducing Pantone colors. (Pantone, Inc.)

or dark a color is. If the red ink just mentioned also contains considerable white pigments, it has a high level of brightness and becomes pink. *Saturation* is the attribute of color defining the color's degree of cleanliness, or purity. A color loses its saturation when it is mixed with a second color of a very different hue, black, white, or gray. Green ink loses saturation if it is mixed with orange, black, or white ink. See **Figure 16-28.**

Munsell's HSB color model is one of many methods describing or generating colors with three values. Such models are known as *tristimulus*. Other tristimulus methods are RGB, CMY, and the xyY and LAB models, which will be explained next. Breaking color down into three dimensions was a major step toward describing and specifying colors systematically. There was still no method of mapping a color numerically, however—until 1931.

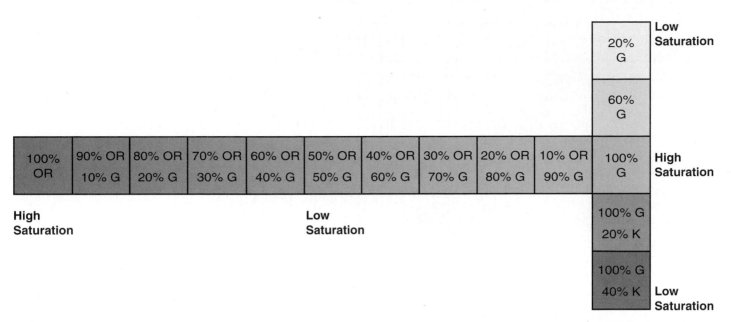

										20% G	Low Saturation
										60% G	
100% OR	90% OR 10% G	80% OR 20% G	70% OR 30% G	60% OR 40% G	50% OR 50% G	40% OR 60% G	30% OR 70% G	20% OR 80% G	10% OR 90% G	100% G	High Saturation

High Saturation   Low Saturation

100% G 20% K

100% G 40% K   Low Saturation

Figure 16-28. Saturation can be reduced by mixing a color (such as orange) with its complementary color (green). This attribute is also reduced when either black or white is added to a color.

The International Commission on Illumination (CIE)

In 1931, the *International Commission on Illumination (CIE)*, or the *Commission Internationale de l'Eclairage*, made two major steps toward measuring color. One was to establish normal human color perception. The other was to create a three-dimensional model to numerically measure the responses of the average human eye to different wavelengths of light.

CIE XYZ values

CIE (pronounced *SEE*) had several people with normal color vision look at a wide range of colors. From their responses, the scientists were able to establish normal human sensitivity to RGB light, which they call the *standard observer*. The eye's sensitivity to RGB light is represented by X, Y, and Z, respectively. The *International Commission on Illumination (CIE) XYZ values* of a color are then used to identify the color. Similar to a fingerprint, the ratio of RGB light making up an individual color is unique. Even today, XYZ values are commonly used as a frame of reference for specifying a color numerically.

The CIE chromaticity diagram

The *International Commission on Illumination (CIE) chromaticity diagram* plots the wavelengths of the visible spectrum in a curve bending across a grid. See **Figure 16-29.** Every color can be mapped on a grid framed by x- and y-axes. For example, a particular orange is found at 0.6 on the x-axis and 0.3

on the y-axis. The A, C, D_{50}, and D_{65} points near the center of the chart represent standard light sources.

The CIE chromaticity diagram uses numerical values to pinpoint the location of a color on three axes—x, y, and Y. To understand how the xyY coordinates work, imagine an airplane flying through the air. If you want to locate the plane precisely, you need only three pieces of data—its latitude, longitude, and altitude. With this system, a color can be specified numerically—no more struggling with

Pantone Matching System® standard: a color book based on the major groups of pigment colors (such as reds, yellows, greens, and blues) common to the printing industry.

saturation: the property of color defining the color's degree of strength, or difference from white. This property is the extent to which one or two of the three additive primaries predominates in a color.

tristimulus: color identification by measuring the amount of the three primary additive colors making up a color.

International Commission on Illumination (CIE): an international organization that establishes specs for the description of color, used as the basis of all color.

International Commission on Illumination (CIE) XYZ value: a method of identifying a color by the amount of RGB light making up the color.

International Commission on Illumination (CIE) chromaticity diagram: a diagram with a plotted curve defining the visible spectrum on an X-Y chart.

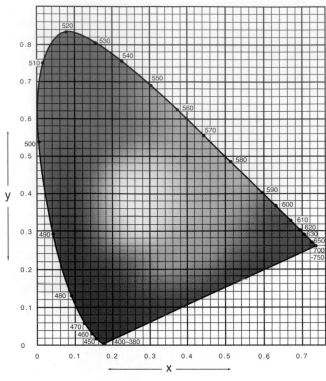

Hue and Saturation Levels

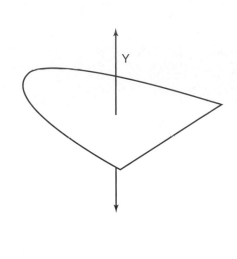

Brightness Levels

Figure 16-29. The CIE chromaticity chart plots the wavelengths of the visible spectrum on a grid. Colors can now be identified by their coordinates on the x- and y-axes. Moving across the horseshoe portion of the chart results in changes in hue. The highest saturation levels are along the outside of the diagram, so moving toward the center reduces saturation. Brightness levels are measured on the Y-axis, which is perpendicular to the x-y plane. Therefore, any visible color can be identified by its x, y, and Y values.

subjective terms, such as *bluish green*. These values, or coordinates, define the **color space**, a three-dimensional representation of color as numerical data. The term *space* is used because color data occurs in three dimensions.

The CIELAB system

In 1976, the Commission Internationale de l'Eclairage, or CIE, developed the **CIELAB system**. Similar to the xyY chromaticity diagram, the CIELAB (pronounced *SEE-lab*) model locates a color on three intersecting axes. The vertical axis (L) represents lightness. A horizontal axis (A) has green at one end and red at the other. A bisecting horizontal axis (B) has blue at one end and yellow at the other. See **Figure 16-30.** CIELAB is also represented as CIE L*a*b and CIE Lab.

The simplicity of CIELAB is based on the fact that a color cannot share the complementary colors of red and green. As a result, a color containing some red has a positive A value (up to +100). If it has some green in it, it has a negative A-axis value (down to –100). Similarly, if the same color has some yellow in it, it will have a positive B-axis value (up to +100). If

it has some blue in it, it will have a negative B value (down to –100). The L-axis values range from 0, for black, to 100, for white—so light colors have L values over 50, and darker colors have L values below 50. For example, examine the six colors and their LAB values shown in **Figure 16-31.** The values for pure white are L = 100, A = 0, and B = 0. The values for pure black are L = 0, A = 0, and B = 0.

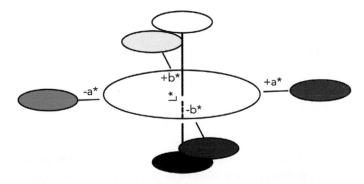

Figure 16-30. CIELAB allows any color to be identified by its values on three axes. L measures its lightness or darkness, A measures its content of green or red, and B measures its content of yellow or blue. (X-Rite, Incorporated)

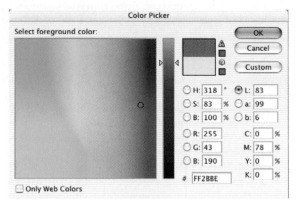

Pink

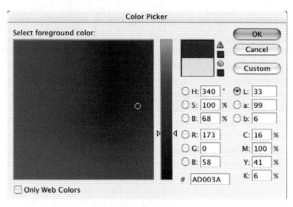

Dark Red

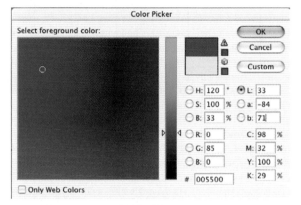

Dark Green

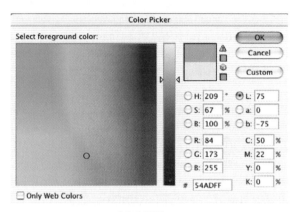

Light Blue

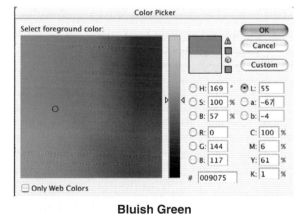

Bluish Green

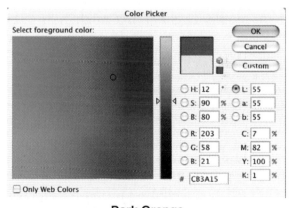

Dark Orange

Figure 16-31. Six colors and their CIELAB values are shown.

An examination of **Figure 16-31** reveals that a color can be defined by four different models—HSB, RGB, LAB, and CMYK. Of these, the CIELAB color model has become an international standard for specifying color with a system that is not dependent on a particular device, such as an individual monitor's version of RGB or a specific press's application of CMYK. In other words, when a color is specified with CIELAB values, it is defined in a pure and universally understood manner. Such a system is termed *device*

color space: a three-dimensional coordinate system that plots three different color qualities on three axes, allowing color samples to be quantitatively measured, plotted, and described by a single point located somewhere on the coordinate system.

CIELAB system: a method of identifying a color by the values on three axes formed by opposing colors (red-green, blue-yellow, and black-white).

independent. Defining a color in CIELAB is at the heart of color management—the process of ensuring that computer monitors, proofers, and printing presses generate the same colors for a job.

Measuring Color

In the twenty-first century, color evaluation is both visual and numerical. The viewing variables just studied require a standardized method of measuring color. As has been explained, color cannot be described and managed unless it can be measured numerically. Instruments for measuring color vary in their approach to this task. Some measure color values, some measure light waves, and others measure density. The most common color-measuring instruments are colorimeters, spectrophotometers, densitometers, and spectrodensitometers.

Colorimeters

The three distinct values must be measurable because the CIELAB model views color as a combination of those three components. *Colorimeters* measure color by generating numerical data that pinpoints a sample on the three CIELAB axes described earlier in this chapter. These axes are the white-black axis, the green-red axis, and the blue-yellow axis, and each number indicates the sample's position on an axis. For example, a light orange might have CIELAB measurements of L = 80, A = 55, and B = 55. A dark green's measurements can be 33, -80, and 70, respectively. A portion of a rose petal is found to be L = 51.18, A = 29.53, and B = 48.88. See **Figure 16-32.**

With a colorimeter, a customer-supplied color image or sample can be measured, and its tristimulus values can be used as a basis of comparison when the same image appears on a monitor, a proof, and the final printed press sheet. An understanding of the CIELAB model allows the prepress operator to know what adjustments are needed to bring the color back to its original values. CIELAB values are based on the tristimulus concept affecting human color perception. In other words, a colorimeter assesses a color in terms of how a human observer perceives it.

Spectrophotometers

The *spectrophotometer* measures light reflectance across the visible spectrum. This instrument measures a color by plotting a curve revealing the amount of light in each wavelength area reflected from a sample. To illustrate how this contour line defines a color, a spectrophotometer is used to read

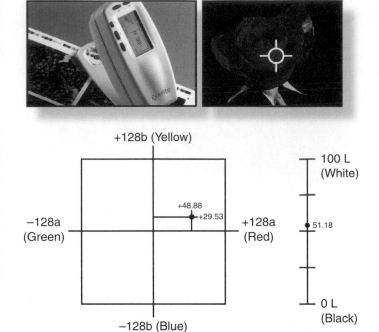

Figure 16-32. A colorimeter quantifies color by displaying its CIELAB values. The red rose petal has the following values: L = 51.18, A = 29.53, and B = 48.88. (X-Rite, Incorporated)

a different portion of the red rose. See **Figure 16-33.** The dots in the curve indicate the percentage of light reflected for that wavelength. A reading is made every 10 nm. The curve indicates modest (26–37%) reflectance of blue light, very little (9–12%) reflectance of green light, and considerable (as high as 71%) reflectance of red light.

The overall curve is comparatively low on the scale because the color being read is a dark red. A lighter red reflects more light and places the curve higher on the scale. For example, if a spectrophotometer were used to measure three very different skin tones, the curves would be at different levels because light skin reflects more light than dark and very dark skin. See **Figure 16-34.** All three skin tones are made up of more red light than any other.

Unlike colorimeters, spectrophotometers do not describe the colors in terms of the tristimulus effect a person viewing the samples perceives. Spectrophotometric curves accurately describe the reflectance of the sample, however, and are very useful in color matching. A client-supplied sample can be measured, and its curve can be graphed and compared with the curve of an ink mixed to match it. Differences between the two curves indicate how the ink can be modified to match more closely.

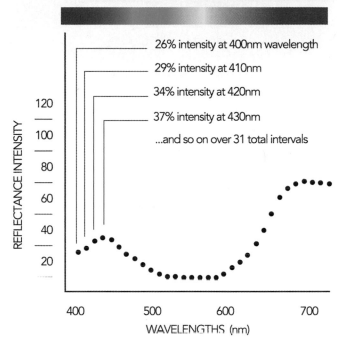

26% intensity at 400nm wavelength

29% intensity at 410nm

34% intensity at 420nm

37% intensity at 430nm

...and so on over 31 total intervals

Figure 16-33. Instead of measuring color numerically, a spectrophotometer profiles it by plotting a curve of its wavelength reflection. (X-Rite, Incorporated)

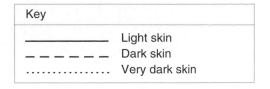

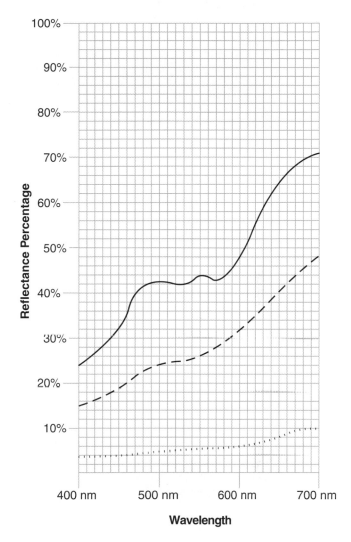

Figure 16-34. The spectrophotometric curves on this graph illustrate the reflectance of light skin, dark skin, and very dark skin.

Densitometers

Although *densitometers* do not measure color, their ability to measure optical density makes them useful in maintaining color consistency throughout a pressrun. Optical density is the light-absorption ability of an image or a surface material. A densitometer uses RGB filters to isolate broad bands of light about 55 nm wide. Depending on the type being used, densitometers can be used on negative or positive transparencies, photographs, or printed images. Reflection densitometers measure the amount of light bouncing off a photographic print or printed sheet at a 90° angle. Transmission densitometers measure the fraction of incident light conveyed through a negative or positive transparency without being absorbed or scattered. Combination densitometers measure both reflection and transmission densities.

A handheld densitometer is used in the pressroom to read the color bars of sample press sheets to ensure consistent color throughout the run by measuring ink density. See **Figure 16-35.** Changes in the ink film thickness during the run affect the color of a process color job. For example, if the magenta ink film thickness starts to increase during the run, the extra magenta imparts a warm or reddish hue to the photograph. Reading ink densities on sample press sheets and adjusting the press when density changes are found can prevent this problem.

A scanning densitometer automates the measurement of press-sheet color bars. See **Figure 16-36.** Scanning densitometers provide these values conveniently and easily by moving across the color bar and immediately displaying the results signaling density

Figure 16-35. Densitometers measure the density of color bars to ensure consistent color across a press sheet. (X-Rite, Incorporated)

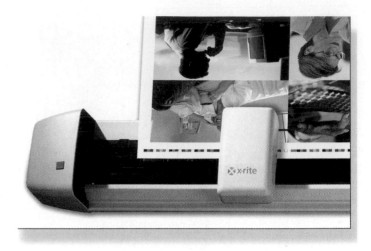

Figure 16-36. Scanning densitometers are installed on-line and allow quick and accurate color measurement. (X-Rite, Incorporated)

changes. Target reference values are easily set for each swatch on the color bar. The reference value might be a standard value, such as a density of 1.30, for a solid magenta swatch, or the recorded values from an approved sheet scan. A typical color bar is shown in **Figure 16-37.**

An examination of **Figure 16-38** reveals the function of a densitometer being used to measure ink film density. From a stabilized light source, the light passes through a lens, where it is focused to fall on the printed surface. Depending on the ink film

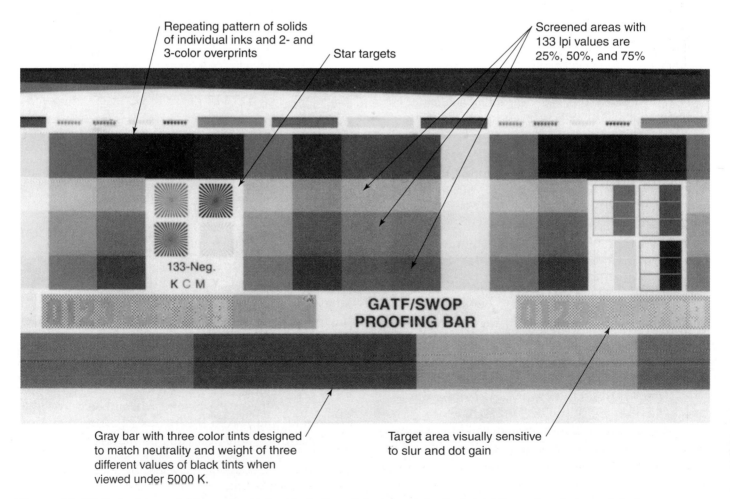

Repeating pattern of solids of individual inks and 2- and 3-color overprints

Star targets

Screened areas with 133 lpi values are 25%, 50%, and 75%

133-Neg.
K C M

GATF/SWOP PROOFING BAR

Gray bar with three color tints designed to match neutrality and weight of three different values of black tints when viewed under 5000 K.

Target area visually sensitive to slur and dot gain

Figure 16-37. Color bars might vary in design, but all contain a swatch of each of the colors being printed.

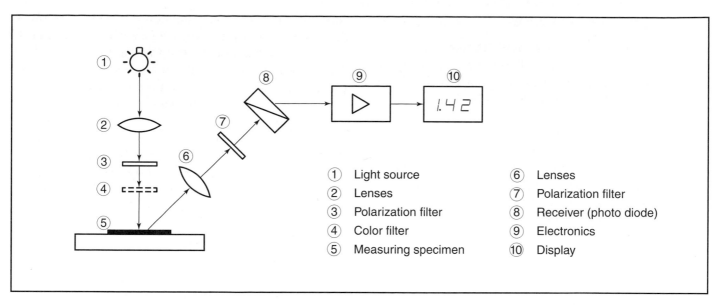

①	Light source		⑥	Lenses
②	Lenses		⑦	Polarization filter
③	Polarization filter		⑧	Receiver (photo diode)
④	Color filter		⑨	Electronics
⑤	Measuring specimen		⑩	Display

Figure 16-38. This schematic diagram illustrates the operating principles of a densitometer. (Heidelberg, Inc.)

thickness and the pigmentation of the ink involved, part of the light is absorbed. The nonabsorbed portion of the light passes through the ink film and is reflected by the surface of the printed paper. A lens system now captures those light rays returning from the ink film at an angle of 45° to the measuring ray and passes them to a photodiode receiver.

The quantity of light the photodiode receives is converted into electricity. The electronics now compare this measuring current with a reference value (reflectance for an absolute white). The difference obtained is the basis for calculating the absorption characteristics of the ink film being measured. The result of the ink-film measurement is shown in the display as a logarithmic number that gives the ratio of the absorbed light for an absolute white to that obtained from the measured ink film.

Color filters in the ray path restrict the light to the wavelengths relevant for the printing ink in question. In addition, some densitometers incorporate polarization filters in the path of the ray, in order to prevent significant differences between dry and wet printing ink. The surfaces of wet and dry printing inks reflect light differently. With freshly printed ink, the smooth surface of the ink reflects a greater proportion of the light the light source emits than when the ink is dry, and therefore, the receiver detects less light.

In order to eliminate the influence of the ink film surface on the measurement results, linear polarization filters are inserted in the path of the rays. These polarization filters allow the light of only one particular vibration direction to pass, while stopping all light waves vibrating in other directions. The ink surface also partially reflects the light rays the polarization filter polarizes, without altering their polarization. See **Figure 16-39.** If this polarized light is now passed through a second polarization filter aligned at an angle of 90°, the light rays cannot pass through the filter. This is because the filter lies on a different polarization plane and, therefore, cannot influence the measurement. Light rays penetrating into the ink film as far as the printing paper and then reflected lose their original polarization and are, therefore, able to pass through the second filter. Hence, only rays that the ink film thickness has influenced (and are, therefore, necessary for the measurement) reach the receiver.

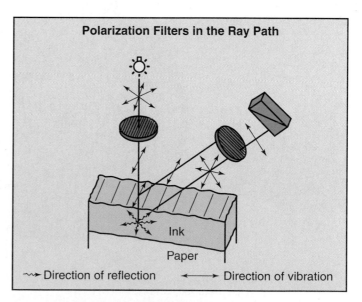

Figure 16-39. The ink surface partially reflects the light rays that the polarization filter polarizes, without altering their polarization. (Heidelberg, Inc.)

Spectrodensitometers

Spectrodensitometers are densitometers that can measure light across the visible spectrum by using a prism or diffraction grating to spread the light and a slit to isolate narrow bands of light between 1 nm and 10 nm. These densitometers are able to measure ink film densities of spot (nonprocess) colors. A spectrodensitometer can serve all the functions of a densitometer and colorimeter in a single instrument. Besides measuring color value and optical density, many instruments can also measure paper attributes and special colors. Unlike the spectrophotometer, the output of the spectrodensitometer is numbers, not curves.

Measuring Color Variation

After a system to measure color has been adopted, the next step is to measure color variation. The degree of difference between the client-supplied swatch and its reproduction on a given proof or press sheet can be expressed numerically as ΔE (pronounced *delta E*) units. The number of ΔE units indicates how far apart the color has drifted from the target. Research suggests that 1 ΔE represents the amount of color shift a person can detect, but staying within 6 ΔEs is often considered acceptable printing.

Color can drift in on the L axis, the A axis, the B axis, or a combination of the three because CIELAB measures colors on three axes. As a result, the ΔE model is also three-dimensional. See **Figure 16-40.** The black dot in the middle of the sphere represents the correct color—the intersection of the LAB axes. The black dot in the upper right of the sphere represents a slight shift from the original color. This second color can result from a color shift occurring on the monitor, proof sheet, or press sheet. The sphere itself represents the customer's tolerance for deviation from the actual color. The second dot is not deviating from the original enough for the customer to see the difference because it is within the sphere. In other words, it is within that customer's tolerance. The black dot outside the sphere represents a color that deviates more than the acceptable ΔE units from the original and is unacceptable. The number of ΔE units defining acceptable color reproduction varies from customer to customer. The value of the ΔE is that it allows an individual customer's color tolerance to be measured and expressed numerically.

The human perception of color difference is not consistent across the color wheel. That is, the human observer is able to see tiny variations among oranges that go unnoticed with greens. In short, human color perception is more acute with oranges than greens. In addition, humans detect shifts in hue quicker than shifts in lightness. See **Figure 16-41.** For this reason, the ΔE sphere is actually an ellipse, instead of a perfect sphere.

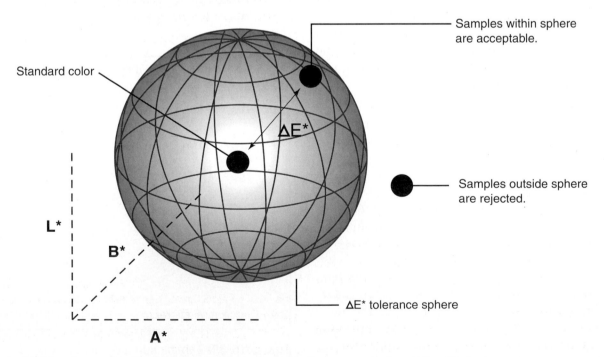

Figure 16-40. The three-dimensional ΔE space represents the amount of variation that can occur on any one of the LAB axes before the difference can be detected. (X-Rite, Incorporated)

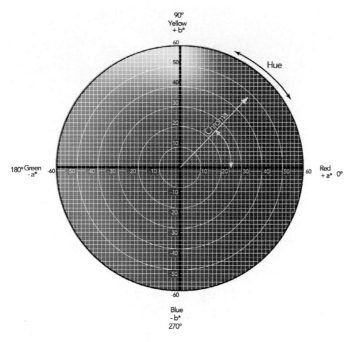

Figure 16-41. This illustration represents how human color tolerances vary. Hue changes in green are less noticeable than in orange, and hue changes are more noticeable than changes in lightness. (X-Rite, Incorporated)

Color Gamuts

The range of colors that can be generated within a color system is called a ***color gamut***, and different systems have different color-gamut sizes. See **Figure 16-42.** The largest color gamut exists in the realm of human vision. A smaller gamut is possible with color film, which means some colors people can perceive with their eyes cannot be captured on color film. Some colors appearing on a color transparency cannot be created on a monitor, and some colors appearing on the monitor cannot be reproduced precisely with the CMYK inks of a printing press. This does not mean a color such as lime green cannot be printed with a press. It simply means a particularly bright lime green might not be reproduced precisely on a press. The loss is seldom noticeable.

Process color, also known as *four color* or *full color,* is the faithful reproduction of color photographs or other art containing colors. In general terms, the wide range of colors making up a color photograph can be reproduced with only four ink colors, referred to as *process ink colors*. This amazing accomplishment results from controlling the absorption and reflection of light by colorants.

Colorants are chemical substances that give color to such materials as ink, paint, and crayons. Such substances that dissolve in liquids are dyes. Colorants that do not dissolve but are distributed

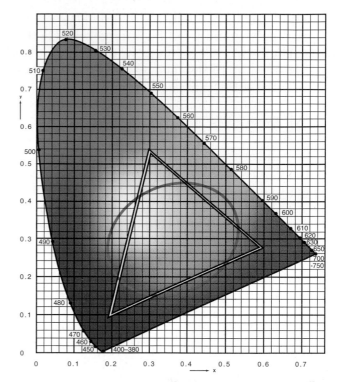

Figure 16-42. The range of possible colors is a gamut. The gamuts of human vision, a color transparency, RGB, and CMYK become progressively smaller. The entire chromaticity chart represents the human vision gamut. The triangle represents the gamut of an RGB monitor. The circle represents the gamut of CMYK on a proofer or press.

as tiny solid particles through a vehicle are called *pigments*. Printing inks use pigments because they are more fade resistant than dyes. A still smaller gamut is available with the RGB of a television screen or computer monitor, and an even smaller gamut is possible with the CMYK inks of process printing. Fortunately, process printing can produce around 1 million distinct colors, so this reduced ability to reproduce colors is too subtle to create a problem for average viewers. Nonetheless, not every color on a color slide can be reproduced on a computer monitor, and not every color seen on the monitor can be created on press.

The color gamut achievable on a printing press using CMYK inks can be enhanced by using three additional colors of ink, a process called *hi-fi color*. By

color gamut: the total range of colors that can be defined by a color model or reproduced with a given set of colorants, on a given paper, and on a given printing press.

colorant: a dye or pigment that gives color to materials such as ink, paint, crayons, and chalk.

hi-fi color: using more inks than CMYK to reproduce a full-color photograph or another graphic.

supplementing CMYK with red, blue, and green inks, the press color gamut can be enlarged to 1,300,000 colors. The extra cost involved in using seven inks, however, usually limits their use to printing photographs with highly saturated colors.

Color Proofs

After the original color image has been separated into its CMYK components, proofs are prepared to check the quality of the separation. A proof is a preview of the printed job, and it allows the printer and the customer to see what the job will look like after the job comes off the press and provides the opportunity to make alterations before the actual pressrun. Soft proofs are simply an examination of the job on a computer monitor. Although soft proofing is quick and economical, the colors on the screen are useful only if the monitor has been properly calibrated. In addition, the RGB colors on the screen are not the CMYK inks that will be used on press. Hard proofs consist of ink or toner on paper and can be made digitally from electronic data, photochemically from film and dyes, or from printing with the actual plates.

Proofs made from film and dyes or electronic data are *prepress proofs*. Those made from the actual plates after they have been mounted on the press are *press proofs*. High-quality prepress proofs can predict the colors of the finished job so well that the printer can use them to accurately predict how the finished job will look and eliminate the need for press proofs. These proofs are called *contract color proofs*.

Depending on the complexity of a project and the arrangement made with the customer, a printing company might produce proofs at more than one stage of production before the job goes to press. Proofs are generated for performing corrections (text, layout, and color) and to avoid visual surprises when the job is delivered to the customer. See **Figure 16-43**. Besides confirming that layout, fonts, and other design elements were not lost or deformed before reaching the output stage, proofs should be checked for color accuracy, resolution, and registration. *Registration* is the overall agreement in the position and alignment of printing detail on a press sheet.

Analog Proofs

Photomechanical proofing systems are categorized into single-sheet, or laminate, color-proofing systems and overlay color-proofing systems. The advantage of single-sheet, or laminate, proofing is that

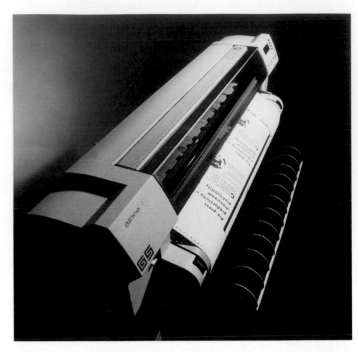

Figure 16-43. A signature proofer prints on both sides of the substrate. (Gerber Systems Corp.)

the viewing light is reflected from a single surface, and light refraction is limited. Film-generated proofs include Matchprint® proofs, bluelines (diazo), the Cromalin® system, and Color-Key® proofs.

- *Matchprint® proofs* are four-color proofs produced from the film that will be used to create the printed pages. They enable accurate evaluation of the film for trapping, moiré, and other printing problems.

- *Color-Key® proofs* are transparent sheets imaged from film and then physically fastened together in register. Proofs can be made from each process color separation or from mechanically separated art to show spot color.

Digital Proofs

When a printing company adopts a CTP work flow, it eliminates the films from which plates and analog proofs have traditionally been made. Without films, proofs are generated directly from digital code, a process called *digital proofing*. Depending on the system's capabilities, digital proofs can simulate results from any type of printing press. Most dye sublimation printers and ink-jet printers are able to simulate both process inks and spot colors. Iris, Agfa® Sherpa 43, and Gerber are examples of ink-jet proofers. These machines produce dotless color images closely simulating the press sheet, at a much lower cost than conventional methods. See **Figure 16-44.**

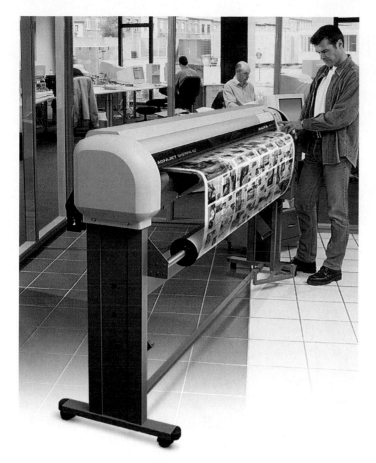

Figure 16-44. Although contract proofs can be either analog or digital, their requirement is that they predict the color of the finished job very closely. (Agfa-Gevaert Inc.)

Some digital proofing systems, such as the PolaProof system, can simulate dot patterns and the dot gain expected on final output. This capability is especially useful because most customers insist on seeing the halftone dots or screen pattern before accepting the proof as a true indication of color and quality. Many digital output devices can be connected to the same RIP that runs the platesetter and output halftone patterns identical to those that will appear on the final sheet.

Some electrostatic printers and high-quality printers and copiers can also simulate the printing inks of a press. They are commonly used for proof production, as well as short-run impressions of finished color printing. The same process used to calibrate printers is used for calibrating proofing devices.

Press Proofs

For some jobs, offset plates are made and run on four-color proof presses to create press proofs. A *proof press* is a printing machine used to produce press proofs, which are proofs printed from plates

prepared from film. This press has most of the elements of a true production machine, but it is not meant for long pressruns. See **Figure 16-45.**

A proof press uses two large cylinders called the *plate cylinder* and the *blanket cylinder.* The plate cylinder holds all four offset plates. The blanket cylinder transfers each ink color to the sheet of paper. A third cylinder, called the *impression cylinder,* makes four revolutions per sheet. This is required to print all four colors in register. Press proofs might be some of the best verification proofs, but press proofing is slow and expensive.

Printing companies without a proof press can have the client present at the start of the pressrun and pull a press sheet for client inspection. These press proofs are the most expensive because of the hourly cost of the long-run press, which must stop production if the client orders color changes requiring new plates to be made and mounted. As was explained earlier in this chapter, color proofs should be viewed under a common light source because any variation in the quality of light affects color perception. Many problems result when the printer and customer use different light sources for viewing the proofs.

Color Correction

Some of the biggest challenges in the printing industry are getting color to reproduce the way it should and even predicting what the printed colors will look like. Color correction is complex because color functions are interconnected. For example, in an RGB system, a change in value changes chroma. For a brighter, more saturated red, the percentages of all three of the primary colors must be adjusted. To merely increase the percentage of red can increase

prepress proof: a proof made from film and dyes or electronic data before the pressrun.

press proof: a proof run on a proof press using the printing inks and substrate for the actual job.

contract color proof: a color proof serving as the basis for whether or not a printing job is acceptable to the customer.

registration: overall agreement in the position and alignment of printing detail on a press sheet.

Matchprint® proof: a color proof produced from the actual film that will create the printed page.

Color-Key® proof: a proof made with transparent sheets imaged from film and then physically fastened together in register.

proof press: a printing machine used to produce photomechanical proofs.

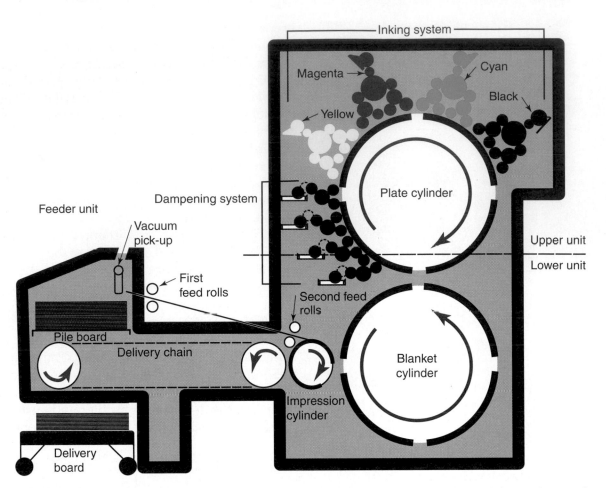

Figure 16-45. This is a four-color proof press. If approval for a color job requires proofing on a four-color proof press, the same plates, paper, and inks that will be used for the actual pressrun should be used to make the proof.

lightness as well. To achieve a brighter red in a CMYK system, the cyan and black need to be reduced, and the yellow and magenta need to be increased.

Color correction is now performed almost exclusively electronically with photo-editing software, such as the Photoshop editor and Paint Shop Pro software. Imaging programs provide tools and filters for setting highlights and shadows, adjusting midtones and color balance, modifying hue and saturation values, sharpening images, and changing brightness and contrast. Although most imaging programs allow the user to perform these types of adjustments, the results in the pressroom still best determine the need for and amount of color correction.

Color Sequencing on Press

In process color printing, the *color sequence,* laydown sequence, or printing sequence is the order in which the colors of ink are printed. In offset lithography, the most common printing sequence on a four-color press is black, cyan, magenta, and yellow. See **Figure 16-46.**

Originally, the standard printing sequence used was yellow, magenta, cyan, and black. This sequence was used for the sake of cleanliness. Yellow is fairly transparent and is muddied if it is printed after the darker or stronger colors. Today, the color sequence used for printing depends on several factors, including the desired ink coverage, the job, the printing process (sheet or web), the substrate, and the type of ink.

The amount of ink coverage needed of each particular color is the most important factor. For example, on a web-fed press, a greater amount of yellow is needed to get sharp, bright colors. Therefore, yellow is the last color printed. If yellow were printed first, printing the other colors on such a thick ink film would be similar to printing "on butter."

Deviations in the color sequence often depend on the predominant color of the job. For example, if cyan is the dominant color of a printed piece (a poster consisting mainly of blue sky), it might be desirable to modify the color sequence and print the cyan last. See **Figure 16-47.** Color sequence is a factor in the formulation of ink. For this reason, ink

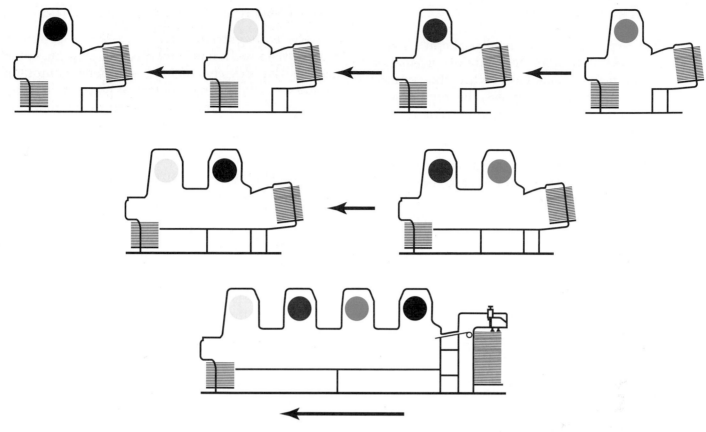

Figure 16-46. The color sequence used depends on many factors, including the desired ink coverage, the job, the printing process, the substrate, the type of ink, and the tack of the ink. (Heidelberg, Inc.)

Standardized Color Sequence for Proofing and Production Run		
Four-color print wet-on-wet	Two-color print wet-on-wet	One-color print wet-on-dry proof press
Four-color press	Two-color press	Single-color press
K + C + M + Y	C + M; K + Y	C; M; Y; K or K; C; M; Y
Special Case Color Sequence for Proofing and Production Run		
Four-color print wet-on-wet	Two-color print wet-on-wet	One-color print wet-on-dry proof press
Four-color press	Two-color press	Single-color press
K + C + M + Y	M + C; K + Y	M; C; Y; (K)

K: black; C: cyan; M: magenta; y: yellow

Figure 16-47. Various standardized printing sequences for single-, two-, and four-color presses. (Heidelberg, Inc.)

manufacturers should be made aware of the color sequence for a given job so each ink color can be formulated to perform well on press.

Color Sequencing on Proof

Depending on the type of proof being generated, color sequencing might not apply. Film-generated and digital proofs do not operate on the same principle as press proofs. Therefore, it is not necessary, and sometimes not even possible, to use the same color sequence that will be used on the press. If a press proof is being used, however, it is wise to use the same color sequence that will be used on the final pressrun.

color sequence: in process color printing, the order in which the colors of ink are printed.

Color Management

As was explained earlier in this chapter, maintaining the original color throughout production is one of the major challenges within the printing industry. In conventional prepress, the key to maintaining accurate color and avoiding color drift is the halftone negative. The dot sizes on the negatives generate the dots on the analog proofs. If color corrections are needed, new negatives are made until the proof is acceptable to the customer. These films are then used to generate the dots on the plates. Therefore, if the proofs have good color, the plates are likely to produce good color on press.

The advent of a completely electronic prepress has eliminated the films, however, and replaced them with scanners, software, monitors, proofers, and platesetters. Each of these components of prepress production is a common cause of *color drift*. This drift is any variation in hue, saturation, or lightness that occurs when a color image moves from one electronic-prepress device to another.

Color drift is a very common occurrence for several reasons. Imagine that a continuous tone color print is scanned. The scanner converts the colors of the photograph into RGB channels, and this transformation is an opportunity for color drift. The digital file is then displayed on a computer monitor. As anyone who has been to an appliance or electronics store and seen a wall of televisions displaying the same broadcast or DVD movie knows, the same image can look very different from one screen to another. Therefore, the monitor itself can produce color drift.

Next, the image can be manipulated with photo-editing software and then placed within a document with page composition software, which converts the data into its own language. The image is also separated—converted from RGB to CMYK. These transitions can produce color drift as well. The next likely step is for the image to be sent to a CMYK-proofing device that applies inks to paper, which is a very different medium than any of the previous displays and still another opportunity for color drift. If the customer accepts the proof, the image is sent to a RIP, which converts it to still another computer language. This language transforms the image into halftone dots, which are then sent to a platesetter. The platesetter images the plates. These four stages are also common sources for color drift. Finally, the four plates are mounted onto a press, which prints the image onto press sheets by overlaying the four process inks.

Color Management Software (CMS)

Color management software (CMS) is designed to coordinate each device involved in printing color images. The devices include scanners, computer monitors, proofers, imagesetters or platesetters, and the press itself. Without CMS, the different color responses of these devices result in an inconsistent display of the image.

In basic terms, CMS assesses each device in the work flow. That is, it sends an image with known color values through the prepress stages and compares the output of each device with the color values of the original image. For example, a scanner might make photographs look too blue, or a proofer might make them look too red.

After the CMS discovers these device idiosyncrasies, it makes allowances for them. For example, it can automatically remove the extra blue the scanner captures so the blue is not passed onto the next stage. CMS can also prevent the proofer from applying the extra red ink onto the proof. This calibration process is applied to software as well as hardware, with the result that the colors of the original photograph appear the same on the monitor, the proof, and the printed sheet.

At the heart of every stage of color management are the device-independent color values—usually CIELAB. Describing color in CIELAB values at every stage of production creates a common language that allows the software to move between very different systems, such as RGB and CMYK. See **Figure 16-48.**

In addition to CMS, the function of controlling color is enhanced by the *International Color Consortium (ICC)*. Founded in 1993, the ICC promotes the creation and use of universal color management systems—that is, cross-platform and device-independent systems. ICC-compliant input devices, display devices, and output devices can seamlessly transfer color data, even if the three devices use different color spaces—such as CIE based, RGB based, or CMY based. Scanners, computers, monitors, proofers, and RIPs can work in harmony because they can translate data defined by one color space (for example, RGB) into another color space (for example, CIELAB) without color drift.

Calibration and Profiling

To *calibrate* an electronic device is to ensure its parameters (settings) are at the manufacturer's specs. To profile a device or software is to measure its color output and compare the output with a device-independent color model, such as CIE XYZ or

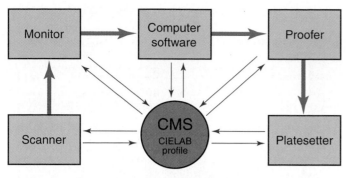

Figure 16-48. During device profiling, CMS uses the CIELAB values of the test target to identify color drift, which occurs at all stages of the process. The way each device interprets the color becomes its profile. Based on these profiles, the CMS then corrects the outputs of each stage to ensure color consistency from the scanner to the press sheet.

Figure 16-49. This monitor is being profiled. As colors appear on the screen, a colorimeter measures their CIELAB values and compares them to the actual CIELAB values. Variations between what is displayed and what should be displayed define the monitor's profile. Once a device is profiled, CMS can correct for inconsistencies.

CIELAB. CMS profiles each device and software package to detect color drift. This software compares the color of a known test form with its original values throughout production.

Calibrating and profiling the monitor

The color-management process begins with the calibration of the computer monitor for RGB balance. Next, CMS displays a series of color squares on the screen. A colorimeter reads each square and compares the square's CIELAB values to the original CIELAB values. See **Figure 16-49.** Both CRT and LCD monitors can be read. The CMS notes any differences between the original color and its display. The pattern of differences forms the monitor's *profile* and tells the CMS how to compensate for any color drift.

Profiling the scanner

After the monitor has been calibrated and profiled, the CMS develops a profile of the scanner. That is, it analyzes how the scanner interprets the colors in the original and calculates how to correct for the differences. An IT-8, a GretagMacbeth ColorChecker® chart, or another target is scanned, and because the monitor already has been calibrated and profiled, any differences between the original images and the images on the screen are due to the scanner. See **Figure 16-50.** As was the case with the monitor, the pattern of differences forms the scanner's profile and tells the CMS how to compensate for any color drift.

Profiling output devices

Both process and spot colors are defined and read by their CIELAB values. See **Figure 16-51.** After an output device has printed an image consisting of several color patches, a colorimeter reads the patches

on the printed sheet. Some software displays the actual output color patch next to a patch representing the actual color. In this manner, the operator can get immediate visual feedback on the performance of the proofer. CIELAB output values for each patch can also be displayed to provide a more objective assessment.

After a profile has been created for an output device, the profile can be edited. Once again, the original CIELAB values are the standard of reference. See **Figure 16-52.** Editing can be performed to remove color cast, replace out-of-gamut colors, and selectively adjust for ink densities. An edited profile makes the CMS aware of the individuality of the output device in question. After all proofers and presses have been profiled, they can be expected to print images matching those on the monitor.

color drift: any change in the color of an image as the image moves through the electronic prepress and press stages.

color management software (CMS): software that prevents color drift by compensating for deviation within one or more devices.

International Color Consortium (ICC): a group of vendors to the printing industry that promote a color management system of devices and software based on universally recognized color profiles.

calibrate: to adjust the scale on a measuring instrument, such as a densitometer, to a standard for specific conditions.

profile: a comparison of the output of a proofer or press against the input data.

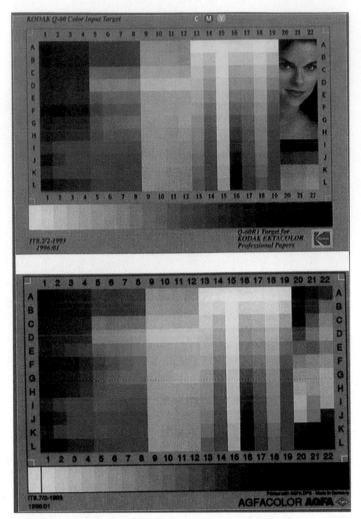

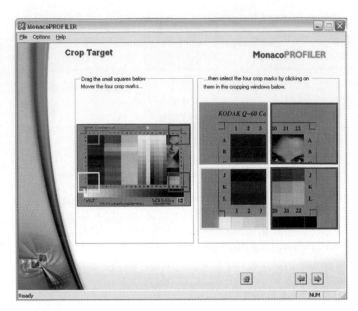

Figure 16-51. During the profiling of proofers and other output devices, CIELAB values of both process color and spot-color inks are used as a basis for identifying color drift. (Monaco Systems, Incorporated)

Figure 16-50. The IT-8 target is an example of an image with numerous colors of known CIELAB values. These targets provide a basis for profiling scanners, monitors, proofers, and platesetters. To profile a scanner, the scanned IT-8 target appears on the monitor screen. Any deviations between the original and displayed colors are attributable to the scanner because the monitor has already been calibrated. (Eastman Kodak Co.; Agfa-Gevaert Inc.; Monaco Systems, Incorporated)

Editing color

In addition to maintaining consistent color throughout the printing process, color-management software can also edit color. One method of performing this tweaking is by adjusting one or more color curves. See **Figure 16-53.** In the example shown, the green color curve has been modified, which explains the different values for the Input Level and the Output Level. Color-management software provides printers with the means of producing color that customers will find acceptable. Being able to match the colors in customer-supplied files on press is a key to being a successful printer in the twenty-first century. The higher output level will increase the ink film thickness.

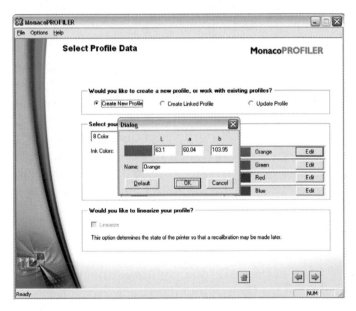

Figure 16-52. To edit an output device's profile, the cursor can be moved over the sample image, and data describing the color appears. (Monaco Systems, Incorporated)

Industry Specs

One of the most challenging requirements of high-quality printing is making color separations that replicate the original image and then maintaining that color throughout the pressrun. In an effort to help enhance and standardize color printing, three divisions of the printing industry have developed standards for the prepress and on-press operations

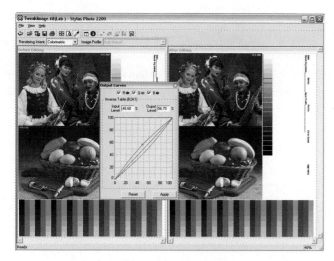

Figure 16-53. Color has been edited by modifying the green curve. The difference in the values of the Input Level and the Output Level will adjust ink densities on the plate. (Monaco Systems, Incorporated)

to follow when CMYK is printed on substrates typically used in their respective sectors of the industry. In 1976, a group of experts published a set of specs for web offset printing. These guidelines became known as the *Specifications for Web Offset Publications (SWOP®) specs*. In 1993, the SWOP specs included specs for the preparation of digital files, and in 1997, they added CTP operations. The SWOP specs also provide standards for proofing, dot gain, solid-ink density, paper, and ink. A summary of the SWOP standards is in Chapter 23.

Printing companies that produce the colorful advertising sections found in newspapers have guidelines the *Specifications for Newsprint Advertising Production (SNAP)* provides. As the name implies, these standards are tailored to printing on newsprint—both coated and uncoated. SNAP includes specs on color separation, proofing, presswork, paper, and ink.

Commercial printing companies can follow standards the *General Requirements for Applications in Commercial Offset Lithography (GRACoL)* provide. First published in the late 1990s, GRACoL is similar to the SWOP specs and SNAP because it also provides guidelines for making color separations, creating digital files, maintaining color on press, and specifying paper and ink. Color is controlled during the pressrun by holding dot gain to specified levels.

In 2006, the GRACoL Committee published a new manual, known as *G7*. This publication introduced the concept of attaining proper color on press and maintaining it throughout the pressrun by monitoring gray balance instead of dot gain. The name *G7* is taken from the technique for calibrating

gray scale and the seven specified, required inks. These three publications can be remembered in this order—SNAP, GRACoL, and the SWOP specs.

Summary

Color is a major factor in graphic communications. Although color is so much a part of our daily lives that we take it for granted, it is a highly complex phenomenon involving light, pigment, and color receptors in the eye and brain. Color is a phenomenon resulting from the interaction of light and pigment. Color perception is determined by the type of light source, the behavior of the light, and the viewer's sensitivity to color.

Visible light is a small portion of the electromagnetic spectrum. Light's visible spectrum is composed of RGB light, and the wavelengths determine the color of the light. The additive system of color involves the creation of various colors by overlapping RGB light. In the printing industry, hundreds of colors are created by combining CMY inks. The application of these pigments involves the subtractive system because they subtract light by absorbing it.

Breaking down a color photograph into its process colors for the purpose of printing is color separation. Whether performed photographically or electronically, color separation uses color filters to isolate colors by their wavelengths. After the separation, the CMY images are carried on different plates, along with a black plate, which is needed because commercial printing inks are contaminated. During the separation process, several adjustments to the image are made to improve the reproduction, including dot gain, USM, UCR, and GCR. UCR and GCR are used to replace equal amounts of the process colors with additional black to reduce the amount of total ink used to print four-color images.

Specifications for Web Offset Publications (SWOP®) specs: a publication containing standards for accurate color reproduction when printing with web lithography.

Specifications for Newsprint Advertising Production (SNAP): a publication containing standards for accurate color reproduction when printing on newsprint.

General Requirements for Applications in Commercial Offset Lithography (GRACoL): a publication containing standards for accurate lithographic color reproduction during commercial printing.

G7: a publication containing standards for accurate color reproduction with an emphasis on monitoring gray balance.

Color management is needed to ensure that the various devices and software languages making up the prepress and press portions of production maintain consistent color. The first step is to measure color numerically, and several color models have been developed to describe color as people perceive it. They include HSB, CIE XYZ, CIE xyY, and CIELAB.

Three types of instruments are used to analyze or measure color. The colorimeter identifies a color by its three CIELAB values. A spectrophotometer plots a curve revealing the amounts of light all the colors reflect. A densitometer indicates the density of a color by measuring the amount of light reflected from it. CMS compares the input and output of each prepress device to an ICC profile, such as CIELAB or CIE XYZ. When scanners, monitors, proofers, and presses define color according to the same color profile, consistent color is the result.

Review Questions

Please do not write in this book. Write your answers on a separate sheet of paper.

1. What does the term *wavelength* mean?
2. To what do the rods and cones in our eyes respond?
3. Define *color* and list the factors determining our perceptions of color.
4. Why does variation in the quantity and quality of light affect our perception of color?
5. In the _____ color system, the primary colors of light are combined to form other colors.
6. In the _____ color system, color is created when pigments absorb light.
7. In two or three sentences, briefly discuss the relationship between primary and secondary colors.
8. Why is black ink used as a fourth color in process printing?
9. What is the color-separation function?
10. What purpose do color-separation filters serve?
11. The adjustment our eyes make when exposed to low light for some time is known as _____.
12. Explain how adjacent colors affect color.
13. List three types of viewing variables affecting color perception.
14. Why are viewing booths used in the printing industry?

15. According to the Munsell system, _____ is the lightness or darkness of a color, as measured against a scale running from white to black.
16. According to the HSB color model, _____ is the attribute of color defining the color's degree of purity.
17. How does the CIE chromaticity diagram measure a color?
18. State the definition of *color space* and the dimensions of color.
19. Identify the three axes that measure a color in the CIELAB system.
20. Distinguish between a colorimeter and a spectrophotometer, in how they measure color.
21. What does ΔE measure?
22. The total range of colors that can be defined by a color model or reproduced with a given set of colorants, on a given paper, and on a given printing press is called the color _____.
23. Use the concept of color gamuts to explain why not all colors on a color slide can be reproduced on a magazine cover.
24. Chemical substances that give color to such materials as ink, paint, crayons, and chalk are called _____.
25. What are press proofs?
26. Compare analog and digital proofs.
27. Summarize the basic methods of color correction.
28. What is color sequencing? What factors influence color sequencing?
29. Summarize the function of CMS.
30. Describe how a scanner is profiled.
31. How is an IT-8 test target used in color management?

Skill-Building Activities

1. Bring up a photographic image with large areas of yellow, red, and blue on a computer. Using a magnifying glass or loupe, look at the phosphors glowing on the screen. Do the same for an image frozen (on tape) on your TV screen at home. What do you see?
2. Obtain several samples of continuous tone color copy (such as photographs and paintings). Using a loupe or magnifying glass, look at the different materials. What do you see? How do your findings compare to those of the previous activity?

3. Using library resources and the Internet, research color science and theory and write a report based on your findings.

4. Open a scanned color photograph in the Adobe Photoshop editor. Zoom in to make the pixels more visible. Enlarge the photograph's dimensions and resolution. Apply USM in varying degrees and examine the results.

Building Bridges

The printing plate shown in this photograph is the bridge between the prepress and press departments. This plate is the most obvious example of the need for perfect communication between the two areas because it is produced in prepress and used in press. The printing plate also represents the need for prepress personnel to have an awareness of printing presses and how they work.

Too often, faulty plates are discovered during the pressrun. Obviously, this situation means press time and paper have been wasted and more press time will be lost while the press is stopped and new plates are made. This chapter acquaints the student with the types of lithographic plates, techniques of producing them, and remedies for common problems associated with faulty plates.

(Goss International Corporation)

Chapter 17
Lithographic Plates

Key Terms

ablation
additive plate
aqueous plate
computer-to-plate (CTP)
conventional lithographic
  plate
deep-etch plate
diazo coating
diazo plate
dry method
electrostatic plate
electrostatic platesetter
gum arabic
halftone scale
image area
ink-jet plate
ink-jet platesetter
lacquer
lithographic plate
multimetal plate

negative-working plate
nonimage area
photopolymer
photopolymer plate
plate blinding
positive-working plate
presensitized plate
silver-halide plate
step-and-repeat
  platemaking
step tablet
subtractive plate
surface plate
thermal-ablation plate
thermal-conversion
  plate
tusche
waterless offset printing
waterless plate
wipe-on plate

Learning Objectives

When you have completed the reading and assigned activities related to this chapter, you will be able to do the following:

◆ Explain the principles on which lithographic plates are designed and made.

◆ Describe basic plate structure.

◆ Name a variety of lithographic plates and explain the processes used to image and develop them.

◆ Summarize manual and automatic processing of conventional plates.

◆ Properly handle and store lithographic plates.

◆ Use a platemaker's gray scale to properly expose presensitized plates.

◆ Expose and process subtractive- and additive-working plates.

◆ Make plate deletions by the dry and deletion-fluid methods.

◆ Explain the various types of CTP systems.

◆ Analyze plate problems and describe how to prevent them from happening in the future.

Of the prepress operations, platemaking is the final stage. The type-composition, page composition, image-assembly, and imposition stages of production culminate with generating the plates that will go onto the press. See **Figure 17-1**. Lithographic plates vary in the way they are made and in the materials from which they are composed. The type of platemaking process and materials used depend largely on the type of press the plates will go on and whether the plates are to be exposed with film or digitally.

The operation of an offset press involves the transfer of images from one surface to another. *Lithographic plates* made from thin sheets of metal, polyester, or paper serve as the image-carrying medium on an offset printing press or duplicator. Plates used on duplicator-size presses are sometimes referred to as *masters*. Regardless of the method or materials used, the surface of a lithographic plate contains image and nonimage areas.

The plates used in letterpress, flexography, and gravure printing place the image and nonimage areas on different levels. In contrast, the image and nonimage areas of a lithographic plate feel the same to the touch because they are essentially on the same level. Instead of being physically higher or lower than one another, the image and nonimage areas of a plate are different in their chemical makeup. Most offset plates in use today are based on the principle that grease and water do not readily mix. The *image areas* are ink receptive (oleophilic) and water-repellent (hydrophobic). The *nonimage areas* are ink resistant (oleophobic) and water receptive (hydrophilic).

After the plate is mounted onto the press, dampening solution and ink are applied to the plate, in that order. The dampening solution transfers to the nonimage areas, but not to the image areas. The ink transfers to the dry image areas, but not to the dampened nonimage areas. The inked images on the plate are transferred (offset) to the rubber blanket and then onto the paper passing between the blanket cylinder and impression cylinder. See **Figure 17-2**. There are too many types of plate characteristics to describe every type of plate, but the following descriptions provide an understanding of the basic imaging and development processes used to make lithographic plates.

Basic Plate Structure

Offset plates are manufactured from many different types of materials. These include cellulose-based paper; plastic-coated paper; acetate; aluminum; a paper base with a laminated aluminum surface; polyester; steel with a plastic surface; and copper on chromium, stainless steel, or aluminum. The most common material used to make plates is aluminum. Aluminum is widely used because it is flexible, is lightweight, can be easily grained, and is more receptive to water than the oil-based ink used in lithography. To be more water receptive, most metal-based offset plates have a textured surface, or grain. Aluminum plates vary in thickness from .008″ to .0015″.

Figure 17-1. The plate represents the culmination of the prepress work flow. (Agfa-Gevaert Inc.)

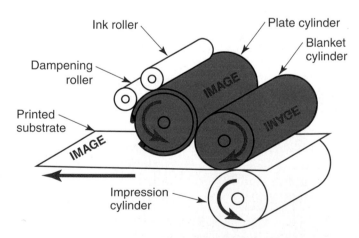

Figure 17-2. The inked image on the rubber blanket is transferred to the sheet of paper passing between the blanket cylinder and the impression cylinder.

Surface Grain

The surface of most metal plates is grained to form a slight texture, which makes them more water receptive. A grained surface is more capable of carrying a film of dampening solution than a smooth surface is. This surface assists in maintaining consistent ink and water balance on the press. Graining is usually performed chemically, but some plates are grained mechanically.

Some metal plates and all plastic and paper plates do not have a grained surface. These plates are referred to as *grainless*. Grainless plates are chemically treated during manufacture so the surface retains a moisture film during the printing operation.

Chemical grains are formed with chemicals that etch into the plate material. Mechanical methods used to produce the grain include sandblasting and brushing. **Figure 17-3** illustrates the differences between grainless and grained plates.

Surface Coatings and Emulsions

Nearly all lithographic plates have some type of surface coating, usually an emulsion. The type of coating used varies with the plate material and processing method to be used. As each type of plate is introduced in the following sections, its surface coatings are also explained.

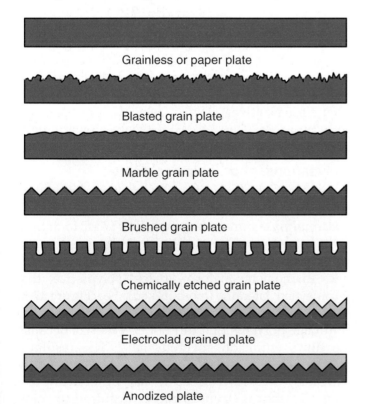

Figure 17-3. Different types of grain are used to form a surface texture on metal offset plates.

Sizes and Shapes

Offset plates are manufactured in sizes to fit the wide range of presses. Plate material might, however, also come in rolls that are cut to size as the plates are processed. Smaller-size (duplicator-size) plates are available with three types of plate ends. These are straight, pin bar, and serrated (slotted). See **Figure 17-4.** These three designs correspond to the three types of plate clamps on different presses.

Conventional Lithographic Plates

As stated earlier, lithographic plates vary in the materials from which they are made, as well as in the processes used to image and develop them. *Conventional lithographic plates* are imaged with

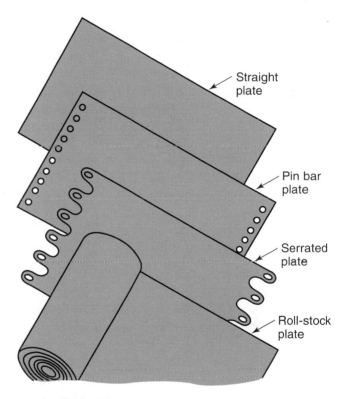

Figure 17-4. Offset plates are available with four types of plate ends. These are straight, pin bar, serrated, and roll stock. (3M Company)

lithographic plate: a metal, plastic, or paper image-carrying surface on an offset printing press or duplicator.

image area: an ink-receptive, water-repellent area on a printing plate.

nonimage area: an ink-resistant, water-receptive area on a printing plate.

conventional lithographic plate: a plate made by exposing it to light through a piece of film.

either negative or positive films, using a contact method. These plates are also categorized as surface or deep-etch, wipe-on or presensitized, additive or subtractive, and negative- or positive-working.

Note

Keep in mind that, whenever more than one color is to be printed, a printing plate must be prepared for each one of the colors. For example, four-color process printing requires a printing plate for each of the process colors (CMYK). Five- or six-color printing requires five or six printing plates, respectively.

Surface Plates

A *surface plate* has a base material on which a light-sensitive coating rests. See **Figure 17-5**. This plate is called a *surface plate* because the image area is formed on the surface of the plate, instead of etched below or added above the surface. Surface plates require exposure to high-intensity light and can be either negative or positive working. The nonimage areas are removed through chemical processing after exposure and during processing.

Surface plates are the most common type of lithographic plate and can be identified by the type of light-sensitive chemicals used to coat them. The two main types of coating used on surface plates are diazo and photopolymer. Surface plates can be presensitized (coating applied by manufacturer) or wipe-on (coating applied by user).

Wipe-on plates

Grained surface plates purchased without the light-sensitive coating are *wipe-on plates*. Just prior to exposing these plates, a *diazo coating* is applied by hand or with a special roller coater. Wipe-on plates are usually negative-working plates, but they can be positive-working plates. They are not widely used.

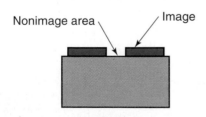

Nonimage area   Image

Figure 17-5. The light-sensitive coating of a surface offset plate rests on the base metal.

Presensitized plates

Much more commonly used than wipe-on plates, *presensitized plates* are purchased with the light-sensitive coating already applied. Presensitized plates are made to fit most duplicator and larger-press sizes. They are also designed for various lengths of pressruns (impressions). Short-run plates are durable for about 5000 to 10,000 impressions. Other presensitized plates are available for printing runs of a million or more impressions. Some plates are manufactured with a light-sensitive coating on both sides of the base, so they can be used twice. Presensitized plates are available for use with both negative and positive films.

Diazo plates

Presensitized surface plates coated with a light-sensitive diazo compound are called *diazo plates*. Exposure to light converts the diazo coating to insoluble resins that receive ink easily and hold up well during pressruns as long as 250,000 impressions. Diazo plates are usually exposed with film negatives. After exposure, these plates are processed with an emulsion developer, and the nonimage (unexposed) areas of the plate are removed. The nonimage areas can be treated and desensitized with *gum arabic* or some other type of gum. Diazo plates exposed with film positives require the addition of a special image-strengthening material, such as *lacquer*, to protect and strengthen the image area.

All plates on which the images are formed from film are either negative working or positive working. Negative-working plates are exposed from film negatives, and positive-working plates are exposed from film positives. The images are produced on both types of plates through high-intensity light exposure and chemical processing.

Conventional photopolymer plates

Surface plates with a light-sensitive photopolymer coating are called *photopolymer plates*. *Photopolymers* are substances that react to actinic light by polymerizing. The light strikes image areas of the emulsion, causing the individual molecules (monomers) to form chains (polymerize) that become tied laterally (cross-linked). See **Figure 17-6**. After exposure, the processing stage removes the nonimage portions that did not polymerize because the film's emulsion covered them. The resultant images are very strong, and the plates generally withstand pressruns of up to one million impressions. Additional strength can be acquired through a special curing process.

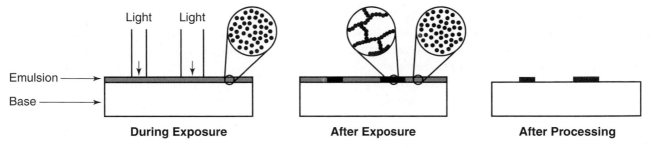

Figure 17-6. When actinic light strikes the photopolymer emulsion of a plate, the individual monomers immediately polymerize and cross-link. The unexposed emulsion areas remain monomers. Processing then removes the unexposed emulsion.

In the previous description of the exposure and processing steps, a negative-working plate is described. Photopolymer plates, however, can be either negative working or positive working. Positive-working photopolymer plates come with a prehardened emulsion. During exposure, the light strikes the nonimage areas and causes them to lose their bonds. Processing washes away the coating in these areas. Changes in temperature and relative humidity do not easily affect photopolymer-coated plates. The plates can be precoated and stored for long periods of time before use.

Negative-Working and Positive-Working Plates

Another way of categorizing plates is whether they are exposed from film negatives or positives. *Negative-working plates* are imaged from film negatives placed over the unexposed plates and exposed to high-intensity light. The light passing through the transparent portions (image areas) of the film hardens the coating on the surface of the plate and makes these areas insoluble in the developer. See **Figure 17-7.** The areas on the plate not exposed

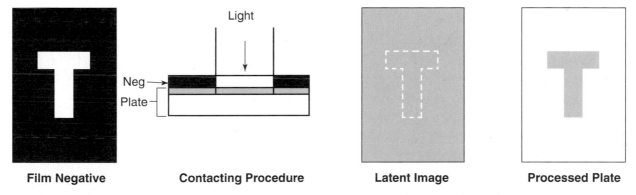

Figure 17-7. A film negative placed over a negative-working plate allows light to expose the image areas of the plate and create a latent image. Processing removes the unexposed emulsion in the nonimage areas to produce a visible image.

surface plate: a printing plate on which the image area is formed on the surface of the plate.

wipe-on plate: a printing plate similar to a presensitized plate in that specially treated metal is needed and diazo coatings are used, except the coatings are applied by hand or with a special roller coater.

diazo coating: a light-sensitive printing-plate coating made from condensation products of formaldehyde and diazo diphenylamine, stabilized with a compound such as zinc chloride.

presensitized plate: a printing plate that the manufacturer has pretreated with a light-sensitive coating.

diazo plate: a surface plate coated with an emulsion of a light-sensitive, organic compound called *diazo*.

gum arabic: a gummy, water-soluble substance obtained from certain types of trees. This substance is used in fountain solutions to desensitize the nonimage areas of the printing plate and prevent them from accepting ink and to protect printing plates from humidity and chemical attack when the press is not running or when the plates are in storage.

lacquer: a clear or colored resin-based solution added to the image area of a printing plate to increase its durability.

photopolymer plate: a surface plate with a light-sensitive photopolymer coating.

photopolymer: an organic substance that undergoes physical changes when exposed to light.

negative-working plate: a printing plate that is exposed with a film negative and in which the image areas harden when exposed to light.

to light (nonimage areas) are not hardened, and the coating dissolves when the plate is developed. With the coating gone, these nonimage areas become water receptive, while the hardened image areas are ink receptive. The nonimage areas can be treated and desensitized with a solution such as desensitizing gum to increase hydrophilic properties. The most commonly used plates are negative-working plates.

Positive-working plates are exposed from film positives and a high-intensity light. Light passing through the transparent portions (nonimage areas) of the film begins decomposing the coating. The coating in the exposed areas of the plate becomes soluble and is dissolved during processing. The exposed, or nonimage, areas become water receptive. See **Figure 17-8.** Coating in the areas not exposed to light remain hard and insoluble during development, and these areas become the ink-receptive image areas.

Many positive-working plates can be cured after processing to make the image areas harder and more durable for long pressruns. As with negative-working plates, the nonimage areas can be treated and desensitized with a solution such as desensitizing gum to make them more water receptive. An advantage of positive-working plates is that the harder image areas tend to reproduce halftone images with less dot gain than negative-working plates do.

Subtractive and Additive Plates

Just as the terms *negative-working* and *positive-working* describe whether light exposes the image or nonimage areas of the plate, the terms *subtractive* and *additive* describe how the exposed plates react to the developer. *Subtractive plates* require a developer to dissolve the unexposed coating so the coating can be easily removed (subtracted) from the base material. Areas with the coating removed become the nonimage, dampening solution–receptive areas. The areas of the light-sensitive coating exposed to light

are hardened and become insoluble when the developer contacts them. These exposed areas are the ink-receptive image areas of the plate.

Pressruns of 15,000 to 200,000 impressions or more are possible with subtractive plates. Subtractive plates are popular because they are easy to process and do not use lacquer-based chemicals. **Figure 17-9** provides information that is helpful when processing subtractive plates.

Additive plates are imaged with a high-intensity light and a film negative. The light shines through the transparent (image) areas and hardens the image areas on the plate. During processing, a special image-strengthening lacquer is applied (added) to the image areas, and the coating in the nonimage areas is removed from the plate.

Most lacquers perform two functions. These functions are the removal of the unexposed coating to make the nonimage areas water receptive and coating the exposed (image) areas with an oleophilic lacquer to make these areas ink receptive. **Figure 17-10** provides information that is helpful when processing additive plates.

Deep-Etch Plates

Surface plates carry the light-sensitive coating on the surface. *Deep-etch plates* carry the coating slightly below the plate surface. These plates are exposed from film positives, rather than film negatives. After exposure and processing, the ink-receptive, or unexposed, areas are chemically etched, making the image areas lower than the nonimage areas. See **Figure 17-11.** The preparation of deep-etch plates requires considerable skill, but these plates have a greater ink-carrying capacity than surface plates do. Pressruns over 500,000 impressions are common with deep-etch plates. Most deep-etch plates use aluminum, zinc, or stainless steel as the base, or carrier.

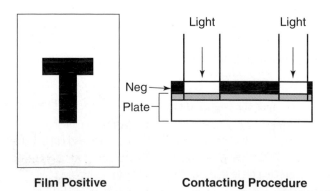

Film Positive **Contacting Procedure** **Latent Image** **Processed Plate**

Figure 17-8. A film positive placed over a positive-working plate allows light to expose the nonimage areas of the plate and create a latent image. Processing then removes the exposed nonimage areas.

Problem	Probable Cause	Remedy
Weak or faint images (usually due to lacquer developer not applying evenly).	Diazo coating on wipe-on plate too thin for grain.	Try using higher dye load (diazo concentration) coating or relieve tension on roller coater.
	Insufficient exposure.	Increase exposure time (use gray scale and shoot for a step 5-6).
	Diazo coating not completely dissolved.	Reshake bottle of coating mix; let sit 30 minutes at room temperature (65°–85°F) until completely dissolved.
	Contamination.	Use clean wipes when applying diazo; make sure rollers are clean on roller coaters; film should be clean when exposing.
	Diazo decomposed. Plates out-of-date or allowed to get too warm and /or too wet.	Use fresh bottle of diazo; use new plates and improve storage conditions.
	Diazo deactivated. Diazo came in contact with ammonia fumes (glass cleaner, film cleaner, floor cleaner).	Use new coating/plates; avoid ammonia.
	Lacquer developer has settled out in container.	Shake or stir lacquer developer until uniform color is achieved. If problem continues, use new developer.
	Lacquer developer damaged in shipment or storage.	Developer may have been frozen or overheated during shipment or storage; discard.
	Lacquer developer out-of-date.	Developer too old, check shelf life recommendation of manufacturer; use new batch.
Black spots on background area (black marks on plate).	Plates stored too long and/or under hot humid conditions.	Check shelf life and batch number of presensitized plates; if out-of-date, use new plates (counter etching or use of desensitizer before lacquering may help).
	Plates stored with slip sheet paper. Paper chemicals plus humidity react with diazo and/or aluminum surfaces.	Avoid storage with slip sheet paper, especially during hot, humid weather.
	Diazo decomposed or contaminated.	Check age of diazo coating solution; diazo solutions should be stored cool (40°–70°F) for only a few days; used and recycled coating decomposes faster, avoid use of old coating; check cleanliness of roller coater. Old decomposed diazo (staining on rollers) can catalyze the decomposition of fresh coating; clean rollers frequently with approved cleaners; use fresh wipes for hand application; if you must use a sponge, make sure it's clean.
	Developer imbalance.	If condition worsens with age of developer, discard and use fresh developer.
	Old developer redepositing from processor.	Clean brushes, belts, pans, lines, pump, etc., with approved cleaner.
	Pinholes in negative	Check negative for holes and opaque.

Figure 17-9. Subtractive-working plates are preferred because of the ease in processing. This chart provides helpful processing data.

positive-working plate: a printing plate that is exposed with a film positive and in which the plate coating in the nonimage areas begins decomposing when exposed to light.

subtractive plate: a printing plate that is processed by the developer removing the nonimage areas of the plate's coating.

additive plate: a printing plate requiring the addition of a special image-strengthening lacquer to the image areas to retain their durability.

deep-etch plate: a printing plate that is exposed with film positives and on which the ink-bearing image area is slightly etched below the nonprinting area.

Problem	Probable Cause	Remedy
Plugging, bridging (images fill with developer), piling (lacquer buildup on images).	Too much developer.	Reduce quantity used by hand or reduce flow rate in processor.
	Too much water in sponge or brush.	Some developers are very sensitive to the quantity of water present while developing; monitor carefully.
	Developer too concentrated.	Make sure developer is shaken or stirred uniformly; using the bottom portion of developer in a bottle that has settled will cause problems.
	Developer has lost too much solvent and/or is too old.	Check shelf life recommendations of manufacturer; solvents evaporate right through the plastic bottle; they will evaporate faster through an open bottle or in a processor and in hotter temperatures; avoid conditions that lead to evaporation; use fresh developer.
Development too fast or too slow (causes symptoms similar to piling and plugging).	Same causes as piling and plugging	See cures recommended for piling and plugging.
Developer scums, deposits on background (lacquer adheres to nonimage areas).	Diazo coating not uniform, blank spots on plate.	Make sure diazo completely coats plate; check to see if a wetting agent is included in the diazo coating; adjust rollers.
	Plate, diazo too old.	Use fresh plates or diazo coating.
	Plate contamination.	Oil spots, fingerprints, defoamers, other chemicals can cause scumming; coat, expose, and develop plates in clean areas.
	Faulty plates.	Improper anodization or silication can result in developer scumming.
White spots in image (light specks on type and solid images).	Dewetting of diazo on plate.	Oil or chemicals can cause diazo to be repelled from plate leaving a void; clean rollers; use fresh wipes, new diazo.
	Water spots on diazo.	Water spraying on plates or sneezing can cause white spots.
	Dust and dirt on negative, plate, or exposure frame glass.	Carefully clean away any debris that can block light.
Halation (halftone dots plug or gain size; dark, hotspot in tone areas).	Dirt or debris between plate surface and negative.	Carefully clean all surfaces.
	Kinks in plate or film.	Carefully handle plates and film to avoid kinking.
	Insufficient vacuum.	Check vacuum gauge (25–27); allow longer times for pump-down (the larger the plate, the longer the time); check for vacuum leaks.
	Film flopped.	The emulsion side of the film should be in contact with the coated side of the plate.
	Overexposure.	Use a gray scale and shoot for a step 5–6; a contact scale or dot gain scale may be useful.

Figure 17-9. *(Continued)*

Problem	Probable Cause	Remedy
Blinding on press (some images do not take ink fully).	Too much gum on image.	Gum arabic must be buffed very thin on plate; use a lower Baumé concentration; for example: cut a 14 Bé to 10 Bé or 7 Bé (too thin a gum will cause scumming or tinting); use a gum asphaltum (must be shaken well and buffed properly); use a nonblinding, nongum finisher.
Streaking on press (marks across image).	Same as blinding, but in streaks.	Same as blinding.
Scumming on press (nonimage areas of plate pick up ink and transfer it to sheet).	Insufficient gumming.	Use a heavier concentration of gum on the plate.
	Insufficient desensitizing.	Anodized plates are often harder to desensitize; use more acidic gum; use a nongum desensitizer.
Difficulty in achieving ink/water balance on press (poor halftones, washed out solids).	Image not ink receptive enough (partial binding).	Use less gum; buff down thinner; use gum asphaltum; use a nongum finisher.
	Background not water receptive enough.	Use a more powerful desensitizing finisher.
Heavy linting (uniform light colored tint over nonimage areas).	Background requires too much water to stay clean due to insufficient desensitizing.	Use a more powerful desensitizing finisher.
Short plate life (image failure, short length of run, plate not properly processed and images break down to produce loss of detail).	Insufficient exposure.	Use a gray scale, shoot for a step 5–6.
	Coating insufficient to fill grain.	Use a heavier dye-load (concentration) diazo coating.
	Lacquer coating from developer too thin or too thick.	Shake developer thoroughly; use proper amounts while developing; use proper speed and brush pressure in plate processor to give uniform color in solids without piling.
	Plate faulty (poor graining, poor anodizing, poor silication).	Check another batch of plates.
	Weak diazo coating (see weak image).	Use fresh diazo or freshly coated plates.
	Harsh solvents, plate cleaners, roller cleaners, etc.	Avoid using or splashing harsh solvents and cleaners on plates; some plate cleaners will etch and undercut dots.
Poor tonal reproduction (loss of halftone dots and image detail).	Faulty exposures.	Check gray scale; check integrator, replace bulbs.
	Dots on film too soft, too much veil or fringe.	Use harder dots; change exposure level on film; change film or film developer; dupe the negative.
	Images too thick (piling).	See remedies for piling.
	Improper desensitizing.	Use a stronger desensitizing finisher.

Figure 17-9. *(Continued)*

Problem	Probable Cause	Remedy
Slow development (excess time in development during plate preparation).	Developer temperature too low.	Most developers must be between 65°–90°F to operate properly, but even at 65°F, development is much slower than at 90°F; cold sinks, cold plates, or developer just in from the warehouse need to be warmer; check heater and thermostat on processor.
	Developer activity too low.	In a processor, developer may have already processed too many plates (square feet of area subtracted); either replace part of developer, or flush and start a new batch; increased temperature may help but will lead to alcohol evaporation with some developers; slowing down throughput speed may be sufficient; in some cases, increasing replenisher concentration may help (too much replenisher will undercut highlights).
	Developer too old.	Out-of-date developer may have lost to much solvent (alcohol); increasing replenisher concentration may help (too much replenisher will undercut highlights); change to a newer batch.
	Overexposure (negative plates).	Use gray scale; shoot for step 5–6; overexposure will fill in shadows.
	Film flopped, out of contact.	Make sure film emulsion side is in contact with plate coating.
	Poor platemaker vacuum.	Check vacuum gauge (25–27); check for leaks; poor vacuum causes light striking (fogging, halation) with negative-working plates.
	Plate exposed to light (negative plates).	Check safe light (yellow light) condition for source of stray ultraviolet light (doors, fluorescent fixtures, exposure frame, skylight, etc.); partially exposed plates are hard to develop; store plates in dark area.
	Plate too old.	Check shelf life date from manufacturer; use new lot.
	Developer diluted by rinse water.	Check for leaks in processor; adjust roller pressures to prevent feedback.
Dot loss on plate (failure of halftone dot structure).	Underexposure (negative plates).	Use of gray scale; shoot for step 5–6.
	To much replenisher (alcohol).	Reduce replenisher concentration.
	Developer too hot.	Reduce temperature control on processor, temperature should read 80°–90°F.
	Development time too long.	Reduce development time to manufacturer's recommendation; make sure shadows are clean; speed up processor throughput.
	Too much development pressure.	Reduce brush pressure; use a less abrasive developing pad.
	Overexposure (positive plate).	Use gray scale; shoot for a clear 2–3.
	Light striking or undercutting (positive plate).	Work in good yellow light; check for sources of light leaks; check for good contact between film and plate.
	Developer too acidic (negative plates).	Check pH; it should be between 4.5–9.5.
	Developer too alkaline (positive plates).	Check pH; it should be between 9.5–12.5; check plate manufacturer's recommendations.

Figure 17-10. Additive offset plates require a lacquer to be applied to exposed image areas. Information in this chart provides helpful processing data.

Problem	Probable Cause	Remedy
Dot gain on plate (enlargement of halftone dots).	Overexposure (negative).	Use gray scale; shoot for step 5–6; use a dot gain scale.
	Under development (see causes of slow development).	Same cure for slow development.
	Improper contact, vacuum problems.	Check vacuum gauge (25–27); look for leaks; clean glass and gaskets; increase draw-down time.
	Film flopped.	Emulsion side of film should be in direct contact with coated side of plate.
	Dots in film too soft, too much veil or fringe.	Use contact/dupe films; change film or film developer.
	Combination of too much replenisher and too long of an exposure.	Cut back on both exposure time and alcohol amount.
Spots on background (dark areas on plate).	Pinholes in film.	Check film; opaque all pinholes.
	Image polymer depositing on background.	Check developer or replenisher levels (see causes/cure of slow development).
	Weak developer.	Check developer or replenisher levels (see causes/cure of slow development).
Redepositing (developer deposit on image solids and screens).	Weak developer.	Check developer age; add fresh developer or replenisher.
	Developer solution too cold.	Check developer temperature; should be between 80°–90°F in processor.
	Developing pad, brushes, or rollers dirty.	Use new pad; clean brushes and rollers.
	Filter clogged.	Change filter.
Halation (halftone dots plug, hot spots in tone areas).	Dirt on film or plate.	Clean thoroughly with appropriate cleansers.
	Kinks on plate or film.	Handle plates, film more carefully; use two hands, grasping opposite two corners.
	Insufficient vacuum, uneven background.	Check vacuum gauge; check for leaks; adjust backboard.
	Air trapped between plate or film.	Change filter.
White spots in image (light specks on type and solid images).	Dirt on film, plate, or glass of vacuum frame.	Clean thoroughly with appropriate cleaners.
Heavy linting (uniform light tint over nonimage areas).	Background requires too much water to keep clean.	Increase development time; use stronger developer or finisher with stronger desensitizer.

Figure 17-10. *(Continued)*

Problem	Probable Cause	Remedy
Blinding (image not taking ink).	Too much gum on image.	To prevent, gum must be buffed down thoroughly; use a lower concentration of gum (too little gum can cause scumming, toning); use a nongum, nonbleeding finisher; to correct, wet wash plate with hot water or mild acid solution; use gum asphaltum or plate cleaner to restore ink receptivity; make new plate.
	Contamination from sponge or brushes.	Use thoroughly rinsed clean sponge; clean brushes; avoid other chemicals in sink while developing or gumming.
Scumming on press (tinting or toning on restart)	Insufficient gumming or desensitizing.	Ensure complete coverage of plate with gum or finisher; allow sufficient time for developer and/or finisher to desensitize plate.
	Light struck plate (negative plates).	Check for sources of ultraviolet light leaks; film density too low, masking is burning through; check all light blocking materials for adequate performance.
Short plate life (short length of run causes image on plate to deteriorate).	Insufficient exposure (negative plate).	Use gray scale; shoot for 5–6; check center to edge difference; may require change of distance from light source; use light source with higher UV output.
	Lightstruck.	Check masking for light blocking ability; check for light leaks.
	Overdevelopment, developer temperature excessive.	Cut back on development time and/or brush pressure in processor; temperature in processor too high, lower to 80°–90°F.
	Developer too harsh, too much replenisher.	Cut back on replenisher concentration.
	Water pH too high (positive plate).	Check manufacturer's recommendations (typically keep between 9.5–12.5).
	Harsh solvents in contact with plate.	Keep film cleaner, blanket wash, etc., from contacting plate.
	Insufficient baking (positive plate).	Check baking time and temperature; one or both may require increase.

Figure 17-10. *(Continued)*

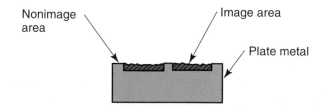

Figure 17-11. Deep-etch offset plates are exposed with film positives, rather than film negatives. The ink-bearing image area is etched below the nonprinting surface area.

Multimetal Plates

Multimetal plates are made with two layers of metal (bimetal) or three layers of metal (trimetal). See **Figure 17-12.** Multimetal plates are sturdy and useful for long pressruns because, unlike other lithographic plates, they carry the image above the plate surface. The metals used to make the plates are selected for their ink- and water-receptive characteristics. The most common metals used for multimetal plates are copper plated onto aluminum or stainless steel.

On most multimetal plates, copper is electroplated onto an aluminum base or a stainless steel base, and a light-sensitive coating is applied to the copper surface. The plate is imaged with a film negative and high-intensity light. The image areas are exposed to the light, and the coating on top of the copper is hardened. The unexposed coating remains soluble and is removed during processing, exposing the copper. This exposed copper is also removed during processing, baring the metal beneath it.

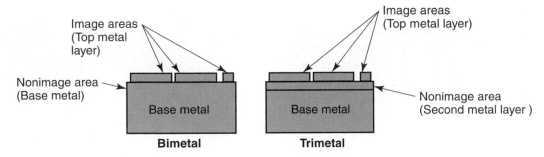

Figure 17-12. Multimetal plates provide excellent durability and print well, but they are expensive.

Metals used for multimetal plates are often referred to as *nonimage metals* and *image metals*. The skills and cost required to prepare multimetal plates are considerable. Although multimetal plates are extremely durable and can withstand pressruns exceeding one million impressions, they are not as commonly used as photopolymer plates are.

Electrostatic Plates

Electrostatic plates are imaged by a photoelectrostatic process that uses light and electrostatic properties. The principles on which the process is based are the same as those used in most photocopying machines and laser printers—a surface must be selectively charged. The process begins when light is reflected from a black-and-white original. When the light reflected from the white nonimage areas of the original light strike portions of a positively charged surface, the light causes those portions to lose their charge and become neutral. Unexposed parts of the surface (the image areas) remain positively charged. Negatively charged toner particles are then attracted to only the positively charged areas of the surface. See **Figure 17-13.**

Electrostatic platemaking systems vary in design, and either the drum or plate surface is coated with chargeable photoconductors. In systems in which the drum is coated with the photoconductors, light exposure changes the charge in the nonimage areas on the drum. The image areas are not exposed to the light and retain the charge, which then attracts the oppositely charged toner. The special cylinder receives the image and transfers it to the plate surface.

The imaging process is slightly different if the plate, rather than the drum, is coated with the photoconductors. The same electrostatic principle applies, but the toner is fused directly to the surface of the plate. The plate material has a light-sensitive coating formulated to accept the electrostatic charge. The photoconductive coating must be removed from the nonimage areas before printing. The nonimage areas

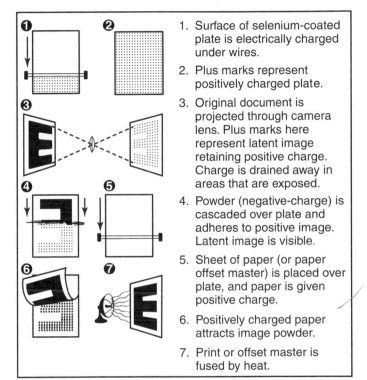

1. Surface of selenium-coated plate is electrically charged under wires.
2. Plus marks represent positively charged plate.
3. Original document is projected through camera lens. Plus marks here represent latent image retaining positive charge. Charge is drained away in areas that are exposed.
4. Powder (negative-charge) is cascaded over plate and adheres to positive image. Latent image is visible.
5. Sheet of paper (or paper offset master) is placed over plate, and paper is given positive charge.
6. Positively charged paper attracts image powder.
7. Print or offset master is fused by heat.

Figure 17-13. Electrostatic offset plates are prepared in seven steps. (Xerox Corp.)

also need to be treated and desensitized to become water receptive.

Original copy consisting of a pasteup, typewritten copy, drawn or printed images, or even photographic prints can be used to image the plate. As with a copying machine, the image can be reproduced on the plate at the same size, an enlarged size, or a reduced size. Electrostatic plates can also be referred to as *electrophotographic plates*.

multimetal plate: a printing plate made with two or three layers of metal, each selected for its ink- or water-receptive characteristics.

electrostatic plate: a printing plate that is imaged electrostatically.

Electrostatic platemakers

Electrostatic plates are prepared on automatic processors. The processor's lighttight magazine holds a quantity of unexposed plates that are either precut to size or in roll form. The plate processor is prepared by first loading the copyboard with camera copy. The operator then sets the lens and copyholder distances for the desired reproduction size. The lights, aperture, timer, and plate length are set. After pressing a button, the processor automatically begins a series of steps, including charging, exposing, developing and fusing.

Suitable substrates and inks

These plates are intended for use with uncoated papers. They should not be used when running clay-coated enamel papers or nonporous materials, such as plastics, foils, or pyroxylin-coated cover papers. This is because the special fountain solutions required for electrostatic plates severely inhibit oxidation drying of the ink.

Electrostatic fountain chemistry poses no problem when running uncoated papers because printing inks designed for use with uncoated papers dry primarily by absorption (ink is absorbed into the paper similar to how water is absorbed into a blotter). When running coated papers and nonabsorbent plastic and foil papers, however, the inks depend on oxidation to dry. The use of electrostatic plates is becoming increasingly rare. Instead of making plates for short pressruns, printing companies are using high-speed photocopiers.

Aqueous Plates

Aqueous plates are developed with chemistry that is primarily water based, instead of solvent based. See **Figure 17-14**. Aqueous plate developer is the result of environmental regulations that seek to reduce the use of organic solvent-based chemistry in the United States. Spent solvents can contain large amounts of alcohol and other harmful substances. In some areas of the United States, spent organic solvents can be flushed down the drain, but only after they have been extensively treated or diluted. In many states and municipalities, it is illegal to flush this used chemistry at all, necessitating an EPA-approved hauler to remove it.

Figure 17-14. Many digital plate systems use aqueous-based processing. The plate illustrated here is aluminum based, with a photopolymer coating. (Fuji Photo Film USA, Inc.)

Conventional Platemaking Equipment

Conventional platemaking processes are photomechanical processes. In these processes, light-sensitive coatings on the plate surface physically change after exposure to a high-intensity light source. After exposure, the plate is processed so the nonimage portions of the emulsion are receptive to dampening solution and the image areas are receptive to lithographic ink.

Caution

Be certain that adequate mechanical exhaust ventilation and a supply of clean air are available and operating properly in the platemaking area.

Most platemaking machines use a light source to expose the plate from film negatives or positives. The platemaker has a vacuum frame with a rubber blanket and a glass cover. The blanket is bordered by a rubber sealing gasket and contains an outlet fitting connected to the vacuum pump by a rubber hose. A flip-top platemaker is one example of a self-contained unit. See **Figure 17-15**.

The offset plate is placed on the rubber blanket in the frame, with the stripped-up flat on top of the plate. When the plate and flat are precisely aligned, the glass cover is closed and locked in place. The vacuum blanket compresses the plate and the flat to produce an airtight contact. The vacuum frame containing the plate and flat is then introduced to a UV light source. The light source generally consists

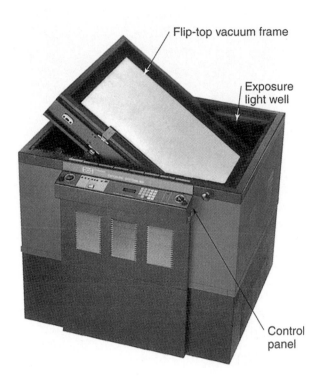

Figure 17-15. A typical platemaker that uses a light source to expose plates from film negatives or positives. (nuArc Company, Inc.)

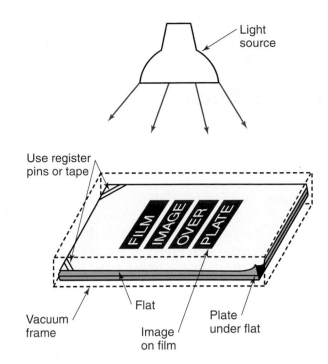

Figure 17-16. A vacuum frame compresses the plate and flat to form an airtight contact. The light source shines through the image on the film and exposes the light-sensitive surface of the plate.

of pulsed xenon or mercury vapor. See **Figure 17-16.** The light source must provide even illumination across the entire plate area. A computerized control panel on the front of the platemaker houses controls for vacuum and exposure time.

Uniform contact is essential when using the vacuum frame. When exposing the plate, it is essential for the film intermediate to be in firm, even contact with the plate. A soft, pliable vacuum blanket ensures good contact. If firm contact is not made between the film and plate, the image will be larger than the original because the light will spread out under the edges. Film that is improperly stripped on the flat or an excessive amount of tape can cause poor contact. See **Figure 17-17.** After the plate is exposed, it is either developed manually in a plate-developing sink or by an automatic plate processor. In either case, the processing of offset plates is done under subdued room light or in an area illuminated with a yellow light.

To overcome the difficulties of controlling the variables and slowness of manual plate processing, automatic plate processors have become the preferred method in the printing industry. The automatic plate processor develops, rinses, dries, and gums the plate in one continuous operation. Many systems are available that use aqueous-based chemistries, which are nonflammable and can be disposed of

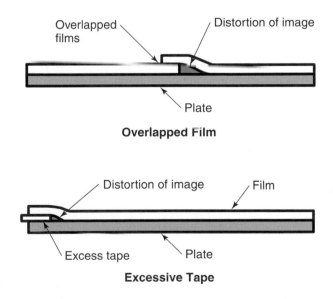

Figure 17-17. Overlapped film causes a distorted image on the plate. An excessive amount of tape can cause poor film-to-plate contact.

aqueous plate: a printing plate that uses coatings that can be processed by developing chemistries that are primarily, if not entirely, water based.

in conventional wastewater treatment systems. The internal parts of a typical plate processor are shown in **Figure 17-18.**

Exposure Control

A platemaker's *gray scale* is used to determine the correct exposure time of a presensitized offset plate. The gray scale is a measuring device used to obtain consistent exposure and development of offset plates. See **Figure 17-19.** A gray scale can be supplied on film as either continuous tones or halftone dots. If it is on film and contains discrete stages of gray, it is called a **step tablet.** If it is a single continuous strip of progressively dense gray, it is called a **halftone scale.**

A step tablet is a piece of film with 10 or 21 separate steps, ranging in densities from clear to completely black. Each density is referred to as a

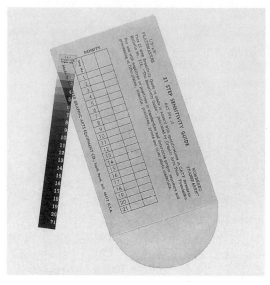

Figure 17-19. A platemaker's gray scale is used to determine the correct exposure time of an offset plate. (Stouffer Graphic Arts Equipment Co.)

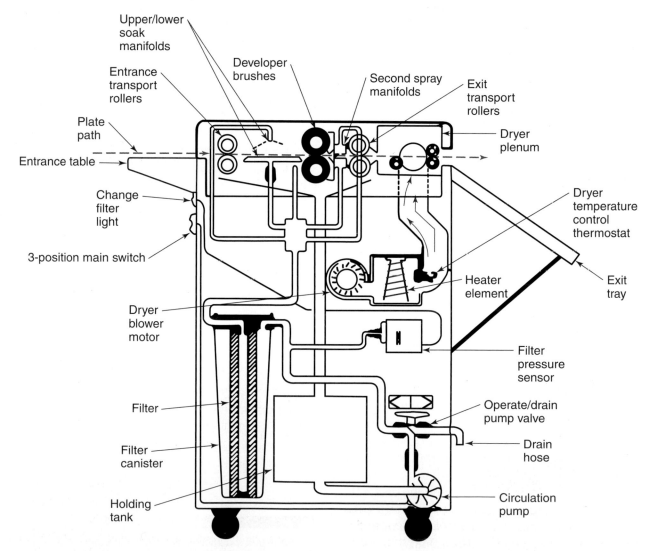

Figure 17-18. The components of an automatic plate processor. Automatic plate processors have replaced most manual plate-processing methods.

step. The intensity of the light, transparency of the negative, and thickness of the plate coating influence the exposure time. The distance from the light source to the plate is kept constant. To determine the correct exposure time for any given plate, the manufacturer's instructions should be followed.

The gray scale should be placed along the gripper or tail edge of the flat. To do this, a window opening is cut in the flat so the gray scale is not covered. In this way, the gray scale receives the same amount of exposure as the rest of the image. See **Figure 17-20.**

After exposure, the plate image and gray scale areas are chemically processed. If the plate has been properly exposed, the correct numbered step appears as shown in **Figure 17-21.** In this example, step six should be as dark as step one. If the plate is underexposed, the gray scale reading can be increased by increasing the exposure time. If the plate is overexposed, the gray scale reading can be reduced by reducing the exposure time. Charts are available to determine corrected exposure times. See **Figure 17-22.**

To increase original gray scale reading by:	1 Step	2 Steps	3 Steps	4 Steps
Multiply your original exposure time by:	1.4	2.0	2.8	4.0

To decrease original gray scale reading by:	1 Step	2 Steps	3 Steps	4 Steps
Multiply your original exposure time by:	0.7	0.5	0.36	0.25

Figure 17-22. This exposure-modification chart can be used for correcting underexposed and overexposed offset plates. (3M Company)

As a rule, a gray scale reading of solid step six for a negative-working plate indicates a properly exposed and developed plate. A higher gray scale reading usually means the image has spread (become larger) enough to plug up (fill in) any halftones or screen images on the plate. A plate containing only coarse line work generally does not plug up, even when taken to step seven or eight.

Preparing Presensitized Plates

When removing a plate from the package, care should be taken not to scratch the presensitized coating, and fingers should be kept off the plate surfaces. The plate should be handled by its outer edges and lifted, rather than slid, from the package. Plates must not be bent or creased in any way. Unused plates need to be stored in their containers in a cool, dry place.

Caution

Avoid looking directly at the platemaker's light source while the plate is being exposed. Such an exposure can temporarily harm your vision.

When exposing a plate, it should be placed emulsion side up on the rubber blanket of the platemaking unit. The flat is positioned over the plate with the emulsion side of the negative or positive down. This

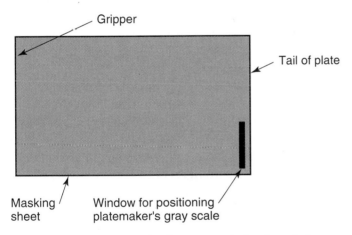

Figure 17-20. A platemaker's gray scale is placed along the tail or gripper edge of the flat. The gray scale receives the same amount of exposure as the rest of the image.

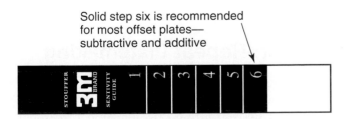

Solid step six is recommended for most offset plates—subtractive and additive

Figure 17-21. The correct exposure of the plate reveals the desired gray scale step. For most subtractive- and additive-working plates, solid step six is recommended. Always check the manufacturer's recommendations for the gray scale step. (3M Company)

step tablet: a piece of film with 10 or 21 steps ranging in densities from clear to completely black. This tablet is used to obtain consistent exposure and development of offset plates.

halftone scale: a measuring device made of film that is a single continuous strip of progressively dense gray. This scale is used to obtain consistent exposure and development of offset plates.

places the flat in direct contact with the emulsion side of the plate. As previously stated, a platemaker's (film) gray scale should be placed in a cutout portion of the flat along the gripper or tail edge of the plate, outside the printing area. Expose the plate to a solid step six, as shown in **Figure 17-23.** Step six is the recommended reading for most negative-working, additive and subtractive plates. **Figure 17-23** also shows how a gray scale appears before developing.

Note

A solid step six means step six is just as dense as step one on the developed image of the gray scale.

For most positive-working plates, the gray scale reading should be an open step three or four. This

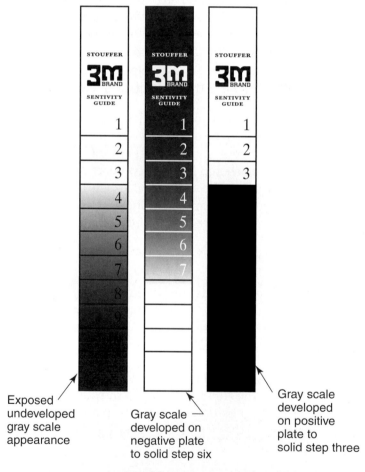

Exposed undeveloped gray scale appearance

Gray scale developed on negative plate to solid step six

Gray scale developed on positive plate to solid step three

Figure 17-23. The platemaker's gray scale is used to verify the correct exposure time. Step six is recommended for negative-working plates. Step three is recommended for positive-working plates. The example on the left illustrates how an exposed undeveloped gray scale appears in a flat. When developed, it looks similar to the example in the middle. (3M Company)

means step three or four should be just as open as step one. If a positive-working plate does not develop satisfactorily, it is probably underexposed. If the plate is underexposed, the gray scale should indicate this with an open step one or two. If exposure is made through more than one layer of film, increase the exposure time. One extra layer of film usually requires one-half step more exposure.

The lead edge of the flat should be aligned with the lead edge of the plate. In addition, the flat is generally aligned along the left-hand edge of the plate. When using a pin register system, be certain the tabs fit snugly over the pins.

Always check the glass on the top of the plate-making machine for cleanliness. When the plate and flat are in position, lower and lock the glass cover. Turn the vacuum switch on, and the vacuum blanket compresses the plate and flat to produce a tight contact. Set the timer for the recommended exposure time and expose the plate and flat to the UV light source by pressing the exposure button.

After the exposure is complete, move the vacuum frame back to its normal position and turn off the vacuum. Open the glass frame carefully. A certain amount of vacuum resistance might be present and cause the flat and plate to stick to the glass. After removing the flat and plate, close and lock the glass frame to avoid glass breakage.

Process the plate by hand or with an automatic plate processor. If the plate has been correctly exposed, the recommended numbered gray scale step appears. The processing methods for both additive- and subtractive-working, presensitized plates are described here because these plates are handled differently.

Caution

Some plate-processing solutions are toxic and can cause irritation or inflammation on fingers and hands.

Step-and-Repeat Platemaking

It is frequently desirable to run a job with two or more identical images on the plate—in other words, printing more than one at a time. Ordinarily, these extra images require additional negatives to be used. An alternative procedure known as *step-and-repeat platemaking* is used to prepare one negative to be exposed in two or more different positions on the plate.

With step-and-repeat platemaking, a single negative or positive is stripped and fitted into a special chase and frame on the platemaking machine. The chase can be moved back, forth, up, and down to any series of preset dimensions. An unexposed, presensitized offset plate is loaded into the machine.

For exposure, the frame is closed, the vacuum is turned on, and the frame is moved to a vertical position so it faces the exposure light. The step-and-repeat platemaking machine automatically moves to each required position on the plate, and an exposure is made. During each exposure, all areas of the plate except the portion under the chase are covered and receive no exposure. After all exposures have been made onto the plate, it is removed and processed manually or in a plate processor.

Figure 17-24 illustrates how a step-and-repeat plate appears after multiple exposures and processing. This procedure greatly increases productivity in the platemaking department. The result is maximum utilization of press time in printing items such as posters, cartons, letterheads, brochures, labels, shipping tags, business cards, and business forms.

Processing Additive Plates

The processing of additive plates involves removing the unexposed coating and hardening the image areas to improve the plate's durability on press.

1. Apply a desensitizing gum to the entire surface of the plate. See **Figure 17-25.** Use a small cellulose sponge for this purpose, moving the sponge back and forth. This gum removes the unexposed coating.

Figure 17-24. A step-and-repeat plate being manually processed. Note the multiple images of the same form on a single plate. (Enco Products)

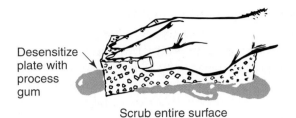
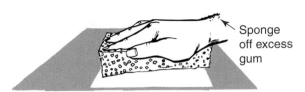

Figure 17-25. An additive-working offset plate is processed by first desensitizing the entire surface with gum. (3M Company)

2. Apply the developing lacquer to the plate by pouring it onto the surface of the plate in a small pool about 1 1/2″ (38 mm) in diameter. Move a clean cellulose sponge in a circular motion to develop the image and gray scale to a ruby-red color. This lacquer hardens the image areas. See **Figure 17-26.**

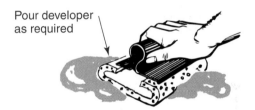

Figure 17-26. After desensitizing the surface of an additive-working plate, developer is applied, and a circular motion is used to develop the image and gray scale. (3M Company)

step-and-repeat platemaking: the means by which multiple images from a single image are exposed onto a printing plate in two or more positions.

3. Rinse the plate with tap water in a plate sink. This removes all the excess chemicals. If the plate is going directly on the press, no additional preparation is necessary. The plate must be preserved if it is to be stored for a period of time, however, to protect it from oxidation, dirt, and handling.

4. To preserve the plate, apply a thin coating of gum arabic or plate gum solution to the surface of the plate. Apply the gum solution with a lint-free cotton pad or soft, disposable paper wipe. Buff the gum in the direction of the length of the plate. Continue the buffing action until the plate is completely dry.

The entire sequence of steps involved in processing an additive-working, presensitized plate is illustrated in **Figure 17-27.** Both sides of the plate can be exposed and processed, if desired. If an automatic plate processor is used, follow the instructions given by the manufacturer.

Note

Never dry a plate under forced-air heat, since this action penetrates the gum application and destroys the gum's usefulness.

1. Apply a developing solution evenly over entire plate surface. Use a clean, soft cellulose sponge. Remove the excess gum, leaving only a thin film on plate. Gum removes unexposed diazo coating on plate or renders it water receptive.

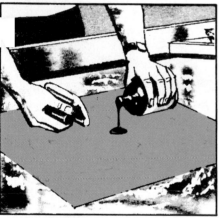

2. A special lacquer emulsion is applied before gum dries. Size of image area determines how much lacquer to use so that all image areas are covered. Continue rubbing lacquer until strong, uniform image appears.

4. Squeegee plate dry with a squeegee made expressly for this purpose.

5. Apply a small amount of special gum solution with a soft, clean cellulose sponge. Polish gum dry with clean, soft cheesecloth. Plate is ready for press or storage.

3. Flush off excess lacquer with water and inspect plate. Image should not be streaked and should not rub off with fingers.

Figure 17-27. The steps necessary to process an additive-working, presensitized offset plate. (3M Company)

Processing Subtractive Plates

A subtractive, presensitized plate is exposed in exactly the same way as an additive plate. A subtractive plate, however, has a colored, light-sensitive coating over its entire surface. This coating must be removed from all the unexposed areas of the plate's surface. Two solutions are required for subtractive plate processing. These are the subtractive developer and the plate gum.

1. Place the exposed plate on a smooth, firm surface and pour a small quantity of subtractive developer over the surface of the special pad. Pour a liberal amount of the developer on the surface of the plate. Spread the developer evenly over the entire surface with the pad. Use firm pressure on the pad with a tight circular motion to remove the coating from the nonimage areas. See **Figure 17-28.**
2. The image areas, including the gray scale, must be completely developed. Fresh developer can be used to clean out halftone and tint areas that appear filled in. Do not allow the developer to dry on the nonimage areas of the plate.
3. Use a squeegee on the plate. Remove any remaining developer from the plate's surface with a soft, disposable paper wipe. This prevents image loss, ink specks, and streaks in nonimage areas when the plate is run on the press.
4. Rinse the image side of the plate in the plate sink with tap water, and then rinse the plate on the reverse side to remove any stray developer and dirt.

Figure 17-28. Developing solution is rubbed over the plate with a pad to bring out the image. (3M Company)

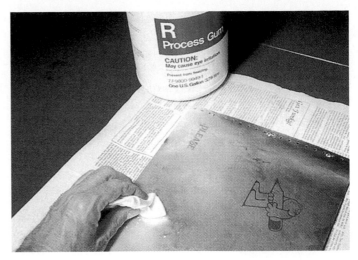

Figure 17-29. Protective gum is applied to the plate after development.

5. Use a soft, disposable paper wipe to completely dry the surface of the plate. Pour a small pool of plate gum on the plate's surface and spread it with a soft, disposable paper or cotton wipe. See **Figure 17-29.** Buff the surface dry with a fresh paper wipe and wipe the reverse side of the plate dry.

Some subtractive-working plates can be exposed and processed on both sides, if desired. If a plate processor is used, follow the instructions given by the manufacturer.

Plate Corrections

After processing, a surface plate should be checked to determine the overall quality of its image and nonimage areas. This must be done before the plate is released to the press department to avoid problems when on press. Plate corrections are categorized as either additions or deletions. Additions and deletions might be needed to repair minor problems on the plate.

Additions

Simple additions to lines, solids, and other image parts of an offset plate can be made either on or off the press. This is done by applying a tusche solution to the affected area of the plate. *Tusche* is a form of greasy lithographic developing ink. Tusche pens are available for this purpose.

To make minor additions on the press, be sure the area to be treated is free of ink and completely dry. Apply tusche to the affected area with a tusche

tusche: a liquid-emulsion ink painted or drawn on a lithographic plate to form an image.

pen or cotton-tipped swab. The area tusched turns a brown color in 20 to 40 seconds. Neutralize the area immediately with water. Dry the area, and then apply offset ink to the area with your finger. If the ink does not adhere to the affected area after resuming the pressrun, tusche the area again. This procedure can be repeated as many times as necessary, but it might require a plate remake.

Deletions

After developing a surface plate, it might be necessary to make deletions to unwanted words, lines, spots, or solid image areas. The *dry method* of deleting small image areas uses a simple rubber eraser. Ironically, the dry method can include wetting the image with water or a lubricant. First, dampen the area to be deleted. Moisten the eraser and rub it on the unwanted area carefully. This is done by alternately wetting and then erasing the unwanted area. Keep the treated area wet with water throughout the deletion process. The deleted area is then desensitized with fountain solution and rinsed with water. The plate should be preserved if it is not used on the press immediately. In most instances, deletions are needed after the plate is on the press and running.

Besides the method just described, a solution called *deletion fluid* can be used to remove large areas of image on a plate. Apply the fluid using a cotton swab when the plate is clean and completely dry. After the fluid is allowed to work on the area for about one minute, clean the area with water.

Deletions on paper plates during a pressrun should be handled with care, since the surface is easily damaged. Use only the recommended deletion procedure for the type of plate being used. In most instances, apply full-strength etch solution to the affected areas before resuming the pressrun.

Digital Plates

In conventional platemaking, camera-ready copy is photographed, and the images are captured on film, which is used to expose the plate. Today's technology allows plates to be imaged directly from digital files in a process known as *computer-to-plate (CTP)* or *direct-to-plate (DTP)*. Most lithographic plates used today are digitally generated. In a digital prepress operation, there are no camera-ready art boards, process cameras, film negatives, or contact platemaking equipment. Instead, the electronically imposed images are sent to platesetters, high-quality devices that expose and process plates. See **Figure 17-30.** With the exceptions of paper

Figure 17-30. Platesetters image plates with a laser driven by the digital data prepared in prepress. (Agfa-Gevaert Inc.)

and ink-jet plates, CTP plates consist of a base coated with a light-sensitive emulsion. Important characteristics of digital plates are the base material, emulsion type, emulsion's reaction to exposure, and degree of processing required.

CTP plates, similar to conventional plates, can be either negative or positive working. A negative-working plate is imaged as the platesetter's laser strikes the image areas, and a positive-working plate is imaged as the laser strikes the nonimage areas, because there are no films involved in CTP. There are several types of plates manufactured especially for platesetters.

Base Material

Similar to conventional plates, digital plates can be aluminum, polyester, or paper. The main distinction among the three materials is their durability during the pressrun. Aluminum plates have a grained surface to improve the retention of a thin film of dampening solution. Depending on the emulsion, aluminum plates can print between 100,000 and 2 million impressions.

Before the development of platesetters, imagesetters were capable of outputting polyester plates, as well as films used to expose metal plates. These early polyester plates were limited to one- or two-color jobs and short pressruns. The introduction of platesetters brought a new generation of polyester plates that can print up to 25,000 impressions and are appropriate for four-color jobs.

Polyester plates are not grained. Instead, they are treated chemically to improve their hydrophilic characteristic. Polyester plates are available in thicknesses ranging from 0.004" to 0.008". Thicker plates are more appropriate for longer pressruns because polyester plates can stretch on the press cylinder over time.

Paper plates do not carry a light-sensitive emulsion. Instead, they are imaged electrostatically. A laser beam strikes portions of a positively charged drum, causing those portions to lose their charge and become neutral. Unexposed parts of the surface (the image areas) remain positively charged. Negatively charged toner particles are attracted to only the positively charged areas of the surface. The drum then rolls against the plate materials and transfers the toner to it. The surface of these plates is chemically treated to make it hydrophilic. Paper plates are usually limited to offset duplicators and short-run jobs.

Imaging Technologies

Several types of emulsions are available on digital plates. Some emulsions are formulated to react to visible light. Others react to invisible light. Still others react to heat. Emulsions are also different in whether the laser exposes the image areas (negative working) or nonimage areas (positive working). They vary in the amount of exposure required to generate an image. Some types of emulsions are more durable than other emulsions are. Some emulsions are capable of higher resolutions than others are. Last, some emulsions require processing, and others do not.

Silver-halide plates

Both metal and polyester plates can carry a light-sensitive emulsion containing a silver halide—making them similar to the emulsion of photographic film. Known as *silver-halide plates*, they are positive-working plates that are processed in a manner similar to processing photographic film. Therefore, the spent chemistry contains enough silver to be a contaminant. Silver recovery needs to be performed before the spent chemistry can be sent down the drain.

Aluminum silver-halide plates are panchromatic. Most types of visible light lasers can expose them. These plates can carry 300-lpi screen rulings and print over 250,000 impressions.

Digital photopolymer plates

Instead of silver, the emulsions on photopolymer plates contain light-sensitive plastic molecules that form strong bonds through polymerization. Whereas conventional photopolymer plates are exposed by light moving through the clear areas of film, digital photopolymer plates are exposed by light generated and directed by lasers. Refer back to **Figure 17-6**. The spent processing chemistry requires no special treatment because there is no silver involved. The hardness that polymerization imparts allows these emulsions to print up to 250,000 impressions. If they receive a baking treatment, they are capable of over 1 million impressions.

Thermal-conversion plates

In contrast to silver-halide and photopolymer emulsions, *thermal-conversion plates* have a polymer coating that reacts to heat instead of light. The heat of an IR laser beam converts the image areas of the coating to a polymerized material, which resists the processing chemistry that dissolves the unexposed coating in the nonimage area to reveal the hydrophilic base. Thermal-conversion plates are usually baked to extend their lives during pressruns of up to 1 million impressions. A thermal-conversion, negative-working plate requiring no processing and having a pressrun capability of 1 million impressions is available. See **Figure 17-31**.

Figure 17-31. This thermal-conversion, negative-working plate is capable of a 100,000-impression pressrun. (Agfa-Gevaert Inc.)

dry method: a method of deleting small image areas that uses a simple rubber eraser.

computer-to-plate (CTP): a platemaking process that allows plates to be imaged directly from electronic data.

silver-halide plate: a printing plate with a light-sensitive emulsion of silver and iodine, bromine, or another halogen.

thermal-conversion plate: a printing plate with a coating that is imaged by being exposed to heat instead of light.

Thermal-conversion plates are available in metal and polyester. Polyester thermal-conversion plates have the highest resolution of all CTP plates, with 300 lpi and a 10-micron stochastic dot. Thermal-conversion plates can be processed automatically with water-based chemistry. The plate material is purchased in rolls and automatically cut to length after exposure. Thermal-conversion plates can also be referred to as *heat-sensitive plates* or *thermal plates*.

Thermal-ablation plates

Ablation is the process of removing a material by any one of several means—cutting, melting, vaporizing, or erosion. ***Thermal-ablation plates*** are made by ablating the plate's top coating layer with a laser that vaporizes it. Removing the top coating exposes the bottom coating layer. See **Figure 17-32**. If a positive-working plate is imaged, the top layer is oleophilic, and the bottom layer is hydrophilic. The laser exposes the nonimage areas to remove the top layer and reveal the surface that will carry the dampening solution. If a negative-working plate is being imaged, the layers are reversed. The top layer is hydrophilic, and the bottom layer is oleophilic. The laser removes the top layer in the image areas to reveal the surface that will carry the ink. Each type of plate must be imaged in a platesetter designed for it.

Thermal-ablation plates have a metal or polyester base and are imaged with a computer-controlled laser diode. A small vacuum nozzle moves along with the laser beam and removes the tiny particles caused by ablating the top coating layer. There is no processing to be performed because the exposure has actually created the image and nonimage areas of the plate. The plate is wiped down and mounted on the press. The elimination of the plate-processing stage saves time and eliminates the need to purchase, handle, and dispose of chemistry. Thermal ablation can be found in both CTP and CTPr systems. Baking the processed metal plates can make them capable of up to two million impressions.

Waterless plates

Unlike conventional offset printing, ***waterless offset printing*** does not use dampening solution (water). For this reason, waterless offset printing plates are designed differently from conventional offset plates. See **Figure 17-33**.

Waterless plates are made with an aluminum base and three to four coatings. The first coating applied to the base serves as a primer to which the next layer can adhere. The second coating is a light-sensitive photopolymer, which the next layer (silicone rubber) adheres to or releases from when exposed

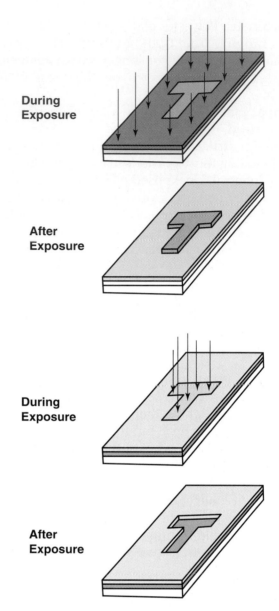

During Exposure

After Exposure

During Exposure

After Exposure

Figure 17-32. Positive-working, thermal-ablation plates are imaged as the laser's heat strikes and vaporizes the nonimage areas of the oleophilic top coating layer (red). Removing the top layer in the nonimage areas exposes the hydrophilic bottom layer (blue). Negative-working, thermal-ablation plates are imaged as the laser's heat strikes and vaporizes the image areas of the hydrophilic top coating layer (blue). Removing the hydrophilic top layer in the image areas exposes the oleophilic bottom layer (red), which carries the ink.

to UV light, depending on whether the plate is positive or negative working. The top layer is a protective layer of transparent film, which is removed during developing.

Negative-working waterless plates are imaged as UV light strikes the image areas. The UV light weakens the bond between the rubber silicone and the photopolymer in the image areas. After exposure,

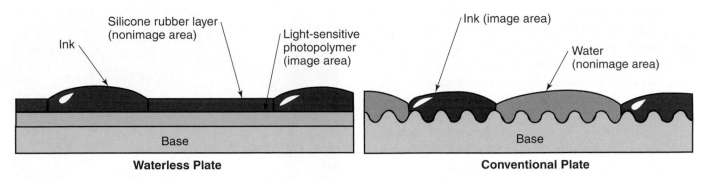

Figure 17-33. The image area of the waterless plate is slightly below the nonimage area and is receptive to ink. (Polychrome Corp.)

the plate material is treated to bond the silicone and the photopolymer in the unexposed nonimage areas. The silicone is then washed off the image areas.

Positive-working waterless plates are imaged as UV light strikes the nonimage areas. Exposure to UV light causes the silicone to adhere to the photopolymer layer in the nonimage areas. During developing, the silicone layer is washed away from the image area, revealing the photopolymer layer.

Electrostatic plates

Electrostatic (or electrophotographic) CTP polyester and metal plates are used in printing facilities with small-format presses. The metal plates are six mils thick and range in size from 10″ × 15″ to 13.4″×25″. These plates have a resolution equivalent to a 150-line screen and a run length of 25,000 impressions. The polyester plates are four mils and can also be as large as 13.4″ × 25″. These plates require nochemical processing.

Ink-jet plates

Metal CTP plates can be imaged without exposure to light. *Ink-jet plates* are imaged with platesetters that create image areas on the plate surface with ink-jet technology. These plates are intended for small printing facilities. Ink-jet plates have a resolution equivalent to 150–175 lpi and can handle pressruns up to 100,000 impressions. These plates in 6-, 8-, and 10-mil thicknesses and as large as 24″ × 29.5″ can be imaged.

Computer-to-Plate (CTP) Equipment

CTP systems use an automatic processor called a *platesetter* to image and process plates. Platesetters vary in size and output capabilities, but many can image and process eight-page flats in a matter of minutes. Some CTP systems eliminate the need for chemical processing, are environmentally friendly, and improve print quality. Depending on the particular job and processing method, plates created with a CTP system can handle run lengths of 40,000 to a million or more impressions. See **Figure 17-34.**

Figure 17-34. Platesetters vary in size and output capabilities. The platesetter illustrated here can produce six-page imposition plates. (Gerber Systems Corp.)

ablation: the physical removal of a material by cutting, vaporizing, or erosion.

thermal-ablation plate: a printing plate with a coating that is ablated by a laser's heat.

waterless offset printing: an offset printing process that eliminates water or fountain solution from the offset lithography printing equation.

waterless plate: a printing plate made with an aluminum base and three to four coatings and designed for waterless offset printing.

ink-jet plate: a plate with image areas that are applied with an ink-jet printer.

These systems require the use of platesetters and RIPs to process information before plate imaging can take place. Most CTP systems are modified to suit the printer's needs. CTP systems usually include software that performs trapping, imposition, and image replacement. Many systems include a densitometer, for calibrating and monitoring the quality of plate output, and a transfer punch, which notches and trims the plate to fit a specific press format. CTP systems also allow proofs to be generated from the same data that will be used to generate the plate. Advantages of CTP technology include the following:

- The excellent print quality in both color and black-and-white.
- A reduction in work-flow and material cost, based on the elimination of the film-based cycle.
- The elimination of bad plates resulting from dust and scratches on film.
- A reduction in processing time and storage space.
- The suitability for short printing runs, as well as long commercial and publication runs.

The costs of plate materials and proofing devices are issues for printers using CTP technology. The cost of many CTP plates is higher than the cost of conventional plates, and the initial investment in platesetters and other necessary equipment is substantial. The cost of film materials and film processing is eliminated, however, thereby reducing the cost of materials and labor.

Electrostatic Platesetters

Printing facilities with small-format presses can use CTP systems that image plates with *electrostatic platesetter* (or electrophotographic platesetter) technology. The digital data drives a laser, which images a drum by selectively charging its surface so electrically charged, dry toner particles are attracted to the image areas. The toner is then transferred to either a metal or polyester plate. See **Figure 17-35.** This technology can output 60 plates an hour.

Ink-Jet Platesetters

A CTP technology for small-to-medium presses is the *ink-jet platesetter*. Plates are imaged as digital data directs the application of the image coating onto metal plates through ink jets. The technology uses conventional development. These platesetters can output 12 plates an hour. See **Figure 17-36.**

Blank Plate

Imaged Plate

Figure 17-35. A blank plate is fed into the electrostatic platesetter. The imaged plate is output. (Xante)

Plate Precautions on Press

When an offset plate is attached to the plate cylinder of the press, the operator should remove the gum coating from the surface of the plate before inking it. Removal is performed with a damp sponge or cotton wipe. If the pressrun is interrupted for more than a few seconds, the plate can dry. This is especially true when the fountain solution contains alcohol. The operator must dampen the plate again before proceeding. Such dampening is essential with ungrained plates, such as a photodirect paper plate. If the press operator must leave the press for an extended time, the plate should be gummed immediately.

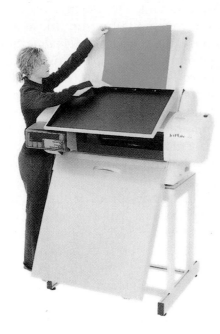

Figure 17-36. A blank plate is placed into an ink-jet platesetter. (JetPlate Systems)

When the press operator is ready to resume the run, the gum coating must be removed with a sponge or cotton wipe. This procedure prevents deterioration of the nonimage areas of the plate. If this procedure is not followed, the ability of the nonimage areas of the plate to repel ink can be destroyed.

Handling and Storage

Offset plates are manufactured under rigid quality-control conditions. The manufacturer guarantees consistent printing qualities, as long as the plates are handled and processed according to directions. The following points should be observed when working with offset plates:

- Handle presensitized offset plates in subdued yellow light. Never subject plates to room white light or sunlight.
- Plates should be kept in their original containers and stored in a dry, cool drawer near the platemaking equipment.
- Plates should be removed from their containers by lifting, not sliding, to avoid scratching one plate with the surface of another.
- Handle plates by the ends, being careful to keep fingers away from the printing surface. Acid and moisture from fingers cause marks on the surface of the plates.

Thin metal and plastic plates can cause severe cuts. Use care when removing plates from packages and handling them during processing.

When offset plates are retained for future printing, they must be stored to avoid damage and oxidation. See **Figure 17-37.** Following the pressrun, the plate should be gummed to preserve it. To gum a plate is to give it a thin coating of gum arabic solution or a similar gum preservative. Gum arabic is a gummy, water-soluble substance obtained from certain African acacia trees.

The gum coating acts as a preservative, preventing oxidation of the otherwise bare nonimage areas of the plate. Plates should be stored in a dry area in a hanging position. Plate cabinets and hanging systems are provided for this purpose. See **Figure 17-38.** Plates must be kept dry because moisture attacks the protective gum coating and can cause oxidation of the metal. Oxidized plates need to be replaced because ink will be attracted to the affected nonimage areas.

Plate-Related Problems

The printing plate is one of the most critical components governing the quality of the final printed product because it carries the image to be

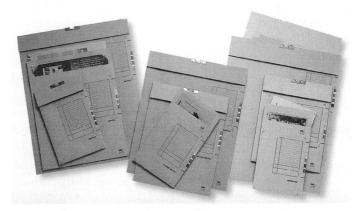

Figure 17-37. Special filing systems include envelopes varying in size and design. Special color-coding labels can be used for more efficient filing. (Jalema Inc., Filing Systems Division)

electrostatic platesetter: a platesetter that digitally images plates by charging the plate's image areas so they attract dry toner.

ink-jet platesetter: a platesetter that images printing plates by using ink-jet technology to apply image areas to the plate surface.

Figure 17-38. When metal offset plates are to be reused, they should be stored in a hanging position or placed in a plate cabinet. (Jalema Inc., Filing Systems Division)

placed on the paper or substrate. Various problems can result if the plates are processed or used improperly. **Figure 17-39** is a list of plate-related problems and some of their causes.

Plate blinding is a situation in which clearly visible image areas of the offset plate do not accept ink. There are three distinct types of plate blinding. These are roll up blinding, makeready blinding, and into-the-run blinding.

Roll Up Blinding

In roll up blinding, the plate appears to not take any ink in certain solids, small type, and some halftone midtone areas at press start-up. Washing with various solutions and cleaning compounds does not easily improve the situation. Plate cleaners often damage the image surface and shorten the run length.

The plate surface can be contaminated with a surfactant (surface-active agent) or roller and blanket cleaning products. This condition has the effect of capping the image area, and no amount of cleaning removes these surfactants or detergents. The primary causes are the transferring of chemicals from dampeners, rollers, and the blanket and poor press-area housekeeping. Old or contaminated plate developer can also contribute to roll up blinding. A number of plate manufacturers suggest using a finisher with a higher acid content to help prevent roll up blinding.

Makeready Blinding

Some blinding can occur when a press operator has started a press as part of the makeready for a job and stops the press to make adjustments for register and image placement. On starting up again, if the plate does not resume taking up ink in some areas, the situation is called *makeready blinding*. Some of the major causes of makeready blinding are contamination from the rollers, dampeners or surfactants in the washes, and failure to remove all the excess wash from the dampening rollers and blanket. In many cases, the press does not exhibit makeready blinding at the first part of a run. This can be attributed to the proper removal of ink and fountain solution after the previous run.

When cleaning with press or blanket washes, use clean water in the last stage to remove any surfactants, detergents, or soaps contained within the cleaning fluids. This step is extremely important, as it dramatically reduces roller glazing and the deterioration of all the rollers and blankets on a press. The safest and most effective cleaner is a two-stage wash product, used according to the manufacturer's recommendations.

Into-the-Run Blinding

An ink-related problem causes most into-the-run blinding. A buildup of calcium salts in the fountain solution can transfer onto the plate surface and attach themselves to screened areas, eventually making the plate less attractive to ink. Into-the-run blinding frequently occurs with highly pigmented inks, such as magenta and cyan, although ink manufacturers have made progress on improving the situation with magenta blinding.

Solving into-the-run blinding is not easy. Some suggestions are to change the brand of ink and to ask the ink manufacturer to reformulate the ink causing the problem. There are fountain solutions on the market claiming to solve the calcium problem, and a number of well-known products alleviate much of this problem. These fountain solutions contain a chemical additive that keeps the salts suspended within the fountain solution and reduces the possibility of mineral deposits building up on the plate surface.

Once a plate that has blinded from calcium salts and other trace elements has been cleaned, it will quickly blind again. This occurs because it is not possible to completely remove buildup from the complex grained and anodized surface of today's presensitized plates. The quickest remedy is to make a new plate.

Hydrogen peroxide can remove calcium buildup from plates. This is only a short-term measure, however, and blinding will reoccur at approximately 2000 to 3000 impressions, if the same ink and

Problem	Cause
Black spots	Plates not printing well on press, due to age, poor storage and handling, or a combination of these factors
Bridging	Developer solution reacts to connect two or more image areas on the plate
Contamination	Loss of purity and intrusion of dirt or unwanted material in the developer solution or other materials
Decomposition	Plate developer undergoes a chemical breakdown
Acidic developer	Developer has a high acid content
Alkaline developer	Developer is more alkaline than acidic
Dot gain	Poor vacuum between the negative and the plate
Faulty developer	Developer is outdated or improperly mixed
Gum blinding	Excessive amount of gum applied to the plate's image
Halation	Soft, fuzzy, unwanted circles, similar to halos, occurring in screened highlight areas of the plate
Hot spots	Improper contact of the negative and plate
Overdevelopment	Exposure time or developer solution used to excess
Piling	Excessive amount of developer solution allowed to build up on certain image areas of the plate
Pinhole	Unwanted, pinhead-size opening in the film
Plate blinding	Clearly visible areas of the plate that do not accept ink
Plugging	Images on the plate fill in where they should be open and clean
Shadow plugging	Poor vacuum contact between the negative and the plate
Soft image	Outside edges of an image on the plate contain less density or tone quality than the inside portion of the image does
Spotty image	Air pockets or dust between the plate and the glass
Streaking	Excessive amount of gum on the image area of the plate
Streaky image	A processor artifact, such as contaminated chemistry
Underdevelopment	Exposure time or developer solution is inadequate
Weak image	Inadequate development
White spots	Parts of image areas have pinhead-size openings where there is no image

Figure 17-39. A list of plate-related problems and some of their causes.

fountain solution are used. For more information on plate-blinding cures, refer to the troubleshooting chart at the end of Chapter 24.

Summary

Lithographic platemaking is the culmination of all prepress operations. The plates used for offset printing vary in the way they are made and the materials from which they are composed. The type of platemaking process and materials used depend largely on the configuration of the press or duplicator on which the job will be run.

Lithographic plates are thin sheets of metal, plastic, or paper used to duplicate an image on a press. Most offset plates in use today are based on the principle that grease and water do not readily mix. The image and nonimage areas of a plate are kept separate chemically. This successful separation is necessary because the image and nonimage areas are essentially on the same plane of the plate's surface. Lithographic plates can be imaged conventionally with negative or positive film using a contact method, or they can be imaged directly from digital data using lasers. Conventional lithographic plates

plate blinding: the effect occurring when the acid eats away the image areas of a printing plate and causes a lack of ink receptivity.

are categorized as additive or subtractive, negative- or positive-working, and presensitized or wipe-on.

Automatic processing machines and CTP systems have largely replaced manual plate-processing techniques. CTP systems are capable of automatically imaging and processing various types of plate materials for specific kinds of applications. Most CTP systems image plates categorized as silver-halide, photopolymer, thermal-conversion, or thermal-ablation plates. Electrostatic and ink-jet plates are also imaged digitally. CTP systems are environmentally friendly, are less time-consuming than conventional systems, and provide excellent print quality.

Review Questions

Please do not write in this book. Write your answers on a separate sheet of paper.

1. The term for water receptive is _____.
   A. oleophobic
   B. oleophilic
   C. hydrophobic
   D. None of the above.

2. What purpose does the surface grain on a lithographic plate serve?

3. _____ plates can be purchased to be exposed with either negative or positive films.

4. Surface plates carry the emulsion _____ the plate surface.
   A. on
   B. above
   C. below
   D. Both B and C.

5. Negative-working photopolymer plates form an image when monomers become _____.

6. _____-working offset plates are exposed with film negatives.

7. Conventional positive-working plates are imaged when the light strikes the _____ areas of the plate.

8. Subtractive plates are processed with chemistry that removes the _____ portions of the emulsion.
   A. hardened
   B. image
   C. exposed
   D. unexposed

9. Deep-etch plates carry the _____ areas below the plate surface and are exposed with film _____.

10. Multimetal plates are well suited to _____ pressruns.

11. Explain how conventional electrostatic plates are imaged.

12. Aqueous plates use coatings that can be processed by primarily _____-based developing chemistries.

13. Describe manual and automatic processing of conventional plates.

14. Explain how offset plates should be handled.

15. How should offset plates be stored?

16. A platemaker's _____ is used to determine the correct exposure time for a presensitized offset plate.

17. A(n) _____ is an exposure-control device made on film and containing discrete stages of gray.

18. A negative-working plate should be developed to a solid step _____.

19. Explain how a plate can carry eight images of the same business card with only one film negative of the card.

20. The two solutions required for processing a subtractive-working, presensitized plate are subtractive _____ and plate _____.

21. A(n) _____ pen can be used for simple additions to lines, solids, and other image areas of a lithographic printing plate.

22. How do you make a plate deletion by the deletion-fluid method?

23. Explain what CTP technology means.

24. Give two advantages of CTP systems.

25. What base material used in digital platemaking makes plates for the longest pressruns?

26. How are thermal-conversion plates different from silver-halide and photopolymer plates?

27. What effect does heat have on thermal-ablation plates?

28. How do waterless offset plates keep ink away from the nonimage areas of the plate?

29. Summarize the various types of CTP systems.

30. _____ blinding is an absence of ink in image areas of the plate during the press start-up phase of the pressrun.

Skill-Building Activities

1. Obtain a stripped flat. Cut and tape a platemaker's 21-step gray scale along the bottom edge (tail) of the flat. Make the exposure to a presensitized plate of the type and size your instructor specifies. Process and preserve the plate for future use.

2. Using resources in the library and on the Internet, research and write a report on xerography. If possible, prepare a simple demonstration of the electrostatic principles used to make electrostatic plates. Prepare a plate using an electrostatic platemaker system.

3. With a partner, obtain a single negative flat for a step-and-repeat job. Make the step-and-repeat exposures. Process and preserve the plate for future use.

4. Gain experience in adding, deleting, and repairing images on presensitized metal plates. Use the solutions and tools discussed in this chapter.

Forest, Fibers, Formation, and Finish

The paper in the photograph is nearing the end of its production. Its journey began, however, in a distant forest. Selected trees were harvested and sent to pulp mills, where the wood was reduced to individual fibers. After the fibers were refined, they were formed into a sheet. This formation was critical to the sheet's quality. Next, the sheet received a finish—perhaps textured or glossy. The photograph was taken at this point. This chapter takes the student on a more detailed study of paper—its manufacture, physical properties, classifications, and uses. The graphic designer who selects the paper, the planner who orders it, and the press operator who prints on it need a solid understanding of paper.

(Smurfit-Stone)

Key Terms

absorbency
alkaline paper
antique finish
baronial envelope
blank
bleaching
bond paper
book paper
bristol
business paper
cancellation method
carbonless bond paper
category
chemical-mechanical pulp
chemical pulp
chipping
classification
coated back (CB)
coated front (CF)
coated front-and-back
  (CFB)
coated groundwood paper
coated offset paper
combination cut
cover paper
cut size
deckle edge
digester
dimensional stability
dull finish
eggshell finish
elemental chlorine–free
  (ECF) bleaching
embossed finish
enamel finish
external sizing
fiber puffing
filler
fine
finish
finishing
flatness
fold strength
forming wire
fourdrinier machine
gloss finish
grain
groundwood pulping
hardwood tree
hickey
index bristol
internal sizing

label paper
linting
long-grain paper
machine finish
machine finished
matte finish
mechanical pulp
mineral paper
newsprint
offset paper
opacity
opaque paper
oxygen delignification
paperboard
paper classification
picking
pick resistance
piling
postconsumer waste
powdering
preconsumer waste
pulping
recycled paper
recycled pulp
refiner groundwood
refining stage
scumming
sheets per carton
short-grain paper
slurry
softwood tree
splicing
spoilage allowance
substance weight
supercalendering
synthetic paper
tagboard paper
tear strength
text paper
thermal-mechanical
  pulp (TMP)
totally chlorine-free
  (TCF) bleaching
twin-wire paper machine
uncoated offset paper
universal basic size
utility paper
vellum finish
washer
watermark
wet end
whiteness

Chapter 18
Paper

Learning Objectives

When you have completed the reading and assigned activities related to this chapter, you will be able to do the following:

❧ Summarize the papermaking process and list the various stages involved.

❧ Identify paper requirements for sheetfed and webfed presses.

❧ Give examples of various paper properties and explain how they affect a paper's printability, print quality, and runnability.

❧ List the paper classifications and indicate their identifying characteristics.

❧ Explain basic size, substance weight, ream weight, and M weight (Mwt).

❧ Describe the various sizes and styles of envelopes.

❧ Determine the number of sheets required for a printing job.

❧ Calculate the purchase price for an order of paper.

❧ Determine the appropriate paper for various printing jobs.

The material on which a job is printed, called the *substrate*, plays several roles in influencing the effectiveness of the finished job. The substrate usually contributes to the visual impact of the job, often represents 35%–55% of the final cost of a printed job, and might even determine which printing process is used. For example, the designs printed on drinking glasses are generally applied by screen printing, and clear plastic bread wrappers are commonly printed by flexography. The wide range of printing substrates includes paper, paperboard, glass, ceramics, metal, cloth, plastics, and wood. For offset lithographic printing, however, paper products are most commonly used. To select a substrate—whether it is paper, paperboard, or a synthetic paper—that is cost-effective and meets the aesthetic and printing requirements of a particular job, a working knowledge of paper is necessary. An inadequate awareness of paper from the graphic designer, print buyer, and even press operators often is responsible for major production problems and their resulting material waste, lost production time, late deliveries, and poor-quality products.

Paper and paper products are so much a part of everyday life that people take the material for granted. Sheets of paper that appear identical to the casual observer, however, actually can be different in many crucial ways. Very often, the problems just mentioned result from selecting the wrong type of paper for a particular application. The many different categories and subcategories of printing papers have complicated the paper-selection process. The demands of twenty-first-century consumers require these papers for packaging and communication. Consumers require printing products that work well, are inexpensive, and are environmentally friendly.

As the printing industry's technology and processes have evolved and improved, the paper industry's size and processes have evolved as well. See **Figure 18-1.** The United States produces 90 million tons of paper a year and consumes even more—100 million tons. To meet this need, the paper industry has developed massive high-speed machinery, exacting science, high technology, and precise quality control processes. Therefore, the graphic designer and the printer must have an understanding of various papers' capabilities to select the right sheet for a given job and work with it properly. This chapter begins with a brief history of papermaking, explains the modern-day papermaking process, and also provides information on paper characteristics and requirements that will help you identify and choose the proper substrate for specific work.

Figure 18-1. A pulp and paper mill is a massive manufacturing facility that converts trees into a variety of paper products. (MeadWestvaco)

Paper Origins

The word *paper* comes from the word *papyrus*, a reed the ancient Egyptians used for making a writing material. As early as 2000 BC, the Egyptians cut papyrus stalks into thin strips, which were soaked in water before being laid out in crisscrossed layers and then pressed into sheets that dried to form a thin surface on which to write. Although papyrus somewhat resembled paper, it did not qualify as paper because the reeds were not boiled and beaten to reduce them to their tiny, individual fibers before the sheet was formed. As a result, papyrus was rougher and stiffer than true paper.

It was not until over 2000 years later that papermaking was developed in China. Ts'ai (pronounced *SY*) Lun, a Chinese court official, is generally credited with the discovery of making paper in 105 AD. This official mixed debarked mulberry branches, hemp, and rags with water. The resulting slurry was cooked, beaten, poured onto molds, and pressed into flat sheets, which were hung to dry in the sun. See **Figure 18-2.**

This new product and the process of making it became very popular as several paper products were devised. Paper mills were established throughout the vast Chinese empire, but the techniques of paper manufacture were a secret the Chinese guarded closely for over 600 years. In 750 AD, however, the Muslim culture learned how to make paper, and during the next 500 years, paper mills became established in Syria, in Egypt, and across northern Africa. The Muslims substituted linen fibers for wood fibers because linen fibers produced stronger paper.

Figure 18-2. Eighth-century Chinese workers boiled mulberry branches in water to produce pulp for papermaking.

Figure 18-3. The original fourdrinier machine allowed paper to be formed into a continuous ribbon, which was immediately cut into sheets to be dried. The conveyor mesh moved from right to left.

Meanwhile, Europeans were still writing on expensive animal skins or wood.

Although there is a legend that a Crusader who was captured and forced to work in a Damascus paper mill escaped and returned to Europe with the centuries-old secret, history records that the Europeans did not learn of the secret of papermaking until the thirteenth-century conquest of Muslim-held provinces in southern Spain. After papermaking began in Europe, paper was used only as a material for handwriting because printing was not invented for another 200 years.

Although paper mills were built throughout Europe, the method of making paper from wood had long ago been lost, and paper was made exclusively from discarded rags. Each sheet was individually made by dipping a wire screen into a vat of water-suspended fibers, lifting it until the water drained through the screen to form a mesh of intertwined fibers, and then placing the wet sheet between pieces of felt and pressing out most of the water. Finally, the sheets were hung out to dry.

In 1798, Frenchman Nicolas Louis Robert invented a papermaking machine that made paper by pouring a slurry of pulp over a continuous conveyor belt made of wire screen. See **Figure 18-3.** As the wire screen slowly moved forward, water drained out and was then squeezed out, as the continuous sheet passed between rollers. Robert struggled with technical and financial troubles, however, and the London-based Fourdrinier brothers purchased the rights to it. After considerable financial investment, the efforts of these brothers were rewarded in 1812, when they put into operation the world's first paper machine,

known as the *fourdrinier machine.* Although the first fourdrinier machine was less than 9' long and was powered by hand, its descendents in use today are massive and operate at amazing speeds. Yet, they are still known as fourdrinier machines. See **Figure 18-4.** After the drum drier was invented in 1839, paper could be formed and dried to form a continuous roll.

Making Paper

The manufacture of paper for printing involves two processes: pulp production and paper manufacture. Pulp production includes debarking, chipping, pulping, bleaching, beating, refining, adding nonfibrous ingredients, and cleaning the pulp. Paper manufacture includes forming the paper, producing watermarks, removing water, drying the paper, and finishing the paper. Each of these stages is described later in this chapter.

Paper is made with what are known as *cellulose fibers*—the basic structure of plants. For the first 16 centuries of papermaking, the primary sources of cellulose fibers were cotton and linen rags. Today, wood fibers have largely replaced these sources, with the exception being the use of some cotton and linen fibers in the production of papers in which extra strength or permanence is required. Wood-fiber sources are divided into softwoods (coniferous)

◼◻◼◼◼◻◼◻◻

fourdrinier machine: a papermaking machine that forms a continuous web of paper on a moving, endless wire belt.

Figure 18-4. The wet end of a modern-day paper fourdrinier machine can form a 24′-wide stream of paper at a speed of 3000′ per minute. (MeadWestvaco)

Figure 18-5. Paper companies use greenhouses to raise millions of seedlings, which are later transplanted and allowed to reach maturity before being harvested. (Smurfit-Stone)

and hardwoods (deciduous). *Softwood trees* include pine, fir, spruce, and hemlock. *Hardwood trees* include oak, poplar, gum, beech, maple, birch, and chestnut. Fibers from both types of wood are used in most papers because the long and thick softwood fibers give the sheet strength, and the shorter and thinner hardwood fibers fill in the low places between the softwood fibers and make the sheet smoother.

It is important that the nation's timber supply is maintained because over 95% of America's paper is made from wood fiber. Many large paper manufacturers and other forest-product industries operate their own tree farms. See **Figure 18-5.** These companies plant selected seeds in containers and nurture the seedlings until they are large enough to transplant outdoors. When the trees are around 20 years old, they are cut and transported to the pulp mill. See **Figure 18-6.** Fortunately, several advancements in forest genetics, management, and harvesting techniques have allowed the nation's volume of timber to actually increase over the last several decades, despite a reduction in total forest acreage. Fewer acres are producing larger volumes of timber.

Pulping

Pulping is the process of reducing wood to individual fibers, and the product of the pulping process is called *pulp.* The mixture of water and dissolved

Figure 18-6. Mature trees can be cut and delimbed with the same machine. Delimbed trees are cut into uniform lengths and stacked in preparation for transportation to the paper mill. (Smurfit-Stone)

paper pulp is called *slurry*. *Mechanical pulp* is produced entirely by mechanical means—that is, no chemicals are used. The most simple and inexpensive procedure for producing mechanical pulp is *groundwood pulping*. Debarked logs are cut to 5' lengths and forced against a grindstone, which tears the fibers away from one another. See **Figure 18-7**. The tearing action produces short and badly damaged fibers, which result in weak paper. Groundwood papers are also subject to *fiber puffing*. This puffing causes the paper surface to become rough and abrasive. All methods of pulping, except for groundwood pulping, begin with *chipping*—the reduction of the debarked logs to chips approximately 1/4" thick and 1 1/2" long. See **Figure 18-8**. A method of mechanical pulping that produces stronger paper is

Figure 18-8. After their bark has been removed, logs are reduced to chips. This truckload of chips is being emptied at the paper mill. (MeadWestvaco)

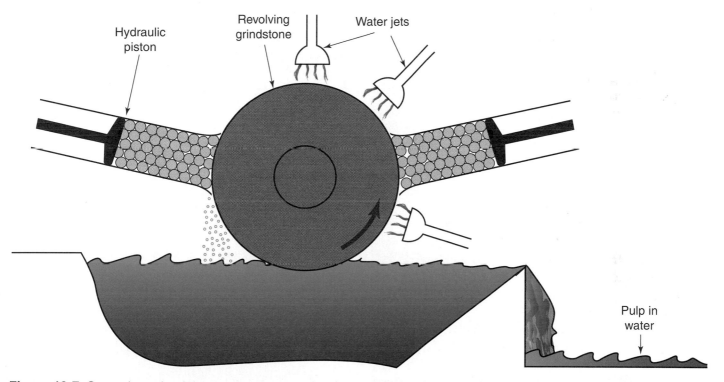

Figure 18-7. Groundwood pulping pushes logs against a revolving stone, which reduces the wood to fibers. Water is sprayed to prevent fire.

softwood tree: a coniferous tree, such as pine, fir, spruce, or hemlock.

hardwood tree: a deciduous tree, such as poplar, gum, beech, maple, birch, or chestnut.

pulping: liberating cellulose fibers from other impurities and chemicals in the wood and producing pulp for papermaking.

slurry: a mixture of water and dissolved paper pulp.

mechanical pulp: inexpensive paper pulp produced entirely by mechanical means and used for newspapers, directories, catalogs, magazines, and paperback books.

groundwood pulping: low-quality paper pulp produced by grinding debarked logs. The resulting fibers contain a high level of impurities, tend to be shortened from the pulping, and produce weak paper.

fiber puffing: the exploding of paper fibers that have not been completely ground during heatset drying. This puffing causes the paper surface to become rough and abrasive.

chipping: cutting wood into waferlike pieces called chips.

refiner groundwood. Debarked logs are reduced to chips, which are then mixed with water and pumped into refiners, where they are forced against counter-rotating disks.

Thermal-mechanical pulp (TMP) is produced by a process that uses heat to soften the chips before they go into the refiners, with the result that the softened chips come apart more easily and less fiber damage results. **Chemical-mechanical pulp** uses both heat and chemicals to soften the chips even more than with heat alone. The process generates pulp with even less fiber damage than producing TMP does.

Chemical pulp is prepared by pressure-cooking chips in a large enclosed container called a *digester.* See **Figure 18-9.** Heat, water, and cooking chemicals dissolve the lignin that bonds the fibers, thereby allowing the fibers to fall away undamaged. The resultant pulp produces strong paper. In fact, the first paper made from chemical pulping was called *kraft*

paper because *kraft* is German and Swedish for *strong.* Chemical pulping is a complex and comparatively expensive process. This pulping results in lower yields but higher-quality wood pulp than any other process because it removes almost all the lignin. Paper made from **chemical pulp** is often referred to as *free sheet* because it is essentially free of lignin, and it is used to print books, brochures and other promotional pieces, annual reports, maps, labels, stationery, and other applications requiring good quality. The presence of lignin causes newspaper to eventually turn brown and brittle.

Recycled pulp is made from repulped wastepaper. The wastepaper is reduced back to individual fibers in a hydropulper—a large tank that works similarly to a giant blender. Contaminants such as staples, paper clips, and rubber bands are then screened out, and ink is separated from the fibers through the use of solvents, detergents, other chemicals, and more screening. After the ink and other impurities are washed away from the fibers, the pulp is bleached. **Fines** are fibers that have become too short from repeated repulpings. They are also washed away because short fibers reduce paper's strength. See **Figure 18-10.**

Figure 18-9. Wood chips, water, and chemicals are cooked at a high temperature and under high pressure in a digester. (Hammermill Paper Co.)

Figure 18-10. As a dilute mixture of fibers and water pours over sidehill washers, dirt, ink, and short fibers fall through the holes in the screens.

Treating the Pulp

The stages of making high-quality paper are represented in **Figure 18-11**. After logs have been debarked, they are reduced to chips, which are cooked in a *digester* to separate them into individual fibers and stored in the blow pit before moving onto further treatment stages—washing; bleaching; refining; and the addition of fillers, sizing, dyes, and pigments. Depending on the type of pulp and the paper being manufactured, some of the steps might be omitted.

The pulp goes to *washers*, which remove spent chemicals used in the digester, and then is sent over a series of screens and centrifugal cleaners that remove small pieces of uncooked wood and grit. In a series of carefully controlled operations, the pulp passes through four stages of *bleaching* to whiten the paper fibers. The pulp is then given a final series of washings and sent to storage towers, where it awaits the addition of fillers, sizing, and dyes.

The *refining stage* (also known as the *beating stage*) plays a major role in affecting several physical characteristics of the finished sheet. During the refining process, pulp fibers are flattened, frayed, and sometimes shortened. Many additives (such as fillers, sizing, and dyes) are incorporated into the pulp during the refining process. *Fillers* are finely ground particles of clay or chalk added to pulp to improve the paper's opacity (reduce the passage of light). See **Figure 18-12**. Filler content is highest in book paper and other papers intended for two-sided printing. This content is much lower in bond, writing, xerographic, and other sheets expected to carry images on only one side.

Sizing is used to make paper less absorbent. Writing on newsprint with an ink pen demonstrates how excessive *absorbency* allows feathering, which hurts image quality. In lithographic printing, paper receives dampening solution, as well as ink. An excessive absorption of dampening solution can weaken the sheet and slow the drying of ink. Solving both problems requires two types of sizing—internal sizing and surface sizing. *Internal sizing* is achieved when the fibers are coated during the refining process with rosin or other substances that reduce their absorbency. Lithographic papers receive a large amount of sizing to greatly increase their water-repellent qualities. Excessive absorption of dampening solution weakens the fiber-to-fiber bond. External, or surface, sizing occurs after the sheet has been formed. *External sizing* usually consists of applying a starch to both sides of paper before the paper is removed from the paper machine.

This sizing improves print quality by reducing the absorption and feathering of ink. Paper is made in a variety of colors, from light tints to dark shades. Dyes and pigments are added to the pulp during refining to give the paper color.

Manufacturing Paper

The forming of paper starts at the *wet end* of the fourdrinier machine, where a slurry of 99% water and 1% fiber flow from the head box across a continuously forward-moving mesh wire screen called a *forming wire*. See **Figure 18-13**. The water drains from the pulp through the wire screen as it moves along, leaving a mat of fibers on the surface of the wire. Rollers and suction boxes under the wire screen support the screen and accelerate the removal of water. The side of the paper against the screen is called the *wire side*, and the top side is called the *felt side*.

refiner groundwood: chips and water pumped through refiners, where they are forced between counterrotating disks.

thermal-mechanical pulp (TMP): a type of mechanical pulp made by pumping preheated chips and water through refiners, where they are forced between counterrotating disks.

chemical-mechanical pulp: pulp produced using a combination of mechanical and cooking separation processes.

chemical pulp: pulp that uses chemical action to dissolve some of the wood's substances. This pulp results in lower yields, but higher-quality pulp, than the groundwood process.

recycled pulp: pulp made from fibers reclaimed from used paper and paper products.

fine: a cellulose fiber that is too short for papermaking.

digester: a pressurized kettle that breaks down the lignin in the cellulose fibers as part of the papermaking process.

washer: a large tank that uses water to flush away spent cooking chemistry from chemical pulp.

bleaching: a papermaking step in which pulp is treated with chlorine and similar chemical solutions to whiten the paper fibers.

refining stage: the stage in the papermaking process during which the fibers are flattened and abraded.

filler: a material added to pulp to smooth the paper surface, provide a better bond for ink, brighten color, and increase opacity.

absorbency: the physical characteristic of being porous.

internal sizing: the application of materials to wet paper pulp to provide the desired degree of resistance to water and increase the surface strength.

external sizing: material added to the surface of paper near the end of the papermaking process to give the paper greater stiffness.

wet end: the forming section of a papermaking machine.

forming wire: the continuously moving mesh wire screen on a papermaking machine on which the pulp is formed into paper.

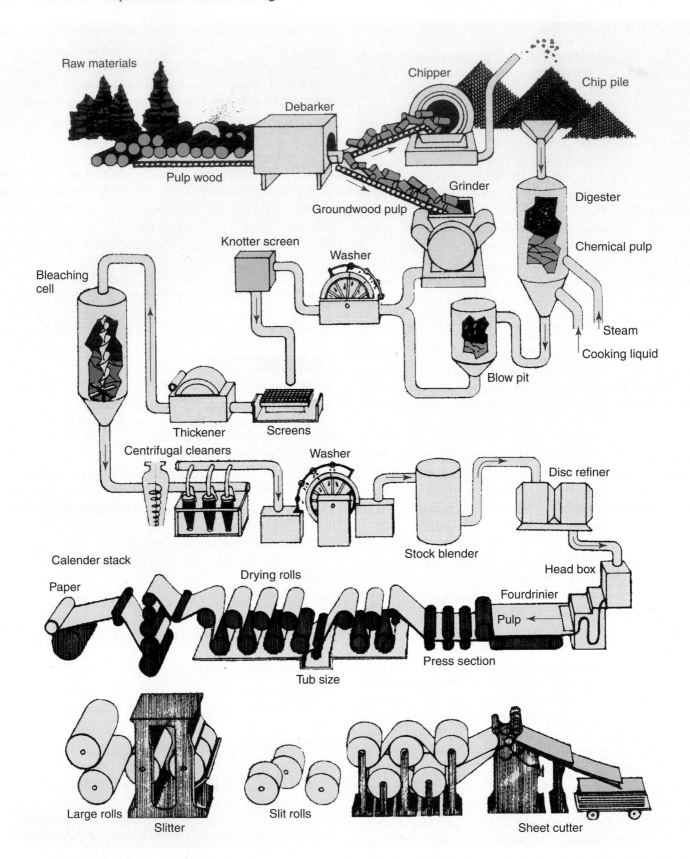

Figure 18-11. Wood enters the pulping stage, where it is chipped and pulped. The fibers are then washed, bleached, cleaned, and refined, before matting together on a moving wire to form a sheet that is dried, slit, sheeted, and wrapped.

Figure 18-12. Fillers are added to pulp to strengthen its properties. (Hammermill Paper Co.)

At this point, the pulp passes under a dandy roll to break up any bubbles that might have formed. The *dandy roll* also produces watermarks when it carries designs on raised metals. See **Figure 18-14.** A *watermark* is a symbol or logo identifying the brand of paper. At this point, the web of paper leaves the wire with 75% water content and is supported by a felt conveyor as it enters what is known as the *wet press section*, where it is squeezed between felt blankets that absorb much of the water. The web of paper leaves the wet press section with a 65% water content, and it is ready for the dryer section. In what is known as the *dryer section*, the web passes over and under steam-heated drums to remove most of the moisture. Surface sizing is performed at this point, and the now wet-again web goes through what is called a *second dryer section*, which reduces the water content to around 5%. As the web of paper emerges from the dryer section of the papermaking machine, it is forced between heavy iron *calender rollers*, which

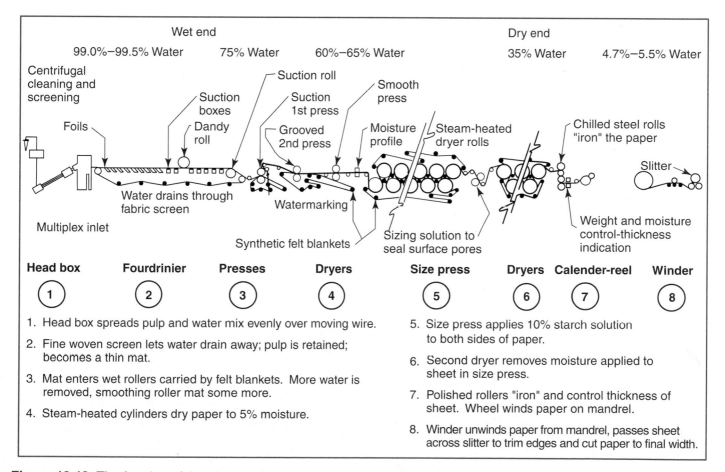

Figure 18-13. The forming of the sheet involves several steps. Note the lowered moisture content shown at the top of the diagram as the sheet moves through the process. (Hammermill Paper Co.)

watermark: a symbol or logo produced by a raised pattern on the dandy roll that identifies the brand of paper or trademark of a company.

Recessed design gives dark work

Raised design gives light work

Dandy roll

Figure 18-14. A watermark is a symbol or logo formed by a dandy roll on the papermaking machine. (MeadWestvaco)

make the paper's caliper (thickness) more consistent. If the paper manufacture is considered complete at this point, the paper is called *machine finished*.

In addition to being made on the fourdrinier machine, paper is also made on *twin-wire paper machines*, which function in much the same way, except the pulp slurry is forced upward between two wire screens. See **Figure 18-15.** Twin-wire machines can run considerably faster than fourdrinier machines because the coming together of the two wires eliminates foaming and air bubbles and water is removed from both sides.

If glossy paper is required, the rolls are taken to the coating room, where a liquid coating is applied to the paper and dried. Air-knife coaters apply a uniform thickness of the coating for uniform ink

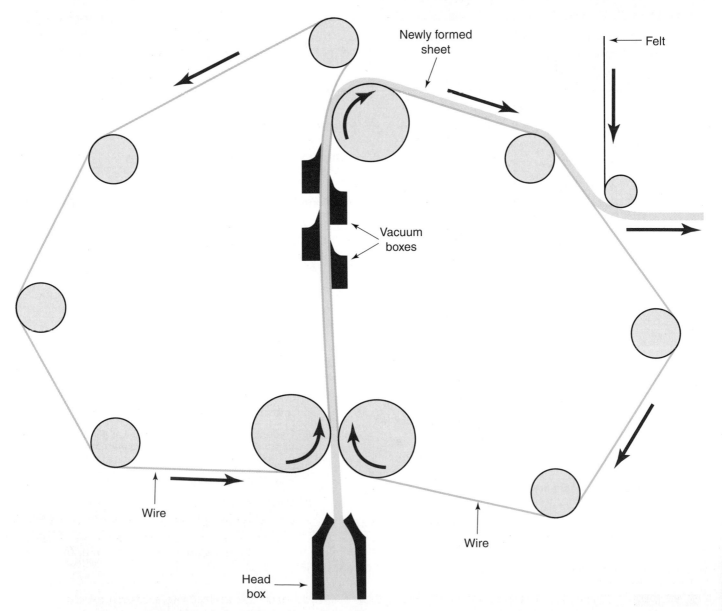

Newly formed sheet

Felt

Vacuum boxes

Wire

Head box

Wire

Figure 18-15. A twin-wire machine forms paper at a faster rate than a fourdrinier machine does because water is removed in two directions.

holdout and printing, while trailing-blade coaters produce a sheet with a high degree of smoothness and gloss. See **Figure 18-16.** The newly coated paper is then *supercalendered* by being run through another series of rollers that polish the coating and impart the desired gloss to the sheet. *Supercalendering* is the process of sending coated paper through a series of rollers that polish the coating to form a glossy

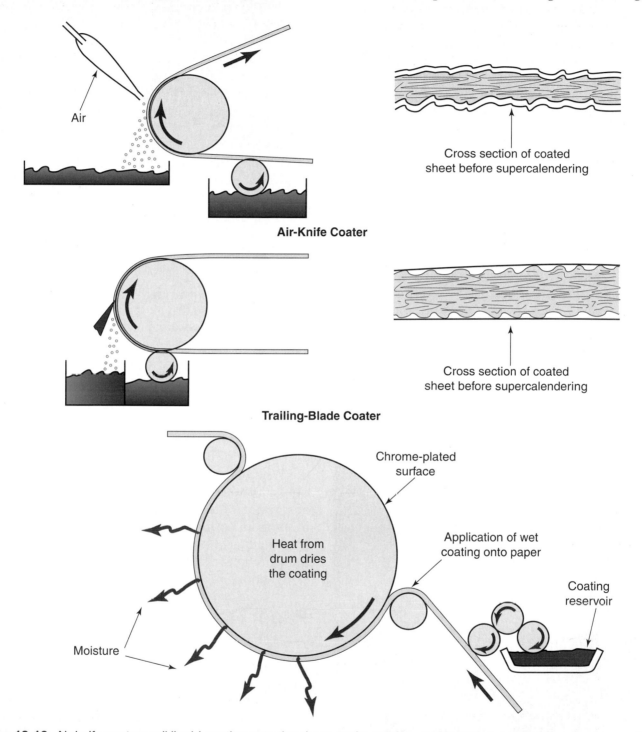

Air-Knife Coater

Cross section of coated
sheet before supercalendering

Trailing-Blade Coater

Cross section of coated
sheet before supercalendering

Chrome-plated
surface

Heat from
drum dries
the coating

Application of wet
coating onto paper

Coating
reservoir

Moisture

Figure 18-16. Air-knife coaters roll liquid coating onto the sheet, and a continuous blast of air blows off excessive coating to leave a uniform thickness. Trailing-blade coaters remove excessive coating with a metal blade to create a smooth surface.

machine finished: a high-gloss paper finish produced by allowing the wet-paper web to dry against a highly polished metal cylinder.

twin-wire paper machine: a papermaking machine that forms a sheet by sending the pulp between two moving wire screens.

supercalendering: the process of sending coated paper through a series of rollers that polish the coating to form a glossy finish.

finish. When leaving the papermaking machine, the finished web of paper is wound on huge steel reels. See **Figure 18-17.** Paper that is *caste coated* dries the coating against a slowly turning drum with a heated chrome surface. The coating dries to the same glossiness as the chrome, so it does not need to be polished by the supercalender rollers. The web is moved to a slitter machine, where it is cut into several smaller rolls. See **Figure 18-18.** Paper that needs to be sold as sheets goes on to a sheeter. Whether paper is sold as rolls or sheets, it must be wrapped to maintain the ideal moisture content.

Receiving, Handling, and Storing Paper

Paper represents a large financial investment and should be given the proper attention. Shipments of paper should be inspected for damage during transit as soon as they arrive. An inexpensive single-use camera should be kept on hand to document any damage while rolls, skids, or cartons are still on the truck or receiving dock. If the wrapping is torn but the paper is undamaged, the wrapping should be repaired or replaced before the paper is placed in inventory. Wintertime shipments of paper that were chilled by sitting in a cold truck should be allowed to warm to indoor temperature before they are unwrapped.

Figure 18-18. The rewinder-slitter machine in the background is used to cut the web into desired widths and rewind it onto separate rolls. (MeadWestvaco)

The rolls of paper used on web presses can be easily damaged by being dropped only a short distance. They can also be damaged by being rolled across a rough floor or a floor with clutter that can cut into them. Paper rolls should be stored on their ends to avoid flattening one side of the roll.

Whether in rolls or sheets, paper should be kept out of contact with concrete floors to prevent the absorption of moisture. Also, paper should be stored away from sources of heat or cold. Most important, stored paper should not be allowed to absorb or lose moisture to the surrounding air. Opened cartons and skids should be rewrapped to protect unused sheets.

Paper Requirements

Small and large offset presses can print on almost any kind of paper. For quality work, however, paper should meet certain basic requirements. Mills manufacture **offset paper** (or litho paper)—sheets manufactured specifically for lithography—because of the demands offset lithographic printing places on paper.

Sheetfed-Offset Requirements

The ink has a high tack level and can exert enough pull against the paper to pull away part of the surface because offset printing uses a paste ink, instead of a liquid ink. For this reason, offset paper must have a

Figure 18-17. A new log of paper is checked for uniformity before moving on to be slit into smaller rolls. (Smurfit-Stone)

stronger fiber-to-fiber bond than is needed for other printing processes, such as gravure, screen, or flexography. In offset lithography, the paper receives both ink and dampening solution. To prevent the softening and weakening of the sheet by excessive absorption of dampening solution, offset paper receives internal sizing, as well as surface sizing.

The softening and weakening of the paper surface can cause *picking* (the lifting of clumps of paper fibers) and a transfer of fibers or coating to the blanket. The complete contact of rubber blanket and paper and the inherent tendency of the blanket to lift any loosely bound materials from the paper demand an exceptionally clean and strongly bonded surface. Excessive moisture pickup of the dampening system can also cause the sheet to curl and expand across both dimensions.

Webfed-Offset Requirements

Paper requirements for web-offset lithography include those for sheetfed-offset lithography. The tension involved in pulling the web of paper through the press at high speeds and the differences in press operation, however, place additional demands on paper made for web-offset presses. Webfed paper must have a high *tear strength* to prevent web breaks resulting from the tension of being pulled through the press. Coated papers must be made to prevent blistering and to fold without cracking during heatset drying.

Web-offset inks generally have lower tack, so paper used on web-offset presses can have lower moisture and pick resistance than paper run on sheetfed-offset presses. Web-offset printing systems also use less moisture, and less time exists during the print run for the paper to pick up moisture. Paper rolls that unwind with even tension and flatness across the web and without localized distortion are required for good register and to prevent wrinkling. Rolls free of defects and with proper *splicing* (joining of two ends of rolls) are essential for good runnability and for minimizing web breaks.

Physical Properties of Paper

Paper is manufactured in many different forms and for many uses—the more specialized the paper is, the more unique its properties are. To be able to choose the proper substrate for a specific job, you must understand the properties of paper and how they affect printability, print quality, and runnability. The various physical properties that determine a paper's printability, print quality, and runnability

include grain, finish, pick resistance, whiteness, basis weight, flatness, ink setting and drying, moisture absorbency and resistance, and opacity. The interaction of these properties is also extremely important.

Grain

As the paper moves from the wet end of the papermaking machine toward the dry end, the fibers tend to align themselves in the direction they are traveling, and this alignment of fibers is referred to as the *grain* of the paper. *Long-grain paper,* or paper that is grain long, is paper that is cut into sheets with the fibers aligned parallel to the sheets' longer dimension. If the fibers are aligned parallel to the sheets' shorter dimension, the paper is called *short-grain paper* or grain short. See **Figure 18-19.**

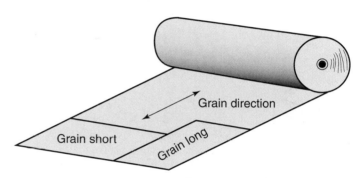

Figure 18-19. Paper is made with the grain in the direction of its travel on the wire. Depending on how it is sheeted from the roll, it might be either grain long or grain short. In this illustration, if the roll is slit and sheeted to produce horizontal sheets, the paper will be grain short. If the roll is slit and sheeted to produce vertical sheets, the paper will be grain long.

offset paper: a paper classification of papers with internal sizing to reduce its absorbency of dampening solution.

picking: the lifting of paper fibers caused by the softening and weakening of the paper surface or when the pulling force of the ink is greater than the surface of the paper. This lifting is the lifting of paper fibers by the offset rubber blanket.

tear strength: a paper property that takes into account the work required to tear a paper sample through a specified distance once the tear has started and starting the tear at an edge of the sheet.

splicing: in papermaking, the joining together of two rolls of paper, end-to-end.

grain: the alignment or structure of paper fibers.

long-grain paper: paper cut into sheets with the fibers aligned parallel to the sheet's longer dimension.

short-grain paper: paper cut into sheets with the fibers aligned parallel to the sheet's shorter dimension.

Dimensional Stability

One of the most important factors for paper being used in sheetfed-offset lithography is the paper's *dimensional stability*, the ability of the paper to retain its original length and width when exposed to moisture. The dimensional stability of a paper is greatly determined by the paper's grain direction. Lightweight sheets are ordinarily run with the grain in the direction of travel to take advantage of the stiffness imparted by the grain and reduce the sheets' buckling. In contrast, a press sheet for a close-register job requiring more than one pass per side will likely be run with the grain perpendicular to the direction of travel to help the press operator deal with sheet growth between passes, due to moisture pickup. See **Figure 18-20.**

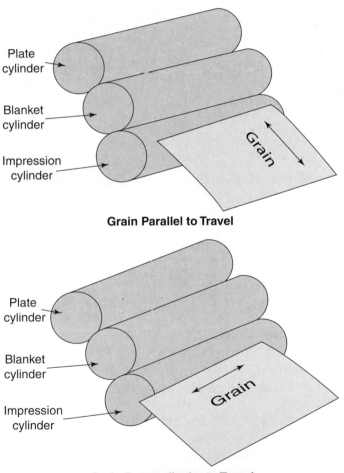

Grain Parallel to Travel

Grain Perpendicular to Travel

Figure 18-20. Lightweight sheets are often fed through the press with the grain in the direction of travel to assist feeding because paper is stiffer in the grain direction. Close-register jobs requiring multiple passes through the press for the same side are commonly run with the grain perpendicular to the direction of travel to allow the operator to hold register, despite sheet growth due to moisture pickup.

Fiber Length

Fiber *length* is important to paper's tear strength, its resistance to tearing. A sheet's tear strength is proportional to the length of its fibers. Longer fibers require more effort to tear the paper. As already noted, tear strength is especially important on web presses. Fiber length also contributes to *fold strength*—the resistance to weakening and coming apart at the fold. Papers with long fibers can better stand the severe strain of mechanical folding.

Finish

When the paper leaves the papermaking machine, it is likely to be wound into a huge roll weighing nearly 10,000 lbs. (4500 kg). Several operations must take place before this raw paper is ready for use. The term *finishing* refers to any action performed on the sheet after it has been removed from the paper machine. Finishing operations affect the sheet's surface. The word *finish* is also used to refer to the degree of smoothness of a paper's surface. For example, uncoated book papers are made in a variety of finishes—including antique, eggshell, vellum, machine, and embossed:

- Paper with an *antique finish* is characterized by a rough surface intended to simulate old, handmade paper.
- An *eggshell finish* attempts to simulate the rough surface of an egg.
- A *vellum finish* is characterized by a rough, absorbent surface intended to simulate the texture of ancient vellum (a printing material made from the split skin of livestock).
- A *machine finish* has a smooth, calendered, low-gloss finish.
- *Embossed finishes* are created when the paper is sent between the counterrotating rollers of a rotary embosser. Commonly used embossing patterns are tweed, linen, and pebble.

Coated papers are available in matte, dull, and gloss (enamel) finishes. One of the primary benefits of coating paper is to improve ink holdout—the ability to prevent ink from sinking into the paper and feathering out. Coated papers are popular for magazines and promotional pieces because color photographs appear more vibrant when the ink remains on the surface. All coated papers provide improved ink holdout, but their degree of gloss varies greatly:

- A *matte finish* is created by applying coating to the paper but not polishing it on the supercalender machine.

- A *dull finish* results from giving the coating moderate polishing.
- A *gloss finish* or *enamel finish* receives a high level of polishing.

Gloss-coated paper is a favorite in magazines because the maximum ink holdout enhances the advertising. Matte-coated paper and dull-coated paper are commonly used in books and other publications in which the glare of a glossy finish would interfere with reading.

Pick Resistance

The ability of a paper to resist surface rupturing during printing is its *pick resistance*, or surface strength. During lithographic printing, the ink film on the blanket splits. Roughly one-half stays on the blanket, and the other half transfers to the paper. Picking occurs when the ink fails to split, and the surface of the paper ruptures. When uncoated paper picks, clumps of fibers are pulled from the paper's surface and held by the ink on the blanket. When coated paper picks, portions of the coating separate from the paper. When these lifted materials, known as *hickies*, stick to the blanket, they accept dampening solution and then repel ink. They do not transfer ink to the paper, creating small nonimage areas on the sheet where ink should be, because they do not accept ink from the plate. See **Figure 18-21.** *Hickey* is also the term given to a speck that appears in an inked area of the press sheet. When picking occurs, the press must be stopped, and the hickies must be removed from the blanket.

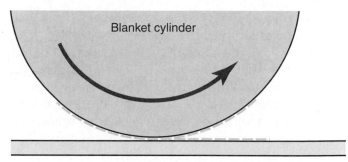

Proper Ink-Film Split

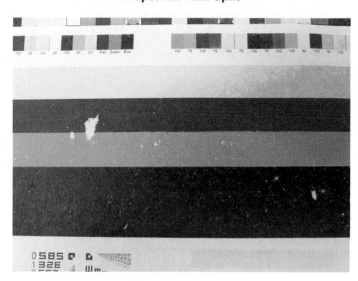

Result of Picking

Figure 18-21. When the ink film splits properly in contact with the paper, one-half transfers to the paper, and the other one-half remains on the blanket. Picking occurs when a portion of the paper's surface is pulled out by the tack of the ink and adheres to the blanket as a hickey. This press sheet lost hundreds of individual fibers (from linting) and also is picked in approximately a dozen places.

dimensional stability: the ability of a paper to retain its original length and width when exposed to moisture.

fold strength: the ability of a sheet of paper to be folded and unfolded repeatedly without tearing.

finishing: the many operations carried out during or following printing, such as cutting, folding, slitting, perforating, creasing and scoring, die cutting, embossing, stamping, numbering, drilling and punching, varnishing, and laminating.

finish: any action performed to the surface of the sheet of printing paper affecting its structure. A finish is the degree of smoothness of a paper's surface.

antique finish: a paper finish characterized by a rough surface intended to simulate old, handmade paper.

eggshell finish: a finish attempting to simulate the rough surface of an egg.

vellum finish: a relatively absorbent paper finish characterized by a rough, absorbent surface intended to simulate the texture of an ancient printing material made from the split skin of livestock.

machine finish: the finish imparted to a sheet as it leaves the calender rollers of a paper machine.

embossed finish: a paper surface with an obvious texture created by embossing.

matte finish: a finish possessing a generally flat, smooth surface, free from shine or highlights.

dull finish: a finish that is smoother than matte but still without gloss.

gloss finish (enamel finish): a surface sheen or brilliance.

pick resistance: the ability of a paper to prevent fibers from rupturing during printing.

hickey: a doughnut-shaped speck caused by dirt, hardened ink, or another unwanted particle that sticks to the press plate and appears in the inked image areas of the printed sheets.

The effect of picking is immediately visible on each press sheet until the hickies are removed from the blanket because picking is the lifting of a clump of fibers or coating. In contrast, *linting* is the ink's lifting of an individual paper fiber from the surface. *Powdering* is the ink's lifting of a filler particle. Neither linting nor powdering creates an immediate problem because the lifted materials are so tiny. An accumulation, however, of even tiny materials on the blanket will eventually impair print quality. *Piling* is the lifting of individual filler or coating particles by the dampening solution, instead of by the ink. The accumulation of these particles can abrade the nonimage areas of the plate because dampening solution pulls and holds particles onto the nonimage areas of the blanket. A wearing of the nonimage areas of the plate can cause them to lose their ability to resist ink, and traces of ink begin to appear in the nonimage areas of the printed sheet—a condition known as *scumming*.

Whiteness and Brightness

A paper's *whiteness* refers to the extent to which it reflects nearly equal amounts of RGB light from its surface. White light is formed from roughly equal parts of the visible spectrum. Therefore, in order for a paper to be pure white, it has to reflect nearly equal amounts of RGB light. A sheet reflecting extra amounts of blue light is referred to as a *cool white*, and a sheet reflecting more red and green light than blue light is said to be a *warm white*.

Brightness can be defined as the percentage of striking light a surface reflects. For example, a sheet with a brightness of 88 reflects 88% of the light striking it. The brightness of an uncoated white sheet results from bleaching the fibers and removing pigments that absorb light, instead of reflect it. Obviously, paper that has been dyed with a color has lower brightness than a white sheet. Coated papers derive their brightness from the white coating layer. This paper can attain higher brightness levels than uncoated sheets because prolonged bleaching can destroy cellulose fibers.

Substance Weight

Paper mills produce paper in various weights. The weight of a paper is measured by its *substance weight*, or basis weight. The substance weight is the weight, in pounds, of a ream (500 sheets) in a specified size, known as the *basic size*. For example, the basic size for offset paper is 25″ × 35″. Therefore, a ream of 70-lb. offset paper cut to 25″ × 38″ in size weighs 70 lbs. In this example, the paper can be described as Sub. 70 or Basis 70.

The basic size is not the same for all *classifications* of paper. For example, the basic size for bond and other business papers is 17″ × 22″. The basic size for cover paper is 20″ × 26″, and the basic size for index bristol is 25 1/2″ × 30 1/2″. **Figure 18-22** displays the basic sizes and typical substance weights of many types of paper. A paper merchant's price book lists the colors, sheet sizes, and substance weights available for a given brand of paper. See **Figure 18-23**.

Flatness

Paper *flatness* is a measurement of how much the paper curls or becomes wavy. Offset papers should be delivered perfectly flat because the surfaces of both the offset plate and impression cylinder are flat. Exposure to excessive humidity in the pressroom or dampening solution can cause paper to curl. An uneven or wavy sheet is likely to wrinkle when it is pressed between the plate and the impression cylinder. Similarly, tight edges result from moisture loss in dry air. Papers are packaged at 4–6% moisture content for best printing results under normal conditions. Pressrooms should have controlled humidity levels.

Squareness

A sheet's squareness describes the sheet being exactly 90° at all four corners. Squareness is important for press sheets that will be printed with a work-and-turn or work-and-tumble imposition. A sheet's squareness can be checked by folding it in half, with care taken to keep the sides perfectly aligned. The ends are then checked to see if they also align.

Ink Drying

Ink drying can be a serious problem when paper quality is poor or in cases where paper and ink are not compatible. Offset inks are formulated to print and dry on a wide range of papers—newsprint, bonds, and coated and uncoated offset sheets. For papers to be compatible with any of the dozens of brands of offset ink an individual printing company might use, however, the paper must be manufactured within a quality control program that produces a consistent product every day. Variations in paper quality often result in slow drying. In an effort to ensure that their paper will perform well on press, paper mills take samples from every newly made roll and test for several physical characteristics.

Type	General Uses	Basic Size (Inches)	Substance Weights (Pounds)
Business	Business forms, letterheads, envelopes, direct-mail ads	17 x 22	9, 13, 16, 20, 24
Book/offset	Catalogs, books, brochures, pamphlets, direct-mail ads	25 x 38	Coated: 60, 70, 80, 90, 100 Uncoated: 33, 40, 50, 60
Bristol (card)	Tickets, postcards, covers, menus, novelty items	22 1/2 x 28 1/2	67, 80, 100, 120, 140, 160
Bristol (index)	Index cards, folders, records	25 1/2 x 30 1/2	90, 110, 140, 170
Carbonless	Business forms, stationery, statements	17 x 22	
Cover	Covers, binders, menus, posters, tags	20 x 26	Coated: 60, 65, 80, 100, 125 Uncoated: 50, 65, 80, 130
Label	Labels	25 x 38	50, 60, 70
Ledger ruled forms	Graphs, maps, bookkeeping	17 x 22	24, 28, 32, 36
Newsprint	Newspapers, advertisements	24 x 36	28, 30, 32, 34, 35
Onionskin	Carbon copies, airmail letterheads	17 x 22	7, 8, 9, 10
Safety	Checks, securities	17 x 22	24

Figure 18-22. Different categories of paper have different basic sizes. For example, the basic size of business paper is 17″ × 22″, but the basic size of cover paper is 20″ × 26″.

Moisture Absorbency and Resistance

In order for ink to transfer and bond with both coated and uncoated offset paper, it must be capable of penetrating the sheet's surface enough to become part of the sheet. The ink should not be capable, however, of penetrating the surface enough to feather out or disappear into the sheet. Achieving this delicate balance between inadequate and excessive absorbency is necessary for paper to produce quality printing.

Opacity

A paper's *opacity*, or show-through, refers to the extent to which light passes through the sheet. A sheet with high opacity allows the passage of very little light, and sheets with poor opacity allow printed images to show through to the reverse side. Book paper has more opacity than bond paper because two-sided printing requires a higher level of opacity than letterheads and other one-sided jobs do. A sheet's opacity can be increased by limiting the amount of refining the fibers receive, increasing the sheet's caliper, increasing the substance weight, and increasing the filler content. *Opaque paper* is the term given to lightweight sheets with a high filler content to improve opacity.

linting: the result of loosely bonded fibers that break off and are carried by the offset blanket to the ink rollers.

powdering: the lifting by ink of individual filler particles from paper during printing.

piling: a printing problem characterized by the accumulation of paper fibers, bits of detached coating particles, and other debris on the printing plate or blanket in both the image and nonimage areas. This problem occurs when ink tack or one of various other press problems overcomes the paper's pick resistance.

scumming: the adhering of ink to the nonimage areas of the plate.

whiteness: the extent to which paper equally reflects all wavelengths of light from its surface.

substance weight: the actual weight of a ream of a paper.

classification: an organized arrangement in groups or types according to established standards.

flatness: a measurement of how much the paper curls, waves, or bends.

opacity: the ability of a sheet of paper to block the passage of light.

opaque paper: paper with high filler content to improve its ability to block the passage of light.

Hammermill Bond Hammermill Paper
No. 1 Sulphite, Watermarked
Packaged: 500 Sheets

| | Pkg | Price Per CWT | | |
		1 Ctn	4 Ctn	16 Ctn
White Bond, 13#	88.90	77.75	68.00	62.65
White Bond, 16#	72.20	63.20	55.25	50.90
White Bond, 20 & 24#	69.20	60.55	52.90	48.75
Colors Bond, 16#	76.25	66.75	58.35	53.75
Colors Bond, 20#	73.20	64.05	56.00	51.60
White Rippletone, 20#	78.30	68.50	59.90	55.20
Ivory Rippletone, 20#	82.30	72.05	62.95	58.05

17 × 22 Basis	Size	M Wt	Ctn	Price Per 1000 Sheets			
White							
13	17 × 22	26	5000	23.11	20.22	17.68	16.29
	17 × 28	33	4000	29.34	25.66	22.44	20.67
	22 × 34	52	2500	46.23	40.43	35.36	32.58
16	17 × 22	32	4000	23.10	20.22	17.68	16.29
	17 × 28	41	3000	29.60	25.91	22.65	20.87
	22 × 34	64	2000	46.21	40.45	35.36	32.58
	24 × 38	78	1500	56.32	49.30	43.10	39.70
	28 × 34	82	1500	59.20	51.82	45.31	41.74
20	17 × 22	40	3000	27.68	24.22	21.16	19.50
	17 × 28	51	3000	35.29	30.88	26.98	24.86
	17½ × 22½	42	3000	29.06	25.43	22.22	20.48
	19 × 24	49	3000	33.91	29.67	25.92	23.89
	22 × 34	80	1500	55.36	48.44	42.32	39.00
	22½ × 35	84	1500	58.13	50.86	44.44	40.95
	24 × 38	98	1500	67.82	59.34	51.84	47.78
	28 × 34	102	1500	70.58	61.76	53.96	49.73
24	17 × 22	48	3000	33.22	29.06	25.39	23.40
	17 × 28	61	2000	42.21	36.94	32.27	29.74
	22 × 34	96	1500	66.43	58.13	50.78	46.80
	24 × 38	118	1000	81.66	71.45	62.42	57.53
White Rippletone							
20	17 × 22	40	3000	31.32	27.40	23.96	22.08
	22 × 34	80	1500	62.64	54.80	47.92	44.16
Ivory Rippletone							
20	22 × 34	80	1500	65.84	57.64	50.36	46.44
Colors:							
Blue, Canary, Green, Pink							
16	17 × 22	32	4000	24.40	21.36	18.67	17.20
Buff, Gray, Ivory							
16	17 × 22	32	4000	24.40	21.36	18.67	17.20
Colors:							
Blue, Buff, Canary, Ivory, Cherry, Gray							
20	17 × 22	40	3000	29.28	25.62	22.40	20.64
Green, Pink, Russet, Cafe							
20	17 × 22	40	3000	29.28	25.62	22.40	20.64
Goldenrod, Greentint, Orchid, Melon, Salmon							
20	17 × 22	40	3000	29.28	25.62	22.40	20.64

Figure 18-23. Paper merchants sell paper in more sizes than the basic size.

Testing Methods

After production, paper is tested for several of the physical characteristics just described. To ensure meaningful results, the Technical Association of the Pulp and Paper Industry (TAPPI)—an international organization devoted to paper research and development—has established these tests. Some physical characteristics can be measured by more than one testing method, so test results usually specify the TAPPI test used.

Paper Classifications

Paper classifications are used to identify and categorize the hundreds of different types of paper. The five classifications of paper are business, book, cover, bristol, and utility. Most of these classifications are broken into *categories*. For example, the book classification includes the categories of offset, text, and label paper.

Business Paper

As the name suggests, *business papers* include sheets commonly found in the business world. The basic size for all business papers is 17″ × 22″. The most common category of business paper is *bond paper*, which is used primarily for letterhead stationery, business forms, writing, typing, and photocopying. Bond paper got its name when the Bank of England approved it for the printing of bonds. Since that time, bonds have been created to function well in a range of applications. For example, xerographic bond is designed to resist curling in a photocopier; business-forms bond (register bond) is typically sold in rolls to be run on webfed-offset presses; carbonless bonds are pressure sensitive to produce copies in two-, three-, or four-part sets; dual-purpose bond can work in offset duplicators or photocopiers; and translucent bond is nearly transparent. Bond paper intended for letterhead stationery accepts not only offset ink, but also ink and toner from computer printers, copying machines, typewriters, and pens.

These papers are available in several cost levels and grades. The primary cost factors are the fiber content, finish, and brightness level. Sulfite bonds are made entirely of wood fiber. These bonds are used for invoices and other business forms. To increase strength and permanence, cotton fibers are substituted for wood fiber in high-grade bonds, and the percentage of cotton content is always identified in the watermark. Cotton content, also known as *rag content*, increases the cost significantly.

Both sulfite and cotton-content bonds are available in different finishes. Wove finish is the most basic and commonly used. A laid finish is both watermarked and embossed to simulate the appearance of paper made by hand. A cockle finish simulates the uneven surface of paper dried by hand, is most common in sheets containing cotton fibers, and is typically used for high-quality letterheads and resumés.

Bond papers have low filler content and low opacity because they are not intended for two-sided printing. Both sulfite and cotton bonds are made in

Bond Papers											
Brand Name and Manufacturer	Brightness	Opacity	Basis Weight	Caliper	Finish	Rec Cont	Post Cons	Alkaline	Color	Sold In	Comp With
Premium—Brightness Range 88 and Above											
Timberline Laser Bond—Boise Paper Solutions	91	78	20	4.0		100			W	R	
Torchglow Multipurpose—Fraser Papers Inc.	92	86	Sub. 20		ST	30	30	Y	C		DI, IJ, LR
No. 1—Brightness Range 85—87.9											
Boise™ Hibrite Opaque—Boise Paper Solutions	87	86	11.5	2.2				Y	W	R	
No. 2—Brightness Range 83—84.9											
Boise™ MOCR Laser Bond—Boise Paper Solutions	84	89, 92	24, 28	4.8, 5.35				Y	W	R	
Boise™ OCR Laser Bond—Boise Paper Solutions	84	87	20	4.2				Y	W	R	
Boise™ RC MICR (30R/30PC)—Boise Paper Solutions	83	88	24	4.0		30	30	Y	C	R	
Private Label Brands											
Brand Bond—Paper Mart Inc.											
Papmar Bond—Paper Mart Inc.											
Roosevelt Bond— Roosevelt Paper Co. (1932)	84		10, 12, 15 16, 18, 20 24					Y			

Figure 18-24. Bond papers are assigned to grades based on factors such as brightness, opacity, and cost. (Adapted from Walden's Paper Catalog)

four grade levels—Premium #1, #1, Premium #4, and #4—with the Premium #1 grade having the highest brightness and opacity, as well as the highest price. See **Figure 18-24.** Premium #1 and #1 sulfite bonds are watermarked. Bond paper is available in 16-, 20-, and 24-lb. substance weights. Bond can also be purchased with 25, 50, 75, and 100% cotton fiber to give the sheet more strength and permanence.

Carbonless bond papers are used to transfer and copy written, printed, or typed images between sheets. These papers simplify paperwork; produce clean, smudge-free copies; and long ago eliminated the messiness associated with the use and disposal of carbon papers. Unlike regular papers, carbonless papers use a chemical transfer system to create images. Pressure from a pen or typewriter applied to

paper classification: a group of related types of paper.

category: regarding paper, a subdivision of a paper classification.

business paper: a classification of types of paper commonly used in business.

bond paper: paper with a medium-finish surface that accepts ink and toner easily from computer printers, copying machines, typewriters, and pens.

carbonless bond paper: bond paper coated with microcapsules that, under pressure, transfer an image to a sheet or sheets underneath it.

the top sheet activates a chemical reaction between the sheets in the set. The back side of the top sheet is designated *coated back (CB)* because this sheet in the carbonless set is coated with encapsulated chemicals. All sheets between the first and last sheets have a receptor coating on top and an encapsulated coating on the back. These sheets are designated *coated front-and-back (CFB)*. The last sheet has a receptor coating only. This type of sheet is called *coated front (CF)*. When pressure is applied to the top sheet of the set by typing or writing, an image is formed when an activator chemical escapes from the broken capsules on the underside of the top sheet to activate the chemistry on the top of the second sheet. See **Figure 18-25.**

Other business papers include onion skin, envelope, and safety paper. Onion skin is a very light-weight paper, in which some cotton and linen fibers have been added to the wood fibers to impart strength. Envelope paper is manufactured to enhance burst, fold strength, strength, opacity, and the ability to be gummed and moistened with a minimum of curl. Safety paper is commonly used to add security to certificates of title and bank checks. This paper carries a printed image to thwart alteration by erasure and carries an image in invisible ink that becomes visible if bleach is used to chemically alter an image.

Book Paper

Book is a classification containing several categories of paper—most of which are intended for two-sided printing. *Book papers* carry comparatively high filler content to improve opacity because of the need to carry printing on both sides. These papers are available in a wide range of finishes, weights, colors, and cost levels because they are used to print very different products, such as annual reports, pamphlets, magazines, textbooks, posters, newsletters, journals, menus, and brochures. The basic size for all book papers is 25″ × 38″.

Offset paper

The most popular of the book papers is offset paper. Offset paper has been internally sized to resist being weakened from absorbing too much dampening solution during lithographic printing. In the case of both uncoated and coated offset paper, a sheet's grade is primarily determined by its brightness, opacity, and cost. See **Figure 18-26.**

Uncoated offset paper

Uncoated offset paper is commonly used to print newsletters, direct-mail pieces, journals, and fliers. Uncoated sheets are available with antique, smooth, vellum, or embossed finishes. Lightweight uncoated offset papers containing extra amounts of filler to provide adequate opacity despite their light weights are opaque sheets. Catalogs and other mailed jobs are often printed on opaque offset paper to reduce postage costs. For example, a college that has traditionally printed its catalog on a 50-lb. uncoated sheet could switch to a 40-lb. opaque sheet to reduce the catalog's weight and the school's annual mailing expense. The high filler content provides more opacity than a normal 40-lb. sheet does.

Coated offset paper

Posters, magazines, brochures, fliers, and other jobs requiring four-color printing are typically printed on *coated offset paper*. Coated offset carries a layer of coating on one or both sides and is available with a variety of finishes, ranging from matte to gloss. Magazine publishers desiring a low-cost sheet that still has good ink holdout often use a *coated groundwood paper*.

Text paper

The classification known as *text paper* contains a very diverse range of sheets typically used in brochures, menus, announcements, annual reports, and any other piece intended to convey a richness of

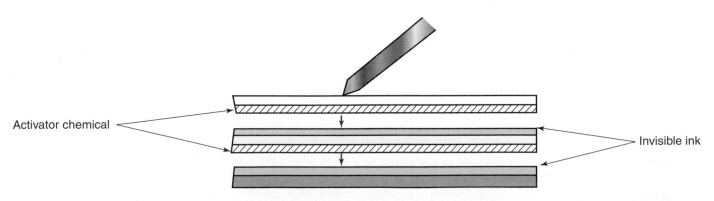

Figure 18-25. Carbonless paper transfers an image when pressure ruptures capsules on the underside of the sheets that activate invisible ink contained in capsules on top of the next sheets.

C1S Label–Litho											
Brand Name and Manufacturer	Brightness	Opacity	Basis Weight	Caliper	Finish	Rec Cont	Post Cons	Alkaline	Color	Sold In	Comp With
Premium—Brightness Range 88 and Above											
All Purpose Litho—Smart Papers	88	88–95	60–100	3.2–5.8	ST, EM			N			
All Purpose Litho-Hi Brite—Smart Papers	91	88–95	60–100	3.2–5.8	ST			N			
All Purpose Litho-Recycled—Smart Papers	88	88–95	60, 70, 80, 100	3.2–5.8	ST	50	10		W	SR	
Brightwhite C1S—Pasadena Paper Co.	91		60–100					Y		SR	DI, LR
Felxo Fold®—Boise Paper Solutions	89	92, 94, 97	24, 28, 36	4, 4.6, 6.8				Y			
FelxoGloss™—Boise Paper Solutions	91	93	70	4.0					W	R	
Go-Line—Gruppo Cordenons Intermills-Cordenons, Inc.	89	79–94	40–81					N	W		
Interflash–Gruppo Cordenons Intermills-Cordenons, Inc.	89	83–90	45–60					N	W		
Kromekote Litho Coverting—Smart Papers	90	88–91	55–70	3.5–4.9	CC			Y	W	R	
Kromekote Litho Xtra Gloss—Smart Papers	90	90	57	3.9	CC				W	R	
KromekotePlus Litho—Smart Papers	90	93–95	60–70	4.0–5.1	CC				W	S	
Pasadena C1S FWS (Full Wet Strength)—Pasadena Paper Co.	88		47, 51, 54		GL			Y	W	SR	
Pasadena C1S SWS (Semi Wet Strength)—Pasadena Paper Co.	88		47, 51, 54		GL			Y	W	SR	
Sterling® Ultra C1S—MeadWestvaco Papers Group	90		60, 70, 80, 100					Y			
Sterling® Ultra C1S Text—MeadWestvaco Papers Group	90		60, 70, 80, 100						W	S	
No. 1—Brightness Range 85–87.9											
Chromolux C1S Label—M-Real Alliance USA	87		60, 68								
Pasadena C1S—Pasadena Paper Co.	87		50–100					Y		SR	DI, LR

Figure 18-26. Offset papers are assigned to grades based on factors such as brightness, opacity, and cost. (Adapted from Walden's Paper Catalog)

coated back (CB): the back side of the top sheet in the carbonless set coated with encapsulated chemicals.

coated front-and-back (CFB): a carbonless paper sheet between the first and last sheets with a receptor coating on top and an encapsulated coating on the back.

coated front (CF): the last sheet of carbonless paper with a receptor coating only on the front.

book paper: a grade of paper used primarily in the printing of texts and trade books.

uncoated offset paper: offset paper that has not been coated.

coated offset paper: offset paper that has been coated on one or both sides.

coated groundwood paper: groundwood paper that has been coated on both sides.

text paper: a grade of paper made from either wood or cotton fibers popular for use in products such as brochures, menus, announcements, and annual reports. This paper is similar to book paper and is available with a variety of surface textures, attractive colors, and finishes.

Brand Name and Manufacturer	Brightness	Opacity	Basis Weight	Caliper	Finish	Rec Cont	Post Cons	Alkaline	Color	Sold In	Comp With
No. 2—Brightness Range 83–84.9											
Boise™ C1S Label—Boise Paper Solutions	83	88, 89	60, 70	3.3, 3.8				Y	W	R	
Sterling® Litho C1S Text—MeadWestvaco Papers Group	83		60, 70, 80, 100						W	S	
Brightness Not Furnished by Company											
Algro-Baress—Sappi Fine Paper Europe			47–100					Y			
Algro-Finess—Sappi Fine Paper Europe			47–100					Y			
Astralux H.T. Label—Sappi Fine Paper Europe			56					N			
Astralux Litho Label—Sappi Fine Paper Europe			57–68					Y			
Bladonart Label—Sappi Fine Paper Europe			47-100					Y			
OCR—Miami Wabash Paper LLC											
Plated Papers—Hampden Papers, Inc.								N	C	SRC	
Val-Glo Fluorescent C-1-S—Miami Wabash Paper LLC			60					N			
Private Label Brands											
Bindakote®— CTI Paper USA, Inc.	91		60, 68					N		SR	
Mailbrite C1S Envelope—E. Aaron Enterprises Inc.	86	93.5–94.5	60, 70								
Roosevelt Coated One Side Litho—Roosevelt Paper Co. (1932)	88		55–100					Y		SR	

Figure 18-26. (Continued)

texture or finish. Text paper is similar to uncoated book paper and is available with a variety of surface textures, attractive colors, and finishes. This paper is often watermarked and can be purchased deckle-edged. A *deckle edge* is a feathered edge created during manufacture to resemble the look of handmade paper. See **Figure 18-27.**

Cover Paper

Cover paper is used primarily to cover and protect other printed material. This paper is heavy, strong, easy to fold, and available in a wide variety of colors. Cover paper is able to withstand rough handling. This paper is used for business cards, booklets, catalogs, pamphlets, covers, programs, and mailing pieces.

Cover sheets are available in the same colors and finishes as most offset and text sheets because they are usually manufactured to match offset and text sheets. See **Figure 18-28.** Cover sheets can be uncoated, coated on one side (C1S), or coated on two sides (C2S).

Cover paper is available as what is known as a *duplex sheet*—a single sheet of paper consisting of two laminated, thin sheets of different colors. For example, a duplex sheet can be navy blue on one side and ivory on the second side. Cover paper is commonly made in 65-, 80-, and 100-lb. substance weights. The basic size of cover paper is 20″ × 26″.

Figure 18-27. Some text sheets, such as this black one, are available with a deckle edge simulating the look of handmade paper.

50 / 20 lb. Texte / Text		65 lb. Couverture / Cover	
50 / 20 lb. Texte / Text		65 lb. Couverture / Cover	
50 / 20 lb. Texte / Text		65 lb. Couverture / Cover	
50 / 20 lb. Texte / Text		65 lb. Couverture / Cover	
50 / 20 lb. Texte / Text		65 lb. Couverture / Cover	
50 / 20 lb. Texte / Text		65 lb. Couverture / Cover	
50 / 20 lb. Texte / Text		65 lb. Couverture / Cover	

Figure 18-28. As shown on these swatch books, most text papers are available with a matching cover-weight sheet.

Bristol

Heavy papers at least .006″ thick are termed *bristols* (or *bristol boards*), and they come in several categories. *Index bristol* is a heavyweight paper used for index cards, menus, and mailing pieces. This bristol is used when rigidity, ruggedness, and erasability are important. Index bristol is manufactured in both smooth and antique finishes and in many different colors. This bristol is made in 90-, 110-, and 120-lb. substance weights, and the basic size is 25 1/2″ × 30 1/2″. Postcard bristol is C1S paper at least .007″ thick, to meet U.S. Postal Service requirements.

Tagboard paper is a heavy paper used primarily for jobs requiring sturdiness. Tagboard can contain jute and other long fibers, which make it very strong. *Paperboard* is strong, thick paper or cardboard used for boxes and other types of packaging. This paper can be bleached or unbleached, coated or uncoated, and produced in a variety of thicknesses up to 0.056″ (1.4 mm).

A *blank* is paperboard made up of two or more sheets laminated together. These cardboards are used in package printing, outdoor and transit advertising, point-of-purchase displays, and many commercial advertising programs. *Railroad board* is the term given to colored blanks. The basic size of paperboard is 22″ × 28″. The various categories and calipers of paperboard are shown in **Figure 18-29**.

Utility Paper

Papers that do not belong in these first four classifications are grouped together and termed *utility papers*. These papers are also known as *miscellaneous papers*. Newsprint, label paper, synthetic paper, and mineral sheets are included.

Newsprint is a popular utility sheet made primarily from groundwood pulp. Although groundwood pulp has high opacity and good printing

deckle edge: a feathered edge left untrimmed when the paper is manufactured.

cover paper: a classification of heavy, easily folded paper available in a variety of finishes and commonly used for business cards and booklet covers.

bristol: a classification of paper that is heavy, rigid, and used for programs and index cards.

index bristol: a type of cover paper available in smooth and antique finishes used for business forms, menus, index cards, booklet covers, postcards, and mailing pieces. This bristol is a lightweight cardboard used when rigidity, ruggedness, and erasability are important.

tagboard paper: a strong cover paper with long fibers; excellent folding qualities; good water resistance; and a surface adaptable to writing, stamping, or printing. This paper is used primarily for jobs requiring sturdiness.

paperboard: a strong, thick paper or cardboard used for boxes and other types of packaging. This paper is available bleached, unbleached, coated, uncoated, and in a variety of thicknesses.

blank: a very heavy sheet of paperboard.

utility paper: a classification containing types of paper that do not belong in any other classification.

newsprint: an inexpensive grade of paper with high opacity and good printing qualities made primarily from groundwood pulp, usually blended with chemical pulp to increase the paper's tear strength. Newsprint is used primarily for the printing of newspapers, but it is also used for direct-mail advertising, sketch pads, comic books, catalogs, and all types of directories.

Number of Plies	Caliper	Approximate Weight (1000 Sheets)
Plain blanks		
3	.015	280
4	.018	330
5	.021	360
6	.024	420
8	.030	520
10	.036	600
Coated blanks		
3	.015	340
4	.018	420
5	.021	460
6	.024	530
8	.030	650
10	.036	760
Railroad board		
4	.018	400
6	.024	530
8	.030	650
Tough check		
3	.012	310
4	.018	430
6	.024	550
8	.030	680
Thick china		
	.011	300

Figure 18-29. Paper manufacturers provide charts listing the various grades and thicknesses of paperboard available. (Boise Cascade Paper Group)

qualities, it lacks strength, permanence, and brightness. Sheets manufactured for label applications are called *label papers*. Labels must be able to accept ink on one side and gumming on the other, without curling. Label paper is commonly found in substance weights of 60, 70, 80, and 100 lbs. *Synthetic paper* is a thin sheet of plastic with a clay coating on both sides that accepts the ink. These papers are popular with menus, maps, and other applications requiring resistance to stains and tearing. *Mineral paper* is paper made from pulverized limestone particles a binding agent holds together. This paper has no grain direction, is waterproof, and resists tearing because it is not made from cellulose fibers. Marketed by ViaStone® paper, mineral paper is available for business cards, greeting cards, and postcards. Mineral paper is also available as photo paper and in rolls for wide-format ink-jet printers.

Environmentally Friendly Paper

Many graphic designers and print buyers specify papers that are considered environmentally friendly. Current environmental concerns include a paper's content of recycled fiber and the chemistry used in its bleaching. *Recycled paper* is produced from pulp made from recovered paper and paper products, manufacturing waste, nonpaper materials, and wood residues. This paper is not a paper classification because paper in all classifications can be made from recycled fiber.

Recycled Paper

At the present, the paper industry recycles about 50% of the fibrous waste materials that might otherwise enter the solid waste stream. Cellulose fibers suffer physical deterioration after each recycling, however, as they lose some of their length and physical strength. Even the strongest wood cellulose loses most of its value as a papermaking material after several recyclings. For this reason, recycled fiber is not a replacement for virgin pulp. Generally, recycled fiber is used to supplement virgin pulps in the manufacture of new paper. Recycled-paper production is a two-step process involving the following:
1. The collection of wastepaper at the point of generation, sorting, accumulation, and delivery to the point of conversion.
2. The conversion of collected wastepaper into reusable pulp by deinking (if necessary), washing, and bleaching.

Growing concern over the shortage of landfills has encouraged the use of recycling wastepaper. To distinguish which recovered fibers are actually reducing landfill demand, the federal government has created two categories of wastepaper. *Preconsumer waste* is obtained from materials such as subpar paper, mill waste, and repulped obsolete inventory. These materials have always been repulped, so their use in making new paper does not ease the strain on landfill space. *Postconsumer waste* is obtained from used office paper, old newspapers, old magazines, mixed wastepaper, and corrugated boxes that have served their intended purpose and would otherwise enter the waste stream. In other words, postconsumer wastepaper represents materials that would otherwise be disposed of in a landfill. To date, all printing and writing papers the government purchases must contain at least 50% waste fibers and 30% postconsumer fibers. See **Figure 18-30.**

Surprisingly, paper products carrying the recycling logo are not necessarily made from recycled fiber. Dark "chasing arrows" indicate the paper is made from paper that has been recycled, and light arrows indicate the paper is appropriate to be recycled. See **Figure 18-31.**

Figure 18-30. Swatch books for paper with recycled-fiber content indicate the percentage of postconsumer and total recycled or reclaimed fiber.

Figure 18-31. A recycle symbol with dark arrows indicates that the paper contains recycled fiber. Outlined arrows indicate that the paper can be recycled.

Paper Made with Alternative Chemicals

A second environmental concern involves the chemistry used in the bleaching of wood pulp to produce white paper. During the history of papermaking, the primary bleaching chemical has been chlorine gas. During the 1980s, it was discovered that the wastewater from paper mills contained tiny amounts of dioxin, a man-made carcinogen that can result when chlorine combines with the lignin on the fibers during bleaching. Despite the miniscule amounts of dioxin in mills' wastewater, the health risks even small traces of dioxin pose prompted the U.S. EPA, in 1994, to order the elimination of any dioxin from paper mills' effluent. Mills have sought out alternative methods of bleaching pulp because most dioxin is produced when elemental chlorine (pure chlorine not combined with another element) is used as a bleaching agent.

Elemental chlorine–free (ECF) bleaching substitutes chlorine dioxide or sodium hypochlorite in place of chlorine gas as a bleaching agent. Even though chlorine dioxide has chlorine in its name, its chemistry is very different from that of elemental chlorine gas. By substituting chlorine dioxide, mills can reduce dioxins to undetectable levels. Papers bleached without elemental chlorine are labeled ECF.

Totally chlorine-free (TCF) bleaching uses no chlorine—neither in its elemental state, nor as part of a compound such as chlorine dioxide or sodium hypochlorite. At present, TCF bleaching is not necessary to eliminate dioxin. Paper mills that adopt TCF bleaching often do so as insurance against future wastewater-testing instruments becoming capable of detecting traces of dioxin not found with present-day technology. Papers bleached with no chlorine are labeled TCF.

With chlorine-free paper production, there is no change in the sheet's printability or runnability in either sheetfed or webfed operations. On the printing press, chlorine-free papers print well and, for the most part, exhibit excellent surface strength and ink holdout. Chlorine-free papers do, however, tend to have lower brightness levels than traditionally bleached papers do.

Oxygen delignification is an approach to eliminating dioxin formation that allows chlorine bleaching. Some mills remove the lignin instead of the chlorine because dioxin can result from lignin in the presence of chlorine. This approach treats the pulp with oxygen to remove lignin prior to the bleaching stage. As a result, many papermaking

label paper: paper made to accept adhesive without curling.

synthetic paper: paper made without cellulose fiber.

mineral paper: a type of synthetic paper.

recycled paper: paper produced from pulp made from used paper and paper products, manufacturing waste, nonpaper materials, wood residues, and fibers recovered from mill wastewater.

preconsumer waste: wastepaper that results from papermaking and printing operations and is free from ink.

postconsumer waste: recycled material collected from the end user or consumer.

elemental chlorine–free (ECF) bleaching: an alternative bleaching process that uses chlorine dioxide or sodium hypochlorite instead of chlorine gas as a bleaching agent.

totally chlorine-free (TCF) bleaching: any method of bleaching that uses no chlorine.

oxygen delignification: the use of oxygen to remove lignin from pulp in preparation for bleaching.

mills are able to use a final chlorine-based bleaching stage to achieve high whiteness levels.

Alkaline paper (or acid-free paper) is a response to concerns over problems with permanence that develop when rosin is used to internally size paper. Traditionally sized paper becomes acidic when exposed to oxygen over a period of several years. As a result, tens of thousands of old books in America's libraries are being chemically treated or microfilmed because they are too brittle to be handled. In response to this tragedy, many book publishers now specify alkaline paper for their first editions. Alkaline sizing uses a synthetic sizing agent in place of the traditional rosin. Printing on alkaline paper usually requires a modification in the pH of the dampening solution.

Paper-Swatch Books

Paper-swatch books are valuable sources of information because they provide samples of every color and weight of paper for a particular sheet. Not every combination, however, of available weight and color is always shown as a sample. Therefore, someone using a swatch book should refer to the complete listing of available combinations of weight and color.

The chart shown in **Figure 18-32** represents one way standards might appear in a swatch book. The information states the substance weight and the category for the paper being described in the swatch book (examples include Sub. 50 offset, Sub. 20 bond, Sub. 67 cover, and Sub. 70 text). The basic size for the particular category often follows this information.

The available sheet sizes for each substance weight are listed. The underlined dimension is the grain direction. All the sheets listed have the grain running in the long direction and, thus, are grain long. Grain direction can also be indicated by setting the dimension in a boldface type or by the letters *L* and *S*, for *long* and *short*. When both dimensions are underlined or in boldface type, the paper is available with either grain direction.

Following the sheet dimensions, the M weight (Mwt) is provided. The Mwt is the weight of 1000 (1M) sheets of paper in the size being ordered. For 23" × 35" Sub. 80 text paper, it is 136 lb. A sheet's Mwt is necessary in estimating the cost for paper priced by the pound. For example, 10,000 sheets of 23" × 35" Sub. 80 text weigh 1360 lbs. Printers use the *sheets per carton* information to calculate the number of cartons making up an order. The number of cartons is needed because the price charged per pound decreases as the number of cartons increases.

Certain colors can cost more than other colors. Paper merchants do not always keep certain combinations of color, weight, and size on hand. In such an instance, the merchant needs to order the paper from the mill, and a longer delivery time results.

International Organization for Standardization (ISO) Metric Sizes of Paper

Standard U.S. paper sizes have evolved over many years. Some sizes exist to satisfy a particular end-use requirement. For example, bond paper is often sold in a 17" × 22" size because it cuts down to 8 1/2" × 11". The most popular size for multicolor printing on coated paper is 25" × 38" because it accommodates a 16-page, 8 1/2" × 11" signature, with space left over for bleed and trim.

There are other influencing factors in paper sizes. Today, nearly all printing presses are manufactured outside the United States, and their sizes are expressed in metric terms. For instance, printers commonly refer to a 40" press, which is actually 102 cm, or 40 1/4". See **Figure 18-33**.

To standardize printing-paper sizes, the ISO has developed a system, being adopted in many countries, using the metric standard. The system is based on a rectangle in the ratio of 1:2. In the A Series, for

Weight and Size	Sheets per Carton	Weight per Carton	White Ivory Natural	Gray Blue Brown	Yellow Red Black
Basis 80 text (25" x 38")					
23" x 35" (136M)	1000	136	X		
25" x 38" (160M)	750	120	X	X	X
Basis 80 cover (20" x 26")					
23" x 35" (201M)	750	150	X	X	
26" x 40" (320M)	400	128	X	X	X

Figure 18-32. Paper merchants' catalogs contain important information about each brand of paper carried—including the available sizes, weights, and colors, as well as Mwts and the number of sheets in a carton. This information is essential for printers and graphic designers. (*Step-by-Step Graphics* Magazine)

inches	=	mm	inches	=	mm	inches	=	mm	inches	=	mm
6		152	14 1/4		362	22 1/2		572	30 3/4		781
6 1/4		159	14 1/2		368	22 3/4		578	31		787
6 1/2		165	14 3/4		375	23		584	31 1/4		794
6 3/4		171	15		381	23 1/4		591	31 1/2		800
7		178	15 1/4		387	23 1/2		597	31 3/4		806
7 1/4		184	15 1/2		394	23 3/4		603	32		813
7 1/2		191	15 3/4		400	24		610	32 1/4		819
7 3/4		197	16		406	24 1/4		616	32 1/2		826
8		203	16 1/4		413	24 1/2		622	32 3/4		832
8 1/4		210	16 1/2		419	24 3/4		629	33		838
8 1/2		216	16 3/4		425	25		635	33 1/4		845
8 3/4		222	17		432	25 1/4		641	33 1/2		851
9		229	17 1/4		438	25 1/2		648	33 3/4		857
9 1/4		235	17 1/2		445	25 3/4		654	34		864
9 1/2		241	17 3/4		451	26		660	34 1/4		870
9 3/4		248	18		457	26 1/4		667	34 1/2		876
10		254	18 1/4		464	26 1/2		673	34 3/4		883
10 1/4		260	18 1/2		470	26 3/4		679	35		889
10 1/2		267	18 3/4		476	27		686	35 1/4		895
10 3/4		273	19		483	27 1/4		692	35 1/2		902
11		279	19 1/4		489	27 1/2		699	35 3/4		908
11 1/4		286	19 1/2		495	27 3/4		705	36		914
11 1/2		292	19 3/4		502	28		711	36 1/4		921
11 3/4		298	20		508	28 1/4		718	36 1/2		927
12		305	20 1/4		514	28 1/2		724	36 3/4		933
12 1/4		311	20 1/2		521	28 3/4		730	37		940
12 1/2		318	20 3/4		527	29		737	37 1/4		946
12 3/4		324	21		533	29 1/4		743	37 1/2		953
13		330	21 1/4		540	29 1/2		749	37 3/4		959
13 1/4		337	21 1/2		546	29 3/4		756	38		965
13 1/2		343	21 3/4		552	30		762			
13 3/4		349	22		559	30 1/4		768			
14		356	22 1/4		565	30 1/2		775			

* To obtain other sizes, multiply inches by 25.4, and round to the nearest whole number.

Figure 18-33. This table displays inch-to-mm conversions.

example, A3 is half the area of A2 and double the area of A4. The A Series has the unique advantage that the proportion of height to width remains the same, regardless of size. See **Figure 18-34.** Therefore, a design prepared for one size can be reduced or enlarged to fit the smaller or larger sizes in the same series. While the United States still thinks of 8 1/2″ × 11″ as a standard letterhead and flier size, ISO promoters have adopted the A4 size, which is 8 1/4″ × 11 1/2″.

Metric sheet dimensions are stated in millimeters (mm). To convert inches to mm, multiply the number of inches by 25.4 and round off to the nearest whole mm. For example, to convert 8 1/2″ × 11″ to mm, follow these steps:

1. 8 1/2″ × 25.4 = 215.9 mm = 216 mm (rounded off)
2. 11″ × 25.4 = 279.4 mm = 279 mm (rounded off)

Therefore, the familiar 8 1/2″ × 11″ size becomes 216 × 279 mm.

The ISO sizes for envelopes are shown in **Figure 18-35.** They are designed to hold the A-Series sheets unfolded or folded. For example, an A1 sheet fits unfolded into a C1 envelope. If it is folded in half, it fits in a C2 envelope.

ISO Basic Weight System

Paper using the U.S. customary system of measurement is presently sold by the pounds per ream. The international paper sizes relate all basic weights to the A0 sheet size. The ISO metric basic weight system for paper is expressed in grams per square meter (g/m^2). A rough conversion of U.S.

alkaline paper: paper that has a pH above 7.

sheets per carton: the number of sheets in a carton of paper.

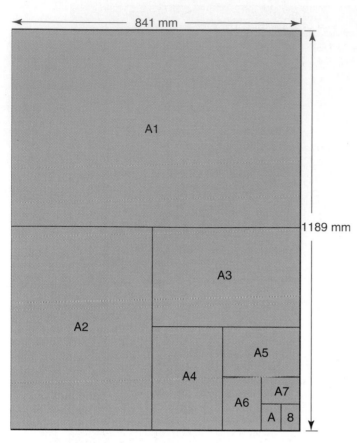

Figure 18-34. The metric system used for paper is based on the principle that a rectangle's dimensions have a ratio of 1:2. This example shows the A-Series ISO sizes for paper.

customary weights to ISO metric for basic book weights can be made by multiplying the weight, in pounds, by 1.5. For example, a 50-lb. book paper is about the same as 75 g/m².

Universal Basic Size

For a number of years, printers and paper manufacturers have proposed to substitute a *universal basic size* for the current practice of having a different basic size for each paper classification. A universal size of 25″ × 40″ (1M square inches) would become the standard for weighing 1M sheets of any paper—business, book, cover, bristol, or utility. See **Figure 18-36.**

The weight of 1M sheets in the universal size, 1M square inches, would be used as an identifying number for each type of paper. This weight would also be a simple method of calculating any amount and size of paper of that number and would be a means of comparing different kinds of paper by weight. As is the current practice, different basic sizes among classifications give similar sheets very different substance weights. As seen in **Figure 18-37,** Sub. 50 book paper is comparable to Sub. 20 bond. Although many people think a universal basic size should be adopted, at this point, it is only an idea.

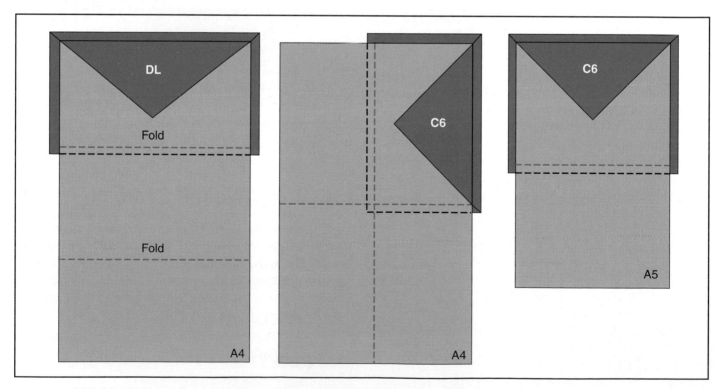

Figure 18-35. ISO sizes for envelopes are designed to hold A-Series sheets unfolded or folded.

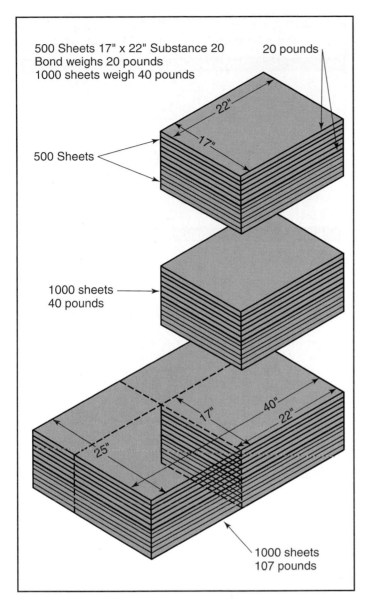

500 Sheets 17" x 22" Substance 20 Bond weighs 20 pounds
1000 sheets weigh 40 pounds

20 pounds

22"

17"

500 Sheets

1000 sheets
40 pounds

17"   40"

22"

25"

1000 sheets
107 pounds

Figure 18-36. The proposed universal basic size would eliminate the current system of different basic sizes for different paper classifications.

Equivalent Weights   (Pocket Pal)

In reams of 500 sheets, basis weights in bold type

Grade of Paper	BOOK 25 x 38	BOND 17 x 22	COVER 20 x 26	BRISTOL 22½ x 28½	INDEX 25½ x 30½	TAG 24 x 36	GRAMMAGE (gsm)
BOOK	**30**	12	16	20	25	27	44
	40	16	22	27	33	36	59
	45	18	25	30	37	41	67
	50	20	27	34	41	45	74
	60	24	33	40	49	55	89
	70	28	38	47	57	64	104
	80	31	44	54	65	73	118
	90	35	49	60	74	82	133
	100	39	55	67	82	91	148
	120	47	66	80	98	109	178
BOND	33	**13**	18	22	27	30	49
	41	**16**	22	27	33	37	61
	51	**20**	28	34	42	46	75
	61	**24**	33	41	50	56	90
	71	**28**	39	48	58	64	105
	81	**32**	45	55	67	74	120
	91	**36**	50	62	75	83	135
	102	**40**	56	69	83	93	151
COVER	91	36	**50**	62	75	82	135
	110	43	**60**	74	90	100	163
	119	47	**65**	80	97	108	176
	146	58	**80**	99	120	134	216
	164	65	**90**	111	135	149	243
	183	72	**100**	124	150	166	271
BRISTOL	100	39	54	**67**	81	91	148
	120	47	65	**80**	98	109	178
	148	58	81	**100**	121	135	219
	176	70	97	**120**	146	162	261
	207	82	114	**140**	170	189	306
	237	93	130	**160**	194	216	351
INDEX	110	43	60	74	**90**	100	163
	135	53	74	91	**110**	122	203
	170	67	93	115	**140**	156	252
	208	82	114	140	**170**	189	328
TAG	110	43	60	74	90	**100**	163
	137	54	75	93	113	**125**	203
	165	65	90	111	135	**150**	244
	192	76	105	130	158	**175**	284
	220	87	120	148	180	**200**	326
	275	109	151	186	225	**250**	407

Figure 18-37. The equivalent-weight chart displays the substance weights of a paper classification in boldface. The weights shown in the same horizontal row are the equivalent weight in other classifications. For example, Sub. 50 book paper has nearly the same caliper as Sub. 20 bond paper.

Envelopes

Envelopes are manufactured in many styles. See **Figure 18-38.** Most styles are available in several sizes, usually ordered by number. See **Figure 18-39.** For example, a No. 10 envelope is for business use and measures 4 1/8″ × 9 1/2″. A No. 6 3/4 commercial envelope measures 3 5/8″ × 6 1/2″. Envelopes having a transparent window are used for business purposes, such as mailing statements and invoices.

Styles used for social invitations and wedding announcements are called *baronial envelopes.* Cards and blank sheets are available in sizes matching the envelopes. Heavy kraft or manila envelopes are manufactured for mailing magazines, pamphlets, reports, books, and similar materials. One of the most common types is the manila clasp envelope, which comes in several standard sizes.

Envelopes are also available in different colors and vary in thickness according to their construction and the weight of paper. Depending on style

universal basic size: a metric system of measurement in which a universal size of 25″ x 40″ would become the standard for weighing 1M sheets.

baronial envelope: an envelope used for social invitations and wedding announcements.

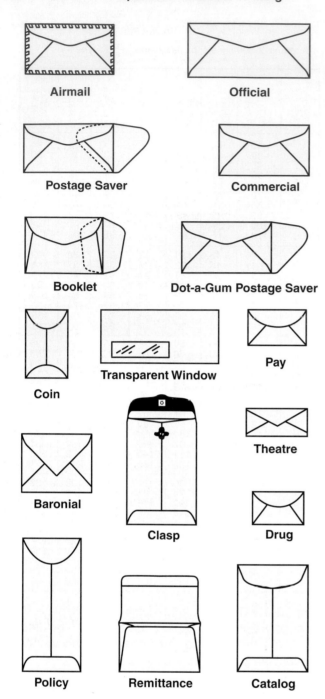

Figure 18-38. Each style and size of envelope fits a specific purpose. (Leslie Paper Co.)

Size	Dimensions (Inches)
Office and Commercial	
5	3 1/6 x 5 1/2
6 1/4	3 1/2 x 6
6 3/4	3 5/8 x 6 1/2
7	3 3/4 x 6 3/4
7 3/4	3 7/8 x 7 1/2
8 5/8	3 5/8 x 8 5/8
9	3 7/8 x 8 7/8
10	4 1/8 x 9 1/2
11	4 1/2 x 10 3/8
12	4 3/4 x 11
14	5 x 11 1/2
Baronial	
4	3 5/8 x 4 11/16
5	4 1/8 x 5 1/8
5 1/2	4 3/8 x 5 5/8
5 3/4	4 5/8 x 5 15/16
Booklet	
2 1/2	4 1/2 x 5 7/8
3	4 3/4 x 6 1/2
5	5 1/2 x 8 1/8
6	5 3/4 x 8 7/8
6 1/2	6 x 9
7	6 1/4 x 9 5/8
7 1/2	7 1/2 x 10 1/2
9	8 3/4 x 11 1/2
9 1/2	9 x 12
10	9 1/2 x 12 5/8
Clasp	
0	2 1/2 x 4 1/4
5	3 1/8 x 5 1/2
10	3 3/8 x 6
15	4 x 6 3/8
11	4 1/2 x 10 3/8
25	4 5/8 x 6 3/4
35	5 x 7 1/2
14	5 x 11 1/2
50	5 1/2 x 8 1/4
55	6 x 9
63	6 1/2 x 9 1/2
68	7 x 10
75	7 1/2 x 10 1/2
80	8 x 11
83	8 1/2 x 11 1/2
87	9 3/4 x 11 1/4
90	9 x 12
93	9 1/2 x 12 1/2
94	9 1/4 x 14 1/2
95	10 x 12
97	10 x 13
98	10 x 15
105	11 1/2 x 14 1/2
110	12 x 15 1/2

Figure 18-39. U.S. envelope sizes and dimensions in inches. (EMA)

and size, envelopes are usually sold in boxes of 250 or 500. European envelope measurements are listed in **Figure 18-40.**

Estimating and Cutting Paper

Paper is an expensive material and can account for up to one-half of the total cost of a printed job. The printer must calculate the amount of required paper and how images will be arranged on the press sheet to avoid waste. Many quick printers use *cut sizes* of paper, such as 8 1/2″ × 11″, 8 1/2″ × 14″, and 11″ × 17″, for their jobs. These cut sizes, as well as much larger sizes, can be purchased from local paper merchants. Before paper is ordered, however, calculations must

Number	Height	mm Width	Inches Height	Inches Width
C7	81	114	3.19	4.49
C7/6	81	162	3.19	6.38
DL	110	220	4.33	8.66
C6	114	162	4.49	6.38
B6	125	176	4.92	6.93
1/2BC4	125	324	4.92	12.75
E6	140	200	5.51	7.87
C5	162	229	6.38	9.02
B5	176	250	6.93	9.84
E5	200	280	7.87	11.02
C4	229	324	9.02	12.75
B4	250	353	9.84	13.09
E4	280	400	11.02	15.75

Figure 18-40. European-envelope measures used in all European countries, except Great Britain. In Great Britain, A5 is the standard size for folded letterheads 4.25″ × 8.625″. (EMA)

be made on the number of finished units (such as fliers, business cards, or posters) that can be carried on a press sheet and the number of press sheets that can be cut from the purchase sheet. For example, a printer might print four 5″ × 8″ cards on an 11″ × 17″ press sheet after splitting two press sheets from a 17″ × 22″ purchase-sheet size. The *cancellation method* is used to determine the greatest number of sheets that can be cut from a single, full-size sheet. To do this, the dimensions of the small (cut) sheet are written under the dimensions of the large (parent) sheet, and each cut-size dimension is divided into the parent-size dimension above it. The two resulting whole numbers are then multiplied to reveal the number of cut sheets that can be cut from the parent sheet.

To see this method applied, imagine that the order just described calls for 2000 5″ × 8″ cards run on an 11″ × 17″ press sheet. The paper is available in only one size—17″ × 22″. 5 goes into 11 twice, and 8 goes into 17 twice. The 2s are then multiplied to reveal that 4 cards can be printed on a single press sheet. The cutting pattern and yield are shown to

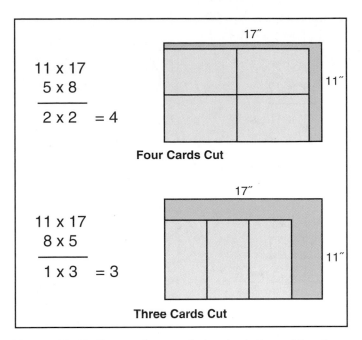

Figure 18-41. Depending on their orientation, either four or three cards can be cut from each press sheet. The blue areas represent waste.

the right. At this point, the cut-size dimensions are reversed to see if the reorientation produces a better yield. See **Figure 18-41.** This imposition gets only 3 cards on each press sheet and creates a large amount of waste, however, as seen in the cutting pattern and yield shown on the right. As this example shows, it is important to calculate with both orientations to determine the better imposition. With 4 cards coming out of each press sheet, only 500 press sheets are needed to produce 2000 cards.

The same procedure is performed to find the number of press sheets that can be cut from a purchase sheet. For this calculation, the press sheet becomes the cut size. As shown in **Figure 18-42,** each 17″ × 22″ purchase sheet can yield a maximum of 2 11″ × 17″ press sheets. Therefore, the needed 500 press sheets require only 250 purchase sheets. In summary, the printer orders 250 sheets of 17″ × 22″ paper, which are cut to produce 500 11″ × 17″ press sheets. After printing, these sheets are cut again to produce 2000 5″ × 8″ cards.

In this example, the customer did not specify a grain direction for the cards. If the cards had to be delivered grain long (5″ × 8″) and the purchase

cut size: a sheet size that fits into the printing press.

cancellation method: a paper-estimating method used to determine the greatest number of pieces of paper that can be cut from a single, full-size sheet.

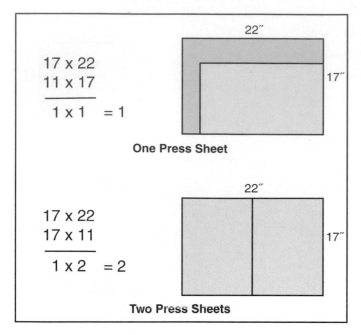

Figure 18-42. The blue area represents the waste resulting from a yield of only one press sheet from the purchase sheet. A different orientation yields a maximum of two press sheets from each purchase sheet, with no waste.

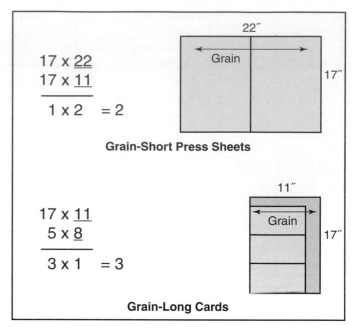

Figure 18-43. When grain direction is important, the grain-direction dimensions are stacked, and division is straight up. Two grain-short press sheets can be cut from the grain-long purchase sheets with no waste. The blue area represents the waste required if grain-long cards are to be cut from a grain-short press sheet.

sheet was available only grain long (17″ × 22″), the press sheets would be grain short (11″ × 17″). The calculation for cards out of each press sheet would require the dimensions with the grain direction to be stacked, as shown in **Figure 18-43.** This limitation would allow only 3 cards from each press sheet, and so 667 press sheets and 334 purchase sheets would be needed. In short, when grain direction is a factor, calculations must be performed with the grain directions aligned.

Estimating Spoilage Allowance

The paper calculations shown above did not take into consideration the reality of spoilage. In calculating the amount of paper needed for a job, it is necessary to add in a certain percentage of press sheets, to allow for spoilage. This percentage is called the *spoilage allowance* and is included to allow for the sheets needed to set up the press (makeready) and for the sheets that are printed badly during the run. Spoilage allowance is made for each pass the sheets make through the press, as well as any necessary finishing operations, such as trimming, folding, drilling, or embossing. A table of allowances for sheetfed spoilage is shown in **Figure 18-44.** A table for webfed presses is shown in **Figure 18-45.**

For example, assume the 2000 5″ × 8″ cards described earlier carry one color of ink on both sides and are printed on a single-color sheetfed

press. If the job is run with 4 cards on each press sheet, the resulting net 500 press sheets require two passes through the press. Using the "1000" column in **Figure 18-44,** the spoilage allowance for the first pass through the press is 8%, and for the second pass is 6%, for a total of 14%. Multiplying 500 net press sheets by 14% gives 70—the number of press sheets that can be expected to be spoiled during production. Adding 90 to the 500 net press sheets gives 590 total press sheets and, by extension, 295 purchase sheets. Spoilage allowances vary among printing companies, depending primarily on the type of equipment and the competency of the press and finishing operators.

Estimating Combination Cuts

On occasion, a printer imposes images on a press sheet in a *combination cut* (or stagger cut), which means images are aligned in both directions on the press sheet. A combination cut is used when such an arrangement squeezes more finished units onto the press sheet and grain direction is not important to either the customer or the production of the job. As an example, if a 32″ × 44″ sheet must be cut into the greatest number of 8 1/2″ × 11″ sheets with the least amount of waste, a combination cut can be used because neither dimension of the finished size

**Sheetfed-Offset
Spoilage Allowances**

Sheetfed Offset*	1000	2500	5000	10,000	25,000+
Single–color equipment					
One color, one side	8%	6%	5%	4%	3%
One color, work–and–turn or work–and–tumble	13%	10%	8%	6%	5%
Each additional pass (per side)	6%	5%	4%	3%	2%
Two–color equipment					
Two colors, one side	–	–	5%	4%	3%
Two colors, work-and-turn or work–and–tumble	–	–	8%	6%	5%
Each additional pass (per side)	–	–	4%	3%	2%
Four–color equipment					
Four colors, one side only	–	–	–	6%	5%
Four colors, work–and–turn or work–and–tumble	–	–	–	8%	7%
Bindery spoilage					
Folding, stitching, trimming	4%	3%	3%	2%	2%
Cutting, punching, or drilling	2%	2%	2%	2%	2%
Varnishing and gumming	7%	5%	4%	3%	3%

* Percentage represents press-size sheets, not impressions. Figures do not include waste sheets used to run up color, as it is assumed that waste stock is used for this purpose.

Figure 18-44. This table gives spoilage allowances for sheetfed-offset pressruns. (S.D. Warren Co.)

**Web-Offset
Spoilage Allowances**

Web Offset	Waste % of Total Impressions*
Pressrun	
Up to 25M	18
Over 25M to 50M	15
Over 50M to 100M	13
Over 100M to 200M	11
Over 200M	9
Penalties to be added:	
For each additional web over 1	1
For using 2 folders	1
For 3, 4, or 5 colors	1
For coated paper	5
For light papers under 40 lbs.	2
For heavy papers over 60 lbs.	2

* Includes waste for core, wrappers, and damaged paper, which is estimated at 2 1/2%. The chart is for blanket-to-blanket presses running two colors on two sides of the web, on uncoated paper 40–60 lbs., and using one folder. The chart includes makeready spoilage.

Figure 18-45. This table gives spoilage allowances for web-offset pressruns. (S.D. Warren Co.)

is underlined to indicate a preferred grain direction. **Figure 18-46** shows the amount of waste involved. Drawing a cutting diagram reveals that the accumulated waste permits printing four more pieces of 8 1/2″ × 11″ paper, if they are rotated. When grain direction is not a factor in the job, drawing a cutting diagram before planning the press sheet avoids unnecessary waste.

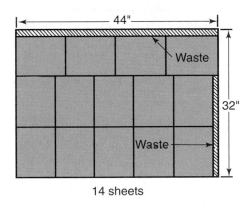

14 sheets

Figure 18-46. A cutting diagram reveals the best cut with the least amount of waste when calculating combination cuts.

Calculating the Purchase Price

After calculating the number of total purchase sheets, the next step is to calculate the price for the order. Many printers simply telephone the local paper merchant and inform a customer service representative (CSR) of the order's specs. The CSR then calculates the price and informs the printer, who includes

spoilage allowance: the percentage of extra sheets added to the total pieces needed for a job to compensate for replacing soiled or misprinted sheets and for use during makeready or when setting up the press.

combination cut: a paper-cutting method for jobs that do not divide evenly into the basic-size paper from which they are to be cut. This method provides the greatest number of press-size sheets, while reducing waste to a minimum.

the cost of the paper into the estimate being prepared for the customer.

It is also common for printers to have their own copy of the paper merchant's catalog and calculate the paper cost themselves. A paper merchant's catalog contains all the information needed to calculate the cost of a paper order, but the procedure is somewhat complicated. To demonstrate the method, imagine ordering 6200 sheets of Skylark dull offset Sub. 80, 23″ × 35″. See **Figure 18-47.**

The two columns on the far left list the available substance weights and sheet sizes, respectively. The third and fourth columns contain the Mwts and the number of sheets in a carton for Sub. 80 Skylark dull offset in the 23″ × 35″ size. Dividing the number of sheets in the order (6200) by the sheets in a carton (1100) reveals that this order consists of over five cartons. The size of the order—as measured by the number of cartons—is important because larger orders receive lower prices per pound. The

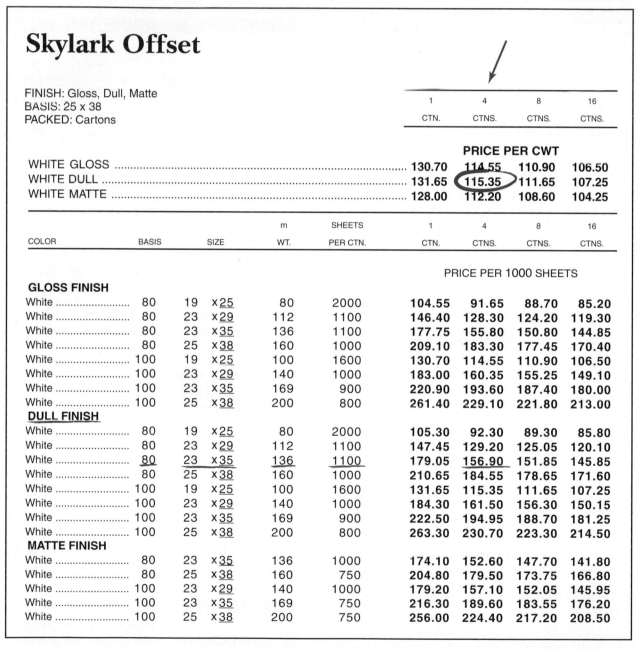

Figure 18-47. This sample page from a paper merchant's catalog contains all the information needed to calculate the cost of a given article.

four-carton price applies because this order is for at least four cartons (note the arrow). The circled $115.35 is the price per hundredweight (cwt), which is the cost per 100 lbs. (C is the Roman numeral for *100*). The price per cwt is converted to the price per pound by dividing by 100, or simply moving the decimal point two places to the left, to reveal the price per pound to be $1.1535.

Next, multiplying the number of thousand sheets in the order (6.2 Ms) by the Mwt (136#) gives the total weight of the order in pounds, which is then multiplied by the price per pound ($1.2325) to give the total cost ($1895.09).

Ms	×	Mwt	×	$/#	=	Total Cost
6.2		136#		$1.1535	=	$972.63

This paper merchant also lists prices per thousand sheets ordered. In the eight-carton column of the "Price per 1M Sheets" section, the price per M is $156.90. If the cost is calculated by using this M-sheet price, a different formula is used—Ms multiplied by the Mwt.

Ms	×	$/M	=	Total Cost
6.2	×	$156.90	=	$972.78

People use the formula they prefer because any difference in total cost between the two procedures is negligible.

Selecting and Ordering Paper

When selecting paper for a particular printed piece, the following factors should be considered:

- Select paper that is compatible with the printing process and ink to be used. Think about durability, permanence, foldability, and exposure to various weather conditions.

- Price is extremely important. Expensive paper is not always necessary. The intended use is usually the key to determining quality and price.

- Paper that is heavier than necessary leads to high mailing costs. A number of lightweight papers are available that have good opacity and exceptional printability.

- The paper surface and finish should be selected on the basis of the printing process to be used and the aesthetic qualities desired. Rough-textured paper gives a different feel and appearance from a smooth-textured paper.

- Paper is available in many sizes. The finished size and the maximum press-sheet size should be considered for maximum efficiency and minimum waste.

- Colored paper can add to the aesthetics of a printed piece, but it might also add cost.

- Four-color printing reproduces most accurately on neutral white paper, but type is most easily read when printed on a soft white paper.

- The finish of the paper selected can affect the mood of the completed job. Select a paper that prints well and harmonizes with the type and tone of the message.

- Paper-grain direction is most important when planning folded pieces. Paper tears and folds most easily with the grain. When a job is folded in both directions, the grain should be parallel to the last fold.

Printers usually place their order to the paper merchant by telephone after consulting the merchant's price catalog. Orders for most types of paper specify the following information:

- The stock number as it appears on the catalog page.

- The quantity, or number of sheets, packages, cartons, bundles, skids, or carload lots.

- The sheet size (chosen from the sizes available in the catalog).

- The substance weight.

- The exact name of the color, as shown in the catalog.

- The brand name of the manufacturer.

- The desired finish (matte, dull, or gloss coated or smooth, vellum, antique, linen, or eggshell uncoated).

- The grain direction, especially for jobs in which folding is involved.

- Packing—whether the paper should be delivered in cartons or on skids.

- The delivery date. When it is important, indicate the time of day—early morning, midmorning, early afternoon, or late afternoon.

When the printing facility has a railroad siding, include that information. Identify the railroad. When the printing facility has a receiving platform, be sure to indicate if over-the-road trailers can be accommodated. When the paper is being shipped into a warehouse, identify its location. **Figure 18-48** and **Figure 18-49** illustrate two checklists for ordering paper in flat sheets and rolls. By using these forms, the printer ensures that the paper merchant is supplied all the information needed to deliver the order at the assigned destination and proper time.

Checklist for Ordering Paper in Flat Sheets

GRADE _____

QUANTITY _____ (Sheets) _____ (Pounds)

SIZE & WEIGHT _____ M; _____ basis weight

COLOR _____ FINISH _____ DESIGN _____

CALIPER THICKNESS _____ 1-sheet _____ 4-sheets _____ pages-to-inch

☐ WATERMARKED   ☐ UNWATERMARKED

GRAIN DIRECTION   ☐ long   ☐ short   ☐ optional (one dimension)

DESIGN OR PATTERN NUMBER   ☐ long   ☐ short   ☐ optional (one dimension)

TRIMMING   ☐ machine   ☐ trimmed-2-sides

TO ONE SIZE   ☐ trimmed-2-ends   ☐ trimmed-4-sides

PRESS SHEET   ☐ Sheetwise   ☐ Work-and-Turn   ☐ Work-and-Tumble

REPRODUCTION METHOD (indicate which)

☐ Letterpress   ☐ 1-color   ☐ 2-colors   ☐ 3-colors   ☐ 4-colors

                 ☐ wet   ☐ dry

☐ Lithography   ☐ 1-color   ☐ 2-colors   ☐ 3-colors   ☐ 4-colors

                 ☐ wet   ☐ dry

☐ Gravure   ☐ High-gloss inks   ☐ Metallic inks

☐ Photogelatine ☐ Finishing ☐ Varnishing ☐ Lacquering ☐ Embossing

☐ Acetate laminating   ☐ Liquid laminating   ☐ Polyethylene laminating

PLANT HUMIDITY REQUIREMENTS_____

PURPOSE FOR WHICH THIS PAPER IS INTENDED _____

PACKING   ☐ Ream-marked in cartons   ☐ Ream-marked in bundles

           ☐ Ream-sealed in cartons   ☐ Ream-marked on single-tier skids

           ☐ Ream-marked on double-tier skids ☐ Ream-marked on 4-tier skids

           ☐ Felt-side-UP ☐ Felt-side-DOWN   ☐ Cast-side-UP   ☐ Cast-side-DOWN

SKID SPECIFICATIONS   ☐ 4-way-entry   ☐ 2-way-entry

runners   ☐ short-way   ☐ long-way

minimum distance between runners .. inches maximum height .. inches maximum weight .. pounds

        Note — MARK SKID NUMBER AND ORDER NUMBER ON RUNNERS

SHIPPING   siding on _____ RR

                 plant can accommodate trailers up to _____ feet long

                 ☐ sidewalk delivery by winch truck

Most satisfactory delivery hours _____ AM to _____ AM   _____ PM to _____ PM

Receiving platform closed _____ to _____

SPECIAL MARKINGS ON SKID WRAPPERS _____

SPECIAL INSTRUCTIONS NOT IDENTIFIED ABOVE_____

SAMPLE FOR MATCHING ACCOMPANYING

Figure 18-48. A checklist for ordering paper in flat sheets provides the paper merchant with all the information regarding an order. (Walden-Mott Corp.)

Checklist for Ordering Paper in Rolls

GRADE _____

QUANTITY _____ pounds

Maximum Basis weight _____ pounds

Maximum Thickness_____ pages-to-inch _____

Maximum Roll Width _____ inches

Maximum Roll Diameter _____ inches

Core Inside Diameter _____ inches

Type of Core

☐ returnable   ☐ non-returnable

☐ slotted   ☐ non-slotted

☐ slot in juxtaposition   ☐ Dimensions of Keyway _____ x _____

Roll winding   ☐ felt-side OUT   ☐ felt-side IN

Note — MARK DIRECTIONAL ARROWS ON WRAPPERS

Splicing   Maximum acceptable to roll _____

flag ☐ one side   ☐ two sides

☐ diagonally across roll

☐ use 3-M splicing material for heat-set reproduction

Wrapping ☐ moisture proof   ☐ non-moisture proof

Delivery ☐ on side   ☐ on end

PLANT HUMIDITY REQUIREMENTS

Special instructions

☐ Rolls must be wound uniformly firm   ☐ Indicate weight of each roll on wrapper

☐ Surface of paper must be free from lint and   ☐ Indicate roll-number and winding direction on
   other extraneous materials   ends of rolls

☐ Provide roll cards in core of each roll   ☐ Provide packing slips complete with roll-number,

☐ Number each roll on wrapper   weight-per-roll, and number-of-splices-per-roll

SHIPPING   ☐ siding on _____RR

                        plant can accommodate trailers up to _____ feet long

☐ sidewalk delivery by winch truck

Most satisfactory delivery hours _____AM to _____AM   _____PM to _____PM

Receiving platform closed _____ to _____

SPECIAL MARKING ON ROLL

WRAPPERS_____

_____

_____

SAMPLE FOR MATCHING ACCOMPANYING

Note — Be sure to send out-turned samples in advance of shipment

---

Type of press _____

Speed of press _____

Maximum ink-drying temperature _____

Type of Delivery _____

Figure 18-49. A checklist for ordering paper in rolls is used by web-offset printers. (Walden-Mott Corp.)

Summary

Paper has been around since around 105 AD. This product was made by hand into the early 1800s, before Nicolas Louis Robert invented a paper-making machine that produced paper in continuous rolls, rather than individual sheets. The Fourdrinier brothers financed improvements on Robert's invention, and the innovation became known as the *fourdrinier papermaking machine*—a device that revolutionized paper production and is widely used today.

Although the Chinese originally used wood fibers in the production of paper, there was a period of time when this art was lost. Most paper was manufactured from pulp made from old rags. Today, wood is the basic raw material used to manufacture most printing papers.

When selecting paper for a particular job, a working knowledge of paper is extremely important. The buyer must understand paper characteristics defined in terms of classification, weight, printability, and runnability. It is important to understand the stages of papermaking to better understand how desired sheet characteristics are achieved.

Mechanical, chemical, and semichemical pulping processes are used to convert wood into pulp. Pulping reduces wood into individual cellulose fibers and removes most impurities and chemicals in the wood to produce virgin pulp. Recycled pulps are made using many of the same processes, but they require additional steps, such as deinking, to purify the pulp. The pulping process used determines many of the paper's properties.

As the offset-printing process has evolved and improvements in printing technology have occurred, papers have been developed with specific printing properties. Paper is grouped into paper classifications, categories, and grades. The classifications are business, book, text, cover, and utility. Estimating the paper requirements for a given job involves planning how the press sheet will be imposed to avoid unnecessary waste, figuring the number of net press sheets needed, calculating adequate spoilage allowance, and figuring the number of purchase sheets to be ordered.

Review Questions

Please do not write in this book. Write your answers on a separate sheet of paper.

1. What is the function of the pulping stage of the papermaking process?
2. Groundwood pulp is an example of _____ pulping because it has been reduced to fibers without the use of chemicals.
3. The process of treating pulp with chemicals to whiten the cellulose fibers is called _____.
4. The addition of fillers to pulp improves which property of the finished sheet?
5. Sizing added to the pulp during refining is _____ sizing.
6. Why is good water resistance needed with offset papers?
7. The absorption of ink by a sheet of paper is controlled by _____ sizing.
8. The side of the paper touching the screen on the papermaking machine is called the _____.
9. As paper begins to form on the papermaking machine, it passes under a(n) _____ roll.
10. A(n) _____ is a symbol or logo identifying the brand of bond paper or trademark of a company.
11. Explain the calendering stage of the papermaking process—both the process and its effect on the sheet.
12. What advantages do twin-wire paper machines have over fourdrinier machines?
13. What is the function of the supercalendering stage?
14. The alignment of fibers is referred to as the _____ of the paper.
15. What is dimensional stability?
16. Distinguish among matte, dull, and gloss finishes on coated paper.
17. Good _____ resistance is required of offset papers because offset inks tend to be tacky.
18. _____ is the lifting of individual particles by the dampening solution.
19. The weight, in pounds, of a ream of paper in its basic size is called its _____.
20. What causes tight edges in a pile of paper?
21. Moisture _____ is needed so the surface of the paper can accept and bond with the ink.
22. Bond paper is part of which classification?
23. A(n) _____ edge is an untrimmed, feathery edge remaining on some kinds of paper.
24. The bristol classification contains sheets sharing what characteristic?
25. Distinguish between preconsumer and postconsumer wastepaper.
26. _____ is an alternative bleaching process that uses chlorine dioxide or sodium hypochlorite instead of chlorine gas.

27. What is alkaline paper, and what is the benefit to using it?

28. Give three examples of envelope sizes and styles.

29. How many 7″ × 9″ cards can be printed on a 20″ × 26″ press sheet?

30. How many purchase sheets are needed for a job to print 48,000 fliers, if each purchase sheet yields two press sheets and each press sheet carries six finished units?

31. The percentage of extra sheets to replace those ruined during a printing operation is called the _____.

32. Under what conditions can a combination cut be used?

33. Referring to **Figure 18-47,** how many sheets of Sub. 80 19″ × 25″ Skylark dull offset are in a carton?

34. Referring to **Figure 18-47,** what would be the total weight of 4000 sheets of Sub. 100 23″ × 29″ Skylark gloss offset?

35. Referring to **Figure 18-47,** calculate the cost to order 4000 sheets of Sub. 100 23″ × 29″ Skylark gloss offset.

36. Referring to **Figure 18-47,** calculate the cost to order 9340 sheets of Sub. 100 25″ × 38″ Skylark matte offset.

37. Compare three different types of paper and their appropriateness for certain printing jobs.

Skill-Building Activities

1. Determine the grain direction and felt and wire sides of several kinds of paper used in your lab. Use the methods listed below and those TAPPI recommends:
   A. Tear a sheet of paper in one direction and then the other. The straightest tear is with (parallel to) the grain.
   B. Cut two strips of paper, each in a different direction. Lay the strips over a rod or straight surface. The sheet curving the most is across (at a right angle to, or opposite) the grain.
   C. Dampen one side of the sheet. The dampened paper curls with the grain. Usually, a sheet of paper folds easier and forms a more even edge with the grain.

2. Gather samples of ten different letterheads. Check each of the letterheads for watermarks. Write your findings on the back of each sample.

3. Determine the maximum number of pieces that can be cut from the parent sizes listed below. Prepare a cutting diagram for each problem:

Finish Size	Parent Size
5″ × 8″	25 1/2″ × 30 1/2″
8 1/2″ × 11″	17″ × 22″
8″ × 10″	20″ × 26″
9″ × 12″	26″ × 38″
11″ × 17″	17 1/2″ × 22 1/2″
6″ × 9″	20″ × 28″

4. Determine the cost of paper for the following orders:
   A. 8 reams of 17″ × 22″—20 bond at $1.18 per pound
   B. 7000 sheets of 25 1/2″ × 30 1/2″—90 index at $1.40 per pound
   C. 40 reams of 17″ × 22″—24 bond at $1.36 per pound
   D. 2500 sheets of 25″ × 38″—70 book at $1.53 per pound
   E. 5000 sheets of 20″ × 26″—80 cover at $1.21 per pound

5. Give the mm sizes for the sheets listed below:
   A. 5″ × 8″
   B. 8 1/2″ × 11″
   C. 10″ × 12″
   D. 11″ × 17″
   E. 17″ × 22″
   F. 20″ × 26″
   G. 25 1/2″ × 30 1/2″
   H. 25″ × 38″

6. In groups of four to five students, collect samples of each of the following paper groups: bond, book, text, cover, newsprint, paperboard, and carbonless. Assemble the information relating to surface finish, thickness, opacity, strength, and general quality of each paper. Use a magnifying glass (loupe) if necessary. Each group will report their findings to the entire class.

7. Prepare a paper sample chart of all the paper stocks used in your school lab. This chart will be useful when trying to determine what paper to use for a job.

Think Ink

The ink colors in this large photograph represent only 10 of the more than 1000 colors a graphic designer can specify. Amazingly, a printer can produce any of these colors from an inventory of only 20 inks. As shown in the sequence of smaller photographs, a specific ink color is achieved by mixing carefully measured portions of two or more of these stock colors. As the mixing continues, the red and yellow inks begin to form the exact hue of orange the designer wants. Just as a thorough mixing operation is needed to produce a uniform color, this operation is also necessary to evenly distribute all the other ingredients.

Driers, resins, and other necessary components you will learn about in this chapter are as necessary as the color. For example, some lithographic inks adhere to paper; others adhere to plastics; and still others adhere to metal, ceramics, or glass. There are lithographic inks that dry in less than a second. A package of frozen peas must be printed with inks formulated to remain flexible at very cold temperatures. There are inks resistant to fading in sunlight. With all these available formulations, people in the printing industry need to be aware of the many ink properties in order to avoid using the wrong ink on the wrong substrate or in the wrong application. In other words, they need to think ink.

(Flint Ink Corp.)

Key Terms

absorption
additive
antifoaming agent
antioxidant
back trapping
coldset ink
color strength
conductivity
corrosion inhibitor
crystallization
dampening solution
degree of contamination
drier
drying oil
drying stimulator
dry trapping
electron-beam (EB) curing
fill-in
fluorescent ink
fungicide
grayness
heatset ink
high-solids ink
hue error
hybrid ultraviolet (UV) ink
infrared (IR) radiation
ink
ink body
ink film thickness
ink formulation
ink length
ink mileage
inkometer
ink permanence
ink rub-off
invisible ink
leafing
lightfastness
liquid ink
lubricant
magnetic ink
mechanical ghosting
metallic ink
milling
mottling
news ink
nonporous ink
opaque ink
optical density

overprint varnish
oxidation
oxidative
  polymerization
paste ink
pH level
polymerize
poor binding
poor color
pseudoplasticity
quick-set ink
radiation curing
radiation-curing ink
resin
rubber-based ink
scuff-resistant ink film
selective absorption
semidrying oil
set
setoff
shot mill
show-through
solvent
soy ink
soy news ink
specific gravity
spot varnish
sticking in the pile
strike-through
tack
tack modifier
thermochromic ink
three-roll mill
through drier
tinting
tinting strength
top drier
ultraviolet (UV)-cured
  ink
ultraviolet (UV) fade-
  resistant ink
vehicle
viscosity
viscosity modifier
waterless offset ink
wax
wetting agent
wet trapping
yield value

Learning Objectives

When you have completed the reading and assigned activities related to this chapter, you will be able to do the following:

❖ Describe the three basic ingredients of lithographic-printing inks.

❖ Explain how ink is manufactured.

❖ Name and explain lithographic-ink properties.

❖ Define and explain various ink-drying methods.

❖ State and describe the types of lithographic-printing inks.

❖ Summarize the use of dampening solutions and their effect on ink performance.

❖ List the specs to supply when ordering lithographic ink.

❖ Identify the factors affecting quantity when estimating the amount of ink needed for a given printing job.

❖ Discuss how ink should be packaged, handled, and stored.

❖ Mix and color-match ink.

Although the printing-ink industry is relatively small, it is one of the most complex and technologically advanced in the nation. The quality of its products and services is maintained through the industry's high level of technical competence. Most ink companies have research laboratories staffed by chemists, ink technicians, and color specialists. These laboratories are equipped with a variety of testing equipment. See **Figure 19-1.**

The Purpose of Printing Inks

Ink is the most common material used to print images on substrates. Modern printing inks are either pastes or liquids. *Paste inks* are thick and tacky. *Liquid inks* are fluid and watery. The printing process requires inks with specific properties to ensure optimum performance and high-quality results. Most inks designed for use on sheetfed-offset presses are paste inks. See **Figure 19-2.** Inks formulated for web-offset presses have a more liquid consistency. This chapter discusses the characteristics of offset-printing inks and explains how ink affects a print job.

Printing-Ink Ingredients

All inks consist of three basic components—the pigment, a vehicle, and additives—that determine an ink's characteristics and performance. See **Figure 19-3.** The nature of these ingredients and their ratios vary greatly across the spectrum of printing inks. Gravure, flexography, and screen printing require inks that are liquid and dry very quickly by evaporation. Letterpress and lithography require paste inks that

Figure 19-2. Yellow and brown lithographic inks are mixed on a slab with a knife to achieve the desired orange color. (Flint Ink Corp.)

dry much more slowly through a complex process called *oxidative polymerization*. Even within the category of lithographic inks, there are different drying mechanisms, and different formulations are needed to adhere to different substrates.

Pigments

An ink's pigment—solid particles suspended, not dissolved, within the liquid vehicle—supplies its color. In addition to providing an ink's color, pigments impart properties such as opacity; resistance to light, heat, chemicals, water, or oils; and

Figure 19-1. Ink chemists and technicians use a variety of test equipment for research and to maintain consistent product quality. (Flint Ink Corp.)

Figure 19-3. An ink's ingredients determine its characteristics and performance. The yellow powder at the back of the paper is the pigment, the gold disks are the resin, and the third pile on the left contains additives and modifiers. (Van Son Holland Ink Corp.)

suitability to lithographic printing. Pigments are divided primarily into three classifications: black, white, and color pigments.

- Black pigments are made from organic ingredients such as lampblack.
- White pigments can be either opaque or transparent.
  - Opaque pigments are made from organic compounds such as zinc sulfide and zinc oxide. These pigments reflect the light from their surface and are used to hide the background on which they are printed.
  - Transparent pigments are made from magnesium carbonate, calcium carbonate, and clays. These pigments allow light to pass through and are used to reduce the color strength of other inks and to produce tints.
- Color pigments are made from inorganic and organic compounds.
  - Inorganic color pigments are typically made from minerals and are classified according to their chemical makeup—chromes, cadmiums, irons, and earth colors.
  - Organic color pigments are derived primarily from coal tar and are the most widely used pigments. Organic pigments are classified by color—yellows, oranges, reds, blues, violets, greens, and browns.

Pigments also determine if the ink is safe (nontoxic) enough for such printed products as butter and meat wrappers. These inks also must be water-resistant so they do not bleed through the paper and affect the food.

Vehicles

Ink pigment requires a liquid *vehicle* to carry it through the ink train and onto the substrate because it is finely ground powder. See **Figure 19-4.** The ink's vehicle determines its stiffness, degree of gloss, drying speed, ability to adhere to the intended substrate, and appropriateness to a particular printing process. Vehicles for lithographic inks must resist water and the slight acidity of *dampening solutions*. These vehicles must allow just the right amount of dampening solution to emulsify into the ink. Although a small degree of emulsification improves an ink's performance, a lithographic ink with excessive dampening solution must be removed from the press and replaced with fresh ink.

In addition to delivering the pigment particles to the substrate, the vehicle's *resins* (or binders) must permanently adhere them to it. The substrate

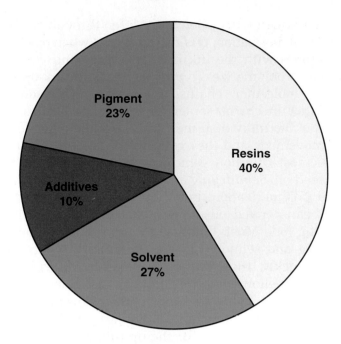

Figure 19-4. An ink's vehicle (resins and solvent) makes up the majority of it composition.

with which the ink will be used—paper, metal, or plastic—determines its binder. Ink resins are solid materials *solvents* must dissolve before they can become part of the liquid vehicle. Once the ink reaches the substrate, the solvent evaporates, and the resin reverts back to its solid state, contributing to the ink's drying.

Commonly used components in lithographic ink are drying oils and semidrying oils. *Drying oils* are linseed, tung, and other vegetable oils that assist in

ink: a color coating specially formulated to reproduce an image on a substrate. This coating is a combination of pigments, vehicles, resins, and additives used in printing.

paste ink: a thick and tacky printing ink.

liquid ink: a fluid and watery printing ink.

oxidative polymerization: the bonding of molecules into chains called *polymers*, when exposed to oxygen.

vehicle: the fluid part of the ink that carries the pigment and works as a binder to hold the pigment on the printed surface after drying.

dampening solution: a mixture of water and other chemicals (such as an acid, a buffer, and gum) the dampening system of an offset press distributes.

resin: a solid or semisolid organic substance used as a binder in printing ink vehicles.

solvent: a typically fluid material able to liquefy or dissolve one or more other materials.

drying oil: a vegetable oil that readily transforms to a solid when exposed in a film to oxygen.

the drying process when they stiffen through oxidative polymerization. *Oxidation* occurs when oxygen combines with the ink oil's molecules and causes them to polymerize. To *polymerize* is to link up to form molecular chains. By linking themselves together in chains somewhat similar to strings of pearls, the individual molecules lose their freedom of movement, and they collectively become a solid. The most common vehicle in lithographic inks is linseed oil. *Semidrying oils* also dry through oxidative polymerization, but they do so more slowly. Soybean-derived oil (known as *soya oil*) is a semidrying oil. Most lithographic inks contain both drying and semidrying oils. Although drying oils dry quickly, their darkness makes it difficult to produce yellow and other light colors. Semidrying oils are much lighter in color, but their slow polymerization rate lengthens the ink's drying time. Therefore, the ink maker strives for the optimum blending of drying and semidrying oils to produce inks with vibrant color and an adequate drying rate.

Additives

A lithographic ink's *additives* might include driers, waxes, lubricants, wetting agents, antiskinning agents, and viscosity and tack modifiers. Some modifiers are added to the vehicle as it is being prepared, while others are added while the ink is being manufactured. Many modifiers can be added to the finished ink to change it for special conditions during a pressrun.

Driers are chemical catalysts that accelerate the ink oil's rate of oxidative polymerization. In other words, they make the ink dry faster. There are two types of driers—top driers and through driers—because lithographic ink dries in two stages, known as *setting* and *drying*.

Ink has *set* when the top of the ink film has hardened or, phrased differently, when the ink has skinned over. Properly set ink does not set off (transfer) to the paper that falls over it in the delivery unit of a sheetfed press, but it can smudge with lateral pressure. *Top driers* (cobalt) are added to accelerate the polymerization rate of the top of the ink film and reduce the setting time. Ink has dried only after the entire ink film has hardened. This ink must have dried before sheets can be fed back through the press or a folder, or they smudge as they are pulled across the top of the pile. *Through driers* (manganese) are added to accelerate the polymerization of the remainder of the ink film and reduce the drying time.

Usually, a sufficient amount of drier is placed in the ink when it is manufactured. There are occasions, however, when the press operator adds drier to the ink. Great care should be taken when adding driers because too much can cause the ink to dry on the press or fill in halftones.

Waxes can be added to the ink during manufacture to help prevent setoff and perform other functions. Wax can increase the ink's scuff resistance. A *scuff-resistant ink film* has a tough, hard surface that can withstand the scrapes and shocks from shipping and handling. Waxes also are used to control the slip of the printed product. For example, it is important that a bag of dog food or fertilizer can be pulled from the top of a pile without excessive friction bringing other bags with it.

Lubricants are added to reduce ink tack (stickiness) and to cause the ink to dry more quickly. These ingredients also help lubricate the ink so it distributes more consistently on the plate, blanket, and substrate. Adding too much lubricant causes an ink to become greasy and print poorly.

Wetting agents (also known as *surfactants*) perform a similar function in ink as a detergent does in water. These agents reduce the surface tension of the vehicle and enable it to more thoroughly mix with the pigment particles. *Antioxidants* (or antiskinning agents) are added to ink to ensure that the ink does not oxidize and form a skin while still on the press. *Tack modifiers* allow the ink formulation to attain the optimum level for the ink's tack characteristics. *Viscosity modifiers* allow the ink formulation to attain the optimum level for the ink's flow characteristics.

The Manufacture of Lithographic Ink

The majority of lithographic inks are mixed and processed in batches. The vehicle, which contains the important performance, setting, and consistency properties, is prepared first, and then the pigment and additives are mixed in. Lithographic inks are prepared in two stages—mixing and milling.

Mixing

In the mixing stage, the pigment is introduced into and distributed throughout the vehicle. Mixing is performed as blades (impellers) slowly rotate to stir ink inside metal containers that can be large enough to hold over 500 gallons (1900 liters) of ink. See **Figure 19-5.**

Milling

Lithographic inks require a second operation, called *milling*, to grind down the tiny clumps of pigment particles called *agglomerates* and more

Figure 19-5. Ink ingredients are mixed in a large metal tub. (Flint Ink Corp.)

uniformly distribute the pigment through the vehicle because the inks are so viscous (thick). In a *three-roll mill*, lithographic ink moves across three steel rollers that revolve in opposing directions at different speeds. See **Figure 19-6.** These combined actions create a friction that breaks down tiny clumps of pigment particles and disperses them through the ink's vehicle. Some pigments require more than one pass through the mill. After the proper amount of milling, the ink is removed by a knife-edged apron and directed into a tub. See **Figure 19-7.**

Small orders of ink prepared at local ink facilities usually receive only three-roll milling. A significant

Figure 19-6. After mixing, ink is milled to break up pigment agglomerates on a three-roll mill, which has steel rollers revolving in opposite directions. The rollers revolve at three speeds. (Van Son Holland Ink Corp.)

portion of ink shipped from large production facilities also goes through a shot mill. A *shot mill* (or bead mill) forces ink through a cylinder containing small metal pellets (similar to steel shot) and rotating metal impellers. See **Figure 19-8.** The friction from passing through the swirling shot breaks up the pigment agglomerates that survived the three-roll mill. The fineness of the particles can be adjusted by reducing the rotation speed of the disks. If a slower speed is used, the slurry remains in the mill longer, and the particles are ground finer. Milling is critical to lithographic-ink quality because of the need to break down pigment agglomerates. These tiny clumps of

oxidation: a chemical reaction involving the combination of oxygen with another substance. This is an ink-drying method in which there is a chemical reaction involving the combination of oxygen with the varnishes in the printed ink film.

polymerize: to form chains immobilizing each molecule and collectively hardening and forming a solid layer, binding the pigment to the printed surface.

semidrying oil: a vegetable oil that transforms to a solid when exposed in a film to oxygen, but at a slower rate than drying oils do.

additive: an ingredient, such as a drier, lubricant, wax, or starch, added to ink to impart special characteristics, improve desirable properties, or suppress undesirable properties.

drier: a liquid or paste additive used in the formulation of printing inks that accelerates drying.

set: the point at which an ink is dry enough to be lightly touched without smudging.

top drier: a catalyst that accelerates the oxidative polymerization of the top portion of an ink film.

through drier: a catalyst that accelerates the oxidative polymerization of an entire ink film.

wax: an ink additive used to improve a dried ink's resistance to rubbing and scuffing.

scuff-resistant ink film: an ink film with a tough, hard surface that can withstand the scrapes and shocks from shipping and handling.

lubricant: an oil used as an ink additive to reduce tack and improve the ability to cover the image areas uniformly.

wetting agent: a substance such as IPA, glycerin, or glycol, added to a fountain solution to lower its surface tension.

antioxidant: a material inhibiting oxidation or reactions promoted by oxygen or peroxides.

tack modifier: an ink additive that adjusts an ink's tack.

viscosity modifier: an ink additive used to adjust an ink's viscosity.

milling: a process used to crush and further blend the ink pigment into the vehicle.

three-roll mill: a machine that uses three steel rollers revolving in alternating directions to break up the solid pigment particles and disperse them into the ink's vehicle.

shot mill: a machine that uses small metal pellets (similar to steel shot) to chop up ink-pigment particles and mix them into the vehicle.

Figure 19-7. After sufficient milling, lithographic ink is removed from the rollers by an apron and directed into containers. (Flint Ink Corp.)

pigment particles can have an abrasive effect on the lithographic plate's emulsion, which ruins the plate.

Lithographic-Ink Properties

There are many factors influencing the printing performance of a lithographic ink. The ability of ink to print well, however, depends primarily on how appropriate the ink's numerous properties are for the press, printing speed, and surface being printed. Generally, these conditions require a careful selection of pigment, resin, varnish, drier, and modifiers.

Inks used in lithography must have many different properties from inks used in the other printing processes. Lithographic inks must work well with water because of the dampening solution unique to offset presses. The ink manufacturer must select ingredients that are more readily moistened by greasy varnish than by water. The pigments in lithographic ink cannot dissolve in water. Likewise, the vehicle should not emulsify—break down and mix—with the water.

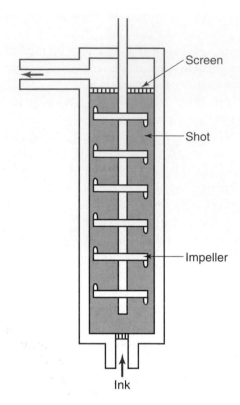

Figure 19-8. A shot mill consists of a large cylinder in which turning blades keep shot in constant motion. Ink is pumped through and milled by the friction and heat.

There are two types of ink emulsification that can occur in offset lithography, and only one of them is good. The first involves a small amount of dampening solution becoming part of the ink—a desired state that actually improves the ink's performance. The other type of emulsification, however, where ink becomes part of the dampening solution, is to be avoided because it results in ink appearing in nonimage areas.

No component of a lithographic ink can react chemically with the printing plate. There should be no grit in the form of tiny clumps of pigment particles in a lithographic ink because the grit can act as an abrasive and wear at the printing plate's surface. Formulating a lithographic ink for a printing job requires knowledge of the press, dampening system, paper, and end use of the product. Each of these factors can determine the formulation of the ink to achieve the desired levels of properties, such as body, viscosity, length, tack, opacity, color, and permanence.

Body

Ink body is a term many press operators use to describe an ink's stiffness. *Body* is an imprecise term that is not a true ink property. In general, the term *body* is used to describe an ink's viscosity or length.

Viscosity

An ink's *viscosity* is its resistance to flowing under applied force. Lithographic inks have a high viscosity because they are paste inks. In fact, they must be removed from their containers and placed into the ink fountain of the press with an ink knife. See **Figure 19-9.** This high viscosity changes, however, as the ink moves through the ink train because friction in the ink rollers creates heat, which lowers the ink viscosity. The same principle of temperature affecting viscosity applies to many other fluids, such as engine oil in an automobile.

Pseudoplasticity (or *shear thinning*) is the name for the loss of viscosity as the result of being stirred or otherwise agitated. Lithographic ink becomes more fluid as it moves through the ink train because it is a pseudoplastic material, but it reverts to its more solid state when the agitation stops. Pseudoplasticity is one reason offset presses have so many ink rollers to agitate the ink, reduce viscosity, and improve flow until the ink comes to rest on the comparatively cool surface of the paper, where it solidifies.

An ink's *yield value* is a measure of the amount of force required before it begins to flow. An ink with a low viscosity, but a high yield value, resists flowing until the necessary amount of force is applied, and then it flows freely. A high yield value can prevent an ink from flowing forward in the fountain to replenish ink the fountain roller has removed. See **Figure 19-10.** This phenomenon is incorrectly described as the ink's "backing away," because the ink is not moving away from the form roller.

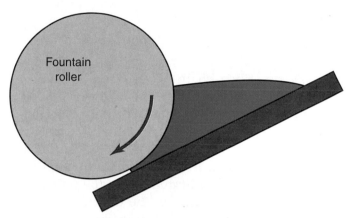

Ink with a Proper Yield Value

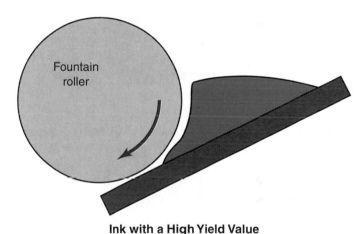

Ink with a High Yield Value

Figure 19-10. An ink with the proper viscosity and yield value flows forward and replaces ink the fountain roller removed. One with a high yield value does not maintain contact with the form roller and appears to move away from it.

ink body: the consistency or degree of softness or hardness of an ink. Body is the covering power and flow of the ink or vehicle.

viscosity: the degree to which ink resists flow under applied force.

pseudoplasticity: the property of a material causing it to lose viscosity when stirred and regain viscosity when left to stand.

yield value: the force required to initiate flow of a pseudoplastic material.

Figure 19-9. An ink knife is used to remove ink from the can and fill the fountain. (Van Son Holland Ink Corp.)

Length

Ink length describes the ability of an ink to form threads or strings when stretched. The test for length is its ability to form a string when drawn (spread out) by an ink knife. Some length is necessary to allow an ink to feed properly to the fountain roller and then transfer. Too much length can cause an ink to mist or fly around in the press area. The length of an ink changes when used on the press, due to heat and friction. See **Figure 19-11.**

Tack

Tack describes an ink's resistance to splitting when pulled from two directions. Lithographic inks have the highest tack levels of all printing inks. High tack helps to print clean, sharp halftone images and prevent excessive emulsification of the ink by the dampening solution. If the ink has too much tack, however, it does not split and cannot be transferred from one roller to another in the ink train or to the plate. Instead of splitting and transferring from the blanket to the paper, ink with excessive tack is likely to remain on the blanket and pull away part of the paper's surface. See **Figure 19-12.** An *inkometer* is used to measure the tack of an ink to determine if it is too great for the surface strength of the paper.

Opacity

Opacity refers to the covering ability of an ink. High opacity means very little light is transmitted, and opaque is the opposite of transparent. Most lithography inks are transparent so two colors can be overprinted to create a third color. See **Figure 19-13.** Process-color (or four-color) printing is dependent on light passing through all the layers of ink. If a design calls for a color to be printed on a colored paper, however, an opaque ink is needed to prevent

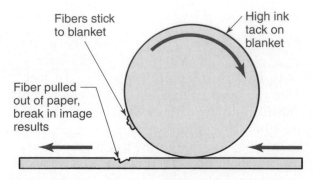

Figure 19-12. Picking can result when ink tack is not matched to stock. High tack can pull off fibers of paper.

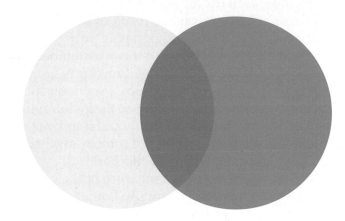

Figure 19-13. Nearly all inks are transparent so they can be overlapped to create other colors. In this example, yellow and cyan have been applied to the same area of the page to create green.

the paper's color from altering the color of the ink. Ink opacity is also referred to as *covering power.*

Color

Three factors influence an ink's color on the substrate. These factors are the color strength, the ink film thickness applied to the substrate, and the process ink's degree of contamination. They must be understood and monitored because any one or all three of these factors can alter color.

Color and tinting strength

The *color strength* of an ink is the pigment-to-vehicle ratio of the ink. One way for an ink maker to lower manufacturing cost is to reduce the amount of pigment because pigment is an expensive ink ingredient. Understandably, an ink's color strength determines its opacity, so inks with poor color strength must be printed with a thicker (heavier) ink film in order to get enough pigment on the paper to attain the proper color. An increase in ink film thickness increases the usage rate and slows drying time. Therefore, inks with poor color strength are no bargain.

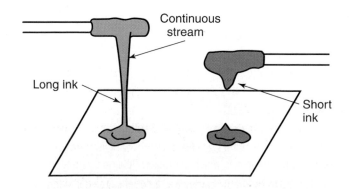

Figure 19-11. The ink on the left is a long ink because it stretches and resists snapping after the short ink on the right has already broken.

One method of comparing the color strength of two different ink brands of the same color is to assess them relative to their tinting strength. The *tinting strength* (or tinctorial strength) of an ink is the ink's ability to maintain its color, despite the addition of white pigment. In other words, it is a measure of how much white pigment must be added to the ink in order to produce a tint of a given strength. Recall that a tint results from the addition of white to a color. For example, pink is a tint of red. The addition of the same amount of white to two red inks—one with high tinting strength and one with low tinting strength—reveals that the first one maintains its original color better than the second one does.

Ink film thickness

The color of a printed image depends, to a certain degree, on the *ink film thickness*, the thickness of the ink's application onto the substrate. All other factors being equal, a thicker ink film appears darker because it contains more pigment than a thinner ink film does. The correct amount of ink film thickness varies with the absorbency of the substrate. For example, uncoated paper is more absorbent than coated paper, so more ink is needed to allow for the amount of ink penetrating the surface.

The term *optical density* describes the light-absorption behavior of a printing-ink film. With transparent primary colors, changes in ink film thickness during a pressrun create differences in the color of the printed images. Densitometers are used to measure film thickness by measuring ink density because the human eye is a poor judge of ink film thickness and the ink density resulting from it.

Process-ink contamination

A densitometer can also be used to assess a process color's *degree of contamination*. As explained in Chapter 16, each of the process colors—CMY—should absorb one-third and reflect two-thirds of the visible spectrum. Actual inks, however, cannot meet this theoretical perfection. In reality, all commercial process inks contain some degree of contamination preventing them from reflecting the full one-third of the light they should reflect. As a result, one ink manufacturer's cyan might reflect light differently than another manufacturer's cyan. In fact, there can be differences between two batches of ink from the same manufacturer. These differences in light reflection can create problems in achieving the desired color on press, and they can be measured by two methods—grayness and hue error. Both measurements allow a process ink's actual reflection to be compared against its theoretical reflection.

A process color's *grayness* is a measurement of its contamination due to the absorption of unwanted light. The amount of light the pigment should have reflected, but did not, determines an ink's grayness. For example, theoretically pure yellow ink would reflect all the green and red light and absorb all the blue. Any green or red light not reflected from a process yellow ink contaminates the yellow and is its grayness. To calculate the grayness of a process ink, the densitometer reads the light reflected from the ink three times—once with a blue filter, once with a green filter, and once with a red filter. Using the formula L/H × 100, the lowest density reading is divided by the highest density reading, and the answer is multiplied by 100.

The other measurement of a process ink's degree of contamination is *hue error*—the imbalance between the two reflected colors. See **Figure 19-14**. The greater reflection of red light than green light does not produce a true yellow. In other words, the yellow appears somewhat orange. All commercial inks have some degree of hue error because none are pure. Yellow is the least contaminated, followed by magenta and cyan. Hue error is calculated by dividing the difference between the middle reflection value and the lowest reflection value by the difference between the highest reflection value and the lowest reflection value. The answer is multiplied by 100.

ink length: the ability of an ink to flow and form threads, or strings, when stretched.

tack: the stickiness of an ink, measured by its ability to split between two surfaces.

inkometer: an instrument (a meter with rollers) that measures the tack of printing inks, in terms of the torque required to split an ink film.

color strength: a measure of the concentration of pigment in the ink to the total weight or volume of the ink. This strength determines the opacity, or covering power, of the ink.

tinting strength: the amount an ink can be reduced or diluted with a white-pigment dispersion to produce a tint of a given strength.

ink film thickness: the thickness of ink when printed onto a substrate.

optical density: the light-absorption behavior of a printing-ink film.

degree of contamination: the amount of unwanted foreign matter in a substance.

grayness: the degree to which equal amounts of overlapping CMY inks produce a neutral gray.

hue error: the degree of unequal reflection by a process color of the two RGB colors making it up.

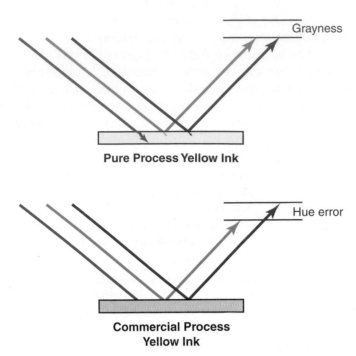

Figure 19-14. An unrealistically pure process yellow ink would absorb all the blue light and reflect all the green and red light, producing a true yellow. Contaminations in a commercial process yellow ink, however, do not allow it to reflect all the green and red light. The difference between the desired reflection and the actual reflection is an ink's grayness. In the bottom drawing, note the greater reflectance of red light than green light. This difference is the ink's hue error and shifts the ink's color toward orange.

Permanence

Ink permanence refers to the ability of a printing ink to resist changes from exposure to light, weather, and time. The permanence of an ink generally depends on the lightfastness of the pigment used. *Lightfastness* is the ability of a printing ink to resist fading due to long-term exposure to light. High-permanency ink should be used on material being printed for window or outdoor display.

Lithographic-Ink Drying Mechanisms

An ink that does not dry is of no use to anyone. There are several methods for getting the ink to dry. Actually, the word *dry* is used loosely in this chapter and in the printing industry in general. The act of drying occurs when a liquid becomes a solid through one or more chemical methods. Some inks solidify so instantly, however, they are said to cure, instead of dry. Still other inks do not actually dry. These inks merely set. Nonetheless, this portion of the chapter uses the word *dry* to include any method of an ink becoming solid. Some common means of drying ink are absorption, oxidative polymerization, selective absorption, evaporation, and radiation curing.

Absorption

When ink dries through *absorption*, it soaks into the paper as though the paper is a sponge. See **Figure 19-15.** Inks that dry by absorption do not dry hard, but they remain on the surface as a powdery substance. As a result, a two-week-old image still smears if it is rubbed. The inks on newspapers are a good example of lithographic inks that dry by absorption. Absorption-drying inks, also called *penetrating inks*, are the least inexpensive lithographic inks, so they are used to print newspapers, telephone directories, and some paperback books to reduce costs.

Oxidative Polymerization

Inks that dry through oxidative polymerization become solid when the oxygen in the air combines with the ink film's drying oils. The oxygen causes the individual molecules in the ink to polymerize—to form chains immobilizing each molecule and collectively hardening and forming a solid layer, binding the pigment to the printed surface. See **Figure 19-16.** Oxidative polymerization is the most common ink-drying mechanism used in offset lithography.

Using *infrared (IR) radiation*, which is nothing more than passing the just-printed substrate under a strong source of IR light, can hasten the oxidation-polymerization process. IR radiation can also be used with quick-set inks to produce what is called *superquick-set IR ink*. The IR radiation's heat accelerates the penetration of the quick-set ink's solvent into the paper, with the result that the image can be smearproof in less than a minute. IR radiation is not a drying mechanism. This radiation merely accelerates other drying mechanisms.

Figure 19-15. When ink "dries" through absorption, most of the vehicle soaks into the paper and leaves the pigment on the surface. These inks smear because they do not actually dry.

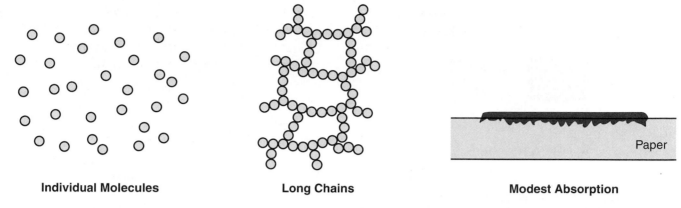

Individual Molecules **Long Chains** **Modest Absorption**

Figure 19-16. When ink dries through oxidative polymerization, oxygen causes the freely flowing molecules of the ink's vehicle to polymerize—that is, individual molecules connect to form long chains. There is only modest absorption.

Selective Absorption

A faster mechanism was sought that would allow a newly printed job to be printed on the second side or receive a finishing operation right away because the oxidation-polymerization drying mechanism can require several hours. The result was the concept of the *selective absorption* of a single component of the vehicle—the key to quick-set inks. The rapid setting of *quick-set inks* depends on a marginally stable solution of a heavy resin in a light oil. When a quick-set ink reaches the substrate, the light oil immediately leaves the solution to penetrate the substrate's surface, thereby leaving behind the resin to quickly return to its solid state. See **Figure 19-17.**

Quick-set inks can solidify rapidly enough to increase the tack of the printed ink between units on the press. If they set sufficiently between units, it is possible to print process colors using four inks that all have the same tack rating, allowing the printer to use a set of process colors in any printing sequence. Ordinarily, the tack levels of subsequent inks must increase. In other words, the second ink color has a higher tack level than the first color, the third is higher than the second, and the fourth is the highest. Quick-set inks are used in both sheetfed and webfed lithography.

Evaporation

High-speed web presses require a faster drying mechanism than oxidative polymerization, and one such method is evaporation—the passage of a liquid to a gaseous state. *Heatset inks* dry through evaporation, as paper carries the still-wet ink film through ovens. The high temperature causes the ink resin's solvent to evaporate, and then chill rollers solidify the pigment-in-resin film left on the paper. Heatset inks are commonly used to print magazines, newspaper advertising inserts, and other high-volume printing on gloss-coated paper.

Radiation Curing

Radiation curing causes a wet ink to become solid in about a second—so fast that the process is called *curing* instead of *drying*. There are two types of radiation curing—UV and electron beam (EB). UV-curing inks are more common because they require less costly equipment and use less power.

After being applied to the paper, *ultraviolet (UV)-cured inks* pass under a strong source of UV light while still on the press. The UV light activates special molecules in the ink, called *photoinitiators*, to give up electrons that, in turn, cause the ink's individual molecules to lock together (or cross-link) and solidify immediately. UV curing is compatible with both sheetfed and webfed lithographic presses. See **Figure 19-18.**

ink permanence: the ability of a printing ink to resist changes from exposure to light, weather, and time.

lightfastness: the ability of a printing ink to resist discoloration and fading when exposed to light or over time.

absorption: an ink-drying method in which the ink soaks into the paper as though the paper were a sponge.

infrared (IR) radiation: exposure of ink to high doses of IR light.

selective absorption: the absorption of one or more, but not all, components of a solution.

quick-set ink: a rapid-drying printing ink made with a balanced solvent, resin, and an oil vehicle.

heatset ink: an ink that dries when hot air accelerates the evaporation of solvents.

radiation curing: the instant solidification of an ink film, due to exposure to high doses of UV light or electron beams.

ultraviolet (UV)-cured ink: ink that instantly solidifies when exposed to high doses of UV light.

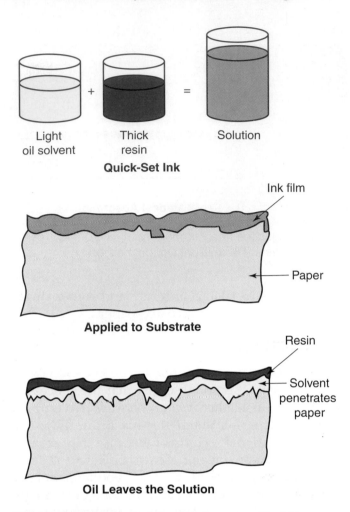

Figure 19-17. When quick-set inks are applied to paper, the resin's solvent immediately leaves the ink to penetrate the surface and leave behind the resin to solidify and hold the pigment.

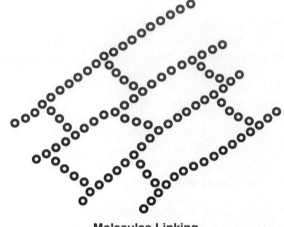

Molecules Linking

Radiation Curing between Printing Units

Figure 19-18. Radiation curing causes individual molecules to link up and lose their mobility. This curing can occur between printing units of an offset press. (Prime Systems, Inc.)

Electron-beam (EB) curing is similar to UV curing, except it radiates electrons directly onto the fresh ink, so no photoinitiators within the ink are needed. EB-curing inks cure more thoroughly than UV-curing inks do because electron beams are able to penetrate and activate the entire ink film. Most of the light that strikes UV-cured ink is absorbed by the pigments before it reaches the lowest part of the ink film. Therefore, a complete cure of UV-cured ink takes longer, although the ink is essentially cured and presents no production problems. An interesting feature of all radiation-cured inks is they dry only when radiated. As a result, if one of these inks is spilled on the floor, it will remain in its wet state for several days.

Ink Formulation

Ink formulation refers to the recipe of the ink—the ingredients and their ratios. There are many lithographic-ink formulations because there are several combinations of substrates and drying mechanisms. The following presentation is limited to the most common formulations. The use of nontraditional lithographic, sheetfed inks, such as metallics, waterless inks, fluorescents, and opaques, has increased in popularity as a graphic-design element and an internal productivity enhancement. When nontraditional inks are on press, it is important to keep each ink's qualities in mind so press settings can be adjusted accordingly to achieve the best results.

Sheetfed Inks

Sheetfed, lithographic inks dry primarily by oxidative polymerization, which cobalt and manganese driers accelerate. These inks have a higher tack than web inks. The relatively low speed of the press permits use of a high-tack ink, which is required for sharp image definition. This also helps to avoid filling in of halftone dots and avoids *setoff* in the printed pile of paper.

Rubber-Based Inks

The vehicle in *rubber-based inks* contains cyclized rubber that allows these inks to remain on the ink train of the press for several hours without drying. As a result, the press does not have to be washed up at the end of the day. These inks dry quickly on the paper, are commonly used with small sheetfed presses called *duplicators*, and are compatible with different dampening systems.

When leaving rubber-based ink on the press, several precautions should be taken. After standing overnight, the ink on the rollers might appear to be drying. To overcome this problem, leave a heavy ink film on the rollers. This can be done by placing extra ink on the large oscillating roller and running the press. Run the press slowly when starting. If the press has an aquamatic system, remove the dampening system. Should the press be overinked, manually feed (with the power off) paper in and out of the ink train. The paper collects the excess ink and brings the press back to normal.

When using rubber-based inks on aquamatic systems, use just enough ink to cover the ink rollers and run low on the dampening solution. Increase both the ink and water to acquire the desired density. Avoid overinking and overdampening. Keep the *pH level* of the dampening solution between 4.5 and 5.5. This pH factor keeps the nonimage areas of the printing plate clean.

Web-Offset Heatset Inks

Web-offset heatset inks require the application of high temperature immediately after the ink film reaches the substrate. The resin solvent is a petroleum distillate that evaporates quickly as the substrate passes through in-line ovens or another heat source, leaving behind the resin and pigment mixture. The web then passes over low-temperature chilling rollers, which cool and harden the resin, binding the pigment to the substrate.

Web-Offset Coldset Inks

Web-offset *coldset inks* (nonheatset inks) are used to print business forms and other materials not requiring coated paper. Although these inks dry by oxidation, they usually are printed on highly absorbent papers because they depend on good absorption for drying. Coated papers provide too much ink holdout and usually cannot be printed with coldset inks. Newly introduced inks have been formulated, however, to print not only the newspaper, but its coated inserts as well. Still another innovation is the use of UV curing to prevent *ink rub-off* when coldset inks are printed on coated paper.

News Inks

News inks are formulated to dry by absorption (or penetration). These inks are made of mineral oil (a colorless petroleum product) and carbon black and are generally thin and fluid. News inks are the least expensive formulation, usually used with web presses, and susceptible to smearing when they are rubbed.

Nonporous Inks

Nonporous inks are used to print on nonabsorbent metal or plastic-coated papers. This ink dries by oxidation, rather than by absorption. It is important not to overdampen this ink because the dampening solution remains in the ink when the substrate is nonporous. Excessively dampened ink does not dry or set and easily smears or sets off to other sheets. Using an acid level of less than 4.5 also retards drying. Ink additives are not recommended with this type of ink. Piles should be kept short, and only a small amount of spray powder should be used.

electron-beam (EB) curing: the use of equipment to produce and direct electrons at a wet coating or printing ink to create a solid film.

ink formulation: the amount and types of ingredients mixed together to make an ink.

setoff: an unwanted transfer of ink from one sheet to the back of the next.

rubber-based ink: ink that can stay on the ink train of a press for several hours without drying because it contains cyclized rubber.

pH level: the potential of the hydrogen ion. The pH level of a fountain solution is the measure of how acidic or alkaline the solution is.

coldset ink: an ink that needs to be printed on absorbent paper in order to properly dry.

ink rub-off: the smearing of an ink film from applied pressure.

news ink: generally thin and fluid ink made of mineral oil and carbon black and formulated to dry by absorption.

nonporous ink: ink designed for metallic or plastic-coated papers. This ink dries by oxidation.

High-Solids Inks

Heatset inks produce VOCs, which are a form of air pollution, because they dry through evaporation. In an attempt to reduce the amount of VOCs given off by heatset printing, ink manufacturers have created *high-solids inks* with 30 to 35% less solvent. These inks are also known as *low-solvent inks*. In addition, with careful treatment of the solvent, it is possible to remove both the components carrying odor and those known to react with sunlight to create smog or irritating air contaminants. Printers who use evaporation inks usually must capture the VOC fumes at the drier and incinerate them, however, in order to comply fully with stringent environmental laws.

Radiation-Curing Inks

Radiation-curing inks use complex vehicles that instantly polymerize and harden when exposed to radiation from UV light (UV curing) or electrons (EB curing). Unlike heatset inks, radiation-curing inks do not require high temperatures to dry. These inks are more expensive than conventional inks because the active ingredients in them are more costly than the solvents they replace in conventional inks. Radiation-curing inks are made of 100% solids and do not discharge solvents into the air.

Do not confuse UV-curing inks with UV fade-resistant inks. *Ultraviolet (UV) fade-resistant inks* are not cured with UV light. Instead, they are conventional inks with a high degree of lightfastness. They resist fading or color change when exposed to the UV rays of the sun. Common uses for these types of inks include posted property signs, "For Sale" signs, bumper stickers, and "No Hunting" signs.

Hybrid Ultraviolet (UV) Inks

Special rollers must be installed because the chemistry of UV-curing inks makes these inks incompatible with conventional offset-press ink rollers. To allow lithographic presses to be able to use both UV-cured and conventional lithographic inks, hybrid inks were developed. *Hybrid ultraviolet (UV) inks* are a blend of conventional lithographic and UV-cured inks. They cure when exposed to UV light, but they are compatible with conventional rollers, allowing the same press to print a job with conventional inks and then print a second job with hybrid inks.

Magnetic Inks

Magnetic inks are designed primarily for printing products such as checks, banknotes, and business forms that are sorted or read electronically.

See **Figure 19-19.** Magnetic inks are formulated with iron-oxide pigments that can be magnetized after printing. Electronic scanning equipment can then recognize the printed characters. The magnetic properties of the ink are derived from a special crystalline form of magnetic iron oxide, and proper performance requires careful and precise formulation of the ink. Magnetic inks can be formulated as conventional, heatset, quick-set lithographic, or letterpress inks.

Invisible Inks

Other security-type inks include invisible inks and thermochromic inks. *Invisible inks* print clear, but they show up as fluorescent blue or yellow when placed under a black light. These inks are often used to mark a winning ticket to prevent fraudulent claims.

Thermochromic Inks

Thermochromic inks allow an image to change as the ink temperature changes. They can enable the printer to hide a message that does not appear on a printed piece until a simple rub or touch warms the ink. The color changes back to its original color after it cools to its original temperature.

These inks are used with commonly seen battery testers, maple syrup bottles, forehead thermometers, and novelty coffee mugs. In the case of the battery tester, the amount of electrical current flowing through the tester produces heat, which affects the layer of thermochromic ink. Heating a bottle of syrup can reveal a message that the syrup is hot. Similarly, a novelty coffee mug can reveal images when a hot liquid is poured into it.

Soy Inks

Soy inks use oil extracted from the soybean as part of the vehicle. Soybean (also known as *soya*) oil can be found in several types of lithographic ink, but in very different ratios. The appropriateness of soybean-oil content in inks varies widely with the type of ink, and the complexity of the topic has generated many misconceptions regarding the relative benefits of ink made with soybean oil.

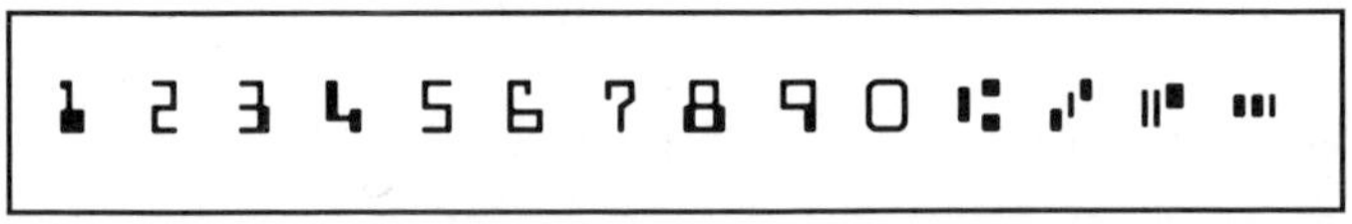

Figure 19-19. Magnetic inks are formulated with pigments that can be magnetized after printing. They are designed and used primarily for printing bank products, such as checks. (International Paper Co.)

In an effort to promote the inclusion of soybean oil in printing ink, the American Soybean Association (ASA) has created requirements for inks qualifying for the SoySeal trademark. See **Figure 19-20.** The following minimum percentages of soybean oil are shown for the various types of lithographic ink:

- Black news ink: 40%.
- Color news ink: 30%.
- Coldset web ink: 30%.
- Business-forms ink: 20%.
- Sheetfed ink: 20%.
- Heatset ink: 7%.

Soy news inks

The American Newspaper Publishers Association (ANPA) developed soy inks in the 1970s, soon after a shortage of imported petroleum threatened industries in the United States that were dependent on petroleum-based chemicals and refined-oil products. ANPA discovered that *soy news inks*, news inks made with soya oil instead of petroleum-based oil, produced more vibrant colors and less dot gain, got better mileage, and emitted less VOCs. The clarity of soy oil allows pigments to excel in their brightness and produce more vibrant colors. The bright reds and yellows available in soy-ink formulations do not exist in petroleum-based inks. Improved color has become increasingly important in the growing trend toward more color in newspapers. Newspaper presses can use less ink because soy news ink provides brighter colors. Soy oil is free of environmentally harmful substances. Therefore, printing with soy ink results in less release of VOCs within the pressroom.

Sheetfed lithographic inks

Soy inks are an acceptable replacement for petroleum-derived mineral oil that does not actually dry because news inks solidify largely by absorption.

Figure 19-20. Printers and companies publishing materials use this version of the SoySeal trademark when printing with soy ink. (National Soy Ink Information Center)

Soybean oil is less appropriate, however, for lithographic inks that dry by oxidative polymerization. Linseed oil and tung oil are vegetable oils that are classified as drying oils because of their comparatively fast rate of oxidation. In contrast, soybean oil is a semidrying oil with a slower rate of oxidation. As a result, linseed and tung oil are the vegetable oils traditionally used in sheetfed lithographic inks. When they are replaced with soybean oil, the ink's drying speed suffers. As a result, the ASA allows soy ink to contain other vegetable oils, but it stipulates that soybean oil must be the predominant vegetable oil. Unfortunately, replacing linseed oil with soybean oil in sheetfed litho inks does not help the environment because one vegetable oil is replacing another.

The environmental impact of soy inks

In 1989, soy ink represented 5% of all printing ink used in the United States, and by 2002, it represented nearly 25%. It is estimated that one-quarter of the nation's commercial printing firms and one-third of the newspaper firms use soy ink. Much of the promotion has emphasized soy ink's environmental advantages, but these vary greatly with the type of ink used. Replacement of the petroleum-based oils in news inks with vegetable oils clearly reduces VOC levels in the pressroom, but soybean oil is one of many vegetable oils that can be used. Although vegetable oils are biodegradable, vegetable oil–based inks removed from the press are still considered

high-solids ink: an ink with a lower than normal content of solvent.

radiation-curing ink: ink that uses complex vehicles that harden and polymerize when exposed to radiation from UV light, beams of electrons, or IR light.

ultraviolet (UV) fade-resistant ink: ink designed with a high degree of permanence to resist fading or color change when exposed to the UV rays of the sun.

hybrid ultraviolet (UV) ink: UV-curing ink that is compatible with the rollers used for conventional lithographic ink.

magnetic ink: ink formulated with iron-oxide pigments that can be magnetized after printing.

invisible ink: ink that prints clear but shows up as a fluorescent blue or yellow when placed under a black light.

thermochromic ink: ink that does not appear until it is warmed by a simple rub or touch.

soy ink: ink that uses oil extracted from the soybean as the vehicle to carry the pigment.

soy news ink: ink used to print on newsprint that contains 40% soy oil for black ink and 30% soy oil for color ink.

hazardous waste because these inks contain pigment and other chemicals and are contaminated with washup solvents and fountain chemistry.

Opaque Inks

On occasion, almost all printers need to print on dark or colored surfaces. *Opaque inks* are required for these types of papers, to hide the color of the underlying substrate and prevent the color of the substrate from influencing the ink color. Achieving a bright color when printing on a dark paper is a challenge. Some very pleasing effects can be achieved, however, by simply adding 50% opaque white. If you use more than 50%, the color has a pastel look. Less than 50% produces inadequate opacity. When you are using custom-matched colors or Pantone-mixed color inks requiring Pantone Transparent White in the formulation, opaque white can be substituted with minimal loss of color strength. In most cases, it is not necessary to replace the entire amount of transparent white with opaque white.

Waterless Offset Inks

Waterless offset inks are formulated for offset presses that do not use dampening solution—a process called *waterless offset*. They allow for faster makeready and drying than many conventional inks. Higher color density and good adhesion to nonabsorbent plastic substrates also make them attractive.

In conventional lithography, the dampening solution helps cool the surface of the plate. This cooling effect is lost, however, because waterless offset removes the water from the offset process. Therefore, waterless offset requires the use of precise temperature-control systems within the printing press. Water is pumped through hollow-core vibrator rollers in the ink train to carry away the heat and maintain proper ink viscosity.

Fluorescent Inks

Fluorescent inks are made with fluorescent pigments that transform UV light into visible light. These inks appear to glow under a UV light source because they absorb invisible UV light waves and reflect visible light waves. See **Figure 19-21.** By reflecting more visible light than it receives, fluorescent ink appears to glow.

The semitransparency of fluorescent inks allows overprinting to achieve brighter, cleaner colors. For example, fluorescent pink ink can be used as a fifth color in four-color printing to enhance skin tones and magentas. Pantone's Hexachrome® color inks also use fluorescent colors to brighten the conventional yellow, magenta, and orange process-color inks.

Note

Clean your press thoroughly when printing with fluorescent inks. Even small amounts of residual black or nonfluorescent ink on the rollers greatly reduce the glow.

Metallic Inks

Metallic inks are made with small metal flakes or particles (aluminum for silver and bronze or brass for gold) that leaf together on the printed surface as the ink dries. *Leafing* occurs when metallic pigments

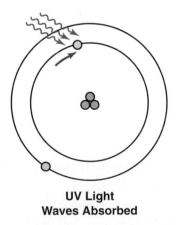
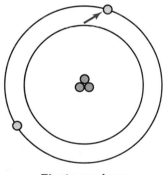
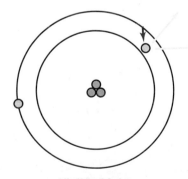

UV Light Waves Absorbed

Electrons Jump to Higher Level

Visible Light Waves Reflected

Figure 19-21. Fluorescent pigments transform invisible UV light into visible light. UV-light energy strikes electrons. The now-excited electrons immediately accelerate and jump to a higher level. Unable to sustain this speed for more than a split second, they slow down and fall back to their original level. As they fall back, their lost mechanical energy is transformed into visible light. This cycle occurs thousands of times a second.

form a layer parallel to the surface of the print, causing a high metallic luster of silver or gold. The shade of the gold color can be changed from reddish to yellowish by varying the pigment's metallic composition or by adding a tinting varnish. In an attempt to produce the maximum metallic effect, press operators can apply too much ink and overpower the dampening system, causing *tinting* (ink emulsifying in the dampening solution) or scumming (ink adhering to the nonimage areas of the plate).

Note

Specialty inks can be used underneath process colors to enhance the effect of the colors. This is referred to as *bumping the color*. The necessary extra plates are referred to as *bump plates*.

Caution

Some specialty inks do not work well with some inks or printing processes. Designers or publishers should always discuss the project in depth with the printer to avoid any problems or surprises.

Overprint Varnishes

Overprint varnishes are transparent coatings applied over ink. They are used to protect the printed surface from moisture, abrasion, or other potential sources of damage. Overprint varnishes are also applied to create a gloss, matte, or satin finish. Important characteristics of overprint varnishes include stability on the press, quick-drying ability, and good adhesion to the printed piece.

A *spot varnish* is an overprint varnish applied only to portions of a printed piece, instead of to the entire piece. Spot varnishes are typically used for aesthetic purposes. One such use is highlighting an image by giving it a high gloss that contrasts it from the background.

Dampening Solutions

Dampening solutions are mixtures of water and other chemicals distributed by the dampening systems of offset presses. Dampening systems, inking units, and fountain operation are discussed in Chapter 21. Dampening solutions greatly affect ink performance and should be carefully set and maintained during a pressrun. Most dampening solutions are made with basic ingredients, each of which are designed to perform a specific function. These ingredients include water, acid, gum arabic, wetting agents, corrosion inhibitors, antifoaming agents, fungicides, and drying stimulators.

The type of dampening solution used depends greatly on the type of ink and stock being used. Inks with nonstandard bases are not compatible with some types of dampening solutions. For example, many vegetable oil–based inks dry by oxidation and have slow setting and drying times. An alcohol dampening solution can speed up drying of the vegetable oil–based ink, but nonevaporative wetting agents should be avoided. Ink manufacturers provide recommended pH levels for the different types of ink they produce. Refer to Chapter 20 for additional information on dampening solutions.

Water

The quality of the water used in dampening solutions greatly affects the performance of the dampening solution and ink. If tap water is used, it is important to determine its purity and whether it is soft or hard. Most dampening-solution manufacturers perform tests on tap water to determine its hardness. Hard water typically has a great deal

opaque ink: ink that does not transmit light. This ink is the opposite of transparent ink.

waterless offset ink: ink made for offset presses that use no dampening solution.

fluorescent ink: ink that appears to glow under black light and is made with pigments that naturally absorb UV light waves that other inks cannot use.

metallic ink: ink made with small metal flakes or particles (aluminum for silver and bronze or brass for gold) that leaf together on the printed surface as the ink dries.

leafing: an effect that occurs when metallic pigments in an ink form a layer parallel to the surface of the print, causing a high metallic luster of silver or gold.

tinting: a contamination problem that occurs when ink emulsifies in the dampening solution, causing a slight tint of ink to appear on the nonimage area of the printed sheet.

overprint varnish: a clear coating applied over ink to protect the printed surface from moisture, abrasion, or other potential sources of damage.

spot varnish: an overprint varnish applied only to portions of a printed piece, instead of the entire piece. This varnish is typically used for aesthetic purposes.

of mineral content, leaves deposits on the press, and causes a multitude of printing problems, including roller stripping and plugged halftones. Printers with hard tap water should use deionized or distilled water.

Distilled water is colorless, tasteless, and odorless and should have a pH of 7.0 (a neutral acid and alkaline balance). This water should be pH tested before it is used to prepare the dampening solution because it can become contaminated and, therefore, not pH neutral. Controlling water quality makes it easier to maintain the dampening solution's pH, and ultimately it gives you better reproduction and print quality.

Acid

The acid used in a dampening solution varies according to the desired pH. The pH of a dampening solution is the measure of how acidic or alkaline the solution is. An excess of hydrogen ions (H+) makes the solution acidic. An excess of hydroxyl ions (OH–) makes the solution alkaline, and an alkaline dampening solution is referred to as a *base*. An equal concentration of both ions produces a neutral solution.

The pH scale begins at 0 (very strong acid) and ends at 14 (very strong base). A neutral solution has a pH of 7. See **Figure 19-22.** Each step on the pH scale represents a 10× change in acidity or alkalinity. For example, a solution with a pH of 4 is 10 times more acidic than one with a pH of 5 and 100 times more acidic than one with a pH of 6. The pH of the dampening solution used on offset presses should be kept between 4.0 and 5.5. The chart in **Figure 19-23** illustrates how different pH values can influence ink-drying time.

Both the initial pH and the maintenance of the dampening solution's pH during the pressrun are extremely important to the production of high-quality output. If the pH of the solution is allowed

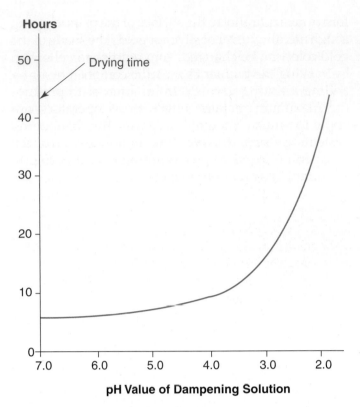

Figure 19-23. Changes in the pH value of the dampening solution can greatly influence ink-drying time and cause a variety of printing problems.

to rise (become less acidic), the gum arabic loses its effectiveness. If the gum arabic loses its ability to adhere to the plate, a problem known as *scumming* occurs. Scumming describes the presence of ink on nonimage areas of the plate. An excessive amount of acidity can cause both scumming and plate blinding, which occurs when the acid eats away the image areas of the plate and reduces the image areas' ink receptivity.

Measuring pH

The pH of a dampening solution can be determined using pH-indicator paper (sometimes called *litmus paper*) or with an electronic pH meter. When

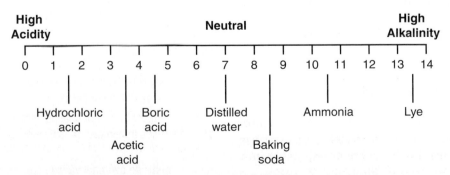

Figure 19-22. The pH scale measures acidity and alkalinity. An increase of 1.0 represents a 10-fold increase because the scale is logarithmic. A pH of 7.0 reveals a neutral material.

using pH-indicator paper, it is necessary to dip only a short strip of test paper in the solution for a second or two. The color of the wet test paper is matched with the paper's color chart to reveal the pH value. See **Figure 19-24**.

All pH test papers are made with special indicator dyes that change color at specific pH values. The useful limit of color change for most individual indicators is about 2 pH units. Beyond this limit, no additional color change takes place, regardless of a change in pH. For example, with a 6.0 to 8.0 pH range–indicator paper, a reading of a solution falling within these points can be taken correctly. If the pH of the solution is lower than 6.0 or higher than 8.0, however, the indicator paper cannot indicate the correct pH value. Nonetheless, it shows the 6.0 or 8.0 color from the chart.

Some materials, such as proteins and alkaloids, interfere with the indicator color changes. Strong salt solutions (2% or more) might also have an adverse effect. In these cases, pH test papers might not give reliable results.

Conductivity

In addition to pH level, dampening solution should be consistent in its *conductivity*—the amount of electricity the solution will carry. Attaining and maintaining the correct concentration of dampening solution is very important in achieving consistent printing. Conductivity is a more accurate means of measuring concentration than pH is.

Pure (distilled) water has a conductivity level of nearly 0, but soft tap water can have a conductivity of 200. Hard water can exceed 400, depending on which minerals are present. The conductivity of the water

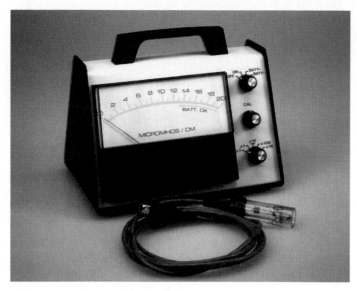

Figure 19-25. A conductivity meter measures the ability of a dampening solution to conduct electricity. (Industrial Chemical Measurement Co.)

used to make the solution should be controlled and monitored because a dampening solution's conductivity is related to maintaining the solution's pH level. See **Figure 19-25**.

During the pressrun, water evaporates from the dampening solution, but the additives remain. Just as adding water dilutes a solution, removing water increases the concentration and conductivity. A more accurate assessment of a dampening solution's concentration is its conductivity because most dampening solutions contain buffers that maintain the pH level as water evaporates. Increases in the conductivity level indicate a need to replace evaporated water.

Gum Arabic

Gum arabic is a gummy, water-soluble substance obtained from certain types of trees. This substance is used in dampening solutions to desensitize the nonimage areas of the printing plate and prevent them from accepting ink. Gum arabic is also used to protect printing plates from humidity and chemical attack when the press is not running.

Wetting Agents

Wetting agents are substances, such as IPA, glycerin, and glycol, added to a dampening solution to lower its surface tension. In other words, they make the water "wetter" by allowing it to spread over the nonimage area of the plate more quickly, maintain

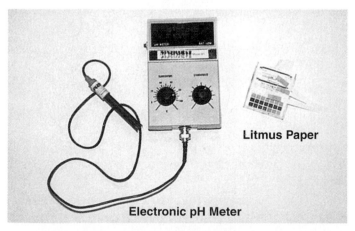

Litmus Paper

Electronic pH Meter

Figure 19-24. The pH value of a dampening solution can be measured with an electronic pH meter. When litmus paper is dipped into the solution, the paper changes color and is compared to a range of color tones to determine the pH value.

conductivity: the property of a material to transmit electricity.

the water's wetting ability, and allow the operator to run less water. Wetting agents are also referred to as *surfactants* because they are added to alter a liquid's surface properties.

Besides lowering surface tension, the use of alcohol in dampening solutions also increases the viscosity of the solution. This increase in viscosity allows a thicker film to be applied to the rollers and plate. Alcohol evaporates quickly and tends to emulsify the ink to a lesser extent than other liquids do.

Although the use of alcohol is cost-effective, its expense, toxicity, and flammability are causing an increase in alcohol-substitute dampening solutions. Using glycol instead of IPA greatly reduces the air pollution within the pressroom resulting from the VOCs that the IPA's volatility creates. There are also on-press advantages to replacing alcohol. Using an alcohol-substitute dampening solution allows less ink to be used to achieve the same density because IPA tends to dilute the ink. In addition, because alcohol substitutes are not nearly as volatile as IPA is, they do not evaporate and alter the dampening solution's conductivity levels.

Switching to an alcohol-substitute dampening solution, however, requires some on-press adjustments. Alcohol substitutes do not increase the dampening solution's viscosity as alcohol does, with the result that less solution is supplied to the plate. This problem can be corrected by using softer rollers, lighter stripes, and less roller-to-roller pressure.

Corrosion Inhibitors

Corrosion inhibitors are compounds used in dampening solutions to prevent or minimize damage to the printing plate through oxidation or other chemical reactions. These inhibitors increase print quality and extend the life of the plates. A commonly used inhibitor is magnesium nitrate.

Antifoaming Agents, Fungicides, and Drying Stimulators

Antifoaming agents are typically silicone-based fluids or emulsions added to dampening solutions to reduce the tendency of the solution to foam or bubble. Foaming of the dampening solution can cause distribution problems on the press. Dampening solutions might also contain a fungicide and drying stimulators. Offset printing involves a great deal of water and might create a breeding ground for mold. *Fungicides* help kill any organic growth in the fountain or elsewhere in the dampening system. *Drying stimulators* enhance the effectiveness of the drier in the ink.

Purchasing Offset Ink

The high cost of printing supplies—including printing ink—makes it very important that they be purchased in the best possible way. Decisions regarding ink purchase should involve the pressroom personnel because of their experience. See **Figure 19-26**. It will be helpful, therefore, to review some of the considerations that should be made when purchasing lithographic ink. These include the following:

- Purchasing ink to do the job required, with particular reference to quality definitions and specs.
- Purchasing ink in the most economical way, including consideration of price, quality, and coverage.
- Establishing and maintaining inventory goals of good inventory turnover, in relation to realistic and flexible reorder levels.

To ensure the proper formulation, it is important to tell the ink manufacturer as much as possible about the proposed printing job. See **Figure 19-27**. This information includes the make of the press, dampening system, running speeds, color sequence, type of substrate, drying method being used, and end use of the product. It is also useful to establish basic specs for color strength and tack preference. Optional specs for gloss, rub-off properties, and fade resistance can also be requested.

Figure 19-26. Ink purchasing is usually left to pressroom personnel. (Van Son Holland Ink Corp.)

Figure 19-27. Printers can be more certain about the type of ink needed for a given job by telling the ink manufacturer as much as possible about the type of work being printed. (Van Son Holland Ink Corp.)

Figure 19-28. Printers buy ink in various-size containers. Newspaper and magazine publishers use tanker-truck quantities. (Flint Ink Corp.)

Buying ink in the optimum quantities affects the price per pound. The larger the batch is, the less the cost of production for the ink manufacturer will be. Ink can be obtained in a wide range of quantities, including by the pound in 1-, 3-, 5-, and 10-lb. cans and by the gallon in 2-, 3-, 5-, 15-, 30-, and 55-gallon containers. Inks are also available in 2500-lb. reusable tote bins. Examples of containers are shown in **Figure 19-28.**

Ink is priced by the pound. Lithographic ink is used, however, by the square inch. Therefore, the true value of a pound of ink is not how much it costs, but instead, how far it will go.

Estimating Ink Coverage

Ink mileage is a measurement of the number of square inches a pound of ink covers. With the ink mileage, the total amount of ink required for a job can be estimated after allowance is made for makercady, spoilage, and washups. Several factors affect ink mileage—the absorption of the substrate, as well as the ink's film thickness, covering power, and specific gravity. An ink's *specific gravity* is a measure of its density, which is its weight divided by its volume. See **Figure 19-29.** Water is the basis of comparison for all materials. The specific gravity of water is 1.0. Any material with a higher specific gravity (such as 1.1 or 2.7) is denser and sinks if placed in water, while any material with a lower specific gravity (such as 0.88 or 0.63) floats. As specific gravity increases, a material becomes denser.

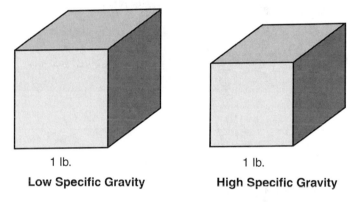

1 lb.	1 lb.
Low Specific Gravity	**High Specific Gravity**

Figure 19-29. Inks with a low specific gravity occupy a larger volume than inks with a higher specific gravity and greater density. Larger volume translates to more mileage.

corrosion inhibitor: a compound used in fountain solutions to prevent or minimize damage to the printing plate through oxidation or other chemical reactions.

antifoaming agent: a silicone-based fluid or emulsion added to a fountain solution to reduce the tendency of the solution to foam or bubble.

fungicide: a substance added to a fountain solution to help kill any organic growth in the fountain or elsewhere in the dampening system.

drying stimulator: a substance added to a fountain solution to enhance the effectiveness of the drier in the ink.

ink mileage: a measurement of how much area a specific amount of ink will print over.

specific gravity: the weight of a given volume of ink, compared to the weight of an equal volume of water.

A pound of ink with a high specific gravity occupies less volume than a pound of ink with a lower specific gravity. Low volume translates to a smaller can. A 1-lb. can of one ink is smaller than a 1-lb. can of an ink with a lower specific gravity.

The density of an ink's pigment largely determines the ink's specific gravity. Inks requiring a high percentage of pigment have high specific gravities and comparatively low volumes, so they cannot cover as much area. For this reason, two different colors of the same ink can have different mileage. For example, light colors such as white and yellow require high quantities of pigment to achieve opacity. Dark colors such as black and brown, however, can achieve opacity with much less pigment.

The ink-mileage chart in **Figure 19-30** shows the coverage for certain colors of ink on various types of paper using a sheetfed press. The figures listed are the number of thousand square inches that 1 lb. of ink will cover. The type of paper finish and surface characteristics influence the amount of ink required. A smooth, hard-surfaced paper requires less ink film thickness than a rough-textured paper. The absorbency rate is higher for a rough-textured paper than for a smooth, hard-finished paper. To estimate the amount of ink a job requires, use the following procedure:

1. Multiply the width and height of the job's dimensions to determine the number of square inches in a single copy.
2. Estimate the percentage of coverage for the ink color in question. For example, light text is around 15%, medium text is around 35%, and heavy text and halftones are usually around 50%.
3. Multiply the square inches by the percentage of coverage to get the number of square inches to be covered by the ink.
4. Multiply the square inches of coverage by the number of copies to be printed to get the total square inches of coverage for the job.

Grade of Stock	Enamel	Litho Coated	Dull Coated	Machine Finished	Antique
	Figures below represent 1000 square inches that 1 lb. of ink will cover				
Black	425	380	375	400	275
Rubberbase black	445	430	425	435	335
Purple	360	350	320	350	235
Process and transparent blue	355	340	335	340	220
Transparent green	360	350	335	350	235
Process and transparent yellow	355	355	340	340	220
Chrome and lemon yellow	285	260	250	250	150
Persian orange	345	325	310	325	225
Process and transparent red	350	345	340	340	225
Semitransparent red	350	340	325	340	175
Brown	345	335	325	335	225
Silver	335	300	285	295	220
Gold	125	115	115	115	75
Opaque white	200	175	165	175	135
Tint base	400	380	375	385	250
Fluorescent	135	120	120	120	85
Overprint varnish	450	425	415	425	—

Figure 19-30. Printers use ink-mileage charts to estimate the amount of ink required for a job.

5. Divide the total square inches of coverage by the ink-mileage factor (from the ink-mileage chart) to determine the number of pounds needed to cover the total area.

6. Add in the amount of ink needed to cover the ink train of the press (for example, 1/4 lb. for an 11″ × 17″ duplicator and 1/2 lb. for a 19″ × 25″ press). This ink will be removed during washup.

7. Add a percentage for the extra sheets that will be printed during the press makeready. Web presses usually require more paper for makeready than sheetfed presses do.

Most estimating software includes a module for estimating the amount of ink required for a specific job. It is also possible to use estimating software dedicated to ink. See **Figure 19-31.**

Use and Storage of Printing Inks

Ink can be bought in tubes, cartridges, cans, pails, drums, and tanks. The proper storage and use of inks prolong their shelf life and maintain their printing quality. The following information is recommended for general storage and use. Always refer to the manufacturer's recommendations for storage conditions (such as temperature and humidity) for optimum results.

Ink containers should be stored in a clean, dry place that is relatively free of airborne contaminants and extreme temperature fluctuations. An enclosed, fire-resistant cabinet is ideal for ink storage. Before opening a can of ink, wipe the outside surface with a lint-free rag. Ink cans must be opened in a manner that does not bend the lid, or it will be difficult to close the can tightly. A small amount of oil placed on the inside rim of the lid helps to seal the can.

If the can is not sealed properly, the ink forms a hard, dry skin. Pieces of this skin cause hickies if they are part of the ink loaded into the press. Another strategy for avoiding hickies is to remove ink from the can by smoothly scraping from the top with an ink knife.

Before closing the can, the ink surface should be smoothed and covered with heavy-duty plastic wrap. Some kitchen heavy-duty plastic wraps work well to prevent air from coming in contact with the ink. If the ink can has a cardboard donut, the donut should be placed firmly over the plastic wrap when closing the container.

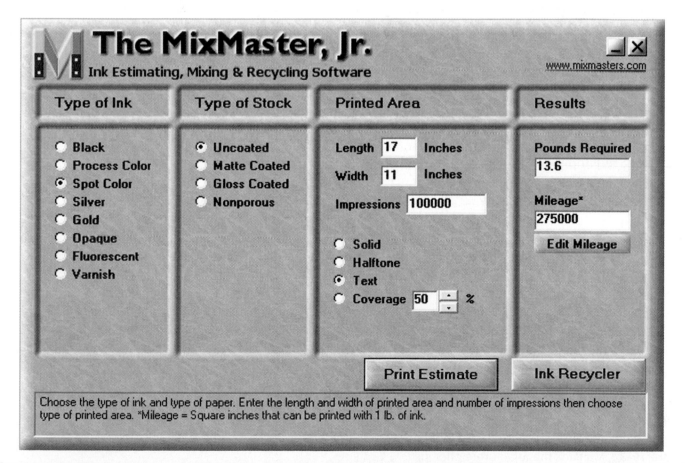

Figure 19-31. The type of ink and paper, the job's dimensions and quantity, and the area of ink coverage are required for estimating the amount of ink needed for a job. (MixMasters, Inc.)

Most ink manufacturers offer inks in disposable cartridges. See **Figure 19-32.** Only a trace amount of ink remains in the tube, so less ink is wasted. When using a cartridge, the first 1/4″ of ink pushed through the spout should be discarded. To prevent ink from drying in the cartridge, the cap should always be replaced. Dried or lumpy ink should never be placed on an offset press.

Inks have a limited shelf life. Although a can of ink might appear to be fine, one or more of its chemical properties might have deteriorated. A lithographic ink's driers are usually the first of its components to break down with time—causing ink to dry too slowly. An unopened can of ink can stay fresh for five years, but a can that has been opened is good for one year. It is important to rotate inks so the older inks are used first. To avoid the unnecessary opening of ink containers, the amount of ink left in a can or cartridge should be indicated with pencil marks on the outside of the container. It then is easy to determine if enough ink is left to complete a particular job without having to open the container. Inks should be grouped according to color and usage. Labels should not be destroyed.

Mixing Colored Inks

A wide assortment of ready-mixed colored inks is available. Sometimes, however, it might be necessary to prepare special colors and tints before placing the ink in the press. Yellow, red, and blue are the primary pigment colors and can be mixed together to produce any other colors needed. Understanding the following basic combinations is useful when mixing inks:

- Mixing red and yellow produces orange.
- Mixing red and blue produces purple.
- Mixing blue and yellow produces green.

As was explained in Chapter 16, color results from the interaction of light and pigment. Black and white are not considered colors because black results from the absence of light, and white results from the absence of pigment. They can be added to colors, however, to lighten or darken them. When black ink is added, the color becomes a shade. If a color is added to white, a tint results. The color should always be added to the white, instead of white being added to the color. If the lighter color is added last, it takes much more ink than is necessary for the job.

Ink mixing must be done on a clean table near the press area. The following equipment should be used for this purpose:

- A piece of glass or plastic on which to mix the ink.
- Ink knives to handle and mix the ink.
- An ink scale to weigh the inks. See **Figure 19-33.**
- A color chart or sample of the ink required.

To mix a desired ink color, follow these steps:

1. Compare the color chart and the sample to be matched.
2. Select an ink from the chart that most closely matches.
3. Prepare a small test batch. Make the first color comparison using an ink knife to form a swatch of ink. Do this on the paper that will be used for the printing.
4. After the test, add what is needed to match the color desired. When the color has been mixed, reducers, body gum, or drier can be added as needed.

To mix a tint, follow this procedure:

1. Start with mixing white ink in an amount that will complete the printing job.

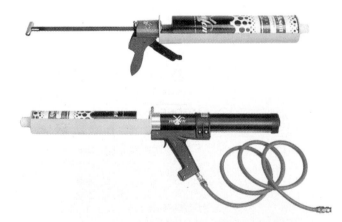

Figure 19-32. Most ink manufacturers offer ink in disposable cartridges that can be used with manual or automatic feeding systems. (Van Son Holland Ink Corp.)

Figure 19-33. A computerized ink scale can be used when mixing ink for a job. (Ohaus Corp.)

2. Add color in small amounts.
3. Continue to add color until the correct tint is achieved. Never start with a colored ink and add white ink. This results in mixing far more ink than is required. Several small mixed batches might be needed to achieve the correct match.

When mixing a small batch of ink, mix less than is needed for the job. It is best to weigh all ingredients. Maintain a record of all additions until the color is correct. The ingredients must mix well and remain stable. Ink should be mixed thoroughly before placing it in the ink fountain. Never mix an ink in the press ink fountain, or there can be a matching problem later because ink cannot be thoroughly mixed and matched in the fountain. All ink going into the fountain must be well mixed to avoid streaking. Ink fountains on offset presses are not designed for ink mixing.

After ink has been mixed, it is stored in a small metal or plastic container. The need for cleanliness when mixing and storing the ink is important because, if the ink becomes contaminated or dirty, the color changes. All inks should be stored on shelves at a stable temperature. They should also be marked by kind, color, and delivery date. All cans should be checked for leaks. New containers might be required if cans are damaged. Proper storage and handling are required to preserve ink and maintain its printing qualities.

The Pantone Matching System Standard

The Pantone Matching System standard is a well-established method for specifying and mixing ink colors. See **Figure 19-34.** Using this system, printers, graphic artists, and print buyers can select any of the more than 1000 colors from a swatch book. Each color sample is identified by a number and accompanied by a formula the printer can follow to achieve a match. The Pantone Color Formula Guide contains simple formulas for colors on coated and uncoated papers. A color formula uses a specific number followed by a letter *C* for coated or *U* for uncoated paper. By simply mixing the formula given, the user can achieve the same color every time and in any quantity.

Under each standard color is the mixing formula divided proportionally and identified in parts, followed by the percentage of the total for each ingredient. Every displayed Pantone color in the formula guide can be matched using various combinations of 12 Pantone basic colors, plus Pantone Black and Pantone Transparent White. The color formulas

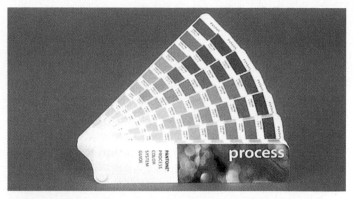

Figure 19-34. The Pantone Process Color Guide displays over 3000 CMYK color combinations. Colors are chromatically arranged and displayed with their CMYK percentages. (Pantone, Inc.)

shown in **Figure 19-35** are examples illustrating the simplicity of mixing and matching a specified color. The formula guide allows a graphic designer in Maryland to specify an ink color to a printer in Texas by merely identifying the desired Pantone number. Colors can be matched by using the volume or weight and following these basic steps:

1. Gather the following equipment: a measurement device, a mixing slab, ink knives, test papers, cleaning solvents, and utensils. Be sure all equipment is clean to avoid color contamination.

Color	Color Combination	Ratio
PANTONE 163C	2 parts PANTONE Yellow	12.5%
	2 parts PANTONE Warm Red	12.5%
	12 parts PANTONE Transparent White	75.0% (Ratio 1:1:6)
PANTONE 164C	4 parts PANTONE Yellow	25.0%
	4 parts PANTONE Warm Red	25.0%
	8 parts PANTONE Transparent White	50.0% (Ratio 1:1:2)
PANTONE 165C	8 parts PANTONE Yellow	50.0%
	8 parts PANTONE Warm Red	50.0% (Ratio 1:1)
PANTONE 168C	8 parts PANTONE Yellow	40.0%
	8 parts PANTONE Warm Red	40.0%
	4 parts PANTONE Black	20.0% (Ratio 2:2:1)

Figure 19-35. Examples of color formulas used in the Pantone Matching System standard. (Pantone, Inc.)

2. Choose the desired Pantone color that best meets the specs of the printing job.
3. Analyze the formula for that color and determine the proportion of each ink needed, as indicated under parts or percentages.
4. Gather the necessary basic color inks at your workstation, and prepare them for mixing the required color. Be sure to review the basic ink colors for possible contamination or dried ink and to make sure there is a sufficient amount for the job.
5. Using a clean ink knife, measure the required amount of ink (by volume or weight) as indicated in the formula and place it on the ink-mixing slab or ink-mixing equipment.
6. Record all ingredients on the formula card (electronic or hard copy) for this particular printing job and customer. File it for future use.
7. Mix the ingredients until all the ink colors are thoroughly blended.
8. After the mix is blended properly, test it against the standard (the sample in the Pantone Color Formula Guide). Pull a prepress proof or complete a drawdown (swatch) test, and compare it to the approved ink sample.

There will be a visual difference between wet ink and the dry ink in the formula guide. In addition, the color of the paper used affects the final color because the matching system is a transparent ink system. This means there is always a slight degree of show-through on colored papers.

Volatile Organic Compounds (VOCs)

Regulatory agencies in the United States unilaterally apply a chemical process to many printing substances to determine their potential or actual impacts on air quality. Known as *Method 24*, this process is the tool the EPA uses to measure printing solutions' real or potential contributions to air pollution. Method 24 subjects inks, dampening solutions, and other similar chemicals to a temperature of 230°F (110°C) for one hour. During that time, all substances that evaporate from the solution are captured and analyzed. Any evaporating substance that is not water is considered a VOC. The combined weight of all the VOCs divided by the weight of the original formula equals the percentage of VOCs in the formula. The rating system makes press solutions seem more dangerous to the environment than they actually are because most printing inks are never heated to that extreme temperature on the printing

press. The printing process most dependent on ink evaporation is high-speed heatset web printing.

Ink Ecology

As a service to their printers, some ink suppliers accepted returns of waste inks. The EPA now classifies such inks as hazardous materials because they are often contaminated with dampening solutions, press washes, and other chemicals. Current federal and state waste-disposal regulations, however, make it illegal for ink suppliers to accept returns. The responsibility for waste-ink disposal now rests with the printer. The printer must dispose of the waste safely and economically. It has been estimated that printers accumulate more than 1.7 million pounds of waste ink annually. The National Association of Printing Ink Manufacturers (NAPIM) cooperates with ink-reclaiming firms by helping to inform their printer customers of safe and economical ways to dispose of waste inks. There are three methods of ink-waste reduction currently being used in the printing industry:

- A reduction in the amount of ink put into use so printers automatically minimize their disposal problems. See **Figure 19-36.**
- The reuse of the ink in excess of a current job's needs. Only inks returned directly from the ink fountain are designated for reuse.
- The reclamation of inks (principally paste inks) by physically reworking and converting them back to their original state.

Recycling Mixed Inks

Printing companies can accumulate a considerable inventory of leftover inks mixed for past jobs. A mixed color is likely to lose its properties before there is another job requiring that color because the shelf life of an opened can of ink is one year. A practical solution involves software that allows a printing company to use leftover mixed inks to create different colors. See **Figure 19-37.** In the example shown, 10 lbs. of Pantone 469 are needed. The operator can examine the list of mixed inks (shown on the right of the screen) that can be used to produce 469. When choosing an ink color left over from a previous job, the software displays formulas using the surplus color.

Pantone 469 can be achieved with a very high percentage of surplus inks. Refer to **Figure 19-37.** With this formula, three mixed inks in inventory are used with a small amount of new black ink. Of course, this application requires a printing company to have adequate amounts of all three mixed inks on hand. Recycling surplus inks before they become too old reduces the need for new inks and reduces ink-disposal costs. It also improves productivity by ensuring that drying time is not increased by using old inks with deteriorated driers.

Ink-Related Problems

There are a number of common ink-related problems on press that occur largely because of changes or variations in the dampening solution used for offset printing. Problems also arise due to an inaccurate setting of the press roller pressures. Ink problems can affect the efficiency of the printing operation because ink performance is such a vital factor in the printing process. Some of the common ink problems encountered include poor color, mottling, slow drying, picking, sticking in the pile or rewind, fill-in, poor binding and rub-off, setoff, piling and caking, trapping, show-through, strike-through, ink not flowing from the fountain, mechanical ghosting, ink drying on rollers, plate wear, and crystallization.

Poor Color

Poor color occurs when the color of the printed image does not match the original image. Printers need to be aware of the factors affecting color, in addition to proper color mixing, because the correct color is critical for most jobs. These conditions include the following:

- **Improper ink film thickness.** Too much or not enough ink is being carried on the paper.
- **Contamination.** The press rollers and fountain are not properly cleaned.
- **Paper variation.** A variation in the paper on which the ink is printed on can cause color problems.
- **Color drift.** Some pigments used to obtain the correct color have a tendency to change shade (called *drift*) when aging or used in tints.

To keep color problems to a minimum, the press operator should always check the printed results against a known standard at the start of and during a pressrun. If variations exist, the press operator should check the factors listed above.

Mottling

A condition known as *mottling* occurs when the solid portions of the dried print appear uneven and speckled. The ink does not produce a uniform film. See **Figure 19-38.** There are several causes for mottling:

- Hard-surfaced, nonabsorbent papers.
- Faulty distribution of the ink on the printing plate.
- Poor wetting or dispersion of the ink.
- Ink that is too soft.
- Uneven ink absorption.

The mottling problem can be improved or eliminated by using a more opaque ink or making the ink heavier by adding a body gum. In some cases, use of a flat ink instead of a glossy ink overcomes the problem.

Figure 19-36. Efficient ink-dispensing systems help reduce ink waste and often provide biodegradable packaging (tubes). This system uses a vacuum-sealed cardboard tube and a dispensing nozzle that prevents oxygen from contacting the ink. (Van Son Holland Ink Corp.)

poor color: a reproduced color that is noticeably different from the original.

mottling: a blotchy or cloudy appearance of an image, instead of a smooth, continuous appearance.

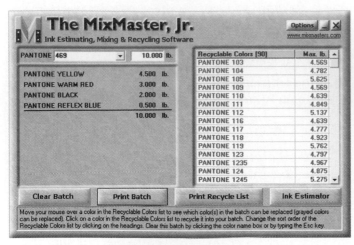

Colors That Can Be Used

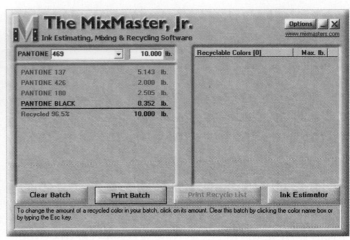

Surplus Inks in Inventory

Figure 19-37. The standard formula for mixing Pantone 469 is shown on the left of the left screen. The list on the right of the left screen shows Pantone colors that can be used to make 469. The right screen shows the formula for mixing Pantone 469 with surplus inks in inventory. (MixMasters, Inc.)

Figure 19-38. Mottling has occurred on the press sheet on the right. A better press sheet is on the left.

Slow Drying

Slow-drying problems are evident when the ink smears or sets off onto the back of the next sheet. Depending on the type of ink and printing process, ink drying occurs by one of the following methods:

- **Absorption into the paper.** If slow drying occurs in inks that dry by absorption, the best solution is to apply a thinner film of ink.
- **Solvent evaporation.** Slow drying occurring in solvent-evaporation inks can be improved by adding a more volatile solvent to the ink. The drying-oven temperature can be increased on web-offset presses.
- **Oxidation.** Slow-drying problems in oxidizing inks require the addition of more drier.
- **Precipitation.** The drying speed of inks that dry by precipitation (evaporation) can be increased by the use of steam or the addition of a faster glycol solvent.

Paper can also contribute to slow drying, especially if it contains excessive moisture or has high acidity. Temperature and humidity can also have an influence on proper drying. See **Figure 19-39.**

Picking

Picking is the lifting of clumps of paper fibers or coating from the paper by the offset rubber blanket. See **Figure 19-40.** These particles collect on the blanket, accept dampening solution, repel ink, and print as white specks (hickies) in the image areas of subsequent sheets. The lifting of individual fibers is called *linting*. The most common causes of picking include the following:

- Too much body and tack in the ink.
- Ink that is drying too fast.
- Poor paper coating.

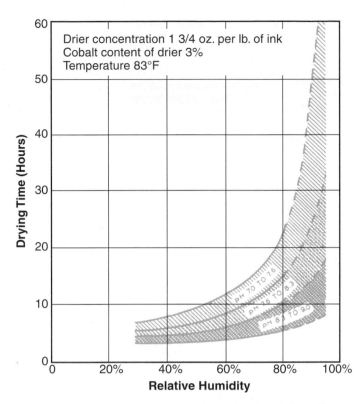

Figure 19-39. Temperature and relative humidity affect ink-drying time. (Graphic Arts Technical Foundation)

- Rollers that are too hard.
- Pressroom, press, and ink temperatures that are too low.

To remedy picking, reduce the ink tack or use a paper with a higher-rated pick resistance.

Sticking in the Pile

Ink *sticking in the pile* (also known as *blocking in the pile*) occurs when a pile of printed sheets stick together, as the wet ink film serves as an adhesive. The condition is an extreme case of both setoff and poor drying. Prints become marred by the transfer of ink or by picking of paper fibers when the sheets are separated. Sticking in the pile can result in white specks appearing in image areas that resemble sheets that have picked. Closer inspection reveals, however, that the white areas are above the surface, instead of below it. The white areas have been pulled away from the above sheet. See **Figure 19-41.** Steps to avoiding sticking in the pile are keeping piles in the delivery unit from getting high, winding (fanning) the pile to increase the supply of oxygen to the printed sheets, and using as thin an ink film as possible because thin ink films tend to dry more rapidly or penetrate into the paper more completely.

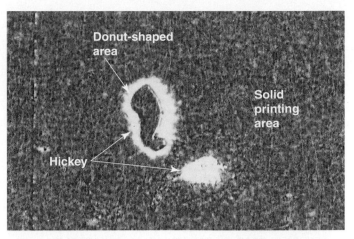

Figure 19-40. Hickies are created when high-tack ink pulls clumps of fiber onto the blanket from a sheet. The fibers promptly absorb dampening solution and repel ink. Donut hickies result from small pieces of dried ink adhering to the blanket. The thickness of the dried ink prevents nearby contact between the blanket and the plate. Both types of blanket contamination hurt print quality until they are removed from the blanket. (Graphic Arts Technical Foundation)

Fill-in

The problem of *fill-in*, or specking, produces a muddy look in the midtones and shadows. This problem is often detected in the printing of the small, normally nonprinting areas between the halftone dots, giving the screen highlights a speckled appearance and a loss of detail. Fill-in also can occur in the open area in fine type and line work and might be caused by the presence of foreign material in the ink, such as lint, fibers, or paper-coating particles. Other foreign material, such as dirt or spray dust, might have also worked back into the ink.

Poor Binding and Rub-off

The problem of *poor binding* and rub-off should not be confused with ink drying slowly. Poor binding and rub-off result when the ink is dry on the printed paper but does not hold to the surface when rubbed under pressure. The possible causes of rub-off include the following:

sticking in the pile: the sticking together of recently printed sheets, due to slowly drying ink.

fill-in: an undesirable effect producing a muddy look in the midtones and shadows. This effect is caused by the presence of foreign material in the ink.

poor binding: inadequate adhesion of an ink to the substrate.

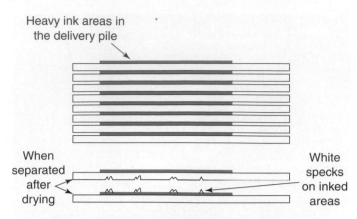

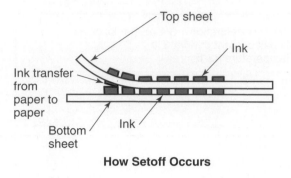

How Setoff Occurs

Figure 19-41. Sticking in the pile occurs when inadequately dried ink adheres to the bottom of the above sheet. In this situation, what appears to be hickies are actually tiny pick outs from the above sheet.

- Insufficient binder in the ink for the particular paper being used.
- Excessive penetration of the vehicle portion of the ink into the paper, leaving only the pigment on the surface.
- Ink that is too soft.
- Paper that is too absorbent.

Setoff

The problem of setoff occurs when ink transfers to the underside of the next sheet of paper in the delivery pile or rewind roll. See **Figure 19-42.** There are several causes for setoff:

- Ink sets too slowly.
- Static electricity in the paper.
- Too much ink is being carried.
- Too much impression.

Setoff can be decreased by adding offset compound to the ink or by using antisetoff spray.

Piling

A buildup of individual fibers, coating particles, or ink pigment on the printing plate or blanket in both image and nonimage areas is called *piling*, or *caking*. Contaminants lifted by the ink accumulate on the image areas, and contaminants lifted by the dampening solution accumulate on the nonimage areas of the plate or blanket. Printed sheets show blotchy areas outlined by a thin, nonprinted line, and frequent press washups are needed to eliminate fill-in of screens and reverse type. Piling can occur when the pigment is too coarse or poorly wetted, preventing the vehicle from carrying the pigment properly and resulting in a short, pasty ink.

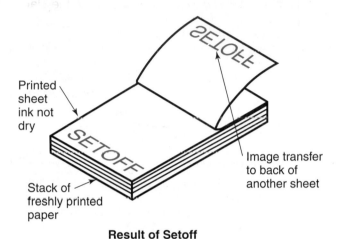

Result of Setoff

Figure 19-42. Setoff occurs when freshly printed images transfer to the above sheet. The improper drying of ink usually causes setoff, but excessively thick ink film, paper stacked too high, or an improper substrate and ink combination can also cause setoff.

The buildup on the plate or the rubber blanket in offset printing might be due to cutter dust or paper coating. A paper coating with insufficient binder or with a weak binder that attracts moisture might cause trouble when humidity is high. The simplest remedy is to change the paper.

Trapping

Wet trapping is the successful application of an ink color over a just-printed color, and its success is necessary when printing on multicolor presses. In contrast, *dry trapping* is printing a color over a different color that has had plenty of time to dry. Clearly, wet trapping is a more challenging task because it involves printing over wet ink. If the first ink to be printed has not adequately set to the paper, the second ink film might lift it from the paper. See **Figure 19-43.** In other words, instead of the second ink transferring onto the first ink, the first ink transfers to the second ink, which remains on the blanket—a problem known as *back trapping*.

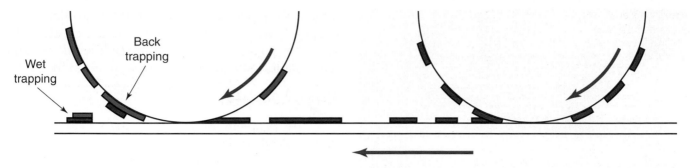

Figure 19-43. Wet trapping requires an ink to transfer to a just-printed ink film. If the second ink (green) fails to split properly, the first-down ink (red) is lifted onto the blanket of the next unit—a condition known as *back trapping*.

Show-through

The lack of opacity in a paper might cause *show-through*, which allows the printed image to be seen from the opposite side of the sheet. Show-through is generally a fault of the paper and not the ink. The best remedy is to use a more opaque paper. A strong heavy-bodied ink printed with a thin film helps reduce the show-through, but it does not eliminate the show-through.

Strike-through

The problem of *strike-through* occurs when the ink or vehicle penetrates through the paper. The image becomes visible on the reverse side of the sheet. The excessive penetration is usually due to the ink being too soft or too slow when drying. The ink might also contain an excessive amount of nondrying oils. When the ink film is too heavy, it causes strike-through. To improve the strike-through problem, a heavier ink should be used, and a thinner ink film should be printed.

Ink Not Flowing from the Fountain

When ink does not flow to the fountain roller, difficulty is encountered in holding proper color. The printing is streaky or uneven, and the color is light. Improper ink body causes this problem. To remedy this condition, the ink should be stirred while it is in the fountain. Many presses have conical agitators that automatically supply enough force to overcome the ink's yield value.

Mechanical Ghosting

A faint reappearance of an image from another part of the plate is referred to as *mechanical ghosting*. Mechanical ghosting (also known as *ink-starvation ghosting* or *press ghosting*) occurs when the plate removes ink from areas of the form rollers that the ink train does not adequately replace before the form

rollers make a complete revolution. See **Figure 19-44.** When ink removed from a form roller is not replaced immediately, these ink-starved areas on the form roller are repeated as faint ghosts in trailing image areas of the plate.

Ink Drying on Rollers

Ink drying on rollers might increase the ink tack to the point that the ink on the blanket picks or tears the sheet. This drying might pull sheets from the grippers or break the web on a web press. An examination of the ink on the rollers, besides revealing the tack level, might show that the ink is skinning or drying, particularly on the ends. If so, the ink might have a dull, dry look, rather than the shiny, wet appearance seen toward the center of the rollers. See **Figure 19-45.**

With oxidizing inks, this difficulty might indicate the use of too much drier or a vehicle that dries too fast. This difficulty might be corrected by adding small amounts of an antioxidant. Nondrying compounds can be added at the ends of the rollers. With heatset inks or quick setting–type inks, solvents that are too volatile might cause drying on the rollers.

Plate Wear

In offset lithography, the problem of plate wear is often noticed when halftones lose contrast and fill-in

wet trapping: applying an ink film onto another ink film that is still wet.

dry trapping: applying an ink film onto another ink film that has dried.

back trapping: the lifting of a wet ink film from the substrate while trying to wet trap.

show-through: the ability of a sheet of paper to block the passage of light. This is an undesirable effect of poor opacity in which the image on one side of a sheet of paper is seen on the other side.

strike-through: a problem occurring when the ink or vehicle penetrates through the paper and shows through the opposite side of the sheet.

mechanical ghosting: the uneven printing of an image because of an uneven replenishment of ink on the plate and blanket.

Ghosting

Figure 19-44. Mechanical ghosting shows up as a faint repetition of an image printed near the lead edge of the press sheet.

Figure 19-45. An examination of the ink on the rollers reveals the degree of tackiness and whether or not the ink is skinning or drying, particularly on the ends.

occurs. In severe cases, the plate's emulsions are actually worn off, and the plate must be replaced. The ink might be at fault in four ways—it was poorly ground, contains too much pigment, lacks lubrication, or contains an excessively acidic vehicle. Press faults contributing to wear include excessive or uneven

impression, poor makeready, and form rollers set too tightly to the plate. In addition, coating or slitter dust from the paper can be picked up by the ink or dampening solution and begin to wear against the plate.

Crystallization

The problem of *crystallization* can occur in multicolor printing when the second ink down does not adhere to the dried first ink because wax in the ink migrated to and became concentrated at the top of the ink film. This form of crystallization occurs when the two colors are printed on separate pressruns, and the cause is excessive wax content. A second type of crystallization occurs when the second ink tends to mottle or rub off when dry. The usual cause is too much drier, especially if cobalt is used in the first-down ink, and the remedy is to retard the drying of the first-down ink or any ink that is to be overprinted by reducing the drier content and eliminating the cobalt drier.

Summary

Printing inks are colored coating materials applied to the surface of paper or other substrates, such as plastic, metal, glass, and wood. In the ink-manufacturing process, the ingredients are first mixed and then milled or ground. Ink ingredients include pigments, a vehicle, and modifiers. Both organic and inorganic pigments are used to provide color, opacity, and permanence to inks. Vehicles carry and bind the pigment to the substrate. Modifiers such as driers, waxes, oils, and varnishes are used to adjust the basic ink characteristics for special conditions during a pressrun.

The selection of ink for a job requires knowledge of ink characteristics such as viscosity, body, tack, length, opacity, color, and permanence. Ink is manufactured to meet the specific requirements of each printing process. The use of nontraditional inks, such as metallics, waterless inks, fluorescents, and opaques, requires special dampening solutions and press adjustments.

An ink's ability to dry is important to the quality of the finished product. Some common means of drying ink are absorption, oxidative polymerization, evaporation, and radiation curing. Dampening solutions affect an ink's drying ability, as well as its performance on press.

Before ordering ink, the purchaser should know the quality definitions and specs for a particular job. It is wise to tell the ink manufacturer as much as possible about the proposed printing job. This includes the type of work being printed, type and make of the press, running speeds, type of substrate, drying method being used, and product's end-use requirements. Variables that must be considered when estimating ink coverage for a job include color strength, specific gravity, paper finish, type of job, and press makeready.

A number of common printing problems occur largely because of the dampening solution and the roller pressures on the offset press. Other press problems might include poor color, mottling, nondrying ink, sticking in the pile, picking, fill-in, setoff, piling, and caking. Most press and ink manufacturers provide troubleshooting charts that can be used to solve or eliminate these common problems.

Review Questions

Please do not write in this book. Write your answers on a separate sheet of paper.

1. Most inks used in lithography are (paste/liquid) inks.
2. The solid coloring in lithographic ink is the _____.
3. The _____ in lithographic inks carries the pigment.
4. _____ oil is an example of a drying oil, and _____ oil is an example of a semidrying oil.
5. Driers, waxes, greases, lubricants, reducing solvents, and antiskinning agents are all called _____.
6. Distinguish between the roles of cobalt and manganese in ink.
7. What are two stages of production that can be used to manufacture ink after the vehicle is prepared?
8. Explain the objective of the ink-mixing function.
9. How is a three-roll mill used in the manufacture of lithographic ink?
10. What is ink viscosity? Why is viscosity altered while moving through the ink train?
11. Why does lithographic ink qualify as a pseudoplastic material?
12. The ability of an ink to flow and to form threads when stretched is its _____.
13. What is an ink's color strength?

14. Optical density describes the _____-absorption behavior of a printing-ink film.
15. Calculate the grayness and hue-error values for the following set of process inks, using these densitometer readings:

Ink	Blue Filter	Green Filter	Red Filter	Grayness	Hue Error
Magenta	0.43	1.19	0.06	_____	_____
Cyan	0.09	0.28	1.05	_____	_____
Yellow	1.01	0.09	0.04	_____	_____

16. Ink _____ is a required ink characteristic for jobs meant for outdoor displays.
17. List at least four common methods of ink drying.
18. Name and describe five types of lithographic-printing inks.
19. Explain the principle behind hybrid UV inks and their primary benefit.
20. _____ occurs when metallic pigments form a layer parallel to the surface of the print and cause a high metallic luster of silver or gold.
21. What can happen if too much metallic ink is used on an offset press?
22. What is an overprint varnish? What purpose does it serve?
23. What ingredients are used in a dampening solution?
24. What purpose does the gummy substance added to dampening solutions serve?
25. Surfactants lower the _____ of a dampening solution.
26. List at least three considerations that should be taken into account when purchasing offset ink.
27. Identify the specs to supply when ordering lithographic ink.
28. Give three examples of factors affecting quantity when estimating the amount of ink needed for a given printing job.
29. Ink-_____ charts show the coverage in square inches for certain colors of ink on various types of paper.

crystallization: a problem occurring in multicolor printing when the first ink printed dries too hard and the second ink printed does not adhere to the dried ink surface.

30. Use the ink-mileage chart in **Figure 19-30** to calculate the amount of ink (in pounds) required to cover 26,000 20″ × 30″ posters printed on dull, coated paper with 35% coverage of brown ink. Add 1/2 lb. of ink for the washup and 1/8 lb. for the makeready.

31. When estimating ink mileage, allowance must be made for _____.
    A. washups
    B. ink coverage
    C. makeready
    D. All of the above.

32. Why should an ink be smoothly scraped from the top and not gouged out from the middle of a can?

33. If a color is added to white ink, the ink color becomes a(n) _____.

34. What can a printing company do to reduce its inventory of mixed inks left over from past jobs? Remember that surplus ink's performance begins to weaken after one year, and ink disposal can be expensive.

35. Uneven and speckled ink drying in solid areas of the printed sheet is called _____.

36. An incorrect balance between the tack of the ink and the strength of the paper surface can cause _____.

37. How can sticking in the pile be prevented?

38. The unwanted transfer of ink from one printed sheet to the back of the next is called _____.

39. A buildup on the plate or blanket of paper fibers, coating, or pigment is known as _____.

40. Distinguish between show-through and strike-through.

41. The problem of ink _____ occurs in multicolor printing when the first ink printed contains too much wax, and the second ink printed does not adhere to it.

Skill-Building Activities

1. Familiarize yourself with an ink swatch book. Learn the terms and procedure for ordering lithographic ink.

2. Mix and match three colors your instructor provides. Be careful not to mix too much ink for the job.

3. Obtain a printed one-color flier. Estimate how much ink would be used to print 10,000 fliers. Use the ink-coverage chart in this chapter.

4. Use a densitometer to calculate the grayness and hue-error values of two cans of the same process ink color—such as two cans of cyan from different manufacturers. Which manufacturer's ink contains less contamination?

5. Make a peanut butter and jelly sandwich. Spread the peanut butter onto the bread first, and then spread on the jelly. Now, try reversing the sequence. What does this experiment reveal about the proper tack sequence during wet trapping?

Nine skids of printed press sheets wait to be taken to the finishing department, where they will be cut and folded. (Hopkins Printing)

Dispelling a Myth

Many people think most press operators work around noisy, dirty machines and are up to their elbows in ink. This photograph should dispel that image. This press operator is running a four-color sheetfed press with an aqueous coater. After he finishes adding ink, he will start the press and operate it from the console shown on the left. The operator can pull a press sheet, lay it on the console, read color bars with a densitometer, and adjust the amount of ink being applied to the paper, without leaving the console.

Modern, large presses are amazingly automated, but the presses students are trained on are usually just the opposite. Schools usually introduce students to press operation with small presses that require plenty of hands-on operator intervention. This is how it should be—manual presses for teaching and automated presses for optimal productivity.

Both large and small lithographic presses are included in this chapter. As you read it, keep in mind that nearly all the press principles you are learning apply to both basic and complex machines. In fact, the operator in the photograph probably first ran a duplicator.

(Heidelberg, Inc.)

Key Terms

alcohol dampening system
antisetoff spray
bearer
blanket
blanket cylinder
carcass
common impression cylinder
common impression
  cylinder press
compressible blanket
computer-to-press (CTPr)
continuous dampening
  system
continuous feeding
conventional blanket
conventional dampening
  system
dampening unit
delivery chain
delivery cylinder
delivery gripper
delivery pile
delivery platform
delivery unit
direct imaging (digital)
direct imaging (digital)
  offset press
direct imaging press
distributing roller
double-sheet detector
ductor roller
duplicator
dwell
ejector delivery system
fanning out
feedboard
feeding unit
feed-roll system
finger-type pull guide
form roller
fountain blade
fountain key
fountain roller
front guide
gripper
gripper edge
guide
impression cylinder
ink agitator
ink fountain
inking system
inking unit
ink train
integrated dampening system
intermediate roller
intermittent dampening
  system
jogging

keyless inking
low-lift gripper
metering roller
molleton
multicolor press
night latch
offset duplicator
offset press
on impression
oscillating roller
paper table
perfecting press
pile feeder
pile height regulator
piling bar
plate cylinder
preregistering
printing unit
pull guide
push guide
receding delivery table
register board
ribbon
rider
right-reading
roll-to-sheet feeding system
rotary (roller) guide
sheetfed press
sheet separator
side guide
skeleton wheel
smart fountain
squeeze
stop
stream feeder
stream feeding
stripper finger
successive feeding
successive feeding system
suction foot
swing-feed assembly
swing-feed system
table
three main cylinder press
three-point guide system
Townsend Color Head
transfer-cylinder system
transfer roller
tumbler gripper
two main cylinder
  duplicator
underblanket
undercut
waterless offset press
water stop
web
webfed press
wrong-reading

Chapter 20
Offset-Press Fundamentals

Learning Objectives

When you have completed the reading and assigned activities related to this chapter, you will be able to do the following:

❖ Distinguish between an offset press and an offset duplicator.

❖ Explain the function of a waterless offset press.

❖ Describe the features common to offset presses and duplicators.

❖ Give examples of the controls of an offset press and an offset duplicator.

❖ Define the six major operating units of offset presses and duplicators.

❖ Identify the roller and cylinder locations on offset presses and duplicators.

❖ Summarize blanket properties and proper installation and care.

❖ Discuss the capabilities of a direct imaging press.

❖ Explain the concept of VDP.

Nearly all the preceding chapters deal with getting a job ready for press. The plans and efforts of the graphic designer, the people who work in the various stages of prepress production, and those who acquire the paper and ink come together in the press department. In addition to this prominence, the press department usually occupies the most floor space and receives the largest investment in equipment. For these reasons alone, it is important that people who work in departments such as sales, customer service, estimating, and prepress have a basic understanding of how presses work. Also, learning about press operation is the first step in preparing for a career in the press department. To understand press operation, the student must become familiar with the major systems of the press, the location and function of the press controls, and the proper operation and adjustment of each part of each major system of the press. See **Figure 20-1.**

This chapter describes the systems making up offset presses and duplicators. The general procedures used in setting up these systems prior to operation are also provided in this chapter. The operation of specific presses commonly found in commercial and quick printing is covered in Chapter 21.

Conventional-Press Classifications

Conventional *offset presses* are not tied directly to the prepress function. Plates are imaged—either conventionally or digitally—away from the press and then carried to it. In contrast, digital offset presses use *direct imaging (digital)*. That is, blank plates are mounted onto the press and then imaged by

digital-driven lasers. Direct imaging offset presses are described later in this chapter.

There are many conventional offset-press classifications. Metropolitan newspapers are printed on two-story presses as long as a basketball court, while a company's one-color newsletter is likely to be printed on a press taking up less floor space than a freezer. Offset printing presses are categorized according to different criteria:

- The maximum-size sheet the press will handle.
- The number of colors that can be applied in a single pass.
- Whether one or both sides of the paper can be printed in a single pass.
- How paper feeds into the press.
- Special features.

For example, a 25″ × 38″ four-color perfecting sheetfed press can apply four ink colors to both sides of individual sheets measuring as large as 25″ × 38″.

Duplicators and Presses

Small sheetfed offset presses printing up to a maximum sheet size of about 11″ × 17″ (28.0 cm × 43.0 cm) or slightly larger are generally referred to as *offset duplicators*. See **Figure 20-2.** Presses printing on sheets significantly larger than this are referred to as *offset presses*. See **Figure 20-3.** Offset presses are larger

Figure 20-1. Press operators must understand the major operating systems of offset duplicators and presses. (Heidelberg, Inc.)

Figure 20-2. Duplicators are small offset presses with a maximum sheet size of between 11″ × 17″ and 13 7/8″ × 17 3/4″. (A.B.Dick Co.)

and usually more sophisticated in their features and capabilities than *duplicators* are.

Historically, duplicators were limited to a maximum press-sheet size of 11″ × 17″, which can carry two 8 1/2″ × 11″ forms or other publications. In the last decade, however, an increasing percentage of short-run jobs were being designed with bleeds and other features requiring a larger (augmented) press sheet. In response to this trend, some duplicators are able to accommodate press sheets as large as 13 7/8″ × 17 3/4″ (34.0 cm × 45.0 cm). Offset duplicators are commonly used for printing one-color and two-color jobs and are excellent for teaching press operation because the basic operating principles are the same for both duplicators and presses.

Sheetfed Presses

Offset presses and duplicators designed to print a single sheet of paper at a time are referred to as *sheetfed presses*. These presses pick up individual sheets of paper from a feed table. See **Figure 20-4**. Sheets are delivered, one at a time, down a *feedboard* to the printing unit. A small space separates the tail of one sheet and the head of the next sheet. This type of feeding system is referred to as *successive feeding*.

On other sheetfed presses, the sheets of paper overlap one another as they travel down the feedboard. See **Figure 20-5**. This is referred to as *stream feeding*. By overlapping the sheets, it is possible to run the sheets of paper down the feedboard at a slower speed than required for individually fed sheets. This improves the registration of each sheet as it enters the *printing unit*. The sheets are less likely to bounce

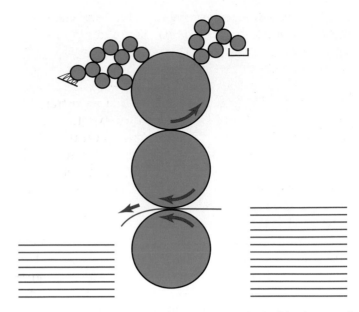

Figure 20-4. Sheetfed presses are loaded with sheets of paper. The sheets are placed in the feeding unit, printed, and then moved to the delivery unit.

away when they strike the register guides at the end of the feedboard.

Webfed Presses

Presses that feed from a roll of paper are referred to as *webfed presses* or *web presses*. See **Figure 20-6**. These presses are used for work requiring long runs, such as magazines, newspapers, and other similar publications. Although the method of feeding and the design of web presses are different from those of sheetfed presses, the operating principles are the same.

offset press: a press that prints on sheets larger than 11″ × 17″ (28 cm × 43 cm).

direct imaging (digital): imaging a plate with a laser while the plate is on the press.

offset duplicator (duplicator): a small offset press that prints up to a maximum sheet size of about 11″ × 17″ (28 cm × 43 cm).

sheetfed press: an offset press or duplicator designed to print a single sheet of paper at a time.

feedboard: a conveyor platform that uses a set of rollers, balls, or brushes to press the sheet to the front guides at the head of the platform.

successive feeding: a system in which the substrate is fed into the press one sheet at a time.

stream feeding: sending sheets into a press with a stream-feeder system.

printing unit: the part of the printing press where printing takes place. This unit contains the plate cylinder, blanket cylinder, and impression cylinder.

webfed press: a press that prints with one long continuous web of paper fed from a roll.

Figure 20-3. Presses larger than duplicators are referred to as *offset presses*. The operating principles are basically the same for both kinds. (Sakurai USA, Inc.)

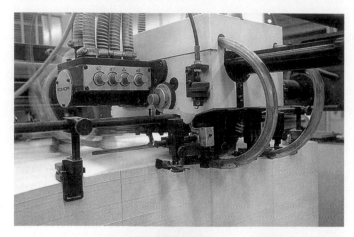

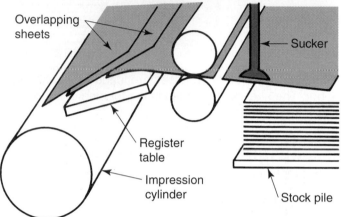

Figure 20-5. In a stream feeder, the sheets of paper overlap one another as they travel down the feedboard.

Webfed presses are extremely large, sometimes half the length of a football field and one or two stories in height. A smaller press, called the *miniweb*, is popular with in-plant and small commercial printers. Webfed presses are discussed in Chapter 23.

Multicolor Presses

Many offset presses and duplicators have only one printing unit and, therefore, can print only one color at a time. If a second or third color is required on a job, the sheets are allowed to dry after the first color is printed and then run through the press again to print the next color. This process is repeated until all the colors have been printed. This is a slow process, but it is acceptable for short pressruns.

Presses that print more than one color during a single pass are referred to as *multicolor presses*. These presses consist of a series of single printing units connected in tandem to form one press. Each unit can be set up with a different plate and a different color of ink. The paper can be fed in either sheets or rolls. See **Figure 20-7.**

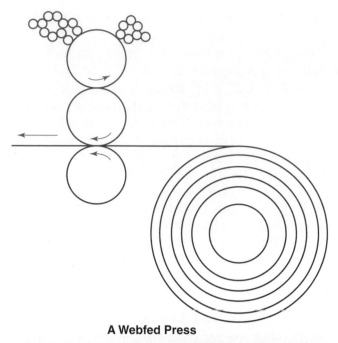

A Webfed Press

A Large Multicolor Web Press

Figure 20-6. Offset presses that feed from a roll of paper are referred to as *webfed presses*. Note the ribbon of paper moving through this large multicolor web press. (Miehle Products, Graphic Systems Division; Rockwell International)

Figure 20-7. This in-line multicolor press consists of six printing units the substrate passes through in a single pass. (Heidelberg, Inc.)

Perfecting Presses

Most offset presses print on only one side of the paper at a time. In order to print on the reverse side of the paper, the ink from the first side is allowed to dry, and the paper is turned over and run through a second time. Presses that print on both sides of the paper at the same time are known as *perfecting presses* or *perfectors*. Both sheetfed and webfed presses can be perfecting. The operating principle of one type of perfecting press is illustrated in **Figure 20-8**.

Townsend Color Head Units

The *Townsend Color Head* unit is a unique self-contained printing unit allowing second-color printing on most offset duplicators. See **Figure 20-9**. The unit permits two colors to be printed in one pass through the press. The Color Head unit is capable of good registration and affords one- and two-color flexibility. These color heads are used largely by quick printers and in-plant printers.

Before the Townsend Color Head unit was invented, a color head was available only as a bolt-on unit specifically made to fit on several models of offset duplicators. With this version, the entire unit

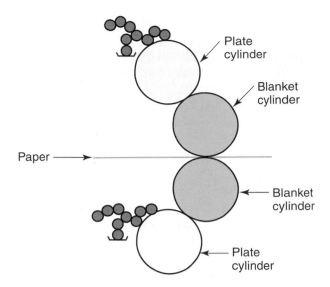

Figure 20-8. Perfecting presses print on both sides of the substrate at the same time. There is no impression cylinder in this configuration. Each blanket cylinder functions as the impression cylinder for the other blanket cylinder.

Figure 20-9. This duplicator uses a self-contained second-color printing unit that can be swung away from the press when it is not in use. (A.B.Dick Co.)

multicolor press: a press that prints more than one color at the same time.

perfecting press: a press that prints on both sides of the paper at the same time.

Townsend Color Head: a unique self-contained printing unit allowing second-color printing on most offset duplicators.

requires removal when it is not needed for two-color work. When the unit is bolted on the press again for color work, several adjustments must be made. The latest version is a swing-away model that eliminates the necessity of installing and removing the unit each time two colors are required. Similar to the older version in operation, the newer swing-away model is a self-contained printing unit with its own plate cylinder, ink, and dampening system. The image is transferred from its plate to the duplicator's *blanket* in register with the image from the duplicator's plate.

The swing-away color head has a single-lever control. This head also features a variable-control water dampening system. The swing-away capability, along with the ability to remove and replace the color head without going through the old readjustment steps, makes the unit easier to operate.

Waterless Offset Presses

As was explained in Chapter 17, *waterless offset presses* do not use dampening solution to keep the plate's nonimage areas free of ink. These presses function because the plate's nonimage areas consist of a layer of silicon that repels ink. A waterless press resembles a conventional offset press, except the dampening system might be missing. See **Figure 20-10.** A more common design, however, includes a dampening system to allow the press to function conventionally when needed. ***Direct imaging (digital) offset presses*** are waterless, with no dampening system.

Waterless offset inks have a higher tack and viscosity (thickness) and are generally stiffer than conventional offset inks. The temperature of the inks must be strictly controlled to maintain the correct viscosity because the plate surface is designed to repel inks of a specific viscosity. This temperature distinction is achieved by running chilled water through tubing in the hollow cores of two or more vibrating rollers in the *ink train* on the printing press.

The imaged surface of a waterless plate is intaglio (recessed), allowing the plate to carry a greater volume of ink than a conventional plate does and allowing extremely high screen rulings, ranging from 300 to well over 800 lpi. Waterless printing yields higher ink densities and a broader color spectrum than conventional offset printing does. Waterless plates used on sheetfed presses are commonly rated for runs of 100,000 to 200,000 impressions. The plates designed for use on web-offset presses can yield 300,000 to 500,000 impressions.

Waterless printing provides for easier and faster makeready, a sharper dot structure, and greater flexibility in ink lay down. In addition, waterless lithography

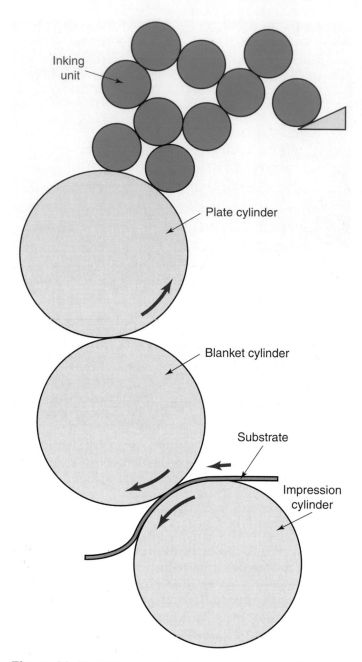

Figure 20-10. Waterless offset presses appear similar to conventional offset presses, with the exception of not having a dampening unit.

provides the benefit of less paper stretch, lower dot gain, and more consistent process control. Finally, the elimination of alcohol-based dampening systems greatly reduces VOC emissions in the pressroom.

When a job is to be run again, the plate can be rehung on the press, and although the register must be achieved manually, a portion of the makeready is simplified, since the ink-key profiles could have been saved and reloaded. A more likely option is that the original prepress files or the plate-format bitmaps are saved or RIPped again. The bitmap data can be reloaded via the direct imaging server, reimaged on press, and run normally on press. Direct imaging plates are nonphotographic, contain no hazardous waste, and can be recycled through normal aluminum-recycling channels. A compact list of the advantages of waterless printing includes the following:

- Higher screen rulings, resulting in better image definition, increased print contrast, and the elimination of rosette patterns.

- Greater color range than conventional offset plates.

- Higher ink densities with excellent ink holdout on any paper.

- More consistency of color during the run.

- Sharper dots and more highlight and shadow detail.

- Makeready time is cut in half.

- Elimination of ink-and-water balance variables yields reduced running time and waste.

- Better register control (elimination of paper stretch caused by fountain solution).

- Elimination of dampening solution results in no emission of hazardous VOCs or wastewater.

Main Printing-Unit Classifications

The main printing unit of an offset press or duplicator usually includes three large cylinders. The *plate cylinder* carries the printing plate. This cylinder brings the inked plate image into contact with the rubber blanket on the *blanket cylinder*. The inked image on the plate is transferred to the blanket. The inked image on the blanket is then transferred to the paper as the paper passes between the blanket and the *impression cylinder*, a smooth metal cylinder that presses the paper against the blanket cylinder with the correct pressure. The operation and arrangement of the cylinders in the main printing unit vary.

Three Main Cylinder Presses

The *three main cylinder press*, or duplicator, has a plate cylinder that holds the image (plate) to be printed. A blanket cylinder carries a rubber blanket, onto which the image is transferred, or offset, from the plate. An impression cylinder presses the paper against the blanket. The image is then transferred from the rubber blanket to the paper. See **Figure 20-11.**

On the plate, the image is *right-reading*, or reads left to right. When transferred to the blanket, the image is backward, or *wrong-reading*. When the image is transferred from the blanket to the

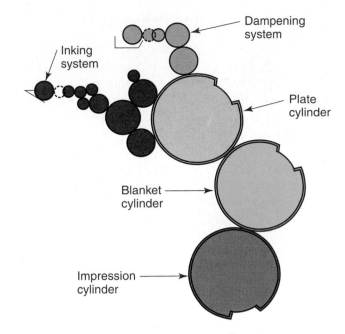

Figure 20-11. A three main cylinder offset press or duplicator includes a plate cylinder, a blanket cylinder, and an impression cylinder.

paper, it is right-reading once more. Of the main printing processes—letterpress, offset lithography, gravure, and flexography—only offset plates are right-reading.

blanket: a synthetic rubber mat that transfers, or offsets, the image from the plate to the substrate as the impression cylinder presses the image against the mat.

waterless offset press: an offset press that does not use dampening solution.

direct imaging (digital) offset press: an offset press on which the plates are on the plate cylinder when they are imaged.

ink train: the system of rollers that carries the ink from the fountain to the plate cylinder.

plate cylinder: the part of a printing press holding the printing plate.

blanket cylinder: the part of an offset press holding the rubber blanket that accepts images from the plate.

impression cylinder: the part of an offset press or duplicator carrying the stock through the printing unit and forcing it against the inked blanket, where the image is transferred to the stock.

three main cylinder press: the standard offset lithographic press configuration, in which the plate, blanket, and impression cylinders are all the same size.

right-reading: capable of being read from left to right.

wrong-reading: backward.

Two Main Cylinder Presses

The *two main cylinder duplicator* that ATF Davidson produces has a double-sized upper cylinder containing a plate section and an impression section. The smaller, lower cylinder is called the *blanket cylinder*. The blanket cylinder is half the diameter of the upper cylinder. Refer to **Figure 20-12**.

The blanket cylinder revolves twice for each revolution of the upper cylinder because it is half the diameter of the upper cylinder. On the first revolution, the plate portion of the upper cylinder transfers ink to the blanket cylinder. At the same time, the impression segment of the upper cylinder grips a sheet of paper and pulls it between the two cylinders. As the blanket cylinder continues to turn, it transfers the ink to the paper the impression cylinder is holding. At about the same time, the plate receives a new supply of water and ink for the revolution. This press configuration has not been produced for 20 years. Although it had the advantage of being able to print heavier sheets than conventional duplicators can, it was more difficult for the press operator to monitor the job because the press sheets emerged from the press with the printed side down.

Double-Sized Impression Cylinders

The two-color offset press in **Figure 20-13** illustrates a double-sized impression cylinder. Often referred to as a *common impression cylinder press*, this press design features a double-diameter impression cylinder fitted with two sets of grippers, so the sheet never changes grippers between color units,

thereby eliminating register shift. A second benefit is this design requires less floor space than a conventional two-color press does.

Single-Lever Control Devices

Most offset duplicators have a single-lever control device used to operate the dampener and ink form rollers and to provide blanket-to-blanket contact. See **Figure 20-14**. The control panels on most offset duplicators and presses are automated to allow easy setup and operation. Clustering the low-profile, easy-to-read controls on one panel further simplifies operation. See **Figure 20-15**.

A Double-Sized Impression Cylinder

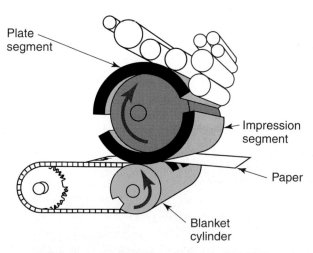

Figure 20-12. A two main cylinder offset press or duplicator has a double-sized upper cylinder containing plate and impression segments. The lower cylinder, which is half the diameter of the upper cylinder, acts as a blanket cylinder. (A.B.Dick Co.)

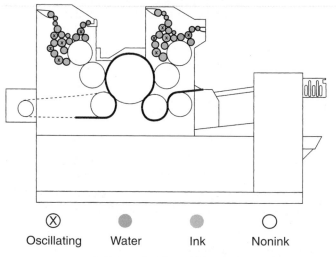

A Cross-Sectional View

Figure 20-13. A double-diameter impression cylinder is used with two sets of grippers. A cross-sectional view shows press cylinders oscillating, water, and ink rollers. (Hamada)

Figure 20-14. Duplicators generally are equipped with a single-lever control arm, allowing the press operator ease of operation. (Ryobi Xpedx Impact Group)

Figure 20-15. The operating control panel on a typical offset duplicator has easy-to-read buttons. (A.B.Dick Co.)

Operating Units

Offset presses and duplicators are divided into six operating units. These are the feeding unit, register board, printing unit, inking unit, dampening unit, and delivery unit. Nearly all presses require all six

units. The exception is the waterless offset press, which has no dampening system. Briefly, each press sheet is individually sent forward from the feeding unit, positioned on the register board, and imaged within the printing unit as the paper receives dampening solution and ink from the dampening unit and inking unit, respectively. Finally, the printed sheet is placed into the delivery unit.

The Feeding Unit

The *feeding unit* of a press is responsible for sending the substrate into the press properly. With sheetfed presses, the feeding unit is responsible for picking a single sheet from the top of the pile of paper that has been loaded into the press. With webfed presses, the feeding unit sends a long *ribbon* of paper into the press.

Continuous feeding means that long ribbons of paper or individual sheets are fed into the press constantly. Continuous feeding systems used on sheetfed presses are commonly referred to as *stream feeders*. When the substrate is fed into a sheetfed press with a *successive feeding system*, it is fed one sheet at a time. See **Figure 20-16.** Successive feeding systems are also referred to as *single-sheet feeders*. Webfed offset presses use continuous feeding systems, whereas sheetfed offset presses use either continuous or successive sheet feeding. Although the principles remain the same, feeding systems vary in design and operating details. The following descriptions are a general overview of the various types of feeding systems.

two main cylinder duplicator: an offset-press design featuring a double-sized cylinder, which carries a plate component and a blanket component.

common impression cylinder press: an offset-press design featuring a single oversized impression cylinder that contacts all the blanket cylinders.

feeding unit: the system on a press that transfers paper (or some other substrate) from a stack or roll to the registration unit.

ribbon: the continuous roll of paper that forms on a papermaking machine or is fed into a web press.

continuous feeding: a system in which a ribbon or individual sheets of paper are fed into the press constantly.

stream feeder: a feeding system in which a web or overlapped sheets are fed into the press.

successive feeding system: a system that performs successive feeding.

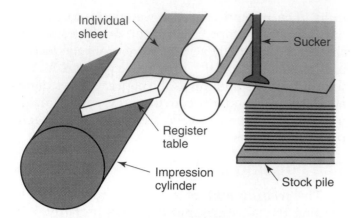

Figure 20-16. In a successive feeding system, the press feeder picks up a single sheet at a time and delivers it down the feedboard to the printing unit. The paper is moving from right to left.

Caution

Exercise extreme care when working with belts, chains, rollers, cylinders, grippers, joggers, and fountains on offset presses and duplicators.

Webfed-press feeding units

Webfed offset presses use large rolls of paper that unwind as the length of paper makes its way through the series of rollers in the press. The paper winding through the press is referred to as a *ribbon* or *web*. Most webfed presses feed at least two rolls at a time. As the web feeds through the press, its tension must be closely regulated. A paper-tension device is used to control the movement of the paper. A brake mechanism is one of the most commonly used tension-control devices. This mechanism is attached to the paper roll and is designed to produce a slight amount of friction, or drag, on the web. Improper web tension can alter the registration of the paper and affect print quality or cause the web to break and force shutdown of the press.

Offset presses can also use a *roll-to-sheet feeding system*, in which the substrate comes from a roll, enters as a ribbon, is cut into sheets, and is then fed into the press. This type of system is used to reduce paper costs, as rolls of paper are less expensive than precut sheets. Unlike precut sheets, which are guaranteed to have square corners, the sheets cut on press might not have square corners because they are not usually cut on all four sides. A roll-to-sheet feeding system might also require the paper to be fed grain short. This type of feeding configuration is often referred to as a *roll sheeter* or *sheeter*.

Sheetfed-press feeding units

A continuous feeder on a sheetfed press (a stream feeder) sends the sheets to the press on a conveyor platform called the *feedboard*, which uses a set of rollers, balls, or brushes to move the sheets forward. Individual sheets are picked up from the pile and sent forward slowly in an overlapping fashion. Refer back to **Figure 20-5.** Compared to single-sheet feeders, stream feeders allow greater control over sheet positioning as the paper is fed into the press. The slower speeds keep the paper from moving around on the feedboard, which in turn, helps prevent paper jams and misregister.

An important requirement of feeding units is to ensure that only one sheet at a time enters the press. If two sheets are lifted at the same time and fed into the press, only the top one receives ink. In addition to causing paper jams and loss of time, more than one sheet entering the press at a time can cause damage. Extra-sheet detectors, or *double-sheet detectors*, are used with both stream and successive feeders to detect when more than one sheet of paper is being fed. See **Figure 20-17.**

The double-sheet detector is positioned near where the sheets leave the feeder. This detector is usually set to the thickness of a single sheet of the kind of paper being used. When more than one sheet of paper is fed through the feeder, the double-sheet detector automatically rejects all but one sheet. The rejected sheets fall into a metal tray beneath the feedboard. Differences in sheet size determine

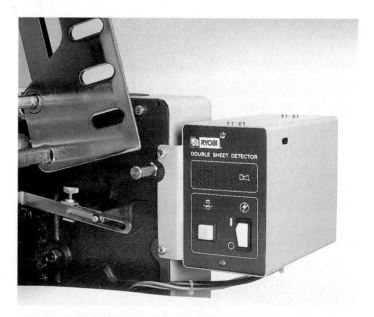

Figure 20-17. Offset presses and duplicators are equipped with double-sheet detectors to avoid jamming on the press and damaging the rubber blanket. (Ryobi Xpedx Impact Group)

the number of sheets overlapping on the feedboard at any one time, requiring the operator to calibrate the detector according to paper thickness and size. There is no metal tray beneath the feedboard on larger offset presses. Double-sheet detectors can be mechanically or electrically operated.

In addition to increased productivity, continuous feeding systems produce less spoilage and more consistent quality than successive feeding systems do. The more steadily an offset pressruns, the easier it is to maintain consistent color. This is because the ink-and-water balance can be set for optimum productivity, without the need for stopping to reload the press.

Pile feeders

A **pile feeder** is a mechanism used to lift individual sheets from the pile and feed them into the press. This mechanism is the most versatile and flexible method for handling sheets. The pile feeder can be a successive or continuous sheet-feeding system. See **Figure 20-18.**

The sheets of paper are stacked on a platform called a *pile table* or **paper table**. See **Figure 20-19.** Most pile tables allow both manual and electronic adjustment. The pile of paper must be straight and neat when placed on the **table**. All defective sheets (such as those with wavy edges and those that are curled or folded) should be removed from the pile. The paper must also be fanned out and jogged, prior to placing it on the pile table. **Fanning out** allows for easier separation and feeding by introducing a blanket of air between the sheets. *Jogging* refers to squaring and aligning all the sheets just before loading them onto the feed table.

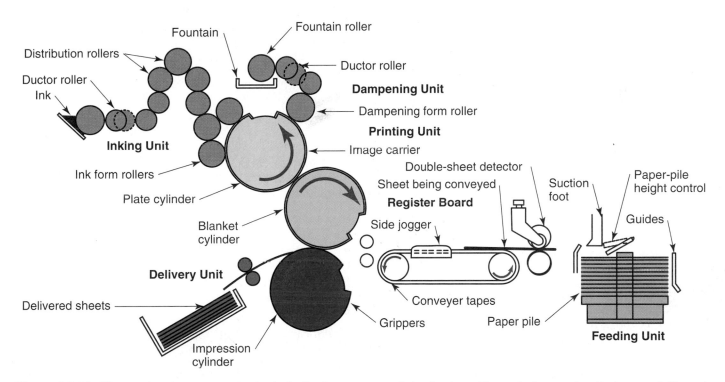

Figure 20-18. These six systems are typical of offset presses and duplicators. Paper to be run is piled on a platform in the feeder. (A.B.Dick Co.)

web: a roll of paper or other substrate used uncut on a webfed offset press.

roll-to-sheet feeding system: a feeding system in which the substrate comes from a roll, enters as a ribbon, is cut into sheets, and is then fed into the press.

double-sheet detector: a printing-press device used to detect when multiple sheets of paper are being fed at the same time.

pile feeder: a mechanism used to separate the sheets of paper and feed them into the press.

paper table: a platform on which the sheets of paper are stacked as they are delivered from the press.

table: the platform in the feeder of a sheetfed press on which the pile of paper sits.

fanning out: the progressive widening of the web or sheet as it goes from unit to unit. This widening is normally caused by tension differences between the roll and printing units or water pickup of the stock.

jogging: the squaring and aligning of sheets before loading onto the feed table or in the delivery pile.

Figure 20-19. The pile table automatically rises and maintains the correct feeding height as sheets are removed. Note the suction feet suspended above the paper and the platform wheels below the stack of paper. (A.B.Dick Co.)

The pile must be positioned in correct relationship with the settings of the register and insertion devices. The pile table automatically rises and maintains the correct feeding height as sheets are removed from the top. The amount of paper loaded on the pile table depends on the length of run and type of press. For example, most duplicators are equipped to handle a stack of 20-lb. bond paper approximately 20″ deep.

Traditionally, the use of a pile feeder required the press to be stopped for loading more paper. This is a drawback with long runs, but not with runs short enough that the feeder can hold all the paper. Fortunately, new press configurations allow printers to transform most single-sheet pile feeders into continuous sheet-feeding systems.

Additional stock can be placed in feeding position before the current pile runs out through the use of a secondary pile table or flat metal elevator strips or bars. If the system uses a secondary pile table, precision timing moves it into place just as the stock on the first table is about to run out. As long as the second table is placed at the same height, there is no interruption to the pressrun. **Figure 20-20** shows a continuous feeder.

Elevator strips or bars can also be used to replace the stock before the first pile runs out. These strips or bars are used to support the weight of the paper remaining from the first load, while the pile table is lowered and refilled. The new pile of stock is moved up to the bottom of the preceding load, the rods are withdrawn, and a single pile is left on the pile table. If care is used in these operations, there is no

Figure 20-20. This continuous feeder makes it possible to reload the feeder with paper while the press is running. (Omnitrade Industrial/Omni Adast)

interruption to the pressrun. The elevator strips or bars are referred to as *piling bars*. Their position corresponds to the width of the paper to be run. Piling bars steady the paper as it moves up and is fed into the press.

A *pile height regulator* controls the speed of elevation of the pile table or piling bars, allowing the table or bars to run higher or lower, depending on the thickness of paper being used. As the paper is fed into the press, the pile height regulator rides lower and lower. This action moves the table or bars up one notch at a time—the thicker the paper, the faster the table or bars rise.

Sheet transfer

A vacuum blower pump inside the press forces air through plastic tubes near the front of the paper stack to separate the top sheets and improve feeding. A set of *suction feet* drops down against the front edge of the top sheet of paper on the pile and lifts it to the edge of the feedboard. See **Figure 20-21**. The suction feet are commonly referred to as *suckers* or *sucker feet*. Sometimes, when the suction feet pick up the top sheet of paper, the sheet below it is lifted

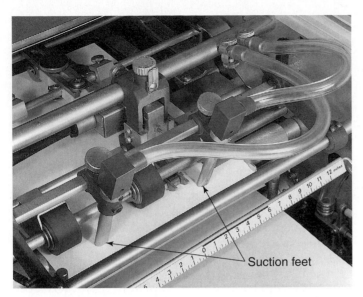

Figure 20-21. The suction feet on an offset-press feeding unit drop down against the front edge of the top sheet of paper on the pile and lift the sheet to the edge of the feedboard.

along with it. This phenomenon can result from the static electricity a dry pressroom causes. A double-sheet detector is then needed to prevent jamming the press or damaging the rubber blanket.

On smaller presses, the suction feet are positioned at the leading edge of the sheet. Suction feet can also be located at the rear edge of a sheet. The rear feet draw the paper to the pullout rollers, which move the sheet ahead to the register table.

The amount of forced air and suction is usually adjusted with controls on the side of the press. The blower is usually adjusted to separate five to six sheets of paper in the pile. The amount of vacuum the suction feet provide must be adjusted for each type of stock. Light suction is used for thin paper, and heavy suction is used on thick paper and cardboard. See **Figure 20-22.** Once the suction feet direct a sheet to the pullout rollers, the sheet is then guided to the register unit for entry to the press.

Note

Check the oil level in the vacuum blower pump jars weekly. Clean the filters and add oil as the manufacturer specifies.

Sheet separators

Most offset duplicators and some offset presses are also equipped with sheet separators. *Sheet separators* are springy, steel fingers extending over

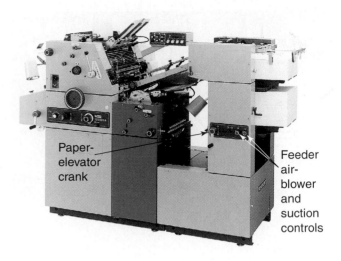

Figure 20-22. The operator can control the amount of suction and feeder air-blower force with simple hand controls. (Ryobi Xpedx Impact Group)

the lead edge of the pile of paper in the feeder. See **Figure 20-23.** Sheet separators hold down the side edge of the top sheet, as the front blowers separate the sheet from the stack. When the suction feet grip the top sheet on the pile and pull it upward and away from under the sheet separators, the sheet separators prevent the next sheet from being picked up at the same time. In order to have the separator devices function properly, the pile must be at the proper height in the feeder, and the top of the pile must be reasonably flat—especially on offset presses that run large sheets.

The sheet separators must be adjusted to provide the correct amount of resistance. If the separators drag too heavily against the paper, they might interfere with the action of the suction feet. If the tension is too light, the separators might fail to prevent more than one sheet from entering the press. At this point, the difference in feeders of various designs is most noticeable. The manufacturer's instructions must be followed in all instances. It is well, however, to keep in mind several principles that apply, generally speaking, to all feeders.

piling bar: an elevator strip or bar used to replace the stock on a pile feeder before the first pile runs out.

pile height regulator: a device used to control the speed of elevation of the pile table or piling bars.

suction foot: a rubber suction cup used on a printing-press sheet-separation unit to feed paper into the press.

sheet separator: a springy steel finger extending over the lead edge of the pile of paper in the feeder.

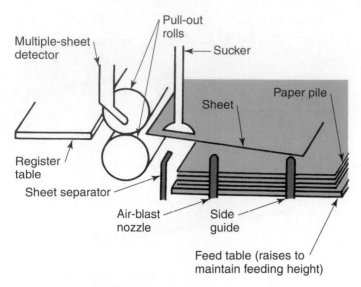

Figure 20-23. Sheet separators are springy steel fingers that extend over the lead edge of the paper pile in the feeder unit. These fingers hold the top sheet down as the front blowers separate it from the pile.

On many offset presses, separation and the moving forward of sheets can be accomplished entirely by air. Air-blast nozzles fluff the rear corners of several sheets on the top of the pile. Suckers drop down and pick up the top sheet. Another set of air nozzles moves under this top sheet and floats it on a cushion of air. The same suckers or a set of separate forwarding suckers then guide the sheet into the pullout rollers or other forwarding mechanism at the top of the feed ramp. Some type of combing device usually starts separation at the rear corners of the sheet on most feeders, especially the larger ones. See **Figure 20-24.**

Telescopic suckers come down and pick up the corners of the top sheet while it is being combed. Blower tubes, shaped similarly to feet, descend and enter under the top sheet, resting firmly on the pile. A blast of air from the blower feet then separates the entire top sheet and floats it up to a second set of suckers, while the first pair still has the sheet under control. The suckers in the second set are generally the ones that advance the sheet to the forwarding mechanism.

While the principles remain the same, there are considerable variations in the structure and operating details of the feeders the various manufacturers supply. Even within the line of presses of one manufacturer, there are wide differences, especially between the larger and smaller offset presses. The brief descriptions given of the two basic types apply generally to the larger presses. Most of the modern smaller presses and duplicators use other separation devices.

Control of the amount of air and the direction of the blower tubes or feet is critical. The sheet must be floated without riffling, waving, or flapping. The one

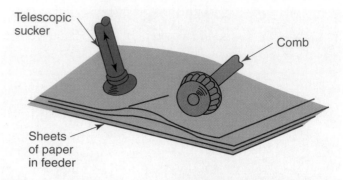

Figure 20-24. On large sheetfed offset presses, a combing device initially separates the sheets in the feeder. Telescopic suckers descend on a sheet and lift it to a second set of forwarding sucker feet. (Graphic Arts Technical Foundation)

being forwarded must be completely separated from the pile, so as not to drag the next sheet or stumble on its leading edge, especially in feeders where no blower-foot device is provided.

The sheet must be under such complete control that it reaches the forwarding mechanism at the right time and perfectly straight. If both of these conditions are not met, the proper timing of the sheet is lost. Also, a sheet coming down the ramp or board in a cocked position will likely jam and stop the press.

The Register Board and Insertion Unit

After the sheets are separated and forwarded from the feeder unit, a different set of devices takes control of the sheet. On most duplicators and small presses, the *register board*, or table, accepts a sheet from the feeder unit and inserts it in register, ready for printing. Register is the proper positioning of the sheet, with respect to the image on the blanket. In other words, to register the sheet is to precisely align it so the inked images contact it at the intended locations—within 1/100th of an inch.

On large offset presses and some duplicators, the press inserts and aligns the sheet so, when the impression-cylinder grippers draw the sheet through the printing nip, the front edge of the paper is a set distance from the image area of the plate. This distance is determined when the plate is clamped into proper position and the *front guides* are set. One side edge is also a fixed distance from the edge of the image area. This distance is also determined when the plate is mounted onto the press and the *side guide* is set in its proper position.

To ensure good register, it is important that each of these operations be performed properly. Each and every sheet must be aligned exactly alike. With the sheets under proper control and the registering devices properly set and operating, good register will be achieved.

In general, there are three press register and insertion methods—the three-point guide system, the feed-roll system, and the swing-feed (transfer-gripper) system.

The three-point guide system

With the *three-point guide system,* the sheet is forwarded to the front guides (two to four). While it is held against the front guides, a side guiding mechanism pushes or pulls the sheet into proper side alignment. In the three-point guide system, the sheet is held in this position until the impression-cylinder grippers take hold of it. At this time, the front guides are lifted out of the sheet's path of travel. As soon as the entire sheet clears the feedboard, the *guides* drop back into position to align the next sheet.

In the simple three-point guide system, the guides are mounted on a shaft above the feedboard. See **Figure 20-25.** These guides can be moved sideways along this shaft to properly balance the particular size of the sheet being run. The guide itself is essentially a flat faceplate. In the registering (lowered) position of this guide, the sheet's bottom edge straddles a metal tongue protruding under the feedboard or a register plate.

The three-point guide system is not an insertion device. The system does, however, fix the sheet in printing position, just as is done for any insertion device. On presses equipped with insertion devices, the positioning of the sheet before the insertion device starts its cycle of operation is generally referred to as *preregistering.*

When an insertion device supplements the three-point register system, the general principle and construction are similar. The front guides, however, are typically constructed so as to drop down out of the forward path of the sheet after the *grippers* on the insertion device take hold of the sheet. See **Figure 20-26.**

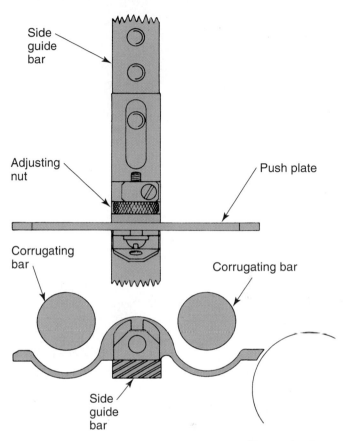

Figure 20-26. This cross-sectional view shows the parts of a push-type offset-press side guide. (Graphic Arts Technical Foundation)

register board: a platform that accepts a sheet from the feeder unit and inserts it in register, ready for printing.

front guide: a metal tab or plate attached to the front end of the feedboard on a sheetfed printing press that stops the sheet of paper and holds it on the feedboard while the side guide moves the sheet into position.

side guide: a roller, pivoting foot, or suction-powered plate that aids in the lateral positioning of a sheet of paper before the sheet is transferred into the printing unit.

three-point guide system: a method of registering a press sheet by contacting the sheet on the front and two sides.

guide: a device attached to the feedboard that aids in the proper positioning of a sheet of paper before the sheet is fed into the printing unit.

preregistering: the positioning of a sheet before the insertion device starts its cycle of operation.

gripper: a metal tab or clip located on an impression cylinder, a transfer cylinder, or another device of the feeding system that grabs a sheet of paper and feeds it through the printing press.

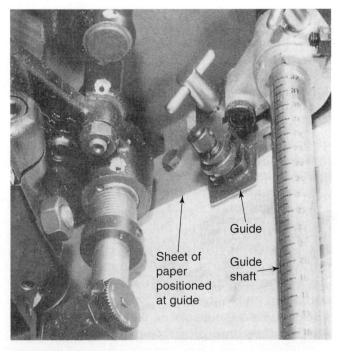

Figure 20-25. Note the three-point offset-press register system. Guides are mounted on the shaft above the feedboard. (Heidelberg, Inc.)

The swing-feed system

The *swing-feed system* is one of three methods of inserting the press sheet into the grippers of the impression cylinder. In this system, the sheet is moved forward down the feedboard and brought to rest against front *stops* (guides). The side guides then align the sheet. After being properly guided, the sheet is picked up by a set of grippers, usually mounted over the feedboard. See **Figure 20-27.** The front guides move out of the way, and the arm swings forward, carrying the sheet into the grippers on the impression cylinder. Positive control over the sheet is maintained during the transfer of the sheet from the swing arm to the impression cylinder. This pickup mechanism is called a *swing-feed assembly.*

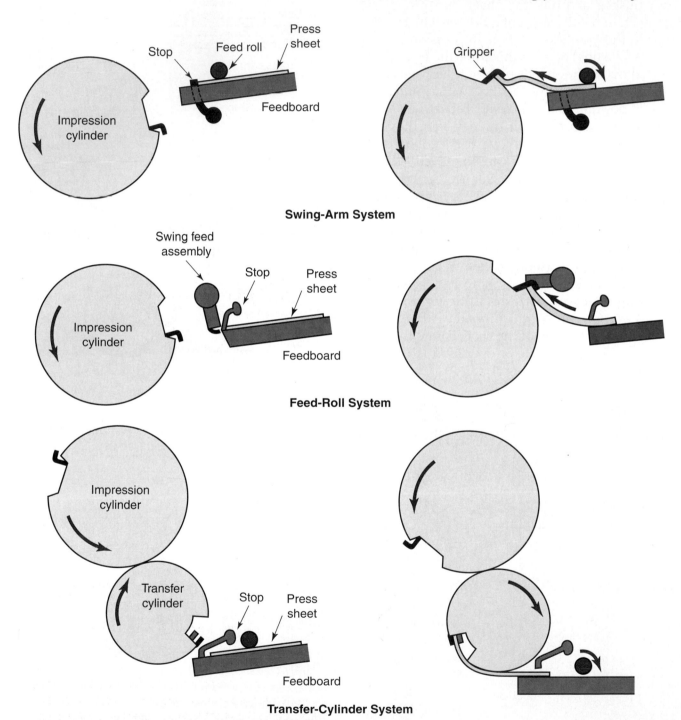

Swing-Arm System

Feed-Roll System

Transfer-Cylinder System

Figure 20-27. The swing-arm system uses an intermediate device to grip the press sheet and swing the sheet over to be gripped by the impression cylinder. The feed-roll system pushes the press sheet forward, with feed rolls, and into grippers on the impression cylinder. The transfer-cylinder system uses a rotating cylinder (drum) to grip the sheet and transfer it to the impression cylinder's grippers.

The feed-roll system

With a *feed-roll system*, the sheet is moved down the feedboard, preregistered against stops, and side guided. While the sheet is at rest, it is firmly gripped in its preregistered position by being pinched between upper and lower feed rolls or cams. Refer to **Figure 20-27**. At a precise moment, the front guides move out of the way, and the feed rolls start rotating to drive the sheet forward and into the grippers on the impression cylinder. The sheet buckles slightly to ensure complete insertion into the grippers.

The transfer-cylinder system

The *transfer-cylinder system* is similar to the feed-roll system, except the feed rolls send the sheet forward into grippers on an intermediate transfer cylinder, which carries the sheet into the grippers on the impression cylinder. Refer to **Figure 20-27**. The grippers on the transfer cylinder do not release the sheet until the grippers on the impression cylinder have closed on the sheet.

Guides

Guides are devices attached to the feedboard that aid in the proper positioning of a sheet of paper before it is fed into the printing unit. See **Figure 20-28**. Guides are divided into front and side guides.

Front guides

Front guides are metal tabs or plates attached to the front end of the feedboard on a sheetfed printing press. These guides stop the sheet of paper and hold it on the feedboard while the side guide moves it into position. See **Figure 20-29**. When the sheet is in

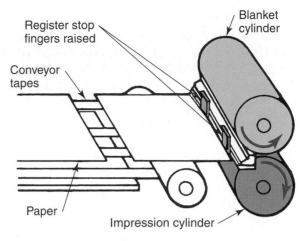

Stopping and Holding the Sheet

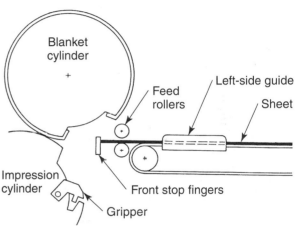

Moving the Sheet into Position

Figure 20-29. The register stop fingers place sheets in register. Stop fingers are metal posts or pins that stop a sheet of paper and hold it on the feedboard while the side guide moves it into final position. (Multigraphics)

swing-feed system: a register-and-insertion method in which a sheet is advanced forward, stopped, and then gripped and swung forward by arms, in time to connect with the grippers on the impression cylinder.

stop: a metal tab or finger attached to the front end of the feedboard on a sheetfed printing press that stops the sheet of paper and holds it on the feedboard while the side guide moves the sheet into position.

swing-feed assembly: the pickup mechanism used in the swing-feed system.

feed-roll system: a register-and-insertion method that advances a sheet forward, stops the sheet, and then propels it forward with rollers, in time to connect with the grippers on the impression cylinder.

transfer-cylinder system: a feeder design in which the press sheet is fed to the grippers of an extra cylinder, which carry the sheet to the grippers of the impression cylinder.

Figure 20-28. A photosensor on this press safeguards correct sheet delivery prior to the final positioning at the guides. (Omnitrade Industrial/Omni Adast)

position at the sides, the front guides either rise above or drop below the surface of the feedboard and allow the sheet to pass. The paper is then caught by the impression cylinder and carried into the printing unit.

On some duplicators and most larger offset presses, the front guides can be adjusted forward or backward to regulate the gripper on the paper. If the image is slightly crooked on the plate, the press operator can move the front guide in or out on one end. This changes the position of the image on the sheet. Some presses have other types of devices for the same purpose. The sheet of paper is made to skew slightly as it feeds into the printing unit. Front guides are further classified as multiple-stop guides, two-point drop guides, or stops. These guides can also form part of the insertion device.

Side guides

The type of front guides, insertion device, or gripper action on the press does not affect the design and style of operation of side guides. See **Figure 20-30**. *Push guides* push the sheet into its predetermined position, after the sheet is moved forward into the front guides or insertion device. The side-guiding operation is the same whether it is done on the near or far side of the press. Push guides are typically found on smaller presses or those running heavy, rigid material, such as metal and cardboard. They do not handle large-sized, lightweight paper very well. Some type of corrugating or stiffening device is usually used along with the push guide–type mechanism to slightly buckle the sheet, to stiffen it against the action of the push guide.

Pull guides are either finger type, rotary (roller), or a combination of the two. All pull guides use a side-guide plate, which is fixed in the desired position, where the sheet is pulled up against the side guide after being positioned at the front guides, or stops. The *finger-type pull guide* advances over the sheet, closes on it by pinching the sheet against a lower plate, and pulls the sheet to the side-guide plate. The *rotary (roller) guide* is common on most presses. This guide has a built-in lower roller that constantly rotates when the press is running. The sheet is forwarded to the front stops so the side edge rides over this lower guiding roller. After front register has been accomplished, a second spring-loaded roller (mounted above the lower one) drops down and pinches the sheet against the rotating lower roll. Friction causes the sheet to be pulled against the side-guide plate.

Grippers

Grippers are the row of metal tabs or clips that grab a sheet of paper and feed it through a printing press. They can be located on an impression cylinder, a transfer cylinder, or another device of the feeding system. See **Figure 20-31**. Grippers are classified as

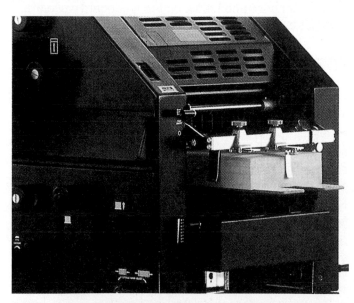

Figure 20-30. This type of duplicator has no conveyor board. Instead, sheets are transferred directly from the feeder pile to the feed rolls. (A.B.Dick Co.)

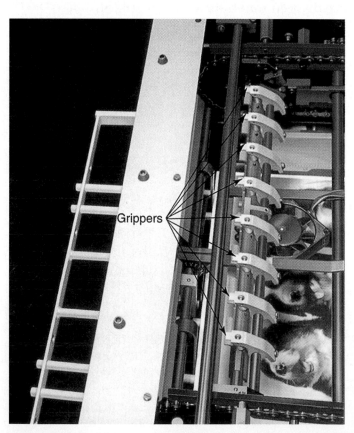

Figure 20-31. Grippers are used at various points on an offset press or a duplicator. (Omnitrade Industrial/Omni Adast)

tumbler grippers or low-lift grippers. Presses using a three-point guide system without an insertion device require **tumbler grippers**. Those that have either a feed-roll or swing-feed (rotary-gripper) insertion device use **low-lift grippers**.

Tumbler grippers rotate through a rather large arc when they open and drop back into the impression-cylinder gap. The term *tumbler* is derived from the mechanism imparting the opening and closing motions to the gripper shaft. Tumbler grippers must drop below the cylinder surface to clear the **gripper edge** of the sheet as the impression cylinder comes around to its sheet-taking position. At this point, the grippers rotate into the closed position, pinching the sheet against gripper pads and pulling the sheet into the impression nip. Grippers on presses with insertion devices that open just enough to allow the sheet to be inserted are known as *low-lift grippers*. Instead of a mechanism that imparts a complete tumbling action, low-lift grippers are mounted on a shaft rotated slightly through a cam and cam-roller device at the end of the gripper shaft.

A one-piece gripper has its finger constructed as an integral part and extension of the base or gripper clamp. The base is often a solid piece of metal drilled to fit snugly on the gripper shaft. In other cases, the base might be a split collar around the shaft. In the construction of two-piece grippers, the finger and collar are each a separate piece. A two-piece gripper is designed so provision is made for spring-loading the gripper finger, attaining a more uniform gripper bite pressure on the sheet, while the finger opens and closes as an integral part of the assembly. This same objective is accomplished in the case of some one-piece grippers by spring-loading the gripper pad set in the top of the gripper post. Three common types of gripper construction are shown in **Figure 20-32.**

Some offset presses use grit-faced grippers to prevent slippage of the sheet during the printing cycle. See **Figure 20-33.** On older presses, the grippers or gripper pads might be faced with lightweight emery cloth, if proper bite pressure cannot be developed through the spring-loaded grippers or gripper pads.

Duplicator register systems

Having covered the topic of register and insertion devices on larger offset presses, the following discussion concerns register as it relates to duplicators and small offset presses. During the feeding cycle on many offset duplicators, the suction stops briefly. This releases the top sheet to a pair of rubber forwarding rollers, which deliver the sheet to a set of moving conveyor tapes that feed each sheet to the grippers.

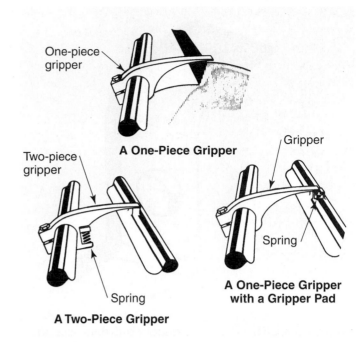

Figure 20-32. There are three common types of gripper construction: one-piece grippers; two-piece, spring-loaded grippers; and one-piece grippers with spring-loaded gripper pads. (Graphic Arts Technical Foundation)

Note

A few press designs do not have conveyor tapes. Instead, the sheet of paper is delivered directly to the grippers.

push guide: a side guide on a press that pushes the sheet into its predetermined position after the sheet is forwarded into the front guides or insertion device.

pull guide: a mechanism that uses a finger or roller (or a combination of the two) to move the sheet against the side guide after the sheet has been positioned at the front guides, or stops.

finger-type pull guide: a side guide that advances over the sheet, closes on it by pinching the sheet against a lower plate, and pulls the sheet to the side-guide plate.

rotary (roller) guide: a device that uses rollers to position the sheets against the side guide.

tumbler gripper: a device that rotates through a rather large arc when it opens and drops back into the impression-cylinder gap. This gripper is used to grab a sheet of paper.

low-lift gripper: a gripper on a press with an insertion device that opens just enough to allow the sheet to be inserted.

gripper edge: the lead edge of a sheet of paper passing through a sheetfed press containing the gripper margin.

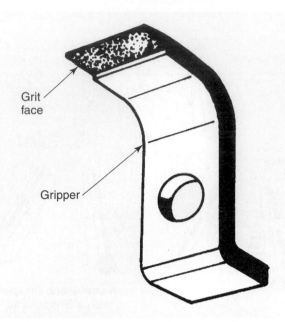

Figure 20-33. This grit-faced gripper prevents slippage of the sheet during the printing cycle. (Graphic Arts Technical Foundation)

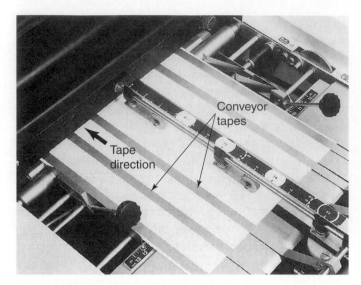

Figure 20-34. Most duplicators are equipped with conveyor tapes transporting each sheet from the feeder to the front guides. (Multigraphics)

The narrow belts or *conveyor tapes* are located on the feedboard. The fabric tapes are threaded over a roller at each end of the feedboard. When the press is operating, the rollers turn, and the tapes travel down the feedboard and back under it in one continuous motion. Individual pulleys located under the feedboard keep the tapes tight. The tapes can be adjusted individually inward or outward to handle any width paper and are moved by sliding the pulleys from side to side or rotating a knob. **Figure 20-34** shows a set of conveyor tapes on a duplicator.

The front guides stop the sheet of paper and hold it on the feedboard, while the side guide pushes the sheet into position. Some duplicators have only one side guide, while others have one on each side of the feedboard. Only one guide is used at a time, and the guide not being used is locked out of operation or moved to the edge of the feedboard. See **Figure 20-35.**

The impression-cylinder grippers are small metal fingers attached to the impression cylinder and operated by a cam. See **Figure 20-36.** The gripper fingers open to receive and close along the sheet's lead edge. Duplicators are equipped with up to six gripper fingers. The grippers pull the paper into the printing unit between the nip of the blanket and impression cylinders.

The Printing Unit

The printing unit is the heart of the offset press. Everything about the actual printing cycle centers on the three cylinders in the printing unit. The three

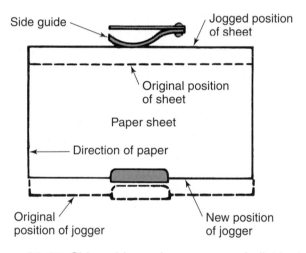

Figure 20-35. Side guides or joggers move individual sheets into position against side guides once the sheet is aligned against the stop fingers.

cylinders are the plate cylinder, the blanket cylinder, and the impression cylinder. The surfaces of these three cylinders must travel at the same speed (the same distance during each cylinder revolution). The cylinders must be adjusted for the minimum cylinder-to-cylinder pressure capable of producing accurate printed reproduction and long plate life.

The plate cylinder

The plate cylinder holds the printing plate and its image. The components of a plate cylinder include the body, bearers, bearings, and a gear that drives the cylinder. Most duplicators can use offset plates ranging in thickness from about 0.0025" to 0.006" (0.06 mm to 0.15 mm), while large offset presses use

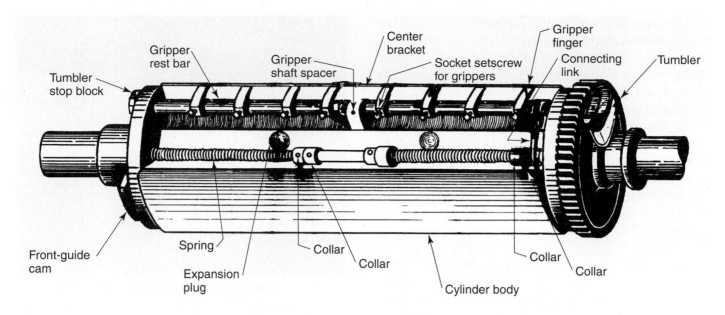

Figure 20-36. Impression-cylinder grippers are metal fingers attached to an offset press or a duplicator impression cylinder and operated by a cam. (U.S. Government Printing Office)

thicker offset plates. The attaching device on duplicators is usually a pinbar clamp, but other types of plate-end attaching methods can be used instead. See **Figure 20-37.**

The plate clamps are set so one holds the leading edge of the plate, while the other holds the tail edge of the plate firmly. Both clamps are designed for a slight sideways cocking movement of the plate, which is sometimes necessary when a plate must be shifted to obtain proper register. On large presses, there is also some latitude for forward and backward movement.

The procedure of attaching an offset plate to the plate cylinder of a duplicator is illustrated in **Figure 20-38.** The lead edge of the plate is attached to the lead-edge clamp of the plate cylinder. The cylinder is then rotated to draw the plate around the

cylinder. The tail clamp is raised by pushing up on a lever and locking the tail edge of the plate over the pins. When the lever is released, spring tension on the tail clamp is enough to hold most paper and foil plates tightly. For metal plates, the tail clamp is tightened slightly by turning the tightening dial clockwise. This process is reversed when removing a plate from the plate cylinder.

Figure 20-38. The first step in attaching a duplicator plate to the plate cylinder is fitting it to the lead-edge clamp of the plate cylinder. The tail edge of the plate is then attached to the tail clamp. (Ryobi Xpedx Impact Group)

Figure 20-37. Press and duplicator plate-end attaching methods include serrated, straight, slotted, and pinbar.

On some duplicators and larger presses, the plate can be twisted slightly on the cylinder to compensate for an image that is not exactly square on the plate. Other presses are equipped with a paper-stop bar, which can be adjusted so one end is set farther in than the other. The paper registers against the fingers on the bar when it reaches the end of the feedboard. Setting the bar at an angle causes the sheets of paper to feed into the printing unit at a slight angle, or skew, aligning the paper with the image on the plate and producing a square image on the paper. The paper-stop bar can also be adjusted slightly forward or backward to raise or lower the printing image on the paper.

Adjusting the image more than about 3/16″ (5 mm) means the plate cylinder must be moved by turning it manually. Turning the cylinder moves a scale containing an indicator pin. See **Figure 20-39.** When the cylinder has been turned the proper distance along the scale, it is locked in place. After adjusting the plate cylinder, the rubber blanket on the blanket cylinder must be thoroughly cleaned before making another impression.

On large offset presses, the bases of the plate cylinder and the blanket cylinder are each *undercut.* This means they are made smaller in diameter than the narrow band or metal ring at each end, called the *bearer.* When properly adjusted, the bearers maintain the two cylinders parallel to each other at the correct level. See **Figure 20-40.** The amount, in thousandths of an inch, that the cylinders are undercut below the bearers is stamped in the cylinder gutters.

The undercut allows for adding packing sheets beneath the plate and blanket, compensating for variations in the thickness of plates and blankets, and it also maintains the two cylinders at virtually equal diameters. If one is larger than the other, the image size can be changed during image transfer. The total thickness of the packing sheets, plus the thickness of the blanket and the plate, should equal 0.003″ (0.08 mm) more than the combined undercut of the two cylinders. A packing gauge is used for this purpose. See **Figure 20-41.** This excess is referred to as *squeeze.*

The blanket cylinder

The blanket cylinder is located between the plate and impression cylinders. This cylinder holds the rubber blanket, a synthetic rubber mat that accepts the image from the plate cylinder and transfers, or offsets, it to the substrate. The blanket attaches to a set of pins at each end of the cylinder. See **Figure 20-42.** The rubber blanket is attached to the upper, or lead-edge, pins first. The cylinder is turned manually to draw

Raising or Lowering the Image

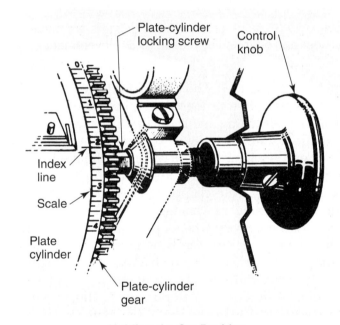

Holding the Set Position

Figure 20-39. Offset duplicators are equipped with a control device for raising or lowering the image on the paper. The image-positioning device has a control knob and plate-cylinder locking screw to hold the set position tightly. (Multigraphics)

the blanket around. The blanket is then attached to the tail end of the cylinder. This mat is drawn tight by turning the clamp-tightening dial counterclockwise.

Note

The blanket might stretch when it is first used on the press. After several hundred impressions, the press should be stopped, and the blanket should be retightened.

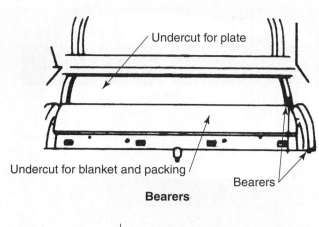

Undercut for plate

Undercut for blanket and packing

Bearers

Bearers

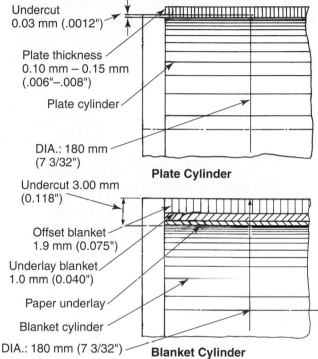

Undercut
0.03 mm (.0012")

Plate thickness
0.10 mm – 0.15 mm
(.006"–.008")

Plate cylinder

DIA.: 180 mm
(7 3/32")

Plate Cylinder

Undercut 3.00 mm
(0.118")

Offset blanket
1.9 mm (0.075")

Underlay blanket
1.0 mm (0.040")

Paper underlay

Blanket cylinder

DIA.: 180 mm (7 3/32")

Blanket Cylinder

Figure 20-40. Offset-press bearers maintain the plate cylinder and blanket cylinder parallel to each other at the correct level. (Heidelberg, Inc.)

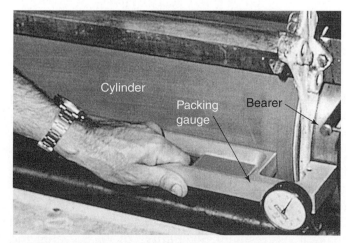

Cylinder

Packing gauge

Bearer

Figure 20-41. A packing gauge is used to check the height of plate- and blanket-cylinder packings. (Baldwin Technology)

Figure 20-42. The green rubber blanket on this offset duplicator attaches to a set of pins at each end of the blanket cylinder. (Ryobi Xpedx Impact Group)

Cleaning the blanket cylinder

By following the proper cleaning methods, blanket life is extended, and print quality remains sharp and clean. See **Figure 20-43.** Use the following guidelines to maintain print quality and extend blanket life:

1. Remove any ink and adhesive residue with an appropriate cleaning solvent, such as a regular blanket wash.
2. Use detergent and water to remove any oily residue from the cylinder surface. Soap and water work very well and do not cause VOC problems.
3. Clean the surface with IPA to remove any oily film or water left on the surface of the cylinder. Some printers successfully use spray glass cleaners.
4. Use clean, dry rags for drying the cylinder surface. Do not wipe the blanket cylinder with a shop rag that has an oily residue from the cleaning process. Using a disposable paper towel for the final cylinder wipe ensures there is no oily residue transmitted to the clean blanket cylinder.

undercut: the difference between the radius of the plate and blanket cylinders' bearers and the radius of the cylinders themselves.

bearer: a narrow metal band at the end of a press cylinder used to allow packing and easy alignment.

squeeze: the pressure exerted between the offset-press plate cylinder and the blanket cylinder.

Figure 20-43. The proper care of a quality offset-press blanket ensures quality impressions and a longer blanket life. (Van Son Holland Ink Corp.)

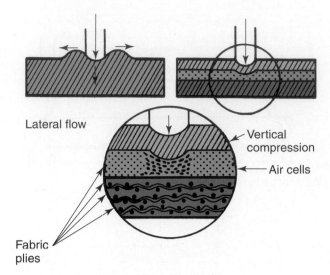

Figure 20-44. Note the cross-sectional view of a compressible offset blanket. This type of blanket compresses and instantly rebounds, returning to its original shape.

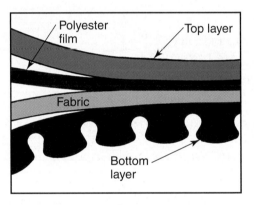

Figure 20-45. This cross-sectional view of an offset blanket shows the four primary layers of material.

In summer and high-humidity conditions, solvents that evaporate quickly cool the blanket cylinder, and condensation forms on the cooled cylinder. This is why steps 3 and 4 are important in helping to prevent adhesion problems.

Offset blankets

The *carcass* is the back side of the blanket and is specially woven to maintain the quality and strength of the blanket. The two basic types of offset blankets are conventional and compressible blankets. *Conventional blankets* tend to bulge at the impact point. *Compressible blankets* are designed to compress (squeeze) and instantly rebound to their original shape and thickness. See **Figure 20-44.** The compressible blanket allows the press operator to increase packing height without increasing printing pressure, thus allowing for better image transfer without distortion and producing a better printing job. Compressible blankets are the most common and widely used blankets. Conventional blankets are less forgiving, but they allow for a more uniform dot formation.

The bottom layer on many blankets is a "waffle" design formed from rubber or a synthetic material. See **Figure 20-45.** The backing on a compressible blanket includes at least one layer of a soft, resilient material, such as foam rubber, cork, or loose fabric fibers, that gives the blanket its compressible characteristic and prevents minor blanket *smashes* from affecting print quality. *Underblankets*, or underlay blankets, made of foam rubber, cork, or loose fabric fibers can be used under the blanket to improve its performance. Some of the benefits from the use of underblankets include reduced downtime, sharper definition of fine images, and reduced roller and cylinder pressures that lead to reduced plate wear.

The surface of the offset blanket receives the image from the plate and transfers it to the substrate. Therefore, the condition of the blanket surface is crucial to print quality. It is important to handle a printing blanket with extreme care because its surface is very delicate. When storing blankets, place them face to face (or back to back) in tubes rolled up tightly or lying flat.

If the duplicator or press will not be used for several days, the tension on the blanket should be released to keep it resilient. All ink should be removed after each pressrun. To keep the blanket clean and ready for the next job, fluids should not be allowed to dry on the blanket. Instead, it should be wiped with a clean dry cloth. To lengthen the life of the blanket, a high-quality blanket wash is best because inexpensive brands can dry out a blanket and make it less resilient. See **Figure 20-46.** Solvents and inks should be used with extreme care. For example,

Figure 20-46. Offset blankets should be cleaned with a high-quality solvent to preserve the life and resiliency of the blanket. (Van Son Holland Ink Corp.)

solvent-soaked rags need to be stored in a metal safety can with a tight metal lid because spontaneous combustion is always a threat.

Caution

Never use gasoline as a blanket wash. Make sure the blanket wash you are using is of high quality and not a flammable material.

When a blanket is ordered, the converter cuts the blanket specifically to meet the needs of the blanket cylinder. Regardless of how the blanket is attached to the cylinder, it is always mounted with the pinstripe on the carcass going around the cylinder. Blankets have an around direction and an across direction. The around direction is always stated first when giving a size. Blankets are mounted with the pinholes or bars going along the across direction.

They can be mounted on the press with pinholes that go into sprockets or with bars mounted by a clamp. Straight-edge blankets require the press to have a special mounting mechanism.

If blanket bars are used instead of pinholes, the blanket must be attached to the blanket bars at each end. Bars are made for each kind and size of press and duplicator. They tightly grip the blanket at all points of the lead and trailing edges. Some bars use bolts to apply pressure, while others use special teeth and gripping devices. Blanket thickness must be measured with care at a number of key points. See **Figure 20-47.**

Note

Most duplicators do not require packing under the blanket or plate.

Any number of adverse results can occur from poor or incorrect packing. Too little packing can cause snowflaky solids, moiré patterns, doubling,

	Plies	Gauge	Hardness
Conventional	2	.052″	81
	3	.066″–.067″	78–81
	4	.076″–.077″	78–81
	5	.010″	78–81
Compressible	3	.067″	70–79
	4	.077″	70–78
	5	.101″	78

Figure 20-47. The number of plies determines the gauge (thickness) of blankets.

carcass: the back side of the blanket, which is specially woven to maintain the integrity of the blanket.

conventional blanket: a blanket used in an offset press made without a layer of foam allowing the blanket to compress when two sheets are fed at a time.

compressible blanket: a rubber printing blanket with backing made of at least one layer of foam rubber, cork, or nonwoven fabric fibers that allows the blanket to squeeze and instantly rebound to its original shape and thickness.

underblanket: packing material made of foam rubber, cork, or loose fabric fibers used under printing blankets to improve the blanket's performance.

piling, linting, or low spots. Excessive packing can cause slurring, fill-in, embossing, ink-film scum, gear marks and streaks, or plate wear. In addition, register problems can result from unequal packing from cylinder to cylinder.

Cylinders on a press might not have a good chromed surface. Scratched or rough cylinders can cause blanket removal to be difficult. Normally, blanket removal is simply a matter of peeling off the blanket by pulling it at 180° to the cylinder surface while jogging the press. If it has been a long time since the blanket was installed, use the following procedure to aid blanket removal:

1. Carefully cut the blanket into 1″ to 2″ strips. Be careful not to score the cylinder.
2. Peel the blanket from the cylinder one strip at a time. The removal should be done at a very sharp angle (as close to 180° as possible).

Blanket removal from scratched or rough cylinders can be simplified by using a good quality blanket with a tough, fibrous backing. A strong reinforcing layer also makes the blanket more tear resistant.

The impression cylinder

The impression cylinder carries the paper through the printing unit and presses it against the inked blanket, where the image is transferred to the paper. This cylinder is also called the *back cylinder* because it is usually located behind the blanket cylinder. See **Figure 20-48.**

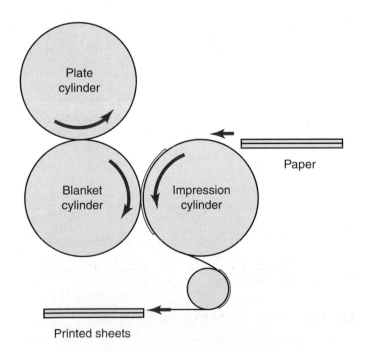

Figure 20-48. On an offset press or duplicator, the impression cylinder forces the sheet of paper against the blanket to transfer the image to the paper.

This cylinder uses a set of grippers to grab the lead edge of the press sheet when the sheet reaches the end of the feedboard. The paper is drawn around the impression cylinder and forced against the blanket to make the impression. The grippers then open to release the sheet to the next printing unit or to the delivery pile.

The pressure between the blanket and impression cylinders must be adjusted each time a change in paper thickness is made. When going from a thin paper to a thick paper, the pressure between the blanket and impression cylinders is decreased so the rubber blanket is not smashed from the increased thickness of paper. Setting the press *on impression* means bringing the impression cylinder into contact with the paper and blanket, which causes the image to print on the paper.

A *common impression cylinder* is frequently used in multicolor printing. This cylinder is an impression cylinder that contacts more than one blanket, passing a single sheet beneath successive blankets. Refer back to **Figure 20-13.**

Cylinder and roller pressures

There are several pressure checks that must be made to cylinders and rollers on a daily basis. These checks should also be made whenever rollers, roller coverings, blankets, plate thicknesses, and paper thicknesses are changed. All adjustments should be made to the manufacturer's specific recommendations. The sequence of pressure checks is given below and in **Figure 20-49:**

1. Check dampener form roller–to-plate pressure.
2. Check ink form roller–to-plate pressure.
3. Check plate cylinder–to–blanket cylinder pressure.
4. Check impression adjustment (squeeze).

Make sure you have properly installed and gummed the plate on the duplicator or press. Place the dampener form rollers in the off position. Place the ink rollers in the on position, and allow the gummed plate to ink up over its entire surface. Stop the press and place the ink rollers in the off position. Allow the plate cylinder to come into contact with the blanket cylinder. Take the plate cylinder out of contact. Do this in several different locations on the blanket. You should have a uniform ink-band line 1/8″ to 3/16″ (3.2 mm to 4.8 mm) wide. If an adjustment is required, correct the parallel first and then the overall pressure adjustments. See **Figure 20-50.**

Duplicators typically have a self-compensating adjustment that is a spring-loaded impression. This adjustment provides for variations in paper thicknesses. The following method can be used to test impression:

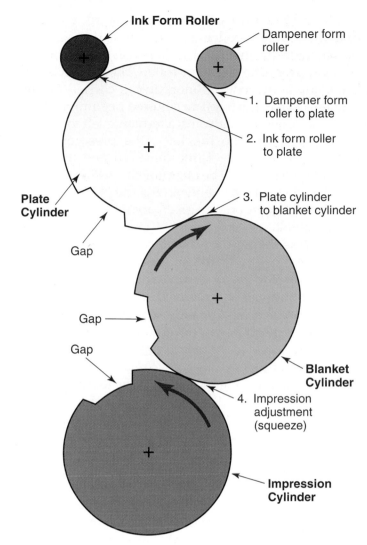

Figure 20-49. Learn offset-press and duplicator pressure checks. These pressure checks should be performed each day before starting presswork. (Multigraphics)

1. With the press stopped, insert two 2″ × 8″ (50 mm × 200 mm) test strips between the blanket and the impression cylinders. Insert one strip near each end. The test strips should be cut from the same stock that will be used for the printing job.
2. Adjust for parallel impression until the pull on each strip indicates the strips are held firmly and equally between the cylinders.
3. Add approximately 0.003″ (0.08 mm) more squeeze either by adjustment or the addition of packing sheets.

The Inking Unit

The *inking unit* (also referred to as the *ink train*) consists of an ink fountain and several rollers that control the feeding of the ink. See **Figure 20-51.** The *ink fountain* is a reservoir that holds the ink before the rollers transfer the ink to the printing plate. The

Ink band swollen at ends: Setting roller too tightly against the vibrator causes rubber to break loose from the roller shaft. This allows solvent to swell rubber at roller ends. Grind rollers or replace.

Too heavy at one end, too light at other end: Uneven setting. Reset rollers to obtain uniform medium.

Heavy in center, light at ends: Roller bowed or worn at ends. Caused by form roller being set too tightly against vibrator roller. Correct by resetting rollers. Regrind or replace rollers if it's no longer possible to obtain the desired setting.

Light areas in ink band: Indicates improper grinding or manufacture of roller. Regrind or replace.

Ideal setting: Uniform parallel bands.

Figure 20-50. The parallel adjustment of ink form rollers is essential for uniform ink distribution.

various rollers making up the train leading back to the ink fountain include the fountain roller, the ductor roller, three or four metal oscillating rollers, four or more rubber intermediate rollers, and two to four rubber form rollers. The inking unit is also referred to as the *inker* or *inking system*.

On conventional systems, a set of screws, called *fountain keys*, regulate the supply of ink to the plate at the ink fountain. By adjusting the keys, the press

on impression: into contact with the paper and blanket.

common impression cylinder: an impression cylinder that contacts more than one blanket, passing a single sheet beneath successive blankets.

inking unit: the portion of the press consisting of the ink fountain and rollers that control the feeding of the ink.

ink fountain: the reservoir in the inking system holding the ink before the rollers transfer the ink to the printing plate.

inking system: the portion of the press transferring ink from the ink fountain to the printing plate.

fountain key: a screw on a conventional inking system used to regulate the ink at the ink fountain.

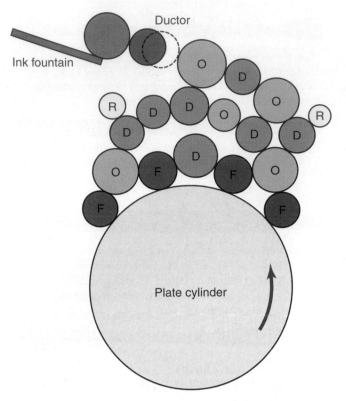

Figure 20-51. The inking unit on an offset press or a duplicator consists of an ink fountain, a fountain roller (brown), a ductor roller (green), oscillating rollers (blue), distributing rollers (purple), and form rollers (red).

operator moves the fountain blade against or away from the *fountain roller*. The *fountain blade* is a metal plate or plastic strip forming a barrier between the ink fountain and the fountain roller. The fountain roller is a metal roller found in the ink fountain.

There is a thin gap between the ink fountain and the fountain roller. The width of this gap can be changed by moving the fountain blade toward or away from the fountain roller. The farther away the blade is moved, the more ink is carried on the fountain roller. The keys are adjusted beginning at the center and working outward, alternating left to right.

By adjusting the ink keys, the press operator controls the amount of ink delivered and the ink's level of distribution. The operator can adjust the keys so ink is distributed evenly across the plate or so it is heavier or lighter on any given area of the plate. See **Figure 20-52.**

Keyless inking uses a metering roller to deliver a uniform coating of ink to the plate. Once this is done, a *ductor roller* scrapes off excess solution. Ink is continuously circulated, and little evaporation takes place. The process is much simpler than the process used with conventional ink fountains, and it produces acceptable press sheets and fewer makeready sheets.

A gear controlling the speed of the fountain roller can further regulate the supply of ink. Turning the control dial clockwise allows a maximum amount of ink. Turning the control counterclockwise reduces the feed. The usual procedure is to operate with a minimum of ink on the fountain roller. The ink-feed control dial is then regulated as needed. The ink supply can be completely stopped by turning a lever.

When the press is in operation, the metal fountain roller revolves in the fountain, mixing the ink and picking up a measured amount of ink. Many offset presses also use an ink agitator for this purpose.

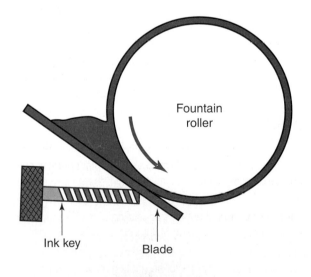

Adjustable Ink Keys

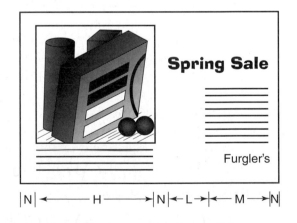

A Design's Ink Requirements

Figure 20-52. The ink fountain is equipped with a set of keys for adjusting the flow of ink to the fountain roller so each portion of the plate can receive the proper amount of ink. Portions of this design require very different amounts of ink to cover the images areas. These ink requirements can be described as none (N), light (L), moderate (M), and heavy (H).

See **Figure 20-53.** An *ink agitator* is a motorized, revolving metal cone running along the ink fountain, continuously stirring the ink. Ink agitators keep the ink at a workable consistency and help reduce the formation of dried ink skins. As the ink leaves the fountain roller, it is transferred to the ductor roller. Modern offset-ink formulations do not require these ink agitators.

Ink-feed control

The ductor roller is the first roller in the train. This roller comes in alternate contact with the fountain roller and the first oscillator or distributing roller. The length of time the ductor roller is in contact with the fountain roller is referred to as *dwell*. The ductor roller's rate of movement between the fountain roller and the rest of the ink train is adjustable. This rate is usually timed to the revolution of the plate cylinder. Refer back to **Figure 20-51.**

The ductor roller should contact the next roller only while the *form rollers* are over the plate-cylinder gap, allowing the inking system time to renew itself and the form rollers to smoothly return to the plate. The plate-cylinder gap is the recessed portion of the plate cylinder where the plate is clamped. Refer back to **Figure 20-51.** No ink is being applied to or removed from a plate because there is no plate in this portion of the cylinder. The form rollers are in direct contact with the printing plate and are used to transfer ink to the plate.

To prevent various printing problems, the form rollers must be set properly. Setting the form rollers with too much pressure against the plate can cause slurring, dot gain, accelerated plate wear and damage, and streaking. Unequal pressure between the form rollers and the oscillator can also cause skidding and streaking. Too much pressure between the form rollers and the oscillator can cause the form rollers to warp. Warped form rollers bounce against the plate and cause a variety of printing defects. Refer to the manufacturer's specs and instructions for setting the form rollers.

Most of the rollers in the ink train are *intermediate rollers*. The two types of intermediate rollers are distributing rollers, which contact two other rollers, and riders, which contact only one other roller. *Distributing rollers* not only carry ink forward in the ink train, but they also reduce the ink's viscosity at the contact points between rollers. *Riders* often collect debris, such as coating or filler particles. The *oscillating rollers* move from side to side as they rotate. This dual action works the ink and spreads it evenly over the form rollers. The action of these rollers also helps prevent mechanical ghosting on the printed piece.

---

fountain roller: a metal roller used in the ink fountain of inking systems and some dampening systems to transfer ink or fountain solution from the ink fountain to the ductor roller.

fountain blade: a metal plate or plastic strip that forms a barrier between the ink fountain and the fountain roller.

keyless inking: an inking system that uses a metering roller to deliver a uniform coating of ink to the plate.

ductor roller: the first roller in the inking system that comes in alternate contact with the fountain roller and the first oscillator. This roller is the roller in a dampening system that transfers the solution to a distributing roller.

ink agitator: a motorized, revolving metal cone running along the ink fountain, continuously stirring the ink. This agitator keeps the ink at a workable consistency and helps reduce the formation of dried-ink skins.

dwell: the length of time the ductor roller is in contact with the fountain roller.

form roller: a roller in inking and dampening systems that comes in direct contact with the printing plate and is used to transfer ink or fountain solution to the plate.

intermediate roller: one of the nonoscillating rollers in the ink train between the ductor roller and the form rollers.

distributing roller: an intermediate roller in the ink train that contacts two other rollers.

rider: an intermediate roller in the ink train that contacts only one other roller.

oscillating roller: a roller in the inking system of a press that moves from side to side as it rotates to work the ink and spread it evenly over the form rollers.

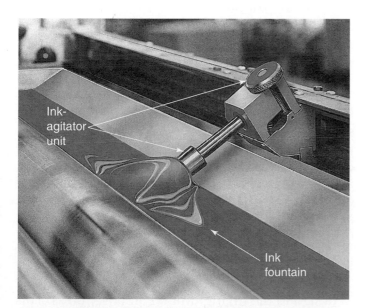

Figure 20-53. Many large offset presses are equipped with ink agitators. These devices continuously mix ink in the fountain and provide good distribution and dispersion. (Baldwin Technology)

The number of distributor, intermediate, and form rollers used in an inking system varies according to the press. The number of rollers in the design provides an indication of the quality of the system. The greater the number of rollers is, the more uniform the distribution of ink to the plate will be. In addition, presses with more ink rollers—especially form rollers—are better able to print designs containing large solid areas. These presses can better replenish the volume of ink large solid areas remove from the blanket. One of the differences between duplicators and presses is the number of rollers in the ink train. The ink trains of most duplicators are too small to handle very large solid image areas.

Controlling ink form rollers

Duplicators generally have two to three ink form rollers, while larger offset presses have three or more. A handle, called the *night latch*, allows the press operator to lower the rollers against the plate and lift them out of contact with the plate. The night latch is usually used to raise the rollers at the end of the working day. On some duplicators, the ink form rollers operate automatically. These rollers rest against the plate when the duplicator begins to print and rise when it is not printing.

On some duplicators, the ink-fountain roller is turned off when sheets of paper are not being fed through the press, preventing excess ink from accumulating on the rollers. An automatic control lever allows the operator to distribute ink over the rollers without turning on the paper feeder. When the lever is pushed down, the fountain roller turns, even though no paper is feeding through. Raising the lever brings the automatic control back into use.

Remote ink control

Students often learn press operation on duplicators or presses with ink keys that must be adjusted manually. Large modern presses, however, usually allow the operator to adjust the ink keys from a console. Remote-press ink-fountain control systems generally use one or more smart fountains controlled by a computer system. These systems are usually equipped with a video monitor, an ink ratchet, remote water control, segmented blades, and a modem housed in the printing-control operation stand.

The *smart fountain* uses a standard ink fountain fitted with custom ink keys, motor-driven ink-key actuators, an electronic circuit board, associated wiring, and a gasket-sealed housing. The ink-key actuator uses a low-voltage direct current (DC) motor, a potentiometer coupling to the ink key, clutches, and a push-and-turn manual knob (for the manual setting of keys). The potentiometer provides precise key-position information to the press operator.

In most remote ink-control systems, the ink-fountain blades are divided into zones, with an individual motor for each. The ink-supply volume for each zone is digitally controlled from the printing-control operation stand. The ink fountains can be opened and closed for easy cleaning and maintenance.

Presetting fountain keys

Press makeready time is significantly reduced when the fountain keys are automatically set for the next job. In many pressrooms, this function is performed by scanning the plate to analyze the pattern of images and determine the demand for ink. These data are then converted to the percent of coverage for each ink zone. An ink zone is the portion of the plate controlled by one of the fountain keys. See **Figure 20-54.**

Newer technology eliminates the plate-scanning stage. Instead, data describing the plate's placement of images is taken from the digital files that were sent to the platesetter. Analysis of the plate's imaging in each ink zone is converted to the proper fountain-key settings, and the keys are set automatically. These settings can reflect the print characteristics of the substrate for that job. After the first sheets are printed, the press operator can pull a press sheet, assess the color, and make any minor adjustments from the control console.

The Dampening Unit

The *dampening unit* is designed to function in much the same way as the inking unit. Rather than applying ink, however, the dampening unit moistens the nonimage areas of the plate with fountain solution so ink does not adhere to them. See **Figure 20-55.** The fountain roller rotates in a pan containing the fountain solution. Depending on the dampening system being used, the fountain roller transfers a thin film of fountain solution either to the ductor roller or directly to the form rollers. If a ductor roller is used, it transfers the solution to a distributing roller and onto the form roller. Offset-press dampening systems are classified as one of three types—intermittent, continuous, or integrated (combination).

Intermittent systems

The *intermittent dampening system* is similar in design to the inking unit on an offset press. This system uses oscillator rollers, form rollers, a ductor roller, and a fountain roller. The dampening system uses fewer rollers than the inking system does

A Smart Fountain

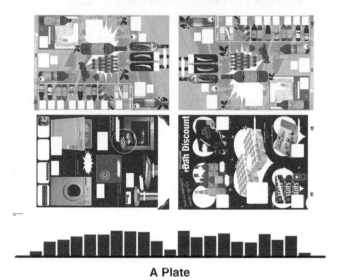

A Plate

Figure 20-54. Smart fountains are set automatically by data that assesses the amount of ink each zone of the plate requires. The device shown can be retrofitted to a press with manual ink keys. The bars below this plate represent the different amounts of ink each zone requires. (EPG, Inc.)

because the fountain solution is more fluid than the ink and does not need to be worked to the same degree.

The fountain on this type of system is a simple pan. Unlike the inking system, it has no blade or keys for controlling the distribution and flow of the solution. Instead, the disbursement of the fountain solution is controlled by regulating the rotating speed of the fountain roller in the solution. The amount of solution transferred to the plate can also be controlled by adjusting the length of time the ductor roller contacts the fountain roller. Some dampening systems use water stops to regulate flow. *Water stops* are small rollers or plastic or metal tabs that press against the fountain roller. These stops squeeze or scrape solution from the fountain-roller surface before it contacts the ductor.

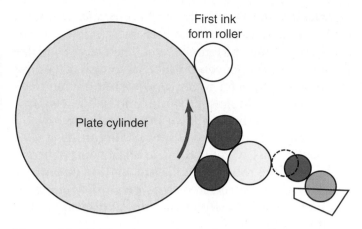

Figure 20-55. The dampening unit on an offset press or a duplicator consists of a fountain-solution source, a fountain pan and solution, a fountain roller (blue), a ductor roller (green), a distributing or oscillating roller (yellow), and one or two form rollers (red).

A common problem with intermittent systems is their inability to quickly adjust the level of solution on the plate. If the roller covers retain too much solution, they must be allowed to sit until the excess water evaporates. Printing must be halted to allow evaporation or to remove and change the rollers or covers. The movement of the ductor roller can also cause the fountain solution to surge through the system. The intermittent system is typically referred to as the *conventional dampening system*.

Continuous systems

Continuous dampening systems do not use ductor rollers to transfer fountain solution from the pan. Instead, continuous systems use a metering roller to move the solution to a transfer roller. The

night latch: a handle provided for lowering the rollers against the plate and lifting them out of contact with the plate.

smart fountain: a standard ink fountain fitted with custom ink keys, motor-driven ink-key actuators, an electronic circuit board, associated wiring, and a gasket-sealed housing.

dampening unit: a press system that moistens the nonimage areas of the plate with fountain solution so ink does not adhere to them.

intermittent dampening system: a system that uses oscillator rollers, form rollers, a ductor roller, and a fountain roller.

water stop: a small roller or a plastic or metal tab that presses against the fountain roller to squeeze or scrape solution from the fountain-roller surface before it contacts the ductor.

conventional dampening system: a system in which the movement of the ductor roller prevents the continuous flow of fountain solution from the fountain to the plate.

continuous dampening system: a system that uses a metering roller to move the fountain solution to the transfer roller.

metering roller is usually made of or covered with rubber and serves the same purpose as the fountain roller in an intermittent system. The *transfer roller* is a hard, chrome-covered roller. In some dampening systems, the transfer roller can be used as the fountain roller. The biggest advantage to using a continuous system is that it allows the operator to quickly make adjustments and see immediate results.

Continuous systems can use a spray bar or brush to dampen the rollers. See **Figure 20-56.** Continuous systems are often referred to as *alcohol dampening systems* because alcohol was commonly used in the fountain solution.

Integrated dampening systems

Integrated dampening systems link the dampening rollers and the inking rollers to the ink fountain. The fountain solution and ink are fed to the plate from the same set of form rollers. See **Figure 20-57.** The fountain solution is distributed, not only to the rollers in the dampening system, but also to some of the ink rollers. Since the fountain solution repels the ink, it can ride on the ink to the plate. This type of system is also referred to as a *combined dampening system* or a *combination dampening system.* Proper formulation of the fountain solution is vital to the functioning of a combination system because this system is more likely to suffer from emulsification problems.

Alcohol dampening systems

Two alcohol dampening systems commonly found in industry are Dahlgren and Varn Kompac. The Dahlgren and Varn Kompac alcohol systems recirculate the fountain solution, thereby making it possible to maintain pH consistency in the fountain solution. These systems also assist the press operator in maintaining the proper fountain-solution level in the fountain pan. The entire fountain system generally runs more cleanly than a conventional dampening unit does.

Dahlgren units

The duplicator version of the Dahlgren dampening unit is a scaled-down, simplified version of the units made for large offset presses. See **Figure 20-58.** This version consists of a large-diameter form roller that is gear driven from the plate-cylinder gear. A rubber fountain roller spins in the fountain solution and is mated against a chromed metering roller.

Varn Kompac units

The Varn Kompac dampening unit is designed to give automatic ink-and-water balance to offset duplicators and presses. The unit is installed after the original dampening system is removed. This dampening unit can be used with duplicators or presses equipped with conventional or integrated systems. The Varn Kompac unit is shown in **Figure 20-59.**

This unit is a continuous-flow, two-roller system that dampens the plate directly from a plate form roller. The plate form roller is gear driven by the plate-cylinder gears to operate at the same surface speed as the plate. Once the Varn Kompac unit is

Figure 20-56. A spray bar can be used to dampen the rollers. (Omnitrade Industrial/Omni Adast)

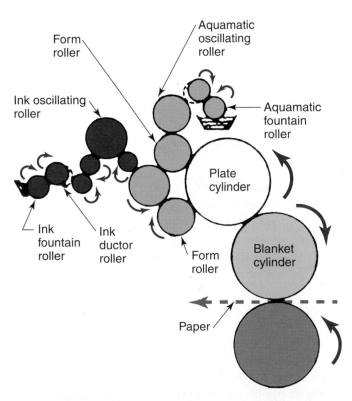

Figure 20-57. In an integrated dampening system, or a combination dampening system, water and ink are fed to the plate from the same set of form rollers. (A.B.Dick Co.)

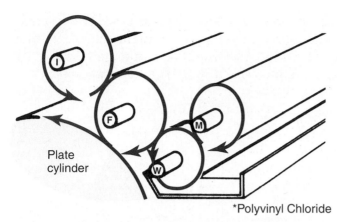

Plate cylinder

*Polyvinyl Chloride

F–Ink water form roller (*PVC blend)
I–Inking oscillator (copper)
M–Metering roller (*PVC blend)
W–Water pan roller (chrome)

Figure 20-58. A Dahlgren system makes it possible for a press operator to maintain consistency in the pH of the fountain solution. The entire fountain system generally runs cleaner than a conventional dampening unit does. (Graphic Arts Technical Foundation)

installed, no other adjustments are necessary from job to job or paper to paper.

Rollers and roller covers

The dampener rollers are either solid metal, solid rubber, or cloth-covered rubber. See **Figure 20-60.** Fountain rollers are usually solid metal, while ductor and dampener form rollers are usually cloth covered.

Figure 20-59. This Varn Kompac dampening unit is designed to give automatic ink-water balance to offset duplicators and presses. In this system, fountain solution is milled (combined) into ink under pressure, thus delivering an extremely thin and uniform film of both fountain solution and ink. (Varn Products Company, Inc.)

Figure 20-60. Rubber rollers can be used with or without cloth covers, as form rollers. Ductor rollers are always cloth-covered rubber rollers. (Jomac, Inc.)

The dampener form and ductor rollers on most duplicators are covered with a cloth, called *molleton*. Molleton covers are available ready cut in tubular or wraparound strip form, as well as in continuous tubular rolls. The molleton in **Figure 20-61** has a seam. The cloth in **Figure 20-62** is seamless.

metering roller: a roller usually made of rubber or covered with rubber and serving the same purpose as the fountain roller in an intermittent system.

transfer roller: a hard, chrome-covered roller. This roller can be used as the fountain roller in some dampening systems.

alcohol dampening system: a dampening system that uses alcohol in the fountain solution.

integrated dampening system: a dampening system in which dampening solution is applied to one of the ink form rollers.

molleton: thick fabric made from cotton used as a covering on dampener form and ductor rollers.

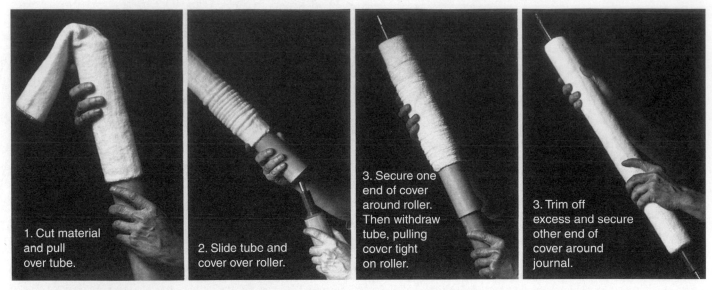

Figure 20-61. This is the correct procedure for installing a molleton cover with a seam. (Jomac, Inc.)

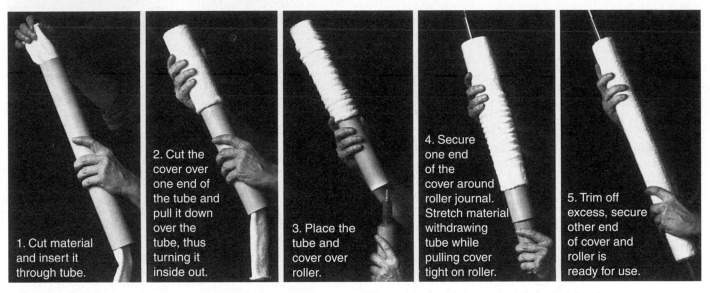

Figure 20-62. Note the correct procedure for installing a molleton cover with no seam. (Jomac, Inc.)

Cover installation

Molleton covers must be installed with care. See **Figure 20-63.** An uneven cover does not spread the fountain solution smoothly over the plate. The steps listed below can be used to install a new molleton cover:

1. Remove the old cover. Do this carefully, so the roller is not damaged.
2. Clean the roller using soap and water. Use solvent to remove ink buildup.
3. Slide the new cover over the roller. An acetate sheet can be placed around the roller to make it easier to pull the molleton sleeve over the roller.
4. Tie both ends of the sleeve. Do this with care so the molleton is smooth. Cut off the extra string. See **Figure 20-64.**
5. Wet the entire molleton in a sink. Smooth down the nap with a cellulose sponge.

6. Install the roller in the press.
7. Run the press to let the roller run in and smooth the surface.

Pressure settings

New dampener covers must be set for proper pressure after they are installed. A pressure check must also be made after the new dampener covers have been run in for a while. The press manufacturer's instructions should be followed for plate packing (if used), order of procedure, rollers to be checked, and pressure required. The following procedure can be used to check dampener-roller pressure settings:

1. Prepare the dampening system for operation. Check for dampness of the form roller. Let the dampener form roller run against the plate on the plate cylinder for a few minutes. Lift the form roller and stop the duplicator.

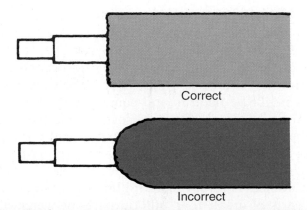

Correct

Incorrect

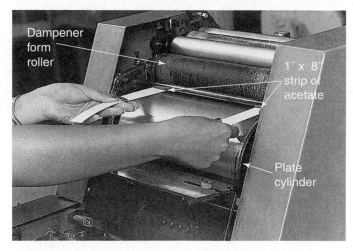

Figure 20-65. New dampener covers must be set for the proper pressure after they are installed on a press or duplicator. Thin strips of acetate can be used to check the pressure between the dampener form roller and the plate cylinder.

3. Drop the form roller to the on position.
4. With one hand holding each test strip, pull toward yourself with a slow, uniform tension. There should be a slight, even drag on both strips. If one strip pulls easier than the other or if there is too much or too little drag on both, adjust the roller on one end or both as the test procedure indicates.
5. After pressures seem satisfactory, drop the form roller to the plate and lift it up again. You should see a faint damp line across the entire width of the plate.

Fountain solutions

As discussed in Chapter 19, fountain solutions greatly affect ink performance and should be carefully set and maintained during a pressrun. Printing quality and press performance depend on the proper mixture of ingredients. As the fountain solution serves to dampen the rollers and plate, it is commonly referred to as the *dampening solution*.

Figure 20-63. When installing molleton dampener sleeves, the ends of the sleeves must be square. The extra string is cut off. (Graphic Arts Technical Foundation; Jomac, Inc.)

2. With the duplicator stopped, place two 1″ × 8″ (25 mm × 200 mm) strips of 0.005″ (0.13 mm)–thick acetate between the form roller and the plate. Place one strip near each end, as illustrated in **Figure 20-65.**

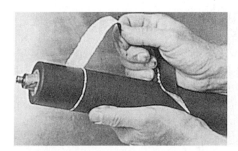

1. Remove old sleeve from rolls.

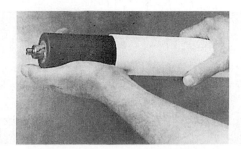

2. Slide seamless sleeve onto roller.

3. Install dampening sleeve and dampen completely.

Figure 20-64. Study the correct procedure for removing an old sleeve and installing a new seamless fiber sleeve. (3M Company)

Mixing

Water is the main ingredient of the fountain solution. When the duplicator is running, it is normal for water to become mixed with the ink to a slight degree. Running an excess amount of water, however, reduces the quality of printing and weakens the ink's color. The distinction between printing areas and nonprinting areas becomes blurred. An excessive amount of water can also lead to excessive emulsification—that is, the ink becomes saturated with water. The press operator must stop the press and change the ink. Not enough water or too much ink causes the plate to ink in the nonprinting areas. Too much ink can also cause characters to thicken and halftone dots to fill in. To help the water keep nonprinting areas free of ink, a small amount of concentrated acid is added to the fountain solution. The concentrated acid is added to the total volume of distilled water required, usually in a ratio of 1 or 2 parts of concentrate to 15 parts of water.

The importance of water

Ordinary tap water usually contains a great variety of chemical compounds, such as salts of calcium, magnesium, iron, and sodium, occurring in the form of chlorides, silicates, or carbonates. Some salts might be neutral, and some might be acid or alkaline. The ideal water for use in offset lithography is distilled water because it is neither acid nor alkaline. There is a numerical formula for expressing the hardness or softness of water. For example, if a water is classified as 70 parts per million (ppm), there are 70 parts of a salt in 1 million parts of water. The degrees of softness and hardness of water in the 48 contiguous states are illustrated in **Figure 20-66.**

The exact degree of acidity or alkalinity is expressed in terms of pH. The pH values are measured on a scale running from 0.0 (strong acids) to 14.0 (strong alkali). The halfway point (7.0) represents a neutral solution. See **Figure 20-67.** In scientific terms, the pH scale measures acidity as expressed by the number of hydrogen ions. The weight of hydrogen ions in a liter of solution for each pH is illustrated in **Figure 20-68.**

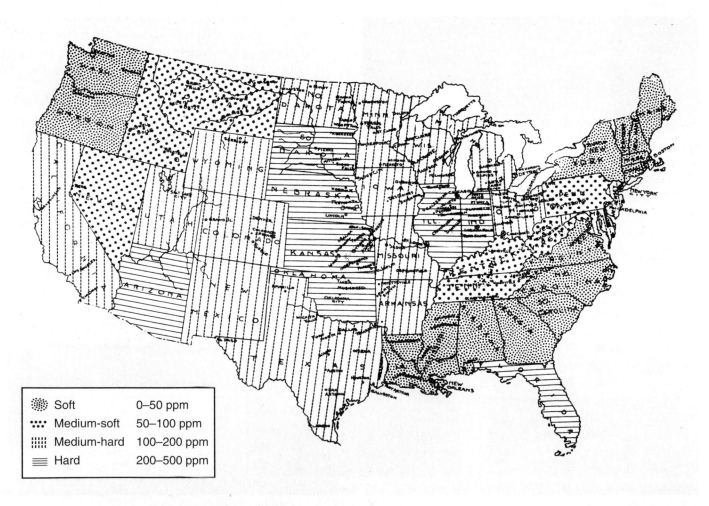

	Soft	0–50 ppm
	Medium-soft	50–100 ppm
	Medium-hard	100–200 ppm
	Hard	200–500 ppm

Figure 20-66. This map of the 48 contiguous states shows the degrees of water softness and hardness. Water quality is an important factor in offset lithography.

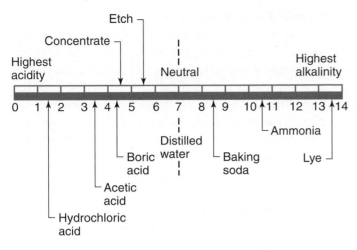

Figure 20-67. The pH scale measures acidity and runs from 0.0 for strong acids to 14.0 for strong alkalis. The halfway point represents a neutral solution. (A.B.Dick Co.)

Weight of Free Hydrogen Ions in a Liter of Solution in Grams		pH
1.0	(10^0)	0.0
0.1	(10^{-1})	1.0
0.01	(10^{-2})	2.0
0.001	(10^{-3})	3.0
0.0001	(10^{-4})	4.0
0.00001	(10^{-5})	5.0
0.000001	(10^{-6})	6.0
0.0000001	(10^{-7})	7.0
0.00000001	(10^{-8})	8.0
0.000000001	(10^{-9})	9.0
0.0000000001	(10^{-10})	10.0
0.00000000001	(10^{-11})	11.0
0.000000000001	(10^{-12})	12.0
0.0000000000001	(10^{-13})	13.0
0.00000000000001	(10^{-14})	14.0

Figure 20-68. This chart shows the weight of hydrogen ions in a liter of solution for each pH. (Micro Essential Laboratory, Inc.)

Clarifiers

Clarifiers are added to the dampening system to remove contaminants that can cause problems for press operators, using a recirculating or spray-bar fountain-solution system. Removing these contaminants enables the operator to increase press productivity, decrease press maintenance, and improve overall print quality. By using a clarifier, the life of the fountain solution is significantly extended, in turn minimizing waste-disposal costs, due to less frequent disposal and decreasing press downtime. Cleaner dampening rollers and fountain-solution trays result in decreased hickey defects and less image-area plate wear. Ink emulsification is also reduced

because clarifiers are constructed of ink (oil)–loving materials, resulting in reduced plate scumming and image tinting. The reduction in contamination leads to improved conductivity control of the fountain solution. Clarifiers reduce nozzle pluggage in spray dampening systems.

Alcohol solutions

On some duplicators and most offset presses, alcohol is used in the fountain solution. Alcohol is added to fountain solutions to reduce surface tension and increase viscosity. The use of alcohol in the fountain solution offers several advantages:

- Using alcohol eliminates the problem of too warm a solution during hot weather.
- Alcohol lowers the surface tension of the water, allowing a finer film of water to be fed to the plate.
- The use of alcohol causes faster evaporation of moisture from the offset plate and ink rollers, resulting in less ink emulsification and faster drying of printed sheets.

No more than 20%–25% alcohol should be added to the fountain solution. **Figure 20-69** shows that the use of more than 25% alcohol has little effect. Alcohol addition up to 20% achieves drastic reductions of surface tension, but adding more produces a minimal effect. It is therefore useless and

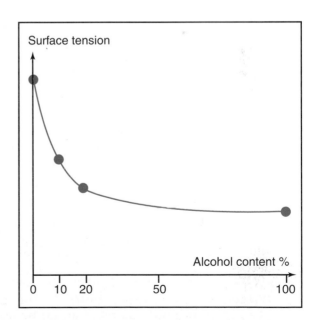

Figure 20-69. Adding alcohol to the dampening system makes the dampening film more uniform and allows a thinner application. The chart illustrates that, beyond a certain percentage, the addition of alcohol has no significant effect on the plate's surface tension. (Heidelberg, Inc.)

unnecessarily costly to add more than 20%–25% alcohol to the fountain solution. For the best results, follow the manufacturer's instructions when mixing a fountain solution containing alcohol.

Alcohol alternatives

With the ever-increasing concern for our environment, the printing and publishing industry is increasingly recognizing the benefits of running presses with alcohol-free solutions. The main environmental benefit of alcohol-free solutions is lower VOC emissions. Most alcohol replacements are used in lower concentrations and do not evaporate as easily as the alcohol. As a result, vapors are not released as easily or in as great amounts. In addition to the environmental benefits, alcohol-free solutions offer many technical advantages:

- **Truer, brighter colors.** Alcohol is a solvent that attacks the ink itself, dulling out the true color of the ink. In order to achieve acceptable color in operations using IPA, the press operator must carry a heavier ink film on the press rollers.

- **Improved dot quality.** By reducing the amount of ink and water carried to the sheet, a cleaner, sharper dot is produced. The dot also has less of a tendency to bleed or spread when alcohol is not dissolving the ink.

- **Cost savings.** In most cases, it is less expensive to use an alcohol replacement. Although IPA is less expensive than most replacements, only 2–3 oz. of replacement are used per gallon of fountain solution, as compared to 20–32 oz. of IPA.

- **Reduced fire risks.** Most alcohol replacements have a flash point near 140°F (60°C). This makes the product much safer to work with and eliminates many storage problems associated with a flammable liquid product.

- **No replenishment required.** Unlike IPA, replacements are mixed with the water and fountain solution at the time the tanks are filled and do not require replenishment.

Alcohol-free operations

Eliminating alcohol from the fountain solution does not require you to rebuild the offset presses. Some adjustments can be made on press, however, to ensure a smooth transition. To minimize disruption, a printer should work with one press at a time and perform the following operations:

- **Clean the press rollers thoroughly and regularly.** Use a good-quality, two-step water-miscible (mixable) wash. Glazed or gummed rollers do not carry a good film of ink and alcohol replacement.

- **Check form-roller stripes.** Set stripes on the low side of the recommended settings. If the stripes are too wide, the alcohol replacement has a tendency to build up in the roller nips, rather than spreading evenly to the plate. The buildup can actually be viewed as globs of residue in the nip. Stripes must be uniform from side to side. Inaccurate settings cause water-control problems.

- **Check roller durometers.** Ink forms should be in the 24 to 26 range, and the water forms should be in the 20 to 22 range. Rollers climbing into the high 20s and low 30s hinder you from achieving zero alcohol. A softer roller carries ink and water more readily than a hard roller does and, therefore, does a more effective job of distributing the less viscous alcohol replacement. Hard rollers might require you to still use 5%–8% alcohol until the rollers are upgraded during routine press maintenance.

- **Adjust metering roll nips, if necessary.** An alcohol replacement at 2%–3% of solution does not flow the same as IPA mixed at 15%–20% of solution. In some cases, the nips might have to be opened to allow better water flow, and in other cases, the nips might have to be squeezed down to help control streaking.

- **Be aware that dampener speeds will probably increase.** An increase in speed does not mean you are using more water. Alcohol replacements are not as viscous as IPA and, therefore, require faster roller speeds to transfer the product. An increase of 10 to 12 points on the speed dial is not uncommon.

- **Check recirculators.** Replace worn filter elements with good-quality, clean elements; tighten the hose connection; and replace missing screws on filter-element canisters. Alcohol replacements use a variety of surfactants (surface-active agents) to lower the surface tension of the fountain solution, and these additives have a tendency to foam more than an alcohol mixture does.

- **Increase the temperature in the recirculators to 55°F–60°F.** Replacements do not evaporate the way IPA does and, therefore, do not require as much chilling. By raising the temperature, you also help reduce foaming.

- **Mix fountain solution and replacement carefully.** Alcohol replacements lower the conductivity readings of a fountain-solution mix, but not as dramatically as IPA does.

- **Reduce the amount of ink fed to the roller train.** Less ink flow is required with the alcohol replacement than is normally run with alcohol. If ink flow is not reduced, the water settings will be abnormally high, and the result will be plugged screens and reverses.

- **Advise your ink and plate suppliers.** Tell them you are operating alcohol free, in case they need to make changes in the products they regularly provide. In addition, do not hesitate to ask for information or help either from your suppliers or directly from chemical companies.

Dampening with just water

Conventional lithographic inks require dampening solution to be used to keep the nonimage areas of the plate free of ink. The chemistry added to water to create dampening solution, however, can emit VOCs into the air and dry out ink and dampening rollers. In addition, the chemistry can lift calcium from press sheets onto the blanket and plate, as well as retard ink drying. As a result, Midwest Ink Company, Flint Group, Braden Sutphin, and Kohl & Madden are among the ink companies with inks formulated to work with tap water in place of dampening solution.

The Delivery Unit

The *delivery unit* on most duplicators and presses consists of a chain delivery, a receding delivery table, joggers, and some type of antisetoff-spray attachment. On some duplicators, the delivery unit consists of a simple ejector mechanism, in which the printed sheets of paper are forced into a paper-receiver tray. The delivery unit transfers the printed sheets from the final impression cylinder to the *delivery pile*. This unit uses a *delivery cylinder* to transfer the sheets. The delivery cylinder carries the printed sheet from the impression cylinder to the delivery grippers attached to the *delivery chains*. This cylinder is usually covered with *skeleton wheels* (adjustable disks holding the sheet as it travels). The delivery cylinder is also known as the *skeleton cylinder*.

Chain delivery

Most duplicators and all large presses are equipped with *delivery grippers* consisting of a series of small metal fingers attached to a bar extended between two continuous delivery chains. See **Figure 20-70**. The delivery chains are belts or chains used to transfer the printed sheet from the impression cylinder to the delivery pile.

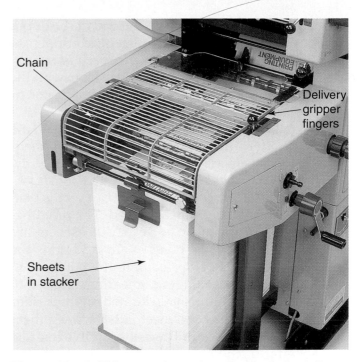

Figure 20-70. This press is equipped with chain delivery and a receding stacker. Small metal gripper fingers are attached to a bar extended between two continuous chains. (Ryobi Xpedx Impact Group)

A pair of sprockets guides and drives the delivery chains. The chains contain segments and special devices for preventing the sheet from rubbing, whipping, or waving during the delivery. Depending on the speed of the press and the distance between the delivery platform and the impression cylinder, there might be two or more sets of these grippers. The grippers are spaced at regular intervals along the chains so one set of grippers is receiving a sheet while another set is delivering the preceding sheet.

Spring pressure usually holds the grippers closed. As the chains carry the grippers toward the impression cylinder, they pass over a cam that forces the grippers open long enough to receive the sheet. The

delivery unit: a system on offset presses and duplicators that delivers the printed sheets.

delivery pile: a platform or tray on which the printed sheets are stacked.

delivery cylinder: a cylinder in the delivery unit of a press that transfers the printed sheets from the impression cylinder to the delivery pile. This cylinder is usually covered with skeleton wheels.

delivery chain: a belt or chain the delivery system of a press uses to transfer the printed sheet from the impression cylinder to the delivery pile.

skeleton wheel: an adjustable disk on the delivery cylinder that holds the sheet as it travels. This disk is a paper-guide wheel.

delivery gripper: a small metal finger attached to a bar extended between two continuous delivery chains.

grippers then carry the sheet to the end of the duplicator or press, where a trip cam forces the grippers to open and release the sheet to the *delivery platform*. The sheet comes to the delivery pile faceup, with the gripper edge toward the front of the duplicator or press.

On most duplicators and larger presses, the delivery platform is constructed to lower automatically as the sheets are delivered. This is part of the *receding delivery table*, called the *receding stacker*. See **Figure 20-71**. The press operator can set the platform to operate at any suitable speed. The receding-stacker mechanism must be set so the sheets are jogged as perfectly as possible. In addition, the printed sheets must be floated onto the pile in such a way as to prevent smudging, smearing, and setoff. The adjustable joggers, usually located on three sides of the sheet, are set so the sheet falls between them when it drops downward. The delivery table can also be referred to as the *delivery pile*.

Most offset presses and duplicators use what are known as *static eliminators* to reduce static electricity. These might be located near the delivery area or plate cylinder. See **Figure 20-72**.

Ejector delivery

On duplicators using an *ejector delivery system*, also referred to as a *chute delivery system*, a simple ejector mechanism is used to deliver the printed sheets to a tray. After impression takes place, a cam on the impression cylinder causes the cylinder grippers to open and release the sheet. Ejector fingers then rise to lift the edge of the sheet away from the cylinder and force it out over a set of stripper fingers.

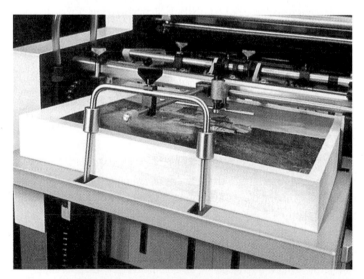

Figure 20-71. The press delivery platform is constructed to lower automatically as the printed sheets are delivered. (Omnitrade Industrial/Omni Adast)

Figure 20-72. Most offset presses and some duplicators are equipped with static eliminators (arrow). Static eliminators make it possible to overcome paper-feeding and delivery problems caused by static electricity buildup within the press. (Pederson Group)

The *stripper fingers* separate the sheet from the impression cylinder and direct it under two ejector rollers that force the sheet into the paper-receiver tray. See **Figure 20-73**.

Paper guides and a paper retainer in the receiving tray help direct the sheets into the tray. On some duplicators, the left paper guide does not move. The right guide moves back and forth with a jogging action while the duplicator is operating. The front paper guide can be adjusted for the depth of paper size being run.

On some presses, the delivery cylinder is coated with a frictionless substance and a frictionless cloth. The cloth is allowed to slide freely over the surface of the cylinder. This ensures the wet ink is not smudged. Some delivery units use a vacuum and rollers to pull the sheet away from the skeleton wheels. The ink is not smeared because it does not contact the wheels. The vacuum pulls the sheet from one side and cannot be used on systems that simultaneously print both sides of the sheet.

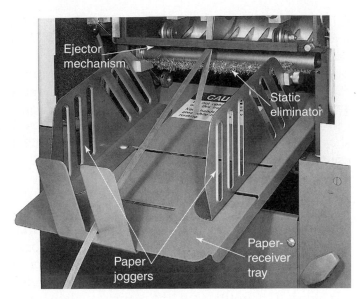

Figure 20-73. Some duplicators are equipped with ejector paper-receiver trays and stripper fingers that separate the printed sheets from the impression cylinder. Stripper fingers direct the sheet under two ejector rollers that force the sheet into the paper-receiver tray. (Multigraphics)

Antisetoff spray

The delivery system on some presses uses an antisetoff sprayer. *Antisetoff spray* is a powder made from fine starch particles that is sprayed on the surface of the printed sheets. The powder prevents setoff, or the transfer of wet ink from one sheet to another. Many printers prefer not to use antisetoff sprays, so most ink manufacturers incorporate an antisetoff compound into the ink.

Direct Imaging Presses

A *direct imaging press* applies the image to plates after they have been mounted onto the plate cylinder. A laser images the plates directly from electronic files, using technology similar to the CTP technology used with platesetters. See **Figure 20-74.** The plates are automatically imaged in register with one another because they are already on the plate cylinder of the press. Each plate is imaged with its own laser. Direct imaging technology is also referred to as *computer-to-press (CTPr)*.

Prepress to Press Workflow

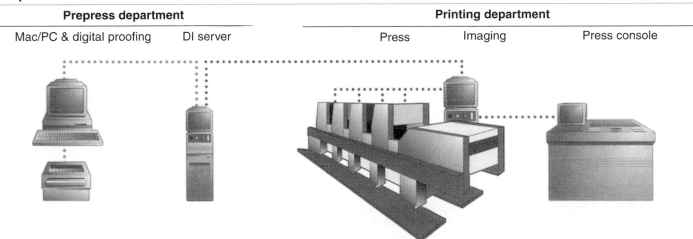

Figure 20-74. Direct imaging press systems eliminate film, film processing, and photographic-plate exposure and processing. (Omnitrade Industrial/Omni Adast)

delivery platform: a platform constructed to lower automatically as the sheets are delivered.

receding delivery table: a delivery table that automatically adjusts the platform height as the sheets are delivered.

ejector delivery system: an offset-duplicator delivery system in which a simple ejector mechanism is used to deliver the printed sheets to a tray.

stripper finger: a device used in an ejector delivery system to separate the sheet from the impression cylinder and direct it under two ejector rollers that force the sheet into the paper-receiver tray.

antisetoff spray: a powder made from fine starch particles sprayed on the surface of printed sheets to prevent setoff.

direct imaging press: a press that uses a laser to image printing plates directly from electronic files.

computer-to-press (CTPr): the technology of laser imaging a plate mounted on a press.

A direct imaging system uses a workstation in the prepress department called a *direct imaging server*. The server captures the post-RIP bitmap pages from the RIP and stores them for plate exposure. The imaging components include a customized computer system to buffer and control the imaging process via an IR-based laser that images the plate material. See **Figure 20-75.** After the plates are imaged, an automatic cleaning system removes the loosened silicon.

The digital files of the images exposed onto the plates are scanned to determine how much ink various portions of each plate require, and this information is sent to each ink fountain for automatic ink-key adjustment. The sheets are then printed using waterless printing. Several digital color-proofing technologies that can include a wide range of devices, such as laser and ink-jet printers, support most direct imaging systems. When used within a color-management system, the proofs can be excellent predictors of the final job because the plates are exposed with the same digital data that exposed the proofs.

Typically, plates are good for 20,000 or more impressions. Plate life is dependent on the paper type, blanket composition, amount of antisetoff powder used during previous runs, bearer settings, and other press variables. The Ryobi 3404DI and the Heidelberg Quickmaster DI-46-4 Pro can print the four process colors onto one side of a maximum 13.39" × 18.11" press sheet with one pass. Both sheetfed presses use a common impression cylinder, four plate-and-blanket units, and no dampening system. See **Figure 20-76.** The four blue circles represent the plate cylinders, and the orange devices above them are the lasers. The black circles are the blankets, and the large gray

impression cylinder grips the press sheet and moves it against each blanket cylinder, before releasing it to the delivery unit.

Direct imaging offset presses are highly automated. At the touch screen on the console, the operator selects from the jobs in the queue and indicates the desired quantity, as well as the number of test sheets. Four blank plates are automatically spooled onto the plate cylinders and imaged and cleaned of excessive silicone while the ink keys are set—all in less than 10 minutes. The operator can then read the final test sheet with a densitometer and use these readings to automate any ink-key adjustments that might be needed, before starting the pressrun. Some direct imaging presses do not require the operator to input specs of the job. Instead, the press can receive the desired quantity and the paper's caliper and grain direction from job-ticket information.

This press design features automatic plate loading. Polyester plates can stretch during the run, thereby impairing registration among colors. To prevent stretching after imaging, direct imaging presses prestretch the plate with the tension the feeder and take-up spools inside the plate cylinder exert. The plate consists of three layers—a polyester base, a titanium layer in the middle, and a silicon layer on top. During exposure, the laser heats the titanium layer, causing the silicone layer to separate from it. After imaging, a cloth and vacuum combine to remove the top two layers from the polyester base in the image areas.

The application of ink to the substrate is accomplished as a conventional common impression–cylinder offset press. The sheet receives four colors on one side with a single pass. As the printed sheet moves into the delivery unit, it can receive IR heat to accelerate ink drying.

Some digital offset lithographic presses are also capable of VDP, which means the photoimaging (plate) cylinder can be reimaged between impressions. The result is that thousands of printed pieces can be printed with different combinations of text and color photographs on each one. One of the many applications of VDP is direct-mail promotion, in which each piece is tailored to its recipient. Colleges are sending promotional mailings to prospective students reflecting each student's interests. For example, a student who has indicated an interest in music sees a color photograph of the university's band, while a student interested in biology sees, instead, a photograph of students in a science lab. The text also reflects each student's goals. The key to VDP is the ability to reimage the plates after each

Figure 20-75. Looking down onto this direct imaging press reveals the image on the plate, as well as the array of lasers that generated the image. (Presstek, Inc.)

A Direct Imaging Press

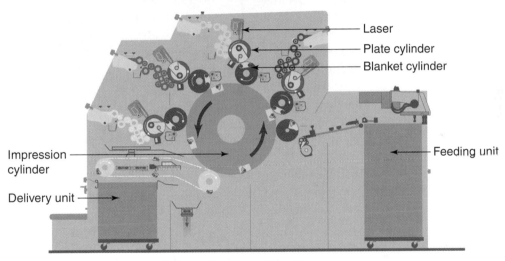

Laser
Plate cylinder
Blanket cylinder
Impression cylinder
Delivery unit
Feeding unit

A Cross Section of the Press

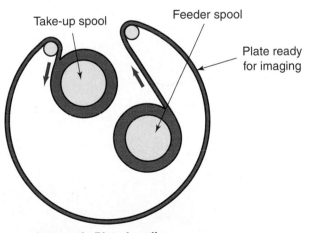

Take-up spool
Feeder spool
Plate ready for imaging

Automatic Plate Loading

Figure 20-76. This direct imaging press prints four colors in a single pass. Note the console on the right. A cross section of a direct imaging press reveals a common impression cylinder. One method of automatic plate loading is to place both the feeder and take-up spools within the plate cylinder. (Heidelberg, Inc.; Presstek, Inc.)

revolution. The cleaning station removes the just-printed image and prepares the "plate" cylinder for the next imaging that will occur as the image moves under the laser.

One model of a variable data press is a webfed perfector-press design. See **Figure 20-77.** The two printing units allow this press to print as many as seven colors to both sides of the web in a single pass. The large green cylinder is the photoimaging cylinder, which functions as a plate cylinder, without having an actual plate. See **Figure 20-78.** As the cylinder moves under the charging unit, the entire surface receives a negative electrical charge, and then the laser applies a positive electrical charge only to the image areas. As the cylinder moves forward, the negatively charged ink is attracted to the image areas and repelled by the nonimage areas. The inked image covers only one-half of the cylinder because the photoimaging cylinder is twice as large as the blanket cylinder. As the cylinder moves forward, the other half is imaged and inked with a second ink.

Both inks are transferred to the more positively charged blanket cylinder. Unlike in conventional printing, the ink films do not split. Nearly all the ink transfers to the blanket. The impression cylinder has an even higher charge, which pulls the ink from the blanket cylinder to the substrate.

As the photoimaging cylinder continues its rotation, any traces of ink are scraped off and recycled to their respective ink fountains, and the imaging

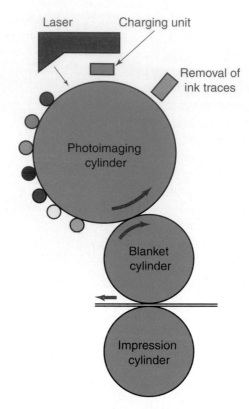

Figure 20-78. The printing cycle of the HP Indigo 3200 allows VDP. The photoimaging cylinder is electrically charged prior to the laser reversing the charge in the image areas. Electrically charged ink is attracted to the image areas and then attracted to the charged blanket cylinder.

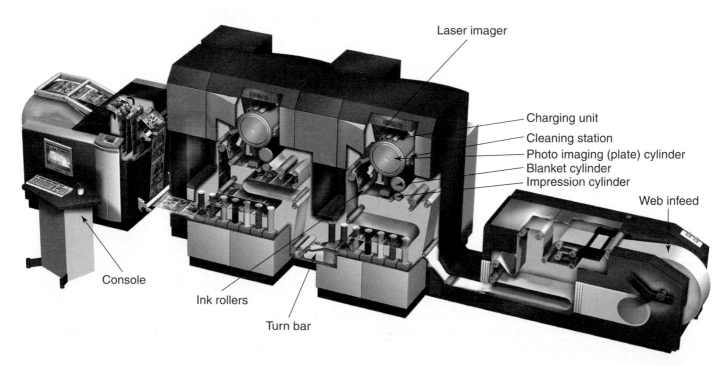

Figure 20-77. The turn bar between the two printing units allows this web press to print up to seven colors on both sides of the web. (HP/Indigo)

process is repeated for the next two ink colors. After the third and fourth inks are applied to the blanket, the impression cylinder pushes the substrate in contact with the blanket cylinder, and all four colors are transferred to the substrate. A complete revolution of the photoimaging cylinder takes less than a second, so a four-color job takes less than two seconds to image and print on one side.

This press can apply as many as seven colors to both sides of a ribbon of paper in a single pass because the web moves over turn bars between the two print units. The printed web can then be cut into sheets or rewound for off-press finishing. The seven ink rollers allow printing the four process colors, as well as three spot colors, or printing with six process colors (CMYK with orange and violet) to achieve a larger color gamut. Press speed can reach 8000 8 1/2″ × 11″ four-color, two-sided sheets an hour.

A sheetfed offset press with VDP capabilities is the Kodak NexPress 2100® digital production color press. See **Figure 20-79.** This press can print a 13.8″ × 18.5″ press sheet, uses dry toner, and features five in-line printing units that can apply either five colors or four colors and a clear toner. The Kodak NexPress 2100 digital production color press can print either one- or two-sided jobs. A sheet requiring two-sided printing is turned over and sent through the printing units a second time.

Printed sheets are passed through a fuser that melts the toner particles and fuses them to the substrate. This press has three paper feeders, so it can print jobs consisting of more than one type of substrate. In addition, the use of a blanket allows it to print on a wide variety of paper surfaces, as well as on some plastics.

Figure 20-79. Both variable and static data printing with five colors on both sides of a 13.8″ × 18.5″ sheet are possible with this sheetfed press. (Kodak NexPress)

The imaging (plate) cylinders are imaged with a laser that identifies image and nonimage areas with different electrostatic charges. The toner is attracted electrostatically to the image areas only and transferred electrostatically to the blanket cylinder. Image transfer to the substrate is achieved by applying a charge to the impression cylinder.

Digital presses have several advantages. They can have shorter makeready times than conventional presses, waste less paper, and are more economical for short-run jobs. The equipment is expensive to purchase, however, and the press-sheet sizes are smaller than are available with conventional presses. Conventional presses are capable of running at faster speeds, as measured in impressions per hour (iph). Of course, if VDP is needed, digital presses are the only option.

Auxiliary Press Functions

In addition to printing, many offset duplicators and presses can be fitted to perform additional operations. Numbering, perforating, slitting, scoring, pasting, folding, tipping, and trimming attachments can be added to the duplicator or press. Attachments for auxiliary press functions might consist of circular knives or disks operating against a mating knife disk or spacers. These operations should never be performed against the press blanket unless special precautions are taken.

Summary

Offset presses are classified by size and function. Duplicator-size presses typically print sheets 12″ × 18″ or smaller. Presses that print sheets larger than 12″ × 18″ are referred to as *offset presses*. These large-format presses are capable of producing a full range of large printed materials in one or more colors. In addition, duplicators and presses are classified as sheetfed, webfed, multicolor, or perfecting.

Duplicators and presses are designed with either two or three main cylinders. All duplicators and presses have six main units. These units are the feeder, register, printing, inking, dampening, and delivery units.

Offset duplicator and press systems deliver ink and dampening solution to the plate in the proper metered quantity, usually through the use of computerized operating systems. A conventional dampening system wets the plate independently of the inking rollers. A combined or integrated dampening system combines the dampening solution with the ink to wet the plate.

Direct imaging uses a laser to image plates already mounted on the press. VDP allows the imaging cylinder to be reimaged between impressions, with the result that no two press sheets need to be exactly the same. In addition to their primary function of printing, many offset duplicators and presses can be equipped to perform operations such as numbering, perforating, slitting, scoring, pasting, folding, tipping, and trimming.

Review Questions

Please do not write in this book. Write your answers on a separate sheet of paper.

1. Small offset presses up to 11″ × 17″ are usually referred to as _____.

2. When the sheets of paper overlap as they travel down the feedboard of a sheetfed press, it is called _____.

3. Webfed offset presses feed from a(n) _____ of paper.

4. Offset presses that can print more than one color at the same time are called _____ presses.

5. Offset presses that can print on both sides of the sheet of paper at the same time are called _____ presses.

6. Identify the function of a waterless offset press.

7. What three types of cylinders does a three main cylinder offset press have?

8. Describe a two main cylinder offset press.

9. Summarize the controls of an offset press and an offset duplicator.

10. _____ feeding means the ribbon or individual sheets of paper are fed into the press constantly.

11. What is a roll-to-sheet feeding system?

12. The safety device that allows only one sheet of paper at a time to enter the press is called the _____.

13. Make a drawing of the plate, blanket, and impression cylinders, as well as the form rollers, of the ink and dampening systems. Label these components and add arrows showing the direction of rotation.

14. Squaring and aligning the sheets of paper before they are loaded into the feeder unit of the press is called _____.

15. What purpose do piling bars serve?

16. _____ hold the edge of the top sheet in the stack down as the front blowers separate the sheet from the stack.

17. As the blowers separate the sheets of paper, a set of _____ drop down and lift the top sheet to the edge of the feedboard.

18. _____ are metal tabs or plates that stop the sheet of paper and hold it on the feedboard while the side guide moves it into position.

19. Small metal _____ attached to the impression cylinder hold the sheet of paper as it is printed.

20. The printing unit on an offset press consists of all the following, *except* the _____ cylinder.
    A. plate
    B. chain
    C. blanket
    D. impression

21. The _____ cylinder holds the printing plate and its image.

22. Why are some press cylinders undercut?

23. The _____ cylinder holds the rubber mat that offsets the image from the plate to the substrate.

24. The _____ is the back side of the blanket.

25. A(n) _____ offset blanket has the ability to squeeze and return to its original shape.

26. What are some of the benefits of using underlay blankets?

27. How should press blankets be stored?

28. The _____ cylinder carries the substrate through the printing unit and forces it against the inked blanket.

29. Explain the function of the ink-fountain keys.

30. The length of time the ductor roller comes in contact with the ink-fountain roller is referred to as _____.

31. What purpose do the distributing rollers serve in the ink train?

32. The _____ of an offset press or a duplicator moistens the nonimage areas of the plate so ink does not adhere to them.

33. _____ systems use a metering roller to move the fountain solution to a transfer roller.

34. In an inker-feed system, water and ink are fed to the plate from the same set of _____ rollers.

35. Rollers in a conventional dampening system are covered with _____.

36. What is the main ingredient in a dampening solution?

37. How is water hardness or softness measured or expressed?

38. The _____ value represents the alkalinity or acidity of the fountain solution.

39. _____ are added to the dampening system to remove contaminants that can cause problems for press operators using a recirculating or spray-bar fountain-solution system.

40. On some offset duplicators, the _____ unit consists of a simple ejector mechanism that delivers printed sheets to a tray.

41. On large offset presses, the delivery gripper fingers are part of the _____ delivery mechanism.

42. On large offset presses, the receding _____ is part of the delivery platform.

43. Plates on _____ presses are imaged after they have been loaded onto the press.

44. Paraphrase the capabilities of a direct imaging press.

45. Plates can be reimaged after each impression on a(n) _____ press.

Skill-Building Activities

1. Ask your instructor for a press-operating manual for each press and duplicator in the lab. Familiarize yourself with the basic operating controls and systems of each.

2. Draw a schematic diagram of the six operating systems of each press and duplicator in the lab. Include the following:
   A. Feeder unit.
   B. Register board.
   C. Printing unit.
   D. Inking unit.
   E. Dampening unit.
   F. Delivery unit.

3. With your instructor's assistance, perform the following:
   A. Install dampener covers on an offset press and a duplicator.
   B. Make the necessary dampening-system pressure checks and adjustments.
   C. Mix fountain solution to specs your instructor gives. Test the solution for the correct pH.
   D. Install and remove a blanket on one of the offset presses or duplicators in the lab.
   E. Install and remove a plate on one of the offset presses or duplicators in the lab.
   F. Perform all the necessary pressure checks and adjustments on an offset press or duplicator in the lab.
   G. Install the proper-thickness packing on the plate and blanket cylinders for a given job. Use the micrometer for determining proper packing thicknesses.
   H. Clean and check the vacuum blower pump jars. Refill with nondetergent SAE 10 weight oil.

4. Write a report on the impact of direct imaging press technology on the printing and advertising industries. Be sure to give examples of how VDP can create new marketing strategies.

Control Center

The newest generation of commercial presses is so automated and computerized that these presses can be run from the kind of console shown here. This console controls a newspaper press. The monitor the operator is watching can indicate the press speed, ink and dampening-solution application levels in each printing unit, and many other pieces of data.

Of course, data alone is of no value unless the operator is knowledgeable enough to make sense of it, interpret it, and act wisely. This is the human component in all technologies. Although airline pilots and weather forecasters require plenty of data, it is their education and training that make the data useful. This chapter explains the basic operations of lithographic presses. The lessons learned here are essential in preparing for a career in any pressroom because the fundamentals of lithography apply to all presses.

(Goss International Corporation)

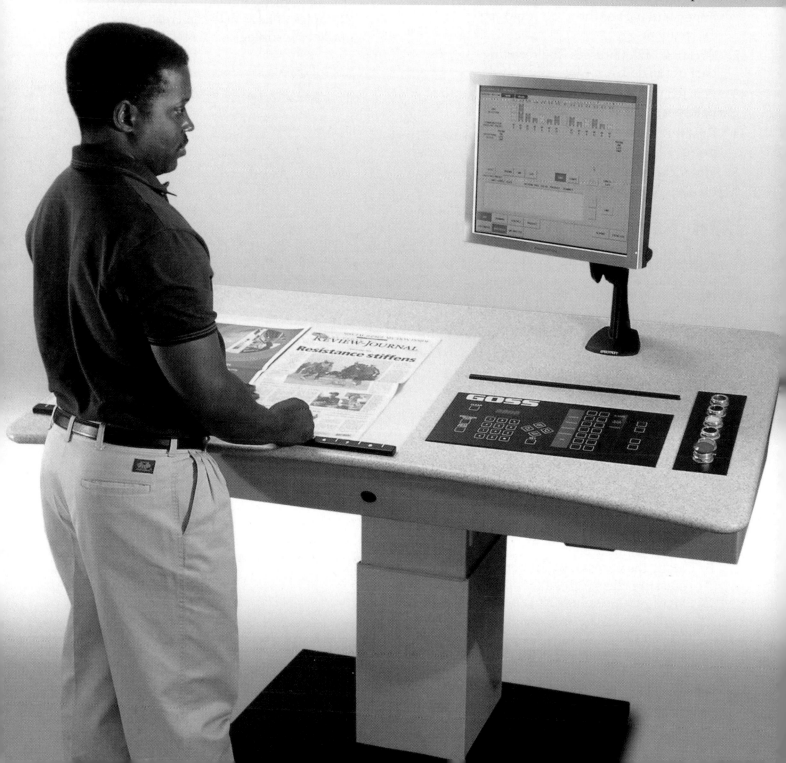

Chapter 21
Offset-Press Operation

Key Term

test plate

Learning Objectives

When you have completed the reading and assigned activities related to this chapter, you will be able to do the following:

- Prepare the feeder unit and register board of an offset duplicator, in preparation for running a job.
- Set up the printing, inking, dampening, and delivery units of an offset duplicator.
- Successfully complete jobs on an offset duplicator and a small offset press.
- Clean and secure an offset duplicator and a small offset press at the end of a job or the working day.
- Operate an offset duplicator or a small press while following safe work procedures.

The previous chapter explained the six main operating systems of offset duplicators and small- to medium-size offset presses. Although press-operating procedures vary from one press to another, they are similar in the fundamental principles. The following material provides an understanding of the sequence of operations involved in setting up and running a job on a duplicator.

Keep in mind that press instructors are the experts in this area. There is no substitute for their qualified professional guidance, especially regarding procedures and safety precautions. Instruction manuals should be available for the particular duplicators and presses in the lab. The first step is to become familiar with the manual for the duplicator or press you are using. An instructor should supervise all press adjustments. It is better to ask questions first, rather than to make adjustments that could result in personal injury and damage to the press.

Caution

Never operate a press or duplicator until you have been instructed in its safe operation. You should always obtain the instructor's permission before operating a press. Unauthorized personnel should not be allowed around a running press.

The Preliminary Inspection

To complete a preliminary inspection, examine the press to make sure all safety devices and operating components are in place. See **Figure 21-1**. Set all controls in the off position. Remove any loose articles from the press.

Install any rollers and fountains that might have been removed earlier. If necessary, remove any protective gum coating from cylinders or plates. Adjust and tighten the blanket if it has been loosened to allow it to rest.

Wipe away any lint or paper dust from the feeder and register board. In addition, wipe off any dust and dirt from the rollers, cylinders, and blanket. You can use a cloth dampened in solvent for this purpose.

Turn the handwheel on the press two or three revolutions by hand. Check to see that nothing interferes with the operation of the press. If all is clear, turn on the power. Set the speed selector at a slow speed. Check to see that all parts are functioning properly.

Caution

Never adjust the speed selector while the press is stopped.

Hinged metal
safety guards

Figure 21-1. No job should be printed until the press is examined to ensure that guards and other safety devices are in place. (A.B.Dick Co.)

Pressure checks must be made before the pressrun. The proper sequence of checks is given in the operator's manual. General instructions for doing these checks are found in Chapter 20. You should use either the gummed plate for the job or a *test plate* of the same thickness to do the pressure checks. Once all press checks have been made, determine the specs for the job you are running using the information on what is called the *job ticket*, or docket. These specs should include the following:

- The correct ink and color.
- Adequate fountain solution.
- The correct paper stock, plus makeready and waste sheets.
- Printing plates on hand.
- Washup solvent and blanket wash.
- Special instructions.

If you are in doubt about any part of the job, consult your instructor before proceeding. Do not make any assumptions about what the customer is asking for on the job ticket. Clarifying the instructions takes only a moment, whereas running the entire job over to correct mistakes is costly and time-consuming.

Makeready Activity	Why and How
Oil the press or duplicator according to the manufacturer's recommendations.	Properly lubricated mechanisms function efficiently and dependably. Mechanisms that are not lubricated correctly cause frequent problems and shortened service life.
Clean the press of dirt, dried ink, grease, and excess oil.	Cleaning the press in this manner helps to guard against paper spoilage and improves the machine's performance.
Check pressure settings of all rollers and cylinders.	Pressure requirements and checking procedures are described in your press or duplicator operating manual.
Examine the blanket for defects.	Repair or replace the blanket as required. Procedures for removing glaze and correcting smashes are in the operating manual.
Examine the inking rollers for glaze.	Glazed rollers will not transfer a uniform film of ink to the offset plate. If glaze has developed, remove it with one of the commercial deglazing compounds available for this purpose. Directions for use are provided with the deglazing compound. After deglazing, roller surfaces should exhibit the velvety, nonsmooth appearance that is required for efficient ink transfer.
Examine dampener roller covers and change them if required.	Replacements for molleton and fiber covers are available for most of the common-size dampening rollers. Complete installation instructions are usually supplied by the manufacturer of the replacement covers.
Check the pH of the fountain solution.	Improperly maintained fountain solution greatly affects press performance and printing quality.
Mix or otherwise prepare the ink that is to be used for the immediate job.	Follow manufacturer guidelines for preparing and using ink.
Examine the image and nonimage areas of the plate to be printed.	Repair or replace the plate if defects are found.

Figure 21-2. The activities listed here should be done before the press or duplicator is made ready for printing.

Figure 21-3. Proper press lubrication reduces wear on all moving parts and lengthens press life. Study the manufacturer's lubrication chart to locate all points of lubrication.

Makeready refers to the procedures preparing the press to print a particular job. The term *makeready* covers all the activities the press operator performs between beginning the job and actually running the job. Use the checklist in **Figure 21-2** when preparing the press for a print run.

Press Lubrication

Correct press lubrication reduces wear on all moving parts and lengthens press life. Lack of lubrication, use of inferior lubricants, or carelessness in the use of lubricants shortens the productive life of the press. See **Figure 21-3**. Study the manufacturer's lubrication chart to locate each oil hole, grease fitting, and point of lubrication. These locations on the press should be marked with red paint for easy identification.

test plate: a printing plate used for performing pressure checks before a pressrun.

Figure 21-4. Always begin your lubrication at a certain point on the press and work your way back to the same point.

Always begin your lubrication at a certain point on the press and work your way back to the same point. Use a good nondetergent, lightweight oil—Society of Automotive Engineers (SAE) No. 20, for example. Wipe off excess oil with a clean cloth.

Lubricate the feeder and delivery drive chains once a week. Use gear grease compound on all gears. Use penetrating oil where applicable. Motors should be oiled sparingly during the weekly lubrication. Those with grease fittings require grease at least twice yearly. Follow the manufacturer's recommendations when lubricating motors. See **Figure 21-4.**

Check the oil level in the vacuum-blower pump jars weekly. SAE No. 10–weight oil is recommended for most pumps. Clean the air-inlet holes and pump filters.

Paper and Ink

Verify the paper supplied for the job. Make sure the grade, size, and quantity are correct. It is assumed the paper conditioning, so far as moisture content is concerned, has been taken care of, within the limitations of the lab or shop. Paper that has been in an unheated warehouse during winter months should be in the press-operating area long enough before the pressrun for the entire pile to reach room temperature. The minimum amount of time for this purpose is 24 hours.

Make sure the press sheet's grain direction is appropriate to the job. Lightweight sheets are usually printed with the grain parallel to the direction of travel through the press to add stiffness to the sheet and avoid buckling. Cover stock and other heavyweight sheets are often run with the grain perpendicular to the direction of travel to reduce the sheet's stiffness and help the sheet to bend around the

impression cylinder. Press sheets run with this grain orientation can absorb enough dampening solution to expand head to tail because paper is less dimensionally stable across the grain. The most important consideration, however, is that the grain direction of the press sheet be appropriate for the imposition of the job and the client's specification for the final job. For example, it is important that business cards are delivered grain long.

Obtain the required ink for the job. A job might require a Pantone-numbered ink or a special color that must be mixed. If color mixing is necessary, mix the proportions on a piece of glass or an ink palette. An ink knife is used for this purpose. See **Figure 21-5.** If ink driers or other modifiers are required, add them at this time. Never mix inks in the press ink fountain. Refer to Chapter 19 for a review of lithographic-ink properties and manufacture.

The Starting Procedure

A standard procedure for starting the press should always be followed. In this way, a minimum of time is consumed in setting up the press. A standard procedure results in a uniform quality of work. The following is the general sequence of steps in setting up and running a job on an offset duplicator.

Preparing the Inking Unit

The ink rollers should be cleaned of all lint and dust before filling the ink fountain. If the duplicator has been standing idle for several days, look over the rollers carefully for accumulated dust. Clean the rollers with blanket and roller wash.

Remove the fountain and clean it thoroughly with solvent. Clean the fountain roller with blanket

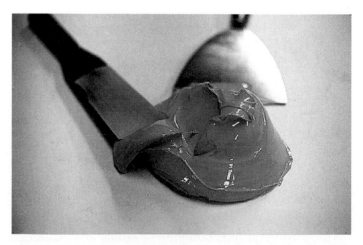

Figure 21-5. When mixing ink, use the proper tools and begin with the minimal amount, so as to minimize waste.

and roller wash. Replace the fountain and turn the duplicator by its handwheel until the ink ductor roller is out of contact with the ink fountain roller.

Caution

Most solvents are flammable and must not be used near an open flame. Make sure solvents are used in well-ventilated areas. Do not splash solvent in your face or breathe fumes for an extended time. Dispose of solvent-covered rags or paper in the proper container.

Fill the ink fountain by applying small amounts of ink with an ink knife against the fountain roller. Before removing ink from the can with an ink knife, skim any hardened crust from the top. See **Figure 21-6.** The ink fountain should be at least half full.

This fountain is equipped with a number of adjusting keys, or screws. See **Figure 21-7.** Turning these keys inward (clockwise) decreases the flow of ink, and turning the keys outward (counterclockwise) increases the flow of ink. While turning the ink fountain-roller control knob, adjust the fountain keys, starting at the center of the fountain. Establish an even flow or pickup line between the ductor roller and the fountain roller across the width of the fountain.

Turn the duplicator on and set the ink-feed volume control to the third or fourth notch. Hold the ink fountain-roller automatic-control lever in the down position. Let the duplicator run until all ink rollers are properly coated with a thin film of ink. Make final adjustments of the fountain screws to establish the desired flow of ink.

Note

If the revolving ink rollers sound similar to "eggs being fried," there is too much ink on the rollers. Turn the press off and remove some ink from the rollers with a clean cloth and a slight amount of solvent. Restart the press and recheck the ink. Push up on the automatic-control lever to release and turn the press off. The ink unit is now ready for use.

Preparing the Dampening Unit

The dampener fountain and fountain roller should be clean and free of dirt. Fill the fountain bottle with the proper mixture of fountain solution.

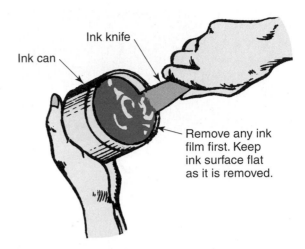

Figure 21-6. Ink should be removed from the ink can with an ink knife. Skim any hardened crust from the top before removing ink.

Figure 21-7. The flow of ink on offset duplicators and presses is controlled by adjusting the fountain keys, or screws. (Heidelberg, Inc.)

Hold the bottle with the spout down over a sink, to be sure it does not leak. Bring it over the side of the press, but not over the ink rollers, and insert it into the holder. See **Figure 21-8.** If there is a night latch for the dampener roller, turn it to the off position to drop the rollers into operating position. The dampener form roller should remain off and should not contact the plate.

Figure 21-8. Make sure the fountain bottle is properly inserted into its holder. (Omnitrade Industrial/Omni Adast)

Figure 21-9. The printing plate is attached to the plate clamp on most offset duplicators.

Start the press, allowing the rollers to pick up moisture. Operate the fountain-roller knob by hand to help the moisture along. If necessary, you can also use a sponge to drip a little fountain solution on the oscillating roller. You can also predampen the dampener ductor roller. With the press stopped, turn the handwheel to bring the water ductor roller into contact with the fountain roller. Turn the fountain-roller knob by hand to transfer fountain solution from the water fountain roller to the ductor roller. Continue this procedure until the ductor roller is sufficiently dampened.

When the form rollers are sufficiently damp, stop the press. You can touch the form roller with your knuckles to determine proper form-roller dampness—but only after the press has stopped. Your instructor can demonstrate the preferred method of determining proper form-roller dampness.

You should now set the ratchet control for the fountain roller at its normal setting. Be sure the ductor control lever is on. The dampening unit is now ready for use.

Attaching the Plate

Always be sure the plate cylinder is clean before attaching a plate. A small particle of dirt under a plate can ruin a halftone or solid in only a few impressions. The plate cylinder should be dry.

Note

Moisture under a paper master causes wrinkles and deterioration of the image.

Turn the handwheel until the lead plate clamp is in position. Attach the lead (gripper) edge of the plate to the plate clamp. See **Figure 21-9.** Start at the right side of the clamp and work over to the left side. Hold the tail of the plate square, tight, and down near the feedboard, to prevent the plate from becoming detached.

Holding the tail end of the plate with your right hand, turn the handwheel clockwise until the tail clamp is in position for attaching the plate. Hold the plate with your left hand and bring the tail clamp up to position with your right hand. Attach the plate to the clamp. Tighten the plate clamp by turning the plate-clamp tightening dial clockwise.

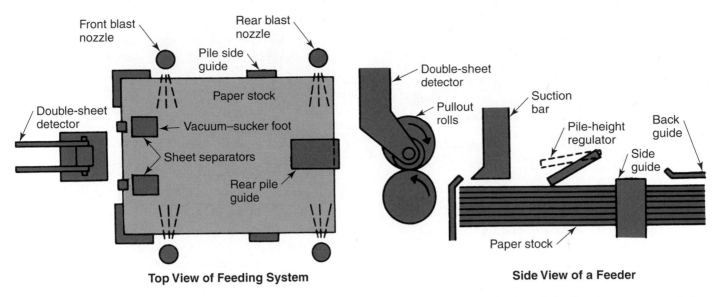

Top View of Feeding System **Side View of a Feeder**

Figure 21-10. Study the component parts of a duplicator feeder unit. Proper positioning of the feeder components is essential to trouble-free feeding. (A.B.Dick Co.)

Note

If a paper master is being used, the spring tension of the clamp alone holds it in place.

Preparing the Feeder Unit

With your right hand, depress the paper-platform lock release. With your left hand, turn the paper-platform crank counterclockwise to lower the platform. Set the inside of the left paper-stack side guide to the position indicated on the scale for the size sheet to be run. **Figure 21-10** illustrates the various parts of the feeder unit.

Lay a sheet of paper on the platform close to the front and left side guide. Set the right paper-stack guide so it is about 1/16" (1.6 mm) away from the edge of the paper. For a quick, accurate way of positioning the front guide and center blower, fold a sheet of paper for the job in half (lengthwise). Fold it in half again, parallel to the first fold. Unfolding the paper reveals creases as represented by lines A and B in **Figure 21-11.** Lay the open sheet on the platform and center the front guides on line B, with the center blower on line A.

Setting the front guides

The front pile guides are on a line representing one-quarter of the front edge of the sheet. Suction feet should be centered on the front guides directly above the sheet separators, called *cat's whiskers*. The front air blowers should be in the center of the sheet.

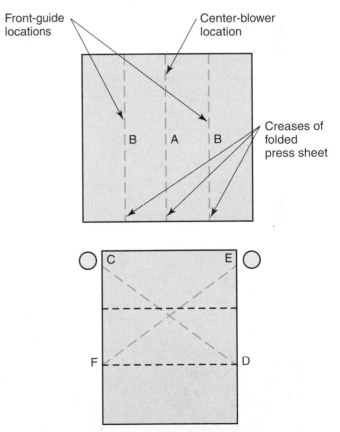

Figure 21-11. Examples of a press sheet folded to locate front guides on line B and the center blower on line A. The location and positioning of the front side blowers should be C to D and E to F. (A.B.Dick Co.)

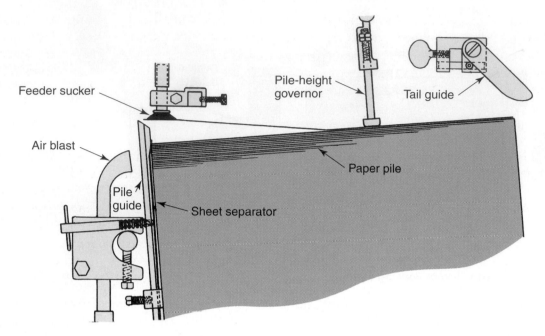

Figure 21-12. Study the relative positioning of the vacuum feeder and paper platform.

Figure 21-12 illustrates the relative positioning of the vacuum feeder and paper platform.

Loading the paper feeder

Fan and jog the sheets of paper to separate any that might be sticking together. See **Figure 21-13.** Place the paper in the center of the feed table using the scale as a guide for centering. This scale corresponds with a similar scale on the head clamp of the plate cylinder. Move the paper stack forward so it touches, but does not press too heavily against, the separator blocks.

Bring the paper stack to within 1/4″ (6.4 mm) of the sheet separators. Set the paper-stock back guide

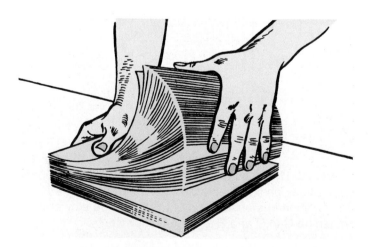

Figure 21-13. Before being loaded in the press feeder, all paper should be fanned and jogged to separate any sheets sticking together. (U.S. Government Printing Office)

so the front set of wings is on top of the paper stack. The back set of wings should be behind and up against the stack.

Setting the side guides

The feeder side guides are set so they are about 1″ (25 mm) from the back of the sheet. Set the side air-blower paper separators so they blow about two-thirds of the way back and across the paper. The second hole in the air-blower tube should be in line with the top of the paper when the paper is 1/4″ (6.4 mm) below the sheet separators. See **Figure 21-14.**

Positioning the paper platform

The paper platform should be lowered about 1″ (25 mm). Turn the duplicator on, to permit the paper platform to rise automatically. Adjust the elevator control knob so the paper stack stops about 1/4″ (6.4 mm) below the sheet separators. Turning this knob clockwise increases the height, and turning it counterclockwise decreases the height.

Positioning the pullout roller and double-sheet detector

The paper pullout roller and double-sheet detector (eliminator) are attached to the same unit. Whenever possible, the unit should be positioned so the pullout roller is close to the center of the paper. A thumb screw controls the pressure of the paper pullout roller. This screw should be set so there is just enough pressure to move the sheet of paper through to the feedboard.

Too much paper pullout-roller pressure distorts the sheet. If printed sheets are run for a second color, the pullout roller might mark the sheet if it is too tight. Insufficient pressure causes sheets to delay or arrive late at the paper stops. A pullout-roller release lever is provided, should paper jam under the pullout roller.

A thumb screw also controls the double-sheet detector. This detector should be set by starting up the duplicator and vacuum motors and feeding sheets through the duplicator. The screw should be turned counterclockwise until single sheets are ejected. The thumb screw is then turned slightly clockwise until the ejector does not act on single sheets. On some duplicator presses, the sheet is delivered directly and precisely to the register point, after the sucker feet pick it up, eliminating the need for a register board or table setup. See **Figure 21-15.** After passing through the double-sheet detector, the sheet is then conveyed down the register board until it reaches the front stop fingers. Stopped at this point, the sheet is pushed by the side jogger across the board to a predetermined register position.

Setting the register board and sheet controls

Paper can be jogged from either the left or right side on the register board. The right-hand jogger (stationary guide) should be used only when running jobs to be printed on both sides of the paper. In this case, it is desirable to use the left-hand jogger the first time through and the right-hand jogger the second time through. In this way, the second (backup) pass through the press uses the same paper edge used the first time through.

For jobs to be printed on one side only, the left-hand jogger is used. The stationary jogger should be set to act as a guide. If it has a leaf spring, it should be set to compress slightly as the sheet is jogged against it.

On most duplicators, the jogger control knob moves the side jogger, ball race, and paper-feed tapes all at one time. These components should be adjusted only when the duplicator is running. Otherwise, the tapes will be distorted, which can cause inaccurate positioning (register) of the paper.

Setting the feedboard joggers

To set the left jogger into action, start the press. Hold the right jogger with your left hand and pull it toward you, while moving the jogger selector back toward the feeder. This sets the left jogger into action.

To set the right jogger into action, start the press. Hold the left jogger with your left hand and push it away from yourself, while moving the jogger selector into its forward position. This procedure sets the right jogger into action. Both joggers can be set into action

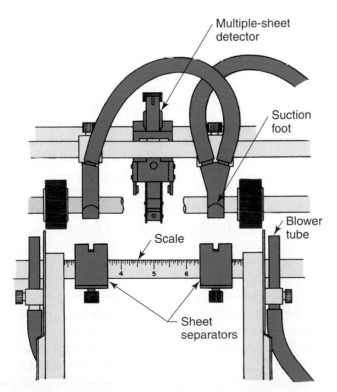

Figure 21-14. This is the correct positioning for the multiple-sheet detector, suction feet, sheet separators, and side blower tubes.

Figure 21-15. On this duplicator, the sheets are delivered directly to the register point, thereby eliminating the need for a register board or table. (Ryobi Xpedx Impact Group)

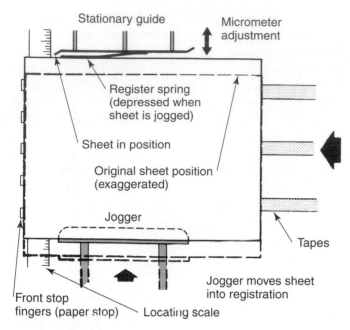

Figure 21-16. Study the parts of jogger and leaf-spring mechanisms. For most printing applications, one of two joggers is locked in a stationary position with the leaf spring lowered. (Multigraphics)

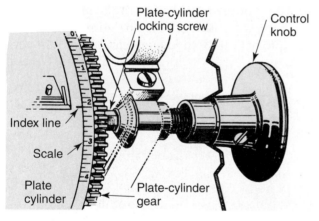

Figure 21-17. Vertical movements of the image on the press sheet are made by moving the plate cylinder. A plate-cylinder lock control is provided for this purpose. (Multigraphics)

by moving the jogger selector into a position midway between the left-hand and right-hand positions, an adjustment often used for small cards and envelopes.

Setting the leaf springs

When the jogger leaf springs are used, the spring on the jogger being used should be raised by pressing down on the back end of the spring retainer. The spring on the stationary jogger should be lowered by pressing down on the front end of the spring retainer. **Figure 21-16** shows the jogger and leaf spring.

When in use, the stationary jogger should be set so it does not move the spring more than 1/16" (1.6 mm) when the paper is moved against the spring. On most duplicators, the angle of either jogger can be regulated by turning the jogger angle-control screw. Feed a few sheets of paper through the duplicator to check jogger action. The paper must be square with the edge of the jogger.

Positioning the image on the paper

The image must be positioned squarely on the paper by adjusting the control knob of the stop bar. This bar can be tilted in either direction. Moving the stop bar eliminates any need for adjusting the angle of the plate on the plate cylinder.

Note

Some duplicators are not equipped with an adjusting stop bar, thereby requiring an adjustment of the plate on the plate cylinder to change the position of the printed image.

Setting gripper-bite control

Small vertical movements of the image can be made by moving the paper stop bar forward or backward, allowing a larger or smaller gripper bite. This movement is limited to about 3/16" (4.8 mm), or 3/32" (2.4 mm) in each direction off center (zero). Larger vertical movements of the image on the paper are made by moving the plate cylinder. These adjustments are made by turning the handwheel until the zero position on the plate-cylinder scale is opposite the mark on the plate-cylinder guard. See **Figure 21-17.** The press plate-cylinder lock control is pressed until it sits on the plate-cylinder lock nut. The lock control is then turned to the left to unlock the nut, while the handwheel is held. While the lock control is held in position, the handwheel is turned until the indicator line shows the cylinder has been moved to the desired position on the scale. The lock control is then turned to the right to lock the cylinder in position.

After the sheet has registered properly against the side guide and stop fingers, the front stop fingers drop down. The feed rolls propel the sheet forward into grippers of the impression cylinder. The timing is adjusted so the leading end of the sheet usually buckles slightly as it meets the gripper stops. This buckling ensures positive positioning at the gripper. See **Figure 21-18.** At this point, the impression-cylinder grippers close on the sheet to carry it between the blanket and impression cylinders under pressure. At this point, the sheet receives the inked image from the blanket.

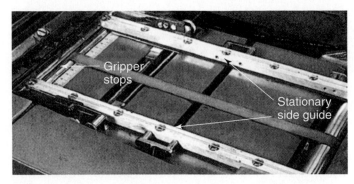

Figure 21-18. Once a sheet of paper has registered against the side guide and stop fingers, the lead end of the sheet buckles slightly as it meets the gripper stops. (Multigraphics)

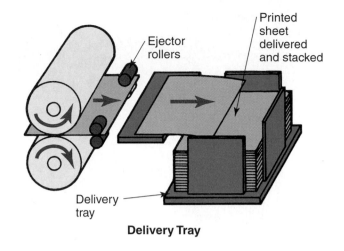

Delivery Tray

Setting the Delivery Unit

Set the delivery tray, jogger, and stacker for the sheet width and length required. See **Figure 21-19.** Feed a sheet of paper into the duplicator. Stop the sheet short of the delivery tray, just as the jogger reaches the closed position. Set the jogger, tray, or stacker to the sheet position.

The lower ejector wheels on a duplicator equipped with a delivery tray must be moved to at least 1″ (25 mm) inward from the sides of the sheet. See **Figure 21-20.** The upper ejector wheels should be moved outward 1/2″ (13 mm) from the lower wheels. Positioning the ejector wheels directly over each other causes the sheets to become wrinkled.

A chain delivery system has gripper bars mounted across two endless chains that revolve between a delivery cylinder and the delivery end of the duplicator. See **Figure 21-21.** Chain-delivered printed sheets are released into the stacker and jogged automatically. The stacker descends automatically to accommodate a large quantity of printed sheets. The chain delivery system might also be equipped with an antisetoff-spray attachment. When adjusted properly, the antisetoff-spray attachment prevents smudging and the transfer of wet ink to the back side of the next sheet.

If the duplicator is equipped with a chain delivery system, make the necessary adjustments to the unit. Use extreme care when working around the chain-delivery gripper fingers because they are somewhat pointed and sharp. The chain delivery system should be protected with safety covers.

Feeding Test Sheets

Assuming the duplicator has been prepared as described, several test sheets should be run through the press to determine if any adjustments

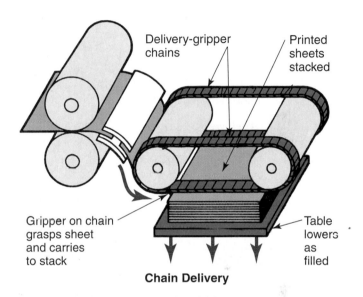

Chain Delivery

Figure 21-19. Two kinds of paper-delivery systems include a delivery tray and chain delivery with a receding stacker. A delivery-tray system is used exclusively on some models of duplicators.

are required. With the duplicator set up according to the previous directions, feed several test sheets as follows:
1. Using a cotton pad, moisten the plate with fountain solution.
2. Start the duplicator under power.
3. Lower the dampener form roller to the plate cylinder.
4. Allow the duplicator to run for several more revolutions, while checking the plate for dampness.
5. Lower the ink form rollers to the plate cylinder.
6. Start the vacuum and blower motor.
7. Set the duplicator on impression.
8. Run a sheet of paper through the duplicator.

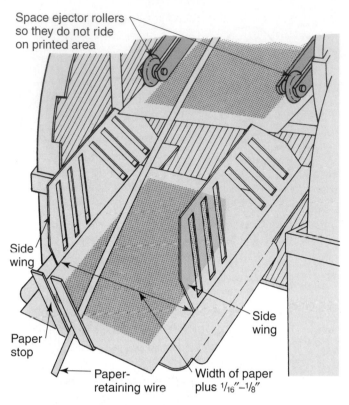

Figure 21-20. The lower ejector wheels of a delivery tray–equipped duplicator should be positioned, if possible, at least 1″ inward from the sides of the press sheet.

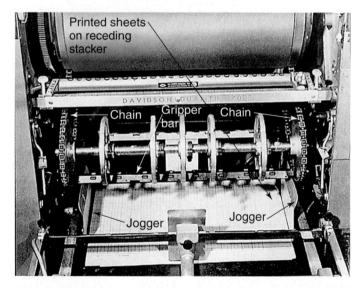

Figure 21-21. A press sheet emerging from the printing unit of this press is pinched by grippers mounted on a bar attached to revolving chains. The sheet is then carried over the delivery pile and released. (ATF Davidson Co.)

9. Take the duplicator off impression.
10. Raise the ink form rollers.
11. Turn off the vacuum and blower motor.
12. Stop the duplicator.
13. Check the position of the image on the sheet.

14. Make all necessary adjustments to achieve the position, ink-and-water balance, and ink coverage desired. This step might take additional trial runs to achieve the desired results.

Checking Test Sheets

Inspect the test sheets carefully. See **Figure 21-22**. The image on the paper should be clear, well inked, and free from background tone. There are important points to examine on the test sheets.

If the plate tends to pick up ink in the nonimage areas, this indicates an excessive amount of ink or insufficient amount of dampening solution. The ideal ink-and-water balance occurs when each printed sheet removes exactly the same amount of ink and water as is being metered to the plate. Too little ink or water shows up immediately on the copy and is easily remedied. Too much ink or water is harder to detect, however, and this situation can cause constant quality problems.

If toning occurs, turn the dampener fountain-roller knob one or two turns clockwise at the instant the ductor roller contacts the fountain roller to momentarily supply more moisture to the plate. If the toning disappears, advance the fountain-feed control lever one or two notches. If the image appears overinked and toning remains, retard the ink-feed control. An excessive amount of ink causes toning of the nonimage area and filling in of the image. An excessive amount of moisture or lack of ink tends to produce a gray, washed-out image. The ideal point of balance is to run the plate as dry as possible, using the minimum amount of moisture, with only enough ink to produce a dark image.

Figure 21-22. When checking the printed sheets, the image should be clear, well inked, and free from background tone. (Van Son Holland Ink Corp.)

The initial symptoms might appear very similar to ink starvation, in which the copies are light and washed-out. In attempting to correct this condition, the press operator can begin a vicious cycle. The print looks too light, so the operator adds more ink, which causes the background to start toning. So the operator adds more water, which causes the ink to print light again. Eventually, the action of the rollers whips together the excess ink and water, and the ink printing the copy encapsulates excess water and air bubbles. A mottled and washed-out print results. The water in the fountain picks up bits of emulsified ink, causing dirty copy and, in severe cases, a buildup of ink on the blanket outside the paper area. On duplicators equipped with integrated dampening systems, in which the same form rollers carry both the ink and water to the plate, the emulsified ink builds up and piles on the top water roller, instead of going to the plate, causing the copy to print light again.

As previously mentioned, the press operator should feed only the amount of ink to the plate that the paper can pick up with each impression. This result is accomplished by cutting back slightly on the water setting and watching the copy closely. Keep cutting back on water until the background begins to tone. Bring the water setting up slightly, so it is just barely enough to keep the background clean. Cutting back on the water results in denser, smoother copy, even though no ink has been added.

Check the position of the image. See **Figure 21-23**. The test sheets should be checked for image position using a line gauge. These checks should include lateral (left-to-right) and vertical (up-and-down) positions.

Figure 21-23. Press test sheets should be checked for image position and proper impression. (Van Son Holland Ink Corp.)

When a position adjustment is necessary for the plate or plate cylinder, wash the image from the blanket, or the next print will show a double impression.

Although an impression check should have been done before running test sheets, periodically check that proper impression is maintained. Impression that is too heavy results in image spread, especially in the case of halftone dots. Too little impression results in a light image, faint halftone dots, or uneven solids. Refer to the duplicator instruction manual for specific impression requirements. If the job carries two or more colors on the same side of the press sheet, register marks need to be checked as part of the makeready and periodically throughout the run.

Handling the Delivery

Observing the run on a duplicator involves more than maintaining specific settings and adjustments. The problems concerning specific components of the duplicator have been discussed. The press operator must also be concerned with maintaining the appearance and quality of the job produced on the duplicator.

It is assumed that the mechanical aspects of running the duplicator are correct. These aspects include that the feeder is functioning properly, the sheet is registering, the color is consistent with customer specs, and the printed sheets are being delivered and jogged in a satisfactory manner. Observing the run then involves seeing to it that no hickies or spots appear on the printed sheets and that the proper amount of ink is being deposited.

Note

Some duplicators are equipped with an automatic washup device. Refer to **Figure 21-24**.

Cleaning and Caring for the Press

The ink train of offset duplicators must be washed at the end of the day or pressrun or when a color change is required. During the washup, students might want to keep ink off of themselves by wearing an apron and rubber gloves. In addition, safety glasses can be useful in protecting the eyes from solvent splatter. To wash the duplicator, follow these steps:

1. Remove the fountain-solution bottle.
2. Remove the fountain solution from the fountain with a sponge or syringe.

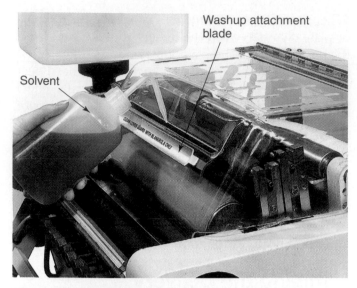

Figure 21-24. A press washup attachment should be used only at a slow press speed. Blanket and roller wash is applied sparingly to rollers. (Baldwin Technology)

3. Use an ink knife to remove and discard the ink from the ink fountain.

4. Remove the ink fountain from the duplicator by lifting it up to a vertical position. Clean the ink fountain with a cloth moistened with an appropriate solvent.

Caution

Make sure solvents are used in well-ventilated areas. Do not splash solvent in your face or breathe fumes for an extended time. Wear eye protection. Dispose of solvent-covered rags or paper in a safety container.

5. Clean the ink-fountain roller with blanket and roller wash.

6. Remove the excess ink from the rollers by manually feeding a sheet of paper into the rollers. Hold on to the end of the sheet while manually turning the handwheel. Back the sheet out and discard it. Repeat this process several times to make the washup easier and faster.

7. Attach a cleanup mat to the plate cylinder and start the duplicator. Turn the speed down to slow.

8. Squirt a small amount of blanket and roller wash over the ink oscillating roller, allowing it to work into the ink system.

9. Move the two form rollers to the on position. Continue to add small amounts of wash until the rollers appear clean. Do not use too much wash at one time. Work one side of the rollers at a time so the rollers do not slip and slide.

10. Turn the ink form rollers (and aquamatic control, if applicable) to the off position. Stop the duplicator, remove the cleanup mat, and discard it. Repeat the operation with another cleanup mat, and a third if necessary.

11. After all ink is removed, moisten a soft, lintless cloth with blanket and roller wash. Wipe all the rollers clean of any ink residue or lint. Wipe the ends of all ink rollers to prevent the rollers from cracking and hardening on the ends.

12. Use a cloth to clean the duplicator of any ink that might have accumulated on interior and exterior parts. Clean off spots caused by fountain solution. Wipe off all chrome-plated parts, including the cylinders and trim. Wipe the ejector rollers and collars, and lubricate them so they move freely along the shaft.

13. Clean the floor around the duplicator of all ink, solvents, and loose papers. Check beneath the duplicator by opening the motor access doors or covers. Visually check the vacuum-pump fluid level and fill it, if necessary.

14. Check the ink and fountain rollers for glaze, or a shiny, glossy accumulation on the surface of the rollers. Ink and fountain solution combining during a pressrun causes glaze. The ink rollers should be treated with a deglazing solution or mild pumice. The fountain roller should be removed and scrubbed with a deglazing agent made for this purpose.

15. At the end of the day, loosen the tension on the blanket to rest it. Tighten the blanket at the start of the next day.

16. Also at the end of the day, set the night latch to release pressure on the form rollers.

17. Gather all tools and articles around the press.

Safe Operation

Safe duplicator and press operation means the duplicator or press is always operated in a sensible manner. Personal safety, as well as mechanical and general shop conditions, should be considered. Always dress appropriately when operating an offset duplicator or press. See **Figure 21-25.**

- Remove coats and sweaters, and store them properly.
- Roll shirt sleeves above the elbows and keep shirttails tucked in.

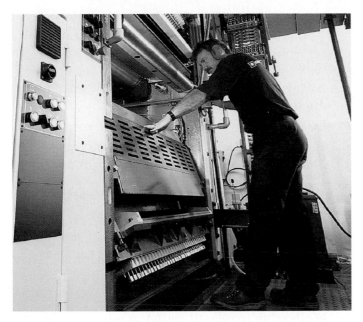

Figure 21-25. When operating a duplicator or press, always dress appropriately. Wearing loosely fitting clothes and carrying wiping cloths in pockets are unsafe practices. (Goss International Corporation)

- Remove neckties and tie back long hair.
- Remove all jewelry, including chains, bracelets, and rings. (The desire to keep one's hands intact should take precedence over appearance or sentiment.)
- Do not carry wiping cloths in your pockets.
- Wear eye protection when needed.

    You should always be aware of your surroundings and keep alert for coworkers and fellow students. Using common sense in the pressroom helps prevent accidents. Keep the following safe practices in mind and apply them whenever possible:

- Never lean against the duplicator or press or rest your hands where there is any chance of getting them caught in moving parts.
- Use hand tools appropriately and keep them in a secure area near the press.
- Place knives in safety sheaths when not using them for cutting, packing, or other press operations. If razor blades are used, they should have holders on them.
- Never carry tools in your pockets. They can cause puncture wounds or be dropped into the duplicator or press and cause personal injury or damage to the machinery.
- Use the proper-size tools when making adjustments. Keep wrenches and other hand tools in good condition.

- Watch finger clearance when lifting rollers in and out of the duplicator or press.
- Inspect the edges of the plate before handling it, especially if it has been cut down from a larger size. Rough metal edges should be filed smooth so they do not cut your hands. See **Figure 21-26.**
- Oiling the duplicator or press should not be attempted unless the press is standing still. Wipe up oil from floors and platforms to reduce slipping hazards.
- Never reach into the duplicator or press while it is running! Stop the machine to clear jams, lubricate, make adjustments or repairs, or clean the press. See **Figure 21-27.**
- Never attempt to remove hickies while the duplicator or press is running. Always stop the machine before picking off the hickies.
- All guards should be in place before the duplicator or press is started.

Figure 21-26. Always inspect the edges of the plate before handling it. (Van Son Holland Ink Corp.)

Figure 21-27. Always stop the press to clear jams, lubricate, make adjustments or repairs, or clean plates and blankets. (Kimberly-Clark Corp.)

Guards

Offset duplicators and presses are equipped with adequate mechanical safeguards when the manufacturer ships them. In the process of transferring equipment from one owner to another, however, the guards might become misplaced or lost. Also, through experience and use, the operator might find additional areas needing mechanical protection. Sometimes, guards are removed because of their inconvenience. The equipment might then, however, be in violation of OSHA regulations. A good operator learns what type of mechanical protection the machine provides, noting especially the following danger points:

- Nip points in running cylinders and rollers.
- Blanket-cylinder and plate-cylinder interface.
- Gears at the edge of the plate and blanket cylinders and near the bearers.
- The footboard and rear of the blanket and plate cylinders.
- The feeder end over insertion devices.
- Chain delivery. See **Figure 21-28.**
- The cam controlling the height of the pile in the feeder.

Caution

Never operate a press unless all its guards are in place!

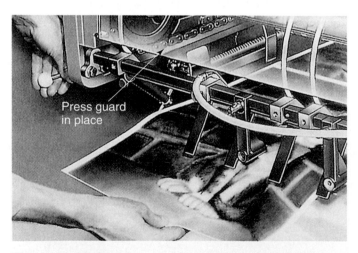

Press guard in place

Figure 21-28. Removing a sheet from a chain delivery press with a receding stacker. Note the transparent safety guard covering the gripper-bar cylinder. (Heidelberg, Inc.)

Washing

Cleaning parts of the duplicator or press requires the following precautions:

- Always turn the power off before cleaning the duplicator or press.
- Do not use solvents near an open flame.
- Take only small amounts of solvent to the duplicator or press and then only in approved safety containers.
- Avoid spilling flammable liquids. The vapors can flow long distances along the floor or ground before they are ignited and flash back.
- Never pour used solvents down a drain. They should be disposed of properly in approved containers.
- Do not inhale solvent fumes. Make sure the area is well ventilated and wear a mask if necessary.
- Do not use solvents on your body and always use protective gloves when handling solvents.
- Place rags and materials used with solvents into approved safety containers.
- When removing paper stuck to the blanket, first use water and a sponge, and then clean with solvent and a rag.
- Operators using bichromate fountain solutions should report any skin irritations promptly. Nonbichromate fountain solutions for use with aluminum plates are helpful to those press operators who are sensitive to bichromate. See **Figure 21-29.**

Housekeeping

Poor housekeeping in and around duplicators and presses contributes to many accidents, especially falls. For your safety and for the safety of those who work around you, check the area for the following conditions:

- Are the oil drip pans emptied periodically?
- Do you have safety containers for solvents?
- Are metal containers for cleaning rags available?
- Are waste containers for paper provided?
- Are there ink cans on the floor or platforms that could be spilled?
- Are there tools left on walkways that could cause an accident?
- Are aprons or shirts hanging dangerously on control boxes or press frames?

Figure 21-29. Nonbichromate fountain solutions can be used with aluminum plates. The use of such solutions is helpful to press operators who are sensitive to bichromate. (Heidelberg, Inc.)

- Are rollers properly racked so they cannot be accidentally knocked from their holders?
- Are the floor, platform, and steps free of grease and oils?
- Are there any empty skids standing on edge or leaning against equipment, walls, or columns?
- Are the air hoses in reels or racks?
- Are all aisles free of debris?

Create a checklist to suit your particular lab or pressroom, to ensure all areas are inspected. See **Figure 21-30.**

	Cleanup Task Checklist
✓	**Task**
	Remove printed sheets from the delivery tray and place them in a rack to dry.
	Remove unprinted sheets from the feed table. Also, remove any deflected sheets from beneath the register table.
	Remove the fountain-solution bottle from the duplicator; empty and wash it.
	Drain the fountain-solution tray and wipe it dry.
	Remove excess ink from the ink fountain by wedging it between two cards. Discard the excess ink.
	Remove the ink fountain from the duplicator and clean it with blanket wash.
	Remove the ink ductor roller and clean it with a cloth moistened with blanket wash.
	Wipe the ink fountain roller clean with a cloth moistened with blanket wash.
	Attach a cleaner sheet (plate-size blotter) to the plate cylinder. Turn on the press and set it to run at its slowest speed. With the form rollers contacting the cleaner sheet, apply a small amount of blanket wash to the uppermost ink rollers. Use a plastic squeeze bottle to apply the wash to the rollers. Continue to add small amounts of wash to the rollers until they appear clean. Note: Repeat this step several times, using a fresh cleaner sheet each time, until all traces of ink have been removed from the rollers. Used cleaner sheets should be set aside to dry. When thoroughly dry, these sheets may be reused on the reverse side.
	With the duplicator stopped, inspect all rollers, especially their ends. Clean as required, by hand. Do not allow a film of blanket wash to remain on the rollers, as this can cause glazing. Dry the rollers with a clean cloth.
	Clean all dampening rollers.
	Clean the blanket with blanket wash.
	Clean the impression and plate cylinders with blanket wash.
	Replace fountain-solution bottle, ink fountain, and rollers. Make sure that the rollers are returned to their correct positions.
	Turn off all duplicator controls and set the form rollers to the night-latch position.
	Wipe the outside of the machine clean with a cloth moistened with an appropriate solvent. Then polish dry.
	Turn master switch off at end of shift or day.

Figure 21-30. Include the items listed here in your cleanup checklist.

Summary

Press operator's manuals are available for all offset duplicators and presses. The operator should be thoroughly familiar with the procedures as found in the manual for the specific press. Before starting a duplicator or press, it is important that the operator prepare the machine by checking for loose articles on or in the machinery. Press pressure checks should be made before running the unit at the start of a day or shift. All paper required for a pressrun should be conditioned. Paper should be delivered to the pressroom area in advance, so it can reach the proper temperature balance.

The press operator should prepare the duplicator or press for operation. This includes preparing the dampening and inking systems, printing unit, feeder system, double-sheet detector, register board, and delivery system. When the duplicator or press has been prepared for operation, several test sheets should be run. Adjustments should be made as required.

When the pressrun has been completed, the press operator must clean the duplicator or press of all ink, paper, lint, and setoff-spray powder or liquid residues. The machine should then be ready for the next job. Proper housekeeping in and around the press area is essential to safe operating conditions.

Review Questions

Please do not write in this book. Write your answers on a separate sheet of paper.

1. Never operate any press or duplicator until you have been thoroughly instructed in the _____ operation of that machine.

2. What type of information can be found on the job ticket?

3. Describe the various operations that are part of the preliminary, offset-press or duplicator inspection.

4. Why is the lubrication of the moving parts on a press or duplicator so important?

5. The press feeder and delivery drive chains should be lubricated _____.
   A. once a week
   B. twice a week
   C. once every two weeks
   D. once a month

6. Most vacuum-blower pumps require SAE No. _____–weight oil.

7. What is the minimum amount of time that should be allowed for paper to reach a temperature balance?

8. Why should solvents not be used near an open flame?

9. Explain how ink should be placed in the offset-press or duplicator ink fountain.

10. Turning the fountain keys clockwise (increases/decreases) the flow of ink.

11. The _____ is used to lift the rollers out of contact with the plate when the press is not in use.

12. The lead edge of the offset plate is attached to the plate _____.

13. Press-feeder side guides should be set so they are about _____" from the back of the sheet.

14. The _____ jogger should be used only when running jobs to be printed on both sides of the paper.

15. For jobs to be printed on one side only, the _____ jogger is used.

16. A stationary paper jogger should be set so, when the paper is moved against the spring, it moves the spring no more than _____.
    A. 1/32" (0.8 mm)
    B. 1/16" (1.6 mm)
    C. 1/8" (3.2 mm)
    D. 1/4" (6.4 mm)

17. Small _____ movements of the image can be made by moving the paper stop bar forward or backward.

18. What are some things that should be done at the end of a job or the working day to clean and secure a duplicator or press?

19. What safety precautions regarding personal dress must be observed when operating an offset press or duplicator?

20. List some important areas of the duplicator protected by guards.

21. Give examples of some of the important essentials of good housekeeping in the pressroom.

Skill-Building Activities

1. Under the supervision of your instructor, lubricate an offset duplicator or press to prepare for a print job. Inspect for loose tools, paper, and other objects in and around the machine. As you lubricate the press and inspect it for loose tools and paper, prepare a checklist. From your notes, create a checklist similar to the one in **Figure 21-30** to be used by other operators.

2. Obtain a copy of the duplicator operating manual. Review the duplicator's steps of operation. If necessary, request assistance from your instructor.

3. With your instructor's assistance, perform the necessary duplicator pressure checks.

4. Install an offset plate on the duplicator plate cylinder. Check to be sure the tail clamp is secure.

5. With your instructor's help, set up an offset duplicator for operation. Feed test sheets through the duplicator and check for proper water-and-ink balance and image position. Get a press sheet OK from your instructor. Complete the pressrun for the required number of impressions.

6. When the duplicator run has been completed, remove the plate, and clean it thoroughly. Preserve the plate and store it for future use. Remove the fountain solution and either save or dispose of it properly. Wash the duplicator thoroughly and have your instructor check it for cleanliness. Be sure roller ends are clean of ink.

Looking Good

All the efforts of the graphic designer, prepress people, paper and ink technicians, and press operator come together when the ink hits the paper. The operator shown here has reason to smile. He has pulled a press sheet for inspection and sees bright colors, precise registration, and crisp contrast. The sheet is looking good. Of course, this kind of press sheet requires considerable skill and expertise. Toward that goal, this chapter takes the student through the actual procedures involved with operating two presses that operators typically work on early in their careers.

(Heidelberg, Inc.)

Chapter 22
Sheetfed Offset Presses

Key Terms

delivery ring
feed position
image position
ink position
neutral position
night-latch position

Learning Objectives

When you have completed the reading and assigned activities related to this chapter, you will be able to do the following:

- Describe the general procedures for running a duplicator and a sheetfed offset press.
- Discuss the common components among the various duplicators and sheetfed offset presses.
- Adjust the impression cylinder on a duplicator and an offset press for various weights of paper.
- Analyze and test the plate-to-blanket pressures on a duplicator and an offset press.
- Set the inking and dampening controls on a duplicator or an offset press to their proper settings.
- Make copy adjustments by repositioning the plate.

This chapter continues your study of duplicators and small sheetfed offset presses. Chapters 20 and 21 summarize the major parts and operation of these presses. This chapter describes the adjustments and methods needed to operate presses properly.

Note

Press manufacturers' instruction manuals are helpful for further study of this topic. The press manual gives information that is more specific, or possibly even unique, to the particular press.

There are many models of duplicators and small sheetfed offset presses in operation. All are equipped with features representing the latest technology at the time they were built. It is impossible to include all the duplicator and press models or detail the operating features of a particular machine. The basic components are, however, present in all press designs. See **Figure 22-1.** For this textbook, two duplicators have been selected for a detailed explanation of their operating procedures. Their inclusion was based on their being commonly used in schools and commercial shops throughout the United States.

The A.B.Dick® 9800 Series

Duplicators in the A.B.Dick 9800 series are sheetfed with vacuum feeders. These duplicators are derivatives of earlier models, such as the A.B.Dick 360. They are equipped with combined (integrated) dampening systems. The ink and the dampener solutions originate in separate fountains and are then combined and fed through the same form rollers to the plate. See **Figure 22-2.**

These duplicators have a single control lever for operating the dampener and ink form rollers and for providing plate-to-blanket contact. The 9835 is equipped with chute delivery. The 9840 is equipped with chain delivery and a receding stacker. The 9850 is basically the same as the 9840, except it is equipped with additional rollers and adjustments for alcohol use in the fountain solution. Duplicator specs are listed in the chart in **Figure 22-3.**

The Operating Procedure

The locations of the operating controls and major components for the A.B.Dick 9840 and 9850 are shown in **Figure 22-4.** Students will want to familiarize themselves with these components so the following

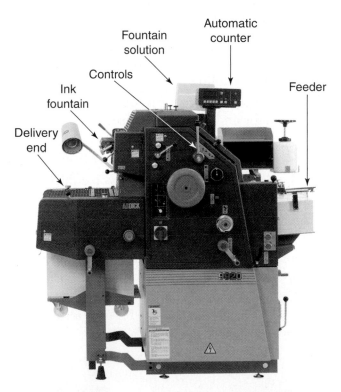

Figure 22-1. Many kinds of duplicators are manufactured, but they all have the basic components shown here. The best source of in-depth information on the characteristics of a particular offset press or duplicator is the operator's manual. (A.B.Dick Co.)

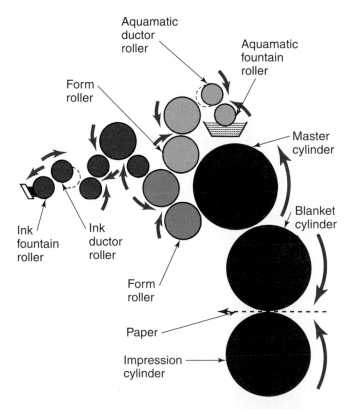

Figure 22-2. In an integrated dampening system, the ink and dampener solutions originate in separate fountains. The ink and fountain solution are then combined and fed through the same form rollers to the plate. (A.B.Dick Co.)

Specifications for A.B.Dick 9800 Series

Paper size: 3″ x 5″ to 13 1/2″ x 17 3/4″(76 x 127 mm to 343 x 451 mm).

Paper weight: Minimum 12-pound bond to maximum 110-pound index (5.4 kg to 50 kg).

Printing area: 12 1/2″ x 17 1/4″ (318 x 438 mm).

Metal plate size: 13″ x 19 3/8″ (330 mm x 492 mm).

Gripper margin: 1/4″ (6.4 mm).

Blanket size: 12 5/8″ x 19 3/16″ (321 mm x 487 mm).

Feed-table capacity: 20″ or 5,000 sheets of 20-pound bond paper.

Receiving-tray capacity (9835 only): 3″ or 500 sheets of 20-pound bond paper.

Chain-delivery capacity (9840/9850 only): 21″ or 5,000 sheets of 20-pound bond paper.

Speed: 4,500 to 9,000 impressions per hour (iph).

Figure 22-3. Specs for the A.B.Dick 9800 series duplicators. Similar specs are available for all duplicators and presses.

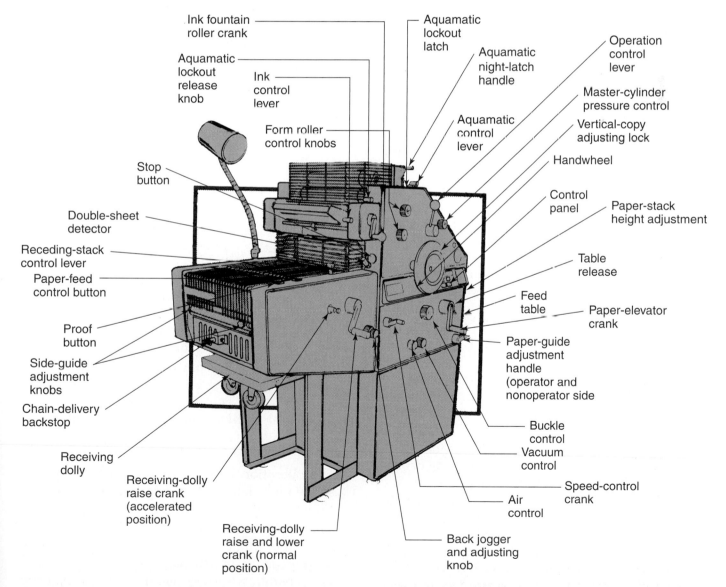

Figure 22-4. The operating controls and major components of the A.B.Dick 9840 and 9850 series duplicators. (A.B.Dick Co.)

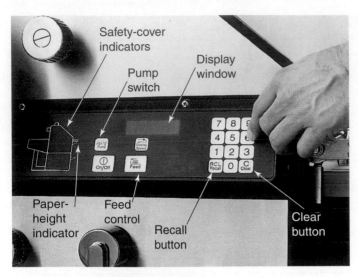

Figure 22-5. The 9840 and 9850 series A.B.Dick duplicators are equipped with keypad control panels. (A.B.Dick Co.)

operating instructions are meaningful. The control panel contains a series of panel switches and indicator lamps for copy count, machine speed, fault detection, and low-paper conditions. See **Figure 22-5.**

A panel clear switch is used to clear the LED count-and-speed display or to reset jam and double-sheet indicators. The jam and double-sheet indicators remain illuminated, disabling the feed, until the paper path is clear and the indicators are reset by pressing the clear switch. Once the indicators are reset, pressing the switch a second time clears the copy count in the LED display. Pressing the clear switch during machine operation turns off the paper feed and resets the LED display to zero.

During machine operation, the initial copy count can be recalled for several seconds by pressing the recall switch. The counting function continues uninterrupted while the initial count is being displayed. The numbers on the keypad are used to select the number of copies to be printed.

The display window has a five-digit LED display indicating copy count and machine speed. When a count is entered, the duplicator counts down until it reaches zero. The paper feed and vacuum pump turn off, and the LED display resets to the initial copy count. If no count is entered, the duplicator counts up until paper feeding is manually stopped.

The rotations per hour (rph) are displayed (to the nearest hundred) in the count display for 8–10 seconds. To return to the count mode prior to this delay, press the clear button. Counting is not interrupted while the duplicator speed is displayed.

The feed switch turns the vacuum pump and paper feed on and off. This switch does not override the pump switch. If the vacuum pump is turned on

using the pump switch, it can be turned off only by reengaging the pump switch. The on-and-off switch is used to turn the drive motor on and off.

The jam indicator shows that the paper feed is shut off, and the indicator illuminates when a sheet does not exit the duplicator within a preset time period. When a jam occurs in the duplicator, turn off the machine before clearing the paper path. Press the clear button to reset the jam indicator, and restart the duplicator.

The double-sheet indicator illuminates the panel when more than one sheet is sensed entering the duplicator and the paper feed shuts off. When a double is fed through the duplicator, turn the machine off (unless the extra sheet is accessible, as with duplicators equipped with receiving trays). Remove the extra sheets. Press the clear button to reset the double-sheet indicator, and restart the duplicator if it stopped. The pump switch turns the vacuum pump on and off. If the pump is turned on using this switch, it can be turned off only by this switch.

The safety-cover indicators are five LEDs that illuminate to show the location of an open safety cover. Only one guard is displayed at a time, even if more than one guard is open. After the first guard is secured, the next open guard (in a clockwise sequence) is displayed.

Caution

> The drive motor does not operate when any safety guard is open. If any guards are opened during machine operation, the drive motor turns off automatically.

A paper-low indicator flashes when there are fewer than 100 sheets (20-lb. bond paper) remaining on the feed table. An audible beep is provided to indicate this condition. The machine continues to print copy when a low-paper condition is detected. The audible signal can be shut off by pressing the clear button once. The indicator lamp continues to flash, however, until the feed table is lowered.

The Operation Control Lever

The operation control lever has five positions. These are night latch, neutral, ink, image, and feed. See **Figure 22-6:**

- **The *night-latch position.*** This lever position pulls the inner oscillating roller away from making contact with the form rollers. The purpose of this separation is to prevent the form rollers from flattening from the pressure of the oscillating roller when the press is not in operation.

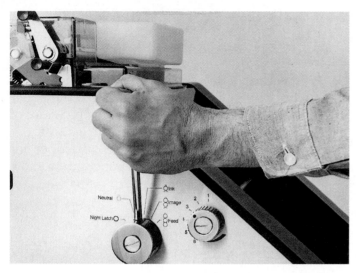

Figure 22-6. The operation control lever has five positions, including night latch, neutral, ink, image, and feed. (A.B.Dick Co.)

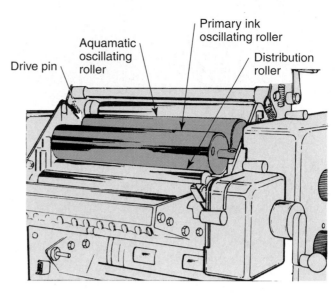

Figure 22-7. Identify the parts of the duplicator before beginning operation. (A.B.Dick Co.)

- The *neutral position.* This lever position brings the inner oscillating roller into contact with the form rollers. The neutral position is used for inking or cleaning the roller system without applying ink to the plate.
- The *ink position.* This lever position moves the form rollers against the plate cylinder to apply ink and dampening solution to it.
- The *image position.* This lever position moves the plate cylinder against the blanket cylinder to transfer the image to the blanket.
- The *feed position.* This turns on the paper feed and vacuum pump to engage paper feed. The operation control lever is spring-loaded and, after the feed position is engaged, normally returns to the ink position after being released from the feed position for producing printed sheets. There is a small detent in the image position, however, so if the operation control lever is returned to the image position from the feed position, the alternate sheet feed is actuated.

Duplicator Setup

Setting up the duplicator properly ensures that the rollers are in proper position.
1. Raise the ink-roller safety guard. Rinse the ink-roller safety guard to begin duplicator setup. Refer to **Figure 22-7.**
2. Place the Aquamatic oscillating roller in position in the ink system. Make sure the hole in the roller shaft is placed over the drive pin on the nonoperator side, with the rounded side of the shaft up. The opposite end of the shaft seats in the channel on the operator side of the inside frame.

3. Position the primary ink oscillating roller in contact with the two distributor rollers.
4. Position the lock levers in the down position to lock the primary ink oscillating roller in place. See **Figure 22-8.**
5. Install the secondary distributor (or rider) rollers in the brackets over the ink and water oscillators. See **Figure 22-9.**
6. Install the secondary ink oscillator and position it in the channel above both distributor rollers.
7. Move the Aquamatic night-latch handle toward the receiving end of the duplicator (9835 and 9840 only).
8. Move the operation control lever from the night-latch position to the neutral position and turn the ink form roller knobs to on.
9. Move the ink-ductor lockout lever toward the receiving end of the duplicator to allow the ink ductor to come into contact with the ink fountain roller.
10. Lower the ink-roller safety guard and turn on the main power switch.

night-latch position: the setting of an A.B.Dick's operation control lever that moves the inner oscillating roller out of contact with the form rollers.

neutral position: the setting of an A.B.Dick's operation control lever so the inner oscillating roller is in contact with the form rollers.

ink position: the setting of an A.B.Dick's control lever that brings the ink form rollers in contact with the plate, thereby inking the plate.

image position: the setting of an A.B.Dick's operation control lever that moves the plate cylinder in contact with the blanket cylinder, thereby inking the blanket.

feed position: the setting of an A.B.Dick's operation control lever that causes the feeder unit to send press sheets into the printing unit.

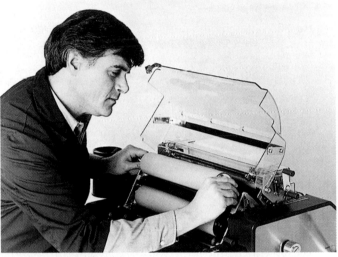

Figure 22-8. Placing the lock levers in the down position locks the primary oscillating roller against the distributing rollers. (A.B.Dick Co.)

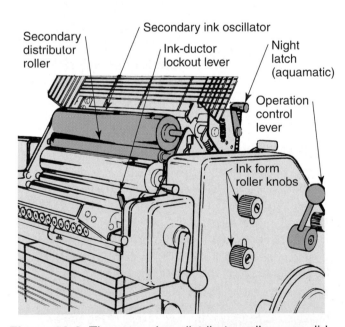

Figure 22-9. The secondary distributor rollers are slid into brackets above the ink and dampening oscillator rollers. (A.B.Dick Co.)

Paper Feed

Setting up the paper properly ensures that only single press sheets will enter the press smoothly.

1. Using the paper-guide handle on the non-operator side of the duplicator, move the paper guide to the correct scale setting for the width of the paper being used. Refer to **Figure 22-10.**
2. Using the paper-guide handle on the operator side of the duplicator, move the paper guide to the correct scale setting for the width of the paper.
3. The paper-support rails slide from side to side. These rails should be positioned to clear both backstops when the table is at its maximum height. See **Figure 22-11.**

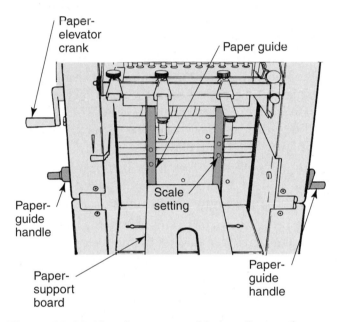

Figure 22-10. Use the paper-guide handles on the nonoperator and operator sides of the duplicator to move the paper guide to the correct scale setting for the width of the paper being used. (A.B.Dick Co.)

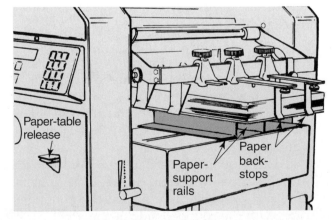

Figure 22-11. The paper-support rails are placed so they cannot contact the backstops. (A.B.Dick Co.)

4. Place the paper-support board on the paper-support rails. The paper-support board should be slightly smaller than the paper size.

5. Press down on the upper lever of the table release until it locks to disengage the automatic table-raise mechanism. Push in the paper-elevator crank to engage it, and then turn the crank counterclockwise to lower the feed table.

6. Turn the handwheel until the paper-height regulators are in the lowest position. See **Figure 22-12.**

7. Fan the paper and load it on the feed table, being careful to keep the reams neatly stacked. See **Figure 22-13.** The assembly holding the backstops, spring guides, and micromatic can be lifted and latched out of the way to assist in paper loading. The micromatic is a thumbscrew that makes minute lateral adjustments to the feeder pile of paper. This thumbscrew moves the paper left or right to better center the image on the press sheets. When loading is completed, release the latch and bring the assembly down to its operating position. See **Figure 22-14.**

8. Squeeze the two levers of the table release and raise them to engage the automatic table-raise mechanism. Push in the paper-elevator crank to engage it, and then turn the crank clockwise to raise the feed table until the top sheets contact the paper-height regulators. Pull out the paper-elevator crank to disengage it.

9. Square the top few sheets of paper and adjust the micromatic paper guide so it just touches the stack of paper on the nonoperator side. See **Figure 22-15.** The lead edge of the paper stack should be flush with the front plate.

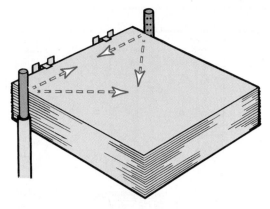

Figure 22-13. Front blowers are positioned to blow air diagonally across and toward the rear of the paper pile. (Multigraphics)

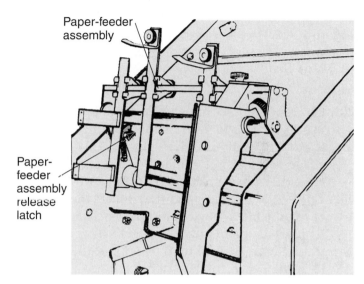

Figure 22-14. The feeder assembly holding the backstops, spring guides, and micromatic can be lifted and latched out of the way to assist in paper loading. (A.B.Dick Co.)

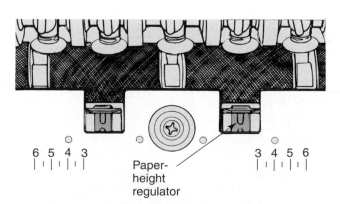

Figure 22-12. Turn the handwheel until the paper-height regulators are in the lowest position. Fan the paper and load it on the feed table. (A.B.Dick Co.)

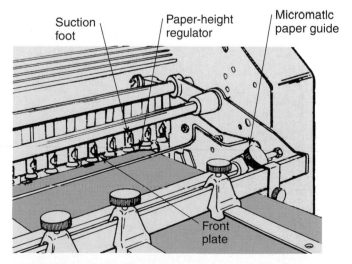

Figure 22-15. Squeeze the two levers of the paper-feeder table release and raise them to engage the automatic table-raise mechanism. (A.B.Dick Co.)

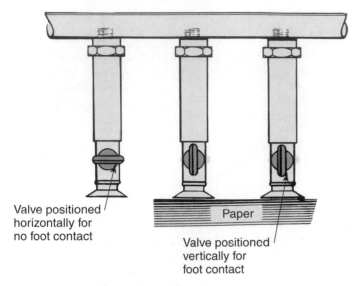

Valve positioned horizontally for no foot contact

Paper

Valve positioned vertically for foot contact

Figure 22-16. Each suction foot has a valve that can be positioned vertically or horizontally to control vacuum. (A.B.Dick Co.)

10. Each suction foot has a valve to control vacuum. See **Figure 22-16.** The feet contacting the sheet should have their valves positioned vertically, while the feet not contacting the sheet should have the valves positioned horizontally.

11. Adjust the backstops so they touch the tail end of the stack, but do not bind the stack against the front plate. See **Figure 22-17.** On heavy card or index stock, there should be approximately 1/8" (3 mm) between the backstop and the paper stack. There are two positions for attaching the backstop to the retaining bar. The bar and stop can also be reversed. Use the best position for the length and type of paper stock being used.

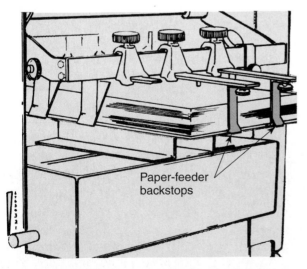

Paper-feeder backstops

Figure 22-17. Adjust the backstops so they make contact with the back of the pile, but do not force it against the front plate. (A.B.Dick Co.)

12. Place the paperweight in a forward notch for light papers and farther back for heavier papers. See **Figure 22-18.**

13. The feeding level of the paper stack should generally be low for lightweight papers and high for heavier-weight papers and card stocks. The automatic raising mechanism can be used to control the stack by raising or lowering the paper-height control lever. This lever has eight gradations, with position eight representing maximum table raise. See **Figure 22-19.** The paper height–control lever settings indicate the approximate position for optimum feeding. With a particular paper or card stock, slight deviations might be necessary.

14. Make sure all safety guards are closed.

15. Momentarily press the on-and-off switch on the control panel and allow the paper stack to reach the proper height. Press the on-and-off switch again to stop the duplicator.

16. Place the spring guide equidistant between the lead and trail edges of the sheet. The spring, for most stocks, should be depressed about 1/8" (3 mm) by the paper stack. Make any necessary final adjustments to the rear guide and backstop.

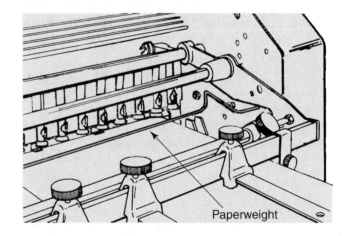

Paperweight

Stock	Paperweight Settings
12-pound bond	1 (special light paperweight)
13-pound bond	2
16- to 20-pound bond	2–3
24-pound bond	3
60-pound book	3
65-pound cover	4
110-pound index	4 (or remove paperweight)

Figure 22-18. Place the paperweight in a forward notch for light paper and farther back for heavier papers. Selecting the correct paperweight setting is important to proper feeding. (A.B.Dick Co.)

Air and Vacuum Control

Proper settings for the air blast and the vacuum are essential for consistent single-sheet feeding.

1. Turn the air and vacuum control knobs clockwise as far as possible to the full position.
2. Turn both knobs counterclockwise three half turns. Close all safety guards.
3. To check the feed operation, press the pump switch momentarily. Turn the handwheel until the paper-height regulators are at their highest position at the top of the front apron. The top few sheets of the paper stack should fluff up and follow the paper-height regulators. It might be necessary to increase the air setting by turning the air control knob clockwise until the sheets fluff up and follow the regulators. Turn the pump switch off.
4. To check the operation of the sucker feet, press the feed switch and turn the handwheel counterclockwise to manually feed one sheet of paper through the duplicator. If the suction feet do not pick up the paper properly, increase the vacuum setting by turning the vacuum control knob clockwise. See the air and vacuum control-knob settings in **Figure 22-20.**

Paper spring guide

Paper-height control lever

Stock	Paper Height Control Lever Settings
12-pound bond	1–3
13-pound bond	2–4
16- to 20-pound bond	4–6
24-pound bond	5–7
60-pound book	5–7
65-pound cover	6–8
110-pound index	7–8

Figure 22-19. The automatic raising mechanism can be used to control the stack by raising or lowering the paper-height control lever. The spring guide, for most papers, should be depressed about 1/8″ by the paper stock. The feeding level of the paper stack should generally be set low for lightweight papers and high for heavier papers and card stocks. (A.B.Dick Co.)

Stock	Air Adjustment Knob Settings
13-pound bond	2–3 half-turns counterclockwise
16- to 20-pound bond	2 half-turns counterclockwise
24-pound bond	2 half-turns counterclockwise
60-pound book	2 half-turns counterclockwise
65-pound cover	2 half-turns counterclockwise
110-pound index	1 half-turn counterclockwise
Stock	**Vacuum Adjustment Knob Settings**
13-pound bond	3–4 half-turns counterclockwise
16- to 20-pound bond	3–4 half-turns counterclockwise
24-pound bond	2–3 half-turns counterclockwise
60-pound book	2–3 half-turns counterclockwise
65-pound cover	2–3 half-turns counterclockwise
110-pound index	1 half-turn counterclockwise

Figure 22-20. The tubes in the photograph carry air to the back of the paper pile to separate the top sheets. Refer to the table for the proper air and vacuum settings for the paper's substance weight.

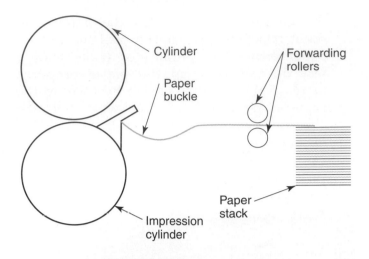

Stock	Buckle Settings
12-pound bond	15
13-pound bond	12
16- to 20-pound bond	7–8
24-pound bond	5–6
60-pound book	5–6
65-pound cover	3–4
10-pound index	0–2

Figure 22-21. Adequate paper buckle is required to deliver each sheet firmly against the paper stops in the paper grippers. On the buckle control, 0 produces minimum buckle, and 15 produces maximum buckle. Refer to the table for the proper buckle setting for the substance weight of the paper. (A.B.Dick Co.)

Buckle Control

Adequate buckle is required to deliver each sheet firmly against the paper stops in the paper grippers. See **Figure 22-21.** This adjustment ensures accurate vertical registration. The buckle control produces minimum buckle when it is set at 0, and it produces maximum buckle when it is set at 15. The buckle is set too high if the stock is being nicked at the lead edge. Changing the buckle might slightly alter the registration. Therefore, the buckle control should not be changed during a pressrun when close registration is required. A normal buckle setting is between 7 and 8.

The Receiving Tray (9835 Only)

Setting up the receiving tray provides a properly jogged pile of printed sheets.

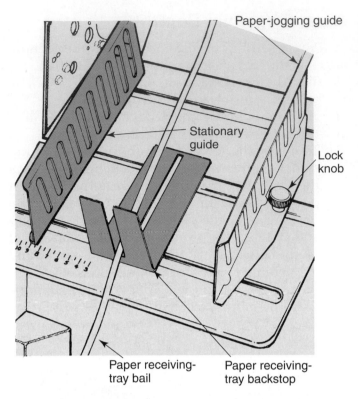

Figure 22-22. Position the stationary side guide so the pile of paper will be centered in the delivery tray. (A.B.Dick Co.)

Caution

The drive motor must be off whenever an adjustment is made to the receiving tray or the delivery wheels and rings.

1. Set the stationary guide on the nonoperator side of the duplicator for the selected width of paper. Look at **Figure 22-22.**
2. Place one sheet of paper in the receiving tray. Adjust the backstop for the length of paper being used and position the sheet against the stationary guide.
3. Rotate the handwheel so the jogging guide is in the inward position. Using the lock knob, adjust the guide so it just touches the paper.
4. Position the tray bail into the slot in the backstop and shape it to provide the best stacking for the type of paper being used.
5. Open the safety guard over the delivery system. Turn the feed switch on.

6. Turn the handwheel counterclockwise to manually feed one sheet of paper through the duplicator until it is just past the upper delivery wheels. Turn off the vacuum-pump motor. See **Figure 22-23.**

7. The upper and lower delivery wheels control the paper as it leaves the cylinders and guide it into the receiving tray. The delivery arms are movable so the wheels can be positioned over the margins of the paper. The wheels should not ride over the image area. In cases where it is necessary for the delivery wheels to travel over portions of the image, an optional wiper kit, which keeps the delivery rollers free of ink, is available.

8. After the delivery wheels are set, turn the handwheel to forward the paper until it is just under the lower delivery wheels.

9. Position the *delivery rings* either to the inside or outside of the delivery wheels and as close as possible to the wheels without crimping the paper.

10. The purpose of the delivery rings is to control paper curl so the paper is delivered properly into the receiving tray. When using flat or curl-down paper, position the rings to the outside of the delivery wheels. For paper that curls up, position the rings to the inside of the delivery wheels.

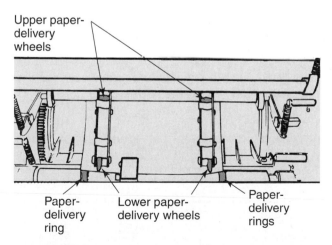

Upper paper-delivery wheels

Paper-delivery ring

Lower paper-delivery wheels

Paper-delivery rings

Figure 22-23. Manually turn the handwheel counterclockwise to feed one sheet of paper through the duplicator until it is just past the upper paper-delivery wheels. (A.B.Dick Co.)

Sheet feeding is better if the paper is fed in the direction of the grain (long grain). When paper is fed against the direction of the grain (short grain), it has a tendency to tumble or flip when entering the receiving tray. It is not always possible to identify curl-up or curl-down paper until it is fed through the duplicator. Curl-up and curl-down paper can most often be identified by the way the lead edge of the paper lifts (curl up) or drops (curl down) into the receiving tray.

11. Continue turning the handwheel until the sheet falls into the receiving tray.

12. Close the safety guard.

Chain Delivery and the Receding Stacker

Setting the chain-delivery controls ensures that the printed press sheets will fall into a properly jogged pile.

1. Place the dolly on the yoke assembly with the swivel wheels in toward the duplicator. See **Figure 22-24.**

2. Place the two-position handle on the raise-and-lower stud (for accelerated raise) and lift the dolly until it is just below the guides of the chain delivery. Be careful not to jam the dolly into the jogging arms. Seat the handle on the normal raise-and-lower stud and place the table-raise lever fully toward the delivery end of the duplicator. Raise the dolly until it is flush with the bottom of the chain-delivery guides.

3. Press the feed switch on, hand-feed one sheet into the duplicator, and then press the feed switch off. Turn the handwheel counterclockwise until the chain grippers hold the paper.

4. Open the delivery-end safety screen, exercising caution while the screen is open.

delivery ring: a ring used to control paper curl so the paper is delivered properly into the receiving tray.

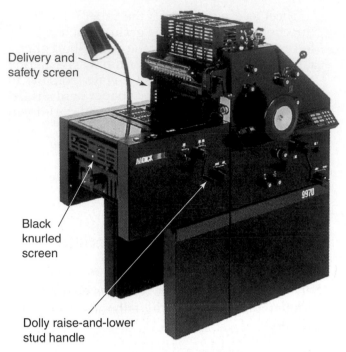

Figure 22-24. When using a chain-delivery operation, place the dolly on the yoke assembly with the swivel wheels in toward the duplicator. (A.B.Dick Co.)

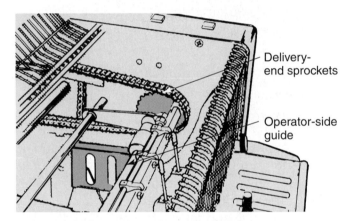

Figure 22-25. Before hand-feeding the sheet into the duplicator, locate the delivery-end sprockets and operator-side guide. (A.B.Dick Co.)

5. Continue to turn the handwheel until the gripper bar reaches the delivery-end sprockets. See **Figure 22-25.** Loosen and move the black knurled screw at the delivery end of the duplicator and adjust the guide on the nonoperator side to just touch the edge of the paper.

6. Turn the handwheel counterclockwise until the chain grippers hold the paper. Open the delivery-end safety screen. Exercise caution while the screen is open. Turn the handwheel until the gripper bar reaches the delivery-end sprockets.

Adjust the side guides on both the nonoperator and operator sides of the duplicator.

7. Again, continue to turn the handwheel until the paper is released and drops on the receiving dolly. Adjust the operator-side guide so it just touches the paper.

8. As the gripper releases the paper, the back jogger is still away from the paper. Turn the handwheel until the jogger moves fully toward the paper and loosen the center locking knob of the back jogger control. See **Figure 22-26.**

9. Turning the outer adjusting knob of the back jogger control, position the back jogger until the jogger is almost touching the trail edge of the paper. See **Figure 22-27.** Lock the back jogging guide in place and make sure the back jogger and side guides do not bind on the dolly.

10. Loosen the knurled knob on the hinged lead-edge stop and adjust the stop so the back jogger can fully stack the sheet without forcing the backstop to move.

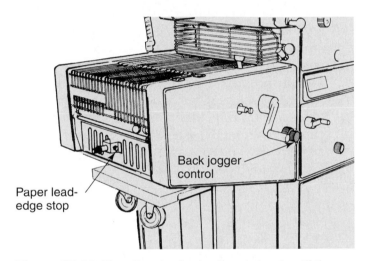

Figure 22-26. Turn the duplicator handwheel until the jogger moves fully toward the paper. (A.B.Dick Co.)

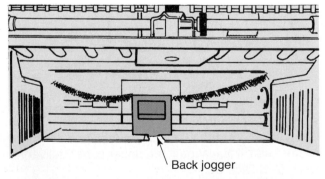

Figure 22-27. Adjust the back jogger so it stacks sheets without forcing the backstop to move. (A.B.Dick Co.)

11. Pull the knurled knob toward the nonoperator side of the sprocket shaft and position the cam of the variable paper-release sprocket so the pin is in the center hole (position four). See **Figure 22-28.** When feeding lightweight paper, position the cam at a higher number and reseat the pin in another hole. This allows the gripper to hold the paper longer and provides better stacking on the dolly. When feeding heavier stock, rotate the cam to a lower number.

12. The paper guides are normally positioned 1″ to 2″ (25.4 mm to 50.8 mm) from the edges of the printed sheet. They can be adjusted in or out for various types of copy and stocks. See **Figure 22-29.**

Note

The delivery wheels must be installed correctly to avoid damage to the grippers. If the wheels are removed, reinstall them as follows:
a. Turn the handwheel until the groove of the delivery-roller shaft is facing up (12 o'clock position).
b. Place the open delivery wheels onto the shaft so the spring-loaded latches are on the nonoperator side of the delivery wheels.
c. Lock the delivery wheels on the shaft and slowly rotate the handwheel to ensure the grippers clear the shaft.

13. Adjust the receding control lever toward the feed end of the chain delivery for heavier stocks and toward the receiving end for lighter-weight stocks. For normal lever position, center the lever in its slot, and then bring the lever back toward the receiving end of the duplicator five to six notches. Since the lever controls the rate of descent of the dolly, readjust the lever after running 400–500 sheets so the top of the paper stack is centered between the top and bottom of the paper joggers when producing printed sheets.

The Double-Sheet Detector

The double-sheet detector prevents two sheets from entering the printing unit at the same time.
1. Turn the double-sheet detector knob clockwise three to four turns. See **Figure 22-30.**
2. Press the on-and-off and feed switches to power the drive and feed systems.
3. Turn the double-sheet detector knob counterclockwise until the feed stops.

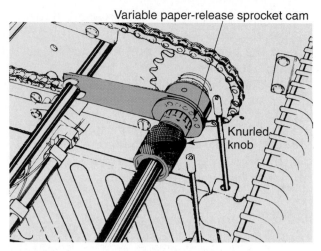

Figure 22-28. Pull the knurled knob toward the nonoperator side of the sprocket shaft. Position the cam of the variable paper-release sprocket so the pin is in the center hole (position four). Lightweight paper requires a higher-number setting. (A.B.Dick Co.)

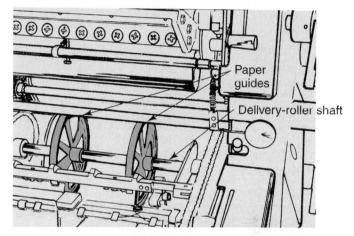

Figure 22-29. The paper guides should be placed inside the press-sheet edges 1 to 2. (A.B.Dick Co.)

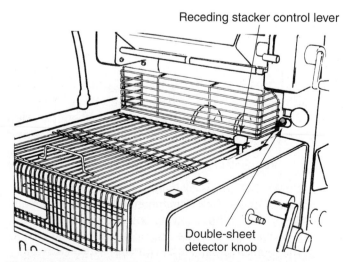

Figure 22-30. The double-sheet detector knob should be turned clockwise three to four turns. (A.B.Dick Co.)

4. Turn the adjusting knob clockwise 1/8 turn.
5. Press the clear switch on the control panel to reset the detector and press the feed switch to resume feeding.
6. Repeat steps 4 and 5 until the feed is uninterrupted.

Inking

Taking the time and care to place ink into the ink fountain and set the inking controls is essential for printing a good image.

Note

If setting up a 9850, always be sure to add the fountain solution before inking the rollers.

1. Turn the ink-fountain keys all the way clockwise, shutting off the ink supply. See **Figure 22-31.**
2. Turn all the keys one-half turn counter-clockwise. These keys provide an even flow of ink to the rollers.
3. Using an ink knife and the required can of ink, dispense ink evenly across the ink fountain. Keep a smooth, level surface in the ink can.
4. Spread the ink in the ink fountain. Using the ink fountain roller handle, rotate the ink fountain roller counterclockwise at least one revolution to carry the ink down into the ink fountain and coat the roller with ink.

5. Rotate the handwheel counterclockwise until the ink ductor roller contacts the ink fountain roller. While rotating the ink fountain roller counterclockwise, adjust the ink-fountain keys until an even, finely stippled effect is obtained on the ink ductor roller (similar to an orange-peel texture).
6. Raise the Aquamatic lockout lever toward the receiving end of the duplicator to allow full contact between the ductor and oscillating rollers (9835 and 9840 only).
7. Lift the ink fountain control up to the full (number 11) position and the Aquamatic control to number 45.
8. Make sure all safety covers are closed.
9. Press the on-and-off button to turn the duplicator on.
10. The speed should be adjusted only when the duplicator is running. Adjust the speed control to the slowest speed (this range is from 4500 to 9000 iph).
11. Allow the duplicator to run until all the rollers are evenly covered with a thin film of ink.
12. Move the ink-fountain control to one or two notches above the off position.
13. Move the Aquamatic control to the operating position (usually number 20).
14. Move the Aquamatic lockout latch toward the receiving end of the duplicator to allow automatic ducting while printing. See **Figure 22-32.**

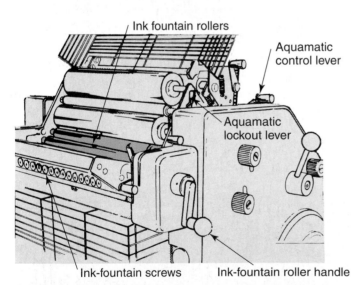

Figure 22-31. Set up the ink fountain and adjust the ink-fountain keys for even ink distribution. Raise the Aquamatic lockout lever toward the receiving end of the duplicator to allow full contact between the ductor and oscillating rollers. Set the ink-fountain control to the number 11 position and the Aquamatic control to 45. (A.B.Dick Co.)

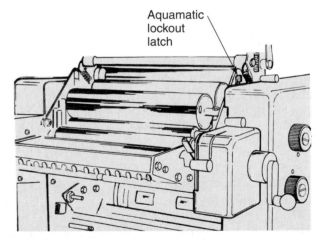

Figure 22-32. Push the Aquamatic lockout latch toward the feeder unit and away from the ink fountain to allow the ductor roller to move back and forth during printing. (A.B.Dick Co.)

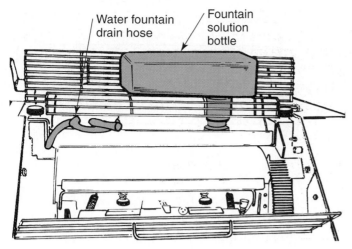

Figure 22-33. Make sure the drain hose is properly secured before placing the filled bottle in position. (A.B.Dick Co.)

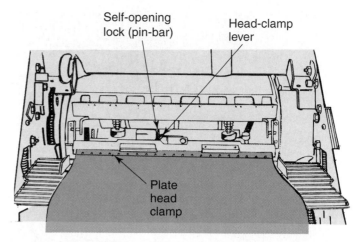

Figure 22-34. Attach the lead edge of the metal plate or master to the head clamp. Use your finger or thumb to crease the plate at the head clamp while holding it taut. (A.B.Dick Co.)

The Fountain Solution (9835 and 9840)

Care should be taken that the dampening solution flows properly into the dampening fountain.

Note

Always be sure the ink rollers, including the two in the Aquamatic unit, are inked before fountain solution is added.

1. Fill the fountain-solution bottle with properly mixed fountain solution.
2. Make sure the drain hose is properly secured. See **Figure 22-33.**
3. Close the safety cover and place the filled bottle in position in the Aquamatic unit.

Attaching the Metal Plate (Pin Bar)

Properly positioning and clamping the plate protects the plate and enhances print quality.
1. Open the safety guard over the plate cylinder.
2. Attach the lead edge of the master or metal plate to the head clamp. While holding the master or plate taut, use your finger or thumb to crease it at the head clamp. See **Figure 22-34.**
3. While still holding the master or plate taut with the right hand, rotate the handwheel counterclockwise until the tail clamp is about 3" (75 mm) from the Aquamatic fountain. Hold the master or plate taut to avoid contact between it and the form rollers.
4. Holding the master or plate against the cylinder surface, crease its tail end on the anvil of the

cylinder. Lift the tail clamp and insert the pins of the clamp over the holes of the pin-bar master or plate. Look at **Figure 22-35.**

Caution

Keep fingers clear of the tail-clamp spikes.

5. Finger tighten the two knurled knobs to secure the master or plate on the plate cylinder.
6. Apply the correct type of etch for the master. If you are using a metal plate, remove the gum coating with a cotton wipe and water. Close the safety guard. See **Figure 22-36.**

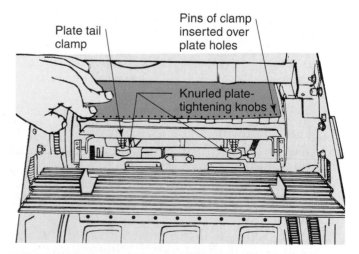

Figure 22-35. Crease the tail end of the plate or master on the anvil of the cylinder while holding it against the cylinder surface. Lift the tail clamp and insert the pins of the clamp over the holes of the plate. (A.B.Dick Co.)

Figure 22-36. Prior to making a trial press copy, moisten the plate with a thin even film of fountain solution (or plate etch, for a paper master) using a cotton pad. (Van Son Holland Ink Corp.)

Note

When using the pin-bar clamp, the self-opening lock must engage the lever.

The Self-Opening Clamp

Models with the self-opening plate clamp have the following procedure to be followed for proper plate mounting:
1. Open the safety guard over the plate cylinder. The side guides on the inside of the open guard are used as a master- or plate-loading table.
2. Set the side guides to the width of the master or plate, using the scale on the loading table to center the master or plate. Actuate the self-opening clamp by disengaging the lock from the clamp latch. See **Figure 22-37**.

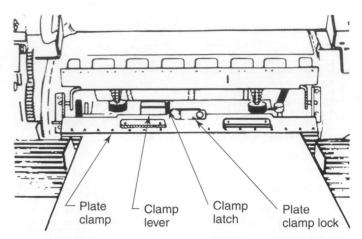

Plate clamp — Clamp lever — Clamp latch — Plate clamp lock

Figure 22-37. Secure the plate or master to the cylinder by tightening the two knurled knobs. (A.B.Dick Co.)

Note

The self-opening clamp can also be actuated by pushing in on the clamp lever.

3. When using the pin-bar clamp, the self-opening lock must engage the lever. To use the self-opening plate clamp, use the side guides on the inside of the open guard as a plate- or master-loading table. The side guides are set to the plate width, and the self-opening clamp is actuated. The plate is inserted into the clamp until it closes. The clamp snaps closed as the handwheel is rotated.
4. Position the straight-edge master or plate on the loading table.
5. Turn the plate cylinder clockwise until the clamp opens.
6. Slide the master or plate squarely into the clamp and continue turning the cylinder clockwise until the clamp closes.

Caution

Since the clamp snaps shut as the handwheel is rotated, keep fingers clear of the clamp area.

7. Apply the correct type of etch (using a master) on a cotton pad and thoroughly wet out the master. If using a metal plate, use fountain solution to thoroughly dampen the surface.

The Sequence of Operation

Once the paper is feeding well, the ink and dampening trains are ready, and the plate is positioned, the actual printing can begin. The operation control level becomes the main control during the run.

1. Close all safety guards. Be sure the Aquamatic control is at 20 and the ink fountain control is between 4 and 5.
2. Press the on-and-off switch to start the duplicator. Depress the Aquamatic lockout release for three to five revolutions to apply fountain solution to the rollers. Refer to **Figure 22-38.**
3. Move the operation control lever to the ink position. Check the master or plate as the duplicator is idling in the ink position to be sure the master or plate is clean of ink in the nonimage areas. If it tends to pick up ink in the nonimage areas, there is too much ink or too little water in the ink system, and adjustments should be made as required.
4. Move the operation control lever to the image position and hold it there for several revolutions (generally two to four revolutions are required).
5. Move the operation control lever to the feed position. When released, the lever automatically returns to the ink position. Allow one sheet of paper to be fed, and then press the feed switch off. If operating a chain-delivery model, single-sheet feed can be accomplished by pressing the proof button after imaging the copy.

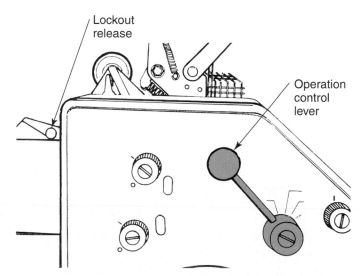

Figure 22-38. Turn the duplicator on after closing all safety guards. Move the operation control lever to the ink position, and then move the control lever to the image position. When ready, move the control lever to the feed position, allow one sheet to be fed, and then press the feed switch off. (A.B.Dick Co.)

6. Remove the copy from the receiving tray, or if operating a chain-delivery model, place the control lever in the neutral position and press the on-and-off switch to shut the duplicator down before removing the copy from the hinged lead-edge stop door.

Caution

Always exercise caution when removing printed sheets from the hinged lead-edge stop door.

7. Inspect the copy for position, clarity, and general acceptability. If copy adjustments are necessary, make sure the operation control lever is in the neutral position and the duplicator is off, and then see the section on copy adjustments later in this chapter.
8. If the trial copy is acceptable, enter the count for the required number of impressions. Turn the duplicator on. Place the operation control lever in ink. Press the feed switch on. If necessary, lighter and darker copy in various areas of the master or plate can be compensated for by adjusting the ink-control screws. Clockwise decreases the ink supply, and counterclockwise increases the flow of ink.
9. If a count has been entered, once the required number of copies has been printed, the feed automatically shuts off. Move the operation control lever to the neutral position.
10. If the master or plate is to be retained, remove the excess ink from it and preserve it.
11. Clean the blanket after the run using a cloth dampened with blanket wash.

Caution

Blanket wash is usually highly flammable! Do not use it near fire or open flame and avoid prolonged skin contact. Always use with adequate ventilation.

The Stop Button

The duplicator can be stopped during a printing cycle by pressing the feed switch off and engaging the red stop button. The stop button interrupts the safety circuit and cuts current to the drive motor. Place the operation control lever in the neutral position in order to move the form rollers out of contact with the master or plate while the duplicator is idle.

To restart the duplicator, press the on-and-off switch. Move the operation control lever to the ink position until the nonimage areas of the master or plate are clean. Press the feed switch on.

Copy Adjustments

The image can be modified in how it is positioned on the press sheet. Angular, lateral, and vertical adjustments can be made to the plate.

Caution

The duplicator must be stopped when making any copy adjustments.

1. Angular copy adjustments can be made by removing the tail end of the master or plate from the clamp and rotating the shaft and pin assembly right or left. See **Figure 22-39.**
   If the copy is running downhill from left to right, turn the pin counterclockwise to raise the right side of the copy. If the copy is running uphill, turn the pin clockwise to lower the right side of the copy. Reinsert the tail end of the master or plate in the tail clamp. Always clean the blanket after making this adjustment.
2. Lateral copy adjustments of up to 1/4″ (6.3 mm) can be made by removing the tail end of the master or plate from the clamp and turning the knurled knob so the head clamp moves in the desired direction. See **Figure 22-40.** Reinsert the

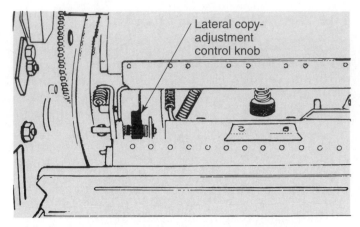

Figure 22-40. Lateral copy adjustments can be made by removing the tail end of the plate or master from the clamp and turning the knurled knob so the head clamp moves in the desired direction. (A.B.Dick Co.)

tail end of the master or plate in the tail clamp and always clean the blanket after making this adjustment. For a lateral adjustment greater than 1/4″ (6.3 mm), move the paper stack.

3. To make a vertical copy adjustment, lift the safety cover over the blanket and rotate the handwheel until the locking gear lines up with the built-in print-adjusting tool. See **Figure 22-41.** Push the print-adjusting lock knob in and loosen the locking gear by turning it counterclockwise. Holding the knob in, move the scale on the opposite side of the blanket cylinder by turning the handwheel and following the arrows to raise or lower the copy.
4. After the adjustment is made, tighten the locking gear. It is not necessary to clean the blanket after raising or lowering the copy image, as the relationship of the plate cylinder to the blanket

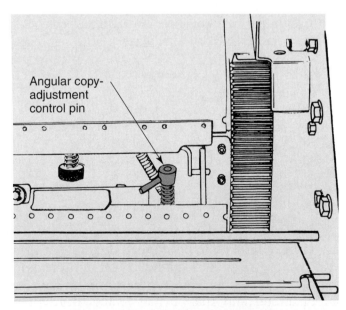

Figure 22-39. Angular copy adjustments can be made by removing the tail end of the plate or master from the clamp and rotating the shaft and pin assembly. (A.B.Dick Co.)

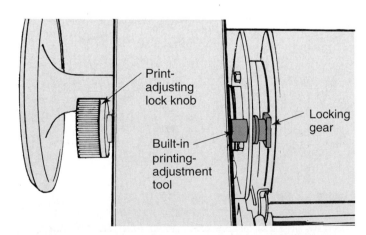

Figure 22-41. You must lift the safety cover in order to reach the handwheel to make a vertical copy adjustment. (A.B.Dick Co.)

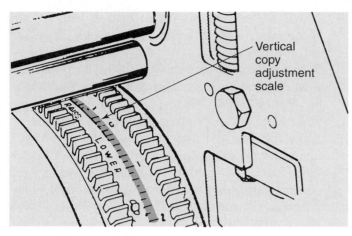

Figure 22-42. Set the vertical copy adjustment scale at zero for normal operating procedures. (A.B.Dick Co.)

cylinder remains the same. For normal operating procedures, set the scale at zero, as no change should be necessary. See **Figure 22-42.**

Adjusting Paper Control

The micromatic paper control allows very precise adjustments to be made to the lateral positioning of the image. This control can move the image a maximum of only 3/16".

1. To adjust the micromatic, loosen the outer guide knob and turn the inner knob toward the mounting bar to move the stack to the nonoperating side. Look at **Figure 22-43.**
2. To move the guide to the operating side of the duplicator, loosen the inner guide knob and turn the outer guide toward the mounting bar.

3. Hold the knob used to make the adjustment and tighten the opposite knob to secure the micromatic. When adjusting the feed-table side guides, be sure the guides clear the paper stack, support rails, and paper board before raising the feed table. For adjustments greater than 3/16" (5 mm), the guide-plate assembly and the paper guide must be moved before the fine adjustment can be made.

Cylinder Adjustments

The impression and plate cylinders automatically adjust to the blanket cylinder to compensate for changes in master, plate, or paper thickness. Some applications, however, might require an adjustment in the impression- or plate-cylinder control. For instance, the copy quality in rough-textured papers, particularly copy containing halftones and solids, can be improved with increased pressure from the impression cylinder. Make these adjustments when the master or plate is on the plate cylinder:

Caution

Keep hands and the Allen wrench clear of the rotating handwheel while making the impression-cylinder adjustment.

1. Insert the Allen wrench into the control-dial opening. Turn the dial to a lower number (clockwise) to increase pressure and to a higher number to decrease pressure. Refer to **Figure 22-44.**

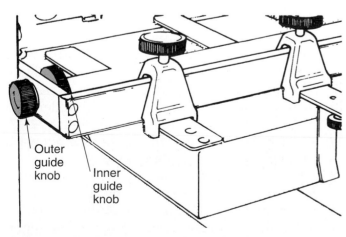

Figure 22-43. To adjust the micromatic paper control, the outer guide knob is loosened, and the inner knob is turned toward the mounting bar. This moves the stack to the nonoperating side. (A.B.Dick Co.)

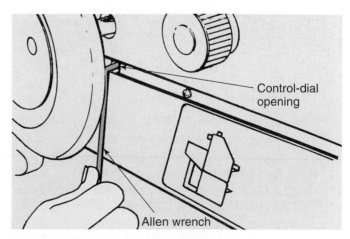

Figure 22-44. Impression-cylinder adjustment is accomplished by inserting an Allen wrench into the control-dial opening and turning the dial. A lower number increases pressure, and a higher number decreases pressure. (A.B.Dick Co.)

Ink fountain

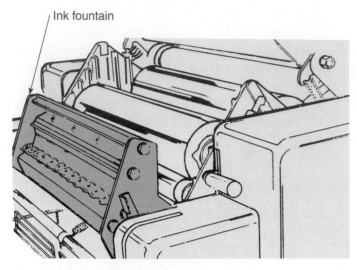

Figure 22-45. Remove the ink fountain by turning it up to a vertical position and lifting it off the duplicator. The ink fountain and fountain rollers are cleaned, and the blanket is washed. (A.B.Dick Co.)

2. While running the required copy, turn the dial counterclockwise to decrease the cylinder pressure until the copy becomes broken (not printing fully). Turn the dial clockwise until an optimum copy image is achieved. Adjust only until the optimum copy is achieved.

The plate-cylinder adjustment is specifically designed for adjusting to different thicknesses of masters and plates. As the number is increased, the pressure is decreased.

Note

On 9850 duplicators, be sure the night-latch lever is positioned toward the feed end to keep the Aquamatic rollers out of contact with the rest of the ink system.

Cleaning the Duplicator

Cleaning ink from the ink train prevents color contamination of the next ink color to be printed and plays an essential role in press maintenance.

1. Remove the fountain-solution bottle.
2. On the 9835 or 9840 only, raise the safety guard and unfasten the hose to drain fountain solution from the fountain. Discard any unused solution. Close the safety cover.
3. Remove the ink from the ink fountain. Wedge the ink between two strips of card stock and remove. Discard the ink.

4. Move the ink-ductor lockout lever up and toward the feed end to lock the ductor away from the ink fountain.
5. Remove the ink fountain by turning it up to a vertical position and then lifting it off the duplicator. See **Figure 22-45.** Clean the ink fountain and fountain roller with a cloth moistened with blanket wash.
6. Move the Aquamatic lockout latch and night-latch lever toward the receiving end of the duplicator (9835 and 9840 only). Position the Aquamatic control to number 45 (9835 and 9840 only).
7. Attach a cleanup mat to the plate cylinder just as you would a master or plate.
8. Be sure all safety covers are closed, and press the on-and-off switch to start the duplicator. Turn the speed down to minimum. From a container filled with blanket wash, apply a small amount to the ink oscillating roller through the opening in the guard with a squeeze container.
9. Move the operation control lever to the ink position.
10. Continue to apply small amounts of blanket wash over the ink rollers until the cleanup mat is saturated. This occurs almost immediately with the first cleanup mat.
11. Move the operation control lever to the neutral position. Stop the duplicator. Remove the cleanup mat. When thoroughly dry, the mat can be reused on the reverse side.
12. Install another cleanup mat and repeat steps 8–11 until the last mat is clean and the rollers are dry.

Note

Do not allow a film of blanket wash to remain on the rollers, as the film causes glazing or sensitizing of the rollers.

13. Move the Aquamatic night-latch lever toward the feed end of the duplicator. See **Figure 22-46.**
14. Remove the secondary ink oscillator and distributor rollers. Place them in a support-cradle accessory.
15. Remove the Aquamatic oscillating roller and place it on its support bracket. See **Figure 22-47.**
16. Unlatch the lock levers by moving them toward the feed end of the duplicator.
17. Lift and tilt the ink oscillating roller toward the ink fountain so it does not contact any other rollers.
18. Drain the fountain solution from the 9850 only.
19. Move the operation control lever to the night-latch position and turn the upper form roller off. Remove the two knurled knobs, lift the

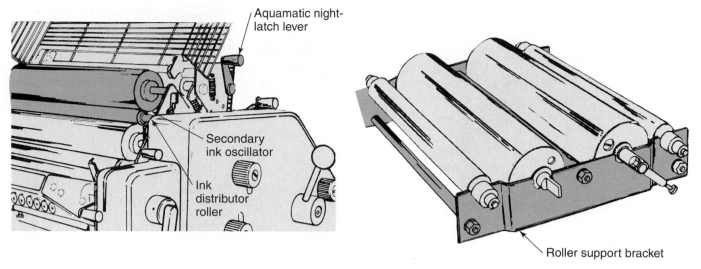

Figure 22-46. Move the Aquamatic night-latch lever toward the feed end of the duplicator. Remove the secondary ink oscillator and distributor rollers. Place them in the roller support cradle. (A.B.Dick Co.)

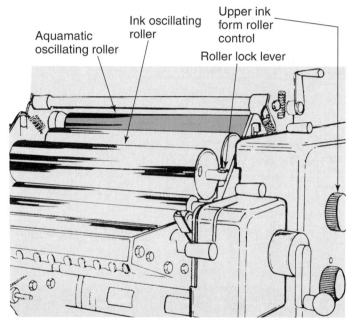

Figure 22-47. Remove the Aquamatic oscillating roller and store it. (A.B.Dick Co.)

Aquamatic tray up and away from the ink system, and clean thoroughly. Replace the tray.

20. Thoroughly clean and polish the plate and impression cylinders.
21. Remove all ink from the blanket.
22. To keep the finish of the impression and plate cylinders clean, apply hand cleaner to the stained areas and let it stand for a few minutes. Rub the area with a soft cloth or cotton pad until the stain dissolves. Remove the residue with a damp cotton pad.

23. If the duplicator is to be secured for the day, set the night latch and turn off all electrical power.

The Ryobi® 3200

Two Ryobi duplicators are commonly found on the floor of printing facilities—the Ryobi 2800 and the Ryobi 3200. The main difference between the two models is the maximum press-sheet size. The 2800 can accommodate a wider sheet. Both models are equipped with a combined dampening system, similar to that of the A.B.Dick 9800. Refer back to **Figure 22-2.** In addition, both models use a single-control lever to control the dampening, inking, image-transfer, paper-feed, and printing functions. The specs for the 2800 and 3200 are listed in **Figure 22-48.** The 3200 has a

Specs for the Ryobi 2800 and 3200	
Paper size	2800—3 9/16″ × 5 1/8″ to 12″ × 17 3/4″ (9.0 × 13.0 cm to 30.5 cm × 45.0 cm); 3200—3 9/16″ × 5 1/8″ to 13 3/8″ × 17 3/4″ (9.0 × 13.0 cm to 34.0 × 45.0 cm)
Paper caliper	0.0016″–0.012″ (0.04–0.3 mm)
Printing area	2800—11″ × 17 1/4″ (28.0 × 43.8 cm); 3200—13″ × 17 1/4″ (33.0 × 43.8 cm)
Metal-plate size	2800—11.26″ × 19.37″ (28.6 × 49.2 cm); 3200—13 3/16″ × 19 6/16″ (33.5 × 49.2 cm)
Gripper margin	0.8 cm
Feed-pile capacity	17 3/4″ (45.0 cm)
Delivery capacity	2800— 23 1/4″; 3200—20 1/2″
Speed	3000–10,000 iph

Figure 22-48. Specs for the Ryobi 2800 and 3200 duplicators.

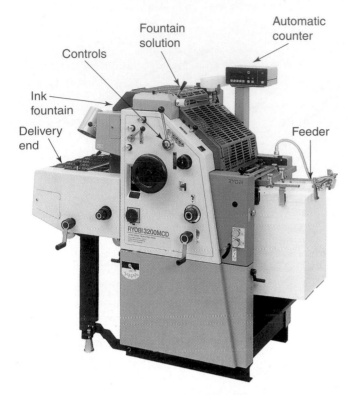

Figure 22-49. The control side of the 3200 contains nearly all the control mechanisms. (Ryobi Xpedx Impact Group)

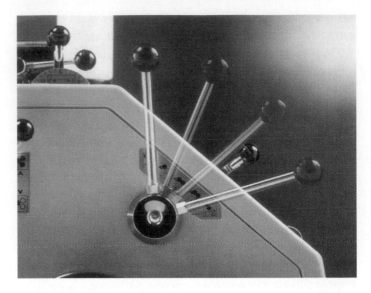

Figure 22-50. Similar to most duplicators, the 3200 has a single-lever control. (Ryobi Xpedx Impact Group)

chain-delivery system, while the 2800 was manufactured in both a chute model and a chain-delivery model.

The basic operating procedures for the Ryobi 3200 are summarized below. These procedures should be conducted only after the operator has been thoroughly oriented to the duplicator. The Ryobi 3200 has an operation panel, which sits above most of the press, and a switch panel, located to the left of the handwheel. See **Figure 22-49.** The operation panel has a display for the preset number of sheets to be printed and, above it, a display that counts the sheets as they are printed. The blanket-jam and double-sheet detector switches are located on the back of the panel. The switch panel has two toggle switches—the drive switch, which activates the cylinders' rotation, and the vacuum pump, which activates the suction to the feeder.

The operating lever has five settings that bring the form rollers in contact with the plate cylinder, bring the plate cylinder in contact with the blanket cylinder, begin the paper feed, and bring the blanket cylinder in contact with the impression cylinder to begin printing. See **Figure 22-50.** The side of the press with most of the controls is known as the *operation side* of the press.

Preparing the Feeder Unit

Making the correct settings in the feeder prevents double feeds and jammed press sheets.

1. The paper-feed table is lowered by moving the release lever to its high position and turning the crank handle. See **Figure 22-51.**
2. After a small pile of paper is placed onto the paper-feed table, move the metal vertical guides toward the sides of the pile by the vertical side-guide handles. These guides keep the pile straight. See **Figure 22-52.**
3. Add the remainder of the paper to the paper-feed table.

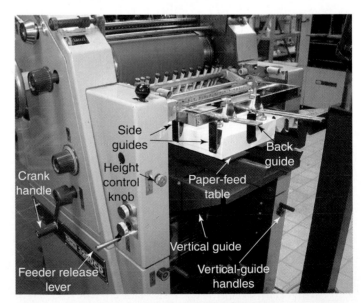

Figure 22-51. The feeder unit has several components and controls. (Zipf Lock Co.)

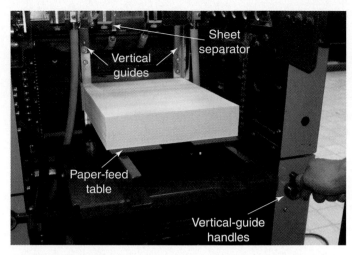

Figure 22-52. The vertical guides are placed against both edges of the paper by turning the vertical-guide handles.

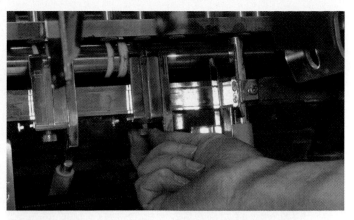

Figure 22-53. After loosening the set screw, position the sheet separators. The outer separators should be inside the outermost suction feet.

4. With the press stopped, position the sheet separators by loosening the screw at the bottom of each sheet separator. See **Figure 22-53.** Four separators are usually used and positioned inside the edges of the paper pile.
5. Turn the height-control knob three clockwise turns. Move the release lever to its low position so the paper-feed table will be raised automatically during printing. Moving the lever to the high position halts this function.
6. Adjust the paper-pile height by turning the height-control knob counterclockwise until the top of the pile is aligned with the appropriate line of the pile-height scale. See **Figure 22-54.**
7. If the pile is too high, move the release lever to the high position and lower the pile by turning the crank handle. Repeat steps five and six.
8. Set the two side guides and the back guide against the pile. Move the side guide on the operation side of the press against the paper until the flat springs bend slightly (about 1/10″, or 2–3 mm). Use the side-guide microadjustment knob if a very minor modification is required.
9. Rotate the black control knobs at the top of the suction feet to activate the feet over the paper, and deactivate the suction feet that are partially or completely outside the paper.
10. Flip the pump switch (in front of the handwheel) to its highest position, and then turn the vacuum control clockwise to create the proper amount of suction. Turning the control clockwise increases suction. Heavyweight paper requires more vacuum than lightweight sheets do.
11. Turn the blower control knob clockwise to increase the amount of air blown against the pile to separate the top five or six sheets.

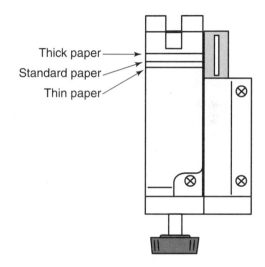

Figure 22-54. The top sheet of the pile should be lined up with the appropriate mark on the pile-height scale.

12. If the paper is lightweight, position and activate the back blower to lift the entire top sheet. The back-blower control knob is on the nonoperator (right) side of the pile of paper.

Setting the Delivery Unit

Making the correct settings to the delivery unit produces a well-jogged pile of undamaged press sheets.
1. Raise the delivery-table dolly by moving its automatic-lower control lever to the zero position, while turning the crank handle. See **Figure 22-55.**
2. Set the position of the side guide. Feed a sheet of paper into the delivery unit by turning the handwheel until the sheet enters the delivery unit. Loosen the knob that locks the side guide and move the side guide so it sits 1/10″ (3 mm) from the edge of the paper. See **Figure 22-56.** Tighten the knob.

Delivery-table dolly automatic-lower control lever   Feed lever

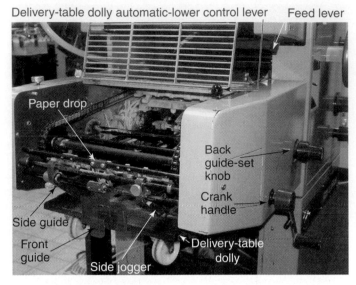

Figure 22-55. The delivery unit of the 3200 has many components and controls.

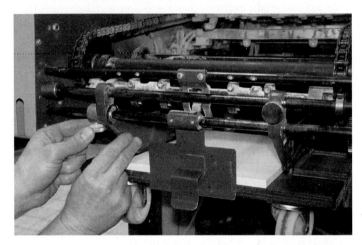

Figure 22-56. After loosening the control knob, the side guide should be positioned 3 mm away from the edge of the paper.

Figure 22-57. Loosen the side jogger. Turn the handwheel until a sheet of paper has been moved as close to the side jogger as it will go. Position the side jogger against the paper.

Figure 22-58. The back guide is moved by loosening the set handle and turning the knob until the guide is against the paper.

3. Feed another sheet of paper into the delivery unit until the sheet falls onto the table dolly. Move the sheet against the side guide and front guide.
4. Turn the handwheel until the side jogger and back guide are closest to the paper. Loosen the knob and move the side jogger in contact with the paper. See **Figure 22-57.** Tighten the knob.
5. Set the back guide by loosening the set handle and turning the knob until the back guide contacts the paper. See **Figure 22-58.** Tighten the set handle.
6. Set the delivery air blower by turning the control knob clockwise to increase the volume of air. The sheets should fall flat.
7. Turn off the pump.

Mounting the Plate

Mounting the plate on this press is not a difficult operation.

1. Place the holes on the plate's lead edge over the pins on the plate cylinder. After the plate is hooked, feed the plate onto the plate cylinder by rotating the handwheel with one hand while pulling at the trailing edge of the plate with the other hand.
2. Hold the trailing edge of the plate against the plate cylinder while lifting the pin-bar clamp and pushing the pins through the holes.
3. Tighten the plate by turning the plate-tension bolts. See **Figure 22-59.**

Figure 22-59. Plate tension is created by turning the tension bolts until the tail edge is pulled down.

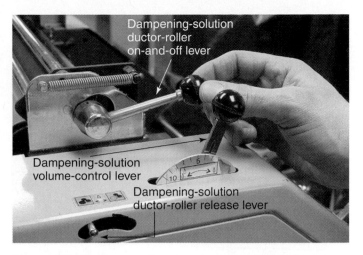

Figure 22-60. Turn on the dampening-solution ductor on-and-off roller lever, move the dampening-solution ductor-roller release lever to the left, and set the dampening-solution volume-control lever at zero.

Setting the Ink and Dampening Units

A careful setting of the controls for the inking and dampening units saves both makeready time and paper.

1. If the ink fountain is not already in place, set the ink rollers by moving the ink form roller release lever (located in front of the operating lever) to its top position.
2. Lift out the ink-rider oscillating roller and place it on the other ink rollers.
3. Wipe off the ink fountain and the ink fountain roller. Apply oil to the sides of the ink fountain roller.
4. Push the ink fountain against the ink fountain roller, insert the fixing screws into the brackets, and screw in the ink fountain.
5. Place ink into the ink fountain.
6. To control the dampening solution, adjust the three controls situated near the top of the press. Move the dampening-solution ductor-roller on-and-off lever toward the feeder. See **Figure 22-60.** Set the dampening-solution ductor-roller release lever to the left. Set the dampening-solution volume-control lever at 0. Turn the drive switch (to the left of the handwheel) to the on position, and push the feed lever forward. See **Figure 22-61.**
7. After the ink rollers are covered with ink, transfer ink to the dampening-solution rollers by moving the water volume-control lever from 0 to 10.
8. Stop the press and manually apply a uniform coating of ink to both ends of the water ductor roller, but do not apply ink to the sides of the roller.

9. Adjust the ink-fountain keys to ensure that the ink feed to the plate is proportional to the amount of image area.
10. Pull back the feed lever to stop feeding.
11. Pour dampening solution into the plastic dampening fountain, tighten the bottle cap, and place the bottle into the bottle bracket at the top of the press.
12. During the pressrun, use the dampening-solution feeding lever to control the amount of solution transferred to the plate.

Adjusting the Press Speed

Set the press running speed by turning the speed-adjustment handle. See **Figure 22-62.** Turning the handle clockwise increases the speed. The press speed is shown on the speed indicator. The numbers above the curved line indicate speeds below 6000 iph, and numbers below the line indicate speeds above 6000 iph.

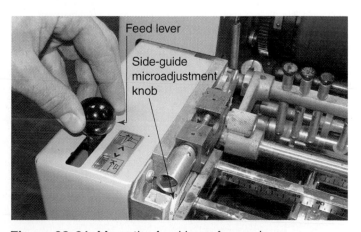

Figure 22-61. Move the feed lever forward.

Figure 22-62. The press speed is set by turning the handle next to the press-speed indicator.

Note

Moving from slow to fast speeds or from fast to slow speeds requires that the press be turned off, the nonoperator-side cover removed, the drive belt moved, and the cover replaced. When the press speed is changed, the dampening-solution speed must also be changed. Refer to the operator's manual for instruction.

Adjusting Impression Pressure

Setting the impression-pressure adjustment dial to "auto" allows the press to adjust the pressure the impression cylinder applies to the blanket cylinder. The paper caliper determines this pressure. The operator has the option of setting the impression pressure by choosing "fixed impression pressure."

Test Printing

The test printing quickly indicates modifications that might need to be made to the ink system, dampening system, or plate positioning.
1. Apply water to the plate with a sponge to remove the gum solution.
2. Flip the drive switch up to on and the pump switch down to its lowest position.
3. Transfer ink and dampening solution to the plate by moving the operating lever to position two.
4. Transfer ink and dampening solution to the blanket by moving the operating lever to position three.
5. After five impressions, move the operating lever to position four.

6. Slide the feed lever forward to print a few test sheets.
7. To end the test printing, return the feed lever to the off position and the operating lever to position one.

Adjusting the Image

It is common for the image to require being moved on the press sheet. These adjustments fall into three categories. The categories are vertical, lateral, and diagonal.

Vertical adjustments

If the image is too high or low on the press sheet, a vertical adjustment is made by pushing in the vertical-microadjustment dial, while pushing down the clutch lever with the other hand. Releasing the clutch lever engages the adjustment dial. Turning the dial in the "+" direction moves the image toward the lead edge of the press sheet. This dial can move the image forward or backward a maximum of approximately 3/4" (2.0 cm). Depressing the clutch lever a second time releases the dial lock and allows the press to be operated.

Lateral adjustments

Moving the image horizontally on the press sheet begins with releasing the vertical guide slightly and turning the side-microadjustment knob. The paper in the feeder unit is reset by adjusting the paper guides. Substantial lateral image adjustment might require the entire feeder and delivery units to be reset.

Diagonal adjustments

If the image is skewed on the press sheet, the image can be rotated by removing the plate and turning the diagonal-position adjustment bolt. See **Figure 22-63.** Turning the bolt clockwise rotates the image clockwise on the press sheet. In other words, the operation side of the image is raised. Turning the bolt counterclockwise rotates the image counterclockwise on the press sheet.

Printing

When the makeready stage is finished, the pressrun begins. The press-sheet counter is set at the beginning of the pressrun.
1. With the delivery-table dolly in place, move the rotary guides in the delivery unit outside the image area. See **Figure 22-64.**
2. Set the press-sheet counter to all zeroes.
3. Set the operation panel with the number of press sheets needing to be printed.

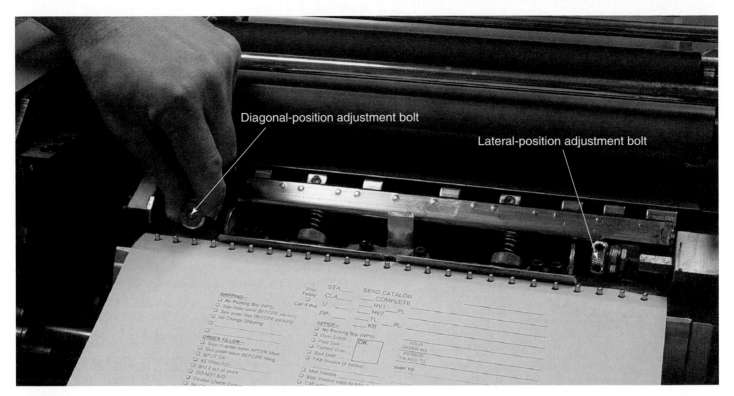

Figure 22-63. If the image is skewed on the press sheet, it can be corrected by adjusting the diagonal-position bolts. (Zipf Lock Co.)

Figure 22-64. Rotary guides should be positioned away from the image areas.

4. Turn on the blanket-jam detector switch and the double-sheet detector switch.
5. Push the double-sheet detector button. A light comes on and stays on until the setting is complete, which is after four sheets have gone through the press.
6. When the thickness of the paper is changed or when printing the second side of a press sheet, reset the double-sheet detector by pressing the set button.

Note

The double-sheet detector cannot function when printing paper that is too dark to transmit light because it works by measuring the amount of light passing through a sheet. When printing on very dark paper, do not activate the double-sheet detector.

7. Wipe off the blanket.
8. Turn on the drive switch and the pump switch.
9. Shift the operating lever to the second, third, fourth, and last positions to begin printing.
10. If necessary, turn on the setoff-spray switch. Set the spray nozzle so the spray is directed at the image areas. Turn the spray-control lever, located on the top of the powder bottle, to adjust the amount of spray. If the timing of the spray needs to be adjusted to match the length of the press sheet, that operation can be performed by opening the small door near the delivery-unit crank handle and adjusting a cam. Refer to the operator's manual.

Cleaning the Press

A thorough press cleaning, or washup, is essential to establishing a good maintenance program and avoiding color contamination of the next ink to be used.

1. After removing the dampening fountain-solution bottle, use the rubber hose to drain the dampening solution from the fountain tray into a bucket or similar container.
2. Secure the ink-roller cleanup attachment onto the pins located beneath the ink oscillating roller. Make sure the attachment is hooked properly over the pins, or it will fall when the rollers rotate. Turn the fixing knobs on the bottom of the ink-roller cleanup attachment.
3. Set the dampening-solution ductor-roller release lever to the right or left. Set the water-control lever to position 10.
4. Turn on the drive switch.
5. Through the safety cover, squirt washup solution.
6. If the rollers do not become adequately clean, open the safety cover and tighten the fixing knobs on the bottom of the ink-roller cleanup attachment.
7. After the rollers become clean, turn off the press at the drive switch.
8. Remove the ink-roller cleanup attachment and immediately clean it thoroughly.
9. Release the ink form roller release lever and the dampening-solution ductor-roller release lever. Lift the ink-rider oscillating roller and release it.
10. Use an ink knife to remove ink from the ink fountain.
11. Loosen the ink-fountain fixing knobs and allow the ink fountain to swing downward. Thoroughly clean the ink fountain with a cloth.
12. Use a rag and washup solution to clean the dampening-fountain tray of accumulated paper dust.
13. Wipe ink from the ends of the dampening-solution ductor roller and the fountain roller. Clean the plate cylinder, the blanket cylinder, and the impression cylinder with a rag and washup solution.

Summary

Sheetfed offset presses are classified on the basis of press size, feeding arrangement, number of colors (units), and whether they are one sided or perfecting. Small offset presses that print on a maximum sheet size of approximately 11″ × 17″ (27.9 cm × 43.2 cm) are classified as duplicators. Presses that print on sheets larger than 11″ × 17″ (27.9 cm × 43.2 cm) are classified as offset presses. Although most offset duplicators perform the same basic functions, their designs and mechanisms vary. For this reason, press operators often need to become familiar with the controls and settings of a new machine. Fortunately, knowing the basic principles of lithographic printing makes this task manageable. The operating procedure for running a small press includes mounting the plate, achieving smooth paper feeding and delivery, controlling ink and dampening solution, adjusting the image as needed, and cleaning the press at the end of the run. Students who can perform these functions on one press are in a good position to learn the operation of other presses they might encounter in their careers.

Review Questions

Please do not write in this book. Write your answers on a separate sheet of paper.

1. In a(n) _____ dampening system, the ink and fountain solution originate in separate fountains but are fed through the same rollers to the plate.
2. What function does a clear switch (button) on an A.B.Dick 9840 or 9850 serve?
3. What are the five positions of the operation control lever on most duplicators?
4. The _____ control should not be changed during a pressrun because it can alter the registration.
5. The _____ are used to control paper curl so the paper is delivered properly into the receiving tray.
6. Why should blanket wash not be used near an open flame?
7. Pressing the _____ button interrupts the safety circuit and cuts current to the drive motor.
8. The quality of images being printed on rough-textured paper can be improved with increased pressure from the _____ cylinder.
9. The parts of the ink fountain that can be adjusted to allow more or less ink flow are fountain _____.
10. How do you adjust the dampener form rollers on a duplicator?
11. Select a type of duplicator and describe what determines the impression pressure.
12. Select a type of duplicator and describe how to adjust the copy by adjusting the plate position.

Skill-Building Activities

1. Plan to visit a commercial printer to observe a press operator. Closely watch what is happening. Should problems develop, observe how the operator solves them. Do not disturb the operator during press operation. Write a short report on your findings.

2. Find examples of the following dampening systems: conventional, integrated, alcohol, no molleton, and "bareback." Examine each system and familiarize yourself with its operating features.

3. Obtain several printing trade journals. Check for articles featuring new presses, press modifications, and accessories for presses. Learn to use the journals for research and information gathering.

4. Pick one of the duplicators or presses in the lab and list the features you like and dislike. What is it about this particular machine that impresses you more than the others?

5. Try to arrange a meeting with a press technician. Ask questions that will assist you in operating the equipment more proficiently, and ask the technician for tips on running more difficult jobs, such as those on onionskin, carbonless paper, and envelopes. Make a chart of the technician's recommendations for future use.

Don't Stop the Press

When high speed and high volume are needed, the web press is the way to go. Unlike sheetfed presses that feed individual sheets, a web press feeds only one sheet—a very long sheet. As can be seen in the photograph, a webfed press pulls a continuous ribbon of paper from a large roll through the units. The simplicity of the feeding function allows the press to run much faster than sheetfed presses do.

Magazines, newspapers, and other deadline-based publications are printed on webfed presses. In fact, when the supply of paper nears the end, the roll can be replaced with a new one without stopping the press. The whole point is to maintain production and to deliver on time. Don't stop the press.

(Goss International Corporation)

Chapter 23
Web Offset Presses

Key Terms

angle bar
back-trap mottle
chill roll
cutoff
delivery conveyor
double ending
drum common impression web offset press
dryer
festoon
flying paster
former folded web
in-line
in-line open web offset press
jaw cylinder
keyless fountain
miniweb
ninety-degree bump turn
numbering tower
pattern gluer with plow
pattern perforator
perfecting blanket-to-blanket web offset press
pinless folder
plow tower
prefolder
remoistenable gluer
roll stand
rotary die cutter
single-knife rotary trimmer
slab waste
splicer
tension control
tucker blade
turning bar
variable folder
variable rotary cutter
web-break detector
web guide
zero-speed paster

Learning Objectives

When you have completed the reading and assigned activities related to this chapter, you will be able to do the following:

- Describe the basic components of a four-unit blanket-to-blanket web offset press.
- Discuss the purpose and operational differences between a flying splicer and a zero-speed splicer on web offset presses.
- Give examples of common methods used to achieve register on web offset presses.
- Identify various types of web offset inks and ink-drying systems.
- Explain the function of web-press management systems.
- Name several in-line web finishing systems.
- Summarize desirable paper qualities and explain proper paper-handling procedures.

Much of the expansion in the offset-lithography industry over the past 30 years is credited to the growth of web offset printing. Web offset presses produce single-color and multicolor work for small- and medium-run newspapers, magazines, business forms, mail-order catalogs, gift wrapping, books, inserts, and all types of commercial printing. See **Figure 23-1.**

Web offset presses feed from a roll, or web, of paper—instead of individual sheets. The term *webfed* is commonly used to distinguish these presses from sheetfed presses. Web offset presses are extremely fast—two to four times faster than the fastest sheetfed offset presses. For this reason, they are typically used for long runs. For example, 50,000 copies of a promotional mailer would likely be printed on a sheetfed press, but 500,000 copies would likely be run on a web that can print four colors on both sides, such as the one shown in **Figure 23-2.** Speeds of 1800 feet per minute (9.14 m/s) are common because the paper moves through the press as a roll. Sheetfed presses must run more slowly because the feeding unit must separate, pick up, and grip each sheet individually. Each sheet provides the chance for a misfeed. After a webfed press is underway, however, feeding is a seamless operation.

Large daily newspapers are printed on web presses that pull paper from more than one roll of

Figure 23-1. This large web press can produce 40,000 newspapers or inserts in an hour. (Goss International Corporation)

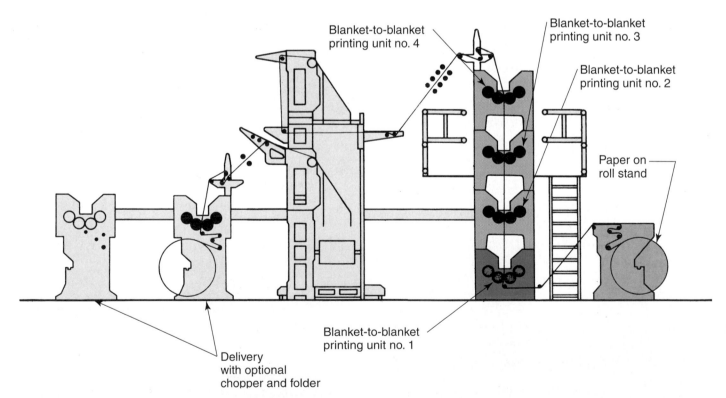

Figure 23-2. The blanket-to-blanket design of this press prints four colors on both sides of the web in one pass. During this run, the paper feeds from one roll and is taken up by another.

paper at a time. In fact, the term *web* was applied to these presses because the maze of ribbons of paper moving in different directions and at different heights was thought to resemble a spider web. Most web offset presses print on rolls 36″ to 38″ (914 mm to 965 mm) wide, but some print on rolls up to 76″ (1930 mm) wide. Large web presses usually feature sophisticated control consoles to maximize efficiency because they are designed for high productivity. See **Figure 23-3.**

An advantage of webfed presses is that finishing operations can be performed *in-line*. That is, operations are performed without leaving the press. For example, much of the work produced on web offset presses proceeds to a folder, which is an integral part of the press. At this point, various combinations of folds convert the web into folded signatures ready to be gathered, bound, and trimmed. A variety of finishing operations can also be incorporated into the pressrun with in-line adjunct mechanisms. In-line finishing operations are performed with the press running at the same high speeds used for printing.

Web-Press Construction

The construction of a web offset press can be described as modular, or unitized. A particular unit built into the press performs each step of a print run. For example, when printing a four-color job, the web enters the first printing unit, and the black ink is printed. The web continues to the second, third, and fourth printing units, where the CMY inks are

printed. At this point, the web enters the next unit of the press, which might be a folder or some type of finishing unit.

The printing units on web offset presses are set up in a line so the web moves through them in a straight line. See **Figure 23-4.** A press can have up to eight or more printing units and might be capable of printing both sides of the web in four or more colors in one pass through the press. Additional units for applying varnish or overprinting with fluorescent or metallic inks can follow the printing units.

A web press can be constructed to feed from one or more rolls at the same time, allowing large runs to be printed with little or no interruption. Depending

Figure 23-4. Most web offset presses are constructed of printing units in tandem. This double-decker configuration is designed to print magazines, catalogs, and books. (Goss International Corporation)

Figure 23-3. To optimize the speed of web presses, they are highly automated. Note the console in the background. (Goss International Corporation)

in-line: the continuous work flow that results from connecting a press with finishing devices such as folders, trimmers, gluing units, and bindery units.

on the design, web presses can print on one or both sides of the web. As was mentioned, the paper is pulled through the press in a continuous ribbon, so unlike a sheetfed offset press, a web offset press has no transfer or cylinder grippers. The absence of sheet grippers allows for narrower cylinder gaps (as small as 3/8″ [9.5 mm]) and faster running speeds.

Gapless blankets are also used on some web offset presses. Conventional blanket cylinders are designed with a gap, or space, between the head and tail of the blanket. The gapless, tubular-type blanket design stabilizes the press, allowing faster running speeds, the use of wider paper, and less paper waste.

The circumference of the plate cylinder on a web offset press, the *cutoff*, determines the length of the printed page. The cutoff is a fixed dimension on most web offset presses. A plate-bending fixture is used to accurately make the leading- and trailing-edge bends in the plate. See **Figure 23-5.**

Automatic plate-changing systems can be installed to automatically mount and remove plates without the use of tools. In most applications, the new plate is inserted into a cartridge, a button is pressed, the old plate is unloaded, and the new one is mounted. A plate change takes only a few minutes and can be performed without breaking the web of paper. Most web offset presses use computers to automatically control every function on the press. The controls for speed, temperature, water flow, ink flow, register, and power are usually located at a single console.

Many web offset presses are equipped with in-line finishing operations, such as folding, cutting, perforating, slitting, imprinting, varnishing, paste binding, numbering, rotary slitting and cutting, and gluing. In-line operations are performed while the job is still on the press. Web presses can be designed to deliver printed work as signatures, as single sheets, or rewound on rolls. See **Figure 23-6.**

Web-Press Designs

Web offset presses are usually custom-built to the specific needs of a printer or publisher because they can be so versatile. Considerable thought and planning go into the design, size, and function of a press.

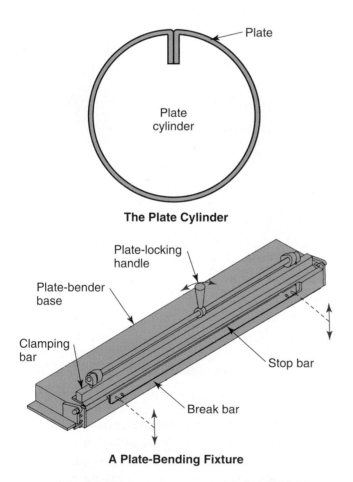

Figure 23-5. Both the leading and trailing edges of a web offset plate fit into the same slot in the plate cylinder. A plate-bending fixture is used to accurately bend both edges of the plates. (Harris Corp.)

Figure 23-6. This high-speed newspaper press prints, folds, cuts, and delivers newspapers ready for distribution. (Tensor Group, Inc.)

The cost and time involved in the installation of a new web offset press require the printer or publisher to determine the type of infeed, number of printing units, and types of finishing and delivery units needed. Printers and publishers must also determine what type of web offset press best suits their requirements. There are three types of web offset presses. These are the perfecting blanket-to-blanket, the in-line open, and the drum common impression presses.

Perfecting Blanket-to-Blanket Presses

As discussed in Chapter 20, most sheetfed presses print on only one side of the paper at a time. To print on the reverse side of the paper, the ink from the first side is allowed to dry, and the paper is turned over and run through a second time. Sheetfed presses printing on both sides of the paper at the same time are known as *perfecting presses* or *perfectors*.

A *perfecting blanket-to-blanket web offset press* does not have impression cylinders. Instead, the blanket cylinder of one unit serves as the impression cylinder for the other unit, and vice versa. See **Figure 23-7**. Each printing unit has two plate cylinders and two blanket cylinders. The paper is printed on both sides at the same time as it passes between the two blanket cylinders. The rubber-faced blanket cylinders transfer plate images from the printing plates to the web.

The design of the plate cylinders on a perfecting blanket-to-blanket press allows for quick plate changes. One-, two-, or four-page (tabloid) plates are locked into position by means of a quick set-and-release plate lockup. See **Figure 23-8**.

Each printing unit has an upper and a lower ink fountain. See **Figure 23-9**. Ink flow from these fountains is adjustable through a series of fountain keys. Newer web offset inking systems have *keyless fountains* (no conventional ink keys) an operator controls at the console.

Most web offset presses use a remote color-control system for inker control and presetting that typically accommodates up to 20 ink fountains per console. Many systems use a touch-screen display for quick inker presetting and simultaneous preset of all fountain keys. See **Figure 23-10**. Job storage of inking profiles and recall capabilities are standard with these types of systems. A separate gear motor drives each ink fountain roller to provide close control of inking. The inking system consists of one ink fountain roller that rides in the ink fountain, one transfer roller that conveys ink from the fountain roller to the rest of the system, three distributor rollers, one vibrator roller, and two form rollers.

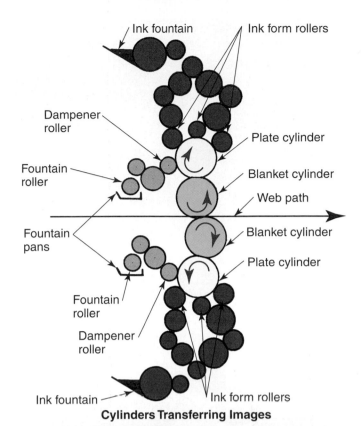

Cylinders Transferring Images

Web Running Between Cylinders

Figure 23-7. This diagram illustrates the principle of how the rubber-faced blanket cylinders on a perfecting blanket-to-blanket offset press transfer plate images from the printing plates to the web of paper. Note the web running between the blanket cylinders on this commercial press. (Goss International Corporation)

cutoff: the length of the printed page as determined by the circumference of the plate cylinder on a web offset press.

perfecting blanket-to-blanket web offset press: a press that uses blanket cylinders acting as impression cylinders and prints on both sides of the paper at the same time as the paper passes between the two blanket cylinders.

keyless fountain: an electronic inking system that does not use conventional fountain keys.

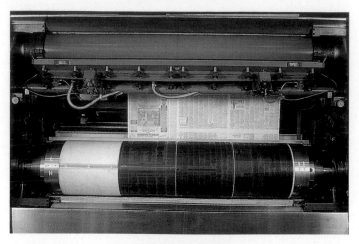

Figure 23-8. The plates on this web press are locked into position by means of a quick set-and-release mechanism. (Man Roland, Inc.)

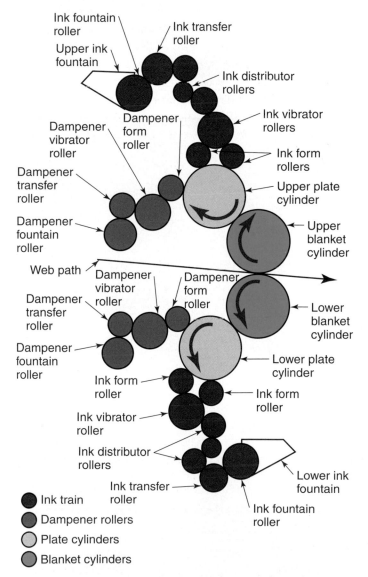

- ● Ink train
- ● Dampener rollers
- ◐ Plate cylinders
- ◐ Blanket cylinders

Figure 23-9. A perfecting blanket-to-blanket web offset press has upper and lower ink fountains. This diagram illustrates how ink is transferred from the ink fountains to the plates. (Harris Corp.)

Figure 23-10. Most web offset presses use fully automated computer control. Computerized press controls on this console regulate speed, temperature, water, ink, register, and color. (Koenig & Bauer)

Each printing unit also has an upper and a lower dampening system that applies the proper amount of fountain solution to the nonimage areas of the plate surface. Refer back to **Figure 23-9**. The fountain solution repels ink, thus enabling the nonimage areas to run clear.

The folder on a newspaper web offset press is capable of producing standard, tabloid, or quarter-folded printed pieces. Separate clutches on the lower folder assembly engage and disengage the folder and quarter folder. One clutch is for the folder assembly, and the other is for the quarter folder. An electrical counter registers the quantity of folded signatures produced.

The standard folding operation begins when the web is routed over the web lead-in rollers. The web then moves under the gathering roll, over the roller top of the former, through the trolleys (where a slitter blade cuts the web to tabloid width, if desired), and down the former, into the nipping rollers. See **Figure 23-11**.

Six pins spaced across the width of the cutting cylinder pull the *former folded web*, or slit web, for tabloids, around the cutting cylinder. A cam mechanism projects these pins from the cylinder to pierce the web and keep the sheets correctly positioned until they pass through the cutting mechanism. *Pinless folders* are equipped to produce quarterfold, tabloid, digest, and broadsheet printed products at speeds of over 3000 feet per minute (fpm). These folders work in conjunction with gapless technology to minimize trim waste. See **Figure 23-12**. Pinless folders reduce paper waste because the space normally allocated for pins on the cutting cylinder is not required. This space can be used as additional print area, or the sheet size can be reduced.

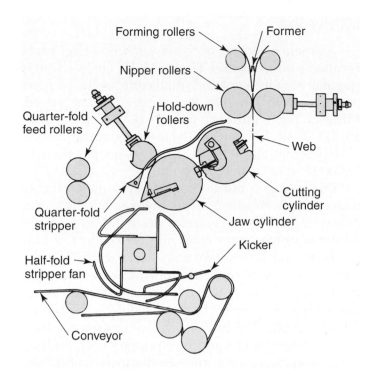

Figure 23-11. The folder on a web offset press is capable of producing a standard, tabloid, or quarter-folded printed piece. This schematic diagram illustrates the operation of a folding unit. (Harris Corp.)

The *tucker blade* on the cutting cylinder tucks the web into the jaw blades of the jaw cylinder. The cutting knife then slices the former-folded web at the proper point. The *jaw cylinder* takes the cut and folded signature from the cutting cylinder. This cylinder next carries the paper around and through the hold-down roller and either into the fan, which lays it down on the conveyor assembly, or to the quarter-folder table.

In-Line Open Presses

Each printing unit of an *in-line open web offset press* has its own plate, blanket, and impression cylinder, meaning each unit prints one color on one side of the web. To print the reverse side, the web of paper is turned over (180°) between printing units by means of *turning bars* that expose the unprinted side of the web to the remaining units. See **Figure 23-13.** Turning bars are also referred to as *angle bars*.

Most in-line open web offset presses operate in much the same way. The web is brought down and under the platforms between the units. These platforms allow the press operator to walk between the units and service them, thus the term *open*. In-line open web offset presses use a very narrow cylinder gap. This press design is commonly used for printing business forms.

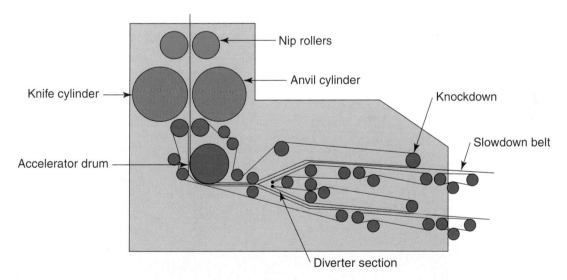

Figure 23-12. The latest web-folding units are pinless, meaning the web remains free of pinhole marks in the margins.

former folded web: a web of paper folded by being run over a triangular-shaped device that causes the web to fold when the web conforms to the wedge.
pinless folder: a folder that uses pressure instead of pins to hold the paper web as it passes through the folder.
tucker blade: a metal blade on a jaw folder used to tuck the web into the jaws of the jaw folder.
jaw cylinder: the cylinder on a jaw folder used to fold the web.
in-line open web offset press: a press on which each printing unit has its own plate, blanket, and impression cylinder.
turning bar: a stationary bar on a web press that guides the moving web so it is flipped over, allowing it to be printed on the reverse side.
angle bar: a metal bar placed horizontally at a 45° angle to the feed direction of a printing press and used to turn the web when feeding from the side or to bypass the former folder.

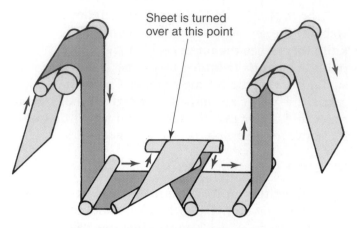

Sheet is turned
over at this point

Figure 23-13. The turning bars turn the web of paper over between printing units on a web offset press.

Drum Common Impression Presses

The *drum common impression web offset press* has all the blanket cylinders grouped around a large common impression cylinder. This type of press is also called a *satellite press*. Up to five colors are printed at the same time on one side of the web. See **Figure 23-14.** The web is immediately dried and turned, and the reverse side is printed on the same printing unit by a process known as *double ending*. A web, one-half the width of the drum, is printed, dried, turned over, and brought back through the other half of the drum for printing the reverse side.

Miniwebs

A smaller version of the larger web offset press is called a *miniweb*. See **Figure 23-15.** This version is popular with in-plant and small commercial printers because of its smaller size and excellent speed. Miniweb roll widths are usually 14″ (355 mm), with an 8 1/2″ or 17″ cutoff. These presses are capable of delivering 30,000 8 1/2″ × 11″ sheets per hour or 15,000 11″ × 17″ sheets per hour.

The cost of a miniweb offset press is similar to that of most sheetfed offset presses, and it varies depending on the accessories desired. For example, a fully equipped, four-color miniweb can print four colors on one side or two colors on each side of the web (two over two). This miniweb can also print three colors on one side and one color on the other side (three over one). The press would be equipped with a turn bar for printing both sides (perfecting). This miniweb might also be equipped with folding, perforating, punching, and numbering attachments.

A miniweb offset press requires about the same space as a multicolor, sheetfed press does. Similar to most larger web offset presses, miniwebs are built in modular form. Printing units, folders, and other attachments can be added as work demands. A miniweb offset press can turn out the same amount of work as two to four duplicators can. Besides having a competitive speed, a miniweb offset press can be more cost-effective than a sheetfed press. The chart in **Figure 23-16** compares the costs of sheetfed

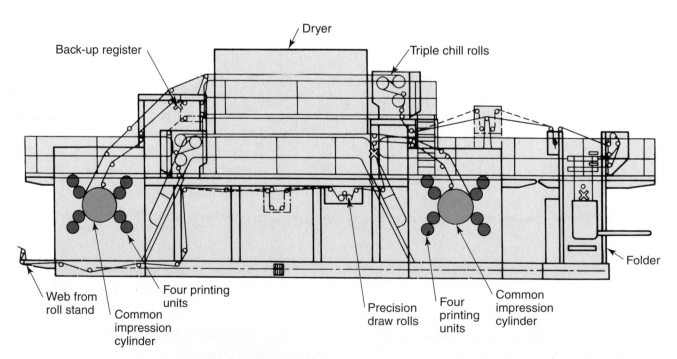

Dryer

Back-up register

Triple chill rolls

Web from roll stand

Four printing units

Common impression cylinder

Precision draw rolls

Four printing units

Common impression cylinder

Folder

Figure 23-14. A drum common impression web offset press. All the blanket cylinders are grouped around a large common impression cylinder. (Baker Perkins Limited)

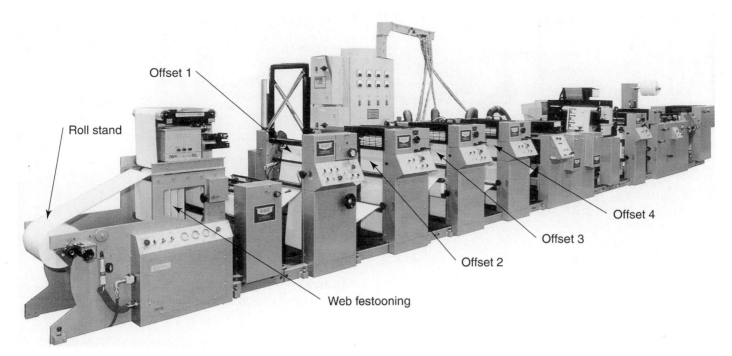

Figure 23-15. This smaller version of a web offset press is called a *miniweb*. (Pederson Group)

	Single-color 25″	Two-color 38″	Four-color miniweb press 11″ x 17 1/2″ roll width
	19″ × 25″	25″ × 38″	11″ × 17″
Press makeready	.50	1.00	1.00
Running speed	7500	7500	30,000
Number of makereadies	4	2	1
Sheet run	25,000–17″ × 22″	12,500–22″ × 34″	50,000–11″ × 17″
Pressrun	100,000	25,000	50,000
Total makeready time	2.00	2.00	1.00
Total running time	13.33	3.33	1.66
Total press time	15.33	5.33	2.66
Finishing	2 out 17″ × 11″	4 out 22″ × 34″	0
Cutting time	1.06	1.30	0
Total time	17.39	6.63	2.66
Total operators	2	3	1
Total labor hours	17.39	11.96	2.66

Figure 23-16. Study this example of a common-size commercial printing job comparing sheetfed operations to web operations for a two-color, two-sided, 11″ × 17″ sheet. What benefits are derived from running the job on a miniweb?

drum common impression web offset press: a webfed offset press in which all the blanket cylinders are grouped around a large common impression cylinder and the double-ending process is used to print on both sides of the web.

double ending: a process in which the web is immediately dried and turned and the reverse side is printed on the same printing unit.

miniweb: a smaller version of the larger web offset press.

Figure 23-17. A new roll is placed on the feeder. (Hammer Packaging)

Figure 23-19. A roll stand can be constructed to hold one or two rolls of paper. (Goss International Corporation)

operations to web operations for a common-size commercial-printing job (two-color, two-sided, 11" × 17" sheet).

Besides the savings shown in the chart, other benefits can be realized from a miniweb press. For example, paper purchased in rolls costs at least 10% less than sheetfed paper does. See **Figure 23-17.** Paper inventory for a miniweb takes up no more space than storing flat sheets for sheetfed presses. Most in-plant firms print 80% or more of their work on one type of paper and would not have to store more than one type of paper.

Web-Press Operation

The following is a summary of operation for a typical eight-page, miniweb, heatset offset press. See **Figure 23-18.** Paper is fed into the press from large rolls on a *roll stand*, replacing the pile feeder of a sheetfed press. See **Figure 23-19.** When a roll begins to run out, a new roll can be spliced onto the old, using an automatic *splicer*. The web is threaded into

the press while the press continues to run at full speed. The large *festoon* is a paper-storage device that unwinds paper to keep the press running at the same speed while the splice is made and the new roll accelerates to press speed. See **Figure 23-20.**

One of the keys to high-quality web printing is *tension control*, regulating the amount of pull needed to keep the paper from having slack. To run a continuous web of paper at high speed between numerous rollers and cylinders, it is necessary to control the tension of the web precisely. Proper tension control ensures accurate register of the sequential colors as they are laid down and prevents web jams and breaks. Tension-control devices vary from press to press and usually accommodate a variety of add-on devices. See **Figure 23-21.** *Web guides* control the side-to-side register of the web as it passes through the press, just as a side guide exercises this control on a sheetfed press.

To get the ink's drying rate to keep up with the speed of a web press, the paper web flows from the printing units into the *dryer*. Hot air causes ink

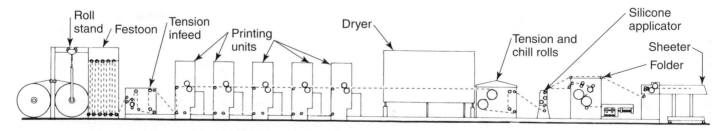

Figure 23-18. This diagram illustrates the operating components of a miniweb offset press. The roll stand on the left allows the web to travel through the printing units, dryer, chill rolls, and folder, and finally into the sheeter at the right. (Harris Corp.)

Figure 23-20. A festoon unwinds the paper to keep the press running at the same speed while a splice is made and the new roll is brought up to press speed.

solvents to evaporate and leave a soft ink film on the substrate. Automatic controls ensure that the proper temperature is maintained, regardless of the paper weight and the speed of the web through the press. Emission-control systems are designed to capture the solvent vapors and convert harmful air pollutants to carbon dioxide and water. See **Figure 23-22.** After the web exits the dryer, *chill rolls* are used to cool the web to room temperature and harden the ink film the dryer has softened.

Flying Pasters

A unique mechanism for bringing a new roll of paper into the feed cycle without stopping the press is called a *flying paster* or *splicer.* As the main feeding roll nears its end, the roll stand is rotated to bring the next full roll of paper into running position without slowing the running speed of the press. Double-sided tape is applied to the leading edge of the new roll. The full roll is then moved into contact with the running roll of paper, and the taped edge of the full roll is pressed against and immediately adheres to the running roll. The paper from the depleted roll is cut off, and the roll is brought to a stop. The new roll begins feeding the press at normal running speed.

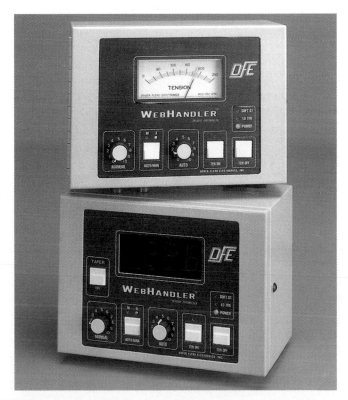

Figure 23-21. Tension controllers reduce production waste, web breakage, stretching problems, and registration inaccuracy. (Dover Flexo Electronics, Inc.)

roll stand: a stand used with web presses to hold one or more paper rolls and feed each in turn with consistent and controlled tension into the printing unit of the press.

splicer: a machine that joins the ends of two webs of paper to make a continuous roll.

festoon: a paper-storage device that unwinds paper to keep the press running at the same speed while the splice is made and the new roll accelerates to press speed. This device also gives the web a long lead time into the press.

tension control: the regulation of the amount of pull needed to keep the paper from having slack.

web guide: a guide on a web press, similar to a side guide on a sheetfed press, that controls the side-to-side register of the web as it passes through the press.

dryer: a type of ink-drying device on a web press that heats the web up to a temperature of about 330°F.

chill roll: an internally cooled metal roller or cylinder located just beyond a web-press dryer, used to lower the temperature of the printed web and harden the ink film before rewinding.

flying paster: a device on a webfed press used to splice a fresh roll of paper to an expiring roll without stopping the press.

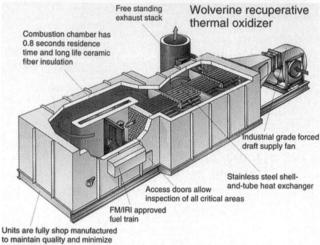

Free standing exhaust stack

Wolverine recuperative thermal oxidizer

Combustion chamber has 0.8 seconds residence time and long life ceramic fiber insulation

Industrial grade forced draft supply fan

Stainless steel shell-and-tube heat exchanger

Access doors allow inspection of all critical areas

FM/IRI approved fuel train

Units are fully shop manufactured to maintain quality and minimize installation time

Figure 23-22. The emission-control system illustrated here can effectively destroy 99% of the harmful air pollutants created as solvent-based inks dry. These types of emission-control systems are custom designed and should meet or exceed all local, state, and federal clean-air regulations. (Wolverine Corporation)

On newer web offset presses, paste is used instead of double-sided tape. See **Figure 23-23.** Regardless of the type of paster used, improperly handled webs cause problems. **Figure 23-24** illustrates an efficient method of handling webs in the pressroom. After a new roll has been automatically loaded, an advanced camera system is used to scan the paper surface as the roll unwinds during splice preparation. Once the camera detects that all damaged paper has been wound off, unwinding is stopped, thereby minimizing paper waste on the outside of each roll (called *slab waste*) and ensuring that the paper after the splice is free of defects.

Zero-Speed Pasters

A *zero-speed paster* or splicer differs from a flying paster because the rolls of paper are stopped momentarily, but the press continues to print. See **Figure 23-25.** Amazingly, the old roll of paper is replaced with a new roll without interrupting production. When the feeding roll nears its end, it is stopped, but the web continues to move into the press as the festoon's top and bottom rollers begin moving closer. The end of the new roll is taped, a splice is made, the paper is cut from the old roll, and the new roll is brought up to press speed. The splice must be performed before all the slack in the festoon has been taken up.

Web-Break Detectors

Web offset presses are equipped with web-break detectors. See **Figure 23-26.** A *web-break detector* activates a control that automatically stops the press if the web breaks during operation. At the same instant,

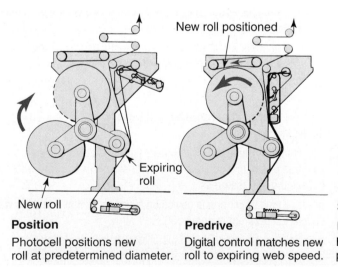

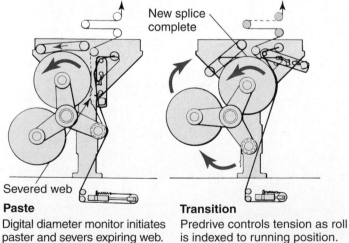

New roll positioned

New splice complete

Expiring roll

New roll

Severed web

Position
Photocell positions new roll at predetermined diameter.

Predrive
Digital control matches new roll to expiring web speed.

Paste
Digital diameter monitor initiates paster and severs expiring web.

Transition
Predrive controls tension as roll is indexed to running position.

Figure 23-23. A photocell positions a new roll of paper at a predetermined diameter on this web offset press. Digital control then matches the new roll to the expiring web-roll speed. An automatic controller initiates the paster unit and adjusts the tension on the roll for running speed. (Rockwell International)

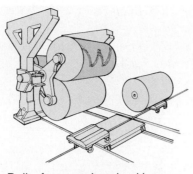

1. Dolly from previous load is held for retrieval of spent core. Under computer guidance, a new roll of proper width and kind arrives on entrance spur and waits.

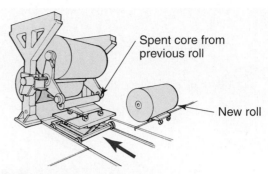

2. After paste, spider rotates to "load" position. Empty dolly is brought back onto transfer table and centered under core. Tabletop is elevated and pneumatic chuck releases spent core onto dolly.

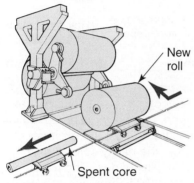

3. Transfer tabletop is lowered and table recenters in pit to exit dolly with core, which the MHS system routes for disposition. New roll is then pulled onto table and centered between spindles by edge scanner.

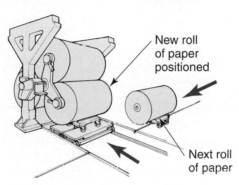

4. Table and roll advance to core location sensors where horizontal and vertical axis are located; then roll proceeds to pneumatic chucks where it is chucked.

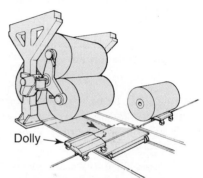

5. When limit switches verify chucking, tabletop is lowered and dolly and table recenter in pit where dolly exits to park position to await spent core. Flat tabletop is now convenient for operator to apply paste pattern to roll.

Figure 23-24. An automated paper-web handling system. These systems are used for large newspaper, magazine, and commercial web offset operations. (Rockwell International)

the web-break detector activates a mechanism that cuts the web just ahead of the printing unit, propelling the oncoming paper out of the printing unit. The detector also prevents any free paper from whipping back and wrapping around the cylinders. This entire procedure is accomplished in a fraction of a second. The five main causes for web breaks are wet spots on the web; edge cuts; felt-hair, calender, and fiber cuts; tension-control malfunction; and humidity:

- Wet spots from fountain solution or washup are a principal cause of web breaks, particularly at start-up. Wet-spot breaks should diminish as the press crew gains experience in handling washups neatly.

- Edge cuts on the web occur from careless handling. This calls for some training effort with paper handlers.

- Felt-hair, calender, and fiber cuts are closely related to edge cuts. These types of cuts usually originate at the paper mill and are a cause of complaint to the supplier.

- Tension-control malfunction can cause web breaks, but this is relatively infrequent, as compared to the previous three causes of web breaks.

---

slab waste: paper waste taken from the outside portion of a roll. This waste often results during splicing.

zero-speed paster: a device in the infeed section of a webfed press that splices a fresh roll to an expiring roll by stopping the expiring roll briefly, but not stopping the press.

web-break detector: a device that automatically detects the site of a web break and immediately shuts down the press.

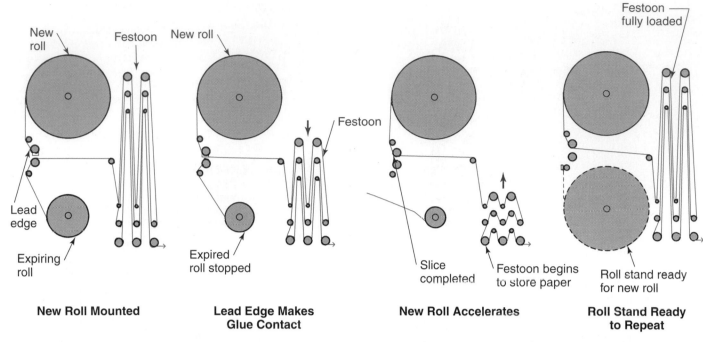

New Roll Mounted   **Lead Edge Makes Glue Contact**   **New Roll Accelerates**   **Roll Stand Ready to Repeat**

Figure 23-25. Note the sequence of operation of a zero-speed automatic splicer. A festoon stores paper. The new roll has been mounted with its lead edge ready for splicing. The expired roll has stopped, and paper is being fed into the press from the festoon. The lead edge of the new roll has been moved under pressure against the expiring roll to make glue contact. The splice has been completed, the expired roll has been cut free, the newly spliced roll has been accelerated to press speed, and the festoon is again storing paper. The festoon is fully loaded. The roll stand is ready for the mounting of a new roll and the repetition of the splicing sequence. The press has remained at a constant speed during the entire splicing operation. (Harris Corp.)

Figure 23-26. When a break occurs in the web of paper, an electronic detector automatically stops the press. (Koenig & Bauer)

- Humidity problems in dry winter climates cause a seasonal increase in web breaks. Some paper manufacturers have increased moisture content to counter the problem.

Image Alignment and Register

Image alignment and register are important in all types of printing. The web-press system is especially demanding on image-alignment and register systems because of its basic design. Unlike on the sheetfed press, rolls of paper must be run through the web press perpendicular (square) to the axes of the press cylinders. On a sheetfed press, the sheet can be twisted considerably and run through the press with little difficulty.

For the purposes of illustrating web alignment, the press can be viewed as a series of precisely parallel printing units. A web of paper traveling exactly perpendicular to the cylinder axes intersects the units. The printing cylinders at each unit and the web of paper create an imaginary perpendicular intersection. See **Figure 23-27**. The folding and sheeting units fold and cut the web of paper parallel and perpendicular to the cylinder axes. Therefore, they form their own imaginary perpendiculars. Proper

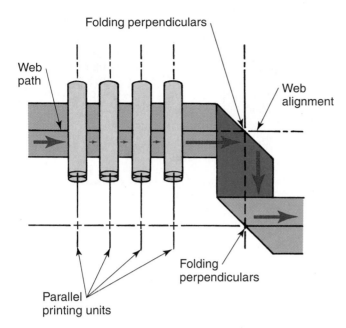

Figure 23-27. To achieve perfect web alignment, the web press consists of a series of parallel printing units that a web of paper traveling perpendicular to the cylinder axes intersects. Folding and sheeting units fold and cut the web of paper parallel and perpendicular to the cylinder axes. (Raden® C, Inc.)

preparation procedures for web offset press plates are essential because there are some web offset presses that have no adjustment for image squareness.

An ideal register-control system for the web offset press is a unit that can consistently align images with the exact imaginary perpendiculars formed on the press. This exact alignment can be tested on any press. A horizontal line is printed on the front and back of the sheet, parallel to the cylinder axis. Two plates are used, with one printing on the front of the sheet and the other printing the identical line on the back. In this test, as with production runs, the backup plate is turned over when placing it on the bottom unit. Any alignment error is doubled by turning the backup plate over. Alignment error is easily determined by the amount the lines vary from being parallel. See **Figure 23-28.**

Printing-Unit Adjustments

There is a number of printing adjustments that can be made to place printed images correctly on the paper web and achieve register in backup and with other colors. The plate cylinder can be angled, moved laterally, or be packed. The entire printing unit can be advanced or retarded. See **Figure 23-29.**

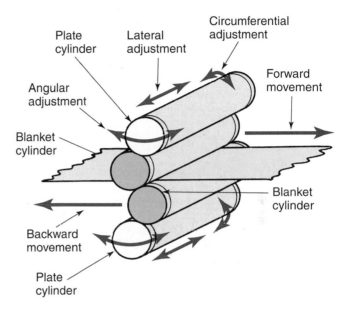

Figure 23-29. The standard adjustments that can be made to web-press printing units to achieve register. A forward or backward movement of the entire printing unit allows for register with other printing units. An angular (plate-cocking) adjustment of the plate cylinder rotates the plate slightly, similar to straightening a crooked picture on a wall. A lateral (side-lay) adjustment of the plate cylinder moves the plate slightly to the side. A circumferential adjustment of the plate cylinder moves the plate slightly up or down. In all instances, the plate cylinder is moved, but the point is to move the plate and, by extension, the image because the plate is attached to the plate cylinder. (Didde Graphic Systems Corp.)

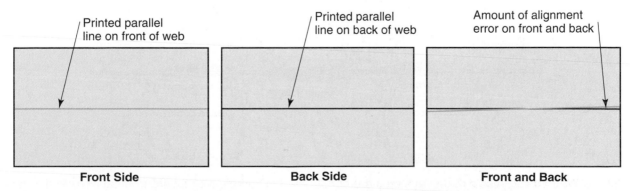

Figure 23-28. Web-press alignment can be checked by printing an identical line on both sides of the web. Alignment error is easily determined by the amount the lines vary from being parallel. (Raden® C, Inc.)

Whereas a sheetfed-press operator can monitor print quality by periodically pulling a printed sheet from the delivery unit and checking it, a web-press operator is watching images speed by on a continuous ribbon. The operator can check the image quality and register on one or both sides of the web while the press is running, however, with fixed or portable high-intensity strobe lights positioned above and below the running web of paper. See **Figure 23-30.** After checking the register and alignment, the press operator might be required to make any one of the following adjustments:

- Unit-to-unit register.
- Angular or skewing adjustment.
- Lateral adjustment of plate cylinder.
- Circumferential register (back-to-back register with the opposite plate image).

Web offset presses do not use plate clamps.

Ink and Drying Systems

Inks used on web offset presses must dry quickly to prevent problems during the pressrun and to prevent setoff on the finished sheets. Heatset inks are the most commonly used inks in web offset printing. The composition of heatset ink requires the use of heat, for drying, and chilling, or coldsetting, to bond the pigments to the paper. Heatset inks are formulated with synthetic resins and petroleum oils with very different boiling points. When the web enters the dryer and the ink is heated at temperatures of 400°F–500°F (204°C–260°C), the petroleum oils' low boiling points cause them to evaporate, leaving the resins (with higher boiling points) to remain on the paper. See **Figure 23-31.** Web offset presses using heatset inks must be fitted with an exhaust system to eliminate solvent vapors from the dryer.

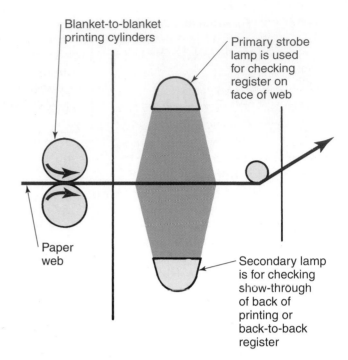

Figure 23-30. Strobe lamps are used to check the printing quality and register on both sides of the web. The primary strobe lamp is used for checking the register on the face of a web. The secondary lamp is used for checking show-through on the back of the printing or back-to-back register.

Nonheatset inks do not require the use of heat from a dryer. Nonheatset web offset inks are usually used on highly absorbent, uncoated, groundwood-pulp papers because they require a certain level of penetration into the paper. Coated papers provide too much ink holdout and usually cannot be printed with nonheatset inks.

Sheetfed and webfed inks can be made into quick-set inks by incorporating a quick-set varnish into the

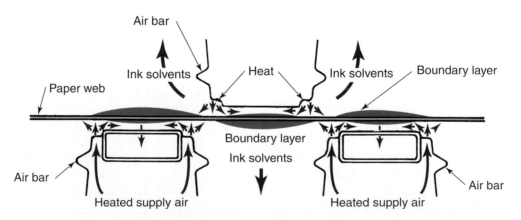

Figure 23-31. Web offset press exhaust systems are constructed to comply with environmental air-pollution control regulations. This schematic diagram of a web-press exhaust system illustrates how ink-solvent vapors are exhausted. (TEC Systems)

formulation. A quick-set varnish consists of a thick resin dissolved in a low-viscosity, high–boiling point hydrocarbon oil. When the ink film is applied to the paper, the light oil immediately leaves the solution to penetrate the paper, leaving the resin to return to its original thickness and rapidly increasing the ink film's viscosity. Quick-set inks can set rapidly enough to increase the tack of the printed ink between printing units and permit the printed sheets to be handled more quickly. When inks set between units, they can all have the same tack rating, allowing the printer to use one set of process colors in any printing sequence. The use of quick-set inks can produce back-trap mottle when printing on multiunit offset presses. *Back-trap mottle* occurs when the inks do not set sufficiently between printing units.

Radiation-curing inks use complex vehicles that instantly harden when exposed to radiation from UV light (UV-curing ink), beams of electrons (EB-curing ink), or IR light (superquick-set IR ink). Unlike heatset inks, radiation-curing inks do not require high temperatures to dry. Radiation-curing inks are more expensive than conventional inks because the active ingredients in these inks are more costly than the solvents they replace in conventional inks. These inks are made of 100% solids and do not discharge solvents into the air. As with heatset inks, the "drying unit" immediately follows the last printing unit. See **Figure 23-32.**

Web offset inks classified as thermal-curing inks are similar to UV-curing inks, but they are formulated to dry instantly with heat. Thermal-curing inks are highly reactive formulas containing little or no solvent. These inks contain special catalysts that allow the ink to dry quickly with the application of heat.

Filtration Systems

Ventilation and filtration systems are commonly found in the press area to overcome ink misting and flying. In severe cases of ink misting and flying, a spray, fog, or mist of ink is visible in the air. This problem typically occurs on high-speed presses used in newspaper pressrooms. The ink mist settles and covers press frames, floors, and walls with a fine deposit of ink.

Commercial ink-mist suppressors are used when conditions require them. These are typically electrically charged devices that repel the charged ink back to the ink roller. Electrical grounding of the press helps eliminate static and often reduces ink mist. Air-conditioning in the pressroom can help remove the ink mist from the air.

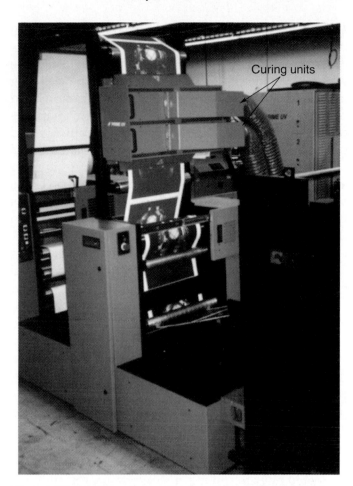

Figure 23-32. After the web has passed through all the printing units, it passes between UV-curing stations. (Prime Systems, Inc.)

Dampening Systems

Most web offset presses use either conventional or continuous dampening systems, similar to sheetfed presses. As discussed previously, a conventional dampening system uses a series of rollers to distribute fountain solution from the fountain to the plate when the plate is positioned on the press. A continuous dampening system uses rollers that distribute a continuous flow of fountain solution to the plate, eliminating the use of a ductor roller. Some web offset presses are capable of short-run waterless printing, using special relief printing plates. These presses can produce up to 40,000 iph with full folding capabilities.

back-trap mottle: a printing defect caused by nonuniform ink setting when the paper is still moving through the press.

Web-Press Management Systems

Web-press management systems must keep pace with the accelerated rate of change in the printing industry. To effectively monitor production and develop methods to improve efficiency, management systems must provide information quickly and constantly. Computerized management systems and specialized software programs are used to monitor and control the web-press printing operation. These systems are usually personalized to match a printer's needs and differ somewhat in the type of information they collect. See **Figure 23-33.** The information monitored includes items such as running time, running speed, downtime, cause of downtime, number of good copies, number of poor copies, makeready time, and cause of web breaks. Most software programs also allow for reporting of press delays by the day, week, or month. Items such as ink and plate problems and press stops for customers and maintenance can also be input and processed. In a plant with several web presses, a press-monitoring and analysis console is located at each press. Each console collects data from sensors on the press and accepts input from the press operator and production supervisors.

At the beginning of a job, an electronic job ticket is created by entering the customer's information. See **Figure 23-34.** This document follows all aspects of production—from layout and design (if provided at the printer) to shipping and handling of the finished product. As the job passes from each production step, workers input the appropriate data. Information entered at the beginning of a run includes the job number, kind of paper, number of webs, quantity to be run, press layout, folding specs, quality level, and type of ink.

During the pressrun, information is transferred automatically from press sensors to the console. See **Figure 23-35.** Included are data such as running speed, good and poor sheet counts, web breaks (including location), production versus standard, waste, and downtime. Some details, such as the cause of a web break or the reason for a press stop, are entered manually. The information collected is reviewed by the production manager and can be used to produce reports on every aspect of production.

In-Line Finishing Systems

In-line finishing is an adjunct system used by many high-volume commercial web printers and finishing specialists. These high-speed systems are capable of performing many finishing operations that cannot be accomplished on some regular web offset presses. See **Figure 23-36.** A typical in-line system offers the following combination of finishing operations:

- *Remoistenable gluer.* This part prints remoistenable adhesives in any pattern for the production of stamps, envelopes, and other "lick-to-stick" products. The gluer also prints spot or full-coverage varnish and microencapsulated materials, such as "scratch and sniff."

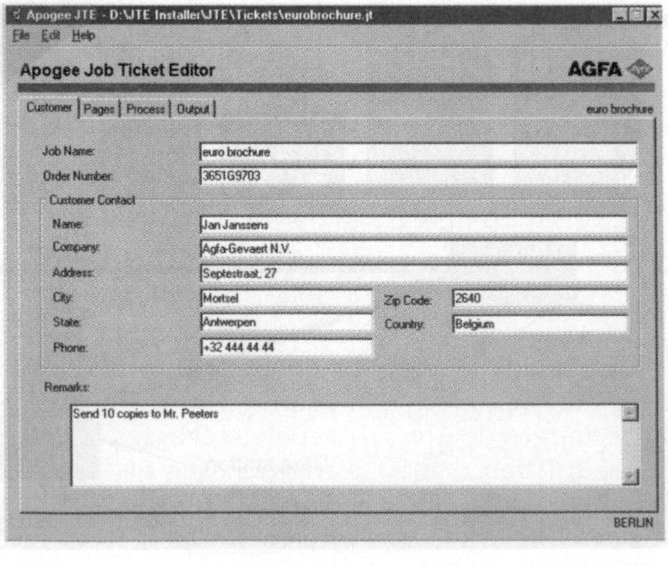

	Makeready Hours	Run Hours	Delay Hours	Total Labor Hours	% Delay
Goreville Plant					
Press #101	22.2	460.4	45.4	528.0	8.5
Press #105	37.2	433.9	56.0	528.0	10.7
Press #106	8.0	417.2	78.8	504.0	15.0
Vienna Plant					
Press #200	98.3	394.2	11.5	504.0	2.2
Press #205	31.3	448.1	25.6	504.0	5.0
Press #206	45.8	323.9	135.3	504.0	26.8
Simpson Plant					
Press #302	6.7	515.5	5.8	528.0	1.0
Press #305	53.4	414.9	49.7	528.0	9.4
Press #306	75.0	413.9	29.1	528.0	5.5
Cairo Plant					
Press #403	82.8	327.9	69.3	480.0	14.4
Press #404	69.4	273.7	136.9	480.0	28.5
Press #407	10.1	249.6	196.3	456.0	43.0

Figure 23-33. The computerization of web-press management is essential for maximum production and cost efficiency. This data table shows information relating to several presses at various locations.

Figure 23-34. An electronic job ticket informs management and production personnel of all the specs for a given job.

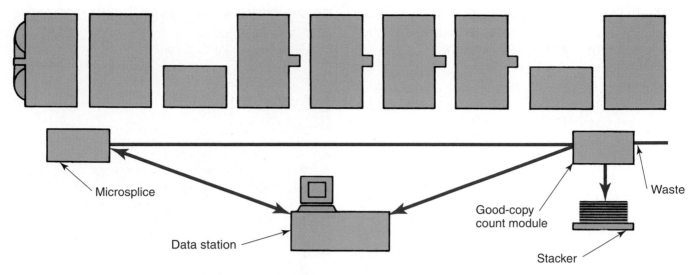

Figure 23-35. A typical web offset pressroom configuration. In the closed-loop process-control concept, an on-line module automatically counts and diverts waste from a splice, blanket washup, or other cause. This ensures that each skid contains only a known quantity of acceptable printed sheets.

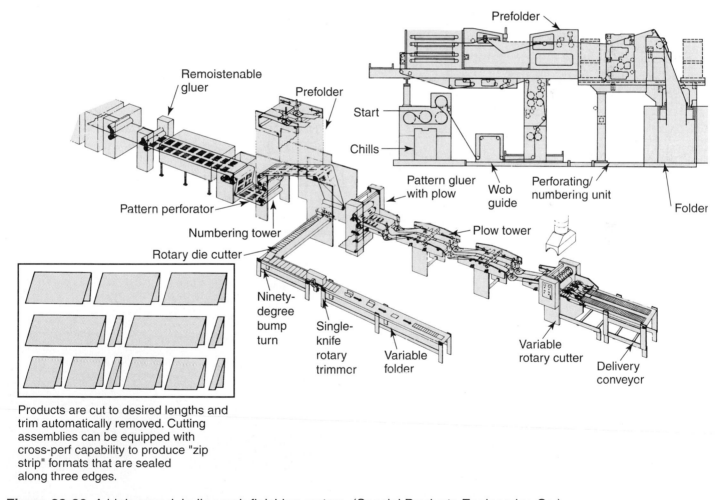

Products are cut to desired lengths and trim automatically removed. Cutting assemblies can be equipped with cross-perf capability to produce "zip strip" formats that are sealed along three edges.

Figure 23-36. A high-speed, in-line web finishing system. (Special Products Engineering Co.)

remoistenable gluer: a device that applies a liquid adhesive to a web or sheet that dries but can be moistened later.

- *Pattern perforator.* This operation scores, slits, and perforates any desired pattern in-line, without tying up a printing unit.

- *Numbering tower.* This part is designed for sequential numbering on one side of the web or both sides of the web simultaneously. The unit is used for numbering coupons, newspaper inserts, security products, lottery products, and direct-mail pieces.

- *Rotary die cutter.* This operation produces many special effects, such as knockouts, pop-ups, tabs, envelope windows, and contoured edges. The cutter can score, slit, and perforate in any desired pattern.

- *Prefolder.* This part consists of an angle-bar section and a plow-folding section. The purpose of the prefolder is to prefold or reposition and prefold the web before it enters the combination folder.

- *Pattern gluer with plow.* This gluer prints glue in-line for the production of return envelopes, return postcards, lottery and game-card products, and spot gluing in trim areas for binding assistance.

- *Plow tower.* This part produces single or multiple folds in the direction of web travel. The tower produces folds in the full web or slits the web into ribbons and produces single or multiple folds in each ribbon.

- *Variable rotary cutter.* This operation produces bleed or nonbleed products in increments of the press repeat. The cutter incorporates a digital registration system for fast makeready.

- *Delivery conveyor.* This part is designed to efficiently transport the product from the rotary cutter to the stackers and bundlers. See **Figure 23-37**.

- *Ninety-degree bump turn.* This operation accommodates the product delivery of folders to the rotary trimmer and the variable folder.

- *Single-knife rotary trimmer.* This part is designed for accurate, clean-cut, high-speed trimming of eight-page press products.

- *Variable folder.* This operation is used in conjunction with all combinations of double-former folders, finishing lines, and especially, narrow web presses. The folder produces, at high speeds, a wide variety of delta folds, #10 envelope stuffers, mail folds, and double parallel folds.

Web Offset Printing Papers

Good-quality papers are essential to web offset printing. Cleanliness and uniformity of moisture content, caliper (thickness), substance weight, and

Figure 23-37. These delivery conveyors transport the printed materials from the rotary cutters to the stackers and bundlers. (A.B.Dick Co.)

finish over the entire paper surface are critical. The ink receptivity of the paper should be highly compatible to the quick-drying qualities of the inks. The paper rolls must possess no weak areas and must be able to withstand the great stresses the press equipment imposes. See **Figure 23-38**. The rolls should arrive well protected and be wound to the proper tension on well-constructed cores of a suitable diameter.

Figure 23-38. Web offset paper rolls must be capable of withstanding the great stresses the press equipment imposes. (Koenig & Bauer)

Web offset papers should measure up to the standard requirements of sheetfed papers. Paper manufacturers make papers with special qualities for each printing process because of the different mechanical characteristics of the two processes and certain demands placed on the offset papers for each. See **Figure 23-39.**

For example, less moisture is present on web offset plates and blanket cylinders during the printing cycle, so the web of paper picks up less moisture than sheetfed paper does. This factor, combined with the high speeds at which webs move through the press, tends to lessen the danger of excessive paper softening. Therefore, the inherent water resistance of web paper can be lower than might be considered satisfactory for sheetfed papers.

Paper is always made with the grain running in the direction of the web. See **Figure 23-40.** In sheetfed offset, the mechanical stress the paper undergoes as it peels from the blanket cylinder is across the grain, so excessive mechanical stretch can be a real problem. Little or no stretch takes place in web offset because the stress is parallel to the grain.

Web-press paper undergoes a different kind of tension than sheetfed paper does because of the way it separates from the blanket cylinder. The paper on a web press releases from the blanket without the severe bend and flex paper on a sheetfed press must undergo. This paper receives severe surface scuffing, however, when passing through the blanket cylinders.

Rolls of paper represent a substantial cost and can be easily ruined. For this reason, there are several recommended procedures, as well as practices to be avoided, when handling and storing rolls of paper. See **Figure 23-41.**

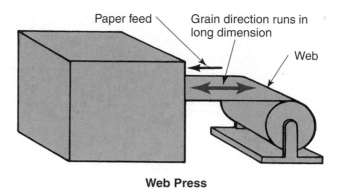

Web Press

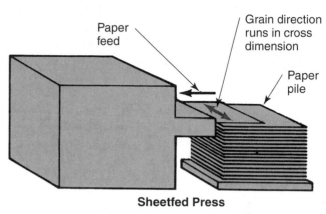

Sheetfed Press

Figure 23-40. On web presses, paper is always fed with the grain running in the long direction (the direction of the web). In sheetfed work, paper is normally fed with the grain running crosswise.

pattern perforator: an in-line device that can perforate, score, or slit the printed web.

numbering tower: an in-line device that can print sequential numbers to the printed web.

rotary die cutter: an in-line device that can slit or cut holes in the printed web.

prefolder: an in-line device that can slit the web into two ribbons, which can then be positioned so one is over the other before they move into a folder, to double the number of pages in the signature resulting from the folding operation.

pattern gluer with plow: an in-line device that can apply a strip of glue and then fold part of the sheet onto the wet glue.

plow tower: an in-line device containing a plow folder, which folds at high speed by lifting part of the moving paper by sending it up a ramp shaped similarly to the blade of a plow.

variable rotary cutter: an in-line device consisting of a rotary knife that can trim the bleed area from a moving web.

delivery conveyor: conveyor belts or tubes that transport the printed product to the area where it is stacked, bundled, or boxed for shipment.

ninety-degree bump turn: an in-line device that serves as the transition between two conveyor belts moving at a right angle to one another.

single-knife rotary trimmer: an in-line device used to trim a bound signature at high speed.

variable folder: an in-line device that can apply multiple parallel folds to a sheet at high speed.

Figure 23-39. A web-press operator examines a roll of paper before loading it on the press. (Hammer Packaging)

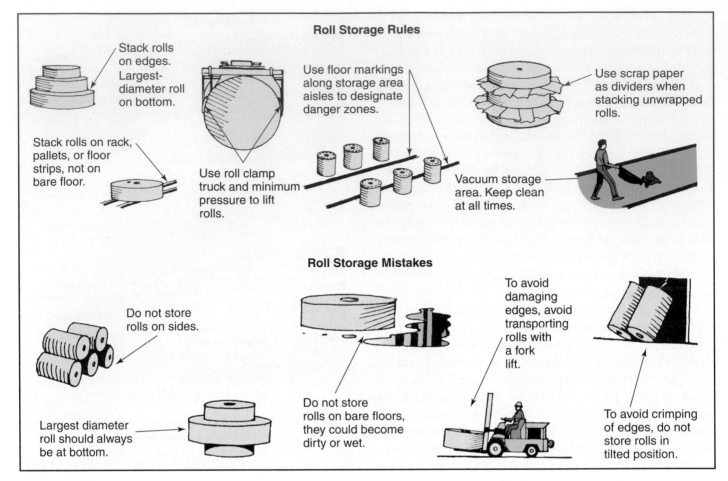

Figure 23-41. Study these recommended procedures and these practices to be avoided when handling and storing rolls of paper. (Hammermill Paper Co.)

These rolls are marked on their wrappers with the date, paper mill, and paper machine of their manufacture. Also included is the position across the width of the paper machine, as the roll was being formed. Consistency in the paper's physical characteristics is usually improved if a job is printed with rolls from the same position.

Web-Press Specs

In 1975, a review committee was formed to establish specs to help standardize the materials prepress service bureaus supply to printers. In 1976, the committee adopted its present name and created the SWOP specs. Although they are not mandated as such, the SWOP specs are accepted as printing-industry standards.

Initially, the specs covered only the production of film and proofs for web offset printing. As electronic technology has become more integrated in the production process, however, the specs now concentrate on the use of electronic files and their impact on publication production. Electronic files are expected to meet the same high-quality standards that have been expected of the graphic arts films and proofs supplied to the printer under SWOP specs. Areas covered under the specs include standard lighting for viewing proofs, electronic-file formats, register marks, film requirements, ink measurement and control, and proofing (on and off the press). For your convenience, the specs have been included at the end of this chapter.

Summary

Web offset presses are used to print single-color and multicolor work for newspapers, magazines, business forms, mail-order catalogs, gift wrappings, books, inserts, and many types of commercial printing. These presses can be equipped to fold signatures, paste, bind, perforate, number, slit, cut, and apply coatings. The three basic types of web offset presses are the perfecting blanket-to-blanket, in-line open, and drum common impression presses. A smaller version of the larger web offset press is called a *miniweb*. Miniwebs are popular with in-plant and small newspaper and commercial printers. These presses can also be equipped to fold, perforate, punch, number, cut, glue, imprint, die cut, and apply coatings.

Two common methods used to bring a new roll of paper into the feed cycle are the flying paster and zero-speed paster. Both methods allow the press to remain running while a new roll of paper is prepared and pasted to the expiring roll. Most web offset presses use a web-break detector to activate a control that automatically stops the press if the paper web breaks during operation. Web presses are equipped with image-alignment and register mechanisms to keep the paper perpendicular, or square, to the axes of the press cylinders. There is a number of adjustments that can be made to the press printing units of a web offset press.

The fast running speeds of web offset presses require fast-drying inks and the use of dryers. Ventilation and filtration systems are also part of the inking system on web offset presses. The proper handling and storing of paper rolls is essential in web offset press printing operations. Cleanliness and uniformity of moisture content, caliper, basis weight, and finish over the entire paper surface are critical factors. SWOP specs cover web printing and production, including standard lighting for viewing proofs, electronic-file formats, register marks, film requirements, ink measurement and control, and proofing (on and off the press).

Review Questions

Please do not write in this book. Write your answers on a separate sheet of paper.

1. Why is the construction of a web offset press described as modular, or unitized?

2. Web offset presses do not have sheet _____.

3. The length of a page printed on a web press is determined by the _____ of the press.

4. Identify other operations, besides printing, done on a web-press system.

5. What is a perfecting blanket-to-blanket web offset press?

6. Perfecting blanket-to-blanket web offset presses use two _____ cylinders and two _____ cylinders.

7. To print on the reverse side of the paper on an in-line open web offset press, the web is turned _____ degrees between the printing units.

8. The drum common impression web offset press is also known as a(n) _____ press.

9. Describe the construction and operation of a common impression cylinder web press.

10. The _____ offset press is popular with in-plant printers because of its smaller size and speed.

11. _____ is the adjustment of the amount of pull needed to keep the paper from developing slack.

12. _____ control the side-to-side register of the web as it passes through the press, just as a side guide exercises this control on a sheetfed press.

13. After the web exits the dryer, _____ are used to cool the web to room temperature and harden the ink film.

14. A(n) _____ paster brings a new roll of paper into the web-press feed cycle without stopping the press.

15. On a(n) _____ paster, the paster-unit rollers draw out slack in the running web, the end of the new roll is taped, and a splice is made while both rolls are stationary.

16. A(n) _____ detector activates a control that automatically brings the press to a full stop.

17. Rolls of paper are run through a web press _____ to the axes of the press cylinders.

18. Why is the exact alignment/registration of images on the plate an extremely important factor in web offset press operation?

19. Briefly discuss a method used to achieve register on a web offset press.

20. High-intensity lights positioned above and below the running web of paper check for image _____ and _____.

21. Web offset presses do not use plate _____.

22. Why must inks used on web offset presses dry quickly?

23. Web offset presses that use heatset inks must be fitted with an exhaust system to eliminate _____.

24. Sheetfed and webfed inks can be made into quick-set inks by incorporating a quick-set _____ into the formulation.

25. Explain the purpose of web offset press management systems.

26. List five types of in-line finishing operations.

27. The _____ direction of paper rolls should be parallel to the web direction on the press.

28. Why can the water resistance of web paper be lower than what might be considered satisfactory for sheetfed papers?

29. List five recommended procedures for handling and storing rolls of paper.

30. What areas are covered under the SWOP specs?

Skill-Building Activities

1. Gather examples of web-press printing. Try to get a broad selection of items, such as throwaway publications, magazines, and expensive four-color work. Prepare a bulletin board that attractively illustrates the products of web offset presswork.

2. Prepare schematic diagrams of various web presses showing the rollers, cylinders, and sheet-flow arrangements of each.

3. Divide the class into four groups. Each group should elect a leader who will assign tasks within the group. Each group should prepare a short report (including printed samples) on the application of web offset printing in the following production environments:
   • Miniweb in-plant printing.
   • Newspaper-publication printing.
   • Magazine-publication printing.
   • Commercial printing.

4. Prepare a short report on the application of miniweb presses for in-plant and commercial printing operations. You need to examine printing journals and other print-related media to obtain information on this subject.

A printing student adjusts the web offset press, which is printing the school newspaper. (Ferris State University)

Press On

At this point, the student has learned about the intricacies of lithographic printing. There are many variables and controls to consider. Even the most sophisticated press technology, such as the touch-screen controls shown here, cannot replace the ability of the human operator to know which part of the screen to touch.

This is the focus of this chapter. When problems arise—and they do—the operator's skill set includes the ability to examine the problem and methodically identify the cause: poor paper, excessive dampening solution, inadequate roller pressure, or too much drier in the ink? Whatever the cause, the operator is counted on to systematically isolate and eliminate it, to stay with the problem, and to press on.

(Heidelberg, Inc.)

Chapter 24
Press Problems and Troubleshooting

Key Terms

antistatic solution
dot doubling
dot gain scale
gray balance patch
slur
slur gauge
test form

Learning Objectives

When you have completed the reading and assigned activities related to this chapter, you will be able to do the following:

- Identify desirable paper characteristics for use on offset presses and duplicators.

- Describe and correct printing problems due to mechanical problems.

- Recognize problems caused by incorrect cylinder-pressure settings.

- Perform preventive maintenance on offset presses and duplicators.

- Give examples of quality-control devices and use the devices to achieve optimum printing results.

- Summarize the role GRACoL plays in achieving press quality.

- Solve and recognize problems related to static electricity.

- Use a troubleshooting chart to identify and correct common printing problems.

Once the product has been designed and the layout has been completed, the printer must turn all the preparatory work into finished printed sheets that meet the customer's expectations and approval. There are many factors that determine the quality of the finished printed product, the most important of which is a competent press operator. Strict attention to press-operating fundamentals is required for quality printing. See **Figure 24-1.**

Understanding each system of the duplicator or press is essential so problems that occur can be identified and analyzed in a logical and timely manner. Problems on press are due to a variety of factors, including pressure settings, feed and delivery adjustments, the substrate being used, and the maintenance demands of the duplicator or press itself. Due to the vast number of makes and models of presses and duplicators in use today, exact procedures for every situation cannot possibly be included. The information in this chapter covers many common problems and their causes, however, and the suggested corrective actions given can be applied to most situations.

Figure 24-1. There are many factors entering into the quality of the finished printed product, the most important of which is a competent press operator. (Van Son Holland Ink Corp.)

Printing problems are due to situations involving the substrate, the ink, or the press—or any combination of the three. See **Figure 24-2.** When scratches occur in the offset plate, it is necessary to prepare a new

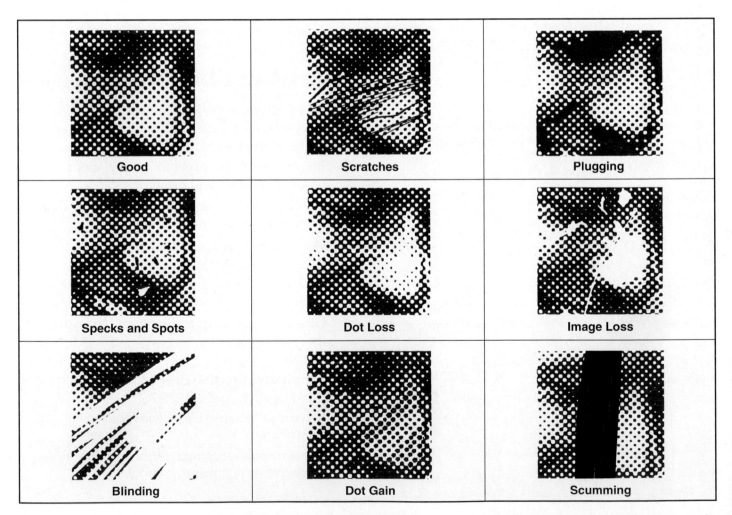

Figure 24-2. Results from some of the most common printing problems encountered on duplicators and presses. (3M Company)

plate. Care should be taken to avoid scratching the plate with your fingernails and dry particles of dirt or developer in the plate-processing pad or sponge. Plugging is a condition in which the image areas are filling in with ink on the printed sheets and plate. Specks and spots are usually referred to as *hickies*, which are particles of foreign matter that attach themselves to the offset plate and blanket. They cause undesirable black or white spots on the printed sheet or image. Dot loss usually occurs in halftones and screened image areas. The dots disappear in the highlight (light) areas of the offset-plate image. Image loss is the gradual disappearance of some lines and some halftone dots from the plate image. Blinding appears as weak spots in the image areas. Dried plate gum, strong fountain solution, and a glazed blanket generally cause blinding. Dot gain usually occurs in halftone and screened image areas of the printed sheet. This gain is due to too much impression pressure, too much ink, or excessive pressure causing a slippage of the blanket against the paper just before the impression stroke. Scumming occurs when the plate picks up ink in the nonimage areas and transfers ink to the nonimage areas of the sheet. Glazed ink rollers, a glazed blanket, too much ink form roller pressure, or too much dampener form roller pressure can cause this. See **Figure 24-3.**

Offset Papers

Most printing papers run satisfactorily on a duplicator or larger offset press. The press operator should recognize, however, that there are a wide variety of papers made specifically for the offset process. There are considerable differences between papers made for offset printing and those made for flexographic, gravure, and letterpress printing. These differences are due primarily to the use of water in offset lithography and the close contact of the rubber blanket to the paper. There are also differences in offset papers designed for sheetfed presses and those designed for web presses.

Offset papers are made with a strong, tough pulp blended with fillers for good running properties and opacity. These papers are also internally sized and surface sized to reduce the excessive absorption of dampening solution that would soften the paper and permit picking by tacky offset inks. The careful elimination of paper dust and stray fibers also helps ensure quality impressions. See **Figure 24-4.**

Sheetfed Papers

Paper used for sheetfed offset lithography must have higher surface and internal-bonding strength than that used for other printing processes. This paper must be able to withstand the tackier ink films and water used in sheetfed offset lithography.

- Good water resistance is needed to prevent the softening and weakening of the paper surface and to avoid excessive moisture pickup from the dampening system.

- The paper must not release active materials that react unfavorably with the chemistry of the plate, ink, and dampening system.

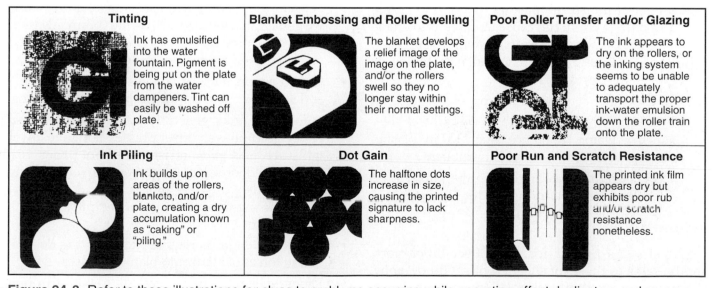

Tinting	Blanket Embossing and Roller Swelling	Poor Roller Transfer and/or Glazing
Ink has emulsified into the water fountain. Pigment is being put on the plate from the water dampeners. Tint can easily be washed off plate.	The blanket develops a relief image of the image on the plate, and/or the rollers swell so they no longer stay within their normal settings.	The ink appears to dry on the rollers, or the inking system seems to be unable to adequately transport the proper ink-water emulsion down the roller train onto the plate.
Ink Piling	**Dot Gain**	**Poor Run and Scratch Resistance**
Ink builds up on areas of the rollers, blankets, and/or plate, creating a dry accumulation known as "caking" or "piling."	The halftone dots increase in size, causing the printed signature to lack sharpness.	The printed ink film appears dry but exhibits poor rub and/or scratch resistance nonetheless.

Figure 24-3. Refer to these illustrations for clues to problems occurring while operating offset duplicators and presses.

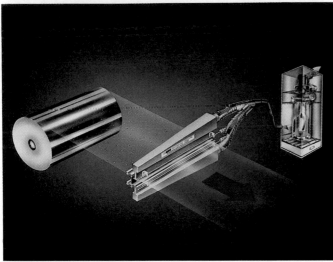

Figure 24-4. Many web-cleaning systems are designed to neutralize static and vacuum away dust particles. (SIMCO)

Figure 24-5. Differences in press operation allow some variance in the basis weight, coatings, and moisture-resistance requirements of paper run on a web offset press. (Heidelberg, Inc.)

- Excessive moisture pickup from the press dampening system can cause curl and intolerable changes in paper dimension. To maintain register, the paper must remain flat and not change its dimensions during printing.
- The moisture content of the paper must be in balance with the relative humidity of the pressroom.
- Excessive water resistance, such as in plastic-coated papers, can also present problems.
- Faster operating speeds require the paper to be stiffer than the paper designed for letterpress.

Webfed Papers

Paper requirements for web offset lithography are the same as those for sheetfed offset lithography. Differences in press operation allow some variance, however, in the paper basis weight, coatings, and moisture-resistance requirements. See **Figure 24-5**.

- The uniform tension maintained on web presses permits the feeding and printing of lower basis weights, or thinner papers, than are commonly used on sheetfed presses. The basis weights of paper used on web presses range from about 20 to 80 pounds.
- Coated papers must be designed to resist blistering and to fold without cracking during heatset drying.
- Web offset inks generally have lower tack, so paper used on web offset presses can have lower moisture and pick resistance than paper run on sheetfed offset presses. Web offset printing systems also use less moisture, and less time exists during the print run for the paper to pick up moisture.
- Internal strength is required to resist the delamination forces of blanket-to-blanket presses.
- Paper webs must be flat enough to pass through the squeeze impressions of the printing units without wrinkling or becoming distorted.

- Paper rolls that unwind with even tension and flatness across the web and without localized distortion are required for good register and to prevent wrinkling.
- Paper rolls free of defects and with proper splicing are essential for good runnability and for minimizing web breaks.

Carbonless Papers

Printing on carbonless papers can sometimes create problems on the duplicator or press. For best results, follow these typical procedures:

1. Fan the paper from the corners (not the ends) before loading. Check (using the CFB test sheet in the carton) to assure the printing side is up.
2. The paper height should be set to about 1/8" to 1/2" (3.175 mm to 12.7 mm) below the sheet separators. The blower tubes should be adjusted to evenly float sheets just below the separator fingers. The suction feet should be positioned about 2" (50.8 mm) from the edges of the paper.
3. The pullout roller should be centered on the paper stack in order to forward the sheet without cocking:

   A. Place the paperweight bar in one of the two forward notches, which helps control the amount of air separating the sheets. Use the lightweight paper kit for best results.

   B. The air should be adjusted to float the top three or four sheets. The vacuum and air might have to be adjusted as the duplicator speed increases.

   C. Set the buckle control at 7 and move up as far as 12, until the paper runs smoothly.

4. The side-register guide should barely tap the side of the sheet. Pushing the sheet excessively can cause it to buckle and wrinkle as it passes through the duplicator.
5. Reduced impression pressure and quick-release compressible-type blankets are recommended to minimize the capsule damage of the sheets. This also reduces any tendency for the paper to stick to the blanket. Results can be checked by spraying a CB surface with instant-replay damage indicator.
6. Use quality inks that dry by oxidation and have a lower tack (in the 10–12 range on a GATF Inkometer) to reduce the possibility of setoff and coating buildup on the blanket.
7. Run with the minimum amount of fountain solution necessary for quality printing.

Heatset printing can encounter a problem called *blistering*. Blistering occurs when the heat of the drying ovens causes moisture within the paper to turn to steam and rapidly expand. The moisture cannot escape, due to the coating layers. See **Figure 24-6.** Blistering can be avoided by ensuring that the web is not unwrapped in a room with excessive relative humidity, where the web will absorb moisture. Excessive oven temperatures can also cause blistering.

Bagginess describes a roll of paper bulging at either the center or the edges. Moisture pickup in a room with high humidity can cause bagginess at the edges. Bagginess can also be caused during manufacture. A baggy roll cannot be printed because it is not flat and is prone to wrinkling as it passes between the blanket and impression cylinders.

Offset Inks

Similar to paper, inks are also designed specifically for the offset process. There are considerable differences between inks made for offset printing and those made for flexographic, gravure, screen, and letterpress printing. As with the differences in paper, these differences are due primarily to the use of water in offset lithography and the close contact of the rubber blanket to the paper. There are also differences in offset inks designed for sheetfed presses and those designed for web presses.

Sheetfed Inks

Sheetfed lithographic inks have a higher tack than webfed offset inks do. The relatively low speed of the press permits the use of a high-tack ink, which is required for sharp image definition. This also helps to avoid the filling in of halftone dots and avoids setoff in the printed pile of paper.

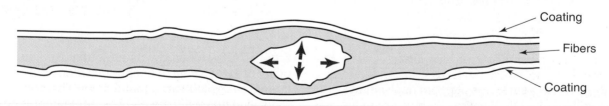

Figure 24-6. Blistering results from moisture trapped by the coating layers flashing to steam within the paper.

Webfed Inks

There are a variety of inks designed for use on web offset presses. Each type is designed for use with specific types of paper and different drying processes. Web offset inks include heatset, nonheatset, quick-set, and superquick-set.

Ink Problems

Setoff (inked image prints on the back of another sheet) usually occurs as a result of running too much ink on the duplicator or press. See **Figure 24-7.** For example, in order to achieve the desired ink color, a press operator runs the ink heavy (thick). In most instances, however, the problem is too much water. Instead of increasing the ink, the press operator should reduce the amount of water. It might be necessary to use a deeper ink color in order to permit the running of a thinner ink film to get the correct color results.

There are times when it is desirable to add a small amount of a cobalt drier or combination cobalt-and-manganese paste drier to the ink. In most cases, the only time it is necessary to add driers is when high-humidity situations are encountered. Care must be taken because adding too much drier can actually retard the drying of the ink. Ink drying can be accelerated through the use of dryers. The size and design of the press determine the type of dryer that can be used. See **Figure 24-8.**

A problem related to ink-and-water balance is called *scumming* (the ink prints lightly in nonimage areas). Although scumming is due to insufficient dampening solution, the first problem leading to scumming can be running an excessive amount of dampening solution. This sequence usually starts out as the press operator gets a light print on the sheets. As the amount of ink is increased, a filling, or scumming, problem begins. The problem is made worse by adding more water, which again produces a light print. The recommended procedure is to carefully reduce the amount of water until a sharp full-density print is obtained. If this produces the filling of fine letters, halftones, or other fine detail, the water should be carefully increased until the condition disappears. The same procedure should be followed if the background begins to pick up ink.

Hickies (unwanted white or black spots) usually result from a small piece of foreign matter that attaches itself to the offset blanket or plate. The small particles of foreign matter can be fibers from a molleton cover, dried ink, paper coating, paper dust, or dirt. The press operator can prevent hickies by practicing the following methods of operation:

- Avoid excessive ink tackiness.
- Pay careful attention to the condition of the molleton rollers.
- Replace damaged and cracked ink rollers.
- Do not use setoff-spray powder or liquid excessively.
- Avoid ink skinning in cans and in the duplicator or press fountain.
- Keep all rollers clean, especially at the ends.
- Use cleaner mats with care. They can leave paper particles on ink rollers.

There are no problems with unwanted patterns, such as ghosting, because of good inking qualities of the roller. Proper care of all dampening rollers on a press or duplicator is essential to achieve optimum print quality. See **Figure 24-9.**

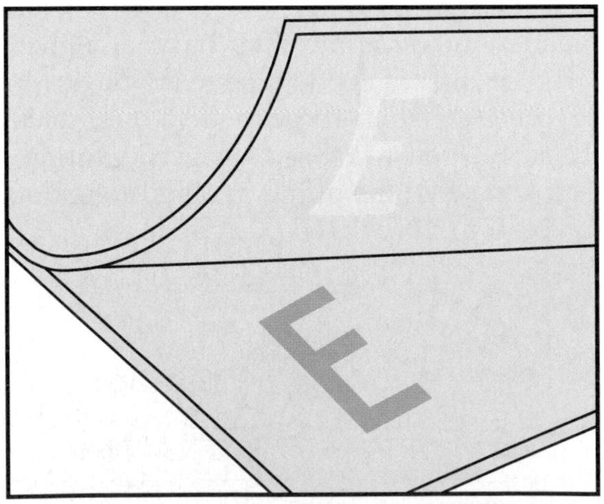

Figure 24-7. Setoff usually results from applying so much ink to the substrate that the ink transfers to the sheet above before it can dry.

Figure 24-8. Hot-air dryers are often used on smaller offset presses. Heat is generated when an electrical current is applied to the thermistors. The dryer is self-regulating and maintains a constant temperature without the need for a thermostat. (ACCEL Graphic Systems)

Offset Presses and Duplicators

The many setup procedures and variables involved in offset lithographic printing greatly affect offset-press and duplicator operation and output. Each component must be functioning properly to achieve quality results. Before making mechanical adjustments to the press, the problem should be

analyzed, and all ink or paper variables should be eliminated as the cause.

Press problems that can contribute to poor printing include plate failure, improper packing of the plate or blanket, and improper roller pressure. If the plate is at fault (damaged or worn), it should be replaced. If improper packing is the problem, the packing should be measured and adjusted according to the proper specs. Roller pressure should also be checked and adjusted to the proper specs.

Roller-Pressure Settings

Offset presses and duplicators rely on accurate pressure settings of the various rollers and cylinders. Roller pressure should be set to the recommended settings listed in the press-operating manual as part of the daily setup routine. Problems caused by improper roller-pressure settings include the following:

- Too little pressure between the ink form rollers and the plate can cause incomplete transfer of ink to the plate. Too heavy a setting can result in image spread and slur. This can also cause excessive plate wear.

- Too little pressure between the plate and blanket cylinders can cause an improper transfer of the image to the blanket. This results in a light print. Excessive pressure or blanket slippage can cause image spread, horizontal streaks, and slurred dots.

- Too little impression between the blanket and impression cylinders can result in a broken or light print. Excessive pressure can cause spread of the image.

- If the pressure between the dampener form roller and plate is too light, the dampening of the plate will not be uniform. The tendency is to run too much water, due to the poor transfer of moisture to the plate. In addition, any variation in the diameter of the dampener rollers shows up very quickly. Excessive pressure can produce slurring of the image. This condition can also cause a bounce of the dampener form roller as it goes through the gap of the plate cylinder.

Most of the newer presses and duplicators are equipped with control devices that monitor and automatically make adjustments or alert the operator to the problem. Many older presses and duplicators have been retrofitted with these same types of devices. Manual adjustments are often needed, however, to correct a printing problem. Operators commonly use troubleshooting charts similar to the one in **Figure 24-10** to analyze and solve printing problems.

A Synthetic Roller

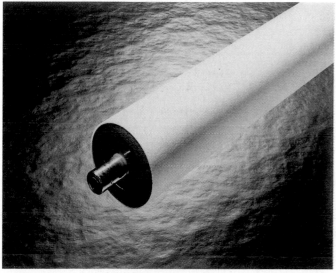

A Seamless Sleeve

Figure 24-9. Many dampener rollers are now constructed of a proprietary synthetic material that is both softer and more resilient than rubber. Seamless dampener sleeves are used for both webfed and sheetfed press applications. (Jomac, Inc.; American Roller Company)

VAN SON'S PROBLEM SOLVING

Condition		Cause	Cure
Backing	Ink lacking "flow" backs away from the fountain roller and is not delivered to ductor rollers	• ink too short and buttery • insufficient ink in fountain	• add Varnish No. 30 • add more ink to fountain and agitate with clean ink knife
Chalking INK	Pigment not properly bound to the paper is easily rubbed off as a powder when dry	• ink unsuitable for absorbent stock • fountain solution or paper too acidic • moisture content of paper too high	• use an oil base ink (such as Van Son's CML-Oil Base Plus) for absorbent coated stock. If print run is completed, job can be salvaged by reprinting the sheet with overprint varnish • adjust fountain solution pH to 5.0–5.5; change to a less acidic stock • condition paper before printing
Crystallization	The failure of a dried ink film to accept overprinting	• too much time has elapsed between printing of succeeding colors or Cobalt Drier was used in first ink down	• run succeeding colors promptly within a week to 10 days. If a job is planned to be imprinted later, leave the area to be printed later blank so imprint is done on plain paper. An ink such as Van Son's Tough Tex will often print and adhere where conventional inks will not
Filling In	A condition in which halftones, tints, and reverses "fill in" producing a muddy or solid appearance	• excessive ink being run • ink too soft • press pressures incorrect • paper coating is of poor quality	• cut back ink flow • add varnish No. 30 to ink • correct pressure settings • change to another type of paper
Gloss Ghosting loss of gloss	Uneven drying rate causes loss of gloss in areas of a printed sheet Large solids printed on back-up form	• the drying of the ink on the second side is retarded or accelerated by the fumes given off by the ink on the first side	• thoroughly wind sheets and allow extra drying time for the first side before printing the second–varnish second side with overprint varnish after printing • print the heavy form first, and the light form on the back-up side
Hickies	Defects in print appearing as specks of ink surrounded by a white halo	• particles of dried ink or skin from can • paper dust and other contaminants get into ink and stick to blanket	• remove hardened ink and skin from can before putting ink in fountain • keep press area clean; brush or vacuum paper pile edges and keep cutter blades sharp
Misting	A condition which occurs when a fine mist or spray of ink particles is thrown off a rapidly moving ink roller	• ink too soft • ink fountain feeding too thick an ink film to fountain roller • ink rollers cracked, nicked, pitted, or out-of-round • speed of press too fast	• add varnish No. 30 to ink • tighten fountain blade and adjust ink ratchet to give ductor roller more sweep • inspect rollers and replace defective ones • reduce press speed
Mottling Tr	An uneven appearance in printed solids characterized by small light and dark areas	• too much water • ink is not sufficiently water repellent • plate image is not sufficiently receptive to ink or partially blind	• reset ink/water balance • add varnish No. 30 to fresh ink in fountain • check plate and remake if necessary
Picking	Removal of parts of the paper surface or coating during printing	• ink too tacky • blanket is tacky and pulling sheet surface • weak stock or poor paper coating	• reduce tack with a tack reducer • exchange blankets, allow old blanket a few days rest to remove solvent from pores • cut ink tack and reduce press speed if necessary to get poor stock through press
Piling	The buildup of ink on the rollers, plate, or blanket	• ink too stiff or tacky • ink has emulsified with water	• add tack reducer to ink • clean up and readjust for proper ink/water balance; add varnish No. 30

Figure 24-10. A troubleshooting chart operators use to analyze and solve printing problems. (Special thanks to Printing Consulting, Inc. for allowing the use of several graphics from their *Printing Ink Complaint Handbook*.)

GUIDE FOR OFFSET PRINTERS

Condition		Cause	Cure
Roller Stripping	Failure of the ink to adhere to the rollers of the press	• fountain solution is too acidic • rollers glazed • rollers have become desensitized • rollers out-of-round • uneven distribution at ink fountain, or fountain blade is buckled • dried ink or dirt has accumulated between fountain roller and blade	• adjust fountain pH to 5.0–5.5 • deglaze rollers with a liquid deglazer. For steel rollers, use a copperizing solution to improve receptivity • pumice and etch ink rollers as recommended by manufacturer • replace worn rollers • adjust fountain keys for even distribution, or replace buckled fountain blade • keep fountain roller and blade clean at all times
Scumming	An undesirable adhesion of ink to the nonimage areas of the printing plate	• ink too soft • too much ink • fountain solution pH is incorrect • molleton cover is dirty or worn • excess pressure on ink form rollers	• add 1 to 2 ozs. of varnish per pound of ink • adjust for better ink and water balance • adjust pH to read 4.5–5.0 • clean or replace molleton cover • readjust pressure
Set-off 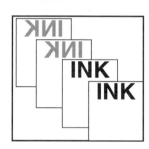	An undesirable transfer of the ink film from the front of one sheet to the back of the adjacent sheet	• too much ink on paper • fountain solution is too acidic • wrong ink for stock • not enough drier • paper coating is of poor quality • delivery pile is too high • pressman squeezes paper when removing from press • static in the delivery pile is attracting sheets to one another	• reduce ink by adjusting fountain keys • use a pH tester, adjust to 4.5–5.0 • determine right ink for stock being used • add drier to ink, or fountain drying stimulator to fountain solution, to speed up drying time • use paper of different quality • reduce height of delivery pile and remove smaller piles from press • use a board under pile and lift paper from press on the board • use static eliminator tinsel across ejector wheel, spray paper pile and delivery area with antistatic spray
Slow Drying	Excessive drying time can delay run of succeeding colors or folding	• fountain solution or paper stock is too acidic • too much ink being run • wrong ink for stock being run • cold paper	• adjust fountain pH to 4.5–5.0, add fountain drying stimulator; change to a less acidic stock • reduce amount of ink being run • determine correct ink for stock • condition paper to room temperature before running
Slur	A condition caused by slippage at the moment of impression between the paper, plate, or blanket	• blanket is loose • blanket is packed to greater diameter than plate cylinder resulting in different surface speeds between plate and blanket • excessive play in the gears and bearings of plate and blanket cylinders	• tighten blanket clamps • change packing to equalize diameters • replace worn parts
Streaking	Streaks or bands which appear across the plate	• molletons dirty or improperly set • loose blanket or improper ink roller pressures or rollers slipping or out-of-round	• use a new molleton and reset roller pressure • tighten blanket or reset roller pressures
Tinting	A uniform discoloration of the background caused by emulsification of ink pigment in the fountain solution	• ink too soft • plate not properly processed • fountain solution too acidic • ink and water out of balance • surface active chemicals in paper coating dissolve in fountain solution causing ink to emulsify or ink pigment to dissolve in the fountain solution	• add varnish No. 30 to your ink • prepare a new plate • use a pH tester and adjust to 5.0–5.5 • clean up and readjust ink and water settings • add varnish No. 30 and change stock if problem persists

Figure 24-10. *(Continued)*

Preventive Maintenance

Offset presses and duplicators are precision machines requiring a great deal of preventive maintenance. Appropriate preventive maintenance greatly reduces the unexpected downtime that results from neglected equipment requiring emergency maintenance or repair. The use of proper setup procedures, proper ink formulation, and quality offset paper, as well as the use of proper cleanup procedures, increases production and maintains printing quality. See **Figure 24-11.** Press and duplicator settings should not be taken for granted just because everything ran well on the last job printed. Different conditions affect press operation and image quality. This is especially true if the previous job was run using a different paper, ink, or plate.

Caution

Before operating a press or duplicator, make sure it is safe for operation. Check that all safety guards are in place and operating properly. Wipe up excess oil, grease, and solvents. See **Figure 24-12.**

All settings should be checked before and during the run. Use a checklist to ensure you have not overlooked any detail. The following items should receive careful attention when preparing to run a job on a press or duplicator.

- Oil the press periodically. Refer to the press operator's instruction manual for lubrication requirements.
- Inspect duplicator or press cleanliness. Check fountains, rollers, and all surfaces for dried ink, gum, dirt, or mechanical contamination. See **Figure 24-13.**

Figure 24-11. Proper maintenance extends the life of a duplicator or press and produces quality work. (Van Son Holland Ink Corp.)

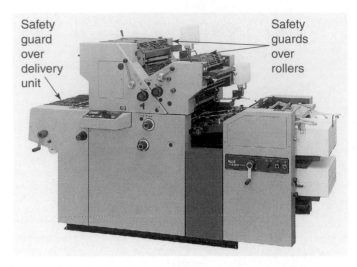

Figure 24-12. Check that all safety guards are in place and operating properly before beginning work on a duplicator or press. (Ryobi Xpedx Impact Group)

- Check the printing plate. Inspect for exposure, development, completeness of image, and damage.
- Adjust the plate clamps back to the same position each time.

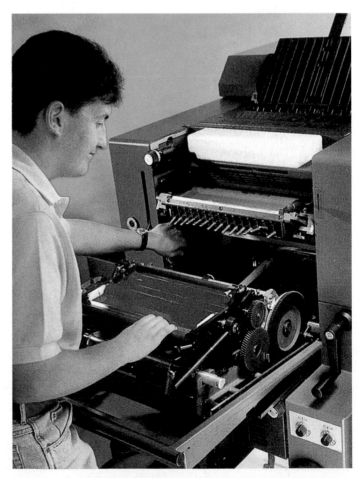

Figure 24-13. Inspect the ink train and dampening trains for contaminants. (Heidelberg, Inc.)

- Mount the plate carefully. When required, pack the cylinder to the manufacturer's specs. Check the tightness of the plate at the edge of the cylinder gap. Register all plates to the same cylinder gutter.

- Properly apply the ink. Discard any ink skin that has formed in the can.

- Set the ink fountain. Adjust the ink-fountain keys to average-image ink-flow requirements using just over half the catches on the ratchet. Check the evenness of the ink film as the fountain roller turns while it is in contact with the ductor roller.

- Test the fountain solution. Check the pH with litmus paper or an electronic pH meter. If using alcohol, also check the specific gravity. Clean the fountain completely every day.

- Measure dampener pressures. When testing dampener form roller-to-plate pressure, a uniform, firm pull should be attained on plastic gauges or paper strips at two points along the rollers.

- Inspect ink form roller-to-plate pressure. Gently drop the inked form rollers to the plate surface. Check the printed bands for uniformity and thickness. See **Figure 24-14.**

- Check plate-to-blanket pressure. Transfer the ink band from the plate to the blanket. The band of ink on the blanket should perfectly match the band of ink on the plate.

- Adjust the impression-cylinder setting. Set for the thickness of paper being run.

Caution

Keep fingers clear of all pressure (nip) points, clamps, and cylinders.

Quality Control

A *test form* is a compilation of quality-control devices on a single sheet or page. See **Figure 24-15.** The reproduction of the test form allows the operator to evaluate the print quality of the particular press, duplicator, printer, or proofer being used.

Test forms are available in printed, film-based, or electronic formats and as negative or positive images. They are designed for many types of presses and duplicators and for a variety of digital printers and proofers. Test forms can be used to check press problems, calibrate equipment (such as monitors, printers,

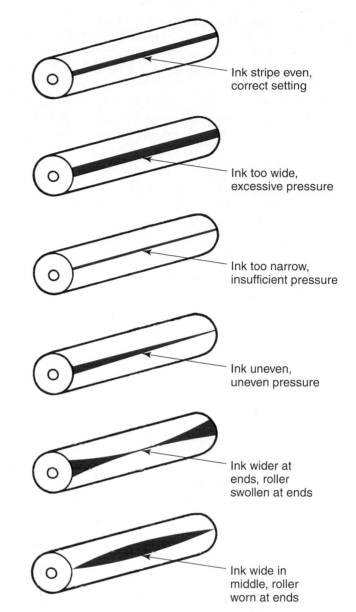

Ink stripe even, correct setting

Ink too wide, excessive pressure

Ink too narrow, insufficient pressure

Ink uneven, uneven pressure

Ink wider at ends, roller swollen at ends

Ink wide in middle, roller worn at ends

Figure 24-14. The parallel adjustment of ink form rollers is essential for uniform ink distribution.

and scanners), and evaluate press performance. Some common quality-control devices include color bars, star targets, gray-balance charts, and dot gain scales. These devices, as well as many others, are available as separate elements or as part of a test form.

A color bar is a strip of colors printed in the trim area of a press sheet. This strip usually consists of overprints of two- and three-color solids and tints; solid and tint blocks of CMYK; and additional aids, such as resolution targets and dot gain scales. See **Figure 24-16.** Press operators can monitor uniform

test form: a compilation of quality-control devices on a single electronic, printed, negative, or positive sheet or page.

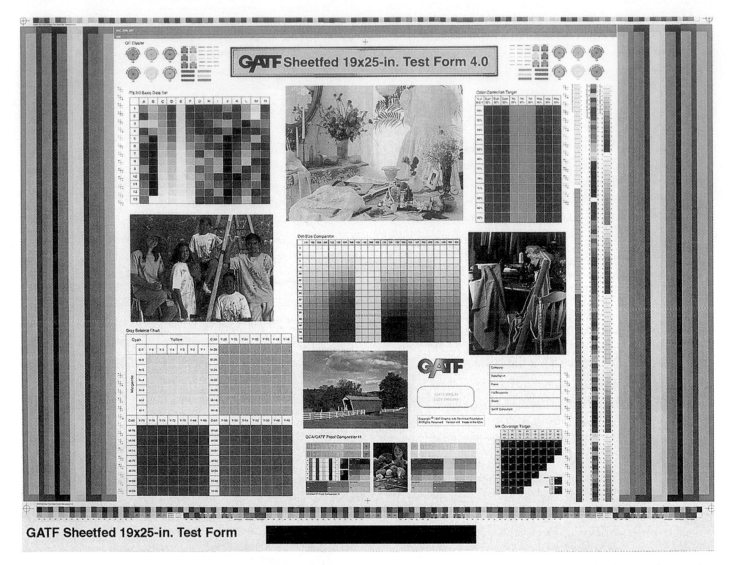

GATF Sheetfed 19x25-in. Test Form

Figure 24-15. This Graphic Arts Technical Foundation (GATF) form is designed to assist printers in diagnosing and calibrating color reproduction on 25″ presses with up to six printing units. The form includes a dot gain scale, a color-correction target, a dot-size comparator, a gray-balance chart, a ladder target, a proof comparator, and two control bars. (Graphic Arts Technical Foundation)

ink distribution across the press sheet by measuring the density of the CMYK patches. Proper ink trapping is revealed by measuring the density of the green, red, and blue patches. A color bar also is used to monitor printing variables such as trapping, ink density, dot gain, and print contrast. They can usually identify the cause of a poorly printed image. Color bars can also be referred to as *color control bars*, *color control strips*, or *proofing bars*.

Usually included with color bars are what are known as *star targets*—circular patterns of lines primarily used to detect dot gain, slur, and dot doubling. Dot gain is the enlargement of the printed dot due to excessive ink film or pressure between cylinders. *Slur* is a stretching of halftone dots caused by a slippage of the cylinders, usually in the around-the-cylinder direction. When this type of slippage occurs, the *slur gauge* indicates dot gain by ink spreading in one direction. *Dot doubling* is printing the same dot twice. Whereas slur is revealed by an oval-shaped center of the star target, dot doubling creates two overlapping dots, and dot gain is revealed by a symmetrical center that is too large. See **Figure 24-17.** When any one of these problems occurs in one of the process colors, the dots of that color grow, and the overall hue of the image is shifted to that color. See **Figure 24-18.**

The *dot gain scale* is a quality-control device used to indicate dot reproduction of halftones and process colors. This scale consists of a series of numbers (zero through nine) that are finely screened and graduated from light to dark. As dot gain increases, the numbers become more visible.

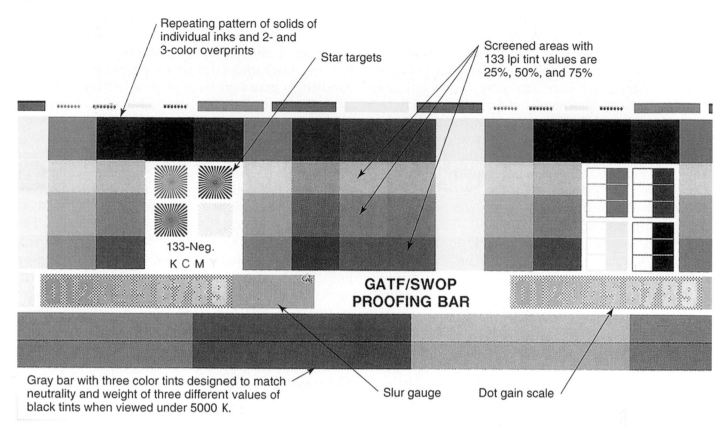

Repeating pattern of solids of individual inks and 2- and 3-color overprints

Star targets

Screened areas with 133 lpi tint values are 25%, 50%, and 75%

133-Neg.

K C M

GATF/SWOP PROOFING BAR

Gray bar with three color tints designed to match neutrality and weight of three different values of black tints when viewed under 5000 K.

Slur gauge

Dot gain scale

Figure 24-16. Color bars contain numerous quality-control devices. (Graphic Arts Technical Foundation)

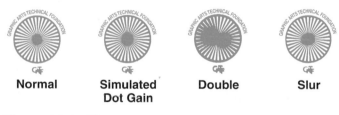

Normal

Simulated Dot Gain

Double

Slur

Figure 24-17. The camera department can use the star target to check for copy resolution. This illustration compares how the printed target appears normal, with dot gain, with doubling, and with slur. (Graphic Arts Technical Foundation)

The slur gauge is usually located to the right of the number nine on the dot gain scale. Its primary use is to indicate slur. The slur gauge is composed of high-resolution horizontal and vertical lines. The horizontal lines spell *slur* within the vertical lines. Under normal printing and viewing conditions, the

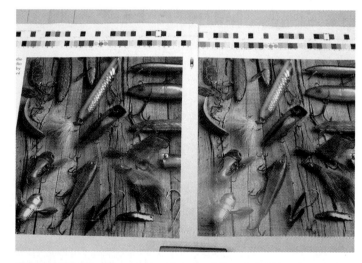

Figure 24-18. The press sheet on the right has been printed properly, but the press sheet on the left has a red cast. Slur occurred on the magenta unit to enlarge the magenta dots and create color imbalance.

slur: a change in sharpness caused by a slippage of the cylinders, usually in the around-the-cylinder direction.

slur gauge: a quality-control device on a color bar used to indicate slur caused primarily by cylinder slippage.

dot doubling: a printing defect characterized by halftone dots printing twice, a type of visual stuttering or echo. This defect is commonly caused by a loose blanket, excessive pressure between the blanket and the substrate, or excessive ink on the plate.

dot gain scale: a quality-control device consisting of a series of numbers used to indicate dot reproduction of halftones and process colors.

word *slur* is not very visible. As slur occurs, however, the word becomes highly visible.

Gray balance is measured by overprinting screen tints of the three process colors to see if they produce a *gray balance patch* of neutral gray. If gray balance is not achieved, the patch will have a tint. The midtone percentages are usually 50% cyan and 40% for magenta and yellow. The cyan dots are larger to compensate for its being the only cool color in the presence of two warm colors and to compensate for impurities in the inks. Gray balance strips can be judged visually or with a colorimeter. If a colorimeter is used, the CIELAB values should be A = 0 and B = –2.0.

Several instruments are available to check dot gain, slur, doubling, and ink coverage on press sheets and proofs. See **Figure 24-19.** These devices can be used to check halftone-dot sizes, as well as the texture

of the paper in cases where mottling appears to be a problem. Colors reflected from other sources, such as the paper or room lighting, are filtered out. Color-viewing instruments must be properly stored and handled to maintain their level of accuracy. Always follow the manufacturer's instructions for cleaning.

Many presses use a built-in scanning densitometer to measure ink density on the printed piece. See **Figure 24-20.** The scanning densitometer scans the color bars in the margin of the printed sheets as they enter the delivery pile of the press. Any color problems that might be occurring on the sheets are instantly indicated on the scanning device. The densitometer can also be used to determine if there is dot gain in the halftones and if the ink is trapping properly. Polarization filters or programming adjustments can be used to make allowance for differences in wet and dry ink. Handheld or table-mounted densitometers or spectrodensitometers can also be used to check color reproduction on printed sheets.

General Requirements for Applications in Commercial Offset Lithography (GRACoL)

Densitometers are often used to achieve standards known as *GRACoL*. GRACoL includes guidelines and specs for achieving consistent quality in

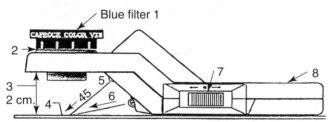

Blue filter 1

2 cm

1. Slip-on, slip-off blue filter for viewing hard-to-see yellow dots and other colors. Optional red and green filters for dropping out other colors.
2. Ten power, flat-field, color-corrected lens.
3. Open area for retouching.
4. Surface area to be examined.
5. 45 illumination for normal viewing.
6. Horizontal illumination for inspecting surfaces and checking roughness and mottle due to recycled papers.
7. Slide switch for activating the upper or lower lightbulbs.
8. Battery compartment for two AA batteries and no. 243 standard lightbulbs.

Figure 24-19. This color viewer and mottle checker is used to check halftone-dot sizes and paper texture. By removing the filter, the instrument can also be used as a 10×, flat-field, color-corrected magnifier. (Caprock Developments, Inc.)

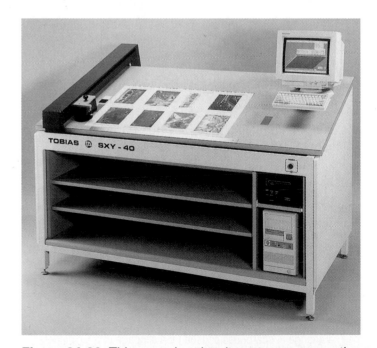

Figure 24-20. This scanning densitometer measures the density of the ink on the printed sheets so a comparison can be made to the original approved color proof. Color bars are included along the edges of the press sheets for this purpose. (Tobias Associates, Inc.)

sheetfed lithographic printing. Published in 1997, GRACoL became the third standard for lithography. Already in existence were SWOP and the Specifications for Non-Heat Advertising Printing. Together, the Specifications for Non-Heat Advertising Printing, GRACoL, and SWOP provide guidelines for quality printing in three distinct types of lithographic printing. They provide standards for printers who want to optimize their equipment, paper, ink, and operators to consistently produce excellent color reproduction and visual contrast. See **Figure 24-21.** The SWOP and GRACoL standards are on the Student CD.

The goal of GRACoL is to coordinate color management with the prepress and press functions by providing numerical targets for several factors affecting print quality—density, dot gain, slur, trap, and print contrast. When the press operator is able to maintain these factors within GRACoL tolerances, the overall print quality is maintained. GRACoL identifies the following guidelines to quality lithographic printing:

- Purchase paper, ink, and other materials from vendors maintaining consistent standards.
- Monitor ink densities on press sheets.

- Consistently calibrate scanners, monitors, proofers, and plate-imaging devices.
- Use CIELAB or spectrophotometer readings to monitor press performance.
- Print IT8 targets to determine the capability of each press.
- Place color bars on proofs and press sheets to identify color drift.

The G7 Approach to Proofer and Press Control

Introduced by IdeAlliance in 2004, G7 is a new specification that outlines methods to calibrate proofing systems and presses based on principles of DI, spectrophotometry, and CTP technologies. The G in the name comes from the specification's gray scale calibration technique, and the 7 represents the seven ink colors (CMYK and RGB) that serve as the basis for the gray scale measurement. G7 is intended to produce a closer match between a proof and the printed product, even when the product is printed on different presses.

Suggested Input Variables															Output Print Characteristics							
Paper Substrate	lpi	TAC	Paper Lab			Solid Ink Density*				Dot Gain				Print Contrast			
			L	a	b	K	C	M	Y	K	C	M	Y	K	C	M	Y
Grades 1 and 2 premium gloss and dull coated	175	320%	95.27	0.67	-1.71	1.70	1.40	1.50	1.05	22	20	20	18	40–45	35–40	35–40	30–35
Grades 1 and 2 premium matte coated	150–175	300–320%	92.00	0.00	-3.00	1.60	1.30	1.40	1.00	24	22	22	20	40–45	35–40	35–40	30–35
Premium text and cover	150–175	260%				1.30	1.15	1.15	0.90	26	22	22	20	35–40	30–40	30–41	25–35
Grade #3	150	310%	87.00	-1.00	3.00	1.65	1.35	1.45	1.02	22	21	22	18	45	40	41	35
Grade #5	133	300%	88.69	-0.33	3.65	1.60	1.30	1.40	1.00	22	20	20	18	35–40	30–40	30–41	25–35
Supercal SCA+	133	280%				1.50	1.25	1.35	1.00	28	26	26	24	23	21	21	20
Supercal SCA	120	260–280%				1.40	1.15	1.20	0.95	28	26	26	24	23	21	21	20
Supercal SCB	120	240–260%				1.35	1.10	1.15	0.995	28	26	26	24	23	21	21	20
Uncoated	110	240–260%	92.00	0.00	-3.00	1.25	1.00	1.12	0.95	28	26	26	24	20	17	16	17
Newsprint	85	240%	82.00	0.00	3.00	1.05	0.90	0.90	0.85	30	30	30	30	16	13	12	15
Newsprint (heatset and Supercal SCC)	100	240%				1.20	1.08	1.15	0.95	32	32	32	32	16	13	12	15

*Solid ink density was measured on dry press sheets.

Figure 24-21. A portion of the GRACoL Print Characterization Chart provides suggested input variables (lpi, total-area coverage, LAB values, and solid ink densities) and output print characteristics.

gray balance patch: a small area where screen tints of the three process colors are printed.

Before G7, press operators relied on controlling dot gain (or tone-value increase) for press control. The G7 approach replaced dot gain with gray balance as the primary means of quality control. This approach relies on measuring color with a spectrophotometer, instead of measuring dots with a densitometer. By measuring gray balance, the output of both proofers and presses can be evaluated by the same standard.

The first step in the G7 methodology is to ensure that both the proofer and press are operating in a stable manner. Next, a Press2Proof (P2P) target is printed by the press and measured with a spectrophotometer. See **Figure 24-22**. These measurements are then used to plot a curve that reveals the values needed to correct the output of the proofer and the CTP RIP. This single Neutral Print Density Curve (NPDC) replaces the separate dot gain curves for CMY. The rationale for the NPDC is that, when both the proofer and the press are printing CMY to achieve a neutral gray, the press sheets should match the proof very closely.

Static Electricity

Although the presence of water in the offset process helps reduce static electricity, static electricity can still be a problem in the pressroom. Static electricity is created when press equipment and the substrate pick up free electrons during operation and become charged. The high production level of a pressroom can cause an excessive buildup of static electricity, in which workers can receive painful shocks when touching the equipment. In extreme cases, fires and explosions can occur. Static electricity can cause feeding and delivery problems and attract dust and lint that can end up in the ink and on the plate. This electricity can also increase the occurrence of ink setoff. Static electricity can be reduced or eliminated from the pressroom in various ways:

- Properly grounding the press and related equipment.
- Installing ionized-air devices on the press to remove free electrons from the equipment and surrounding air.
- Maintaining the proper relative humidity and temperature in the pressroom.

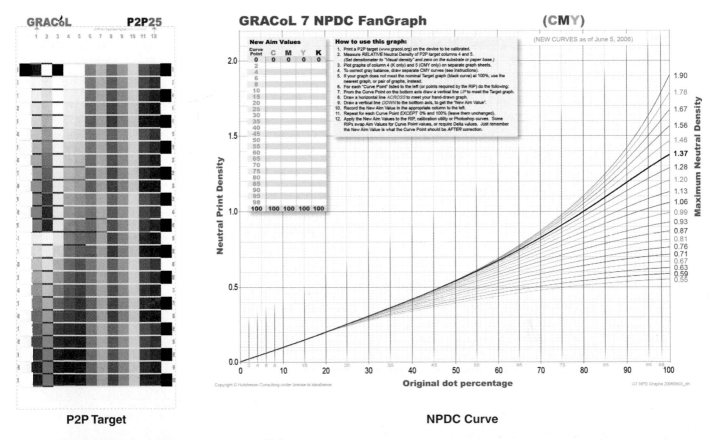

P2P Target

NPDC Curve

Figure 24-22. After this P2P target is printed on press, its patches are read with a spectrophotometer to produce a profile of how the press prints CMY. These data generate the NPDC curve that modifies the proofer and the CTP RIP to match the press.

- Installing static eliminators on the press. See **Figure 24-23.**
- Stringing metallic tinsel across the guide rollers in the delivery system.
- Applying *antistatic solutions* to the paper.

Troubleshooting

Most press manufacturers provide maintenance and troubleshooting guides to help the press operator analyze and correct printing problems. The troubleshooting guide in **Figure 24-10** has been included to help you correct and eliminate common problems associated with duplicator and press operations. This guide is divided into three columns: the condition or problem, the probable cause, and the cure.

Summary

Offset presses and duplicators are precision machines requiring a great deal of maintenance. The use of proper setup procedures, proper ink formulation,

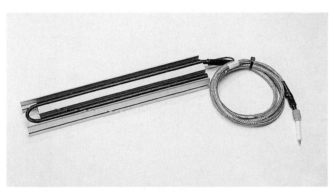
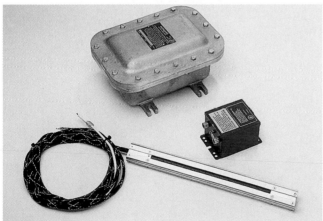

Figure 24-23. Static eliminators can be installed on a press to reduce the amount of static electricity. Some static eliminators are designed specifically for use in hazardous environments where normal static eliminators cannot be used, due to risk of fire or explosion. (Chapman Corp.)

and quality offset paper, as well as the use of proper cleanup procedures, increases production and maintains printing quality. Different conditions affect press operation and image quality, and the press operator should have a thorough understanding of offset-paper and ink characteristics and requirements.

Printing problems can often be attributed to various factors that must be considered while operating the press. During a pressrun, the operator must be able to recognize different problems, understand how they are caused, and determine how they can be solved. Press operators should take advantage of the numerous quality-control devices available, including color bars, test forms, and densitometers. The use of quality-control devices helps the operator understand the operation and performance limitations of the particular press or duplicator being used.

Troubleshooting and maintenance play a critical part in operating a press or duplicator. Operating and troubleshooting guides are available from press manufacturers. Regular press maintenance helps increase production and printing quality.

Review Questions

Please do not write in this book. Write your answers on a separate sheet of paper.

1. The differences in paper designed for the offset process and other types of printing processes are due primarily to the use of _____ and the close contact of the _____ to the paper.
2. Name two desirable characteristics for paper used on an offset press.
3. What happens if an offset paper does not have good water resistance?
4. The uniform _____ used on web offset presses permits feeding and printing of thinner paper than is commonly used on sheetfed offset presses.
5. What can cause paper wrinkling?
6. A problem called _____ occurs when a printed sheet picks up an image on its reverse side from the sheet below it in the delivery pile.
7. Too much ink and not enough water on the plate causes _____.
8. List at least five ways in which the press operator can prevent hickies.

antistatic solution: a compound applied, commonly a coating, on a substrate as a means of preventing the buildup of static electricity.

9. Give two examples of printing problems that can be caused by mechanical problems.

10. Explain three printing problems that improper roller-pressure settings can cause.

11. What is a test form?

12. What purpose does a color bar serve?

13. A(n) _____ is a circular pattern of lines primarily used to detect ink slur.

14. _____ is a change in sharpness caused by a slippage of the cylinders.

15. What is the usual effect of slur, dot doubling, and excessive dot gain on a color photograph?

16. _____ can be used to determine if there is dot gain in the halftones and if the ink is trapping properly.

17. What does GRACoL stand for, and what is its purpose?

18. Why is static electricity a problem in the pressroom? How can it be reduced or eliminated?

19. What can cause uneven printing?

4. Gather samples of printed jobs that show misregister, hickies, smudges, poor ink coverage, ghosting, and other problems. Label each sample and make a display that can be used in the classroom or lab.

5. Prepare a set of 3″ × 5″ reference cards that give the symptoms, probable cause, and remedy for most of the problems commonly occurring during a pressrun. Place one problem on each card and fasten the set together with one screw-post binding device in the upper-left corner. The pack of reference cards will then be accessible and handy to use.

6. Working with your instructor, develop a schedule for preventive maintenance to be performed on your presses.

Skill-Building Activities

1. Check the ink rollers on all duplicators and presses for glaze. Thoroughly clean and deglaze all suspect rollers.

2. Under the direction of your instructor, form groups of two to work as a team on a duplicator or larger press. Using a previously prepared plate, perform all steps necessary to print 25 quality sheets per student. Change the ink-and-water balance so it is no longer correct. Print 25 sheets with a gray, washed out appearance, and then print 25 sheets that show scumming (a dirty background). Finally, adjust the ink-and-water balance back to normal and run 25 more sheets. Save all test sheets for comparison and for instructor review. When the pressrun is completed, gum the plate, thoroughly wash the press, and engage the night latch.

3. Check the impression (back) cylinder on all duplicators and presses. Any ink accumulation and glaze should be removed according to the manufacturer's directions.

A print buyer and press operator confer on a job being printed on the digital press seen behind them. (Heidelberg)

The Finishing Touches

The postpress function includes everything done to the job after presswork. Postpress is typically made up of finishing, binding, and distribution, and these departments are as essential to a perfect job as any other department. For example, after being printed, the direct-mail catalogs shown here are being bound, but they first had to be folded into signatures, which had to be assembled. After binding, a mailing-address label will be placed on each catalog, and the catalogs will be bundled according to zip code and taken to the post office. The finishing, binding, and distribution functions include several operations presented in this chapter.

(Heidelberg, Inc.)

Chapter 25
Finishing, Binding, and Distribution

Key Terms

accordion fold
aqueous coating
assembling
back gauge
barrel fold
bed
binding
blind embossing
buckle folder
burst binding
case binding
casing in
clamp
collate
collating
collating mark
comb binding
cornering
counter die
cutting stick
debossing
die
die cutting
embossing
female die
finished size
foil embossing
foil stamping
fold plate
fold roller
French fold
gatherer-stitcher-trimmer
  (GST)
gathering
guillotine cutter
insert

jog
knife
knife folder
letter fold
lift
loose-leaf binding
mechanical binding
numbering
off-line
padding
parallel fold
perfect binding
perforating
punching
regular embossing
relief die
right-angle fold
saddle sewing
saddle stitching
scoring
short fold
side sewing
side stitching
slitting
slotting
Smyth sewing
spiral binding
stop gauge
thermal binding process
thermography
three-knife trimmer
tipping
trim
varnishing
wire stitching

Learning Objectives

When you have completed the reading and assigned activities related to this chapter, you will be able to do the following:

- Determine the number of sheets of paper and the cutting sequence required for a given printing job.
- List, describe, and perform basic finishing operations.
- Use a guillotine paper cutter to cut and trim paper.
- Identify the various types of folding equipment and types of folds.
- Summarize the various types of binding and indicate their appropriate applications.
- Describe methods used to package printed products for distribution.

Transferring the image to the paper is sometimes thought of as the end of the printing process. In truth, the piles of printed press sheets probably require other production steps before they are ready for delivery to the customer. See **Figure 25-1.** The final processing of a printed product generally includes postpress finishing operations such as cutting, trimming, embossing, die cutting, numbering, laminating, folding, and binding. The equipment used to perform these operations is either automatic or semiautomatic. Finishing operations require strict attention to detail. A mistake in this phase of production can lead to a costly rerun of the job.

Finishing is the term used to describe all operations performed on printed materials from the delivery end of the printing press to the final shipment to the customer. One or more finishing operations are used on most printed jobs. Finishing operations include, but are not limited to, cutting, folding, drilling, perforating, die cutting, foil stamping, embossing, varnishing, and packaging. Depending on the configuration of the press, many finishing operations are performed in-line. The order in which they are performed also depends on the configuration of the press and the end product.

Cutting

The cutting function is required when the press sheet is larger than the dimensions of the finished job and when the press sheet carries more than one finished unit. Paper can be cut either in-line or off-line. In-line cutting is performed in conjunction with web presses. As the web moves out of the last printing unit, it needs to be converted to sheets by being cut into the desired lengths. Off-line cutting is performed in conjunction with sheetfed presses. Sheets can be cut into sizes to be fed into presses (press sheets), or the printed sheets can be cut to produce finished pieces, such as business cards.

In-Line Cutting

On a web press, the cutting function can be performed in-line—meaning while connected to the press in a continuous operation. If the web press is printing business forms, a rotary knife cuts the web into sheets of the desired size. If the job is a newspaper, standard folding operations take place before the web reaches the cutter. In the case of a newspaper press, the web is routed over the web lead-in rollers and moves under the gathering roll, over the roller top of the former, through the trolleys (where a slitter blade cuts the web to tabloid width, if desired), and down the former into the nipping rollers. See **Figure 25-2.** When and how cutting operations are performed varies by press configuration and the desired output.

Figure 25-1. Printed press sheets are usually far from being completed jobs. These piles of printed sheets will move on to the finishing area where they will receive one or several more operations. (Heidelberg, Inc.)

Figure 25-2. A slitter blade is used to cut the web to tabloid width. (J. Walker)

Pins spaced across the width of the cutting cylinder pull the slit web around the cutting cylinder. These pins are projected from the cylinder to pierce the web and keep the sheets correctly positioned until the sheets pass through the cutting mechanism. Typically, the printed sheets are cut so they can be folded into signatures of 4, 8, 16, 32, or 64 pages. See **Figure 25-3.** Many presses now use pinless folders.

The tucker blade on the cutting cylinder tucks the web into the jaw blades of the jaw cylinder. The cutting knife then slices the former-folded web at the proper point. The jaw cylinder takes the cut and folded signature from the cutting cylinder. This cylinder carries the paper around and through the hold-down roller and either into the fan, which lays the paper down on the conveyor assembly, or to the quarter-folder table.

Off-Line Cutting

Paper printed on sheetfed presses is cut *off-line*—as a separate operation. Sheetfed paper is often cut twice—before and after it is printed. For example, imagine 8 1/2″ × 11″ letterheads being printed two-up on an 11″ × 17″ duplicator. If the paper is ordered 17″ × 22″, the purchase sheets have to be cut in half to become 11″ × 17″ press sheets. After printing, the two-up press sheets need to be cut again to separate the two letterheads into the *finished size*—also known as the *trim size*. The term *trim* refers to the strips of excess paper left over after the cutting operation.

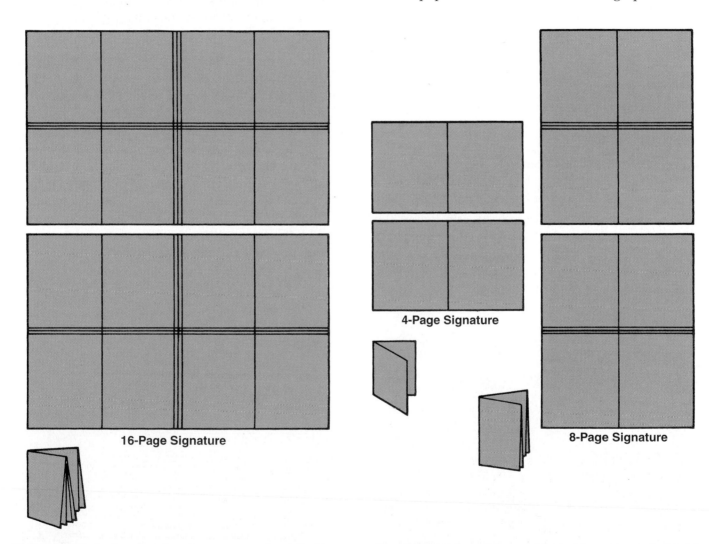

16-Page Signature

4-Page Signature

8-Page Signature

Figure 25-3. A signature is a large press sheet that is generally printed on two sides and folded to make 4, 8, 16, 32, or 64 pages. These examples illustrate 4-, 8-, and 16-page signatures.

off-line: any finishing operation performed away from the press.

finished size: the dimension of the job as delivered to the customer.

trim: the outside dimensions of a sheet of the finished printed piece.

The job just described would be cut twice on a *guillotine cutter*, also known as a *single-knife trimmer*. These machines range in design from hand operated through semiautomatic and fully automatic. See **Figure 25-4.** The guillotine cutters paper manufacturers use are massive machines that can cut large paper sizes and vast quantities of paper. These cutters are designed to simultaneously cut all four sides of the sheet to ensure the paper is square.

A guillotine cutter can cut though as much as a 4″ stack of paper, known as a *lift*. Even the most basic cutter consists of a bed (or table), side guide, cutting stick, back fence, clamp, and blade. See **Figure 25-5.**

- The *bed* is the flat surface on which the lift sits.
- The side guide is the wall against which the left side of the lift is placed.
- A movable *back gauge* (along with side guides) holds the lift firmly in place in the desired position on the bed. This gauge is also known as the *back fence*.
- The *clamp* is a metal bar that moves downward against the lift to force out air and hold the lift while it is being cut.
- The *knife* is made of steel or steel-carbide and is mounted to a bar located near the front of the machine, just in front of the clamp.
- The *cutting stick* is located directly below the blade, beneath the table's surface. When the blade moves through the lift, it cuts slightly into the cutting stick, which is made of wood or plastic, to avoid dulling the knife.

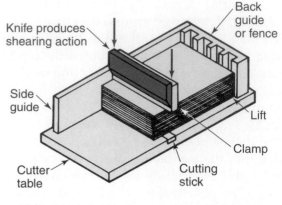

Figure 25-5. After the back gauge has been positioned the proper distance from the knife, the lift is slid on the cutter table until it is against the side guide and back gauge. The clamp is then lowered, and the knife slices through the paper to contact the cutting stick.

All automatic single-knife trimmers should protect the operator by requiring two-hand knife control and a shield to prevent the operator from accidentally touching the knife blade. Numerous accessories have been designed to increase safety and productivity. Low-pressure air tables are used to improve the movement of paper to and from the cutter. See **Figure 25-6.** A line of light can visually preview where a cut will be made on the paper. A split back gauge (divided into three parts) is used to allow trimming of three sides of a stack of paper without having to change the trim settings.

Figure 25-4. A cutter operator blocks a lift of labels against the back fence. He has programmed the machine to automatically move the back fence for several successive cuts. (Heidelberg, Inc.)

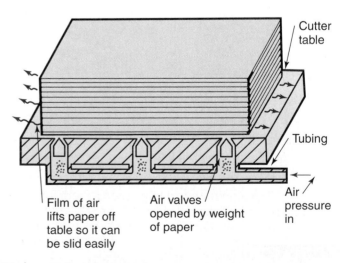

Figure 25-6. Large paper cutters are equipped with an air table—one with dozens of small holes through which air passes to help the operator slide lifts.

Caution

Exercise extreme care when handling sheets of paper because the edges can be as sharp as a razor blade.

Caution

Treat the paper cutter with respect. The cutting blades are razor sharp, and fingers must be kept clear of the cutting edge. Keep steel and wood objects, such as metal line gauges and rulers, from under the blades.

Caution

Keep hands away from the pressure clamp and cutting blade on the paper cutter. Most accidents on a paper cutter occur as a result of misusing the paper clamp.

Cutter maintenance

Paper cutters must be properly maintained. Keeping the paper cutter lubricated and dust free is essential. Paper dust can transfer to the press and cause hickies on the finished product. This dust usually comes from loose fibers or bits of paper lying between sheets. Improper cutting or trimming and a dull blade that tears the paper, rather than cutting it cleanly, cause this.

In large plants, cutter blades are sometimes changed at the end of each shift, depending on how much the blade is used and the type of paper being cut. For example, cutting paperboard, chipboard, and similar heavy papers dulls the blade very quickly. Inaccurate trimming of paper also causes trouble on the press. Misregister, jamming of paper as it feeds, and improper stacking are often the results of bowed, off-square paper or paper cut with a dull or nicked blade.

To check for cutter-blade sharpness, use a piece of black velveteen cloth soaked with a little glycerin. Wipe the cut edges of the paper pile. If the cloth is full of dust, the blade is dull. In addition, if the paper pulls or twists as the knife passes (under normal clamp pressure) the blade is dull. A dull blade makes a smacking noise when it strikes the pile of paper. A sharp blade makes very little sound as it cuts through the pile of paper.

The cutter stick should be kept in perfect condition. Worn wooden cutter sticks ruin the last few sheets in every stack or leave the bottom sheets uncut. Plastic cutting sticks are more expensive than wood. They stay fresh longer, however, and provide an excellent return on investment.

Paper-cutter safety

Paper cutters are commonplace in most printing firms. Unfortunately, there are still many injuries associated with this part of the bindery. To help prevent injuries, keep the following safety tips in mind:

- Check workplace conditions. Remove any debris or foreign objects from the paper-cutter area and make sure the floor is clean and dry to prevent slipping. Make sure only one person is near the paper cutter to prevent distractions.
- To prevent clamp accidents, cover the foot pedal with a hood, where appropriate.
- Never place hands under a knife or clamp, even when it is locked or turned off. Old and worn parts can self-activate.
- Do not rely solely on antirepeat devices. To prevent the knife from continuing on more than one cutting cycle, stop the cutter and repeat as necessary.
- Make sure all guards are in place before operating the paper cutter.
- On paper cutters with two handheld controls, always hold both hands in place. Never bypass or rewire two-handed controls. Modifications to free one hand are dangerous and illegal. To prevent this, install an antibridge device.

guillotine cutter: a trimming and cutting device with a single cutting blade used to cut paper to size.

lift: a pile of paper, usually the amount cut or drilled in a single operation.

bed: a smooth or level surface.

back gauge: a guide on a cutting device used to hold a stack of sheets firmly in place on the bed.

clamp: the part of a guillotine cutter that holds down a lift of paper to be cut.

knife: a razor-sharp cutting blade or instrument in a piece of equipment.

cutting stick: a plastic or wooden piece located directly below the cutting blade to protect the blade from damage.

- Consult the operator's manual before changing the blade. All paper cutters are different, and this can be a difficult operation. Only authorized and experienced personnel should perform this maneuver.

- Do not leave tools (such as metal line gauges) on the cutter work surface when cutting paper.

- Keep repairs up-to-date. Have qualified service technicians perform all service, adjustments, and repairs.

- Turn the paper cutter off if you hear unusual sounds.

- Turn off the power when you are finished with the paper cutter.

- Do not talk with others while operating the paper cutter. Stay alert at all times.

Trimming

Trimming is performed to booklets, magazines, or other publications after they have been bound. Trimming operations remove a small, predetermined amount of paper from the three outside edges of the bound product. The amount of paper to be trimmed is determined at the beginning of a project so it can be included in the layout and design. Trim marks for the commonly found 16-page signature are shown in **Figure 25-7.**

The type of trimming device used depends on the materials being trimmed and the type of *binding* being applied. For example, a softcover book or pamphlet can be trimmed after the signatures have been bound and the cover has been applied. The bound signatures of a hardcover book, however, are trimmed before the cover is attached.

Single-knife trimmers can be used for booklets consisting exclusively of 4-page signatures because these booklets require only a face trim. See **Figure 25-8.** Almost all publications consisting of 8-page or 16-page signatures, however, require a head, foot, and front trim. In most cases, using a single-knife trimmer to make all three cuts would be impractical, so three-knife trimmers are used on most publications.

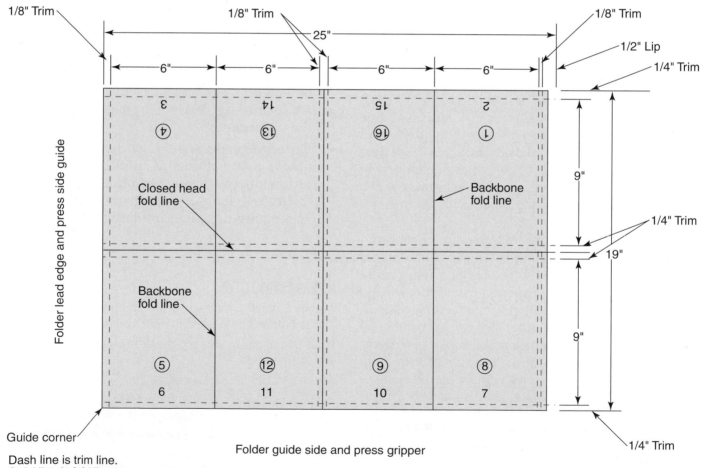

Dash line is trim line.
Solid line is fold line.
The number in the circles is the number of the page on the back of the sheet.

Figure 25-7. This illustration shows the various elements of the press sheet as they relate to binding operations, including trimming and folding.

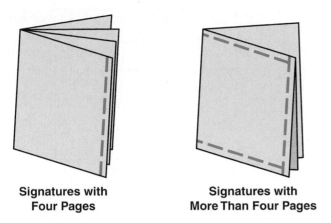

Signatures with Four Pages **Signatures with More Than Four Pages**

Figure 25-8. This publication consisting of two four-page signatures requires only a front trim. Signatures with more than four pages receive a head trim (across the top of the pages), a foot trim (across the bottom of the pages), and a front (or face) trim.

A Cutting Plan

Efficient and accurate cutting begins with developing a cutting plan that includes the optimum cutting pattern, number of sheets required to be cut, number of cuts needed, and cutting sequence to be followed. The optimum cutting pattern maximizes the number of cut sheets the parent sheet can yield. As was explained in Chapter 18, the cut sheets can be oriented on the parent sheet differently. For example, imagine a job in which 7500 5″ × 8″ press sheets must be cut from 25″ × 38″ press sheets. See **Figure 25-9.** The cancellation method reveals that one orientation yields 20 cut sheets and the other orientation yields 21. A combination cut, however, yields 23. Of course, a combination cut cannot be considered if the grain direction of the finished unit is important to the customer. Grain direction is not a concern because this job is for simple leaflets, so a combination cut can be used.

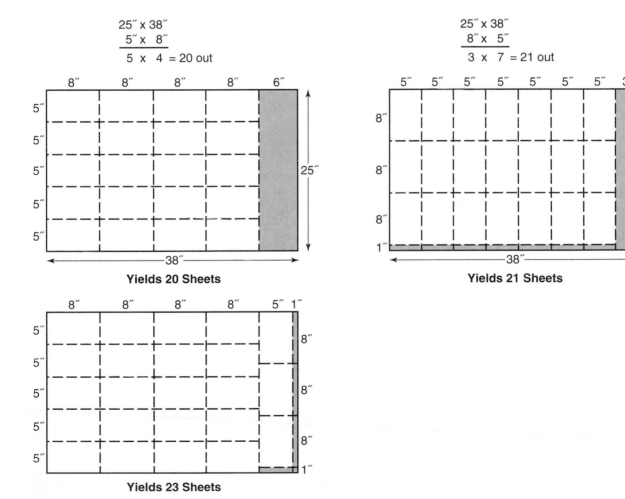

Figure 25-9. The first orientation of the 5″ × 8″ press sheets produces 20 sheets. The other orientation produces 21. The combination cut produces 23.

binding: the act of attaching multiple pages of a printed product together using various methods.

The best cutting sequence minimizes the number of times the back fence of the cutter has to be moved. In this example, the back fence is set to remove 8″, and all cuts of 8″ are made. The fence will next be set for 5″, and the remainder of the cuts will be made. See **Figure 25-10.** If each parent sheet yields 23 press sheets, the 7500 press sheets (including spoilage) require 327 parent sheets (7500/23). Any decimal is always rounded up.

Three factors determine the minimum number of cuts: whether or not all four edges of the parent sheet are to be trimmed, the cutting pattern, and whether or not bleeds are involved. See **Figure 25-11.** All four edges of the parent sheet are often trimmed if the resulting press sheet will be run work and turn or work and tumble. This

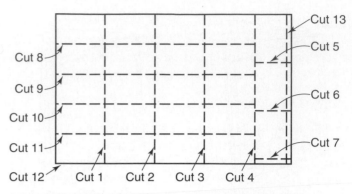

Figure 25-10. The goal of the cutting sequence is to maximize efficiency. The numbers on this diagram indicate the order in which the cuts will be made. The twelfth cut will probably remove only a sliver of excess paper.

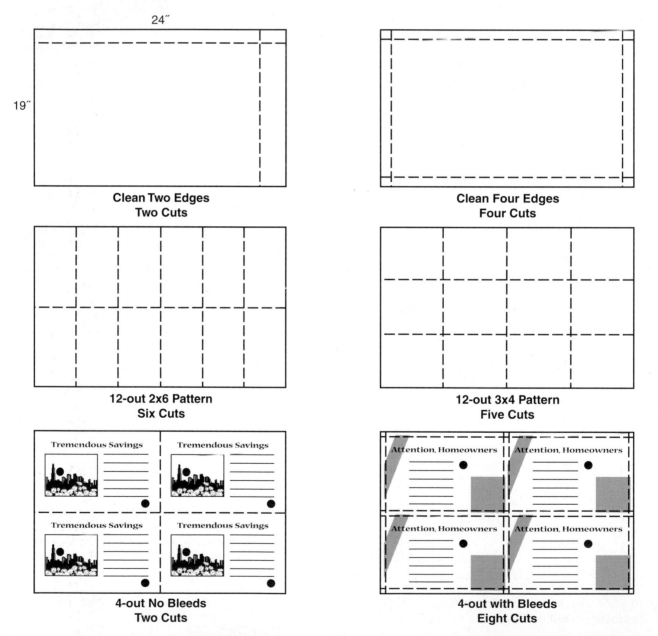

Figure 25-11. A 17″ × 22″ press sheet can be cut from a 19″ × 25″ parent sheet with only two cuts, but cleaning the four edges needs four cuts. A 2 × 6 pattern yields 12 out with six cuts, but a 3 × 4 pattern needs only five cuts. A 2 × 2 pattern of a design with no bleeds can require only two cuts, but bleeds on all four sides require a double trim and eight cuts.

procedure ensures that the four corners are precisely 90°. Also, the four edges are cleaned if they are marred. This combination of variables is best managed by taking the time to draw a diagram and label it carefully.

Three-Knife Trimmers

A *three-knife trimmer* operates in much the same way as a single-knife trimmer, except it has three knives. This trimmer uses two parallel knives and one right-angle knife to trim three sides of the printed publications, such as magazines. See **Figure 25-12.** All three knives do not cut at the same time. The two parallel knives cut together, and the right-angle knife cuts individually. Three-knife trimmers can be stand-alone units or part of collating, folding, and binding systems. They are generally computer controlled and designed to monitor every step of the trimming process, checking for errors and providing information for smooth, continuous operation.

Depending on the trimmer, a single alignment-tab system can control size adjustments for different booklet sizes. The clamps can be adjusted to the weight and delicacy of the paper stock being used by applying the correct pressure. The three cutting blades perform precise, clean cuts as they descend against plastic cutting sticks similar to those used in single-knife cutters. Some three-knife trimmers use air holes in the cutting blades to blow paper trimmings into a collection bin under the machine. All three-knife trimmers use safety knife control and some type of shield to prevent the operator from accidentally touching the knives.

Trim Removal and Dust Collection

Trimming and cutting large amounts of paper results in trim waste and paper dust. Many firms have installed systems that combine trim removal with dust and mist filtration. See **Figure 25-13.** These

Removing Trim

A Trim-Removal System

Figure 25-13. Removing the quarter-inch bleed trim between images creates thins strips of waste. This trim-removal system includes an autotie baler; three press-located, high-speed signature-removal systems; and the ability to handle trim from multiple web-press, in-line cutters and stand-alone flat cutters. (Hammer Packaging, Ohio Blow Pipe)

Figure 25-12. A three-knife trimmer cleans the top and bottom edges of a booklet at the same time, with two parallel knives, and a third knife trims the face.

three-knife trimmer: a paper-cutting device with three blades.

customized systems are designed to meet all OSHA requirements to provide a healthier work environment. Most systems eliminate manual handling of the collected dust and include automated control systems that monitor system functions and air emissions. Some cutting tables are designed to open up to accommodate paper waste and scraps automatically. The trimmed materials fall below the table into a removable receptacle for quick and efficient disposal.

Folding

Most printed materials require some type of folding on automated folding equipment. Tabletop folding machines are used for light- to medium-duty folding by in-plant and quick printers. See **Figure 25-14.** Heavy-duty folders are designed to handle large sheets of paper. See **Figure 25-15.** Some folding

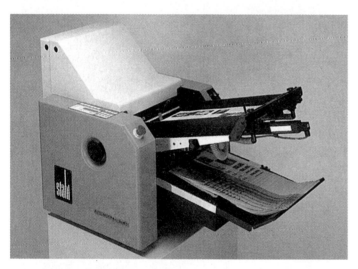

Figure 25-14. Tabletop folders are adequate for light- to medium-duty folding of small signatures. (Heidelberg, Inc.)

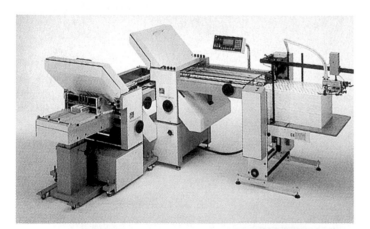

Figure 25-15. Various available attachments allow this machine to be used as a buckle folder or a combination buckle-and-knife folder. (Matthias Bauerle GrmbH)

machines are capable of folding, stitching, and trimming all in one operation.

A complete listing of all combinations of folds would fill several chapters in a book. All possible folds are combinations of two basic folds, however—parallel and right-angle folds. A *parallel fold* is made parallel to the previous fold. A *right-angle fold* is made at a right angle to the preceding fold by changing the direction of the sheet 90° before the second fold is made. **Figure 25-16** illustrates typical applications of parallel and right-angle folds.

Types of Folds

In designing a printed piece, the different types of folds and the limitations of mechanical folding devices should be carefully considered. The various types of common folds are illustrated in **Figure 25-17.** The terms *panel* and *page* are interchangeable.

- **4-page fold.** The 4-page (or four-panel) fold is the simplest type and can be used for greeting cards, price lists, programs, bill stuffers, menus, and instruction sheets.

- **6-page fold.** This type of fold is made with two parallel folds and is used for envelope stuffers, letters, circulars, and promotional folders. The 6-page fold can be used with a letter fold or an accordion fold. A *letter fold* sends one panel to nest between the other two. This inside panel must be slightly narrower than the outside panels. An *accordion fold* consists of two or more parallel folds resembling one or more of the letter Z. All panels of an accordion fold can be the same width.

- **8-page fold.** There are three types of 8-page folds. The first type consists of two right-angle folds and is called a *French fold* when printing is only on one side. The second type consists of two parallel folds. The third type makes a three-parallel accordion fold and is used for ease of opening.

- **12-page fold.** There are two ways to make a 12-page fold—regular and accordion. These folds are often used as a 4-page letter, with the two right-angle folds folding letter size to fit a mailing envelope.

- **16-page fold.** A 16-page fold can be made with three right-angle folds or with three parallel folds. The latter is used for easy-to-open transportation schedules. This fold can also be bound into a 16-page booklet.

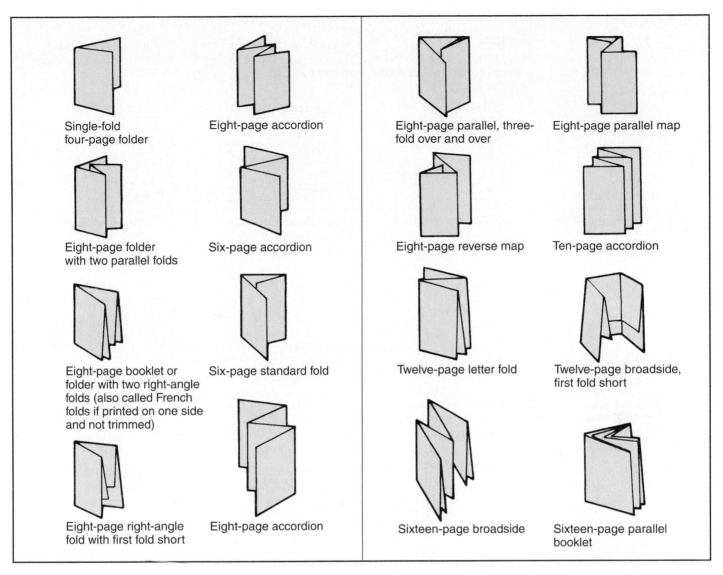

Figure 25-16. Only a few of the many applications of parallel and right-angle folds are shown. (A.B.Dick Co.)

- **32-page and 64-page folds.** It is possible to make a 32-page or 64-page fold by simply adding one or two additional right-angle folds to a 16-page fold. In all cases, make a signature-layout dummy to check for accuracy of imposition.

- *Barrel fold.* This fold is similar to a letter fold, but it has more than three panels.

- *Short fold.* This is any fold resulting in uneven panels.

Caution

Keep hands and fingers away from all roller nip points on the folder. Serious accidents occur because of extreme folder speed.

parallel fold: a basic folding pattern in which all folds being made are parallel to each other.

right-angle fold: a basic folding pattern in which each fold is made at a right angle to the preceding fold.

letter fold: a folding pattern with two parallel folds applied to a sheet, as done to an 8 1/2″ × 11″ sheet to fit into a business envelope.

accordion fold: a pattern of parallel folds in which the angle of the folds alternates.

French fold: a type of fold in which a sheet printed on one side is folded first vertically and then horizontally.

barrel fold: a pattern of parallel folds starting at one end of the sheet and progressing toward the opposite end, as if the sheet were being rolled.

short fold: a single fold applied to a sheet in which one panel is much shorter than the other.

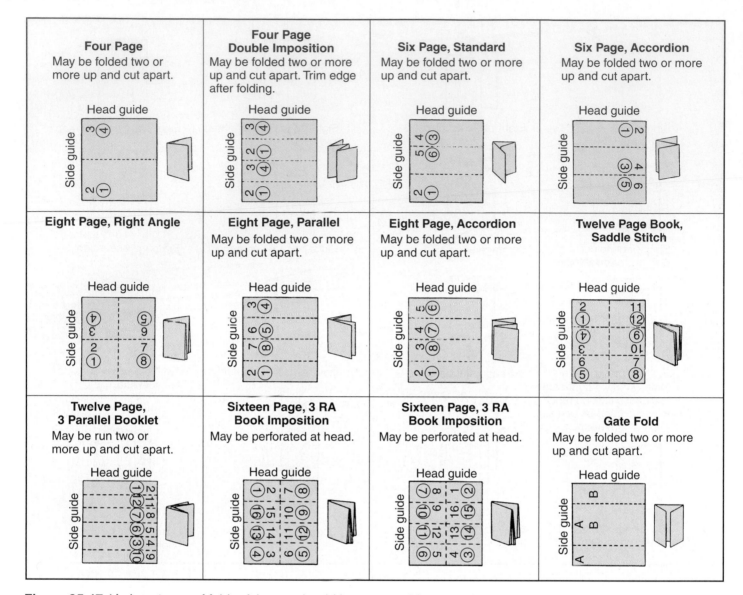

Figure 25-17. Various types of folds. A layout should be prepared for every job requiring folding. (U.S. Government Printing Office)

Types of Folders

Folding equipment can be divided into two basic types. These types are knife folders and buckle folders. More versatile folders use a combination of knife and buckle folder configurations.

Knife folders

A *knife folder* uses a thin blade and fold rollers to create a fold. See **Figure 25-18.** The paper is fed into the folding unit with moving tapes or belts. Side guides keep the paper aligned, and a fold gauge stops the paper in position above the nip of the *fold rollers.* It is important that the sheet is accurately positioned above the fold rollers, or off-center folds and inaccurate trimming and binding will result.

As the knife is lowered, it pushes the paper into the rotating fold rollers that crease the sheet. If additional folds are required, one or more folding units are added, and the folded sheet is carried to them automatically. Additional folding units can be configured to make either parallel or right-angle folds. Knife folders are the most accurate for producing right-angle folds.

Knife folders vary in design by manufacturer and press configuration. Some common design names include the jobber, the double-sixteen, and the quadruple. Each of these designs is capable of producing different numbers and angles of folds:

- The jobber has one or two parallel folding sections and four folding units. This design allows up to four right-angle folds, two right-angle folds and one fold parallel to the second, or three right-angle folds and one fold parallel to the third.

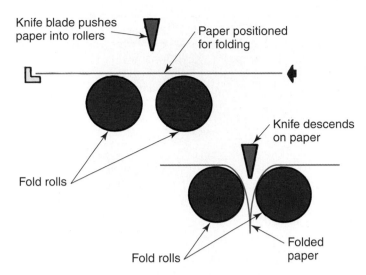

Figure 25-18. In a knife folding design, a descending knife blade creases the paper and forces the paper between the fold rolls. (John F. Cuneo Co.)

- The double-sixteen can produce 16-page or 32-page signatures.
- A quadruple can produce four 16-page or two 32-page signatures.

Perforating units can also be installed on most knife folders. These units lightly pierce the folds to allow air to escape. Removing this air helps prevent problems such as wrinkles and paper jams.

Buckle folders

A *buckle folder* uses tapes or belts to carry a sheet of paper. This folder carries the sheet toward a *fold plate* consisting of two metal plates positioned at a slight incline above the drive and fold rollers. See **Figure 25-19.** The drive roller feeds the sheet into the fold plate and continues to move the sheet after it hits the *stop gauge* at the top of the fold-plate assembly. The sheet buckles downward, and the fold rollers catch it in a predetermined spot. The rollers grab the sheet at the buckle, pull the sheet downward, and create a fold. The location at which the fold occurs can be adjusted by moving the fold gauge slightly. Additional folds are made by connecting additional folding units.

The weight of the paper should also be considered when using a folder. Lightweight papers fold better on buckle folders, and heavier-weight papers perform well on knife folders. Many folders, however, allow adjustment for different weights of paper.

Punching

Punching involves cutting rectangular or specially shaped holes in paper to accommodate plastic and spiral bindings. Punching machines are designed for this purpose. **Figure 25-20** shows a

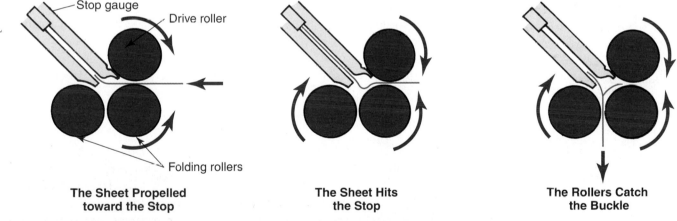

The Sheet Propelled toward the Stop   **The Sheet Hits the Stop**   **The Rollers Catch the Buckle**

Figure 25-19. The principle of the buckle folder. The sheet is propelled toward the stop, hits the stop, and buckles downward. The folding rollers catch the buckle and complete the fold. (John F. Cuneo Co.)

---

knife folder: a folding device that uses a metal blade to force a sheet through a set of folding rollers.

fold roller: a metal roller that transports a sheet through a folder.

buckle folder: a folding device that uses a fold plate to force a sheet to buckle so the sheet can be pulled through a set of folding rollers.

fold plate: a metal plate on a buckle folder positioned at a slight incline above the drive and fold rollers, into which the substrate is fed to create a buckle in the sheet.

stop gauge: the metal bar in a buckle folder that stops the movement of the sheet and causes the sheet to buckle.

punching: an operation in which rectangular or specially shaped holes are cut in paper to accommodate plastic and spiral bindings.

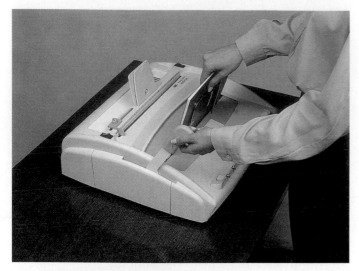

Figure 25-20. The punching-inserting machine is used to cut holes in printed sheets and insert plastic bindings to form small booklets. (General Binding Corp.)

punching-inserting machine used to cut rectangular holes in printed sheets and insert plastic bindings in the punched sheets. Automatic punching machines are used for long production runs.

Drilling, Slotting, and Cornering

Paper drilling makes round holes in paper. This drilling is usually performed on a machine called a *paper drill*. Paper-drilling machines vary in size and capacity from the single-drill models to multiple-drill models. See **Figures 25-21.**

Some paper-drilling machines can also slot and corner paper. *Slotting* involves making holes that are

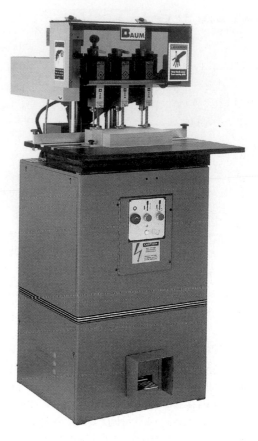

Figure 25-21. This paper-drilling machine is equipped with multiple spindles. (Baum USA)

not round. *Cornering* is any operation performed on the corners of paper. **Figure 25-22** shows common drilling, slotting, and cornering operations. Punching machines also perform drilling, slotting, and cornering operations. With the proper attachments,

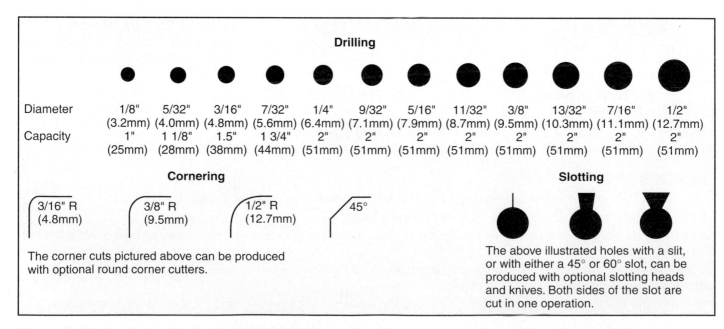

Drilling

Diameter	1/8" (3.2mm)	5/32" (4.0mm)	3/16" (4.8mm)	7/32" (5.6mm)	1/4" (6.4mm)	9/32" (7.1mm)	5/16" (7.9mm)	11/32" (8.7mm)	3/8" (9.5mm)	13/32" (10.3mm)	7/16" (11.1mm)	1/2" (12.7mm)
Capacity	1" (25mm)	1 1/8" (28mm)	1.5" (38mm)	1 3/4" (44mm)	2" (51mm)	2" (51mm)	2" (51mm)	2" (51mm)	2" (51mm)	2" (51mm)	2" (51mm)	2" (51mm)

Cornering

3/16" R (4.8mm)   3/8" R (9.5mm)   1/2" R (12.7mm)   45°

The corner cuts pictured above can be produced with optional round corner cutters.

Slotting

The above illustrated holes with a slit, or with either a 45° or 60° slot, can be produced with optional slotting heads and knives. Both sides of the slot are cut in one operation.

Figure 25-22. Examples of one manufacturer's drilling, cornering, and slotting capabilities. (Baum USA)

many power paper drills can be used for cornering and rounding.

Paper-drilling machines use a hollow drill. See **Figure 25-23.** Drilling bits can be fluted on the inside, beveled on the outside, or specially hardened on the tip. Fluted bits compress the paper and permit it to travel up the barrel of the bit more freely.

Drilling

To drill paper on a single-spindled paper drill, follow the steps listed below:

1. Mark the proper location of the holes on the test sheet. Be sure to use an accurate three-hole master when attempting to drill three-hole paper.
2. Select the correct drill bit for the job.
3. Insert the drill bit into the machine following the equipment-manufacturer directions.
4. Align the bit with the hole-location marks on the paper. Apply holding pressure with the bit and the paper hold-down device to keep the test paper from moving. Place the edge of the paper guide against the test paper, and align the guide with the guide stop. Tighten the guide-stop device.
5. Repeat step four for every hole location desired.
6. Set the back gauge for depth. The back gauge locates the distance the hole is drilled from the edge of the paper. The gauge markings are the distance from the center of the hole to the back gauge.
7. Adjust the bit pressure. Use only enough pressure to drill cleanly through all the paper while the foot pedal is at the lowest comfortable position.
8. Change the cutting block if it is worn.

Figure 25-23. Paper-drill bits are hollow to allow waste pieces to be carried up through the drill, out a chute, and into a waste bin.

9. Adjust the hold-down device (clamp) to touch the top of the paper. The clamp holds the paper in place while the paper is being drilled.
10. To drill the paper, insert the pile of paper securely against both guides. Lower the rotating bit with the foot pedal. Use a small amount of stick lubricant on the bit at regular intervals.

Round Cornering

Round cornering can be done on a paper-drilling machine set up to corner paper. The paper is cornered on a paper-drilling machine with a device that replaces the drill bit and paper hold-down clamp. Two corner guide rails are added to the drill table to guide the paper accurately under the cornering device. To corner paper, the operator sets up the machine, makes all final adjustments, and makes the corners by lowering the cornering blade through the pile of paper. Paper should be cornered in small piles to avoid inaccurate cuts and premature dulling of the blade.

Caution

Keep hands and fingers clear of the paper-drill bit and paper hold-down when operating this equipment.

Jogging

An operation known as *jogging* vertically aligns the edges of a pile of paper. Sheets must be **jogged** when loaded into a paper cutter, press, folder, or gathering machine. An automatic jogging machine is usually equipped with a two-sided slanting table. See **Figure 25-24.** The table vibrates and straightens the pile of sheets in a matter of seconds. Large-format joggers are used in high-production environments.

Scoring

Placing a crease in a sheet of thick paper or cardboard to aid in folding is referred to as *scoring.* The crease produces an embossed, or raised, ridge on the

---

slotting: a method of making holes for a binding that are not round.

cornering: any operation performed on the corners of paper.

jog: to bend into a curve and square up to ensure all sheets are aligned.

scoring: compressing a line across a heavy sheet of paper to improve the sheet's ability to be folded on that line.

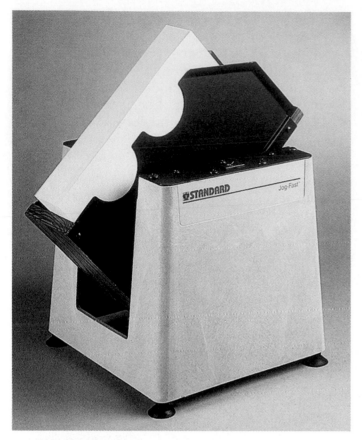

Figure 25-24. This small-format jogging device is adequate for quick-printing operations. (Standard Finishing Systems)

sheet. The fold is made with the ridge on the inside of the sheet to prevent stretching. Scoring can be performed by pressing a steel rule against the paper or by sending the sheet under a scoring wheel. See **Figure 25-25.**

• The width of the crease is varied according to the thickness of the paper being scored. A thicker paper requires a wider crease, which gives a bigger groove to help make a cleaner fold. Scoring is usually done on automatic equipment. See **Figure 25-26.**

• When using string, wire, or single- and double-rule, the objective is to create a male-female *die* that properly stretches the paper without cutting or damaging it. The following points should be observed when scoring paper:

  • The thicker the paper is, the thicker the scoring element should be to prepare for a good fold.

  • Scoring wheels are usually not as effective as the steel rule. To be as effective as possible, scoring wheels should ride over a notched roller into which they press the paper fibers.

  • Scoring wheels must be used with extreme care on coated papers, or they will mar the surface and contribute to a poor-quality fold.

Perforating

Printed products such as tickets, receipt books, and school workbooks require a part of the product to be removable. An operation known as *perforating* is performed to enable easy removal of all, or part, of a printed product. In a perforating operation, a small series of very short slits or holes is cut in the paper. A small bridge of paper remains intact between each hole. See **Figure 25-27.** A perforated sheet can be easily removed or torn by pulling. Perforating

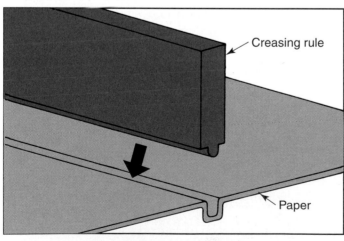

A Steel Rule

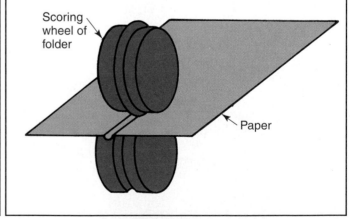

A Scoring Wheel

Figure 25-25. Creasing or scoring can be done by a steel rule using letterpress equipment or specially designed finishing equipment. Scoring can be done on a folder using a scoring wheel. (A.B.Dick Co.)

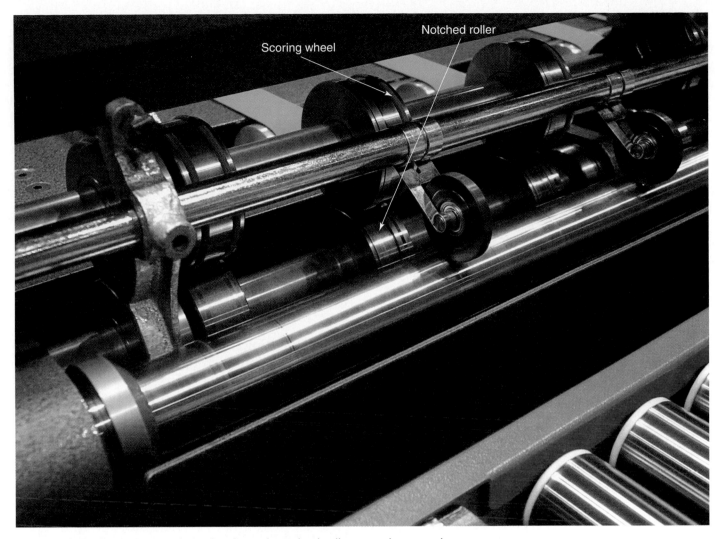

Figure 25-26. Both the scoring wheels and notched rollers can be seen here.

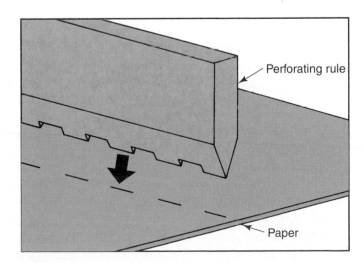

Figure 25-27. Perforating operations place a series of small cuts or slits in the paper. A steel perforating rule is commonly used for this purpose. (A.B.Dick Co.)

can be done on both offset and letterpress presses. This operation is done on an offset press by means of a metal perforating strip attached to one of the cylinders.

Caution

Care should be taken when using perforating material. The sharp cutting teeth can easily cut fingers and hands.

die: a cookie cutter–like device that cuts a sheet of paper into irregular shapes.

perforating: an operation in which a small series of very short slits or holes is cut in the paper and a small bridge of paper remains intact between each hole, as in the case of a ticket stub.

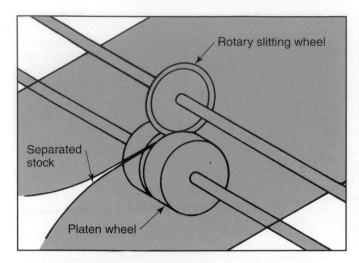

Figure 25-28. Slitting is commonly done by a sharp wheel that cuts paper as the paper passes against the wheel.

Figure 25-30. A sheet that has been die cut to create a window. This sheet will be folded next.

Slitting

Slitting is the process of separating material by a rotary shearing action. See **Figure 25-28.** Printed materials can be slit to a specific size during folding or on special press setups. Slitting is used to separate two or more products from a large sheet or web. This process is also used in place of cutting when it is more economical to integrate slitting as other operations are being performed. It is possible to slit press sheets in both directions. See **Figure 25-29.**

Die Cutting

Any irregular shape or design that cannot be cut with a straight cut is done by a process known as

Figure 25-29. These press sheets will be slit into playing cards on a machine that slits in both directions.

die cutting. Since there is no standard design used in this operation, each metal die is custom-made to match the requirements of the job. See **Figure 25-30.**

The die has a metal cutting edge that matches the outline shape of the design being used. This die is mounted on a wooden die board with the cutting edge up, similar to a cookie cutter. Sponge rubber is glued near the cutting rule to assist in stripping the paper from the die on each press impression.

Die-cutting presses are similar to letterpress printing presses. In some instances, traditional letterpress printing presses are used for die cutting. Examples of die-cut products include boxes, cartons, children's pop-up books, and point-of-purchase containers.

Foil Stamping

Foil stamping is a letterpress process that uses relief images, heat, and foil (or film) to produce shiny gold, silver, or colored images on products such as book covers and wine labels. See **Figure 25-31.** In the foil-stamping process, a heated die containing the relief image presses down on a roll of foil passing above the product to be stamped. The die presses against the foil, and the combination of heat and pressure transfers the image to the product.

The film or foil used for foil stamping is very thin and made entirely of metal or a tissuelike material coated with metal. In most cases, the metals used to create the silver and gold metallic appearance are aluminum and brass, respectively. Gold leaf made with 18–22 carat gold, however, can also be used.

Foil-stamping machines vary in size and function. A hand-operated foil-stamping machine can

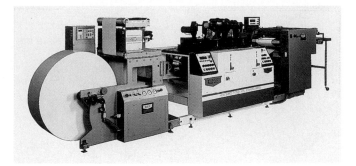

Figure 25-32. This computerized rotary foil press is used for high-volume operations. (Brandtjen & Kluge, Inc.)

Embossing

Embossing creates a three-dimensional (raised) image on a printed product. The two types of embossing are regular and blind. Embossing made over a printed image is known as a *regular embossing*. When the embossing is produced without a printed image or other type of coloration, it is called *blind embossing*. An embossing is made with a male die and a *female die*. See **Figure 25-33.** The dies are three-dimensional molds that press their image into the paper under great pressure to make a raised design.

The desired image or design is first cut or etched into the surface of a piece of brass, magnesium, or copper to create the female die, or *relief die*. The

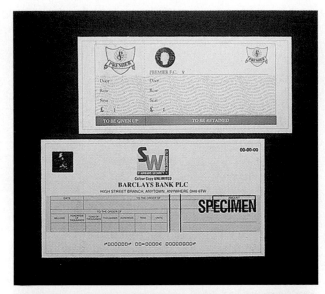

Figure 25-31. Foil stamping and embossing are used on products such as bank checks, letterheads, promotional materials, and book covers. (Brandtjen & Kluge, Inc.)

be used for small volumes of work. Webfed rotary presses can be used for high-volume operations. See **Figure 25-32.** Webfed rotary presses can handle large and oversized sheets. When used with embossing, foil stamping is known as *foil embossing*.

Caution

Caution should be exercised when working around hot stamping equipment, since pressure and extreme heat are used in the process.

slitting: cutting printed sheets or webs into two or more sections by means of a cutting wheel on a printing press, a folding machine, or a slitter-rewinder.

die cutting: a finishing operation that uses a sharp steel rule or knife to cut a specific pattern into a substrate or to cut the substrate into a specific pattern.

foil stamping: a letterpress process that uses relief images, heat, and foil to produce gold, silver, or colored images on products such as book covers, letterheads, and business cards.

foil embossing: the use of dies and foil or film to create a colored, raised image.

embossing: the use of dies to create a three-dimensional image on a printed product.

regular embossing: the imparting of a relief image to a printed sheet.

blind embossing: the stamping of a relief image into a substrate without additional color or decoration of the image.

female die: an embossing die with a sunken image made to fit the male die.

relief die: a metal plate with an image carved into it.

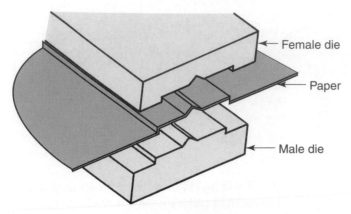

Figure 25-33. Embossing requires the use of two dies. One die is in relief, while the other is recessed. The paper is placed between the dies. When the dies are brought together, the clamping force creates a raised image on the paper.

female die is mounted above the substrate to be embossed. A male or ***counter die*** can be formed on the press when the female die impresses its image into an epoxy-type material the first time it strikes the material. The male die is mounted directly below the substrate, opposite the female die.

Sunken images can also be created on substrates using relief and counter dies. This process is the reverse of embossing and is referred to as ***debossing***. The dies used in either process can be heated.

Note

Mechanical requirements must be built into the design of products that will be die cut, embossed, coated, or finished. For example, some coatings produce excellent results, but not all ink colors take coating well. The printer should be informed of all finishing plans, whether or not the printer is coordinating the whole project.

Numbering

The process of imprinting tickets, checks, certificates, or other items with consecutive figures (numbers and letters) is called ***numbering***. Using a device called a *numbering machine*, the figures are transferred from an inked relief image onto the substrate. See **Figure 25-34.** The printing press or dedicated numbering equipment automatically depresses a plunger to ratchet the numbering head to a different figure or digit, thereby permitting

Figure 25-34. In addition to numbering, many special-event tickets also have foil-stamped or embossed images. (Brandtjen & Kluge, Inc.)

forward or backward numbering. Quite frequently, the numbering machine is set to start on the last number of the job so the last figure printed is the beginning number. This prevents an overrun and places the tickets, forms, or other numbered materials in the correct numerical sequence.

Varnishing

Varnishing is a process that places a coating, or surface finish, on printed sheets to impart resistance to chemicals, heat, scuffing, water, or other elements that would otherwise damage the paper. Varnish can be applied over an entire press sheet or printed selectively as a clear ink. An image printed in a dull varnish over a gloss sheet is visible, due to the difference in reflection.

Normally, varnish is applied on press during the printing process, but it can, instead, be performed as a finishing operation. Various kinds of coatings are available, including print varnish, spirit varnish, copal varnish, shellac solutions, and naphtha varnish. *Aqueous coatings* (water-based coatings) are replacing varnish as a protective layer. Multiple-color presses typically are purchased with a coater unit placed immediately after the last printing unit.

Thermography

Thermography is a process producing raised printing. The word *thermography* is a combination of the word parts *thermo*, meaning "heat," and *graphy*, meaning "to write"—therefore, it means "writing with heat." Thermography is a process that is widely used to simulate the slightly raised images resulting from engraving, a much more expensive printing process. This process is commonly used on business cards, letterheads, and business envelopes.

Several steps are required to produce a thermographic effect. First, a fine resin powder is sprinkled over a freshly printed sheet. Second, the excess powder is removed from the noninked areas. Third, the powder remaining on the wet inked areas is heated. The heat melts the powder and creates a raised effect when the powder cools. A thermography machine is attached to the press because the sheets must move under the powder while the ink is still wet.

Clear powders allow the color of the base ink to show through, whereas opaque powder colors have complete hiding power. Fine powders should be used with images made with fine lines. Coarse powders can be used with images with heavy lines and elements.

Thermography can be used on illustrations, halftones, and type. Finely detailed messages can be created by carefully combining the correct ink and powder. Almost any kind of ink can be used because the ink serves only as an adhesive for the powder. Type smaller than six points in size and letters with delicate serifs should be avoided because they both tend to fill in.

There are several models of automatic thermographic machines for high-speed operations. See **Figure 25-35.** For smaller applications, hand-fed thermography machines are available.

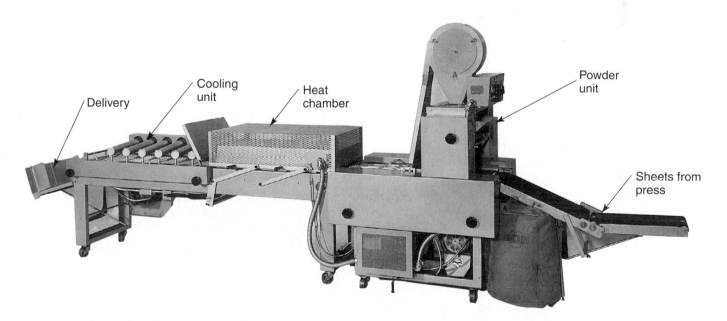

Figure 25-35. Specially designed machines are used to perform thermography. (Virkotype Corp.)

---

counter die: an epoxy plate with a relief image emerging from it.

debossing: the use of dies to stamp or press a depressed image into a substrate.

numbering: the process of imprinting tickets, checks, certificates, or other items with consecutive figures.

varnishing: a process that places a coating, or surface finish, on paper to impart resistance to chemicals, heat, scuffing, water, or other elements that would otherwise damage the paper.

aqueous coating: a clear, water-based, fast-drying coating that can be applied over printed materials to improve resistance to scuffing. These coatings are available in gloss and matte finishes.

thermography: a process that produces raised printing through the application of powder and heat.

Assembling for Binding

Books, booklets, magazines, and notepads are examples of sheets bound together to form a product. *Assembling* is the general term for bringing together the components in preparation for binding. There are three terms for this assemblage process—*collating*, *gathering*, and *inserting*.

Collating

Assembling individual sheets of paper is called *collating*. Collating is performed by placing piles of paper in the correct order along the edge of a work surface. One sheet at a time is picked up from each pile and assembled in proper sequence. Automatic collating machines are used for high-volume production. See **Figure 25-36.**

Gathering

Assembling signatures for hardcover or softcover (perfect) binding is *gathering*, a process similar to collating, except folded signatures are assembled, instead of flat sheets. Signatures are lifted one at a time from their respected piles and stacked in the correct order. The term *collate* is also used to ensure that the correct number of signatures has been gathered in the correct sequence. To assist this process, *collating marks* are printed in different positions on the binding fold of signatures. See **Figure 25-37.** After the signatures have been gathered, a stair-step pattern is visible on the spine so errors can be seen and corrected before the signatures are bound.

Inserting

Signatures to be bound with saddle stitching are assembled by being *inserted*. Instead of being placed alongside one another, they are slipped inside one another so the wire stitch goes through all the signatures. See **Figure 25-38.**

Binding Operations

When a printed job is a book, magazine, booklet, or notepad, it needs to go though binding—the process of fastening together pages or signatures.

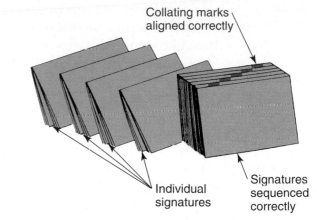

Figure 25-37. Collating marks are black rectangles printed on the signatures so, when the sheets are folded, the marks appear on the spine. After the signatures are gathered, a stair-step pattern indicates that the signatures are in the proper sequence.

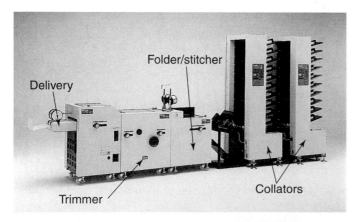

Figure 25-36. The two bin stacks on the right are the collators that hold flat sheets. After being collated, the sheets are folded, stitched, and trimmed. (Duplo USA)

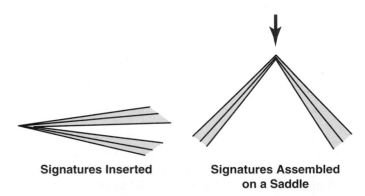

Figure 25-38. Signatures to be saddle stitched must be inserted instead of gathered. After they are assembled on a saddle, a wire stitch goes through the signatures' spines.

Binding serves two purposes—it holds everything together and protects the printed material inside. The binding method can affect both the visual appeal and functionality of the job.

Mechanical Binding

Mechanical binding fastens individual sheets of paper together with metal or plastic wire or strips inserted through punched or drilled holes. Pages bound together with removable rings or posts are classified as having a *loose-leaf binding*. A ring binding such as the one shown in **Figure 25-39** allows pages to be opened flat and removed or added as needed. No other binding method permits this flexibility.

Spiral binding requires a long series of small holes to be punched or drilled along the edge of the product through which a continuous wire or plastic coil is wound. See **Figure 25-40.** A *comb binding* uses a strip of solid plastic with curved teeth or prongs extending out of it. See **Figure 25-41.** A variation of spiral binding is double-wire binding, which consists of a single wire bent to resemble and function similarly to the plastic comb.

Wire Stitching

Wire stitching is a binding method that uses staples to bind pages together. *Saddle stitching* uses wires inserted on the fold line, or saddle, of the sheets to bind the pages together. See **Figure 25-42.** Commercial-printing facilities typically saddle stitch on a machine that automatically picks up and opens each signature and then pulls it over a moving

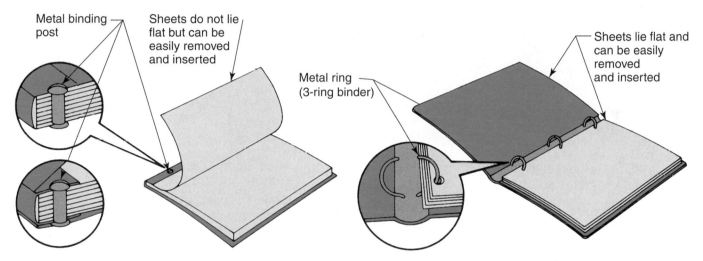

Figure 25-39. Loose-leaf binding includes the use of binding (screw) posts and ring binding because both methods allow pages to be removed and added. (A.B.Dick Co.)

assembling: any finishing operation that brings together, in the proper sequence, the sheets or signatures, in preparation for binding.

collating: assembling individual pages in their correct sequence. Collating is also ensuring that signatures are in their correct order for binding.

gathering: assembling individual sheets of paper or signatures in the correct sequence.

collate: to assemble individual pages into their correct sequence.

collating mark: a symbol printed on the folded edge of a press signature as a means of indicating the proper collating or gathering sequence.

insert: the assembling of signatures for saddle stitching.

mechanical binding: various methods used to fasten together individual sheets.

loose-leaf binding: pages bound together with removable rings or posts.

spiral binding: a binding method requiring a long series of small holes to be punched or drilled along the edge of the product through which a continuous wire or plastic coil is wound.

comb binding: a mechanical binding method in which pages are bound together with a strip of solid plastic with curved teeth or prongs extending out of it.

wire stitching: a binding method that uses staples to bind pages together.

saddle stitching: a sewing method that uses wires or staples inserted on the fold line, or saddle, of the sheets to bind the pages together.

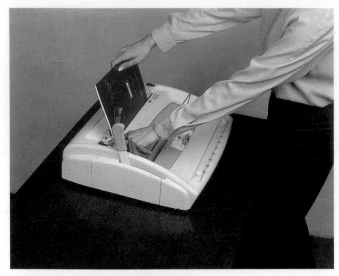

Punching Holes

Inserting Wire

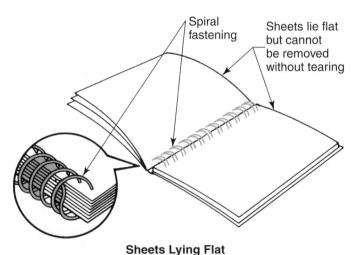

Sheets Lying Flat

Figure 25-40. The first step in spiral binding is to punch the holes. The plastic or metal wire is then inserted into the holes. After binding, the sheets lie flat and cannot be easily removed from the binding.

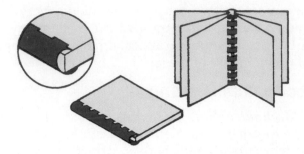

Figure 25-41. The plastic comb locks into the holes that have been punched into the sheets.

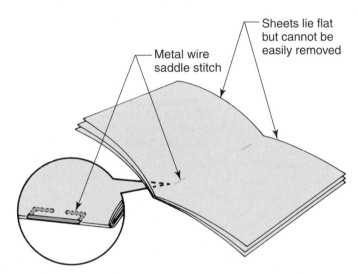

Figure 25-42. The saddle-wire method of binding allows the booklet to be opened fully. This method is not practical for binding thick volumes because it lacks strength. (A.B.Dick Co.)

conveyor called a *saddle*. As the saddle moves the signature forward, other signatures are similarly opened and placed over it, a process that continues until all signatures and the cover are in place. See **Figure 25-43.** The booklet is bound as two or three wire stitches are placed through the spine. A three-knife trimmer then removes the excess paper from the three edges other than the spine. This device is called a *gatherer-stitcher-trimmer (GST)*. See **Figure 25-44.**

Caution

When operating stitching equipment, keep fingers clear of the stitching heads. Staples are capable of being driven through material 1″ (25.4 mm) thick on some types of equipment and would easily penetrate fingers or hands.

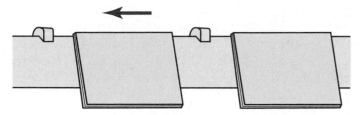

Figure 25-43. Two signatures have been pulled onto the saddle and are being carried forward so the other signatures in the publication can be pulled over each one.

In *side stitching*, staples are inserted close to the fold and clinched at the back. See **Figure 25-45.** This method is not popular because pages of a side-wire stitched book cannot be opened flat, and extra margin allowance must be provided for the staples.

Perfect Binding

With *perfect binding*, the signatures of paper are held together with a flexible cement. Pocket-size books, telephone directories, thick magazines, and mail-order catalogs are examples of perfect binding. Books commonly referred to as *paperbacks* have received perfect binding. This binding is fast

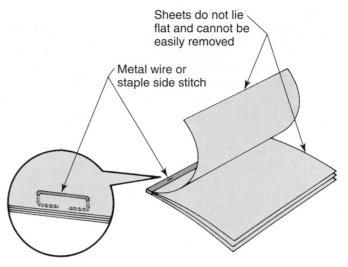

Figure 25-45. The side-wire binding method does not allow the booklet to be opened fully because of the 1/4″ lost to the binding edge. (A.B.Dick Co.)

and economical and results in an attractive printed product.

Signatures are gathered side by side, not inserted, as with saddle stitching. The cover is formed into a *U* shape, hot glue is placed on the inside of the spine,

Figure 25-44. Signatures are moving from left to right and into the stitching unit. Note the shiny spools of wire that will be cut into short lengths, bent to form staples, and pushed through the signatures. The bound signatures then turn left and move into the large trimming unit. (McCain Manufacturing Corp.)

▉▉▉▉▉ ▉□□□

gatherer-stitcher-trimmer (GST): a finishing device that inserts, saddle stitches, and trims three sides of signatures to produce booklets.

side stitching: a binding method in which staples are inserted close to the fold and clinched at the back.

perfect binding: a binding method in which the sheets of paper are held together with a flexible adhesive.

burst binding: a form of perfect binding, used on reference books and some textbooks, in which the spine of the book body is notched or perforated and a high-strength adhesive is applied under pressure.

thermal binding process: a binding process similar to perfect binding that uses heat and a special adhesive applied to the edges of the sheets.

and the gathered signatures are placed against the glue. The binding edges of the signatures have been previously perforated to allow the glue to contact the inside pages of each signature. High-speed automatic equipment is used for perfect binding. See **Figure 25-46.** *Burst binding* is a form of perfect binding used on reference books (dictionaries and encyclopedias) and some textbooks. This binding involves notching the spine of the book body and applying a high-strength adhesive under pressure.

Thermal Binding

The *thermal binding process* is similar to perfect binding because it uses heat and a special adhesive applied to the edges of the sheets. Books or booklets made of cut pages and covers are fed spine down through a thermal binding machine. A strip of heated adhesive material is applied to the spine in one operation. A wraparound cover can also be applied to the spine, if desired.

Case Binding

Case binding is a means of binding pages together with thread and then encasing the sewn

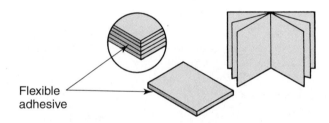

Flexible adhesive

Figure 25-46. Perfect binding holds sheets of paper together with a flexible adhesive. Pocket-size books are almost exclusively bound in this manner. (A.B.Dick Co.)

signatures with a sturdy cardboard cover. See **Figure 25-47.** Case binding creates a strong, durable hardcover book that can withstand extensive use and handling. Terms such as *edition binding, job binding,* and *library binding* are used to describe various types of case binding:

- Edition binding describes the use of fully automated equipment for large quantities of books.
- Job binding is the binding of smaller quantities of books that usually involves some handwork.
- Library binding is used to create reinforced bindings in reference-type books that must withstand a large amount of handling.

The first step in case binding is gathering the signatures in the correct order. A needle and strong thread are then used to sew them together. See **Figure 25-48.** The side sewing method is performed by passing the thread from signature to signature through the side of the book so the stitches run parallel to the binding edge. *Side sewing* creates a very strong binding that is preferred for books sold to public libraries. When signatures are bound with the *saddle sewing* method, the thread passes through the signature fold at the spine of the book. Saddle sewing is commonly known as *Smyth sewing.* The procedure of positioning and attaching the sewn signatures to the case is known as *casing in.* The various elements of a case-bound book are shown in **Figure 25-49.**

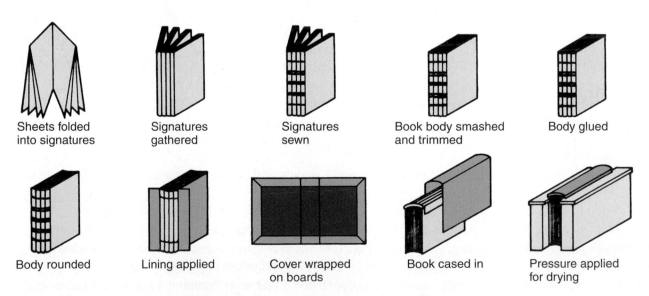

| Sheets folded into signatures | Signatures gathered | Signatures sewn | Book body smashed and trimmed | Body glued |

| Body rounded | Lining applied | Cover wrapped on boards | Book cased in | Pressure applied for drying |

Figure 25-47. There are 10 basic stages to binding a case-bound (hardback) book.

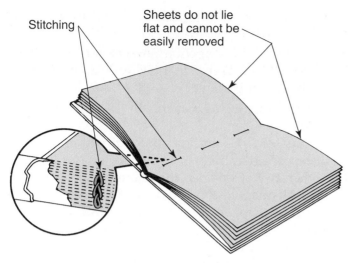

Figure 25-48. The signatures are sewn together using a strong needle and thread. (A.B.Dick Co.)

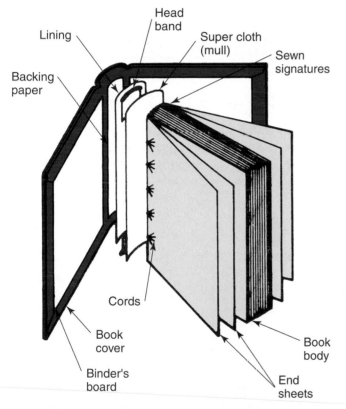

Figure 25-49. The basic elements of a case-bound book. The end sheets serve as the link between the book body and the cover.

Tipping

Tipping involves including a separate piece of printed material in the pages of a printed product. An example of tipping would be gluing an advertising insert to the page of a magazine. In tipping, liquid adhesive is usually applied along one edge of the insert before it is adhered near the spine of a page in a magazine, book, or booklet.

Padding

When simple tablets and notepads are produced, padding is used to hold the sheets together. *Padding* consists of applying a liquid adhesive to one edge of a stack of paper. Usually, a piece of chipboard is included as a backing for each pad. A flexible cement coating is applied to one edge of the pile of sheets and backings. Padding allows easy removal of individual sheets and is usually used for notepads or stationery-type products.

The padding cement is a water-soluble liquid with a thick, creamy appearance. This cement is available in clear and red colors to suit the requirements of the job. The padding cement is applied in two coats to the edges of the paper with an ordinary paintbrush. When dry, the pads are cut apart and trimmed to their final size on a paper cutter. High-speed padding equipment is available for large bindery operations. The steps for hand padding are listed below:

1. Depending on what type of padding device is being used, prepare it for loading. If a device is not available, any flat surface, such as a countertop, can be used. In this method, weights must be placed on top of the paper to be padded.
2. Load the jogged paper into the guide edge of the padding device. Continue to load until the device is full. All sheets must be aligned perfectly, whether using a padding device or a tabletop. See **Figure 25-50.**
3. Apply holding pressure to the paper pile. Remove or open the guide edge of the padding device.
4. With a brush, apply the padding compound evenly across the entire area to be padded. Let the compound dry thoroughly for about 30 minutes. Apply a second coat of padding compound.

case binding: a means of binding pages together with thread and then encasing the sewn signatures with a cardboard cover.

side sewing: a binding method in which the thread is passed from signature to signature through the side of the book so the stitches run parallel to the binding edge.

saddle (Smyth) sewing: a binding method in which the thread passes through the signature fold at the spine of the book.

casing in: the procedure of positioning and attaching the sewn signatures to the case.

tipping: the insertion of a separate piece of printed material into the original pages of a printed product.

padding: a form of perfect binding in which a flexible adhesive is used to hold the sheets together and allow easy removal.

Figure 25-50. Sheets to be padded are jogged in a padding press against the backstop. Pressure is applied to the leading edge of the paper pile with a clamp. The pile is then positioned with the binding edge out. Adhesive is applied to the binding edge with a brush. (Champion Manufacturing Company, Inc.)

5. Remove the padded material from the padding device. Use a padding knife to separate each pad from the pile.
6. Use a paper cutter to trim the pads as necessary.

Bindery Planning

Communication among departments is necessary because most printing jobs move through multiple stages of production. For example, the people in the press and finishing departments depend on the people in prepress to impose the job properly, relative to grain direction, guide edges, and appropriate bindery considerations. Prepress workers must understand the various binding methods because adequate margin allowance must be provided during prepress operations. Just as prepress operators must consider gripper margins and trim allowances, they must consider adequate margin allowance for binding purposes. Common binding classifications include mechanical binding, wire stitching, perfect binding, thermal binding, case binding, sewn softcover, tipping, and padding.

Grain Direction

Grain direction is a major consideration throughout production for several reasons:

- The customer often specifies the grain direction of the finished product.
- Paper's grain direction affects stiffness, and stiffness is a factor in how well a sheet feeds through equipment.
- Grain direction is a factor in how easily paper folds.

Unfortunately, the correct grain direction for one of these considerations is wrong for one or both of the other two. Consider this example, a 10″ × 16″ menu with one fold is printed on an offset duplicator and run one-up on an 11″ × 17″ press sheet. See **Figure 25-51.** The press operator wants a grain-long press sheet so the added stiffness in the direction of travel improves feeding. The folder operator wants a grain-short press sheet, however, because the fold is better if it is not made against the grain. The solution might be to print the job on a grain-long press sheet to enhance feeding into the press and then score it to allow a good fold across the grain. This simple example illustrates why grain direction must be planned for before the job enters production.

Side-Guide and Lead Edges

As was discussed in Chapter 20, a press sheet is positioned for registration purposes at the side-guide edge and lead edge. See **Figure 25-52.** If possible,

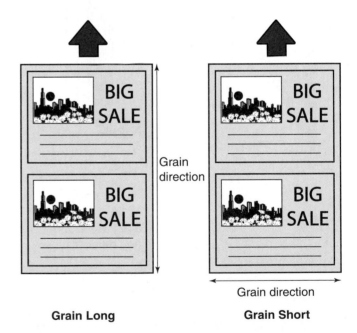

Figure 25-51. The press supervisor might want to run this two-up press sheet with the grain parallel to the direction of travel (grain long) to improve stiffness and feeding. The finishing supervisor might want the grain to be parallel to the fold (grain short), however, to improve fold quality.

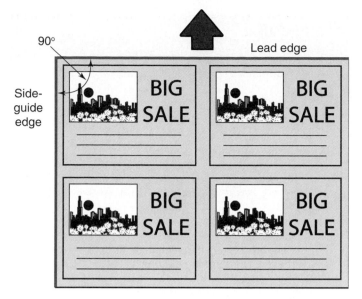

Figure 25-52. The lead edge and side-guide edge of this press sheet form a perfect 90° corner. When this sheet moves through the finishing machines, one of these two edges should be the lead edge.

the same lead edge and side-guide edge of the press sheet is used when the sheet is cut or fed through a folder or other finishing equipment to maintain registration. If the press sheet is not perfectly square, using a wild side—an edge opposite the lead or side-guide edge—would misalign the image. When the press sheet must feed into a folder or other finishing machine at a right angle to the way it fed into the press, the side-guide edge is used as the lead edge.

Note

The press sheet's guide corner is the intersection of the side-guide and gripper edges. The folder's guide corner is the intersection of the side-guide and lead edges.

If the guide edge is damaged and cannot be used, a new guide can be made by either removing the damaged portion or squaring the wild side. When a sheet is cut or folded using the original guide edge, new guide edges are created—the edge on either side of the cut or fold. They are then used to make additional folds or cuts.

Signature Lips

It is necessary to consider the need for a signature-assembling extender, known as a *lip*, *lap*, or *pickup*. This extender is an extension of one side of a signature and results from the signature's last fold being off center. See **Figure 25-53**. The lip is needed if the signatures will be saddle stitched because grippers need to open each signature in order to drag it over the saddle. Without a lip, grippers would close down on the entire signature and prevent it from opening. If the first pages of the signature form the lip, it is a low-page lip. A high-page lip is formed by the pages with the higher page numbers.

A 1/2″ (12.7 mm) lip is generally used for automatic assembly and binding machines. A 1/4″ (6.4 mm) lip is used for hand-assembling operations. Signatures that are not saddle stitched do not require a lip because they are not inserted.

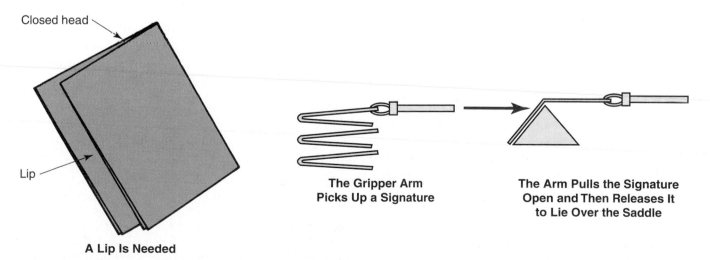

Figure 25-53. A lip (or lap, or pickup) is an extension of one side of a signature. The extension is needed so the gripper arm can pick up the signature and pull it open for positioning on the saddle.

Bindery Dummies

As you learned in Chapter 12, a dummy refers to a paper model of the job folded and assembled in the same way the finished product will be folded and assembled. The dummy shows the size, shape, form, and general plan of the printed piece. Preparing a dummy is a very important planning step because it helps the planner visualize the complete job by indicating the locations of folds, trims, imposition, bleeds, and guides. All the printing and finishing requirements must be visualized before making the dummy. Factors to be considered include the number and size of pages, number of signatures, number and type of inserts, cover requirements, basic imposition, folding requirements, assembly, and binding requirements.

Planning is necessary at every stage in the printing process. Accurate and complete instructions on every job must be made and adhered to before going to the bindery. The bindery department should be given all essential information to handle a job efficiently. A simple set of guidelines for the bindery is shown in **Figure 25-54.**

Every job schedule for bindery operations should include full instructions and a dummy as to page numbers, trim size, crop marks, and side-guide or gripper marks. If changes are made in the original specs or mistakes are found in positioning, the bindery personnel should be alerted. Be sure a plan is established for cutting and trimming the paper, both before and after the job is printed. A simple form for this purpose is shown in **Figure 25-55.**

Bindery Guidelines for Print Shops

1. Kind and weight of stock..
2. Size of sheet to be run..
3. Direction of the grain..
4. Number of each page in signature................................
5. How job is to be run streetwise
   One-sided Two-sided Work-and-turn Work-and-tumble
   Other...
6. Will there be bleeds.........split pages.........hairline line-up? (If so, the pressroom should consult the bindery before work begins to determine the best way to lay out the job.)
7. What kind of packaging is desired?................................
8. Are deliveries to be bulk.........or split? What date?.........
9. Is delivery to be in bulk..........or skids.........
   or packages..........Transported by elevator..........
   or stairs..........
10. Will addressed office supply labels be provided or be furnished by the bindery?...
    ....
    Who supplies bill of lading or delivery...........................
    ....
11. Any other special instructions...
    ....
    ....
    ....
    ....

Figure 25-54. The bindery department uses these guidelines to plan and handle each job efficiently. (Hammermill Paper Co.)

Distribution

A growing trend within the printing industry is for commercial printers to include distribution (also called *mailing*) among the services offered to customers. The customer merely supplies the printer with a CD with the mailing list, and the printed materials are inserted into envelopes, addressed, and bundled by zip code without leaving the shop. Personnel prepare the printed materials using sophisticated packaging and addressing technologies for both domestic and international delivery. See **Figure 25-56.** In addition, computerized inventory-control warehouse systems are maintained for customers who want shipments made periodically.

For many advertisers who buy print materials, target advertising is a critical consideration. Advertisers use customized and personalized materials for niche demographic groups, different geographic regions, and even individual households to gain an advantage in the marketplace. Competition from television and other electronic sources requires shorter production times for printed materials and lower shipping costs. The growth of VDP is expected to increase the demand for short turnaround times for printing and distribution even more in the future.

Packaging

The printer is responsible for the packaging and delivery of the printed product. The main purpose of packaging is protection of the contents. Customers typically specify how the job is to be packaged.

Cartons

Special cartons are used for some printed materials. The products are often banded or wrapped before they are placed in cartons, which are often

| Date_____ | | | | | | | | Stock Requisition | | | | | No. 000 |

The following stock is to be used on:

Job order no._____ Customer_____ Description_____

Paper			Buy out	Warehouse location	Sheet size or roll width	Weight (rolls)	No. sheets	Cutting Instructions				Amount returned to inventory
Name	Sub.	Color						Cut to	Grain	Pcs. out	Total	

➡ Paper bought from _____ P.O. #_____

Deliver to ☐ Cutter on_____ and press #_____ on_____

Figure 25-55. The bindery department uses a stock requisition to cut and trim paper, both before and after the job is printed. (National Association for Printing Leadership)

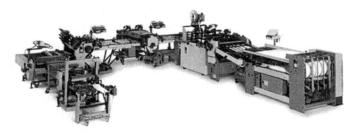

Figure 25-56. This self-mailing system is capable of folding, perforating, trimming, slitting, labeling, and gluing in any programmed sequence. (Heidelberg, Inc.)

banded themselves. Wrapping, banding, and boxing operations are usually done on hand-mechanical, semiautomatic, or automatic equipment. Printed products can be tied with inexpensive, but strong, string. Printed sheets and publications can be tied by hand or with automatic tying equipment.

Shrink-Wrap

Shrink-wrap is a transparent plastic film used to wrap or contain printed parcels or products. This film is one of the most efficient packaging methods used in the finishing department. The process makes the finished products easy to handle, makes the products attractive to the customer, and provides some protection to the bundled product. Shrink-wrapping can be

performed manually or with automated equipment. See **Figure 25-57.**

Special transparent, plastic film is used in the shrink-wrap packaging method. Heat is applied to the plastic material to cause it to shrink tightly around the printed material. Larger equipment can shrink-wrap packages approximately 12″ (30.48 cm) wide, 18″ (45.72 cm) long, and 8″ (20.32 cm) high. Individual packages are placed in cartons for shipment to the customer. Automated machines are used to wrap, bundle, stack, and move the packaged product.

Caution

Use caution around shrink-wrap equipment, since it uses extremely high temperatures to shrink and bond the plastic material.

After packaging, finished products are usually stacked on pallets or skids. A pallet is a low, portable, double-faced platform. Automatic equipment, such as the palletizer shown in **Figure 25-58,** is used to secure or band printed sheets and other printed products for storage or further production handling.

Figure 25-57. A roll of transparent plastic film is fed to the wrapping device on shrink-wrap packaging machines. (SIG Packaging Technology)

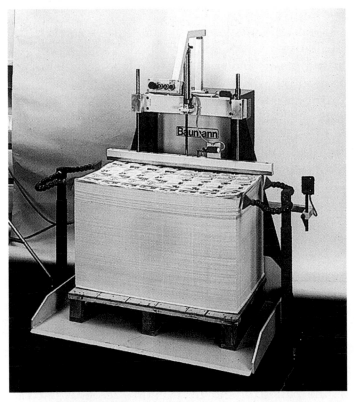

Figure 25-58. A paper palletizer is used to secure bundles of printed or unprinted sheets to a pallet. (Man Roland, Inc.)

Summary

Finishing is the term used to describe all operations performed on printed materials from the delivery end of the press to the final shipment to the customer or consumer. Finishing operations include cutting and trimming, folding, punching, drilling, slotting and cornering, round cornering, gathering, collating, jogging, scoring, perforating, slitting, die cutting, foil stamping, embossing, varnishing, thermography, and packaging. Binding operations serve two general purposes. First, the binding holds everything together by fastening one element to the other. Second, the binding helps protect the printed material inside. Common binding methods include mechanical, wire stitching, case bound, sewn softcover, perfect, padding, and thermal.

Bindery planning is an important first step in printing. Specific requirements for the job must be determined here. Bindery-planning requirements include the placement and relationship of the press, folder, and cutter guides. Consideration is also given to the placement of the press side guide and press gripper, with respect to the edge of the press sheet. Signature lips provide a means of opening signatures in the center for assembling or saddle stitching.

A bindery dummy is prepared to show how the finished product will be folded and assembled. This dummy shows the order of assembly and the relationship of folds, trims, imposition, bleeds, and guides needed for the job. Mailing and distribution operations generally encompass work functions related to computerized ink-jet imprinting, mailing, and the shipping of printed materials to the customer or consumer.

Review Questions

Please do not write in this book. Write your answers on a separate sheet of paper.

1. _____ is the term used to describe all operations performed on printed materials from the delivery end of the printing press to the final shipment to the customer.

2. Printed sheets with several pages are prepared so they can be folded into _____.

3. What are two standard safety features on paper cutters?

4. How do the blades on a three-knife trimmer work?

5. _____ folds run in the same direction as one another.

6. In _____ folds, each fold is made at a right angle to each preceding fold. After the first fold is made, the sheet is turned 90° before the second fold is made.

7. The two basic kinds of folding machines are the _____ folder and the _____ folder.

8. The _____ on a buckle folder is made up of two metal plates positioned at a slight incline above the drive and fold rollers.

9. The cutting of rectangular or specially shaped holes for plastic binding and spiral binding is called _____.

10. Holes for a ring binder are made with a paper _____.

11. What is cornering?

12. Placing a crease in sheets of thick paper or cardboard to aid in folding is called _____.

13. In a(n) _____ operation, a small series of very short slits or holes is cut in the paper, leaving a small bridge of paper intact between each hole.

14. An irregular shape or design can be cut in paper or cardboard by _____.

15. A letterpress process that uses pressure and heat to make permanent images on objects with gold, silver, or colored film material is called _____.

16. _____ creates a raised image on a printed product.

17. _____ is the process of imprinting tickets, checks, certificates, or other items with consecutive figures.

18. The process that places a coating on paper to impart resistance to chemicals, heat, and other elements is called _____.

19. Placing individual sheets or signatures in the correct sequence is called _____.

20. Signatures that are going into a saddle-stitched booklet are assembled by being _____.
    A. collated
    B. inserted
    C. gathered
    D. tipped

21. What are collating codes? What purpose do they serve?

22. Pages bound together with removable rings or posts are called _____.

23. Spiral binding and comb binding are two common methods of _____ binding.

24. Explain saddle stitching.

25. In _____ stitching, staples are inserted close to the fold and clinched at the back.

26. What is perfect binding?

27. _____ binding involves notching the spine of the book body and applying a high-strength adhesive under pressure.

28. Describe the process and applications of case bindings.

29. When signatures are bound with the _____ sewing method, the thread passes through the signature fold at the spine of the book.

30. The procedure of positioning and attaching the sewn signatures to the case is known as _____.

31. What is tipping?

32. _____ is a form of perfect binding used to hold the sheets of a tablet or notebook together.

33. The assembling extension on a signature is known as a(n) _____.

34. A(n) _____ shows the size, shape, form, and general plan of the printed piece.

35. Transparent plastic film and heat are used in a packaging method called _____.

Skill-Building Activities

1. Obtain samples of at least 10 kinds of bindings described in this chapter. Be prepared to discuss the advantages and disadvantages of each binding method.

2. Prepare a paper-cutting waste-factor chart that can be posted near the paper cutter in your lab. Use the standard sheet sizes used in your lab.

3. Prepare a chart or bulletin board display with samples of finishing operations, including collating, gathering, folding, punching, drilling, round cornering, jogging, perforating, die cutting, scoring, and slitting. Label each sample, giving its name and application.

4. Familiarize yourself with carbonless papers. What is meant by precollated? For what purposes would a printer use several different reams and colors of uncollated carbonless paper?

5. Prepare a bindery dummy for a job scheduled to be produced in your lab.

6. Create the necessary folding dummies for a saddle-stitched, 48-page booklet consisting of three 16-page signatures and a separate cover.

It Can Happen

Few students see themselves as someday owning or managing a business. It should be remembered, however, that every owner and manager was once a student. Shown here are Gene Scott (left) and Danny Robinson. Gene is the owner of PXP Ohio. PXP Ohio is a 31-employee printing company located in the Midwest. Gene has owned the company since 1971. Danny has been the prepress supervisor since 1977. During their time together, they have witnessed many changes in the printing industry. One of the largest changes has been the emergence of electronic work flow.

PXP Ohio is not a large printing company. Gene has always recognized the need to stay competitive, however, in both technology and skilled personnel. The six-color Komori press seen in the background and the completely electronic prepress work flow are examples of the need to continuously invest in new equipment and software. This chapter identifies many of the issues with which Gene and other owners deal and is important even for people who never become owners or supervisors. Employees who have an awareness of the issues facing management are often better members of the team.

(PXP Ohio)

Chapter 26
Operating a Printing Business

Key Terms

brokering
corporation
entrepreneur
existing business
franchising
new business
partnership
profit
sole proprietorship

Learning Objectives

When you have completed the reading and assigned activities related to this chapter, you will be able to do the following:

◆ Identify the professional and personal traits of an entrepreneur.

◆ Describe three basic business organizational structures.

◆ Discuss the tasks administrative, sales, accounting, and production personnel perform in a typical printing company.

◆ List and describe the categories of business costs.

◆ Summarize the methods of starting a business.

◆ Explain how regulatory laws affect businesses.

Small businesses play an important role in the printing and publishing industry. In fact, the industry is made up mostly of small establishments. Over 60,000 of them employ a total of about a million people. The service sector of the U.S. economy is expected to grow. This makes printing a good choice for a business venture. Owning a business can be an exciting and rewarding experience. Business ownership, however, is hard work and creates emotional, financial, and legal issues. This chapter covers various aspects of owning and operating a printing business.

Entrepreneurship

Becoming the owner of a printing company is an entrepreneurial endeavor. An *entrepreneur* is a self-starter who organizes and manages a business undertaking, while assuming the risks involved in making a profit. See **Figure 26-1.**

Business owners are called on to demonstrate leadership capability in several areas:

- Planning and goal setting.
- Organizing and managing.
- Record keeping and accounting.
- Hiring employees and training.
- Complying with governmental laws and regulations.

A basic education in business, finance, or management is important. Knowledge of and experience in the printing business are also important. Personal traits describing an entrepreneur are optimistic, energetic, responsible, industrious, and decisive.

Figure 26-1. The owner is ultimately responsible for the success of an enterprise.

Types of Businesses

The type of printing business someone starts requires a great deal of thought and planning. The first step is to examine personal abilities and interests. Those personal traits are then applied to considering several questions:

- What aspect of printing should be pursued: commercial printing, publication printing, quick printing, or specialty printing?
- What printing process should be used: offset lithography, letterpress, flexography, or screen printing?
- Most importantly, what specific product line or specialty will be delivered: business cards, booklets, promotional pieces, packaging, or labels?

Market demand, combined with your skills and qualifications, generally dictates the type of business, printing process, and product line you choose. A person might decide, for example, to start an offset printing business specializing in short-run business forms for local, small businesses. Sources such as the Small Business Administration (SBA), the American Management Association (AMA), the U.S. Government Printing Office (GPO), and PrintImage International can provide guidance during this exploratory stage.

Funding the Business

The amount of funding required to start a small business varies and is largely determined by the type of business and the business's intended purpose. Location plays an important role when considering whether to build, purchase, rent, or lease a structure. Certain geographic areas are more desirable (and thus more expensive) than others.

Adequate capital means having enough money to purchase equipment, supplies, and furnishings, while maintaining a reserve sufficient to operate the business for at least the first 12 months. The amount of reserve depends on expenses. Expenses include wages, building mortgage or rent, utilities, ongoing expenses, and required services. See **Figure 26-2.** Banks, venture-capital organizations, and government agencies such as the SBA are sources of loans for *new businesses*.

Business Start-Up Expenses Proposal

Start-Up Expenses $ _____

Initial investment (purchase, rent, lease)   _____

Inventory   _____

Equipment, fixtures   _____

Equipment and fixture installation   _____

Remodeling   _____

Permits and licenses   _____

Professional services (attorneys, etc.)   _____

Cash reserve   _____

                                        Total start-up $ _____

Estimated 12-Month Operating Expenses

Mortgage, rent, lease $ _____ mo. x 12 _____

Wages, salaries   _____ mo. x 12 _____

Utilities (heat, lights, telephone) _____ mo. x 12 _____

Supplies for office   _____ mo. x 12 _____

Supplies for shop   _____ mo. x 12 _____

Advertising   _____ mo. x 12 _____

Taxes   _____ mo. x 12 _____

Accounting, legal   _____ mo. x 12 _____

Insurance (workers' comp., fire, etc.) _____ mo. x 12 _____

Interest on debt   _____ mo. x 12 _____

Maintenance   _____ mo. x 12 _____

Miscellaneous   _____ mo. x 12 _____

                            Total 12-month operation $ _____

Figure 26-2. A form similar to this one should be used to calculate business start-up expenses for the first 12 months.

entrepreneur: a self-starter who organizes and manages a business undertaking, while assuming the risks involved in making a profit.

new business: a for-profit organization that is originated.

Business Organizational Structures

A *sole proprietorship* is a single-owner business in which the profits belong to the owner. A *partnership* is made up of two or more owners. This arrangement can be highly motivating when the people involved work together to realize a *profit*. Incompatibility of partners is a potential drawback. Liquidating the partnership interests for whatever reason can also be problematic.

A *corporation* is a legal venture a group of shareholders owns. Elected officers who report to an elected board of directors manage the business operations. This arrangement has the advantages of drawing on experts within the organization and eliciting large amounts of capital. Higher operating expenses are one disadvantage of a corporation. Furthermore, profits are taxed twice. First, corporate taxes are paid on profits. Second, taxes are paid on dividends paid to shareholders.

Company-Personnel Hierarchy

Every business enterprise, no matter its size, has a hierarchy of personnel to perform specific tasks that can be divided into four categories:

- **Administrative.** Coordinates and manages all operations within the company structure.
- **Sales and marketing.** Acquires customers to buy the company's products or services.
- **Accounting.** Handles the financial operations of the company.
- **Production.** Performs the operations required to produce goods or services for customers.

In a small business, a single proprietor and two to five workers might perform all the responsibilities of a larger organization. For example, a business could be structured so the owner handles both administrative and sales tasks. An office manager sends out invoices, pays bills from suppliers, and keeps business records. The production manager operates press equipment and supervises the work of the prepress worker and the press and bindery helper. See **Figure 26-3.**

In a medium-sized company, these same responsibilities are divided among more people. The company whose organization chart is shown in **Figure 26-4** has approximately 50 employees in four departments. The organization of a large printing company with 125 employees is shown in **Figure 26-5.** This company is a corporation. Stockholders elect

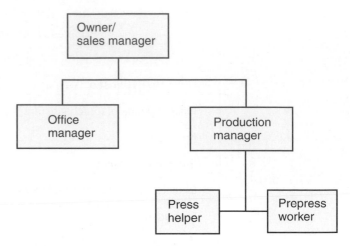

Figure 26-3. An organizational chart for a small printing company of five employees.

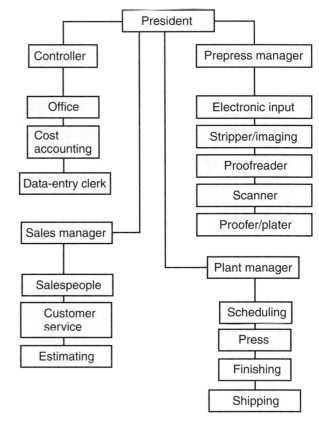

Figure 26-4. An organizational chart for a medium printing company with approximately 50 employees.

members of the company's board of directors to oversee the business.

Business Costs

The primary goal of business is to make a profit. This means more income must be acquired from the sale of products and services than is spent on salaries, materials, mortgage or rent, utilities, and other

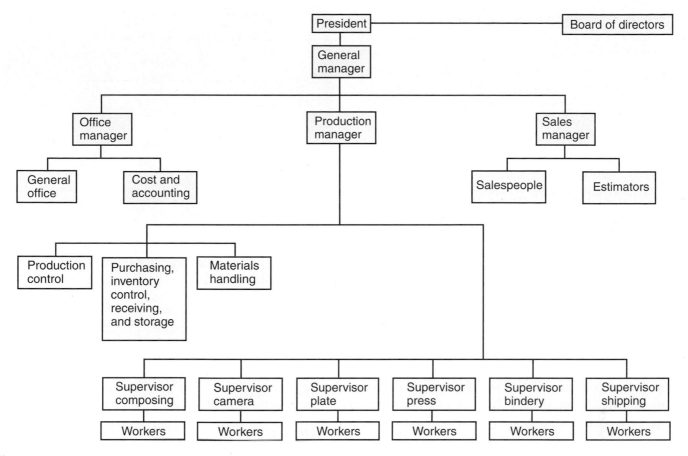

Figure 26-5. An organizational chart for a large printing company with approximately 125 employees.

costs of conducting business. The difference between income and expenses is profit.

Identifying and controlling costs is essential to realize a desired profit. If a company does not accurately determine its costs and sets its prices too low to make a profit, it will quickly fail. In most businesses, costs are usually categorized as labor, material, and fixed:

- **Labor costs.** The largest expenditure of most business enterprises is labor. Costs include not only the wages and salaries of workers. They also include the cost of health insurance, retirement benefits, paid holidays and vacations, and other fringe benefits.

- **Material costs.** Paper, ink, chemicals, and packaging are examples of material costs. Materials are items used in the manufacture of a product.

- **Fixed costs.** Regardless of the volume of business, these costs remain constant. Fixed costs include utilities such as natural gas, electricity, and the telephone. Office supplies, advertising, and equipment are also fixed costs.

Methods of Starting a Business

An enterprise can be started by purchasing an existing business, creating a new business, franchising, or brokering. Each method of starting a business is described briefly:

- *Existing business.* One advantage of purchasing an existing business is not having to fully equip and stock it as if it were a new business. Another benefit is inheriting the former owner's customer base. Price, location, and reputation are important considerations when deciding whether to buy an existing business.

sole proprietorship: a single-owner business in which the profits belong to the owner.

partnership: a business owned by two or more owners.

profit: the income acquired from the sale of products and services above and beyond the costs of salaries, materials, mortgage or rent, and utilities and the other costs of conducting business.

corporation: a legal venture owned by a group of shareholders.

existing business: a for-profit organization that has been in existence.

- **New business.** Choosing to start a new business brings the challenge of creating something from scratch and, perhaps, being the first such business in an area. Such an enterprise requires purchasing or constructing a building, obtaining equipment, and stocking the business with supplies. Location is an extremely important factor in any business. A complete analysis of the intended location is necessary. Becoming established and building a customer base are two challenges the new business owner faces.

- *Franchising.* The U.S. Department of Labor defines franchising as a licensing agreement. The franchiser provides the franchisee with training in technical, management, and accounting practices. Also, the franchiser assists the franchisee in securing financing, selecting a site, and marketing. In most cases, the franchiser provides the equipment necessary for operation and offers ongoing sales, promotional, and technical support. For these services, the franchisee pays a lump sum, plus a predetermined monthly royalty on gross sales of the operation. See **Figure 26-6.**

- *Brokering.* Another way to get started in the printing business is through brokering. A printing broker is a person who acts as an agent in the sale and purchase of printing products and services. See **Figure 26-7.** Instead of working for a printing company, a broker works for several

Figure 26-7. Most printing brokers have had experience in the production or managerial department of a printing firm. (Jack Klasey)

clients and seeks out the best printing company for a client's given job. Brokering takes advantage of others' expertise, equipment, and personnel. A brokerage house is typically an office or a home-based site.

The key to this business enterprise is good customer service. Personal contacts and telephone solicitation are the broker's principal means of doing business. Brokers deal directly with commercial and specialty printers to arrange services for their customers. A printing broker must be an astute businessperson who is skilled in communication, organization, and coordination.

Regulatory Laws

Business owners are required to understand and comply with local, state, and federal regulations. An owner should always seek the counsel of a qualified business attorney. The following areas must be considered in the acquisition and operation of a business:

- **Business licenses.** A local or state business license or similar operating assessment is required annually.

- **Insurance.** Some of the more obvious types of insurance are liability, fire, workers' compensation, vehicle, life, disability, and health for you and your workers.

- **Taxes.** As a business owner, you will be required to pay local, state, and federal taxes. In addition, taxes must be paid on the Federal Insurance Contributions Act (FICA), employee income, unemployment compensation, sales, and property.

Figure 26-6. This print shop was started with the assistance of a franchiser who provides ongoing sales, promotional, and technical support.

- **Labor laws.** The Fair Labor Standards Act was implemented to regulate and specify minimum wages and hours for employees. Most businesses are subject to fair-labor regulations. Owners must check with the Department of Labor, however, for specific requirements.

- **Health and safety.** OSHA governs the health and safety of workers in business and industry. See **Figure 26-8.** Business owners and managers should be knowledgeable of the OSHA regulations pertaining to their operations. OSHA officials frequently make unannounced inspections.

- **Environmental impact.** Almost all businesses are restricted by local, state, and federal environmental-protection laws and ordinances. The printing industry is particularly subject to regulation because of the volatile waste its operations generate. See **Figure 26-9.** Common regulations cover chemical removal and storage of flammable liquids, paper, wiping rags, and solvent-soaked materials.

The local fire department usually has jurisdiction over a printing facility and periodically inspects the facility.

Staying in Business

Entrepreneurs must understand that they are a part of a vast information industry that is constantly changing and evolving. For example, the rapidly increasing number of companies marketing their products on the Internet has reduced the need for business forms. Therefore, many printing companies that specialized in producing business forms have chosen to diversify their operations.

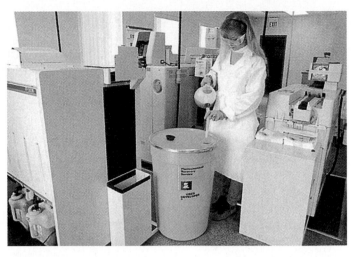

Figure 26-9. Waste-management companies specialize in the removal and reclamation of waste from industries. (Safety-Kleen)

It is imperative that printing entrepreneurs and their employees remain aware of the changing technology in the areas of business and administrative operations. At the same time, they must facilitate a high level of employee skill through on-the-job, in-service, and equipment-manufacturer educational programs. They understand that the customer is the boss. All these factors, in addition to knowing what the competition is doing, play a crucial role in the production of a quality product at a fair price, delivered on time. This challenge can ultimately lead to business success, future growth, and increased profits within the company.

Figure 26-8. Business owners need to be aware of workplace-health and -safety regulations that protect people while on the job.

franchising: granting the right or authorization to a person or group to market a company's merchandise or services in a particular region.

brokering: acting as an agent or intermediary in the sale of goods or services.

Summary

Owning and operating a printing business can be a challenging and rewarding endeavor. Being an entrepreneur means working long hours and accepting full responsibility for all business activities, including the risks involved in making a profit. Not only must you be creative in the establishment of an enterprise. As an owner, you must also possess the knowledge, people skills, and ability to carry out a business plan.

The amount of funding required to start a business varies and depends on the type of enterprise and its purpose. Capital is adequate when you have enough money to purchase equipment, supplies, and furnishings, while maintaining a reserve allowing you to operate the business for at least the first 12 months. The essential ingredient to success is identifying and controlling costs to realize a desired profit. If a company fails to accurately determine its costs (labor, material, and fixed) or sets its prices too low, it will not succeed. Owners of printing companies must be aware of the numerous regulatory laws affecting their businesses.

Review Questions

Please do not write in this book. Write your answers on a separate sheet of paper.

1. Describe a typical entrepreneur.
2. In addition to your skills and qualifications, what factor dictates the type of business you might choose?
3. How much capital reserve should a business owner have?
4. Briefly discuss the three types of organizational structures.
5. Explain the four categories of tasks personnel perform in a business enterprise.
6. _____ is the difference between income and expenses.
7. Identify the three categories of business costs. Give an example of each.

8. _____ is a licensing agreement in which one party provides the other with training in technical, management, and accounting practices, plus assistance in securing financing, selecting a site, and marketing.
9. A printing _____ is anyone who acts as an agent in the sale and purchase of printing products and services.
10. What areas of business do regulatory laws affect?

Skill-Building Activities

1. Visit a franchised quick printer, an independent quick printer, and a small commercial quick printer. Obtain a price sheet from each printer. Compare the pricing. Prepare a short written report describing your findings.
2. Contact an official at the SBA in your community. Find out what services are available for a new printing-business entrepreneur and what important points must be considered in starting a business in the community. Prepare a summary report for the class.
3. Prepare a list of advantages and disadvantages of owning a franchised shop, compared to a nonfranchised shop. Discuss these issues with the class. What is the general conclusion?
4. Prepare a report on Total Quality Management (TQM), Six Sigma, or Dr. W. Edwards Deming. Focus on the main principles and how those principles have made businesses more productive and profitable.
5. Make a photocopy of the Business Start-Up Expenses Proposal form in **Figure 26-2.** Alternatively, use the form your instructor provides. Using the following expenses, carefully complete the form by using a pencil to neatly write the figures on the appropriate lines. Determine the final start-up and 12-month operational totals. Print your name in the upper right-hand corner of the form. Submit the form to your instructor for evaluation.

Start-Up Expenses

Initial investment:	$2985.00 (lease, 1200 sq. ft.)
Inventory:	$20,900.00
Equipment, fixtures:	$81,500.00
Equipment and fixtures installation:	$3395.00
Remodeling:	$1075.00
Permits and licenses:	$325.00
Professional services:	$325.00
Cash reserves:	$25,000.00

Estimated 12-Month Operating Expenses

(All costs listed are on a per-month basis.)

Lease:	$995.00
Wages:	$6370.00
Utilities:	$449.00
Office supplies:	$150.00
Shop supplies:	$1850.00
Advertising:	$175.00
Taxes:	$159.00
Accounting:	$250.00
Insurance, workers' comp.:	$595.00
Interest on debt:	$433.00 ($125,000)
Maintenance:	$125.00
Miscellaneous:	$100.00

Two owners of printing companies in a midwestern city are presented here to show how very different career paths can lead to ownership. Also, their stories illustrate the potential for young people who have an entrepreneurial attitude and solid work ethic. Although students might find it difficult to think beyond getting their first job, they should recognize that they will continue to learn skills and develop professionally in the workplace. For this reason, they should keep an open mind about their career potential.

Mark Carro

When he graduated from high school, 17-year-old Mark Carro thought he would like to operate a camera at a television station. The local technical institute, however, did not teach this skill. When the admissions representative mentioned the printing program, Mark immediately imagined a man wearing an eyeshade and inky apron. "It's not like that," he was told. When he learned more, he enrolled in the first class of the new graphic communications program at Columbus Technical Institute in Columbus, Ohio.

While a student, Mark decided that eventually he wanted to become the owner of a printing company. When he graduated two years later, the 19-year-old went into sales because he thought that career would give him the best opportunity to earn enough money to fulfill his dream. Even though he was competing against much older salespeople, Mark's technical education gave him an advantage in answering questions and advising customers on how they could design their jobs to reduce production costs. His customer base grew. He soon gained a reputation for being customer oriented and highly conscientious. In time, he left his first employer for a printing company with greater production capabilities and sales potential. By saving his money and working steadily toward his goal, Mark became a partner in Fine Line Graphics before his thirtieth birthday. Three years later, he became president and guided the company's growth to 175 employees.

Jim Hopkins

Jim Hopkins had worked as a machinist for 10 years when he helped a friend who was in the printing business. He soon discovered that printing was the field for him. In 1974, he purchased a used press, paper cutter, and platemaker for $3000. After his shift at a factory was over, he called on local businesses to get printing orders that he would produce in his garage at night and during the weekends. Sometimes, he would sleep on the floor for an hour before going to work in the morning.

After two years of working two jobs, Jim had learned enough to become a full-time printer. With the help of his wife, he opened a quick-copy shop that produced letterhead stationery, business cards, and forms. The fledgling operation was committed to personal service, fast turnaround, and high quality. Four years later, in 1980, the quick-copy shop had become a full-service commercial printing company. The shop was producing full-color sheetfed work. In 2001, the company expanded to a new 75,000-square-foot facility with over 100 employees. Hopkins Printing has nationally-known clients, such as The Limited and Nationwide Insurance. Jim did not have the opportunity to learn printing and business practices in a school. He is committed, however, to promoting and assisting printing programs at both the high school and college levels. For young people who would like to become entrepreneurs, he offers the following advice: "Recognize the fact that most of us don't have all the talents that we need in order to succeed in business, so we need to find out those things that we are not good at and then hire skilled people to do those things for us."

In Addition to Skills...

Operators of today's offset presses bring a different skill set than was needed only 15 years ago. This operator is able to take advantage of technology that allows the ink keys to be set automatically by the data imaging the plate. He can make adjustments during the pressrun at his touch screen. Digital presses and color management are other technologies that have brought the pressroom into the digital age and integrated it with the prepress areas.

This chapter identifies a wide range of other job titles within the printing and publishing industries. Some are creative. Others are technical. Still others are managerial. Students should realize that only part of career success is based on what a person can do. The rest is based on how well the person does it and how well the person contributes to the organization's overall success. This press operator is able to keep his job and advance within the company because of his willingness to expand his skill set and learn new technology. Also important are punctuality, a professional appearance, a concern for detail, communication skills, a strong work ethic, and a sense of teamwork. This chapter provides a good opportunity for students to assess the work habits they will take with them into the work world. Once students identify areas that could be improved, they can work with teachers and school counselors to enhance their chances for success.

(Heidelberg, Inc.)

Chapter 27
Careers in the Printing Industry

Key Term

résumé

Learning Objectives

When you have completed the reading and assigned activities related to this chapter, you will be able to do the following:

◆ Identify the occupational areas the printing industry offers.

◆ Describe the responsibilities and qualifications of several positions in a printing company.

◆ Draft a personal résumé summarizing your education, employment history, and qualifications.

◆ Discuss the essential steps to follow when seeking employment.

The printing and publishing industry is huge. This industry has more than 43,000 facilities in the United States. One segment of the industry alone—commercial printing—is the nation's fourth largest manufacturing enterprise. This segment has over 500,000 jobs. Over a million Americans are currently working in all sectors of the industry—publishing, commercial printing, packaging, quick printing, and specialty printing. Of the major printing processes, offset lithography employs the most people.

Of the 20 major manufacturing groups in the United States, printing ranks second in the number of establishments and third in the number of employees. The size of printing companies is diverse. Some printing facilities have over 500 employees. Most, however, employ fewer than 25 skilled people.

The printing and publishing industry plays a prominent role in the United States and the world because the words and graphic images it produces both inform and enrich us. We live in an information age and a visual world. As the industry moves from manual to digital technologies, a major shift is occurring in the skills required for workers in all aspects of the industry. These skills are moving away from traditional craftsmanship, toward technical mastery and workplace readiness.

Employment Outlook

The population of the United States is increasing. Every person in our society is or soon will be a consumer of printed products. The printing industry is a strong career choice because of this demand for printed communications. Well-trained and educated workers with a team-oriented attitude can expect to find jobs and earn good wages in the printing industry.

New computer-oriented imaging systems are increasingly in demand for people with electronic-imaging skills. Prepress, press, and postpress operations are seeing greater shifts to an electronic environment. See **Figure 27-1.** Also, front office positions, such as estimating, customer service, and production management, are increasingly computerized.

Earnings of production workers in the printing industry are among the highest in the manufacturing sector. The standard workweek is between 35 and 40 hours, depending on the type of plant and the geographical location of the plant. The industry has fewer seasonal fluctuations than many other industries do. This is the primary reason it offers steadier employment and higher average annual earnings.

Figure 27-1. CTP and CTPr systems are revolutionizing the prepress phase of production. People with electronic-imaging skills can expect good employment opportunities. (Gerber Systems Corp.)

Career Areas

Young people bring a wide range of interests and talents to the printing industry. Creative people often work in prepress. People with interpersonal skills can find careers in sales, customer service, or human resources. People who combine visual and mechanical skills typically find their way into the press area. In addition, people who are multitalented often have careers that begin in one area and move into another, as the person's interests and career expectations evolve.

Administrative Positions

Administrators (also known as *supervisors* or *managers*) are responsible for operating a printing company efficiently and profitably. They function as part of a larger management team. A primary responsibility of a manager is to motivate and coordinate other employees to accomplish the goals of the company. See **Figure 27-2.** Administrative personnel usually are required to have a college degree in an appropriate field.

Owners are entrepreneurs. Entrepreneurs are committed to their work and get satisfaction from being their own boss. See **Figure 27-3.** Estimators predict the production costs for a potential job based on specs the customer supplies. They are in an important position because they often determine the profit or loss margin for the company. See **Figure 27-4.** Planners devise the best route for a job to move through production. They also might be responsible for ordering the paper, ink, and other required

Figure 27-2. Supervisors use their knowledge and experience to solve or avoid problems in their departments. (Color Graphics, Los Angeles)

Figure 27-3. Owners invest their time and money into acquiring and growing the business. (Hammer Packaging)

Figure 27-4. Estimators use computer-assisted programs to predict the cost of producing a job. Their accuracy is crucial to the company's success. (PXP Ohio)

materials. See **Figure 27-5.** After planners decide the route for each job, schedulers coordinate the time all jobs will spend in the prepress, press, and postpress areas.

Sales representatives and CSRs are links between customers and production. The sales manager supervises the sales staff, sales activities, quota, and profit margins. Salespeople represent their company to clients. They also get to know their clients so they can accurately represent the likes and dislikes of each customer. Pressure is constant to maintain existing accounts while building new business. Sales representatives are out calling on clients about 70% of the time. Strong communication skills and self-motivation are necessary qualities. A bachelor's degree is recommended. See **Figure 27-6.** The CSR takes over a project once the salesperson has secured a contract because the sales representatives are away from the printing company so much of the time. This person becomes the link between the client and production, making both aware of changes that occur. See **Figure 27-7.**

Creative Positions

Printed products are designed and produced to deliver information. Those who develop the ideas, images, and words are part of the creative team in a printing firm. They must be able to write copy and form visual images from verbal and visual descriptions. Among the creative positions in an advertising agency or comprehensive printing company are copywriter, graphic designer, and photographer.

Copywriters produce the copy, or manuscript, for the intended printed product. A creative writing style and thorough knowledge of language and grammar are necessary. Graphic designers arrange text and illustrations for printed products. See **Figure 27-8.** Graphic designers have an eye for composition and

Figure 27-5. Planners choose the press and imposition plan for each job. They also order the paper and other materials. (Heidelberg, Inc.)

Figure 27-6. A sales representative and his clients perform a press check. (Heidelberg, Inc.)

Figure 27-7. The CSR works closely with customers as their jobs move through production. (American ColorScans)

color. Computer skills are essential because layout is performed almost exclusively with software. Graphic designers should have a degree in graphic design, as well as experience in designing for print.

Creating high-quality photographic images is the job of the photographer. The photographs must complement the text and draw attention to the printed piece. Extensive knowledge of camera equipment and photo techniques is essential. Many photographers work as independent contractors. Advertising agencies, art studios, newspapers, and magazines employ other photographers.

Production Positions

In some large offset lithography printing plants, technicians play a major role in the operation of the company. Many companies recognize that skilled

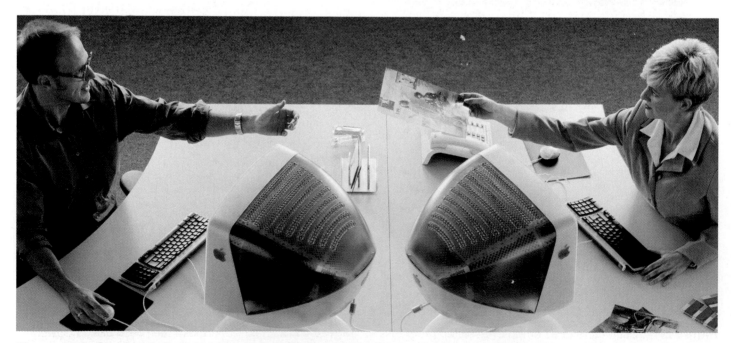

Figure 27-8. Graphic designers use a variety of drawing, image manipulation, and page composition software packages to design and produce digital files of materials to be printed. (Heidelberg, Inc.)

workers possess production expertise that no one else can contribute. These workers might, for example, work on ways to improve production procedures, improve quality, reduce costs, or handle materials.

Prepress positions

When a customer's digital files are received, they receive a preflight examination for missing fonts or other components. See **Figure 27-9.** The color-scanner operator takes the original photograph or piece of artwork and creates digital files using a high-resolution scanner. See **Figure 27-10.** Once the image is digitized, it must be evaluated against the original for color quality. After the illustrations and typeset copy have been photographed, the negatives or positives are sent to a film assembler or stripper. A film assembler must be computer literate and understand the basics of black-and-white and color film assembly. See **Figure 27-11.**

Pressroom positions

The press operator prepares and controls an offset printing press. The work itself can vary, depending on the type and size of press. On sheetfed offset presses, the press operator installs the printing plates; adjusts roller pressures; loads paper; mixes inks; controls ink flow, fountain solution, and press speed; and inspects printed sheets. The web offset–press operator must set up a press using large rolls of paper, rather than sheets. See **Figure 27-12.** Press

Figure 27-9. People who work in preflight examine newly received digital files for any irregularities. (PXP Ohio)

Figure 27-11. The monitor screen displays the imposition plan the image assembler created digitally. He is loading the platesetter with the plate material. (Heidelberg, Inc.)

Figure 27-10. This color-scanner operator is preparing negatives for scanning. (Linotype-Hell)

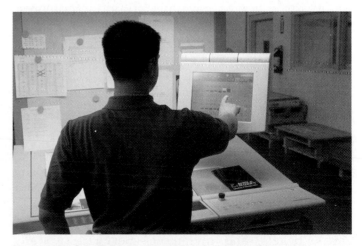

Figure 27-12. Press operators use their skill level and concern for detail to produce high-quality printed products. They also should be comfortable with computer controls.

operators must have excellent color perception because much of the work is in full color. Mechanical ability and artistic appreciation are attributes of a good press operator. Generally speaking, operators of large presses earn more than those who operate small presses because of the increased responsibility associated with expensive equipment. Large presses often require what is known as a *press helper*, who works at the delivery end of the press. He assists the press operator by removing printed press sheets and stacking them on pallets for transfer to the postpress department.

Postpress positions

Binding and finishing operators perform the final operations in the manufacture of a printed product. Binding operations include the assembly and fastening of books, magazines, catalogs, business forms, and calendars. Finishing operations include embossing, drilling, cutting, folding, gathering, collating, sorting, wrapping, labeling, and shipping. The finishing and binding operations are important stages in the manufacture of printed products because an error made here can result in the loss of time, materials, and money. Binding and finishing personnel must have mechanical aptitude and a willingness to perform frequent setups and repetitive tasks on automated equipment. See **Figure 27-13**.

Other Employment Opportunities

In addition to employment at commercial printing companies, people who are knowledgeable about printing can find employment elsewhere. There are in-plant printing facilities, quick-printing facilities, industry vendors, and schools that teach printing. Many students who have an aptitude for prepress work find employment at advertising agencies and in the marketing departments of corporations, as they prepare files for advertisements and promotional materials. They also work for companies that publish books and magazines.

Quick-Printing Facilities

Quick printing consists primarily of businesses with small offset-press equipment and high-speed copiers. See **Figure 27-14**. Quick printers accept many types of jobs. These jobs range from letterheads, reports, and brochures to business forms, cards, tickets, and invitations. Services typically include duplicating, high-speed copying, and simple binding. In addition, most quick printers offer word processing, graphic design, presswork, and basic

Figure 27-13. Work in the postpress department ranges from manual labor to the operation of sophisticated machinery. This cutter operator is preparing a lift of labels. (Hammer Packaging)

Figure 27-14. Quick-print facilities perform prepress, press, and postpress functions with a small staff. Therefore, each employee must be versatile. (The Ink Well)

binding. Workers often have multiple duties because most quick-printing facilities have fewer than 20 employees. This is a definite advantage for people who like varied assignments.

This sector of the printing industry has experienced tremendous growth as the industry has moved toward multiple-color reproduction and electronic printing. Over 40,000 establishments in the United States make $7.9 billion in business a year. As a result, career opportunities are plentiful in every area of production, including design and typesetting, equipment operation, marketing, sales, management, and ownership.

In-Plant Printing Facilities

In-plant printing consists of a printing facility owned and operated within a parent company or organization, such as an airline or insurance company. In-plant printing facilities differ from commercial printers because they print only for the parent company. Companies maintaining in-plant departments use them as a convenience to print such items as invoices, letterheads, newsletters, catalogs, and business forms. Approximately 80,000 in-plant printing departments operate in the United States. Their employment outlook is excellent because many companies can obtain the same professional results in-house as they can from an outside commercial printer.

Printing-Related Fields

An industry as large as printing and publishing requires vast amounts of materials, equipment, and services. As a result, thousands of people work for organizations serving the printing industry. Sales representatives and CSRs work for companies that sell paper, ink, plates, software, equipment, and consumable materials such as blanket wash and shrink-wrap. See **Figure 27-15.** Service bureaus

supply prepress services and, therefore, need people with expertise in image manipulation and page composition software.

Graphic Arts Teachers

Graphic arts teachers prepare people for careers in the printing and publishing industry. They are employed in secondary schools, community colleges, and universities. See **Figure 27-16.** Some teachers work in regional occupational and vocational training centers. Others are employed in private and governmental sectors. Some teachers work in industrial-training and union-sponsored programs within the printing and publishing industry. Graphic arts teachers must have extensive knowledge of offset lithography and the related processes, the ability to communicate their knowledge effectively, and a desire to work with people. In most cases, industrial-printing experience and a college or university degree are requirements for a teaching career.

Finding Employment

People who seek employment in the printing industry and its allied fields enjoy the luxury of choosing from the wide range of companies previously described. Launching a career in any field, however, is an undertaking requiring serious consideration and a proactive approach. Too often, young people do not give much thought to their career until graduation. Much can be done several months before graduation to enhance the process. The key is to match one's personal traits with the most appropriate type of job and work environment. See **Figure 27-17.**

Figure 27-15. Technical representatives work for companies that sell equipment, software, and consumable materials such as plates, blankets, paper, and ink to printers. (Graphpros)

Figure 27-16. Graphic arts teachers share their knowledge with students at the high school and college levels. (Ferris State University, Printing and Imaging Technology Management)

A Prepress Operator

A Press Operator

Figure 27-17. Interests and aptitudes should be assessed when choosing a career. Planners, estimators, schedulers, and prepress personnel work at computer-based workstations. Press operators are responsible for the operation of large, expensive pieces of equipment. (Hopkins Printing, Rockwell International)

A good job rewards an individual in several ways. Salary is the most obvious reward because the income enables a person to provide the basic needs of life and build a savings account. In addition, long-term job satisfaction usually requires feeling a sense of achievement, contributing to the organization and society at large, and growing as a person.

Students can learn about the requirements and job market for a given career by talking with people who work in that field, as well as owners or managers of companies who do the hiring. They can also become aware of the job market in their locality or region of interest. Some possible leads to employment are the following:

- Personnel offices in business and industry.
- Civil-service announcements.
- Employment agencies.
- Newspaper help-wanted classified advertising.
- School placement offices.
- Web sites of printing companies.
- The Web site for a region's printing association.

As graduation approaches, the next step is to begin the process of becoming a candidate for the type of job you have chosen. A current *résumé* that tells what you can do for a potential employer is essential, along with finding out as much as possible about potential employers. Filling out application forms and questionnaires will be easier, and a better impression is likely to be made on prospective

employers, if the candidate has some familiarity with the company. People who have thought carefully about what they would bring to a potential employer gain self-confidence and are better prepared for the interviewing process.

Personal Résumés

A personal résumé is a typed summary representing the candidate to people the candidate has never met. A résumé is an outline of education, employment history, and qualifications. A well-written résumé can make a good first impression and generate an invitation to come in for an interview. Résumés need to be kept up-to-date as the people acquire additional education, take on new duties, or change jobs.

The contents and layout of a personal résumé vary as widely as the individuals who apply for jobs. Certain types of information, however, are required. See **Figure 27-18.** A résumé should be tailored to the job being sought. For example, vague objectives such as "To obtain a challenging position with a good company" do not indicate that the candidate has given much thought to the process. Employers generally agree that a résumé has three primary uses:

- To allow an employer to screen for essential qualifications.
- To introduce a prospective employee. A résumé serves as an expanded business card.

Patricia White

Address	3131 Glenwood Avenue Frankfort, IL 60423 815/599-4212
Objective	To obtain a position as a graphic designer in a medium-sized printing or publishing firm.
Education	Eastern Illinois University, Charleston, IL Bachelor of Arts in Graphic Design, May 2008
Work Experience	8/06 to present Pepco Print, Charleston, IL Type of business: Small quick printer serving mostly walk-in trade. Produces bound/collated copies, letterheads, reports, brochures, cards, tickets, and invitations. Job duties: Electronic and manual layout and design; document center equipment operation; customer service at front counter.
Special Skills	Experienced in the following design applications: QuarkXpress, Adobe Illustrator, Adobe Photoshop, Director, Fractal Design Detailer.
Organizations and Activities	*Member*, Graphic Design Association, Eastern Illinois University, *Committee Member*, University Board Graphics, Eastern Illinois University. *Conference Attendee*, American Center for Design Conference, Chicago, 2008.
	References available upon request.

Annotations:
- Let employers know how well your needs match theirs. *(pointing to Objective)*
- Provide most recent employment information, including starting and ending dates. *(pointing to Work Experience)*
- Briefly describe your areas of responsibility. *(pointing to Job duties)*
- List skills most appropriate to the job you are seeking. *(pointing to Special Skills)*
- Get permission from references before giving out their names and addresses. *(pointing to References)*

Figure 27-18. Examine this sample one-page résumé. The information on a résumé should acquaint a prospective employer with its author's career goal, work experience, education, and skill set. The goal of the résumé is to secure an interview.

- To serve as a guide for a follow-up interview.

In planning the layout and writing of your résumé, remember these important points:

- Keep the résumé simple and only one page.
- Word process the résumé, with detail to a professional appearance.
- Print the résumé on a quality paper.
- Make sure the résumé is neat and accurate in every detail.
- Remember that the person reading the résumé works in the field of graphic communications. Correct spelling, punctuation, spacing, and tabbing are crucial.

Filling out an application and being interviewed are parts of the employment process. Candidates should have already thought about questions they might encounter in either stage, such as why they should be hired, what personal qualities they bring, and where they would like their career to be in five years.

Researching the Company

Learning about the company in question protects the candidate's interests. Information gathered about the company provides applicants with something to talk about besides themselves during an interview and helps them generate thoughtful questions. Knowledge about the company also helps the candidate to make a wise decision if the job is offered.

résumé: a typed summary of a job applicant's education, experience, and previous employment.

Information about a large company can be located through company brochures and annual reports obtained from the company or a public library. Valuable data can also be obtained via the Internet. Important information to know about a prospective employer includes the following:

- The location of the employer's plants and offices and the territory the employer covers.
- The length of time the employer has been in business.
- Products or services the employer provides.
- The name of the owner or president.
- The name and title of the person in charge of hiring.
- Whether the employer is a union or nonunion shop.
- Employee benefits.
- The rate of growth and future prospects.

Applying for Employment

After information has been learned, the candidate is ready to contact the employer. Methods for making initial contact include mailing a letter of application and résumé, inquiring in person about openings, and inquiring about openings by telephone. The decision regarding which method to use depends on how the candidate learned of the position. If it is known that the employer is currently not hiring, the candidate might elect to follow up monthly by inquiring in person or by telephone. Judgment should be used, however, because many employers frown on telephone calls. Candidates should always contact the company's human-resources office.

Summary

A modern offset lithographic printing plant is equipped and staffed to handle all phases of print manufacturing. In these comprehensive operations, employees do everything from initial planning to shipping of the printed product. A very wide range of potential employers exists. Employees of large firms usually specialize in a particular kind of work. In smaller printing companies, each employee typically handles a variety of duties.

Success in today's printing and publishing job market requires preparation and means knowing how to get a job, keep it, and move to another job when appropriate. It is up to the candidate to take the initiative to succeed in building a career. Making the effort to search for rewarding opportunities will pay excellent dividends in the future.

Review Questions

Please do not write in this book. Write your answers on a separate sheet of paper.

1. Moving from manual to _____ technologies has brought a major shift in the skills required for workers in all aspects of the printing industry.
2. _____ are responsible for operating a printing company efficiently and profitably and function as part of a larger team.
3. _____ are responsible for preparing cost figures for every job a printing company handles. They largely determine the profit or loss margin for the company.
4. Distinguish between the estimating and planning functions.
5. Coordinating the time each job will spend in each production center is the work of the _____.
6. A(n) _____ serves as the link between the client and production after the contract is signed.
7. Copywriters, graphic designers, and photographers hold _____ positions.
8. The offset lithography industry offers opportunities to work in administrative, creative, and _____ occupations.
9. Prepress and press operators belong to the _____ occupational group within printing.
10. Why are press operators required to have excellent color perception?
11. Explain why the finishing and binding operations are some of the most important phases in the manufacture of printed products.
12. To a potential employer, the résumé is *not* used to _____.
    A. learn about the applicant
    B. screen for applicants with essential qualifications
    C. provide a basis for the interview
    D. select which applicant will be hired
13. Describe the essential steps that should be followed when seeking employment in the offset lithography industry.

Skill-Building Activities

1. Prepare a one- to two-page report on one of the offset lithography occupations. Also, list what you would like and dislike about the job.

2. Study the help-wanted advertisements in your daily newspaper. Prepare a list of the available offset lithography jobs, including qualifications and salaries. Discuss your findings with other graphic arts students in your class.

3. Prepare a list of occupations with the printing industry. Contact the human-resource people at local printing companies. Ask them to rate the jobs in terms of being in high demand, moderate demand, or low demand. Creative occupations should be evaluated by advertising agencies.

4. Visit a commercial offset lithography firm. Talk with employees in the areas of production, management, and sales concerning the career opportunities, working conditions, salaries, and opportunities for advancement and promotion available.

5. Visit your local or school library. Find a copy of the Occupational Outlook Handbook. Study the information relating to offset lithography. Summarize the information. Share it with other graphic arts students in your class.

6. Talk with owners of local printing companies. Ask what personal traits they look for in potential employees.

7. To identify saturated job markets, cut out local help-wanted ads for creative, administrative, and production positions in the printing and advertising industries. Wait three weeks. Call each employer to ask for the number of applications received and the education and experience of the person who was hired.

Where the Jobs Are (In the Contiguous United States)

New England
(Connecticut, Maine, Massachusetts, New Hampshire, and Rhode Island)
Over 2500 business establishments employ more than 72,000 people. Boston alone has some 700 graphic-communications companies.

Mid-Atlantic
(New Jersey, New York, and Pennsylvania)
The mid-Atlantic area has nearly 197,000 individuals working in over 7600 businesses. The New York City area has more than 1700 operations. Nearby Newark, New Jersey has over 500 operations. Philadelphia has more than 1000 operations.

South Atlantic
(Delaware, District of Columbia, Maryland, West Virginia, Virginia, North Carolina, South Carolina, Georgia, and Florida)
More than 6000 establishments employ more than 152,000 people. Washington DC has over 700 printing facilities employing more than 18,000 people. Printing is the largest manufacturing industry in Washington DC. Atlanta has more than 550 plants employing more than 16,000 people. The Greensboro-Winston Salem, North Carolina area's 230 establishments employ around 8500 people.

East South Central
(Alabama, Kentucky, Mississippi, and Tennessee)
More than 1900 businesses employ over 56,000 people. Nashville has over 200 facilities with more than 7600 employees.

East North Central
(Illinois, Indiana, Michigan, Ohio, and Wisconsin)
Nearly 9000 businesses, the most in any region of the country, employ more than 245,000 people. Chicago alone has over 2000 operations. Detroit has more than 600 operations. Greater Cincinnati has more than 375 operations.

West North Central
(Iowa, Kansas, Minnesota, Missouri, Nebraska, North Dakota, and South Dakota)
Nearly 4000 businesses employ more than 109,000 people. Minneapolis-St. Paul has over 700 businesses with nearly 30,000 employees. In St. Louis, over 450 plants employ around 11,000 people. In-plant operations employ an additional 3000 people.

Mountains
(Arizona, New Mexico, Colorado, Idaho, Montana, Nevada, Utah, and Wyoming)
More than 2300 plants employ over 46,000 people. In Denver alone, over 6500 people work at more than 260 facilities.

West South Central
(Arkansas, Oklahoma, Louisiana, and Texas)
Nearly 4000 plants employ more than 75,000 people. Dallas has over 650 facilities employing more than 16,000 people. Houston's 475 establishments employ more than 9000 people.

Pacific
(California, Oregon, Washington, Hawaii, and Alaska)
More than 7000 businesses employ more than 144,000 people. California has the most graphic-communications firms of any state—more than 6800 firms. This state ranks second only to New York in the number of people employed. Los Angeles has nearly 2000 printing companies. Orange County has more than 600 companies. The greater Portland-Vancouver area's 350 shops employ 9750 people. The Seattle area's 425 companies employ more than 9760 people.

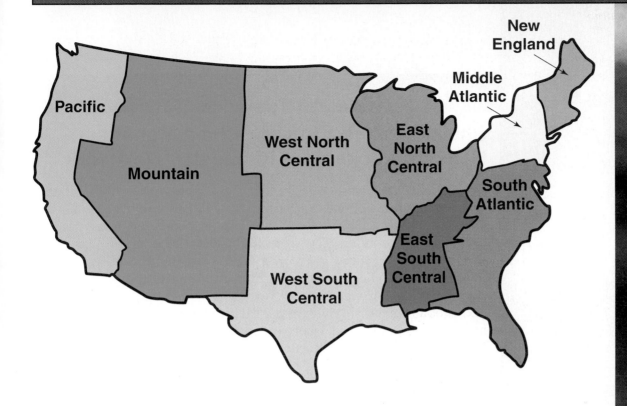

Sheila Soehner; Supply-Chain Manager; Hammer Packaging; Rochester, New York

Sheila's older brother suggested she enroll in her high school's graphic-communications course because the instructor was a very good teacher. In fact, the instructor was so good that, after graduation from a Rochester, New York high school, Sheila enrolled at the University of Northern Iowa on a track scholarship and majored in industrial technology, with a graphic-communications concentration. Her first job was back in Rochester as a lithographic stripper and proofer. Later, she interviewed with Hammer Packaging. Sheila, however, was not hired. She worked as a lithographic stripper for a business-forms printer. During the next several months, she kept in touch with Hammer Packaging because she had been very impressed with the company's product quality and organization.

Hammer Packaging had been impressed with her, as well. Soon, she was hired as the assistant to the prepress supervisor. She coordinated schedules, made sure proofs got out to customers on time, and calculated the x- and y-coordinates for the automatic platemaker. Sheila later accepted an opening in customer service and then became an estimator because she "was always good at math." After 8 years in estimating, she became the supply-chain manager and supervises purchasing for the three printing facilities that are part of the corporation. She has been with Hammer Packaging for 20 years.

Sheila's career path is an example of three concepts. First, acquiring a solid technical background and performing a job well usually lead to new opportunities and advancement. Second, that same solid background prepares a person for a wide range of job titles and duties. Third, not being hired for a particular job should not be interpreted as rejection. If an applicant is impressed with an organization, maintaining a relationship with the company might very well lead to being hired when another position opens.

Bill Fedus, President of Mitchell Graphics

When Bill Fedus graduated from high school in Detroit, he took the opportunity to learn press operation through a trade-union apprenticeship program. In a few years, he became a journeyman press operator. He decided to broaden his skill set and learned estimating.

Bill then relocated from Detroit to Traverse City, Michigan. There, he worked for a small printing company as a press operator. When business became slow, Bill went into sales to generate more business. Later, he learned lithographic stripping and other prepress skills.

He next moved to Petoskey, Michigan. Here, he decided he would like to own a printing company. He remortgaged his home and used the equity to start Mitchell Graphics in 1972. During his career, Bill had learned that the three keys to a successful printing business are quality, service, and price. He strove to keep those three factors at the core of his company.

Bill realized the company could not grow by limiting itself to the local region because Mitchell Graphics was located in a small town. In 1981, he decided to develop a national client base by specializing in postcards for art galleries and other high-end clients. The marketing decision worked. In 1981, Mitchell Graphics had 13 employees. By 1990, however, the company had grown to 45 employees. Today, the company prints for customers from coast to coast. Bill's impressive career demonstrates what can come from taking advantage of opportunities to learn about printing—both in production and in the front office. Each of the many positions he held helped to prepare him for starting his own company and making it successful.

Dominic Pangborn, Owner of Pangborn Design

He was 10 years old when he boarded an airplane in his homeland of South Korea to come to the United States to meet his adoptive family. "To me, America promised to be like Disney World. I had never seen it, but I had learned and heard a lot about it," says Dominic Pangborn. Before long, a Jackson, Michigan family adopted him.

Chances are that the little boy, whose birth mother thought he would have a better life in the United States, would have become a farmer if he had stayed in the tiny Korean village. Instead, he spent the second decade of his life with his Michigan family and became intrigued with color and graphic arts design. By the time he graduated from the Academy of Fine Arts in Chicago, Dominic already had apprenticed at a graphic-design firm. He moved to Detroit and began his career at a multimedia company. There, he designed promotional materials for the 75th anniversary of Ford Motor Company. In 1984, using personal savings, he launched Pangborn Design. Pangborn Design is a company that now has $3 million in annual revenues. His team of 13 employees designs everything from company logos and annual reports to restaurant menus.

Dominic relies on a simple management style. He does not believe in a multilevel reporting structure. Everyone on his staff reports directly to him. In fact, at his headquarters in Detroit River Town, the only levels one finds are among the open offices tucked in and around staircases, lofty corners, and catwalks. No cubicles are allowed. "We're in the communications business, so we need to communicate," says Dominic. Levels are also taboo in dealing with clients. "We don't put account executives between the client and the graphic designer," says Dominic. "Account executives don't think the same way as a creative person."

Dominic's graphic designers and marketers work amid their prized possessions—festive twinkling lights, old bicycles, antique tables and lamps, and the latest computers. The offices are filled with dozens of awards for excellence in graphic design. Some of Dominic's notable clients include Proctor & Gamble Co., Xerox Corp., Blue Cross and Blue Shield of Michigan, Kmart Corp., and Wolverine Worldwide.

Dominic believes companies need art. "Design is one of the most critical assets for companies," he says. Company logos, themes, annual reports, and other images help to communicate a company's mission. Design helps to define what a company is.

So what does it take to be both an inspiring graphic artist and a skilled businessperson? "When I am talking to a client," says Dominic, "I understand their financial needs. Their objective is to make money."

Planning for a Career

One of the most common mistakes young people make is preparing for a career with very limited job opportunities. People who would never arrive at the airport without a confirmed seat on their desired flight invest years in a program of study, only to learn after graduation that there are no positions in the desired field. Instead of investigating the job market before choosing a program of study, they had merely assumed employment would be waiting for them. Often, these people must return to school to get a second education—one more appropriate to the realities of the job market.

Usually, these students selected a field based solely on their personal interest. In other words, they asked, "What would I like to do?" The problem arises when too many people select the same field because, just as there are only so many seats on an airplane, there are only so many jobs in a field. For example, graphic design is a field that has been saturated for many decades. In fact, is not uncommon for an advertised job opening to generate more than 50 applications. Nonetheless, because an increasing number of young people want a job in which they can be creative, the imbalance between graphic-design jobs and candidates for those jobs is growing.

A more realistic approach is to recognize that personal interest is only one of four components of a successful career:

- **Personal interest.** This is the component most young people are well aware of. Choosing an interesting career is essential to looking forward to going to work every day.
- **Talent.** Anyone who has watched television shows such as *American Idol* knows that many people lack the talent needed for the career they want. Remember that, for the person doing the hiring, the key question is not "Is this person qualified?" Instead, it is "Is this person the most qualified of all the candidates?"
- **Credentials.** Many jobs require certain credentials. These credentials might be in the form of a completed course of study, a passing score on a test, a certified skill level, or a specified level of experience. For example, architects must have a degree in architecture. Registered nurses must pass a state board examination. Airline pilots must be certified by the Federal Aviation Administration (FAA). In printing, some jobs might require a high school education. Others require an associate's degree or a bachelor's degree. Other jobs might require a journeyman card or a certain number of years of experience. Graphic-design jobs are likely to also require a portfolio of the candidate's work. When many candidates apply for a job opening, the requirements often are raised to reduce the number of candidates who are interviewed.
- **A need in the marketplace.** If 50 people apply for one job, at least 49 people will not get it, regardless of their education, skill, and experience. In contrast, if only one qualified candidate applies, that person will probably get the job. For this reason, it is crucial that people become aware of the supply-and-demand situation for careers they are considering. In fact, to ensure a reality-based decision, this fourth component should be considered first. Start with a list of careers in demand. Evaluate their appropriateness to you.

  Alternatively, if a particular career is of interest, you can investigate the job market for it in your area. Begin by watching for advertised job openings. When you see one, cut it out. Wait three or four weeks. Contact the company. Ask how many applications were received and what the qualifications of the person who was hired were. Over a period of time, this procedure will provide you with a good feel for the local market for that job.

The purpose of considering all four of these components is for students to avoid investing time and money in pursuit of unrealistic goals. A person's career is worth doing some investigation. A career is far too important to be left to wishes, hopes, and dreams.

Looking for a Career Change

A press operator at a large printing company wants to become a printing estimator. "I'm interested in the business end of the industry, but before I go back to school, I want to know what kinds of opportunities there are in printing estimating and business management. I plan to keep my present job and go to school part-time until I get the degree. I talked to the placement center at the college that I plan to attend, but didn't get much help."

Print estimating and other front office jobs are good options for people who already have experience in printing production. Estimating experience can lead to many other jobs, such as planning, production management, scheduling, purchasing, and inventory control. The printing and publishing industry has many rewarding jobs for employees who wish to change careers. People who work for a printing company and have an interest in a different position with the firm can share their interest with company officials. These officials might help by adjusting work hours and providing tuition reimbursement if further education is needed. People who do not live near a school offering appropriate courses can seek a school offering distance-learning courses over the Internet.

Graphic Arts and Printing Associations

American Forest and Paper Association (AFPA), 1250 Connecticut Avenue NW, 2nd Floor, Washington, DC 20036, (202) 463-2455

American Institute of Graphic Arts (AIGA), 164 Fifth Avenue, New York, NY 10010, (212) 807-1990

Association for Graphic Arts Training (AGAT), c/o Wanda Breeden, Quebecor Printing Corporation, 2501 Powell Avenue, Nashville, TN 37204, (800) 214-1120

Association for Information and Image Management (AIIM), 1100 Wayne Avenue, #1100, Silver Spring, MD 20910-5699, (301) 587-8202

Association of College and University Printers (ACUP), Pennsylvania State University, 107 Business Services Building, University Park, PA 16802, (814) 863-0580

Association of Graphic Communications, 330 7th Avenue, #9, New York, NY 10001-5010, (212) 279-2100

Binders and Finishers Association, 408 8th Avenue, Suite 10A, New York, NY 10001-1816, (212) 629-3232

Business Forms Management Association (BFMA), 319 SW Washington, No. 710, Portland, OR 97204, (503) 227-3393

Digital Printing & Imaging Association, 10015 Main Street, Fairfax, VA 22031-3489, (703) 385-1339, www.dpia.org, dpi@dpia.org

Envelope Manufacturers Association (EMA), 500 Montgomery Street, Suite 550, Alexandria, VA 22314-2536, (703) 739-2200, www.envelope.org

Flexographic Technical Association (FTA), 900 Marconi Avenue, Ronkonkoma, NY 11779-7212, (516) 737-6020, www.flexography.org

GATF, 200 Deer Run Road, Sewickley, PA 15143-2600, (412) 741-6860, info@gatf.org

Graphic Communications Association (GCA/ PIA), 100 Daingerfield Road, 4th Floor, Alexandria, VA 22314-2888, (703) 519-8160

Gravure Association of America, 1200-A Scottsville Road, Rochester, NY 14624-5701, (716) 436-2150, www.gaa.org

IAPHC, 7042 Brooklyn Boulevard, Minneapolis, MN 55429, (800) 466-4274

IdeAlliance—International Digital Enterprise Alliance, 200 Deer Run Road, Sewickley, PA 15143-2600, (412) 741-6860, info@gatf.org

International Graphic Arts Education Association, Inc. (IGAEA), 1899 Preston White Drive, Reston, VA 20191-4367, (703) 758-0595

International Prepress Association, 7200 France Avenue S., Suite 327, Edina, MN 55435, (612) 896-1908

International Publishing Mailing Association (IPMA), 710 Regency Drive, Suite 6, Kearney, MO 64060, (816) 902-4762, www.ipma.org

NAPIM, 581 Main Street, Woodbridge, NJ 07095, (732) 855-1525, www.napim.org

National Association for Printing Leadership, 75 West Century Road, Paramus, NJ 07652-1408, (201) 634-9600, public.napl@napl.org

National Association of Desktop Publishers (NADP), 462 Old Boston Street, Topsfield, MA 01983, (508) 887-7900

National Association of Litho Clubs (NALC), P.O. Box 6190, Shalotte, NC 28470, (910) 575-0399, www.graphicarts.org

Newspaper Association of America, 1921 Gallows Road, Suite 600, Vienna, VA 22182, (703) 902-1000, www.naa.org

North American Graphic Arts Suppliers Association (NAGASA), P.O. Box 934483, Margate, FL 33093, www.nagasa.org

PIA, Inc., 200 Deer Run Road, Sewickley, PA 15143, (412) 741-6860, www.gain.net

PrintImage International, 70 East Lake Street, Suite 333, Chicago, IL 60601, (800) 234-0040, www.printimage.org

Rochester Institute of Technology (RIT), Technical and Education Center, 28 Lomb Memorial Drive, Rochester, NY 14623-5604

SkillsUSA, P.O. Box 3000, Leesburg, VA 20177-0300, (703) 777-8810, www.skillsusa.org

Specialty Graphic Imaging Association, 10015 Main Street, Fairfax, VA 22031

TAPPI, Technology Park, P.O. Box 105113, Atlanta, GA 30348-5113, serviceline@tappi.org (include list of TAPPI Official Test Method, TAPPI USEful Test Methods)

Trade Journals

American Printer, Intertec Publishing Co., 330 N. Wabash, Suite 2300, Chicago, IL 60611, www.americanprinter.com

Graphic Arts Monthly, The Cahmers Publishing Company, 2000 Clearwater Drive, Oak Brook, IL 60523, (630) 288-8538, www.gammag.com

Gravure, Gravure Association of America, Inc., 1200A Scottsville Road, Rochester, NY 14624-5703

High Volume Printing, Innes Publishing Co., Box 7280, Libertyville, IL 60048-7280

In-Plant Printer & Electronic Publisher, Innes Publishing Co., Box 7280, Libertyville, IL 60048-7280

Print-Equip News, 215 Allen Avenue, P.O. Box 5540, Glendale, CA 91201-5540, www.print-equip.com

Printing Impressions, North American Publishing Co., 401 N. Broad Street, #501, Philadelphia, PA 19108-1085, www.piworld.com

Printing Manager, NAPL, 780 Palisade Avenue, Teaneck, NJ 07666-3165

Printing Views, Spencer/Cygnus, 30 East Padonia Road, Suite 504, Timonium, MD 21093

Quick Printing, Cygnus Business Media, 3 Huntington Quadrangle, Suite 301N, Melville, NY 11747, (631) 845-2700

Screen Printing, ST Media Group, 407 Gilbert Avenue, Cincinnati, OH 45202, www.stmediagroup.com

Franchise Information

The U.S. Department of Commerce provided most of the franchisors listed below in two reports entitled *Franchising in the Economy* and *Franchise Opportunities Handbook*. This information might be of help to those who desire additional information related to franchising opportunities in the United States. Acquiring a franchise is one way of starting a printing business. Franchise owners have access to training and resources for marketing.

Allegra Network, 21680 Haggerty Road, Northville, MI 48167, (248) 596-8613

AlphaGraphics, Inc., 268 South State Street, Suite 300, Salt Lake City, UT 84111, www.alphagraphics.com

American Speedy Printing Centers, 32100 Telegraph Road, Birmingham, MI 48010

Big Red Q (Quickprint, Inc.), 2545 W. 237 Street, Suite 2, Torrance, CA 90505

Copy Mat, 48 Shattuck Square, Berkeley, CA 94704

Franklin's Copy Service Inc., 135 International Boulevard, Atlanta, GA 30303

Ink Well, Inc., 2323 Lake Club Drive, Columbus, OH 43227

Insty-Prints Inc., 1215 Marshall Road NE, Minneapolis, MN 55413

Kwik-Kopy Corp., P.O. Box 777, 1 Kwik-Kopy Lane, Cypress, TX 77429

Minuteman Press International, 61 Executive Boulevard, Farmingdale, NY 11735, www.minutemanpress.com

PIP, 26722 Plaza Drive, Suite 200, Mission Viejo, CA 92691, www.pip.com

Printmasters, Inc., 370 S. Crenshaw Boulevard, E 100, Torrance, CA 90503

Print Shack, 500 N. Westshore Boulevard, Suite 610, Tampa, FL 33609-1924

Quick Print, 3345 North Webb Road, Wichita, KS 67226

Sir Speedy Inc., 26722 Plaza Drive, Suite 200, Mission Viejo, CA 92691, (949) 348-5000, www. sirspeedy.com

Zippy Print and Imaging, 4087 Harvester Road, Unit 10, Burlington, ON, Canada L7L 5M3, (905) 681-3155, www.zippyprint.com

Ink Manufacturers

American Ultraviolet Company (for info on UV-curing inks and equipment), Murray Hill, NJ, (908) 665-2211

Braden Sutphin Ink Co., 3650 East 93rd Street, Cleveland, OH 44105, (800) 289-6872, www.bsink.com

Chromatic Technologies, 4870 Centennial Boulevard, Suite 126, Colorado Springs, CO 80919, (719) 592-1557, www.interactivecolors.com

Flint Ink, 4600 Arrowhead Drive, Ann Arbor, MI 48105, (734) 622-6000, www.flintgrp.com

Kohl & Madden Ink, 651 Garden Street, Carlstadt, NJ 07072, (201) 939-8011, www.sunchemical.com/ kandm/Home-Index.html

National Soy Ink Information Center, 4554 NW 114th Street, Urbandale, IA 50322-5410, www.soyink. com, soyink@soyink.com

Superior Printing Ink, 70 Bethune Street, New York, NY 10014, (212) 741-3600, www.superiorink.com

Van Son Holland Ink, Corporation of America, 92 Union Street, Mineola, NY 11501, (800) 645-4182, www. vansonink.com

Alternative Paper-Fiber Resources

Arbokem Canada, Box 95014, South Vancouver CSC, Vancouver, BC V6P 6V4, Canada

Costa Rica Natural, 5000 SW 75th Avenue, Miami, FL 33155, hitmanis@aol.com

Crane & Company, 30 South Street, Dalton, MA 01226, lagiusti@crane.com

Ecosource Paper Inc., 111-1841 Oak Bay Avenue, Victoria, BC V8R 1C4, Canada, ecodette@islandnet.com

Esleeck Manufacturing, P.O. Box 717, Canal Street, Turners Falls, MA 01376

Green Field Paper Co., 4149 Cartagene Drive, Suite A, San Diego, CA 92115, (888) 402-9979, www. greenfieldpaper.com

KP Products/Vision Paper Co., P.O. Box 20399, Albuquerque, NM 87154-0399, kenafman@aol.com

Living Tree Paper Co., 1430 Willamette Street, Suite 367, Eugene, OR 97401, livingtree@dnsi.net

Neenah, 1376 Kimberly Drive, Neenah, WI 54957-0211

Watson Paper Co., 1719 5th Street NW, Albuquerque, NM 87102, info@denim-paper.com

Environmental Resources

Alternative Agricultural Research and Commercialization Corporation (AARCC), U.S. Department of Agriculture (USDA), 0156 South Building, 1400 Independence Avenue SW, Washington, DC 20250-0401

American Bamboo Society, 750 Krumkill Road, Albany, NY 12203-5976

American Institute of Graphic Arts, 164 Fifth Avenue, New York, NY 10010, AIGAnswers@aiga.org

Chlorine Free Products Association, 19 North Main Street, Algonquin, IL 60102, www. chlorinefreeproducts.org

Co-op America's WoodWise Consumer Initiative, 1612 K Street NW, Suite 600, Washington, DC 20006, (800) 584-7336, www.coopamerica.org/programs/ woodwise

Green Seal, 1001 Connecticut Avenue NW, Suite 827, Washington, DC 20036-5525, (202) 872-6400, www.greenseal.org

Industrial Ag Innovations (a firm specializing in research and commercial applications for sustainable agricultural fibers, such as hemp, flax, and kenaf), 2725 North Westwood Boulevard, Suite 7, Poplar Bluff, MO 63901, iagi@pbmo.net

International Kenaf Association, P.O. Box 7, Ladonia, TX 75449

Mid-South Fiber Network/Agro-Tech Communications, 7344 Raleigh Lagrange Road, Cordova, TN 38018, fiber@netten.net

Reach for Unbleached! Foundation, Box 39, Whaletown, BC V0P 1Z0, Canada, www.info@rfu.org

Scientific Certification Systems, 1939 Harrison Street, Suite 400, Oakland, CA 94612

TAPPI, 15 Technology Park Way South, Norcross, GA 30092

TerraChoice Environmental Marketing, 1280 Old Innes, Suite 801, Ottawa, ON K1B5M7, Canada, (800) 478-0399, www.terrachoice.com

Appendix B
Typefaces

There are five classifications of typefaces, and within each classification, there are both obvious and subtle differences that make each style unique. Several typefaces are presented here, grouped by classification. First, look for the one or more characteristics members of a classification share. Look for characteristics that make each typeface distinct. Why is Bauer Bodoni a modern serif typeface, but Caslon 540 and Cheltenham are old-style serif typefaces? What differences distinguish Helvetica from Swiss 721? As you study these type designs, refer to the components identified below for features to compare.

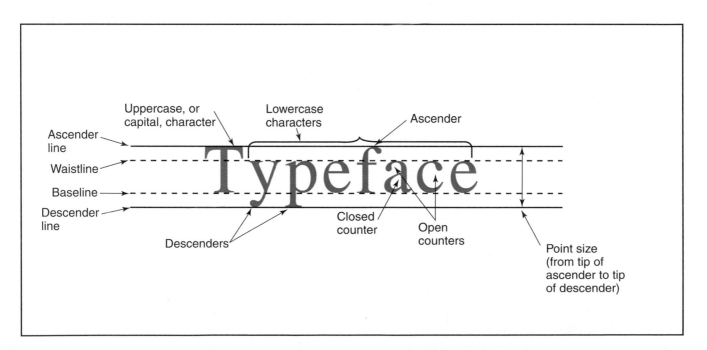

When discussing typefaces, using the correct terminology ensures effective communication.

Serif

Palatino
abcdefghijklmnopqrstuvwxyzABCDEFG

Times
abcdefghijklmnopqrstuvwxyzABCDEFGHIJ

Century Old Style Standard
abcdefghijklmnopqrstuvwxyzABCDEFG

Bauer Bodoni
abcdefghijklmnopqrstuvwxyzABCDEFGHIJKL

Cheltenham
abcdefghijklmnopqrstuvwxyzABCDEFGHIJK

ITC New Baskerville
abcdefghijklmnopqrstuvwxyzABCDEFG

Minion Pro
abcdefghijklmnopqrstuvwxyzABCDEFGHI

Italian Garamond
abcdefghijklmnopqrstuvwxyzABCDEFGHI

Caslon 540
abcdefghijklmnopqrstuvwxyzABCDEFGHI

ITC Garamond
abcdefghijklmnopqrstuvwxyzABCDEFGH

Casablanca
abcdefghijklmnopqrstuvwxyzABCDE

Square Serif

Geometric Slabserif 703
abcdefghijklmnopqrstuvwxyzABCDEF

Courier
abcdefghijklmnopqrstuvwxyzABCD

Playbill
abcdefghijklmnopqrstuvwxyzABCDEFGHIJKLMNOPQRSTUVWXYZ12

Sans Serif

Helvetica
abcdefghijklmnopqrstuvwxyzABCDEFG

Futura
abcdefghijklmnopqrstuvwxyzABCDEFGHIJ

Formata
abcdefghijklmnopqrstuvwxyzABCDEF

Ottawa
abcdefghijklmnopqrstuvwxyzABCDEFGHI

Gothic 812
abcdefghijklmnopqrstuvwxyzABCDEFGHIJKLMNOPQR

KabanaBook
abcdefghijklmnopqrstuvwxyzABCD

News Gothic Standard
abcdefghijklmnopqrstuvwxyzABCDEFGHIJK

Myriad
abcdefghijklmnopqrstuvwxyzABCDEFGHIJ

Swiss 721
abcdefghijklmnopqrstuvwxyzABCDEFGHI

Vogue
abcdefghijklmnopqrstuvwxyzABCDEFGHIJK

Cursive and Script

Ex Ponto
abcdefghijklmnopqrstuvwxyzABCDEFGHIJKL

Amazone
abcdefghijklmnopqrstuvwxyzABCDEFGH

Commercial Script
abcdefghijklmnopqrstuvwxyzABCDEFGHIJ

Freehand 591
abcdefghijklmnopqrstuvwxyzABCDEFGHIJKLM

Berthold Script
abcdefghijklmnopqrstuvwxyzABCDEFGHI

Tekton
abcdefghijklmnopqrstuvwxyzABCDEFGHIJKL

Novelty, Decorative, and Miscellaneous

IRONWOOD
ABCDEFGHIJKLMNOPQRSTUVWXYZABCDEFGHIJKLMNOPQRSTUVWXYZ1

Hollow
abcdefghijklmnopqrstuvwxyzABCDEFG

Lincoln
abcdefghijklmnopqrstuvwxyzABCDEFGHIJ

LIBERTY
ABCDEFGHIJKLMNOPQRSTUVWXYZABCDE

Madrone
abcdefghijklmn

Merlin
abcdefghijklmnopqrstuvwxyzABCDE

Kids
abcdefghijklmnopqrstuvwxyzABC

GEOMETRIC SLABSERIF 703
ABCDEFGHIJKLMNOPQRSTUVWXYZABCD

Caslon Openface
abcdefghijklmnopqrstuvwxyzABCDEFGHIJ

Southern
abcdefghijklmnopqrstuvwxyzABCDEFGH

Orbit-B
abcdefghijklmnopqrstuvwxyzABCDEFGH

PALETTE
ABCDEFGHIJKLMNOPQRSTUVWXYZABCDEFG

Penguin
abcdefghijklmnopqrstuvwxyzABCDEFGHIJKLMN

ROSEWOOD STANDARD
ABCDEFGHIJKLMNOPQRSTUVWXYZABCD

STENCIL
ABCDEFGHIJKLMNOPQRSTUVWXYZ

UMBRA
ABCDEFGHIJKLMNOPQRSTUVWXYZABCD

Appendix C
Useful Information

Prefix	Symbol	Multiplication Factor	
exa	E	$10^{18} =$	1,000,000,000,000,000,000
peta	P	$10^{15} =$	1,000,000,000,000,000
tera	T	$10^{12} =$	1,000,000,000,000
giga	G	$10^{9} =$	1,000,000,000
mega	M	$10^{6} =$	1,000,000
kilo	k	$10^{3} =$	1,000
hecto	h	$10^{2} =$	100
deca	da	$10^{1} =$	10
(unit)		$10^{0} =$	1
deci	d	$10^{-1} =$	0.1
centi	c	$10^{-2} =$	0.01
milli	m	$10^{-3} =$	0.001
micro	u	$10^{-6} =$	0.000001
nano	n	$10^{-9} =$	0.000000001
pico	p	$10^{-12} =$	0.000000000001
femto	f	$10^{-15} =$	0.000000000000001
atto	a	$10^{-18} =$	0.000000000000000001

Figure C-1. U.S. Customary and metric conversion factors and prefixes.

When you know ↓	Multiply by: Very accurate	Approximate	To find ↓
Length			
inches	*25.4		millimeters
inches	*2.54		centimeters
feet	*0.3048		meters
feet	*30.48		centimeters
yards	*0.9144	0.9	meters
miles	*1.609344	1.6	kilometers
Weight			
grains	15.43236	15.4	grams
ounces	*28.349523125	28.0	grams
ounces	*0.028349523125	0.028	kilograms
pounds	*0.45359237	0.45	kilograms
short ton	*0.90718474	0.9	tonnes
Volume			
teaspoons	*4.97512	5.0	milliliters
tablespoons	*14.92537	15.0	milliliters
fluid ounces	29.57353	30.0	milliliters
cups	*0.236588240	0.24	liters
pints	*0.473176473	0.47	liters
quarts	*0.946352946	0.95	liters
gallons	*3.785411784	3.8	liters
cubic inches	*0.016387064	0.02	liters
cubic feet	*0.028316846592	0.03	cubic meters
cubic yards	*0.764554857984	0.76	cubic meters
Area			
square inches	*6.4516	6.5	square centimeters
square feet	*0.09290304	0.09	square meters
square yards	*0.83612736	0.8	square meters
square miles	*2.589989	2.6	square kilometers
acres	*0.40468564224	0.4	hectares
Temperature			
Fahrenheit		* 5/9 (after subtracting 32)	Celsius

* = Exact

Figure C-2. Conversion table—U.S. Customary to SI metric.

When you know	Multiply by:		To find
↓	Very accurate	Approximate	↓

	Length		
millimeters	*0.03933701	0.04	inches
centimeters	*0.3937008	0.4	inches
meters	*3.280840	3.3	feet
meters	*1.093613	1.1	yards
kilometers	*0.621371	0.6	miles
	Weight		
grams	*0.03527396	0.035	ounces
kilograms	*2.204623	2.2	pounds
tonnes	*1.1023113	1.1	short tons
	Volume		
milliliters	*0.20001	0.2	teaspoons
milliliters	*0.06667	0.067	tablespoons
milliliters	*0.03381402	0.03	fluid ounces
liters	*61.02374	61.024	cubic inches
liters	*2.113376	2.1	pints
liters	*1.056688	1.06	quarts
liters	*0.26417205	0.26	gallons
liters	*0.03531467	0.035	cubic feet
cubic meters	*61023.74	61023.7	cubic inches
cubic meters	*35.31467	35.0	cubic feet
cubic meters	*1.3079506	1.3	cubic yards
cubic meters	*264.17205	264.0	gallons
	Area		
square centimeters	*0.1550003	0.16	square inches
square centimeters	*0.001077639	0.001	square feet
square meters	*10.76391	10.8	square feet
square meters	*1.195990	1.2	square yards
square kilometers	*0.3861019	0.4	square miles
hectares	*2.471054	2.5	acres
	Temperature		
Celsius		* 9/5 (then add 32)	Fahrenheit

* = Exact

Figure C-3. Conversion table—SI metric to U.S. Customary.

Measures of Length	Measures of Weight	Measures of Liquid Volume
10 millimeters = 1 centimeter (cm) 10 centimeters = 1 decimeter (dm) 10 decimeters = 1 meter (m) 10 meters = 1 decameter (dam) 10 decameters = 1 hectometer (hm) 10 hectometers = 1 kilometer (km) 10 kilometers = 1 myriameter (mym)	10 milligrams = 1 centigram (cg) 10 centigrams = 1 decigram (dg) 10 decigrams = 1 hectogram (hg) 10 hectograms = 1 kilogram (kg) 10 kilograms = 1 myriagram (myg) 10 myriagrams = 1 quintal (q) 10 quintals = 1 millier or metric ton (MT or t)	10 milliliters = 1 centiliter (cl) 10 centiliters = 1 deciliter (dl) 10 deciliters = 1 liter (l) 10 liters = 1 decaliter (dal) 10 decaliters = 1 hectoliter (hl) 10 hectoliters = 1 kiloliter (kl)

Figure C-4. Metric units.

FRACTION	INCHES	M/M		FRACTION	INCHES	M/M
1/64	.01563	.397		33/64	.51563	13.097
1/32	.03125	.794		17/32	.53125	13.494
3/64	.04688	1.191		35/64	.54688	13.891
1/16	.6250	1.588		9/16	.56250	14.288
5/64	.07813	1.984		37/64	.57813	14.684
3/32	.09375	2.381		19/32	.59375	15.081
7/64	.10938	2.778		39/64	.60938	15.478
1/8	.12500	3.175		5/8	.62500	15.875
9/64	.14063	3.572		41/64	.64063	16.272
5/32	.15625	3.969		21/32	.65625	16.669
11/64	.17188	4.366		43/64	.67188	17.066
3/16	.18750	4.763		11/16	.68750	17.463
13/64	.20313	5.159		45/64	.70313	17.859
7/32	.21875	5.556		23/32	.71875	18.256
15/64	.23438	5.953		47/64	.73438	18.653
1/4	.25000	6.350		3/4	.75000	19.050
17/64	.26563	6.747		49/64	.76563	19.447
9/32	.28125	7.144		25/32	.78125	19.844
19/64	.29688	7.541		51/64	.79688	20.241
5/16	.31250	7.938		13/16	.81250	20.638
21/64	.32813	8.334		53/64	.82813	21.034
11/32	.34375	8.731		27/32	.84375	21.431
23/64	.35938	9.128		55/64	.85938	21.828
3/8	.37500	9.525		7/8	.87500	22.225
25/64	.39063	9.922		57/64	.89063	22.622
13/32	.40625	10.319		29/32	.90625	23.019
27/64	.42188	10.716		59/64	.92188	23.416
7/16	.43750	11.113		15/16	.93750	23.813
29/64	.45313	11.509		61/64	.95313	24.209
15/32	.46875	11.906		31/32	.96875	24.606
31/64	.48438	12.303		63/64	.98438	25.003
1/2	.50000	12.700		1	1.00000	25.400

Figure C-5. A decimal conversion chart.

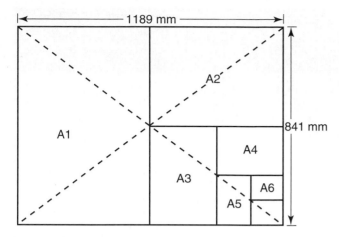

Figure C-6. ISO A-series paper.

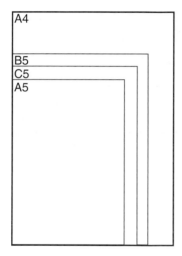

Figure C-7. The relationships among ISO A-, B-, and C-series papers.

ISO Sizes	Millimeters	Inches
2A	1189 x 1682	46.81 x 66.22
A0	841 x 1189	33.11 x 46.81
A1	594 x 841	23.39 x 33.11
A2	420 x 594	16.54 x 23.39
A3	297 x 420	11.69 x 16.54
A4	210 x 297	8.27 x 11.69
A5	148 x 210	5.83 x 8.27
A6	105 x 148	4.13 x 5.83
A7	74 x 105	2.91 x 4.13
A8	52 x 74	2.05 x 2.91
A9	37 x 52	1.46 x 2.05
A10	26 x 37	1.02 x 1.46

Figure C-8. ISO A-series paper sizes (metric and U.S. Customary measurements).

ISO Sizes	Millimeters	Inches
B0	1000 x 1414	39.37 x 55.67
B1	707 x 1000	27.83 x 39.37
B2	500 x 707	19.68 x 27.83
B3	353 x 500	13.90 x 19.68
B4	250 x 353	9.84 x 13.90
B5	175 x 250	6.93 x 9.84
B6	125 x 176	4.92 x 6.93
B7	88 x 125	3.46 x 4.92
B8	62 x 88	2.44 x 3.46
B9	44 x 62	1.73 x 2.44
B10	31 x 44	1.22 x 1.73

Figure C-9. ISO B-series paper sizes (metric and U.S. Customary measurements).

R Series	Bond 17" x 22" (432 mm x 559 mm) (g/m²)	Cover 20" x 26" (508 mm x 660 mm) (lb/ream)	Index 25 1/2" x 30 1/2" (648 mm x 775 mm) (lb/ream)	Newsprint 24" x 36" (610 mm x 914 mm) (lb/ream)	Book 25" x 38" (635 mm x 965 mm) (lb/ream)
20.0	5.32	7.39	11.00	12.29	13.51
22.4	5.95	8.28	12.39	13.77	15.13
25.0	6.65	9.24	13.83	15.36	16.89
28.0	7.44	10.35	15.49	17.21	18.92
31.5	8.37	11.65	17.43	19.36	21.28
45.0	11.97	16.64	24.89	27.66	30.40
50.0	13.30	18.49	27.66	30.73	33.78
56.0	14.89	20.71	30.98	34.42	37.84
63.0	16.75	23.30	34.85	38.72	42.57
71.0	18.88	26.26	39.28	43.63	47.97
85.0	22.61	31.45	46.90	52.27	57.46
100.0	26.60	36.98	55.32	61.46	67.57
112.0	29.79	41.42	61.96	68.83	75.68
140.0	37.24	51.78	77.45	86.04	94.60
180.0	47.88	66.57	99.58	110.62	121.63
200.0	53.20	73.97	110.64	122.91	135.14
250.0	66.50	92.46	138.30	153.64	168.93
400.0	106.41	147.95	221.29	245.83	270.29

Figure C-10. The R20 series of paper weights and equivalent weights.

Trimmed Page Size (Inches)	Number of Printed Pages	Number from Sheet	Standard Paper Size
4 x 9	4	12	25 × 30
	8	12	38 × 50
	12	4	25 × 38
	16	6	38 × 50
	24	2	25 × 38
4 1/4 x 5 3/8	4	32	35 × 45
	8	16	35 × 45
	16	8	35 × 45
	32	4	35 × 45
4 1/2 x 6	4	16	25 × 38
	8	8	25 × 35
	16	4	25 × 38
	32	2	25 × 38
5 1/2 x 8 1/2	4	16	35 × 45
	8	8	35 × 45
	16	4	35 × 45
	32	2	35 × 45
6 x 9	4	8	25 × 38
	8	4	25 × 38
	16	2	25 × 38
	32	2	38 × 50
8 1/2 x 11	4	4	25 × 35
	8	2	25 × 35
	16	2	25 × 45
9 x 12	4	4	25 × 38
	8	2	25 × 38
	16	2	25 × 50

Figure C-11. Cutting charts. Using standard paper sizes can prevent waste, while using odd-size pages can create excess waste and also increase costs, if the correct quantity has not been ordered or there is not enough time to order special-size paper. This chart shows the number of pages to several standard paper sizes. The paper size includes trim top, bottom, and sides. This size does not include bleed.

Grade of Paper	Book 25 x 38	Bond 17 x 22	Cover 20 x 26	Bristol 22 1/2 x 28 1/2	Index 25 1/2 x 30 1/2	Tag 24 x 36	g/m²
Book	**30**	12	16	20	25	27	44
	40	16	22	27	33	36	59
	45	18	25	30	37	41	67
	50	20	27	34	41	45	74
	60	24	33	40	49	55	89
	70	28	38	47	57	64	104
	80	31	44	54	65	73	118
	90	35	49	60	74	82	133
	100	39	55	67	82	91	148
	120	47	66	80	98	109	178
Bond	33	**13**	18	22	27	30	49
	41	**16**	22	27	33	37	61
	51	**20**	28	34	42	46	75
	61	**24**	33	41	50	56	90
	71	**28**	39	48	58	64	105
	81	**32**	45	55	67	74	120
	91	**36**	50	62	75	83	135
	102	**40**	56	69	83	93	158
Cover	91	36	**50**	62	75	82	135
	110	43	**60**	74	90	100	163
	119	47	**65**	80	97	108	176
	146	58	**80**	99	120	134	216
	164	65	**90**	111	135	149	243
	183	72	**100**	124	150	166	271
Bristol	100	39	54	**67**	81	91	148
	120	47	65	**80**	98	109	178
	148	58	81	**100**	121	135	219
	176	70	97	**120**	146	162	261
	207	82	114	**140**	170	189	306
	237	93	130	**160**	194	216	351
Index	110	43	60	74	**90**	100	163
	135	53	74	91	**110**	122	203
	170	67	93	115	**140**	156	252
	208	82	114	140	**170**	189	328
Tag	110	43	60	74	90	**100**	163
	137	54	75	93	113	**125**	203
	165	65	90	111	135	**150**	244
	192	76	105	130	158	**175**	284
	220	87	120	148	180	**200**	326
	275	109	151	186	225	**250**	407

Figure C-12. Equivalent weights, in reams of 500 sheets. Basis weights are in bold type.

Book (25 x 38)	This grade encompasses the widest range of printing papers. As the name implies, book grade is widely used for books. Other uses include magazines, folders, pamphlets, posters, and other commercial printing. The different grades of book paper are coated (enamel), uncoated, offset, text, and label.
Cover (20 x 26)	Many grades of coated, text, and book papers are made in matching cover weights. There are also many special cover papers with a variety of surface textures, coatings, and finishes.
Bond (17 x 22)	Primarily used for stationery and business forms, this category also includes ledger and writing grades. Available in a wide range of colors and weights. Surfaces accept typewriter and writing inks and erase easily. There are two types: sulphite and cotton fiber (rag content). More costly bonds are made with 25% to 100% cotton fiber.
Index Bristol (25 1/2 x 30 1/2)	Characterized by stiffness and receptivity to printing inks, index is used wherever a stiff, inexpensive paper is required.
Printing (Mill) Bristol (22 1/2 x 28 1/2)	Generally stiffer than index, printing bristols are widely used for menus, greeting cards, covers, and tickets.
Newsprint (24 x 36)	This inexpensive grade is limited primarily to cost-critical uses.

Figure C-13. Printing papers. All papers have certain properties and characteristics affecting printability and quality. Printability and quality are not always related. The finest quality of paper might not always print well. Weight, bulk, caliper, grain direction, color, opacity, surface texture, coatings, and strength are some of the factors to consider before selecting paper. Papers are generally classified and defined in terms of use, as suggested by the grade names listed in this chart. Basic sizes are shown in parentheses.

Basis 25 x 38	30	35	40	45	50	60	70	80	90	100	120	150
17½ x 22½	25	29	33	37	41	50	58	66	75	83	99	124
19 x 25	30	35	40	45	50	60	70	80	90	100	120	150
20 x 26	33	38	44	49	55	66	77	88	99	109	131	164
22½ x 29	41	48	55	62	69	82	96	110	124	137	165	206
22½ x 35	50	58	66	75	83	99	116	133	149	166	199	249
23 x 29	42	49	56	63	70	84	98	112	126	140	169	211
23 x 35	51	59	68	76	85	102	119	136	153	169	203	254
24 x 36	55	64	73	82	91	109	127	146	164	182	218	273
25 x 38	60	70	80	90	100	120	140	160	180	200	240	300
26 x 40	66	77	88	99	109	131	153	175	197	219	263	328
28 x 42	74	87	99	111	124	149	173	198	223	248	297	371
28 x 44	78	91	104	117	130	156	182	207	233	259	311	389
30½ x 41	79	92	105	118	132	158	184	211	237	263	316	395
32 x 44	89	104	119	133	148	178	207	237	267	296	356	445
33 x 44	92	107	122	138	153	183	214	245	275	306	367	459
35 x 45	99	116	133	149	166	199	232	265	298	332	398	497
35 x 46	102	119	136	153	169	203	237	271	305	339	407	508
36 x 48	109	127	146	164	182	218	255	291	327	364	437	546
38 x 50	120	140	160	180	200	240	280	320	360	400	480	600
38 x 52	125	146	166	187	208	250	291	333	374	416	499	624
41 x 54	140	163	186	210	233	280	326	373	419	466	559	699
41 x 61	158	184	211	237	263	316	369	421	474	527	632	790
42 x 58	154	179	205	231	256	308	359	410	462	513	615	769
44 x 64	178	207	237	267	296	356	415	474	534	593	711	889
44 x 66	183	214	245	275	306	367	428	489	550	611	734	917
46 x 69	200	234	267	301	334	401	468	535	601	668	802	1000
46½ x 67½	198	231	264	297	330	396	463	529	593	661	793	991
52 x 76	250	291	333	374	416	499	582	666	749	832	998	1248

Book, Offset, Label (Coated and Uncoated), and Text

Basis Size 17 × 12	13	16	20	24	28	32	36	40
8½ x 11	6.5	8.0	10	12	14	16	18	20
8½ x 14	8.3	10.2	12.7	15.3	17.8	20.4	22.9	25.5
11 x 17	13	16	20	24	28	32	36	40
16 x 21	23	29	36	43	50	57	65	72
16 x 42	47	58	72	86	101	115	130	144
17 x 22	26	32	40	48	56	64	72	80
17 x 26	31	38	47	57	66	76	85	95
17½ x 22½	27	34	42	51	59	67	76	84
17 x 28	33	41	51	61	71	81	92	102
18 x 23	29	36	44	53	62	71	80	89
18 x 46	58	71	89	106	124	142	160	178
19 x 24	32	39	49	59	68	78	88	98
19 x 28	37	46	57	68	80	91	102	114
19 x 48	63	78	98	117	137	156	176	195
20 x 28	39	48	60	72	84	96	108	120
21 x 32	47	58	72	86	101	115	130	144
22 x 25½	39	48	60	72	84	96	108	120
22 x 34	52	64	80	96	112	128	144	160
22½ x 22½	35	43	54	65	76	87	97	108
22½ x 28½	45	55	69	82	96	110	123	137
22½ x 34½	54	66	83	100	116	133	149	166
22½ x 35	55	67	84	101	118	135	152	168
23 x 36	58	71	89	106	124	142	159	177
24 x 38	63	78	98	117	137	156	176	195
24½ x 24½	42	51	64	77	90	103	116	128
24½ x 28½	49	60	75	90	105	120	135	150
24½ x 29	50	61	76	91	106	122	137	152
24½ x 38½	66	81	101	121	141	161	182	202
24½ x 39	66	82	102	122	143	164	184	204
25½ x 44	78	96	120	144	168	192	216	240
26 x 35	61	76	94	113	132	151	170	189
28 x 34	66	82	102	122	143	163	184	204
28 x 38	74	91	114	136	159	182	205	228
34 x 44	104	128	160	192	224	256	288	320
35 x 45	109	135	168	202	236	270	303	337

Bond, Business, Writing, and Ledger

Figure C-14. Standard paper sizes and weights. It has been traditional practice to price papers based on a ream (500 sheets). 1M pricing is replacing this. These tables give the weight per 1M sheets for common sizes and weights of different paper grades.

Basis Weights in Boldface

	Bond 17 x 22	Book 25 x 38	Cover 20 x 26	Index 25½ x 30½	Bristol 22½ x 28½
Bond	**13**	33	18	27	22
	16	41	22	34	28
	20	51	28	42	34
	24	61	33	50	42
	28	71	39	58	48
	32	81	45	66	55
	36	91	50	75	62
	40	102	56	83	68
Book	12	**30**	16	25	20
	16	**40**	22	33	27
	18	**45**	25	37	30
	20	**50**	27	41	33
	22	**55**	30	45	37
	24	**60**	33	49	41
	26	**65**	36	53	44
	28	**70**	38	57	47
	30	**75**	41	61	50
	31	**80**	44	65	54
	35	**90**	49	74	61
	39	**100**	55	82	68
	47	**120**	66	98	81
Cover	18	46	**25**	38	31
	25	64	**35**	52	42
	29	73	**40**	60	50
	36	91	**50**	75	62
	40	100	**55**	82	68
	43	110	**60**	90	74
	47	119	**65**	97	80
	58	146	**80**	120	99
	65	164	**90**	135	111
	72	183	**100**	150	123
Index	43	110	60	**90**	74
	53	135	74	**110**	91
	67	171	93	**140**	116
	82	208	114	**170**	140
Bristol	52	133	73	109	**90**
	58	148	81	121	**100**
	70	178	97	146	**120**
	82	207	114	170	**140**
	93	237	130	194	**160**
	105	267	146	218	**180**

**Equivalent Weights in Reams
of 500 Sheets**

Figure C-14. *(Continued)*

Weight per 1000 Sheets

Basis Size 22½ x 28½	67	80	90	94	100	110	120	140	160
22½ x 28½	134	160	180	188	200	220	240	280	320
22½ x 35	165	196	221	231	246	270	295	344	393
23 x 35	168	201	226	236	251	276	301	352	402
26 x 40	217	259	292	305	324	357	389	454	519
28½ x 45	268	320	360	376	400	440	480	560	640

Printing Bristol

Weight per 1000 Sheets

Basis 20 x 26	50	60	65	80	90	100	130
20 x 26	100	120	130	160	180	200	260
22½ x 28½	123	148	160	197	222	247	321
23 x 29	128	154	167	205	231	257	333
23 x 5	155	186	201	248	279	310	403
26 x 40	200	240	260	320	360	400	520
35 x 46	310	372	403	495	557	619	805

Cover

Weight per 1000 Sheets

Basis Size 25½ x 30½	90	120	140	170	220
20½ x 24¾	117	157	183	222	287
22½ x 28½	148	198	231	280	263
22½ x 35	182	243	284	344	446
25½ x 30½	180	240	280	340	440
28½ x 45	297	356	462	561	726

Index Bristol

Formula:	Weight of 1000 sheets x the number of sheets ÷1000 = total weight
Example:	Determine the weight of 1765 sheets of 25 x 38 x 80 (160M) lb stock.
Solution:	160 x 1765 = 282,400 ÷ 1000 = 282.4 lbs.

Figure C-15. Finding the weight of a number of sheets.

Basis Weight	Paper Finish			
	Coated	Smooth	Vellum	Antique
Book				
40		.0025	.0031	.0034
45	.0021	.0028	.0035	.0037
50	.0023	.0031	.0038	.0041
60	.0028	.0038	.0046	.0050
70	.0034	.0044	.0054	.0058
80	.0040	.0050	.0059	.0065
90	.0046	.0057	.0065	.0074
100	.0052	.0063	.0071	.0082
120	.0060	.0076	.0082	.0100
150	.0072	.0095	.0106	.0123
Cover				
50		.0058	.0070	.0075
60	.0056			
65		.0075	.0092	.0097
80	.0072	.0093	.0113	.0120
90		.0106	.0130	.0135
100	.0092	.0116	.0140	.0150
130		.0150	.0184	.0190
Bond				
13		.0021	.0025	.0027
16		.0026	.0031	.0033
20		.0032	.0039	.0042
24		.0038	.0047	.0050
Index				
90		.0080	.0084	
110		.0096	.0104	
140		.0132	.0140	
170		.0144	.0160	
Bristol				
90	.0055	.0069	.0084	.0090
100	.0061	.0076	.0093	.0100
120	.0073	.0092	.0111	.0120
140	.0085	.0107	.0130	.0140
160	.0097	.0122	.0148	.0160
180	.0110	.0137	.0167	.0180
200	.0122	.0153	.0185	.0200
220	.0134	.0167	.0204	.0220

Figure C-17. Caliper equivalents. The numbers provided are averages. Variations occur in mill runs.

Problem: Determine the weight of a roll of coated (2 sides) book paper that is 30" in diameter and 38" wide.

1. Square the diameter: 30 x 30 = 900

2. Multiply the result by the roll width: 900 x 38 = 34,200

3. Multiply by given factor (.034): 34,200 x .034 = 1162.8

Answer: 1163 lbs.

Factors:	(These average factors apply for all weights)
Newsprint	0.016
Antique finish	0.018
Machine finish, English finish, Offset, Bond	0.027
Supercalendered (coated 1 side)	0.030
Coated 2 sides	0.034

Figure C-16. How to find the weight of a roll of paper.

Diameter (Inches)	All Bond	Regular Ledger	Posting Ledger	Regular Offset	Regular Tagboard
10	1.86	2.34	1.98	2.10	2.55
12	2.83	3.37	2.94	3.12	3.74
14	3.92	4.58	4.07	4.32	5.07
16	5.13	5.99	5.38	5.71	6.86
18	6.60	7.58	6.86	7.27	8.01
20	8.23	9.35	8.51	9.04	10.21
22	10.00	11.16	10.28	10.90	12.47
24	11.90	13.34	12.30	13.05	14.56
25	13.10	14.62	13.42	14.22	15.96
26	14.10	15.80	14.53	15.41	17.24
27	15.30	17.05	15.68	16.63	18.60
28	16.40	18.33	16.88	17.90	20.00
29	17.70	19.66	18.12	19.22	21.46
30	18.90	21.05	19.40	20.58	22.96
31	20.02	22.45	20.73	21.99	24.62
32	21.60	23.93	22.10	23.45	26.10
33	22.90	26.52	23.52	24.95	27.78
34	24.20	27.89	24.98	26.49	29.49
35	25.70	29.86	26.48	28.06	31.25
36	27.00	31.60	28.03	29.73	33.06
37	28.70	33.39	29.61	31.41	34.93
38	30.20	35.23	31.25	33.15	36.83
39	31.90	37.13	32.93	34.92	38.81
40	33.70	39.06	34.65	36.75	40.82

Figure C-18. Approximate roll weights per inch of width. (International Paper Co.)

No. Out of Sheet	Quantity of Pressrun									
	500	1000	1500	2000	2500	3000	3500	4000	4500	5000
1	500	1000	1500	2000	2500	3000	3500	4000	4500	5000
2	250	500	750	1000	1250	1500	1750	2000	2250	2500
3	167	334	500	667	834	1000	1167	1334	1500	1667
4	125	250	375	500	625	750	875	1000	1125	1250
5	100	200	300	400	500	600	700	800	900	1000
6	84	167	250	334	417	500	584	667	750	834
7	72	143	215	286	358	429	500	572	643	715
8	63	125	188	250	313	375	438	500	563	625
9	56	112	167	223	278	334	389	445	500	556
10	50	100	150	200	250	300	350	400	450	500
11	46	91	137	182	228	273	319	364	410	455
12	42	84	126	168	209	250	292	334	375	417
13	39	77	116	154	193	231	270	308	347	385
14	36	72	108	144	179	215	250	286	322	358
15	34	67	100	134	167	200	234	267	300	334
16	32	63	94	125	157	188	219	250	282	313
17	30	59	89	118	148	177	206	236	265	295
18	28	56	84	112	139	167	195	223	250	279
19	27	53	79	106	132	158	185	211	237	264
20	25	50	75	100	125	150	175	200	225	250
21	24	48	72	96	120	143	167	191	215	239
22	23	46	69	91	114	137	160	182	205	228
23	22	44	66	87	109	131	153	174	196	218
24	21	42	63	84	105	125	146	167	188	209
25	20	40	60	80	100	120	140	160	180	200
26	20	39	58	77	97	116	135	154	174	193
27	19	38	56	75	93	112	130	149	167	186
28	18	36	54	72	90	108	125	143	161	179
29	18	36	54	72	87	103	121	138	156	173
30	17	34	51	67	84	100	117	134	150	167
31	17	33	49	65	81	97	113	130	146	162
32	16	32	47	63	79	94	110	125	141	157
33	16	31	46	61	76	91	107	122	137	152
34	15	30	45	59	74	89	103	118	133	148
35	15	29	43	58	72	86	100	115	129	143
36	14	28	42	56	70	84	98	112	125	139
37	14	28	41	55	68	82	95	109	122	136
38	14	27	40	53	66	79	93	106	119	132
39	13	26	39	52	65	77	90	103	116	131
40	13	25	38	50	63	75	88	100	113	125

Figure C-19. Paper-stock estimator. Use this chart to determine how many sheets are needed for a particular job. For example, a job calls for 4000 pieces that cut 16 out of 1 sheet. Follow the first column to 16, and then read across that line to the 4000 column. The result is 250 sheets. (No spoilage is included.)

To determine the approximate number of linear feet in a roll of paper, use the formula and factors shown below.

Formula: $\dfrac{\text{Net Weight} \times 12 \times (\text{Factor})}{\text{Basis Weight} \times \text{Width}}$ = Linear Feet

Paper	Factors
Bond	1300
Cover	1805
Book or Offset	3300
Vellum Bristol (22 1/2" x 28 1/2")	2230
Index (25 1/2" x 30 1/2")	2700
Printing Bristol (22 1/2" x 35")	2739
Wrapping, Tissue, Newsprint, Waxing (24" x 36")	3070
Tag	3000

Example: Find the number of linear feet in a roll of form bond (20" width, sub. 16 lbs., net weight 750 lbs.)

$$\frac{750 \times 12 \times 1300}{16 \times 20} = 36{,}562.5 = 36{,}563 \text{ Linear Feet}$$

To obtain a more exact approximation of linear feet, use the formula below:

$$\frac{[(\text{Roll Radius})^2 \times (3.1416)] - [(\text{Core Radius})^2 \times 3.1416)]}{\text{Paper Thickness}} = \text{Linear Inches}$$

$$\frac{\text{Linear Inches}}{12} = \text{Linear Feet}$$

Figure C-20. The approximate number of linear feet in rolls. (Zellerbach Paper Co.)

PROOF SYMBOLS USED TO CORRECT ERRORS IN LINES OF TYPE

⊙ Change this to a period. It marks the

A comma, inserted here will make more

Machinecast is a compound word when

The printers work is most interesting

Place a colon here this is a place to

Semi-colon one should be inserted here

Quotation marks are called "quotes by

Delete, or take out, a characters marked

Sp out The meeting was held in Columbus, Ⓞ.

THE LINES AFTER CORRECTIONS HAVE BEEN MADE

Change this to a period. It marks the

A comma, inserted here, will make more

Machine-cast is a compound word when

The printer's work is most interesting

Place a colon here: this is a place to

Semi-colon; one should be inserted here

Quotation marks are called "quotes" by

Delete, or take out, a character marked

The meeting was held in Columbus, Ohio

⊙	Insert period	tr	Transpose ¹—used in margin	⊏	Move left
	Insert comma	∿	Transpose ²—used in text	⊓	Move up
:/	Insert colon	sp	Spell out	⊔	Move down
;/	Insert semicolon	ital	Italic—used in margin	‖	Align vertically
at?	Insert question mark		Italic—used in text	—	Align horizontally
at!	Insert exclamation mark	b.f.	Boldface—used in margin	⊐⊏	Center horizontally
=/	Insert hyphen		Boldface—used in text		Center vertically
	Insert apostrophe	s.c.	Small caps—used in margin	⌣	Push down space
	Insert quotation marks		Small caps—used in text	⌢	Use ligature
⅟N	Insert 1-en dash	rom.	Roman type	eq.#	Equalize space—used in margin
⅟M	Insert 1-em dash	caps.	Caps—used in margin	∨∨∨	Equalize space—used in text
#	Insert space		Caps—used in text	stet.	Let it stand—used in margin
ld>	Insert lead	c+sc	Caps & small caps—used in margin		Let it stand—used in text
shill	Insert virgule		Caps & small caps—used in text	⊗	Dirty or broken letter
∨	Superior	l.c.	Lowercase—used in margin	run over	Carry over to next line
∧	Inferior	/	Used in text to show deletion or substitution	run back	Carry back to preceding line
(/)	Parentheses	w.f.	Wrong font	out, see copy	Something omitted—see copy
[/]	Brackets	⌒	Close up	??	Question to author to delete
□	Indent 1 em		Delete	∧	Caret—General indicator used to mark exact position of error in text.
⊏⊐	Indent 2 ems		Close up and delete		
¶	Paragraph	↺	Correct the position		
no ¶	No paragraph	⌐	Move right		

Figure C-21. Proofreader's marks.

Appendix D
Examples of Photoshop Applications

Example 1

The surreal image to the left was generated with the Photoshop editor by manipulating and combining the two photographs shown below. Photo 1 was converted to gray scale mode and copied. One copy was layered over the other, side by side.

The bird was isolated from Photo 2 with the magnetic-lasso tool, and two copies were made. One copy was rescaled, and the brightness and contrast were adjusted. A portion of the bird's image was layered over the face, and the smudge tool in the normal mode was used to create the lightened texture around a portion of the face.

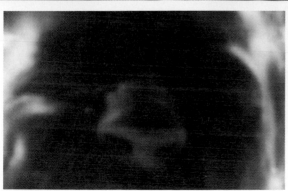

Photo 1

Photo 2

Example 2

The image to the left was created with portions of the three photographs shown below. Photo 1 was converted to gray scale mode. The magnetic-lasso tool was used to isolate the building, and the brightness and contrast were adjusted.

Photo 2 was also converted to gray scale mode. The brightness was adjusted. This photo was then cropped, rescaled, and layered in the upper-left corner of the composite image.

Photo 3 was rescaled. The clone tool was used to place portions of the bird onto a new layer over the lower portion of the building. The contrast was adjusted, and the black portions were treated with the brush tool to create the appearance of tall grass.

Photo 3

Photo 1   **Photo 2**

Example 3

The image to the left was created from portions of the four photographs below. Photo 1 was cropped. The clone tool was used to capture pixels of the sky and hide the hills in the background.

The magnetic-lasso tool was used on Photo 2 to isolate the red ball from the background. The eraser tool was used to remove a portion of the ball. The ball was rescaled.

The lasso tool was used on Photo 3 to isolate the chess piece from the background. The chess piece was then copied three times. The different images of the chess piece were individually rescaled and rotated.

The image of the man in Photo 4 was isolated with the magnetic-lasso tool. The brightness was adjusted. This created a white silhouette.

The images of the red ball, four chess pieces, and silhouette were combined on layers with Photo 1. The texture tool was used on the bottom of the images placed onto the water to create the appearance of partial submersion. Pixels of the water were cloned and layered over the man's feet, and their opacity was adjusted to suggest three dimensions.

Photo 1

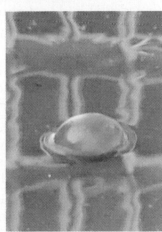

Photo 2

Photo 3

Photo 4

Glossary

A

ablation: the physical removal of a material by cutting, vaporizing, or erosion. (17)

absorbency: the physical characteristic of being porous. (18)

absorption: an ink-drying method in which the ink soaks into the paper as though the paper were a sponge. (19)

accordion fold: a pattern of parallel folds in which the angle of the folds alternates. (25)

achromatic vision: a vision irregularity in which a person can see only in shades of white, gray, and black. (16)

actinic light: light rays that cause photochemical changes. This light is used to harden light-sensitive offset plate emulsions. (12)

additive: an ingredient, such as a drier, lubricant, wax, or starch, added to ink to impart special characteristics, improve desirable properties, or suppress undesirable properties. (19)

additive color system: the forming of colors by combining RGB light in various proportions. (16)

additive plate: a printing plate requiring the addition of a special image-strengthening lacquer to the image areas to retain their durability. (17)

adjacent: bordering. (16)

alcohol dampening system: a dampening system that uses alcohol in the fountain solution. (20)

alkaline paper: paper that has a pH above 7. (18)

American-British system: a system of print measurement used throughout North America and Great Britain. (3)

American Standard Code for Information Interchange (ASCII): an industry-standard code representing text (letters, numbers, punctuation, and sets of basic commands) but not style attributes (bold, italic, and underlined). (8)

AM screening: producing a conventional halftone with equally spaced dots of various sizes. (11)

analog image: an image created by variations in voltage or density, instead of digitized numerical values. (13)

angle bar: a metal bar placed horizontally at a 45° angle to the feed direction of a printing press and used to turn the web when feeding from the side or to bypass the former folder. (23)

antifoaming agent: a silicone-based fluid or emulsion added to a fountain solution to reduce the tendency of the solution to foam or bubble. (19)

antihalation coating: an application to the back of film that prevents light from reflecting back to the emulsion during exposure. (10)

antioxidant: a material inhibiting oxidation or reactions promoted by oxygen or peroxides. (19)

antique finish: a paper finish characterized by a rough surface intended to simulate old, handmade paper. (18)

antisetoff spray: a powder made from fine starch particles sprayed on the surface of printed sheets to prevent setoff. (20)

antistatic solution: a compound applied, commonly a coating, on a substrate as a means of preventing the buildup of static electricity. (24)

aqueous coating: a clear, water-based, fast-drying coating that can be applied over printed materials to improve resistance to scuffing. These coatings are available in gloss and matte finishes. (25)

aqueous plate: a printing plate that uses coatings that can be processed by developing chemistries that are primarily, if not entirely, water based. (17)

artifact: a visible defect within a digital photograph. (14)

artwork: any illustration matter, including hand lettering, that is not text. (7)

ascender: the part of a type character extending above the body height. (3)

assembling: any finishing operation that brings together, in the proper sequence, the sheets or signatures, in preparation for binding. (25)

automatic picture replacement (APR): a process by which high-resolution image files are automatically substituted for low-resolution image files at output time. (13)

automatic trap: a trap set by building art with common colors. (14)

axis: in design, a line actually drawn and used as the origin of dimensions in an effective representation. In image assembly, the axis is the line separating the front images from the back images in a work-and-turn or work-and-tumble imposition. (12)

B

back gauge: a guide on a cutting device used to hold a stack of sheets firmly in place on the bed. (25)

back-trap mottle: a printing defect caused by nonuniform ink setting when the paper is still moving through the press. (23)

back trapping: the lifting of a wet ink film from the substrate while trying to wet trap. (19)

balance: the even distribution of images to create a pleasing visual effect. (7)

baronial envelope: an envelope used for social invitations and wedding announcements. (18)

barrel fold: a pattern of parallel folds starting at one end of the sheet and progressing toward the opposite end, as if the sheet were being rolled. (25)

barrier guard: a plastic or metal safety barrier covering a point of operation on machinery. (2)

base: an alkaline fountain solution. (10)

basic density range (BDR): the tonal-range capability of a halftone screen. (11)

basic size: the size of a sheet of a particular grade of paper at which its basis weight is determined. (3)

basis weight: the weight, in pounds, of a ream of paper cut to the basic size for a particular grade of paper. (3)

Bayer filter pattern: a mosaic of tiny color filters arranged in two array patterns that alternate in rows. (14)

bearer: a narrow metal band at the end of a press cylinder used to allow packing and easy alignment. (20)

bed: a smooth or level surface. (25)

bellows extension: an accordion-shaped component on a process camera that forms a light tunnel from the lens to the film plane. (10)

binary digit (bit): the smallest piece of information used by a computer, consisting of either the number *1* or the number *0*. (3)

binary system: a mathematical system based on two numbers (*1*s and *0*s) and used by computers. (8)

binding: the act of attaching multiple pages of a printed product together using various methods. (25)

bit depth: the number of bits used to represent each pixel of an image. (13)

bitmap font: a set of typographic characters existing as a collection of dots, rather than as outline fonts. (6)

bitmap graphic: a digital representation of an image created with pixels arranged in rows and columns. (13)

black printer: the black component image of process color printing. (16)

blank: a very heavy sheet of paperboard. (18)

blanket: a synthetic rubber mat that transfers, or offsets, the image from the plate to the substrate as the impression cylinder presses the image against the mat. (20)

blanket cylinder: the part of an offset press holding the rubber blanket that accepts images from the plate. (20)

bleaching: a papermaking step in which pulp is treated with chlorine and similar chemical solutions to whiten the paper fibers. (18)

bleed: a printed image extending to the trim edge of a sheet or page. (9)

bleed image: a printed image extending to the trim edge of a sheet or page. (12)

blind embossing: the stamping of a relief image into a substrate without additional color or decoration of the image. (25)

blueline: a light-sensitive proof with a blue image, used for proofing single-color flats. This proof is a single-color photographic proof exposed from film negatives prior to platemaking and used primarily to evaluate pagination and the location or omission of page elements. (12)

blue-sensitive material: a light-sensitive material that records high densities from blue materials, but very little from green or red light. (10)

body type: type sizes ranging from 4-point through 12-point used for setting straight matter. (6)

bond paper: paper with a medium-finish surface that accepts ink and toner easily from computer printers, copying machines, typewriters, and pens. (18)

booklet: a small book, particularly a brochure. (7)

book paper: a grade of paper used primarily in the printing of texts and trade books. (18)

brightness: a value indicating how light or dark a color is. (16)

bristol: a classification of paper that is heavy, rigid, and used for programs and index cards. (18)

broadside: a large, single sheet of paper, printed on two sides and folded down. (7)

brochure: a large elaborate booklet with features such as string binding, embossing, translucent paper, hot-foil stamping, or heavy paper and costing over a dollar per copy to produce. (7)

brokering: acting as an agent or intermediary in the sale of goods or services. (26)

buckle folder: a folding device that uses a fold plate to force a sheet to buckle so the sheet can be pulled through a set of folding rollers. (25)

budgeted hourly rate (BHR): the cost determined from all fixed and variable costs, based on the hourly operation of a particular cost or production center. (4)

burst binding: a form of perfect binding, used on reference books and some textbooks, in which the spine of the book body is notched or perforated and a high-strength adhesive is applied under pressure. (25)

business paper: a classification of types of paper commonly used in business. (18)

butterfly: a register mark cut in a masking sheet. (12)

buyout: the cost of subcontracting outside materials, supplies, and services. (4)

byte: a group of eight digits, or bits. (8)

C

calibrate: to adjust the scale on a measuring instrument, such as a densitometer, to a standard for specific conditions. (16)

caliper: the thickness of a sheet of paper, measured in thousandths of an inch or in points. (3)

camera-ready art: copy that has been prepared for exposure in the camera, in preparation for platemaking. (9)

cancellation method: a paper-estimating method used to determine the greatest number of pieces of paper that can be cut from a single, full-size sheet. (18)

carbonless bond paper: bond paper coated with microcapsules that, under pressure, transfer an image to a sheet or sheets underneath it. (18)

carcass: the back side of the blanket, which is specially woven to maintain the integrity of the blanket. (20)

case binding: a means of binding pages together with thread and then encasing the sewn signatures with a cardboard cover. (25)

casing in: the procedure of positioning and attaching the sewn signatures to the case. (25)

cast removal: the removal of an excessive amount of a color from a photograph or another digital image. (14)

category: regarding paper, a subdivision of a paper classification. (18)

cathode-ray tube (CRT) monitor: a large vacuum tube with an inside surface that is a flat screen on which images appear when light is selectively allowed to strike it. (13)

centered format: a typesetting format centered on the page or column, resulting in uneven line widths. (6)

charge-coupled device (CCD): an array of light-sensitive, solid-state receptors that react electronically when exposed to light. (14)

chemical-mechanical pulp: pulp produced using a combination of mechanical and cooking separation processes. (18)

chemical pulp: pulp that uses chemical action to dissolve some of the wood's substances. This pulp results in lower yields, but higher-quality pulp, than the groundwood process. (18)

chill roll: an internally cooled metal roller or cylinder located just beyond a web-press dryer, used to lower the temperature of the printed web and harden the ink film before rewinding. (23)

chipping: cutting wood into waferlike pieces called *chips.* (18)

choke: a print made in a contact-printing frame that makes the original image slightly smaller. (10)

choke trap: a trap performed by spreading the background under the foreground object. (14)

chroma: the intensity or strength of a color and its saturation. (7)

CIELAB system: a method of identifying a color by the values on three axes formed by opposing colors (red-green, blue-yellow, and black-white). (16)

clamp: the part of a guillotine cutter that holds down a lift of paper to be cut. (25)

classification: an organized arrangement in groups or types according to established standards. (18)

cloning stamp: an image manipulation tool that covers selected pixels with selected pixels from another area of the photograph. (14)

closed counter: a portion of a letter consisting of a closed loop. (6)

closed shop: a company that hires only union members. (5)

coated back (CB): the back side of the top sheet in the carbonless set coated with encapsulated chemicals. (18)

coated front (CF): the last sheet of carbonless paper with a receptor coating only on the front. (18)

coated front-and-back (CFB): a carbonless paper sheet between the first and last sheets with a receptor coating on top and an encapsulated coating on the back. (18)

coated groundwood paper: groundwood paper that has been coated on both sides. (18)

coated offset paper: offset paper that has been coated on one or both sides. (18)

codex: a wax tablet framed and backed with wood and joined with cords on which the Greeks and Romans wrote. (8)

coldset ink: an ink that needs to be printed on absorbent paper in order to properly dry. (19)

cold-type composition: all typesetting that does not use molten metal to cast images. (8)

collate: to assemble individual pages into their correct sequence. (25)

collating: assembling individual pages in their correct sequence. Collating is also ensuring that signatures are in their correct order for binding. (25)

collating mark: a symbol printed on the folded edge of a press signature as a means of indicating the proper collating or gathering sequence. (25)

collimator: an optical instrument used to make sure register marks are properly aligned when two or more overlays are used. (12)

color: a visual sensation produced in the brain when the eye views various wavelengths of light. (7)

colorant: a dye or pigment that gives color to materials such as ink, paint, crayons, and chalk. (16)

color bar: a strip of colors printed in the trim area of a press sheet containing a variety of quality-control devices. (12)

color blindness: the inability to tell colors apart. (16)

color depth: the number of distinct colors that can be represented by a piece of hardware or software. (3)

color drift: any change in the color of an image as the image moves through the electronic prepress and press stages. (16)

color gamut: the total range of colors that can be defined by a color model or reproduced with a given set of colorants, on a given paper, and on a given printing press. (16)

color harmony: the selection of two or more colors that produce a visually pleasing sensation. (7)

colorimeter: a color-measurement device that measures and compares the hue, purity, and brightness of colors in a manner modeling vision. (3)

Color-Key® proof: a proof made with transparent sheets imaged from film and then physically fastened together in register. (16)

color level: an image manipulation tool that allows adjustment of the tonal range and contrast of a bitmap image by using sliders to change the values of highlights, midtones, and shadows. (14)

color management software (CMS): software that prevents color drift by compensating for deviation within one or more devices. (16)

color sensitivity: a measure of how receptive a material is to the colors of light. (10)

color separation: the process of dividing the colors of a multicolored original into the subtractive, or printing, primaries and black. The CMYK color separations are made into films and used to prepare printing plates. (16)

color sequence: in process color printing, the order in which the colors of ink are printed. (16)

color space: a three-dimensional coordinate system that plots three different color qualities on three axes, allowing color samples to be quantitatively measured, plotted, and described by a single point located somewhere on the coordinate system. (16)

color strength: a measure of the concentration of pigment in the ink to the total weight or volume of the ink. This strength determines the opacity, or covering power, of the ink. (19)

color temperature: a means of evaluating color using the temperature to which a black object would need to be heated to produce light of a certain wavelength (or color). (16)

color wheel: a circle containing colors in positions reflective of the colors' relationships to one another. (7)

comb binding: a mechanical binding method in which pages are bound together with a strip of solid plastic with curved teeth or prongs extending out of it. (25)

combination cut: a paper-cutting method for jobs that do not divide evenly into the basic-size paper from which they are to be cut. This method provides the greatest number of press-size sheets, while reducing waste to a minimum. (18)

commercial printing: an important segment of the graphic communications industry, encompassing all sizes and types of printing operations, ranging from small local shops with one or two employees to large companies with several plant locations and hundreds or thousands of employees. This industry segment is dominated by one printing process, offset lithography. (1)

commercial register: an industry standard that does not allow more than 1/100″ of variation between adjacent colors. (9)

common impression cylinder: an impression cylinder that contacts more than one blanket, passing a single sheet beneath successive blankets. (20)

common impression cylinder press: an offset-press design featuring a single oversized impression cylinder that contacts all the blanket cylinders. (20)

communication model: a diagram identifying the components of communication and the sequence it follows. (7)

compact disc–recordable (CD-R): a computer storage disk that can be written to once and then read any number of times. (8)

complementary flat: a film-assembly method in which the line negatives and halftone negatives are stripped separately. (12)

composition: the production and organization of all images and type to be placed in a layout. (8)

comprehensive layout (comp): a detailed drawing of how the final printed piece will appear. (7)

compressible blanket: a rubber printing blanket with backing made of at least one layer of foam rubber, cork, or nonwoven fabric fibers that allows the blanket to squeeze and instantly rebound to its original shape and thickness. (20)

computer platform: the basic computer architecture, or hardware, a particular model uses. (13)

Computer Ready Electronic File (CREF) II guidelines: the guidelines the SGAUA publishes to improve prepress productivity. (13)

computer-to-plate (CTP): a platemaking process that allows plates to be imaged directly from electronic data. (17)

computer-to-plate (CTP) technology: a combination platemaking and printing process that allows plates to be imaged directly from electronic data. (13)

computer-to-press (CTPr): the technology of laser imaging a plate mounted on a press. (20)

conductivity: the property of a material to transmit electricity. (19)

contacting film: graphic arts film used to produce contact reproductions of negatives or positives. (10)

contact printing: a photographic process in which a film negative or positive is placed in direct vacuum contact over a sheet of film or photo-print paper. (10)

contact vacuum frame: a frame used to make prints, negatives, positives, spreads, and chokes by holding the negative or positive in vacuum contact with the photographic material being made. (10)

continuous dampening system: a system that uses a metering roller to move the fountain solution to the transfer roller. (20)

continuous feeding: a system in which a ribbon or individual sheets of paper are fed into the press constantly. (20)

continuous ink-jet printer: a device that emits a steady stream of tiny drops of ink. (13)

continuous tone art: an image containing one or more gray tones. (7)

contract color proof: a color proof serving as the basis for whether or not a printing job is acceptable to the customer. (16)

contract proof: a color proof representing the appearance of the finished printed product that the printer and the client agreed on. (13)

contrast: the principle of design that adds interest and emphasis to the printed page by using different sizes and weights of type and art, using a second ink color, underlining type, or shading backgrounds. (7)

control strip: a sheet of film (about 4″ × 10″) with a preexposed gray scale image used to determine the condition of the chemicals in an automatic film processor. (10)

conventional blanket: a blanket used in an offset press made without a layer of foam allowing the blanket to compress when two sheets are fed at a time. (20)

conventional dampening system: a system in which the movement of the ductor roller prevents the continuous flow of fountain solution from the fountain to the plate. (20)

conventional image assembly: the manual positioning and attaching of films to a flat, with the purpose of exposing the films' images to a plate. (12)

conventional lithographic plate: a plate made by exposing it to light through a piece of film. (17)

conventional prepress: preparing images for platemaking without using electronic software. (8)

conventional screen: a halftone screen that produces a square dot. (11)

copyboard: the part of the process camera on which the copy to be photographed is positioned. (10)

copyboard light: the source of illumination for copy being photographed with a process camera. (10)

copyfitting: the process of fitting copy or text into a specific amount of space. (3)

copy preparation: the process of properly arranging the various elements, or components of a page, (such as type and illustrations) that make up a printed page. (9)

copyright: the exclusive legal right to reproduce, publish, and sell original works of authorship existing in print or another tangible form of expression. (5)

copyright infringement: the unauthorized use of copyrighted work. (5)

cornering: any operation performed on the corners of paper. (25)

corporation: a legal venture owned by a group of shareholders. (26)

corrosion inhibitor: a compound used in fountain solutions to prevent or minimize damage to the printing plate through oxidation or other chemical reactions. (19)

cost center: a production operation that costs money to maintain. (4)

counter die: an epoxy plate with a relief image emerging from it. (25)

counterfeit: to imitate or copy closely with the intent to deceive. (5)

cover flap: a thin sheet of paper taped to the top of a mechanical to protect the mechanical or carry instructions. (9)

cover paper: a classification of heavy, easily folded paper available in a variety of finishes and commonly used for business cards and booklet covers. (18)

creep: a pushing out on the inside of a folded signature or group of signatures, caused by the thickness of the paper. (12)

cropping: a method used to identify the part of an illustration to be used. (7)

cross-platform: the capacity to function with two or more computer platforms, such as the Microsoft Windows operating system, Linux® software, and Mac OS® operating system software. (13)

crystallization: a problem occurring in multicolor printing when the first ink printed dries too hard and the second ink printed does not adhere to the dried ink surface. (19)

cursive typeface: a typeface imitating handwriting with characters that do not touch. (6)

curve adjustment: an image manipulation tool that allows the lightness and darkness of a digital photograph to be modified at the 1/4-tone, halftone, and 3/4-tone levels of the image by altering a diagonal line. (14)

cutoff: the length of the printed page as determined by the circumference of the plate cylinder on a web offset press. (23)

cut size: a sheet size that fits into the printing press. (18)

cutting stick: a plastic or wooden piece located directly below the cutting blade to protect the blade from damage. (25)

cyan: a greenish-blue color formed by combining green and blue light. This color is a primary color of the subtractive color system. (16)

cyan, magenta, yellow, and black (CMYK): the four process colors. (16)

D

dampening solution: a mixture of water and other chemicals (such as an acid, a buffer, and gum) the dampening system of an offset press distributes. (19)

dampening unit: a press system that moistens the nonimage areas of the plate with fountain solution so ink does not adhere to them. (20)

darkroom: a specially lighted room for processing light-sensitive photographic materials. (10)

daylight film: graphic arts film used with very high-intensity light sources. (10)

debossing: the use of dies to stamp or press a depressed image into a substrate. (25)

decibel (dBA): a unit of measure for stating sound levels. (2)

deckle edge: a feathered edge left untrimmed when the paper is manufactured. (18)

decorative typeface: a typeface classification consisting of typefaces that do not fit any other classification. (6)

deep-etch plate: a printing plate that is exposed with film positives and on which the ink-bearing image area is slightly etched below the nonprinting area. (17)

degree of contamination: the amount of unwanted foreign matter in a substance. (19)

delivery chain: a belt or chain the delivery system of a press uses to transfer the printed sheet from the impression cylinder to the delivery pile. (20)

delivery conveyor: conveyor belts or tubes that transport the printed product to the area where it is stacked, bundled, or boxed for shipment. (23)

delivery cylinder: a cylinder in the delivery unit of a press that transfers the printed sheets from the impression cylinder to the delivery pile. This cylinder is usually covered with skeleton wheels. (20)

delivery gripper: a small metal finger attached to a bar extended between two continuous delivery chains. (20)

delivery pile: a platform or tray on which the printed sheets are stacked. (20)

delivery platform: a platform constructed to lower automatically as the sheets are delivered. (20)

delivery ring: a ring used to control paper curl so the paper is delivered properly into the receiving tray. (22)

delivery unit: a system on offset presses and duplicators that delivers the printed sheets. (20)

densitometer: a color-measurement device that computes the light-stopping or light-absorption ability of an image or a surface material. (3)

descender: the part of a type character extending below the body height. (3)

descreening: an electronic means of eliminating or minimizing the halftone-dot pattern of a scanned printed image. (14)

design: the manner in which materials are selected and arranged on a printed page to produce a certain result or effect. (7)

desktop publishing: the process of creating and assembling pages on a desktop computer. (13)

developing: a film-processing step that basically dissolves the light-exposed area of the film. (10)

diazo coating: a light-sensitive printing-plate coating made from condensation products of formaldehyde and diazo diphenylamine, stabilized with a compound such as zinc chloride. (17)

diazo plate: a surface plate coated with an emulsion of a light-sensitive, organic compound called *diazo*. (17)

diazo proofing material: a proofing material with a positive image produced from transparent film positives or negatives. (12)

dichromatic vision: a vision irregularity in which a person can see only yellows and blues. (16)

Didot system: a system of print measurement used primarily in the European printing industry. (3)

die: a cookie cutter–like device that cuts a sheet of paper into irregular shapes. (25)

die cutting: a finishing operation that uses a sharp steel rule or knife to cut a specific pattern into a substrate or to cut the substrate into a specific pattern. (25)

digester: a pressurized kettle that breaks down the lignin in the cellulose fibers as part of the papermaking process. (18)

digital camera: a camera that uses arrays of photosites to convert light into electrical signals and then into digital data. (8)

digital font: a typeface represented and stored as digitized electronic data. (6)

digital image: an image created by a unique combination of numerical values known as *bits*. (13)

digital imaging (DI) technology: the hardware and software that images a plate on the press. (13)

digital printing: any reproduction technology that receives electronic files and uses spots (or dots) for replication. (13)

digital proof: a proof generated by outputting files on a high-resolution, high-quality printer, rather than from film separations. (13)

digital toner-based press technology: a type of DI in which the image is imparted to the plate by electrically charging image areas that attract toner material. (13)

digital videodisc (DVD): a very high-capacity optical storage disk that is the same size as a CD but can hold six times as much data. (8)

dimensional stability: the ability of a paper to retain its original length and width when exposed to moisture. (18)

dimension line: a line drawn in nonphoto blue indicating where type, art, or any other page element is to be placed on a mechanical. (9)

dingbat: an ornamental design used to illustrate and attract attention to specific text matter. (6)

diphthong: the combination of two letters in a single graphic and single sound. (6)

direct imaging (digital): imaging a plate with a laser while the plate is on the press. (20)

direct imaging (digital) offset press: an offset press on which the plates are on the plate cylinder when they are imaged. (20)

direct imaging press: a press that uses a laser to image printing plates directly from electronic files. (20)

direct lithography: a lithographic printing process in which the printed impressions are made on the paper directly from the stone, metal stone, or plate. (1)

disk: a round flat plate on which information for a computer is stored. (8)

display type: a typeface that is 14 points or larger and usually used for headlines, subheadings, and decks added below main headlines in newspapers and magazines. (6)

distributing roller: an intermediate roller in the ink train that contacts two other rollers. (20)

dot doubling: a printing defect characterized by halftone dots printing twice, a type of visual stuttering or echo. This defect is commonly caused by a loose blanket, excessive pressure between the blanket and the substrate, or excessive ink on the plate. (24)

dot gain: the optical increase in the size of a halftone dot during prepress operations or the mechanical increase in halftone-dot size that occurs as the image is transferred from plate to blanket to paper. (13)

dot gain compensation: a reduction of the size of dots on a printing plate in anticipation that the size of the dots will grow when they are transferred to the substrate. (16)

dot gain scale: a quality-control device consisting of a series of numbers used to indicate dot reproduction of halftones and process colors. (24)

dot matrix printer: a low-quality output device that prints dots to form an image. (13)

dot pitch: the measure of the diameter of an individual pixel. (3)

dots per inch (dpi): a measure of the resolution of a computer monitor, a scanner, or an output device. (3)

double ending: a process in which the web is immediately dried and turned and the reverse side is printed on the same printing unit. (23)

double-sheet detector: a printing-press device used to detect when multiple sheets of paper are being fed at the same time. (20)

draw program: a software program used to produce and manipulate vector graphics. (13)

drier: a liquid or paste additive used in the formulation of printing inks that accelerates drying. (19)

drop-on-demand ink-jet printer: a device that emits tiny drops of ink when commanded by digital data. (13)

drum common impression web offset press: a webfed offset press in which all the blanket cylinders are grouped around a large common impression cylinder and the double-ending process is used to print on both sides of the web. (23)

drum scanner: an electronic imaging device that uses a rotating drum and photomultiplier tubes to digitize images. (14)

dryer: a type of ink-drying device on a web press that heats the web up to a temperature of about 330°F. (23)

dry film: graphic arts film that requires no chemical processing. This film is imaged with data from electronic files and a laser. (10)

drying oil: a vegetable oil that readily transforms to a solid when exposed in a film to oxygen. (19)

drying stimulator: a substance added to a fountain solution to enhance the effectiveness of the drier in the ink. (19)

dry method: a method of deleting small image areas that uses a simple rubber eraser. (17)

dry trapping: applying an ink film onto another ink film that has dried. (19)

ductor roller: the first roller in the inking system that comes in alternate contact with the fountain roller and the first oscillator. This roller is the roller in a dampening system that transfers the solution to a distributing roller. (20)

dull finish: a finish that is smoother than matte but still without gloss. (18)

dummy: a folded sheet of paper representing the finished job. (9)

duotone: a two-color halftone produced with two halftone negatives made from the same photograph. (11)

duplicating film: graphic arts film used to produce exact copies of negatives or positives. (10)

duplicator: a small offset press that prints up to a maximum sheet size of about 11″ × 17″ (28 cm × 43 cm). (20)

dust collector: a vacuum system that captures airborne dust and removes it to a storage compartment. (2)

dwell: the length of time the ductor roller is in contact with the fountain roller. (20)

dye sublimation printer: an electronic output device that produces photographic-quality digital color proofs using a sublimable dye. (13)

Dylux® proofing material: a dry-processed proof for single-color printing. (12)

dynamic range: the range of tones of an image or the difference between the minimum and maximum tones a scanner can capture, as measured on a scale of 0.0 to 4.0. (14)

E

E gauge: a device used to measure point sizes and leading of printed type. (3)

eggshell finish: a finish attempting to simulate the rough surface of an egg. (18)

ejector delivery system: an offset-duplicator delivery system in which a simple ejector mechanism is used to deliver the printed sheets to a tray. (20)

electromagnetic spectrum: the entire range of wavelengths of electromagnetic radiation, extending from gamma rays to radio waves. (16)

electron-beam (EB) curing: the use of equipment to produce and direct electrons at a wet coating or printing ink to create a solid film. (19)

electronic color separation: the process of separating the process colors and black with an electronic imaging system. (16)

electronic prepress: the steps prior to printing that use computers and digital technology. (1)

electrostatic plate: a printing plate that is imaged electrostatically. (17)

electrostatic platesetter: a platesetter that digitally images plates by charging the plate's image areas so they attract dry toner. (17)

elemental chlorine–free (ECF) bleaching: an alternative bleaching process that uses chlorine dioxide or sodium hypochlorite instead of chlorine gas as a bleaching agent. (18)

elliptical dot screen: a halftone screen with diamond or oval dots that join only two opposite corners, as the dots reach 50% size. (11)

em: a printer's unit of area measurement equal in width and height to the letter *M* in any selected type body size. This unit is commonly used as an abbreviation of the pica em, in which the em is equivalent to 12 points. (6)

embossed finish: a paper surface with an obvious texture created by embossing. (18)

embossing: the use of dies to create a three-dimensional image on a printed product. (25)

em quad: a nonprinting body in the shape of a square of the type size being used. (6)

em space: a nonprinting fixed space equal in width to the point size of a font. This space is used for indenting paragraphs and aligning type columns. (6)

emulsion: a gelatin or collodion solution holding light-sensitive salts of silver in suspension. (10)

en: a printer's unit of measurement equal to the same height, but half the width, of the em. This unit is sometimes used to specify the area of composition, as its value closely approximates the number of characters in the text. (6)

enamel finish: a surface sheen or brilliance. (18)

Encapsulated PostScript (EPS) file: a file format used to transfer PostScript-image information from one program to another and for outputting to an imagesetter. (13)

engine speed: the maximum number of pages per minute the printer can output in full- or single-color mode. (13)

en quad: an increment equal to half the width of an em quad, used for space between words. (6)

entrepreneur: a self-starter who organizes and manages a business undertaking, while assuming the risks involved in making a profit. (26)

ergonomics: the study of equipment design that improves convenience, ease of use, and operator comfort. (2)

estimating: the process of determining the approximate costs of a printed job, based on quality and quantity specs. (4)

existing business: a for-profit organization that has been in existence. (26)

exposure index: a means of classifying the speed of film. (10)

external sizing: material added to the surface of paper near the end of the papermaking process to give the paper greater stiffness. (18)

F

fair use: exceptions to the law that allow duplication of copyrighted materials without written permission or copyright infringement. (5)

fake duotone: a photograph printed in black ink over an area (usually a rectangle) printed in a color. (11)

fanning out: the progressive widening of the web or sheet as it goes from unit to unit. This widening is normally caused by tension differences between the roll and printing units or water pickup of the stock. (20)

feedboard: a conveyor platform that uses a set of rollers, balls, or brushes to press the sheet to the front guides at the head of the platform. (20)

feeding unit: the system on a press that transfers paper (or some other substrate) from a stack or roll to the registration unit. (20)

feed position: the setting of an A.B.Dick's operation control lever that causes the feeder unit to send press sheets into the printing unit. (22)

feed-roll system: a register-and-insertion method that advances a sheet forward, stops the sheet, and then propels it forward with rollers, in time to connect with the grippers on the impression cylinder. (20)

female die: an embossing die with a sunken image made to fit the male die. (25)

festoon: a paper-storage device that unwinds paper to keep the press running at the same speed while the splice is made and the new roll accelerates to press speed. This device also gives the web a long lead time into the press. (23)

fiber puffing: the exploding of paper fibers that have not been completely ground during heatset drying. This puffing causes the paper surface to become rough and abrasive. (18)

filler: a material added to pulp to smooth the paper surface, provide a better bond for ink, brighten color, and increase opacity. (18)

fill-in: an undesirable effect producing a muddy look in the midtones and shadows. This effect is caused by the presence of foreign material in the ink. (19)

filter: colored material, usually glass or acetate, blocking some wavelengths of the light spectrum and letting others through. (14)

fine: a cellulose fiber that is too short for papermaking. (18)

finger-type pull guide: a side guide that advances over the sheet, closes on it by pinching the sheet against a lower plate, and pulls the sheet to the side-guide plate. (20)

finish: any action performed to the surface of the sheet of printing paper affecting its structure. A finish is the degree of smoothness of a paper's surface. (18)

finished size: the dimension of the job as delivered to the customer. (25)

finishing: the many operations carried out during or following printing, such as cutting, folding, slitting, perforating, creasing and scoring, die cutting, embossing, stamping, numbering, drilling and punching, varnishing, and laminating. (18)

fixed cost: a cost rate that remains constant, regardless of production output in the cost center. (4)

fixing: a step of film development used to make the developed image stable and permanent. (10)

flash exposure: a nonimaging, yellow light exposure made through a halftone screen. This exposure is used to enhance the dots in the shadow regions of the halftone negative. (11)

flash point: the lowest temperature at which a solvent emits vapors supporting combustion if exposed to an open flame. (2)

flat: a complete masking sheet, with its taped-on film negatives or positives. (12)

flatbed press: a lithographic press on which lithographic stone rests on a flat bed. (1)

flatbed scanner: an electronic imaging device in which the original is placed on a flat glass bed and a CCD is used to digitize images. (14)

flatness: a measurement of how much the paper curls, waves, or bends. (18)

flexography: a direct rotary printing method that uses flexible relief image plates of rubber or photopolymer material and relatively thin-bodied, resin-solvent or water-based inks. (1)

fluorescent ink: ink that appears to glow under black light and is made with pigments that naturally absorb UV light waves that other inks cannot use. (19)

flush left/ragged right format: a typesetting format with the type aligned evenly on the left side of the page and ragged on the right side. (6)

flush right/ragged left format: a typesetting format with the copy evenly aligned on the right side of the column and uneven on the left. (6)

flying paster: a device on a webfed press used to splice a fresh roll of paper to an expiring roll without stopping the press. (23)

FM screening: a type of electronic halftone screening using dots that are all the same size but varying in frequency or pattern. (11)

focal length (FL): the distance from the lens's optical center to the film, when the image is in focus. (10)

focusing controls: the wheels on the process camera controlling the distance of the lens and the copyboard from the film plane. (10)

fog: a photographic defect in which a deposit of silver either locally or entirely veils the image. This defect is due either to the action of stray light or to improperly compounded chemical solutions. (10)

foil embossing: the use of dies and foil or film to create a colored, raised image. (25)

foil stamping: a letterpress process that uses relief images, heat, and foil to produce gold, silver, or colored images on products such as book covers, letterheads, and business cards. (25)

folder: a folded, single sheet of paper, printed on two sides. (7)

folding dummy: a sheet of paper folded as the job will be folded in production. This sheet serves as a prototype. (12)

fold plate: a metal plate on a buckle folder positioned at a slight incline above the drive and fold rollers, into which the substrate is fed to create a buckle in the sheet. (25)

fold roller: a metal roller that transports a sheet through a folder. (25)

fold strength: the ability of a sheet of paper to be folded and unfolded repeatedly without tearing. (18)

font: a type family narrowed down to a specific weight, width, and point size. (6)

font library: a collection of fonts, either on a computer's hard drive or available for purchase on a CD or another storage device. (6)

font report: a list of the typefaces used in a document. (15)

font set: the font list for a document. These sets can be created for individual jobs, and only the set needed can be activated. (15)

form: a group of pages printed on each side of the press sheet. (12)

format: the form, dimensions, and general structure of a publication. (15)

former folded web: a web of paper folded by being run over a triangular-shaped device that causes the web to fold when the web conforms to the wedge. (23)

forming wire: the continuously moving mesh wire screen on a papermaking machine on which the pulp is formed into paper. (18)

form roller: a roller in inking and dampening systems that comes in direct contact with the printing plate and is used to transfer ink or fountain solution to the plate. (20)

for position only (FPO) image: a copy of a graphic image placed on a mechanical or in an electronic layout to indicate placement, but not used for reproduction. (14)

fountain blade: a metal plate or plastic strip that forms a barrier between the ink fountain and the fountain roller. (20)

fountain key: a screw on a conventional inking system used to regulate the ink at the ink fountain. (20)

fountain roller: a metal roller used in the ink fountain of inking systems and some dampening systems to transfer ink or fountain solution from the ink fountain to the ductor roller. (20)

fourdrinier machine: a papermaking machine that forms a continuous web of paper on a moving, endless wire belt. (18)

franchising: granting the right or authorization to a person or group to market a company's merchandise or services in a particular region. (26)

French fold: a type of fold in which a sheet printed on one side is folded first vertically and then horizontally. (25)

front guide: a metal tab or plate attached to the front end of the feedboard on a sheetfed printing press that stops the sheet of paper and holds it on the feedboard while the side guide moves the sheet into position. (20)

f-stop: a fixed size at which the aperture of a lens can be set, the value of which is determined by the ratio of the aperture to the focal length (FL) of the lens. (10)

fungicide: a substance added to a fountain solution to help kill any organic growth in the fountain or elsewhere in the dampening system. (19)

G

gatherer-stitcher-trimmer (GST): a finishing device that inserts, saddle stitches, and trims three sides of signatures to produce booklets. (25)

gathering: assembling individual sheets of paper or signatures in the correct sequence. (25)

General Requirements for Applications in Commercial Offset Lithography (GRACoL): a publication containing standards for accurate lithographic color reproduction during commercial printing. (16)

gigabyte (GB): one billion bytes. (8)

gloss finish: a surface sheen or brilliance. (18)

goldenrod paper: yellow-orange masking paper used for preparing flats. (12)

gothic: a sans serif typeface. (6)

grade: a means used to identify and categorize the hundreds of different types of paper. (3)

grain: the alignment or structure of paper fibers. (18)

graphic arts film: any type of film used to capture an image in conventional prepress. (10)

Graphic Communications Trade Customs: the trade customs originally established in 1922 covering such matters as proofs, alterations, press overruns, delivery, and terms of payment. (5)

graphic design: a process that involves the arrangement and organization of graphic elements in a manner pleasing to the eye and conducive to clear communication. (7)

Graphic Design Trade Customs: The general terms and conditions for sales within the graphic-design sector of the graphic-communications industry. (5)

graphics tablet: an input device by which pictographic data can be manually entered into a computer in a way comparable to drawing. (8)

gravure: a printing process that uses engraved cylinders or cylinder-mounted plates to carry the image. (1)

gray balance patch: a small area where screen tints of the three process colors are printed. (24)

gray component replacement (GCR): an electronic technique used to substitute black ink for calculated amounts of CMY inks to produce a clearer, less muddy image. (16)

grayness: the degree to which equal amounts of overlapping CMY inks produce a neutral gray. (19)

gray scale: a measuring device, supplied on film as continuous tones, used to obtain consistent exposure and development of graphic arts film and offset plates. (10)

gray scale method: a method for determining the proper amount of time of development for exposed film by using a gray scale and monitoring when the desired step becomes totally black. (10)

gray scaling: the process of converting a continuous tone image to a monochromatic image with varying shades of gray. (14)

gripper: a metal tab or clip located on an impression cylinder, a transfer cylinder, or another device of the feeding system that grabs a sheet of paper and feeds it through the printing press. (20)

gripper edge: the lead edge of a sheet of paper passing through a sheetfed press containing the gripper margin. (20)

ground glass: a process-camera component used to assist the camera operator in positioning and focusing the image. (10)

groundwood pulping: low-quality paper pulp produced by grinding debarked logs. The resulting fibers contain a high level of impurities, tend to be shortened from the pulping, and produce weak paper. (18)

G7: a publication containing standards for accurate color reproduction with an emphasis on monitoring gray balance. (16)

guide: a device attached to the feedboard that aids in the proper positioning of a sheet of paper before the sheet is fed into the printing unit. (20)

guillotine cutter: a trimming and cutting device with a single cutting blade used to cut paper to size. (25)

gum arabic: a gummy, water-soluble substance obtained from certain types of trees. This substance is used in fountain solutions to desensitize the nonimage areas of the printing plate and prevent them from accepting ink and to protect printing plates from humidity and chemical attack when the press is not running or when the plates are in storage. (17)

H

hairline register: the register setup in which no overlap or white space is allowed to show where elements touch. (9)

halftone: a continuous tone copy formed as a series of fine dots of various sizes and densities. (11)

halftone-block method: the method that uses masking film or black construction paper to indicate the position of photographs on the pasteup base material. (9)

halftone copy: a photograph or another image that must be broken into halftone dots in order to reproduce it in the printing process. (7)

halftone-outline method: a method used to locate the position of photographs on the pasteup base material. (9)

halftone-positive method: a technique for integrating line and halftone copy onto a mechanical during page composition. (9)

halftone scale: a measuring device made of film that is a single continuous strip of progressively dense gray. This scale is used to obtain consistent exposure and development of offset plates. (17)

halftone screen: a sheet of film or clear, flexible plastic with a diffused pattern of dots on it. (11)

hand composition: a typesetting method that creates images by using preprinted type and lettering machines. (8)

hard disk drive: a device that reads data from and writes data to a hard disk. These drives are usually built into the computer system. A hard drive contains one or more permanent aluminum, hard disks coated with a magnetic material. (8)

hard drive: a device that reads data from and writes data to a hard disk. These drives are usually built into the computer system. A hard drive contains one or more permanent aluminum, hard disks coated with a magnetic material. (8)

hard proof: a proof printed onto a sheet of paper or other material. (13)

hardware: the basic computer architecture a particular model uses. (13)

hardwood tree: a deciduous tree, such as poplar, gum, beech, maple, birch, or chestnut. (18)

harmony: the state of design achieved when the placement of elements do not clash with one another or with the theme of the message. (7)

healing brush: a photo-editing technique that improves the blending of pixels that have been placed over pixels with the patch tool. (14)

heatset ink: an ink that dries when hot air accelerates the evaporation of solvents. (19)

hickey: a doughnut-shaped speck caused by dirt, hardened ink, or another unwanted particle that sticks to the press plate and appears in the inked image areas of the printed sheets. (18)

hi-fi color: using more inks than CMYK to reproduce a full-color photograph or another graphic. (16)

highlight area: the darkest area of a negative consisting of small, clear openings in an otherwise solid area. This area is the lightest area on the positive, or printed image. (11)

high-solids ink: an ink with a lower than normal content of solvent. (19)

holding dimension: as part of the sizing process, the new dimension that is known. (3)

horizontal camera: a process camera that has a side-to-side optical axis. (10)

hot-type composition: a typesetting method in which molten metal is used to form pieces of type. (8)

hue: the color perceived by the eye and determined by the dominant wavelengths reflected or transmitted. (7)

hue error: the degree of unequal reflection by a process color of the two RGB colors making it up. (19)

hybrid ultraviolet (UV) ink: UV-curing ink that is compatible with the rollers used for conventional lithographic ink. (19)

I

image area: an ink-receptive, water-repellent area on a printing plate. (17)

image assembly: the process of manually or electronically positioning and assembling line and halftone films into their proper places for exposure during platemaking. (12)

image manipulation program: a graphics program providing a variety of special features for altering bitmap images. (13)

image position: the setting of an A.B.Dick's operation control lever that moves the plate cylinder in contact with the blanket cylinder, thereby inking the blanket. (22)

imagesetter: a high-resolution output device that takes bitmap data generated by a RIP and writes it to film, paper, or printing plates, using a laser that writes the data line by line. (13)

imagesetting system: an imagesetter and its RIP. (13)

imposition: the arrangement of pages so they will be in the proper sequence after the sheet is printed and folded. (12)

impression cylinder: the part of an offset press or duplicator carrying the stock through the printing unit and forcing it against the inked blanket, where the image is transferred to the stock. (20)

index bristol: a type of cover paper available in smooth and antique finishes used for business forms, menus, index cards, booklet covers, postcards, and mailing pieces. This bristol is a lightweight cardboard used when rigidity, ruggedness, and erasability are important. (18)

infrared (IR) light: a range of the electromagnetic spectrum that serves as a source of heat. (2)

infrared (IR) radiation: exposure of ink to high doses of IR light. (19)

initial character: a larger first character in a body of copy set in display type for emphasis or to serve a decorative function. (6)

ink: a color coating specially formulated to reproduce an image on a substrate. This coating is a combination of pigments, vehicles, resins, and additives used in printing. (19)

ink agitator: a motorized, revolving metal cone running along the ink fountain, continuously stirring the ink. This agitator keeps the ink at a workable consistency and helps reduce the formation of dried-ink skins. (20)

ink body: the consistency or degree of softness or hardness of an ink. Body is the covering power and flow of the ink or vehicle. (19)

ink film thickness: the thickness of ink when printed onto a substrate. (19)

ink formulation: the amount and types of ingredients mixed together to make an ink. (19)

ink fountain: the reservoir in the inking system holding the ink before the rollers transfer the ink to the printing plate. (20)

inking system: the portion of the press transferring ink from the ink fountain to the printing plate. (20)

inking unit: the portion of the press consisting of the ink fountain and rollers that control the feeding of the ink. (20)

ink-jet plate: a plate with image areas that are applied with an ink-jet printer. (17)

ink-jet platesetter: a platesetter that images printing plates by using ink-jet technology to apply image areas to the plate surface. (17)

ink-jet printer: a computer output device that forms images with a printhead containing nozzles that shoot tiny dots of ink onto the substrate. (13)

ink length: the ability of an ink to flow and form threads, or strings, when stretched. (19)

ink mileage: a measurement of how much area a specific amount of ink will print over. (19)

ink mist: tiny droplets making up a spray, fog, or mist of ink, created as rotating press rollers throw tiny droplets of ink into the air. (2)

inkometer: an instrument (a meter with rollers) that measures the tack of printing inks, in terms of the torque required to split an ink film. (19)

ink permanence: the ability of a printing ink to resist changes from exposure to light, weather, and time. (19)

ink position: the setting of an A.B.Dick's control lever that brings the ink form rollers in contact with the plate, thereby inking the plate. (22)

ink rub-off: the smearing of an ink film from applied pressure. (19)

ink train: the system of rollers that carries the ink from the fountain to the plate cylinder. (20)

in-line: the continuous work flow that results from connecting a press with finishing devices such as folders, trimmers, gluing units, and bindery units. (23)

in-line open web offset press: a press on which each printing unit has its own plate, blanket, and impression cylinder. (23)

in-plant printing: a printing operation that is part of a company, a corporation, or an association. (1)

input resolution: the amount of detail a digital image contains. (16)

insert: the assembling of signatures for saddle stitching. (25)

inspection method: a method for determining the proper amount of development for exposed film by observing detail during development. (10)

integrated dampening system: a dampening system in which dampening solution is applied to one of the ink form rollers. (20)

intelligent character recognition (ICR): an imaging process that electronically reads handwritten material. (14)

intermediate color: in additive color formation, colors (yellow-green, blue-green, blue-violet, red-violet, red-orange, and yellow-orange) created by combining primary colors and secondary colors. (7)

intermediate roller: one of the nonoscillating rollers in the ink train between the ductor roller and the form rollers. (20)

intermittent dampening system: a system that uses oscillator rollers, form rollers, a ductor roller, and a fountain roller. (20)

internal sizing: the application of materials to wet paper pulp to provide the desired degree of resistance to water and increase the surface strength. (18)

International Color Consortium (ICC): a group of vendors to the printing industry that promote a color management system of devices and software based on universally recognized color profiles. (16)

International Commission on Illumination (CIE): an international organization that establishes specs for the description of color, used as the basis of all color. (16)

International Commission on Illumination (CIE) chromaticity diagram: a diagram with a plotted curve defining the visible spectrum on an X-Y chart. (16)

International Commission on Illumination (CIE) XYZ value: a method of identifying a color by the amount of RGB light making up the color. (16)

International Cooperation for Integration of Prepress, Press, and Postpress (CIP3): an association working to produce systems for digital documents that can be created in prepress and used to set up press and finishing devices. (13)

International Organization for Standardization (ISO): the organization that sets international standards on products, services, and testing in nearly all industries. (3)

International System of Units (SI) metric system: the modern version of the metric system, based on seven internationally recognized units of measure. (3)

Internet: a worldwide computer network in which smaller networks and individual computers are connected to each other by means of a complex system of routers and gateways. (13)

interpolated resolution: a measure of the maximum resolution at which a scanner can capture an image using its optics in combination with interpolation software. (14)

interpolation: the increase of image resolution by the addition of new pixels throughout an image. (14)

interpreter: a computer program residing on a controller board in the printer. (13)

invisible ink: ink that prints clear but shows up as a fluorescent blue or yellow when placed under a black light. (19)

iris diaphragm: the device on a process camera for restricting light gradually from the outer edges of the ends toward the center. (10)

ISO series: the standard sizes of paper set by the ISO. (3)

J

jaw cylinder: the cylinder on a jaw folder used to fold the web. (23)

job costing: the process of comparing the estimated production times and costs to the actual production times and costs. (4)

Job Definition Format (JDF): a format that allows data input by customers seeking an estimate to be used by workstations involved in the job's production. (13)

job ticket: an electronic form or a paper form used to track costs for labor, materials, and press time of a given printing job. (4)

jog: to bend into a curve and square up to ensure all sheets are aligned. (25)

jogging: the squaring and aligning of sheets before loading onto the feed table or in the delivery pile. (20)

journalistic convention: an accepted practice newspapers and other publications use, regarding typography and page layout. (15)

jukebox: a device used to store and access information from a collection of electronic storage devices, such as CDs, MOs, and DVDs. (8)

justified format: a typesetting format in which the lines are aligned on both the left and right edges of the column or page. (6)

K

kerning: the process of adjusting the space between certain character pairs to minimize gaps for the best appearance and readability. (6)

keyboard: a computer input device based on the original typewriter keyboard arrangement. (8)

keyless fountain: an electronic inking system that does not use conventional fountain keys. (23)

keyless inking: an inking system that uses a metering roller to deliver a uniform coating of ink to the plate. (20)

kilobyte (KB): about one thousand (1024) bytes. (8)

knife: a razor-sharp cutting blade or instrument in a piece of equipment. (25)

knife folder: a folding device that uses a metal blade to force a sheet through a set of folding rollers. (25)

L

label paper: paper made to accept adhesive without curling. (18)

labor union: an organization of workers formed to advance its members' interests concerning wages, benefits, and working conditions. (5)

lacquer: a clear or colored resin-based solution added to the image area of a printing plate to increase its durability. (17)

laser: a device that produces intense, single-wavelength, unidirectional beams of light. (14)

laser beam: a beam of nearly parallel and monochromatic light moving in phase. (2)

laser printer: a medium- to high-quality computer output device that uses a laser beam to polarize images on the drum. (13)

laser proof: a proof created on a laser printer. (13)

layout: a drawing, a sketch, or another plan indicating how a printed piece will look, including the placement of text, illustrations, and other page elements. (7)

layout line: a straight line drawn on a masking sheet to assist the stripper in placing images. (12)

layout table: a table used to prepare layouts or check finished flats. (12)

lead edge: the part of a sheet entering the printing press first. (12)

leading: the vertical distance separating each line of typeset copy, measured in points from one line to the next. (3)

leafing: an effect that occurs when metallic pigments in an ink form a layer parallel to the surface of the print, causing a high metallic luster of silver or gold. (19)

leaflet: a folded flier intended for free distribution. (7)

legibility: the ease with which a typeface can be read immediately. (6)

lens: the part of a camera through which light passes and is focused on the film. (10)

lensboard: the part of a process camera that acts as the carrier of the lens. (10)

letter fold: a folding pattern with two parallel folds applied to a sheet, as done to an 8 1/2″ × 11″ sheet to fit into a business envelope. (25)

letterpress: the process of printing from a raised surface. (1)

letterspacing: the spacing placed between individual characters. (6)

library: a set of reference resources. (15)

lift: a pile of paper, usually the amount cut or drilled in a single operation. (25)

ligature: a combination of characters in one unit. (6)

lightfastness: the ability of a printing ink to resist discoloration and fading when exposed to light or over time. (19)

light integrator: a device, similar to a light meter, that is capable of making certain that the exposure is correct for originals of any given density. (10)

lightness: the degree to which colors reflect light. (16)

line: a long narrow mark that can be straight or curved. (7)

line art: type or a drawing with no grays or middle tones. (7)

line copy: artwork with no tone variations consisting of solid lines on a white or contrasting background, including pen-and-ink drawings, diagrams, and type composition. (7)

line gauge: a device used to measure type sizes and line widths in picas or inches. (3)

line negative: a film negative produced by line photography. (10)

line photography: original single-color or single-tone camera copy reproduced on film without continuous tones. (10)

line shot: an image captured with a process camera without the use of a halftone screen, usually used for line copy, such as text and line drawings, and occasionally used to reduce an original photograph to only black and white. (11)

line spacing: additional space inserted between lines of type to make the type matter easier to read. (6)

lines per inch (lpi): a term used to describe screen ruling, computer screen resolution, and image resolution. (3)

linting: the result of loosely bonded fibers that break off and are carried by the offset blanket to the ink rollers. (18)

lip: an allowance made for the gripper to pick up and open signatures during saddle-stitching assembly. A lip is also the amount of overlap of one half of a folded signature. This amount is needed for the feeding of signatures into a GST. (12)

liquid crystal display (LCD) monitor: a flat screen on which images appear by the rotation of selected liquid crystals. (13)

liquid ink: a fluid and watery printing ink. (19)

lithographic plate: a metal, plastic, or paper image-carrying surface on an offset printing press or duplicator. (17)

lockout device: a key or combination-type lock to hold an energy-isolating device in the off position to prevent the machine from energizing. (2)

log E curve: a graphical representation of the contrast capabilities of graphic arts film. (10)

long-grain paper: paper cut into sheets with the fibers aligned parallel to the sheet's longer dimension. (18)

loose-leaf binding: pages bound together with removable rings or posts. (25)

lowercase letter: a "small" letter of the alphabet. (6)

low-lift gripper: a gripper on a press with an insertion device that opens just enough to allow the sheet to be inserted. (20)

lubricant: an oil used as an ink additive to reduce tack and improve the ability to cover the image areas uniformly. (19)

M

machine finish: the finish imparted to a sheet as it leaves the calender rollers of a paper machine. (18)

machine finished: a high-gloss paper finish produced by allowing the wet-paper web to dry against a highly polished metal cylinder. (18)

made for hire: a work an employee created or a work that has been specially ordered or commissioned, in writing, as a contribution to a collective work. (5)

magenta: a purplish-red color made by combining equal amounts of red and blue light. This color is a primary color of the subtractive color system. (16)

magnetic ink: ink formulated with iron-oxide pigments that can be magnetized after printing. (19)

main disconnect (master) switch: a switch that allows all power to machinery and small appliances to be turned off when a facility is not in use. (2)

main flat: the flat carrying most of the images, when a complementary flat is needed. (12)

management information system (MIS): a computer-based management tool used to assess data in production planning, inventory control, financial transactions, and sales records. (4)

mask: in line photography, a piece of black construction paper (or similar light-blocking material) placed over the film when making test strips. (10)

masking film: a material with a thin ruby- or amber-colored emulsion on a thicker sheet of clear plastic, creating a clear area when a film negative is exposed. (9)

masking flat: a flat used to cover certain images and prevent their exposure during platemaking. (12)

masking sheet: the thick sheet of paper or plastic that holds the negatives or positives. (12)

master page: a page composition–program feature that can be set up to include the page geometry, typography, and other elements of a page that will recur in a document. (15)

Matchprint® proof: a color proof produced from the actual film that will create the printed page. (16)

material safety data sheet (MSDS): a sheet that gives the chemical name and the name, address, and telephone number of the manufacturer. (2)

matte finish: a finish possessing a generally flat, smooth surface, free from shine or highlights. (18)

mechanical: the camera-ready page elements assembled on an art board. A mechanical is the paperboard on which camera-ready page elements are mounted. (9)

mechanical binding: various methods used to fasten together individual sheets. (25)

mechanical ghosting: the uneven printing of an image because of an uneven replenishment of ink on the plate and blanket. (19)

mechanical pulp: inexpensive paper pulp produced entirely by mechanical means and used for newspapers, directories, catalogs, magazines, and paperback books. (18)

Mediaan system: a system of print measurement used primarily in Belgium. (3)

megabyte (MB): about one million (1,048,576) bytes. (8)

memory: computer data storage that comes in the form of chips. (8)

mercury vapor lamp: an enclosed light source that produces radiation by passing an electrical current through gaseous mercury. (2)

metallic ink: ink made with small metal flakes or particles (aluminum for silver and bronze or brass for gold) that leaf together on the printed surface as the ink dries. (19)

metamerism: the phenomenon of a color appearing differently under light sources with different color balances. (16)

metering roller: a roller usually made of rubber or covered with rubber and serving the same purpose as the fountain roller in an intermittent system. (20)

micrometer: a device that measures the thickness of thin objects, such as paper. (3)

midtone area: the area of an image falling between the highlight and shadow areas. (11)

milling: a process used to crush and further blend the ink pigment into the vehicle. (19)

mineral paper: a type of synthetic paper. (18)

miniweb: a smaller version of the larger web offset press. (23)

modem: an electronic device that converts digital computer data into a form that can be transmitted along telephone lines. A modem also receives transmitted signals from over the phone line and converts them back to digital data. (8)

modern serif typeface: a Roman typeface showing great variation in stroke thickness; thin, straight, and somewhat rectangular serifs; and a very strong contrast between the thin and thick lines of the characters. (6)

moiré pattern: an undesirable wavelike or checkerboard pattern visible across a halftone or screened image. This pattern is usually caused by a misalignment of screens. (11)

molleton: thick fabric made from cotton used as a covering on dampener form and ductor rollers. (20)

mottling: a blotchy or cloudy appearance of an image, instead of a smooth, continuous appearance. (19)

multicolor press: a press that prints more than one color at the same time. (20)

multimetal plate: a printing plate made with two or three layers of metal, each selected for its ink- or water-receptive characteristics. (17)

M weight: the figure representing the weight of 1000 sheets of a paper in the size listed. (3)

N

nanometer (nm): a unit of measurement equal to one-billionth of a meter. (16)

negative film assembly: the preparation of flats containing film negatives. (12)

negative-working plate: a printing plate that is exposed with a film negative and in which the image areas harden when exposed to light. (17)

neutral position: the setting of an A.B.Dick's operation control lever so the inner oscillating roller is in contact with the form rollers. (22)

new business: a for-profit organization that is originated. (26)

news ink: generally thin and fluid ink made of mineral oil and carbon black and formulated to dry by absorption. (19)

newsprint: an inexpensive grade of paper with high opacity and good printing qualities made primarily from groundwood pulp, usually blended with chemical pulp to increase the paper's tear strength. Newsprint is used primarily for the printing of newspapers, but it is also used for direct-mail advertising, sketch pads, comic books, catalogs, and all types of directories. (18)

Newton's rings: an undesirable color pattern resulting from interference between the exposure light and its reflected beam from the closely adjacent surface. (14)

night latch: a handle provided for lowering the rollers against the plate and lifting them out of contact with the plate. (20)

night-latch position: the setting of an A.B.Dick's operation control lever that moves the inner oscillating roller out of contact with the form rollers. (22)

ninety-degree bump turn: an in-line device that serves as the transition between two conveyor belts moving at a right angle to one another. (23)

nip point: the point where two rollers come together. (2)

nominal weight: the basis weight specified when ordering paper. (3)

nonactinic light: rays from fluorescent and incandescent bulbs. (12)

nonimage area: an ink-resistant, water-receptive area on a printing plate. (17)

nonimpact printing: a method of printing in which the substrate is never in contact with the plate. (1)

nonpareil: a unit of measure of the point system equal to one-half pica. (3)

nonporous ink: ink designed for metallic or plastic-coated papers. This ink dries by oxidation. (19)

nonregister: the least exacting color registration in which allowance is made for several different colors to be completely independent of each other. (9)

numbering: the process of imprinting tickets, checks, certificates, or other items with consecutive figures. (25)

numbering tower: an in-line device that can print sequential numbers to the printed web. (23)

O

obscene literature: material considered offensive to morality or virtue. (5)

Occupational Safety and Health Administration (OSHA): the agency of the U.S. Department of Labor that promotes and enforces safe and healthful working conditions. This administration also educates employers and employees about industrial hazards. (2)

off-line: any finishing operation performed away from the press. (25)

offset duplicator: a small offset press that prints up to a maximum sheet size of about 11" × 17" (28 cm × 43 cm). (20)

offset lithography: a printing method in which inked images are offset, or transferred, from one surface to another. (1)

offset paper: a paper classification of papers with internal sizing to reduce its absorbency of dampening solution. (18)

offset press: a press that prints on sheets larger than 11″ × 17″ (28 cm × 43 cm). (20)

old-style serif typeface: a typeface with little contrast between thick and thin lines and pointed serifs that generally slant or curve and extend outward at the top of the capital T and the bottom of the capital E. (6)

one-person proofing: proofreading during which one person is responsible for reading both the galley and the manuscript. (6)

one-piece copy: a mechanical with no overlay. (9)

on impression: into contact with the paper and blanket. (20)

opacity: the ability of a sheet of paper to block the passage of light. (18)

opaque ink: ink that does not transmit light. This ink is the opposite of transparent ink. (19)

opaque paper: paper with high filler content to improve its ability to block the passage of light. (18)

open counter: a portion of a letter consisting of a loop that is incomplete (not closed). (6)

Open Prepress Interface (OPI): a work-flow protocol in which high-resolution images are stored on a server and low-resolution files with corresponding names are placed in the layout. (14)

open shop: a nonunion company. (5)

optical character recognition (OCR): an imaging process that electronically reads typewritten or printed pages and saves the copy in its ASCII format. (14)

optical density: the light-absorption behavior of a printing-ink film. (19)

optical resolution: a measure of the maximum resolution at which a scanner can capture an image using its optics alone, exclusive of software interpolation. (14)

orphan: the first line of a paragraph at the bottom of a column of type. (15)

orthochromatic material: a light-sensitive material sensitive to all areas of the visible spectrum, except red. (10)

oscillating roller: a roller in the inking system of a press that moves from side to side as it rotates to work the ink and spread it evenly over the form rollers. (20)

output device: a target for information held in the central computer unit. (13)

output resolution: the amount of detail in an image that a monitor, a printer, or another output device can produce. (16)

output service bureau: a supplier generally specializing in PostScript output, rather than in a broader range of color separation and prepress service. (13)

output size: the dimensions a digital image becomes when output to a monitor or printer. (16)

outside purchase: a service or material contracted to be performed or supplied by another company. (4)

overlay: a transparent sheet (similar to acetate) to which second-color image elements are attached. The overlay is attached at the top of the pasteup base. (9)

overprint varnish: a clear coating applied over ink to protect the printed surface from moisture, abrasion, or other potential sources of damage. (19)

oxidation: a chemical reaction involving the combination of oxygen with another substance. This is an ink-drying method in which there is a chemical reaction involving the combination of oxygen with the varnishes in the printed ink film. (19)

oxidative polymerization: the bonding of molecules into chains called *polymers*, when exposed to oxygen. (19)

oxygen delignification: the use of oxygen to remove lignin from pulp in preparation for bleaching. (18)

P

packaging: the sector of the printing industry specializing in producing items that contain objects. (1)

padding: a form of perfect binding in which a flexible adhesive is used to hold the sheets together and allow easy removal. (25)

page composition: the process of properly arranging the various elements, or components of a page, (such as type and illustrations) that make up a printed page. (9)

page composition program: computer software that allows the user to determine the page size and format and to assemble the page elements. (13)

page composition software: an application that creates layouts for any type of document by positioning text and graphic elements. (15)

page description language (PDL): a software program consisting of commands that, when translated through a special device, form the desired image on an output device. (6)

paint program: computer software that allows the user to create original bitmap graphics or manipulate existing ones. (13)

panchromatic (pan) film: film that is sensitive to the colors visible to the human eye. (10)

Pantone Matching System® standard: a color book based on the major groups of pigment colors (such as reds, yellows, greens, and blues) common to the printing industry. (16)

paperboard: a strong, thick paper or cardboard used for boxes and other types of packaging. This paper is available bleached, unbleached, coated, uncoated, and in a variety of thicknesses. (18)

paper caliper: a device used to measure paper thickness. (3)

paper classification: a group of related types of paper. (18)

paper gripper margin: the area on the lead edge of a press sheet that grippers hold during printing. (12)

paper size: a metric or conventional measurement that describes the length and width dimensions of paper. (3)

paper table: a platform on which the sheets of paper are stacked as they are delivered from the press. (20)

parallax error: an illusion that can result from a change in the viewing angle. (12)

parallel fold: a basic folding pattern in which all folds being made are parallel to each other. (25)

partnership: a business owned by two or more owners. (26)

paste ink: a thick and tacky printing ink. (19)

patch tool: an image manipulation tool that can be used to cover selected pixels with pixels from another area of the photograph. This tool can be used in conjunction with the healing brush. (14)

pattern gluer with plow: an in-line device that can apply a strip of glue and then fold part of the sheet onto the wet glue. (23)

pattern perforator: an in-line device that can perforate, score, or slit the printed web. (23)

perfect binding: a binding method in which the sheets of paper are held together with a flexible adhesive. (25)

perfecting blanket-to-blanket web offset press: a press that uses blanket cylinders acting as impression cylinders and prints on both sides of the paper at the same time as the paper passes between the two blanket cylinders. (23)

perfecting press: a press that prints on both sides of the paper at the same time. (20)

perforating: an operation in which a small series of very short slits or holes is cut in the paper and a small bridge of paper remains intact between each hole, as in the case of a ticket stub. (25)

personal protective equipment: various types of eye, ear, respiratory, and skin protection devices used to prevent physical injury. (2)

pH level: the potential of the hydrogen ion. The pH level of a fountain solution is the measure of how acidic or alkaline the solution is. (19)

photographic color separation: separating a full-color photograph or piece of art into the process colors of CMY to film, with the use of color filters. (16)

photomechanical transfer (PMT) gray contact screen: a halftone screen used for making screened paper prints. (11)

photometer: a device used to measure light intensity. (3)

photomultiplier tube: a light-gathering sensor composed of highly sensitive photocells that transform variations in light into electric currents. (14)

photopolymer: an organic substance that undergoes physical changes when exposed to light. (17)

photopolymer plate: a surface plate with a light-sensitive photopolymer coating. (17)

photo retouching: a photo-editing tool that alters all or part of a digital photograph. (14)

phototypesetting: the setting of type or the preparation of copy for printing using photographic paper or film. (8)

pica: a principal unit of measurement of the point system equal to 0.166 . (3)

picking: the lifting of paper fibers caused by the softening and weakening of the paper surface or when the pulling force of the ink is greater than the surface of the paper. This lifting is the lifting of paper fibers by the offset rubber blanket. (18)

pick resistance: the ability of a paper to prevent fibers from rupturing during printing. (18)

picture box: a closed figure of any shape used to position a graphic element. (15)

picture element (pixel): the smallest indivisible point of display on a computer monitor. (3)

piezoelectric ink-jet printer: a device that emits tiny drops of ink when the ink chamber is squeezed.13)

pigment: a colorant that does not dissolve, but spreads as tiny particles through liquids or other substances, such as ink. (16)

pile feeder: a mechanism used to separate the sheets of paper and feed them into the press. (20)

pile height regulator: a device used to control the speed of elevation of the pile table or piling bars. (20)

piling: a printing problem characterized by the accumulation of paper fibers, bits of detached coating particles, and other debris on the printing plate or blanket in both the image and nonimage areas. This problem occurs when ink tack or one of various other press problems overcomes the paper's pick resistance. (18)

piling bar: an elevator strip or bar used to replace the stock on a pile feeder before the first pile runs out. (20)

pinhole: a small unwanted transparent opening on a film negative that forms a small dot-size image on the printing plate. (12)

pinless folder: a folder that uses pressure instead of pins to hold the paper web as it passes through the folder. (23)

pin register system: a system that uses punched holes and mechanical devices to produce an accurate register. This register system allows multiple overlays to be created in precise register. (12)

pixels per inch (ppi): the number of pixels making up a digital image. (3)

plasma display monitor: a flat screen on which images appear when electrons strike selected cells and cause the creation of UV light, which in turn, creates visible light. (13)

plate bend: the portion of a plate that is bent to be clamped onto the plate cylinder. A plate bend is also the portion of a flat corresponding to the plate-bend area of the plate. (12)

plate blinding: an effect occurring when the acid eats away the image areas of a printing plate and causes a lack of ink receptivity. (17)

plate cylinder: the part of a printing press holding the printing plate. (20)

platen press: a type of letterpress in which both the form and the substrate remain flat during printing. (1)

platesetter: the platemaking component of a CTP system, used to image plates containing paginated text and graphics. (13)

plow tower: an in-line device containing a plow folder, which folds at high speed by lifting part of the moving paper by sending it up a ramp shaped similarly to the blade of a plow. (23)

pocket CD: a compact disc that is 3 1/8" in diameter, in contrast to a larger CD, which is 4 5/8" in diameter. (8)

point: a principal unit of measure for type and line spacing equal to approximately 1/72 of an inch, or 0.0138". (3)

point size: the vertical measurement used to identify or specify the size of a typeface. This measurement is roughly from the top of the ascender to the bottom of the descender. (3)

point system: a system of print measurement used throughout the printing industry in the United States. (3)

polymerize: to form chains immobilizing each molecule and collectively hardening and forming a solid layer, binding the pigment to the printed surface. (19)

poor binding: inadequate adhesion of an ink to the substrate. (19)

poor color: a reproduced color that is noticeably different from the original. (19)

portable document format (PDF): a file format Adobe Systems developed for representing documents in a manner that is independent of the original program software, hardware, and operating system used to create those documents. (13)

positive film assembly: the preparation of flats containing film positives. (12)

positive-working plate: a printing plate that is exposed with a film positive and in which the plate coating in the nonimage areas begins decomposing when exposed to light. (17)

postconsumer waste: recycled material collected from the end user or consumer. (18)

posterization: the conversion of a continuous tone image to a high-contrast image with only a few distinct tones. This conversion can be performed photomechanically with high-contrast film or electronically in an illustration program, by specifying a set number of gradient steps. (11)

PostScript® font technology: a PDL Adobe Systems, Inc. developed that enables imagesetters different companies have developed to interpret electronic files from any number of personal computers and off-the-shelf programs. (6)

powdering: the lifting by ink of individual filler particles from paper during printing. (18)

preconsumer waste: wastepaper that results from papermaking and printing operations and is free from ink. (18)

preflighting: an orderly review of files to identify things that might cause problems during prepress operations or at the output stage. (13)

prefolder: an in-line device that can slit the web into two ribbons, which can then be positioned so one is over the other before they move into a folder, to double the number of pages in the signature resulting from the folding operation. (23)

prepress proof: a proof made from film and dyes or electronic data before the pressrun. (16)

prepress service: a service bureau offering a full range of prepress services, including everything from manual page composition to high-end scanning and RIPping. (13)

prepress service bureau: a business specializing in prepress operations such as page composition and image manipulation. (1)

preregistering: the positioning of a sheet before the insertion device starts its cycle of operation. (20)

presensitized plate: a printing plate that the manufacturer has pretreated with a light-sensitive coating. (17)

press proof: a proof run on a proof press using the printing inks and substrate for the actual job. (16)

press sheet: a large sheet of paper printed on the front and back. (12)

primary color: in additive color formation, a main color on the color wheel (red, yellow, or blue). (7)

printer: an electronic device that outputs digital information onto a substrate, such as paper. (13)

printing: the production of multiple copies of images and words with the use of another surface to transfer an impression to a substrate. (1)

Printing Trade Customs: the trade customs originally established in 1922 covering such matters as proofs, alterations, press overruns, delivery, and terms of payment. (5)

printing unit: the part of the printing press where printing takes place. This unit contains the plate cylinder, blanket cylinder, and impression cylinder. (20)

Print Production Format (PPF): a format that allows data input at the beginning of a job's production to be read by several workstations throughout the job's production. (13)

process camera: a special graphic arts camera designed to photograph two-dimensional copy and produce high-contrast films used to prepare printing plates. (10)

process color: one of the three ink colors (CMY) used for printing full-color materials. (16)

process color printing: the printed reproduction of full-color images using the transparent inks of CMYK. This color printing is printing from a series of two or more plates in halftone to produce other colors and shades. (16)

production house: a business specializing in one area of printing production, such as prepress or finishing. (1)

production stage: a collection of functions that occur to a design as part of getting the design printed. (7)

production standard: an hourly value representing the average output of a particular operating area under specified conditions. (4)

profile: a comparison of the output of a proofer or press against the input data. (16)

profit: the income acquired from the sale of products and services above and beyond the costs of salaries, materials, mortgage or rent, and utilities and the other costs of conducting business. (26)

proof: a prototype of the printed job made digitally from electronic data, photochemically from film and dyes, or photomechanically from plates. (13)

proof press: a printing machine used to produce photomechanical proofs. (16)

proofreader's mark: a symbol used on manuscript or proof to show when something is to be deleted, added, or changed. (6)

proofreading: the process of checking for typesetting errors and marking them for correction. (6)

proportion: the pleasing relationship between the elements on the printed page and the general dimensions of the page itself. (7)

proportion scale: a device used to determine the percentage of reduction or enlargement an image requires, based on a ratio of the size of the original to the size it needs to fit. (3)

pseudoplasticity: the property of a material causing it to lose viscosity when stirred and regain viscosity when left to stand. (19)

psychology of color: the knowledge of proper color combinations and applications. (7)

publishing industry: the sector of the printing industry specializing in producing books, booklets, catalogs, journals, and magazines. (1)

pull guide: a mechanism that uses a finger or roller (or a combination of the two) to move the sheet against the side guide after the sheet has been positioned at the front guides, or stops. (20)

pulping: liberating cellulose fibers from other impurities and chemicals in the wood and producing pulp for papermaking. (18)

pulsed xenon: a light source designed to light, or pulse, with each half cycle of alternating current applied. (10)

pulsed xenon lamp (PXA): a primary light source in graphic arts photography. This source provides a constant output with a spectral composition resembling sunlight. (2)

punching: an operation in which rectangular or specially shaped holes are cut in paper to accommodate plastic and spiral bindings. (25)

push guide: a side guide on a press that pushes the sheet into its predetermined position after the sheet is forwarded into the front guides or insertion device. (20)

Q

quartz-iodine lamp: a photographic light source that provides even illumination at the film plane and does not grow dimmer with age. This lamp is used primarily for black-and-white photography and as a source of illumination for platemaking equipment. (10)

quick printing: a printing establishment specializing in producing short-run jobs quickly on offset duplicators or digital presses. (1)

quick-set ink: a rapid-drying printing ink made with a balanced solvent, resin, and an oil vehicle. (19)

R

radiation curing: the instant solidification of an ink film, due to exposure to high doses of UV light or electron beams. (19)

radiation-curing ink: ink that uses complex vehicles that harden and polymerize when exposed to radiation from UV light, beams of electrons, or IR light. (19)

ragged: type aligned unevenly on the right or left side. (6)

random-access memory (RAM): the short-term memory a computer uses to store information in process. (8)

rapid access film: graphic arts film used to produce negatives with a process camera and contact negatives and film positives with a contact vacuum frame. (10)

raster image processor (RIP): a hardware-software combination that interprets digital data into an array of dots (a bitmap), which can be output through an imagesetter marking engine. (13)

rasterization: the process of converting mathematical and digital information into a series of dots by an imagesetter or a platesetter for the production of film or plates. (13)

readability: a measure of how difficult or easy it is to read several pages of printed matter before eye fatigue begins. (6)

ream: for most types of paper, 500 sheets of paper of a single size. (3)

receding delivery table: a delivery table that automatically adjusts the platform height as the sheets are delivered. (20)

recycled paper: paper produced from pulp made from used paper and paper products, manufacturing waste, nonpaper materials, wood residues, and fibers recovered from mill wastewater. (18)

recycled pulp: pulp made from fibers reclaimed from used paper and paper products. (18)

refiner groundwood: chips and water pumped through refiners, where they are forced between counterrotating disks. (18)

refining stage: the stage in the papermaking process during which the fibers are flattened and abraded. (18)

reflection densitometer: an electronic device used to measure the amount of light that bounces, or reflects, off a photographic print or printed sheet at a 90° angle. (3)

register board: a platform that accepts a sheet from the feeder unit and inserts it in register, ready for printing. (20)

register mark: a design or shape placed in the nonimage areas of negatives, positives, color separations, and plates to ensure correct register. (12)

register pin: a holding device used to hold punched sheets in place for film assembly and platemaking. (12)

register punch: a device used to make perfectly aligned holes on the masking sheet and printing plate. (12)

registration: overall agreement in the position and alignment of printing detail on a press sheet. (16)

regular embossing: the imparting of a relief image to a printed sheet. (25)

relief die: a metal plate with an image carved into it. (25)

remoistenable gluer: a device that applies a liquid adhesive to a web or sheet that dries but can be moistened later. (23)

remote proofing: sending a digital image across the Internet to a proofer located in a different location. (13)

repeatability: the ability of an imagesetter or another device to achieve exactly the same results each time, given the same data. This ability is a critical specification for accurate color-film separations. (13)

reproduction size: the size of an image after the sizing process, not to be confused with the original size. (3)

repurposing: reusing content intended for one medium by reformatting it for another. (8)

requisite of design: a characteristic that is a necessary component of a design. (7)

resampling: in image manipulation, reducing the file size of an image by lowering the resolution. (14)

resin: a solid or semisolid organic substance used as a binder in printing ink vehicles. (19)

resizing: altering the height and width of a digital image, such as a photograph or another graphic. (16)

resolution: a means of quantifying an image's sharpness of clarity. (3)

respiratory protection device: a mask that prevents harmful matter from entering the respiratory system. (2)

résumé: a typed summary of a job applicant's education, experience, and previous employment. (27)

reverse type: type that drops out of the background and assumes the color of the paper. (6)

rhythm: the state of design created with the repetition of similar elements in a design. Rhythm is the flow or movement of the individual elements in a design. (7)

ribbon: the continuous roll of paper that forms on a papermaking machine or is fed into a web press. (20)

rider: an intermediate roller in the ink train that contacts only one other roller. (20)

right-angle fold: a basic folding pattern in which each fold is made at a right angle to the preceding fold. (25)

right-reading: capable of being read from left to right. (20)

right-reading side: the side of a negative that allows type to be read easily. (12)

roll stand: a stand used with web presses to hold one or more paper rolls and feed each in turn with consistent and controlled tension into the printing unit of the press. (23)

roll-to-sheet feeding system: a feeding system in which the substrate comes from a roll, enters as a ribbon, is cut into sheets, and is then fed into the press. (20)

Roman: a typestyle based on the capital letters the ancient Romans cut into stone monuments. (6)

rotary die cutter: an in-line device that can slit or cut holes in the printed web. (23)

rotary press: a printing press that uses two cylinders rotating in the same direction. (1)

rotary (roller) guide: a device that uses rollers to position the sheets against the side guide. (20)

rough layout: a sketch or an enhanced thumbnail of a page design or layout depicting a somewhat accurate representation of the final size and position of all page elements. (7)

rubber-based ink: ink that can stay on the ink train of a press for several hours without drying because it contains cyclized rubber. (19)

rule: an object formed by directly connecting two points. This object is one of the most basic design elements. (7)

ruler: a representation of a conventional ruler showing increments of linear measurement. (15)

ruler guide: a light blue line that is not output to a printer, but assists in the placement of type or graphic elements during page composition. (15)

runaround format: a typesetting format in which text flows or contours around illustrations and logos. (6)

S

saddle sewing: a binding method in which the thread passes through the signature fold at the spine of the book. (25)

saddle stitching: a sewing method that uses wires or staples inserted on the fold line, or saddle, of the sheets to bind the pages together. (25)

safelight: a special darkroom lamp emitting illumination under which light-sensitive materials can be handled without danger of fogging through exposure to light. (10)

safety color code: a color code established to alert and inform students and workers to take precautionary action around potential hazards. (2)

sampling rate: in digitizing of images, the frequency with which points are recorded. In scanning, the sampling rate is measured as the number of samples taken per inch (or per mm), both horizontally and vertically. (3)

sans serif: a typeface with no serifs and little or no contrast in the thickness of character strokes. (6)

saturation: the property of color defining the color's degree of strength, or difference from white. This property is the extent to which one or two of the three additive primaries predominates in a color. (16)

scaling: the process of reducing or enlarging an image. (3)

scanner: an electronic imaging device that measures color densities of an original, stores those measurements as digital information, manipulates or alters the data, and uses the manipulated data to create color separations. (8)

scanning densitometer: an electronic instrument installed on press that uses a photocell to accurately measure the amount of light reflected from or through different tone values. (3)

scoring: compressing a line across a heavy sheet of paper to improve the sheet's ability to be folded on that line. (25)

screen: a ruled screen used to change continuous tone photographs into dotted halftones for printing. (3)

screen angle: the angular relationship of halftone screens used in making black-and-white halftones and color separations for four-color printing. (3)

screen angle indicator: a device used to determine the screen angles of halftones and screen tints. (12)

screen printing: a printing process that uses a squeegee to force ink through a porous fabric covered by a stencil that blocks the nonimage areas. (1)

screen ruling: the number of ruled grid lpi on a halftone screen. (11)

screen tint: the mechanical or electronic special effect added to certain areas of a layout to add contrast, emphasis, or color or to subdue a background image. (9)

script typeface: a typeface designed to imitate handwriting with characters that touch. (6)

scuff-resistant ink film: an ink film with a tough, hard surface that can withstand the scrapes and shocks from shipping and handling. (19)

scumming: the adhering of ink to the nonimage areas of the plate. (18)

secondary color: in additive color formation, a color (orange, green, or violet) created by the combination of two primary colors. (7)

selective absorption: the absorption of one or more, but not all, components of a solution. (19)

semidrying oil: a vegetable oil that transforms to a solid when exposed in a film to oxygen, but at a slower rate than drying oils do. (19)

sensitivity guide: a narrow, calibrated, continuous tone gray scale with each tone scale numbered. In a platemaking operation, the sensitivity guide is exposed on a sensitized press plate with the rest of the work. The device measures the tone values represented on the plate. (10)

serif typeface: any typeface containing traditional (not square) serifs. (6)

service bureau: a supplier providing services such as high-resolution scanning or film output. (13)

set: the point at which an ink is dry enough to be lightly touched without smudging. (19)

setoff: an unwanted transfer of ink from one sheet to the back of the next. (19)

shade: the alteration of a color created by adding black to the color. (7)

shadow area: the area of least density in a halftone negative. This area is the darkest area on the positive, or printed image. (11)

shadow exposure: a yellow light exposure made through a halftone screen after the main exposure, in making a halftone. This exposure is used to enhance the dots in the shadow regions of the halftone negative and to improve detail. (11)

shape: an elementary form, such as the square, circle, and triangle. (7)

sharpening: the software function of creating the illusion of greater sharpness by increasing the contrast at the edges within an image. (16)

sheetfed press: an offset press or duplicator designed to print a single sheet of paper at a time. (20)

sheet separator: a springy steel finger extending over the lead edge of the pile of paper in the feeder. (20)

sheets per carton: the number of sheets in a carton of paper. (18)

short fold: a single fold applied to a sheet in which one panel is much shorter than the other. (25)

short-grain paper: paper cut into sheets with the fibers aligned parallel to the sheet's shorter dimension. (18)

shot mill: a machine that uses small metal pellets (similar to steel shot) to chop up ink-pigment particles and mix them into the vehicle. (19)

show-through: the ability of a sheet of paper to block the passage of light. This is an undesirable effect of poor opacity in which the image on one side of a sheet of paper is seen on the other side. (19)

side guide: a roller, pivoting foot, or suction-powered plate that aids in the lateral positioning of a sheet of paper before the sheet is transferred into the printing unit. (20)

side sewing: a binding method in which the thread is passed from signature to signature through the side of the book so the stitches run parallel to the binding edge. (25)

side stitching: a binding method in which staples are inserted close to the fold and clinched at the back. (25)

signature: a folded printed sheet in a sequence of 4, 8, 16, 32, or 64 pages. (7)

signature imposition: arranging pages so they will appear on a press sheet in the proper position and so, when the sheet is folded, the pages will be in the proper sequence. (7)

silver-halide plate: a printing plate with a light-sensitive emulsion of silver and iodine, bromine, or another halogen. (17)

silverless film: graphic arts film that uses a diazo compound in its light-sensitive emulsion. (10)

single-knife rotary trimmer: an in-line device used to trim a bound signature at high speed. (23)

single-side imposition: image assembly for a job to be printed on one side only. (12)

size: in graphic design, the dimensions of an element within a design. (7)

sizing: the process of reducing or enlarging an image. (3)

skeleton wheel: an adjustable disk on the delivery cylinder that holds the sheet as it travels. This disk is a paper-guide wheel. (20)

skew: text that contours around a jagged illustration. (6)

skin protection device: gloves or other clothing that protects the skin from contact with harmful materials. (2)

slab waste: paper waste taken from the outside portion of a roll. This waste often results during splicing. (23)

slitting: cutting printed sheets or webs into two or more sections by means of a cutting wheel on a printing press, a folding machine, or a slitter-rewinder. (25)

slotting: a method of making holes for a binding that are not round. (25)

slur: a change in sharpness caused by a slippage of the cylinders, usually in the around-the-cylinder direction. (24)

slur gauge: a quality-control device on a color bar used to indicate slur caused primarily by cylinder slippage. (24)

slurry: a mixture of water and dissolved paper pulp. (18)

small cap: an uppercase letter slightly smaller than the normal capitals of the font. (6)

smart fountain: a standard ink fountain fitted with custom ink keys, motor-driven ink-key actuators, an electronic circuit board, associated wiring, and a gasket-sealed housing. (20)

Smyth sewing: a binding method in which the thread passes through the signature fold at the spine of the book. (25)

soft proof: a proof displayed on a computer screen. (13)

software: a computer program that initiates the functions of a computer, such as word processing, page composition, and image creation and manipulation. (13)

software piracy: the use of unlicensed computer software programs. (5)

softwood tree: a coniferous tree, such as pine, fir, spruce, or hemlock. (18)

sole proprietorship: a single-owner business in which the profits belong to the owner. (26)

solvent: a typically fluid material able to liquefy or dissolve one or more other materials. (19)

soy ink: ink that uses oil extracted from the soybean as the vehicle to carry the pigment. (19)

soy news ink: ink used to print on newsprint that contains 40% soy oil for black ink and 30% soy oil for color ink. (19)

specifications (specs): written information relating to typestyle, type sizes, and line or column width for a project. (7)

Specifications for Newsprint Advertising Production (SNAP): a publication containing standards for accurate color reproduction when printing on newsprint. (16)

Specifications for Web Offset Publications (SWOP®) specs: a publication containing standards for accurate color reproduction when printing with web lithography. (16)

specific gravity: the weight of a given volume of ink, compared to the weight of an equal volume of water. (19)

spectrodensitometer: a color-measurement device that serves all the functions of a spectrophotometer, densitometer, and colorimeter in a single instrument. (3)

spectrophotometer: the most accurate type of color-measurement device. A spectrophotometer measures light intensity and different colors or wavelengths of light. (3)

spherical aberration: the loss of focus when the outer edges of the process lens transmit light. (10)

spiral binding: a binding method requiring a long series of small holes to be punched or drilled along the edge of the product through which a continuous wire or plastic coil is wound. (25)

splicer: a machine that joins the ends of two webs of paper to make a continuous roll. (23)

splicing: in papermaking, the joining together of two rolls of paper, end-to-end. (18)

spoilage allowance: the percentage of extra sheets added to the total pieces needed for a job to compensate for replacing soiled or misprinted sheets and for use during makeready or when setting up the press. (18)

spot color: a color added to a layout to add interest, highlight important information, accent line art, and create duotones. (9)

spot varnish: an overprint varnish applied only to portions of a printed piece, instead of the entire piece. This varnish is typically used for aesthetic purposes. (19)

spread: a print made in a contact-printing frame that makes the original image slightly larger. (10)

spread trap: a trap created by spreading the foreground over the background color. This trap is used when a lighter object knocks out of a darker background. (14)

square dot screen: a halftone screen producing square dots that join in all four corners, as the dots reach 50% midtone size. (11)

square-serif typeface: any typeface containing serifs that do not come to a sharp or rounded point. (6)

squeeze: the pressure exerted between the offset-press plate cylinder and the blanket cylinder. (20)

standard size: a commonly available sheet dimension. (3)

star target: a circular pattern of lines on a color bar, primarily used to detect ink slur. (12)

static eliminator: a press attachment used to reduce the amount of static developing on a press because of low relative humidity and the movement of paper over metal surfaces. This attachment is also used to eliminate ink setoff or paper-feeding problems. (2)

step-and-repeat film assembly: the means by which multiple images from a single image are exposed onto a printing plate in two or more positions. (12)

step-and-repeat platemaking: the means by which multiple images from a single image are exposed onto a printing plate in two or more positions. (17)

step tablet: a piece of film with 10 or 21 steps ranging in densities from clear to completely black. This tablet is used to obtain consistent exposure and development of offset plates. (17)

sticking in the pile: the sticking together of recently printed sheets, due to slowly drying ink. (19)

stochastic screening: a type of electronic halftone screening using dots that are all the same size but varying in frequency or pattern. (11)

stop: a metal tab or finger attached to the front end of the feedboard on a sheetfed printing press that stops the sheet of paper and holds it on the feedboard while the side guide moves the sheet into position. (20)

stop bath: a film-processing solution consisting of a mild solution of acetic acid and water used to immediately stop the action of the developer. (10)

stop gauge: the metal bar in a buckle folder that stops the movement of the sheet and causes the sheet to buckle. (25)

stopping: a film-processing step used to halt the developing action. (10)

stream feeder: a feeding system in which a web or overlapped sheets are fed into the press. (20)

stream feeding: sending sheets into a press with a stream-feeder system. (20)

strike-through: a problem occurring when the ink or vehicle penetrates through the paper and shows through the opposite side of the sheet. (19)

stripper: the person who handles the task of film assembly. (12)

stripper finger: a device used in an ejector delivery system to separate the sheet from the impression cylinder and direct it under two ejector rollers that force the sheet into the paper-receiver tray. (20)

style sheet: a formatting tool used in page-composition programs that combines a number of attributes, such as type size, alignment, and other factors. (15)

substance weight: the actual weight of a ream of a paper. (18)

substrate: any surface to be printed to which ink will adhere. This surface is the material being printed on. (1)

subtractive color system: the forming of colors by combining CMY pigments. (16)

subtractive plate: a printing plate that is processed by the developer removing the nonimage areas of the plate's coating. (17)

successive feeding: a system in which the substrate is fed into the press one sheet at a time. (20)

successive feeding system: a system that performs successive feeding. (20)

suction foot: a rubber suction cup used on a printing-press sheet-separation unit to feed paper into the press. (20)

supercalendering: the process of sending coated paper through a series of rollers that polish the coating to form a glossy finish. (18)

surface plate: a printing plate on which the image area is formed on the surface of the plate. (17)

swing-feed assembly: the pickup mechanism used in the swing-feed system. (20)

swing-feed system: a register-and-insertion method in which a sheet is advanced forward, stopped, and then gripped and swung forward by arms, in time to connect with the grippers on the impression cylinder. (20)

synthetic paper: paper made without cellulose fiber. (18)

T

table: the platform in the feeder of a sheetfed press on which the pile of paper sits. (20)

tack: the stickiness of an ink, measured by its ability to split between two surfaces. (19)

tack modifier: an ink additive that adjusts an ink's tack. (19)

tagboard paper: a strong cover paper with long fibers; excellent folding qualities; good water resistance; and a surface adaptable to writing, stamping, or printing. This paper is used primarily for jobs requiring sturdiness. (18)

tagged image file format (TIFF): a bitmap file used for exchanging raster images between applications. (14)

tagged image file format for image transfer (TIFF/IT-P1): a device-dependent format used for describing four-color documents, including specs for printing presses. (14)

tagout device: a prominent warning attached to an energy-isolating device to prevent power from being restored to a particular circuit. (2)

tear strength: a paper property that takes into account the work required to tear a paper sample through a specified distance once the tear has started and starting the tear at an edge of the sheet. (18)

template: a reusable form incorporating all the master pages and other formatting for a document. (9)

tension control: the regulation of the amount of pull needed to keep the paper from having slack. (23)

test form: a compilation of quality-control devices on a single electronic, printed, negative, or positive sheet or page. (24)

test plate: a printing plate used for performing pressure checks before a pressrun. (21)

text box: a closed figure of any shape used to position text. (15)

text paper: a grade of paper made from either wood or cotton fibers popular for use in products such as brochures, menus, announcements, and annual reports. This paper is similar to book paper and is available with a variety of surface textures, attractive colors, and finishes. (18)

text type: a typeface that is 13 points or smaller and usually used for newspapers and books. (6)

texture: the visual surface characteristics and appearance of an element in a layout. (7)

thermal-ablation plate: a printing plate with a coating that is ablated by a laser's heat. (17)

thermal binding process: a binding process similar to perfect binding that uses heat and a special adhesive applied to the edges of the sheets. (25)

thermal-conversion plate: a printing plate with a coating that is imaged by being exposed to heat instead of light. (17)

thermal ink-jet printer: a device that emits tiny drops of ink through the use of heat. (13)

thermal-mechanical pulp (TMP): a type of mechanical pulp made by pumping preheated chips and water through refiners, where they are forced between counterrotating disks. (18)

thermal printer: a computer output device that uses the thermal transfer process to output color images. (13)

thermochromic ink: ink that does not appear until it is warmed by a simple rub or touch. (19)

thermography: a process that produces raised printing through the application of powder and heat. (25)

three-knife trimmer: a paper-cutting device with three blades. (25)

three main cylinder press: the standard offset lithographic press configuration, in which the plate, blanket, and impression cylinders are all the same size. (20)

three-point guide system: a method of registering a press sheet by contacting the sheet on the front and two sides. (20)

three-roll mill: a machine that uses three steel rollers revolving in alternating directions to break up the solid pigment particles and disperse them into the ink's vehicle. (19)

through drier: a catalyst that accelerates the oxidative polymerization of an entire ink film. (19)

thumbnail sketch: a small rendering in the same shape and proportion as the printed piece being planned. (7)

time-and-temperature method: a method for determining the proper amount of development for exposed film by relying on the film manufacturer's recommendations. (10)

tint: the alteration of a color created by adding white to the color. (7)

tinting: a contamination problem that occurs when ink emulsifies in the dampening solution, causing a slight tint of ink to appear on the nonimage area of the printed sheet. (19)

tinting strength: the amount an ink can be reduced or diluted with a white-pigment dispersion to produce a tint of a given strength. (19)

tipping: the insertion of a separate piece of printed material into the original pages of a printed product. (25)

tonal range: the range of tones in an original continuous tone image or a halftone reproduction, expressed as the difference between the areas of maximum and minimum density. (11)

tone: lightness or general quality of a color. To tone is to alter a color by adding some of its complement. (7)

tone break: an uneven blend of the dots in the 50% region of a halftone. (11)

tone compression: a reduction of the tonal range of an original image to make the image compatible with the capabilities of a press or an output device. (14)

top drier: a catalyst that accelerates the oxidative polymerization of the top portion of an ink film. (19)

totally chlorine-free (TCF) bleaching: any method of bleaching that uses no chlorine. (18)

touch pad: an input device typically found on laptop computers to move the cursor by sliding a fingertip across the surface of the pad. (8)

Townsend Color Head: a unique self-contained printing unit allowing second-color printing on most offset duplicators. (20)

trackball: a mounted, movable ball that can be rotated to move and position the cursor on a computer screen. (8)

tracking: a feature of computer-typesetting programs that allows the user to control the character and word spacing together. (6)

transfer-cylinder system: a feeder design in which the press sheet is fed to the grippers of an extra cylinder, which carry the sheet to the grippers of the impression cylinder. (20)

transfer roller: a hard, chrome-covered roller. This roller can be used as the fountain roller in some dampening systems. (20)

transitional serif typeface: a Roman typeface with characteristics of both old-style and modern typefaces. (6)

transmission densitometer: an electronic instrument that measures the fraction of incident light conveyed through negative or positive transparency without being absorbed or scattered. (3)

trap: an allowance of color overlap in multicolor printing. This allowance helps prevent gaps between colors. (10)

trapping: how well one color overlaps another without leaving a white space between the two or generating a third color. (14)

trim: the outside dimensions of a sheet of the finished printed piece. (25)

trim edge: the outside dimensions of the finished printed piece. (12)

tristimulus: color identification by measuring the amount of the three primary additive colors making up a color. (16)

TrueType® font technology: a fully scaleable font operating from a single file format, as opposed to the older format in which both printer and screen font files were needed. This technology was originally developed by Apple. (6)

tucker blade: a metal blade on a jaw folder used to tuck the web into the jaws of the jaw folder. (23)

tumbler gripper: a device that rotates through a rather large arc when it opens and drops back into the impression-cylinder gap. This gripper is used to grab a sheet of paper. (20)

tungsten filament: a photographic light source that uses the same metal found in regular lightbulbs. (10)

tungsten-halogen lamp: a low-voltage, high-current tungsten light. (14)

turning bar: a stationary bar on a web press that guides the moving web so it is flipped over, allowing it to be printed on the reverse side. (23)

tusche: a liquid-emulsion ink painted or drawn on a lithographic plate to form an image. (17)

twin-wire paper machine: a papermaking machine that forms a sheet by sending the pulp between two moving wire screens. (18)

two main cylinder duplicator: an offset-press design featuring a double-sized cylinder, which carries a plate component and a blanket component. (20)

two-person proofing: proofreading during which one person reads the manuscript aloud, while another person compares what is heard to what is being read on the galley. (6)

type: the letters and other characters (numerals and punctuation) used in printed messages. (6)

typeface: a type family narrowed down to a specific weight and width. (6)

typeface classification: a basic category into which typefaces are grouped. (6)

type family: a collection that includes a typeface and its variations. (6)

type series: the range of point sizes available for a specific font of a specific typeface in a specific type family. (6)

typesetting format: a way in which type can be displayed or set on the printed page. (6)

type specifications (specs): directions written on rough layout or on a manuscript informing the compositor about alphabet style, series, size, and amount of leading, or space between lines. (8)

typography: the selection and arrangement of type to be used in the design of a printed piece. (6)

U

ultraviolet (UV)-cured ink: ink that instantly solidifies when exposed to high doses of UV light. (19)

ultraviolet (UV) fade-resistant ink: ink designed with a high degree of permanence to resist fading or color change when exposed to the UV rays of the sun. (19)

ultraviolet (UV) radiation: a range of electromagnetic radiation lying outside the visible spectrum. In the printing industry, UV rays are used for producing various types of proofs, curing ink, or exposing plates. (2)

uncoated offset paper: offset paper that has not been coated. (18)

underblanket: packing material made of foam rubber, cork, or loose fabric fibers used under printing blankets to improve the blanket's performance. (20)

undercolor addition (UCA): a means of lightening dark areas of a reproduction and adding warmth or coldness to the dark areas by adding CMY to the shadow areas after removing some of the black. (16)

undercolor removal (UCR): a technique used to reduce the amount of CMY in shadows and neutral areas of an image and replace it with an appropriate amount of black. (16)

undercut: the difference between the radius of the plate and blanket cylinders' bearers and the radius of the cylinders themselves. (20)

uninterruptible power supply: a battery that supplies temporary power to a computer when there is a power loss. (13)

unit system: a counting system used with typesetting methods that specifies type sizes and spacing. (6)

unity: the proper balance of all elements in an image so a pleasing whole results and the image is viewed as one piece. (7)

universal basic size: a metric system of measurement in which a universal size of 25″ × 40″ would become the standard for weighing 1M sheets. (18)

unsharp masking (USM): the increase of tonal contrast where light and dark tones come together at the edges of an image to create a sharper image. (14)

uppercase letter: a capital letter. (6)

U.S. Customary system: the system of weights and measures used in the United States. This system establishes the values of units such as inches, feet, ounces, pounds, and gallons. (3)

utility paper: a classification containing types of paper that do not belong in any other classification. (18)

V

vacuum back: a process-camera component at the rear of the camera that uses a vacuum device to hold the photographic film in position during the exposure. (10)

value: the lightness or darkness of a color as measured against a scale running from white to black. (7)

variable cost: a cost rate generated by items such as labor and utilities, when production occurs in a cost center. (4)

variable data printing (VDP): a type of digital printing that allows different type and images to be printed on consecutive press sheets because the plate is reimaged between impressions. (13)

variable folder: an in-line device that can apply multiple parallel folds to a sheet at high speed. (23)

variable rotary cutter: an in-line device consisting of a rotary knife that can trim the bleed area from a moving web. (23)

varnishing: a process that places a coating, or surface finish, on paper to impart resistance to chemicals, heat, scuffing, water, or other elements that would otherwise damage the paper. (25)

vector font: type characters and symbols generated from mathematical formulas corresponding to the curves and lines of the characters, as opposed to collections of dots. This font is similar to an outline font, in that it can be proportionally sized and rotated. (6)

vector graphic: an electronic image represented as mathematical formulas that define all the shapes in the image, as well as their placements on a page. (13)

vehicle: the fluid part of the ink that carries the pigment and works as a binder to hold the pigment on the printed surface after drying. (19)

vellum finish: a relatively absorbent paper finish characterized by a rough, absorbent surface intended to simulate the texture of an ancient printing material made from the split skin of livestock. (18)

vertical camera: a process camera that has an up-and-down optical axis. (10)

video digitizer: a component that converts analog video signals into digital data. (8)

viewing booth: a viewing area with color-balanced lighting so anyone viewing the same printed materials is seeing them under the same lighting conditions. (16)

viscosity: the degree to which ink resists flow under applied force. (19)

viscosity modifier: an ink additive used to adjust an ink's viscosity. (19)

visible spectrum: the portion of electromagnetic waves visible to humans. (16)

vision fatigue: the tiring of the eyes from excessive reading. (16)

volatile organic compound (VOC): an organic compound that significantly participates in photochemical reactions and is released as hazardous emissions. A VOC eventually vaporizes and reacts with the atmosphere and sunlight to create smog and other pollutants. (2)

W

washer: a large tank that uses water to flush away spent cooking chemistry from chemical pulp. (18)

washing: a step in the film-development process used to remove any remaining processing chemicals. (10)

waterless offset ink: ink made for offset presses that use no dampening solution. (19)

waterless offset press: an offset press that does not use dampening solution. (20)

waterless offset printing: an offset printing process that eliminates water or fountain solution from the offset lithography printing equation. (17)

waterless plate: a printing plate made with an aluminum base and three to four coatings and designed for waterless offset printing. (17)

watermark: a symbol or logo produced by a raised pattern on the dandy roll that identifies the brand of paper or trademark of a company. (18)

water stop: a small roller or a plastic or metal tab that presses against the fountain roller to squeeze or scrape solution from the fountain-roller surface before it contacts the ductor. (20)

wax: an ink additive used to improve a dried ink's resistance to rubbing and scuffing. (19)

web: a roll of paper or other substrate used uncut on a webfed offset press. (20)

web-break detector: a device that automatically detects the site of a web break and immediately shuts down the press. (23)

webfed press: a press that prints with one long continuous web of paper fed from a roll. (20)

web guide: a guide on a web press, similar to a side guide on a sheetfed press, that controls the side-to-side register of the web as it passes through the press. (23)

wedge spectrograph: a device that splits a beam of light into the beam's spectrum. The spectrograph varies the intensity of the light passing through the entrance slit by moving an optical wedge. (10)

wet end: the forming section of a papermaking machine. (18)

wetting agent: a substance such as IPA, glycerin, or glycol, added to a fountain solution to lower its surface tension. (19)

wet trapping: applying an ink film onto another ink film that is still wet. (19)

What You See Is What You Get (WYSIWYG): the ability of computers to display text, graphics, color, and other page elements almost exactly the way they will print. (13)

What You See Is What You Print (WYSIWYP): software that adjusts printers and other output devices to output the same colors seen on the monitor. (13)

whiteness: the extent to which paper equally reflects all wavelengths of light from its surface. (18)

white space: the total amount of nonimage area on a page. (7)

widow: the last line of a paragraph at the top of a column of type. (15)

wipe-on plate: a printing plate similar to a presensitized plate in that specially treated metal is needed and diazo coatings are used, except the coatings are applied by hand or with a special roller coater. (17)

wire stitching: a binding method that uses staples to bind pages together. (25)

word processing program: computer software that allows the user to compose the text, or body matter, of a page. (13)

word processing software: a computer application for creating and editing text in various typestyles, sizes, and formats. (8)

word spacing: the spacing between words. (6)

work-and-back imposition: positioning films for a two-sided job in which the fronts will be carried on one plate and the backs will be carried on a different plate. (12)

work-and-flop imposition: a layout similar to a work-and-turn imposition, in which the press-sheet size must be twice the size of the finished signature sheet, but in which the axis is perpendicular to the direction of travel. (12)

work-and-tumble imposition: a layout similar to a work-and-turn imposition, in which the press-sheet size must be twice the size of the finished signature sheet, but in which the axis is perpendicular to the direction of travel. (12)

work-and-turn imposition: a layout producing two or more identical, perfected pieces using one printing plate in two impositions. (12)

World Wide Web (WWW): an interlinked collection of pages corresponding to files on widely separated computers. (13)

wrong-reading: backward. (20)

X

xenon lamp: a high-pressure, gas-discharge lamp that emits a constant high-intensity light. (14)

Y

yellow: a color whose hue bears a resemblance to that of ripe lemons or sunflowers or is that of the part of the spectrum lying between green and orange. This color is light with a wavelength of 570–580 nm. (16)

yield value: the force required to initiate flow of a pseudoplastic material. (19)

Z

zero-speed paster: a device in the infeed section of a webfed press that splices a fresh roll to an expiring roll by stopping the expiring roll briefly, but not stopping the press. (23)

Index

S